The North Carolina Gazetteer

The Classic Reference Updated for a New Generation—
With More Than 20,000 Entries

The North Carolina
Gazetteer

A Dictionary of Tar Heel Places and Their History

SECOND EDITION

WILLIAM S. POWELL AND MICHAEL HILL

The University of North Carolina Press   Chapel Hill

Library of Congress Cataloging-in-Publication Data
Powell, William Stevens, 1919–
The North Carolina gazetteer: a dictionary of Tar Heel places and their history / William S. Powell and Michael Hill.—2nd ed.
p. cm.
"The classic reference updated for a new generation—with more than 20,000 entries."
Includes bibliographical references.
ISBN 978-0-8078-3399-5 (cloth: alk. paper)—ISBN 978-0-8078-7138-6 (pbk.: alk. paper)
1. North Carolina—Gazetteers. 2. Names, Geographical—North Carolina.
I. Hill, Michael R., 1954– II. Title.
F252.P6 2010
975.6—dc22   2009045021

cloth   14 13 12 11 10   5 4 3 2 1
paper   14 13 12 11 10   5 4 3 2 1

For
my mother
and in memory of
my father,
who from summer to summer took
me on vacation trips from one
end of North Carolina to the other.
I cannot remember when I did not
know and love the coast, the
mountains, and many special places
in between.
—William S. Powell, 1968

Preface to the Second Edition

It is remarkable to consider the number of place names that derive from the difficulties that North Carolinians had in crossing creeks. Pig Basket Creek in Nash County, for example. It seems that an early settler, headed home with a basket of newborn pigs, dropped them into the water as he tried to cross the creek, which was swollen by recent rains.

Then there are the place names with unusual—often wildly so—derivations: Asey Hole, Bandana, Black Ankle, Calico Creek, Cat Square, Dixie, Easy Street, Enola, Haoe, Handy, Hanging Dog, Huggins Hell, Ivanhoe, Lawyers Spring, Naked Mountain, Observer, Oriental, Revolution, Rhodo, Shakerage, Tater Hill, Virgilina, Whynot.

Look a little further and you will find 12 Concords, 11 Gum Swamps, 10 Big Laurels, 9 Tarkilns, 8 Silvermines, 7 Frying Pans, 6 Vances, 5 Milksicks, 4 Whetstones, 3 Sengs (as in ginseng), 2 Kill Quicks, and 1—and only 1—Shit-Britches Creek. Add to that 149 Bears, 103 Beavers, 85 Chestnuts, 85 Horses, 68 Wolfs, 68 Grassys, 66 White Oaks, 51 Turkeys, 49 Saints, 46 Hogs, 38 Buffalos, 35 Little Creeks, 34 Forts, 30 Wildcats, 32 Rattlesnakes, 28 mentions of Sassafras, 22 Ravens, 14 Jumping Runs, and 13 Town Creeks.

We know all of this because of William S. Powell's work on *The North Carolina Gazetteer*. Published in 1968, the book set a new standard for guides to place names. It is the most consulted book in my office and in many offices and libraries. No other state has anything to approach it. Powell's *Gazetteer* is a classic, a work of use to historians, genealogists, librarians, journalists, creative writers, geographers, urban planners, armchair travelers, and anyone with an interest in the Old North State. In working on a revised edition, I did so with the knowledge that the book is a gem, and, aside from a new polish and a few new facets, it should remain largely intact. To my mind, the *Gazetteer* provides no greater service than to preserve the memory of places already gone or in danger of disappearing due to urban growth and development—what might be called suburban swallowups.

Indeed, the question may arise about the need for this type of reference book in the Digital Age of the twenty-first century, when information is a few keystrokes away via Google Earth, MapQuest, WorldCat, and other Internet marvels. Global Positioning System (GPS) units are now inexpensive and widely used. I would argue that these new technologies and databases make the *Gazetteer* all the more valuable. New technologies can locate with precision the places we live, work, and play, but technology alone cannot tell their stories. With its focus not just on locating but on describing the origins and naming of North Carolina's cities, towns, crossroads communities, waterways, peaks, and other places and physical features, the *Gazetteer* is as valuable today as it was when first published more than forty years ago. And given the state's rapid growth over the last decades, there are many new readers who can learn from and enjoy the information contained herein.

In 2007 Professor Powell and editors at the University of North Carolina Press asked me to take on the responsibility of producing this revised edition. With 19,638 entries in the original edition, I commenced my search for additional entries. In the end, I added about 1,200. The work would involve updates of existing entries and a close examination of the criteria to determine which new entries would be logical fits. Some of these were obvious. Jordan Lake, for example, did not exist when the original edition was published but undoubtedly belonged in the *Gazetteer*. Most readers would join me in recognizing that, for the most part, we stopped making a significant number of new place names a long time ago. Some modern names do not belong in the book. This would include residential subdivisions, the kinds of communities that spell harbor with a *u* and town with an *e*.

This matter of list making, of course, did not begin with Professor Powell. Mapmakers have been at work describing, depicting, and inventorying the landscape since the days of John White and the Roanoke colonies. A substantial number of Tar Heel place names from Chicamacomico to Nantahala have Native American origins. Successive waves of settlers—the Moravians to name just one group—assigned names to places. The Revolutionary War generation left the greatest imprint on place names, having the distinction of selecting most county names. Arnold Guyot, the Harvard scientist who came south to survey the North Carolina mountains in the 1850s, kept such a list in his notebooks along with altitudes. Today, Mount Guyot, named in his honor, stands in Haywood County and is duly recorded in the *Gazetteer*.

Professor Powell made wide use of maps in producing his original work. One that he did not consult is the 1901 *Historical Map and Gazetteer of North Carolina*, prepared by D. C. Mangum of Durham and issued by Rand McNally. It is the type of old wall map that once decorated classrooms, depots, and public buildings. For this project, the utility of the beautifully designed and richly detailed Mangum map derives from the year of its issue: 1901. The map was prepared during the heyday of small, unincorporated communities in North Carolina, after the rise of the railroads and the proliferation of post offices but, importantly, before the consolidation of post offices and the use of rural free delivery, which came about after 1915. Interested readers are invited to examine the Mangum map and other digitized maps at the North Carolina Maps project website (*http://www.lib.unc.edu/dc/ncmaps/index.html*).

In his preface, Professor Powell explained why he elected not to include most post offices. In short, it was because in many cases these were not true communities but rather a store, a gristmill, or just someone's house. Still, there was inconsistency with respect to post offices. For Warren County and Caswell County, every post office is included in the original edition. Mangum's map helped separate the wheat from the chaff among the 6,900 post offices that have operated in North Carolina over the years. From the Mangum map, I could detail the section of the county where the community was located. If it was on a creek or a railroad, I could determine that. Of course, it was silent with respect to name derivation. But with a list of place names in hand from the Mangum map, I then could turn to the four-volume guide to post offices issued by the North Carolina Postal History Society in 1997 to record the years of operation.

Since 1968 other reference works have appeared that proved useful. The *Omni-Gazetteer of the United States*, a massive tome published in 1990, is among these. The *National Gazetteer of the United States*, issued by the U.S. Geological Survey and updated regularly, is another. The former includes churches, water towers, dams, cemeteries, airports, schools, bridges, broadcast towers, and a host of sites not documented in Powell's book. The latter is authoritative. But these reference sources are, despite their inclusiveness, dry as dust compared to the *Gazetteer*. The stories attached to place names are at the core of Powell's book and the reason why it has stood the test of time.

In conducting an entry-by-entry examination of the old volume, I found that a few necessary changes were quickly apparent. In listings for counties and towns, for example, principal agricultural and industrial products were indicated. These include, for places both large and small, textiles, the industry so long associated with the state and one that was still relatively healthy in 1968. In many cases, I simply struck the word; in others, I changed the reference to the past tense. You cannot profile Kannapolis without noting the role of Cannon Mills and the production of towels. And, to bring the entry up to date, the town's new research campus, with its focus on nutrition, needs to be mentioned.

Other commodities are treated similarly. The updating of the agricultural and industrial production, surprisingly, was among the toughest nuts to crack. The N.C. Departments of Agriculture and Commerce keep detailed statistics, but their abstracts did not translate well to the county and town level. At any rate, I reviewed all such entries—everything from gravel to strawberries—but I know that some items must have slipped by. The presence of textile production, literally hanging by a thread in so many communities, likely will go misrepresented in some instances.

Streams and other waterways are treated fully in the original edition. I wish that I could have done more with landings and with plantation names. I am convinced that a book (or at least a scholarly article) could be written on the variations of Indian names such as Torhunta and Ocracoke. Transliteration in the seventeenth and eighteenth centuries was not an easy or simple matter.

Occasionally, I would correct an entry. The *Gazetteer*, for example, indicates that the word "lynch" is taken from Lynch Creek, but most etymologists now agree that such is not the case. A number of terms of personal interest are also now included. These include Speculation Land, the story of Tench Coxe and the disposition of a half million acres in Henderson, Polk, and Rutherford Counties. The story of Joara, the Indian village in Burke County, upon which Juan Pardo's men built Fort San

Juan, is another. I created entries for Back of Beyond, Backcountry, and Cackalacky, a popular nickname for Carolina with obscure roots. Dry Hill was a long-gone, one-room school and community in the area where I grew up in Henderson County.

The naming of a county can provide a lesson in North Carolina history. What is now Greene County was once part of Johnston, but in 1758 it became Dobbs County for royal governor Arthur Dobbs. In 1791 that name was "expunged from our map," as historian Kemp Battle phrased it, and a new county was named for Secretary of State James Glasgow. After Glasgow met an ignominious end involving land fraud, in 1799 the name was changed to Greene County to honor Nathanael Greene, the hero of Guilford Courthouse.

With details from the Mangum map and the post office guide, I was able to create about 600 new entries for the *Gazetteer*, about half of my total number of new additions. And these turned out to be some of the more fascinating place names. Moore County, for some reason, was particularly rich. There was a post office called Tempting, no doubt selected to lure the late nineteenth-century tourist trade. In 1882 in northwest Moore, there was a community with the unlikely name of Noise. The next year, just ten miles away, neighbors founded Quiet. Some post office names recall faraway places: Bombay, Klondike, Oswego, Bismarck, Shanghai, Moscow, Pomona, Berlin, Nebraska. One of those was Japan in Graham County, a community inundated by the waters of the lake behind Fontana Dam. Before it disappeared, locals during World War II began calling it MacArthur. Others paint their locality as a little piece of heaven on earth: Bliss, Breeze, Splendor, Sweet Home.

At the outset of my work, I prepared an appeal for assistance and distributed it by e-mail listservs and other means. Like Professor Powell, I pinned my hopes largely on the community of local historians and librarians. I did not get a response from all 100 counties, but those who helped out did so with enthusiasm and respect for Powell's work. "Viva the *Gazetteer*," wrote one.

I wish to thank the dedicated researchers who responded to my call and, in some cases, shared details that they had amassed over many years working on their county: Carole Troxler and Lisa Kobrin (Alamance); Clarence Horton (Cabarrus); Victor Jones (Craven); Barbara Snowden (Currituck); David Stick and Naomi Rhodes (Dare); Jane McAllister and James Wall (Davie); Sonny Sikes (Duplin); Monika Fleming (Edgecombe); Leonard Dean (Granville); Helen Snow and Gwen Gosney Erickson (Guilford); Ronnie Faulkner (Harnett); Mary Lowder (Haywood); John Ward (Hertford); Jean Krause and Anne Swan (McDowell); Jack Thomas (Madison); Jane Johnson, Shelia Bumgarner, Linda Blackwelder, and James Williams (Mecklenburg); Sharon Faulkner (Montgomery); Mary and Charles Prevost (Moore); Bob Carter (Rockingham); Steve Shelton (Stokes); Ken Badgett (Surry); Marcy Thompson (Transylvania); Patrick Valentine (Wilson); and Andrew Mackie and Barbara Norman (Yadkin). James Wall, David Stick, and H. G. Jones were contributors to the original edition and I thank them for returning to the task. All were generous in sharing information.

Offering assistance of a more general nature were Robert Anthony, Tom Beaman, Matthew Brown, Robert Cain, Steve Case, Beth Hayden, Charles Heath, Joy Heitman, Josh Howard, H. G. Jones, Jay Lester, Vivian McDuffie, Cheryl McLean, Chris Meekins, Lynn Roundtree, Druscie Simpson, Jason Tomberlin, Pam Toms, Walter Turner, Ansley Wegner, and Ashley Yandle. Colleagues at the Office of Archives and History, at the State Library of North Carolina, and in the North Carolina Collection in Chapel Hill were always willing to lend a hand. A special debt of gratitude is owed to Professor Powell and his wife, Virginia. George Stevenson, assistant to Powell in the North Carolina Collection and key to development of the original book, pointed me toward valuable source material. Mark Simpson-Vos of UNC Press assisted with the loan of a laptop computer with the original text installed in Filemaker Pro. Jay Mazzocchi completed the time-consuming and tedious task of copyediting the manuscript. The foregoing deserve no responsibility for any errors which arise; such remain my doing alone. Readers who wish to share information or point out the need for a correction are invited to contact Michael Hill at the N.C. Office of Archives and History, 4610 Mail Service Center, Raleigh, NC 27699-4610.

My habit, as I worked on this project, was to highlight entries in the old edition with an exclamation point if a humorous or intriguing story was attached. My copy therefore is dotted with such marks. Two new ones came to me from my correspondents in Davie County: Bullhole, a site on the Yadkin River where an early settler fell through the crude bridge with his team of cattle; and Turkeyfoot, the convergence of several roads that, when viewed from the air, resembles a gobbler's appendage. I invite the reader to dip into the new edition for such revelations.

MICHAEL HILL
May 2009

Preface

The North Carolina Gazetteer is a geographical dictionary in which an attempt has been made to list all of the geographic features of the state in one alphabet. It is current, and it is historical as well. Many features and places that no longer exist are included; many towns and counties for which plans were made but which never materialized are also included. Some names appearing on old maps may have been imaginary, but many of them also appear in this gazetteer.

Each entry is located according to the county in which it is found. I have not felt obliged to keep entries uniform. The altitude of a place, the date of incorporation of a city or town, may appear in the beginning of one entry and at the end of another. Some entries may appear more complete than others. I have included whatever information I could find. If there is no comment on the origin or meaning of a name, it is because the information was not available. In some cases, however, resort to an unabridged dictionary may suggest the meaning of many names.

Names of former post offices have been included only when the name was more than a convenience for delivering mail. If a post office name was attached to a community, it probably will appear. In the days before rural free delivery, however, hundreds of post offices existed in private homes or in stores. When a postmaster died or retired, the post office would be moved to the home or the store of the new postmaster, and frequently this meant that it would be in another county. The post office name was nothing more than a means of distributing mail. Lists of post offices will be found in postal directories. I do not consider them of importance in a gazetteer.

How the Gazetteer Developed

In 1951, when I was a member of the staff of the State Department of Archives and History, I read an interesting manuscript journal kept in the early eighteenth century by a British merchant who visited North Carolina seeking a suitable location for a retail store. He mentioned several people with whom he talked and a number of creeks and small communities. The journal was unsigned, the people it mentioned were obscure, and the place names are no longer shown on maps. I returned the journal to its proper box and gave up my hopes of editing it for publication.

A few months later a commercial airplane exploded over eastern North Carolina, and a small community whose name appeared on no maps of the state suddenly was in newspaper headlines throughout the United States. At about the same time, the name of a mountain in western North Carolina appeared in the state newspapers for some reason that I no longer remember; perhaps it was mentioned in a syndicated feature story on moonshiners. My attempts to locate the mountain on maps or in books was fruitless.

As a member of the Archives staff and later at the North Carolina Collection in Chapel Hill, I realized how futile it was to search for the names of small communities, streams, and other geographical features in any logical manner. No national gazetteer lists them. Many maps, even county maps, do not name them.

It was to meet such needs as this that I began the compilation of *The North Carolina Gazetteer* some fifteen years ago. I cannot recall the circumstances of its beginning. For more than thirty years, I have maintained an organized card file of notes on subjects of historical and bibliographical interest to me, and at first I simply dropped possible gazetteer entries into this file. Somewhere along the way, the idea for a more serious use of these cards developed, and I began to think about how to proceed.

In response to a request from a patron directed to the North Carolina Collection for information concerning townships in the state, I compiled an alphabetical list of all townships. I do not think that such a list had been compiled previously. It was made from census reports in which townships are listed only by county. Entered on cards, this list soon became a part of the developing gazetteer file.

A request for information concerning the colonial parishes of eighteenth-century North Carolina led me to examine the laws creating counties and parishes. (The parish as a unit of local administration was abolished in 1776 with the adoption of the state constitution and the disestablishment of the Church of England.) A list of parishes was the result, and this also was soon incorporated into my file.

Piecemeal work would accomplish little and might even be wasted, so I decided to approach the problem of compiling a gazetteer county by county. With a manageable unit, I undertook to gain some experience and to work out some standards. I began with Iredell County, where I grew up, and with Johnston County, where I was born. My personal knowledge of the face of the land in these counties was helpful in attempting to work out a plan for writing descriptions from information shown on maps. I next undertook an unfamiliar county—Alamance, the first in the alphabet and also conveniently nearby so that I could easily visit with map and note card in hand for an on-the-scene comparison.

Since soil survey maps are available for nearly all of the counties and show a large amount of detailed information, they became the basic map with which I worked. Although rather uniform in the amount and type of information shown, their chief drawback is that they have appeared sporadically from the early twentieth century until 1967. I supplemented them with large county maps prepared by the State Highway Commission, and for the county whose soil survey map was quite old, the highway map was of great importance. These two maps were used in compiling the basic entries for each county. Supplementary entries were prepared from such diverse sources as the reports of the U.S. Board on Geographic Names, county histories, geological surveys, lists of post offices, lists of streams compiled by the N.C. Department of Water Resources, entries in the North Carolina Guide, and other general printed works. Federal and state reports listing altitudes were combed for supplementary information. Inscriptions of historical markers along the highways of the state frequently provided additional facts. When I happened to be traveling in the state, I made notes for entries on named communities, streams, and other features as I encountered them.

During this period, the county remained the basic unit by which I worked. Cards containing entries for each county were filed in alphabetical order by county. In 1960 I sought out men and women who were authorities on local history and geography in each county and asked that each examine my file for the particular county. Many new entries resulted from their contributions, but many were also eliminated. The problem of the changing of county lines through the years, as well as the creation of new counties from old, meant that I had not always properly located geographic features. Many errors were corrected.

When the cards were returned to me from the counties, they were microfilmed in their original county arrangement for security purposes and to provide a means of checking them in this order at a later date if that became necessary. The cards for all of the counties were then filed in one alphabet. At this stage it became possible to combine entries for streams flowing through one or more counties and for mountains that cross county lines. Many duplications and errors were discovered and eliminated.

At this time, historical maps were examined and entries were made showing the earliest appearance of a name, changes in name that could be determined from maps, and the names of features that no longer appear on modern maps. Although the state is inadequately covered by U.S. Geological Survey and Army Map Service maps, they were also examined at this stage of the development of the *Gazetteer*. They were not a major source of information, however, because to take detailed information from those that were available would have produced an unbalanced coverage of the state. Nevertheless, the place names (streams and communities, for example) that seemed to be of Indian origin and suggested early settlement were included because of their particular interest to historians, folklorists, geologists, and botanists. These were included in the *Gazetteer* as they were discovered by chance while comparing soil survey and state highway maps with geological survey or army map-service maps. It is hoped that this arbitrary decision will not make use of the *Gazetteer* difficult.

Terms

Numerous generic terms form a part of the specific name of many geographic features in North Carolina. A few of them will be unfamiliar to some readers, but reference to a dictionary will provide definitions of most. Among these might be considered bald; butt or butte; cove (both in the mountains and along the bank of a stream or the ocean); face (generally an exposed rock surface on a mountain); flat (often any level place in the mountains); hollow (in the sense of a valley or mountain cove); knob; lead (which may be unique to North Carolina and for which I have been unable to get an entirely satisfactory definition, although it seems to be a mountain term for a lesser mountain or spur "leading" off the larger mountain); pocosin (a swamp or boggy place that may also run or flow as a stream); run (generally an eastern term to be equated with creek or branch); spur; stamp (in the mountains, apparently a place devoid of trees); and top.

The term "brook" occurs only three times in the *Gazetteer*; creek and branch are the forms used for small streams. The term "village" apparently was used a few times before the Civil War, but in a very loose way, and it is not used today as applied to a municipality. All municipalities are incorporated either as cities or as towns, and I have attempted to use the proper term in the descriptions. Apparently the term "city" was first used in North Carolina in the laws of 1881. Unincorporated places dignified by a name are described simply as communities.

A number of general entries have been made that may be found useful. They include Coastal Plain, fall line, General Assembly (listing the places at which the legislature has met), geographic center, Mountain Region, Piedmont, thermal belt, and Welsh Tract, among numerous others.

Alphabetizing, Spelling, and Abbreviations

The *Gazetteer* is arranged in straight, letter-by-letter alphabetical order whether the name consists of one word or more. The generic term is considered in this arrangement to be part of the name, as in Collett Creek and Collett Ridge. Collinstown follows Collins Mountain because *t* follows *m*. The fact that Collinstown is one word and Collins Mountain two is not considered. In the case of duplicate names (Grassy Branch, for example), the arrangement under the name is alphabetical by county: Grassy Branch in Buncombe County will precede Grassy Branch in Cleveland County. If there were a community named Grassy Branch, it would follow all of the entries for branches of that name. The feature described by the generic name is listed before all other uses of the name: all mountains named Black Mountain are entered ahead of the town named Black Mountain.

An effort has been made to use the spelling preferred at or near the feature described. When obvious errors have been made in recent years by mapmakers in Raleigh, New York, or Chicago, I have followed the local usage, often with mention of the error. Sometimes historical precedent for a different form than that used on modern maps is so strong that I have commented on it.

A few abbreviations have been used: Alt.—altitude; approx.—approximate or approximately; Inc.—incorporated; n—north; s—south; e—east; w—west; ne—northeast; etc.

Maps

Throughout the *Gazetteer*, references will be found to early usage of names or locations of features on certain maps. Further information on these maps will be found in William P. Cumming, *The Southeast in Early Maps* (Chapel Hill: University of North Carolina Press, 1962) or in standard bibliographies of American maps

available in most libraries of the state. A number of the maps cited have been repro-
duced in facsimile by the State Department of Archives and History, Raleigh.

The maps that I have most often cited are: White (1585), De Bry's engraving of
White (1590), Velasco (1611), Smith (1624), Comberford (1657), Ogilby (1671), Hack
(1684), Moll (1729), Moseley (1733), Collet (1770), Price (1808), and MacRae (1833).
The *Gazetteer* may be found to be virtually an index to these maps. In addition,
many other maps are cited in occasional entries.

Other Sources

The need for a reference book such as this has been recognized for many years.
The *Peoples Press* (Salem) for March 7, 1856, and the *American Advocate* (Kinston)
for September 11, 1856, contained an advertisement in which William D. Cooke
of Raleigh sought information for a North Carolina gazetteer. He asked for lists of
post offices by county with distance and direction of each from the "county town,"
the names of rivers and creeks with the direction in which they flowed, the names
and locations of mills and factories, the schools and colleges with the number of
teachers and pupils, and the churches and their denominations. There is no evidence that Cooke's interest in the subject ever produced a book.

North Carolina entries in national gazetteers have always been brief and lim-
ited. The first publication to do more than list the counties and the larger cities and
rivers was *How They Began: The Story of North Carolina County, Town, and Other Place
Names*, compiled by workers of the WPA Writers' Program and published in New
York in 1941 under the sponsorship of the State Department of Conservation and
Development. Long out of print, it contained only 73 pages and numerous errors.

A useful source for information on counties and county seats is D. L. Corbitt's
The Formation of the North Carolina Counties (Raleigh: State Department of Archives
and History, 1950). Based on the laws of North Carolina and on the published Colonial and State Records, it contains detailed information on both the formation of
the counties and the subsequent changes in their boundaries.

Corrections

In a work such as this, opportunities for error abound. I can only hope that I have
avoided careless errors. Poor judgment may account for some, but in the face of
conflicting evidence, I have often had to make arbitrary decisions. Many possible
entries have been omitted simply because I was uncertain of the reliability of the
information.

WILLIAM S. POWELL
Chapel Hill
March 30, 1968

Acknowledgments

For assistance in many phases of the compilation of this gazetteer, my greatest indebtedness is to George Stevenson Jr. and to my wife, Virginia Waldrop Powell. With tireless devotion to the project, they have compiled long lists of entries from assorted sources. My special thanks go to George Stevenson for his careful work in comparing numerous historic maps with contemporary maps and preparing notes on early locations of geographic features and the changes in name that can best be discovered by this process. From published lists of altitudes, post offices, streams, and many shorter lists of various kinds, my wife prepared and interfiled hundreds of cards.

Two grants from the University Research Council made it possible for me to have the services at various times of four student assistants: George M. Beasley III, James A. Chesnutt III, William H. Salling Jr., and George Stevenson Jr. I am grateful to the University Research Council for its generosity and to these young men for the personal interest they took in their work. Without them, the *Gazetteer* would have been delayed many years.

Individuals throughout the state willingly answered my questions about specific places; others, hearing of the *Gazetteer*, voluntarily contributed information. My indebtedness to them is great and my regret is sincere that I cannot acknowledge their contributions by name simply because they were so numerous.

Those on whom I called frequently for specific help include: C. Ritchie Bell, for botanical information; Sanford Boswell; Richard Bryson, especially for the preparation of the county maps; Myra Champion; Fred Coker; D. L. Corbitt; Christopher Crittenden; L. Polk Denmark; Louise McG. Hall; U. T. Holmes, for translations of foreign words, particularly Gaelic; Thomas Hyatt; Roy Johnson; J. O. Kilmartin, for information from the files of the U.S. Board on Geographic Names; Mrs. Pattie B. McIntyre; Elizabeth McPherson; Mrs. Elizabeth Merritt; Thomas C. Parramore; Mrs. Mary J. Rogers; Bill Sharpe; Frederick Symmes: Gary Trawick; Mae Tucker; and Mrs. Elizabeth Wilborn. They responded with enthusiasm to all of my pleas for assistance.

Hardly a state or municipal agency escaped my persistent search for facts, and many private business concerns fared little better. County agricultural agents, registrars of deeds, mayors, city and town clerks, as well as postmasters displayed admirable civic spirit in their attempts to furnish me with the information I sought. The office of the secretary of state, the State Highway Commission, the Department of Conservation and Development, and especially the staffs of the State Department of Archives and History and of the State Library were generous with the time they devoted in replying to my letters and telephone calls. Chambers of commerce throughout the state and the North Carolina League of Municipalities in Raleigh willingly supplied data and showed not the least sign of annoyance at my repeated requests for their services. To many members of the staff of the Institute of Government in Chapel Hill I am deeply indebted for information and advice, but especially to the director, John Sanders, and to Marion Benfield, a former staff member. At my request, they asked a team of researchers working through all of the Session Laws of North Carolina for another purpose to record also the date of incorporation of municipalities. This information, I feel, is a valuable part of the *Gazetteer*. Officials of the Carolina Power & Light Company, Duke Power Company, and the Virginia Electric and Power Company proved to be generous sources for geographical facts, as did officials of the railroads operating in the state. Attorneys and surveyors in many counties came forward with information they had gleaned from years of experience in working with local records. Editors of every newspaper in the state came to my aid. They published many "letters to the editor" in my desperate attempts to find persons with specific information.

At a critical stage in the preparation of *The North Carolina Gazetteer*, I sent the file of county entries to one or more knowledgeable persons in each county. To these people my debt is great. They added much new information and saved me from many errors. Those errors that remain, however, should in no wise be considered the fault of anyone but me. In all fairness, it must be pointed out that for various reasons based on editorial policy I could not always accept the advice offered me.

Without the help of the following North Carolinians, this work would be less complete and less accurate:

Alamance County	Howard White
Alexander County	Charles E. Echerd, Homer M. Keever, J. P. Lentz
Alleghany County	J. K. Doughton
Anson County	Mary Louise Medley
Ashe County	Colonel A. L. Fletcher, Mrs. Jesse A. Reeves
Avery County	Horton Cooper
Beaufort County	Mrs. Pauline Worthy
Bertie County	Dr. W. P. Jacocks
Bladen County	Mrs. Carl C. Campbell
Brunswick County	Cornelius Thomas
Buncombe County	D. Hiden Ramsey, Colonel Paul A. Rockwell
Burke County	Dr. Edward W. Phifer
Cabarrus County	Eugenia Lore, Harold Nash
Caldwell County	James B. Dula, Allan L. Poe
Camden County	Jesse F. Pugh
Carteret County	Tucker Littleton, F. C. Salisbury
Caswell County	H. G. Jones

Catawba County	Mrs. J. M. Ballard, Dr. J. E. Hodges
Chatham County	Wade Barber, John H. London, Lawrence F. London
Cherokee County	John C. Christie
Chowan County	Elizabeth Vann Moore
Clay County	Mrs. J. Walter Moore
Cleveland County	Mrs. O. Max Gardner
Columbus County	Jim High
Craven County	Rose B. Carraway, Elizabeth Moore
Cumberland County	Frank H. Jeter
Currituck County	Dudley W. Bagley
Dare County	David Stick
Davidson County	Wade H. Phillips, M. Jewell Sink
Davie County	Flossie Martin
Duplin County	Mrs. Fred D. Hamrick Jr., Mrs. Christine W. Williams
Durham County	A. B. Markham
Edgecombe County	Mabrey Bass Jr.
Forsyth County	Mary C. Wiley
Franklin County	Hamilton H. Hobgood, Phil R. Inscoe
Gaston County	Brice T. Dickson
Gates County	William T. Cross, Mrs. O. C. Turner
Graham County	W. M. Sherrill
Granville County	Claude A. Renn
Greene County	Charles R. Holloman
Guilford County	James G. W. MacLamroc
Halifax County	Mrs. Quentin Gregory
Harnett County	Malcolm Fowler
Haywood County	Hiram C. Wilburn
Henderson County	Mrs. Sadie S. Patton
Hertford County	Mrs. W. D. Boone
Hoke County	Mrs. Kate B. Covington, Admiral A. M. Patterson
Hyde County	Tommie Gaylord
Iredell County	Homer M. Keever, Mrs. W. B. Knox
Jackson County	J. R. Buchanan
Johnston County	Mrs. W. B. Beasley, T. J. Lassiter
Jones County	John D. Larkins Jr., Tucker Littleton
Lee County	Paul J. Barringer
Lenoir County	Charles R. Holloman
Lincoln County	Mrs. Joseph Graham
Macon County	Thomas A. Henson, Weimar Jones, Lake V. Shope
Madison County	Mrs. J. B. Tweed
Martin County	R. H. Goodmon
McDowell County	Ruth M. Greenlee
Mecklenburg County	Charles R. Brockmann

Mitchell County	Jason B. Deyton
Montgomery County	Colonel Jeffery F. Stanback
Moore County	R. E. Wicker
Nash County	L. S. Inscoe
New Hanover County	Louis T. Moore
Northampton County	Mrs. Nancy Froelich
Onslow County	J. Parsons Brown, Tucker Littleton
Orange County	L. J. Phipps
Pamlico County	Dallas Mallison
Pasquotank County	L. S. Blades Jr.
Pender County	Clifton L. Moore
Perquimans County	Mrs. J. Emmett Winslow
Person County	R. B. Griffin
Pitt County	D. L. Corbitt
Polk County	Alan T. Calhoun, Mrs. Sadie S. Patton
Randolph County	Cleveland Thayer
Richmond County	Isaac S. London
Robeson County	Penn Gray
Rockingham County	Mrs. Bettie Sue Gardner, Mrs. S. R. Prince
Rowan County	William D. Kizzah
Rutherford County	Mrs. Fred D. Hamrick Jr.
Sampson County	Mrs. Taft Bass
Scotland County	A. B. Gibson
Stanly County	Fred T. Morgan
Stokes County	Mrs. Grace T. Rodenbough, L. H. van Noppen
Surry County	J. S. Gentry
Swain County	Kelly E. Bennett
Transylvania County	O. H. Orr
Tyrrell County	Sara L. Taft
Union County	S. Glen Hawfield, W. S. Tarlton
Vance County	S. T. Peace
Wake County	Christopher Crittenden, Mrs. Mary J. Rogers, Mrs. Louis Woodward
Warren County	J. Edward Allen
Washington County	Mrs. Tom Grier, Mrs. L. E. Hassell
Watauga County	D. J. Whitener
Wayne County	Mrs. E. Charles Powell, Mrs. S. R. Prince
Wilkes County	Johnson J. Hayes, Allan L. Poe, T. E. Story
Wilson County	Hugh B. Johnston Jr.
Yadkin County	William Rutledge
Yancey County	H. Grady Bailey

For help with the tremendous task of alphabetizing some 20,000 cards, I am grateful to Mrs. Elizabeth Merritt; George Stevenson Jr.; Mrs. Pattie B. McIntyre; Mrs. Archibald Henderson; Miss Florence Blakely; Miss Mary L. Thornton; Mrs. Jane C. Bahnsen; my mother-in-law, Mrs. John B. Hill; my sons, John and Charles; and my wife, Virginia.

It is with a real sense of loss that I must say that a number of people with whom I have worked on *The North Carolina Gazetteer* have died. I miss their friendship, and their knowledge of local history is also a loss to the state and to their home communities.

Finally, it remains my pleasure to acknowledge sincere appreciation to the Z. Smith Reynolds Foundation of Winston-Salem and to the University Research Council for generous grants to the University of North Carolina Press, which made possible the publication of this book.

WILLIAM S. POWELL
March 30, 1968

The North Carolina Gazetteer

A

Aaron. *See* Hood Swamp.

Aaron. *See* Montezuma.

Aaron Branch rises in n Mitchell County and flows se into Bean Creek.

Aaron Creek rises in ne Cherokee County and flows nw into Taylor Creek.

Aaron Duff. *See* Iron Duff.

Aarons Corner, community in n Stokes County. Named for a church.

Aarons Creek rises in nw Granville County and flows ne into Virginia, where it enters Dan River.

Aaron Swamp rises in w Robeson County and flows s into Ashpole Swamp.

Abbots Island. *See* Croatoan Island.

Abbot Top, mountain in central Cherokee County between Hiwassee River and West Prong Grape Creek.

Abbottsburg, town in sw Bladen County. Inc. 1903. Alt. approx. 99. Named for Joseph C. Abbott (1825–81), president of the Cape Fear Building Company there.

Abbotts Creek rises in ne Davidson County and flows sw into Yadkin River. Appears as Abbots Creek on the Collet map, 1770.

Abbott's Creek rises in n Wake County and flows ne into Neuse River.

Abbotts Creek, community in ne Davidson County. A Primitive Baptist church was founded there in 1756. Gen. Nathanael Greene camped there in February 1781 before the Battle of Guilford Courthouse.

Abbotts Creek Township, ne Davidson County.

Abbotts Creek Township, se Forsyth County.

Abbotts Township, sw Bladen County.

Abbs Creek rises in n Jackson County and flows s into Caney Fork.

Abe Creek rises in s Macon County and flows se into West Fork Overflow Creek.

Abel Bay, sw Hyde County in the mouth of Pungo River.

Abells, community in ne Johnston County served by post office, 1880–1900.

Abel's Creek rises in North River Pocosin in s Camden County and flows e into North River.

Aberdeen, town in s Moore County. Inc. 1893. Known originally as Blue's Crossing after settler Malcolm Blue. Renamed in 1887 by resident John Graham, who had formerly lived in Aberdeen, Miss., which in turn was named for the seaport in Scotland. Economy caters to golf and tourist industry and area military bases. Produces carpets, hosiery, textiles, furniture, and canned foods. Alt. 339.

Aberdeen Creek rises in s Moore County and flows sw into Lumber River. Known as Devil's Gut Creek or Devils Creek until early in the twentieth century.

Aberly, community in e Onslow County.

Abernethy, community in w Iredell County.

Abernethy Creek rises in sw Gaston County and flows ne and se in an arc into Crowders Creek.

Abes Mountain, sw Cleveland County near Broad River. Alt. 950.

Abi, community in central Stanly County served by post office, 1894–1907.

Abier Creek rises in se Burke County and flows n into Henry Fork.

Abigails Islands appear on the Smith map, 1624, as the cluster of islands in Pamlico Sound off s Hyde County between Rose Bay and Swanquarter Bay. Now Bell, Great, Judith, Marsh, and Swanquarter Islands, *which see*.

Abingdon Creek rises in sw Caldwell County and flows se into Lower Creek. Sometimes called Greasy Creek. Originally Aventon Creek for Aventon Sherrill, early settler.

Abner, community in n Montgomery County formerly known as Saunder's Hill and served by post office, 1859–98. Took Abner name in 1898. Post office by the name operated until 1953. By tradition named for local principal.

Abraham Bay, small bay in the mouth of Turnagain Bay in n Carteret County.

Abraham's Plains, former district in ne Granville County. It had 62 heads of families in 1790 at the time of the first census. Took its name from the home, built 1766, of Col. Samuel Smith, who had fought in the battle at Abraham's Plains at Quebec, Canada.

Abrams Branch rises in s Transylvania County and flows ne into French Broad River.

Abshers, community in n Wilkes County between Harris Creek and Middle Prong Roaring River.

Academy Crossroads. *See* Nahunta.

Acconeechy. *See* Hillsborough.

Ace Enloe Ridge, ne Swain County in Great

Smoky Mountains National Park, a short spur of Hughes Ridge.

Acme, town in ne Columbus County on Livingston Creek. Known originally as Livingston for the creek. Inc. 1905 as Cronly and named for local landowner; name changed to Acme in 1911 for Acme Manufacturing Company, producer of fertilizer. Produces fertilizer and paper. Alt. 37.

Acorn, community on Jones Pond e Gates County. Sometimes also known as Acorn Hill.

Acorn Hill. *See* Acorn.

Acre, community in n central Beaufort County. Long Acre appears on the Collet map, 1770, as a ridge in the Dismal Swamp of ne Beaufort and s Washington Counties. It supported a post road from Plymouth to Bath. It is called Long Acre on various maps until Kerr, 1882, where it is marked "Long Acre Ridge." Long Acre community grew up at the s end of the ridge, and a post office there from 1883 to 1907 was called Acresville. By 1917 it was called Acre from the railroad name, and the ridge was no longer recorded on maps. Alt. 32.

Acresville. *See* Acre.

Acton, community between Enka and Sulphur Springs, central Buncombe County.

Adair, community in n Gates County.

Adake, community in w Caldwell County on Wilsons Creek.

Adams, community in central Watauga County.

Adams Branch rises in n Cleveland County and flows se into Knob Creek.

Adams Branch rises in s central Transylvania County and flows s into French Broad River.

Adams Creek rises in central Cabarrus County and flows se into Dutch Buffalo Creek. Named for John Adam Blackwelder, an early settler.

Adams Creek rises in central Carteret County and flows n into Craven County, where it enters Neuse River. A canal connecting the headwaters of Adams Creek with Newport River provides access between Newport and Neuse Rivers for the Intracoastal Waterway. For a part of its course, Adams Creek forms the boundary between Carteret and Craven Counties.

Adams Creek rises in e Swain County and flows s between Cooper Creek and Owl Branch into Oconaluftee River.

Adams Crossroads, community in w Wake County between Brier Creek and Sycamore Creek.

Adams Hollow, in nw Swain County extends s on a tributary of Ekaneetlee Creek to Grill Cove.

Adams Mountain, w Caldwell County. Alt. 1,500.

Adams Point, point of land in e Beaufort County on Pamlico River near the mouth of Pungo River. Appears on the Moseley map, 1733.

Adams Run, community in e Henderson County on Big Hungry Creek.

Adams Store, community in n Halifax County.

Adam's Store, community in nw Mecklenburg County served by post office, 1852–55.

Adams Store. *See* Adamsville.

Adamsville, former community in central Wayne County on the e edge of Goldsboro. At one time known as Adams Store. Now within the corporate limits of Goldsboro.

Adcock Creek rises in s Granville County e of Stem and flows e into Tar River. Named for Adcock family.

Addie, community in n Jackson County, on Scotts Creek. Located about 3 mi. ne of town of Sylva. Alt. 2,249.

Addor, town in s Moore County. Inc. 1881 as Keyser; named for an officer of the Raleigh and Augusta Airline Railroad. During World War I, the name became unpopular because of the similarity to "Kaiser." Name changed in October 1918 to Addor in honor of Felix Addor, local resident, who had been killed on the troopship SS *Leviathan* in March. Long inactive in municipal affairs. Served by post office, 1877–1918.

Adelaide, community in s Rockingham County served by post office, 1883–1905.

Adkin Branch rises in n Lenoir County and flows se through the city of Kinston into Neuse River. Named for Robert Atkins, who had land grants there in 1729.

Adkins, community in n Yancey County.

Adkins Branch rises in n Buncombe County and flows nw into Madison County, where it enters Ivy River.

Adkins Falls, rapids in Cape Fear River in central Harnett County e of the town of Lillington and near the confluence of Buies Creek with the river. Mentioned as early as 1819 in a survey of the rivers of North Carolina.

Adlai, community in se Union County served by post office, 1896–1900.

Adley, community in s Wilkes County on the s side of Yadkin River. Home of Capt. John Brown, in which the Wilkes County government was organized in March 1778, is across the river. The W. Kerr Scott Dam is there.

Adoniram, community in n Granville County served by post office, 1889–1906.

Ad Tate Knob, on Utah Mountain in central Haywood County.

Advalorem Branch rises in n Swain County between Jumpup Ridge and Bald Ridge and flows se into Forney Creek.

Advance, town in e Davie County. Known as Shady Grove as early as 1816. When a post office was est. in 1877, a new name was required because there was already a Shady Grove post office in the state. Named because local citizens expected progress with the addition of a post office to the community. Inc. 1893. Alt. 810.

Affinity. *See* Marietta.

Afton, community in sw Warren County between Lees Branch and the head of Richneck Creek. Post office est. 1874 but discontinued in 1919.

Afton Run, stream, rises in n Cabarrus County and flows s into Coddle Creek. Also appears in early documents as Ashton Run and Astin's Run.

Agate, community in nw Hertford County served by post office, 1892–1906.

Aggie Run is formed in nw Beaufort County by the junction of Old Ford Swamp and Snoad Branch. It flows s into Tranters Creek.

Agiqua. *See* French Broad River.

Agnela, community in sw Hertford County.

Aho, community in s Watauga County near the heads of Stony Branch, Moore Branch, and Buffalo Creek. It is said that a group of men gathered to select a name for the community but, being unable to agree on a name, decided that the next word spoken by any one of them would be accepted. After a long silence, B. B. Dougherty arose, stretched, and said "Aho!"

Ahoskie, town in s Hertford County. Post office as early as 1828 named Ahosky Ridge. Inc. 1893. Name of Indian origin, spelled Ahostsky and Ahostskey as early as 1719. Produces apparel, lumber, and wooden containers. Alt. 59.

Ahoskie Creek rises in se Northampton County and flows ne into Hertford County, where it enters Ahoskie Swamp.

Ahoskie Swamp rises in s Hertford County and flows se and ne into Bear Swamp. Appears as Ahotskey Swamp on the Collet map, 1770.

Ahoskie Township, s Hertford County.

Ahosky Ridge. *See* Ahoskie.

Ahostsky, Ahostskey, Ahotskey. *See* Ahoskie.

Ai, community in se Person County served by post office, 1887–1907.

Aiken Branch rises in nw Swain County and flows se into Lake Cheoah.

Aiken Mill Creek rises in s Transylvania County and flows n into French Broad River.

Aiken Mountain, s Transylvania County between Aiken Creek and Carson Creek.

Airbellows, former community in s Alleghany County, now an entrance to the Blue Ridge Parkway. Alt. 3,800.

Air Bellows Gap, on the Alleghany-Wilkes county line. An early road across the Blue Ridge Mountains passed through the gap. Alt. 3,744.

Airlie, community in w Halifax County. Named for plantation home of jurist Walter Clark (1846–1924).

Airlie, community in e New Hanover County on the n side of Bradleys Creek.

Akwetiyi, a spot on Tuckasegee River in nw Jackson County, about 1 mi. nw of town of Dillsboro, and between mouth of Dicks Creek and mouth of Laurel Branch. According to Indian tradition there was a dangerous water monster in the river. The meaning of the name is lost.

Alamance, community in w Alamance County. A post office est. there as early as 1828; cotton mill built in 1837 by E. M. Holt. Alt. 454. Post office name for many years was Allemance.

Alamance Battleground State Historic Site, w central Alamance County. Markers and a museum on the 40-acre site tell the story of the battle on May 16, 1771, in which the North Carolina militia under Gov. William Tryon defeated the Regulators.

Alamance Church, community in se Guilford County. Second Ulster Scots Presbyterian Church in Guilford County, founded in the second half of eighteenth century.

Alamance County was formed in 1849 from Orange County. Located in the central part of the state, it is bounded by Orange, Chatham, Randolph, Guilford, and Caswell Counties. Named for Great Alamance Creek, *which see*, or the Battle of Alamance, May 16, 1771. The name appears as Aramancy River in the writings of William Byrd, 1728. Area: 434 sq. mi. County seat: Graham, with an elevation of 656 ft. Townships, now numbered 1 to 13, were formerly Patterson, Coble, Boon Station, Morton, Faucette, Graham, Albright, Newlin, Thompson, Melville, Pleasant Grove, Burlington, and Haw River. Produces auto parts, tobacco, poultry, dairy and beef cattle, pecans, textiles, electronics, paper boxes, apparel, crushed stone, pyrophyllite, and bricks.

Alamance Creek. *See* Great Alamance Creek.

Alarka, community in s Swain County on Yalaka Creek, from which it takes its name.

Alarka Creek. *See also* Yalaka Creek.

Albans, community in ne Union County.

Albemarle, city and county seat in n central Stanly County. Alt. 505. Post office opened there as Smith's Store in 1826; name changed to Albemarle, 1841. Inc. 1857. Named for George Monck (1608–79), Duke of Albemarle, one of the original Lords Proprietors of Carolina in 1663.

Albemarle, The, or the **Albemarle Section**, a term applied to ne North Carolina. It was the location of the first county, Albemarle County, *which see.*

Albemarle Beach, nw Washington County on Albemarle Sound, w of the town of Mackeys. Formerly known as Reas Beach.

Albemarle City Lake, central Stanly County on Long Creek. Formed in 1915. Covers 75 acres; max. depth 40 ft. Fishing, swimming, boating.

Albemarle County was est. in 1664 in the ne portion of the Lords Proprietors' new province of Carolina covering a poorly defined 1,600 sq. mi. The first governor of the county was appointed in October 1664, and it soon also had a legislature and courts. By 1668 it was divided into Chowan, Currituck, Pasquotank, and Perquimans precincts. The county ceased to exist as a unit of government in Carolina in 1689, when Governor Seth Sothel departed. The next governor had his commission for "that part of our province of Carolina that lyes north and east of Cape feare," which was basically the whole of modern North Carolina.

Albemarle River. *See* Albemarle Sound.

Albemarle Section. *See* Albemarle, The.

Albemarle Sound, ne North Carolina, separated from the Atlantic Ocean by a part of the Outer Banks. Approx. 52 mi. long and 5 to 14 mi. wide. Max. depth 25 ft. Sea level; freshwater not affected by tide. Waters from the Chowan and Roanoke Rivers enter the sound on the w; it drains into Roanoke, Croatan, and Pamlico Sounds. Explored by Ralph Lane, 1586; known as Sea of Rawnocke (Roanoke Sea) in 1609. Appears as Roanoke Sound on the Comberford map, 1657. Known briefly in 1663 as Carolina River and appears as Albemarle River on the Locke map, 1671, and the Blome map, 1672. The John Barnwell map of about 1722 was one of the first to use the name Albemarle Sound. First permanent settlements in North Carolina were made along its n shore. Named after 1663 for George Monck, Duke of Albemarle, one of the Lords Proprietors of Carolina. *See also* Weapemeoc.

Albemarle Township. *See* North Albemarle Township; South Albemarle Township.

Albert Mountain, s Macon County between Bearpen Gap and head of Hurricane Creek. Alt. 5,207.

Albertson, community in ne Duplin County. Earlier known as Holt's Store for Marion Holt. Post office est. there as early as 1828.

Albertson Township, ne Duplin County.

Alberty. *See* Fairview.

Albright Township, former township in s central Alamance County, now township no. 7.

Albright Township, nw Chatham County.

Albrittons, community in w Lenoir County.

Alco, community in e Montgomery County served by post office, 1889–1915.

Alder Branch, community in s Camden County.

Alt. 10. Probably named for the alder bush, which grows in profusion in the vicinity. The branch, called Cross Branch in colonial days, connects a swamp that drains into Pasquotank River to another swamp that drains into North River.

Alderman, community in s Cumberland County served by post office, 1885–1907.

Aldridge Creek rises in sw Person County and flows se into South Flat River.

Ale, community in sw Stokes County served by post office, 1898–1903.

Alert, community in n Franklin County. Alt. 300. Settled about 1900. Name chosen by first postmaster, Thomas D. Farrow.

Alexander, town in n Buncombe County on French Broad River. Settled about 1828; inc. 1905, but long inactive in municipal affairs. Named for James Mitchell Alexander, who built and operated a stagecoach tavern there. Alt. 1,791.

Alexander Branch rises in n Buncombe County near Lovelace Gap and flows nw into Paint Fork.

Alexander County was formed in 1847 from Iredell, Caldwell, and Wilkes Counties. Located in the w central section of the state, it is bounded by Iredell, Catawba, Caldwell, and Wilkes Counties. It was named for William Julius Alexander (1797–1857), member of the General Assembly from Mecklenburg County and Speaker of the House of Commons. Area: 259 sq. mi. County seat: Taylorsville, with an elevation of 1,247 ft. Townships are Ellendale, Gwaltneys, Little River, Millers, Sharpes, Sugar Loaf, Taylorsville, and Wittenburg. Produces cattle, poultry, barley, apples, corn, bearings, textiles, furniture, and paper boxes.

Alexander Knob. *See* Jess Knob.

Alexander Mills, town in s Rutherford County. Inc. 1925. Named for textile mill est. by J. F. Alexander.

Alexander's Store, community in e Mecklenburg County also known as Lawyers and Hornet's Nest. Named for postmaster Guy Alexander.

Alexandriana. *See* Croft.

Alexis, town in n Gaston County. Inc. 1899, but long inactive in municipal affairs. Formerly known as Alex's Cross Roads for a man named Alexander who owned land there.

Alex's Creek. *See* Grants Creek.

Alex's Cross Roads. *See* Alexis.

Alfordston, town authorized to be laid off and inc. 1793 on land of Thomas Matthews. Site approx. 1 mi. s of Carthage, central Moore County. The town was never laid off.

Alfordsville, community in w Robeson County. A post office operated there from 1800 to 1922.

Alfordsville Township, sw Robeson County.

Alfred, community in se Beaufort County. Settled about 1910 and named for Fred R. Alfred, large landowner. Alt. 25.

Alfred Creek rises in ne Cherokee County and flows nw into Taylor Creek.

Algood, community in s Yadkin County served by post office, 1886–1904.

Alkalithia Springs. *See* All Healing Springs.

Allan Branch rises in n Yancey County and flows e into Nolichucky River.

Allan Creek rises in s Duplin County and flows s into Island Creek.

Allan Creek rises in n Madison County and flows se into Little Laurel Creek.

Allanstand, community in n Madison County on Martin Creek. In the days when stock was driven to market, a drover's station or stand was operated there by a man named Allen. Since 1897 site of Allanstand Cottage Industries, handicraft shop est. by Frances Goodrich.

Allbone Branch rises in w Clay County and flows sw into Hiwassee River.

Alleghany County was formed in 1859 from Ashe County. In the nw part of the state, it is bounded by the state of Virginia and by Surry,

Wilkes, and Ashe Counties. The name is a
corruption of the Delaware Indian name for
the Allegheny and Ohio Rivers and is said to
have meant "a fine stream." Area: 230 sq. mi.
County seat: Sparta, with an elevation of 2,939
ft. Townships are Cherry Lane, Cranberry,
Gap Civil, Glade Creek, Piney Creek, Prathers
Creek, and Whitehead. Produces corn, barley,
apples, hay, pipes, turkeys, Christmas trees,
Irish potatoes, dairy products, livestock,
textiles, apparel, and crushed stone. There
are manganese and granite deposits in the
county.

Alleghany Township, s Davidson County.

Allegheny, community n Madison County on
Shelton Laurel Creek.

Allegheny Mountains. *See* Appalachian
Mountains.

Allemance. *See* Alamance.

Allen, community in ne Mecklenburg
County.

Allen Branch rises in n Cherokee County and
flows se into Davis Creek.

Allen Branch rises in ne Cherokee County and
flows s into Junaluska Creek.

Allen Branch rises in central Henderson County
and flows nw into Clear Creek.

Allen Branch rises in n Macon County and flows
w into Burningtown Creek.

Allen Branch. *See* Bill Allen Branch.

Allen Creek rises in se Brunswick County and
flows ne into McKenzie Pond, *which see*. It is
drained by Lilliput Creek. Named for Eleazer
Allen (1692–1750), founder of Lilliput Plantation. Name appears on the MacRae map,
1833. *See also* Lilliput Creek.

Allen Creek rises in s Catawba County and flows
nw into Maiden Creek.

Allen Creek rises in s Haywood County and flows
ne into Richland Creek. Named for Allen
family, pioneer settlers in Haywood County,
approx. 1812.

Allendale Township, se Hoke County.

Allen Gap, n Cherokee County near the headwaters of Allen Branch.

Allen Mountain, ne Buncombe County.

Allen Mountain, in s Macon County between
Ball Creek and Coweeta Creek.

Allens Branch rises in n Jackson County and
flows se into Scott Creek.

Allens Branch rises in e Orange County and
flows ne into New Hope Creek.

Allens Creek rises in e Haywood County and
flows nw into Pigeon River. Named for Allen
family, pioneer settlers in Haywood County,
approx. 1812.

Allen's Creek. *See* Lilliput Creek.

Allen's Crossroads, community in s Granville
County w of Hester Station.

Allen's Crossroads, community in sw Johnston
County.

Allen's Fall. *See* Ramseur.

Allens Level, community in s Person County.

Allensville, community in e Person County.
Formerly known as Trilby.

Allensville Township, e central Person County.

Allenton, community in e Robeson County.
Alt. 131. Settled about 1868. Named for
W. H. Allen, trainmaster. Bear Bay, post office
1 mi. e, abandoned with the development of
Allenton.

Allenton, former town in se Stanly County on
Pee Dee River. Laid off in 1-acre lots on an 85-
acre tract on the lands of William and James
Allen and John Davison in 1799. A post office
operated there from 1813 to 1831; Allenton
ferry operated there into the twentieth century. Site now under waters of Lake Tillery.

Allents Cove Branch rises in e Transylvania
County and flows n into Crab Creek.

All Healing Springs, community in w Alexander
County. Springs discovered in 1882 by Milt
Milstead and developed as a resort that was
popular as late as 1911. Named for supposed
healing qualities of water; known also as
Alkalithia Springs. Alt. 1,225.

All Healing Springs, community in sw Gaston
County near the ne slope of Crowders Mountain. A health resort flourished there in the
late nineteenth and early twentieth centuries
because of the mineral springs.

All Healing Springs. *See* Crumpler.

Alliance, community in n Pamlico County, in
the center of an area that produces potatoes
and tobacco. Settled in the 1890s and named
for the Farmers' Alliance movement. Former
railroad station there was known as West
Alliance.

Alliby Creek. *See* Ellerbee Creek.

Alligator, farming and grazing community in
ne Tyrrell County on the Big Savanna near
Alligator Creek.

Alligator Bay, swamp in nw Brunswick County.
A part of Green Swamp, *which see*.

Alligator Bay, in s Onslow County at the e end of Stump Sound.

Alligator Creek, a tidal stream on Eagles Island in e Brunswick County. It flows s into the Cape Fear River.

Alligator Creek rises in e central Camden County and flows e into North River.

Alligator Creek rises in central Pamlico County and flows n into Bay River.

Alligator Creek rises in n Tyrrell County and flows se and ne into the mouth of Alligator River. Appears on the Moseley map, 1733.

Alligator Dismal Swamp. *See* Great Alegator Dismal Swamp.

Alligator Lake, a natural lake in n Hyde County, 3½ mi. in diameter, almost a perfect circle. Not shown on the Collet map, 1770, or the Mouzon map, 1775; a map in *The Political Magazine* (November 1780) shows an enlarged area at the head of Alligator River. Not until 1812, on a map published in Boston, is the lake clearly shown. Within a few years it was being labeled Alligator Lake on maps. The lake now is filled by swamp drainage; its two outlets are the New Lake Fork of Alligator River and a drainage ditch leading into Pungo River. Alligator Lake, known locally as New Lake, covers approx. 6,000 acres and is 6 to 7 ft. at its deepest.

Alligator Pond, built beside McClendon's Creek 2 mi. s of Carthage, Moore County. 1 acre.

Alligator River rises in central Hyde County and flows e and n to the Hyde-Tyrrell county line, se to the Dare-Tyrrell county line, and n into Albemarle Sound. In part, the Intracoastal Waterway follows the Alligator River. Appears as Layn Flu[ve] on the Smith map, 1624, undoubtedly named for Ralph Lane, governor of the first Roanoke colony. Appears as Alligator River on the Ogilby map, 1671.

Alligator River Bridge. *See* East Lake Landing; Sandy Point.

Alligator Swamp rises in nw Brunswick County and flows n into Juniper Creek.

Alligator Township, ne Tyrrell County.

Alligoods, community in central Beaufort County. Alt. 37.

Allison, community in w central Caswell County. A post office operated there from 1886 to 1909.

Allison Creek rises in s Macon County and flows ne into Cartoogechaye Creek.

Allison Creek rises in s central Transylvania County, just s of Elk Lodge Mountain, and flows se into French Broad River.

Allman Branch rises in n Buncombe County and flows nw into Madison County, where it enters French Broad River.

Allman Branch rises in s Madison County and flows nw into French Broad River.

Allmon Branch rises in ne Cherokee County and flows se into Morris Creek.

Allmon Creek rises in n Cherokee County in the Snowbird Mountains and flows s into Hyatt Creek.

Allreds, community in ne Montgomery County served by post office, 1880–1953. Took its name from Allred family, operators of gristmill on Little River.

Alma. *See* Daystrom.

Almond, community in w Swain County on Little Tennessee River. Inc. 1905, but no longer active in municipal affairs. Named for Bud Almond, donor of original town site. Alt. 1,613.

Almond Township, w Stanly County.

Alora, community in e Buncombe County served by post office, 1900–1906.

Alpha, community in n Rowan County served by post office, 1894–1904.

Alpine, community in s Sampson County served by post office, 1894–1915.

Alspaugh, community in central Forsyth County.

Alston, community in central Warren County. Post office est. there in 1903 but discontinued in 1918.

Altamahaw, community in w Alamance County on Haw River. Founded about 1860 with the establishment of a cotton gin there. Later the site of several textile mills. The community of Ossipee lies directly s. Name of Indian origin, meaning unknown.

Altamont, community in s Avery County. Name means high mountain. Thomas Wolfe adopted name for his fictitious Asheville in *Look Homeward, Angel* (1929).

Altamont Township, s Avery County.

Altan, community in s central Union County. Served by post office from 1890 to 1904.

Altapass, community in se Mitchell County on Little Rose Creek. Alt. 2,623.

Alto. *See* Lasker.

Alum Knob, between Caney Fork and Tuckasegee River in central Jackson County.

Alum Knob, n Madison County between Alum Ridge and Shelton Laurel Creek.

Alum Ridge, nw Madison County parallel to Pounding Mill Branch.

Alum Spring, mineral waters in w Onslow County near Southwest Creek.

Aman's Store. *See* Verona.

Amantha, community on Cover Creek in w Watauga County. Settled 1870. First known as McBrides Mill for Hiram McBride, first postmaster; post office by that name, 1869–87. Name later changed to honor Amantha Combs, local resident; post office by that name, 1887–1937.

Amboy, community in n Chowan County served by post office, 1880–1904.

Amelia, community in nw Alleghany County.

Ames Turnout. *See* Wingate.

Amherst, community in s central Caldwell County. Site of Amherst Academy in nineteenth century, named by Robert Logan Patton, principal, for Amherst College in Massachusetts, of which he was a graduate.

Amherst. *See* Roberson Store.

Amity Hill, community in s Iredell County.

Ammon, community in nw Bladen County.

Ammon Bottom, e Cherokee County between Elliott Branch and Piper Branch.

Ammon Knob, on the Cherokee-Clay county line in the Valley River Mountains.

Ammons Branch rises in se Macon County and flows se into Chattooga River.

Ammons Branch rises in se Macon County and flows sw into Cullasaja River.

Ammons Branch rises in e Macon County and flow sw into Rabbit Creek.

Ammons Branch rises in s Madison County and flows w into Walnut Creek.

Ammons Branch rises in w Swain County and flows e into Little Tennessee River.

Ammons Knob, s Macon County between the head of Hayes Mill Creek and Nickajack Creek. Alt. 3,916.

Amorita, community in n Alleghany County served by post office, 1899–1906.

Amos Creek rises in nw Caldwell County and flows s into Mulberry Creek. Probably named for Amos Green, a nineteenth-century resident of the area.

Amos Creek rises in ne Madison County and flows sw into Spillcorn Creek.

Amos Mill Pond. *See* Weldons Millpond.

Amos Plott Balsam. *See* Waterrock Knob.

Amour. *See* Armour.

Amy, community in n central Ashe County.

Añadales Chase, an otherwise unidentified designation appearing on the Smith map, 1624, shown between what is now Tar and Roanoke Rivers, nw of the head of Pungo River, probably in what is now n Pitt and Martin Counties.

Anderson, community in s central Caswell County, known earlier as Anderson's Store. A post office was operated there during the approx. period 1820 to 1905.

Anderson Branch rises in w Clay County and flows nw into Hiwassee River.

Anderson Branch rises in s Graham County and flows ne into Tulula Creek.

Anderson Branch rises in sw Macon County and flows ne into Lowery Creek.

Anderson Branch rises in sw Madison County and flows ne into French Broad River.

Anderson Cove, valley through which Shelton Branch flows in n Buncombe County.

Anderson Cove Branch rises in w Madison County and flows nw into Puncheon Camp Branch.

Anderson Creek rises in s Cabarrus County and flows e into Rocky River. Appears on the Mac-Rae map, 1833.

Anderson Creek rises in a bend of Hiwassee River below the Hiwassee Dam in w Cherokee County and flows sw into Hiwassee River.

Anderson Creek rises in s Craven County and flows e into the mouth of Slocum Creek.

Anderson Creek rises in s Harnett County and flows se into Little River. Named for Thomas Anderson, an early settler.

Anderson Creek rises in e Haywood County and flows ne into Burnett Creek.

Anderson Creek rises in n Lincoln County and flows se into Killian Creek.

Anderson Creek Township, s Harnett County.

Anderson Mountain, se Catawba County. Alt. 1,547.

Anderson Mountain, e Haywood County between the headwaters of Stamey Cove Branch and Sally Haines Branch.

Andersons Crossroads, community in n Halifax County.

Anderson's Mountain, ne Lincoln County. Also known as Little Mountain.

Anderson's Store. *See* Anderson.

Anderson Swamp Creek rises in central Vance County and flows n into Kerr Lake.

Anderson Township, s central Caswell County.

Andreas Branch rises in n central Swain County and flows w into Noland Creek.

Andrews, town in ne Cherokee County. Inc. 1905. First known as Valley Town, a name still applied to an adjacent community. Renamed for Alexander Boyd Andrews (1841–1915), leader in the development of the Western North Carolina Railroad. Alt. 1,825. Produces textiles and apparel.

Andrews Bald, n Swain County in Great Smoky Mountains National Park between Forney Creek and Salola Branch. Alt. 5,860.

Andrews Geyser, sw McDowell County, in Horseshoe Bend of the Southern Railway, was constructed in the 1880s, restored in 1911 and 1975, as a tribute to Col. Alexander Boyd Andrews, builder of the Western North Carolina Railroad into Asheville. Water from a higher mountain lake about 2 mi. away is piped to the site. Natural pressure forces the water upward in a 100-ft. jet from the center of a stone fountain. Formerly passenger trains stopped there for 20 minutes to enable those interested to visit the site.

Andy, community in n Polk County on the head of Bullin Creek.

Andy Branch rises in nw Haywood County in Great Smoky Mountains and flows about 2 mi. se to join Woody Branch, which then joins Conrad Creek in forming Little Cataloochee Creek. Named for Andy Bennett, a former homeowner in the area.

Andy Gap, s Macon County between Cedar Cliff Mountain and Mulberry Gap.

Angelico Gap, sw Cherokee County at the sw end of Angelico Mountain.

Angelico Mountain, sw Cherokee County extending ne from Angelico Gap to Bowmans Gap. *See also* Rocky Face.

Angeline, community in n Henderson County between McDowell Creek and North Fork.

Angel Mountain, sw Macon County between Bryson Branch and Moore Creek.

Angier, town in n Harnett County. Inc. 1901. Named for Col. John C. Angier, one of the town's founders. Produces apparel. Alt. 301.

Angle, community in se Wayne County served by post office, 1888–1902.

Anglin Branch rises in w Yancey County and flows se into Jacks Creek. Named for Manon Anglin, an early settler.

Anglin Knob, central Yancey County near the head of Bailey Branch.

Anglins Mill, community in nw Rockingham County. Named for Anglin family, members of which operated gristmill on Mayo River in mid-eighteenth century.

Angola, community in w Onslow County.

Angola. *See* Maple Hill.

Angola Bay, pocosin in s Duplin and n Pender Counties. Angola Bay Game Preserve there is maintained by the N.C. Wildlife Resources Commission; bear, deer, and other wildlife abound. *See also* Holly Shelter Bay.

Angola Creek rises in Angola Bay in ne Pender County and flows s into Holly Shelter Creek.

Anna, community in central Alleghany County served by post office, 1890–1921.

Annandale, community in se Pender County. Alt. 44.

Annie Mountain, e Henderson County s of Bradley Mountain. Alt. 2,731.

Ann Mountain, on a branch of Cabin Creek in s Henderson County.

Anson County was formed in 1750 from Bladen County. In the s central section of the state, it is bounded by the state of South Carolina and by Union, Stanly, and Richmond Counties. It was named for George Anson, Lord Anson (1697–1762), a British admiral who, for a number of years, was assigned to protect the commerce of the Carolina coast from pirates. Area: 536 sq. mi. County seat: Wadesboro, with an elevation of 423 ft. Townships are Ansonville, Burnsville, Gulledge, Lanesboro, Lilesville, Morven, Wadesboro, and White Store. Produces lumber, bricks, soybeans, oats, corn, milo, cotton, broilers, turkeys, hosiery, textiles, and wooden boxes. Sand, gravel, and crushed stone are also produced, and there are deposits of granite, sandstone, and shale for brick.

Ansonville, town in n central Anson County. Alt. 324. Settled 1844, named in 1857 for the county. Inc. 1885. Carolina Female College, 1850–67, est. by local planters and later operated by the Methodist Church, was there.

Ansonville Township, n central Anson County.

Anthony Bolick Branch rises in nw Caldwell County on nw slopes of Rocky Knob and flows w into Johns River.

Anthony Branch rises in n Swain County and flows s into Proctor Creek.

Anthony Branch. *See* Auntery Branch.

Anthony Creek rises in e Avery County and flows se into Caldwell County, where it enters Johns River.

Anthony Creek rises in central Catawba County and flows sw into Clark Creek.

Anthony Creek rises in s central Gaston County, about 2 mi. se of community of South Gastonia, and flows n through Robinwood Lake and empties into Catawba Creek.

Anthony Mountain, s central Avery County.

Anthony's Creek rises in nw Caldwell County and se Avery County and flows se into Johns River.

Antioch, community in s Hoke County on Raft Swamp.

Antioch Township, s Hoke County.

Antioch Township, e Wilkes County.

Antler, community in central Moore County served by post office, 1891–1907.

Antone. *See* Concord.

Apalachia Lake, nw Cherokee County on Hiwassee River at the Tennessee state line. Formed by Tennessee Valley Authority dam completed in 1943. Covers 1,123 acres, max. depth 120 ft., approx. 10 mi. long. Spelling with single *p* contrary to accepted manner.

Apex, town in w Wake County on the head of Beaver Creek. Inc. 1873. Named because it was supposed to be the highest point on the railroad between Richmond, Va., and Jacksonville, Fla. When first settled, the area was an important producer of turpentine and rosin. The town now produces apparel, plywood, and chemicals.

Appalachian Creek rises in nw Rutherford County and flows ne into Broad River.

Appalachian Mountains include all of the e mountains of the United States from Alabama to northern Maine. The name was given by Spaniards under Hernando De Soto in 1539 for the Apalachee Indians, whose name meant "people on the other side" (presumably of a river). In North Carolina the Blue Ridge, Black Mountains, and Great Smoky Mountains are part of the Appalachian Mountains. At one time, both Appalachian and Allegheny were names applied to the range from Georgia to New York, but a study by Arnold Guyot, "On the Appalachian Mountain System," published in 1861, firmly established the present name. *See also* Mountain Region.

Appalachian Trail, a marked footpath extending approx. 2,050 mi. from Maine to Georgia. In North Carolina approx. 70 of the 200 mi. within the state cross the crest of the Great Smoky Mountains. The highest point on the trail is Clingmans Dome, with an alt. of 6,642 ft. Proposed in 1921 and completed in 1937, it has been described as the longest marked footpath in the world.

Appie, community in n Greene County. Named about 1907 for Mrs. Appie (Apelia?) Bynum, local resident.

Apple Grove, community in nw Ashe County. Alt. 3,137.

Appletree, community in nw Greene County served by post office, 1886–98. Later known as Lindell, *which see.*

Appletree Branch rises in nw Macon County and flows sw into Queens Creek.

Appletree Branch rises in w Macon County and flows se into Nantahala River.

Appletree Swamp rises in ne Wayne County and flows se into Nahunta Swamp in Greene County. The name appears in local records prior to 1750.

Applewhite, community in e Columbus County served by post office, 1892–1907.

Aquadale, community in s Stanly County. Inc. 1943; charter repealed 1945. Named by local resident: *aqua* (water) and *dale* (valley). Many springs in the area.

Aquascogoc appears on the White map, 1585, as an Indian village near the head of Pungo River estuary, not far from either modern Scranton in Hyde County or Belhaven in Beaufort County.

Aquascog River. *See* Whipping Creek.

Aquone, community in w Macon County on Nantahala River. Alt. 2,950. Settled on the site of Fort Scott, one of the stockades where Cherokee Indians were housed before being removed to Oklahoma, 1838. Name believed to be a corruption of *egwanul'ti* (by the river).

Arabi, community in n Robeson County served by post office, July–November 1900.

Arabia, community in se Hoke County.

Arabia, nickname applied about 1860 to the desolate Outer Banks of North Carolina.

Aramancy River. *See* Great Alamance Creek.

Aramuskeet, described in 1758 as a part of Hyde County: "That Part of the County is a Peninsula, or rather an Island for three Parts of the Year, and can be entered by foot Passengers only in the Height of Summer, and that with great Difficulty for several Miles together. It was formerly an Indian Settlement, and there are at present about 12 Families of Indians, who live dispersed among the Whites, and dress and live like them, but they have still one whom they call the King among them." *See also* Aromuskek Marshes; Lake Mattamuskeet.

Arapahoe, town in s Pamlico County, inc. 1920. Post office est. 1886. Said to have been named for a local racehorse.

Ararat, community in e Surry County on Ararat River. Named for the river. Alt. 898.

Ararat River rises in Virginia and flows s across Surry County into Yadkin River. Appears on the Collet map, 1770. Named for the biblical Mount Ararat.

Arba, community in s Greene County. Named for the biblical name Kirjatharba (Joshua 14:15).

Arbuckle, community in e Yancey County between North Toe and South Toe Rivers near their junction. A former post office, Dobag [Doe Bag], served the area.

Arcadia, community in n Davidson County.

Arcadia Township, nw Davidson County.

Archdale, town in se Cleveland County. Alt. 943. Settled in the eighteenth century and named for Quaker John Archdale, governor of Carolina, 1694–96.

Archdale, town in nw Randolph County. Settled about 1786 by Quakers. Inc. 1874 as Bush Hill; named for the fact that the area was originally covered with a growth of low bushes. Name changed to Archdale, 1887, in honor of John Archdale (1642?–1717), a Quaker, one of the Lords Proprietors of Carolina, and governor, 1694–96. Original post office was ½ mi. from present site and named Bloomington until moved to Bush Hill in 1865. Archdale is now a residential suburb of High Point.

Archdale County was formed before 1696 "on Pampticoe River without the Bounds of the County of Albemarle." It was named for John Archdale (1642?–1717), governor of Carolina, 1694–96. The precinct of Pampticoe was a part of Archdale County in 1696, at which time it became the County of Bath. The name of Archdale County was changed to Craven, *which see*, about 1712.

Archdale Precinct was formed from Bath County on December 3, 1705, and named in honor of John Archdale (1642?–1717), governor of Carolina, 1694–96. The name was changed about 1712 to Craven County, *which see*.

Archer Lodge, community in n Johnston County.

Arch Hill, a mountain in n Macon County between Tellico Creek and Bird Branch.

Archies Creek rises in ne Surry County and flows e into Stokes County, where it enters Dan River.

Archies Knob, nw Stokes County near Dan River.

Archie's Point, point of land extending from Bogue Banks into Bogue Sound, sw Carteret County. Named for Archibald Smith. Sometimes also called Point of Woods.

Arch Ridge, se Clay County, extends s in arc from Vineyard Mountain to Shooting Creek.

Arcola, community in se Warren County e of Fishing Creek. Post office est. there in 1849, but discontinued in 1954.

Arcot, community in central Sampson County served by post office, 1894–1902.

Arden, town in s Buncombe County. Settled about 1840. Inc. 1883, but long inactive in municipal affairs. Known first as Shufordsville. Renamed for the Forest of Arden in Shakespeare's play *As You Like It*. Alt. 2,225.

Ardreys, community in s Mecklenburg County served by post office, 1898–1902.

Ardulusa, community on Rockfish Creek in s Cumberland County.

Arenuse Creek consists of two branches, both rising in central Camden County and flowing generally sw into Pasquotank River. The branches come together in such a fashion that they seem to form an arrow nose. The fact was noted by the Indians, and the white settlers merely translated their word for "arrownose" when they gave the creek its present name. The present name appears in records as early as 1694. To distinguish between the two branches, local inhabitants sometimes refer to First Milldam (nearest the county seat) and Second Milldam since water mills existed on each.

Argo, former town in n Nash County on Short Swamp Branch. Inc. 1889. Nearby Argo Gold Mine worked from about 1850 until about 1920. Both town and mine are now abandoned.

Argura, community in e central Jackson County on Gladie Creek. Alt. 3,291.

Argyle, former community on Little Rockfish Creek in ne Hoke County. Site now within the Fort Bragg Military Reservation. Named for Argyll, Scotland.

Arington Branch rises in n Madison County and flows sw into West Fork [Bull Creek].

Arlington, community in w Harnett County between the Cape Fear River and Upper Little River.

Arlington, town in ne Mecklenburg County on Clear Creek. Inc. 1930, but long inactive in municipal affairs.

Arlington, town in nw Yadkin County. Chartered 1893; long inactive in municipal affairs and rechartered 1930. Merged with Jonesville, 2001.

Arlington. *See* Coinjock.

Arlington Branch rises in s Swain County and flows nw into Tuckasegee River.

Arm, The, an extension of Big Bald Mountain on the line dividing Unicoi County, Tenn., from Madison and Yancey Counties, N.C.

Armour, community in ne Columbus County. Named Amour (French, "love") for the Love family in the area, but through the years the spelling was changed.

Armstrong, former community in nw McDowell County on Threemile Creek. With the establishment of Little Switzerland, *which see*, 2 mi. nw, the community began to decline.

Armstrong Branch rises in s Lincoln County and flows ne into Dellinger Branch.

Armstrong Creek rises in nw McDowell County and flows e into North Fork [Catawba River].

Arnold, community in w Davidson County near the headwaters of Swearing Creek.

Arnold Branch rises in e Macon County and flows sw into Cullasaja River.

Arnold Knob, se Mitchell County between North Toe River and Rose Creek.

Arnt, formerly a small community and site of Arnt Ferry over the Catawba River, ne Catawba County. Site now covered by waters of Lookout Shoals Lake.

Aromuskek Marshes appear on the Ogilby map, 1671, in the e section of present Hyde County between Lake Mattamuskeet and Pamlico Sound. *See also* Aramuskeet.

Arp Gap, w Cherokee County between Bowman Gap and Wolfpen Gap. Alt. approx. 2,750.

Arrowhead Branch rises in w Macon County and flows sw into Nantahala Lake.

Arrowwood Creek rises in w Macon County and flows se into Wayah Creek.

Arrwood Mill, community in e Cherokee County on Slow Creek.

Artesia, community in central Columbus County.

Arthur. *See* Bellarthur.

Arthurs Creek rises in nw Northampton County and flows s into Roanoke River.

Arthur Township, w central Pitt County, formerly known as Beaver Dam Township.

Art Stewart Ridge, w Graham County n of Wright Creek and parallel to it. Named for an early settler who came from Georgia.

Arturs Knob, e Mitchell County between Snow Creek and Bear Creek. Alt. 3,695. Named for Arthur ("Artur") McFalls (died 1839), who fought as a Tory at the Battle of Kings Mountain in 1780 but afterward joined the Americans. He lived alone for many years on the mountain. Sometimes erroneously called Otters Knob.

Arundells Island. *See* Croatamung.

Asa, community in central Greene County served by post office, March–September 1900.

Asa Cove, s Macon County between Messer Ridge and Betty Creek.

Asahel Creek rises in ne Davidson County and flows se into Abbotts Creek.

Asbury, community in ne Montgomery County. Alt. 624. Auman's Hill post office est. there, 1850. Name of the community changed to Asbury in 1887 for a local Methodist church.

Asbury, community in nw Stokes County between Dan River and Big Creek. Alt. 1,279.

Asbury, community in w Wake County on the

head of Richland Creek. Settled 1900. Named by its founder, Calvin Bridgers, for Asbury, England. Alt. 484.

Asbury Mountain, ne Alexander County. Alt. 1,820. Probably named for local Asbury family, which settled near the head of Snow Creek. Locally known as Big Mountain.

Asey Hole, deep section of White Oak River in e Onslow County near the mouth of Freemans Creek. Named for an old man, Asa Moore, who fell into the river there.

Asgini Ridge, nw Swain County extending as a short spur se from the Great Smoky Mountain ridge centering near lat. 35°32′50″ N., long. 83°46′20″ W.

Ash, community in w Brunswick County.

Ash Bearpen Knob, sw Watauga County on the head of Moodys Mill Creek.

Ash Branch rises in w Jackson County and flows ne into Tuckasegee River.

Ashby Harbor, a bay on the w shore of Roanoke Island, e Dare County, in the waters of Croatan Sound. Site of landing by troops of Union general Ambrose Burnside, February 7, 1862.

Ash Cove, ne Cherokee County in the Snowbird Mountains.

Ash Cove Creek rises in ne Cherokee County and flows sw into Gipp Creek.

Asheboro, town and county seat, central Randolph County. Inc. 1796. Named for Samuel Ashe (1725–1813), governor of North Carolina, 1795–98. Produces hosiery, apparel, textiles, blankets, batteries, furniture, toys, and shoes. Alt. 879.

Asheboro South, unincorporated outskirts of Asheboro, central Randolph County.

Asheboro Township, central Randolph County.

Asheboro West, unincorporated outskirts of Asheboro, central Randolph County. A portion of the area was taken into the town of Asheboro late in 1960 after the census had been taken.

Ashe County was formed in 1799 from Wilkes County. In the nw corner of the state, it is bounded by the states of Tennessee and Virginia and by Alleghany, Wilkes, and Watauga Counties. It was named for Samuel Ashe (1725–1813), Revolutionary patriot, superior court judge, and governor of the state (1795–98). Area: 427 sq. mi. County seat: Jefferson, with an elevation of 2,900 ft. Townships are Chestnut Hill, Clifton, Creston, Elk, Grassy Creek, Helton, Horse Creek, Hurricane, Jefferson, Laurel, North Fork, Obids, Oldfields, Peak Creek, Pine Swamp, Piney Creek, Pond Mountain, Walnut Hill, and West Jefferson. Produces corn, tobacco, Christmas trees, rubber products, wood products, hay, dairy livestock, chemicals, textiles, hosiery, furniture, and electronics. Home to a cheese plant in West Jefferson. Copper and mica are mineral products, and the county has a potential for the production of stone, iron ore, and gem stones.

Ashe Creek rises in e Pender County in Holly Shelter Bay and flows w into Northeast Cape Fear River. Appears as Ashes Mill on the Price map, 1808, and as Ashe's Mill Creek on the MacRae map, 1833. Exeter, *which see*, was nearby.

Ashe Gap, on the Mitchell County, N.C.–Carter County, Tenn., line.

Ashes Creek. *See* Upper Broad Creek.

Ashe's Island, s Onslow County in Stump Sound on the s side of Spicers Bay, a tidal-marsh and coastal-beach island approx. 1¼ mi. long. Named for John Baptista Ashe (1748–1802).

Ashe's Mill Creek. *See* Ashe Creek; Exeter.

Asheville, city and county seat, central Buncombe County on French Broad River. Settled about 1792; inc. 1797. First called Morristown, probably for William Morrison, who cast the deciding vote as one of the commissioners to select a site for the courthouse in 1792. Named Asheville for Samuel Ashe, governor of North Carolina (1795–98). As the city grew, its boundaries were extended to take in a number of adjacent areas, including Kenilworth, Biltmore, Montford, Ramoth (or Woolsey), Sunset Park, Victoria, and West Asheville. Historically a tourist and health resort, the city experienced a renaissance as bohemian mecca in late twentieth century. Alt. 2,216. University of North Carolina at Asheville n of downtown. Industry: publishing, software, apparel electronics, furniture, handicrafts, metalwork.

Asheville Township, central Buncombe County.

Ash Flat Branch rises in s Macon County and flows n into Allison Creek.

Ashford, community in n McDowell County on North Fork [Catawba River]. Alt. 1,762.

Ash Hill, community in e Surry County served by post office, 1881–1907.

Ash Knob, central Clay County between Downing and Licklog Creeks.

Ashland, community in w Ashe County. Est. 1886 and known as Solitude until 1914, when the name was changed to Ashland for the county. Alt. approx. 3,000.

Ashland, community in sw Caswell County. A post office operated there from 1878 to 1915.

Ashley, community in nw Ashe County served by post office, 1888–1905.

Ashley Branch rises in s Buncombe County and flows ne into French Broad River.

Ashley Heights, community in w Hoke County. Alt. 438.

Ashmont, community in w Hoke County.

Ashpole. *See* Fairmont.

Ashpole Swamp, s Robeson County between Ashpole Swamp (stream) and Lumber River.

Ashpole Swamp rises in w Robeson County and flows se and sw into South Carolina.

Ashton, community in s Pender County. Named for a member of the Ashe family who was a railroad official.

Ashton Run. *See* Afton Run.

Ashturn Branch rises in ne Cherokee County and flows n into Junaluska Creek.

Ashwood, s Bladen County, was the home of William Bartram, uncle of the naturalist of the same name. The naturalist lived there 1761–65 and 1770–72. It was called Ashwood by John Baptista Ashe, a previous owner, as early as 1731. It was on the right bank of Cape Fear River, approx. 5 mi. ne of Council. Only a cellar excavation and some chimney brick remain to mark the site.

Ashwood, community in s Pamlico County. Named for the wood burned by a railroad that formerly ran through the community.

Ashworth, community in ne Rockingham County served by post office, 1901–22. Was near Chandler's Mill on Wolf Island Creek.

Ashworth Creek rises in se Buncombe County near Henderson County line and flows nw into Cane Creek.

Ashworth Creek rises in sw Cleveland County and flows n into Broad River.

Askew. *See* Union.

Askew Ridge, s Avery County.

Askewville, town in central Bertie County. Settled in 1890s, named for local family. Alt. 64. Inc. 1951.

Askins, community in ne Craven County. Named for Alec Askins, on whose land a former post office was built. Alt. 18. *See also* Ernul.

Askins Creek, a cove on the Pamlico County side of s Hatteras Island, s Dare County, below the community of Avon.

Aspen, community in e Warren County. Post office est. there in 1908 but discontinued in 1915.

Aspen Grove. *See* Wittys Crossroads.

Assembly. *See* General Assembly.

Assembly Lake, se Buncombe County at Ridgecrest, Baptist assembly grounds, on a tributary of Swannanoa River.

Astin's Run. *See* Afton Run.

Atfa, community in w Johnston County served by post office, 1893–1903.

Athens, community in ne Robeson County served by post office, 1880–1903.

Atherton. *See* Jackson.

Athlone. *See* Bowlens Creek.

Atkin River. *See* Yadkin River.

Atkins Bank. *See* Kinston.

Atkinson, town in w Pender County. Laid out on the lands of W. H. Lewis in 1883 (the year after a station had been est. there on the railroad) and known as Lewis. Inc. 1909 as Atkinson, named for an engineer whose work sped the completion of the railroad. Alt. 65.

Atkinson Pond, approx. 1 mi. long, on Moccasin Creek in se Johnston County.

Atlantic, town in ne Carteret County, inc. 1905, but not now active in municipal affairs. Alt. 15. Settled about 1740; called Hunting Quarters until 1890. Post office est. 1880.

Atlantic Beach, town on the e end of Bogue Banks on the Atlantic Ocean. Inc. 1937.

Atlantic Ocean forms the e boundary of North Carolina. The state has a shoreline of 328 mi.

Atlantic Township, on Core Sound in e Carteret County. Formerly known as Hunting Quarters Township.

Atlantic Township, e Dare County on the Outer Banks.

Atlee, community in e Rockingham County served by post office, 1889–1903.

Atoah Creek rises in s Graham County and flows ne into Long Creek.

Atoah Gap, in s Graham County between Eller Cove and the headwaters of Atoah Creek.

Attakulla. *See* Mount Mitchell.

Atwell Township, sw Rowan County.

Atwood, community in s Forsyth County.

Auberry, community in w Clay County on Hiwassee River.

Auburn, community in e Wake County. Alt. 340.

Augerhole Branch rises in w Swain County and flows sw into Fontana Lake.

Aughburn. *See* Ogburn.

Augusta, community in se Davie County served by post office, 1890–1902.

Aulander, town in nw Bertie County. In existence before the Civil War as Harmon's Crossroads. Inc. as Aulander in 1885. Alt. 73. The intended name was Orlando, but a phonetic spelling was used to distinguish it from Orlando, Fla. Another story is that a local sawmill operator, Andrew J. Dunning, had the town named for himself, i.e. "Ole Ander."

Aumans Crossroads, community in s Randolph County.

Auman's Hill. *See* Asbury.

Auntery Branch, also known as Anthony Branch, rises in se Graham County and flows sw into Tulula Creek. Named for Jack Anthony.

Aurelian Springs, community in w Halifax County. Named aurelian (golden) because the water from the seven springs there was believed to be a cure-all. A popular recreation area of the late nineteenth century.

Aurora, town in se Beaufort County. Alt. 25. Inc. 1880. Named for a former county newspaper, *Aurora Borealis*. Originally a settlement of free African Americans called Betty Town existed there.

Ausbon, community in w Washington County. Alt. 41. Named for C. V. M. Ausbon, clerk of Superior Court, 1906–42.

Austin, community in ne Wilkes County near the headwaters of Little Elkin River.

Austin Creek rises in n central Caldwell County and flows s into Warrior Creek. Named for Thomas J. Austin, who settled nearby during the Civil War.

Austin Creek rises in e Wake County and flows sw into Smiths Creek. Shown on 1870 map as Millstone Creek.

Austin Mountain, w Yancey County near the head of Dryspring Branch.

Austins Mill, community in n Scotland County.

Auston Branch rises in s Madison County and flows s into Morrow Branch.

Autreys Creek Township. *See* Otter Creek Township.

Autro, community in w Cleveland County served by post office, 1883–1904.

Autryville, town in w Sampson County. Settled about 1888; inc. 1891. Named for James L. Autry, who erected stores and est. a trading center there. Alt. 108.

Avalon, former community in w Rockingham County. Built about 1899 as a mill village on the Mayo River. On June 11, 1911, the mill was destroyed by fire, and soon afterward the 60 or so houses in Avalon, a Moravian church, a school, and a company store were moved on horse-drawn rollers to Mayodan, about 2 mi. sw.

Avalon Beach, area of extensive real estate development n of Wright Memorial in e Dare County. Once known as Moore's Shore.

Aventon, community in n Nash County on the head of Crooked Swamp. Named for the Avent family, which settled there about 1738; descendants still live on the original grant. A post office, Aventsville, opened there prior to 1828; Aventon post office operated from 1903 to 1911. Alt. 175.

Aventon Creek. *See* Abingdon Creek.

Avents Creek rises in n Harnett County and flows sw into Cape Fear River.

Aventsville. *See* Aventon.

Averasboro, formerly a town on the Cape Fear River in se Harnett County. Provided for by legislative act in 1791, to be laid off on land owned by Alexander Avera and called Averasburg. Site of a gristmill about 1740 and soon afterward of other public buildings. Site of Confederate attack on Sherman's army, March 15, 1865. Town began to decline soon after Civil War and by 1888 was practically abandoned. Site, 1 mi. s of Erwin, is marked by grove of large oak and beech trees and sets of historic houses and historical markers.

Averasboro Township, se Harnett County.

Avery County was formed in 1911 from Mitchell, Watauga, and Caldwell Counties. In the nw section of the state, it is bounded by the state of Tennessee and by Watauga, Caldwell, Burke, McDowell, and Mitchell Counties. It was named for Colonel Waightstill Avery (1741–1821), Revolutionary soldier and attorney general of North Carolina. Area: 247 sq. mi. County seat: Newland, with an elevation of 3,589. Townships are Altamont, Banner Elk, Beech Mountain, Cranberry, Linville, Roaring Gap, Toe River, Wilson's Creek. Produces corn, dairy and beef cattle, Christmas trees, mica, hay, cabinets, textiles, kaolin, iron, sand and gravel. There are also deposits of olivine and asbestos in the county.

Avery Creek rises in s Buncombe County and flows e into French Broad River.

Avery Creek rises in n Transylvania County and flows se into Davidson River.

Avery Creek, community in s Buncombe County on the e limit of Pisgah National Forest.

Avery Creek Township, sw Buncombe County.

Averys Bald. *See* Big Yellow Mountain.

Avilla, community in w Alexander County on Middle Little River. Served by post office from 1888 to 1906.

Avoca, community in e Bertie County on the site of Avoca Plantation, part of the eighteenth-century Nathanael Duckenfield estate. Name comes from the phrase "sweet vale of Avoca" in Thomas Moore's poem "The Meeting of the Waters." *See also* Black Walnut Point.

Avon, community on Hatteras Island, se Dare County. Post office est. in 1873 as Kinnakeet. Post office renamed Avon in 1883. Alt. 3.

Avondale, community in se Rutherford County on Second Broad River between the communities of Caroleen on the n and Henrietta on the s.

Axe Ridge, in s Graham County, extends n from Panther Cove to Little Snowbird Creek.

Axtell, community in w Warren County between Long Branch and Phoebes Creek. Alt. 400.

Settled during the Revolutionary War and first named Old Shatter, a corruption of Chateau. Shatter Muster Ground, used during the Civil War, was located there. The post office that was located there from 1885 until 1889 was named Shatter. Name changed to Axtell in 1890 for noted race horse.

Aycock, community in n Wayne County and s Wilson County between Great Swamp and Aycock Swamp.

Aycock Creek rises in s Granville County and flows ne into Tar River.

Aycock Crossing, community in sw Wilson County.

Aycock Millpond, in n Wayne County on Great Swamp. Adjacent to Sasser Millpond, named for the original owners. Max. depth 12 ft.; area covered, 30 acres. Fishing and boating open to the public.

Aycocks Pond, sw Warren County on Lees Branch.

Aycock Swamp rises in n Wayne County and flows ne into Wilson County, where it enters Turners Swamp.

Ayden, town in s Pitt County. Inc. 1891. Name changed to Harriston in 1895 but changed back to Ayden in 1899. Alt. 64. Produces canned foods.

Ayden Branch rises in n Swain County and flows s into Beech Flats Prong.

Ayden Township, sw Pitt County.

Aydlett, community on the w shore of Currituck Sound in central Currituck County. Probably named for first postmaster around 1909.

Ayersville, community in ne Stokes County served by post office, 1833–1915. Named for first postmaster, James Ayers.

Ayles Creek rises in e Yancey County and flows ne into Little Crabtree Creek.

Ayr, former community in w Rutherford County near Lake Lure. Site of a pre–Civil War tannery that made saddles for the Confederate army during the war. A Scotsman, Francis Reynolds, operated the tannery and named the community for his native town. Post office est. there 1880, closed 1911.

Azalea, community in central Buncombe County, e of Asheville. Known as Gudger's Ford until renamed for the flowering shrub. Alt. 2,052.

B

Babbit's Pond. *See* Parrish's Pond.

Bacchus, community in e Yancey County.

Bachelor, community in se Craven County on Clubfoot Creek.

Bachelor Creek rises in Great Dover Swamp in ne Jones County, flows ne into central Craven County, and then turns to flow se for approx. 3 mi. along the w border of Hog Island before entering Neuse River approx. 3½ mi. nw of town of New Bern. Approx. 14 mi. long. Appears as Batchellors Creek on the Moseley map, 1733. Formerly called Batchelder Creek. Named for Edward Batchelor.

Bachelor Creek rises in s Randolph County and flows e into Richland Creek. Named for a wild stallion that is reported to have roamed through the section. People called him "Bachelor."

Bachelor's Delight Swamp rises in n Onslow County and flows sw into New River. Mentioned in local records as early as 1744.

Back Bay, a bay formed by the encircling islands of Hog Island in ne Carteret County.

Backcountry, term used during the early settlement and colonial period for the vast interior of North Carolina, located away from the coastline and including both the modern-day Piedmont and Mountain regions.

Back Creek rises in w Alamance County and flows se into Great Alamance Creek.

Back Creek rises in e Beaufort County and flows sw into Bath Creek.

Back Creek rises in se Craven County and flows nw on the Craven-Carteret county line into Adams Creek.

Back Creek, an inlet of North Landing River, ne Currituck County. It forms the n boundary of Mackay Island.

Back Creek rises in central Iredell County a short distance sw of Statesville and flows sw into Third Creek.

Back Creek rises in se Iredell County and flows ne into w Rowan County, where it joins Withrow Creek in forming North Second Creek. Appears as South Fork [Second Creek] on the Collet map, 1770.

Back Creek rises in se Mecklenburg County and flows e into sw Cabarrus County to join Rocky River. So called because it appears to back into Rocky River rather than flow into it. Shown as Buck Creek on Kerr map, 1882, and as Black Creek on recent state highway maps.

Back Creek rises in w Orange County and flows sw into Alamance County, where it enters Haw River. Appears on the Moseley map, 1733, as Buffalo Creek.

Back Creek rises in central Randolph County and flows sw into Caraway Creek. The creek is dammed about 5 mi. w of Asheboro, creating a 250-acre lake that is the chief water supply of Asheboro Township.

Back Creek Mountain, central Randolph County w of Asheboro. One of the principal mountains of the Uwharrie range.

Back Creek Township, w central Randolph County.

Back Lake, a small lake on the mainland of Dare County e of the community of Lake Worth on Stumpy Point Bay.

Back Landing, in nw Tyrrell County on Scuppernong River. *See also* Newport.

Back Landing Creek rises in the highlands of Indian Island, se Camden County, and flows se into North River.

Back Marsh rises in n Duplin County and flows sw into Northeast Cape Fear River.

Back of Beyond, name given to far western counties by Horace Kephart in *Our Southern Highlanders* (1913). Derived from longtime inaccessibility of region.

Back Sound, between Shackleford Banks and Harkers Island in se Carteret County.

Back Swamp rises in nw Nash County and flows se into Big Peachtree Creek.

Back Swamp rises in nw Onslow County and flows sw into Duplin County, where it enters Cypress Creek.

Back Swamp rises in w Robeson County and flows se into Lumber River in central Robeson County.

Back Swamp Township, central Robeson County.

Bad Branch rises in e Macon County and flows sw into Big Creek.

Bad Creek rises in sw Jackson County and flows se into South Carolina, where it enters Chattooga River.

Bad Creek rises in n Mitchell County and flows se into Big Rock Creek.

Bad Fork rises in nw Henderson County and flows s into Wash Creek.

Bad Fork rises in nw McDowell County on the n slopes of Woods Mountain and flows ne approx. 2 mi. into Armstrong Creek.

Badin, community in ne Stanly County on Badin Lake. Alt. 400. Est. 1913 by Adrien Badin, French industrialist who operated aluminum-reduction plant there. Plant opened as Aluminium Francais in 1915, later operated by Aluminum Company of America, closed 2002.

Badin Lake on Yadkin River in Montgomery and Stanly Counties. Covers 5,973 acres; max. depth 40 ft. Completed 1917 by Carolina Aluminum Company to generate hydroelectricity and for recreation. Also referred to as Narrows Reservoir.

Bad Knob, in n Mitchell County between Aaron Branch and Big Ridge.

Bagdad, community in n Davidson County served by post office, 1893–1902.

Bagley, community in ne Johnston County. Named for local family.

Bagley Academy Branch rises in ne Warren County and flows n into Little Stonehouse Creek.

Bahama (ba-HAY-ma), community in n Durham County. Settled about 1880. Originally called Balltown until renamed. Bahama coined from the first two letters of the names of three prominent families—Ball, Harris, and Mangum. For a time in the nineteenth century, the post office name was Hunkadora. Alt. 507.

Bailey, community in w Davie County served by post office, 1890–1902.

Bailey, community in w Mitchell County on Sams Branch.

Bailey, town in sw Nash County. Settled about 1860. Inc. 1908 as Baileys, named for Joe Bailey, an early settler; now known as Bailey. Alt. 233.

Bailey. *See* Center.

Bailey Branch rises in e Madison County and flows s into Gabriels Creek.

Bailey Branch rises in e Madison County and flows s into Middle Fork.

Bailey Branch rises in s Madison County and flows n into French Broad River.

Bailey Branch rises in central Yancey County and flows sw into Pine Swamp Branch. Named for M. A. Bailey, who owned a large tract of land through which it flowed.

Bailey Branch rises in n Yancey County and flows ne into Pigpen Creek. Named for John and Charles Bailey, early settlers.

Bailey Branch rises in n Yancey County and flows se into Jacks Creek.

Bailey Branch rises in w central Yancey County on se slopes of Roland Knob and flows s into Cane River.

Bailey Cove, n central Yancey County near the head of Star Branch.

Bailey Creek rises in se Beaufort County and flows e into South Creek.

Bailey Hill, n Yancey County, extends nw from Locust Rough Mountain to Jacks Creek. Early settlers named Bailey are buried there and the site is reserved for a burying ground.

Bailey Meadows, in e Mitchell County between Sparks Ridge and Beaver Creek.

Bailey Mountain, e Yancey County between Browns Creek and South Toe River.

Bailey Ridge, s Madison County, extends ne from Bull Creek to Gabriels Creek.

Baileys. *See* Bailey.

Bailey's Camp, community in nw Caldwell County.

Bailey's Fork rises in s central Burke County and flows n into Silver Creek.

Bailey Township, se Nash County.

Bain, community in e Davidson County near the headwaters of Beaverdam Creek.

Baines Mountain, in s Swain County between Little Yalaka Creek and De Hart Branch.

Bairds Creek rises in w central Watauga County and flows sw into Watauga River.

Bairds Creek. *See* Beards Creek.

Baird's Forge. *See* Granite Falls.

Baker. *See* Drexel.

Baker Creek rises in w central Yancey County and flows n into Cane River. Named for Sidney Baker, an early settler.

Baker Gap, on the Watauga County, N.C.–Johnson County, Tenn., line in the Stone Mountains.

Baker Island, a sandy island approx. 2 mi. long in the Roanoke River, nw Northampton County. Called Eaton Island on the Price map, 1808, and Lashleys Island on the MacRae map, 1833.

Baker Mill. *See* Wheeler Creek.

Baker Mountain, w Catawba County. Alt. 1,812.

Bakers, community in w central Union County.

Bakers. *See* Ca-Vel.

Bakers Branch rises in n Madison County and flows ne into Spillcorn Creek.

Bakers Creek rises in n Catawba County and flows s into Lyle Creek.

Bakers Creek. *See* Mud Creek.

Bakers Crossroads, community in s Franklin County.

Bakers Crossroads, community in central Rockingham County. Named for Baker family, local farmers. Site of Malloy post office, *which see.*

Bakers Lake, a natural lake in nw Bladen County, approx. 1½ mi. long. Formerly known as Wilkinson's Lake.

Bakers Ridge, w Alleghany County.

Bakers Swamp rises in n Washington County and flows ne into Kendricks Creek.

Bakersville, town and county seat, in central Mitchell County on Cane Creek. Alt. 2,457. Settled prior to 1857 and named for David Baker, who settled on a grant that he had at the site in 1797. During the latter part of the Civil War and until 1868 known as Davis, apparently in honor of Confederate president Jefferson Davis. Inc. 1868.

Bakersville Township, central Mitchell County.

Baker Swamp rises in e Cumberland County and flows sw into Reese Creek.

Balconce Branch rises in w Lee County and flows nw into Little Pocket Creek.

Bald, The, a peak in nw Watauga County in the Stone Mountains.

Bald Beach, island on Atlantic Ocean in sw Brunswick County.

Bald Branch rises in sw Madison County and flows n into Spring Creek.

Bald Branch rises in n Swain County and flows se into Noland Creek.

Bald Branch rises in s Swain County between Rattlesnake Ridge and De Hart Bald and flows w into Wesser Creek.

Bald Cove, on the head of Cove Creek in e Haywood County.

Bald Creek rises in n Cherokee County and flows sw into Davis Creek.

Bald Creek rises in e Haywood County and flows sw into Crabtree Creek.

Bald Creek rises in e Pamlico County and flows ne into Bay River.

Bald Creek rises in w Yancey County and flows e into Cane River.

Bald Creek, community in w Yancey County on the stream of the same name. Alt. 2,576.

Bald Fork rises near Bald Knob in nw Buncombe County and flows sw into Sandymush Creek.

Bald Gap, w Haywood County in Great Smoky Mountains National Park between Canadian Top and Bald Top near lat. 35°39′ N., long. 83°06′22″ W.

Bald Ground Mountain, nw Burke County. Alt. 4,100.

Bald Head. *See* Smith Island.

Baldhead Creek, a tidal waterway extending from just inside the outer coast of Smith Island in Brunswick County in a nw direction into the Cape Fear River. Also known as Lighthouse Creek.

Bald Hill. *See* Intelligence.

Bald Knob, peak at the e end of Peach Bottom Mountain, n Alleghany County. Alt. 3,653.

Bald Knob, n Buncombe County nw of Cherry Log Gap.

Bald Knob, peak on Newfound Mountain on Buncombe-Haywood county line near the headwaters of Bald Fork.

Bald Knob, on the Buncombe-Yancey county line between Swannanoa Gap and Pinnacle. Alt. 5,400–5,420.

Bald Knob, e Caldwell County. Alt. 1,727.

Bald Knob, on Haywood-Madison county line.

Bald Knob on the Jackson-Transylvania county line. Alt. 4,824. Part of Tennessee Ridge, *which see.*

Bald Knob, central Surry County.

Bald Knob, w Transylvania County between Johnnies Creek and Bee Tree Fork.

Bald Knob, w Yadkin County between Dobbins Creek and South Deep Creek.

Bald Knob, e Yancey County near the head of Plum Branch.

Bald Knob Creek rises in n Cleveland County and flows se into Little Knob Creek.

Bald Knob Mountain, w Alexander County. Alt. 1,887.

Bald Knob Ridge, s Yancey County between Left Prong South Toe River and Right Prong South Toe River.

Bald Mountain, on the Alexander-Wilkes county line.

Bald Mountain, central Avery County.

Bald Mountain, on Grassy Ridge near the Avery-

Mitchell county line. Known also as Grassy Ridge Bald.

Bald Mountain, s Davidson County on Yadkin River.

Bald Mountain, n Jackson County between Blackrock Ridge and Sheepback Mountain. Alt. 5,400.

Bald Mountain, sw Jackson County between Flat Creek and Mill Creek. Alt. 4,050.

Bald Mountain, se Orange County about 4 mi. nw of town of Carrboro. Alt. 762.

Bald Mountain, e Watauga County on South Fork New River.

Bald Mountain, community in nw Yancey County on Bald Mountain Creek.

Bald Mountain. *See* Rumbling Bald Mountain.

Bald Mountain Creek rises in central Avery County and flows ne into Banner Elk Creek.

Bald Mountain Creek rises in nw Yancey County and flows ne into Cane River.

Bald Mountain Falls, in Yadkin River opposite Bald Mountain in s Davidson County. Mentioned as early as 1819 in a survey of the rivers of North Carolina.

Bald Mountains, in Haywood, Madison, and Yancey Counties, N.C., and Cocke, Greene, and Unicoi Counties, Tenn., forming the common boundary line of North Carolina and Tennessee from the Pigeon River, near lat. 36°04′20″ N., long. 82°24′30″ W., to the Nolichucky River, near lat. 35°46′15″ N., long. 83°04′50″ W. On 25 of 40 miscellaneous maps, 1795–1930, the section of the mountains between Pigeon River and the French Broad River bears no name; and the names on 15 maps vary between Iron, Great Iron, Smoky, and Great Smoky. There is also some usage of Max Patch.

Bald Mountain Township, ne Watauga County.

Bald of Humpback Mountain, s Mitchell County at the head of Rose Creek.

Bald Point, peninsula extending from s Hatteras Island, s Dare County, into Pamlico Sound.

Bald Ridge, central Avery County.

Bald Ridge, n Swain County between Slab Camp Branch and Advalorem Branch.

Bald Rock, mountain on the Jackson-Transylvania county line at the head of Tucker Creek. Alt. 4,150. Part of Tennessee Ridge, *which see*.

Bald Rock Mountain, s Jackson County, bordered on sw by Fairfield Lake and on n and w by Trays Island Creek. Alt. 4,232.

Bald Spot Mountain. *See* Gregory Bald.

Bald Spring Branch rises in n Clay County and flows sw into Fires Creek.

Bald Top, w Haywood County in Great Smoky Mountains National Park between Little Davidson Branch and Coggins Branch near lat. 35°39′ N., long. 83°06′30″ W. Alt. 3,960.

Bald Top Mountain, n Henderson County between Clear Creek and Kyles Creek. Named by William Mills, first known white settler of the county.

Baldwin, community in sw Ashe County. Named for family of early settlers. Alt. 3,100.

Baldwin Cove, s Buncombe County n of Baldwin Gap.

Baldwin Cove, on Burningtown Creek in central Macon County.

Baldwin Gap, on the Ashe County, N.C.–Johnson County, Tenn., line. Alt. 3,762.

Baldwin Gap, s Buncombe County between Busbee and Butler Mountains. Alt. 3,076.

Baldwin Gap, s Buncombe County between Stradley and Scott Mountains.

Baldwin Gap, n Henderson County between Rich Mountain and Hightop.

Baldwin Swamp rises in central Pitt County and flows se into Moyes Run.

Baldwin Township, ne Chatham County.

Bales Creek rises in sw Anson County and flows e into Deadfall Creek.

Balfour, community in central Henderson County now part of Hendersonville on its n side. Alt. 2,125. Railroad name was Smyth. Named for Capt. William Balfour Troy, who operated a rock quarry there in 1880 and was agent for the newly opened railroad.

Balfours, community in central Randolph County adjacent to Asheboro on the n, formerly known as North Asheboro. Named for an abandoned community of the same name in w central Randolph County, sw of Asheboro, which was the home of Col. Andrew Balfour, Revolutionary patriot. Spero, formerly a community in its own right, is now considered to be a part of Balfours.

Bal-Gra, home of Thomas Pollock, president of the Council and acting governor, 1712–14 and 1722. Located in e Bertie County on the n side of Salmon Creek at its junction with Chowan River and Albemarle Sound. The brick house, named for the Pollock home in Renfrow County, Scotland, is no longer standing. Near site of Edenhouse, *which see*.

Ball, community in nw Ashe County. Formerly a post office.

Ballard, community in n Martin County, named for the plantation of John Bryant located near there in 1734. The first court in Martin County met in the community on the land of John Griffin, 1774.

Ballard Cove, n Buncombe County s of Horse Gap.

Ballard Cove, the valley through which Ballard Creek flows in sw Buncombe County.

Ballard Creek rises in e Buncombe County and flows se into Cane Creek.

Ballard Creek rises in sw Buncombe County near Fork Mountain and flows n into Glady Fork.

Ballard Creek rises in n Lincoln County and flows se into Anderson Creek.

Ballard Crossroads, community in sw Gates County.

Ballard Gap, Swannanoa Mountains, s Buncombe County e of Face Rock peak.

Ballard Gap, e Transylvania County between Fodderstack Mountain and Pine Mountain.

Ballards Crossroads, community in w Pitt County.

Ballast Bank, the point of land in the mouth of South Fork Creek at Scuppernong River, w Tyrrell County.

Ballast Pit, stony area about 1 mi. square, e central Anson County. Worked commercially for construction material.

Ballast Point, peninsula from e Roanoke Island extending into Roanoke Sound s of Shallowbag Bay, e Dare County.

Ball Creek rises in s Macon County and flows ne into Coweeta Creek.

Ballentine's Mills, community in s Wake County.

Ball Gap, s Buncombe County, nw of Ball Mountain.

Ball Island, small tidal-marsh island in the Bay River estuary, e Pamlico County. Used as a target for practice bombing by Marines.

Ball Mountain, s Buncombe County.

Ballou Hill, community near Balsam on Jones Creek in ne Jackson County.

Ball Pocosin, e Lenoir County between Vine Swamp and Southwest Creek.

Balls Creek rises in e Catawba County and flows e into Catawba River.

Balls Creek Camp Ground, e Catawba County. Est. 1853, and trustees inc. 1861. Methodist. Camp meetings held there annually during the last week in August.

Balls Mountain, s Orange County at the head of Mountain Creek.

Ball's Point, point of land extending from w Carteret County into White Oak River.

Balltown. *See* Bahama.

Balm, community in ne Avery County.

Balsam, town in ne Jackson County. Inc. in 1951, but not active in municipal affairs. Named for Balsam Mountains. Has highest standard-gauge railroad e of Rocky Mountains. Alt. 3,315.

Balsam Branch rises in ne Swain County and flows se into Raven Fork.

Balsam Cone, mountain in s Yancey County between the head of Timber Creek and the head of Middle Creek. Alt. 6,611.

Balsam Cone. *See* Mount Craig.

Balsam Corner, mountain on the Haywood-Swain county line. In Great Smoky Mountains National Park near lat. 35°40'17" N., long. 83°10'55" W., near a sharp bend in the county line, hence the name. Alt. 6,020.

Balsam Corner Creek rises in ne Swain County in Great Smoky Mountains National Park and flows sw into Straight Fork Raven Creek.

Balsam Gap, on the Buncombe-Yancey county line w of Walker Knob, near the s end of Bear Wallow Stand Ridge. The Blue Ridge Parkway passes through the gap. Alt. 5,320.

Balsam Gap, at the head of Richland Creek in w Haywood County. It is the lowest gap in the Balsam Mountain. Through it passed a prominent aboriginal Indian trail; a highway and railroad also pass through it now. Alt. 3,347.

Balsam Grove, community in w Transylvania County on North Fork French Broad River.

Balsam High Top, mountain on the Haywood-Swain county line between Beech Gap and Laurel Gap in Great Smoky Mountains National Park. Alt. 5,688.

Balsam Mountain, on the Haywood-Swain-Jackson county line, centering near lat. 35°35' N., long. 83°12' W. Tricorner Knob, *which see*, is at its junction with the main divide of the Great Smoky Mountains. Also known as Chiltoskie Ridge in Swain County. *See also* Richland Balsam.

Balsam Ridge extends e from Huckleberry Knob to Winding Knob in w Haywood County.

Balsam Ridge, ne Swain County in Great Smoky Mountains National Park, a short spur extending sw from Hughes Ridge.

Baltic, community in w Duplin County. Alt. 146.

Baltimore, community in e Davie County. Alt. 828. Site of a community store from the 1880s.

Baltimore, community in e Yadkin County between Forbush and Logan Creeks. Named for a local church. A former post office there was named Tracadia.

Baltimore Branch rises in w Madison County and flows nw into Spring Creek.

Baltimore Landing, a clearing and landing for small boats on the Cashie River in se Bertie County. In use in the 1890s.

Bamboo, community in s Watauga County on Sawpit Branch.

Bandana, community in w Mitchell County on Toe River. Alt. 2,331. Name said to have been given after a railroad brakeman left a bandana tied to a laurel bush to mark the location of a station.

Bandana Hollow, central Mitchell County on a tributary of Toe River.

Bandy, community in e Catawba County. Named for pioneer Bandy family.

Bandy Cove Mountain, nw Burke County. Alt. 2,747.

Bandy Township, se Catawba County. Named for George Bandy, Virginian, who settled in Lincoln County, 1783.

Bangor, community in nw Wake County served by post office, 1888–1904.

Banjo Branch rises in central Avery County and flows s into North Toe River.

Banjo Branch rises in se Mitchell County and flows sw into North Toe River about 1 mi. e of Spruce Pine. Formerly known as Christ Branch; name changed after 1939.

Banjo Fork rises in e Beaufort County and flows nw into Pungo Creek.

Bank Mountain, n Henderson County between Garren Mountain and Kyles Creek.

Bank Point extends from se Pasquotank County into Pasquotank River on the s shore of Little Flatty Creek.

Banks, community in s Wake County.

Banks Branch rises in w Hertford County and flows ne into Meherrin River.

Banks Channel, a channel through a mass of tidal-marsh islands in the extreme w end of Bogue Sound in sw Carteret County.

Banks Channel, in Topsail Sound, s Pender County near New Topsail Inlet.

Banks Creek rises in s Yancey County and flows nw into Price Creek.

Banner Branch rises in n Stokes County and flows sw into Snow Creek.

Banner Elk, town in ne Avery County on Elk River at the mouth of Shawneehaw Creek. Alt. 3,710. Inc. 1891 as Shawneehaw; reincorporated 1911 as Banner Elk. First settlers said to have arrived at the site about 1825. Named for the Banner family, early settlers on the Elk River. Lees-McRae College is there.

Banner Elk Creek rises in e Avery County and flows n into Elk River.

Banner Elk Township, ne Avery County.

Bannerman's or **Bannerman's Bridge**, community in e Pender County on Northeast Cape Fear River. Est. prior to the Revolution, but now largely abandoned.

Banner's Store. *See* East Bend.

Bannertown, community in ne Surry County.

Banner Township, s Johnston County.

Banton Creek rises in ne Washington County and flows ne into Bull Bay; a portion of it forms the boundary with Tyrrell County. Sometimes erroneously called Bunton Creek.

Baptist Church Township, former township in central Cabarrus County. Now township no. 11. In 1945 a part of the township was annexed to Concord, coextensive with Concord township.

Barbacue Creek. *See* Barbecue Swamp.

Bar Banks. *See* Bear Banks.

Barbecue Swamp rises in ne Bertie County and flows ne into Hertford County, where it enters Chinkapin Creek.

Barbecue Swamp rises in w Harnett County and flows ne into Upper Little River. Named by Red Neill McNeill about 1750. Mists rising from the stream early in the morning reminded him of smoke rising from barbecue pits he had seen in the West Indies. In a fit of culinary nostalgia, he named the stream Barbecue. Appears as Barbacue Creek on the Collet map, 1770.

Barbecue Township, sw Harnett County.

Barber, community in w Rowan County. Two lines of the railroad cross there, hence sometimes called Barber's Junction. Named either for W. P. Barber, from whom the railroad purchased land for the station, or for R. L. Barber, first postmaster. Alt. 752.

Barber Creek rises in central Pitt County and flows se into Tar River.

Barber Junction. See Barber.

Barclaysville, community in ne Harnett County. Once the center of the Barclay-Barbee naval stores industry.

Barco, community in central Currituck County. Named for first postmaster. *See also* Coinjock.

Barden Inlet, a passage between Core Banks and Shackleford Banks n of Cape Lookout in se Carteret County. Named for Graham Arthur Barden, a congressman from North Carolina. Formerly known as Bardens Inlet, Lookout Bight Channel, and The Drain.

Barden Pond, w Duplin County on a tributary of Rockfish Creek.

Bardins Bay, a sand-filled bay in w Cleveland County.

Bare Banks. *See* Bear Banks.

Barefoot's Mill Pond. *See* Contentnea Lake.

Bareford Swamp rises in w Bladen County and flows sw through Hesters Pond into Crawley Swamp.

Barfields. *See* Tuscarora Beach.

Bargaw Creek. *See* Burgaw Creek.

Barham, community in ne Wake County.

Barium Springs, community and former health resort in s Iredell County. Known by the Indians as Poison Springs; developed in the 1880s as Linsters Springs. Post office name changed from Poison Springs to Barium Springs in 1889. Named for springs that contain barium salts and other minerals. Presbyterian Orphans Home est. there, 1891.

Barker Butt, e Swain County on Hickory Mountain.

Barker Creek rises in nw Graham County and flows ne into Cheoah River.

Barker Heights, community in central Henderson County on s side of Hendersonville. Home to regional airport.

Barker Road Gap, on the Cherokee-Graham county line.

Barkers Bridge. *See* Stella.

Barkers Creek is formed by junction of West Fork and Middle Fork in w Jackson County and flows ne into Tuckasegee River.

Barkers Creek rises in s Macon County and flows s into Rabun County, Ga., where it enters Betty Creek.

Barkers Creek, community in nw Jackson County. Alt. 1,901.

Barkers Creek Township, nw Jackson County.

Barkers Ferry, on Catawba River at Mecklenburg-Lincoln county boundary. Now under waters of Lake Norman.

Barkerside, community in central Pitt County.

Barker–Ten Mile, community in ne Robeson County. Named for Barker Methodist Church and Ten Mile Baptist Church. A prosperous farming center.

Barkley, community in w Lincoln County served by post office, 1889–1906.

Barlowes, community in se Pender County on Bishop Creek. A former post office there was known as Sloop Point, *which see.*

Barnard, community in central Madison County on French Broad River at the mouth of Brush Creek. Alt. 1,534. Barnard's Station post office est. as early as 1830. Named for Job Barnard, who settled there by 1794.

Barnards Creek rises in central New Hanover County and flows w into Cape Fear River.

Barnardsville, town in n Buncombe County near the junction of North Fork Ivy Creek and Dillingham Creek. Inc. 1959. A post office operated there beginning in 1875. Alt. 2,250. Produces wearing apparel.

Barn Branch rises in s Haywood County and flows n into Jonathans Creek.

Barnes Branch rises in n Haywood County and flows se into Big Creek.

Barnes Branch rises in n Madison County and flows w into Big Laurel Creek.

Barnes Creek rises in central Cleveland County and flows nw and sw in an arc into First Broad River.

Barnes Creek rises in sw Gates County and flows se into Chowan River.

Barnes Creek rises in s Randolph County and flows sw into Montgomery County, where it enters Uwharrie River.

Barnes Crossroads, community in n Johnston County.

Barnes Store, community in w Wilson County. Named for Elias G. Barnes. A post office, 1877–1907.

Barnesville, community in s Robeson County. Alt. 125. Settled 1898. Named for R. R. Barnes, who gave land for the right-of-way for a railroad, now abandoned. Served by post office, 1879–1943.

Barnett Branch rises in central Cherokee County and flows sw into Slow Creek.

Barnett Branch rises in n Mitchell County and flows w into Big Rock Creek.

Barnett Branch rises in n Transylvania County and flows se into South Fork Mills River.

Barnett Branch rises in n Yancey County and flows sw into Unicoi County, Tenn., where it enters Spivey Creek.

Barnett Creek rises in e Clay County and flows ne into Buck Creek.

Barnett Creek rises in sw Currituck County and flows w into North River.

Barnett Knob, on the Jackson-Swain county line near the head of Pigeon Creek.

Barnett Mountain, central Madison County between Brush and Walnut Creeks.

Barnetts Pond. *See* Loch Lily.

Barney Slue, in the waters of Pamlico Sound, n of Hatteras Inlet, s Dare County.

Barns Creek. *See* Bartrams Creek.

Barnwell Mountain, on the Buncombe-Henderson county line.

Barnwell Mountain, ne Henderson County 1½ mi. sw of community of Bat Cave. Alt. approx. 2,700.

Barr Banks. *See* Bear Banks.

Barr Creek rises in sw Iredell County and flows s into Davidson Creek.

Barren Head. *See* Smith Island.

Barren Inlet. *See* Mason Inlet.

Barrett, community in ne Alleghany County.

Barrett Branch rises in se Clay County and flows nw into Right Fork [Eagle Creek], which is also sometimes known as Dave Barrett Creek.

Barrett Cove, n Buncombe County between Chestnut Knob and Reems Creek.

Barrett Mountain, sw Alexander County. Alt. 1,950. Named for Jonathan Barrett, pioneer settler who laid out road from Fort Dobbs to Quaker Meadows.

Barriers Mill, community on Dutch Buffalo Creek in e Cabarrus County.

Barringer Township, se Iredell County. Named for a Civil War muster ground.

Barris Creek rises in central Beaufort County and flows e into Pamlico River.

Barrows Mill Pond, w Northampton County on Gumberry Swamp. Approx. 1 mi. long. Appears as Jones Mill on the Collet map, 1770;

known as Wheeler's Mill by 1833 and more recently by its present name. Boyhood home of Willie and Allen Jones, Revolutionary leaders, was there.

Barry Bay, a small bay in ne Carteret County, w of Core Sound and s of Cedar Island and Thorofare Bay, into which it empties.

Barshavia Creek. *See* Bechewa Creek.

Bart Branch rises in n Jackson County and flows sw into Scott Creek.

Bart Branch rises in w Transylvania County on Brushy Mountain and flows sw into Shoal Creek.

Bartlett. *See* Bluebutton.

Bartlett Creek rises in nw McDowell County and flows se into O'Dear Creek.

Bartlett Mountain, central Buncombe County se of Swan Mountain.

Bartleys Island, narrow sandy strip approx. 2¾ mi. long beside French Broad River, w Madison County.

Barton Creek Township, nw Wake County.

Bartonsville, community in ne Hertford County. Named for local Barton family before the Civil War.

Bartrams Creek rises in sw Carteret County and flows s into Bogue Sound. Also known as Barns Creek. Probably named for William Bartram.

Bartrams Lake. *See* White Lake.

Basal Creek rises in sw Wake County and flows se and then ne through Mills Pond and into Sunset Lake, where it joins Middle Creek.

Basin, The, a body of water at the s tip of New Hanover County. The Cape Fear River on the w is separated from The Basin by a dam; New Inlet on the Atlantic Ocean side permits access from Onslow Bay. The Brunswick–New Hanover county line divides The Basin near its center.

Basin Creek rises in s Alleghany County and flows s through Doughton Park in n Wilkes County to join Lovelace Creek in forming Middle Prong Roaring River.

Basnight, community in w central Washington County midway between towns of Roper and Plymouth. Locally called Macedonia.

Basnights Ditch rises in s Tyrrell County and flows ne into The Frying Pan.

Bason, community in central Rockingham County served by post office, 1885–1904.

Bass. *See* Keener.

Bass Ferry. *See* West Point.

Bass Lake, s Watauga County on String-fellow Branch in Moses H. Cone Memorial Park, *which see*. Formerly known as Cone Lake, it was formed before 1908. Covers 22 acres, with a max. depth of 30 ft. On the Blue Ridge Parkway.

Bass Mountain, peak in the Cane Creek Mountains, s Alamance County.

Bass's Crossroads. *See* Momeyer.

Bat Cave, community in ne Henderson County on Broad River. Alt. 1,250. Named for a nearby cave inhabited by bats and rare animals. The cave is preserved as a natural area. Fans of 1960s *Batman* television series coveted postmark.

Batchelder Creek. *See* Bachelor Creek.

Batchellors Creek. *See* Bachelor Creek.

Batchelor Bay, formed at the mouth of the Roanoke and Cashie Rivers, e Bertie County, at the head of Albemarle Sound. Confederate ironclad *Albemarle* crossed bay to meet seven Union ships 15 mi. e, May 7, 1864.

Bateman Branch rises in nw Macon County and flows sw into Whiteoak Creek.

Bateman Gap, nw Macon County between Batey Branch and Bateman Branch.

Bates, community in se Beaufort County served by post office, 1900–1904.

Bates Branch rises in s Macon County and flows se into Little Tennessee River.

Bates Creek rises in central Cherokee County between Bates and Fain Mountains and flows sw into Hiwassee River.

Bates Gap, s Macon County between Fulcher Branch and Hickory Knoll Creek.

Bates Mountain, central Cherokee County, extends from Hiwassee River to Blackwell Mountain.

Bates Mountain, at the head of Bates Branch in s Macon County.

Bates Ridge, s Macon County between Bristle Ridge and Hickory Knoll Creek.

Batey Branch rises in nw Macon County and flows s into Cold Springs Creek.

Bat Fork rises in se Henderson County and flows nw into Mud Creek.

Bath, town in central Beaufort County at junction of Bath and Back Creeks. Alt. 9. Settled 1690. Inc. 1705. The oldest town in North Carolina, it was the county seat from 1696 to 1785, when it was changed to Washington.

Probably named for Bath County in which it was originally located. Bath is now a State Historic Site and a number of restored buildings are open to the public. St. Thomas Church there, the oldest church in North Carolina, was built in 1734. The colonial assembly met there in 1744 and 1752.

Bath County, formed in 1696 from the territory s of Albemarle Sound, was named in honor in John Granville, Earl of Bath, one of the Lords Proprietors. On December 3, 1705, the territory was divided into Archdale, Pamptecough, and Wickham precincts. Bath County was not abolished with the creation of the precincts but continued to be referred to in records as late as 1724. As the precincts increased in importance, eventually becoming counties themselves, the parent county lost its identity.

Bath Creek rises in central Beaufort County and flows s into Pamlico River.

Bathsheba Creek. *See* Bechewa Creek.

Bath Township, e central Beaufort County.

Baton, community in s Caldwell County.

Bats Grave. *See* Batts Island.

Batson Creek rises in s Transylvania County and flows n into Carson Creek.

Battery Bolles. *See* Fort Fisher.

Battery Island, a tidal-marsh island in the Cape Fear River opposite Southport, se Brunswick County.

Battis Point. *See* Wades Point.

Battleboro, town in ne Nash and sw Edgecombe Counties. Inc. 1872. Had its origin about 1840 as a railroad depot in a rich agricultural area. The station was named for James and Joseph Battle, stockholders in the Wilmington and Raleigh Railroad. Produces lumber. Annexed by Rocky Mount, 2002. Alt. 131.

Battle Branch rises in central Davidson County and flows sw into Abbotts Creek.

Battle Branch rises in e Macon County and flows s into Ellijay Creek.

Battle Branch rises in s Macon County and flows se into North Fork [Skeenah Creek].

Battle Cove, e Swain County between Falls Branch and Fishtrap Branch.

Battle Creek rises in s Swain County and flows ne into Yalaka Creek.

Battle Creek. *See* Johnsons Mill Creek.

Battle Ground, former community in central Guilford County, now within the limits of the city of Greensboro. Served by post office,

1858–1923. Site of Battle of Guilford Courthouse, March 15, 1781.

Battle Royal, community 10 mi. w of Wilmington in Brunswick County. Site of tar manufactory, 1884.

Battle Run Brook rises in e Catawba County and flows se into North Fork Mountain Creek.

Battles Falls, in Cape Fear River in n Harnett County along a rock outcrop between the confluence of Camels Creek and Fish Creek with the river. The n end of the rapids, near Camels Creek, is called Battles Upper Falls; the s end, near Fish Creek, is called Battles Lower Falls. Mentioned as early as 1819 in a survey of the major rivers of North Carolina.

Batts Crossroads, community in ne Wilson County. Named for John Batts before the middle of the nineteenth century.

Batts Grave. *See* Batts Island.

Batts House, the home of Nathaniell Batts, first-known permanent white settler in North Carolina, was built as early as 1655 and stood between Roanoke River and Salmon Creek, e Bertie County, facing Albemarle Sound.

Batts Island, former island in Albemarle Sound near the mouth of the Yeopim River, sw Perquimans County. Named for Nathaniell Batts, who acquired property in the area, September 24, 1660. It is mentioned in local records as early as 1694. In 1749 it was 40 acres in area and had houses and orchards on it; by 1756 it had been reduced to 27 acres. Early in the twentieth century it was a campsite for fishermen, but later it was reduced to a mud flat with a few dead trees. A hurricane in the 1950s completely destroyed the island. Appears as Heriots Island, probably for Thomas Hariot (1560–1621), on the Smith map, 1624; as Hariots Island on the Comberford map, 1657: and as Bats Grave on the Moseley map, 1733, and the Collet map, 1770.

Baucoms, community in n central Union County on the head of Watson Creek.

Baughn Mountain, w Rockingham County e of the Mayo River and n of the Dan River near the junction of the two. Originally known as East Mayo Mountain; renamed for Henry Baughn, who settled there in 1814. By 1897 known as Cedar Point Mountain. Alt. 995.

Baum Creek rises in sw Roanoke Island, Dare County, and flows sw into Oyster Creek.

Baum Point extends from n Roanoke Island into Roanoke Sound, Dare County.

Bawdy Creek rises in e Johnston County and flows se into Neuse River.

Bawdy Swamp rises in central Johnston County and flows se into Bawdy Creek.

Baxter, community in e Henderson County on Tumblebug Creek. Post office operated there, 1881–1914.

Baxter Branch rises in n Madison County and flows se into White Rock Branch.

Baxter Creek rises in s Davie County and flows se approx. 2 mi. into Bear Creek.

Baxter Creek rises in n Haywood County near lat. 35°43′ N., long. 83°06′40″ W., and flows nw into Big Creek. Named for Steven Baxter, a longtime resident and woodcutter in the area. Now in Great Smoky Mountains National Park.

Bay. *See* Bull's Bay.

Bay, The. *See* Turnagain Bay.

Bayboro, town and county seat, central Pamlico County on Bay River. Named for the river, *which see*. Became the county seat in 1876, succeeding Vandemere. Inc. 1881. Alt. 8.5.

Bay Branch rises in sw Beaufort County and flows e into Chocowinity Creek.

Baybush Swamp, a fine sandy loam swamp in n Craven County.

Bay City, community in Bay City Pocosin, n Pamlico County. Est. in the early twentieth century as a farming community by out-of-state developers. Now produces grain.

Bay City Pocosin, muck-filled area approx. 12 mi. wide in n Pamlico and s Beaufort Counties.

Bay Creek, a tidal creek on Smith Island in Brunswick County that extends from its junction with Cape Creek first se and then ne to flow into Buzzard Bay.

Bay Creek, The. *See* Turnagain Creek.

Bayleaf, community in n central Wake County.

Bayley. *See* Shawboro.

Baymarsh Thorofare, waterway between Sheep Island and Portsmouth Island, e Carteret County.

Baymeade, community in ne New Hanover County.

Baynes, community in s Caswell County.

Bay River rises in n Pamlico County and flows ne for approx. 16 mi. into the Neuse River. Named for the bay tree, which flourishes in the vicinity. Appears on the Moseley map, 1733.

Bay River Point, peninsula off e Pamlico County extending into Bay River estuary.

Bays. *See* Carolina Bays.

Baysden Mill Pond, in sw Onslow County on Cypress Creek. Covers approx. 10 acres; max. depth 10 ft.

Bay Shore Park, town in s Carteret County on Bogue Sound. Inc. 1959.

Bayside. *See* Bayview.

Bay Swamp, e Pender County, drains nw into Holly Shelter Bay.

Bayview, community in s Onslow County served by post office, 1895–1902.

Bayview, community on Pamlico River, central Beaufort County. Known earlier as Bayside.

Beach Branch rises in ne Cherokee County and flows se into Right Fork Webb Creek.

Beach Creek rises in s Clay County and flows sw into Brasstown Creek.

Beach Springs, community in w Perquimans County.

Beach Top, s Clay County near the headwaters of Beach Creek and Long Branch.

Beacon Height, mountain in e Avery County.

Beacon Island, in Pamlico Sound, ne Carteret County, is situated between Wallace Channel and Blair Channel leading through Ocracoke Inlet. Approx. 1,200 ft. long. Name derived from two large beacons on the island formerly used by pilots guiding ships through the channels. Jonathan Price wrote in 1795 that a "fort" was built on the s end of the island in 1794–95 pursuant to an act of Congress. Appears on the Moseley map, 1733.

Beacon Island Road. *See* Wallace Channel.

Beacon Island Shoal, in Pamlico Sound in ne Carteret County, obstructing passage through Ocracoke Inlet. Located between Beacon Island and Wallace Channel. Appears on the Moseley map, 1733.

Beal's Knob, n Clay County near the Cherokee County line. Alt. 5,000–5,100.

Beals Mill Pond, e Northampton County on a tributary of Potecasi Creek.

Beaman Run, the s part of Howell Swamp, in n Greene County; it flows sw into Contentnea Creek. Named for the Beaman family, which settled in the vicinity about the time of the Revolution.

Beamans Crossroads, community in n Sampson County between Old Mill Swamp and Marsh Swamp.

Beam Mill, community in e Cleveland County on Magness Creek. Alt. 1,001.

Bean Creek is formed in n Mitchell County by the junction of Right Fork Bean Creek and Left Fork Bean Creek. It flows se into Big Rock Creek.

Bean Shoals, a succession of rocks and loose stones in Yadkin River on Surry-Yadkin county line, approx. 1 mi. s of the confluence of Ararat River. The shoals measure 2 mi. in length. The communities of Shoals (Surry County) and Bean Shoals (Yadkin County) are nearby. Mentioned as early as 1819 in a survey of the rivers of North Carolina.

Beantown Creek rises in central Haywood County and flows se and ne into Jonathans Creek.

Bear Banks, coastal beach in se Onslow County on the Atlantic Ocean between Bogue and Bear inlets. Mentioned in local records as early as 1713; also spelled Bare, Bar, and Barr. Known also as Bear Beach and Heady's Beach for Daniel Heady and four generations of his descendants who owned the area. The Banks are approx. 3½ mi. long.

Bear Bay. *See* Allenton.

Bear Beach. *See* Bear Banks.

Bear Branch rises in ne Cherokee County and flows nw into Junaluska Creek.

Bear Branch rises in central Columbus County and flows se into Waccamaw River. Schulkens Pond, *which see*, is on the branch.

Bear Branch rises in n Craven County and flows sw into Swift Creek.

Bear Branch rises in n Haywood County and flows nw into Cold Springs Creek.

Bear Branch rises in w Haywood County near lat. 35°36′ N., long. 83°10′50″ W., and flows e to join Horse Creek in forming Rough Creek.

Bear Branch rises in nw Henderson County and flows sw into Wash Creek.

Bear Branch rises in s Lee County and flows e into Crane Creek.

Bear Branch rises in e Madison County and flows n into Callahan Branch.

Bear Branch rises in s Madison County and flows ne into Spring Creek.

Bear Branch rises in w Madison County and flows e into Spring Creek.

Bear Branch rises in w Nash County and flows se into Sapony Creek.

Bear Branch rises in w Watauga County and flows nw into Buckeye Creek.

Bear Branch rises in se Wilson County and flows sw into Toisnot Swamp. Approx. 3 mi. long.

Bearcamp Creek rises in sw Transylvania County and flows se into South Carolina and into Toxaway River.

Bear Cove, in w Macon County at the head of Wayah Creek.

Bear Creek rises in e Ashe County and flows nw into South Fork New River.

Bear Creek rises in w Beaufort County and flows n into Tar River.

Bear Creek rises in ne Cabarrus County and flows se into Stanly County, where it enters Big Bear Creek.

Bear Creek rises in sw Chatham County and flows se and ne into Rocky River.

Bear Creek rises in s Cleveland County and flows sw into Shoal Creek.

Bear Creek rises in w Davie County and flows se approx. 14 mi. into South Yadkin River. Daniel Boone and his father, Squire Boone, and other members of the family owned land along the stream. Daniel Boone killed many bears along the creek, hence its name. The Bear Creek watershed is about 15,000 acres in area.

Bear Creek rises in e Franklin County and flows se into Nash County, where it enters Back Swamp.

Bear Creek rises in nw Graham County and flows ne into Cheoah River.

Bear Creek rises in se Graham County and flows sw into Tulula Creek.

Bear Creek rises in central Jackson County and flows ne into Bear Creek Lake on Tuckasegee River. *See also* Bear Creek Lake.

Bear Creek rises in s Madison County and flows nw into French Broad River.

Bear Creek rises in central Mitchell County and flows s into North Toe River.

Bear Creek rises in e Onslow County and flows se into Brown's Sound. Appears on the Moseley map, 1733. Known earlier as Deep Creek.

Bear Creek rises in w Orange County and flows sw into Cane Creek.

Bear Creek rises in ne Pamlico County and flows se into Bay River. *See also* Mesic.

Bear Creek rises in e Pitt County and flows e into Tar River. Appears on the Collet map, 1770.

Bear Creek rises in s Randolph County and flows se into Moore County, where it flows se then ne into Deep River.

Bear Creek rises in s Surry County and flows se into Fisher River.

Bear Creek rises in central Swain County in Great Smoky Mountains National Park and flows se into Forney Creek.

Bear Creek rises in e Wayne County and flows se on the Wayne-Greene county line into nw Lenoir County and se into Neuse River. The name appears in local records as early as 1742.

Bear Creek, community in sw Chatham County. Known as Richmond until 1895. Noted for production of fruitcakes. Alt. 473.

Bear Creek, community in se Graham County at the mouth of Bear Creek.

Bear Creek. *See* Warrior Creek.

Bear Creek Lake, central Jackson County on Tuckasegee River. Formed in 1954 as a reservoir for Nantahala Power and Light Company. Covers 476 acres, with a max. depth of 195 ft. Shoreline is 13.5 mi. Used for generating hydroelectric power. Named for Bear Creek, which feeds it. Also receives the waters of Sols, Flat, and Robinson Creeks. Known for bass and trout fishing. Alt. 2,560.

Bear Creek Township, sw Chatham County.

Beard, community in ne Cumberland County.

Beard Cove, central Buncombe County, between Beard Mountain and Gooch Peak in the Elk Mountains.

Beard Creek rises in s Pamlico County and flows s into Neuse River. Appears on the Moseley map, 1733. Local tradition attempts to associate the origin of the name with Blackbeard, the early eighteenth-century pirate.

Beard Mountain, central Buncombe County in the Elk Mountains.

Beards Creek, community in s Pamlico County on Beard Creek, *which see*, and Neuse River, where a recreational area has been developed. Settled prior to 1750; a post office operated there from 1878 to 1914 as Bairds Creek.

Bearford Bay, a marshy bay in sw Duplin County.

Bear Gap, s Clay County on Chunky Gal Mountain.

Bear Gap, s Yancey County between Blue Sea Creek and Beech Nursery Creek.

Beargarden Pocosin, central Greene County. Named because it was a favorite haunt of bears and numerous flowering plants grow there. Yellow jasmine and honeysuckle were so fragrant that they could be smelled a mile or so away downwind.

Beargrass, town in s Martin County on a tributary of Beargrass Swamp. Settled about 1828. Inc. 1909, but inactive in municipal affairs until 1961, when the General Assembly appointed new officers. Alt. 65.

Bear Grass Creek rises in central Craven County and flows s into Trent River s of New Bern.

Beargrass Swamp rises in s Martin County and flows w into Turkey Swamp.

Beargrass Township, s central Martin County.

Bearhead Creek rises in e Onslow County and flows nw into Wallace Creek.

Bear Inlet, se Onslow County, through which Brown's Sound drains into the Atlantic Ocean. Mentioned in local records as early as 1713 and appears on the Moseley map, 1733. Following the Spanish alarm of 1747, Bear Inlet Fort was constructed there.

Bear Island, not now identifiable, appears on the Moseley map, 1733, in Bogue Sound, s Carteret County w of Dog Island.

Bear Island, a sand island in the w section of Angola Bay, n Pender County.

Bear Knob, on the Cherokee-Graham county line.

Bear Knob, sw Macon County between Little Indian Creek and Nantahala River.

Bear Marsh Branch rises in nw Duplin County and flows sw into Merritt Mill Pond and Goshen Swamp.

Bearmeat Branch rises in se Swain County and flows sw into Yalaka Creek.

Bear Mountain, s Jackson County between Doubletop Mountain and Glassy Rock Creek. Alt. 4,650.

Bearpaw, community in w Cherokee County at the mouth of Bearpaw Creek.

Bearpaw Creek rises in w Cherokee County and flows sw and se into Hiwassee River.

Bearpen Branch rises in s Haywood County and flows w into Allen Creek.

Bearpen Branch rises in w Jackson County and flows ne into Dodgen Creek.

Bear Pen Branch rises in n Madison County and flows sw into Little Laurel Creek.

Bearpen Branch rises in n Swain County and flows se into Little Jonas Creek.

Bearpen Branch rises in n Swain County on Noland Ridge and flows se into Left Fork [Deep Creek].

Bear Pen Branch rises in n Transylvania County and flows ne into South Fork Mills River.

Bearpen Creek rises in s Macon County and flows w into Nantahala River.

Bearpen Creek rises in w Macon County and flows sw into Wine Spring Creek.

Bearpen Creek rises in n Madison County and flows s into Chimney Creek.

Bearpen Creek rises in ne Mitchell County and flows sw into Laurel Creek.

Bearpen Creek rises in n Swain County and flows s into Noland Creek.

Bearpen Gap, n central Avery County.

Bearpen Gap, sw Avery County near the Mitchell County line.

Bearpen Gap, ne Buncombe County w of Bearpen Knob.

Bearpen Gap, n Cherokee County in the Unicoi Mountains between Chestnut Mountain and Hangover Top.

Bearpen Gap, n Cherokee County near the headwaters of Slickrock Branch.

Bear Pen Gap, n Clay County between Tuni Creek and the Cherokee County line.

Bearpen Gap, on the Clay-Macon county line.

Bearpen Gap, n central Graham County on Cables Cove Creek.

Bearpen Gap, on the Jackson-Haywood county line between Spot Knob and Rough Butt. Alt. 2,872.

Bearpen Gap, s Macon County at the head of Shope Fork.

Bearpen Gap, w Macon County between Locust Tree Gap and Ray Branch.

Bearpen Gap, n Swain County between Laurel Branch and Bearpen Creek.

Bearpen Gap, nw Swain County between Cable Branch and Fontana Lake.

Bear Pen Islands Swamp, n central Brunswick County. A part of Green Swamp.

Bearpen Knob, ne Buncombe County between Beartree and Bearpen Gaps.

Bearpen Knob, peak in s Jackson County bordered on nw by Chattooga River. Southern

slope is head for Scotsman Creek. Also called
Bearpen Mountain. Alt. 4,300.

Bearpen Mountain, on the Jackson-Transylvania
county line between Sassafras Mountain and
Horsepasture River. Alt. 4,025.

Bearpen Mountain, s Macon County between
Bearpen Creek and Steeltrap Knob.

Bearpen Mountain, se Macon County between
Little Bearpen Mountain and Saltrock
Branch.

Bearpen Mountain, n Madison County parallel
to Former Camp Branch.

Bear Pen Ridge, se Clay County.

Bearpen Ridge, s Haywood County between
Daniels Cove and Correll Branch.

Bearpen Ridge, w Haywood County between
Bearpen Branch and Caldwell Fork.

Bearpen Ridge, n Madison County between
Hickeys Fork and Rock Branch.

Bearpen Ridge, ne Mitchell County between
Laurel Creek and Bearpen Creek.

Bearpen Ridge, n Swain County in Great Smoky
Mountains National Park, a short spur of
Noland Ridge extending se.

Bearpen Ridge, sw Yancey County between
Sodom Branch and Indian Creek.

Bearpen Rock, a mountain in w Avery County.

Bear Pocosin, ne Sampson County s of Youngs
Swamp and e of Six Runs Creek.

Bear Point extends into Pamlico Sound from e
Hyde County.

Bear Point, se Tyrrell County, extends from the
mainland into Alligator River.

Bearpond, community in s Vance County,
named for a local tradition of a celebrated
bear hunt there. In 1785 a practical joke was
played on Zeke Brown to put an end to his tall
tales of bear killing. A mock bear hunt was
arranged at the present site of Bearpond in
which a local citizen, Jake Sims, dressed in
bearskins and gave Brown such a scare he left
the county for "Orrapeake." The community
is now known locally as Buena Vista, after the
plantation of Dr. Robert Christian Pritchard
(b. 1812) in nearby s Warren County.

Bear Poplar, community in w Rowan County.
Known first as Rocky Mount; present name
adopted in 1878, when a post office was est.
Name came from the nearby location of a
poplar tree in which Capt. Thomas Cowan,
Revolutionary hero, treed a bear in the late
eighteenth century.

Bear Ridge, mountain in w Avery County.

Bear Ridge, between Cashie Branch and Licklog
Creek in n Jackson County.

Bear Ridge, s Yancey County between Blue Sea
Creek and Beech Nursery Creek.

Bear Rock Branch rises in s Yancey County and
flows se into South Toe River.

Bearskin, community in w central Sampson
County near Bearskin Swamp.

Bearskin Creek rises in n Granville County and
flows n into Grassy Creek.

Bearskin Creek rises in w Union County and
flows e through the city of Monroe into
Richardson Creek.

Bearskin Swamp rises in w central Sampson
County and flows sw into Little Coharie
Creek.

Bear Swamp, e Chowan and w Perquimans
Counties. Covered about ⅛ of Chowan
County before being drained to provide
farmland.

Bear Swamp rises in nw Duplin County and
flows ne into Goshen Swamp.

Bear Swamp rises in w Halifax County and flows
sw into Little Fishing Creek.

Bear Swamp is formed in s Hertford County by
the junction of Horse Swamp and Flat Swamp
and flows e into Ahoskie Creek.

Bear Swamp rises in central Northampton
County and flows se into Urahaw Swamp.

Bear Swamp rises in w Robeson County and
flows se into Lumber River.

Bear Swamp Creek rises in n Franklin County
and flows sw into Tar River.

Beartown Mountain, on the Mitchell County,
N.C.–Carter County, Tenn., line. Alt. 5,481.

Beartown Ridge, ne Mitchell County between
Beartown Mountain and Big Rock Creek.

Beartrail Ridge Gap, on the Haywood-Jackson
county line.

Beartrap Knob, s Haywood County between
Raven Hollow and Possum Hollow.

Beartrap Ridge, s Haywood County between Big
Beartrap Branch and Raven Hollow.

Beartree Creek rises in e Chatham County and
flows se into New Hope Creek.

Beartree Gap, ne Buncombe County between
Snowball Mountain and Bearpen Knob.

Bearwallow, community in ne Henderson
County. Named by William Mills, pioneer
settler, because of a nearby, much-frequented
bear wallow.

Bearwallow Bald, peak in n Swain County in Great Smoky Mountains National Park on Welch Ridge. Alt. 4,954.

Bearwallow Branch rises in ne Buncombe County and flows ne into Carter Creek.

Bear Wallow Branch rises in ne Madison County and flows sw into Foster Creek.

Bearwallow Branch rises in ne Swain County and flows sw into Bradley Fork.

Bearwallow Brook rises in n Transylvania County and flows se into South Fork Mills River.

Bearwallow Creek rises in e Jackson County and flows sw into Piney Mountain Creek.

Bearwallow Creek rises in nw Mitchell County and flows sw into Pigeonroost Creek.

Bearwallow Creek rises in sw Transylvania County and flows se into Toxaway River.

Bearwallow Creek rises in e Yancey County and flows n into Little Crabtree Creek.

Bearwallow Gap, se Buncombe County se of Bearwallow Mountain.

Bear Wallow Gap, ne Haywood County on the head of Wesley Creek.

Bearwallow Gap, nw Mitchell County on Bearwallow Creek.

Bear Wallow Knob, s Yancey County at the e end of Bear Wallow Ridge.

Bear Wallow Knob, s Yancey County between Hurricane Gap and Ogle Gap. Alt. 5,085.

Bearwallow Mountain, on the Buncombe-Henderson county line. Alt. 4,249.

Bearwallow Ridge, n Jackson County between Cherry Orchard Branch and Rough Branch.

Bearwallow Ridge, n Swain County, extends ne from the confluence of Proctor Creek and Hazel Creek to Proctor Ridge.

Bear Wallow Ridge, s Yancey County between Middle Fork and Grassy Knob Branch.

Bear Wallow Stand Ridge, s Yancey County between Raven Fork and Blue Sea Creek.

Bearwell Pocosin, se Lenoir County between Joshua Creek and Trent River. Probably a corruption of the family name Burwell. Thomas Burwell was living in the vicinity about 1750.

Beasley, community in n Washington County. Known locally as Holly Neck.

Beasley Bay, in Currituck Sound between Jarvis Channel and Currituck Banks in e Currituck County.

Beasley Branch rises in w Gates County and flows se into Run of Swamp.

Beasley Branch rises in s Transylvania County and flows se into Cherryfield Creek.

Beasley Creek rises in ne Macon County and flows sw into Cowee Creek.

Beasley Creek rises in w Transylvania County and flows s into West Fork French Broad River.

Beasley Gap, s Macon County between Mulberry Creek and Commissioner Creek.

Beasleys Creek rises on the Pender-Onslow county line and flows se into Stump Sound in s Onslow County. Appears on the Collet map, 1770.

Beasleys Mill Pond, on Millers Creek in w Duplin County.

Beason Creek rises in se Cleveland County and flows se into Buffalo Creek.

Beatie's Ford. *See* Beattie's Ford.

Beaton Branch rises in s Buncombe County and flows n into Bent Creek.

Beattie's Ford, across the Catawba River, Lincoln-Mecklenburg Counties near the Iredell County line. Named for John Beatty, who owned land in the area as early as 1749. A post office named Beatie's Ford existed in the vicinity from 1806 to 1838. A part of the British army, in pursuit of Gen. Nathanael Greene, crossed the river there on February 1, 1781. The site is now under the waters of Lake Norman.

Beatty Branch rises in central McDowell County and flows se into Paxton Creek.

Beattys Mill Pond in e Bladen County on Lake Creek.

Beaty Spring Knob, s Haywood County on the head of Inman Branch.

Beaucatcher Mountain, central Buncombe County in e Asheville. Alt. approx. 3,200. About 1850 James W. Patton erected a summer house or arbor there, and it became quite popular with courting couples, hence the name. Highway construction in 1979 opened a cut in the mountain alongside 1929 tunnel despite public opposition.

Beaufort, town and county seat in s central Carteret County. Laid out in 1713 and settled soon afterward. Inc. 1723. Named for Henry Somerset (1684–1714), Duke of Beaufort, one of the Lords Proprietors of Carolina. Built on the site of an Indian village, Wareiock, said to have meant "Fish Town" or "Fishing Village"; the town was first called Fishtown. Home of North Carolina Maritime Museum. Alt. 9.

Beaufort (BOE-furt) County was first called Pamptecough Precinct when it was formed in 1705 from Bath County; the name was changed to Beaufort about 1712 to honor Henry Somerset, Duke of Beaufort (1684–1714), who in 1709 became one of the Lords Proprietors. Located in the e part of the state, it is bounded by Craven, Hyde, Martin, Pitt, Pamlico, and Washington Counties. Area: 957 sq. mi. County seat: Washington, with an elevation of 11 ft. Townships are Bath, Long Acre, Chocowinity, Pantego, Richland, and Washington. Produces tobacco, corn, hogs, cattle, boats, air filters, soybeans, Irish potatoes, peanuts, wheat, oats, sorghum, cotton, canned seafood, lumber, and phosphate.

Beaufort Inlet, s central Carteret County, from the Atlantic Ocean into Bogue Sound, between Bogue Banks on the w and Shackleford Banks on the e. Appears as Topsail Inlet on the De Graffenried map (French text), 1711, and was later known as Old Topsail Inlet.

Beaufort Township, on Taylors Creek and Beaufort Inlet in central Carteret County. For a time called township no. 4.

Beaumont, community in s Chatham County served by post office, 1851–1914.

Beautancus, community in n Duplin County near Bear Marsh Branch.

Beauty Spot, mountain on the Mitchell County, N.C.–Unicoi County, Tenn., line. Alt. 4,254.

Beauty Spot Gap, on the Mitchell County, N.C.–Unicoi County, Tenn., line.

Beaux, community in n Wilkes County near Mulberry Creek.

Beaver Branch rises in ne Wayne County and flows se into Nahunta Swamp in w Greene County. The name dates from colonial times.

Beaver Creek rises in s central Ashe County and flows se into South Fork New River.

Beaver Creek rises in ne Cabarrus County and flows s into Dutch Buffalo Creek about 2 mi. n of town of Mount Pleasant.

Beaver Creek rises in ne Caldwell County and flows n into Wilkes County, where it enters into Yadkin River.

Beaver Creek rises in ne Cherokee County and flows se into Valley River.

Beaver Creek, about 13 mi. long, rises on the ne slope of Vaughn Hill in the Fort Bragg Military Reservation, nw Cumberland County, and flows e then s into Little Rockfish Creek.

Beaver Creek rises in e Forsyth County and flows ne into Reedy Fork Creek in nw Guilford County.

Beaver Creek rises in w Guilford County and flows w into Alamance County, where it enters Great Alamance Creek.

Beaver Creek rises in sw Harnett County near the junction of Harnett-Lee-Moore county lines and flows sw then se into Moore County, where it enters Crains Creek.

Beaver Creek rises in e Hoke County and flows se into Rockfish Creek.

Beaver Creek rises in nw Jones and e Lenoir Counties and flows e into Trent River.

Beaver Creek rises in e Mitchell County and flows se into North Toe River.

Beaver Creek rises in e central Surry County and flows sw into Fisher River.

Beaver Creek rises in n central Wake County and flows sw into Neuse River almost directly opposite the mouth of Reedy Spring Branch.

Beaver Creek rises in w Wake County and flows sw into e Chatham County, where it enters New Hope Creek.

Beaver Creek rises in sw Wilkes County near the Alexander county line in the Brushy Mountains and flows n into Yadkin River.

Beaver Creek, community in s central Ashe County. Alt. approx. 2,990.

Beaver Creek. *See* Cumberland.

Beaver Creek Pond. *See* Beaver Lake.

Beaver Creek Township, n Jones County.

Beaver Creek Township, sw Wilkes County.

Beaverdam, community in sw Buncombe County on Beaverdam Creek ne of Long Mountain.

Beaverdam. *See* Marshville.

Beaverdam Bald, on the Cherokee County, N.C.–Monroe County, Tenn., line in the Unicoi Mountains. Alt. 4,280.

Beaverdam Bay, ne Bladen County.

Beaverdam Bay, sw Bladen County.

Beaverdam Bay, a section of Green Swamp, central Brunswick County.

Beaver Dam Branch rises in e Brunswick County and flows e into Cape Fear River.

Beaverdam Branch rises in ne Franklin County and flows ne into Sandy Creek.

Beaverdam Branch rises in e Johnston County and flows se into Wayne County, where it enters Neuse River.

Beaverdam Branch rises in w Johnston County and flows e into Middle Creek.

Beaverdam Branch rises in s Jones County and flows n into Mill Run.

Beaverdam Branch rises in sw Mecklenburg County and flows sw into Catawba River.

Beaverdam Branch rises in sw Nash County and flows se into Turkey Creek.

Beaverdam Branch rises in w Nash County and flows e into Big Peachtree Creek.

Beaver Dam Branch of Hunting Creek rises n of Calahaln in w Davie County and flows s into Hunting Creek.

Beaver Dam Brook rises in s Catawba County and flows sw into South Fork Catawba River.

Beaverdam Brook rises in Magnolia in w Duplin County and flows ne into Maxwell Creek.

Beaverdam Creek rises in se Bladen County and flows ne into Waymans Creek in Columbus County.

Beaver Dam Creek rises in se Brunswick County and flows s into Cape Fear River.

Beaverdam Creek is formed in the Elk Mountains, central Buncombe County, by the junction of Webb Cove Creek and Linn Cove Creek. It flows w into French Broad River.

Beaverdam Creek rises in sw Buncombe County near the Henderson County line and flows n into South Hominy Creek.

Beaverdam Creek rises in n central Cherokee County and flows sw into Hiwassee River.

Beaverdam Creek rises in central Cleveland County and flows s into First Broad River.

Beaverdam Creek rises in se Cumberland County and flows se into South River.

Beaverdam Creek rises in se Davidson County and flows s into Badin Lake on Yadkin River in nw Montgomery County.

Beaverdam Creek rises in w Davidson County and flows se into Swearing Creek.

Beaverdam Creek rises in w Duplin County and flows e into Maxwell Creek.

Beaverdam Creek rises in nw Gaston County and flows ne into South Fork Catawba River.

Beaverdam Creek rises in n Gates County and flows nw into Virginia, where it enters Somerton Creek.

Beaverdam Creek rises in s Granville County and flows sw into Wake County, where it enters Neuse River.

Beaverdam Creek rises in sw Granville County and flows s into Neuse River in nw Wake County.

Beaverdam Creek rises in e Haywood County at Beaverdam Gap and flows sw into Pigeon River.

Beaverdam Creek rises in e Jones County and flows s into Trent River.

Beaverdam Creek rises in s Martin County and flows n into Conoho Creek.

Beaverdam Creek rises in s Nash County and flows ne into Toisnot Swamp.

Beaverdam Creek rises in n Richmond County and flows sw into Rocky Fork Creek.

Beaverdam Creek rises in w Rowan County and flows ne into Withrow Creek.

Beaverdam Creek rises in n Surry County and flows se into Little Fisher River.

Beaverdam Creek rises in e Union County and flows ne into Lanes Creek.

Beaverdam Creek rises in central Wake County and flows se into Neuse River.

Beaverdam Creek rises in central Wake County in the nw side of the city of Raleigh and flows ne into Crabtree Creek.

Beaverdam Creek rises in se Wake County and flows se into Moccasin Creek.

Beaverdam Creek rises in e Wake County and flows w into Neuse River.

Beaverdam Creek rises in n Watauga County and flows sw into Watauga River.

Beaverdam Creek rises in w Wayne County and flows se then ne into Thoroughfare Swamp.

Beaverdam Dismal, a swampy area in nw Sampson County between the heads of Little Coharie Creek and Beaverdam Swamp.

Beaverdam Gap, sw Buncombe County in Newfound Mountain.

Beaverdam Gap, on the Buncombe-Henderson county line w of Ferrin Knob.

Beaverdam Gap, n Cherokee County at the headwaters of Beaverdam and Cook Creeks.

Beaverdam Gap, on the head of Beaverdam Creek in e Haywood County.

Beaverdam Gap, nw Henderson County on the nw end of Trace Ridge. Alt. 3,500.

Beaver Dam Lake, basin on Falls Lake along the Granville-Wake county line fed by Robertson,

Beaverdam, Smith, and Little Beaverdam Creeks.

Beaverdam Pocosin, nw Bertie County.

Beaverdam Ridge, w Watauga County extends nw from Watauga River, w of Cove Creek and se of Ward Hollow.

Beaverdam Run rises in s Greene County and flows se in an arc into Contentnea Creek.

Beaverdam Swamp rises in central Beaufort County and flows w into Broad Creek.

Beaverdam Swamp rises in nw Bertie County and flows e into Loosing Swamp, which becomes Stony Creek.

Beaver Dam Swamp rises in e central Brunswick County and flows s into Town Creek.

Beaverdam Swamp rises in w Columbus County and flows se to join Gum Swamp in forming Monie Swamp.

Beaverdam Swamp rises in ne Craven County and flows s into Little Swift Creek.

Beaverdam Swamp rises in n central Halifax County and flows se into Beech Swamp. Appears on the Collet map, 1770.

Beaverdam Swamp rises in s Lenoir County and flows ne into Trent River. Appears in local records as early as 1720.

Beaverdam Swamp rises in n Nash County and flows ne into Fishing Creek.

Beaverdam Swamp rises in e central Sampson County and flows se into Six Runs Creek.

Beaverdam Swamp rises in n Sampson County and flows sw into Great Coharie Creek.

Beaverdam Swamp rises in nw Sampson County and flows sw into Mingo Swamp.

Beaverdam Swamp rises in w Wayne County and flows se into Neuse River.

Beaverdam Swamp. *See* Nahunta Swamp.

Beaverdam Swamp Canal rises in s Harnett County and flows s into Cape Fear River.

Beaverdam Township, n Cherokee County.

Beaver Dam Township, se Cumberland County.

Beaverdam Township, e Haywood County.

Beaverdam Township, e Richmond County.

Beaverdam Township, n Watauga County.

Beaver Dam Township. *See* Arthur Township.

Beaver Gap, s Cherokee County n of Sheep Knob.

Beaver Island Creek rises in e Stokes County and flows e into Rockingham County, where it turns s to flow into Dan River.

Beaver Island Township, e Stokes County.

Beaver Lake, in the city of Asheville near its n limits, central Buncombe County. On Beaverdam Creek. Constructed as part of real-estate development.

Beaver Lake is formed by a dam on Beaver Creek, w Cumberland County. Approx. 1 mi. long. Sometimes known as Beaver Creek Pond.

Beaverpond Creek rises in nw Northampton County and flows ne into Virginia, where it turns se to flow back into Northampton County. It again turns ne to flow back into Virginia, where it enters Fontaine Creek. It appears on the map of the North Carolina–Virginia line prepared by William Byrd in 1728.

Beaver Store, community in e Wayne County between Exum Mill Branch and The Slough.

Bechewa Creek rises in w Forsyth County and flows sw into Yadkin River. Appears as Bathsheba Creek on Collet map, 1770, and as Barshavia Creek on MacRae map, 1833.

Beck, community in n Wake County served by post office, 1882–1903.

Beckham Millpond. *See* South Lake.

Beck Mountain, a granite formation in sw Chatham County.

Beckon Mill. *See* South Lake.

Becks Bald, peak on Hughes Ridge, n Swain County in Great Smoky Mountains National Park. Alt. 5,022.

Becks Branch rises in ne Swain County in Great Smoky Mountains National Park and flows s into Oconaluftee River.

Beck Springs. *See* Bennett.

Beckwith, community in e Beaufort County.

Beddingfield Creek rises in e Wake County and flows se into Johnston County, where it turns n and flows into Neuse River.

Bedford County. A bill was introduced in the Assembly on November 23, 1768, to create Bedford County and Trinity Parish from parts of Rowan and Orange Counties, but the bill was rejected on December 1. The Bethabara Diary (*Records of the Moravians*, I, 381) for December 18, however, reports that a county by the name was est. "last year" in "Lord Granville's part of the Province." Another bill to erect a Bedford County and St. John Parish from the upper part of Tyrrell County and the lower part of Halifax County was considered on November 6, 1769, but it was not passed. The name probably was intended to honor John

Russell, Duke of Bedford (1710–71), Lord
President of the Council, 1763–65.

Bee Branch rises in n Buncombe County near
Rattlesnake Ridge and flows sw into Reems
Creek.

Bee Branch rises in nw Buncombe County near
Potato Knob and flows ne into Willow Creek.

Bee Branch rises in e Haywood County and flows
w into East Fork Pigeon River.

Bee Branch rises in nw Henderson County and
flows se into Big Creek.

Bee Branch rises in central Madison County
between Red Hill Knob and Lisenbee Ridge
and flows sw into Ammons Branch.

Bee Branch rises in e Mitchell County and flows
w into Stagger Weed Creek.

Bee Branch rises in central Yancey County and
flows sw into Cane River.

Bee Branch rises in n Yancey County and flows
ne into Toe River.

Beebranch Mountain, central Yancey County
near the head of Bee Branch.

Beech, community in n Buncombe County near
the junction of Maney Branch and Reems
Creek. Alt. 2,413. Named for large grove of
beech trees in the vicinity. Served by post
office, 1885–1919.

Beech Bottom, community in w Avery County.

Beech Branch rises in e Nash County and flows
se into w Edgecombe County and se into Tar
River.

Beech Cove Branch rises in w Macon County and
flows w into Nantahala River.

Beech Creek rises in sw Cherokee County and
flows ne into Hiwassee River.

Beech Creek rises in se Clay County and flows
sw into Towns County, Ga., where it enters
Tallulah River.

Beech Creek rises in e Graham County and flows
w into Sweetwater Creek.

Beech Creek rises in n Granville County and
flows ne into Jonathan Creek. Later known as
Little Johnson Creek.

Beech Creek rises in w Haywood County near lat.
35°39′30″ N., long. 83°11′30″ W., on e slope of
Balsam High Top, and flows se to join Falling
Creek in forming Palmer Creek.

Beech Creek rises in n Mitchell County and
flows se into Big Rock Creek.

Beech Creek rises in sw Watauga County and
forms a part of the Avery-Watauga county
boundary. It flows nw into Watauga River.

Beech Creek, community in n Avery County.
A post office est. there about 1850.

Beech Creek, community in w Watauga County.

Beech Creek. *See* Beech Swamp.

Beechertown, community in nw Macon County
on Nantahala River. A large hydroelectric
power development is there.

Beechflat Creek rises in e Jackson County and
flows sw into Mull Creek.

Beech Flats Prong rises in n Swain County in
Great Smoky Mountains National Park at
Luftee Gap and flows se to join Kephart Prong
in forming Oconaluftee River.

Beech Gap, se Clay County between Scaly Ridge
and Fairfield Ridge.

Beech Gap, on the Clay-Macon county line.

Beech Gap, on the Haywood-Swain county line
between Ledge Bald and Balsam High Top
in Great Smoky Mountains National Park.
Formerly known as Big Swag Gap. Alt. approx.
5,060.

Beech Gap, on the Haywood-Transylvania
county line between Tanasee Bald and Devils
Court House.

Beech Gap. *See* Black Mountain Gap.

Beech Glen, community in e Madison County on
Little Ivy Creek. Alt. 2,105.

Beechgrove, community in nw Washington
County.

Beech Knob, e central Avery County. Alt. 5,067.

Beech Knob, on the Haywood-Transylvania
county line. Alt. 5,160–5,180.

Beech Knob, on the Jackson-Haywood county
line.

Beech Mountain, on the Avery-Watauga county
line. Peak in Avery County. Alt. 5,506.

Beech Mountain, n Yancey County between Bent
Creek and Little Creek.

Beech Mountain. *See* Bucks Peak.

Beech Mountain Township, n Avery County.

Beech Nursery Creek rises in s Yancey County
and flows nw into Cane River.

Beech Nursery Gap, s Yancey County between
Beech Nursery Creek and Big Pine Mountain.

Beechnut Gap, on the Swain County, N.C.–Sevier
County, Tenn., line in Great Smoky Mountains National Park.

Beech Ridge, nw Haywood County between
Seven Mile Ridge and the head of Big Creek.

Beech Ridge, between Lost Bottom Branch and
Beech Creek in w Haywood County, Great
Smoky Mountains National Park. It is a spur

of Balsam Mountain extending se from Balsam High Top.

Beech Spring Gap, s Haywood County between Shining Rock and Dog Loser Knob.

Beech Swamp rises in central Halifax County and flows se into Fishing Creek. Appears as Rogers Creek on the Moseley map, 1733, and as Beech Creek on the Collet map, 1770.

Beechville, community in ne Beaufort County.

Bee Cove Knob, n Graham County on the ne end of Bee Cove Lead.

Bee Cove Lead extends ne from Yellow Creek to Bee Cove Knob in n Graham County.

Bee Creek rises in central Graham County and flows nw into Yellow Creek.

Bee Creek rises in w Mitchell County and flows s into Big Rock Creek.

Beef Market Top, ne Jackson County on Grassy Ridge. Alt. 5,040. Said to have been named (1) because deserters from the Confederate army, hiding in the area, stole and slaughtered cattle there; or (2) because a young man killed cattle there that belonged to the father of his sweetheart when he was forbidden by her father to see her again.

Bee Gap, at sw end of Sassafras Ridge in sw Graham County.

Bee Gum Branch rises in n Swain County and flows se into Hazel Creek.

Bee Gum Branch rises in n central Swain County in Great Smoky Mountains National Park and flows sw into Forney Creek.

Bee Island Bay, swamp in w central Brunswick County. A part of Green Swamp.

Bee Knob, at the head of West Buffalo Creek in w Graham County.

Bee Knob, n Swain County in Great Smoky Mountains National Park on Pilot Ridge. Alt. 4,300.

Bee Log, community in n Yancey County on Bald Mountain Creek. Named when a fallen tree in the vicinity was discovered to contain bees and honey.

Bee Mountain, sw Caldwell County between the headwaters of Husbands and Abingdon Creeks.

Bee Ridge, central Buncombe County ne of Busbee Reservoir.

Bee Ridge, in South Mountains in s Burke County.

Bee Ridge, e Mitchell County between Bee Branch and Stony Valley.

Bee Ridge, n Swain County w of Forney Creek, parallel to Welch Branch.

Bee Ridge, e Yancey County, extends ne parallel to Dobag Creek.

Bee Rock Creek rises in nw McDowell County and flows e into Armstrong Creek.

Beer Rice Gap, on the Madison County, N.C.–Unicoi County, Tenn., line.

Bee Stump Branch rises in s Yancey County and flows n into South Toe River.

Beetree Branch rises in ne Cherokee County and flows nw into Valley River.

Bee Tree Branch rises in n Wilkes County and flows s into Mulberry Creek.

Bee Tree Canal, w Tyrrell County, flows ne from Lake Phelps to a tributary of Scuppernong River. Dug by slave labor to drain swamplands for cultivation.

Beetree Creek rises in ne Buncombe County and flows sw into Swannanoa River. An early settlement w of the Blue Ridge Mountains was est. there in 1785.

Bee Tree Creek rises in s Jackson County and flows s into Cedar Creek.

Beetree Creek rises in e Madison County and flows sw into East Fork [Bull Creek].

Beetree Creek rises in e Mitchell County and flows sw into Little Rock Creek.

Beetree Creek rises in n Swain County in Great Smoky Mountains National Park and flows sw into Right Fork Deep Creek.

Bee Tree Creek rises in s Watauga County and flows ne into Boone Fork.

Bee Tree Fork rises in nw Transylvania County and flows se into North Fork French Broad River.

Bee Tree Mountain. *See* Craggy Knob.

Beetree Reservoir, on Beetree Creek, ne Buncombe County. Alt. 2,669. The 55-acre lake is part of the water system of the city of Asheville.

Beetree Ridge extends se from Candler Knob to Big Creek in nw Henderson County.

Beetree Ridge, e Mitchell County between Reuben Creek and Beetree Creek.

Beetree Ridge, n Swain County in Great Smoky Mountains National Park, a spur extending sw from Thomas Ridge.

Bee Tree Ridge, n Watauga County; extends sw, w of Laurel Branch.

Begonia, community in s Gaston County served by post office, 1880–1905.

Belcross, community in central Camden County named for Bell family. Post office est. 1882.

Belew Creek, community in ne Forsyth County. A post office est. 1870. Originally est. as Belews Creek Mill.

Belews Creek rises in ne Forsyth, ne Guilford, and sw Rockingham Counties and flows ne across the se edge of Stokes County and into the Dan River on the Stokes-Rockingham county line. The creek rises independently of East and West Belews Creeks, both of which flow into it. Belews Creek appears on Collet map, 1770.

Belews Creek Township, ne Forsyth County.

Belews Lake, on Belews Creek, Rockingham County, was constructed 1970–73 by Duke Power Company. The 3,863-acre lake serves as cooling lake for power plant.

Belfast, community in e Davidson County served by post office, 1892–1907.

Belfast, community in central Wayne County. Named by John Robinson, native of Ireland, for his wife's birthplace, Belfast, Ireland. Formerly called Scottsville.

Belford, community in nw Nash County near the Franklin County line. Named by David Sills, who settled there in 1798, for his home in n England. A post office operated there, 1804–55.

Belgrade, community in ne Onslow County. Thousands of tons of limestone marl, used in building road foundations and in concrete, are shipped from there annually.

Belgrade. *See* Bonarva.

Belhaven, town in e Beaufort County on Pungo River and Pantego Creek. Alt. 4. Settled about 1890; inc. 1899. Name a combination of the words "belle" and "haven," meaning beautiful harbor. *See also* Aquascogoc.

Bell, community in central Buncombe County served by post office, 1883–1902. Named for first postmaster, George H. Bell.

Bellair, community in central Craven County.

Bellamy, crossroads community in e Robeson County. Alt. 108. Settled about 1910. Named for John D. Bellamy (1854–1932), counsel for the Seaboard Air Line Railroad. Bellamy station, now abandoned, was 2 mi. s.

Bellamys Lake, about ¾ mi. long, on Rocky Swamp near its confluence with Fishing Creek, sw Halifax County.

Bellarthur, town in w Pitt County. Settled about 1907. Inc. 1907 as Arthur; named for L. C. Arthur, local landowner and farmer. Name changed to Bellarthur, 1933. Alt. 79.

Bell Bay, in the mainland of sw Hyde County on Pamlico Sound immediately w of Rose Bay. Known as Jasper's Creek in the eighteenth century. The courthouse for Hyde County was located on Jasper's Creek in 1791–92.

Bell Branch rises in s central Brunswick County and flows w into Shallotte Creek.

Bell Branch rises in ne Buncombe County and flows se into Beetree Creek.

Bell Collar Cove, on Shining Creek in s Haywood County.

Bellcollar Gap, on the Graham-Swain county line between Little Bald and Cheoah Bald.

Bell Coney Mountain, on the e end of Lizzy Mountain in central Jackson County. Alt. 4,349.

Bell Cove, site of early settlement on the e end of Bogue Banks, s Carteret County. Name is taken from the fact that a bell in the local church was rung for services. Storms drove out early settlers until settlement of Salter Path, *which see.*

Bell Creek rises in sw Anson County and flows s into Deadfall Creek.

Bell Creek rises in central Carteret County and flows sw into Core Creek.

Bell Creek rises in n Cherokee County and flows se into Garreck Creek.

Bellemont, community in w central Alamance County, est. as a mill village prior to 1900.

Bellevedere Pond, n Wayne County in a tributary of Nahunta Swamp.

Bellfont. *See* Russellborough.

Bell Island, a peninsula extending from the e mainland of Currituck County into Coinjock Bay and Currituck Sound. Formerly separated from the mainland and called Willowbies Island on the Ogilby map, 1671, in honor of Peregrine Bertie, Lord Willoughby de Eresby (1555–1601), thought to have been a subscriber to the Roanoke voyage of 1585. On the Collet map, 1770, and subsequent maps until MacRae, 1833, the name Betts Island is used. It is now 1½ mi. long and ½ mi. wide. *See also* Bell's Island.

Bell Island, peninsula that extends from the s mainland of Hyde County into Pamlico Sound between Swanquarter Bay and Rose Bay. *See also* Abigails Islands.

Bell Island. *See* Pittmans Island.

Bell Knob, on the Clay-Macon county line.

Bell Mountain, s Cherokee County between Raminger Creek and Cane Creek.

Bell Mountain, w Henderson County between Little Willow Creek and South Fork.

Bellows Bay, at the n end of Currituck Sound and mouth of North Landing River; extends into the s tip of MacKay Island in ne Currituck County.

Bell Point, peninsula off n Pamlico County extending into Bay River.

Bell River is formed in s Alexander County where Glade Creek enters Lower Little River. It flows s approx. 1½ mi. into Catawba River. Local usage applies the name to Lower Little River s from a point about midway between the mouths of Muddy Fork and Spring Creeks, where N.C. Highway 90 crosses Lower Little River.

Bell's, community in nw Pitt County.

Bells Branch rises in central Hertford County and flows se and ne into Potecasi Creek.

Bells Corners. *See* Newport.

Bells Creek rises in n Richmond County and flows se into Rocky Fork Creek.

Bells Cross Roads, community in sw Iredell County. A post office named Fallstown operated there from 1811 to 1866.

Bells Ferry appears on the Moseley map, 1733, across Lockwoods Folly River on the Brunswick, N.C.–Charleston, S.C., road in New Hanover Precinct of Clarendon County. The site is in what is now s central Brunswick County.

Bells Ferry. *See* Mackeys Ferry.

Bell's Ferry. *See* Grifton.

Bells Island, a marshy island in Core Sound about 1 mi. e of Marshallberg in se Carteret County. Formerly known as Great Marsh.

Bell's Island, a real-estate development, e Currituck County on Bell Island, *which see*. The 1967 General Assembly passed an act under which, by a vote of the residents, Bell's Island may be inc. as a town by resolution of the county commissioners.

Bells Point, the s end of Bells Island, on the w side of Core Sound about 1 mi. e of Marshallberg in s Carteret County. Formerly known as Bell Point, Bell's Point, and Great Marsh Point.

Bell Swamp rises in e Onslow County and flows se and ne into Queens Creek. Probably named for George Bell, who owned land there as early as 1713.

Bell Swamp, community in e central Brunswick County.

Bell Swamp Creek rises in e central Brunswick County and flows e into Rices Creek.

Belltown, community in central Granville County.

Bell View, community in s Cherokee County.

Bellview, community in n Moore County.

Bellvue Mountain, central Avery County.

Belmont, city in e Gaston County. Site of cotton mills in late nineteenth century. Named Garibaldi in the 1870s for the man who built the railroad water tank there. Inc. as Belmont, 1895. Named for August Belmont (1853–1924), New York banker and financier. Roman Catholic St. Mary's College opened there in 1878, chartered 1886; renamed Belmont Abbey College, 1913. Sacred Heart Junior College operated there, 1892–1987. Produces textiles and hosiery. Alt. 685.

Belmont, community in e Nash County. North Carolina Wesleyan College est. there, 1956.

Belmont Mountain, n Henderson County between Clear Creek and Featherston Creek.

Belmont–South Rosemary, community on the w outskirts of Roanoke Rapids, n Halifax County.

Belo, community in central Surry County served by post office, 1886–1905.

Belva, community in n Madison County on Shelton Laurel Creek. Alt. 1,689.

Belvidere, community in w Perquimans County on the Perquimans River. Settled by Quakers early in the eighteenth century. The Moseley map, 1733, shows "G. Newby's Ferry" at about the site; appears as Newbes Bridge on the Collet map, 1770. A post office, Newby's Bridge, est. there, 1827; changed to Belvidere, 1861.

Belvidere Township, n Perquimans County.

Belville, highly developed plantation of 8,000 acres, of which 1,700 were cleared, in Currituck and Pasquotank Counties. Flourished 1757–77. Located on North River, with wharf and shipyard. Owned wholly or in large part by Thomas Macknight. Numerous buildings were scattered throughout the area connected by roads. Canals drained much of the land.

Belville, community in s Brunswick County.

Belvoir Township, nw Pitt County.

Belvoir Township, n central Sampson County.

Belwood, community in ne Cleveland County. Alt. 990. Served by post office, 1882–1954.

Bems Creek rises in w Halifax County and flows se into Little Fishing Creek.

Benaja, community in s Rockingham County served by post office, 1870–1917 and 1921–33. Alt. 687. Store, depot, watering station there served the railroad. Named for the creek.

Benaja Creek rises in ne Guilford County and flows ne into Rockingham County, where it enters Haw River. Original name was Benajar. Believed to have been named for the tropical ben tree, plus *ajar* in the sense of "out of place."

Ben Bolen Creek rises in sw Ashe County and flows w into Three Top Creek.

Bench Mountain, e Macon County between Caler Fork and Mica City Creek.

Bench Mountain, sw Watauga County, extends ne from White Rocks along the head of Spice Bottom Creek.

Ben Cove Branch rises in e Jackson County and flows se into Sols Creek.

Ben Creek rises in n Macon County and flows nw into Cold Spring Creek.

Benge, community in s Ashe County near Benge Gap on the Wilkes County line.

Benge Gap, on the Ashe-Wilkes county line.

Bengle Creek. *See* Wolfpen Creek.

Benham, community in ne Wilkes County between Little Elkin River and Elkin River.

Ben Johnson Lake, on Eno River, central Orange County. Formed 1955. Covers 15 acres; max. depth 12 ft. Source of water for town of Hillsborough. Known as Hillsboro Lake prior to February 1956.

Bennehan, community in s Granville County. Named for Bennehan Cameron, planter and University of North Carolina trustee.

Bennett, community in se Anson County. Alt. 251.

Bennett, town in sw Chatham County. Inc. 1915. Named for J. M. Bennett, superintendent of Southern Railway. Earlier known as Beck Springs and Beck Mountain. Was a terminus of Bonlee and Western Railroad, now abandoned. Alt. 250.

Bennett, community in nw Pamlico County.

Bennett Branch rises in se Haywood County and flows nw into East Fork Pigeon River.

Bennett Branch rises in w Haywood County in Great Smoky Mountains National Park and flows w in Cataloochee Creek. Named for Bennett family, which lived in the area.

Bennett Branch rises in n Transylvania County near Bennett Gap and flows se into Cherry Cove Branch.

Bennett Gap, on the Haywood-Transylvania county line on Pisgah Ridge between Cherry Gap and Green Knob. Alt. approx. 4,420.

Bennett Gap, n Transylvania County between Looking Glass Creek and Avery Creek. Alt. 3,516.

Bennett Knob, n Transylvania County on Seniard Ridge s of Big Bear Pen Branch.

Bennetts Creek is formed by the junction of Duke, Harrell, and Raynor Swamps in central Gates County. It flows sw and se into Chowan River. Named for Richard Bennett, governor of Virginia, 1652–55. Appears on the Ogilby map, 1671.

Bennetts Creek Landing. *See* Gatesville.

Bennetts Millpond, on Rockyhock Creek in central Chowan County. Formed about 1856. 2 mi. long and ⅓ mi. wide, centering near lat. 36°09′10″ N., long. 76°39′40″ W. Covers approx. 50 acres. Max. depth 6 to 8 ft. Probably named for William Bennett (d. 1785), an early owner of the site.

Bennies Branch rises in s Macon County and flows ne into Turtle Pond Creek.

Benn Knob, mountain on Burke-Cleveland county line. Part of South Mountains. Alt. 2,894.

Benny Cove extends nw from Benny Ridge to Vengeance Creek in ne Cherokee County.

Benny Ridge, mountain in Valley River Mountains between Kimsey Cove and Horse Ridge, ne Cherokee County.

Bensalem, community in w Moore County on the head of Dry Creek. A Presbyterian church was organized there in 1813. Former names were Caledonia (post office, 1828–78) and Bigoak (post office, 1878–1906).

Bensalem Township, w Moore County.

Bensborough. *See* Falkland.

Bens Creek rises in e Warren County and flows se into Little Fishing Creek. Mentioned in local records as early as 1764.

Benson, town in sw Johnston County. Inc. 1887 and named for M. C. Benson, pioneer settler and landowner. Alt. 245. Produces lumber and apparel.

Benson Creek rises in n Surry County and flows se into Stewart Creek.

Bens Ridge, sw Buncombe County w of Ripshin Mountain.

Bens Ridge, se Watauga County extends se between Dugger Creek and the head of Flat Branch.

Bent Creek rises near Bent Creek Gap, s Buncombe County, and flows ne into French Broad River.

Bent Creek rises in ne Cherokee County and flows nw into Valley River.

Bent Creek is formed in n Yancey County by the junction of Left Prong Bent Creek and Right Prong Bent Creek. It flows se approx. 1/10 mi. into Cane River.

Bent Creek, community in n Yancey County on Cane River near the mouth of Bent Creek.

Bent Creek Experimental Forest, s Buncombe County, a part of Pisgah National Forest.

Bent Creek Gap, s Buncombe County, near the headwaters of Bent Creek. Alt. 3,270.

Bent Fork Gap, at the head of Bad Fork in nw Henderson County.

Bent Knee Knob, on the head of Stevens Creek, n Haywood County, near lat. 35°38′05″ N., long. 83°02′30″ W., in Great Smoky Mountains National Park. Alt. 4,000.

Bent Knob, central Mitchell County between Ellis Mountain and Toe River.

Bentley, community in s central Alexander County.

Bent Mountain, sw Buncombe County w of Piney Mountain.

Benton Branch rises in sw Caswell County and flows sw into Stoney Creek.

Benton Branch rises in e Lenoir County and flows ne into Dailys Creek. Probably named for Francis Benton, who was living in the vicinity as early as 1760.

Benton Crossroads. *See* Fairview.

Benton Heights, town in central Union County. Inc. 1913. Merged with city of Monroe in 1945. Alt. 595.

Bentonville, community in s Johnston County.

Bentonville Battlefield, State Historic Site, s Johnston County. Scene of Civil War battle, March 19–22, 1865, in which Confederates under Gen. Joseph E. Johnston encountered Federals under Gen. William T. Sherman. Bloodiest battle ever fought on North Carolina soil.

Bentonville Township, se Johnston County.

Bent Ridge, sw Avery County.

Bent Ridge, s Mitchell County in a bend of North Toe River.

Benvenue, community in e Nash County between Horn Beam Swamp and Compass Creek. Took its name from the plantation of Benjamin Hickman Bunn, which was named about 1890 for Ben Venue, a small mountain in Perthshire, Scotland.

Berea, community in w Granville County. Alt. 475. Settled prior to 1870.

Bergaw Creek. *See* Burgaw Creek.

Berkeley County, est. prior to 1691 by the Lords Proprietors of Carolina in what is now e South Carolina. Named for John Berkeley (ca. 1607–78), Baron Berkeley of Stratton, one of the original eight Lords Proprietors.

Berkeley Parish, Church of England, Perquimans County, was est. in 1701, coextensive with the county. In 1767 it was composed of 900 white taxable "inhabitants in midling Circumstances."

Berkeley Precinct. *See* Perquimans County.

Berlin. *See* Bina.

Bermuda Island, in the waters of Kitty Hawk Bay, n Dare County.

Bernal Branch rises in w Johnston County and flows se into Hannah Creek.

Bernice, community in ne Ashe County.

Berry, community in central Rockingham County served by post office, 1880–1903.

Berry. *See* Graham.

Berry Creek rises in e Macon County and flows nw into Corbin Creek.

Berry Gap, on the Jackson-Macon county line.

Berryhill Township, former township in sw Mecklenburg County. Now township no. 2.

Berry Mill, community in e Macon County on Watauga Creek.

Berry Mountain, s Madison County between Dan Payne Mountain and Doctor Mountain.

Berry Mountains, two adjacent mountains in se Gaston County on South Fork Catawba River.

Berrys Gap, sw Buncombe County between Long and Young Pisgah Mountains.

Berryville. *See* Hickory.

Bert Creek rises in se Graham County and flows sw by Bert Creek Lead into Tulula Creek. Named for Bert Wiggins.

Bert Creek Lead, se Graham County between Franks Creek and Bert Creek.

Bertha, community on w shore of Currituck Sound in central Currituck County.

Bertie, former town in se Bertie County. Inc. 1939 and merged with the town of Windsor in 1959. Known earlier as Rosemont.

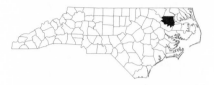

Bertie (BURR-tee) County was formed in 1722 from Chowan County. Located in the ne section of the state, it is bounded by Albemarle Sound, Chowan River, and Washington, Martin, Halifax, Northampton, and Hertford Counties. Area: 721 sq. mi. Named for James Bertie (1673–1735), who held a proprietary share of North Carolina. His brother Henry (1675–1735) appears as a Proprietor in 1728, and it has often been said that the county was named for both men. County seat: Windsor, with an alt. of 10 ft. Townships are Colerain, Indian Woods, Merry Hill, Mitchells, Roxobel, Snake Bite, Whites, Windsor, and Woodville. Site of the home of Nathaniell Batts, first known permanent white settler in North Carolina, which was built by 1655. Produces tobacco, corn, soybeans, peanuts, cotton, hogs, sweet potatoes, poultry, seafood, and lumber. *See also* Society Parish.

Berwick, community in w central Bladen County.

Bessemer City, town in w Gaston County. Inc. 1893. Named for Sir Henry Bessemer (1813–98), discoverer of process for making steel from cast iron. Iron ore had been found in the vicinity, and there were hopes that steel mills might be est. there. Produces textiles, machinery, and chemicals. Alt. 912.

Bessie, community on the head of Flat Creek in sw Jackson County.

Best, community in e Wayne County. Named for Henry Best, who had a grant of land there in 1743. Alt. 126.

Best. *See* Biltmore.

Beston, community in se Wayne County served by post office, 1882–1910.

Beta, community in n Jackson County on Scott Creek. Alt. 2,145.

Bethabara. *See* Old Town.

Bethania, town in w Forsyth County on Muddy Creek. Settled 1759, inc. 1839, but no longer active in municipal affairs. Named by the Moravians, whose second or "new town" it was, for the biblical town of Bethany. Refugees during the French and Indian War found protection within the Bethania stockade, and many of them remained to build homes there. Alt. 789.

Bethania Township, nw Forsyth County.

Bethany, community in n Davidson County. Settled in late eighteenth century by Germans and called Fredericktown. Later known as Possumtown. In 1861 a new church was built and named Bethany, a name soon applied to the community.

Bethany, community in e central Iredell County named for Bethany Presbyterian Church, organized there in 1775. Ebenezer Academy, building still standing, operated there, 1822–57.

Bethany, community in sw Rockingham County.

Bethany. *See* Milwaukee.

Bethany Township, central Iredell County.

Bethel, community in s Alexander County.

Bethel, community in nw Caswell County.

Bethel, community on Peter Cove Branch in s Haywood County.

Bethel, community in sw Hoke County.

Bethel, community in s Perquimans County.

Bethel, town in n Pitt County. Settled before the Civil War. Inc. 1873. Named for Bethel Methodist Church. Alt. 69.

Bethel, community in nw Watauga County on Rube Creek.

Bethel, community in w Wayne County near Bear Creek.

Bethel. *See* Harrellsville.

Bethel. *See* Whortonsville.

Bethel Church Township, a former township in s Cabarrus County. Now township no. 10.

Bethel Creek rises in sw Perquimans County and flows se into Yeopim River.

Bethel Hill, community in n Person County.

Bethel Township, w central Bladen County.

Bethel Township, sw Perquimans County.

Bethel Township, n Pitt County.

Bethesda, community in se Durham County.

Bethlehem, community in s Hertford County.

Bethlehem, community on Town Creek, e Rockingham County, settled by immigrants from Virginia who founded local Methodist church, 1835.

Bethlehem. *See* Redland.

Betsey Gap, on Madison-Haywood county line. Alt. 5,895.

Betsy Branch rises in central Jackson County and flows nw into Trout Creek.

Betsy Ridge, n McDowell County, extends s from Woods Mountain.

Bett Brook rises in s Catawba County and flows se into Clark Creek.

Bettie, community in e Carteret County on e side of North River.

Bettie McGee's Creek rises in w Randolph County and flows sw into Uwharrie River. Said to have been named for the second wife (also known as Martha McGee) of William Bell, first sheriff of the county. Cornwallis and troops camped nearby at mill operated by William McGee. Monument at Guilford Courthouse National Military Park in her honor.

Bettis Branch rises in n Cherokee County and flows s and sw into Valley River.

Bettis Branch rises in n Haywood County near lat. 35°42'54" N., long. 83°97' W., in Great Smoky Mountains National Park and flows nw into Big Creek.

Betts Branch rises in central Swain County and flows sw into Deep Creek.

Betts Island. *See* Bell Island.

Betty Branch rises in w Clay County and flows s into Hiwassee River.

Betty Branch rises in nw Henderson County and flows se into Boylston Creek.

Betty Branch rises in w Jackson County and flows ne into Savannah Creek.

Betty Creek rises in s Macon County and flows se into Rabun County, Ga., where it joins Darnell Creek in forming Little Tennessee River.

Betty Creek Gap, at the head of Betty Creek in s Macon County.

Betty Gap, w Jackson County near the head of Betty Branch. Alt. 3,000.

Betty Noland Cliff, between Norton Branch and the head of Ammons Branch in se Macon County.

Betty Town. *See* Aurora.

Beulah, community in sw Hyde County.

Beulah, community in e central Polk County.

Beulah, community in central Sampson County.

Beulah Township, ne Johnston County.

Beulaville, town in e Duplin County. Alt. 95. Inc. 1915. Produces apparel.

Bevins Branch rises in se Cherokee County and flows se and ne into Brendle Branch.

Bev Jones Crossroads, community in s Wake County s of Swift Creek.

Bewes Ordinary appears on the Collet map, 1770, apparently in what is now w Guilford County s of the community of Colfax, e of Deep River, and near Sandy Ridge Church.

Biddie Toe Creek rises in w Nash County and flows ne into Tar River.

Biddleville, community in central Mecklenburg County. Historically black, the area took its name from Biddle University, predecessor institution of Johnson C. Smith University. Served by post office, 1892–1908.

Big, community in sw Warren County.

Big Abrams Gap, mountain gap on the Swain County, N.C.–Blount County, Tenn., line in Great Smoky Mountains National Park.

Big Alamance Creek rises in se Guilford County and flows ne to join Little Alamance Creek in forming Great Alamance Creek, *which see.*

Big Andy Ridge, ne Buncombe County between Little Andy Creek and Walker Branch. *See also* Point Misery.

Big Arm Creek rises in n Johnston County and flows sw into Marks Creek.

Big Bald, on the Avery-Mitchell county line. Sometimes called Penland Yellow or Big Yellow.

Big Bald, on the Haywood-Swain county line, a peak on Balsam Mountain 2½ mi. sw of Balsam Corner.

Big Bald, on the Haywood-Transylvania county line between Flat Laurel Gap and Frying Pan Mountain. Alt. 5,340.

Big Bald, on the Yancey County, N.C.–Unicoi County, Tenn., line. Peak in Yancey County is at the n end of Hensley Ridge. Alt. 5,516. Known by the Indians as Sasseenohla (white man). Previously called Grier Bald for David Grier, spurned lover of the daughter of Col. David Vance. He lived there from 1802 until 1834, when he was killed for having killed a hunter who "trespassed" on the mountain. Much of the mountain is covered by mounds, ranging from the size of a football to a bushel basket, that emit a hollow sound when struck. Scientists theorize that the mounds are the rotted roots of balsam and spruce trees blown over by a storm centuries ago. *See also* The Arm.

Big Bald Branch rises in w Haywood County and flows nw into Caldwell Fork.

Big Bald Mountain, on the Ashe-Watauga county line e of Long Hope Creek.

Big Bald Mountain, on the Avery-Mitchell county line.

Big Bay, e central Bladen County.

Big Bay, sw Bladen County. *See also* Delightful Plains.

Big Bay, a section of Little Green Swamp, nw Brunswick County.

Big Bay, central Columbus County filled with fine sandy loam.

Big Bay, a loam-filled bay in sw Columbus County.

Big Beach, a section of outer beach in sw Brunswick County between Holden Beach and Shallotte Inlet.

Big Bear Creek rises in nw Stanly County and flows se into Long Creek.

Big Bear Pen Branch rises in n Transylvania County and flows e into Looking Glass Creek.

Big Beartrail Ridge, s Haywood County, between Right Hand Prong and Little Beartrap Branch.

Big Beartrap Branch rises in s Haywood County and flows e into Middle Fork.

Big Bearwallow Creek rises in central Transylvania County and flows s into North Fork French Broad River.

Big Beaverdam Creek rises in se Sampson County and flows e into Duplin County, where it enters Rockfish Creek.

Big Bend, a turn in Pigeon River in n Haywood County near the mouths of Groundhog Creek and Skiffley Creek.

Big Black Pine Ridge, w Watauga County, extends nw to the Avery-Watauga county line n of Grassy Gap Branch.

Big Branch rises in se Alexander County and flows se into Elk Shoal Creek.

Big Branch rises in w Avery County and flows ne into Horse Creek.

Big Branch rises in w Avery County and flows sw into Roaring Creek.

Big Branch rises in ne Brunswick County and flows e into Cape Fear River.

Big Branch rises near Potato Knob in ne Buncombe County and flows s into Right Fork.

Big Branch rises in s Columbus County and flows sw into Grissett Swamp.

Big Branch rises in nw Cumberland County and flows se into Beaver Creek.

Big Branch rises in se Duplin County and flows w into Muddy Creek.

Big Branch rises in s Franklin County and flows ne into Cedar Creek.

Big Branch, swamp in s Gates County that drains e into Cole Creek.

Big Branch rises in e Granville County and flows s into Gibbs Creek.

Big Branch rises in w Harnett County and flows se into Barbecue Swamp.

Big Branch rises in central Haywood County and flows ne into Pigeon River.

Big Branch rises in central Haywood County and flows w into Pigeon River.

Big Branch rises in n Haywood County and flows nw into Big Creek.

Big Branch rises in nw Haywood County and flows se into Big Creek.

Big Branch rises in s Haywood County and flows ne into Little East Fork Pigeon River.

Big Branch rises in n Macon County and flows nw into Cold Spring Creek.

Big Branch rises in e Madison County and flows s into Little Ivy Creek.

Big Branch rises in s Madison County and flows ne into Robert Branch.

Big Branch rises in n Mitchell County and flows e into Right Fork Bean Creek.

Big Branch rises in sw Nash County and flows sw into Turkey Creek.

Big Branch rises in s Randolph County and flows sw into Little River.

Big Branch rises in ne Swain County and flows se into Enloe Creek.

Big Branch rises in e Transylvania County near Shuford Mountain and flows sw into Little Mountain.

Big Branch rises in s Transylvania County and flows sw into East Fork French Broad River.

Big Branch rises in e Wake County and flows n into Walnut Creek.

Big Branch rises in ne Wake County and flows se into Little River.

Big Branch rises in w Wake County and flows s into Whiteoak Creek.

Big Branch rises in w Wake County and flows se into Little Whiteoak Creek.

Big Branch rises in e Warren County and flows sw to join Walkers Creek in forming Little Fishing Creek.

Big Branch rises in w Wilson County and flows
s into Contentnea Creek. Known earlier as
Johnson's Branch.

Big Branch rises in e Yancey County and flows se
and ne into Crabtree Creek.

Big Branch. *See* Mill Branch.

Big Buckeye Cove, se Haywood County on the
head of East Fork Pigeon River.

Big Buffalo Creek rises in central Lee County
and flows nw into Deep River.

Big Bugaboo Creek rises in ne Wilkes County
and flows s into Yadkin River.

Big Butt, s Macon County between Mooney Gap
and Bearpen Gap.

Big Butt, on the Madison County, N.C.–Greene
County, Tenn., line. Alt. 4,836.

Big Butt Creek rises in ne Buncombe County
and flows nw into Straight Creek.

Big Butte, mountain on the Buncombe-Yancey
county line sw of Flat Springs Gap. Alt. 6,001.
Formerly known as Wilson Knob Mountain;
also called Yeates Knob.

Big Butte Mountain, w Avery County.

Big Butt Knob, on the Buncombe-Yancey county
line between Flat Spring Knob and Little Butt
Knob.

Big Butt Mountain, peak of Newfound Mountain
on the Buncombe-Haywood county line. Alt.
4,744.

Big Butt Mountain, w Haywood County in Great
Smoky Mountains National Park. On Mount
Sterling Ridge near lat. 35°40′20″ N., long.
83°10′10″ W.

Big Cataloochee Mountain, w Haywood County
in Great Smoky Mountains National Park.
A Balsam Mountain peak, alt. 6,122, near
lat. 35°40′25″ N., long. 83°10′27″ W. Known
briefly in the 1890s as Nibb's Knob after
a member of the U.S. Geological Survey
party attempted to name the peak for
himself.

Big Chestnut Bald, mountain on the Swain
County, N.C.–Sevier County, Tenn., line in
Great Smoky Mountains National Park. Alt.
4,970.

Big Chinquapin Branch. *See* Chinquapin
Branch.

Big Colington Island. *See* Colington Island.

Big Colly Bay, ne Bladen County, approx. 5½ mi.
long. Colly Creek rises there. Probably named
for the obsolete adjective "colly," meaning
grimy or coal-black.

Big Cove, ne Buncombe County s of Chestnut
Cove Ridge.

Big Cove, sw Buncombe County near the headwaters of Webb Branch.

Big Cove, at the head of Big Cove Branch in the
Snowbird Mountains, ne Cherokee County.

Big Cove lies between Ramp Cove Branch and
Vengeance Creek in the Valley River Mountains, ne Cherokee County.

Big Cove, e Haywood County between Bobs
Ridge and Roland Ridge. Little Creek flows
through the cove.

Big Cove, e Haywood County on Cove Field
Branch.

Big Cove, w Jackson County between Tatham
Creek and Savannah Creek.

Big Cove, ne Swain County on Raven Fork, just n
of the community of Swayney. Alt. 2,452.

Big Cove, ne Transylvania County e of Cat Ridge.

Big Cove Branch rises in ne Cherokee County
and flows sw into Dan Holland Creek.

Big Crabtree Creek rises in se Yancey County
and flows n on the Mitchell-Yancey county
line into North Toe River.

Big Craggy, mountain on the McDowell-Yancey
county line near the head of Big Lost Cove
Creek.

Big Craggy. *See* Craggy Dome.

Big Creek rises in n Carteret County and flows
ne into South River.

Big Creek rises in e Cumberland County and
flows ne and se into South River on the
Cumberland-Sampson county line.

Big Creek rises in s Haywood County and flows e
into West Fork Pigeon River.

Big Creek rises in w Haywood County near lat.
35°42′05″ N., long. 83°14′50″ W., and flows ne
into Pigeon River.

Big Creek rises in nw Henderson County and
flows ne, where it joins Fletcher Creek in
forming North Fork.

Big Creek rises in e Macon County and flows sw
into Lake Sequoyah.

Big Creek rises in se Macon County and flows
sw into Rabun County, Ga., where it enters
Overflow Creek.

Big Creek rises in n Madison County and flows s
into Shelton Laurel Creek.

Big Creek rises in e Montgomery County and
flows nw into Little River.

Big Creek rises in ne Surry County and flows se
into Stokes County, where it enters Dan River.

Big Creek rises in sw Swain County and flows n into Silvermine Creek.

Big Creek rises in n Yancey County and flows ne and se into Cane River.

Big Creek Township, nw Stokes County.

Big Cypress Swamp rises in s Columbus County and flows s to join Monie Swamp in forming Seven Creeks.

Big Dam Branch rises in n Cherokee County in the Snowbird Mountains and flows sw into Hyatt Creek.

Big Deserter Island, a land formation in s Duplin County surrounded by marsh.

Big Dismal, a pocosin at the head of Big Swamp, a stream in w Sampson County.

Big Dog Mountain, in se Macon County between Cullasaja River and Kettle Rock.

Big East Fork, a cove on Dry Branch in e Haywood County.

Big Elk Creek rises in ne Watauga County and flows se into South Fork New River at town of Todd.

Big Elk Mountain, s central Avery County.

Big Fall Creek. *See* Honeycutt Creek.

Big Falls, on Stony Creek in central Alamance County near the confluence with Haw River. A post office existed in the vicinity as early as 1882. *See also* Hopedale.

Big Falls, in Snowbird Creek, sw Graham County. In a series of two or three falls, water drops from approx. 25 to 60 ft.

Big Falls, The. *See* High Falls.

Big Fat Gap, nw Graham County at the head of Bear Creek.

Big Flats, mountain peak in se Buncombe County w of Patton Gap in Swannanoa Mountains.

Big Flats Branch rises in n Swain County and flows sw into Bone Valley Creek.

Big Flatty Creek rises in s Pasquotank County and flows se into Albemarle Sound. Shown on the Hack map, 1684, as Flatt Creek; on the Moseley map, 1733; and the Collet map, 1770, as Flatty Creek.

Big Fork Knob, peak on Big Fork Ridge, ne Buncombe County.

Big Fork Ridge, ne Buncombe County between Mineral and Carter Creeks.

Big Fork Ridge, w Haywood County in Great Smoky Mountains National Park, extending ne from Cataloochee Balsam; a Balsam Mountain summit between Rough Fork and Caldwell Fork. Center near lat. 35°35′40″ N., long. 83°07′30″ W.

Big Fork Ridge, n Swain County, extends ne in a horseshoe shape from between Pilkey Creek and the head of West Fork [Chambers Creek] to Welch Ridge and se between West Fork and North Fork to their junction forming Chambers Creek.

Big Fork Ridge, s Yancey County between Cane River and Cattail Creek.

Big Garland Gap, n Graham County between Sawyer Creek and Stecoah Creek at the sw end of Hogback Mountain.

Biggerstaff Branch rises in se Mitchell County and flows sw into Beaver Creek.

Big Gooseberry Ridge, e Jackson County between Frady Creek and Chastine Creek.

Big Governors Creek rises in e Moore County and flows nw into Deep River on the Moore-Lee county line. Called Millstone Creek in a 1748 grant to Governor Gabriel Johnston. Named for Johnston, who owned 7,000 acres n of the creek. Appears as Governors Creek on the Collet map, 1770.

Big Grassy Creek rises in e central Avery County and flows sw into Linville River.

Big Green Mountain, se Jackson County between Little Green Mountain and Panthertown Creek. Alt. 4,100.

Big Grill Ridge, nw Swain County in Great Smoky Mountains National Park, extending se from Devils Tater Patch.

Big Harris Creek rises in central Cleveland County and flows se into First Broad River.

Big Haw Mountain, central Avery County.

Big Head Branch rises in ne Swain County and flows se into Straight Fork.

Big Hogback Creek rises in se Jackson County and flows sw into Horsepasture River.

Big Horse Creek rises in sw Grayson County, Va. and flows se into n central Ashe County, where it enters North Fork New River.

Big Hungry Creek rises in e Henderson County and flows sw into Green River.

Big Hungry Mountain, e Henderson County at the head of Big Hungry Creek. Alt. 3,006.

Big Indian Creek rises in sw Macon County and flows n into Nantahala River.

Big Island, in Green Swamp, central Brunswick County.

Big Island lies off the sw shore of Roanoke

Island, Dare County, in the waters of Croatan Sound.

Big Island, off the w shore of s Hatteras Island in the waters of Pamlico Sound, s Dare County.

Big Island, a land formation in e Duplin County surrounded by swamp.

Big Island, in Yadkin River, Rowan-Davidson Counties. Area: 100 acres. Trading Ford, *which see*, was located at the e end of Big Island. *See also* Island Borough.

Big Island, 50-acre sandy island in Yadkin River, ne Yadkin County.

Big Ivy Creek. *See* North Fork Ivy Creek.

Big Junction, a mountain on the Graham County, N.C.–Monroe County, Tenn., line.

Big Juniper Creek rises in w Moore County and flows ne into McLendons Creek.

Big Kennedy Creek rises in s Yadkin County and flows s into Iredell County. It enters Flat Rock Creek ne of Houstonville.

Big Kinnakeet Coast Guard Station, se Hatteras Island in Dare County. First est. as lifesaving station in 1878–79. Lifesaving Service and Revenue Cutter Service joined to form U.S. Coast Guard in 1915. Now decommissioned.

Big Kitchens Knob, se Clay County at the nw end of Big Kitchens Ridge.

Big Kitchens Ridge, se Clay County between Sassafras Branch and Holden Cove.

Big Knob, on Snowbird Creek in sw Graham County.

Big Knob, on Haywood-Madison county line.

Big Knob, nw Henderson County between Queen Creek and Davie Mountain.

Big Knob, on the n end of Big Ridge in s Jackson County.

Big Knob, e Madison County on the head of Bear Branch.

Big Knob, n Madison County on the ne end of Bearpen Ridge.

Big Knob, s Watauga County on the head of Buffalo Creek.

Big Lake, The, formed by a large rock dam on Long Creek, w Surry County. Covers approx. 30 acres; max. depth 35 ft.

Big Laurel, peak in se Clay County on the nw end of Little Kitchens Ridge.

Big Laurel, community in n Madison County on Spillcorn Creek. Alt. 2,034.

Big Laurel, community in se Swain County on the head of Yalaka Creek.

Big Laurel Branch rises in s Macon County and flows nw into Kilby Creek.

Big Laurel Creek rises in nw Ashe County and flows se into North Fork New River.

Big Laurel Creek rises in w Macon County and flows nw into Whiteoak Creek.

Big Laurel Creek rises in e Madison County and flows w into French Broad River.

Big Laurel Gap, on the McDowell-Yancey county line near the head of Neals Creek. Alt. approx. 3,700.

Big Laurel Mountain, on the McDowell-Yancey county line.

Big Laurel Township, former township in n central Madison County; now township no. 10.

Big Lick, community in sw Stanly County. Inc. 1879; charter repealed 1919. Named because salt in the ground attracted deer and buffalo. *See also* Oakboro.

Big Lick Creek rises in e central Durham County and flows ne into Neuse River.

Big Lick Township, s central Stanly County.

Big Lost Cove Creek rises in s Yancey County and flows n into South Toe River.

Big Marsh Swamp rises in Hoke County and flows se into Robeson County, where it joins Gallberry Swamp in forming Big Swamp.

Big Meadow Creek rises in w Stanly County and flows w into se Cabarrus County, where it enters Rocky River.

Big Meadows, loamy section between Balls Mountain and Blackwood Mountain on the head of Old Field Creek in s Orange County.

Big Milksick Knob, on the Clay-Macon county line.

Big Mooney Branch rises in s Macon County and flows sw into Kilby Creek.

Big Mountain. *See* Asbury Mountain.

Big Mountain Branch rises in w Transylvania County and flows sw into North Fork French Broad River.

Big Mountain Creek rises in s Montgomery County and flows sw into Richmond County, where it enters Pee Dee River.

Big Mountain Gap, central Transylvania County in Big Mountain Ridge, Pisgah National Forest. Alt. approx. 3,060.

Big Mountain Ridge, central Transylvania County, extends about 2 mi. in a north-south direction. Bounded on the n by Three Forks Mountain. The ridge is a part of Pisgah National Forest.

Bigoak. *See* Bensalem.

Big Oak Gap, w Macon County on Fire Gap Ridge.

Big Peachtree Bald, in the Valley River Mountains on the Cherokee-Clay county line.

Big Peachtree Creek rises in e Franklin County and flows se into Nash County, where it joins Little Peachtree Creek in forming Stony Creek.

Big Pine, community on Big Pine Creek in s Madison County. Alt. 2,500. Post office, Big Pine Creek, est. prior to 1882.

Big Pine Creek rises in ne Alleghany County and flows w into Brush Creek.

Big Pine Creek is formed in s Madison County by the junction of North Fork and South Fork and flows ne into French Broad River opposite Barnard.

Big Pine Creek Township, former township in sw Madison County; now township no. 12.

Big Pine Fishing Gut, a water-filled ditch adjoining the Neuse River in e Durham County.

Big Pine Mountain, s Yancey County between Beech Nursery Creek and Big Poplar Creek.

Big Pine Ridge, s Clay County between Rocking Chair Branch and Pounding Creek.

Big Pine Ridge, n Transylvania County, extends se between Jumping Branch and Pounding Mill Branch.

Big Piney Branch rises in ne Buncombe County and flows se into Flat Creek.

Big Piney Ridge, ne Buncombe County between Big Piney Branch and Little Piney Branch.

Big Pisgah. *See* Mount Pisgah.

Big Pisgah Mountain, w Transylvania County between Panthertail Mountain and West Fork French Broad River.

Big Pocosin, sand and swamp area covering approx. 150 sq. mi. in sw Beaufort and ne Craven Counties. Includes Reedy and Blount Pocosins in its n and nw edges. Drained by many tributaries into Neuse River at the sw end and into Pamlico River at the ne end.

Big Pocosin, a sand and swamp pocosin in ne Craven County and s Beaufort County.

Big Pond Branch rises in central Columbus County and flows sw into Beaverdam Swamp.

Big Poplar Creek rises in s Yancey County and flows ne into Sugar Camp Creek.

Big Porpoise Bay, in Pamlico Sound on the e side of Goose Creek Island, ne Pamlico County.

Big Raft Swamp rises in s Hoke County and flows se into Robeson County, where it enters Lumber River.

Big Rattlesnake Branch rises in ne Buncombe County and flows s into Swannanoa River.

Big Ridge, w Haywood County in Great Smoky Mountains National Park. A short spur of Big Fork Ridge extending se near lat. 35°34′50″ N., long. 83°08′ W.

Big Ridge extends se between Horse Cove and Middle Fork in nw Henderson County.

Big Ridge, central Jackson County, extends se between West Fork Tuckasegee River and Tuckasegee River.

Big Ridge, n Mitchell County between Pigeon-roost Creek and Bean Creek.

Big Ridge, central Mitchell County between Rebel Creek and Snow Creek.

Big Ridge, w Watauga County, extends se from n of Beech Creek.

Big Ridge, se Yancey County parallel to Roaring Fork.

Big Ridge, community in s Jackson County near Lake Thorpe.

Big Ridge. *See* Pups Ridge.

Big Ridge Mine, on the head of Deep Gap Creek, s Haywood County. An old source of feldspar and mica operated most recently during World War II.

Big Roan Ridge, w Avery County.

Big Rock Creek rises in n Mitchell County and flows sw into Toe River.

Big Rocky Branch rises in n Madison County and flows se into White Rock Branch.

Big Rocky Creek. *See* Patterson Creek.

Big Rough Knob, e central Avery County.

Big Sandy Creek rises in ne Wilkes County and flows sw into East Prong Roaring River.

Big Savanna, n Tyrrell County, is a slough extending ne in an arc n of Mills Ridge from near the community of Levels to Alligator Creek.

Big Savannah, central and nw Pender County. Originally covered over 2,000 acres, lying between 50 and 60 ft. above sea level. A flat, treeless area, surrounded by pine woods. Water table generally at or close to the surface. Much of the Big Savannah has been drained and cultivated. Once noted for the large variety of wildflowers that grew among the grasses. Also known as Burgaw Savannah.

Big Scaly, peak in se Clay County at the ne end of Scaly Ridge. Alt. 5,070.

Big Shoal Branch rises in sw Macon County and flows e into Big Indian Creek.

Big Shoeheel Creek rises in n Scotland County and flows s through w Robeson County into South Carolina, where it enters Little Pee Dee River. *See also* Maxton.

Big Snowball Mountain. *See* Snowball Mountain.

Big Spring, community in n Jackson County served by post office, 1852–1903.

Big Spring Branch rises in w Haywood County and flows se into Jonathans Creek.

Big Spring Branch rises in ne Rutherford County and flows se into Cleveland County, where it enters Hinton Creek.

Big Spring Branch rises in Forest City in s central Rutherford County and flows ne into Second Broad River.

Big Spring Creek rises in e Mitchell County and flows s into Hawk Creek.

Bigspring Gap, s Macon County at the head of Pinnacle Branch.

Big Spring Gap, e Mitchell County at the head of Big Spring Creek.

Big Spruce Ridge, w Haywood County, Great Smoky Mountains National Park, extends se from Cataloochee Balsam; a Balsam Mountain peak between Straight Creek and Caldwell Fork, center near lat. 35°34′30″ N., long. 83°08′40″ W.

Big Stamp, a peak in the Valley River Mountains on the Cherokee-Clay county line.

Big Stamp Knob, on the Cherokee-Clay county line.

Big Stonehouse Creek. *See* Stonehouse Creek.

Big Swag, peak of Round Mountain Ridge in nw Swain County in Great Smoky Mountains National Park. Alt. 3,685.

Big Swag Branch rises in central Jackson County and flows n into Bear Creek.

Big Swag Gap. *See* Beech Gap.

Big Swamp rises in nw Brunswick County and flows sw into Juniper Creek for a distance of several mi.; it forms a part of the boundary between Brunswick and Columbus Counties.

Big Swamp is formed in e Robeson County by the junction of Big Marsh Swamp and Gallberry Swamp. It flows sw into Lumber River. Its e high-water line forms the boundary between Bladen and Robeson Counties and a part of the Cumberland-Robeson county line.

Big Swamp rises in w Sampson County and flows s into South River.

Big Tom, peak in Mount Mitchell State Park, s Yancey County. One of two peaks known as Black Brothers until 1947, when renamed in honor of Thomas "Big Tom" David Wilson (1825–1909), bear hunter and guide who found the body of Elisha Mitchell on July 7, 1857, after he had fallen to his death on Mount Mitchell. Known earlier as Hairy Bear Mountain.

Big Tomahawk Creek rises in s Sampson County and flows s to join Little Tomahawk Creek in forming Tomahawk Creek.

Big Troublesome Creek. *See* Troublesome Creek.

Big Warrior Mountain, s Polk County, w of town of Tryon. Named for Big Wayah (wolf), chief of the Cherokee Indians. Alt. 2,466.

Big White Oak Creek rises in w Wake County and flows s and sw into Chatham County, where it enters New Hope River.

Big White Pocosin, sandy pocosin in se Cumberland County.

Big Witch Creek rises in n Jackson County and flows sw into Wrights Creek.

Big Witch Gap, on the Jackson-Swain county line near the head of Moody Branch.

Big Yellow. *See* Big Bald.

Big Yellow Bald Mountain, w Avery County.

Big Yellow Mountain, at the junction of Avery and Mitchell Counties, N.C., and Carter County, Tenn. Alt. approx. 5,600. Known also as Bright Yellow Mountain and Averys Bald. *See also* Rose Ridge.

Bilboa, community in s Durham County near the head of Northeast Creek. Named for the Bilbo family, which lived in the vicinity in the early nineteenth century before moving to Mississippi. Alt. 401.

Bilesville. *See* New London.

Bill Allen Branch rises in e central Yancey County and flows n into Little Crabtree Creek. Named for Bill Allen, an early settler who raised a large family there.

Bill Branch rises in central Catawba County and flows sw into Clark Creek.

Bill Cole Mountain, n Buncombe County between Bradley and Gentry Gaps. Alt. 3,284. *See also* Morgan Ridge.

Bill Cove, e Haywood County between Poplar Cove and James Branch.

Bill Davenport Branch rises in se Mitchell County and flows s into North Toe River.

Billet's Bridge. *See* Shiloh.

Bill Holt Mountains, a short range in the Cane Creek Mountains, s Alamance County.

Billie Top, a peak on Holland Mountain on the Buncombe-Haywood county line between Newfound Gap and Grassy Top.

Bill Moore Creek rises in s Buncombe County near Stradley Mountain and flows n into Hominy Creek. Enka Lake is on Bill Moore Creek.

Bills Branch rises in w Haywood County and flows sw into Evans Creek.

Bills Creek rises in nw Rutherford County and flows e into Cove Creek. Named for Rev. William (Billy) Logan, whose brick house still stands nearby.

Bills Creek, community in w Rutherford County on the stream of the same name.

Bills Knob, n Haywood County on the e end of Cedar Cliff.

Bills Mountain, e Henderson County near Henderson Creek.

Bills Mountain, nw Rutherford County between Bills Creek and Broad River. Alt. approx. 2,450. Named for Rev. William (Billy) Logan.

Bill Wray Gap, s central Yancey County at the sw end of Callaway Mountain.

Billy Branch rises in n Transylvania County and flows sw into South Fork Mills River.

Billy Cabin Ridge, in se Macon County between Big Creek and Cullasaja River.

Billy Cove, valley in se Buncombe County nw of Billy Cove and Billy Cove Knob.

Billy Cove, s Swain County between De Hart Creek and Marr Branch.

Billy Cove Gap, s Buncombe County between Billy Cove Knob and Hickory Top.

Billy Cove Knob, s Buncombe County, sw of Billy Cove Gap.

Billy's Branch rises in central Carteret County and flows w into Black Creek.

Billys Creek rises in n Franklin County and flows ne into Tar River.

Billy's Creek flows between tidal-marsh islands in the mouth of White Oak River in e Onslow County. Named for Billy (William) Russell.

Billy Top, n Haywood County on the head of Laurel Branch.

Biltmore, former town in central Buncombe County. Inc. 1893 but since 1929 within the corporate limits of Asheville. Named for the Biltmore Estate, *which see*. Alt. 1,994. Known as Best as early as 1880, when a post office existed there; named for William J. Best, one of the owners of the Western North Carolina Railroad. Post office operated briefly as Bilton, 1890. *See also* South Biltmore.

Biltmore Estate, central Buncombe County on the s outskirts of Asheville. Built for George W. Vanderbilt (1863–1914); the name combines the last part of his family name with *more*, an old English word for rolling, upland country. The house, in the style of a French chateau, was formally opened in 1895 after 5 years of construction. Handsomely furnished, surrounded by formal gardens, and including adjoining forests, farms, winery, and dairy lands, the estate has been open to the public since 1930.

Biltmore Forest, a part of the Biltmore Estate in s Buncombe County, approx. 11,000 acres along the Swannanoa and French Broad Rivers. Alt. approx. 2,000–2,300. Est. 1890 on land largely cut over; planting continued until about 1911. Gifford Pinchot, the first trained American forester, planned and directed the work. In 1898 Carl A. Schenck founded the Biltmore School of Forestry there, the first such school in the United States. *See also* Carl Alwin Schenck Forest.

Biltmore Forest, town in central Buncombe County, sw of Asheville. Inc. 1923 and named for the experimental forest est. on the Vanderbilt estate. Alt. 2,050.

Bina, community in n central Ashe County. First known as Berlin but name changed during World War I.

Bingham Branch rises in e Alamance County in the n outskirts of Mebane and flows nw into Mill Creek.

Bingham Heights, community in central Buncombe County ne of Emma. Site of Bingham School, 1891–1928, and residence of teacher Robert Bingham.

Bingham Township, sw Orange County.

Birch, community in sw Cherokee County on Beech Creek.

Birch Branch. *See* Birch Creek.

Birch Cove, the valley through which Chairmaker Branch flows in central Clay County.

Birch Creek rises in central Pender County and

flows sw into Rileys Creek. Now often referred to locally as Birch Branch.

Birchfield Branch rises in nw Swain County and flows se into Fontana Lake.

Birchfield Creek rises in w Avery County and flows se into North Toe River.

Birchfield Fork Creek. *See* Birch Fork Creek.

Birch Fork Creek rises in ne Rockingham County and flows e into Wolf Island Creek. Originally known as Birchfield Fork Creek.

Birch Knob, central Clay County at the se end of Birch Cove.

Birch Spring Gap, n Cherokee County in the Snowbird Mountains.

Birch Spring Gap, nw Swain County in Great Smoky Mountains National Park on Twenty-mile Ridge.

Bird Branch rises in n Macon County and flows n into Little Tennessee River.

Bird Creek rises in se Buncombe County and flows ne into McDowell County, where it enters Crooked Creek.

Bird Creek rises in s Haywood County and flows e into West Fork Pigeon River.

Bird Creek rises in w Mitchell County and flows se into Pigeonroost Creek.

Bird Island, on the Atlantic Ocean, sw Brunswick County. The w tip of the island is in South Carolina.

Bird Islands, approx. a dozen small islands on Clam Shoal, in the waters of Pamlico Sound, s Dare County, off the s part of Hatteras Island.

Bird Rock Falls, w Transylvania County on North Fork French Broad River just below where it is formed by junction of Indian Creek and Shoal Creek. Alt. approx. 2,720.

Birdstand Mountain, s Haywood County between Little East Fork Pigeon River and West Fork Pigeon River.

Birdtown, community in e Swain County on Oconaluftee River. Probably named for the Bird Clan, *In-a-cheese-quah*, one of the original seven clans of the Cherokee Indians. Bird Town is one of the five townships of the Cherokees' Qualla Boundary, *which see*. Alt. 1,900. *See also* Oconaluftee River.

Birta, community in s Pender County served by post office, 1894–1905.

Biscoe, town in e Montgomery County. Alt. 609. Inc. 1901. Known as Filo until 1895, when it was renamed for Maj. Henry Biscoe, lumber commission merchant. Produces textiles.

Biscoe Township, e Montgomery County.

Bishop, community in ne Brunswick County.

Bishop Creek rises in se Pender County and flows s into Topsail Sound.

Bishops Cross, a community in e Beaufort County. Alt. 12. Perhaps named for the interesting figure, somewhat like a bishop's staff, formed by former railroad intersection and two highways that crossed it.

Bismarck, community in w Johnston County served by post office, 1886–1903.

Bissett Mill Pond, s Nash County on Beaverdam Creek. About ¾ mi. long.

Biven, community in s Brunswick County served by post office, 1898–1904.

Bixby, community in e Davie County. The first train on that portion of the track ran in 1891. From 1881 to at least 1889, the community was known as Chaplin's Stand. Named by a railroad conductor after he observed a large stock of Bixby Shoe Polish in the community store. Alt. 835.

Bizzell Millpond, e Wayne County on Walnut Creek. Site of the Dobbs County courthouse, jail, and stocks from sometime after 1758 until 1779. After the formation of Wayne County in 1779, the county court met variously on Little River. The old courthouse, jail, and stocks were sold to Col. William McKinne. The McKinne heirs sold the property to Elijah Bizzell of Duplin County, who moved there and erected a mill in 1839.

Black Ankle, derisive name for an area in s central Randolph County and ne Montgomery County. Named because bootleggers operating there during Prohibition would start fires over a large area when they were operating a still so that officers of the law could not find the still. They were said to have "black ankles" from walking through the ashes of old fires to start new ones. Name also said to derive from fact that gold miners in the area stood in muck.

Black Ankle, a strip of deep fertile soil across the s portion of Robeson County. Named for the fact that a plowman's ankles would be black after plowing in the soil.

Black Ankle, community in n Cleveland County.

Black Bald, s Macon County at the head of Dry Branch. Alt. approx. 5,100.

Black Balsam Knob, s Haywood County between

the headwaters of Yellowstone Prong and Flat Laurel Creek.

Black Branch rises in e Clay County and flows sw into Buck Creek.

Black Branch rises in sw Duplin County and flows ne into Rockfish Creek.

Black Branch rises in e Hoke County and flows s into Beaver Creek.

Black Brothers, former name of two peaks approx. 1 mi. n of Mount Mitchell, s Yancey County. Renamed Mount Craig and Big Tom, *which see*, in 1947.

Blackburn, community in sw Catawba County. Alt. 1,000.

Blackburn Knob, s Watauga County between Middle Fork [South Fork New River] and Matney Branch.

Black Camp Gap on the Haywood-Swain county line near the head of Bunches Creek in Great Smoky Mountains National Park on Balsam Mountain. A log-house camp was built there for the use of cattle rangers and hunters. A forest fire partially burned the camp, burning off the bark and charring the logs of the cabins. Later campers lodging there got themselves black from contact with the burnt logs, hence the name Black Camp. Alt. 4,492.

Black Creek rises in e Carteret County and flows s into Newport River. Sometimes called Black River.

Black Creek rises in sw Columbus County and flows sw into Lake Tabor, *which see*.

Black Creek rises in e Hoke County and flows s into Puppy Creek.

Black Creek rises in e Rutherford County sw of Hollis and flows se into Hinton Creek.

Black Creek rises in s Wake County and flows se into Johnston County, where it enters Neuse River.

Black Creek rises in w central Wake County and flows ne into Crabtree Creek.

Black Creek rises in sw Wilson County and flows e into Contentnea Creek.

Black Creek, town in s Wilson County named for nearby stream. Alt. 120. Est. 1840 as a station and post office on the Wilmington and Weldon Railroad. Inc. 1870.

Black Creek. *See* Back Creek.

Black Creek Swamp appears on the Collet map, 1770, as a fork of East Mingo Branch, *which see*, lying completely in modern Harnett

County between Black River and East Mingo Branch. The particular fork is no longer named on maps.

Black Creek Township, s Wilson County.

Black Dome. *See* Mount Mitchell.

Black Fields, an area of black, poorly drained soil in e Washington County, covering an area of approx. 6 sq. mi., w of the community of Scuppernong. Mentioned as early as 1868 in local records.

Black Fox Ridge, s central Burke County.

Black Gap, on the Clay-Macon county line. Alt. 3,841.

Black Gut Creek rises in nw Northampton County and flows s into Roanoke River.

Blackjack, community in e Pitt County. Served by post office, 1882–1907. Spelled as Blackjack after 1895.

Black Jack Branch rises in e Union County and flows e into w Anson County and into Brown Creek.

Blackjack Mountain, w Henderson County at the head of Little Mud Creek.

Black Jack Mountain, w Randolph County just w of Caraway Mountain in a close group with Slick Rock, Vineyard, and Prickly Pear Mountains.

Black Jack Township, w central Richmond County.

Black Knob, se Buncombe County sw of High Windy peak. Alt. 4,240.

Black Knob, e Transylvania County, about 1½ mi. w of Cascade Lake. Alt. approx. 3,220.

Black Lake, a natural lake in e central Bladen County with a max. depth of 71 ft. and covering 1,418 acres. Fishing, boating, and swimming. Part of state park system.

Blackman Crossroads, community in s Johnston County.

Blackman's Landing. *See* Coniott Landing.

Blackman's Mills, community in n Sampson County served by post office, 1858–1914.

Black Mine, former gold mine in w Union County near the town of Indian Trail.

Black Mingle Pocosin, n Gates County.

Black Mingo. *See* East Mingo Branch.

Black Mountain, n central Alleghany County. Formerly known as Carson Mountain.

Black Mountain, a peak on the se end of Laurel Mountain in nw Henderson County. Alt. 3,952.

Black Mountain, n Jackson County, extends ne

from Tuckasegee River between Parker Knob and Fern Mountain.

Black Mountain, w Jackson County on the head of Cagle Branch.

Black Mountain, on the Jackson-Haywood county line. An attempt was made to change the name to Browning Peak in honor of R. Getty Browning, state highway location engineer, but it was not accepted locally. Alt. 6,275.

Black Mountain, at the head of Black Mountain Branch in s Macon County. Alt. 3,735.

Black Mountain, sw Randolph County s of Mill Creek.

Black Mountain, ne Rutherford County at the head of Brier Creek. Alt. 2,614.

Black Mountain, n Transylvania County between Clawhammer Cove and Bear Pen Branch.

Black Mountain. *See* Mount Chapman.

Black Mountain. *See* Mount Hardy.

Black Mountain, town in se Buncombe County. Inc. 1893. Known earlier as Grey Eagle. Named for the Black Mountain range by S. Dougherty, in whose home the first post office was est. Alt. 2,395. Summer resort. Produces lumber. Black Mountain College operated nearby, 1933–56.

Black Mountain Branch rises in s Macon County and flows ne into South Fork [Skeenah Creek].

Black Mountain Gap, about ¼ mi. nw of Bald Knob, between the Black Mountain on the n and the Blue Ridge on the s on the Buncombe-Yancey county line. Lat. 35°43′ N., long. 82°16′45″ W. Known originally as Beech Gap, later as Swannanoa Gap, and finally since 1949 by its present name. Alt. approx. 5,200.

Black Mountain Gap. *See* Mount Hardy Gap.

Black Mountain Natural Area, in Pisgah National Forest, Yancey County. Covers 1,405 acres, the watershed of Middle Creek, a tributary of the South Toe River on the e slope of Mount Mitchell. The area was set aside from all commercial use on October 22, 1932, and reserved for scientific study.

Black Mountains, range extending from the Buncombe-Yancey county line ne to the head of Bowlens Creek in s central Yancey County. Among the peaks are Mount Mitchell, Clingmans Dome, Potato Knob, and Mount Craig. Named for the dark green foliage of Fraser fir,

which covers the top and sides. Known by the Cherokee Indians as *See-noh-ya* (dark; night). *See also* Appalachian Mountains.

Black Mountain Township, e central Buncombe County.

Blacknel, community in n Lee County. Named for Tom Blacknal, a free black. Primarily an African American community centered around a church.

Black Pine Ridge, n Madison County between Dry Creek and Mill Creek.

Black Ridge, s Yancey County between Lower Creek and Camp Creek.

Black River rises in n Harnett County and flows se across the county into e Cumberland County, where, at the Cumberland-Sampson county line, it joins East Mingo Branch in forming South River.

Black River is formed in s Sampson County by the junction of Six Runs Creek and Coharie River. It flows s on the Bladen-Sampson county line, the Bladen-Pender county line, and into w Pender County, where it turns se to flow into Cape Fear River at the New Hanover County line. Approx. 30 mi. long. Appears as Black or Swampy River on the Moseley map, 1733.

Black River. *See* Ivanhoe.

Black River Chapel. *See* Delta.

Black River Township, ne Cumberland County.

Black River Township, ne Harnett County.

Black Rock, a peak in se Jackson County between Rye Mountain and Little Green Mountain. Alt. 4,500.

Black Rock, community and fishery in e Bertie County. Site of Black Rock plantation, home of Thomas Pollock Jr.

Blackrock Branch rises in se Macon County and flows sw into Big Creek.

Blackrock Creek rises in n Jackson County and flows nw into Soco Creek.

Blackrock Gap, s Macon County between Dryman Fork and Ball Creek.

Blackrock Knob, e Swain County in Yalaka Mountains near the head of Piney Wood Creek. Alt. 4,364.

Blackrock Mountain, n Jackson County on the n end of Blackrock Ridge on Plott Balsams. Alt. 6,100.

Blackrock Mountain, on the Jackson-Macon county line between Granite City formations and Wildcat Gap.

Blackrock Mountain, on the Jackson-Macon county line between Hamburg Gap and Buck Gap.

Blackrock Ridge, n Jackson County, extends n from Scott Creek to Soco Creek.

Blacksnake Branch rises in n Transylvania County and flows se into Turkey Creek.

Blackstock Branch rises in n Buncombe County and flows nw into Madison County, where it enters Ivy River.

Blackstock Knob, on the Buncombe-Yancey county line between Balsam and Rainbow Gaps. Alt. 6,325. Probably named for a surveyor, Nehemiah Blackstock, who worked in the vicinity in 1845.

Blackstone, community in ne Caldwell County. Named for Sir William Blackstone (1723–80), English jurist, by Col. George N. Folk, who conducted a law school there after the Civil War.

Black Swamp rises in w Bladen County and flows w into Big Swamp in Robeson County. Bryants Pond is on Black Swamp.

Black Swamp, se tip of Camden County.

Black Swamp rises in n Nash County and flows se into Beaverdam Swamp.

Black Swamp, w Pitt County, drains se into Little Contentnea Creek.

Black Swamp Creek rises in se Jones County and flows s into White Oak River.

Black Wall Street, Parrish Street in Durham, center of African American entrepreneurship, ca. 1905. Black-owned businesses such as Mechanics and Farmers Bank and North Carolina Mutual Life Insurance Co. originated there. Booker T. Washington and W. E. B. DuBois chronicled the area's growth.

Black Walnut Point, e Bertie County on Chowan River between Avoca and Scotch Hall plantations.

Blackwalnut Swamp rises in e Bertie County and flows e into Chowan River.

Blackwater River rises in Virginia and flows sw into North Carolina, where it joins the Nottoway River a short distance s of the Virginia line on the Hertford-Gates county line to form the Chowan River. The name appears on the Comberford map, 1657.

Blackwater Run rises in s Rowan County and flows s into n Cabarrus County, where it enters Dutch Buffalo Creek. The last Indians in Cabarrus County lived along the stream.

Blackwell, community in nw Caswell County. A post office operated there, 1830–1909. A tobacco factory also formerly existed there.

Blackwell Gap, central Cherokee County near the middle of Bates Mountain.

Blackwell Mountain, a peak on Bates Mountain, central Cherokee County.

Blackwell Ridge, sw Macon County between Long Branch and Curtis Creek.

Blackwood, community in s Orange County. Alt. 487.

Blackwood Creek rises in central Gaston County near the sw limits of West Gastonia and flows s into Crowders Creek.

Blackwood Mountain, s Orange County between Mountain Creek and Old Field Creek.

Bladenboro, town in sw Bladen County. Inc. 1903. Alt. 111. Named for the county. Produces textiles. *See also* West Bladenboro.

Bladenboro Township, sw Bladen County.

Bladen County was formed in 1734 from New Hanover County. Located in the se section of the state, it is bounded by Sampson, Pender, Columbus, Robeson, and Cumberland Counties. It was named for Martin Bladen (1680–1746), English soldier and politician who was commissioner of trade and plantations, 1717–46. Area: 891 sq. mi. County seat: Elizabethtown, elevation 121 ft. Townships are Abbotts, Bethel, Bladenboro, Brown Marsh, Carvers Creek, Central, Colly, Cypress Creek, Elizabethtown, French's Creek, Hollow, Lake Creek, Turnbull, White Oak, and Whites Creek. Produces turkeys, chickens, tobacco, corn, soybeans, oats, peanuts, grapes, blueberries, hogs, dairy livestock, wood products, and sand for concrete.

Bladen Lakes State Forest, Bladen County, covers 35,875 acres, of which 1,000 acres around Jones, Singletary and Salters Lakes are reserved for park purposes and in which no cutting is done. Named for the lakes included in the area. Objectives: to build up the growing stock of timber on overcut and previously badly burned areas; to utilize all the resources of the area, including game, forestry demonstration, and recreation. Acquired by the state of North Carolina from the federal government in 1939.

Blades, community in e Craven County on Clubfoot Creek.

Blaine, community in nw Montgomery County. Known as Post Oak prior to 1884, when it was renamed in honor of James G. Blaine (1830–93), Republican nominee for president. Served by post office, 1884–1934.

Blaine Branch rises in central Macon County and flows ne into Cartoogechaye Creek.

Blaine Knob, s Macon County between Jones Creek and North Fork [Skeenah Creek].

Blair Channel, in Carteret and Hyde Counties, a navigable lane in Ocracoke Inlet running n and s between Wallace Channel and Teaches Hole. Appears on the Price survey of Ocracoke Inlet, 1795, as Ship Channel.

Blair Creek rises in s Clay County and flows ne into Hiwassee River.

Blair Fork rises in central Caldwell County and flows s and sw into Lower Creek.

Blake, community in central Sampson County served by post office, 1898–1905.

Blakeley County. On November 28, 1817, the General Assembly attempted to create a county by the name from a portion of Rowan County. It was intended to honor War of 1812 naval hero Johnston Blakely.

Blakeleyville, town authorized to be est. and laid off on the lands of Andrew Polk on Little Creek in nw Anson County in 1817. Probably named for Capt. Johnston Blakely, North Carolina naval hero who lost his life at sea in the War of 1812. There is no evidence that the town was est., nor is it known whether there was any connection with the nearby community of Blakely in Montgomery County.

Blakely, former community in w Montgomery County on Pee Dee River at the mouth of Island Creek. A post office as late as 1822, but abandoned shortly afterward as a result of the depression of 1819. *See also* Blakeleyville.

Blakely, former town in nw Northampton County on the e side of Roanoke River. Inc. 1832–33. To be laid off on 200 acres of land owned by John D. Amis. Named for Johnston Blakely (1781–1814), a naval hero of the War of 1812. Was terminal point in 1833 of the Petersburg Railroad, the first railroad in

North Carolina. Town declined as Weldon, just across the river in Halifax County, flourished.

Blakely's Depot. *See* Garysburg.

Blake Mountain, s Buncombe County n of Skyland.

Blake Mountain, on the Henderson-Polk county line.

Blakley, community in nw Forsyth County served by post office, 1894–1903.

Blalock, community in w McDowell County served by post office, 1898–1906.

Blanch, community in n Caswell County on Dan River. Named for Blanche Moore, niece of D. G. Watkins, who owned the land on which the community developed beginning about 1875. Alt. 750.

Blanchards, community in s Wake County.

Bland, community in se Sampson County served by post office, 1887–1904.

Bland Branch rises in s Duplin County and flows se into Allan Creek.

Bland Crossroads, community in w Lenoir County.

Blankenship Creek rises in s Yancey County and flows nw into Price Creek.

Blanket Bottom Creek. *See* Blanket Creek.

Blanket Creek rises in sw Forsyth County and flows sw into Yadkin River. Appears as Linviles Creek on the Collet map, 1770; called Blanket Bottom Creek in Moravian records, 1778; and appears as Clements Creek on the MacRae map, 1833.

Blanton Branch rises in n Jackson County and flows n into Ochre Creek.

Blantyre, community in e Transylvania County near the mouth of Gash Creek. Named by C. H. Boswell, railway construction engineer, for his birthplace near Glasgow, Scotland.

Blazed Creek rises in ne Macon County and flows sw into Beasley Creek.

Blazed Gap, on the Macon-Swain county line.

Bledsoe Creek rises near Fender Mountain in w Alleghany County and flows se into Little River.

Blennerhassett Island, s Madison County in the French Broad River opposite Marshall. The sandy island, approx. ¼ mi. long, probably was named for the island in the Ohio River below Parkersburg, W.Va., where Harman Blennerhassett and Aaron Burr plotted in 1805–1806 to seize an empire in the West.

Blevin Branch rises in n Buncombe County and flows se and w into Panther Branch.

Blevine Knob, w Yancey County between Edney Branch and Cane River.

Blevins, community in n Ashe County served by post office, 1889–1906.

Blevins Branch rises in n Mitchell County and flows w into Big Rock Creek.

Blevins Creek, community in central Avery County.

Blevins Creek rises in central Avery County and flows nw into Cranberry Creek.

Blevins Crossroads, community in ne Alleghany County.

Blevins Ridge, n central Avery County.

Blewett Falls Lake, on the Pee Dee River in Anson and Richmond Counties. Rockingham Power Co. began development of falls for hydroelectric power, 1907–1908; Carolina Power and Light Co. (now Progress Energy) took over, 1926. A dam 1,470 ft. long impounds a lake 9.4 mi. long covering 2,500 acres. Named for William Bluit or Blewett (1719–1810), native of England, who owned land there in 1758. Falls, now under the lake, dropped 8 or 9 ft. over a distance of about 1,000 ft.

Blewing Creek. *See* Blue Creek.

Bliss, community in e Surry County served by post office, 1880–1902.

Bloat Springs Landing, on Cape Fear River in central Bladen County.

Blockade Branch rises in w Macon County and flows ne into Choga Creek.

Blockade Shoal lies off the nw shore of Roanoke Island, e Dare County, in the waters of Croatan Sound.

Blockers. *See* Stedman.

Blockersville. *See* Stedman.

Block House Creek rises in South Carolina and flows ne into Polk County, where it enters Pacolet River.

Blockhouse Mountain, nw Swain County in Great Smoky Mountains National Park on Jenkins Trail Ridge near lat. 35°33′ N., long. 83°42′35″ W. Alt. 5,425.

Blockhouse Ridge, nw Swain County in Great Smoky Mountains National Park, a spur of Jenkins Trail Ridge extending se from Blockhouse Mountain near lat. 35°32′40″ N., long. 83°41′15″ W.

Blood Camp Ridge, central Avery County.

Blood Creek rises in sw Wilkes County and flows n into W. Kerr Scott Reservoir.

Bloodrun Creek rises in w Chatham County and flows sw into Brush Creek. Local tradition says that a "hot skirmish" occurred between small bands of Whigs and Tories during the Revolutionary War. Each side, not wishing to reveal its losses, buried its dead secretly. One of the sites selected as a burying ground was near the small stream, and it was given its present name to commemorate the shedding of blood in battle.

Bloody Bluff, s Sampson County overlooking Black River.

Bloody Fork rises in n Yancey County and flows nw into Cane River.

Bloody Rock, near Cullasaja, e Macon County. A blood-colored liquid oozing from the granite rock is said by legend to mark the site where a young man of the community was murdered by a jealous rival for the affections of a local lass.

Bloomery Swamp is formed by the junction of Millstone and Juniper Creeks in nw Wilson County. It flows se into Contentnea Creek. Known prior to 1782 as Great Swamp.

Bloomingdale, community in s Robeson County.

Bloomington, community in w Stanly County. Probably named for an early operator of a cotton gin.

Bloomington. *See* Archdale.

Blossie Creek, waterway off Roanoke Bay separating Off Island from Bodie Island, e Dare County.

Blossom Swamp rises in s Pender County and flows ne into Trumpeters Swamp. Probably named for Samuel Blossom, a Portuguese emigrant who operated a ferry across the Northeast Cape Fear River in the late nineteenth and early twentieth centuries.

Blossomtown, community in central Macon County on a tributary of Cartoogechaye Creek.

Blount Pocosin, the n section of Big Pocosin in sw Beaufort County.

Blounts Creek, community in s Beaufort County approx. 2 mi. from the source of the stream for which it is named. Post office est. there about 1894.

Blounts Creek rises in Big Pocosin, s Beaufort County, and flows n approx. 10 mi. into

Pamlico River. Appears as Slade Creek on the Collet map, 1770.

Blounts Creek rises in central Cumberland County and flows se into Little Cross Creek.

Blounts Ford. *See* Grifton.

Blountsville, former town in nw Martin County on the Roanoke River. Est. 1785 on the lands of Whitmel Hill (1743–97) near Hamilton, but probably never developed. A post office, Clark's Store, existed there from 1819 to 1842.

Blowing Rock, town in s Watauga and n Caldwell Counties near the head of Yadkin River. First settled in 1870; inc. 1889. Named for a peculiar rock formation rising above the Johns River valley that creates a current of air that returns to the sender light articles thrown over the void. Known as Ohlanto by the Indians and the subject of many legends. In 1927 the communities of Green Park, *which see*, and Mayview Park were annexed. Fort Rollins, used in the Civil War, was located there. Alt. 3,586.

Blowing Rock Township, s Watauga County.

Blowing Spring, w Swain County near Nantahala Gorge; its waters fall into Nantahala River.

Blue Banks, The, high marl bank along Contentnea Creek below Edwards Bridge, Greene-Pitt county line. The name comes from the distinctive color of the formation. The banks are on both sides of the creek but are more prominent on the Pitt County side.

Blue Branch rises in n Buncombe County and flows w into French Broad River.

Bluebutton, community in s central Camden County, named for the plantation of Stephen Richardson located there in 1722; in turn named for the small periwinkle (*Vinca minor*) commonly called bluebutton and native to the area. The community was the gathering point, in 1840, for families in the area beginning on their w migration. From 1908 to 1929, the post office name of Bluebutton was Bartlett, for a local family.

Blue Creek rises in e Caldwell County and flows ne into Kings Creek.

Blue Creek rises in n Granville County and flows ne into Little Grassy Creek. For a possible source of the name, *see* Blue Wing Creek.

Blue Creek rises in w Onslow County and flows se into New River. Mentioned in local records as early as 1744.

Bluefield, community in s central Bladen County. Named for John Blue.

Blue Gap, sw Buncombe County e of Thompson Knob.

Blue Mud Creek is formed in n Warren County by the junction of Terrapin and Malones Creeks; it flows n into Smith Creek.

Blue Ridge, community in e Henderson County. Alt. 2,270.

Blue Ridge Cove Creek rises in s Yancey County and flows n into South Toe River.

Blue Ridge Gap, s Transylvania County in Blue Ridge Mountains near the head of Toxaway Creek.

Blue Ridge Island, a sandy elevation in the middle of Angola Bay in s Duplin and n Pender Counties.

Blue Ridge Mountains is the name applied to the e portion of the Appalachian Mountains, *which see*, extending from a few mi. n of Harpers Ferry, W.Va., to n Georgia. The average elevation is from 2,000 to 4,000 ft. The highest peaks of the Blue Ridge are in the Black Mountains of North Carolina, *which see*. The name comes from the hazy blue appearance of the mountains. The Cherokee Indians knew the section of the mountains as *Sa-koh-na-gas* (blue).

Blue Ridge Parkway, an elongated park with a scenic motorway following the crest of the Blue Ridge Mountains from Shenandoah National Park in Virginia to the Great Smoky Mountains National Park in North Carolina and Tennessee. It averages more than 3,000 ft. above sea level. There are a number of wayside parks, marked historic sites (including cabins and farm buildings), a mineral museum, scenic overlooks, and other points of interest along the way. Construction began on September 11, 1935, and was completed in 1987 with the opening of the Linn Cove Viaduct, *which see*, around Grandfather Mountain. Extends 469 mi. The parkway enters North Carolina in ne Alleghany County and extends sw for 252.1 mi.

Blue Ridge Pinnacle. *See* Pinnacle.

Blue Ridge Township, se Watauga County.

Blue Rock Branch rises in e Yancey County and flows w into South Toe River.

Blue Rock Knob, se Buncombe County ne of Little Pisgah Mountain.

Bluerock Knob, e Yancey County near the head of George Fork. Alt. 4,859.

Blue Rock Knob, e Yancey County between Blue Rock Branch and Sevenmile Ridge.

Blue's Crossing. *See* Aberdeen.

Blue Sea Creek rises in s Yancey County and flows nw into Beech Nursery Creek.

Blue Sea Falls, on Blue Sea Creek, s Yancey County in Pisgah National Forest.

Blue's Mountain, an elevation in n Hoke County on the Fort Bragg Military Reservation. Named for the Blue family, former owners.

Blues Pond, w Scotland County on Joes Creek. Covers 30 acres. Formed prior to 1909 and known earlier as Gibsons Millpond.

Blue Springs Township, sw Hoke County. A part of Robeson County until 1911.

Blue Valley, joined valleys of East Fork Overflow Creek and West Fork Overflow Creek in se Macon County.

Blue Wing, community in nw Granville County served by post office, 1841–1905.

Bluewing, community in nw Granville County.

Blue Wing Creek rises in e Person County and flows ne into Hyco Creek in Virginia. Mentioned in 1728 by William Byrd. The bluewing was a small duck regarded as a delicacy.

Bluewing Mine, copper mine on branch of Aarons Creek in nw Granville County. First operated 1898–1900; opened again for a short time during World War I.

Bluff, community in w Madison County on Meadow Fork. Alt. 2,150.

Bluff Branch rises in n Clay County and flows sw into Tusquitee Creek.

Bluff Mountain, sw Ashe County. Alt. 5,073.

Bluff Mountain, w Madison County near the head of Hickory Ridge Branch. Alt. 4,640.

Bluff Park. *See* Doughton Park.

Bluff Point, s Chowan County approx. 8½ mi. se of Edenton, extends into Albemarle Sound. Mentioned in local records from the early eighteenth century; appears on the Moseley map, 1733.

Bluff Point extends from the s mainland of Hyde County into Pamlico Sound between East Bluff Bay and West Bluff Bay. Appears as Machapunga Bluff on the Moseley map, 1733.

Bluff Point extends from e Onslow County into White Oak River.

Bluff Point extends from se Pasquotank County into the Pasquotank River on the n shore of Little Flatty Creek.

Bluffs, The, rough, rocky mountain peaks in sw Alleghany County e of the Blue Ridge Parkway near Doughton Park, *which see*.

Bluff Shoal, formed by the merging waters of the Albemarle and Pamlico Sounds, extends from Bluff Point on the s mainland of Hyde County to Royal Shoal on the Carteret-Hyde county line. The name appears as early as the Mouzon map, 1775.

Bly Gap, s Clay County. The Appalachian Trail passes through the gap just n of the Georgia line.

Blythe Branch rises in e Transylvania County and flows sw into Lydia Creek.

Blythe Mill Creek rises in nw Henderson County and flows se into French Broad River.

Blythe Mountain, w Henderson County on Little Willow Creek.

Board Camp Creek rises in n Swain County in Great Smoky Mountains National Park below Broad Camp Gap and flows w into Forney Creek.

Board Camp Gap, n Swain County on Forney Ridge in Great Smoky Mountains National Park.

Board Cove Branch rises in ne Swain County and flows n into Bunches Creek.

Board Gap, on Drymans Branch in s Macon County.

Boardman, town in nw Columbus County on Lumber River. Inc. 1891 as Hub; name changed in 1899 to honor prominent American Baptist clergyman George Dana Boardman (1828–1903). Long inactive in municipal affairs.

Boardtree Creek rises in s Macon County and flows se into Poplar Cove Creek.

Boathouse Creek rises in w Carteret County and flows sw into White Oak River.

Boat Island, e Onslow County just inside Bogue Inlet. Named because early fishermen pulled boats up there.

Boatman Branch rises in n Franklin County and flows se into Sandy Creek.

Bobbitt, community in se Vance County near Lynch Creek.

Bob Branch rises in ne Cherokee County and flows sw into Beaver Creek approx. 150 yds. before the latter stream enters Valley River.

Bob Branch rises in w central Clay County and flows s parallel to and e of Graveyard Ridge into Hiwassee River.

Bob Branch rises in n Randolph County and flows ne into Muddy Creek.

Bob Creek rises in n Cherokee County and flows sw into Tellico River.

Bob Creek rises in ne Pender County and flows s into Angola Creek.

Bob's Cove, site of early settlement on e end of Bogue Banks, s Carteret County. Storms drove out early settlers until settlement of Salter Path, *which see.*

Bobs Creek rises in e Yancey County and flows nw into South Toe River.

Bob's Knob, s Burke County. Alt. 2,000.

Bob's Ridge, e Haywood County between Big East Fork and Big Cove.

Bob Whites Corner, community in s Pasquotank County.

Boby Cove, between Laurel Mountain and Big Creek in nw Henderson County.

Boddies Mill Pond, w Nash County on Stony Creek. Covers more than 100 acres; max. depth 15 ft. Owned by Braswell Milling Company and furnishes power for corn mill.

Bodie Island (pronounced "body"), one of the Outer Banks, e Dare County. N boundary was formerly New Inlet, now the area around Kitty Hawk. Bounded on the s by Oregon Inlet. Mentioned by John Lawson in 1700. Appears on the Moll map, 1729. Cow Island and Duggs Island, also shown on the Moll map, are now joined with and a part of Bodie Island. *See also* Etacrewac.

Boger City, community in central Lincoln County. Named for Robert Boger, who est. a textile mill there. Previously known as Goodsons Store and Goodsonville.

Boggan, community in central Anson County. Alt. 306. Probably named for Patrick Boggan, pioneer settler. *See* Wadesboro.

Bogue, community in w Carteret County. Site of auxiliary air base for Cherry Point Marine Corps Air Station.

Bogue. *See* Swansboro.

Bogue Banks, barrier beach in s Carteret County forming one of the Outer Banks. It is 25 mi. long and from ½ to 2 mi. wide. Fort Macon is at the e end; the towns of Atlantic Beach, Salter Path, and Emerald Isle are on Bogue Banks. The name appears on the Moseley

map, 1733. Josiah Bogue settled in the vicinity in the early eighteenth century. Named for him or for the family.

Bogue Inlet, an inlet from the Atlantic Ocean into Bogue Sound between Dudley's Island, e Onslow County, and Bogue Banks, sw Carteret County. White Oak River enters the Atlantic Ocean through the inlet. Shown on the De Graffenried map (French text), 1711.

Bogue Sound extends from the sw end of Carteret County along its s edge to the se section of the county at Beaufort and Morehead City. The sound drains into the Atlantic Ocean through Beaufort Inlet, *which see.*

Bogue Swamp rises in n central Columbus County and flows se into Waccamaw River.

Bogue Township, central Columbus County.

Boiling Springs, community in n Cherokee County on Hanging Dog Creek.

Boiling Springs, town in sw Cleveland County. Alt. 990. Inc. 1911 and took its name from a boiling spring known to the Cherokee Indians. Site of Gardner-Webb University, an outgrowth of a high school est. there in 1905.

Boiling Springs Lake, town in se Brunswick County. Inc. 1961.

Boiling Springs Township, former township in sw Cleveland County, now township no. 2.

Bold Branch rises in n Henderson County and flows se into Clear Creek.

Bolden Branch rises in ne Cherokee County and flows nw into Junaluska Creek.

Bold Run Branch rises in s Franklin County and flows sw into Wake County, where it enters New Light Creek.

Bolick Branch. *See* Anthony Bolick Branch.

Bolin Creek rises in se Orange County on the s slope of Bald Mountain and flows se, on n side of the town of Chapel Hill, to join Booker Creek in forming Little Creek. Appears as Bollings Creek on a map of Chapel Hill made in 1792 by John Daniel. The Bolling family settled in Orange County in the eighteenth century.

Bolin Knob, mountain at junction of Burke-McDowell-Rutherford county line. Alt. approx. 2,200. Named for a family living in the area by the late eighteenth century.

Bolivia, town in e central Brunswick County. Settled in the late nineteenth century and inc. in 1911. Alt. 40. County seat located nearby in 1978.

Bollens Run rises in s Granville County and flows s into Tar River.

Bollers Knob, central Henderson County at the head of Findley Creek.

Bolling, community in n Halifax County a short distance w of Roanoke Rapids.

Bolling Creek. *See* Bolin Creek.

Bolton, town in nw Columbus County. Settled 1889. Inc. 1915. Named for Bolton Lumber Company. Alt. 66.

Bolton Township, e Columbus County.

Bombay, community in sw Randolph County served by post office, 1889–1917.

Bona, community in sw Chatham County.

Bonaparte Landing, sw Brunswick County on the Intracoastal Waterway.

Bonarva, plantation of the Pettigrew family in se Washington County and w Tyrrell County. Of the various plantation houses of the Pettigrew family, two were on Bonarva. Belgrade, in Washington County, was built about 1796 and is still standing; it was named for the earlier Pettigrew house on Harveys Neck in Perquimans County. Magnolia was built in Tyrrell County, the site of the greater portion of the Pettigrew lands. Scotch Hall was the Pettigrew home in Bertie County. Belgrade is now a part of Pettigrew State Park, *which see*.

Bonarva Canal, w Tyrrell County, flows from Lake Phelps ne into Old Canal. Known also as Magnolia Canal. Dug during antebellum era with slave labor to drain swamplands for cultivation.

Bond Creek rises in se Beaufort County and flows n into the mouth of South Creek at Pamlico River.

Bonds Ferry. *See* Pamlico River.

Bone Camp Branch rises in s Madison County and flows sw into Bull Creek.

Bones Creek rises in nw Cumberland County and flows se and s into Little Rockfish Creek.

Bone Valley, nw Swain County in Great Smoky Mountains National Park. Named after an early settler found the bleached bones of his long-lost cows there.

Bone Valley Creek is formed in nw Swain County in Great Smoky Mountains National Park by the junction of Roaring Creek and Defeat Branch. It flows s into Hazel Creek.

Boney Mill Pond, on Paget Branch in s Duplin County.

Bonlee, community in sw Chatham County.

Est. 1894 and first known as Dunlap's Mill; in 1898 renamed Causey for Joshua Causey, local resident. Renamed Bonlee in 1910, supposedly for a brand of cloth. Inc. 1913; charter repealed 1936. Alt. 526.

Bonner Bay, waterway in e Pamlico County between the mouth of Spring Creek and Bay River.

Bonner Bridge. *See* Oregon Inlet.

Bonnerton, community in se Beaufort County.

Bonnets Points appears on the Moseley map, 1733, from what is now se Brunswick County extending into Cape Fear River between Elizabeth River and Dutchmans Creek.

Bonnie Doone, community in central Cumberland County nw of Fayetteville near limits of the Fort Bragg Military Reservation. Inc. 1941; charter repealed 1953.

Bonsal, community in sw Wake County on the head of Tom Jack Creek. Settled 1900. Inc. 1907; charter repealed 1917. Named for the railroad engineer who drove the first train through the area. Alt. 305.

Bonus, community in n Jones County served by post office, 1888–1903.

Boogertown, community in s Gaston County at the n end of Jackson Knob, about 3 mi. s of Gastonia.

Booker Creek rises in se Orange County and flows through Eastwood Lake to join Bolin Creek just e of town of Chapel Hill to form Little Creek.

Boomer, community in s Wilkes County on Warrior Creek, by which name it was known until renamed for "Boomer" Matheson, local postmaster.

Boomer Branch rises in n Swain County and flows se into Proctor Creek.

Boomer Inn Branch rises in s Haywood County and flows e into Right Hand Prong [Pigeon River].

Boomer Township, sw Wilkes County.

Boone, town and county seat, central Watauga County. Inc. 1871. Named for Daniel Boone (1734–1820) who, according to tradition, camped there while on a hunting trip. Home of Appalachian State University. The outdoor drama *Horn in the West*, by Kermit Hunter, has been produced there each summer since 1952. Produces electronics components, apparel, canned foods, wood products, and shoes. Alt. 3,266.

Boone Branch rises in n Clay County and flows se into Tuni Creek.

Boone Camp Branch rises in e Watauga County and flows se into Elk Creek.

Boone Cove Gap, on the Madison County, N.C.–Unicoi County, Tenn., line.

Boone Creek rises in s Watauga County and flows ne into Flannery Fork [South Fork River].

Boone Fork rises in s Watauga County and flows ne and n into Watauga River.

Boone Ridge, w Yancey County between Wolf Branch and Shepherd Branch.

Boone's Cave, on a high bluff overlooking the Yadkin River in w Davidson County is traditionally said to have been occupied by Daniel Boone. It is near Horseshoe Neck, *which see*, and a park is maintained near the cave by the county.

Boones Crossroads, community in sw Northampton County.

Boone's Fork, stream, rises in nw Caldwell County and flows w into Mulberry Creek. Named for Jesse Boone, pre-Revolutionary settler and nephew of Daniel Boone.

Boones Gap, sw Wilkes County near the head-waters of Warrior Creek. Named for the explorer Daniel Boone.

Boone Township, w Davidson County, named for Daniel Boone, who is said to have lived in a cabin along the banks of the Yadkin River in the area.

Boone Township, central Watauga County.

Boonford, community in e Yancey County on North Toe River. Named for Daniel Boone, who is said to have forded the river there.

Boon Hill Township, se Johnston County. *See also* Princeton.

Boons Ferry appears on the Collet map, 1770, as being on the Meherrin River between ne Northampton County and nw Hertford County. By 1802 it had ceased operation, and by 1833 Boone Bridge existed at the site. A bridge still crosses the river there.

Boons Fork, community in central Northampton County.

Boon's Mill Pond, w Northampton County on Gumberry Swamp. Covers 100 acres; max. depth 20 ft. Confederates repulsed Union march there on July 28, 1863.

Boon Station, community in w central Alamance County.

Boon Station Township, former township in w central Alamance County, now township no. 3.

Boonville, town in n Yadkin County. Inc. 1895. Named for Daniel Boone (1734–1820), who is said to have camped at the site. Produces textiles and processed grain.

Boonville Township, nw Yadkin County.

Bordensville. *See* Mill Creek.

Border, community in w Orange County served by post office, 1880–1905.

Border Creek rises in e Lincoln County and flows se into Catawba River.

Boring Creek rises in s Transylvania County and flows nw into East Fork French Broad River.

Boring Mill Branch rises in s Buncombe County and flows se into French Broad River.

Borough, The, sw Pender County on Black River near the mouth of Moore's Creek, a shipping point for goods sent by water. Dates from prior to the Revolution. Apparently, site was authorized to be laid off in 1798 for the town of Parkersborough on the land of Hardy Parker. It is not known whether the town was actually established. The remains of an old wharf may still be seen a short distance from the bank of the river. A fishing camp is now operated at the site, and three old roads through the woods converge at the wharf site.

Bosley. *See* Wardville.

Bost Creek rises in se Cabarrus County and flows se into Rocky River.

Bostic, town in central Rutherford County between Second Broad River and Puzzle Creek. Alt. 923. Inc. 1893. Named for George T. Bostic, first mayor.

Bostick's Mills, community in n Richmond County served by post office, 1830–1905.

Bosts Mills, community in se Cabarrus County on Rocky River, former site of gristmill and sawmill.

Boswell, community in central Buncombe County w of Asheville near Deaver View.

Boteler Peak, ne Vineyard Mountain, e Clay County. Alt. 4,500.

Bottom, community in n Surry County on Beaverdam Creek.

Bottomless Pools, in Pool Creek, sw Rutherford County at Lake Lure. Formed by whirlpool action of the rushing water in weaker sections of the huge granite rock over which it flows. Three pools now exist, and a fourth apparently is being formed. In 1947 a geologist who studied them reported that the pools may vary in age from 100,000 to a million years.

Boulding Creek rises in central Granville County and flows se into Tar River.

Boushell, community in e central Wake County.

Bowan's Crossing. *See* Icard.

Bowans Gap, sw Cherokee County at the ne end of Angelico Mountain.

Bowden Mountain, e Davidson County between the headwaters of Flat Swamp Creek and Fourmile Branch.

Bowden Pond, on the head of Bear Swamp in w Duplin County.

Bowdens, community in nw Duplin County. Alt. 167. Settled prior to 1872, inc. 1911, but no longer active in municipal affairs. Named for Capt. James Bowden, who owned land in the vicinity. Railroad name is Bowden.

Bowditch, community in e Yancey County on Ayles Creek.

Boween River rises in s Cleveland County and flows sw into South Carolina, where it enters Broad River.

Bowen Point, a point of land on the w side of the mouth of Shallotte River. The channel of the Intracoastal Waterway cuts through the point.

Bower, community in sw Forsyth County served by post office, 1894–1904.

Bowers Creek rises in s Swain County and flows nw into Yalaka Creek.

Bowers Gap, on the Avery-Watauga county line se of Shawneehaw Creek.

Bower's Store. *See* Sparta.

Bowies Falls. *See* Buies Falls.

Bowlens Creek rises in s Yancey County and flows nw into Cane River.

Bowlens Creek, community in central Yancey County. Formerly known as Athlone.

Bowlens Pyramid, peak in s central Yancey County between Jumpoff Gap and the head of George Fork. Alt. 4,908. The northernmost peak in the Black Mountains.

Bowles, community in central Wilkes County served by post office, 1888–1902.

Bowling Green Creek rises in nw Mitchell County and flows se into Hollow Poplar Creek.

Bowman Bluff, an elevation in w Henderson County overlooking French Broad River. Named because it was an Indian lookout site.

Bowman Gap, sw Cherokee County between Angelico Mountain and Pack Mountain. Alt. approx. 3,215.

Bowman Gap, n Yancey County between the head of Shoal Creek and Bailey Hill.

Bowmans Bluff, community in w Henderson County near the mouth of Willow Creek. Settled about 1875–80.

Bowmore, community in s Hoke County.

Box, P[ort]. *See* P[ort] Box.

Box Creek rises in n central Rutherford County at Camel Knob and flows s into Second Broad River.

Boyd, community in sw Rockingham County served by post office, 1884–1905. Mill run by J. Wright Moore was nearby.

Boyd Branch rises near Little Hickory Top in s Buncombe County and flows se into Bent Creek.

Boyd Creek rises in central Alamance County and flows s into Haw River.

Boyden, community in se Surry County on Yadkin River. Alt. 771.

Boyd Mountain, nw Buncombe County between Cherry and Wade Gaps.

Boyds Crossroads, community in e Pitt County.

Boyd's Ferry. *See* Grimesland.

Boyd Township, ne Transylvania County.

Boyette, town in sw Wilson County. Inc. 1887 as Silverboro; name changed 1897 to honor first mayor, Nathan Boyette. Long inactive in municipal affairs.

Boyles' Store. *See* Dalton.

Boylin, community in w Anson County served by post office, 1900–1903.

Boylston, community in nw Henderson County. Site of numerous unsuccessful attempts to mine gold. Named for Revolutionary War soldier.

Boylston Creek rises in ne Transylvania County and flows ne into Henderson County, where it enters French Broad River.

Boza Creek rises in nw Rockingham County and flows sw into Mayo River.

Bracebridge Hall, home of Elias Carr, governor 1893–97, stands 5 mi. se of Pinetops, s Edgecombe County.

Brachcoast Swamp, pocosin in e Cumberland County drained by Reese Creek. One of the Carolina Bays, *which see*.

Brack Branch rises in s Madison County and flows se into Big Pine Creek.

Bracken Mountain, a ridge approx. 1½ mi. long

in w Transylvania County s of and parallel to the headwaters of Tucker Creek. Named for a large coarse fern growing there.

Brackens Creek rises in two forks in central Transylvania County; one flows ne and the other se to join. The creek then flows e into Nicholson Creek.

Brackettown. *See* Demming.

Bracketts Creek rises in s Rutherford County and flows se into Floyds Creek.

Brackett Township, se McDowell County.

Braden Mountain, e Cherokee County, extends from the headwaters of Lamb Branch on the s to Slow Creek on the n, due w of Indian Grave Gap.

Bradey Branch rises in ne Cherokee County and flows se into Valley River.

Bradford Mountain, s Caldwell County. Alt. 1,313. Named for Bennet Bradford, eighteenth-century settler who is buried on its slopes.

Bradford Mountain, se Transylvania County in Blue Ridge Mountains.

Bradley Branch rises in s Macon County and flows se into Norton Branch.

Bradley Butt, e Macon County between Fall Branch and Mica City Creek.

Bradley Creek rises in n Macon County and flows sw into Little Tennessee River.

Bradley Creek rises in central New Hanover County and flows se into Greenville Sound.

Bradley Creek rises in ne Transylvania County and flows se into South Fork in Pisgah National Forest. Site of early ironworks; a forge operated there during the Civil War.

Bradley Creek rises in s Transylvania County and flows sw into East Fork French Broad River.

Bradley Fork is formed in ne Swain County in Great Smoky Mountains National Park by the junction of Chasm Prong and Gulf Prong. It flows se into Oconaluftee River.

Bradley Gap, w Avery County.

Bradley Gap, n Buncombe County between Bruce Knob and Bill Cole Mountain.

Bradley Mountain, e Henderson County between Little Hungry River and Hungry River. Alt. 2,731.

Bradley's Store. *See* Kipling.

Bradshaw, community in sw Orange County served by post office, 1880–1905.

Bradshaw Branch rises in s Lincoln County and flows sw into Leepers Creek.

Bradshaws Millpond, s Sampson County, drains sw into Black River.

Bradshaw Township, nw Mitchell County.

Bragg, community in n Scotland County served by post office, 1888–1912.

Bragg Crossroads, community in s Granville County.

Bragtown, former community in central Durham County n of the city of Durham, now within the limits of the latter. Also spelled Braggtown.

Branchs Store, community in n Duplin County.

Branchville, community in w Robeson County served by post office, 1880–1903.

Branchville. *See* Manson.

Brandle Branch rises in se Cherokee County and flows se into Little Brasstown Creek.

Brandon, community in n Ashe County. Alt. approx. 2,850.

Brand Swamp rises in n Wilson County and flows se into Cattail Swamp. Named for Benjamin Brand.

Brandy Creek rises in w Franklin County and flows ne into Cedar Creek.

Brandy Gap, in nw Mitchell County at the head of Right Fork [Pigeonroost Creek].

Brank Cove, the valley through which Brank Cove Branch flows in n Buncombe County, w of Thurz Mountain.

Brank Cove Branch rises near Brittain Mountain in n Buncombe County and flows nw into Flat Creek.

Brank Mountain, n Buncombe County between Pink Fox Cove and Little Middle Mountain.

Branning, community in n Bertie County served by post office, 1895–1906.

Branon, community in s central Yadkin County near South Deep Creek.

Branson Creek rises in central Onslow County and flows e into New River.

Brant Island, a tidal marsh island approx. ½ mi. long in Pamlico Sound, ne Pamlico County off Goose Creek Island.

Brantley Island, a neck of land in sw Brunswick County between Saucepan Creek and the Intracoastal Waterway.

Brassfield, community in s Durham County. Named for a local family. Formerly known as Flemington; name changed prior to 1865.

Brassfield Township, se Granville County.

Brasstown, community in sw Clay County on Ledford Branch. Alt. 1,650. Reputedly named because of confusion of two Cherokee words of similar sound but different meaning— *itse'yi* (a place made green with vegetation) and *untsai'yi* (brass). The John C. Campbell Folk School, on a 175-acre farm, is there.

Brasstown Creek rises in s Clay County and flows nw to the Cherokee-Clay county line, which it forms for a short distance before flowing into Hiwassee River.

Brasstown Gap, s Clay County on the headwaters of Beach Creek.

Brasstown Knob, n Jackson County on Coward Mountain.

Brasstown Township, se Clay County.

Braswell, community in nw Columbus County.

Braswells Crossroads, community in s Halifax County.

Brave Mountain, on the n end of Buck Mountain in w Haywood County.

Bray. *See* Riddle.

Brazel Creek rises in s Wake County and flows ne into Sunset Lake.

Breakneck Ridge, e central Avery County.

Breakneck Ridge, ne Swain County in Great Smoky Mountains National Park, a spur extending w from Hyatt Ridge.

Breedlove Branch rises in ne Swain County and flows s into Bulldie Creek.

Breeze, community in w Orange County served by post office, 1892–1905.

Brendletown, community in e Macon County on Coon Creek.

Brett Bay, in the waters of Core Sound, ne Carteret County. Formerly known as Britts Bay.

Brevard, town and county seat, central Transylvania County. Est. as county seat 1861 or 1862; inc. 1889. Named for Ephriam Brevard (1744–81), teacher, secretary of the convention that drew up the Mecklenburg Resolves of May 31, 1775, and Revolutionary surgeon. Home of Brevard College, founded 1853 as Rutherford College, *which see*; merged in 1934 with Weaver College and took its present name. Summer music camp, begun in 1936, is there. Noted tourist area. Produces chemicals, textiles, and leather products. Alt. 2,230.

Brevard Station. *See* Stanley.

Brevard Township, central Transylvania County.

Brewer Branch rises in w Swain County and flows s into Tuckasegee River.

Brewers, community in n Wilkes County near Double Creek. Alt. 1,450.

Briar Branch rises in se Buncombe County and flows ne into Wolfpit Branch.

Briar Creek rises in se Durham County and flows s into Wake County and into Stirrup Iron Creek.

Briar Patch Branch rises in n Madison County and flows sw into Culvin Creek.

Briarpatch Ridge, s Mitchell County between Middle Fork Grassy Creek and East Fork Grassy Creek.

Briary Creek rises in sw Henderson County and flows sw into Transylvania County, where it enters Reasonover Creek.

Briary Knob, e Haywood County on the head of Pisgah Creek.

Brice Creek rises in s Craven County and flows nw into Trent River. Appears on the Moseley map, 1733.

Brice Creek Pocosin, sw Craven County.

Brick Church, community in se Guilford County. First German Calvinist (German Reformed) church in Guilford County.

Brickhaven, community in Chatham County. Center of brick manufacturing.

Brickhouse. *See* Savages Crossroads.

Brickhouse Point, e Pasquotank County extends into the Pasquotank River s of Davis Bay.

Brick Kiln Branch rises in ne Onslow County and flows se into White Oak River.

Brickle Inn. *See* Union.

Brickle's Ferry. *See* Brittle's Ferry.

Brick Mill. *See* Hunsucker.

Bricks, community in n Edgecombe County. Named for Joseph Keasbey Brick, in whose honor an agricultural, industrial, and normal school for blacks was est. there by Mrs. Julia Elma Brewster Brick in 1895. School closed, 1933.

Brickton, community in n Henderson County. Took its name from former large brick-manufacturing plant.

Bridal Veil Falls, se Macon County on Cullasaja River. Water falls 120 ft. *See also* Cullasaja River.

Bridal Veil Falls, e Transylvania County on Little River between the mouths of Reasonover Creek and Tom Creek. Height of falls 50 ft.

Bridge Branch rises in n Macon County and flows se into Burningtown Creek.

Bridge Creek rises in central Craven County and flows s into Trent River.

Bridge Creek rises in s Scotland County and flows s to join Leiths Creek in forming the Little Pee Dee River.

Bridge Creek rises in n Swain County and flows se into Deep Creek.

Bridge Falls, se Haywood County on West Fork of Pigeon River. In a series of falls, water drops between 300 and 400 ft. Named because a bridge crosses the river at the top of the falls.

Bridgeport, community in central Stanly County served by post office, 1883–1916.

Bridgers Creek rises in s Northampton County and flows w into Roanoke River. Appears as Bridges Creek on the Moseley map, 1733. Pulhams Ferry, according to the Collet map, 1770, was operated across the Roanoke River at the mouth of Bridgers Creek. By 1808 and as late as 1833, the ferry was known as Pollock's Ferry, and in 1862 it was known as Devereux's Ferry.

Bridgersville, town in e Wilson County. Inc. 1925, but long inactive in municipal affairs. Named for John F. Bridgers. Post office operated there, 1889–95.

Bridges Camp Gap, on the Haywood-Transylvania county line.

Bridges Creek rises in e Montgomery County and flows nw into Little River.

Bridges Creek. *See* Bridgers Creek.

Bridgeton, town in central Craven County. Settled about 1900. Inc. 1907. Named for the bridge across the Neuse River that connected it with New Bern. Alt. 8.

Bridgewater, community in w Burke County on the Catawba River. Originally the name of the plantation of John Rutherford, who named it for Francis Egerton (1736–1803), Earl of Bridgewater, inland navigation expert and canal builder.

Bridgewater Reservoir. *See* Lake James.

Bridle Creek rises in w Warren County and flows e into Fishing Creek. A bridge across the creek is mentioned in local records as early as 1765.

Bridle Creek, former plantation house in w Warren County approx. 3 mi. sw of Warrenton. Two Confederate major generals, Matthew Whitaker Ransom and Robert Ransom, brothers, were born there. Only ruined foundations now mark the site.

Bridle Ridge extends se from Yancey County into nw McDowell County between Bee Rock and Cow Creeks.

Brief, community in n Union County between Red Creek and Duck Creek.

Brier Creek rises in nw Cleveland County and flows sw and s into Rutherford County, where it enters First Broad River.

Brier Creek rises in nw Columbus County and flows nw into Big Swamp in Robeson County.

Brier Creek rises in central Mecklenburg County and flows sw into Little Sugar Creek.

Brier Creek rises in w Wake County and flows s into Stirrup Iron Creek.

Brier Creek rises in s Wilkes County in the Brushy Mountains and flows ne into Yadkin River.

Brier Creek, community in s Wilkes County. Brier Creek Baptist Church there est. in the eighteenth century. A post office by the name served the community from about 1822 until 1882.

Brier Knob, on Swain County, N.C.–Blount County, Tenn., line in Great Smoky Mountains National Park near lat. 35°34′15″ N., long. 83°40′48″ W. Alt. 5,225.

Brier Lick Gap, on Swain County, N.C.–Blount County, Tenn., line in Great Smoky Mountains National Park near lat. 35°32′00″ N., long. 83°49′42″ W.

Brier Ridge, n Jackson County between Licklog Creek and Dark Cabin Creek.

Brier Ridge, n Yancey County e of Coxe Branch.

Briertown Mountain, sw Swain County, extends ne beside Nantahala Gorge.

Briery Bay, a loam-filled bay in s Columbus County.

Briery Hall Point, a point of land in central Dare County near the nw end of South Lake and its junction with Alligator River.

Briery Run rises in n Lenoir County and flows e into Stonyton Creek.

Briery Swamp rises in n Pitt County and flows se into Tranters Creek.

Briggs Hollow, valley in central Avery County.

Briggsville, community in se Madison County served by post office, 1887–1907.

Bright, community in n Polk County on Lake Adger, Green River.

Brights Creek rises in nw Polk County and flows se into Green River.

Brights Mill Creek. *See* Mill Creek.

Brightwater Branch rises in w Henderson County near Jumpoff Mountain and flows n into Shaw Creek.

Bright Yellow Mountain. *See* Big Yellow Mountain.

Brigman Hollow, n Madison County on a branch of Rocky Branch.

Brim, community in ne Surry County near Archies Creek.

Brindletown, community in sw Burke County. In the heart of the former gold-mining area of the county. A post office operated there, 1829–1907. A former township by the name was abolished in 1885 and merged with Silver Creek Township.

Bringles, community in sw Davidson County served by post office, 1879–1905.

Brinkland, community in s Bladen County served by post office, 1874–1903.

Brinkleyville, community in w Halifax County. Named for Joseph Brinkley, who settled there in 1767. A post office as early as 1822.

Brinkleyville Township, sw Halifax County.

Brinkly. *See* Delco.

Bristle Ridge, s Macon County between Bates Ridge and Little Tennessee River.

Bristol, community in n Ashe County. Post office in late nineteenth century.

Bristol Branch rises in n Clay County and flows s into Tusquitee Creek.

Bristol's Mill Creek rises in n central Burke County and flows s into Lower Creek at Chesterfield. Formerly known as White's Mill Creek, Bullinger's Mill Creek, and Kincaid's Mill Creek.

Bristow, community in nw Mecklenburg County.

Brittain. *See* Westminster.

Brittain Cove, se Buncombe County.

Brittain Cove, n Buncombe County on the s side of Brittain Mountain.

Brittain Mountain, n Buncombe County sw of Watershed Ridge.

Brittain Store, community in central Burke County.

Britten Creek rises in nw Polk County and flows se approx. 5½ mi. into Green River. Sometimes known as Bullin Creek.

Brittle Ordinary. *See* Union.

Brittle's Ferry appears on the Collet map, 1770, just above Winton on Chowan River, e Hertford County. Name probably a corruption of the prominent Hertford County name of Brickle.

Britton Creek rises in ne Cherokee County and flows s and sw into Valley River. Panther Den Falls, *which see*, are on Britton Creek n of Andrews.

Britton Creek rises in central Henderson County and flows se into Mud Creek.

Britton Mountain, s Buncombe County. Alt. 2,530.

Brittons Creek rises in nw Bertie County and flows w and s into Roanoke River.

Brittons Crossroads. *See* Roxobel.

Britts Bay. *See* Brett Bay.

Britts Store, community in n Hertford County.

Britts Township, se Robeson County.

Broad, community in w Rutherford County.

Broadbay Township, s Forsyth County. Named for Broadbay, Mass. (now Waldoboro, Maine), the former home of the first settlers of Friedland, a community in the township. *See also* Friedland.

Broad Branch rises in n Mitchell County and flows w into Big Fork Creek.

Broad Creek, fed by several canals from the Dismal Swamp in n Beaufort County, flows s and e into Pantego Creek.

Broad Creek rises in w Beaufort County and flows s into Pamlico River.

Broad Creek rises in se Bertie County and flows e into Cashie River.

Broad Creek, a canal in se Bertie County connecting two sides of a loop in the Roanoke River.

Broad Creek rises in the North River Pocosin of s Camden County and flows e into North River. Appears on the Collet map, 1770.

Broad Creek, stream in Nelson Bay, cuts into mainland in ne Carteret County.

Broad Creek rises in w Carteret County and flows se into Bogue Sound. Appears on the Moseley map, 1733.

Broad Creek, a bay near the nw end of South Lake, central Dare County.

Broad Creek, a tidal creek in the waters of Roanoke Sound on e Roanoke Island in e Dare County.

Broad Creek rises in se Macon County and flows se into Clear Creek.

Broad Creek rises in e Pamlico County and flows e into Neuse River estuary. Appears on the Moseley map, 1733. Known locally as Lower Broad Creek.

Broad Creek. *See* Scranton Creek.

Broad Creek Point, peninsula on the e shore of Roanoke Island, e Dare County, extending se into Roanoke Sound and Broad Creek.

Broad Inlet appears on the Moseley map, 1733, in the beach barrier of e New Hanover County between the present Masonboro and Moore Inlet.

Broadneck Swamp, se Bertie County. Named for its location in a neck of the Roanoke River. *See also* Town Swamp.

Broad River rises in se Buncombe County and flows se across ne Henderson County into w Rutherford County; se to the Polk-Rutherford county line, where it is joined by Green River; se and ne into Cleveland County; and se into South Carolina, where it joins Saluda River at Columbia to form the Congaree River. Sometimes known locally as Rocky Broad River and Main Broad River. Known by the Indians as *Ess-ee-daw*. Lake Lure is on Broad River. Appears on the Collet map, 1770. *See also* Hickory Nut Gorge.

Broad River Township, se Buncombe County. Formerly in McDowell County but annexed to Buncombe County by legislative act in 1925.

Broad Run rises in e Pitt County and flows se into Tar River.

Broad Shoals, community in s Alexander County served by post office, 1881–1904.

Broad Swamp, w Beaufort County, is the lower course of Hall Swamp. It flows s into Pamlico River.

Broadway, town in e Lee County. Inc. 1907. Settled in the 1870s and named for a broad, level opening in the vast pine forest that covered the area.

Broadway Gap, s Macon County between Little Scaly Mountain and Fork Mountain.

Brock, community in n Graham County on Sawyer Creek.

Brock Knob, on French Broad River in w Henderson County.

Brodie, former community in s Warren County on Shocco Creek. A post office was est. there in 1879; apparently the community died out after the post office was discontinued in 1913.

Brogden, community in s Wayne County.

Brogden Township, s Wayne County. Named for the family of Curtis Hooks Brogden (1816–1901), governor of North Carolina and a native of the county.

Brokeleg Branch rises in ne Cherokee County and flows s into Gipp Creek.

Broke Yoke Gap, on Graham-Swain county line between Tyre Knob and Peachtree Gap.

Bromine-Arsenic Springs. *See* Crumpler.

Brompton, central Bladen County on Cape Fear River, 4 mi. n of Elizabethtown. Started as a home by Governor Gabriel Johnston (1699–1752) but not completed. Evidence remains of unfinished building.

Brook Branch rises in w Jackson County and flows se into Greens Creek.

Brook Cove, community in se Stokes County.

Brookford, town in w Catawba County, on Henry Fork at site of former Hanging Rock Bridge. Inc. 1907. Alt. 1,000. Named for parts of the name of joint owners of a local mill, Hol*brook* and Shu*ford*.

Brookland, community in central Person County served by post office, 1899–1901.

Brookride, community in ne Watauga County.

Brooks Branch rises near Potato Knob in sw Buncombe County and flows se into Newfound Creek.

Brooks Cove, sw Buncombe County near the headwaters of Little Pole Creek.

Brooks Cove, the valley through which South Hominy Creek flows in sw Buncombe County.

Brooks Cove, e Cherokee County on the headwaters of Messer Branch.

Brooks Cove. *See* Welch Cove.

Brooks Creek rises in e Hertford County and flows se into Wiccacon River.

Brooks Crossroads, community in w Yadkin County. Alt. 1,072.

Brooksdale, community in central Person County. Named for the Brooks family, local landowners and merchants.

Brooks Gap, on the Buncombe-Haywood county line near the headwaters of South Hominy Creek.

Brooks Gap, central Graham County on Santeetlah Lake.

Brooks Knob, on the Surry-Wilkes county line.

Brooks Point, off the n shore of Hatteras Island, opposite Cape Hatteras and extending into the waters of Pamlico Sound, s Dare County.

Brookston, community in e Vance County. Post office est. in 1882.

Broomfield Swamp Creek rises in se Beaufort County and flows e into South Creek.

Broom Straw Mountain, e Madison County between Paint Fork and Crooked Creek.

Browders Branch rises in n Columbus County and flows sw into West Prong Creek.

Brower's Mill (or **Mills**), former community and post office on Fork Creek in se Randolph County. A post office operated there from 1828, when Alfred Brower was postmaster, until 1910. The name appears on a map of 1919 but apparently is not found after that date.

Brower Township, se Randolph County.

Brown, community in s Randolph County served by post office, 1879–1914. Known as Brown's Store until 1895.

Brown Branch rises in sw Beaufort County and flows sw into Chocowinity Creek.

Brown Branch rises in n Buncombe County near Carter Mountain and flows sw into Ivy Creek.

Brown Branch rises in s Buncombe County and flows sw into Fourmile Branch.

Brown Branch rises in e Watauga County and flows nw into South Fork New River.

Brown Branch rises in s Watauga County and flows se into Middle Fork [South Fork New River].

Brown Cove, e Haywood County between Medford Cove and Sorrells Cove.

Brown Creek rises in n Carteret County and flows n into Neuse River.

Brown Creek rises in ne Cherokee County and flows n and nw into Valley River.

Brown Creek rises in e Macon County and flows w into Watauga Creek.

Brown Creek rises in e Pamlico County and flows s into Broad Creek.

Brown Creek rises in w Transylvania County and flows se into Parker Creek.

Brown Creek rises in South Carolina and flows ne through the se corner of Union County and into Anson County, where it enters Pee Dee River in n central Anson County.

Brown Creek, community in se Union County. Nation's first soil conservation district est. there, 1937.

Brown Fork Gap, at the e end of Cheoah Mountains in e central Graham County at the head of Sawyer Creek.

Brown Gap, on the Haywood County, N.C.– Cocke County, Tenn., line. The Appalachian Trail passes there, and Pounding Mill Branch rises a short distance e.

Brown Gap, e Macon County between Corbin Creek and Brown Creek.

Brown Gap, at the head of Henson Branch in se Macon County.

Browning Branch rises in s Haywood County and flows nw into Richland Creek.

Browning Peak. *See* Black Mountain (Jackson-Haywood county line).

Brown Marsh Station. *See* Clarkton.

Brown Marsh Swamp rises in sw Bladen County and flows se into Columbus County, where its name is changed to Red Hill Swamp. Appears as Brown Meadow on the Moseley map, 1733. *See also* Brown Meadow.

Brown Marsh Township, s central Bladen County.

Brown Meadow appears on the Collet map, 1770, in what is now Columbus County, nw of the headwaters of White Marsh. *See also* Brown Marsh Swamp.

Brown Mountain, central Alleghany County.

Brown Mountain, s Buncombe County e of Skyland.

Brown Mountain, on the Burke-Caldwell county line approx. 1½ mi. w of Wilson Creek. Alt. 2,725. Noted for mysterious lights, known since 1833 in many popular legends. Many explanations have been offered for the lights, among them burning marsh gas, foxfire, and light refraction by the atmosphere of train, automobile, or city lights.

Brown Mountain, w Jackson County on the head of Cullowhee Creek.

Brown Mountain, community in w central Stokes County contiguous with mountain of same name.

Brown Mountain Beach, a recreational beach in Wilson Creek in w Caldwell County.

Brown Ridge, n Avery County.

Browns Creek rises in central Bladen County and flows e into the Cape Fear River. Appears as Earthquake Branch on the Moseley map, 1733.

Browns Creek rises in e Yancey County and flows e into South Toe River.

Brown's Creek. *See* Browns Swamp.

Brown's Crossroads, community in nw Randolph County. The former county seat of Johnstonville, *which see*, was there.

Browns Ford, in Yadkin River, sw Wilkes County. Named for Capt. John Brown, Revolutionary War soldier, who lived nearby and in whose home the first county government was organized in 1778. A bridge was built there after 1900, later replaced by a modern highway bridge.

Browns Inlet, se Onslow County between the n end of Onslow Beach and Bear Inlet. Appears on the Moseley map, 1733.

Brown's Island, s Carteret County, approx. 1½ mi. long, n of the e end of Harkers Island and separated from it by Westmouth Bay and Eastmouth Bay.

Brown's Island, a coastal beach island approx. 3 mi. long on the Atlantic Ocean in se Onslow County. Now within the limits of Camp Lejeune. It lies between Brown's Inlet and Bear Inlet. Sometimes referred to locally by an older name, Shacklefoot Island.

Browns Knob, sw Buncombe County between Billy Cove and Sheep Rock. Alt. 3,760.

Browns Landing, U.S. Lock Number 2 on Cape Fear River in central Bladen County.

Browns Mill Creek rises in s Transylvania County and flows ne into French Broad River.

Browns Mountain, sw Wilkes County between Yadkin River and Long Fork of Beaver Creek. Named for James Brown, eighteenth-century resident who lived at its foot. Alt. 2,075. Joins Jerry Mountain in ne Caldwell County.

Browns Siding. *See* Vaughan.

Brown's Sound, s Onslow County. Largely tidal marsh, it lies between Brown's Island and Onslow Beach and the mainland and extends from Bear Inlet to New River Inlet. It empties into the Atlantic Ocean through Bear Inlet, Browns Inlet, and New River Inlet. Now within the limits of Camp Lejeune.

Brown's Store. *See* Locust Hill.

Brown's Store. *See* Brown.

Browns Summit, community in n Guilford County. Alt. 805. Land there acquired by Jesse Brown, 1858. Named for him in 1863 when Richmond and Danville Railroad was built; the Brown farm was the highest point on the line. Also called Brown Summit.

Browns Swamp rises in e Cumberland County and flows se into Big Creek.

Browns Swamp rises in se Onslow County and flows sw into Turpentine Creek. Appears in local records as Brown's Creek as early as 1744.

Browns Turnout. *See* Vaughan.

Brown Summit. *See* Browns Summit.

Brownsville, community in ne Granville County on Grassy Creek. A post office as early as 1822.

Browntown, former town in ne Davidson County. Inc. 1843 at the junction of the Fayetteville-to-Salem and the Greensboro-to-Salisbury roads. A center of trade and furniture making until one of the roads was changed in 1859. The coming of the railroad brought a decline to the town and, after the Civil War, it was abandoned. Many of the people moved to what became High Point.

Browntown, community in s Greene County. Named for the fact that it was a community of residents of mixed race. Settled prior to 1890.

Bruce, community in w Pitt County. Cottendale, the plantation of the Cotten family (Sallie Southall Cotten, Bruce Cotten, and others) is nearby.

Bruce Knob, n Buncombe County between Wolfpen Gap and Middle Mountain.

Bruce Knob, central Macon County between the head of Wallace Creek and Carson Cove.

Bruce Ridge, e Clay County between Glade Branch and Cold Spring Branch.

Bruce's Crossroads. *See* Summerfield.

Bruce Township, nw Guilford County, named for Charles Bruce, early settler, Revolutionary War soldier, and founder of Bruce's Crossroad, now Summerfield.

Brumleys Creek rises in ne Caldwell County and flows se into Lower Creek approx. 3 mi. w of Lenoir.

Brummett Creek rises in w Mitchell County and flows sw into Toe River.

Brummett Creek, community in w Mitchell County. A post office existed there in the 1880s.

Brundana, community in w Mitchell County.

Brunswick, former town in se Brunswick County on Cape Fear River, now a State Historic Site. A museum contains artifacts, and many building sites have been excavated. Settled about 1725 and est. 1745. Named for King George I, Duke of Brunswick and Lunenberg. First abandoned about 1776, but two or three families moved back after the Revolution. By 1830 the town was totally in ruins. During the Civil War, Fort St. Philip (named for St. Philips Church there but also known as Fort

Anderson) was constructed over part of the site. Brunswick was the county seat, 1764–79. Several colonial governors resided there. Modern archaeological work has revealed foundations of 23 of 60 colonial-era structures identified at the site.

Brunswick, town in central Columbus County. Inc. 1925.

Brunswick, community in n Randolph County served by post office, 1884–1903.

Brunswick County was formed in 1764 from New Hanover and Bladen Counties. In the se section of the state, it is bounded by the Atlantic Ocean; South Carolina; Columbus, Pender, and New Hanover Counties; and the Cape Fear River. Named for the town of Brunswick, *which see*. Area: 907 sq. mi. County seat in rural setting near Bolivia. Townships are Lockwood Folly, Northwest, Shallotte, Smithville, Town Creek, and Waccamaw. Produces corn, soybeans, oats, hogs, beef cattle, fishmeal, lumber, fertilizer, hay, tobacco, strawberries, and processed seafood.

Brunswick River, ne Brunswick County, extends s from Cape Fear River along the w side of Eagles Island and empties into Cape Fear River. Approx. 5 mi. long. The waterway undoubtedly is the Hilton's River discovered by William Hilton in 1663 and described by him in an account published the next year.

Brush Creek is formed in e Alleghany County by the waters of Laurel Branch, Little Pine, and Little Glade Creeks. It flows n into Little River.

Brush Creek rises in se Buncombe County near Bearwallow Mountain and flows nw into Cane Creek.

Brush Creek rises in w Chatham County and flows sw into Randolph County, where it enters Deep River.

Brush Creek rises in nw Cherokee County and flows sw and se into Shuler Creek.

Brush Creek rises in w Guilford County and flows ne into Reedy Fork Creek.

Brush Creek rises in e Macon County and flows w into Cullasaja River.

Brush Creek rises in central Madison County and flows se into French Broad River.

Brush Creek rises in s Swain County and flows w into Little Tennessee River.

Brush Creek rises in ne Yancey County and flows n into Toe River.

Brushcreek, community in w Chatham County on Little Brush Creek.

Brush Creek, community in se Randolph County served by post office, 1846–73.

Brush Creek Township, e Yancey County.

Brush Fence Ridge, on the Buncombe-Yancey county line between Point Misery and Balsam Gap.

Brush Fork rises in sw Ashe County and flows ne into North Fork New River.

Brush Fork Creek rises in central Anson County and flows s into Reedy Fork Creek.

Brush Mountain, w Randolph County.

Brush Mountain, nw Rockingham County alongside the Mayo River. Probably named for the fact that it is very rocky and supports little vegetation.

Brushy Branch rises in s Macon County and flows ne into Wayah Creek.

Brushy Branch rises in n Swain County and flows sw into Walker Creek.

Brushy Branch rises in n Transylvania County and flows ne into South Fork Mills River.

Brushy Creek rises in s Avery County and flows sw into North Toe River.

Brushy Creek rises in w Cleveland County and flows se into First Broad River.

Brushy Creek rises in central Forsyth County ne of the city of Winston-Salem near Smith Reynolds Airport and flows s on the e side of Winston-Salem into Middle Fork.

Brushy Creek rises in s Mitchell County and flows nw into Crabtree Creek.

Brushy Creek rises in e Rutherford County and flows se into Cleveland County, where it enters First Broad River.

Brushy Creek rises in central Transylvania County and flows se into Tucker Creek.

Brushy Face, mountain in se Macon County between Horseshoe Mountain and Sassafras Knob.

Brushy Fork rises in n Davidson County and flows s into Abbotts Creek.

Brushy Fork rises in central Watauga County and flows nw into Cove Creek.

Brushy Fork, community in w central Watauga County. Formerly known as Hagaman.

Brushy Fork Branch rises in ne Craven County and flows sw into Little Swift Creek.

Brushy Fork Branch rises in e central Forsyth County and flows s and sw into Salem Creek near the e limits of Winston-Salem.

Brushy Fork Creek rises in w Jackson County and flows ne into Greens Creek.

Brushy Fork Creek rises in w Stokes County and flows se into Town Fork Creek.

Brushy Fork Mountain, w Jackson County between Savannah Creek and Brushy Fork.

Brushy Fork Township, w central Watauga County.

Brushy Gap, ne Swain County in Great Smoky Mountains National Park on Shiltoskie Ridge.

Brushy Head Mountain, ne Cherokee County between Graybeard Creek and Valley River.

Brushy Knob, ne Buncombe County near the headwaters of Walker Branch.

Brushy Mountain, ne Buncombe County near Beetree Reservoir.

Brushy Mountain, se Buncombe County se of Dutchman Mountain.

Brushy Mountain, n Haywood County between Mount Sterling Creek and Dogwood Flats Creek. Alt. approx. 5,600.

Brushy Mountain, s Jackson County between Scotsman Creek and Fowler Creek.

Brushy Mountain, w Polk County, ne of town of Saluda.

Brushy Mountain extends se in w Transylvania County from Gloucester Gap to Tarkiln Branch.

Brushy Mountain. *See* Gilreath.

Brushy Mountains, a low range extending across s Wilkes County, n Alexander County, and into e Caldwell County. Sometimes also described as crossing Yadkin and Surry Counties, with isolated Pilot Mountain included as the e peak. Pore's Knob in Wilkes County, the highest peak, is 2,680 ft.; Hibriten Mountain in Caldwell County is 2,265 ft. Shown on the 1755 ed. of the Fry-Jefferson map.

Brushy Mountain Township, s Wilkes County.

Brushy Ridge, central Buncombe County sw of Wolf Branch.

Brushy Ridge, ne Buncombe County between Sugar Fork and Laurel Branch.

Brushy Ridge, nw Burke County. Alt. 3,600.

Brushy Ridge extends ne between Bear Branch and Bad Fork in nw Henderson County.

Brushy Ridge, e Macon County between Little Salt Rock Creek and the head of Wildcat Creek.

Brushy Ridge, s Macon County between Rock Branch and Falls Branch.

Brushy Ridge, w Madison County between Maple Spring Branch and Meadow Fork.

Brushy Ridge, se Polk County on the South Carolina line.

Brushy Ridge Branch rises in w Transylvania County and flows sw into Cathey's Creek.

Bryan, community in s Chatham County served by post office, 1891–1904.

Bryan, community in e Pitt County.

Bryan Creek rises in central Pitt County and flows se into Tar River.

Bryan's Settlement, area in Yadkin River valley of ne Davie County. In 1748 Morgan Bryan moved there with his large family. Their holdings totaled over 5,000 acres.

Bryant Branch rises in n Davie County near Pino and flows se approx. 4 mi. into Dutchmans Creek. Named for the Bryant family, which settled in the area prior to 1752.

Bryant Mountain, sw Cherokee County between Wolf Creek and Hothouse Branch.

Bryant Mountain, central Watauga County n of Howard Creek.

Bryantown, community in s Northampton County.

Bryan Township, w Surry County.

Bryants Pond, nw Bladen County on Reedy Meadow Creek and Black Swamp. Formed by a dam built about 1860 to create a millpond. Fishing, swimming, and boating.

Bryant Swamp rises in Big Bay in sw Bladen County and flows w into Robeson County, where it enters Big Swamp.

Bryson Branch rises in ne Cherokee County and flows se into Morris Creek.

Bryson Branch rises in ne Cherokee County and flows sw into Valley River.

Bryson Branch rises in s Jackson County and flows se 1 mi. to empty into Scotsman Creek.

Bryson Branch rises in e Macon County and flows ne into Cullasaja River.

Bryson Branch rises in e Macon County and flows se into Joe Creek.

Bryson Branch rises in w Macon County w of

Panther Knob and flows sw into Nantahala River.

Bryson Branch rises in central Swain County and flows se through Bryson City into Tuckasegee River.

Bryson City, town and county seat in central Swain County on Tuckasegee River. Alt. 1,736. Inc. 1887 as Charleston. Name changed to Bryson City in 1889 by act of General Assembly; named in honor of Capt. Thaddeus Dillard Bryson (1829–90), one of the founders of the town.

Bryson Cove, on a tributary of Cowee Creek in n Macon County.

Bryson Creek rises in e Transylvania County and flows se into w Henderson County, where it enters French Broad River.

Bryson Knob, e Macon County between Mashburn Branch and Cullasaja River.

Bryson Lead, nw Cherokee County, parallel to Shular Creek and nw of Chestnut Orchard Ridge, Nin Ridge, and Groundhog Ridge.

Bryson Mountain, n Henderson County between Sitton Creek and Foster Creek.

Bubble Branch rises in w Jackson County and flows se into West Fork Tuckasegee River.

Bubbling Springs Branch rises in s Haywood County and flows n into West Fork Pigeon River.

Buby Gap, on the Jackson-Macon county line.

Buchanan, community in n Granville County served by post office, 1856–1906.

Buchanan Branch rises in sw Clay County and flows sw into Brasstown Creek.

Buchanan Falls on Pee Dee River on the Anson-Richmond county line about 1½ mi. n of the South Carolina line.

Buchanan Ferry. *See* Diggs Ferry.

Buchanan Hollow, e Mitchell County between Mine Hill and Sandy Branch.

Buchanan's Pond, nw Scotland County on a tributary of Gum Swamp Creek. Formed in 1950 and named for owner, D. M. Buchanan. Covers 23 acres; max. depth 12 ft. Fishing, swimming, boating.

Buck, community in s Wilkes County near Millers Creek.

Buck Branch rises in e Duplin County and flows sw into Little Limestone Creek.

Buck Branch rises in s Durham County and flows sw into Burden Creek.

Buck Branch rises in w Edgecombe County and flows ne into Tar River.

Buck Branch rises in s central Rutherford County nw of Forest City and flows ne into Second Broad River.

Buck Branch rises in s Wake County and flows s into Swift Creek.

Buck Branch rises in central Wilson County and flows approx. 3 mi. s into Toisnot Swamp, *which see*. Known as Buckhorn Branch as early as 1754.

Buck Cove, e Haywood County on the head of Thickety Creek.

Buck Cove Mountain, e Haywood County between Buck Cove and Rice Cove.

Buck Creek rises in n central Carteret County and flows w into South River.

Buck Creek rises in se Clay County and flows nw and ne into Nantahala River.

Buck Creek, a tidal marsh creek in s Hyde County, flows sw into Juniper Bay.

Buck Creek rises in e Macon County and flows nw into Cullasaja River.

Buck Creek rises in w McDowell County and flows se into Catawba River. Buck Creek Falls are on the stream near its head.

Buck Creek. *See* Back Creek.

Buck Creek. *See* McLendons Creek.

Buck Creek Falls. *See* Buck Creek.

Buck Creek Gap on the McDowell-Yancey county line between Horse Trail Gap and Hazelnut Gap. Alt. approx. 3,200.

Buckeye Branch rises in e Haywood County and flows se into Bald Creek.

Buckeye Branch rises in ne Swain County and flows se into Raven Fork.

Buckeye Cove, ne Buncombe County on the w side of North Fork [Swannanoa River].

Buckeye Cove, s Buncombe County s of Potato Knob.

Buckeye Cove, on the Cherokee County, N.C.–Polk County, Tenn., line between Rocky Ford Creek and Potato Creek.

Buckeye Cove, e Haywood County on the head of Cove Creek.

Buckeye Cove, e Haywood County on the head of Murray Branch.

Buckeye Cove, nw Haywood County on the head of Big Creek.

Buckeye Cove Creek rises in ne Buncombe County and flows nw into North Fork Ivy Creek.

Buckeye Creek rises at Buckeye Spring on the Avery-Watauga county line and flows nw and n into Beech Creek.

Buckeye Creek rises in s Haywood County and flows nw to join Haywood Gap Stream in forming Middle Prong [West Fork Pigeon River].

Buckeye Creek rises in s Macon County and flows sw into Tessentee Creek.

Buckeye Gap, on the Avery-Mitchell county line.

Buckeye Gap, on the Haywood-Jackson county line.

Buckeye Gap, on Swain County, N.C.–Sevier County, Tenn., line in Great Smoky Mountains National Park near lat. 35°34′43″ N., long. 83°36′05″ W.

Buckeye Gap, central Watauga County s of Norris Branch.

Buckeye Knob, e Haywood County between the head of Bald Creek and the head of Cove Creek.

Buckeye Knob, central Watauga County on the w slope of Rich Mountain.

Buckeye Knob, n Watauga County between the forks of Fork Ridge.

Buckeye Mountain, a peak in the Swannanoa Mountains, s Buncombe County between Cedar Cliff and Face Rock.

Buckeye Ridge, w Madison County between Max Patch Mountain and Roaring Fork Mountain.

Buckeye Spring, on the Avery-Watauga county line. Source of Buckeye Creek.

Buck Forest, mountain, e Transylvania County between Laurel and Tom Creeks.

Buck Gap, on the Buncombe-McDowell county line s of Sourwood Gap.

Buck Gap, on the Jackson-Macon county line. Alt. 3,950.

Buck Gap, s Macon County between Wolf Gap and the head of Evans Creek.

Buck Gap, on the Swain County, N.C.–Blount County, Tenn., line in Great Smoky Mountains National Park near lat. 35°32′03″ N., long. 83°49′20″ W.

Buckhead Creek rises in central Cumberland County and flows s into Little Rockfish Creek.

Buckhead Swamp rises in se Bladen County and flows s into Columbus County, where it enters Slap Swamp.

Buck Hill, mountain peak in sw Avery County.

Buckhill Branch rises in w Duplin County and flows sw into Buster Hall Branch.

Buck Hill Gap, w Avery County.

Buck Hollow Mountain, ne Rutherford County at the head of Duncans Creek.

Buckhorn, community in w Orange County.

Buckhorn. *See* Como.

Buckhorn Bald, n Swain County in Great Smoky Mountains National Park on Forney Ridge. Alt. 4,829.

Buckhorn Branch rises in ne Cherokee County in Swag Cove on Buckhorn Ridge and flows nw into Vengeance Creek.

Buckhorn Branch rises in se Granville County and flows s into Wake County, where it enters New Light Creek. Approx. 4 mi. long.

Buckhorn Branch rises in se Orange County and flows se into Bolin Creek.

Buckhorn Branch rises in n Swain County and flows w into Forney Creek.

Buckhorn Branch rises in w Wilson County and flows n into Contentnea Creek.

Buckhorn Branch. *See* Buck Branch.

Buckhorn Creek rises in nw Cherokee County and flows sw into Copper Creek.

Buckhorn Creek rises in sw Gates County and flows se into Chowan River.

Buckhorn Creek rises in n Hertford County and flows e into Chowan River.

Buckhorn Creek rises in e Transylvania County and flows s into Little River.

Buckhorn Creek rises in sw Wake County and flows sw into se Chatham County, where it enters Buckhorn Lake on the Cape Fear River.

Buckhorn Crossroads, community in w Wilson County s of Contentnea Creek and w of Buckhorn Branch.

Buckhorn Falls, in Cape Fear River at the junction of Chatham, Harnett, and Lee Counties. Mentioned as early as 1819 in a survey of the major rivers of North Carolina. Since 1908 the site of a power-generating plant operated by what is now Progress Energy. Navigation locks built there as early as 1805; iron ore mined nearby during the Civil War.

Buckhorn Gap, se Macon County.

Buckhorn Gap, n Transylvania County between the head of Avery Creek and Rich Mountain.

Buckhorn Iron Furnace. *See* Cokesbury.

Buckhorn Knob, n Caldwell County. Named by Bryson Coffey about 1870 for a big pair of antlers that he found there. Alt. approx. 1,500.

Buckhorn Lake, se Chatham and ne Lee Counties on Cape Fear River. Formed by a dam constructed in 1907, the lake covers 400 acres, with a max. depth of 21 ft. Used to generate hydroelectric power.

Buckhorn Mountain, s Macon County between Buckhorn Gap and Cullasaja River.

Buckhorn Ridge, ne Cherokee County in the Valley River Mountains.

Buckhorn Ridge, e Swain County between First Hurricane Branch and Second Hurricane Branch.

Buckhorn Swamp rises in ne Robeson County and flows se into Gallberry Swamp.

Buckhorn Township, nw Harnett County.

Buckhorn Township, sw Wake County.

Buckingham Mountain, sw Alamance County.

Buck Island, a tidal marsh island about ½ mi. square in North River, sw Currituck County.

Buck Island is a raised area of land surrounded by swamp in Mon Swamp in se Tyrrell County.

Buck Knob, central Cherokee County between Hiwassee River and West Prong Grape Creek. Alt. 2,584.

Buck Knob, w Cherokee County between Shular Creek and Caney Branch.

Buck Knob, w Haywood County, in Great Smoky Mountains National Park near lat. 35°33′ N., long. 83°08′12″ W.

Buck Knob, on Laurel Creek in w Henderson County.

Buck Knob, between Wayehutta Creek and Cane Creek in n Jackson County.

Buck Knob, s Jackson County on the head of Frolictown Creek.

Buck Knob, w Jackson County between Wilson Creek and Tilley Creek.

Buck Knob, w Jackson County on the head of Little Pine Creek.

Buck Knob, sw Macon County at the head of Allison Creek.

Buckland, community in n central Gates County. Alt. 32. Settled prior to 1711.

Buckland Mill Branch rises in n Gates County, flows sw, and joins Hacklan Branch in forming Cole Creek. Formerly known as Knotty Pine Creek.

Buckleberry Pocosin, se Bertie County.

Buckle Creek rises in sw Bladen County and flows se into Pender County, where it enters Lyon Creek.

Bucklesberry Pocosin, nw Lenoir County. Mentioned in local records as early as 1780.

Camp Blackjack (named for the black oak, commonly called blackjack oak), a Civil War training camp on the railroad near La Grange, was in the vicinity.

Buckle Swamp rises in se Bladen County and flows se into Pender County, where it enters Lyon Creek.

Buck Marsh rises in se Wayne County and flows se into Duplin County, where it enters Buck Run.

Buck Mountain, w Haywood County between Fie Creek and Evans Creek.

Buck Mountain, w Lee County. Several very rocky hills, one of which is quite steep, in an area of 3 or 4 acres.

Buck Mountain, w Macon County between Wayah Creek and Camp Branch.

Buck Mountain, w Montgomery County between Cedar Creek and Bundle Mountain.

Buck Mountain, sw Polk County between Pacolet River and Cove Creek.

Buck Mountain, n Surry County between Fulcher Mountain and Round Peak Mountain.

Buck Mountain, sw Transylvania County, extends se between the headwaters of Thompson River and Whitewater River.

Buckner, community in e Madison County on Middle Fork. Alt. 2,400. Named for pioneer settler.

Buckner, community in w Rowan County.

Buckner. *See* Colon.

Buckner Branch rises in n Buncombe County near Wildcat Mountain and flows nw into Ivy Creek.

Buckner Branch rises in e central Madison County and flows nw into Big Laurel Creek.

Buckner Branch rises in s central Swain County and flows ne into Tuckasegee River 1½ mi. w of Bryson City.

Buckner's Knob. *See* Craggy Pinnacle.

Buck Quarter Creek rises in ne Orange County and flows s into Eno River. It is mentioned in land grants as early as 1750. Sometimes called Buck Water Creek.

Buck Ridge, n Avery County.

Buck Ridge, sw Avery County.

Buck Ridge, se Buncombe County between Rocky Fork and Ellison Branch.

Buck Ridge, n Haywood County on Chestnut Branch.

Buck Ridge, e Mitchell County between Gouges Creek and Jackson Branch.

Buck Ridge, s Watauga County, extends se from Sawpit Branch parallel to Days Creek.

Buck Ridge, ne Yancey County between Green Mountain and Brush Creek.

Buck Run rises in ne Duplin County and flows sw into Northeast Cape Fear River.

Bucks Corner, community in w Carteret County n of Pettiver's Creek.

Buck Shoal, on French Broad River in n Henderson County. Named because deer formerly fed on moss growing there. Bill Nye (1850–96), American humorist, lived there from about 1880 until his death.

Buck Shoals, community in sw Yadkin County on North Hunting Creek. Named for the herds of deer that once gathered in the shoals of the creek.

Buck Shoals Township, sw Yadkin County.

Buckskin Branch rises in central Duplin County and flows se into Grove Creek.

Bucks Knob, e Madison County near the head of East Fork [Bull Creek].

Bucks Peak, se Alleghany County and ne Wilkes County. Also appears on maps as Buck Mountain and state highway maps as Beech Mountain.

Buck Spring, e Haywood County, springs forming in part the headwaters of Pisgah Creek.

Buck Spring, ne Warren County between Hubquarter Creek and Stonehouse Creek. Formerly the plantation of Nathaniel Macon (1758–1837), member of Congress (1791–1828) and speaker of the U.S. House of Representatives; he is buried there. House burned by vandals, 1977, and reconstructed. Post office operated there from 1901 to 1905. Site owned and maintained by Warren County.

Buck Spring Gap, on the Haywood-Transylvania county line on Pisgah Ridge just s of Little Pisgah Mountain at the head of Pisgah Creek. Alt. 4,980.

Buck Swamp rises in s Wayne County and flows nw into Thoroughfare Swamp.

Buck Swamp Township, nw Wayne County.

Buck Water Creek. *See* Buck Quarter Creek.

Buck Water Mountain, e Macon County between Little Buck Creek and Katie Creek.

Buckwheat Knob, n Transylvania County on the head of Avery Creek.

Bud, community in n Ashe County served by post office, 1894–1906.

Buddy Gap, s Macon County between Coweeta Creek and Little Tennessee River.

Budget Falls, in Yadkin River in se Surry County, w of the junction of Ararat River. Mentioned as early as 1819 in a survey of the rivers of North Carolina.

Bud Lowe Gap, s Wilkes County near the head of Rocky Creek.

Bud Ridge, s Buncombe County e of Billy Cove.

Buena Vista, community in n central Bertie County.

Buena Vista, community in s Buncombe County e of Biltmore Forest. Inc. 1891; charter repealed 1903.

Buena Vista, community in e Duplin County served by post office, 1847. Named by Capt. Zacheus Smith, local Mexican War veteran, for site of battle in the conflict. Named changed in 1891 to Leon, and post office discontinued in 1916.

Buena Vista, sw Warren County near the Franklin County line, was formerly the home, office, and tavern of Dr. Robert Christian Pritchard. *See also* Bearpond.

Buffalo, community in ne Cherokee County at the mouth of Gipps Creek.

Buffalo, community in ne Stokes County near the head of Buffalo Creek.

Buffalo Branch rises in w Johnston County and flows s into Middle Creek.

Buffalo Branch rises in s Wake County and flows s into w Johnston County, where it enters Middle Creek.

Buffalo Branch rises in w Warren County and flows s into Shocco Creek. Mentioned in local records as early as 1764.

Buffalo City, community on the mainland, w Dare County. Settled 1888. Named for Buffalo City Mills, former sawmill there. Alt. 10.

Buffalo Cove, community in n Caldwell County. Named for the cove in which many buffalo were killed. Settled late eighteenth century.

Buffalo Creek rises in nw Anson County and flows e into Pee Dee River.

Buffalo Creek rises near Bluff Mountain in se Ashe County and flows ne into North Fork New River.

Buffalo Creek rises in n Caldwell County and flows s into Yadkin River.

Buffalo Creek rises in n Cleveland County and flows sw through Cleveland County into South Carolina, where it enters Broad River.

Buffalo Creek rises in nw Cleveland County and flows sw into Rutherford County, where it enters Brier Creek.

Buffalo Creek rises in ne Davie County and flows sw approx. 3 mi. into Dutchman Creek about 4 mi. from its mouth in the Horseshoe of Yadkin River.

Buffalo Creek rises in n Forsyth County and flows ne into s Stokes County, where it enters Town Fork Creek.

Buffalo Creek rises in central Franklin County and flows sw into Tar River.

Buffalo Creek rises in n Franklin County and flows se into Sandy Creek.

Buffalo Creek rises in nw Franklin County and flows ne into Tar River.

Buffalo Creek is formed by the junction of North Buffalo Creek and South Buffalo Creek in ne Guilford County. It flows ne into Reedy Fork Creek. Named after 1755 but before 1758.

Buffalo Creek rises in sw Harnett County and flows s into e Moore County (formerly Hoke County), where it enters Little River.

Buffalo Creek rises in w Hoke County and flows sw into Lumber River.

Buffalo Creek rises in w Moore County and flows ne into Deep River.

Buffalo Creek rises in ne Orange County and flows se into Durham County, where it enters North Fork Little River.

Buffalo Creek rises in n Richmond County and flows sw into Little River.

Buffalo Creek rises in nw Rutherford County and flows s into Broad River.

Buffalo Creek rises in e Stokes County and flows into Rockingham County and into Mayo River.

Buffalo Creek rises in ne Stokes County and flows ne into Rockingham County, where it enters Mayo River.

Buffalo Creek rises in s Union County and flows sw into South Carolina, where it enters Lynches Creek.

Buffalo Creek rises in s Vance County and flows s into Tar River. Water-ground corn meal is produced commercially on the creek.

Buffalo Creek rises in e Wake County and flows se into Johnston County, where it enters Little River.

Buffalo Creek rises in s Warren County and flows s into Fishing Creek.

Buffalo Creek rises in s Watauga County and flows se into Caldwell County.

Buffalo Creek. *See* Back Creek.

Buffalo Creek. *See* Irish Buffalo Creek.

Buffalo Creek. *See* Warrensville.

Buffalo Ford, community in se Randolph County served by post office, 1850–1904. Known as Buffaloford after 1894.

Buffaloford. *See* Buffalo Ford.

Buffalo Island, swampy land formation on Potecasi Creek in central Hertford County.

Buffalo Island Creek rises in n Rockingham County and flows se into Dan River.

Buffalo Knob, a stony elevation on the Cleveland-Lincoln county line.

Buffalo Lake, w Harnett County on the head-waters of Reedys Swamp. Approx. ½ mi. long. Alt. 293.

Buffalo Race Path. *See* Bute County.

Buffalo Shoals Creek rises in w Iredell County and flows s into Catawba River.

Buff Creek rises in n Jackson County and flows s into Scott Creek.

Buffeys Branch rises in s Transylvania County and flows sw into East Fork French Broad River.

Buford. *See* Canton.

Buford Township, s central Union County.

Buggs Island Lake. *See* Kerr Lake.

Bug Hill, community in se Columbus County.

Bug Hill Township, se Columbus County.

Buie, community in n Robeson County. Inc. 1909. Charter repealed 1947, though previously long inactive in municipal affairs. Railroad name was Buies.

Buies. *See* Buie.

Buies Creek rises in ne Harnett County and flows sw into Cape Fear River. Known as Archie Buie's Creek on early maps of the region.

Buies Creek, community in e central Harnett County. Settled in the latter part of the nineteenth century. Inc. 1903; charter repealed 1967. Campbell University is there. Alt. 210.

Buies Falls, rapids in Cape Fear River in central Harnett County at the junction of Buies Creek with the river. Called Bowies Falls by Hamilton Fulton in his 1819 survey of the rivers of North Carolina.

Buies Pond, n Robeson County on a branch of Richland Swamp. Covers approx. 150 acres, with a max. depth of 10 to 12 ft.

Buladean, community in n Mitchell County

on Big Rock Creek. Known first as Magnetic City for its location near large deposits of magnetic iron ore. Present name said to have been for Beulah Dean, daughter of the first postmaster.

Bulla, community in central Randolph County served by post office, 1882–1903.

Bull Bay, nw Tyrrell County and ne Washington County, formed by the Scuppernong River estuary in Albemarle Sound. Surface area approx, 10,000 acres; max. depth 14 ft.

Bull Branch rises in ne Bertie County and flows sw into Chinkapin Swamp.

Bull Branch rises in ne Burke County and flows sw into Linville River.

Bull Branch is formed in ne Pender County by the junction of Bullhead Branch and Bull Tail Branch. It flows se into Moore's Creek.

Bull Branch rises in w Robeson County and flows s into Little Pee Dee River.

Bull Branch rises in e Union County and flows nw into Richardson Creek.

Bull Branch. *See* Millers Creek.

Bull Cove, se Clay County between Bear Pen Ridge and Fairfield Ridge.

Bull Cove, sw Macon County on a tributary of Big Indian Creek.

Bull Creek rises in n Buncombe County near Bull Mountain and flows s into Swannanoa River. The last buffalo seen in the county was killed by one of the first white settlers in the vicinity, Joseph Rice.

Bull Creek is formed in s Madison County by the junction of East Fork and West Fork and flows s into Ivy River.

Bull Creek rises in ne Washington County and flows ne into Bull Bay.

Bull Creek Gap, n Madison County between Big Laurel Creek and the head of West Fork [Bull Creek].

Bull Creek Township, former township in s central Madison County, now township no. 3.

Bulldie Creek rises in ne Swain County and flows se into Raven Fork.

Bulldie Ridge, ne Swain County in Great Smoky Mountains National Park, a spur extending ne from Katalsta Ridge.

Bullfrog Creek rises in central Currituck County in Great Swamp and flows s into North River.

Bull Gap, n Buncombe County at the w end of Bull Mountain. Alt. 3,177.

Bullhead, community in w Greene County s of Nahunta Swamp near the Wayne County line. Settled as early as 1769. During the Revolution, as British soldiers approached, a ferocious bull was turned loose to frighten them. The soldiers, however, killed the bull, cut off his head, and placed it on a fence post.

Bullhead Branch rises in ne Pender County and flows s to join Bull Tail Branch in forming Bull Branch.

Bullhead Creek rises in s Alleghany County and flows s into Wilkes County, where it enters East Prong Roaring River.

Bullhead Gap, ne Buncombe County between Craggy Dome and Bullhead Mountain.

Bullhead Mountain, se Alleghany County near Blue Ridge Parkway. Alt. 3,784–3,800.

Bullhead Mountain, ne Buncombe County in the Great Craggy Mountains. Named for its resemblance to a bull's head. Alt. 5,958.

Bullhead Ridge, ne Buncombe County between Waterfall and Peach Orchard Creeks.

Bull Head Township, nw Greene County.

Bull Hill, community in sw Northampton County.

Bull Hill Mill Pond, sw Northampton County on Wheeler Creek. Covers approx. 400 acres; max. depth 12 ft. Partly a natural lake but enlarged by a dam on the creek. Originally known as Lake Witheranna.

Bullhole, The, section of the shoals on the South Yadkin River bordering Davie and Rowan Counties. Lumbering along the river included use of oxen and mule teams to assist work at sawmills. Heavy rains and a swollen river led to loss of a bull ox, swept into a whirlpool. Area now part of park at Cooleemee Falls.

Bullin Creek. *See* Britten Creek.

Bullinger Mountain, e Caldwell County. Alt. 1,595. Probably named for Henry Bullinger, eighteenth-century settler.

Bullinger's Mill Creek. *See* Bristol's Mill Creek.

Bull Mountain, n Buncombe County between Lane Pinnacle and Bull Gap. *See also* Lane Pinnacle.

Bull Mountain, s Watauga County s of Sims Creek and e of Laurel Creek.

Bullock, community in ne Granville County. Settled about 1750. Alt. 429.

Bullpen Cove, se Haywood County on East Fork Pigeon River.

Bull Pocosin, n Sampson County bounded on the s by Goshen Swamp, on the w by Ward Swamp and Craddock Swamp, and on the n by Kill Swamp.

Bull Point, ne Washington County, extends into Bull Bay from the n shore of Bull Creek estuary.

Bull Ruffin Mountain, se Watauga County. Alt. approx. 4,100.

Bull Run Creek rises in s Guilford County and flows sw into East Prong Deep River.

Bull Run Creek rises in e central Surry County and flows se into Ararat River.

Bull's Bay, community in nw Tyrrell County. Called Bay when a post office was there. It is on Bull Bay.

Bullscrape Gap, central Avery County. Alt. 3,882. A salt lick there once attracted cattle; bulls scraped the ground with hooves, pawing before charging one another in combat. *See also* Montezuma.

Bull Tail Branch rises in ne Pender County and flows s to join Bullhead Branch in forming Bull Branch.

Bulltail Swamp rises in se Sampson County and flows se into Duplin County, where it enters Doctors Creek.

Bumgardner Branch rises in n Swain County and flows sw into Deep Creek.

Bumgardner Ridge, n Swain County in Great Smoky Mountains National Park, a spur extending sw from Sunkota Ridge.

Bumgarner Branch rises in n Jackson County approx. 2 mi. se of Sylva and flows sw 1½ mi. into Mill Creek.

Bumgarner Gap, n Wilkes County between North Fork Reddies River and Burke Mountain. Named for Daniel Bumgarner, early nineteenth-century resident.

Bumgartner Mountain, peak in South Mountains on Burke-Rutherford county line.

Bumplanding Creek rises in sw Currituck County and flows w into North River.

Buna Ridge, e Madison County parallel to Holland Branch.

Bunch, community in sw Randolph County served by post office, 1888–1901.

Bunches Bald, on the Jackson-Swain county line near the head of Madcap Branch.

Bunches Creek rises in ne Swain County in Great Smoky Mountains National Park and flows s, w, and nw into Raven Fork.

Buncombe County was formed in 1791 from Burke and Rutherford Counties. Located in the w section of the state, it is bounded by McDowell, Henderson, Haywood, Madison, and Yancey Counties. Named for Col. Edward Buncombe (1742–78), a Revolutionary War soldier. Area: 770 sq. mi. County seat: Asheville, with an elevation of 2,216 ft. Townships are Asheville, Avery Creek, Black Mountain, Broad River, Fairview, Flat Creek, French Broad, Ivy, Leicester, Limestone, Lower Hominy, Reems Creek, Sandy Mush, Swannanoa, and Upper Hominy. Produces tobacco, corn, cattle, printed products, engines, cutlery, wine, apparel, electronics, textiles, nursery products, lumber, and crushed stone. Rep. Felix Walker (1753–1828), in "speaking for Buncombe," gave rise to term "bunk."

Buncombe Hall, the home of Col. Edward Buncombe of the Continental Line, who was captured at Germantown and died a prisoner in 1778. Stood 1 mi. w of Roper, nw Washington County.

Buncombe Horse Range Ridge, s Yancey County between South Fork Upper Creek and Right Prong South Toe River.

Bundle Mountain, n Montgomery County between Buck Mountain and Morris Mountain.

Bunn, town in s Franklin County. Alt. 295. Settled about 1909; inc. 1913. Named for Green Bunn, local resident.

Bunnlevel, community in s Harnett County. Est. in 1904 or 1905 around railroad depot. Originally called Bunn's Level after a local resident's flat plot of land. Inc. 1921 as Bunlevel, but recently inactive in municipal affairs. Authorized by General Assembly in 1961 to est. municipal government if approved by vote, but the proposition was defeated.

Bunton Creek. *See* Banton Creek.

Bunton Island lies off the sw shore of Roanoke Island, e Dare County, in the waters of Croatan Sound.

Bunyan, community in w Beaufort County. Alt. 14. A post office operated there from 1880 to 1902.

Burch, community in s Surry County. Alt. 881. A former post office named Rusk operated there, 1851–1951.

Burcham, community in e Wilkes County served by post office, 1882–1901.

Burden, community in nw Bertie County.

Burden Branch rises in w Wayne County and flows sw into Moccasin Swamp.

Burden Creek rises in s Durham County and flows sw into Northeast Creek.

Burdett, community in ne Mecklenburg County. Served by post office, 1880–1903.

Burd Gap, sw Macon County at the head of Anderson Branch.

Burgaw, town and county seat, central Pender County. When the county was formed in 1875, it was directed that the place chosen as a county seat should be named Cowan, but an act of 1877 directed that it should be named Stanford. Burgaw was chosen, however, and an act of the General Assembly of 1879 changed the name Stanford to Burgaw and inc. the town. Burgaw appears on maps as early as 1861. *See* Burgaw Creek for early uses of the name. Alt. 49.

Burgaw Creek rises in s Graham County and flows ne into Long Creek.

Burgaw Creek rises in central Pender County ne of the town of Burgaw and flows se into Northeast Cape Fear River. Appears on the Collet map, 1770, as Bargaw Creek and on the Mouzon map, 1775, as Bergaw Creek. Burgaw Plantation in the vicinity appears in records of 1764.

Burgaw Savannah. *See* Big Savannah.

Burgaw Township, central Pender County.

Burger Mountain, w Cherokee County between Shoal Creek and Apalachia Lake.

Burgess, community in n side of Harveys Neck in s Perquimans County.

Burgin Cove, se Buncombe County between Black Mountain and Ridgecrest.

Burgin Cove Branch rises in se Yancey County and flows nw into Three Forks Creek.

Burgoin Gap, e Macon County between Rough Knob and Moses Branch.

Burke County was formed in 1777 from Rowan County. Located in the w central section of the state, it is bounded by Catawba, Cleveland, Rutherford, McDowell, Avery, and Caldwell Counties. It was named for Thomas Burke (1744–83), member of the Continental Congress and governor of North Carolina. Area: 517 sq. mi. County seat: Morganton, with an elevation of 1,182 ft. Townships are Drexel, Icard, Jonas Ridge, Linville, Lovelady, Lower Creek, Lower Fork, Morganton, Quaker Meadow, Silver Creek, Smoky Creek, Upper Creek, and Upper Fork. Produces corn, soybeans, hay, oats, wheat, poultry, medical supplies, baked goods, textiles, furniture, sand, gravel, and mica.

Burkemont, mountain peak in the South Mountains of s Burke County.

Burkemont, community in s Burke County near the headwaters of Bailey's Fork.

Burke Mountain, n Wilkes County extending n between North Fork Reddies River and Mulberry Creek. Probably named for James Burke (died 1776), pioneer settler.

Burkes Creek rises in s Caswell County and flows ne into Pinson Creek.

Burkeville, community in s Forsyth County served by post office, 1898–1902.

Burl Branch rises in e Cherokee County and flows s and se into Peachtree Creek.

Burleson Bald, sw Avery County.

Burleson Branch rises in ne Buncombe County and flows sw into North Fork Ivy Creek.

Burleson Branch rises in central Yancey County and flows n into Cane River.

Burlington, city in central Alamance County. About 1851 the North Carolina Railroad built its repair shops there and the name Company Shops was applied to the community until 1887, when a list of names suggested by local citizens was referred to a committee for decision. Burlington is said to have been suggested by Katherine Scales, daughter of Governor Alfred M. Scales. Inc. 1893. Railroad shops moved to Spencer in 1896. A Civil War training camp was est. at Company Shops.

Alt. 658. Produces textiles, hosiery, electronics, and paper boxes.

Burlington Crossroads, community in s Hoke County.

Burlington Township, former township in central Alamance County, now township no. 12.

Burl Mountain, w Henderson County between French Broad River and Johnsons Mill Creek.

Burl Mountain, n central Transylvania County between King Creek and Southern Mountain.

Burnett Bear Pen Ridge, s Yancey County near the head of Big Lost Cove Creek.

Burnett Cove, e Haywood County on Burnett Creek.

Burnett Creek rises in e Haywood County and flows nw into East Fork Pigeon River.

Burnett Reservoir, ne Buncombe County on North Fork [Swannanoa River] w of Walkertown. A part of the Asheville water system.

Burnett Siding, community in s Haywood County on West Fork Pigeon River.

Burney, community in nw Bladen County.

Burney Mountain, on the Buncombe-Henderson county line.

Burningtown, community in central Macon County on Burningtown Creek.

Burningtown Bald, n Macon County between Copper Bald and Burningtown Gap. Alt. 5,115.

Burningtown Creek rises in w Macon County and flows ne and nw into Little Tennessee River.

Burningtown Falls, in Downes Branch in central Macon County.

Burningtown Gap, n Macon County at the head of Burningtown Creek. Alt. approx. 3,700.

Burningtown Township, n central Macon County.

Burns Creek rises in w Henderson County and flows se into French Broad River.

Burns Gap, sw Cherokee County near the headwaters of Shoal Creek.

Burns Mountain, central Mitchell County between Bandana Hollow and Snow Creek. Appears as Burns Mountain on maps but is known locally as Burnt Mountain.

Burnsville, community in nw Anson County. Area settled by 1753; known as Burnsville by 1836. Probably named for Walter Burns, who operated an early tavern there.

Burnsville, town and county seat, central Yancey County. Alt. 2,817. Est. 1833 at the creation of the county. Named for Otway Burns (1775–1850), privateer of the War of 1812 and later member of the General Assembly. Although he was an easterner, he supported the political ambitions of the westerners around the time Yancey County was created. Burnsville was chartered in 1857 but repealed in 1921; rechartered 1922. Produces hosiery, carpets, textiles, and minerals.

Burnsville Township, nw Anson County.

Burnsville Township, central Yancey County.

Burnt Branch rises in ne Cherokee County and flows nw into Valley River.

Burntcabin Creek rises in e Clay County and flows s into Shooting Creek.

Burnt Cabin Gap, in se Jackson County between Panthertown Creek and Little Hogback Mountain.

Burnt Chimney. *See* Forest City.

Burnt Coat Branch rises in ne Duplin County and flows sw into Northeast Cape Fear River.

Burnt Coat Swamp rises in w central Halifax County and flows sw into Beech Swamp. Appears on the Collet map, 1770.

Burnthill, community in e Ashe County served by post office, 1899–1914.

Burnt Hill. *See* Burnthill.

Burnt Mill Creek rises in Bear Swamp, se Chowan County, and flows se on the Chowan-Perquimans county line into Yeopim River. The Collet map, 1770, shows Mingo Mill on the headwaters of Yeopim River; the present name appears in local records as early as 1800.

Burnt Mills, community in n central Camden County. Tradition says watermills were destroyed by fire in the vicinity, hence the name. Last mill there discontinued about 1910, but water still flows down the mill race.

Burnt Mountain, e Transylvania County on the head of McCrary Branch.

Burnt Mountain. *See* Burns Mountain.

Burnt Ordinary, formerly an inn on the post road in what is now n central Warren County, about ¾ mi. ne of the present town of Macon. Appears on the Collet map, 1770. The correct name for the inn is thought to have been Burnet Ordinary.

Burnt Pocosin, n Sampson County between Little Coharie Creek and Sevenmile Swamp.

Burnt Ridge, e Yancey County between the head

of Browns Creek and the head of Shuford Creek.

Burnt Rock Ridge follows the course of Sassafras Creek in sw Graham County.

Burnt Shanty Branch rises in ne Cherokee County and flows s into Valley River.

Burntshirt Mountain, ne Henderson County.

Burnt Shop. *See* Melville.

Burnt Spruce Ridge, n Swain County in Great Smoky Mountains National Park, a short spur extending se from Noland Ridge near lat. 35°32′30″ N., long. 83°26′20″ W.

Burnt Stocking Branch rises in e Johnston County and flows se into Little Creek. Mentioned in local records as early as 1779.

Burnt Swamp rises in w Robeson County and flows se into Richland Swamp.

Burnt Swamp Township, central Robeson County.

Burnt Tavern. *See* Clarksville.

Burnt Timber Branch rises in e central Avery County and flows s into Wilson Creek.

Burris Creek rises in w Surry County and flows e and ne into Fisher River.

Burr Mountain, n Buncombe County between Dillingham Creek and North Fork Ivy Creek.

Burrtown. *See* Erwinsville.

Bursted Rock Creek rises in s Transylvania County and flows nw into East Fork French Broad River.

Burt, community in sw Wake County.

Burthen Channel flows through a mass of tidal marsh islands in the extreme w end of Bogue Sound in sw Carteret County. Probably originally known as Borden Channel for William Borden, who owned the neighboring section of Bogue Banks and a plantation on the mainland. The local pronunciation of Borden is Burden, and from Burden the name Burthen derived.

Burton, community in e Durham County. Alt. 300.

Burton Creek rises in e Pamlico County and flows s into Broad Creek.

Busbee, community in s Buncombe County. Named for the nearby mountain.

Busbee Mountain, s Buncombe County near the headwaters of Robinson Creek. Named for one Busby, hunter, whose cabin was on its slopes.

Bush Arbor, community in s Caswell County.

Bush Creek rises in s Avery County and flows sw into North Toe River.

Bush Creek rises in ne Chatham County and flows ne into Overcup Creek.

Bush Creek rises in e Lee County and flows ne into Cape Fear River.

Bush Creek rises in n Randolph County and flows sw into Deep River.

Bush Hill. *See* Archdale.

Bushnell, former town in w Swain County on Tuckasegee River. Inc. 1913. Site now under the waters of Fontana Lake.

Bushy Fork rises in sw Person County and flows ne into South Flat River.

Bushy Fork, community in sw Person County.

Bushy Fork Township, sw Person County.

Bushy Ridge, w Jackson County between Hog Cove Branch and Sassafras Branch.

Busick, community in ne Guilford County. Alt. approx. 850.

Busick, community in se Yancey County on Three Forks Creek. Post office serving the community in the late nineteenth century was named Three Forks.

Bussels Creek rises in s Wilkes County and flows ne into Hunting Creek.

Buster Hall Branch rises in w Duplin County and flows s into Stewarts Creek.

Butcher. *See* Stony Knoll.

Bute County was formed from Granville County in 1764; named in honor of John Stuart (1713–92), Earl of Bute, who until his resignation in 1763 had been First Lord of the Treasury. The county was divided in 1779 to form Franklin and Warren Counties. The courthouse was ordered to be built on Jethro Sumner's land at a place called Buffalo Race Path; the site is in Warren County approx. 6 mi. se of Warrenton. *See also* St. John's Parish, Granville County.

Butler. *See* Oakland.

Butler Creek rises in w Surry County and flows se into North Fork Mitchell River.

Butler Gap, e Yancey County near the head of Long Branch.

Butler Island, ne Tyrrell County in the mouth of Alligator Creek.

Butler Knob, peak in the South Mountains, s Burke County. Alt. 2,062.

Butler Mountain, s Buncombe County between Baldwin Gap and Chestnut Mountain.

Butler Mountain, se Henderson County.

Butlers, community in central Bertie County.

Butlers Crossroads, community in s central Sampson County.

Butler's Mills, community in central Montgomery County served by post office, 1827–47.

Butner, community in sw Granville County. State hospital, training school, and factories are there. Camp Butner, *which see*, activated 1942, closed 1946, named for Maj. Gen. Henry Wolfe Butner (1875–1937), was there. Produces textiles, hosiery. *See also* Hampton; Knap of Reeds.

Butte Mountain, n Caldwell County on Little Kings Creek. Alt. 2,500.

Butte Mountain, e Madison County between Holland Branch and Middle Fork.

Butter Gap, w Transylvania County between Stone Mountain and Cedar Rock Creek.

Buttermilk Creek rises in s Caswell County and flows se into Alamance County, where it enters Haw River.

Buttermilk Mountain, on Bradley Creek in nw Henderson County.

Butters, community in w Bladen County. Butters Lumber Company was located there. Alt. 111.

Butterwood Creek rises in nw Halifax County and flows sw into Bear Swamp.

Butterwood Township, w central Halifax County.

Butt Mountain, se Henderson County.

Butt Mountain, w Henderson County in Great Smoky Mountains National Park, a spur extending se from Big Butt Mountain on Mount Sterling Ridge, near lat. 35°39′20″ N., long. 83°09′10″ W.

Button Bay, a loam-filled bay in n Columbus County.

Button Branch rises in nw Columbus County and flows sw into Dunn Swamp.

Buxton, community on Hatteras Island, se Dare County. One of the most thickly populated sections of the Outer Banks. Formerly known as The Cape (for Cape Hatteras), but the post office was changed to Buxton, 1882. Named for Judge Ralph P. Buxton (1826–1900).

Buxton, plantation house in s Warren County s of the community of Inez; home of John Buxton Williams, a local planter. The house, built in 1850, is still standing.

Buxton Woods Coastal Reserve. *See* Hatteras Woods.

Buzzard Bay, an inlet of the Cape Fear River and the Atlantic Ocean (through Corncake Inlet) in the n part of Smith Island, Brunswick County.

Buzzard Bay, in South River near site of former Lukens community, n central Carteret County.

Buzzard Bay, on the sound side of n Bodie Island in e Dare County; opposite the town of Kill Devil Hills and on s coast of Colington Island. *See also* Colington Island.

Buzzard Branch rises in n Franklin County and flows ne into Sandy Creek.

Buzzard Knob, s Buncombe County nw of Hickory Top.

Buzzard Knob, sw Buncombe County w of Stony Fork community.

Buzzard Knob, s Macon County between Nickajack Creek and Stansfield Branch.

Buzzard Knob, sw Macon County at the sw end of Horse Ridge.

Buzzard Point, a large neck of marsh land on the Roanoke River, se Halifax County.

Buzzard Rock, peak in central Buncombe County between Roaring Gap and Sassafras Gap.

Buzzard Rock, peak between Wildcat Cliffs and Blackrock Mountain on the Jackson-Macon county line.

Buzzard Rock, peak on Sevenmile Ridge, e Yancey County near the head of Murphy Branch.

Buzzard Roost, mountain in South Mountains in s Burke County.

Buzzard Roost, a mountain on the Cherokee-Graham county line at the n end of Hanging Dog Mountain. Alt. 4,081.

Buzzard Roost, peak in n Haywood County w of Pigeon River near Big Bend.

Buzzardroost Mountain, central Swain County between Middle Peachtree Creek and Canebrake Branch.

Buzzard Roost Ridge, n Macon County parallel to Mason Branch.

Buzzards' Rocks, near Shulls Mill, s Watauga County.

Buzzardtown. *See* Darlington.

Byarsville, community in s Cleveland County served by post office, 1875–1903.

Byers Branch rises in central Clay County and flows sw into Shooting Creek.

Byers Creek rises in e Henderson County and flows sw into Lewis Creek.

Byers Creek rises in n Henderson County and flows sw into Mud Creek.

Byers Creek rises in sw Iredell County and flows s into Davidson Creek.

Byers Mountain, n Henderson County on Byers Creek.

Bynum, community in n Chatham County on Haw River. Named for the Bynum family, which est. a cotton mill there. Alt. 322.

Bynum Mill Creek rises in s Edgecombe County and flows ne into Town Creek.

Bynum's Bluff, ne Burke County, promontory alongside Linville Gorge.

Byrd, community in ne Wilkes County served by post office, 1882–1912.

Byrd Pond, s Harnett County on Stewarts Creek. Approx. ½ mi. long.

Byrds Branch rises in n Yancey County and flows se into Jacks Creek.

Byrds Creek rises in s Person County and flows ne into South Flat River.

Byrdsville, community in ne Columbus County.

C

Cabarrus, community in s Cabarrus County.

Cabarrus County was formed in 1792 from Mecklenburg County. Located in the s central section of the state, it is bounded by Stanly, Union, Mecklenburg, Iredell, and Rowan Counties. It was named for Stephen Cabarrus (1754–1808), member of the General Assembly and speaker of the House of Commons. Area: 360 sq. mi. County seat: Concord, with an elevation of 704 ft. Townships are nos. 1–12, formerly Rocky River, Poplar Tent, Odell School, Kannapolis, Mount Gilead, Watts Cross Roads, Earnhardts, Mount Pleasant, Smiths, Bethel Church, Baptist Church, and Concord. Reed Gold Mine in the county was the site of the first discovery of gold in North Carolina, 1799. Produces wheat, barley, corn, cigarettes, plastics, cattle, oats, corn, cotton, poultry, dairy products, textiles, and apparel.

Cabbage Branch rises in n central Anson County and flows s into Brown Creek.

Cabbage Inlet appears on the Moseley map, 1733, in the barrier beach of e New Hanover County between what is now Masonboro Sound and Myrtle Sound. It was still open in 1775 but closed by 1808.

Cabe Branch rises in s Swain County and flows nw into Little Tennessee River.

Cabin, community in e Duplin County on Cabin Creek.

Cabin Branch rises in nw Anson County and flows se into Brown Creek.

Cabin Branch rises in ne Bertie County and flows sw into Chinkapin Swamp. A Cabin Creek is mentioned in local records as early as 1723.

Cabin Branch rises in central Durham County and flows e into Little River.

Cabin Branch rises in w Hoke County and flows ne into Rockfish Creek. Now within the Fort Bragg Military Reservation.

Cabin Branch rises in s Pitt County and flows se into Cow Swamp.

Cabin Branch rises in ne Swain County and flows sw into Bradley Fork.

Cabin Branch rises in w Swain County and flows se into Hazel Creek.

Cabin Branch rises in e central Wake County and flows w into Marsh Creek near its junction with Crabtree Creek.

Cabin Branch rises in n Wilson County and flows approx. 3 mi. s into Bloomery Swamp.

Cabin Branch rises in n Wilson County and flows se into Rocky Ford Branch.

Cabin Cove, se Buncombe County, e of Garren Mountain.

Cabin Creek rises in se Davidson County and flows sw into Yadkin River.

Cabin Creek rises in e Duplin County and flows s into Limestone Creek.

Cabin Creek rises in s Henderson County and flows se into Green River.

Cabin Creek rises in ne Jackson County and flows sw into Dark Ridge Creek.

Cabin Creek rises in e Macon County and flows sw into Rabbit Creek.

Cabin Creek rises in e Montgomery County and flows ne into Moore County and into Bear Creek.

Cabin Creek. *See* Candor.

Cabin Ridge Plantation, the home of Col. Thomas Lee of Lees Mills (now Roper, *which see*), used as the first courthouse for Washington County; county court met there from 1800 until sometime in 1801.

Cabin Swamp, community in central Tyrrell County near Second Creek.

Cable Creek rises in central Randolph County and flows sw and nw into Back Creek.

Cable Gap, n Graham County at the e end of Yellow Mountain between the headwaters of Yellow Creek and Cables Cove Creek.

Cable Gap, ne Graham County at the head of Panther Creek.

Cables Cove Creek rises in n central Graham County and flows n into Fontana Lake.

Cabo de Trafalgar. *See* Cape Fear.

Cabot, community in s Cleveland County served by post office, 1898–1902.

Cackalacky, modern variant homonym of Carolina that gained use in popular culture after World War II. Origin variously attributed to *tsalaki*, Cherokee word for native people, and to cocklaleechie, a traditional Scottish soup.

Cadon Branch rises in s Macon County and flows sw into Tessentee Creek.

Cadon Gap, s Macon County at the head of Whiterock Branch.

Cadwell Creek rises in Virginia and flows sw into n Stokes County. Turning slightly to the nw, it flows back into Virginia.

Caesar Austin Branch rises in central Clay County and flows se into Tusquitee Creek. Named for an early black settler who lived on the branch.

Caesar's Branch rises in n Franklin County and flows ne into Little Shocco Creek.

Caesar Swamp rises in w Sampson County and flows se into Little Coharie Creek.

Caffey Gap, s Watauga County on the head of Laurel Creek.

Caffey's Inlet, former inlet n of present town of Duck, e Dare County. In 1788 George Caffee bought a tract in the area but lost much of it when a small inlet cut through his property. Also known as Providence Inlet.

Caffey's Inlet Station was built by the U.S. Lifesaving Service in 1874 at Caffey's Inlet. Destroyed by fire, its replacement, built 1899, later served U.S. Coast Guard. Later housed restaurant.

Cagle Branch rises in w Jackson County and flows se into Savannah Creek.

Cagles Mill, community in ne Montgomery County served by post office, 1876–1921.

Cahaba, community in sw Bertie County.

Cahoogue Creek rises in se Craven County approx. 3 mi. nw of North Harlowe and flows approx. 3½ mi. nw into Hancock Creek.

Cahoon Point extends from e Onslow County into White Oak River. Named for John Cahoon, early settler.

Caintuck Township. *See* Canetuck Township.

Cairo, community in se Anson County. Served by post office, 1878–1904. Center of rich farming land. Named for Cairo, Egypt, also a center of rich farming land.

Cairo, community in s Wake County. Named for the city in Egypt.

Cajahs Mountain, s Caldwell County. Alt. 1,342. Said to have been named for a man named Micajah who was hanged there.

Calabash, community in sw Brunswick County. Settled prior to 1880. Original name was Pea Landing. Changed to Calabash in 1880 for the gourds that hung outside wells in the vicinity. Noted for its seafood restaurants.

Calabash Creek rises in sw Brunswick County and flows w into South Carolina, where it enters Little River.

Calahaln, community in w Davie County. Probably named for William Callahan (or his descendants), who was in the area as early as 1778. Post office est. there 1858.

Calahaln Mountain, w Davie County. Signs of excavations made on the mountain are said to be the result of Indians digging for gold.

Calahaln Township, w Davie County.

Cal Cove, s Graham County between Willie Knob and Little Snowbird Creek.

Caldwell, community in n Mecklenburg County between towns of Cornelius and Huntersville. Named for Joseph Caldwell (1773–1835), first president of the University of North Carolina.

Caldwell, community in ne Orange County.

Caldwell Branch rises in sw Madison County and flows w into Spring Creek.

Caldwell County was formed in 1841 from Burke and Wilkes Counties. Located in the w central section of the state, it is bounded by Alexander, Catawba, Burke, Avery, Watauga, and Wilkes Counties. It was named for Joseph Caldwell (1773–1835), first president of the University of North Carolina. Area: 480 sq. mi. County seat: Lenoir, with an elevation of 1,182 ft. Townships are Globe, Judson, Johns River, King's Creek, Lenoir, Little River, Lovelady, Lower Creek, Mulberry, North Catawba, Patterson, Wilson Creek, and Yadkin Valley. Produces poultry, dairy products, hogs, furniture, apparel, textiles, hosiery, and gravel. Center of trucking industry.

Caldwell Creek rises in se Mecklenburg County and flows n into Cabarrus County and Reedy Creek. Named for family of David Caldwell (d. about 1780).

Caldwell Fork rises in w Haywood County in Great Smoky Mountains National Park and flows ne to join Palmer Creek in forming Cataloochee Creek.

Caldwell Institute, community in w Orange County served by post office, 1877–1904.

Caldwell Township, se Catawba County. Named in 1868 for Caldwell family, members of which were large landowners.

Caleb Branch rises in w Carteret County and flows w into Hadnot Creek.

Caleb's Creek rises in e Onslow County and flows ne into White Oak River.

Caledonia, state prison farm since 1892 on the Roanoke River, e Halifax County. It consists of 3,700 acres. Named before 1713 for an early plantation that took its name from the Latin term for northern Scotland. Dikes were built along the river to control flooding. The plantation was later owned by Samuel Johnston of Edenton. Numerous Indian relics have been found there.

Caledonia. *See* Bensalem.

Caledonia Creek rises in sw Pender County and flows s into Black River.

Caler Cove, at the head of Caler Cove Branch in n Macon County.

Caler Cove Branch rises in n Macon County and flows s into Little Tennessee River.

Caler Fork rises in e Macon County and flows sw into Cowee Creek.

Caler Knob, on Macon-Swain county line near the head of Gibby Branch.

Cales Creek rises in nw Carteret County and flows sw into White Oak River.

Calf Branch rises on Fort Bragg Military Reservation in n Hoke County and flows sw into Rockfish Creek.

Calf Creek rises in sw Beaufort County and flows n into Pamlico River.

Calfpen Gap, ne Graham County.

Calhoun, community in e Transylvania County between Little River and McCall Branch.

Calhoun Branch rises in w Cherokee County and flows s into Hiwassee River.

Calhoun Branch rises in nw Swain County and flows s into Desolation Branch.

Calhoun Branch rises in w Swain County and flows sw into Fontana Lake.

Calhoun Island, formerly a 15-acre island in Little Tennessee River in ne Graham County. Now under the waters of Fontana Lake.

Calico, community in s Pitt County. Named for the fact that a local store, owned by Henry Venters and his father, sold more calico cloth than any other store in Pitt County. The store also housed the local post office.

Calico Bay, a loam-filled bay in sw Duplin County.

Calico Creek rises in central Carteret County and flows e and se into the mouth of Newport River. An English ship, loaded with calico, is said to have wrecked near Beaufort in a storm. Afterward, pieces of calico were found draped over bushes growing along the creek.

California, community in central Hertford County on the head of Mill Branch.

California, community in ne Madison County. A post office, California Creek, est. there prior to 1882.

California, community in w Pitt County.

California Branch rises in n Cabarrus County and flows n into Rowan County, where it enters South Second Creek.

California Creek rises in e Madison County and flows s to join Paint Fork in forming Little Ivy Creek.

California Gap, s Macon County between Gold Mine Branch and California Ridge.

California Knob, central Surry County.

California Ridge, s Macon County between California Gap and Henderson Mountain.

California Township. *See* Falkland Township.

Call, community in s Wilkes County on Mill Creek. Named for a local family.

Callaghan Creek rises in central Dare County on the mainland and flows e into Croatan Sound.

Callahan, community in n Granville County.

Callahan. *See* Calahaln.

Callahan Branch rises in e Madison County and flows ne into Laurel Creek.

Callaway Mountain, central Yancey County parallel to Cane River.

Callisons, community in central Pamlico County.

Call Millpond, s Wilkes County on Fishing Creek. Covers two acres; max. depth 12 ft. A grain mill and a sawmill operate there.

Caltolina, former lumbering community in e Person and w Granville Counties. A 1,300-acre tract belonging to the John Pomfret Webb family and later to the Calton family, from which the name was developed. The tract was divided into 15 farms about 1919.

Calvander, community in se Orange County. Formed from the name of Calvin Andrews, who operated Andrews's Academy there. The post office was first known as Faucette. Andrews's wife was Elizabeth Faucette.

Calvert, community in s Transylvania County between Calloway Creek and French Broad River.

Calvin. *See* Carbon City.

Calypso, town in nw Duplin County. Settled about 1890, inc. 1913. Alt. 167. Named for the sea nymph in Homer's *Odyssey*. Produces lumber.

Calypso Community Pond, on the head of Dicks Branch in nw Duplin County.

Cam Branch rises in n Duplin County and flows e into Northeast Cape Fear River.

Cambridge. *See* Ostwalt.

Camden, unincorporated county seat in w central Camden County. Known as Plank Bridge as early as 1740; inc. as Jonesborough, 1792. As early as 1840, the name "Camden" was being used. From the end of the Revolution until about 1830, the community was a port of entry for customs collection. Alt. 10.

Camden County was formed in 1777 from Pasquotank County. Located in the ne section of the state, it is bounded by the state of Virginia, Albemarle Sound, and Pasquotank, Gates, and Currituck Counties. It was named for Sir Charles Pratt, Earl of Camden (1716–94), English jurist and political leader who opposed taxation of the American colonies and believed the Stamp Act to be unconstitutional. Area: 308 sq. mi. County seat: Camden, with an elevation of 10 ft. Townships are Court House, Shiloh, and South Mills. Produces corn, soybeans, Irish potatoes, wheat, steel products, concrete products, seafood, and hogs.

Camden Point, the se tip of Camden County that extends into the Albemarle Sound. *See also* Poquoson Point.

Camel Field, cove in n Buncombe County between North Knob and Reems Creek.

Camel Hump Knob, a peak in Great Smoky Mountains National Park on the line between Haywood County, N.C., and Cocke County, Tenn., near lat. 35°43′33″ N., long. 83°13′ W. Alt. 5,200–5,250.

Camel Knob, n Rutherford County n of Camp Creek. Alt. 2,124.

Camels Creek rises in w Harnett County and flows ne into Cape Fear River. Named for "Surveyor John" Campbell, who settled along its banks about 1770.

Camera. *See* Willard.

Camerer Ridge, on the Haywood County, N.C.–Cocke County, Tenn., line in Great Smoky Mountains National Park. Extends ne from Low Gap to Mount Camerer, then e approx. 2½ mi. to the valley of Pigeon River. Named in honor of A. B. Camerer, formerly of the U.S. Department of Interior, who was active in promoting the park.

Cameron, town in e Moore County. Inc. 1876 and named for a civil engineer who surveyed the Raleigh and Augusta Airline Railroad. Alt. 304.

Camerons Hill. *See* Johnsonville.

Camp Alamance, Civil War training camp near

Company Shops, now Burlington, central Alamance County.

Campania, an estate of 19,000 acres in Currituck, Pasquotank, and Perquimans Counties owned by Thomas Macknight. Being developed at the time of the Revolutionary War.

Camp Ashe, a Civil War training camp in New Hanover County, described in contemporary records as being "12 miles from Wilmington."

Camp Bay, a bay in central Columbus County filled with fine sand.

Camp Beauregard, Civil War training camp in w Warren County near the community of Ridgeway.

Campbell, community in n Stokes County near the head of Little Creek.

Campbell Creek rises in se Beaufort County and flows e to join Upper Spring Creek in forming Goose Creek.

Campbell Creek rises in s Graham County and flows ne into Tulula Creek.

Campbell Creek is formed in w Haywood County by the junction of East and West Forks and flows ne into Jonathans Creek.

Campbell Gap, central Macon County between Iotla Branch and Iotla Creek.

Campbell Island, e Brunswick County on the Cape Fear River. Once known as Crane Island. Named for William Campbell (1745–81), a general in the Revolution.

Campbells Creek rises in e Mecklenburg County and flows s into McAlpine Creek.

Campbell's Creek, community in se Beaufort County in the center of an Irish potato–growing area. Phosphate deposits exist in the vicinity.

Campbell's Crossroads. *See* Semora.

Campbells Falls, rapids in Cape Fear River in se Harnett County near the confluence of Juniper Creek with the river. Mentioned as early as 1819 in a survey of the rivers of North Carolina.

Campbell's Mill on Waterhole Swamp. *See* Pembroke.

Campbellton. *See* Fayetteville.

Camp Blackjack. *See* Bucklesberry Pocosin.

Camp Branch rises in w Avery County and flows s into Horse Creek.

Camp Branch rises in se Buncombe County and flows nw into Swannanoa River.

Camp Branch rises in ne Clay County and flows se into Clear Creek.

Camp Branch rises in e Durham County near the Wake County line and flows ne into Lick Creek.

Camp Branch rises in n Haywood County and flows sw into Pigeon River.

Camp Branch rises in s Haywood County and flows nw into Browning Branch.

Camp Branch rises in nw Macon County and flows sw into Nantahala River.

Camp Branch rises in w Macon County and flows se into Wayah Creek.

Camp Branch rises in nw Surry County and flows sw into Fisher River.

Camp Branch rises in e Swain County and flows ne into Connelly Creek.

Camp Branch rises in s Wake County and flows s into Middle Creek.

Camp Branch rises in e Watauga County and flows ne into Elk Creek.

Camp Branch rises in n central Wilkes County and flows ne into Roaring River.

Camp Branch, community n central Brunswick County.

Camp Branch Falls, 360-ft. waterfalls on the Nantahala River, Clay-Macon county line.

Camp Butner, former army post in Durham, Granville, and Person Counties. Est. 1942; closed 1946. Infantry training center, convalescent hospital, and reassignment center. Housed Axis prisoners of war. Named for Maj. Gen. Henry Wolfe Butner (1875-1937), native of Surry County. *See also* Butner.

Camp Call, community in central Cleveland County on Little Harris Creek.

Camp Campbell, a Civil War training camp near Kinston in e Lenoir County.

Camp Canal, Civil War training camp in Carteret County, probably at or near Morehead City.

Camp Chronicle, a World War I training camp located on the w side of present S. Linwood Street, Gastonia, central Gaston County. Operated in connection with an artillery range at the foot of Crowders Mountain. Named for Maj. William Chronicle, killed at the Battle of Kings Mountain, 1780.

Camp Clingman, former Confederate camp in Asheville (French Broad Avenue near Philip Street), central Buncombe County. Named for Thomas L. Clingman, U.S. senator and brigadier general in the Confederate army.

Camp Crabtree, Civil War training camp located approx. 3 mi. n of Raleigh on "Crabtree," the plantation of Kimbrough Jones Sr.

Camp Creek rises in n Burke County and flows nw into Avery County, where it enters Linville River. Named for three brothers—Everette, Howard, and Arthur Camp—of Chicago, who were railroad builders in the vicinity.

Camp Creek rises in se corner of Burke County and flows ne into Jacob Fork.

Camp Creek rises in se Burke County and flows se into Catawba County, where it enters Jacob Fork.

Camp Creek rises in w Cherokee County and flows nw and ne into Apalachia Lake.

Camp Creek rises in sw Cleveland County and flows n into Broad River.

Camp Creek rises in se Henderson County and flows ne into Polk County, where it enters Green River.

Camp Creek rises in e Jackson County and flows sw into Tanasee Creek.

Camp Creek rises in nw Jackson County and flows sw into Tuckasegee River.

Camp Creek rises in w Johnston County and flows s into Black Creek.

Camp Creek rises in s McDowell County and flows sw into Rutherford County, where it continues sw and then turns se to enter Second Broad River.

Camp Creek rises in s Person County and flows se across the ne corner of Durham County into Granville County, where it enters Knap of Reeds Creek.

Camp Creek rises in w Stokes County and flows ne into Cascade Creek.

Camp Creek rises in sw Surry County and flows se and ne into Mitchell River.

Camp Creek rises in s Yancey County and flows se into South Toe River.

Camp Creek Bald, on Madison County, N.C.–Greene County, Tenn., line. Alt. 4,844.

Camp Creek Mountain, s central Avery County.

Camp Creek Township, n central Rutherford County.

Camp Davis, a Civil War training camp near Wilmington, w New Hanover County.

Camp Davis, World War II antiaircraft training base at Holly Ridge, s Onslow County. Opened April 1941 and attained a maximum of 60,000 men and women; closed October 1944. Reopened briefly in the summer of 1945 as an air force convalescent hospital and redistribution station. Named for Maj. Gen. Richmond Pearson Davis (1866–1937), a native of North Carolina.

Camp Fisher, Civil War training camp near High Point, sw Guilford County.

Camp Gap, nw Macon County at the head of Camp Branch.

Camp Glenn, National Guard camp, 1907–13, in Morehead City on site of Carolina City, *which see*. Also site of first U.S. Coast Guard air station, 1920–21.

Camp Greene, World War I training camp, 6,000 acres in area. Est. July 1917 and located in sw Charlotte; named for Gen. Nathanael Greene.

Camp Grier Lake, w McDowell County on a tributary of Mill Creek; 1/5 mi. long, about 1 mi. nw of Old Fort. A summer camp is operated there by the Presbyterian Church. Formerly known as Lake Refuge.

Campground, The, sw Gates County approx. 3 mi. nw of Gatesville, the site of religious camp meetings from the 1820s until the early 1900s. Popular with the people from Hertford, Bertie, and Chowan Counties. An artesian well at the site supplied water.

Campground Gap, on the Buncombe-Yancey county line between Campground Knob and Rocky Knob.

Campground Knob, on Buncombe-Yancey county line between Sugartree Gap and Campground Gap.

Camp Hebron, s Watauga County on Boone Fork, operated for girls.

Camp Hill, a Civil War training camp described as being near Garysburg in Northampton County. It was also referred to as a "camp of instruction."

Camping Creek rises in sw Franklin County and flows ne into Cedar Creek.

Camping Fork rises in n Mitchell County and flows sw into Right Fork Bean Creek.

Camping Island Creek rises in central Stokes County and flows ne between Hanging Rock and Flat Shoal Mountain into Dan River.

Camp Jeter, former Confederate camp in Asheville (Cherry Street–Flint Street section), central Buncombe County.

Camp Johnston, a Civil War training camp in the vicinity of Kinston, named for Gen. Joseph E. Johnston.

Camp Knob, n Cleveland County between Cove and Cox Creeks.

Camp Lamb, a Civil War training camp near Wilmington, w New Hanover County.

Camp Lejeune, Marine base in s Onslow County on both sides of New River, adjacent to Jacksonville. Construction began in 1942. Known first as New River Marine Base; later named for Maj. Gen. John A. Lejeune (1867–1942), World War I Marine commandant. The base covers 173 sq. mi., of which 26,000 acres are under water. Onslow Beach, a part of the base, is used for amphibious assault training.

Camp Mackall, World War II training camp, the second-largest Airborne training center in the nation. Site in e Richmond and nw Scotland Counties. *See also* Hoffman.

Camp Macon. *See* Macon.

Camp Mangum, Civil War training camp in central Wake County about 3 mi. w of Raleigh on site of present state fairgrounds.

Camp Mason, Civil War training camp near Graham, central Alamance County.

Camp Mason, Civil War training camp near Goldsboro in central Wayne County.

Camp Mountain, e Jackson County between Tanasee Creek and the Transylvania County line.

Camp Patton, Civil War training camp in Asheville (East Chestnut Street e of Charlotte Street), central Buncombe County. Probably named for Capt. Thomas W. Patton, who served with distinction in the Confederate army. The camp was probably on land that he owned, as his home was nearby.

Camp Point, at the nw tip of the largest island in the Hog Island group, ne Carteret County. Earlier known as Whale Camp Point and was the site of an early settlement.

Camp Polk, World War I tank camp of 1,600 acres located in Raleigh and named for William Polk, Revolutionary War colonel. Camp had two sections: administrative, housing, and assembly grounds on Hillsborough Street and tank training grounds on Blue Ridge Road.

Camp Ridge, mountain in w Avery County.

Camprock Branch rises in s Macon County and flows se into Shope Fork.

Camp Springs, community in sw Caswell County. Believed to have been named because Cornwallis's troops camped there during the American Revolution.

Camps Store. *See* Gaston.

Camp Swamp rises in s Columbus County and flows se into Horry County, S.C., where it enters Buck Creek.

Camp Tuscarora, Boy Scout camp and lake in s Wayne County s of Sleepy Creek.

Camp Two Branch rises in s Haywood County and flows nw into Middle Prong.

Camp Vance, a Civil War training camp near Sulphur Springs, central Buncombe County. Named for Col. Robert B. Vance of the 29th N.C. Regiment, which trained there.

Camp Vance, central Burke County, site of camp for state troops, 1861–64; named for Col. Zebulon B. Vance, Civil War governor. Raided by Federal troops in 1864.

Camp Whiting, a Civil War training camp at Wilmington, w New Hanover County.

Camp Wilson. *See* Vaughan's Springs.

Camp Wyatt, a Civil War training camp in s New Hanover County about 2 mi. n of Fort Fisher. Named for Henry Lawson Wyatt, first North Carolina soldier killed in action in the Civil War, at Bethel Church, June 10, 1861.

Cana, community in n Davie County. Made a post office in 1875 and named for James H. Cain, first postmaster.

Canada Township, se Jackson County.

Canadian Hole, deep trough just offshore in Pamlico Sound, n of Buxton, e Dare County. Frequented by windsurfers, many of them Canadian. Term also used by N.C. Department of Transportation to describe section of highway 12 subject to frequent washouts.

Canadian Top, peak in w Haywood County, Great Smoky Mountains National Park, near lat. 35°38′55″ N., long. 83°06′13″ W.

Canady Creek rises in n Guilford County and flows nw into Rockingham County. Name is a variation of Thomas Kennedy, pioneer settler.

Canal A, in central Washington County, drains ne from East Dismal Swamp into Main Canal.

Canal B, in central Washington County, drains ne from East Dismal Swamp into Main Canal.

Canal Gut rises in sw Bertie County and flows s into Roanoke River.

Canal Swamp rises in e Northampton County and flows se into Hertford County, where it enters Potecasi Creek.

Canby, community in s Montgomery County on Thickety Creek. Served by post office, 1900–1932. Named by Chesley Greene for Fort Canby, Wash., where he served during the Spanish-American War.

Candills, community in w Johnston County served by post office, 1891–1903.

Candle Branch rises in w Forsyth County and flows sw into Yadkin River.

Candler, community in sw Buncombe County at the junction of South Hominy and Hominy Creeks. Alt. 2,108. Named for George Candler, an early settler.

Candler Knob, on Buncombe-Henderson county line, sw of Cutthroat Gap. Alt. 4,548.

Candon, community in w Mecklenburg County served by post office, 1833–75. Also operated as Clear Creek post office.

Candor, town in e Montgomery County. Alt. 729. Inc. 1891. Named by three local merchants who envisioned a "town of frankness and sincerity." Post office est. as Cabin Creek in 1873; name changed in 1885. Also once called Lamond's Old Field.

Candy Creek rises in ne Guilford County and flows n into Rockingham County, where it enters Haw River. Known as Kenady's Branch and as Kanady Creek prior to 1800, named for an early settler.

Cane, community in s Alamance County.

Cane Bottom, community in n Yancey County on Nolichucky River.

Canebrake Branch rises in w central Swain County and flows s into Tuckasegee River.

Cane Brake Creek rises in s Rutherford County and flows s into Broad River.

Cane Branch rises in Angola Bay, n Pender County, and flows se into Holly Shelter Creek.

Cane Branch rises in e Yancey County and flows n into Little Crabtree Creek.

Cane Creek rises in sw Alamance County and flows e into Haw River. Cane Creek Friends (Quaker) Meeting House was est. along its banks in 1751. Named for canebrakes on the banks of the stream.

Cane Creek rises in se Buncombe County near Cane Creek Gap and flows sw into Henderson County, where it enters French Broad River.

Cane Creek rises in s Cherokee County and flows ne into Nottely River.

Cane Creek rises in n Jackson County and flows sw into Tuckasegee River.

Cane Creek rises in sw Jackson County and flows se into Chattooga River.

Cane Creek rises in se Macon County and flows se into Chattooga River.

Cane Creek rises in se McDowell County and flows s into Rutherford County, where it turns sw to flow into Second Broad River.

Cane Creek rises in w McDowell County and flows ne into Catawba River.

Cane Creek rises in e Mitchell County and flows w into Toe River.

Cane Creek rises in w Orange County and flows sw into Haw River.

Cane Creek rises in sw Person County and flows e into the Hyco River.

Cane Creek rises in w Rutherford County and flows ne into Lake Lure.

Cane Creek rises in s Union County and flows sw into Catawba River in South Carolina.

Cane Creek rises in n Wilkes County and flows se into North Prong Roaring River.

Cane Creek. *See* Crane Creek.

Cane Creek Gap, se Buncombe County near the headwaters of Cane Creek.

Cane Creek Mountains, s Alamance County. Among the named peaks are Huronian Mountain and Stafford Hill. Alt. approx. 1,033.

Cane Creek Township, e Mitchell County.

Canedy Gap, w Cherokee County at the se end of Chestnut Gap Mountain.

Canedy Mountain, w Cherokee County s of Canedy Gap between Shoal and Bearpaw Creeks.

Cane Island, sandy island approx. ¼ mi. long in French Broad River, w Madison County.

Cane Mountain, between Foster Creek and McDowell Creek in nw Henderson County.

Cane Mountain extends from Cane River in n Yancey County ne to the junction of Toe and Cane Rivers.

Cane River rises in the Black Mountains of s Yancey County and meanders n to join Toe River on the Mitchell-Yancey county line to form Nolichucky River.

Cane River, community in w central Yancey County.

Cane River Gap, on Buncombe-Yancey county line se of Ivy Gap. Also known as Little Cane River Gap.

Cane River Township, nw Yancey County.

Canetuck, community in sw Pender County on Buckle Creek.

Canetuck Township, sw Pender County, formerly Caintuck Township.

Caney Bottom Creek rises in n Transylvania County and flows se into Cove Creek.

Caney Branch rises in w Cherokee County and flows se and sw into Hiwasee River.

Caney Branch rises in n McDowell County on the e slopes of Witness Rock Ridge and flows ne about 2 mi. into Armstrong Creek.

Caney Fork, stream formed in ne Jackson County by the junction of Piney Mountain Creek and Rough Butt Creek; flows sw into Tuckasegee River.

Caney Fork Bald, on Haywood-Jackson county line nw of Lone Bald. Alt. 5,926.

Caney Fork Branch rises in s Madison County and flows nw into Robert Branch.

Caney Fork Township, e central Jackson County.

Caney Lead extends ne from Hangover Lead to Cheoah River in nw Graham County.

Canie Creek rises in central Buncombe County and flows se into Hominy Creek.

Cannon, community in w Henderson County. Settled soon after the Revolutionary War.

Cannon Branch rises in n Avery County and flows e into Buckeye Creek.

Cannon Branch rises in s Watauga County and flows sw into Boone Fork.

Cannon Creek rises in e Transylvania County and flows se into Buckhorn Creek.

Cannon Gap, n Avery County near the head of Cannon Creek.

Cannon Gap, in s Watauga County on the head of Payne Branch.

Cannon Lake is fed by several small streams in sw Rowan County. Covers 100 acres. Used as a source of water by former Cannon Mills and the town of Kannapolis.

Cannons Crossroads, community in central Pitt County.

Cannon's Ferry, community on the Chowan River in nw Chowan County.

Cannon Swamp rises in central Pitt County and flows se into Moyes Run.

Canoe Creek rises in w Burke County and flows se into Catawba River in central Burke County.

Cansadie Top, central Haywood County between Shook Gap and Jolly Gap.

Canterbury Creek. *See* Southwest Creek.

Canto, community in nw Buncombe County near the Madison County line.

Canton, town in e Haywood County. Inc. 1889 as Buford. Name changed to Pigeon River in 1891 and to Canton in 1893. Named for Canton, Ohio, source of the steel used in the bridge being built across Pigeon River. Produces paper. Alt. 2,609.

Cantrell Creek rises in n Transylvania County and flows se into South Fork Mills River.

Cantrell Creek rises in s Transylvania County and flows n into French Broad River.

Cantrell Mountain, w Henderson County between North Fork and South Fork.

Cantrell Top, nw Cherokee County.

Cape, community in se Randolph County served by post office, 1886–1904.

Cape, The. *See* Buxton.

Cape Amidas. *See* Cape Hatteras.

Cape Carteret, town in sw Carteret County on Bogue Sound. Inc. 1959.

Cape Creek, a tidal creek on Smith Island in se Brunswick County rising about 1 mi. n of Cape Fear just inside the outer beach and extending nw to the main outlet on the w shore of Smith Island.

Cape Fair. *See* Cape Fear.

Cape Fear, the southernmost tip of Smith (Bald Head) Island, s Brunswick County, at the mouth of Cape Fear River in the Atlantic Ocean. Discovered by Verrazzano in 1524. Appears as *Promontorium tremendum* on the De Bry map, 1590, and as Cape of Feare on the Molyneux map, 1592. The name apparently originated in 1585 when the *Tiger*, en route to Roanoke Island, was nearly wrecked "on a breache called the Cape of Feare." John White had a similar experience and mentioned the name again in 1587. Spanish maps of the same period mark the point as Cabo de Trafalgar. At a later time, when it was desirable to attract colonists to the Carolina region, the name Cape Fair was substituted but not permanently accepted.

Cape Fear, community in central Harnett County near the n bank of Cape Fear River.

Cape Feare. *See* Cape Lookout.

Cape Fear River is formed by the junction of Deep and Haw Rivers on the Chatham-Lee county line. It flows se along the Chatham-Lee county line and through Harnett County, s through Cumberland County, se through Bladen County, and along the Columbus-Pender, Brunswick-Pender, and Brunswick–

New Hanover county lines into the Atlantic Ocean. It had a succession of names after it was first discovered by Europeans. Spanish explorers in 1526 named it Rio Jordan; a Barbadian colony in 1664 named it Charles River; and between 1664 and 1667, when Clarendon County existed in the area, it was known as Clarendon River. It appears as Clarendon River on the Ogilby map, 1671; as "C. Fear R. or Clarendon R." on the Gascoyne map, 1682; as Cape Fear River on the Barnwell map, 1722; as Clarendon River on the Moll map, 1729; and as Cape Fear River on the Moseley map, 1733, and thereafter on others.

Cape Fear Section, a term applied to se North Carolina along the Cape Fear River. Appears as Pine Plains on the Ogilby map, 1671.

Cape Fear Township, se Chatham County.

Cape Fear Township, former township in e Lee County, now township no. 3.

Cape Fear Township, n New Hanover County.

Cape Hatteras, the easternmost point in North Carolina, is at the s tip of Hatteras Island, se Dare County. Diamond Shoals, extending into the Atlantic Ocean se from the Cape, reach to the Gulf Stream at the notorious "Grave-yard of the Atlantic." Called Cape St. John on the Velasco map, 1611; Cape Amidas on the Smith map, 1624; and its present name on the Ogilby map, 1671. The word "Hatteras" apparently is an English rendition of the Algonquian Indian expression of "there is less vegetation." Archaeological evidence indicates that the sixteenth-century Indian village of Croatoan may have been located there. *See also* various entries under Hatteras; Diamond Shoals.

Cape Hatteras National Seashore, est. 1953, consists of the s part of Bodie Island and most of Ocracoke and Hatteras Islands, except the settled areas. First U.S. national seashore, it was authorized by Congress in 1937. Campsites provided. On the Outer Banks of se Dare and Hyde Counties.

Cape Hatteras Woods. *See* Hatteras Woods.

Cape Kenrick in the sixteenth and early seventeenth centuries extended into the Atlantic Ocean from Hatteras Island in e Dare County between the present communities of Rodanthe and Salvo. Appears on the Velasco map, 1611. It disappeared later in the seventeenth century, either through erosion or in a storm. Wimble Shoals, *which see*, are now at the site. Kenrick is believed to have been derived from the Algonquian Indian word for "sinking-down-sand."

Capella, community in w Stokes County between Quaker Gap and East Prong Yadkin River.

Capell Mills, community in n Richmond County served by post office, 1869–1905.

Cape Lookout, the southernmost tip of Core Banks in se Carteret County. A lighthouse, coast guard station, and a few summer cottages are there. The De Bry map, 1590, marks the point as "Promontorium tremendum." On the Velasco map, 1611, it is Cape Feare. On the Ogilby map, 1671, it appears as Cape Lookout.

Cape Lookout National Seashore was authorized to be est. by U.S. Congress in 1966 on Core Banks, Portsmouth Island, and Shackleford Banks on the Outer Banks of e Carteret County. Area contains approx. 16,400 acres.

Cape Lookout Shoals, in the Atlantic Ocean off Cape Lookout, *which see*, se Carteret County.

Capelsie, community in s Montgomery County on Little River. Named for A. W. Capel and M. Elsie Shamburger, owners of a cotton mill est. there about 1870. Served by post office, 1902–16.

Cape of Feare. *See* Cape Fear.

Cape Point, the extreme tip of land at Cape Hatteras, extends into the Atlantic Ocean, se Dare County.

Capernium, community in sw Forsyth County.

Cape St. John. *See* Cape Hatteras.

Capps Hill, community in n Mecklenburg County on the head of Stuarts Creek.

Caraleigh, former community in central Wake County now within the city of Raleigh.

Caraway, community in central Randolph County served by post office, 1845–1932.

Caraway Creek rises in nw Randolph County and flows s into Uwharrie River near town of Farmer. Appears on the Collet map, 1770. Traditionally an Indian name, probably a survival of Keyauwee, the name of an Indian tribe that inhabited the area when white men first entered it. *See also* Keeauwee.

Caraway Mountain, w Randolph County between Black Creek and Caraway Creek, *which see*. Appears on the Collet map, 1770, as a name applied to all of the small mountains between the Uwharrie and Deep Rivers.

Carbon City, community in w central Burke County. Formerly known as Calvin but renamed following the construction of the Great Lakes Carbon Company plant at the site.

Carbonton, community in s Chatham County on Deep River at the junction of the Chatham-Lee-Moore county lines. Named by Mrs. Peter Evans, daughter of Gov. John Motley Morehead, for the element carbon, a constituent of coal, abundant in the vicinity. Alt. 260.

Cardenas, community in s Wake County.

Careening Point extended into North River estuary of Carteret County from the mainland on Moseley map, 1733. The name has fallen into disuse, though the point still exists.

Carl, community in e central Montgomery County served by post office, 1893–1909.

Carl Alwin Schenck Forest, central Wake County, approx. 3 mi. w of North Carolina State University. Covers 245 acres. Est. 1936 and afterward named in honor of Schenck (1865–1955) who, in 1898, founded the first forestry school in the United States at Biltmore Forest, *which see*. The school was closed in 1912. The Schenck Forest, owned and operated by the Department of Forestry and Environmental Resources, N.C. State University, is used for demonstration, research, and forest genetics. Schenck's ashes are scattered in the forest.

Carlile Island. *See* Colington Island.

Carlisle, community in nw Davidson County served by post office, 1886–1905.

Carlos, community in n Cumberland County.

Carlton, community in w Granville County.

Carlton. *See* Carroll.

Carmel, community in w Montgomery County served by post office, 1884–1915.

Carmen, community in n Madison County on Shelton Laurel Creek.

Carolana, a province proposed to be est. in America and named in the charter of King Charles I to Sir Robert Heath, October 30, 1629. The province was to extend from 31° to 36° N. lat. along the Atlantic Ocean and presumably w to the Pacific Ocean. No settlements were made, and the charter was considered vacated in 1663 when Carolina was

granted to eight Lords Proprietors by King Charles II. *See also* County of Norfolk.

Carolarns Islands, presumably the Outer Banks, *which see*, named in the charter of King Charles I to Sir Robert Heath, October 30, 1629.

Caroleen, community in se Rutherford County on Second Broad River. Alt. 805. Named in honor of Caroline, wife of Simpson B. Tanner Sr., industrialist. The Post Office Department ruled that Caroline was too similar to Carolina to be acceptable, so Caroleen was selected instead. The communities of Avondale and Henrietta lie directly s.

Carolina was named by King Charles II of England in his own honor in the charter that he granted in 1663 to eight Lords Proprietors. It was applied to the region between Florida and the Virginia colony extending from the Atlantic to the Pacific Ocean. *See also* Carolana.

Carolina, community in central Alamance County on Haw River. A textile mill est. there prior to 1901.

Carolina Bays, oval-shaped lakes, swamps, pocosins, savannahs, and peat beds in se North Carolina, e South Carolina, and ne Georgia. Several explanations have been advanced as to the origin of the Carolina Bays, but the most generally accepted one is that they were formed thousands of years ago by a shower of meteorites. White Lake, Jones Lake, Singletary Lake, and Lake Waccamaw are Carolina Bays. There also are numerous others, many of which no longer contain water.

Carolina Beach, town in se New Hanover County on the Atlantic Ocean. Alt. 5. Settled about 1885; inc. 1925. Sugar Loaf, a former community at or near the site, was the scene of an engagement between Confederate and Union forces after the capitulation of Fort Fisher, January 15, 1865.

Carolina Beach Inlet, se New Hanover County, an artificially created inlet from the Atlantic Ocean through the barrier bar about 2½ mi. n of the town of Carolina Beach. A dredged channel extends from the inlet to the Intracoastal Waterway.

Carolina City was laid out in 1855 in s central Carteret County by Carolina City Land Company to be terminal point of Atlantic and

North Carolina Railroad. Opening of Morehead City on adjacent land to the e and the
coming of the Civil War brought about its
demise. Union army camped at the site for
3 years and afterward the State Guard trained
there. *See* Camp Glenn.

Carolina Island. *See* Conine Island.

Carolina Power Lake, nw Person and ne Caswell
Counties on Hyco River. Formed in 1964 by
the construction of Hyco Dam by Carolina
Power and Light Company to condense
turbine exhaust steam at its electricity-
generating plant there. The lake is approx.
10 mi. long and covers 3,750 acres. It is also
used for public recreation. Sometimes referred to as Roxboro Lake and Hyco Lake.

Carolina River. *See* Albemarle Sound.

Carolina Shoal Beach, extreme s tip of the mainland of New Hanover County between the
Atlantic Ocean and the Cape Fear River.

Carolina Township, ne Pitt County.

Caroon Point, a point extending from mainland
of n Dare County, near Mashoes, into Albemarle Sound.

Carpenter, community in w Wake County settled
1865. Named for William Carpenter, early
settler. Alt. 325.

Carpenter Branch rises in w Haywood County
and flows s into Jonathans Creek.

Carpenter Knob, in n Cleveland County between
Poundingmill and Knob Creeks. Alt. 1,619.

Carpenters Branch rises in s Macon County and
flows n into Allison Creek.

Carpenters Knob, w Lincoln County. Alt. 1,500.

Carr, community in nw Orange County.

Carraway Creek rises in s central Wayne County
and flows nw approx. 5 mi. into Neuse River.
First known as Michael's Creek for the owner
of surrounding land, Michael Rosher. Land
sold to John Carraway in 1743 and the name
of the creek changed.

Carrboro, town in se Orange County immediately w of Chapel Hill. Alt. 500. Settled 1898.
Inc. 1911 as Venable; named for Francis P.
Venable (1856–1934), president of the University of North Carolina. Changed to Carrboro,
1913, for Julian S. Carr (1845–1924), who est.
a textile mill there.

Carrell Knob, on the Cherokee-Clay county line
in the Valley River Mountains.

Carrikers, community in s Cabarrus County
named for local family.

Carringer Gap, n Graham County between
Yellow Creek and Cochran Creek.

Carrol Gap, near the se base of Carroll Mountain, w Clay County between the headwaters
of Sweetwater and Qualls Creeks near lat.
35°02′45″ N., long. 83°51′20″ W.

Carrol Knob, s Macon County between Jones
Creek and the head of North Fork Coweeta
Creek.

Carroll, community in w Duplin County served
by post office, 1899–1902. Named for Charles
Carroll, postmaster.

Carroll Branch rises in w Clay County on the e
slope of Carroll Knob and flows s into Carroll
Lake near lat. 35°03′45″ N., long. 83°54′53″
W., in Nantahala National Forest.

Carroll Gap, e Watauga County on the head of
Long Branch.

Carroll Knob, on the Cherokee-Clay county
line at the sw end of Valley River Mountains,
Nantahala National Forest. Alt. 2,540.

Carroll Lake, a spring-fed lake in w Clay County,
n of Hiwassee River, formed about 1920.
Covers 30 acres; max. depth 20 ft. Privately
owned. Named for John C. Carroll, first
owner.

Carroll Mountain, w Clay County, s of Hiwassee
River and n of Qualls Creek. *See also* Jim
Carroll Top.

Carrolls Branch rises in se Moore County and
flows e into Mill Creek.

Carroll's Creek rises in n Burke County and
flows s into Johns River.

Carrot Island, a marshy island about 1.5 mi.
long se of Beaufort in s Carteret County and
separated from the mainland by Taylor Creek.
Long refuge for wild horses. Formerly Cart
Island.

Carrs Creek rises in s Lee County and flows s
into Little River.

Carr's Mount, community in central Anson
County on n outskirts of Wadesboro. Alt. 445.
Site of a silk mill in the early twentieth century. Other mills operated there from early
nineteenth century; early fairgrounds and
racetrack were there.

Carrs Township, ne Greene County. Named for
the Carr family, prominent in the area from a
time prior to 1804.

Carr Township, e Durham County.

Carson, community in central Catawba County.
Alt. 1,000.

Carson Cove, on a tributary of Iotla Creek in central Macon County.

Carson Creek rises in s Transylvania County and flows nw into French Broad River.

Carson Mountain, n Buncombe County n of Wildcat Knob.

Carson Mountain, n Rutherford County, extends ne between Cane Creek and Lookadoo Mountain.

Carson Mountain. *See* Black Mountain.

Carson's Creek, community in se Transylvania County near the South Carolina line.

Carter, community in ne Buncombe County near the junction of Mineral and Carter Creeks.

Carter, community in s Gates County.

Carter Branch rises in n Macon County and flows sw into Little Tennessee River.

Carter Cove, the valley through which Beaverdam Creek flows in sw Buncombe County.

Carter Cove, the valley through which Carter Cove Creek flows in central Buncombe County.

Carter Cove, s Clay County near Brasstown Gap.

Carter Cove, community in s Clay County in the cove of the same name.

Carter Cove Creek rises in the Elk Mountains, central Buncombe County, and flows sw into Beaverdam Creek.

Carter Creek rises in the Great Craggy Mountains, ne Buncombe County, and flows generally nw to join Mineral Creek in forming Stony Creek.

Carteret, town est. 1723 to be laid out on the ne side of Roanoke Island, then Bertie, later Tyrrell, and now e Dare County. An act of 1715, without naming the town, attempted to encourage its establishment. A few lots may have been sold by 1733, when it was referred to as "Roanoak Town," but it never developed as planned.

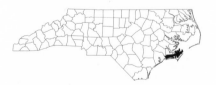

Carteret County was formed in 1722 from Craven County. Located in the e section of the state, it is bounded by the Atlantic Ocean, by Onslow, Jones, and Craven Counties, and by Neuse River and Pamlico Sound. Bogue and Core Sounds separate the Outer Banks from the mainland of the county. It was named for John Carteret (1690–1763), later second Earl Granville, one of the Lords Proprietors. Area: 1,063 sq. mi. (532, land; 531, water). County seat: Beaufort, with an elevation of 9 ft. Townships are Beaufort, Cedar Island, Davis, Harkers Island, Merrimon, Harlowe, Marshallberg, Morehead, Newport, Portsmouth, Smyrna, Straits, and White Oak. Produces corn, soybeans, Irish potatoes, Irish potatoes, hogs, apparel, boxes, boats, and seafood.

Carteret Precinct, Albemarle County, formed by 1681, composed of present Currituck, Pasquotank, and Camden Counties.

Carteret Township, former township of ne Carteret County. Previously a part of Straits Township, now largely Merrimon Township.

Carter Gap, on the Clay-Macon county line.

Carter Mill Ridge, n Madison County between Big Creek and Mill Creek.

Carter Mountain, n Buncombe County near the Madison County line.

Carter Pond, s Wayne County in Yellow Swamp.

Carters Creek rises in ne Davie County near Hillsdale and flows 3 mi. se into Yadkin River. Formerly known as Linville Creek.

Carters Falls, sw Surry County on the Yadkin River near Elkin.

Carters Mills, community in n Moore County on Bear Creek. Named for S. M. Carter, in whose house the post office was first opened. A mill there was est. about 1790 by Nicholas Nall, who also had a tavern there on the old Salem-Fayetteville road.

Carters Mountain extends nw in n Wilkes County between North Prong Roaring River and Middle Prong Roaring River.

Carters Ridge, s Mitchell County between Grassy Creek and North Toe River.

Cartersville, community in s Duplin County.

Carter Top, on the n end of Rich Mountain in nw Jackson County.

Carthage, town and county seat, central Moore County. Authorized to be laid off and inc. 1796. Name changed to Fagansville in 1806 for Richardson Fagin, sheriff of Moore County, 1785–87, and on whose land the town was located; changed back to Carthage, 1818. Produces textiles. Alt. 575.

Carthage Township, central Moore County.

Cart Island. *See* Carrot Island.

Cartledge Creek rises in central Richmond County on w edge of town of Ellerbe and flows sw into Pee Dee River. Named for Edmund Cartledge, who owned land in the vicinity prior to 1758.

Cartoogechaye Creek rises in s Macon County and flows ne into Little Tennessee River. The name is believed to be the Cherokee Indian word for "corn fields."

Cartoogechaye Township, w Macon County.

Cartwheel Branch rises in e Onslow County and flows ne into Holland Mill Creek.

Carver Creek rises in nw Clay County and flows sw into Hiwassee River.

Carver Creek rises in n Cumberland County and flows se into Cape Fear River.

Carver Gap, nw Clay County in Tusquitee Mountains.

Carver Knob, s Madison County between Morrow Branch and Worley Cove.

Carver Mountain between Cope Creek and Blanton Branch in n central Jackson County. Alt. 3,600.

Carvers, community in se Bladen County.

Carvers Branch rises in s Mitchell County and flows sw into East Fork Crabtree Creek.

Carvers Creek rises in se Bladen County and flows e into Cape Fear River. Appears as Livingswood Creek on the Collet map, 1770.

Carvers Creek rises in n Cumberland County and flows se into Cape Fear River.

Carvers Creek, community in n Cumberland County.

Carvers Creek Township, in se Bladen County.

Carvers Creek Township, n central Cumberland County.

Carvers Falls, on Carver Creek, central Cumberland County, approx. 7 mi. ne of Fayetteville at the junction of the forks of Carver Creek near its mouth in the Cape Fear River.

Carvers Gap, on the Mitchell County, N.C.–Carter County, Tenn., line.

Carvers Gap Creek rises in e Mitchell County and flows se into Fall Creek.

Cary, town in w Wake County, settled about 1863 as the site of Frank Page's lumber operations and known as Page's Turnout or Page's Tavern. Later, when the railroad was built, it became Page's Siding. Inc. 1871 as Carey; named for Senator Samuel Fenton Carey

(1814–1900) of Ohio, a Prohibition leader. The spelling became Cary as early as 1899.

Cary Branch rises in sw Wake County and flows sw into Buckhorn Creek.

Cary Creek rises in w Wake County and flows sw into Chatham County, where it enters White-oak Creek.

Cary Flat Branch rises in e central Avery County and flows s into Wilson Creek.

Cary Township, w central Wake County.

Casar, town in n Cleveland County. Settled about 1870 and inc. 1903, but long inactive in municipal affairs. Alt. 1,145. Intended to be named for Julius Caesar but an error was made in the spelling.

Casar Township, former township in nw Cleveland County, now township no. 11.

Cascade, community in nw Guilford County served by post office, 1892–1903.

Cascade Branch rises in n Madison County and flows se into Spring Creek.

Cascade Creek rises in s Virginia and flows se into Rockingham County, where it enters Dan River. Named by William Byrd, surveyor of region in 1728, for small rapids near boundary.

Cascade Creek rises in w central Stokes County and flows nw into Dan River. Named for the falls in the creek. Mentioned by William Byrd in 1728.

Cascade Falls, on Cascade Creek, w central Stokes County in Hanging Rock State Park. From a high rock precipice, water falls about 200 ft. in an "Upper Cascade" and then falls another 60 ft. in a "Lower Cascade." The falls are s of Tories Den.

Cascade Lake, in e Transylvania County in Little River. Covers 150 acres and has max. depth of 75 ft. Used for hydroelectric power and recreation.

Cascoponung River. *See* Scuppernong River.

Case Camp Ridge, n Transylvania County, extends e in an arc from Pisgah Ridge to Case Ridge Gap.

Case Cove, the valley through which Wise Branch flows in sw Buncombe County.

Case Ridge Gap, in n Transylvania County at the e end of Case Camp Ridge.

Cases, community in w Rockingham County served by post office, 1882–1905.

Casey Bay, on Pamlico Sound side of Portsmouth Island w of community of Portsmouth, e Carteret County.

Casey Branch rises in sw Polk County and flows ne into Cove Creek.

Casey Island, in Pamlico Sound off Portsmouth Island, e Carteret County.

Cash Corner No. 2, community in s Pamlico County se of Arapahoe. Named because a store at the crossroads there sold goods cheaper for cash than on credit. *See also* Hollyville.

Cash Creek rises in w Henderson County and flows se into French Broad River.

Cashie Branch rises in n Jackson County and flows nw into Scott Creek.

Cashie Neck, swampy region of se Bertie County between the Roanoke and Cashie Rivers opposite Plymouth.

Cashie River (ca-SHY) rises in nw Bertie County and flows se into Batchelor Bay and Albemarle Sound. One of the few rivers in the state to have its complete course in one county, Cashie was originally named Kesiah, the present name being a gradual corruption. *See also* Connaritsa.

Cashiers (CA-shers), town in s Jackson County beside Cashiers Lake. Inc. 1927. Post office est. 1851 as Cashiers Valley; named changed to Cashiers in 1881. The origin of the name is uncertain, but there are many stories, some concerning a horse named Cash that grazed there. Other stories concern a hermit named Cashiers who lived there.

Cashiers Lake, an artificial lake in s Jackson County formed in 1922 on Chattooga River. Covers 30 acres, with a max. depth of 50 feet. Used for fishing, boating, and power generation. Named for nearby town of Cashiers.

Cashiers Township, s Jackson County.

Cashiers Valley. *See* Cashiers.

Cashoke Creek rises in se Bertie County and flows se into Cashie River.

Cason Old Field, community in s central Anson County. Named for local family.

Castalia, town in nw Nash County. Settled about 1850. Named about 1853 by David S. Richardson, local schoolmaster and native of Cornish, N.H., for Castalian Springs (of Greek mythology) located near Mount Parnassus. Alt. 319.

Castalia Township, nw Nash County.

Castle, The, an island of approx. 1/10 acre in the Pamlico River, w Beaufort County, about 350 yards offshore from the town of Washington. Site of shipbuilding activity in nineteenth century.

Castle Creek rises in n Person County and flows n into Hyco River.

Castle Dobbs. *See* Russellborough.

Castle Hayne, community in n New Hanover County. Est. by 1861 and known as Spring Garden for a number of years. Appears as such on the Colton map, 1861, and on other maps through the 1870s. By 1882 (Kerr map) it was called Castle Hayne. Named for Capt. Roger Haynes, who built a "castle" nearby prior to the Revolutionary War. Originally Castle Haynes but shortened to Castle Hayne by the railroad and later adopted by the post office. A 6,000-acre agricultural colony est. there by Hugh MacRae in the early twentieth century included a number of Dutch families. Produces commercial flowers and bulbs, vegetables, and chemicals. Alt. 20.

Castle of Thundertontrenck. *See* Lenox Castle.

Castletons Creek. *See* Raccoon Creek.

Castle Tryon. *See* Russellborough.

Castoria, community in n central Greene County. A noted pre–Civil War plantation house of the name still exists there and gave its name to the community. Probably named for Castor, one of the Greek mythological Dioscuri twins.

Casville, community in w Caswell County. Known as Dove's Crossroads until about 1962.

Caswell, community in n Jones County. Alt. 46.

Caswell. *See* Kinston.

Caswell. *See* Point Caswell.

Caswell Beach, the s beach front on Oak Island, se Brunswick County.

Caswell Branch rises in sw Warren County and flows s into Shocco Creek.

Caswell County was formed in 1777 from Orange County. In the n central section of the state, it is bounded by the state of Virginia and by Person, Orange, Alamance,

and Rockingham Counties. It was named for
Richard Caswell (1729–89), member of the
First Continental Congress, major general in
the Revolutionary War, and first governor of
the state of North Carolina. Area: 435 sq. mi.
County seat: Yanceyville, with an elevation
of 619 ft. Townships are Anderson, Dan
River, Hightowers, Leasburg, Locust Hill,
Milton, Pelham, Stony Creek, and Yanceyville.
Produces wheat, oats, corn, tobacco, live-
stock, hogs, textiles, meat, clothing, lumber,
crushed stone, and sand.

Caswell Court House. *See* Yanceyville.

Caswell District, one of the districts into which
Caswell County was divided at the time of
the 1790 census. It contained 201 heads of
families.

Caswells Branch. *See* Poorhouse Run.

Caswells Landing. *See* Hookerton.

Caswell Township, w Pender County.

Cataloochee, community on Cataloochee Creek
in w Haywood County. Now almost entirely
in Great Smoky Mountains National Park.
Alt. 2,620. Population formerly around 250.
Cataloochee is a corruption of the Indian
word *gad-a-lu-sti*, a descriptive exclamation
that means "standing in a row." It is what the
Indians saw from Cove Creek Gap—timber
standing up on the distant mountains near
the head of the watershed.

Cataloochee Balsam, mountain on the Haywood-Swain county line between Horse Creek
Gap and Pauls Gap. Alt. 5,940.

Cataloochee Creek is formed in w Haywood
County by the junction of Caldwell Fork and
Palmer Creek. It flows se and e into Waterville
Lake on Pigeon River.

Cataloochee Divide, w Haywood County, Great
Smoky Mountains National Park, extending
ne from Whim Knob. It forms the e boundary
of the park for more than 10 mi. It also marks
the Cataloochee Creek and Johnson Creek
drainage line.

Cataloochee Township, ne Haywood County.

Catawba, town in e Catawba County on the
Catawba River. Inc. 1893. Alt. 834. Post office first est. as Chestnut Grove in nearby
Iredell County, but the name was changed
to Catawba Station when it was moved to e
Catawba County in 1859. Became Catawba
in 1877.

Catawba County was formed in 1842 from Lincoln County. Located in the w central section
of the state, it is bounded by Iredell, Lincoln,
Burke, Caldwell, and Alexander Counties.
It was named for the Catawba Indians, who
once inhabited the region. Area: 412 sq. mi.
County seat: Newton, with an elevation of 996
ft. Townships are Bandy, Caldwell, Catawba,
Clines, Hickory, Jacobs Fork, Mountain
Creek, and Newton. Produces wheat, oats,
barley, hay, poultry, corn, cattle, hogs, hosiery, furniture, fiber-optic cable, textiles,
electronics, fabricated metals, lumber, paper
boxes, crushed stone, and brick.

Catawba Creek rises in central Gaston County
within the limits of Gastonia and flows se into
South Carolina, where it enters the Catawba
River near the state line.

Catawba Falls, on the headwaters of Catawba
River in sw McDowell County near Ridgecrest.
Water falls in a continuous spray down five
levels of rock. Sometimes called Rocky Glen
for one of the upper falls where water plunges
over a ledge 200 ft. high.

Catawba Ferry operated on Catawba River at
Lincoln-Mecklenburg county line in nw
Mecklenburg County.

Catawba Lake. *See* Lake Wylie.

Catawba Land. *See* Piedmont.

Catawba River rises in the Blue Ridge Mountains
in sw McDowell County near the Buncombe-
McDowell county line. It flows ne through
McDowell and e through Burke County;
forms successively the Caldwell-Catawba,
Alexander-Catawba, Iredell-Catawba,
Iredell-Lincoln, Mecklenburg-Lincoln, and
Mecklenburg-Gaston county lines. It enters
South Carolina w of Charlotte and flows s
to join Big Wateree Creek in Wateree Pond
to form the Wateree River about 20 mi.
above Camden. From its headwaters to the
South Carolina line, it flows approx. 150 mi.
Catawba was an Indian word that may have
meant "people of the river banks" or "people
of the river [Catawba] with broken banks."

For some of the named fords across the river, *see also* Beattie's, Cowan's, Island, Sherrills, Tools, and Tuckasege.

Catawba Springs, community in n Catawba County. Former resort, popular in late eighteenth and early nineteenth centuries. Est. as Elliott Springs on June 10, 1859, and became White Sulphur Springs on August 1, 1860. The Sparkling Catawba Springs Company was inc. in 1869 to erect buildings and open and maintain the mineral springs. Became Sparkling Catawba Springs in 1877.

Catawba Springs, popular pre–Civil War resort on Killian Creek, e Lincoln County. Owned by Capt. John Reid, Revolutionary soldier, and known first as Reid's Springs.

Catawba Springs Township, e Lincoln County.

Catawba Station. *See* Catawba.

Catawba Township, e Catawba County. Name changed in 1879 from Hamilton Township.

Catawba Vale. *See* Old Fort.

Cat Creek rises in e Macon County and flows nw into Rabbit Creek.

Catechna. *See* Snow Hill.

Cateechee Branch rises in e central Transylvania County and flows se into French Broad River.

Caterpillar Creek rises in se Alamance County and flows se into Orange County, where it enters Cane Creek.

Cates Creek rises in central Orange County and flows ne into Eno River.

Catfield Point, s Onslow County in Stones Bay.

Catfish, community in w Catawba County served by post office, 1886–1903.

Catfish Lake, a natural lake in Croatan National Forest, e Jones and sw Craven Counties. Covers 950 acres, with a max. depth of 4 to 5 ft. It is in the Lakes Pocosin, *which see*.

Catfish Point, e Tyrrell County, extends from the mainland into Alligator River.

Cat Gap, central Transylvania County near the head of King Creek.

Catharine Creek rises in e Hertford County and flows n into Chowan River. Undoubtedly a corruption of Cautaking, Catokinge, or Cataking, an Indian village of the sixteenth century located in the area. The Indian name probably meant "at the land that pushes" or "bulges out," as if into the river.

Catharine Lake, a natural lake in nw Onslow County. Covers approx. 45 acres, with a max. depth of 15 ft. Alt. 17. A community by the name existed as early as 1861, but the lake itself apparently is not shown on early maps. Local tradition says that it was named by John Avirette for his fiancée, Catharine Cole. Another source relates that it was named for the Cothran family in the vicinity.

Catherine Creek is formed on the Gates-Chowan county line by the junction of Trotman and Warwick Creeks and flows sw into Chowan River. Appears on the Collet map, 1770, as Catharines Creek.

Cathey, community in e Jackson County served by post office, 1883–1901.

Cathey Cove, s Haywood County on a tributary of Little East Fork Pigeon River.

Cathey Creek rises in nw Mecklenburg County and flows w into Davidson Creek.

Cathey Gap, e Haywood County between Rocky Knob and Pressly Mountain.

Cathey Gap, in the middle of Wolf Mountain, e Jackson County.

Cathey Ridge, s Haywood County between Cathey Cove and Hemlock Branch.

Cathey's, community in w Rowan County. Named for George Cathey, who had a grant of land there in 1750.

Catheys Creek rises in n Rutherford County and flows se into Second Broad River.

Catheys Creek rises in w Transylvania County and flows se into French Broad River.

Catheys Creek, community in central Transylvania County; centered on Limekiln Branch approx. 1 mi. nw of French Broad River. Named for Joseph Cathey (1803–74), one of the first settlers in the area. Alt. approx. 2,160.

Cathey's Creek. *See* Kerr Creek; Sloans Creek.

Catheys Creek Falls is located on Catheys Creek in central Transylvania County between King Mountain and Kagle Mountain. Falls are 40 ft. high. Alt. approx. 2,520.

Catheys Creek Township, central Transylvania County.

Cathey's Fort. *See* Woodlawn.

Cat Island, a small island in sw Carteret County in Bogue Sound.

Caton. *See* Zorah.

Cat Pen Branch rises in w Madison County and flows s into Roaring Fork.

Cat Pen Gap, n Transylvania County between Cat Gap and Horse Cove.

Cat Point, central Onslow County in Farnell Bay.

Cat Ridge, ne Transylvania County n of McCall Mountain.

Catskill Creek. *See* Catskin Creek.

Catskin Creek rises in s Pender County and flows sw into Merricks Creek. Formerly Catskill Creek until corrupted by local usage into present name.

Cat Square, crossroads community in nw Lincoln County. Named after unwanted cats and kittens were left there on several occasions.

Catstair Branch rises in ne Cherokee County and flows nw into Ashturn Branch.

Catstairs, The, a very rough and steep trail followed by wildcats from one mountain to another near the head of West Fork Overflow Creek in s Macon County. *See also* Winding Stairs for another use of the name.

Cattail Bay, a loam-filled bay in central Columbus County.

Cattail Branch rises in n Wilson County near Cliftonsville and flows s approx. 1 mi. into Toisnot Swamp.

Cattail Creek rises in central Granville County and flows sw into Tar River.

Cat Tail Creek rises in n Johnston County and flows se into Little River.

Cattail Creek is formed in s Yancey County by the junction of North Fork Cattail Creek and South Fork Cattail Creek. It flows nw into Cane River.

Cattail Peak, s Yancey County between Balsam Cone and Potato Hill in the Black Mountains. Alt. 6,583.

Cattail Swamp rises in n central Wilson County and flows e into Town Creek.

Causey. *See* Bonlee.

Cavanaugh Ditch, a drain in s Duplin County to carry the waters of Kenan Pocosin into Northeast Cape Fear River.

Ca-Vel, community in central Person County. Post office est. 1948. Formerly known as Bakers. Produces textiles.

Caves, The, natural subterranean caves in nw Rutherford County between Broad River and Buffalo Creek in Rumbling Bald Mountain, *which see.*

Cawcaw Bay, shallow mucky area about 5 mi. long and about 2 mi. wide near sw edge of Green Swamp, sw Brunswick County.

Cawcaw Swamp rises in Cawcaw Bay, sw Brunswick County, and flows sw into Waccamaw River.

Cecil, community in s Haywood County served by post office, 1898–1914.

Cecils Harbor appears on the Smith map, 1624, applied to the three bays in s Hyde County now called Rose Bay, Swanquarter Bay, and Juniper Bay. Perhaps named for William Cecil, Lord Burleigh (1520–98), or Robert Cecil, first Earl of Salisbury (1563?–1612).

Cecil Township, s Haywood County.

Cedar, community in nw Bladen County served by post office, 1882–1903.

Cedar Bay is formed by waters of Neuse River and the n tip of Carteret County.

Cedar Bay, in the waters of Currituck Sound on the nw side of Church Island in central Currituck County.

Cedar Bay, off the sw shore of Roanoke Island, e Dare County, in the waters of Croatan Sound.

Cedar Bay Point, a point on the s shore of the Neuse River about 4 mi. upstream from its mouth and n of the entrance to Cedar Bay in ne Carteret County.

Cedar Branch rises in central Columbus County and flows e into Soules Swamp.

Cedar Branch rises in se Wilson County and flows s approx. 3½ mi. into Black Creek.

Cedar Cliff, peak in the Great Craggy Mountains, ne Buncombe County, between Eagle Rock Cove and Wolf Branch. Alt. 4,400.

Cedar Cliff, peak in the Swannanoa Mountains, s Buncombe County. Alt. 3,846.

Cedar Cliff, e Haywood County between Panther Creek and Rust Fork.

Cedar Cliff, n Haywood County, extends e from Snowbird Creek to Bills Knob.

Cedar Cliff, on Jackson-Swain county line near junction of Chestnut Cove Creek and Connelly Creek in e Swain County.

Cedar Cliff, at the head of Shepherd Creek in n Macon County.

Cedar Cliff, s Macon County between Buckeye Creek and Hickory Knoll Creek.

Cedar Cliff, community in se Alamance County on Haw River. A post office operated there, 1877–1908.

Cedar Cliff Knob, ne Buncombe County w of Sheepwallow Knob.

Cedar Cliff Lake, central Jackson County on Tuckasegee River, 14 mi. s of Sylva. Covers 121 acres; max. depth 150 ft. Dam constructed 1952; used to generate hydroelectric power for Nantahala Power and Light Company. Named for Cedar Cliff Mountain at the upper end of the lake. Alt. 2,330.

Cedar Cliff Mountain, on Buncombe-Rutherford county line between Harris View and Cedar Knob. Alt. 3,829.

Cedar Cliff Mountain, central Jackson County between Cedar Valley Creek and Gladie Creek.

Cedar Cliff Mountain, s Macon County between Andy Gap and Buddy Gap. Alt. 4,824.

Cedar Cliff Ridge, n Macon County at the head of Shepherd Creek.

Cedar Cliff Ridge, ne Macon County parallel to Huckleberry Creek.

Cedar Cliffs, at the s end of Cullowhee Mountain in w Jackson County.

Cedar Cove, w Graham County between Cedar Top and Santeetlah Creek.

Cedar Creek rises in e Anson County and flows n into Pee Dee River.

Cedar Creek rises in se Buncombe County and flows se into Rutherford County, where it enters Cove Creek.

Cedar Creek rises in se Caldwell County on the slopes of Hibriten Mountain and flows e into Upper Little River at Cedar Valley.

Cedar Creek rises in n Carteret County and flows sw into Adams Creek.

Cedar Creek rises in s Cumberland County and flows sw into Cape Fear River.

Cedar Creek rises in w Franklin County and flows se into Tar River.

Cedar Creek rises in s Granville County and flows sw into Robertson Creek.

Cedar Creek rises in w Harnett County and flows ne into Cape Fear River.

Cedar Creek rises in s Jackson County and flows w into Lake Thorpe.

Cedar Creek rises in se Rowan County and flows ne for about 3 mi. into Yadkin River.

Cedar Creek rises in s Stanly County and flows se and ne into Lake Tillery.

Cedar Creek rises in n Wake County and flows ne into Neuse River.

Cedar Creek rises in s Yadkin County and flows s into Davie County, where it turns se to enter Dutchmans Creek. Approx. 13 mi. long.

Cedar Creek, community in s Cumberland County on the stream of the same name. Appears as Terebinthe on the Kerr map, 1882.

Cedar Creek Township, e central Cumberland County.

Cedar Falls, community in central Randolph County on Deep River. Inc. 1899; charter repealed 1901. Once known as Everett's Mill for Col. Benjamin Everett. The first cotton mill in the county, Sapona Cotton Mill, was built there in 1836. Produced underwear for Confederate troops.

Cedar Fork rises in ne Wake County and flows e into Little River at Mitchells Millpond. Also known as Cedar Prong of Little River.

Cedar Fork, community in e Duplin County.

Cedar Forks, community in w Northampton County.

Cedar Fork Township, former township in se Durham County. Combined with Patterson Township to form Triangle Township.

Cedar Fork Township, w Wake County.

Cedar Grove, community in nw Orange County. A post office was est. there in 1826.

Cedar Grove Township, nw Orange County.

Cedar Hammock, an island in Bogue Sound, sw Carteret County.

Cedar Hill, community in n Anson County.

Cedar Inlet, an inlet approx. in the middle of Core Banks in e Carteret County on Outer Banks.

Cedar Island, large island in ne Carteret County between West Bay and Core Sound. Appears on Moll map, 1729.

Cedar Island, a small island in Bogue Sound, s Carteret County.

Cedar Island, a two-acre uninhabited tidal-marsh island in Cedar Island Bay on the w side of Church Island, central Currituck County.

Cedar Island, in the waters of Roanoke Sound off the sw tip of Bodie Island, e Dare County.

Cedar Island, tidal-marsh island approx. ½ mi. long in n Pamlico County. Appears on the Lawson map, 1709, and the Moseley map, 1733.

Cedar Island, community on the island of the same name, ne Carteret County.

Cedar Island. *See* Smith Island.

Cedar Island Bay, approx. 4 mi. long and 1½ mi. wide, ne Carteret County. Bounded by Cedar Island, Back Bay, and Core Sound.

Cedar Island Bay, in the waters of Currituck Sound on the w side of Church Island in central Currituck County. Named for the small tidal-marsh island in the bay.

Cedar Island Point, ne Carteret County; easternmost point of Cedar Island on s side of entrance from Core Sound into Cedar Island Bay.

Cedar Island Township, on Pamlico and Core Sounds, ne Carteret County, formerly a part of Hunting Quarters (now Atlantic) Township.

Cedar Knob, on Buncombe-Rutherford county line s of Cedar Cliff.

Cedar Knob, e Macon County between the head of Indian Camp Branch and Walnut Creek.

Cedar Knob, w Madison County between Granger Mountain and Friezeland Creek.

Cedar Lodge, community in e Davidson County. Named for the home of John W. Thomas, founder of Thomasville, who lived there, 1825–52. A nineteenth-century post office serving the community was Fair Grove, a name by which the community is also sometimes known.

Cedar Mountain, a peak in the South Mountains, s Burke County. Alt. 2,160.

Cedar Mountain, sw Polk County. Alt. 2,200.

Cedar Mountain, community in se Transylvania County on Walker Creek near its junction with Little River, approx. 7 mi. se of town of Brevard. Includes former community of Loftis.

Cedar Point, a point extending from the n mainland of Carteret County into Neuse River.

Cedar Point, point of land in sw Carteret County extending into the mouth of White Oak River and Bogue Sound. Appears on the Moseley map, 1733.

Cedar Point, point of land on the w shore of Bodie Island in the waters of Roanoke Sound, a short distance n of Oregon Inlet, e Dare County.

Cedar Point, s Onslow County, extends into n Howards Bay.

Cedar Point, community in sw Carteret County.

Cedar Point Mountain, w Rockingham County near Mayo River. *See* Baughn Mountain.

Cedar Prong of Little River. *See* Cedar Fork.

Cedar Rock, e Transylvania County between Buck Forest and Little River.

Cedar Rock, community in e central Caldwell County named for cedar trees growing from a rock formation.

Cedar Rock, community in e Franklin County.

Cedar Rock Creek rises in w Transylvania County near Cedar Rock Mountain and flows n into Davidson River.

Cedar Rock Creek rises in w Transylvania County near Cedar Rock Mountain and flows sw into Catheys Creek.

Cedar Rock Mountain, w Randolph County.

Cedar Rock Mountain, n central Transylvania County between Sandy Gap and Butter Gap. Alt. 4,056.

Cedar Rock Township, former township in e Franklin County, now township no. 8.

Cedar Run. *See* Vashti.

Cedar Run Creek rises in ne Alexander County and flows s into South Yadkin River. Considered the head stream of South Yadkin River.

Cedar Swamp Creek rises in central Carteret County and flows ne into Newport River.

Cedar Top, mountain in w Graham County between Hooper Mill Creek and Hooper Cove. Alt. approx. 4,000.

Cedar Valley, community in s Caldwell County on Upper Little River.

Cedar Valley Creek rises in central Jackson County and flows sw into Tuckasegee River. Formerly known as Niggerskull Creek; name changed in 2006 by U.S. Board on Geographic Names.

Cedar Valley Knob, in central Jackson County between Cedar Valley Creek and Gladie Creek. Alt. 3,500. Formerly known as Niggerskull Mountain; name changed in 2006 by U.S. Board on Geographic Names.

Cefare, community in nw Wilson County between Turkey Creek and Marsh Swamp. Named for Cefare Bissett. A post office existed there, 1899–1904.

Ceffo, community in nw Person County. Served by post office, 1881–1907.

Celia Creek rises in sw Caldwell County and flows se into Husbands Creek. Originally named Sealeys Creek for George Sealey, eighteenth-century settler.

Celo, community in e Yancey County on Browns Creek. Alt. 2,735. Named for nearby Celo Knob.

Celo Knob, e Yancey County near the head of Browns Creek. Alt. 6,326.

Celo Ridge, e Yancey County between Ayles and

Browns creeks. Named for the Indian word *seeloo* (corn).

Cemetery Branch rises in central Wake County within the limits of Raleigh and flows n into Pigeon House Branch.

Center, community in w Davie County. Est. in the 1820s as a camp-meeting ground. A post office est. there operated under the name Selena in 1889–90; changed to Bailey, 1890–1902. Community retains original name.

Center, community in central Yadkin County. A post office there named Chestnut Ridge operated from 1857 to 1920.

Center, community in w Yadkin County e of Cranberry Creek.

Center Grove, community in central Granville County.

Center Grove Township, n central Guilford County.

Center of North Carolina. *See* Geographic Center.

Center Township, central Chatham County.

Center Township, se Stanly County.

Centerville, community in ne Franklin County. Alt. 300. Settled about 1882. Named because of its central position between Warrenton, Louisburg, and Littleton.

Centerville. *See* Kelly.

Central Falls, community on Deep River, central Randolph County. Long the site of one or more textile mills. Named for minor falls on the river, now obliterated by dams constructed for water power.

Central Township, central Bladen County.

Centre, community in s Guilford County. Named for Centre Friends Meeting, begun in 1757.

Centre Hill, town in e Chowan County. Inc. 1935, but no longer active in municipal affairs. A post office est. there in 1886 was first known as Centre Hill but was renamed for James N. Tyner (1826–1904), a former postmaster general. Tyner is still the post office name.

Cerro Gordo, town in w Columbus County. Inc. 1874 and named for the Mexican battleground where Gen. Winfield Scott, in 1847, was victorious. In Spanish the name means "big hill." Alt. 95.

Cerro Gordo Township, w Columbus County.

Chacandepeco. *See* Chancandepeco Inlet.

Chadbourn, town in n Columbus County. Inc. 1883. Named for a family of lumber mer-

chants. Produces lumber and textiles. Alt. 105.

Chadbourn Township, w central Columbus County.

Chadwick, former mill community in w Mecklenburg County.

Chadwick Acres, in s Onslow County on Chadwick Bay. Inc. 1961, but now inactive in municipal affairs. Planned as a resort development. Covers 308 acres.

Chadwick Bay, se Carteret County, the mouth of Chadwick Creek. Named for Samuel Chadwick, eighteenth-century whaler who lived in the vicinity.

Chadwick Bay, in s Onslow County in New River.

Chadwick Creek rises in s Carteret County and flows s into Chadwick Bay. Appears as Larler Creek on the Collet map, 1770.

Chadwick Creek rises in ne Pamlico County and flows se into Bay River.

Chafin, community in w Harnett County served by post office, 1890–1908.

Chainshot Island, ne Carteret County in Core Sound, midway between Hog Island and Harbor Island. Named for a kind of shot consisting of two balls or half balls united by a short chain, formerly used in naval warfare to cut a ship's rigging or to sweep its decks. Named as early as the Moseley map, 1733. *See also* Hunting Quarter Sound.

Chairmaker Branch rises in central Clay County and flows nw into Tusquitee Creek.

Chairman, community in ne Brunswick County.

Chalk Creek rises in n Rutherford County and flows sw into Cove Creek.

Chalk Level, community in n Harnett County served by post office, 1855–1908.

Chalk Mountain, s Mitchell County between Brushy Creek and North Toe River. Alt. 3,558.

Chalk Mountain. *See* Toms Mountain.

Chalybeate (ka-lib-e-ate), community in n Harnett County. Settled 1760. Named for nearby springs containing salts of iron. Former health resort. Alt. 175.

Chambers, community in sw Burke County.

Chambers Branch rises in e Haywood County on Chambers Mountain and flows s into Pigeon River.

Chambersburg Township, se Iredell County. Named for local Chambers family.

Chambers Cove, s Haywood County on a tributary of West Prong Pigeon River.

Chambers Creek rises in w Cherokee County and flows sw into Hiwassee Lake.

Chambers Creek rises in n Swain County and flows sw into Fontana Lake.

Chambers Creek Gap, n Swain County on Welch Ridge near the head of Bear Creek. Named for John Chambers, an early settler.

Chambers Mountain, e Haywood County, extends ne from the head of Long Branch to the head of Rogers Cove Creek.

Champion, community in sw Wilkes County near South Prong Lewis Fork Creek.

Chancandepeco Inlet, from the Atlantic Ocean into Pamlico Sound through Hatteras Island n of Cape Hatteras, se Dare County. Opened prior to 1585 and closed prior to 1657. Appears as Chacandepeco on the Velasco map, 1611. The name is possibly a Spanish spelling for an Algonquian Indian word meaning "it dips and disappears as shallows."

Chance, community in w Sampson County served by post office, 1889–1904.

Chandler, community in ne Montgomery County served by post office, 1875–1927. Known as Chandler's Grove until 1894.

Chandler Creek rises in e Madison County and flows se into California Creek.

Chandler Knob, n Madison County near the head of Revere Creek.

Chandler's Grove. *See* Chandler.

Chaney Creek rises in central Onslow County and flows sw into New River.

Chapanoke, community in e Perquimans County. Named for an Indian village, Chepanoc, the site of which probably is on Wade Point, Pasquotank County. The name apparently was an Indian word for "land of the dead." Alt. 15.

Chapel Branch rises in w Beaufort County and flows n into Bear Creek.

Chapel Branch rises in sw Hertford County and flows nw into Cutawhiskie Swamp. *See also* St. Johns (community).

Chapel Creek rises se of the town of Chapel Hill, se Orange County, and flows se into Morgan Creek.

Chapel Creek rises in n Pamlico County and flows s into Bay River.

Chapel Creek rises in s Pasquotank County and flows se into Big Flatty Creek.

Chapel Hill, town in se Orange County, seat of the University of North Carolina, which opened January 16, 1795. A committee to lay out the town was authorized by the trustees of the university on December 8, 1792, and lots were first sold on October 12, 1793. Appears on the Samuel Lewis map published in Carey's atlas in 1795. Inc. 1819. Named for the Church of England New Hope Chapel, which once stood at the crossroads on the wooded hill. Alt. 501.

Chapel Hill Township, se Orange County.

Chapel Swamp, nw Tyrrell County on the w side of Scuppernong River. Named for St. Paul's Church, which stood in the vicinity in the eighteenth century.

Chaplin's Stand. *See* Bixby.

Chapman, community in n Alexander County.

Chapmans Creek rises in central Surry County and flows se into Fisher River.

Chappel Creek appears on the Moseley map, 1733, rising in e Beaufort Precinct and flowing e into Machapungo River. The water course probably is either modern Jordan or Satterthwaite Creek.

Chappels Creek rises in s Person County and flows s into North Flat River.

Chappel Swamp, n Washington County on the head of Whites Creek, drains nw into Kendricks Creek.

Charity, community in s Duplin County.

Charity, community in n central Yadkin County. Named for Charity Baptist Church.

Charles, community in n central Iredell County.

Charles Creek rises in ne Mitchell County and flows sw into Little Rock Creek.

Charles Creek rises in w Transylvania County and flows se into Catheys Creek.

Charles Creek. *See* Muddy Creek.

Charles River. *See* Cape Fear River.

Charleston, community in se Halifax County.

Charleston. *See* Bryson City; Waughtown.

Charleston Township, e Swain County. Enlarged between 1934 and 1940 with the establishment of Great Smoky Mountains National Park to include the e part of Forneys Creek Township and all of Oconalufty Township.

Charles Town, center of a colony from Charlestowne, Mass., est. in 1662 under the leadership of William Hilton, on Town Creek, e Brunswick County. Abandoned in 1663. In 1664 a colony from Barbados under the leadership of Sir John Yeamans occupied the site, but they abandoned it in 1665. New Town on the Ogilby map, 1671, apparently was intended to designate the settlement. *See also* Clarendon County.

Charley Bald, a peak at the n end of Charley Ridge on Rich Mountain in e Jackson County. Alt. 5,530.

Charley Branch rises in w Madison County and flows se into Spring Creek.

Charley Branch rises in w Swain County and flows se into Wiggins Creek.

Charley Creek rises in e Jackson County and flows s into Wolf Creek.

Charley Knob, on the s end of Charley Ridge in e Jackson County.

Charley Ridge, e Jackson County between Gage Creek and Charley Creek.

Charlie Creek rises in n Yancey County and flows s into Little Creek.

Charlie Ridge, n Buncombe County w of Brittain Mountain.

Charlies Bunion Mountain, on Swain County, N.C.–Sevier County, Tenn., line in Great Smoky Mountains National Park. Alt. 5,375. So named because Charles Connor remarked to George Masa that the peak looked "like a bunion on Old Smoky's foot."

Charlies Island, a land formation in s Duplin County that is surrounded by swamp.

Charlies Ridge, on the Avery-Mitchell county line between Wolf Ridge and Spear Tops.

Charlone Creek. *See* Shelton Creek.

Charlotte, city and county seat, central Mecklenburg County. Settled about 1750; est. 1768. Named for Queen Charlotte Sophia of Mecklenburg-Strelitz (1744–1818), wife of George III. Appears as Charlottesburgh on the Collet map, 1770. Home of University of North Carolina at Charlotte, Queens University of Charlotte, Johnson C. Smith University, and Central Piedmont Community College. Center for banking services. Produces fabricated metals, textiles, dairy and bakery products, industrial machinery, canned foods, paper products, hosiery, processed meat, primary metals, aircraft parts, apparel, furniture, electronic components, boxes, and chemicals. Alt. 795.

Charlotte Branch rises in w Madison County and flows ne into Spring Branch.

Charlotte Cove, n Cherokee County between Moss Branch and Little Dam Branch.

Charlotte Crossing. *See* Claremont.

Charlottesburgh. *See* Charlotte.

Charlotte Township, former township in central Mecklenburg County, now township no. 1.

Charm, community in central Robeson County served by post office, 1888–1903.

Chasm Prong rises in n Swain County in Great Smoky Mountains National Park and flows e to join Gulf Prong in forming Bradley Fork.

Chasteen Creek rises in ne Swain County in Great Smoky Mountains National Park and flows sw into Bradley Fork.

Chasteen Mountain, sw Clay County between Trout Cove Branch and Greasy Creek.

Chastine Creek rises in e Jackson County and flows s into Caney Fork.

Chatham, community in sw Surry County served by post office, 1894–1906.

Chatham. *See* Pittsboro.

Chatham County was formed in 1771 from Orange County. Located in the central section of the state, it is bounded by Wake, Harnett, Lee, Moore, Randolph, Alamance, Orange, and Durham Counties. It was named for William Pitt, Earl of Chatham (1708–78), who vigorously opposed the harsh measures taken in England with regard to the American colonies in 1774–75 and who advocated cessation of hostilities in 1777. Area: 707 sq. mi. County seat: Pittsboro, with an elevation of 409 ft. Townships are Albright, Baldwin, Bear Creek, Cape Fear, Center, Gulf, Hadley, Haw River, Hickory Mountain, Matthew, New Hope, Oakland, and William. Produces wheat, oats, livestock, poultry, hay, corn, furniture, plywood, bricks, mobile homes, nursery products, textiles, hosiery, crushed stone, and clay for brick.

Chattoka, a Tuscarora Indian village appearing on the Lawson map, 1709, and the Moll map, 1729, between the Neuse and Trent Rivers, central Craven County. The name meant "where the fish are taken out." When the Tuscarora Indians moved to New York, they took the name with them and it has survived as Chautauqua.

Chattooga Ridge, s Jackson County, extends se in an arc from Little Terrapin Mountain to Heddie Mountain. The name is a variation of the Cherokee word *chatawga* (chicken).

Chattooga River rises in sw Jackson County and flows s to the Jackson-Macon county line, which it forms for a short distance before flowing into South Carolina, where it enters Savannah River.

Chatuge Lake, se Clay County on Hiwassee River. Created 1942 by a dam in the river at the mouth of Shooting Creek. Lake about 10 mi. long, covers over 8,000 acres; max. depth 144 ft. Forms a holding reservoir in the Tennessee Valley Authority system. Used for power, boating, swimming, and fishing.

Chawanoac, an Indian village near the junction of the present Chown-Gates-Hertford county lines on the Chowan River. Appears on the White map, 1585. *See also* Chowan.

Cheathamville. *See* Manson.

Cheaves, community in se Franklin County served by post office, 1898–1903.

Cheaves Mill, formerly a homestead and mill in sw Vance County located approx. a mile upstream from the mouth of Tabb Creek, below the junction of Long Creek. Appears on the Collet map, 1770.

Cheecods Creek. *See* Chicod Creek.

Cheek Creek rises in se Montgomery County and flows sw into Richmond County, where it enters Little River.

Cheek Creek Township, s central Montgomery County.

Cheek Mountain, grass-covered peak in the Peach Bottom Mountain range, w central Alleghany County.

Cheeks, community in se Randolph County on Deep River.

Cheeks Crossroads, community in w Orange County.

Cheeks Township, w central Orange County.

Cheeohwa. *See* Cheoah.

Cheeweo, a Tuscarora Indian village, appears on the Moseley map, 1733, on the Roanoke River. Site probably near the present town of Williamston in n central Martin County.

Chemway, community in w Mecklenburg County.

Cheney Bay, s Carteret County, lying between Turner Creek and North River Thorofare.

Cheoah, community in e central Graham County on Sweetwater Creek. Alt. 2,300. Named for the Indian word *tsiyahi* or *cheeohwa*, meaning "otter."

Cheoah Bald, on the Graham-Swain county line between Bellcollar Gap and Sassafras Gap. Alt. 5,062.

Cheoah Branch rises in nw Swain County and flows sw into Fontana Lake.

Cheoah Mountains extend across central Graham County e in an arc from the headwaters of Gladdens Creek to the headwaters of Sawyer Creek.

Cheoah River is formed in central Graham County by the junction of Sweetwater and Tulula Creeks. It flows nw into Little Tennessee River at Cheoah Dam. Santeetlah Lake is on Cheoah River.

Cheoah Township, s Graham County. *See also* Qualla Boundary.

Cheoah Valley. *See* Robbinsville.

Chepanuu, two Indian villages of the Weapemeoc tribe shown on the De Bry map, 1590, in what is now sw Pasquotank County on the Little River estuary.

Cheraw, community in central Caldwell County, named for the Cheraw (or Saura) Indians that formerly roamed the area.

Cherokee, town in e Swain County on Oconaluftee River that is the governmental and spiritual center of the Eastern Band of Cherokee Indians. Alt. 1,955. The name probably is from the Muskogee Indian word *tciloki*, meaning "people of a different speech." The outdoor drama Unto These Hills, written by Kermit Hunter, has been produced there each summer since 1950; the Museum of the Cherokee Indian and the Oconaluftee Indian Village Living History Museum are also there.

Cherokee County was formed in 1839 from Macon County. Located in the w section of the state, it is bounded by the states of Georgia and Tennessee and by Graham, Swain, Macon, and Clay Counties. It was named for the Cherokee Indians, some of whom still live in the region. Area: 467 sq. mi. County seat: Murphy, with an elevation of 1,535 ft. Townships are Beaverdam, Hot House, Murphy, Notla, Shoal Creek, and Valley Town. Produces corn, poultry, dairy products, livestock, hogs, hay, textiles, apparel, tools, lumber, marble, talc, and crushed stone.

Cherokee Creek rises in se Rutherford County and flows n into Second Broad River.

Cherokee Gap, on Jackson-Swain county line near Oconaluftee River.

Cherokee Indian Reservation. *See* Qualla Boundary.

Cherry, town in e Washington County on Scuppernong River. Inc. 1907. A post office from 1898 until 1908.

Cherry, community in e Wayne County between Nahunta Swamp and The Slough, settled prior to 1833. Name is a corruption of the former name, Sherard, by which it appears on the MacRae map, 1833, or Sherards Crossroads, as it was known as recently as 1915. Named for a local family that settled in the area in the eighteenth century.

Cherry Branch rises in nw Macon County and flows nw into Otter Creek.

Cherry Branch rises in n Swain County and flows w into Forney Creek.

Cherry Cove, s Haywood County on the head of Cherry Cove Creek.

Cherry Cove, sw Macon County at the head of Allison Creek.

Cherry Cove Branch rises in s Clay County and flows nw into Hothouse Branch.

Cherry Cove Branch rises in n Transylvania County and flows ne into Looking Glass Creek.

Cherry Cove Creek rises in s Haywood County and flows ne into Allen Creek.

Cherry Creek rises in n Haywood County and flows s into Cold Springs Creek.

Cherry Creek rises in central Henderson County and flows w into Mud Creek.

Cherry Creek rises in n Swain County and flows s into Right Fork.

Cherryfield, community in s Transylvania County between Morgan Mill Creek and Cherryfield Creek. Alt. 2,180.

Cherryfield Creek rises in w Transylvania County on s slopes of Three Forks Mountain and flows se into French Broad River.

Cherry Flats, e Haywood County on the head of Cove Creek.

Cherry Gap, on the Buncombe-Haywood county line between Grassy Gap and Boyd Mountain.

Cherry Gap, on the Haywood-Transylvania county line on Pisgah Ridge s of Bennett Gap.

Cherry Gap, on the Mitchell County, N.C.–Unicoi County, Tenn., line.

Cherry Gap, n Swain County near the nw end of Pilot Ridge, between North Fork [Chambers Creek] and Bear Creek.

Cherry Gap, w Watauga County w of Pond Branch.

Cherry Gap Branch rises in w Jackson County and flows w into Cullowhee Creek.

Cherry Glade, community in nw Pasquotank County.

Cherry Grove, community in sw Caswell County.

Cherry Grove, community in sw Columbus County.

Cherry Hill, plantation in s Warren County near the community of Inez, the home of George W. Alston. The house built in 1852 is still standing.

Cherry Knob, on Cullowhee Mountain in w Jackson County.

Cherry Knob, nw Swain County in Great Smoky Mountains National Park on the w side of Jenkins Trail Ridge and at the ne end of Big Fork Ridge. Alt. 4,420.

Cherry Lane, community in se Alleghany County, settled about 1838 and named for cherry tree–bordered lane leading to home of Frank Bryan. Alt. 2,810.

Cherry Lane Township, se Alleghany County.

Cherry Log Gap, n Buncombe County between Bald Knob and Little Snowball Mountain.

Cherry Log Ridge, s Yancey County between Left Prong South Toe River and Hemphill Creek.

Cherry Mountain, s Clay County, extends ne in an arc from Joe Knob. *See also* Davie Mountain; Joe Knob.

Cherry Mountain, mountain range in e Rutherford County. Called Flint Hill prior to the Civil War, when flint for rifles was obtained there. Acquired the name Cherry Mountain after the war when Amos Owens, Confederate veteran, made corn liquor and "cherry bounce" from cherry trees growing there. *See also* Sweezy Mountain.

Cherry Mountain, s Yancey County between

Middle Fork [Upper Creek] and South Fork [Upper Creek].

Cherry Orchard Branch rises in n Jackson County and flows nw into Hornbuckle Creek.

Cherry Point, a point of land extending into the Neuse River near the mouth of Hancock Creek in se Craven County.

Cherry Point Marine Air Station, se Craven County on Neuse River. Begun in July 1941; opened March 1942. On 12,000 acres, it is the largest Marine air station in the world. The Overhaul and Repair Department of the U.S. Marine Air Corps there is the largest industrial defense plant in the state. A small community, Cherry Point, existed there prior to the est. of the station. The town of Havelock is adjacent.

Cherry Pond, a marsh in central Duplin County.

Cherry Ridge Landing, s Tyrrell County on Alligator River approx. 2 mi. e of its confluence with Northwest Fork [Alligator River]. The Indian village Tramaskecooc, *which see*, was at or near the site.

Cherry Run rises in w Beaufort County and flows sw into Tranters Creek.

Cherryville, town in nw Gaston County. Post office est. there in 1854 as White Pine. Named changed to Cherryville in 1865; inc. 1872. Named for a row of cherry trees planted along an old rail fence parallel to the post road. Produces textiles. Alt. 971.

Cherryville Township, nw Gaston County.

Chesnut Ridge. *See* Wilson's Store.

Chesquau Branch rises in w Swain County and flows s into Fontana Lake.

Chesson, community in n central Washington County.

Chester Branch rises in s Jackson County and flows s into Fowler Creek.

Chesterfield, community in n central Burke County. Formerly known as Hoodsville.

Chesters Creek rises in w Carteret County and flows se into White Oak River.

Chestnut, community in w Catawba County served by post office, 1887–1904.

Chestnut Bald, on the Haywood-Transylvania county line between Devils Court House and Silvermine Bald. Alt. 6,040.

Chestnut Branch rises in n Clay County and flows ne into Tuni Creek.

Chestnut Branch rises in n Haywood County near lat. 35°45′15″ N., long. 83°09′45″ W., and flows e into Big Creek.

Chestnut Branch rises in n Mitchell County and flows e into Left Fork Bean Creek.

Chestnut Branch rises in e Watauga County and flows ne into Elk Creek.

Chestnut Branch rises in ne Yancey County and flows ne into Toe River.

Chestnut Cove, s Buncombe County sw of Truckwheel Mountain.

Chestnut Cove, the valley through which Chestnut Cove Branch flows in ne Buncombe County.

Chestnut Cove, e Swain County between Deep Gap and Camp Branch.

Chestnut Cove Branch rises in ne Buncombe County near Middle Mountain and flows w through Chestnut Cove into North Fork [Swannanoa River].

Chestnut Cove Creek rises in nw Haywood County and flows se into Big Creek.

Chestnut Cove Creek rises in e Swain County and flows ne into Connelly Creek.

Chestnut Cove Gap, s Buncombe County near Chestnut Cove.

Chestnut Cove Knob, on the Jackson-Macon county line.

Chestnut Cove Ridge, ne Buncombe County between Chestnut Cove and Big Cove.

Chestnut Creek rises near Candler Knob on the Buncombe-Henderson county line and flows n into Stony Fork.

Chestnut Creek rises in nw Transylvania County and flows s into Court House Creek.

Chestnut Crossroads. *See* Macon.

Chestnut Flat, a relatively level area in n Buncombe County near Coles Cove.

Chestnut Flat Cove, s Haywood County on Little East Fork Pigeon River.

Chestnut Flat Ridge, central Haywood County parallel to Laurel Branch.

Chestnut Flats, a relatively level area in se Buncombe County ne of Blue Rock Knob.

Chestnut Flats, a relatively level valley in ne Cherokee County near the head of Alfred Creek in the Valley River Mountains.

Chestnut Flats, central Haywood County on Chestnut Flat Ridge.

Chestnut Gap, on Buncombe-Madison county line between Little Sandy Mush Bald and North Fork Gap.

Chestnut Gap, on the Jackson-Macon county line.

Chestnut Gap, in w Macon County at the head of Pierce Creek.

Chestnut Gap Mountain, w Cherokee County extending se from Shoal Creek to Canedy Gap.

Chestnut Grove, community in sw Stokes County.

Chestnut Grove. *See* Catawba.

Chestnut Hill, community in ne Ashe County.

Chestnut Hill, former town in e central Rowan County immediately s of Salisbury and now a part of that city. Inc. 1863.

Chestnut Hill Township, ne Ashe County.

Chestnut Knob, n Buncombe County between Brank Mountain and Windy Gap.

Chestnut Knob, on the Graham County, N.C.–Monroe County, Tenn., line.

Chestnut Knob, w Macon County between Roaring Fork Creek and Jarrett Creek.

Chestnut Knob, ne Rutherford County.

Chestnut Knob, n central Transylvania County near the head of Shutin Branch. Alt. approx. 3,860.

Chestnut Knob, n Yancey County on Sugarloaf Mountain.

Chestnut Knob, s Yancey County near South Fork Upper Creek.

Chestnut Log Branch rises in central Cherokee County and flows s into Pace Branch.

Chestnut Log Gap, n Graham County between Tuskeegee Creek and Sawyer Creek.

Chestnut Log Spring Gap, on the Madison County, N.C.–Greene County, Tenn., line.

Chestnut Mountain, at the junction of Avery-Burke-Caldwell county lines. Alt. 3,173.

Chestnut Mountain, s Buncombe County s of Minehole Gap.

Chestnut Mountain, n central Caldwell County. Alt. 2,555.

Chestnut Mountain, s Caldwell County. Alt. 1,760.

Chestnut Mountain, n Cherokee County in the Unicoi Mountains. *See also* Hawk Knob.

Chestnut Mountain, e Haywood County between Burnett Cove and Hominy Creek.

Chestnut Mountain, central Jackson County between Shoal Creek and Little Trout Creek.

Chestnut Mountain, se Jackson County between Laurel Knob and Bald Rock Mountain. Alt. approx. 4,160.

Chestnut Mountain, s Macon County between Rattlesnake Ridge and the head of Nichols Branch.

Chestnut Mountain, se Macon County between Big Creek and the head of Cane Creek.

Chestnut Mountain, on the Madison-Yancey county line. Alt. 3,749.

Chestnut Mountain, s Polk County between Round Mountain and Tryon Mountain. Alt. approx. 2,100.

Chestnut Mountain, n Transylvania County on the head of Grogan Creek. Alt. approx. 3,700.

Chestnut Mountain, sw Transylvania County between Toxaway River and Horsepasture River. Alt. approx. 2,820.

Chestnut Mountain, w Transylvania County between North Fork Flat Creek and Morton Creek. Alt. approx. 3,340.

Chestnut Mountain, e central Watauga County s of the community of Meat Camp, extends se from South Fork New River. Alt. approx. 3,520.

Chestnut Mountain, n Wilkes County between Mulberry Creek and Herald Mountain.

Chestnut Mountain, ne Yancey County between the head of Chestnut Creek and Brush Creek.

Chestnut Oak Flats, level valley in w Avery County.

Chestnut Oak Ridge, w Avery County.

Chestnut Orchard Branch rises in n Haywood County and flows sw into Groundhog Creek.

Chestnut Orchard Branch rises in w Macon County and flows n into Choga Creek.

Chestnut Orchard Ridge, nw Cherokee County extending se from Bryson Lead to Turkey Pen Hollow and Copper Creek.

Chestnut Ridge, n central Avery County.

Chestnut Ridge, n Buncombe County between Reems Creek and Main Creek.

Chestnut Ridge, on the Cleveland-Gaston county line.

Chestnut Ridge, a high strip of ground in Big Pocosin in sw Gates County.

Chestnut Ridge, e Haywood County between Ugly Creek and Shining Creek.

Chestnut Ridge, se Haywood County between East Fork Pigeon River and the Haywood County line.

Chestnut Ridge, e Jackson County between Rough Fork Creek and Piney Mountain Creek.

Chestnut Ridge, se Macon County, extends s from Cullasaja River to Dog Mountain.

Chestnut Ridge, sw Macon County between Little Lyman Branch and Devils Prong.

Chestnut Ridge, nw McDowell County between Threemile and Cox Creeks.

Chestnut Ridge, ne Mitchell County between Feeding Ridge and Bearpen Creek.

Chestnut Ridge, ne Surry County between Rutledge Creek and the head of Big Creek.

Chestnut Ridge, n Swain County in Great Smoky Mountains National Park, extends sw from Little Chestnut Bald between Desolation Branch and Defeat Branch.

Chestnut Ridge, nw Yancey County near the head of Little Creek.

Chestnut Ridge. *See* Center.

Chestnut Ridge Creek rises in e Jackson County and flows sw into Piney Mountain Creek.

Chestnut Stamp Knob, n Clay County at the ne end of Evans Ridge.

Chestnut Top, on Buncombe-Henderson county line. Alt. 3,069.

Chestnutwood Ridge, w Avery County.

Chetola Lake, s Watauga County on Middle Fork [South Fork New River] n of town of Blowing Rock. Formed by a dam constructed in 1920; also fed by Stringfellow Branch. Covers 15 acres, with a max. depth of 20 ft.

Chicamacomico, the name given to three communities on n part of Outer Banks, e Dare County, s of Pea Island: formerly North Rodanthe, South Rodanthe, and Clarks, now known as Rodanthe, Waves, and Salvo.

Chicamacomico Banks, the name commonly given to Pea Island in e Dare County. The name appears on John Lawson's map, 1709, as Chickinnaccomac. A portion of the word is believed to be derived from an Algonquian word for "sinking-down sand."

Chicamacomico Coast Guard Station, in the community of Rodanthe on n Hatteras Island in e Dare County. Est. in 1874 as Lifesaving Station. Lifesaving Service and Revenue Cutter Service joined to form U.S. Coast Guard in 1915. Decommissioned, 1954.

Chickasaw Knobs, n Henderson County near Clear Creek. Alt. 2,686.

Chickehauk. *See* Kitty Hawk.

Chickinacommock. *See* New Inlet.

Chickinnaccomac. *See* Chicamacomico Banks.

Chickorack River. *See* South Creek.

Chicod. *See* Simpson.

Chicod Creek rises in w Beaufort County and flows nw into Pitt County, where it enters Tar River. Appears as Cheecods Creek on the Collet map, 1770.

Chicod Township, se Pitt County.

Chicora, a name applied to the Carolina coastal area, probably from the Cape Fear River to the Savannah River, explored by the Spaniard Louis Vázques de Ayllón in 1526.

Chiking Indian Fort was referred to in grants made in 1730 for land in what is now Greene County. It was located 3 to 4 mi. downstream from Hookerton, se Greene County, on the n side of Contentnea Creek, approx. ¾ mi. above the mouth of Polecat Branch.

Childsburgh. *See* Hillsborough.

Chiloe, community in central Moore County served by post office, 1891–1907.

Chiltoes Mountain, on Haywood-Swain county line in Great Smoky Mountains National Park. Located at ne end of Balsam Mountain near lat. 35°35′56″ N., long. 83°11′09″ W. Alt. 5,888.

Chiltoskie Ridge. *See* Balsam Mountain.

Chimney Creek rises in n Madison County and flows e into Big Creek.

Chimney End Ridge, e Mitchell County between Reuben Creek and Powers Branch.

Chimney Knob, s Macon County between Carpenters Branch and Jones Creek.

Chimney Mountain, nw Burke County. Alt. 3,657. Known by the Cherokee Indians as Connatara.

Chimney Rock, a resort community in w Rutherford County s of Broad River. Named for nearby granite monolith rising 225 ft. from the shoulder of Chimney Rock Mountain and overlooking Hickory Nut Gorge (*see* Hickory Nut Gap) and Lake Lure. Alt. 1,050. A post office by the name existed there as early as 1843. Long owned by the Morse family, monolith and surrounding area were acquired for a state park in 2007.

Chimney Rock Mountain, w Rutherford County.

Chimney Rock Township, w Rutherford County.

Chimney Top, peak on Piney Mountain, w central Polk County. Ostin Creek rises there. Alt. 1,500.

Chimneytop Mountain, in s Jackson County 1 mi. e of Hampton Lake and s of Rocky Mountain. Alt. 4,618. Known by the Cherokee Indians as *Kayoo-lanta* (a chimney).

China Creek rises in s Watauga County about

1 mi. w of town of Blowing Rock and flows s into Thunderhole Creek in n Caldwell County.

China Grove, town in s Rowan County. Post office est. there in 1823; name changed to Luthersville in 1846, but in 1849 it was changed back to China Grove. Named for chinaberry trees growing there. Inc. 1889. Alt. 867.

China Grove Township, s Rowan County.

China Hill, community in sw Mecklenburg County served by post office, 1829–40.

Chinkapin Creek rises in ne Bertie County and flows ne into Hertford County, where it turns n to enter Wiccacon River. Appears on the Moseley map, 1733.

Chinkapin Creek rises in n Union County and flows se into Stewarts Creek.

Chinquapin, community in se Duplin County, 1 mi. e of Northeast Cape Fear River. Name is an Algonquian Indian word for a kind of small chestnut. Produces tobacco, corn, and poultry. Birthplace of Caleb Bradham, inventor of Pepsi-Cola.

Chinquapin Branch rises in e Haywood County and flows sw into Pisgah Creek.

Chinquapin Branch rises in w Jones County and flows e 4½ mi. to empty into Trent River. Also known as Big Chinquapin Branch.

Chinquapin Creek rises in w Stokes County and flows sw into Surry County, where it enters Toms Creek.

Chinquapin Creek rises in s Yadkin County and flows s into n Davie County, where it turns sw to flow into Dutchmans Creek.

Chinquapin Cross Roads. *See* Courtney.

Chinquapin Mountain, s Macon County between East Fork Overflow Creek and Little Scaly Mountain.

Chinquapin Mountain, central Transylvania County between Gladys Branch and Country Club Lake.

Chinquapin Ridge, high ground in Pantego Swamp, e Beaufort County.

Chinquapin Ridge, a loamy section in n Pitt County between Great Swamp and Gum Pond (swamp).

Chinquapin Township, w Jones County.

Chip, community in ne Craven County.

Chip, community in s Montgomery County between Thickety Creek and Little River. Served by post office, 1920–32. Likely named for byproducts of local sawmills.

Chisholm's Store. *See* Pekin.

Chiska Creek rises in w central Bertie County and flows e into Cashie River. Hills Mill on the creek is shown on the Collet map, 1770, but not on later maps.

Chisman, community in se Stokes County.

Chockeyotte, town in n Halifax County. Inc. 1901.

Chockoyotte Creek rises in n Halifax County and flows se into Roanoke River. Name believed to be a Tuscarora Indian word. A stone aqueduct, part of the pre–Civil War Roanoke Navigation Canal, remains over the creek. It appears as Chocolate Creek on the Collet map, 1770.

Chocolate Creek rises in se Guilford County and flows ne into Stinking Quarter Creek.

Chocolate Creek. *See* Chockoyotte Creek.

Chocolate Drop Mountain. *See* Foster Mountain.

Chocowinity, town in w Beaufort County. Known as Godleys Crossroads until renamed for nearby creek. Inc. 1917; charter repealed 1947; reincorporated 1959. Railroad station name was Marsden, adopted in 1917 for Marsden J. Perry, a railroad official. Alt. 35.

Chocowinity Bay formed by the mouth of Chocowinity Creek in Pamlico River, w Beaufort County.

Chocowinity Creek rises in sw Beaufort County and flows n into Chocowinity Bay and Pamlico River. Called Worsley Creek on the Collet map, 1770; by 1808 (Price's map) it was called by its present name, though MacRae's map in 1833 called it Chocowinity Swamp. The name is said to be Indian in origin and to mean "fish from many waters."

Chocowinity Swamp. *See* Chocowinity Creek.

Chocowinity Township, sw Beaufort County.

Choffington, traditional site of the first courthouse of Cumberland County, located at the mouth of Little River near the present site of Linden in the n part of the county. The courthouse was there from 1755 until it was moved to Campbellton in 1765. The name may be derived from the old English word "chuff," meaning a rustic or rude, coarse fellow, and may have been applied by people of English descent to the recently arrived Scots.

Choga Creek rises in w Macon County and flows ne into Nantahala Lake.

Choggy Butte Mountain, in e Jackson County on the head of Mull Creek.

Chokeberry Branch rises in n Swain County and flows w into Forney Creek.

Choowatic Creek rises in se Bertie County and flows e into Roquist Creek.

Choratuck Inlet. *See* Currituck Inlet.

Chowan, an Indian town, shown on the Moseley map, 1733, as lying in the s central part of present Gates County between Bennetts Creek and Trotman Creek.

Chowan Beach, on Chowan River s of the mouth of Meherrin River on the e border of Hertford County. First named Mount Gallant for John Gallant, who operated a ferry there about 1720. Known as Mount Zion in the latter half of the eighteenth century.

Chowan Beach. *See* Mount Gallant.

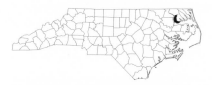

Chowan County was formed by 1668 as Shaftesbury Precinct of Albemarle County. Renamed Chowan Precinct about 1681. Located in the ne section of the state, it is bounded by Albemarle Sound, Chowan River, and Bertie, Hertford, Gates, and Perquimans Counties. It was named for the Chowan River. Area: 234 sq. mi. County seat: Edenton, with an elevation of 16 ft. Townships are nos. 1–4, formerly Edenton, Middle, Upper, and Yeopim. Produces corn, soybeans, peanuts, cotton, hogs, textiles, tires, boats, sweet potatoes, sorghum, cantaloupes, lumber, and processed seafood.

Chowanoke. *See* Croatoan Island.

Chowan River is formed on the Hertford-Gates county line a short distance s of the Virginia state line by the junction of the Nottoway and Blackwater Rivers. It flows se on the Hertford-Gates and Bertie-Chowan county lines into Albemarle Sound. Named for the Chowanoc tribe of Indians who lived in the area. The word is a variant of the Algonquian *sorwán* (south). It may have derived from *sowánohke* (south country). The river was referred to by the Roanoke explorers, 1584–85, but given no specific name except as the location of the tribe. Appears as Choan River on the Comberford map, 1657.

Chrissawn Knob, se Yancey County on South Toe River near the mouth of Rock Creek.

Christ Branch. *See* Banjo Branch.

Christ-Church Parish. *See* Craven Parish.

Christian Creek rises in se Buncombe County and flows nw into Swannanoa River.

Christie Ford. *See* Murphy.

Chronicle, community in se Catawba County. Est. 1857. Named for Maj. William Chronicle, killed at Battle of Kings Mountain. Alt. 1,048.

Chublake, community in central Person County served by post office, 1884–1905.

Chuckle, community in n Wilkes County near East Prong Roaring River.

Chum Creek rises in ne Rutherford County and flows s into Duncans Creek.

Chunky Gal Mountain, se Clay County, extending se from Riley Knob to Big Laurel. Alt. 4,986. Named by slim Indian maidens who delighted in the capture (by her father) of a heavyset Indian lass who had run away to marry a young brave against her family's wishes.

Chunky Pipe Creek rises in central Durham County and flows e into Little Lick Creek.

Chunn Cove, central Buncombe County near the headwaters of Ross Creek.

Chunn Cove Creek. *See* Ross Creek.

Church Branch rises in central Clay County and flows s between Matlock Creek and Moores Branch into Tusquitee Creek.

Churchill, community in ne Warren County. Post office est. there in 1884 but discontinued in 1905.

Church Island, a peninsula in e Currituck County extending into Currituck Sound. Coinjock Bay lies between its w shore and the mainland of the county. It is 5 mi. long, 1 mi. wide. Shown as Emperors Island on the Comberford map, 1657; as White Island on the Ogilby map, 1671; and as Church Island on the Moseley map, 1733. The w portion of the peninsula is known as Piney Island.

Churchland, community in w Davidson County.

Churchville, community in sw Montgomery County served by post office, 1830–36.

Cid, community in e Davidson County. Est. 1885. Named either for Sidney Muffley, superintendent of silver mine nearby; or for Cid, Scotland, by miners who came from there.

Cilley. *See* German's Hill.

Cindy Branch rises in central Cherokee County and flows se into Morgan Creek.

Cindy Edwards Branch rises in sw Beaufort County and flows w into Chocowinity Creek.

Cipo River. *See* Pamlico River.

Cisco, community in central Chowan County served by post office, 1891–1907.

Cisco Cove, central Buncombe County s of Cisco Mountain.

Cisco Mountain, central Buncombe County between Piney Mountain and Randall Gap.

Citron, community in sw Alleghany County. Known as City until some time after 1918.

Citte Weeks Branch, stream about 3 mi. long, rises in w Carteret County and flows w into White Oak River. Also known as Godfrey Branch.

Cittys Store, community in se Rockingham County.

City. *See* Citron.

Clabber Branch rises in sw Clay County and flows se into Pinelog Creek.

Clam Shoal, in the waters of Pamlico Sound, s Dare County, off the s part of Hatteras Island. Bird Islands are on Clam Shoal.

Clanpit Cove, on Burningtown Creek in central Macon County.

Clara, community in sw Stokes County served by post office, 1888–1904.

Claremont, town in ne Catawba County. The earliest name was Charlotte Crossing; later Setzer's Depot. Changed to Claremont in 1892. Inc. 1893. Alt. 969. Named for Clare Sigmon, daughter of Jones Sigmon, an early settler. Produced furniture.

Clarendon, community in e Brunswick County.

Clarendon, community in sw Columbus County. Inc. 1907 as a town; charter repealed 1921.

Clarendon County, one of 3 counties (Albemarle and Craven being the other two) set up in 1664 by the Lords Proprietors of Carolina. It embraced the territory around the mouth of Cape Fear River (then known as Charles River). Named for Edward Hyde (1609–74), Earl of Clarendon, one of the Lords Proprietors. *See also* Charles Town, a settlement that existed in the colony, 1662–65.

Clarendon River. *See* Cape Fear River.

Clargeons Creek. *See* Yeopim Creek.

Clarissa, community in e Mitchell County on Cane Creek.

Clark, community in w Haywood County.

Clark Branch rises in n central Buncombe County and flows nw into Flat Creek.

Clark Branch rises near Yellow Mountain in nw Buncombe County and flows se into Sandy Mush Creek.

Clark Branch rises in w Swain County and flows se into Fontana Lake.

Clark Creek rises in n Catawba County and flows se and sw through Catawba County into Lincoln County, where it enters South Fork Catawba River.

Clark Creek, on Goose Creek Island, ne Pamlico County, flows nw between Mouse Harbor on the e and Pamlico River on the w.

Clark Creek rises in s Watauga County and flows n into Dutch Creek.

Clarke Creek rises in ne Mecklenburg County and flows se into w Cabarrus County, where it enters Rocky River. Named for a family of early settlers, one of whom was scalped by Indians.

Clark Gap, between Cunningham Mountain and Couch Mountain in n Henderson County.

Clark Point, point of land extending into Goose Creek, se Beaufort County.

Clarks, community in central Craven County. Alt. 31.

Clarks. *See* Salvo.

Clarks Bay, a small bay in the waters of Pamlico Sound off n Hatteras Island, e Dare County s of Salvo.

Clarksberry, community in nw Rockingham County served by post office, 1857–66. Named for local Methodist church.

Clarks Branch rises in a small pond in s central Brunswick County and flows s into Lockwoods Folly River.

Clarks Creek is formed in n Mecklenburg County by the junction of North Prong and South Prong. It flows e into Cabarrus County, where it enters Rocky River.

Clarks Creek rises in w Montgomery County and flows sw into Pee Dee River.

Clarks Island, a small tidal-marsh island off the se tip of Eagles Island in the Cape Fear River, ne Brunswick County.

Clarks Little River. *See* Upper Little River.

Clarks Mills, community in se Montgomery County served by post office, 1885–1902.

Clarks Mountain, e central Anson County. Alt. approx. 525.

Clarks Store. *See* Blountsville.

Clarksville, community in nw Davie County. John Pinchback operated Burnt Tavern or Pinchback's Tavern nearby after 1797. Before the Civil War, the stagecoach from Salem to Statesville stopped there for the night. Hinton Rowan Helper (1829–1909), author of *The Impending Crisis* (1857), was born nearby on a farm on Bear Creek. A post office operated there from 1855 until 1869.

Clarksville. *See* Salvo.

Clarksville Township, nw Davie County.

Clarkton, town in s Bladen County. Alt. 93. Inc. 1901. Known earlier as Brown Marsh Station and Dalton. Renamed after 1863 for John Hector Clark (1821–98).

Clarrissa, community in s Mitchell County served by post office, 1887–1952.

Clawhammer Cove, n Transylvania County, extends s from Clawhammer Mountain to Avery Creek.

Clawhammer Creek rises in n Transylvania County and flows e into South Fork Mills River.

Clawhammer Mountain, in n Transylvania County between Clawhammer Cove and Clawhammer Creek.

Clay, community in e Granville County.

Clay. *See* Linville.

Claybrook, community in nw Rockingham County served by post office, 1890–95.

Clay County was formed in 1861 from Cherokee County. In the w section of the state, it is bounded by the state of Georgia and by Cherokee and Macon Counties. It was named for Kentucky senator Henry Clay (1777–1852). Area: 219 sq. mi. County seat: Hayesville, with an elevation of 1,893 ft. Townships are Brasstown, Hayesville, Hiwassee, Shooting Creek, Sweetwater, and Tusquittee. Produces corn, cable, cattle, hay, poultry, lumber, and apparel.

Clay Fork, community in se Cumberland County served by post office, 1875–1906.

Clay Knob. *See* Nigger Head.

Claypole Branch rises in s Transylvania County and flows ne into Middle Fork French Broad River.

Clayroot, community in se Pitt County.

Clayroot Swamp rises in se Pitt County and flows sw and se into Swift Creek. For a part of its course, it forms the boundary between Craven and Pitt Counties.

Clayton, town in nw Johnston County. Inc. 1869. Known previously as Stallings Station. Named for a local school, Clayton Academy, or for Senator John M. Clayton (1796–1856) of Delaware, coauthor of the Clayton-Bulwer Treaty of 1850 with Great Britain. Alt. 345. Produces textiles and apparel.

Clayton Bay, swamp nw Brunswick County. A part of Green Swamp.

Clayton Branch rises in se Cherokee County and flows nw into Little Brasstown Creek.

Clayton Creek rises in s Buncombe County and flows ne into French Broad River.

Clayton Hall. *See* Rocky Point.

Clayton Township, nw Johnston County.

Clear Branch rises in n central Avery County and flows ne into Elk River.

Clear Branch rises in se Buncombe County and flows sw into Broad River.

Clear Branch rises in e Columbus County and flows se on the Brunswick-Columbus county line into Honey Island Swamp.

Clear Branch rises in Green Swamp in e central Columbus County and flows se into Big Swamp. For a little over 2 mi., it forms a part of the boundary between Brunswick and Columbus Counties.

Clear Branch rises in nw Macon County and flows s into Queens Creek.

Clear Branch rises in sw Macon County and flows ne into Lowery Creek.

Clear Branch rises in s Madison County and flows ne into Little Sandymush Creek.

Clear Branch rises in e Watauga County and flows se into Elk Creek.

Clear Creek rises in s Avery County near Doe Hill Mountain and flows sw into North Toe River.

Clear Creek rises in w Avery County near Little Buck Hill and flows s into North Toe River.

Clear Creek rises in sw Burke County and flows n into Silver Creek.

Clear Creek rises in ne Clay County and flows ne into Nantahala River.

Clear Creek rises in e Henderson County and

flows sw into Mud Creek. Known by the Cherokee Indians as *Os-quee-ha-ha*.

Clear Creek rises in se Macon County and flows se into Georgia, where it enters West Fork [Chatooga River].

Clear Creek rises in w McDowell County and flows se into Catawba River.

Clear Creek rises in e Mecklenburg County and flows e into s Cabarrus County and then sw into n Union County, where it enters Rocky River at coincident corners of Cabarrus, Stanly, and Union Counties. Formerly known as Red Creek.

Clear Creek rises in Greenville County, S.C., and flows ne into Transylvania County, where it enters Little River.

Clear Creek rises in se Yancey County and flows w into South Toe River.

Clear Creek, community in s Cabarrus County.

Clear Creek, community in w Mecklenburg County. Later known as Candon, *which see*.

Clear Creek Ridge, s Yancey County, extends ne from South Toe River to East Branch.

Clear Creek Township, ne Henderson County.

Clear Creek Township, former township in e Mecklenburg County, now township no. 6.

Clear Pond, natural lake in se Brunswick County. Max. depth 12 ft.; 2 acres in area.

Clear Run, community in s Sampson County on Black River.

Clear Run Swamp rises in se Sampson County and flows sw into Black River.

Clear View, community in e New Hanover County.

Cleaveland County. *See* Cleveland County.

Clegg, community in s Durham County.

Cleghorn Creek rises in w central Rutherford County and flows sw into Broad River. The name occurs in deeds as early as 1764; perhaps named for John Cleghorn, pioneer settler.

Cleghorn Mountain, n Rutherford County at the head of Catheys Creek.

Clement, community in w Sampson County near Jones Swamp.

Clement Grove, park setting in Mocksville, Davie County. Site of annual Masonic picnic, benefit for Oxford orphanage since 1883. Land once belonged to Herbert Clement.

Clements Creek. *See* Blanket Creek.

Clemmons, town in sw Forsyth County. Known as Clemmonstown as early as 1816; inc.

1824 as Clemmonsville but later known simply as Clemmons. Alt. 792. Named for Peter Clemmons, who moved there from Delaware in 1777. Clemmons was the author of *Poor Peter's Call to His Children*, printed in Salisbury in 1812.

Clemmonsville Township, sw Forsyth County.

Clems Beech Ridge, e Jackson County between Oak Ridge Creek and Chestnut Ridge Creek.

Clems Branch flows through sw Mecklenburg County and into South Carolina.

Cleone, community in w Union County served by post office, 1886–1905.

Cleveland, town in w Rowan County. Inc. 1883 as Third Creek; name changed in 1887 to honor Grover Cleveland (1837–1908), president of the United States. Alt. 788.

Cleveland County was formed in 1841 from Rutherford and Lincoln Counties. Cleaveland was originally used, but the present spelling was adopted in 1887. In the sw section of the state, it is bounded by the state of South Carolina and by Rutherford, Burke, Lincoln, and Gaston Counties. It was named for Col. Benjamin Cleveland (1738–1806), noted partisan leader of the w frontier and one of the heroes of the Battle of Kings Mountain. Area: 466 sq. mi. County seat: Shelby, with an elevation of 85 ft. Townships, now numbered 1 to 11, were formerly River, Boiling Springs, Rippys, Kings Mountain, Warlick, Shelby, Sandy Run, Polkville, Double Shoals, Knob Creek, and Casar. Produces wheat, oats, corn, dairy products, hogs, livestock, poultry, soybeans, nursery products, squash, honey, glass products, textiles, bakery products, limestone, and mica.

Cleveland Mills, inc. 1877 as a town between Lawndale and Casar in n central Cleveland County. No longer in existence.

Cleveland Township, w Johnston County.

Cleveland Township, nw Rowan County.

Clifdale, community in w Cumberland County. Formerly known as Clifton. Alt. 237.

Cliff Branch rises in n Swain County and flows ne into Oconaluftee River.

Cliffield Mountain, on the Polk-Henderson county line.

Clifford, community in e Rutherford County served by post office, 1891–1901.

Cliffs. *See* Rhodhiss.

Cliffside, community in se Rutherford County on Second Broad River. Founded by Raleigh B. Haynes, who est. a textile mill there. High Shoals, former community in the vicinity, was a post office as early as 1828.

Cliffside Lake, at the junction of South Skitty Branch and Skitty Creek in se Macon County.

Cliffs of the Neuse State Park, se Wayne County. Est. 1945 on 355 acres given to the state by the Weil family of Goldsboro and others. Cliffs 90 ft. above the Neuse River are an unusual geological feature in e North Carolina. Galax, laurel, and other mountain plants grow there. It is a scenic and recreational park with a nature museum, trails, etc. Swimming and fishing.

Clifton, community in central Ashe County. Alt. approx. 2,900.

Clifton. *See* Clifdale.

Cliftons Pond, on Crooked Creek in sw Franklin County. Formed about 1890. Covers approx. 55 acres. Max. depth 16 ft. Named for owners.

Clifton Township, nw Ashe County.

Cliftonville, community in n Wilson County near the head of Cattail Branch. Named for Clifton Parker. Post office, 1895–1902.

Climax, community in se Guilford County. Alt. 824. Est. 1853. Named for its location on high ground.

Clinchcross, community in e McDowell County. Probably named for the nearby Clinchfield Railroad.

Cline Creek rises in central Catawba County and flows sw into Clark Creek.

Cline Mine, former copper and gold mine near the community of Watts Crossroads, ne Cabarrus County approx. 8 mi. ne of Concord. Last worked about 1901–1902; later explored by the U.S. Bureau of Mines and by the Tennessee Copper Company.

Clines Township, n Catawba County.

Clingman, community in e Wilkes County near West Swan Creek. Named for Senator Thomas L. Clingman (1812–97). Known also as Frog Level.

Clingman Mine Branch rises in n Avery County and flows e into Buckeye Creek on the Avery-Watauga county line.

Clingmans Creek rises in n Swain County near Clingmans Dome and flows se into Noland Creek.

Clingmans Dome, mountain on the Swain County, N.C.–Sevier County, Tenn., line in Great Smoky Mountains National Park. Named approx. 1860 by Harvard professor Arnold Guyot for Thomas L. Clingman (1812–97), member of the party that first measured it in 1858. Clingman was a soldier, mountain climber, geologist, congressman, and senator from North Carolina. Alt. 6,642, the highest point in the park. A 45-ft. observation tower has been built at the peak. Known to the Indians as *Ku-wa-hi*, meaning "mulberry place." Early settlers called it Smoky Dome.

Clinton, former town in se Davie County (then Rowan) at the junction of South Yadkin and North Yadkin Rivers. Inc. 1818 by Yadkin Navigation Co. About 100 lots were sold before a panic in 1819 stopped work at the site. A post office existed there in 1822, but the town was abandoned soon afterward.

Clinton, town and county seat, central Sampson County. Authorized to be laid out, 1818; inc. 1822. Courthouse est. there about 1784 on land owned by Richard Clinton (1721–96), for whom the town was later named. Alt. 158.

Clinton Township, former township in central Sampson County, now divided into North Clinton and South Clinton Townships.

Clio, community in e central Iredell County. Site of Clio's Nursery, a classical school est. in 1778 by Rev. James Hall (1744–1826). His attempt to make the sciences a part of academic training was the first in North Carolina.

Clontz Branch rises in w Haywood County and flows nw into Caldwell Fork.

Closs, community in e Lenoir County. A post office from 1888 to 1905.

Clotho, community in ne Transylvania County served by post office, 1887–1906.

Cloudland, community in ne Mitchell County on ne Roan Mountain.

Clover Branch rises in nw Madison County and flows n into French Broad River.

Cloverdale, community in n Henderson County.

Clover Garden, former community in sw Orange

County near Haw River. A post office was est. there as early as 1822. Clover Garden Methodist Church is there.

Clover Orchard, community in s Alamance County served by post office, 1849–1906.

Clubfoot Canal, about 2½ mi. long extending from the head of Clubfoot Creek to the head of Harlowe Creek, n Carteret County and n Craven County, affording a waterway from the Neuse River to Newport River. Planned 1797; completed about 1828.

Clubfoot Creek rises near the Carteret-Craven county line and flows n into Neuse River. A canal connects the stream with Harlowe Creek in central Carteret County, affording a waterway from the Neuse River to Newport River. Appears on the Moseley map, 1733. The Indian name for the stream was Irisquoque.

Club Gap, n Transylvania County at the sw end of Rich Mountain.

Club Lake, se Macon County on Monger Creek.

Clum, community in sw Chowan County served by post office, 1897–1902.

Clun Seat, 10,000-acre estate in se Warren County between Great Fishing and Shocco Creeks. Granted to Edward Moseley in 1728, and after his death in 1749, sold by his sons to Joseph Montfort. Mentioned in local records as late as 1765. Probably named for the Clun River or the town of Clun in England.

Cluster, community in s Mecklenburg County served by post office, 1893–1903. Successor to Maxwell's Store, *which see*.

Clyde, town in central Haywood County. Inc. 1889. Named for a member of a firm of railroad construction engineers. Known previously as Lower Pigeon. Alt. 2,539.

Clyde Township, central Haywood County.

Coahoma, community in ne Lenoir County served by post office, 1888–1902.

Coakley, town in e Edgecombe County. Inc. 1903, but not now active in municipal affairs.

Coalglen, community in s Chatham County on Deep River. Known earlier as Farmville. Site of former Carolina Coal Mine, from which the name is derived.

Coalville, community in ne Cherokee County in Nantahala National Forest.

Coastal Plain, e North Carolina, extends inland from the Atlantic Ocean 100 to 150 mi. to the fall line of the rivers. The w limit extends from Northampton and Halifax Counties on

the n in a sw direction through Anson County on the s. In altitude the area ranges from sea level to approx. 500 ft. Generally the soil is sand and black loam. *See also* Tidewater Area.

Coats, town in e Harnett County. Inc. 1905 and named for Elder Tom Coats. Previously known as Troyville for a Fayetteville lawyer. Alt. 314.

Cobb Bluff, s central Cherokee County on the Nottely River at the mouth of Moccasin Creek.

Cobb Creek rises in nw Yadkin County and flows ne into Martin Creek.

Cobb Point, e Pasquotank County, extends into the Pasquotank River between Forbes Bay and Davis Bay.

Cobbs Creek rises in e Caswell County and flows ne into Person County, where it enters North Hyco Creek.

Cobbs Crossroads, community in n Wilson County near Town Creek.

Cobb's Shop, community in w Caswell County.

Cobb Town, community in s Edgecombe County.

Cobb Town, community in nw Rockingham County named for Pleasant Cobb, local blacksmith.

Cobin Branch rises in the Cane Creek Mountains, s Alamance County, and flows nw into Rock Creek.

Coble Township, former township in sw Alamance County, now township no. 2.

Coburn, community in sw Buncombe County.

Coburn Knob, n central Swain County in Great Smoky Mountains National Park near the head of Lands Creek. Alt. 4,370.

Coburn's, community in nw Union County.

Cochran Branch rises in s Swain County and flows ne into Tuckasegee River.

Cochran Creek rises in central Graham County and flows w into Cheoah River.

Cochrane Cove, on Burningtown Creek in central Macon County.

Cochrum, community in w Yadkin County served by post office, 1891–1905.

Cockerne Ferry. *See* Colerain.

Cockey Swamp rises in ne Nash County and flows se into sw Edgecombe County, where it enters Town Creek.

Cockey Township, former township in sw Edgecombe County, now township no. 13.

Cockle Point, peninsula extending from e Pamlico County into Neuse River.

Cockrells Crossroads, community in central Nash County.

Cod Camp Creek rises in sw Cumberland County and flows se on the Cumberland-Robeson county line before entering Robeson County, where it flows into Gallberry Swamp.

Coddle Creek rises along the Rowan-Iredell county line and flows s through Cabarrus County into Rocky River. Appears on the Collet map, 1770, as Codle Creek.

Coddle Creek, community in nw Cabarrus County.

Coddle Creek Township, se Iredell County.

Cody, community in s Surry County served by post office, 1888–1914.

Cody Branch rises in central Graham County and flows nw into Yellow Creek.

Cody Creek rises in w central Surry County and flows se into Fisher River.

Cody Gap, central Graham County at the head of Cody Branch.

Coefield Branch rises in ne Cherokee County and flows ne into McClellan Creek.

Coefield Creek rises in ne Cherokee County and flows nw into Radder Creek.

Coenjock. *See* Coinjock.

Coffee Branch rises in e Haywood County and flows n into Garden Creek.

Coffee Creek rises in w Caldwell County e of Rocky Knob and flows se into Mulberry Creek.

Coffee Creek, a tidal creek in n central Carteret County that flows into South River.

Coffee Ridge, n Haywood County parallel to Laurel Creek.

Coffer, community in n Moore County served by post office, 1892–1905.

Coffey Cove, central Cherokee County between Mason Branch and Rhea Branch.

Coffey Creek rises in w Mecklenburg County and flows s into Sugar Creek.

Cofield, community in e Hertford County.

Cogdell, community in s Wayne County served by post office, 1888–1903.

Coggins Bend, n Macon County in Little Tennessee River.

Coggins Branch rises in w Haywood County, Great Smoky Mountains National Park, near lat. 35°39'08″ N., long. 83°06'12″ W., and flows ne into Little Cataloochee Creek.

Coggins Mine, community in n Montgomery County named for local gold mine operated on Coggins farm.

Coglin Creek rises in s Onslow County and flows w into New River.

Cognac (cog-nack), community in e Richmond County. Settled about 1890 and first known as Eighty-Nine Mile Siding for its distance from Raleigh. Renamed for the town in France or the brandy produced there. Alt. 400.

Coharie River is formed in s Sampson County by the junction of Little Coharie and Great Coharie Creeks and flows se for approx. 6 mi. to join Six Runs Creek in forming Black River.

Cohary Swamp. *See* Great Coharie Creek.

Cohooque, community in se Craven County served by post office, 1880–1914.

Coinjock, community in s central Currituck County. Inc. 1893 as Arlington but dissolved by court order, March 1894, because of technical inaccuracy in description of the boundary. As early as 1830, a post office there was called Coenjock, the same name used by Bishop Thomas Coke in writing of a visit there in 1785. On Intracoastal Waterway. Originally located where Barco is today; moved s when Albemarle and Chesapeake Canal was built. Other early spellings were Cornjack and Cowenjock. Alt. 5.

Coinjock Bay, in the waters of Currituck Sound, central Currituck County, between Church Island and the mainland.

Cokes, community in e Granville County.

Cokesbury, community in n Harnett County. Early center of Methodism in Cape Fear area. Named for Thomas Coke (1747–1814) and Francis Asbury (1745–1816), Methodist bishops. Nearby, Buckhorn Iron Furnace operated during Civil War and until 1873.

Cokesbury, community in e Vance County on the head of Rocky Branch; named for Methodist bishops Thomas Coke and Francis Asbury.

Cokey Swamp rises in se Nash County and flows se into w Edgecombe County, where it enters Town Creek. An Indian village, Tiancok, *which see*, appears on the site on the Comberford map, 1657. Tyanocka Creek appears on the Collet map, 1770, at the location, and the spelling Tincoco and Tiancoco are used on other maps. *See also* Redmans Old Field.

Cokey Township. *See* Edgecombe County.

Colbert Creek rises in s Yancey County and flows se into South Toe River.

Colbert Ridge, s Yancey County between Locust Creek and Colbert Creek.

Coldass Creek rises in nw Caldwell County and flows e into Johns River. Both it and Pinchgut Creek were named by two men hunting in the area. They followed a stream until it came to a fork. There they separated, each following one of the forks; they agreed to meet later and name each stream according to their feelings toward it. One man carried the food and the other the sleeping equipment. They became lost but finally met the next day, when they named the creeks. Sometimes shown as Cold Water Creek on modern maps.

Cold Branch rises in central Clay County and flows nw into Tusquitee Creek.

Cold Branch rises in w Graham County and flows se into Santeetlah Creek.

Cold Camp Creek rises on the Cumberland-Robeson county line and flows se into Gallberry Swamp.

Cold Creek rises in e Haywood County and flows ne into East Fork Pigeon River.

Cold Creek rises in e Jackson County and flows sw into Tanasee Creek.

Cold Knob, on Buncombe-Henderson county line between Bent Creek Gap and Pine Mountain.

Cold Mountain, on Avery-Burke county line. Alt. 3,830.

Cold Mountain, s Haywood County, is parallel to Little East Fork Pigeon River. Alt. 6,030. According to Cherokee legend, some children played on a large rock at the foot of the mountain, and their footprints are said to be there still. Their name for the mountain was *Da-tsu-la-gun-yi,* meaning "where they made tracks." Eponymous novel by Charles Frazier in 1997 and later film led tourists to seek out site.

Cold Mountain, on the Jackson-Transylvania county line w of Panthertail Mountain. Alt. 4,500.

Cold Mountain Branch rises in s Transylvania County and flows ne into East Fork French Broad River.

Coldside Mountain in s Jackson County between Heddie Mountain and Terrapin Mountain.

Cold Spring, community is nw Burke County.

Coldspring Branch rises in e Cherokee County and flows nw into Peachtree Creek.

Coldspring Branch rises in ne Cherokee County and flows nw into Vengeance Creek.

Cold Spring Branch rises in e Clay County and flows sw into Shooting Creek.

Cold Spring Branch rises in n Clay County and flows se into Long Branch.

Cold Spring Branch rises in s Haywood County and flows nw into Shiny Creek.

Cold Spring Branch rises in n Madison County and flows ne into Allan Creek.

Cold Spring Branch rises in se Swain County and flows nw into Yalaka Creek.

Coldspring Branch rises in nw Swain County and flows se into Lost Cove Creek.

Coldspring Branch rises in w Swain County and flows w and nw into Hazel Creek.

Cold Spring Creek rises in n Burke County and flows s into Carroll's Creek.

Cold Spring Creek rises in n Macon County and flows sw into Whiteoak Creek.

Coldspring Gap, on Cherokee-Graham county line in e end of Unicoi Mountains.

Cold Spring Gap, on the Jackson-Transylvania county line.

Cold Spring Gap, n Swain County in Great Smoky Mountains National Park near the head of Bear Creek. Called in Cherokee *A-ha-lu-na* (ambushed) or *U-ni-ha-lu-na* (where they watched). Cherokees are said to have ambushed a large party of invading Iroquois, slaying all but one. His ears were cut off, as was the custom, and he was sent home to take the news to his people.

Cold Spring Knob, nw Graham County in the middle of Hangover Lead.

Cold Spring Knob, s Haywood County on Lickstone Ridge. Alt. 5,960.

Cold Spring Knob, on the Swain County, N.C.–Sevier County, Tenn., line in Great Smoky Mountains National Park at the junction of Miry Ridge and the main divide of the Great Smoky Mountains. Alt. 5,240. Named for spring of cold water near the summit.

Coldspring Mountain, on the Madison County, N.C.–Greene County, Tenn., line.

Cold Springs Creek rises in n Haywood County and flows sw into Pigeon River.

Coldwater Creek rises in s Rowan County and flows s into Cabarrus County, where it enters Rocky River. Appears on the Collet map, 1770.

Cold Water Creek. *See* Coldass Creek.

Cole Cove, s Buncombe County between Pine Mountain and Fannie Ridge.

Cole Creek is formed by junction of Hacklan Branch and Buckland Mill Branch in w Gates County. Flows s through Lilleys Millpond and empties into Sarem Creek. Formerly known as Sarem Creek.

Cole Creek rises on the e side of Rendezvous Mountain, w Wilkes County, and flows s approx. 3 mi. into North Prong Lewis Fork Creek.

Cole Gap, sw Cherokee County at the sw end of Damons Mountain.

Cole Gap, se Macon County w of Houston Branch and approx. 3 mi. n of town of Highlands.

Cole Gap Mountain, w central Stokes County between Indian and Neatman Creeks.

Coleman, community in s McDowell County near Old Fort; former station on Western North Carolina Railroad.

Coleman Branch rises in w Johnston County and flows sw into Black Creek.

Coleman Creek rises in s Clay County and flows e into Hyatt Mill Creek.

Coleman Gap, se Cherokee County at the headwaters of John Mason Branch.

Coleman Gap, on the Clay-Macon county line. The Appalachian Trail passes through the gap.

Cole Mountain, e Macon County at the head of Houston Branch.

Cole Mountain Gap, at the head of Skitty Creek in e Macon County. Alt. 4,100.

Colerain, town in ne Bertie County. Settled by 1700; inc. 1794. Named by its founder, John Campbell, for his hometown of Coleraine, County Londonderry, Ireland. The post office, est. in 1818, dropped the final letter of the name in the mid-nineteenth century. Cockerne Ferry across the Chowan River n of the site of Colerain appears on the Collet map, 1770, but it apparently ceased operation by 1808.

Colerain Township, ne Bertie County.

Coleridge, community in e Randolph County on Deep River. Originally known as Foust's Mill. A cotton mill est. there in 1883. Named for James A. Cole, local storekeeper.

Coleridge Township, e central Randolph County.

Colers Ordinary. *See* Ridgeway.

Coles Cove, the valley through which Coles Creek flows in n Buncombe County.

Coles Creek rises in n Buncombe County near Watershed Ridge and flows nw into Flat Creek.

Colesville. *See* Coleville.

Coleville, community in n Stokes County near Cadwell Creek. Post office there in the late nineteenth century was Colesville.

Coley Gap, w Madison County between Puncheon Camp Branch and Divide Mountain.

Coleys Branch rises in n Gaston County and flows ne into South Fork Catawba River.

Coleys Crossroads. *See* Vicksboro.

Colfax, community in w Guilford County. Alt. 972. Named for Schuyler Colfax (1823–85), vice president of the United States (1869–73).

Colfax Township, e Rutherford County. Named for Vice President Schuyler Colfax (1823–85).

Colington, scattered fishing community on Colington Island, ne Dare County.

Colington Creek, a waterway between Kitty Hawk Bay and Buzzard Bay; e of Colington Island and separating it from n Bodie Island, e Dare County.

Colington Island, in Roanoke Sound, ne Dare County. About 2 mi. from n to s and from e to w, it is separated from Bodie Island by Colington Creek. Consists of two islands, Little Colington and Big Colington. Named for Sir John Colleton (1608–66), one of the Lords Proprietors, to whom it was granted in 1663. Settled by the winter of 1664–65. Earlier known as Carlile Island in honor of Christopher Carleill, stepson of Sir Francis Walsingham, who accompanied Sir Francis Drake on his 1586 Florida-Virginia expedition as Drake's lieutenant general. Appears as Carlile Island on the Ogilby map, 1671, and as Colleton Island on both the Blome map, 1672, and the Moseley map, 1733. The Collet map, 1770, and the Mouzon map, 1775, have Collintons Island.

Colington Island Shoal lies off the nw tip of Roanoke Island, Dare County, in the waters of Albemarle and Croatan Sounds.

Colkins Neck, a sandy area about 2 mi. long and 1 mi. wide, almost surrounded by tidal marsh, sw Brunswick County along the South Carolina line.

Colleton County was est. prior to 1691 by the Lords Proprietors of Carolina in what is now se South Carolina. Named for Landgrave James Colleton, who resided in the area.

Colleton Island. *See* Colington Island.

Collett Camp Branch rises in n Clay County and flows sw into Long Branch.

Collett Creek rises in ne Cherokee County and flows nw into Tatham Creek.

Collett Ridge, ne Cherokee County in the Valley River Mountains.

Collettsville, town in w Caldwell County on Johns River. Inc. 1897, but no longer active in municipal affairs. Named for James H. Collet, on whose land the town was laid out. Settled as early as 1837, when post office was est.

Collie Swamp rises in w Martin County and flows s into Tranters Creek. Appears as Huskanaw Swamp on the Price map, 1808, and the MacRae map, 1833.

Collins Canal. *See* Somerset Canal.

Collins Creek rises in s Orange County and flows sw into Chatham County, where it enters Haw River.

Collins Creek rises in ne Rutherford County and flows s into North Fork.

Collins Creek rises in n Swain County in Great Smoky Mountains National Park and flows ne into Oconaluftee River.

Collins Crossroad. *See* Dixie.

Collins Crossroads. *See* Hollemans Crossroads.

Collins Gap, on the Swain County, N.C.–Sevier County, Tenn., line in Great Smoky Mountains National Park. Alt. 5,720.

Collins Mountain, w central Swain County on the nw end of Jackson Line Mountain.

Collinstown, community in n Stokes County n of Dan River. Name likely derived from that of early settlers Roger Collins and his kin. Also known as Stateline.

Collinsville, community in s Polk County on Hughes Creek. Settled about 1875. Named for Thomas G. Collins, local planter.

Collinwood, former community in w Swain County on Little Tennessee River; the site is now under the waters of Fontana Lake.

Colly, community in ne Bladen County.

Colly Creek rises in Big Colly Bay in ne Bladen County and flows se into Pender County, where it enters Black River.

Colly Swamp, an arm of Big Colly Bay in ne Bladen County.

Colly Township, e central Bladen County.

Colmans Gap, central Haywood County on the head of Big Branch.

Colon, community in n Lee County. Coal from Egypt mine formerly delivered to the Seaboard Railroad there; later the center of a large gas-fired brick industry. Post office est. in 1891 as Buckner; changed to Colon in 1892.

Colonial Assembly. *See* General Assembly.

Colson's Mill. *See* Coulson Ordinary.

Colt Creek rises in se Henderson County and flows ne into Polk County, where it enters Pacolet River.

Columbia, town and county seat in n Tyrrell County on Scuppernong River. Alt. 10. Originated as a trading post, Shallop's Landing; inc. 1793 as Elizabeth Town. Name changed to Columbia in 1801. Became county seat in 1802. Name is poetic appellation for the United States. Produces lumber.

Columbia. *See* Ramseur.

Columbia Township, ne Pender County.

Columbia Township, e central Randolph County.

Columbia Township, n central Tyrrell County.

Columbus, town and county seat, s Polk County on the head of Whiteoak Creek. Inc. 1857. Named for Dr. Columbus Mills, state legislator who was instrumental in the formation of the county. Alt. 1,145.

Columbus, town authorized to be est. on the lands of Jesse Nixon, ne Randolph County, in 1812. Apparently the town was never laid out. A post office at the proposed site on Sandy Creek in 1828 was called Nixon's.

Columbus County was formed in 1808 from Brunswick and Bladen Counties. Located in the se section of the state, it is bounded by the state of South Carolina and by Robeson, Bladen, Pender, and Brunswick Counties. It was named for Christopher Columbus. Area: 954 sq. mi. County seat: Whiteville, with an elevation of 59 ft. Townships are Bogue, Bolton, Bug Hill, Cerro Gordo, Chadbourn, Fair Bluff, Lees, Ransom, South Williams, Tatums, Waccamaw, Welch Creek, Western Prong, Whiteville, and Williams. Produces tobacco, corn, soybeans, oats, peanuts, pecans, cotton, cucumbers, cotton, poultry, livestock, hogs, fish, sweet potatoes, wood products, tires, air filters, chemicals, packaging, watermelons, fertilizer, paper, lumber, textiles, and catfish.

Columbus Township, s central Polk County.

Colvard Creek rises in n Cherokee County on Hanging Dog Mountain and flows se into Valley River.

Colvard Creek rises in ne Cherokee County and flows ne and nw into Gumflats Creek.

Colvin Creek rises in ne Madison County and flows sw into Spillcorn Creek.

Colvins Creek rises in w Pender County and flows se into Black River.

Combs Knob, n Wilkes County between Big Sandy Creek and Little Sandy Creek. Named for George Combs, a Revolutionary soldier who lived nearby.

Comet, community in n central Ashe County.

Comfort, community in s Jones County. A post office existed there as early as 1828.

Commissary Branch rises in s Transylvania County and flows nw into Little River.

Commissary Hill, s Yancey County approx. 9/10 mi. se of Mount Mitchell. Alt. 5,780. Named for a commissary located there by the Carolina Spruce Lumber Company during lumbering operations in the early 1900s.

Commissary Ridge, s Yancey County between Mount Mitchell and Commissary Hill.

Commissioner Gap, s Macon County between Rich Knob and Commissioners Creek.

Commissioners Creek rises in s Macon County and flows se into Little Tennessee River. Likely named in honor of the commissioners who surveyed the North Carolina–Georgia state line in 1819.

Como, town in n Hertford County. First known as Buckhorn. Post office est. in 1883 was named Como for Lake Como in Italy. Inc. 1967.

Company Mills, community in ne Guilford County served by post office, 1873–1903.

Company Shops. *See* Burlington.

Compass Bald Mountain, ne Clay County at the head of Compass Creek. Alt. 3,296.

Compass Creek rises in n Clay County between Julie Ridge and Deadline Ridge and flows s into Tusquitee Creek. Received its name when Robert Henry, a surveyor and Revolutionary War veteran, dropped his compass in the stream as he was crossing it.

Compass Creek rises in central Nash County, flows se into Edgecombe County, and enters Tar River 1 mi. e of Edgecombe-Nash county line.

Complex, community in se Davidson County.

Conaby Creek rises in w Washington County s of the town of Plymouth and flows ne into Roanoke River. It appears as Conalis Creek on the Collet map, 1770, and as Conaly Creek on maps as recent as the 1932 soil survey map. Shown as Coneby Creek on the MacRae map, 1833, and referred to as Conoby Creek in Doc. No. 259, House of Representatives, 63d Congress, 1st Session, 1913.

Conalis Creek. *See* Conaby Creek.

Conaly Creek. *See* Conaby Creek.

Concave, community in sw Scotland County.

Concord, city and county seat, central Cabarrus County. Inc. 1798; alt. 704. Named for the harmonious settlement of a dispute over the site for the town. Home of Barber-Scotia College. Produces textiles, hosiery, and poultry products.

Concord, community in sw Duplin County.

Concord, community in nw Person County.

Concord, community in w Sampson County between Bearskin Swamp and Great Coharie Creek.

Concord, community in s central Yancey County on Cane River. Two former communities, Antone and Dellingers, are now considered to be a part of Concord.

Concord. *See* Seaboard.

Concord Lake, n Cabarrus County on the e edge of Kannapolis. Formed in 1926 by a dam on Patterson Branch. Covers 85 acres, with a max. depth of 25 ft. Owned by the city of Concord and used for fishing and as a municipal water source.

Concord Mountain, s Buncombe County sw of Fairview Gap.

Concord North, unincorporated outskirts of the city of Concord, central Cabarrus County.

Concord Township, former township in central Cabarrus County, now township no. 12. In 1945 parts of townships nos. 4, 5, and 11 (Cooks Cross Roads, Mount Gilead, and Baptist Church) were added to the township.

Concord Township, w central Iredell County. Named for Concord Presbyterian Church, located near its center, est. 1775.

Concord Township, w central Randolph County.

Coneat. *See* Coniott Landing.

Coneby Creek. *See* Conaby Creek.

Coneghta. *See* Conetoe.

Cone Lake. *See* Bass Lake.

Cone Memorial Park. *See* Moses H. Cone Memorial Park.

Conetoe (cuh-NEAT-uh), town in se Edgecombe County, inc. 1887. Known earlier as Warren's Station. Named for nearby Conetoe Creek. Produces tobacco, cotton, and peanuts. Alt. 49.

Conetoe Creek rises in e Edgecombe County and flows s, where it forms a part of the Edgecombe-Pitt county line. It then flows s and sw into Tar River in Pitt County. The Collet map, 1770, shows Great Coneghta Pocosin as a swampy area on the w side of present-day Conetoe Creek in Edgecombe County. The name appears in county records as early as 1745.

Coney Creek rises in se Caswell County near Ridgeville and flows n into North Hyco Creek. Coney is an old word for rabbit.

Coneyhoe Creek. *See* Conoho Creek.

Confederate Memorial Forest, in Pisgah National Forest along the Haywood-Transylvania county line on the West Fork Pigeon River and the Blue Ridge Parkway. Dedicated July 12, 1942. Sponsored by the N.C. United Daughters of the Confederacy, the forest contains 125 acres planted with 125,000 red spruce and balsam trees.

Cong Branch rises in w Sampson County and flows s into Little Coharie Creek.

Congleton, community in ne Pitt County at the head of Great Branch. Inc. 1885 as Keelsville, with members of both the Congleton and Keel families appointed temporary officers. The name, however, was not adopted, nor was a municipal government continued.

Congo, community in w Wilkes County between Lewis Fork Creek and Fishdam Creek.

Conine Bend, in the Roanoke River, s Bertie County, at the w mouth of Conine Creek.

Conine Creek, s Bertie County, is a canal connecting two bends in the Roanoke River and creating Conine Island.

Conine Island, s Bertie County, formed in a bend of the Roanoke River by Conine Creek, which cuts across a neck formed by the river. Appears as Caroline Island on the Collet map, 1770. *See also* Purchace Islands.

Coniott Creek rises in sw Bertie County and flows se into Roanoke River. The name is a Tuscarora Indian word meaning "making cloth."

Coniott Landing, on the Roanoke River in se Bertie County at the mouth of Coniott Creek. Possibly the site of the extinct town Wimberly, which was est. in 1752. Joseph Wimberly petitioned to operate a ferry across the Roanoke River at "Coneat," and the town was built on his land. Site has also been known as Blackman's Landing; Blackman and Wimberly families were owners of large tracts of land in the county.

Conley Branch rises in w Macon County and flows sw into Jarrett Creek.

Conley Branch rises in n McDowell County and flows approx. 2 mi. se into North Fork [Catawba River] near Sevier.

Conley Ridge, s Macon County between Wheatfield Branch and Stillhouse Branch.

Connaritsa, community in nw Bertie County. The name Conneritsat appears in local records as early as 1729 with reference to the location of a bridge across Cashie River.

Connaritsa Pocosin, nw Bertie County.

Connaritsa Swamp rises in nw Bertie County in Connaritsa Pocosin and flows se into Cashie River.

Connatara. *See* Chimney Mountain.

Connelly Creek rises in se Swain County and flows nw into Tuckasegee River.

Connelly Mountain, e Swain County, between Chestnut Cove Creek and Improvement Creek.

Connelly Springs, town in e central Burke County on Island Creek approx. 2 mi. e of Valdese. Settled before the Civil War and named Happy Home. Later, the Connelly family developed a resort there around mineral springs. Named for Mrs. William L. Connelly. Inc. 1920. Alt. 1,195.

Conner Mill Branch rises in central Haywood County and flows n into Pigeon River.

Connestee Falls, in s Transylvania County in Carson Creek. Said to have been named for Indian Princess Connestee.

Connor, community in w Wilson County near Turkey Creek. Post office, 1890–1904.

Conoby Creek. *See* Conaby Creek.

Conoconary Creek. *See* Conoconnara Swamp.

Conoconnara Swamp rises in central Halifax County and flows ne into Roanoke River. It appears as Conoconary Creek on the Collet map, 1770. Conoconnara, the 2,500-acre plantation of Thomas Pollock Sr., was located there in 1721. Before the American Revolution, a Church of England chapel stood near the banks of the stream.

Conoconnara Township, e Halifax County.

Conoho. *See* Oak City.

Conoho Bend, in the Roanoke River at the mouth of Conoho Creek in n Martin County.

Conoho Creek rises in nw Martin County and flows se into Roanoke River. Appears as Coneyhoe Creek on the Collet map, 1770. The headwaters of Conoho Creek are called Fort Branch on the Collet map.

Conover, town in central Catawba County. Settled 1871. Inc. 1877. Alt. 1,060. Named by Mrs. John Seitz, local resident, for Canova, the Italian sculptor whose statue of George Washington was destroyed by the fire that leveled the capitol in Raleigh in 1831. Produces furniture, lumber, and textiles.

Conoway Knob, on the McDowell-Rutherford county line. Alt. 2,144.

Conrad Branch rises in nw Haywood County on the n side of Cooks Knob and flows ne approx. 1½ mi to join Woody Branch in forming Little Cataloochee Creek.

Conrad Hill, former site of a gold mine, central Davidson County near Holly Grove community.

Conrad Hill Township, e central Davidson County.

Conrads, community in e Yadkin County served by post office, 1880-1905.

Contara. *See* Whitewater Falls.

Contaroga. *See* Whitewater Falls.

Contentnea, town in central Greene County on Contentnea Creek. Inc. 1877, but long inactive in municipal affairs. Name derived from the Iroquoian/Tuscarora phrase meaning "fish passing by." Similarly named village of Cotechney (thief; rogue) is 4 mi. upstream.

Contentnea Creek is formed in w Wilson County by the junction of Moccasin and Turkey Creeks. It flows se into Greene County across the county and onto the Lenoir-Pitt county line, which it follows into Neuse River. Contentnea is from the Iroquoian/Tuscarora phrase meaning "fish passing by." Formerly known as Great Contentnea Creek, it is referred to in the De Graffenried account of the founding of New Bern, 1709-10. Appears as Great Cotecktney Creek on the Collet map,

1770. Cotechney was an Indian village on the creek banks in present Greene County. Other eighteenth-century references to the stream use the name Quotankney Creek. *See also* Moccasin River.

Contentnea Lake, central Wilson County on Contentnea Creek. Formed 1773. Covers 450 acres; max. depth 15 ft. First known as Cobb's Mill Pond (1773); later as Hadley's Mill Pond (named for Thomas Hadley), Barefoot's Mill Pond (1863), Wiggins Pond (1886), and David Daniel's Pond (1897). Acquired by Wilson Power and Light Co., 1904.

Contentnea Neck Township, ne Lenoir County.

Contentnea Township. *See* Winterville Township.

Conway, town in e Northampton County. Settled about 1835 and known first as Martin's Crossroads; later, by the early 1880s, as Kirby; and finally as Conway to honor the wife of an officer of the railroad. Inc. 1913. Alt. 105.

Conway Creek. *See* Little Fishing Creek.

Conwell, community in se Northampton County on the e limits of Rich Square.

Coohooca. *See* Cohoogue.

Cook, community in sw Catawba County served by post office, 1895-1905.

Cook Branch rises in e Graham County and flows ne into Rock Creek.

Cook Branch rises in n Madison County and flows s into Big Laurel Creek.

Cook Branch rises in n Mitchell County and flows s into Little Rock Creek.

Cook Branch rises in s Watauga County and flows ne into Pounding Mill Creek.

Cook Creek rises in central Cherokee County near Beaverdam Gap and flows se into Hanging Dog Creek. *See also* Kilby Cove.

Cook Creek rises in n Cherokee County and flows sw into Garreck Creek.

Cook Creek. *See* Island Creek.

Cook Gap, s Watauga County between the head of Laurel Branch and the head of Flannery Creek. Alt. 3,349.

Cook Mountain, nw Buncombe County between Sugar Creek and North Turkey Creek s of Earlies Gap.

Cooks Creek, w Haywood County in Great Smoky Mountains National Park, rises near lat. 35°40′30″ N., long. 83°09′38″ W., and flows se into Pretty Hollow Creek.

Cooks Creek rises in central Surry County and flows sw into Fisher River.

Cooks Crossing, community in n Cabarrus County.

Cooks Cross Roads Township, former township in nw Cabarrus County, now township no. 4. Formerly also known as Kannapolis Township.

Cooks Knob, w Haywood County, Great Smoky Mountains National Park near lat. 35°39'28" N., long. 83°08'42" W., on Indian Ridge between Short Bung (ridge) and Davidson Branch.

Cooks Wall Mountain, w Stokes County at the head of Indian Creek.

Cooktown, community in n Mitchell County on Holison Creek.

Cooleemee, town in s Davie County on the South Yadkin River. Inc. 1985. Site of former Fisher's Ford. Cotton mill est. there and named for Cooleemee Plantation, *which see*. Post office est. 1900. Produced textiles. Alt. 840.

Cooleemee Plantation, e Davie County overlooking the Yadkin River. Land purchased by the Hairston family in 1817; plantation house, with four wings in the form of a cross from a central hall, begun in 1850, completed in 1854. Still owned by the Hairston family. Origin of the name unknown, but legend says that Revolutionary War major Peter Hairston had fought the Creek Indians in Florida; he returned home with a young Indian captive who could remember only one word of his native tongue, the word *Cooleemee*, believed to mean "place where the white oak grows."

Coolers Knob Mountain, w Randolph County between Cedar Rock Mountain and Brush Mountain.

Cooley Creek rises in central Franklin County and flows ne into Neal Gut.

Coollyconch Mountain, a sandy loam elevation in nw Cumberland County on the Fort Bragg Military Reservation.

Cool Run, community in sw Brunswick County.

Cool Spring, community in e central Iredell County. Began with a store and hotel in the 1850s. An academy there in the 1870s became a high school at the turn of the century.

Cool Spring. *See* Creswell.

Cool Spring. *See* Scuppernong.

Cool Spring Branch rises in se Union County and flows n into Lanes Creek.

Cool Spring Precinct. *See* Scuppernong Township.

Cool Springs Township, se Rutherford County.

Cool Spring Township, e central Iredell County.

Coombs Fork, community in w Jones County.

Coon Creek rises in e Granville County and flows s into Fishing Creek.

Coon Creek rises in e Macon County and flows sw into Watauga Creek.

Coon Hollow, s Haywood County on a tributary of Middle Prong.

Coon Mountain, n central Alexander County. Alt. 1,520.

Coontree Branch rises in n Transylvania County near Coontree Mountain and flows s into Davidson River.

Coontree Mountain, n Transylvania County on the head of Coontree Branch.

Cooper, community in ne Cherokee County.

Cooper, community in ne Cumberland County on South River.

Cooper. *See* Swannanoa.

Cooper Branch rises in w Mitchell County and flows s into Toe River.

Cooper Creek rises in n Swain County in Great Smoky Mountains National Park and flows sw into Tuckasegee River.

Cooper Gap, n Yancey County between Peterson Ridge and the head of Sampson Branch.

Cooper Gap Township, n Polk County.

Cooper Knob, at the sw end of Franks Creek Lead in s Graham County.

Cooper Mountain, w central Swain County, a spur running sw from Jackson Line Mountain.

Coopers Branch rises in n central Avery County and flows nw into Cranberry Creek.

Cooper Store, former community in sw Mecklenburg County.

Coopers Township, s central Nash County.

Coopertown, community in s Nash County between Little Sapony Creek and Sapony Creek. Known also as Deans Community.

Coor Millpond, w Wayne County on Beaverdam Swamp. A mill there was owned by Ollin Coor, sheriff of Wayne County in 1848.

Coot Cove, w Swain County between the forks of Pilkey Creek.

Copal Grove, community in n Stanly County served by post office, 1875–1905.

Cope Branch rises in nw Swain County and flows s into Haw Gap Branch.

Cope Creek rises in n central Jackson County on

the sw slope of Carver Mountain and flows w approx. 4 mi. into Scott Creek on the e limits of Sylva.

Cope Knob, on the Jackson-Macon county line.

Copeland, community in s Surry County near the head of East Double Creek.

Copeland Creek rises in w Ashe County and flows se into North Fork New River.

Cope Mountain, n Jackson County between Soapstone Creek and Scott Creek.

Coppedge Crossroads, community in e Franklin County.

Copperas Bald, mountain in w Avery County.

Copperas Mountain, ne Buncombe County at the nw end of Big Fork Ridge.

Copperas Rock, peak in n Transylvania County on Mills River.

Copper Bald, n Macon County at the head of Big Branch. Alt. 5,249.

Copper Creek rises in n Cherokee County between Groundhog Ridge and Copper Ridge and flows se into Beaverdam Creek.

Copper Gap, on the Swain County, N.C.–Sevier County, Tenn., line in Great Smoky Mountains National Park between Eagle Rock and Mount Sequoyah.

Copper Knob, n Macon County between Rhinehardt Creek and Younce Creek.

Copper Mine Branch rises in central Clay County and flows se into Pounding Creek.

Copper Mine Branch rises in Forest City, s central Rutherford County, and flows se into Broad River.

Coppermine Creek rises in e Jackson County and flows se into Mull Creek.

Copper Mine Creek rises in n Lee County and flows se into Hughes Creek. Named for a copper mine operated near its head. Many broken Indian arrowheads have been found on a knoll near its junction with Hughes Creek; since no perfect arrowheads have been found, it has been suggested that they were made at the site.

Copper Mines, former community in nw Alleghany County. Copper mines operated there during the Civil War.

Copper Neck, w Chowan County s of the mouth of Rockyhock Creek. The name is a corruption of Cowpen Neck, the name of a plantation owned in 1747 by Charles West.

Copper Ridge, nw Cherokee County, extends ne from Nin Ridge.

Copper Swamp rises in e Martin County and flows w into Gardners Creek.

Coquina Beach, part of Cape Hatteras National Seashore on s Bodie Island, e Dare County across from Bodie Island Lighthouse. Remains of shipwreck *Laura A Barnes*, grounded 1921, rest there.

Cora, community in s Caldwell County. Named for daughter of Albert G. Corpening. Alt. 1,224.

Coranine River. *See* Newport River.

Coranine Sound. *See* Core Sound.

Corani River. *See* New River.

Corapeake, community in ne Gates County, settled late seventeenth or early eighteenth centuries. Known as Orapeake until a post office was est. and the Post Office Department made a mistake in the spelling. Alt. 44. *See also* Bearpond.

Corapeake Swamp rises in n Gates County and flows se into Hamburg Ditch in the Dismal Swamp. Appears as Orapeak Creek on the Moseley map, 1733. The lower course of the stream is called Elm Swamp on the Moseley map but Loosen Swamp on the Collet map, 1770. Later maps, until as recently as 1929, use the name Orapeake Swamp.

Corbett, community in se Caswell County. Named about 1880 for J. C. and Calvin Corbett, who operated a store there. Alt. 800.

Corbetts Ferry. *See* Ivanhoe.

Corbin Creek rises in e Macon County and flows sw into Cat Creek.

Corbin Knob, on the Jackson-Macon county line. Alt. 4,445.

Corbin Mountain, on the Henderson County, N.C.–Greenville County, S.C., line.

Corbinton. *See* Hillsborough.

Cordova, community in sw Richmond County on the Pee Dee River. A post office, Steeles Mill, existed there as early as 1828 and became the name of the railroad station. Cordova post office est. 1899. Produces textiles.

Corduroy Swamp rises in n Northampton County and flows e and ne to join Rogers Swamp in forming Kirbys Creek.

Core Banks, outer barrier beach extending from Cape Lookout to Swash Inlet along the se side of Core Sound, e Carteret County. Named for Core Indians. Velasco map, 1611, shows the name Endesoakes at the ne end of Core Banks; the Smith map, 1624, shows the name

Salvage Island. Including Portsmouth Island, the Core Banks are approx. 44 mi. long. *See also* Cape Lookout National Seashore Recreational Area.

Core Beach, a portion of Core Banks, *which see*, in e Carteret County between Core Sound and the Atlantic Ocean. It lies just s of Portsmouth Island.

Core Creek originally rose in central Carteret County and flowed s into Newport River. Dredging and the cutting of a canal now make Core Creek a connecting link between the waters of Neuse and Newport Rivers.

Core Point, s side of Pamlico River central Beaufort County. Named for Coree Indians.

Core Sound, a body of water between the mainland and the Outer Banks extending from Cape Lookout to Pamlico Sound in e Carteret County. Named for the Coranine or Coree Indians who lived in the area. The name Corenines appears on the Comberford map, 1657. The Moll map, 1729, shows Coranine Sound; and the Moseley map, 1773, has Core Sound.

Corine, community in sw Duplin County served by post office, 1894–1903. Named for postmaster Luther Powell's daughter, Corina.

Corinth, community in sw Catawba County.

Corinth, community in se Chatham County. Named for Corinth, town in Greece.

Corinth, community in se Granville County.

Cornatzer, community in central Davie County. Named for local family. Alt. 777.

Corncake Inlet, se Brunswick County from Onslow Bay in the Atlantic Ocean into Buzzard Bay and Cape Fear River n of Smith Island.

Corncob Island, w Bogue Sound, sw Carteret County.

Corncob Mountain extends ne between Seniard Creek and Sitton Creek in nw Henderson County.

Corn Crib Point, se Carteret County, extends into Jarrett Bay se of the community of Davis.

Corndack Creek rises in e Moore County and flows s into Little River. Originally known as Cuidreach Creek, it was named for the Cuidreach McDonald family. Early English mapmakers could only translate its Gaelic pronunciation as Corndack.

Cornelia, community in ne Cumberland County served by post office, 1888–1904.

Cornelius, town in n Mecklenburg County. Est.

1893 as Liverpool. Inc. 1905 and renamed Cornelius in honor of Joe B. Cornelius, principal stockholder in a local mill. Produces textiles. Alt. 833.

Cornelius Creek rises in s Iredell County and flows sw into Catawba River.

Corner Knob, on the Jackson-Macon county line.

Corner Rock Creek rises in ne Buncombe County and flows w to join Walker Branch in forming Dillingham Creek.

Cornet Branch rises in se Macon County and flows se into Clear Creek.

Cornet Knob, se Macon County between Tom Branch and Cornet Branch.

Cornett Branch rises in nw Watauga County and flows se into Rube Creek.

Cornjack. *See* Coinjock.

Cornwall, community in n Granville County served by post office, 1892–1908.

Cornwell Branch rises in e Cherokee County and flows se into Snead Branch.

Corolla, community on Currituck Banks, e Currituck County. Known as Currituck Beach until 1895, when a post office was est. there and named Corolla. Whalehead Club built there in the 1920s, later used as a summer school for boys and now open to visitors as part of park. A lighthouse there, the last major one constructed on the Outer Banks, was first lighted on December 1, 1875.

Correll Branch rises in w Haywood County, Great Smoky Mountains National Park, near lat. 35°42'05" N., long. 83°07'06" W., and flows se into Little Cataloochee Creek. The stream has also been known as North Prong.

Corundum, community in e Clay County on Barnett Branch.

Corundum Hill, e Macon County between Lickskillet Branch and Crows Branch. Named for the mineral found there.

Corys Store, community in s Martin County on Smithwick Creek.

Cosby Knob, on the Haywood County, N.C.–Cocke County, Tenn., line, Great Smoky Mountains National Park, on the Great Smoky Mountains divide near lat. 35°43'47" N., long. 83°11'12" W. Alt. 5,145.

Cosma, community in sw Wake County.

Cossart, term used by Moravians to describe land in what is now Watauga and Wilkes

Counties. Appears on the 1757 Bellin map. Title to the tract was taken by Henry Cossart (1714–63), agent who facilitated purchase of Wachovia.

Costin, community in w Pender County on Moores Creek, formerly called Costins Store.

Costins Store. *See* Costin.

Costner, community in s Gaston County served by post office, 1891–1902.

Cotan. *See* Seco.

Cottage Point, e Pasquotank County, extends into the Pasquotank River within limits of Elizabeth City.

Cottendale. *See* Bruce.

Cotten's Cross Roads. *See* Roxobel.

Cotton Creek rises in e Montgomery County and flows e into Moore County, where it enters Cabin Creek.

Cotton Grove, community in s central Davidson County.

Cotton Grove Township, w central Davidson County.

Cotton Hammock, e Carteret County between community of Stacy and Piney Point.

Cotton Patch, former community on Pigeon River in n Haywood County. A number of years ago, a resident planted a small patch of cotton there, and his wife used it to weave cloth. The patch is now grown over and the place abandoned, but the name persists.

Cotton Patch Bay, an arm of Big Colly Bay in ne Bladen County.

Cotton's Crossing. *See* Tuscarora Beach.

Cottonville, community in s Stanly County. Named prior to the Civil War because of the quantity of cotton grown in the vicinity.

Cottonwood, community in s Mecklenburg County served by post office, 1890–1900.

Cottrell Hill, community in e Caldwell County on Zacks Fork. Named for William Cottrell, who settled there shortly before the Civil War.

Couches Creek rises in ne Swain County in Great Smoky Mountains National Park and flows se into Oconaluftee River.

Couch Mountain, n Henderson County between Clark Gap and Rich Mountain.

Couch Mountain, e Orange County on the head of Little Creek.

Coulson Ordinary appears on the Collet map, 1770, on the Pee Dee River in what is now se Stanly County e of the town of Norwood. At

Colson's Mill nearby, Col. William Lee Davidson's Whig militia defeated Col. Samuel Bryan's Tories in July 1780.

Council, town in s Bladen County. Alt. 64. Inc. 1905. Named for industrialist K. Clyde Council (1886?–1951). Also called Council Station because of depot on railroad.

Council Gap, w central Watauga County near the head of Bairds Creek.

Council Mill Pond, s Bladen County 14 mi. se of county seat; an artificial pond on Friar Swamp owned by Clyde Council estate. Fishing. Not open to the public.

Council Station. *See* Council.

Counterfeit Branch rises in n Haywood County and flows sw into Pigeon River.

Country Line, community in n Granville County.

Country Line Creek rises in se Rockingham County and flows ne across Caswell County into Virginia, where it enters Dan River ne of Milton. Mentioned in local records as early as 1754. Named for the eighteenth-century custom of calling the North Carolina–Virginia line the "country line."

County Line, community in w Davie County served by post office, 1828–1906.

County Line Gap, on the Caldwell-Wilkes county line.

County Line Ridge, on the Caldwell-Wilkes county line.

County of Norfolk was created in 1636 by authorities in Virginia to give Henry Frederick Howard, Lord Maltravers, a specific area for his proposed settlement. Maltravers in 1632 acquired the Heath grant (*see* Carolana). The new county extended from about the site of present Suffolk, Va., to New Bern, N.C. It was into the area that the earliest settlers of what is now North Carolina began to move from Virginia. The County of Norfolk was soon divided into Upper Norfolk and Lower Norfolk Counties, with the latter containing the region that later became a part of North Carolina.

Court House Bald, se Clay County on the se end of Ravenrock Ridge.

Court House Bay, s Onslow County in New River. The county's first courthouse was on the banks of New River there, 1734–35.

Court House Creek rises in nw Transylvania County and flows se into North Fork French Broad River.

Court House Falls, nw Transylvania County in Court House Creek.

Courthouse Knob, n peak of Richland Mountains in n Buncombe County near lat. 35°41′ N., long. 82°27′30″ W.

Courthouse Township, central Camden County.

Courtney, community in s Yadkin County. Formerly known as Chinquapin Cross Roads. Named for Courtney Baptist Church, organized there in 1832. A late nineteenth-century post office serving the community was named Cross Roads Church.

Cove, community in e Haywood County on Cove Creek.

Cove Branch rises in s Transylvania County and flows ne into East Fork French Broad River.

Cove City, town in w Craven County. Alt. 48. Settled 1859; inc. 1907. Known earlier as Cove Creek.

Cove Creek rises in n Cleveland County and flows se into Ward Creek.

Cove Creek rises in Great Dover Swamp, w Craven County, and flows ne into Neuse River. Appears as Core Creek on the Moseley map, 1733, and as Moon Creek on the Collet map, 1770.

Cove Creek rises in central Haywood County and flows ne into Jonathans Creek.

Cove Creek rises in e Haywood County and flows w into Fines Creek.

Cove Creek rises in se Henderson County and flows ne into Polk County, where it enters Green River.

Cove Creek rises in s McDowell County and flows sw into Rutherford County, where it enters Broad River.

Cove Creek rises in nw Transylvania County and flows se into Davidson River.

Cove Creek rises in n Watauga County and flows sw into Watauga River.

Cove Creek, community in central Haywood County on Jonathans Creek. Post office from late nineteenth century until mid-twentieth century.

Cove Creek Gap, central Haywood County, Great Smoky Mountains National Park near lat. 35°37′52″ N., long. 83°02′50″ W., at the head of Winding Stair Branch. Alt. 4,071.

Cove Creek Ridge, central Watauga County, forms a semicircle just sw of Buckeye Knob.

Cove Creek Township, w central Watauga County.

Cove Field Branch rises in sw Haywood County and flows ne into Allen Creek.

Covefield Branch rises in se Macon County and flows se into Clear Creek.

Cove Field Ridge, sw Haywood County parallel to Cove Field Branch.

Cove Gap, on the Alexander-Wilkes county line s of Pores Knob.

Covington, community in nw Richmond County. A post office was est. there as early as 1830.

Covington Mountain, nw Cleveland County on Brier Creek. Alt. 2,038.

Cowan. *See* Burgaw.

Cowan Cove, the valley through which the upper course of Smith Mill Creek flows in central Buncombe County.

Cowan Knob, on the w end of Lizzy Mountain in central Jackson County.

Cowan's Ford, over Catawba River at the Lincoln-Mecklenburg county line, now under the waters of Lake Norman. Cornwallis, pursuing Gen. Nathanael Greene, crossed the Catawba there after a sharp fight on February 1, 1781, in which Gen. William Lee Davidson was slain.

Coward Bald, peak at ne end of Coward Mountain in e Jackson County. Alt. 5,200.

Coward Creek, a small tidal stream flowing e through the swampy part of Oak Island into Molasses Creek in se Brunswick County.

Coward Lake formed in 1950 in central Jackson County on Norton Creek. Covers 1 acre and has max. depth of 10 ft. Used for fishing. Not open to the public.

Coward Mountain extends from Moses Creek in central Jackson County ne to Coward Bald.

Cowarts, community in central Jackson County on Caney Fork.

Cow Bog Branch rises in central Columbus County and flows se into Waccamaw River.

Cow Branch rises in n Burke County and flows n into Avery County, where it enters Linville River.

Cow Branch rises in nw Columbus County and flows sw into Porter Swamp.

Cow Branch rises in w Jackson County and flows s into Middle Creek.

Cow Branch rises in sw Wilson County and flows e into Robin Branch.

Cow Branch rises in w Wilson County and flows s into Contentnea Creek.

Cow Camp Branch rises in central Avery County and flows n into North Toe River.

Cow Camp Creek rises in central Avery County and flows n into Kentucky Creek.

Cow Camp Gap, near head of Cow Camp Creek in central Avery County.

Cow Creek rises in the highlands of Garrenton's Island in e Camden County and flows e into North River.

Cow Creek rises in nw McDowell County and flows se into Armstrong Creek.

Cowee, chief town of the Middle Cherokees, destroyed by the Rutherford Expedition, 1776. The mound on which the council house stood is a short distance nw of Franklin in central Macon County. The name is believed to have meant "place of the Deer Clan." Also spelled Keowee.

Cowee Bald, on the Jackson-Macon county line. Alt. 5,085.

Cowee Creek rises in n Macon County and flows sw into Little Tennessee River.

Cowee Gap, on the Jackson-Macon county line.

Cowee Mountains, a range of mountains in se Swain, e Macon, and w Jackson Counties. The Jackson-Macon county line follows the peak of the ridge.

Coweeta, community in sw Macon County between the Nantahala Mountains and Little Tennessee River near Otto. Alt. 2,875. U.S. Forest Service hydrologic laboratory is located there. Older residents and old records use the spelling Coweta. Federal officials adopted the spelling Coweeta, and it now appears on maps and in official records.

Coweeta Creek rises in s Macon County and flows ne into Little Tennessee River.

Coweeta Gap, s Macon County between Carrol Knob and Black Mountain.

Cowee Township, ne Macon County.

Cowee Tunnel. *See* Dillsboro.

Cowell's Bridge. *See* Sligo.

Cowenjock. *See* Coinjock.

Coweta. *See* Coweeta.

Cowford Swamp rises in sw Robeson County and flows ne into Ashpole Swamp.

Cow Gallus Creek rises in e Pamlico County and flows e into Long Creek.

Cowhead Creek rises in se Onslow County and flows sw into Frenchs Creek.

Cow Hole Branch rises in n Duplin County and flows s into Goshen Swamp.

Cowhorn Swamp rises in n Onslow County and flows sw into New River.

Cow Island, higher ground surrounded by swamp, s Duplin County.

Cow Island. *See* Bodie Island.

Cowl Cove, on a tributary of Clear Branch in sw Macon County.

Cowlick Branch rises in w Edgecombe County and flows nw into Tar River.

Cowmire Branch rises in central Cherokee County and flows s into Colvard Creek.

Cowpen Island, a point of land extending from Core Banks into Core Sound in se Carteret County.

Cowpen Neck. *See* Copper Neck.

Cowpen Top, peak on Whiteoak Mountain in n Haywood County.

Cowper's Hill. *See* Maxton.

Cow Pond Branch rises in nw Craven County and flows s into Neuse River.

Cowrock Mountain, s Jackson County between Logan Creek and Long Branch. Alt. 4,240.

Cowstamp Mountain, e Swain County between Long Creek and Hickorynut Branch.

Cow Swamp rises in s Pitt County and flows ne into Chicod Creek.

Cox Branch rises in w Jackson County and flows e into Cullowhee Creek.

Cox Branch rises in e Transylvania County and flows sw into Cascade Lake.

Coxcomb Mountain, on the Buncombe-Yancey county line between Rocky Knob and Ogle Meadows. Alt. 5,443.

Cox Creek rises in n Cleveland County and flows se into Ward Creek.

Cox Creek rises in n Henderson County and flows se into Clear Creek.

Cox Creek rises in nw McDowell County and flows s into Armstrong Creek.

Cox Creek Gap, n Yancey County between the head of North Cox Creek and South Cox Creek.

Coxe Branch rises in n Yancey County and flows se into Little Creek.

Coxe's Store. *See* Newton Grove.

Cox Knob, e Yancey County between the forks of Long Branch and Crabtree Creek.

Cox Mill. *See* Mill Grove.

Cox Millpond, on the Johnston-Wayne county line on Mill Branch, just before its confluence with Mill Creek. Named for an early Quaker family of Wayne County.

Cox Point extends from e Onslow County into White Oak River.

Coxsborough, town authorized to be laid off in 1797 at or near Cox's Mill, e central Randolph County at the junction of Mill Creek and Deep River. Warehouses for inspection of agricultural products were to be est. there in connection with navigation up and down Deep River. Apparently the town was never set. *See also* Cox's Mill.

Cox's Falls, formerly rapids in Neuse River in sw Wayne County but now submerged by Goldsboro Cooling Pond. Mentioned as early as 1819 in a survey of the rivers of North Carolina.

Cox's Knob, e Caldwell County. Alt. 2,430. Probably named for Matthew Cox, eighteenth-century settler.

Cox's Mill, former mill on Deep River, e central Randolph County. Was headquarters of David Fanning, noted leader of N.C. Tories, 1781–82. Appears on the Collet map, 1770. *See also* Coxsborough; Mill Creek.

Cox Store, community in e Polk County between Whiteoak Creek and Green River. Alt. 868.

Coxville, community in s Pitt County.

Cozad Branch rises in ne Cherokee County and flows se into Morris Creek.

Cozad Gap, ne Cherokee County in the Snowbird Mountains.

Cozart, community in sw Granville County served by post office, 1889–1905. Alt. 332.

Crab Creek rises in e Alleghany County and flows nw into Little River.

Crab Creek rises in w Henderson County and flows w into e Transylvania County and nw into Little River approx. 2 mi. n of Cascade Lake.

Crab Creek Township, w Henderson County.

Crab Island, in swampy area of s Currituck County between Sligo and Shawboro. Used by local Confederates under Capt. Caleb Grandy. Target of Union troops under Gen. Edward Wild, 1863.

Craborchard Creek rises in sw Watauga County near Avery county line and flows e into Dutch Creek. Also known as Orchard Creek.

Crab Orchard Fields, an open section in e Haywood County between Crabtree Bald and Gudger Knob.

Crab Orchard Township, former township in e central Mecklenburg County, now township no. 7.

Crab Point, a point of the mainland in central Carteret County extending into waters of Newport River.

Crab Point Bay, in Newport River, Carteret County, near mouth of Calico Creek n of Morehead City.

Crab Point Thorofare, a channel running between Newport Marshes and the mainland in central Carteret County.

Crabtree, community in e Haywood County. Alt. 2,659. Settled about 1809. Named for the creek.

Crabtree Bald, e Haywood County at sw end of Crab Orchard Fields. Alt. 5,320–5,360.

Crabtree Creek rises in n Franklin County and flows ne into Richland Creek.

Crabtree Creek rises in e Haywood County and flows sw into Pigeon River.

Crabtree Creek rises in w Wake County and flows ne and se into Neuse River e of Raleigh. Appears on the Collet map, 1770.

Crabtree Creek State Park. *See* William B. Umstead State Park.

Crabtree Falls, on Long Branch in sw Mitchell County near Big Crabtree Creek.

Crabtree Gap, e Haywood County on the head of Rogers Cove Creek.

Crabtree Mountain, sw Mitchell County at the head of Roaring Branch. Alt. 3,960.

Crabtree Township, e central Haywood County.

Crabtree Township, e Yancey County.

Craddock Swamp rises in n Sampson County and flows sw into Ward Swamp.

Craggy, community in central Buncombe County on the w bank of French Broad River s of Elk Mountain. Alt. 1,944.

Craggy Dome, peak in Great Graggy Mountains, ne Buncombe County. Formerly known as Big Craggy. Alt. 6,080–6,100.

Craggy Gardens, a 675-acre area in ne Buncombe County n of Craggy Knob. Noted for its native purple rhododendron, which blooms in mid-June.

Craggy Knob, peak in Great Craggy Mountains, ne Buncombe County. Sometimes shown on old maps as Bee Tree Mountain or High Top of Bee Tree. Alt. 5,600–5,700.

Craggy Pinnacle, peak in the Great Craggy Mountains, ne Buncombe County. Appears in early records and on old maps as Buckner's Knob. Alt. 5,900–6,000.

Cragnola Gap, at the head of Cabin Creek in s Henderson County.

Craig, community in s McDowell County served by post office, 1896–1912.

Craig Mountain, s Macon County near the heads of Mulberry Creek and Waterloo Branch.

Craigrownie, community in se Montgomery County. Settled by Scots. Area noted for production of naval stores.

Craig's Creek rises in w Caldwell County and flows e into Wilson's Creek.

Craigs Point extends into the e side of Sulliers Bay in se Onslow County.

Crains Creek rises in s Lee County and flows s into Moore County, where it joins Dry Fork Branch in forming Whiteoak Creek. Crains Creek and Whiteoak Creek together were formerly known as North Fork Crains Creek and Little Crains Creek.

Crains Creek, name applied to the lower course of Dunhams Creek, *which see*, e Moore County. It flows se into Little River. Named for the Crain family, which settled along its banks before 1750.

Cramerton, town in se Gaston County on South Fork Catawba River. Est. 1906 when a mill was constructed by J. H. Mayes. Known as Mayesworth until purchased by Cramerton Mills, Inc., founded by Stuart W. Cramer (1868–1940). Inc. 1967. Produces textiles. Alt. 633.

Cranberry, community in n central Avery County. Alt. 3,202. A post office est. there in 1850 as Cranberry Forge; discontinued for a brief period following the Civil War. Name changed to Cranberry after 1882. Named for cranberries that grew abundantly nearby. Cranberry Iron Mine, *which see*, was there.

Cranberry Creek is formed in e Ashe County by the junction of Piney Fork and Mulberry Creeks and flows nw into South Fork New River.

Cranberry Creek rises in w Avery County and flows nw into Elk River.

Cranberry Creek rises in n Jackson County and flows sw into Hornbuckle Creek.

Cranberry Creek rises in se Watauga County and flows n into s Ashe County, where it enters South Fork [New River].

Cranberry Creek rises in w Yadkin County and flows se into South Deep Creek.

Cranberry Gap, central Avery County between Minneapolis and Cranberry. Alt. 3,500.

Cranberry Iron Mine, surface iron mines in n central Avery County. Believed to have been worked by Cherokee Indians. Discovered by white settlers in 1781; worked from 1826, most actively from 1865 to 1930. Supplied iron to the Confederacy. *See also* Cranberry.

Cranberry Island, high ground in n Tyrrell County surrounded by peat lands n of community of Levels.

Cranberry Knob, nw Burke County. Alt. 4,223.

Cranberry Ridge, n Jackson County between Cranberry Creek and Hornbuckle Creek.

Cranberry Township, sw Alleghany County.

Cranberry Township, w Avery County.

Crane Branch rises in central Madison County and flows n into Revere Creek.

Crane Creek rises in s Cherokee County and flows sw into Nottely River.

Crane Creek rises in s Rowan County and flows ne into High Rock Lake (Yadkin River). Mentioned in local records as early as 1728. Appears on the Collet map, 1770, as Cane Creek, but as Crane Creek on the Price map, 1808. Crane Creek has three tributaries, all called Crane Creek; one of them, near Salisbury, is sometimes called Town Creek.

Crane Creek rises in s Sampson County and flows s into Six Runs Creek.

Crane Creek rises in s Wilkes County and flows ne into Rocky Creek.

Crane Creek. *See* Crains Creek. The stream in Lee and Moore Counties has been variously spelled Crane, Crane's, and Crains.

Crane Island. *See* Campbell Island.

Crane Ponds, a cluster of half a dozen small natural lakes in nw Onslow County. Apparently first named on Bache's U.S. Coast Survey map, 1865.

Cranes Island. *See* Eagles Island.

Crane(y) Island. *See* Harkers Island.

Cransford Cove, w Macon County at the head of Wayah Creek.

Craters Mill, community in s Forsyth County.

Craven, community in se Rowan County served by post office, 1882–1915.

Craven County was formed in 1705 as Archdale Precinct of Bath County, although there is evidence that an Archdale County, *which see*, existed as early as 1696. The name was changed to Craven County about 1712. Located in the e section of the state, it is bounded by Carteret, Jones, Lenoir, Pitt, Beaufort, and Pamlico Counties. It has been said that the county was named for William, Earl of Craven (1606–97), one of the original Lords Proprietors and longest lived of the eight. More likely, however, it was named for his grandnephew, William, Lord Craven (who inherited his title and interest in Carolina and who died the year before the name of the county was changed from Archdale to Craven); or for the third William, Lord Craven, one of the Proprietors at the time the change in the name of the county was made. Area: 785 sq. mi. County seat: New Bern, with an elevation of 12 ft. Townships are nos. 1–3, 5–9; all of former township no. 4 was included in Pamlico County when it was created in 1872. Produces tobacco, corn, soybeans, peanuts, hogs, dairy products, processed meat, lumber, boats, and apparel.

Craven County, one of three counties (Albemarle and Clarendon being the other two) set up in 1664 by the Lords Proprietors of Carolina. Its territory embraced what later became South Carolina. The Ashley River settlement, Charles Town (Charleston), was est. in 1670.

Craven Gap, central Buncombe County between Rice Knob and Peach Knob in the Elk Mountains.

Craven Parish, Church of England, Craven County, est. 1715, coextensive with the county. By 1741 it was called Christ-Church Parish. In 1767 there were 1,378 white taxables in the parish. Christ Church Parish of the Episcopal Church, however, still functions in New Bern.

Crawford, community in w Macon County served by post office, 1886–1904.

Crawford. *See* Currituck; Danbury.

Crawford Branch rises in ne Cherokee County and flows nw into Collett Creek.

Crawford Branch rises in central Clay County and formerly flowed s into Licklog Creek. It now flows into Chatuge Lake, and a part of its former course is now partially covered by it.

Crawford Branch rises in w Henderson County and flows ne into Boylston Creek.

Crawford Branch rises in central Macon County and flows se and ne into Little Tennessee River.

Crawford Creek rises in s Clay County and flows se through Wright Cove into Brasstown Creek.

Crawford Creek rises in e Haywood County and flows ne into East Fork Pigeon River.

Crawford Creek Gap, s Haywood County on the head of Crawford Creek.

Crawford Gap, n Haywood County on the ne end of Hurricane Mountain.

Crawford Mountain, sw Orange County on Cane Creek.

Crawford Township, w central Currituck County. *See also* Currituck.

Crawley Creek rises in e Moore County and flows n into Big Governors Creek.

Crawley Creek rises in n Rutherford County and flows se into Camp Creek.

Crawley Swamp rises in w Bladen County and flows w into Robeson County, where it enters Big Swamp.

Creasman Branch rises in s Buncombe County and flows e into Wesley Creek.

Creedmoor, town in sw Granville County. Founded about 1840 by Thomas Lyon. Inc. 1895 as Creedmore; reincorporated 1905 as Creedmoor. Appears as Creedmoor in an 1887 atlas. Said to have been called "Need More" in the earliest days of the community but, with its growth, a more dignified name was desired. Until 1960 "mule capital of North Carolina" because of market for farm animals. Produces apparel.

Creedmoor Lake, se Granville County on Ledge Creek. Formed in 1939 as a source of water for the town of Creedmoor and for recreation. Covers 100 acres. Also called Lake Rogers. Max. depth 30 ft.

Creeds Hill Coast Guard Station, formerly on s Hatteras Island, se Dare County. First formed as a lifesaving station in 1878–79, it became a Coast Guard Station in 1915 but has since been deactivated.

Creed's Hill. *See* Frisco.

Creek, community in s Warren County on Fishing Creek. Settled prior to 1800. Post office located there, 1883–1930.

Creek Mills, community in ne Forsyth County.

Creeksville, community in central Northampton County on Potecasi Creek.

Creeping Swamp rises in sw Beaufort County and flows sw into Clayroot Swamp. For a part of its course, it forms the Beaufort-Pitt and Craven-Pitt county lines.

Cremo, community in n central Bertie County.

Crenshaw's Branch rises in central Wake County and flows ne into Neuse River.

Crescent, community in s Rowan County.

Cressville. *See* Creswell.

Crestmont, former community in nw Haywood County on Big Creek near lat. 35°45′ N., long 83°06′37″ W. A sawmill community, the site is now in Great Smoky Mountains National Park. Inc. 1913, but the charter was repealed in the same year.

Creston, community in w central Ashe County. Alt. approx. 2,850. Post office est. 1830 as North Fork; changed to Creston, 1882. Named for its location near the crest of the mountains.

Creston Township, sw Ashe County.

Creswell, town in e Washington County n of Scuppernong River. Alt. 6. Known as Cool Spring as early as 1826, when a post office by the name was est. there. The name was used locally as late as 1895. When William Atkinson became postmaster in 1874, the post office name was changed to Cressville in honor of John A. J. Creswell, U.S. postmaster general. Inc. 1874 as Cressville; named changed to Creswell in 1885.

Cribs Creek rises in nw Anson County and flows n into Rocky River.

Cricket, community in central Wilkes County. Est. 1888 and named by the Post Office Department.

Cricket Hill, a man-made island in w Bogue Sound, s Carteret County.

Cricket Swamp rises in e central Bertie County and flows s into Eastmont Swamp. Probably named for John Crickett, who owned land in the area as early as 1729.

Crims Crossroads. *See* Grimes Crossroads.

Crimsie, community in n Lincoln County served by post office, 1894–1903.

Crinkley, community in central Warren County served by post office, 1896–1903.

Crisp, community in s Edgecombe County.

Crisp Creek rises in w Martin County and flows sw into sw Edgecombe County. It then flows se and forms a portion of the Edgecombe-Pitt county line before entering Conetoe Creek.

Crit, community in se Clay County served by post office, 1898–1906.

Croaker Channel, w Carteret County in White Oak River. Named for a species of fish. Formerly one of two channels used to reach Swansboro in the days of sailing vessels. Boats moving up Bogue Sound used Croaker Channel, while those approaching from the Atlantic Ocean used Ship (or West) Channel. Croaker Channel is now almost completely filled with sand.

Croatamung, an island shown on the White map, 1585, in what is now a part of Currituck Banks in e Currituck County. Smith, 1624, calls it Arundells Island; Comberford, 1657, makes it Lucks Island. As the latter, is the n boundary of the Carolina territory granted to the Lords Proprietors in 1663. *See also* Lucks Island.

Croatan, community in e Craven County. Settled about 1800. Alt. 28.

Croatan National Forest, in parts of Carteret, Craven, and Jones Counties. Est. 1933. Covers 294,610 acres. Includes the Croatan Cooperative Wildlife Management Area. Headquarters are in New Bern.

Croatan Sound connects Albemarle and Pamlico Sounds between Roanoke Island and the mainland of Dare County. Appears as The Narrows on the Moseley map, 1733. Virginia Dare Memorial Bridge, opened 2002 and 5 mi. in length, spans the sound to connect Roanoke Island to Manns Harbor.

Croatan Township, central Dare County on the mainland.

Croatoan Island, a name applied by John White on his map of 1585 to the s portion of Hatteras Island (Dare County) and a portion of Ocracoke Island (Hyde County). Hatteras Inlet, now dividing this portion of the Outer Banks into two islands, was opened in 1846. Ralph Lane, governor of the first Roanoke colony, named the island "My Lord Admirals Iland" in honor of Lord Howard of Effingham, created Lord High Admiral in 1585. By 1657 Comberford showed the island as "Chowanoke." Smith, in 1624, had called it Abbots Island. The name Croatoan was derived from the Indian village that was on the present Cape Hatteras (Kro-otän [talk town], indicating the chief's residence.) *See also* Portsmouth Island.

Croft, community in n Mecklenburg County. A post office there, Alexandriana, was est. in the home of Joseph McKnitt Alexander in 1804 and continued until 1886. By 1896 the name Croft was in use. Long served by only filling station in n Mecklenburg County.

Cromartie, community in central Robeson County served by post office, 1892–1917.

Cromarties Bridge. *See* Hickory Grove Crossroads.

Cromartys Ferry. *See* Hickory Grove Crossroads.

Cromwell Canal, a stream, rises in s Edgecombe County and flows sw into Tar River.

Cronly. *See* Acme.

Crooked Branch rises in s Richmond County and flows s into South Carolina, where it enters Lightwood Knot Creek.

Crooked Creek rises in e Beaufort County and flows s into Pungo River.

Crooked Creek rises in se Buncombe County and flows ne into McDowell County, where it enters Catawba River.

Crooked Creek rises in Sanderlin's Swamp in central Camden County and flows e through the North River Pocosin into North River.

Crooked Creek rises in w Durham County and flows se into Eno River.

Crooked Creek rises in sw Franklin County and flows se and ne into Tar River.

Crooked Creek rises in nw Jackson County and flows sw into Tuckasegee River.

Crooked Creek rises in s Lincoln County and flows sw into Leepers Creek.

Crooked Creek rises in e Madison County and flows sw into Middle Fork.

Crooked Creek rises in n Stokes County and flows ne into Virginia, where it enters Mayo River.

Crooked Creek is formed in n Union County by the junction of North Fork Crooked Creek and South Fork Crooked Creek. It flows ne into Rocky River.

Crooked Creek. *See* Fork Creek.

Crooked Creek Township, sw McDowell County.

Crooked Fork rises in nw Granville County and flows se in an arc into Aarons Creek.

Crooked Run rises in n Cleveland County and flows se into First Broad River.

Crooked Run rises in w Granville County and flows s into Tar River.

Crooked Run rises in central Jones County and flows n into Trent River.

Crooked Run rises in w Vance County and flows ne into Kerr Lake.

Crooked Run Creek rises in s Stokes County and flows sw into n Forsyth County, where it flows back nw into Stokes County again and into Little Yadkin River.

Crooked Swamp rises in n Nash County and flows se then ne into Fishing Creek.

Cross Branch rises in s Columbus County and flows sw into Horry County, S.C., where it enters Buck Creek.

Cross Branch. *See* Alder Branch.

Cross Canal drains water from nw Camden County (Dismal Swamp) to the e into Dismal Swamp Canal.

Cross Canal. *See* Hamburg Ditch.

Cross Creek rises in n Cumberland County and flows se through Lake Wood and Fayetteville into Cape Fear River. So named because early settlers found that Cross Creek and Little Cross Creek crossed each other. *See also* Fayetteville.

Cross Creek, colonial trading center in central Cumberland County on Cape Fear River begun about 1760. Appears as Cross-creek on both the Collet map, 1770, and the Mouzon map, 1775. Consolidated with Campbellton, approx. 1¼ mi. away, in 1778. In 1783 the name was changed to Fayetteville, *which see*.

Cross Creek Township, central Cumberland County. Coextensive with the city of Fayetteville.

Cross Hill, former community near Carthage, central Moore County. There, at Alexander Morrison's home, Tories gathered before going to the Battle of Moores Creek Bridge, February 27, 1776.

Crossing Knob, w Watauga County w of a bend in Watauga River.

Cross Knob, n Buncombe County between Chestnut Ridge and Rattlesnake Ridge.

Cross Landing, community in w Tyrrell County e of Scuppernong River.

Cross Millpond. *See* Hunters Millpond.

Cross Mountain, on the Buncombe-McDowell county line. Alt. approx. 3,600.

Crossnore, town in s Avery County. Alt. 3,546. Inc. 1925. Settled about 1838 and named for George Crossnore, keeper of general store. Crossnore School, founded in 1913 by Dr. Mary Martin Sloop, since has trained mountain children and promoted crafts.

Cross Roads, community is s Yadkin County served by post office, 1874–1904.

Cross Roads. *See* Maysville.

Cross Roads Church. *See* Courtney.

Cross Roads Township, s central Martin County.

Crossroads Township, central Wilson County.

Cross Rock, community in s Madison County served by post office, 1856–1929.

Cross Swamp rises in e Columbus County and flows se into Waccamaw River.

Crossville, community in e Gates County served by post office, 1870–84.

Crossway, community in s Scotland County on Lytch's Pond.

Crouse, town in s Lincoln County. Settled about 1840. Inc. 1907. Named for W. L. Crouse, a physician who built the first house in the community.

Crow Branch rises in s Jackson County and flows ne into Whitewater River.

Crow Branch rises in se Orange County about 2 mi. n of town of Chapel Hill and flows e into Booker Creek.

Crow Creek rises in s Macon County and flows ne into Cullasaja River.

Crow Creek rises in sw Randolph County and flows se into Montgomery County, where it enters Uwharrie River.

Crowder Mountain Township, sw Gaston County.

Crowders, community in s Gaston County. Nineteenth-century post office there was known as Crowder's Creek. Alt. 775.

Crowders Creek rises in sw Gaston County and flows ne and se into South Carolina, where it enters Catawba River.

Crowders Mountain, sw Gaston County. Named for Ulrich Crowder, an early settler who soon moved away. Some action against Tories took place there during the Revolution. Alt. 1,624. *See also* All Healing Springs.

Crowells, community in central Halifax County between Tillery and Enfield. Named for two brothers, Edward and Joseph Crowell, who settled there about 1730.

Crowells Springs, community in e Stanly County on Mountain Creek.

Crow Hill, point of land w of Straits, e Carteret County, extending into North River.

Crow Island appears on the Collet map, 1770; it existed as late as 1833. In Currituck Sound, ne Currituck County, it was se of Knotts Island and barred the sound side of New Currituck Inlet until the inlet closed. After 1833 Crow Island began disintegrating, so that by 1861 it was only a mass of tidal-marsh islands.

Crown Stream, community in s Pender County. An abandoned railroad station nearby was named Richards.

Crozier Branch rises in se Mecklenburg County and flows e into Cabarrus County, where it enters Ready Creek.

Crumpler, community in ne Ashe County on North Fork New River. Named for Maj. Thomas Newton Crumpler, who died of wounds received in the Civil War. Thompson's Bromine-Arsenic Springs nearby discovered in 1885; hotel and cottages built in 1887. This and nearby All Healing Springs made the region a popular resort in the late nineteenth and early twentieth centuries.

Cruse, community in e Haywood County on East Fork Pigeon River. Est. 1885 and named by first postmaster, who had just read *Robinson Crusoe*. Alt. 2,900.

Cruso, community in central Haywood County served by post office, 1892–1942.

Crusoe Island. *See* River View Community.

Crutchfield, community in sw Surry County on Yadkin River. Alt. 872.

Crutchfields Falls, rapids in Yadkin River, w Surry County near the mouth of Fishers River, s of the community of Crutchfield. The rapids comprise a fall of 4 ft. over a distance of approx. ¼ mi. Mentioned as early as 1819 in a survey of the rivers of the state.

Crystal, community in se Guilford County served by post office, 1880–1903.

Crystal Coast, modern term used to promote tourism on Bogue Banks and surrounding area, Carteret County.

Crystal Lake, e Moore County on Shaddock's Creek at the community of Lakeview. Formed in 1855 when Duncan Blue constructed a dam there; enlarged about 1908. Covers approx. 100 acres. Used for fishing, swimming, and boating.

Cuba, former community in n Rutherford County on Gilkey Creek. Post office from 1850 until 1906. Site of a cotton gin, mill, store, and other buildings; market for cherry bark and herbs.

Cub Branch rises in e Jackson County and flows se into Charley Creek.

Cub Creek rises in e central Burke County and flows se into Henry Fork.

Cub Creek rises in ne Chatham County and flows ne and se into sw Durham County, where it enters Morgan Creek.

Cub Creek rises in ne Davie County and flows sw into Cedar Creek.

Cub Creek rises in central Durham County and flows n into Eno River. Once called Cub Island Creek.

Cub Creek rises in w Granville County and flows ne into Tar River.

Cub Creek rises in n Mitchell County and flows sw into Cane Creek.

Cub Creek rises in e Rutherford County and flows ne into First Broad River.

Cub Creek rises in s Wilkes County and flows n into Yadkin River.

Cub Island Creek. *See* Cub Creek.

Cuccoowink Creek. *See* Dawson Creek.

Cucklemaker Swamp rises in n central Bertie County and flows s into Hoggard Mill Creek.

Cucklers Creek. *See* Cuckolds Creek.

Cuckolds Creek rises in e Beaufort County and flows w into Pantego Creek. Perhaps because of the meaning of the word cuckold, the name Cucklers has been applied to the creek.

Cucumber Creek rises on Noah's Mountain, s Alamance County, and flows s into Wells Creek.

Cucumber Creek. *See* Rock Hole Creek.

Cudda Bum, a creek, rises in ne Davidson County and flows s into Abbotts Creek. Named for Cuddahy Crouch, who lived nearby. "Bum" was his favorite expression and, when Cuddahy Creek was dammed for a mill, he began to speak of it as "a bum creek." From Cuddahy's Bum Creek the name Cudda Bum evolved.

Cuidreach Creek. *See* Corndack Creek.

Culberson, town in sw Cherokee County on South Fork Rapier Mill Creek. Inc. 1911. Named for Henry Culberson, who donated the site for the town and the post office. Alt. 1,618.

Culbert Branch rises in ne Cherokee County and flows nw into Junaluska Creek.

Culbert Ridge, n Yancey County between Hensley Branch and Bald Mountain Creek.

Culbreth, community in central Granville County served by post office, 1892–1907.

Cullasaja, community in e Macon County on Cullasaja River. Once known as Sugar Town. The Cherokee word *Kul-say-gee* meant "sugar" or "sweet."

Cullasaja Branch rises in s Swain County and flows ne into Yalaka Creek.

Cullasaja Falls. *See* Cullasaja River.

Cullasaja River rises in se Macon County and flows nw into Little Tennessee River. Bridal Veil, Dry, and Lower Cullasaja Falls, *which see,* are on the river. Moses Ashley Curtis, writing from Franklin on September 2, 1829, said that the "Falls of Sugar Town Creek" are "very imposing—nearly as high as Linville."

Culler. *See* Pinnacle.

Cullie Creek rises in n central Carteret County and flows nw into Cedar Creek. It is a very short stream.

Cullowhee, community in w central Jackson County on Tuckasegee River. Originally named Kullaughee Valley, an Indian word meaning "place of the lilies." Name changed to Painter, for the first postmaster, when a post office was est. there in 1883 (closed 1908). Renamed Cullowhee about 1900. Home of Western Carolina University, founded in 1889. Alt. 2,066.

Cullowhee Creek rises in w Jackson County and flows n into Tuckasegee River.

Cullowhee Gap, on the Jackson-Macon county line.

Cullowhee Mountain, w Jackson County, extends n from Hunter Jim Creek to Webster Creek. Alt. 4,411.

Cullowhee Township, w central Jackson County.

Cumberland, town in w Cumberland County. Settled 1850. Known as Beaver Creek for the stream on which it is located until 1889, when it was inc. Long inactive in municipal affairs. Alt. 125.

Cumberland County was formed in 1754 from Bladen County. Located in the se section of the state, it is bounded by Sampson, Bladen, Robeson, Hoke, Harnett, and Moore Counties. It was named for William Augustus, Duke of Cumberland (1721–65), second son of George II, who was commander of English troops at the Battle of Culloden in 1746 in which Scottish Highlanders were defeated. His extreme severity earned him the nickname of "The Butcher." It is ironic that the county named for him should have been settled by Scottish Highlanders. Area: 662 sq. mi. County seat: Fayetteville, with an elevation of 107 ft. Townships are Beaver Dam, Black River, Carvers Creek, Cedar Creek, Cross Creek, Eastover, Grays Creek, Manchester, Pearces Mill, Rockfish, and Seventy-First. Produces tobacco, corn, soybeans, wheat, oats, cotton, poultry, bakery products, textiles, dairy products, machinery, and lumber. *See also* Fayette County; Choffington.

Cumberland Gap, central Cherokee County near the junction of Rose and Dockery Creeks.

Cumberland Knob, nw Surry County. Alt. 2,885. Construction on the Blue Ridge Parkway began there September 11, 1935. Cumberland Knob Recreation Area with picnic grounds and hiking trails is there. Said to have been named by Dr. Thomas Walker, a Virginia explorer, for his patron, the Duke of Cumberland, in the 1750s.

Cummins Creek rises in ne Onslow County and flows se into Grants Creek.

Cumnock, community in nw Lee County. The Egypt coal mine is there; it operated at intervals from 1855 until 1928 and supplied coal for Confederate blockade runners. The community was named Egypt because large crops of corn produced in the area brought in buyers from the outside as in the biblical story of Joseph. Post office name changed to Cumnock in 1895 for an official of the mine. Alt. 259.

Cundiff Creek rises in s Surry County and flows se into Yadkin River.

Cunningham, community in nw Person County. Named for John W. Cunningham, local landowner and planter. Post office, Cunningham's Store, operated there from 1816 to 1908.

Cunningham Creek rises in s Macon County and flows ne into Shope Fork.

Cunningham Field, U.S. Marine Corps Air Station, 1941, named for aviator A. A. Cunningham. Renamed Cherry Point, *which see*, 1942.

Cunningham Mill, community is s Rockingham County. Site of grist mill prior to 1759.

Cunningham Mill. *See* Monroeton.

Cunningham Mountain, n Henderson County between Fletcher Branch and Clark Gap.

Cunningham Township, nw Person County.

Curfew, community in sw McDowell County. Site of store, post office, and one-room schoolhouse.

Curl, community in central Montgomery County.

Curl Tail Creek rises in nw Stanly County and flows ne in an arc into Riles Creek. Named for its meandering course. Known in 1903 as Fraley Branch.

Currie, community in sw Pender County. Alt. 33. Settled about 1888. Named for John H. Currie, a director of the Cape Fear & Yadkin Valley Railroad. Battle of Moores Creek Bridge, February 27, 1776, the first battle of the Revolution in North Carolina, was fought nearby. Moores Creek National Military Park, a 30-acre tract with numerous historical monuments and a museum, is at the site.

Curries Branch rises in n Columbus County and flows s into West Prong Creek.

Curriesville, community in s Moore County est. as railroad stop in 1920s.

Currituck, community and county seat, central Currituck County. Mentioned in local records as early as 1755. In 1822 a commission was appointed to purchase 20 acres around the courthouse, if local citizens voted approval, to lay out a town to be named Crawford. The proposal was defeated. Alt. 8.

Currituck Banks, or North Banks of Currituck, in e Currituck County, one of the Outer Banks, extends s from Virginia to Bodie Island in e Dare County. All or a part of

Currituck Banks is shown as Lucks Island on the Comberford map, 1657. *See also* Lucks Island; Croatamung; Point Bacon; Goade Island.

Currituck Beach. *See* Corolla.

Currituck County was formed by 1681 as a precinct within Albemarle County. Located in the ne section of the state, it is bounded by the Atlantic Ocean, Albemarle Sound, Camden County, and the state of Virginia. The name is traditionally said to be derived from *Coratank*, an Indian word for wild geese. Area: 469 sq. mi. County seat: Currituck, with an elevation of 8 ft. Townships are Crawford, Fruitville, Moyock, and Poplar Branch. Produces Irish potatoes, sweet potatoes, corn, soybeans, hogs, cattle, peanuts, steel products, concrete products, seafood, and lumber. *See also* Farmington.

Currituck Creek rises in se Hertford County and flows se into Bertie County, where it enters Chowan River.

Currituck Inlet, through what is now Currituck Banks, e Currituck County, shown on the Comberford map, 1657, as Choratuck Inlet. Closed by a storm in 1828. *See also* Denniss Island.

Currituck Narrows. *See* Poplar Branch.

Currituck Parish, Church of England, Currituck County, coextensive with the county, est. 1715. In 1767 the parish had 400 white taxables.

Currituck Point extends from the sw mainland of Hyde County into the mouth of Pungo River.

Currituck Sound, the body of water between Currituck Banks on the e and the mainland of Currituck County on the w and from Knotts Island on the n to Powells Point on the s. Approx. 30 mi. long; max. width, 4 mi. It appears on the Moseley map, 1733. In 1930 Wright Memorial Bridge, 3 mi. long wooden span, was built across the sound from Point Harbor to n of Kitty Hawk. *See also* Titepano.

Currituck Township, w Hyde County.

Curtis, community in central Alamance County served by post office, 1855–1905.

Curtis Cove, s Haywood County. A tributary of West Fork Pigeon River flows through the cove.

Curtis Creek rises in n central Avery County and flows n into Elk River.

Curtis Creek rises near Doubletop Mountain on the Buncombe-Haywood county line and flows sw into Hominy Creek.

Curtis Creek rises in sw Macon County and flows sw into Nantahala River.

Curtis Creek rises in w McDowell County and flows se into Catawba River.

Curtiss Knob, s Macon County at the head of Piney Knob Creek.

Curtis's Mills. *See* Curtis.

Cuscopang River. *See* Scuppernong River.

Cushing Branch rises in n Henderson County and flows nw into Cane Creek. Also known as Cushion Creek.

Cushion Creek. *See* Cushing Branch.

Cutawhiskie Swamp rises in se Northampton County and flows ne into Hertford County, where it enters Livermans Mill Pond on Potecasi Creek. Named for an Indian village mentioned in local records (with various spellings) as early as 1718.

Cut Laurel Gap, in Stone Mountains, w Ashe County on the Tennessee state line. Named because early settlers encountered such a thick "rhododendron hell" there that they had to cut a tunnel through it for a mile or more. Alt. 3,746.

Cutoff Island, e Dare County, in the waters of Roanoke Sound off the sw tip of Bodie Island.

Cut-off Ridge, n Jackson County, extends n from Scott Creek.

Cutshall Branch rises in n Madison County and flows w into Shelton Laurel Creek.

Cutshalltown, community in n Madison County on a tributary of Shelton Laurel Creek.

Cutthroat Gap, on the Buncombe-Henderson county line between Candler Knob and Stony Bald. Alt. approx. 4,200.

Cuwhiffle Swamp rises in se Sampson County near Delway and flows nw into Six Runs Creek. The name may be derived through faulty pronunciation of the Gaelic *Culmhutar* (pronounced "kul-vú-tar"), meaning "smuggler" or "mutineer." *See also* Quewhiffle.

Cwareunoc, an Indian village shown on the De Bry map, 1590, as being on Bogue Sound, s Carteret County.

Cycle, community in w Yadkin County on Dobbins Creek. Known first as Pea Ridge. Post office est. 1904 and named Cycle from the fact that the patrons it served lived in a circle from the post office. Post office name gradually replaced the older name.

Cynthia Branch rises in n Yancey County and flows w into Cane River.

Cypress Branch rises in central Columbus County and flows ne into White Marsh.

Cypress Creek rises in Cypress Creek Bay in ne Bladen County and flows s and e into South River.

Cypress Creek rises in central Columbus County and flows n into White Marsh.

Cypress Creek rises in e Franklin County and flows s into Tar River. Appears on the Collet map, 1770, as Cyprus Creek.

Cypress Creek rises in sw Harnett County and flows sw into Hoke County, where it enters Crane Creek.

Cypress Creek rises in n Northampton County and flows ne into Virginia, where it enters Meherrin River. Appears on the map of the North Carolina–Virginia line run by William Byrd and others, 1728, and on the Moseley map, 1733.

Cypress Creek rises in n Onslow County and flows n into Jones County, where it enters Trent River. Appears on the Collet map, 1770.

Cypress Creek rises in w Onslow County and flows sw into Duplin County, where it flows nw and ne into Cape Fear River.

Cypress Creek, community in ne Bladen County.

Cypress Creek, community in se Duplin County.

Cypress Creek. See Goodwin Creek.

Cypress Creek Bay, ne Bladen County.

Cypress Creek Bay, a mucky, loam-filled bay in central Columbus County.

Cypress Creek Township, ne Bladen County.

Cypress Creek Township, se Duplin County.

Cypress Creek Township, former township in se Franklin County, now township no. 9.

Cypress Creek Township, s Jones County.

Cypress Landing, community in e Pender County.

Cypress Point, a point of land extending from the mainland of w Dare County s of Mill Tail Creek into Alligator River.

Cypress Run rises in se Beaufort County and flows e into South Creek.

Cypress Swamp rises in w Gates County and flows sw into Taylor Millpond.

Cypress Swamp rises in w Onslow County and flows se into Sandy Run Swamp.

Cypress Swamp. See Goodwin Creek.

Cyprett's Bridge, former bridge over New Hope Creek in ne Chatham County on the road from New Bern by Raleigh to Pittsboro. Also spelled Ceputt's, Cipritz, Cyprits, Cypretz. It was selected in 1793 from seven suggested sites within 15 mi. of which the University of North Carolina was to be located. Later called Prince's Bridge, which see.

Cyrus, community in w Onslow County on Harris Creek.

D

Dabbs, community in s central Caswell County.

Dabney, community in w Vance County. Named for local store operator.

Dabney Township, w Vance County.

Dads Top, mountain peak n of Twelve O'clock Top on the Buncombe-Haywood county line.

Dailys Creek rises in w Lenoir County and flows ne into Neuse River. Probably named for John Dailey, who settled there about 1800.

Dairy Branch flows sw thorough Mecklenburg County into Little Sugar Creek.

Dale, community in se Surry County served by post office, 1894–1904.

Dalila, community in central Sampson County served by post office, 1892–1904.

Dalkeith, plantation house in se Warren County near Arcola. Built in 1824 by Jack Burgess; still used as a dwelling.

Dallas, town in central Gaston County. Authorized to be laid out as county seat by act creating the county, 1846. It remained the county seat until 1909, when Gastonia was selected by popular vote. Inc. 1863. Named for George M. Dallas (1792–1864), vice president of the United States at the time the county was created. The area received postal service as early as 1817 from Hoylesville post office, named for Andrew Hoyle, first postmaster, and located 3 mi. e of site of Dallas. Post office service began in Dallas in 1846.

Dallas Township, n central Gaston County.

Da-loh-no-geh. *See* Yellow Mountain.

Dalton, community in sw Stokes County. Alt. 785. A post office there in 1874 was known as Boyles' Store.

Dalton. *See* Clarkton.

Dalton Branch rises in nw Swain County in Great Smoky Mountains National Park and flows se into Moore Springs Branch.

Dalton Creek rises in e Macon County and flows ne into Caler Fork.

Dalton Gap, on the Swain County, N.C.–Blount County, Tenn., line in Great Smoky Mountains National Park between Sheep Wallow Knob and Parsons Bald. Alt. 2,955.

Dalton Ridge, nw Swain County in Great Smoky Mountains National Park extending nw from the head of Judy Branch to Sheep Wallow Knob.

Dam Creek rises in s Pasquotank County and flows e into Big Flatty Creek.

Damons Mountain, sw Cherokee County, extends from Cole Gap ne to Dickey Branch.

Dana, community in e Henderson County. A post office was est. there in 1892 expressly to serve the Hadley Hotel; named for Dana Hadley, son of the owner of the hotel. Apple growing and packing center.

Danamora, community in n Guilford County served by post office, 1892–1903.

Danbury, town and county seat, central Stokes County on the Dan River. Replaced Germantown as the county seat in 1849 when the county was divided to form Forsyth County. Inc. 1957. Called simply "county town of Stokes" from about 1849 until 1851, when it was given the name Crawford in honor of the wife of John Hill, longtime clerk of court and member of Congress. Changed to Danbury in 1852 for name of plantation of Gov. Alexander Martin (1738–1807) near the mouth of Jacobs Creek on the Dan River in Rockingham County. Martin was governor when Stokes County was created. Alt. 825. *See also* Intelligence.

Danbury Creek rises in sw Stokes County and flows w into Little Yadkin River.

Danbury Township, central Stokes County.

Dandy, community in nw Ashe County. Alt. 3,455.

Danes Creek rises in n Macon County and flows se into Younce Creek.

Dan Gap, s Macon County between Henderson Mountain and Little Fishhawk Mountain.

Dan Holland Creek rises in ne Cherokee County and flows se into Valley River.

Daniel Boone's Cave. *See* Boone's Cave.

Daniel Boone Wildlife Management Area, part of Pisgah National Forest in nw Burke County.

Daniel Ridge in nw Transylvania County between Shuck Ridge Creek and Daniel Ridge Creek.

Daniel Ridge Creek rises in nw Transylvania County and flows se into Right Fork Davidson River.

Daniels Cove, s Haywood County on Shining Creek.

Daniels Creek rises in w Harnett County and flows ne into Cape Fear River. The name is a corruption of Donnelys; named for Arthur Donnelly, who settled on its banks in 1750. Earlier known as McPhersons Creek.

Daniels Gap, on the Ashe-Wilkes county line.

Daniels Marshes. *See* Roanoke Marshes.

Daniels-Rhyne, textile community in central Lincoln County sw of Lincolnton. Originally two separate communities. Daniels named for Daniel Warlick, pioneer settler; Rhyne named for founder of local mill.

Daniel Swash, waterway through a group of unnamed tidal-marsh islands in Pamlico Sound just off Portsmouth Island, e Carteret County.

Daniel Town, community in s Rutherford County. Named for Leonard N. Daniel, who operated a store there, owned adjacent land, and built several houses.

Danover, community in ne Surry County.

Dan Payne Mountain, s Madison County at the head of Caney Fork Branch.

Dan River rises in s Patrick County, Va., and flows se into Stokes County. It flows se and ne into Rockingham County and back into Virginia. It dips back into North Carolina on the Caswell-Rockingham county line and into n Caswell County, then flows ne in Virginia into Kerr Lake, *which see*, on Roanoke River. Mentioned by William Byrd in 1728. Probably an Indian name.

Dan River, community in w Rockingham County served by post office, 1853–66.

Dan River Township, n central Caswell County.

Dans Creek rises in ne Columbus County and flows se and e into Livingston Creek.

Dans Creek rises in ne Swain County and flows sw into Straight Fork.

Dan Sisk Gap, s Burke County in South Mountains.

Dans Knob, e Madison County between Beetree Creek and East Fork [Bull Creek].

Danson's Manor. *See* Shiloh.

Dan's School, community in central Forsyth County.

Danton, town authorized to be est. in 1803 on the lands of Thomas Rivers on the n side of Dan River, Stokes County. Apparently the town never developed.

Danville. *See* Leaksville.

Danville. *See* Startown.

Dan Weeks Point, a point of land extending into White Oak River, sw Carteret County.

Darb Branch rises in n Transylvania County and flows ne into Bradley Creek.

Darby, community in w Wilkes County on Elk Creek. Named for Darby Hendrix, eighteenth-century pioneer landowner.

Dardens, community in ne Martin County. A post office known as Davis' Store served the area from 1827 to 1833. Named Dardens for local family, one of whom, Col. James G. Darden, was a personal friend of Warren G. Harding from as early as 1917 and later, as an oil man, was involved in the Teapot Dome affair. Alt. 46.

Dare County was formed in 1870 from Curri-tuck, Tyrrell, and Hyde Counties. Located in the ne section of the state, it is bounded by the Atlantic Ocean; Pamlico, Croatan, and Albemarle Sounds; and Hyde and Tyrrell Counties. It was named for Virginia Dare, born August 18, 1587, on Roanoke Island in the county; she was the first child of English parents to be born in America. Area: 1,246 sq. mi. (388, land; 858, water). County seat: Manteo, with an elevation of 12 ft. Townships are Atlantic, Croatan, East Lake, Hatteras,

Kennekeet, and Nags Head. Produces boats, concrete products, cabinets, scuppernongs, figs, poultry, processed seafood, corn, soybeans, and lumber.

Darfer, community in s Cleveland County served by post office, 1894–1903.

Darham Creek. *See* Durham Creek.

Dark Branch rises in central Duplin County and flows se into Northeast Cape Fear River.

Dark Branch rises in central Swain County and flows sw into Yalaka Creek.

Dark Corner, reputed bootlegger haven in sw Henderson County. Now part of Greenville, S.C., watershed.

Dark Cove extends nw from Big Butte Mountain to West Cove in e Haywood County.

Dark Mountain, n Montgomery County near Barnes Creek.

Dark Prong rises in s Haywood County and flows e into East Fork Pigeon River.

Dark Ridge, mountain in n Avery County.

Dark Ridge, ne Jackson County between Dark Ridge Creek and Cabin Creek.

Dark Ridge, community in n Avery County.

Dark Ridge Creek rises in n Avery County and flows w into Tennessee, where it enters Elk River.

Dark Ridge Creek rises in ne Jackson County and flows nw into Scott Creek.

Darkridge Gap, mountain gap in n Avery County.

Darlington, community in central Halifax County. Also known as Buzzardtown.

Darlington, community in n Rutherford County served by post office, 1887–1904.

Darnell, community in nw Wilkes County on a tributary of North Fork Reddies River. Named for Abdiel Darnell, who settled in the vicinity shortly after 1800.

Dasemunkepeuc. *See* Manns Harbor.

Dashoga Ridge, ne Swain County in Great Smoky Mountains National Park. Its center is near lat. 35°40'40" N., long. 83°14'55" W.

Da-tsu-la-gun-yi. *See* Cold Mountain.

Dave Barrett Creek. *See* Right Fork [Eagle Creek].

Dave Bellew Top, peak in sw Cherokee County between Wolf Creek and Hot House Creek.

Davenport, community in s Mecklenburg County served by post office, 1888–1903.

Davenport Branch rises in e Clay County and flows sw into Buck Creek.

Davenport Branch rises in s Clay County and flows se into Hiwassee River.

Davenport Forks, community in ne Washington County s of Deep Creek.

Davenport Gap, a wind gap in Great Smoky Mountains where the North Carolina–Tennessee boundary crosses the ne boundary of Great Smoky Mountains National Park, Haywood County, N.C., and Cocke County, Tenn., near lat. 35°46′30″ N., long. 83°6′30″ W. Named in honor of Col. William Davenport, who in 1821 marked a stone on the "north side of Cataloochee Turnpike Road" as the starting point of his survey of the Tennessee–North Carolina state line.

Davenport Mountain, w Henderson County between Johnsons Mill Creek and Shaw Creek.

Dave Rock, in w Transylvania County e of Bart Branch.

Davers Island. *See* Harkers Island.

David Daniel Pond. *See* Contentnea Lake.

Davids Creek rises in e Stanly County and flows se into Cedar Creek.

Davidson, town in n Mecklenburg County. Inc. 1879 as Davidson College; name changed, 1891. Davidson College founded there, 1837, named for Gen. William Lee Davidson (1746–81), Revolutionary War hero killed at the Battle of Cowan's Ford. Alt. 826.

Davidson Branch rises in w Haywood County and flows s into Palmer Creek.

Davidson College. *See* Davidson.

Davidson County was formed in 1822 from Rowan County. Located in the central section of the state, it is bounded by Randolph, Montgomery, Rowan, Davie, Forsyth, and Guilford Counties. It was named for Gen. William Lee Davidson (1746–81), who was killed at the Battle of Cowans Ford on the Catawba River during the Revolutionary War. Area: 560 sq. mi. County seat: Lexington, with an elevation of 810 ft. Townships are Abbotts Creek, Alleghany, Arcadia, Boone, Conrad Hill, Cotton Grove, Emmons, Hampton, Healing Springs, Jackson Hill, Lexington, Midway, Reedy Creek, Silver Hill, Thomasville, Tyro, and Yadkin College. Produces wheat, oats, corn, tobacco, poultry, livestock, glass products, vinyl siding, box springs, voting machines, furniture, apparel, lumber, concrete pipe, batteries, lumber, slate, flagstone, and shale for brick.

Davidson County, now in Tennessee, was created in 1783 and named in honor of Gen. William Lee Davidson (1746–81). Nashville (now the capital of Tennessee) became the county seat. The area was a part of the territory ceded by North Carolina in 1789 to the federal government.

Davidson Creek rises in s Iredell County and flows sw into Mecklenburg County, where it enters Catawba River. Probably named for George Davidson, who owned 500 acres on the creek in 1778.

Davidson Gap, se of Robinson Rough on the Buncombe-Madison county line.

Davidson Gap, w Haywood County, Great Smoky Mountains National Park near lat. 35°39′08″ N., long. 83°06′07″ W., between Bald Top and Cooks Knob.

Davidson River rises in w Transylvania County and flows se into French Broad River.

Davidson River, community in central Transylvania County. *See* Pisgah Forest.

Davidson's Fort. *See* Old Fort.

Davidson Township, sw Iredell County. Named for a local family.

Davidsonville, community in s Cherokee County on Moccasin Creek.

Davids Point, an arm of n Hatteras Island extending into Pamlico Sound, e Dare County. Lies e of Great Island and s of the community of Waves.

Davie, community in central Henderson County. Alt. 2,214.

Davie Academy. *See* Kappa.

Davie Branch rises in nw Henderson County and flows ne into North Fork.

Davie County was formed in 1836 from Rowan County. Located in the central section of the state, it is bounded by Davidson, Rowan, Iredell, Yadkin, and Forsyth Counties. It was named for William Richardson Davie (1756–1820), Revolutionary War soldier, member of the Federal Convention of 1787, governor of North Carolina, minister to France, and one of the founders of the University of North Carolina. Area: 264 sq. mi. County seat: Mocksville, with an elevation of 866 ft. Townships are Calahaln, Clarksville, Farmington, Fulton, Jerusalem, Mocksville, and Shady Grove. Produces corn, wheat, barley, oats, dairy products, livestock, hogs, apparel, furniture, chemicals, garage doors, and textiles.

Davie Crossroads, community in s Davie County at the crossing of U.S. Highway 601 and N.C. Highway 801. Est. 1911–15 when a garage and store opened there. Locally now called Greasy Corner for lube work performed by mechanics at the junction. Alt. approx. 740.

Davie Mountain, s Clay County at the sw end of Cherry Mountain. Alt. 2,958.

Davie Mountain, nw Henderson County near Davie Branch.

Davis, community on Core Sound in e Carteret County on Davis Shore.

Davis. *See* Bakersville.

Davis Bald, on the Macon-Swain county line near the head of Little Laurel Creek. Alt. approx. 4,500.

Davis Bay, e Pasquotank County between Cobb Point and Brickhouse Point on the Pasquotank River.

Davis Branch rises in w Madison County and flows s into French Broad River.

Davis Branch rises in s central Swain County and flows sw into Yalaka Creek.

Davis Cove Branch rises in w Madison County and flows e into Spring Creek.

Davis Creek rises in se Brunswick County and flows sw into tidal marshes that drain into the Atlantic Ocean through Lockwoods Folly Inlet.

Davis Creek rises in n Cherokee County and flows sw and se into Hanging Dog Creek.

Davis Creek rises in s Swain County and flows w into Sawmill Creek.

Davis Ford, former ford over Rocky River, Anson-Stanly county line at the mouth of Richardson Creek. John Davis owned a plantation in the vicinity. Richard Lane Ordinary is located at approx. site on the Collet map, 1770.

Davis Gap, mountain gap in s central Swain County on the head of Davis Branch.

Davis Island, in Core Sound at the s end of Davis Shore, e Carteret County. Named for William Davis, who settled there in 1715.

Davis Landing, on Pungo River, e Beaufort County.

Davis Mill Pond, on Trotters Creek, w Lenoir County. Formed about 1850. Covers 60 acres; max. depth 12 ft.

Davis Mill Pond. *See* Pages Lake.

Davis Shore, e shore of a peninsula in e Carteret County extending into Core Sound.

Davis Slough, e Dare County in the waters of Pamlico Sound sw of Oregon Inlet.

Davis' Store. *See* Dardens.

Davistown, former community in s Edgecombe County. Now only a railroad crossing.

Davis Township, on Core Sound in e Carteret County.

Davis White Sulphur Springs, former resort in e Alexander County. Flourished from about 1883 until early twentieth century. Known also as Sulphur Springs. Davis family operated gristmill there before and after the site was popular as a summer resort.

Dawson, community in s Halifax County. A post office as early as 1830.

Dawson, community in n Lenoir County. Named for a local family. Formerly a depot on the Hines Lumber Company railroad from Kinston to Snow Hill. Once a center for shipping logs and cotton. A school was operated in the vicinity as early as 1793. The Industrial Christian College was operated there from 1906 until about 1921.

Dawson Creek rises in s Pamlico County and flows se into Neuse River. Appears on the Moseley map, 1733. Named for Richard Dawson, who purchased land there in 1706. Prior to 1706 the creek was known as Cuccoowink Creek. *See also* Janeiro.

Dawson's Landing, community in nw Bladen County served by post office, 1873–1903. Formerly Harrison Creek.

Day Book, community in ne Yancey County on Jacks Creek. Alt. 2,350. Post office est. about 1815 and named for a book in which names were recorded of settlers moving west. Another version of the traditional origin of the name is that it came from a time book kept for employees of a local lumber company.

Daylo, community in nw Wilkes County on Middle Fork Reddies River. Est. 1924 by E. N. Vannoy, a merchant, and named for a brand of flashlights that he sold.

Days Creek rises in s Watauga County and flows nw into East Fork [South Fork New River].

Days Crossroads, community in n Halifax County.

Day's Gap. *See* Hugh Day's Gap.

Daystrom, community in w Robeson County. Alt. 179. Known first as Alma for the Alma Lumber Company, which operated there. Name changed about 1950 when Daystrom Laminates, a furniture manufacturer, began operations there.

Dayton, community in se Durham County served by post office, 1881–1905.

Dead Backwater, a sluggish body of water that flows only at high tide between Bird Island and the mainland of Colkins Neck, extending from inside Mad Inlet to Bonaparte Creek in sw Brunswick County.

Deaden Top, peak in central Cherokee County between Hiwassee River and West Prong Grape Creek.

Deadfall Creek rises in sw Anson County and flows ne and s into South Carolina, where it enters Thompson Creek.

Deadline Ridge, central Clay County, extends n from Tusquitee Creek to Chestnut Branch.

Deals. *See* Wash Woods.

Deals Branch rises in nw Swain County and flows s into Lake Cheoah.

Deals Creek rises in n Rowan County and flows ne into Yadkin River.

Deals Gap, mountain gap on the Swain County, N.C.-Blount County, Tenn., line in Great Smoky Mountains National Park. Alt. 1,957.

Dealsville, community in w Alexander County. Alt. 1,150. Named for local family that operated a store and leather tannery.

Dean, community in e Macon County on Lake Emory.

Dean Island, a sandy island approx. ½ mi. long in Little Tennessee River in n Macon County.

Deans Community. *See* Coopertown.

De Armond Bald, mountain in nw Swain County on Jenkins Trail Ridge in Great Smoky Mountains National Park. Alt. 5,100.

De Armond Ridge, nw Swain County in Great Smoky Mountains, a short spur extending sw from De Armond Bald on Jenkins Trail Ridge.

Deavers, former community in central Transylvania County near the confluence of Davidson and French Broad Rivers. Later known as Puella and today as Pisgah Forest.

Deavers Mill Pond, on Poley Swamp in n Duplin County. Alt. 106.

Deaver View, community in central Buncombe County.

Deaver View Mountain, central Buncombe County. Alt. 3,130.

DeBerry's Mill Pond, ne Northampton County on Kirbys Creek. Covers approx. 100 acres; max. depth 10 ft.

Debruhls. *See* Rhems.

Debs Knob, s Wilkes County near the head of East Prong Cub Creek. Probably named for Deborah Riddle, a nineteenth-century resident of the area.

Deck Hill, peak in s Watauga County between Flannery Fork [South Fork New River] and Payne Branch.

Deep Bay, a bay on the se shore of South Lake, central Dare County.

Deep Bay, s Hyde County between Bell Island and Judith Island.

Deep Bottom, stream, rises in w Washington County and flows nw into Welch Creek. Mentioned in local records as early as 1868.

Deep Bottom Branch rises in n Jones County and flows s into Beaver Creek.

Deep Branch rises in ne Cherokee County and flows se into Valley River.

Deep Cove, a channel separating Judith Island and Swanquarter Island in Pamlico Sound, s Hyde County.

Deep Creek rises in n central Alamance County and flows sw into Stony Creek.

Deep Creek rises in sw Anson County and flows s into Deadfall Creek.

Deep Creek rises in e Carteret County and flows s into North River.

Deep Creek rises in n central Carteret County and flows s into Newport River.

Deep Creek rises in central Currituck County in Maple Swamp and flows sw into North River.

Deep Creek rises in w Graham County and flows ne into Cheoah River.

Deep Creek rises in n Halifax County and flows ne into Roanoke River. Appears on the Collet map, 1770, as Great Creek, a name that is still sometimes applied to it.

Deep Creek rises in s Halifax County and flows

se into Fishing Creek in n Edgecombe County. It appears on the Collet map, 1770.

Deep Creek rises in se Halifax County and flows s into ne Edgecombe County, where it flows sw into Fishing Creek.

Deep Creek rises in e Hertford County and flows ne into Chowan River.

Deep Creek rises in Fort Bragg Military Reservation in ne Hoke County and flows ne into Little River.

Deep Creek rises in sw Moore County and flows s into Lumber River.

Deep Creek rises in nw Northampton County and flows se into Roanoke River. Appears as Falling Run on the MacRae map, 1833; name changed after 1862.

Deep Creek rises in central Person County and flows se into Durham County, where it enters Flat River.

Deep Creek rises in Sevier County, Tenn., and flows s through central and e Swain County into Tuckasegee River.

Deep Creek rises in n Washington County and flows ne into Bull Bay.

Deep Creek is formed in s Yadkin County by the junction of North Deep Creek and South Deep Creek. It flows se into Yadkin River. Appears as Fifth Creek on the Collet map, 1770.

Deep Creek, community in sw Anson County. A post office operated there, 1853–1906.

Deep Creek. *See* Bear Creek.

Deep Creek. *See* Indian Creek.

Deep Creek Gap, mountain gap n Swain County on Fork Ridge in Great Smoky Mountains National Park.

Deep Creek Township, former township ne Edgecombe County. Now township no. 4.

Deep Creek Township, sw Yadkin County.

Deep Cut. *See* Eufola.

Deep Ford Creek rises in w Transylvania County and flows e and ne into Toxaway River.

Deep Gap, mountain gap in Bullhead Mountain, se Alleghany County.

Deep Gap, mountain gap in Firescald Mountain, w Avery County.

Deep Gap, on the Clay-Macon county line.

Deep Gap, at nw end of Firescald Ridge in sw Graham County.

Deep Gap, central Graham County in Cheoah Mountains at the head of East Buffalo Creek.

Deep Gap, s Haywood County between Deep Gap Cove and Hickory Flat Cove.

Deep Gap, s Haywood County on Shining Rock Ledge.

Deep Gap, s Haywood County on the head of Deep Gap Creek.

Deep Gap, w Haywood County between Strawberry Knob and Maggie Spring Gap.

Deep Gap, on the head of Plott Creek in w Haywood County.

Deep Gap, on the Henderson-Polk county line.

Deep Gap, s Jackson County on the head of Frolictown Creek.

Deep Gap, n Jackson County between Parker Knob and Steep Mountain.

Deep Gap, e Jackson County between Snaggy Bald and Lynn Gap.

Deep Gap, on Jackson-Haywood county line.

Deep Gap, e Macon County between Round Mountain and Panther Mountain.

Deep Gap, n Madison County at the nw end of Brigman Hollow.

Deep Gap, on the McDowell-Yancey county line between Glass Rock Knob and Green Knob.

Deep Gap, on Big Ridge in n Mitchell County.

Deep Gap, w Polk County on Harm Creek.

Deep Gap, se Swain County between the head of Bowers Creek and Yalaka Creek.

Deep Gap, e Swain County between Deep Gap Branch and Connelly Mountain.

Deep Gap, nw Swain County between Haw Gap Branch and Mill Branch on Forrester Ridge.

Deep Gap, w Swain County between the head of Rowan Branch and Pilkey Creek.

Deep Gap, n Transylvania County on the head of Brushy Branch.

Deep Gap, w Transylvania County on the head of Laurel Fork Davidson River.

Deep Gap, e Watauga County 12 mi. e of Boone. Alt. 4,500.

Deep Gap, s Yancey County near the head of Colbert Creek.

Deep Gap, w Yancey County between Possumtrot and Horton Creeks.

Deep Gap, community in e Watauga County on Deep Gap Creek. Post Office est. 1891 as Yuma. Name changed about 1924.

Deep Gap Branch rises in e Swain County and flows ne into Chestnut Cove Creek.

Deep Gap Cove, s Haywood County on a tributary of Little East Fork Pigeon River.

Deep Gap Creek rises in s Haywood County and flows nw into Allen Creek.

Deep Gap Creek rises in e Watauga County near

Laxon and flows ne into se Ashe County, where it enters South Fork New River. Once known as Gap Creek.

Deep Gap Mountain, e Graham County extends ne from Dry Creek.

Deep Gully rises on Craven-Jones county line and flows se into Trent River.

Deep Gully, a canal on the Jones-Craven county line that flows se into Trent River.

Deep Gully Creek rises in n Onslow County and flows sw into Mill Creek.

Deep Hole Point. *See* Marshallberg.

Deep Inlet appears on the Price map, 1808, in e New Hanover County just n of the present Masonboro Inlet. Deep Inlet closed after 1838 but before 1861.

Deeplow Gap, n Swain County on the e slope of Thomas Ridge in Great Smoky Mountains National Park.

Deep Point, point of land extending into Alligator River, e of junction of Intracoastal Waterway and Alligator River, n Hyde County.

Deep River is formed in sw Guilford County at High Point Lake by the junction of East Fork Deep River and West Fork Deep River. It flows se through Randolph County, continues across the ne edge of Moore County, and forms a part of the Chatham-Lee county line. It joins Haw River in se Chatham County to form Cape Fear River. The junction of Haw and Deep Rivers, site of the town of Haywood, *which see*, was one of six sites suggested in 1788 for the location of the state capital.

Deep River Township, former township in n Lee County. Now township no. 4.

Deep River Township, ne Moore County.

Deep River Township, w Guilford County.

Deep Run, a stream fed by several canals in e Beaufort County, flows w into Broad Creek.

Deep Run rises in sw Lenoir County and flows ne into Southwest Creek.

Deep Run rises in w Onslow County and flows se into Southwest Creek.

Deep Run, town in sw Lenoir County. Inc. 1925. Est. in the 1880s when Ira D. Sparrow and Ike Stroud opened a turpentine distillery and built several stores at the site. A Baptist church erected there about 1850 is still in use. For a time, the place was nicknamed "Red Town" because a number of the earliest houses were painted red.

Deep Run Swamp rises in e Martin County and flows nw into Gardners Creek.

Deep Swamp Branch rises in se Hertford County and flows ne into Chowan River.

Deep Water Point appears on the Moseley map, 1733, in what is now Brunswick County between Elizabeth River and Walden Creek, e of the present town of Southport. Appeared as late as 1851–53 on navigation charts. *See also* Walkersburg.

Deer Branch rises in ne Franklin County and flows e into Sandy Creek.

Deer Branch rises in n Yancey County and flows se into Big Branch.

Deer Creek, a creek in Core Sound near Core Banks in e Carteret County.

Deer Creek rises in sw Carteret County and flows s 2 mi. into Bogue Sound.

Deer Creek rises in nw Haywood County and flows se into Big Creek.

Deer Creek Gap, on the Haywood County, N.C.–Cocke County, Tenn., line in Great Smoky Mountains National Park near lat. 35°43′04″ N., long. 83°15′ W.

Deerfield, community in s Watauga County near East Fork [South Fork New River].

Deer Gap, s Macon County between High Knob and Rich Knob.

Deer Island, se Onslow County w of Swansboro in the mouth of Hawkins Slough. Formerly 3 acres but now considerably reduced. The name is now applied to the nearby peninsula between Swansboro and The Hammock.

Deer Lick Branch rises in s Mitchell County and flows n into East Fork Crabtree Creek.

Deerlick Gap, on the McDowell-Mitchell county line.

Deerlick Knob, in e Macon County between Corbin Creek and the head of Laurel Creek.

Deerlick Ridge extends e from West Buffalo Creek to Snowbird Creek in s Graham County.

Deerlick Ridge, e Haywood County between Rice Cove Creek and Rough Creek.

Deer Mountain, s Yancey County between Winter Star Ridge and the head of Locust Creek. Alt. 6,212.

Deer Park Mountain, w Madison County between Ferry Branch and Spring Creek.

Deerplay Gap, on the Avery-Mitchell county line.

Deer Pond Branch rises in n Granville County and flows ne into Spewmarrow Creek.

Deer Ridge, n Yancey County parallel to Deer Creek.

Deerstand Creek rises in nw McDowell County on the s slope of Woods Mountain and flows s into Slim Creek.

Deets, community in w Jackson County served by post office, 1900–1913.

Defeat Branch rises in n Swain County in Great Smoky Mountains National Park and flows sw to join Roaring Creek in forming Bone Valley Creek. Named after an early hunter there had his shoes burned in the campfire while he slept during a snowstorm.

Defeat Knob, on the Cherokee-Clay county line in the Valley River Mountains.

Dehart, community in n Wilkes County near North Prong Roaring River.

De Hart Bald, in s Swain County on the head of Licklog Creek.

De Hart Branch rises in s Swain County and flows sw into Yalaka Creek.

De Hart Branch rises in s Swain County between Bearpen Ridge and Rattlesnake Ridge and flows w into Wesser Creek.

De Hart Creek rises in s Swain County and flows sw into Little Tennessee River.

Delco, town in ne Columbus County. The site was first known as Brinkly when it was a stop on the Wilmington, Columbia, and Augusta Rail Road. Inc. 1913 as New Berlin when Hugh MacRae of Wilmington attempted to attract German colonists to work surrounding farmlands. In 1918, during World War I, the name was changed to Pershing in honor of Gen. John J. Pershing. After about six months, for an unknown reason, it became necessary to change the name. Delco was chosen because the Delco Light Plant Company had just installed a lighting system in the local high school. Alt. 50.

Delight. *See* Lattimore.

Delightful Plains is shown on the Moseley map, 1733, as extending from the present Big Bay of Bladen County se and parallel with the present Brown Marsh Swamp.

Delk, community in w Forsyth County served by post office, 1889–1907.

Dellaplane, community in s Wilkes County between Brier Creek and Fishing Creek. Col. John Bryan (1753–1842) settled there about 1803.

Dellinger Branch rises in s Lincoln County and flows se into Leepers Creek.

Dellinger Hollow, in e Mitchell County between Long Ridge and the Avery-Mitchell county line.

Dellingers. *See* Concord.

Dellview, town in nw Gaston County. Inc. 1925 by three Dellinger brothers who operated a large chicken farm at the site. They wanted better protection from stray dogs than was provided by the county. By incorporating their farm as a town, they could enact and enforce a town ordinance against stray dogs. About 1930 fire destroyed the chicken business, and by 1967 only a single member of the family was living in the "town."

Dellwood, community in central Haywood County on Jonathans Creek. Alt. 2,771.

Delmar, community in central Halifax County between Halifax and Enfield.

Del Mar Beach, se Pender County on the Atlantic Ocean side of Topsail Island.

Delmont, community in s Henderson County on Little Mud Creek.

Deloach Branch rises in central Edgecombe County and flows sw into Cokey Swamp.

DeLoatche's Mill Pond, central Northampton County on Potecasi Creek.

Delos, community in sw Mecklenburg County served by post office, 1892–98.

De Lozier Gap, n Swain County on Welch Ridge near the head of West Fork [Chambers Creek].

Delphi, community in n Alleghany County served by post office, 1880–94.

Delta, community in s Sampson County served by post office, 1880–1917. Formerly known as Black River Chapel.

Delta, community in e Stokes County.

Delway, community in se Sampson County on the head of Cuwhiffle Swamp.

Demia, community in s Buncombe County served by post office, 1888–1902.

Demming, community in se McDowell County served by post office, 1892–1914. Founded in antebellum period during gold rush and named for mining company officer. Now known as Brackettown.

Democrat, community in n Buncombe County near the junction of Sugar and Ivy Creeks. Alt. 2,119.

Democrat, community on the Madison-Yancey county line on Middle Creek.

Dendron, community in s McDowell County near Old Fort. Named by Western North Carolina Railroad.

Denim, former community in central Guilford County, now within the limits of the city of Greensboro. Est. 1895 and named for the cloth made by the local mill.

Denis Creek, a tidal creek rising in the n part of Oak Island in se Brunswick County and flowing e into Elizabeth River.

Denmark, community in central Buncombe County served by post office, 1890–1902.

Denneysville. *See* New Castle.

Dennis, community in n Forsyth County. Formerly known as Salem Chapel.

Dennis, community in n Polk County.

Dennis Creek rises in s Watauga County and flows se into Caldwell County.

Dennis Crossroads, community in w Wake County between Jim Branch and Buckhorn Creek.

Dennis Mountain, w Montgomery County between Walker Mountain and Dutchmans Creek.

Denniss Island, formerly an island in present Currituck Banks, e Currituck County. It was separated from Currituck Banks by Currituck Inlet on the n and Musketo Inlet on the s, both of which are now closed. Shown on Comberford map, 1657. *See also* Currituck Inlet; Musketo Inlet.

Denny, community in w Wilkes County on Elk Creek. Named in the early twentieth century for John A. Denny, a local citizen.

Dennys Store, community in e Person County.

Denson Creek rises in n Montgomery County and flows se into Little River.

Denton, town in se Davidson County. Inc. 1907. Known as Finch's Crossroads prior to 1875. Post office est. 1878 and name changed to Denton at the recommendation of Samuel Moses Peacock, who had been reading about the town of the same name in Texas and who became the first postmaster.

Denton Gap, on the Graham County, N.C.– Monroe County, Tenn., line.

Dentons, community in s Graham County on Little Snowbird Creek.

Denver, town in ne Lincoln County. Inc. 1877. Settled about 1770 and known as Dry Pond for an adjacent swampy area; in 1873 it was renamed by D. Matt Thompson, school principal, for the capital of Colorado, then being considered for admission to the Union.

Deppe, community in ne Onslow County. Named for Nelson R. Deppe of Pennsylvania, who est. a lumber mill at the site.

Derby, community in ne Richmond County.

Derham Creek. *See* Durham Creek.

Derita, community in central Mecklenburg County. Named for Derita Lewis, a friend of Amos L. Rumple, first postmaster when post office was est. in 1882. Alt. 812.

DeRossett Creek rises in Angola Bay, n Pender County, and flows sw into Northeast Cape Fear River. Named for the DeRossett family, early settlers.

Derr, community in e Lincoln County served by post office, 1883–1904.

Derreberry Branch rises in ne Cherokee County and flows nw into Puett Creek.

Derreberry Gap, ne Cherokee County in the Valley River Mountains.

Desert, The, a pocosin in n Robeson County between Big Raft Swamp and Big Marsh Swamp. Oval shaped and presumed to be one of the Carolina Bays, *which see*. Covers 1,200 acres; water depth varies from 6 in. to 4 ft. Game abounds there, especially deer.

Desert, The, a term sometimes applied locally to that part of the Dismal Swamp that lies in Camden and Currituck Counties. *See* Dismal Swamp.

Deserta Arenosa. *See* Sandhills.

Deserta Montana. *See* Sandhills.

Deserter Island, a land formation in s Duplin County surrounded by swamp.

Desolation Branch rises in nw Swain County in Great Smoky Mountains National Park and flows sw into Roaring Creek. It was named after some early hunters were thoroughly soaked in a cold rain there.

Dester, community in s Union County.

Deuces Quarter. *See* Jews Quarter Island.

Devenport. *See* River Neck.

Devereux's Ferry. *See* Bridgers Creek.

Devil Den Ridge, n Macon County between Matlock Creek and Wests Branch.

Devil Knob, e Madison County on Laurel Creek.

Devils Court House, sw Jackson County, is a n ridge or extension of Whiteside Mountain, *which see*.

Devil's Courthouse, overhang of Whiteside Mountain, *which see*, Jackson County.

Devil's Courthouse, peak in Transylvania County just off Blue Ridge Parkway. Cherokee lore has it that Judaculla, a giant, dwells in a cave on the mountain.

Devils Courthouse, a mountain of jagged black rock in nw Transylvania County near the Haywood County line. Located s of the Blue Ridge Parkway, from which a spectacular overlook affords a fine view of the mountain. Named for its sinister appearance. Alt. 5,740.

Devils Court House Ridge, n Swain County in Great Smoky Mountains National Park, a short spur extending s from Mount Buckley.

Devil's Cradle Creek rises in n Franklin County and flows se into Flatrock Creek.

Devils Creek rises in nw Yancey County and flows ne into Nolichucky River.

Devils Creek Gap, nw Yancey County near the head of Devils Creek.

Devils Den, ridge in s Yancey County extending s between Little Mountain Creek and Long Arm Ridge.

Devil's Den. *See* Pilot Mountain.

Devils Elbow, a sharp bend in the Cashie River, se Bertie County. Appears on the Collet map, 1770.

Devils Elbow Landing on Pungo River, e Beaufort County.

Devils Fork rises in e Henderson County and flows w into Mud Creek.

Devils Fork Gap, on the Madison County, N.C.–Unicoi County, Tenn., line.

Devils Garden, on the Alexander-Wilkes county line. Alt. 3,428. A rough, rocky area in which rattlesnakes and copperheads are commonly found.

Devils Garden, a strip of rough, stony land beside another strip of steep, eroded land, se Buncombe County between Trantham Creek and Laurel Branch.

Devils Gut, stream in ne Martin County connecting a bend in the Roanoke River. Mentioned in local records as early as 1729 and shown on the Collet map, 1770.

Devils Head, w Rutherford County near Chimney Rock, a natural rock formation suggestive of the devil's head.

Devil's Kitchin, pocosin in n Pender County adjacent to Stag Park tract.

Devils Nest, peak in n Mitchell County on Big Ridge.

Devils Prong rises in sw Macon County and flows n into Kimsey Creek.

Devils Race Patch, peak in nw Swain County in Great Smoky Mountains National Park on Jenkins Trail Ridge. Alt. approx. 5,160.

Devils Shoals Ford, former ford across the Catawba River, s Caldwell and ne Burke County. Site now under the waters of Lake Hickory.

Devils Tater Patch, peak on the Swain County, N.C.–Blount County, Tenn., line in Great Smoky Mountains National Park. Alt. 4,752.

Devil's Tramping Ground, w Chatham County 10 mi. s of Siler City, a circular path about 40 ft. in diameter that old-timers say has "always" been there. Legend says the Devil appears there at night to walk in a circle while he plots against the good and thinks up new forms of evil. No vegetation will grow in the path.

Devotion, community in sw Surry County on Mitchell River, served by post office, 1888–1954.

Dewberrie, community in nw Warren County. Post office there from 1900 until 1905.

Deweese, community in nw Cabarrus County.

Deweese Creek rises in w Macon County and flows ne into Burningtown Creek.

Deweese Township, former township in nw Cabarrus County. Now township no. 3. Formerly also known as Odell School Township, *which see*.

Deweese Township, former township, ne Mecklenburg County. Now township no. 9.

Dewey, community in sw Randolph County served by post office, 1898–1911.

Dewey Pier, landing in n Tyrrell County on Albemarle Sound w of Ship Point.

Dewitt, former community in e Henderson County on Henderson Creek.

Dews Creek rises in e central Brunswick County and flows n into Town Creek.

Dews Island. *See* Jews Quarter Island.

Dew's Mill. *See* Silver Lake.

Dexter, community in e Granville County served by post office, 1889–1907.

Dial, community in w Cumberland County served by post office, 1882–1903.

Dial Creek rises in n Durham County and flows s into Flat River.

Diamond City, former community near the e end of Shackleford Banks, s Carteret County. Named for the diamond-shaped design painted on the Cape Lookout Lighthouse. Site of whaling operations in the eighteenth and nineteenth centuries. Several storms in the early twentieth century caused the residents to begin moving to Harkers Island, Morehead City, Beaufort, and elsewhere.

Diamond Creek rises in w Transylvania County and flows se into North Fork French Broad River.

Diamond Grove, community in n Northampton County. A post office operated there, 1827–36.

Diamond Hill, community and former post office, 1837–1905, nw Anson County. So called simply as a "fancy name."

Diamond Shoals, a series of three shoals extending se from Cape Hatteras, *which see*, into the Atlantic Ocean off se Dare County. Hatteras Shoals is nearest to the cape, Inner Diamond Shoal is in the middle, and Outer Diamond Shoal extends farthest into the Atlantic. The channel between Hatteras Shoals and Inner Diamond Shoal is Hatteras Slough; Diamond Slough is the channel between the two Diamond Shoals. There, warm Gulf Stream waters collide with cold arctic waters from the n, causing a constant turbulence in the Atlantic. Area known as the "Graveyard of the Atlantic." Appears as Sholes of Hatteras on the Moll map, 1729.

Diamond Slough. *See* Diamond Shoals.

Diamond Valley, in w Macon County between Chestnut Gap and Dicks Creek.

Dick Branch rises in n Buncombe County and flows sw into Flat Creek.

Dick Branch rises in central Cherokee County in Dick Cove and flows se into Morgan Creek.

Dick Cove, central Cherokee County at the headwaters of Dick Branch.

Dickens, community in e Franklin County. Alt. 250. Settled about 1892. Named for T. H. Dickens, first postmaster.

Dickens Creek rises in w Granville County and flows sw into Knap of Reeds Creek.

Dickerson, community in e Granville County. Named for A. J. Dickerson, who gave land for the railroad right-of-way and depot.

Dickey Branch rises in sw Cherokee County and flows se into Nottely River.

Dickey Mountain, sw Cherokee County, extends ne from Rapier Mill Creek to Dickey Branch.

Dickey Top, peak on Dickey Mountain, sw Cherokee County.

Dick Green Branch rises in s Watauga County and flows n into Middle Fork [South Fork New River]. Named for a farmer in the area.

Dickinson, community in central Harnett County served by post office, 1888–1903.

Dickinson Clearwater Branch rises in ne Brunswick County and flows e into the Cape Fear River.

Dickinson's Branch rises in s Wilson County and flows e into Contentnea Creek.

Dicks. *See* Randleman.

Dicks Branch rises in nw Duplin County and flows s into Goshen Swamp.

Dicks Branch rises in n Haywood County and flows ne into Pigeon River.

Dicks Branch rises in w Johnston County and flows s into Black Creek.

Dicks Branch rises in nw Warren County and flows nw in an arc into ne Vance County, where it enters Kerr Lake.

Dicks Creek is formed in n Jackson County by the junction of West Fork and East Fork and flows sw into Tuckasegee River.

Dicks Creek rises in w Macon County and flows ne into Nantahala River.

Dicks Creek rises in se Mitchell County and flows se into North Toe River.

Dicks Creek rises in e Onslow County and flows ne into Queens Creek.

Dicks Gap, s Yancey County between South Toe River and Three Forks Creek.

Dicks Knob, s Madison County at the head of Little Pine Creek.

Dicks Mountain, a peak in the Peach Bottom Mountain range, w central Alleghany County.

Dickson Creek rises in central Jackson County and flows nw into West Fork Tuckasegee River.

Die Bend, a bend in the Nottely River in sw Cherokee County downstream from the mouth of Walker Mill Creek.

Diggs, community in sw Richmond County.

Diggs Ferry, over the Pee Dee River about 2 mi. n of the South Carolina line. Formerly known as the Buchanan Ferry.

Dillard, community in e Stokes County.

Dillard Creek rises in ne Chowan County and flows sw into Chowan River. The U.S.

Geographic Board in 1933 announced that the stream should henceforth be known as Indian Creek, but the ruling seems to have been ignored locally. Appears as Indian Town Creek on the Moseley map, 1733.

Dillard Top, peak on the Cherokee-Graham county line in the Unicoi Mountains.

Diller Branch rises in s Cleveland County and flows ne into Broad River.

Dillingham, community in ne Buncombe County on Dillingham Creek.

Dillingham Creek is formed in ne Buncombe County by the junction of Corner Rock Creek and Walker Branch. It flows nw and joins North Fork Ivy Creek in forming Ivy Creek.

Dill Knob, se Buncombe County. Alt. approx. 3,790.

Dillon Ridge extends ne and supports a school and a few houses in the middle of swamplands in n Tyrrell County. Alt. 14. Site of commercial timber operations.

Dillsboro, town in n Jackson County on the Tuckasegee River. Inc. 1889 and named for William A. Dills, founder of the town and member of the General Assembly, 1889–91. Post office first est. there in 1852 as Cowee in the home of Dills, whose wife was postmistress. Known as Webster Station from 1882 until 1889.

Dillsboro Township, nw Jackson County.

Dills Branch rises in n Jackson County and flows s into Scotts Creek. Named for Allen B. Dills.

Dills Creek rises in n Jackson County and flows se into Fisher Creek.

Dills Creek rises in s Rutherford County and flows s into Broad River.

Dills Gap, w Jackson County between Black Mountain and Tuckasegee River.

Dills Knob, e Macon County between Buzzard Knob and Cullasaja River.

Dimmette, community in e Wilkes County near the headwaters of Little Elkin River.

Dimond City. *See* Dymond City.

Dimsdale, community in n Polk County between Bullin Creek and Walnut Creek.

Dina Branch rises in s Haywood County and flows ne into North Fork.

Dinah Landing, on Upper Goose Creek, central Beaufort County.

Dingle Creek rises in s Buncombe County and flows w into French Broad River.

Dinkin Branch rises in n Cherokee County and flows sw into Owl Creek.

Dipping Vat Creek rises in e Pamlico County and flows se into Long Creek.

Dirty Britches Creek. *See* Shit-Britches Creek.

Dirty John Creek rises in w Macon County and flows sw into Jarrett Creek.

Dish Knob, ne McDowell County near the Burke County line. Alt. 1,800.

Dismal, community in w Sampson County served by post office, 1869–1904.

Dismal Bay, sand-filled bay in s Sampson County n of Keiths Bay. *See also* Carolina Bays.

Dismal Branch rises in s Johnston County and flows se into Johnson Swamp.

Dismal Branch rises in Little Dismal Swamp, sw Johnston County, and flows sw into Mingo Swamp.

Dismal Cove, sw Macon County at the head of Pat Stable Branch.

Dismal Creek rises in w Henderson County and flows nw into Crab Creek.

Dismal Mountain, e Jackson County, extends ne from Tuckasegee River to Neddie Creek.

Dismal Swamp, marsh, lake, and cypress-filled area approx. 30 mi. long and 10 mi. wide, largely in se Virginia but partially in Gates, Pasquotank, Camden, and Currituck Counties. Appears on the Dudley map, 1647, as "Terra Bassa" (low land) and on the Comberford map, 1657, as "a swampy wilderness." Present name might have been known as early as 1715, when the term "dismal swamp" was applied to the Pasquotank County area by John Talbot in a letter to John Urmston, a missionary to the colony for the Society for the Propagation of the Gospel. Shown on the Moseley map, 1733, as Great Dismal Swamp (the name it is sometimes called today) and as Dismal Swamp on the Mitchell map, 1755. George Washington initiated surveys in 1763 for a canal. The Intracoastal Waterway now passes through the swamp. Also called The Desert in North Carolina.

Dismal Swamp Canal connects the waters of Elizabeth River in Virginia with those of the Pasquotank River. It flows from the state line through nw Camden County. The Intracoastal Waterway is routed through the canal, and there are locks on the w borders of South Mills.

Dismal Township, nw Sampson County.

District of Washington, in the w territory of North Carolina that is now Tennessee; it developed from the Watauga Settlement, *which see*, and was recognized by North Carolina in 1776. Delegates attended the Provincial Congress at Halifax in November 1776. The district was the second place in America to be named for George Washington. In 1777 Washington County was formed from the district, and Jonesboro became the county seat. The district was a part of the area ceded by North Carolina in 1789 to the federal government. *See also* Franklin.

Ditch, The, waterway from Pamlico River to Goose Creek, e Beaufort County. It separates Reeds Hammock from the mainland.

Ditch Branch rises in s Wake County and flows s into w Johnston County, where it enters Middle Creek.

Ditch Creek, ne Pamlico County, connects Jones Bay with the Bay River estuary.

Divide Mountain, w Madison County between Rector Branch and Rocky Branch.

Dividing Ridge, s Avery County.

Dividing Ridge, in ne Henderson County between Burntshirt Mountain and the Buncombe-Henderson county line.

Dividing Ridge, n Transylvania County, extends se from the head of Thompson Creek to Funneltop Mountain.

Dividing Ridge, w Wilkes County between Lewis Fork Creek and Stony Fork Creek.

Dix Creek rises near Dix Creek Gap in sw Buncombe County and flows ne into Newfound Creek.

Dix Creek rises in s Haywood County and flows n into East Fork Pigeon River.

Dix Creek Gap, sw Buncombe County between Suther Knob and Hayes Top.

Dixie, community in w Mecklenburg County. Formerly Collins Crossroad, named for a store at the location. Known as Equality, 1836–46. Named changed to Dixie about 1883, when a community band was formed, the favorite tune locally being "Dixie." Served by post office, 1885–1920.

Dixie, community in s central Wilson County.

Dixon, community in s Onslow County.

Dixon Branch rises in se Cleveland County and flows sw into South Carolina, where it enters Kings Creek.

Dixon Creek, a short stream in n central Carteret County flowing n into South River.

Dixon Creek rises in the w part of Goose Creek Island, ne Pamlico County, and flows w into Goose Creek.

Dixon Gap, n Cleveland County. Alt. 943.

Dixon Mine, former gold mine in s Yadkin County between Courtney and the head of Roby Creek.

Dixon Mountain, w Madison County between Little Creek and Meadow Fork.

Dixon Point, s Onslow County, extends into Stump Sound from the mainland.

Dixons Store, community in ne Person County.

Dobag. *See* Arbuckle; Doe Bag Creek.

Dobbersville, community in sw Wayne County near the Sampson County line.

Dobbin Creek rises in nw Yadkin County and flows s into North Hunting Creek.

Dobbins Mill Pond, central Yadkin County on North Deep Creek, covers approx. 25 acres. Max. depth 30 ft. Formed 1936 by Nelson Dobbins. Used for fishing, boating, irrigation, waterskiing.

Dobbs County, formed from Johnston County in 1758, was named in honor of Arthur Dobbs (1689–1765), governor of North Carolina, 1754–65. Wayne County was formed from Dobbs in 1779, portions of it were added to other counties, and the remainder was divided into Glasgow and Lenoir Counties in 1791. Walnut Creek was the county seat until 1779, and Kingston (Kinston) from 1779 to 1791. *See also* Bizzell Millpond; St. Patrick's Parish.

Dobbs Parish, Rowan County, was est. in 1755 to consist of the Wachovia, *which see*, section of the county settled by the Unitas Fratrum (United Brethren), or Moravians. The area included in Dobbs Parish is now largely in Forsyth County. *See also* St. Luke's Parish.

Dobson, town and county seat, central Surry County. Est. 1851 as county seat after the county had been divided. Inc. 1891. Named either (1) for William Dobson, local justice of the peace in 1776, or (2) for William P. Dobson, member of the General Assembly in 1814. Alt. 1,265.

Dobson Branch rises in central Macon County and flows ne into Cartoogechaye Creek.

Dobson Branch rises in e Mitchell County and flows nw into Sugartree Branch.

Dobson Hill, community in s Graham County on Snowbird Creek.

Dobson Knob, e McDowell County.

Dobson Mount, mountain in central Macon County between Patton Mountain and the head of McKee Branch. Alt. approx. 3,500.

Dobson Mountain, s Jackson County between Little Hogback Creek and Long Branch.

Dobson Ridge between the forks of Wrights Creek and Big Witch Creek in n Jackson County.

Dobson's Crossroads. *See* Kernersville.

Dobson Township, central Surry County.

Doby Creek rises in n Mecklenburg County and flows ne into Mallard Creek.

Dock Branch rises in n Buncombe County near the Madison County line and flows se into Whittemore Creek.

Dockery, community in n Wilkes County near Middle Prong Roaring River.

Dockery Creek rises in central Cherokee County and flows se into Hanging Dog Creek.

Dockerys Store, community in w Richmond County. A post office existed there as early as 1828.

Doc Stewart Ridge extends ne from Little Huckleberry Knob to Santeetlah Creek in w Graham County. Named for an early settler.

Doctor Branch rises in ne Cherokee County and flows s into Valley River.

Doctor Mountain, s Madison County at the head of Bear Creek.

Doctors Creek rises in se Sampson County and flows e along the Duplin-Pender county line into Rockfish Creek.

Dodgen Creek rises in w Jackson County and flows ne into Cullowhee Creek.

Dodgen Ridge, e Jackson County between Gladie Creek and Sols Creek.

Dodgetown, community in e Stokes County.

Dodging Hill, e Henderson County between Bat Fork and Green River.

Dodson Crossroads, community in s Orange County.

Dodsons Creek, formerly a stream in n Vance County; its entire course now lies under the waters of Kerr Lake.

Dodson Store. *See* Gilreath.

Doe Bag Creek rises in e Yancey County and flows ne into Toe River. Sometimes spelled Dobag.

Doe Branch rises in e Jackson County and flows ne into Tuckasegee River.

Doe Branch rises in w Madison County and flows ne into French Broad River.

Doe Branch, community in w Madison County. First settler moved there from Tennessee in 1824.

Doe Creek rises in n central Carteret County and flows w into South River.

Doehead, community in w Edgecombe County served by post office, 1888–1902.

Doe Hill Mountain, s Avery County. Alt. 4,217.

Doe Knob, e Clay County between Buck Creek and Johnson Branch.

Doe Knob, peak on Swain County, N.C.–Blount County, Tenn., line, in Great Smoky Mountains National Park. Alt. 4,520.

Dogback Mountain, part of Linville Mountain, lies on Burke-McDowell county line.

Dogback Mountain, on the Jackson-Macon county line. Alt. 4,950.

Dog Branch rises in central Alleghany County and flows se into Little River.

Dog Branch rises in central Martin County and flows se into Ready Branch.

Dog Cove, e Swain County on the head of Wesser Creek between Middle Ridge and Odear Cove.

Dog Creek rises in e Ashe County and flows se into South Fork New River.

Dog Creek rises in w Henderson County and flows sw into Boylston Creek.

Doggett Gap, s Madison County at the head of Friezeland Creek.

Doggett Knob, s Madison County at the head of Walnut Cove Branch.

Dog Island, formerly a single island in Bogue Sound near Bogue Banks, s Carteret County. Appears on the Moseley map, 1733. Now three small islands.

Dog Loser Knob, s Haywood County between Beech Spring Gap and Old Butt Knob.

Dog Mountain, se Macon County at the s end of Chestnut Ridge. Alt. approx. 4,000.

Dog Ridge Mountain, n Madison County in a bend of Big Laurel Creek.

Dogs' Ears, rock formation near Shulls Mill, s Watauga County.

Dogville Crossroads. *See* Hassell.

Dogwood, community in n Burke County served by post office, 1888–1907.

Dogwood Branch rises in s Virginia and flows

se into Northampton County, where it enters Pea Hill Creek.

Dogwood Flats, e Mitchell County between Beaver Creek and Gouges Creek.

Dogwood Flats, community in n Haywood County on Dogwood Flats Creek.

Dogwood Flats Creek rises in n Haywood County and flows ne into Mount Sterling Creek.

Dogwood Gap, w Madison County at the head of Georgia Branch.

Dogwood Ridge, high ground in s Washington County in East Dismal Swamp. Length from w to e extremity approx. 2½ mi. Soloman Sawyer's plantation, known by the name, was located there as early as 1742.

Dogwood Stump Mountain, in s Burke County between Jacob Fork and Whiteoak Creek. Alt. 2,546.

Dolly Gut, gully cut by stream in central Craven County. Stream rises in central Craven County and flows ne into Neuse River just s of Greens Thorofare.

Dome, community in se Buncombe County near the junction of Flat Creek and Broad River.

Donahues Creek rises in n Caldwell County and flows s into Yadkin River. Named for Henry Donahue, who died in 1775 and is buried nearby.

Donaldson Branch rises in se Cherokee County and flows se into Brasstown Creek.

Donaldson Creek rises in e Person County and flows nw into Maho Creek.

Donegal County was a proposed county in se North Carolina. In 1749 a bill was introduced in the House of the General Assembly to separate the "upper part of New Hanover County" to form Donegal County, but the bill was not passed. The parish would have been called St. Colomb. It would have been named for Donegal County, Northern Ireland.

Donnelys Creek. *See* Daniels Creek.

Donnoha, community in nw Forsyth County on Yadkin River. An Indian village was at or near the place that is named for Donnahee, an Indian chief. The name was applied in 1889 or 1890 by Dr. Samuel Martin of Winston, a descendant of the chief, who accompanied the surveying party that laid out the road from Winston to Wilkesboro and which passes through Donnoha. Richmond, former seat of Surry County, 1774–89, which was destroyed in 1830 by a tornado, was nearby. Alt. 757.

Donoho Creek rises in s Bladen County and flows e into Cape Fear River. Named for David Donoho, who had a grant of land there in 1727.

Doolie, community in sw Iredell County. Takes its name from a local Baptist church.

Doolittle Mill Pond, n Northampton County on Paddys Delight Creek. Covers approx. 75 acres. Max. depth 10 ft.

Doomas Creek. *See* Dumas Creek.

Dora, community in w Lincoln County.

Dora. *See* Midstate Mill; Red Springs.

Dora Mills. *See* Midstate Mill.

Dora's Island, se Onslow County in the mouth of Queens Creek.

Dorithea Creek. *See* Muddy Creek.

Dorsey, former community in w Swain County on Tuckasegee River. Site now under the waters of Fontana Lake.

Dort, community in nw Gates County served by post office, 1879–1910.

Dortches, community in e Nash County near the head of Horn Beam Swamp. Settled about 1890. Named for local family. Alt. 120.

Dosier, community in w Forsyth County.

Doster, community in s central Union County.

Dothan, community in s Columbus County.

Dotmond, community in ne Caswell County.

Dotson Branch rises in central Haywood County and flows ne into Pigeon River.

Double Branch rises in w Forsyth County and flows s into Panther Creek.

Double Branch rises in nw Northampton County and flows se into Black Gut Creek.

Double Branch rises in w Transylvania County and flows se into Parker Creek.

Double Creek rises in w Person County and flows nw into South Hyco Creek.

Double Creek is formed in s Surry County by the junction of East Double Creek and West Double Creek. It flows s approx. ¼ mi. into Yadkin River.

Double Creek rises in n Wilkes County and flows sw into Middle Prong Roaring River.

Double Gap, w Haywood County in Great Smoky Mountains National Park on Cataloochee Divide near lat. 35°34′17″ N., long. 83°06′ W.

Double Gap Branch rises in w Haywood County and flows nw into Caldwell Fork.

Double Gap Ridge, w Haywood County in Great Smoky Mountains National Park, a short spur of Cataloochee Divide extending nw near lat. 35°34′45″ N., long. 83°06′12″ W.

Double Head, a mountain on the Buncombe-Henderson county line. Also known as Double Knob. Alt. 3,399.

Doublehead Creek rises in w Avery County and flows se into North Toe River.

Doublehead Gap, w Avery County.

Double Knob, on the head of Slatten Creek in central Jackson County.

Double Knob. *See* Double Head.

Double Knob Mountain, in s Jackson County on the head of Packs Creek. Alt. 4,412.

Double Knobs, mountain peak in n central Avery County.

Double Knobs, two adjacent peaks s of Lenoir in se Caldwell County. Alt. over 1,200.

Double Knobs, twin peaks in central Clay County near Downing Creek.

Double Shoals, community in central Cleveland County between Big Harris Creek and First Broad River. Settled in the nineteenth century and named for two shoals in the nearby river. Alt. 995.

Double Shoals Township, former township in e central Cleveland County, now township no. 9.

Doubleside Gap, e Haywood County between Long Branch and West Cove.

Double Spring Gap, s Haywood County on Lickstone Ridge. Alt. 4,000.

Double Spring Gap, on Swain County, N.C.–Sevier County, Tenn., line in Great Smoky Mountains National Park e of Silers Bald. Alt. approx. 5,520.

Double Springs, community in n McDowell County near Yancey County line and Blue Ridge Parkway.

Double Springs Gap, s Transylvania County on the head of Morgan Mill Creek.

Double Top, mountain on the Buncombe-Henderson county line n of Dads Top.

Double Top, mountain at the s end of Rich Mountain in nw Jackson County.

Doubletop Branch rises in s Macon County and flows nw into Hickory Knoll Creek.

Doubletop Creek rises in n Jackson County and flows ne into Dark Ridge Creek.

Doubletop Fields, grassy pastureland in s Macon County between Buckeye Creek and Hickory Knoll Creek. An early settler cleared land atop the mountain on which he settled as well as on the next mountain, hence the name.

Doubletop Mountain, on the Haywood-Buncombe county line.

Double Top Mountain, central Jackson County between Johns Creek and Cedar Valley Creek. Alt. 5,481.

Doubletop Mountain, n Jackson County on the head of Cashie Branch.

Doubletop Mountain, s Macon County between Dryman Fork and Mulberry Gap.

Doughton, community in central Pender County served by post office, 1893–1903.

Doughton, community in ne Wilkes County on Elkin River.

Doughton. *See* Sherwood.

Doughton Mountain, peak in the Peach Bottom Mountain range, n central Alleghany County. Alt. 3,650.

Doughton Park, s Alleghany and n Wilkes Counties, a Blue Ridge Parkway recreation area on Basin Creek. Covers approx. 7,000 acres. Est. about 1935 as Bluff Park; renamed to honor Congressman Robert L. Doughton (1863–1954), who worked for the establishment of the parkway. A high, rolling, bluegrass area terminates there in precipitous bluffs, and stands of rhododendron bloom in May and June. Wild Cat Rock is nearby. *See also* The Bluffs.

Douglas, community in central Rockingham County served by post office, 1869–1903. Named for Senator Stephen A. Douglas, whose two sons inherited a large farm in the area on Dan River.

Douglas Ordinary. *See* St. Johns.

Dover, town in nw Craven County. Settled 1879, but the place name dates from as early as 1749, when Francis Stringer owned a plantation there called Dover, probably named for the city in England. Inc. 1901. Alt. 63.

Dover, community in nw Moore County on Wolf Creek.

Dover Branch rises in se Yancey County and flows ne into Crabtree Creek.

Dover Crossroads. *See* Gum Swamp.

Dover Knob, s Macon County between Penson Knob and Norton Branch.

Dover Ridge, se Yancey County between Dover Branch and Crabtree Creek.

Dovers Branch rises in se Yancey County and flows nw into Three Forks Creek.

Dove's Crossroads. *See* Casville.

Dowd, community in central Stanly County served by post office, 1883–1907.

Dowdle Branch rises in s Macon County and flows se into Little Tennessee River.

Dowdle Knob, s Macon County between Little Tennessee River and Porter Cove.

Dowellton, central Yadkin County approx. 1½ mi. w of the present courthouse in the vicinity of modern Harmony Grove Church; was the site of the first court held for the new county in 1851.

Dowgap, community in w Surry County.

Downes Branch rises in central Macon County and flows n into Burningtown Creek.

Downing Creek rises in central Clay County and flows se through Holden Cove into Hiwassee River.

Downingville, community in nw Bladen County served by post office, 1857–1913.

Downs Mountain, s Macon County between Mulberry Creek and Norton Branch.

Downsville, community in e Caldwell County. Named for Downs family, two members of which were postmasters there following the Civil War.

Dowry Island, about ¼ mi. long in Chowan River on the Gates-Hertford county line.

Dowtins Creek. *See* Duncans Creek.

Draco, community in e Caldwell County on the headwaters of Middle Little River. Served by post office, 1888–1915.

Drain, The, a cove on the w shore of Hatteras Island in the waters of Pamlico Sound, s Dare County n of the site of the former Little Kinnakeet Coast Guard Station.

Drain, The. *See* Barden Inlet.

Drakes Crossroads, community in central Northampton County.

Dram Tree Point extends from Eagles Island, w New Hanover County, into Cape Fear River. Named for an old moss-covered cypress tree that stood there; it is said that outgoing mariners, in passing the point, had a drink to the success of their voyage. To those inward bound, it was a welcome signal that port was near.

Draper, former town in n Rockingham County on Dan River. Mill village est. 1905 by Frank Mebane. Arthur J. Draper instrumental in planning village's layout. Inc. 1949; merged with Leaksville and Spray in 1967 to form Eden, *which see*.

Draughn, community in n Edgecombe County.

Dresden, community in central Ashe County. Alt. approx. 2,800.

Drew, community in w central Bertie County. Est. about 1900 and named for a local family.

Drewry, community in e Vance County. Alt. 453. Settled in 1860 and named by G. W. Morrow, president of the Clarksville Railroad, for his father, Drewry Morrow.

Drexel, town in central Burke County. Inc. 1913. Alt. 1,192. Named for the Drexel family of Philadelphia. Originally known as Baker. A large furniture-manufacturing plant is located there.

Drexel Township, e central Burke County.

Drift Branch rises in w Haywood County and flows se into Richland Creek.

Drift Falls, in sw Transylvania County in Horsepasture River just upstream from High Falls.

Drip Off Creek rises in nw Iredell County and flows s into Rocky Creek.

Drivers Store, community in e Wilson County near Whiteoak Swamp.

Driving Creek rises in w Nash County and flows sw into Turkey Creek.

Drowned Bay, mucky swamp, sw Brunswick County.

Drowning Creek rises in e central Burke County and flows ne into Catawba River.

Drowning Creek rises on the Montgomery-Moore county line and flows se across Moore County. At the Moore-Richmond county line, it joins Naked Creek in forming Lumber River.

Drowning Creek Mountains extend from ne Burke County into nw Catawba County.

Drug Store, community in w Johnston County.

Druid, community in n Madison County.

Druid Hills, community in central Henderson County on n side of Hendersonville. Alt. 1,788.

Drum Creek rises in the s part of Goose Creek Island, ne Pamlico County, and flows s into Jones Bay.

Drum Hill, community in n Gates County. Alt. 79. Settled about 1890.

Drum Inlet, between Portsmouth Island on the ne and Core Banks on the sw in e Carteret County. Water from Pamlico and Core Sounds drains into the Atlantic Ocean through the inlet. Also known as Whalebone Inlet. Named for a species of fish. An inlet in the area appears on the De Graffenried map (French text), 1711, as Drum Passage. Another Drum Inlet appears on the Moseley map, 1733, now commonly referred to as Old Drum Inlet. The inlet shown on the Moseley map closed in the late eighteenth century.

Drummersville, community in n Duplin County.

Drummond's Point, se tip of Chowan County extending into the mouth of Yeopim River. Named before 1700 for William Drummond (d. 1677), first governor of Albemarle under the Lords Proprietors. Appears on the Moseley map, 1733. Site of one of the largest early seine fisheries on Albemarle Sound.

Drum Passage. *See* Drum Inlet.

Drum Point, point on mainland of ne Carteret County extending into mouth of Nelson Bay.

Drums Crossroads. *See* Drumsville.

Drumsville, community in se Catawba County, formerly Drums Crossroads. Alt. 946.

Dry Branch rises in ne Buncombe County and flows se into Right Fork [Swannanoa River].

Dry Branch rises in e Haywood County and flows e into East Fork Pigeon River.

Dry Branch rises in n Haywood County and flows s into Groundhog Creek.

Dry Branch rises in central Hoke County and flows ne into Rockfish Creek.

Dry Branch rises in n Macon County and flows sw into Cold Spring Creek.

Dry Branch rises in e Mitchell County and flows s into Cane Creek.

Dry Creek rises in w Alamance County and flows e into Haw River.

Dry Creek rises in n Chatham County and flows ne into Haw River.

Dry Creek, an intermittent stream, rises in e Durham County and flows ne into Ellerbe Creek.

Dry Creek rises in ne Durham County and flows s into Lake Michie.

Dry Creek rises in e Graham County and flows n into Stecoah Creek.

Dry Creek rises in n Harnett County and flows s into Cape Fear River.

Dry Creek rises in n Madison County and flows sw into Big Creek.

Dry Creek rises in w Moore County and flows ne into Cabin Creek.

Dry Creek rises in n Rockingham County and flows e into Cascade Creek.

Dry Creek rises in ne Wake County and flows ne into Moccasin Creek.

Dry Creek, community in se Montgomery County served by post office, 1875–1923.

Dry Falls, waterfall in Cullasaja River, se Macon County nw of Highlands. Water drops approx. 75 ft. from a protruding ledge, making it possible to walk behind it without getting wet, hence the name. *See also* Cullasaja River.

Dry Ford, n Union County in Rocky River.

Dry Fork rises in w Lee County and flows ne into Pocket Creek.

Dry Fork Branch rises in s Lee County and flows sw into Moore County, where it joins Crains Creek in forming Whiteoak Creek.

Dry Gap Ridge, n Haywood County parallel to Skiffley Creek.

Dry Hill, community in e Henderson County w of Dana. Named for fact that a local well ran dry.

Dry Lake, ne Surry County. Formed in 1937 by the construction of a dam across a dry hollow into which a small unnamed stream was diverted. Covers approx. 8 acres; max. depth 15 ft. Municipal water supply for Mount Airy.

Dryman Fork rises in s Macon County and flows ne into Coweeta Creek.

Dryman Mountain, central Buncombe County nw of Asheville.

Drymans Branch rises in s Macon County and flows w into Middle Creek.

Dry Mountain, peak on Newfound Mountain on the Buncombe-Haywood county line s of Haywood Gap.

Dry Pocosin, a muck-filled pocosin in e Duplin County.

Dry Pond. *See* Denver.

Dry Pond Gap, s Watauga County between the heads of Storey Creek, Buffalo Creek, and Joe Creek.

Dry Pond Ridge, w Madison County between Mountain Island Branch and Raccoon Branch.

Dry Sand Shoal. *See* Vera Cruz Shoal.

Drysborough, former town in central Craven County. Inc. 1806 and referred to in the session laws until as late as 1847. The site is now within the limits of New Bern and is the part of town that lies n of Queen Street.

Dry Sluice Gap, mountain gap on the Swain County, N.C.–Sevier County, Tenn., line in Great Smoky Mountains National Park. Alt. 5,375.

Drys Mill, community in ne Cabarrus County.

Dryspring Branch rises in w Yancey County and flows nw into Banks Creek.

Drywells, community in s Nash County served by post office, 1891–1904.

Dry Wells Township, sw Nash County. Created 1903 by act of General Assembly.

Duart, community in nw Bladen County.

Dublin, town in nw Bladen County. Alt. approx. 130. Inc. 1913.

Dublin. *See* Royal.

Dublin Creek rises in w Carteret County and flows sw into White Oak River.

Duck, community near the s end of the North Banks in ne Dare County. Inc. 2002. Situated next to Currituck Sound. Named for wild ducks in the area. Alt. 10.

Duck Branch rises near Cross Mountain on the Buncombe-McDowell county line and flows sw into Broad River.

Duck Branch rises in central Mitchell County and flows s into Mine Creek.

Duck Branch rises in se Mitchell County and flows s into Rose Creek.

Duck Creek rises in central Beaufort County and flows s into Pamlico River. Appears on the Collet map, 1770.

Duck Creek rises in ne Caldwell County and flows se into Alexander County, where it enters Middle Little River.

Duck Creek, short stream in n central Carteret County, flows e into South River.

Duck Creek rises in e Craven County and flows sw into Neuse River.

Duck Creek rises in s Iredell County e of Barium Springs and flows ne into Third Creek.

Duck Creek rises in se Onslow County and flows n into Farnell Bay. Mentioned in local records as early as 1744.

Duck Creek rises in w Person County and flows nw into South Hyco Creek.

Duck Creek rises in n Union County and flows se into Goose Creek.

Duck Creek, community in se Onslow County on Mirey Branch.

Duckenfield Estate. *See* Avoca.

Ducker Creek rises near Ducker Mountain in s Buncombe County and flows sw into French Broad River.

Ducker Mountain, s Buncombe County.

Duckettsville. *See* Roper.

Duckett Top, w Madison County between Meadow Fork and Spring Creek.

Duck Island, in Roanoke Sound at the s end of Bodie Island in e Dare County.

Duckmill Branch rises in n Madison County and flows se into Shelton Laurel Creek.

Duck Mountain, s Macon County between Saltrock Gap and Middle Creek.

Duck Pond Swamp, pocosin in e central Cumberland County drained by Reese Creek. One of the Carolina Bays, *which see*.

Dude Branch rises in w Haywood County in Great Smoky Mountains National Park near lat. 35°41′45″ N., long. 83°07′08″ W., and flows se into Correll Branch.

Dudley, town in s Wayne County. Settled in 1837. Inc. 1897; charter repealed 1899; reincorporated 1903. Named for Edward B. Dudley, governor of North Carolina (1836–41) and president of Wilmington and Raleigh Railroad. Alt. 185.

Dudley Shoals, community on Upper Little River in se Caldwell County.

Dudley's Island, e Onslow County in the mouth of White Oak River at Bogue Inlet.

Duel Hill. *See* Marshall.

Duffey, community in w Robeson County served by post office, 1892–94.

Duffs Creek rises in sw Duplin County and flows s into Rockfish Creek.

Dugar Mountain, se Watauga County between Mast Knob and Little Dugger Mountain. Alt. 3,700.

Duges Island, e Carteret County in Core Sound near Core Banks.

Dugger Creek rises in se Watauga County and flows se into Wilkes County, where it enters Elk Creek at Darby. Appears in eighteenth-century records as Julius Duggar's Rock House Creek.

Duggs Island. *See* Bodie Island.

Duharts Creek rises in central Gaston County and flows se into South Fork Catawba River.

Duke. *See* Erwin.

Duke Forest, w Durham and e Orange Counties, consists of a total of 7,020 acres in 5 main units. Est. 1931, it is owned by Duke University and used for demonstration, an experimental forest, and an outdoor laboratory for students in forestry. There are recreational areas and provisions for picnickers, hikers, and horseback riders.

Duke Hall. *See* Halls.

Duke Power Park, state park in s Iredell County on Lake Norman. Contains 1,328 acres, with 6 mi. of shoreline. Boating, camping, and recreational facilities.

Dukes, community in nw Nash County. Named for Rev. G. W. Duke, local resident.

Dukes Crossroads, community in e Beaufort County.

Dukes Crossroads. *See* Epsom.

Duke Swamp rises in n Gates County and flows s to join Raynor Swamp and Harrell Swamp in forming Bennetts Creek.

Duke Township, se Harnett County. Named for the former community, Duke, now Erwin.

Dukeville, community in e Rowan County on High Rock Lake. Named by A. W. Hicks, editor of the *Spencer News*, for James B. Duke.

Dukie Halls Crossing. *See* Halls.

Dula Knob, s Mitchell County between Middle Fork Grassy Creek and East Fork Grassy Creek.

Dula Springs, community in n Buncombe County on Little Flat Creek e of Weaverville.

Dula Town, an African American community in s central Caldwell County. Named for Alfred Dula, who gave 400 acres of land to his freed slaves. At the close of the Civil War, he also gave a horse, wagon, and cow to each former slave family.

Dulins, community in ne Davie County served by post office, 1877–1905.

Dulin's Grove, community in w Mecklenburg County named for local family.

Dumas Creek rises in n Montgomery County and flows se into Denson Creek. Named for Dumas family, early settlers. Appears on recent maps as Doomas Creek.

Dumplin Creek, short stream in n central Carteret County, flows w into Adams Creek.

Dunbars Landing, in nw Tyrrell County on the n side of Scuppernong River.

Duncan, community in n Harnett County. Alt. 430.

Duncan Creek rises in e Transylvania County and flows sw into Little River.

Duncan Mountain, se Transylvania County s of Duncan Creek.

Duncans Creek rises in ne Rutherford County and flows se into Cleveland County, where it enters First Broad River.

Duncans Creek rises in ne Rutherford County and flows w into Broad River.

Duncans Creek rises in central Warren County and flows e into Walkers Creek. At one time called Dowtins Creek.

Duncans Creek, community in ne Rutherford County. Post office est. there 1829.

Duncans Creek Township, ne Rutherford County.

Dundarrach, town in s Hoke County. Inc. 1911.

Dunfields Creek rises in n central Cumberland County and flows sw into Cape Fear River.

Dunhams Creek rises in e central Moore County and flows se. A short distance above the mouth of Herds Creek, it becomes Crains Creek, *which see*. Named for Joseph Dunham, who settled along its banks in 1760.

Dunlap's Mill. *See* Bonlee.

Dunmoor Branch rises in e central Bertie County and flows n into Cricket Swamp.

Dunn, town in se Harnett County. First known as Tearshirt and later as Lucknow. Renamed Dunn in 1886 for Bennett R. Dunn, construction engineer of the Atlantic Coast Line Railroad. Inc. 1887. Produces apparel, canned foods, lumber, and candy. Alt. 214.

Dunn Creek rises in s Transylvania County and flows nw into French Broad River.

Dunn Mountain, s Rowan County s of Crane Creek and ne of the town of Granite Quarry. Alt. approx. 1,000. Named for John Dunn, early attorney and clerk of Rowan County court.

Dunns Creek rises near Brushy Mountain in w Transylvania County and flows ne into Catheys Creek.

Dunns Rock, peak in ne Transylvania County s of French Broad River.

Dunns Rock Township, se Transylvania County.

Dunnsville. *See* Neuse Crossroads.

Dunn Swamp rises in nw Columbus County and flows nw into Porter Swamp.

Dunn Township, former township in se Franklin County, now township no. 1.

Dunsmore, community in sw Buncombe County on Stony Fork.

Dunsmore Cove, valley of Dunsmore Cove Branch, se Buncombe County near Ridgecrest.

Dunsmore Cove Branch rises near the McDowell County line in se Buncombe County and flows nw into Swannanoa River.

Dunsmore Mountain, sw Buncombe County. Alt. 2,700.

Duplin (DOO-plin) County was formed in 1750 from New Hanover County. Located in the e section of the state, it is bounded by Jones, Onslow, Pender, Sampson, Wayne, and Lenoir Counties. It was named for Thomas Hay (1710–87), Lord Duplin, member of the Board of Trade and Plantations. Area: 823 sq mi. County seat: Kenansville, with an elevation of 127 ft. Townships are Albertson, Cypress Creek, Faison, Glisson, Island Creek, Kenansville, Limestone, Magnolia, Rockfish, Rose Hill, Smith, Warsaw, and Wolfescrape. Produces hogs, turkeys, cotton, cattle, bell peppers, sweet potatoes, hay, wheat, oats, nursery products, cabbage, collards, strawberries, cucumbers, lumber, poultry, textiles, and wine.

Duplin Court House. *See* Kenansville.

Duplin Roads. *See* Wallace.

Dupree Crossroads, community in nw Pitt County.

Durant Island, n Dare County in Albemarle Sound; about 5 m. long from e to w and 3 mi. n to s at the widest. Appears on the Moseley map, 1733.

Durant Point, peninsula extending from the s part of Hatteras Island, s Dare County, into Pamlico Sound n of Sandy Bay.

Durants Neck, peninsula extending into Albemarle Sound between Perquimans and Little Rivers, e Perquimans County. Site of the home of George Durant (1632–94), pioneer settler in the Albemarle about 1662. Appears as Point Durant on the Hack map, 1684, and as Durants Point on the Moseley map, 1733.

Durants Neck, community on Durants Neck peninsula, e Perquimans County. Formerly known as New Hope; a post office by the name was est. by 1820.

Durants Point, point of land extending into Pungo River from w Hyde County opposite Belhaven in e Beaufort County.

Durants Point. *See* Durants Neck.

Durbro, community in s Cleveland County served by post office, 1880–1902.

Durgantown. *See* Vanceboro.

Durgy Mine, former gold and copper mine in e Person County. Operated in late nineteenth century and until about 1920. At its peak operation, approx. 500 persons were employed in the mine.

Durham, city and county seat, central Durham County. A post office est. there in 1851 was named Durhamsville; changed to Durham in 1855. Named for Dr. Bartlett Snipes Durham (1822–58), donor of land for the railroad station. Inc. 1866. Formerly center of tobacco manufacturing. Home of Duke University and N.C. Central University. Produces drugs, bricks, grain products, dairy products, apparel, textiles, hosiery, commercial printing, furniture, corrugated boxes, and industrial machinery. Alt. 406. *See also* Prattsburg.

Durham Branch rises in central Swain County and flows se into Deep Creek.

Durham County was formed in 1881 from Orange and Wake Counties. Located in the central section of the state, it is bounded by Wake, Chatham, Orange, Person, and Granville Counties. It was named for the town of Durham, *which see*. Area: 300 sq mi. The county seat is Durham, with an elevation of 406 ft. Townships are Carr, Durham, Lebanon, Mangum, Oak Grove, and Triangle. Produces tobacco products, pharmaceuticals, software, computers, electronics, plastics, cattle, nursery products, bricks, textiles, machinery, and commercial printing.

Durham Creek rises in ne Craven County and flows se on the Craven-Pamlico county line into Upper Broad Creek.

Durham Creek rises in nw Pamlico County and

flows n into Beaufort County, where it enters Pamlico River. Named for Richard Durham, who acquired land near its mouth in 1706. Appears in local records as early as 1715 as Dereham's Creek, and by 1770 it was being called Derham and Darham Creek. Appears on the MacRae map, 1833, as Derham Creek. The garrison that gave Garrison Point, *which see*, its name was located on Durham's land.

Durham's Creek, community in central Beaufort County served by post office, 1839–1902.

Durham Township, central Durham County.

Dusty Hill, community in central Northampton County.

Dutch Buffalo Creek rises near Organ Church in se Rowan County and flows se through Cabarrus County into Rocky River. Named for the "Pennsylvania Dutch" (German, *Deutsch*) who settled there. *See also* Irish Buffalo Creek.

Dutch Cove, e Haywood County on the head of Dutch Cove Creek.

Dutch Cove Creek rises in e Haywood County and flows nw into Hominy Creek.

Dutch Creek rises in sw Watauga County on n slope of Hanging Rock and flows ne into Watauga River.

Dutch Creek Falls, sw Watauga County on Dutch Creek approx. ½ mi. upstream from the mouth of Pigeonroost Creek. Falls are 85 ft. high and make a perpendicular descent over moss- and lichen-covered rock. Also known as Marianna Falls.

Dutch District. *See* Dutchville Township.

Dutchman Creek rises in se Brunswick County and flows se into the Cape Fear River.

Dutchman Creek rises in s central Wake County and flows ne into Swift Creek.

Dutchman Mountain, peak in w Randolph County.

Dutchman Ridge, mountain peak on the Buncombe-McDowell county line.

Dutchmans Creek is formed in ne Gaston County by the junction of Leepers Creek and Killians Creek and flows se into Catawba River.

Dutchmans Creek rises in w Montgomery County and flows sw into Island Creek.

Dutchmans Creek, approx. 30 mi. long, rises in s Yadkin County and flows s into ne Iredell County and then se across Davie County into Yadkin River near the Horseshoe. Appears on the Collet map, 1770.

Dutch Second Creek. *See* South Second Creek.

Dutchville Township, sw Granville County. A nineteenth-century post office in the sw part of the county was called Dutchville, and in 1790 there was a Dutch District that had 76 heads of families reported in the census for that year.

Dwight, community in w Perquimans County served by post office, 1892–1904.

Dyeleaf Creek rises on the s side of Spring Mountain in ne Buncombe County and flows w through Laughter Cove into Cane Creek. Named for Sweet Leaf or Horse-sugar (*Symplocos tinctoria*), the leaves and bark of which yield a yellow dye.

Dyeleaf Mountain, se Buncombe County between Cane and Garren Creeks.

Dyer Knob, w Watauga County n of Rush Branch and e of Beaverdam Creek. Alt. approx. 3,300.

Dykers Creek rises in w Davidson County and flows w into Yadkin River.

Dymond City, former community in se Martin County in Great Swamp. A post office by the name existed in 1882. Appears as Dimond City on the Kerr map, 1882, located near the head of Deep Run Swamp.

Dysartsville, community in se McDowell County. Alt. 1,262. Named for the Dysart family, early settlers. John Dysart, local militiaman, was a veteran of the Battle of Kings Mountain.

Dysartville Township, se McDowell County.

E

Eads Gap, se Buncombe County between Chestnut Flats and Garren Mountain.

Eagle, community in w Iredell County served by post office, 1848–1907.

Eagle Branch. *See* Spread Eagle Branch.

Eagle Cliff, ne Mitchell County between Fork Mountain and Roan Mountain.

Eagle Creek is formed in se Clay County by the junction of Left Fork and Right Fork and flows nw into Shooting Creek. Known also as Eagle Fork Creek.

Eagle Creek is formed in nw Swain County in Great Smoky Mountains National Park by the junction of Gunna Creek and Tub-Mill Creek.

It flows sw into Fontana Lake. Named for the fact that a nest of eagles was found near its head.

Eagle Falls, a low falls on Dan River, w central Rockingham County. Land adjacent was granted to Charles Galloway in 1745, and early county courts were held on his property. Eagle Falls plantation there, occupied by the Galloway family for many years and later passed to descendants named Carter. The house is now used for farm storage. *See also* Jackson.

Eagle Fork Creek. *See* Eagle Creek.

Eagle Gap, w Cherokee County between Fowler Bend and Hiwassee Dam.

Eagle Knob, in central Graham County between Sweetwater Creek and Mountain Creek.

Eagle Knob, on the Jackson-Macon county line. Alt. 4,500.

Eagle Mills, community in ne Iredell County. Mill operated by the Eagle family there burned by Stoneman's raiders, 1865, later rebuilt. A grain mill is now operated on Hunting Creek at the site.

Eagle Mills. *See* Eagle.

Eagle Mills Township, ne Iredell County.

Eaglenest Branch rises in e Transylvania County near Black Knob and flows ne into Little River.

Eaglenest Creek rises in w Haywood County and flows se into Richland Creek.

Eaglenest Mountain, w Haywood County on the head of Eaglenest Creek.

Eaglenest Ridge, w Haywood County, extends e from Rattlesnake Knob to Eaglenest Mountain.

Eagle Rock, mountain on Swain County, N.C.–Sevier County, Tenn., line between Pecks Corner and Copper Gap. Alt. 5,950–6,000.

Eagle Rock, town in e Wake County. A printing press operated there as early as 1854. Named for a rock on which an eagle fell when shot by Thomas Richard Debnum, around whose home the town developed. Inc. 1911, when lumber industry thrived there. Long inactive in municipal affairs. Alt. 326.

Eagle Rock Cove, valley of Eagle Rock Creek, ne Buncombe County.

Eagle Rock Creek rises in Great Craggy Mountains, ne Buncombe County, and flows sw into Beetree Reservoir.

Eagles Island, a group of swampy islands in w New Hanover County between Cape Fear and Brunswick Rivers opposite Wilmington. Named for Joseph and Richard Eagle, eighteenth-century settlers in the vicinity. *See also* Dram Tree Point. Appears as Cranes Island on the Ogilby map, 1671.

Eagle Springs, community in w Moore County. Settled about 1890. Site of a mineral spring, it probably was named for the Eagle family, which settled in the vicinity in the eighteenth century. Alt. 668.

Eagle Swamp rises in n Lenoir County and flows se into Contentnea Creek.

Eagleton Point, point of land extending nw from Colington Island into the waters of Kitty Hawk Bay, n Dare County. Also known as North Point and Eggleston Point.

Eagletown, community in se Northampton County; an early Quaker settlement. Served by post office, 1887–1907.

Eakers Corner, community on Stoney Run in w Cleveland County.

Earl, town in s Cleveland County. Inc. 1889, but long inactive in municipal affairs. Named for Abel Earl, local landowner. Alt. 925. Produced manufactured fibers.

Earleys, community in s Hertford County. Alt. 65.

Earlies Gap, nw Buncombe County between Cook and Robinson Mountains.

Earl Mountain, ne Rutherford County between the head of Duncans Creek and South Creek.

Earnhardts Township, former township in ne Cabarrus County. Now township no. 7. In 1945 a part of the township was annexed to Concord, coextensive with Concord Township. In 1940 the township was listed as Reed Misenheimers.

Earpsboro, community in n Johnston County near Little River.

Earthquake Branch. *See* Browns Creek.

Easonburg, community in se Nash County, on n side of Tar River.

Eason Crossroads, community in central Gates County.

Eason Millpond, w Pitt County on Kitten Creek.

East Arcadia, community in se Bladen County. Known originally as Marlville for local marl beds. Served by post office, 1900–1919. Formerly known as Marlsville.

Eastatoe Creek rises in ne Pickens County, S.C., in the Blue Ridge Mountains and flows n

into s Transylvania County, N.C., and ne into
Middle Fork French Broad River.

Eastatoe Gap, s Transylvania County between
Shoal Creek and Eastatoe Creek. Alt. 2,686.

Eastatoe Township, s central Transylvania
County.

East Bay, in n Piney Island e of Rattan Bay, ne
Carteret County. Approx. ¾ mi. long and
½ mi. wide.

East Belews Creek rises in e Forsyth County and
flows n into Belews Creek.

East Bend, town in ne Yadkin County between
Logan Creek and Yadkin River. Known as
Banner's Store for a local merchant, Martin
Banner, until the name was changed about
1849 for a nearby e bend in the Yadkin River.
Inc. 1887.

East Bend Township, ne Yadkin County.

East Bluff Bay, s Hyde County in Pamlico Sound
e of Bluff Point.

East Branch rises in s Pitt County and flows s
into Swift Creek.

East Branch rises in se Yancey County and flows
n into Little Whiteoak Creek.

East Branch Chicod Creek formed in w Beaufort County by the junction of Juniper and
Harding Swamps. Flows nw into Pitt County,
where it enters Chicod Creek.

Eastbrook, community in ne Brunswick County.

East Buffalo Creek rises in central Graham
County and flows sw into Santeetlah Lake.

East Buies Creek rises in ne Harnett County and
flows sw into Buies Creek. It appears as Hugh
McCrarey's Creek on early maps of the region
and later as Hugh's Creek.

East Creek rises in central Currituck County and
flows sw into North River.

East Dismal Swamp, a 20,000-acre area of
peat and muck swamp extending ne from n
Beaufort County across s and e Washington
County into w Tyrrell County. *See also* Dogwood Ridge; New Lands.

East Double Creek rises in s Surry County and
flows s to join West Double Creek in forming
Double Creek.

Eastern Channel, a tidal waterway in s Brunswick County extending w from Montgomery
Slough to Lockwoods Folly Inlet.

Eastern Channel, a tidal waterway in sw Brunswick County extending e from Tibbs Inlet
inside Hales Beach for about 3 mi.

East Fayetteville, unincorporated outskirts

of city of Fayetteville, central Cumberland
County 1½ mi. e of Market House.

Eastfield, community in ne Mecklenburg
County served by post office, 1880–1902.

East Flat Rock, former town in central Henderson County. Alt. 2,214. Inc. 1926; charter repealed by local action, 1948, and by act of the
General Assembly, 1949. Est. as a commercial
adjunct to the residential community of Flat
Rock, *which see.*

East Fork, community in s Transylvania County.

East Fork [Barkers Creek] rises in w Jackson
County and flows n to join West Fork in forming Barkers Creek.

East Fork [Bull Creek] rises in e Madison County
and flows sw to join West Fork in forming
Bull Creek.

East Fork [Campbell Creek] rises in w Haywood
County and flows n into Campbell Creek.

East Fork Chattooga River rises in s Jackson
County and flows s into South Carolina,
where it enters Chattooga River.

East Fork [Cove Creek] rises in w Watauga
County and flows s into Cove Creek.

East Fork Crabtree Creek rises in s Mitchell
County and flows nw into Crabtree Creek.

East Fork Creek rises in e Beaufort County and
flows s into Pamlico River.

East Fork Deep River rises in w Guilford County
and flows se into High Point Lake, where it
joins West Fork Deep River in forming Deep
River.

East Fork [Dicks Creek] rises in n Jackson
County and flows sw to join West Fork in
forming Dicks Creek.

East Fork French Broad River rises in s Transylvania County and flows sw and nw into
French Broad River.

East Fork Gap, e Haywood County on the head
of Garden Creek.

East Fork [Goose Creek] rises in n Pamlico
County and flows sw into Goose Creek.

East Fork Grassy Creek rises in s Mitchell
County and flows nw to join Middle Fork
Grassy Creek in forming Grassy Creek.

East Fork [Jenkins Creek] rises in n Jackson
County and flows sw to join West Fork in
forming Jenkins Creek.

East Fork [Kirkland Creek] rises in s Swain
County and flows nw to join West Fork [Kirk-
land Creek] in forming Kirkland Creek.

East Fork Lake, in central Jackson County on

Tuckasegee River. Formed in 1955 to be a reservoir for Nantahala Power and Light Company. Combines with Wolf Creek Lake, *which see*, to generate hydroelectric power. Covers 40 acres, with max. depth of 120 ft. Shoreline is 3.2 mi. Named for East Fork of Tuckasegee River, an old name for the Tuckasegee River.

East Fork [Moses Creek] rises in n Jackson County and flows sw to join West Fork in forming Moses Creek.

East Fork Overflow Creek rises in se Macon County and flows sw to join West Fork Overflow Creek in forming Overflow Creek.

East Fork Pigeon River rises in sw Haywood County near the Transylvania County line and flows n to join West Fork Pigeon River in forming Pigeon River. Known by the Cherokee Indians as Junietta.

East Fork [Savannah Creek] rises in w Jackson County and flows nw into Savannah Creek.

East Fork Shut-in Creek rises in w Madison County and flows nw to join West Fork Shut-in Creek in forming Shut-in Creek.

East Fork [South Fork New River] rises in s Watauga County and flows nw to join Middle Fork and Flannery Fork in forming South Fork New River approx. 2 mi. se of town of Boone.

East Fork [South River], a short stream at the headwaters of South River in n central Carteret County.

East Fork Township, s Haywood County.

East Fork Twelvemile Creek rises in w Union County and flows sw to join West Fork in forming Twelvemile Creek.

East Franklin, community in central Macon County.

East Fruitland. *See* Pores Knob.

East Gastonia, unincorporated outskirts of city of Gastonia, central Gaston County.

Eastham Creek rises near the center of Goose Creek Island, ne Pamlico County, and flows nw into Goose Creek.

East Howellsville Township, e Robeson County.

East Kings Mountain, former town in w Gaston County on the Cleveland County line. Inc. 1907. By popular vote, it was transferred to Cleveland County in 1915. Became a part of Kings Mountain, *which see*, in 1923.

East Lake, lake on the mainland of n Dare County, empties into the mouth of Alligator River.

East Lake, community on the mainland of nw Dare County on South Lake. Settled about 1790. Alt. 10.

East Lake Landing, nw Dare County on Alligator River. State-operated free ferry from the landing to Sandy Point in ne Tyrrell County was replaced by the Lindsay C. Warren Bridge, 2.83 mi. long and opened in May 1962; named for Lindsay C. Warren (1889–1976), former U.S. congressman and comptroller general.

East Lake Township, nw Dare County mainland.

Eastland, community in w Caswell County. A post office operated there, 1887–1905.

East Laport, community in n Jackson County on Tuckasegee River. Developed at the site of an eighteenth-century French trading post that the French considered to be an east gate or door (*la porte*) to the Cherokee country. Alt. 2,186.

East Laurinburg, town in s Scotland County. Inc. 1903 as Scotland Village; name changed, 1909.

East Lumberton, former town in e central Robeson County. Inc. 1901. Charter repealed 1953. Now a part of Lumberton. Was a mill-owned village until 1950, when houses were sold to individuals.

Eastman Creek rises in n Carteret County and flows w into South River.

East Mayo Mountain. *See* Baughn Mountain.

East Mingo Branch rises in sw Johnston County and flows s to join Black River in forming South River on the Cumberland-Sampson county line. For a part of its course, it forms the boundary between Johnston and Harnett Counties and between Harnett and Sampson Counties. Sometimes known as Mingo Swamp. Appears as Black Mingo on the Collet map, 1770. Mingo was an Indian word for a treacherous person. It was also frequently used as a slave name, appearing as such as early as 1680 in Albemarle County. *See also* Black Creek Swamp.

East Monbo, now covered by waters of Lake Norman but formerly a community on the Catawba River in w Iredell County. A cotton mill was est. there in the late nineteenth century and named Mont Beau (beautiful mountain) by its owners. The natives soon corrupted the name to Monbo and, since it was on the e side of the river, it became East Monbo (there being another mill on the w side of the river in Catawba County). East Monbo was long a popular picnic and swimming site.

Eastmost River is formed in se Bertie County by the junction of Middle River and a branch of Roanoke River near its mouth. It flows ne into Batchelor Bay.

Eastmost Swamp rises in e central Bertie County and flows s into Salmon Creek.

Eastmouth Bay, in the waters of Core Sound between the two large islands comprising Harkers Island in se Carteret County.

East Nelson Creek rises in ne Cherokee County and flows se into Valley River.

Eastover Township, e central Cumberland County.

East Prong rises in central Burke County and flows w into Sandy Run Creek.

East Prong rises in w Carteret County and flows sw into Sanders Creek.

East Prong Cub Creek rises in s Wilkes County and flows nw into Cub Creek at the e outskirts of Wilkesboro. Originally known as Little Cub Creek.

East Prong Deep River rises in w Guilford County and flows se into Deep River.

East Prong [Hickory Fork] rises in n Madison County and flows sw into Hickory Fork.

East Prong Little Yadkin River rises in w Stokes County and flows sw to join West Prong Little Yadkin River in forming Little Yadkin River.

East Prong Moon Creek rises in w Caswell County and flows ne into Moon Creek.

East Prong Roaring River rises in ne Wilkes County and flows se into Roaring River.

East Ridge, e Watauga County, extends se between Mary Simmons Ridge and Clear Branch.

East Rockingham, unincorporated outskirts of town of Rockingham, w Richmond County.

East Sanford Township, former township in central Lee County. Now township no. 5.

East Spencer, town in e Rowan County. Originated as Southern City (along the route of the Southern Railway), a real-estate development by John S. Henderson and others. Inc. 1901. The town of Spencer is to the sw. "Spring Hill," plantation of Maxwell Chambers, was there.

East Swan Creek rises in w Yadkin County and flows nw into Wilkes County, where it joins West Swan Creek in forming Swan Creek.

Eastview, community in sw Mecklenburg County served by post office, 1903.

East Wilmington, unincorporated outskirts of the city of Wilmington, w New Hanover County.

Eastwood, community in s Moore County. Named for J. B. Eastwood, lumberman who est. a store there about 1912.

East Woodford, community in se Mecklenburg County.

Eastwood Lake, s Orange County in ne Chapel Hill. Formed in 1937 by a dam on Booker Creek. Approx. ¾ mi. long, covering 58 acres, with a max. depth of about 20 ft. Now the center of a residential area.

Easy Hill, community in ne Brunswick County.

Easy Ridge, n Swain County in Great Smoky Mountains National Park, a short spur extending ne from Noland Divide.

Easy Ridge Gap, s Swain County at the head of First Hurricane Branch.

Easy Street, historically black community in n Sampson County. Said to have been named for the fact that it was easy to purchase illegal liquor there.

Eatman, community in s Nash County served by post office, 1890–1906.

Eaton Island. *See* Baker Island.

Eatons Ferry, in ne Warren County on Roanoke River, was privately owned and operated as early as 1770 and appeared on the Price map, 1808. It was purchased by the state in 1935 and operated until January 1962, when a bridge over Lake Gaston was opened.

Eaves Creek rises in n Franklin County and flows se into Lynch Creek.

Ebenezer, community in central Cherokee County at the junction of Dockery and Hanging Dog Creek.

Ebenezer, community in e Gaston County.

Eby Creek rises in s Transylvania County and flows sw into Little River.

Echo, crossroads community in sw Robeson County.

Echota Mission, n Jackson County, maintained by Holston Conference of Methodist Church for Cherokee Indians about 1840–85. School est. 1850. Missionary's house still stands.

Ecola, former community in w Swain County; site now under the waters of Fontana Lake.

Ecusta. *See* Pisgah Forest.

Edam, community in nw Wilson County.

Eden, town in n Rockingham County on Dan and Smith Rivers. Formed in 1967 by the merger of Leaksville, Draper, and Spray, *which see*. Named for William Byrd's estate, "Land of Eden," *which see*.

Edenhouse, community in e Bertie County on the Chowan River. Site of Eden House, home of Governor Charles Eden, 1714–22, and Governor Gabriel Johnston, 1732–52.

Edenhouse Point, point of land extending into Chowan River, e Bertie County. Location of an early seine fishery.

Edens Pond. *See* Watsons Pond.

Edenton, town and county seat, s Chowan County on Albemarle Sound. Settled by 1710 and known by the Indians as the Town on Matecomack Creek. Town authorized to be laid off in 1712 and the first lot sold in 1714. Known as the Town on Queen Anne's Creek from 1715 until 1723, when it was inc. as Edenton in honor of Charles Eden (1673–1722), governor, who had just died. Edenton was the capital of the colony from 1722 until 1743, and a building was provided for the Assembly by 1733 (and perhaps as early as 1725), though the Assembly met there 1722–36 and 1740–43. The Edenton Tea Party on October 25, 1774, is the earliest known instance of political activity by American women. Alt. 16. Processes peanuts and seafood; produces textiles, veneer, seed, fertilizer, and lumber. *See also* St. Paul's Parish.

Edenton Bay, s Chowan County in Albemarle Sound. Formed by the mouth of Pembroke Creek. Covers approx. 4,000 acres.

Edenton District, at the time of the 1790 census, was composed of Bertie, Camden, Chowan, Currituck, Gates, Hertford, Pasquotank, Perquimans, and Tyrrell Counties and the town of Edenton.

Edenton Township, former township in s Chowan County, now township no. 1. For voting purposes, the township is divided into East Edenton and West Edenton.

Edgar, community in n Randolph County.

Edge, community in n Bladen County served by post office, 1886–1908.

Edgecombe, community in se Pender County.

Edgecombe, Parish of, Church of England, Edgecombe County, later Halifax, est. 1741 with the creation of Edgecombe County.

Coextensive with the county. In 1756 the parish was divided, creating St. Mary's Parish in the s; the Parish of Edgecombe remained in the n. With the creation of Halifax County in 1758, the Parish of Edgecombe became coextensive with the new county. St. Mary's Parish was coextensive with Edgecombe County. Edgecombe Parish in 1767 had 1,500 white taxables.

Edgecombe County was formed in 1741 from Bertie County. Located in the e section of the state, it is bounded by Martin, Pitt, Wilson, Nash, and Halifax Counties. It was named for Richard Edgecumbe (1680–1758), afterward first Baron Edgecumbe, a member of Parliament, lord of the treasury, and holder of other political offices. Area: 511 sq. mi. County seat: Tarboro, with an elevation of 71 ft. Townships, now numbered 1 to 14, were formerly Tarboro, Lower Conetoe, Upper Conetoe, Deep Creek, Lower Fishing Creek, Upper Fishing Creek, Swift Creek, Sparta, Otter Creek, Lower Town Creek, Walnut Creek, Rocky Mount, Cokey, and Upper Town Creek. Produces tobacco, corn, soybeans, peanuts, cotton, sweet potatoes, cucumbers, hogs, livestock, textiles, baked goods, lumber, plastics, paper products, machinery, fabricated metals, and furniture.

Edgemont, community in w Caldwell County.

Edgewater, community in central Beaufort County on the n bank of Pamlico River.

Edgewater, community in s central Carteret County nw of Morehead City. Alt. 19 ft. Formerly named Morehead Bluffs.

Edgewood, community in e Caswell County.

Edgewood, community in e Robeson County served by post office, 1883–95.

Edinburg, former town in sw Montgomery County. Inc. 1807 at the store of, and on the land of, John Billingsly. A post office was there as early as 1828 and as recently as 1882. Site now abandoned. Also spelled Edinborough and Edenboro, 1827–94. Named for the city in Scotland by local residents of Scottish descent. Site of former Edinborough Academy.

Edith, community in se Catawba County. Alt. 1,050.

Edith Lake, s Henderson County on Green River. Approx. 1½ mi. long.

Edmiston. *See* Sunnyside.

Edmonds, community in ne Alleghany County and Virginia.

Edney Branch rises in w Yancey County and flows s into Cane River.

Edneyville, community in e Henderson County. Named for Rev. Samuel Edney, Methodist minister who served as postmaster and magistrate. A post office there since 1842. Former high school now a regional training center for law enforcement. Alt. 2,247.

Edneyville Township, ne Henderson County.

Edonia, community in s Cumberland County served by post office, 1883–1907.

Ed Top, peak in n Haywood County on the head of Laurel Branch.

Edward, town in se Beaufort County. Alt. 25. Inc. 1889 as Edwards' Mill, but long inactive in municipal affairs. Named for Josephus Edwards, who built a mill on nearby Durham Creek about 1868.

Edward Cove, s Haywood County on a tributary of Bird Creek.

Edward Jones Creek. *See* Little Turnbull Creek.

Edwards Branch rises in n Macon County and flows se into Daves Creek.

Edwards Branch, se Mecklenburg County, flows se into Briar Creek.

Edwards Branch rises in n Mitchell County and flows s into Little Rock Creek.

Edwards Bridge, community in e Greene County on Contentnea Creek. Bridge built over the creek as early as the 1850s.

Edwards Creek rises in se Macon County and flows se into Big Creek.

Edwards Crossroads, community in n Alleghany County. Alt. approx. 2,800.

Edwards Crossroads, community in central Northampton County.

Edwards' Mill. *See* Edward.

Edwards Mountain, peak in the Peach Bottom Mountain range, central Alleghany County. Alt. approx. 3,400.

Edwards Mountain, ne Chatham County.

Edwards Pocosin, s Northampton County between Lily Pond Creek and Quarter Swamp.

Edwards Township, e Wilkes County.

Edwardsville, community in w Surry County served by post office, 1871–1905.

Effie, community in s Jackson County served by post office, 1888–1902.

Efird's Mills, community in central Stanly County served by post office, 1848–1916.

Efland, community in w Orange County. Alt. 658.

Eggleston Point. *See* Eagleton Point.

Egg Shoal, in the waters of Pamlico Sound, s Dare County off the s part of Hatteras Island.

Eggtown, community in nw Anson County.

Egypt, community in w Alleghany County served by post office, 1899–1903.

Egypt. *See* Cumnock.

Egypt Land, a name applied to the s portion of Vance County because of its reputation at one time as a land of slaves and corn.

Egypt Township, n Yancey County.

Eight-Foot Ditch, canal in nw Pasquotank County that drains ne into Shepherd Ditch.

Eighty-Nine Mile Siding. *See* Cognac.

Ekaneetlee Creek rises in nw Swain County in Great Smoky Mountains National Park and flows se into Eagle Creek.

Ekaneetlee Gap, on the Swain County, N.C.–Blount County, Tenn., line in Great Smoky Mountains National Park. Alt. 3,852.

Ela, community in e Swain County on Tuckasegee River. Name is a Cherokee word meaning "earth." Alt. 1,830.

Elah or **Eliah,** community in ne Brunswick about 2 mi. sw of Leland. Settled prior to 1882. Inc. 1903 as Myrtle to meet the requirement that whiskey stills could be operated only in incorporated towns. Charter repealed 1905. Took name Elah from local Elah Baptist Church.

Ela Lake, on Oconaluftee River in e Swain County. Covers 20 acres; max. depth 15 ft. Formed in 1925. Owned by the Aluminum Company of America and used to generate electric power. Formerly known as Onitalooga Lake.

Elams, community in ne Warren County between Walker Creek and Lizard Creek. Settled in 1880 and named for James Elam, local resident. Alt. 400.

Elbaville, community in e Davie County. Name derived from the first syllables of names of two local families, Ellis and Bailey. Post office est. 1870. Alt. approx. 808.

Elberon, community in s Warren County

between Lees Branch and Buffalo Branch. Post office est. in 1897 but discontinued in 1954.

Elberta, community in w Moore County. A peach-growing center named for the Elberta peach. Alt. approx. 661.

Elbethel, community in se Cleveland County. Named for El Bethel Methodist Church.

Elbow, community in central Columbus County served by post office, 1894–1910.

Elbow Branch rises in n Swain County and flows nw into Hazel Creek.

Elbow Creek rises in nw Cherokee County and flows s into Shuler Creek.

Elbow Landing, on Pungo River, e Beaufort County.

Elbow Ridge, n Swain County in Great Smoky Mountains National Park, a short spur extending w from Welch Ridge between Elbow Branch and Hazel Creek.

Elder Branch rises in central Duplin County and flows se into Maxwell Creek.

Eldorado, community in nw Montgomery County served by post office, 1875–1953. Earlier known as Tan Yard. Formerly a center of gold mines of varying productivity. Named for a legendary South American king who owned much gold. A post office in the late nineteenth century. Now a residential community.

Eldorado Township, nw Montgomery County.

Eldora Township, e central Surry County.

Eleanors Crossroads, community in central Gates County.

Elease, community in s Cumberland County.

Eleazer, community in sw Randolph County on Uwharrie River. Served by post office, 1883–1933.

Elerbe, community in sw Granville County.

Elevation Township, sw Johnston County. Named for the fact that it is in a hilly section of the county.

Elf, community in s Clay County on Chatuge Lake.

Elgin, plantation house in central Warren County. Built in 1832 and named by a Scottish immigrant, Peter Mitchel, for his native city, Elgin, county seat of Elginshire (or Moray County). The house is still used as a dwelling.

Eli, community in s Rowan County served by post office, 1892–1902.

Elise. *See* Robbins.

Elisha, community in s Pasquotank County.

Elisha Creek, approx. 5 mi. long, rises in central Davie County and flows se into Dutchmans Creek. Appears in local records, 1815, as "Lisha, formerly called Licking Creek."

Eli Whitney, community in se Alamance County. Named for inventor of cotton gin. Public quilting bee held there since 1931.

Elizabeth City, city and county seat, e Pasquotank County on Pasquotank River. Settled in 1790; inc. as Redding in 1793. In 1794 named changed from "Reading" to Elizabethtown; became Elizabeth City in 1801. Probably named for Elizabeth Tooley, wife of Adam Tooley, on whose land the town was est. Elizabeth City State University and College of the Albemarle are there. Produces textiles, ships, lumber, hosiery, apparel, paper boxes, and industrial machinery. Alt. 12.

Elizabeth City Township, e central Pasquotank County.

Elizabeth River rises in se Brunswick County and flows e into the Cape Fear River.

Elizabethtown, town and county seat, central Bladen County. Alt. 121. Est. 1773, chartered 1843, and inc. 1895. Named either for Queen Elizabeth I of England or for the sweetheart of Isaac Jones, on whose land the town was laid out. In the Battle of Elizabethtown, August 27, 1781, Whigs broke Tory power in Bladen County by driving them into Tory Hole, a deep ravine along the banks of Cape Fear River in the middle of the town.

Elizabeth Town. *See* Columbia.

Elizabethtown. *See* Elizabeth City.

Elizabethtown Township, in central Bladen County.

Elk Branch rises in e Mitchell County and flows s into Cane Creek.

Elk Creek rises in w Alleghany County and flows n into New River.

Elk Creek rises in s central Ashe County and flows s into South Fork New River on the Ashe-Watauga county line.

Elk Creek rises in ne Stokes County and flows s into Dan River.

Elk Creek rises in e Watauga County and flows e and se into Wilkes County, where it enters Yadkin River.

Elk Creek rises in e Watauga County and flows se into w Wilkes County, where it enters Yadkin River.

Elk Creek, community in w central Alleghany County.

Elk Fork rises in sw Yancey County and flows ne into Little Creek.

Elk Hollow Branch rises in w Avery County and flows e into Roaring Creek.

Elk Hollow Ridge, w Avery County.

Elkin, town in sw Surry County on Yadkin River near the mouth of Elkin River. Alt. 947. Inc. 1889. Named for the river. Immediately s, separated by Yadkin River, is the town of Jonesville in Yadkin County. Produced woolen goods.

Elkin River rises in ne Wilkes County and flows se across the sw corner of Surry County and into Yadkin River on the Surry-Yadkin county line near the town of Elkin. Appears on the Collet map, 1770.

Elkinsville. *See* Elkton.

Elkin Township, sw Surry County.

Elk Knob, n Graham County between Tuskeegee Creek and Sawyer Creek.

Elk Knob, n Watauga County near the head of Hoskin Fork.

Elkland. *See* Todd.

Elk Lodge Mountain, s central Transylvania County between Allison Creek and Lamb Creek.

Elk Marsh. *See* Marsh Swamp.

Elk Mountain, community in central Buncombe County w of Woodfin. Alt. 1,950.

Elk Mountains, central Buncombe County ne of Asheville, extend from Peach Knob to Roaring Gap. Alt. 3,149–3,190.

Elko, community in n Stokes County served by post office, 1882–1904.

Elk Park, town in nw Avery County. Inc. 1885. First county court held there while the courthouse at Newland was under construction. Named for elk that once roamed the region. Alt. 3,182.

Elk Ridge extends s from Bluff Mountain in sw Ashe County.

Elk Ridge, s Watauga County, extends ne between Dutch Creek and Clark Creek.

Elk Ridge, w Wilkes County between Elk Creek and Stony Fork Creek.

Elk River rises in ne Avery County near Banner Elk and flows w into Tennessee, where it enters Watauga River. For most of its course, it flows in a deep gorge.

Elk River Falls, in Elk River, nw Avery County,

a drop of about 85 ft.; for the next 4 mi. downstream, there is a fall of about 100 ft. per mile.

Elks Crossroads. *See* Todd.

Elk Shoal, community in w Yancey County on Cane River. A nineteenth-century post office serving the community was named Wampler.

Elk Shoal Creek rises in w Yancey County and flows e into Cane River.

Elk Shoals, former community in e Alexander County near headwaters of Elk Shoals Creek. Post office est. there in 1852 was discontinued in 1901 with postal service transferred to Stony Point. Named for shoals in creek at which elk crossed.

Elk Shoals Creek rises in se Alexander County and flows s and sw into Catawba River. The name occurs in local records as early as 1760, and the stream is shown on Collet map, 1770.

Elk Shoals Creek rises in n Catawba County and flows se into Catawba River.

Elk Spur, central Avery County.

Elk Spur, n Wilkes County near Little Sandy Creek.

Elkton, community in s Bladen County. Alt. 90.

Elkton Swamp rises in s Bladen County and flows s into Brown Marsh Swamp.

Elk Township, s Ashe County.

Elk Township, se Watauga County.

Elk Township, sw Wilkes County.

Elkville, community in sw Wilkes County on Yadkin River. Alt. 1,200.

Elk Wallow Creek rises in w Yancey County and flows se into Bald Creek.

Elk Wallow Gap, central Buncombe County in Elk Mountains.

Elk Wallow Knob, on the Madison-Yancey county line near the head of Elk Wallow Creek. Alt. approx. 4,600.

Elkwallow Knob, nw Mitchell County between Leatherman Fork and Bearwallow Creek.

Elkwood. *See* Weaverville.

Elk X Roads. *See* Todd.

Ell Branch rises in s Jackson County and flows se into Robinson Creek.

Ellenboro, town in e Rutherford County. Alt. 1,046. Founded 1886; inc. 1889. Said to have been named for Ellen Robinson, daughter of the president (or engineer) of the Carolina Central Railroad. Robinson gave a bell to the school there with his daughter's name engraved inside. May have been named by Burwell Blanton Byers, owner of much local property, for himself and his wife, Ellen— Ellenburwell, which later became Ellenboro.

Ellenburwell. *See* Ellenboro.

Ellendale, community in w Alexander County. Formerly known as Ellendale Chalybeate Springs, a summer resort. Named for Ellen Reid, daughter of the owner of the spring.

Ellendale Township, w Alexander County.

Eller, community in n Davidson County. Alt. 902. Named for one Eller, who settled in the vicinity about 1753. Also known locally as Midway because of its position between Lexington and Winston-Salem.

Ellerbe, town in n central Richmond County. Scottish settlers in the eighteenth century had a fair at the site each May and November, and it came to be known as The Fair Grounds. After W. T. Ellerbe developed a popular watering place at nearby Ellerbe Springs, the present name began to be applied. Inc. 1911. Produced hosiery.

Ellerbee Creek rises in w Durham County about 2 mi. w of Durham and flows e and ne about 11 mi. into Neuse River. Known earlier as Alliby Creek and Elliby Creek.

Eller Branch rises in n Buncombe County and flows nw into Madison County, where it enters Ivy River.

Eller Cove, n Buncombe County between Little Davis and Lydie Mountains.

Eller Cove, n Buncombe County between McDairies Ridge and Greenfield Ridge.

Eller Cove, s Graham County between Horse Range Ridge and Atoah Gap.

Elliby Creek. *See* Ellerbee Creek.

Ellicott Mountain, s Jackson County near the head of East Fork Chattooga River. Alt. 3,800. Named for Andrew Ellicott (1745–1820), who surveyed the North Carolina–Georgia state line in 1813.

Ellicott Rock, on the e side of Chattooga River in sw Jackson County at the North Carolina–South Carolina–Georgia state line. A granite boulder indicating the junction was marked in 1813 by and named for Andrew Ellicott (1754–1820), surveyor.

Ellijay, community in e Macon County on Ellijay Creek. Alt 2,200. Name is from a Cherokee word meaning "verdant earth."

Ellijay Creek rises in e Macon County and flows sw into Cullasaja River.

Ellijay Township, e central Macon County.

Ellington Branch rises in nw Warren County and flows ne into Smiths Creek.

Elliott, community in e Sampson County. Alt. 137. A post office was opened there in 1886 but closed in 1940. Named for Dr. Elliott Lee of Clinton. An early stop on the railroad there was known as Summit. The community is at the site of "Mt. Pleasant," the plantation of James Faison.

Elliott Branch rises in e Cherokee County and flows s into Peachtree Creek.

Elliott Cove, n Swain County between Sunkota Ridge and Deep Creek.

Elliott Springs. *See* Catawba Springs.

Ellis, community in n Bladen County served by post office, 1885–1907.

Ellisboro, community in sw Rockingham County. Est. 1889 with extension of Cape Fear and Yadkin Valley Railroad. Named for Ellis Roberts, relative of developer. Failed to develop and was abandoned in 1936. Alt. 829.

Ellis Creek, nw Bladen County, drains s from Suggs Mill Pond, *which see*, into Cape Fear River.

Ellis Creek rises in s Davidson County and flows w into Yadkin River.

Ellis Cross Roads, community in ne Rowan County. Settled about 1885.

Ellis Lake, a natural lake in Croatan National Forest, s Craven and n Carteret Counties. Covers 1,500 acres; max. depth 4 to 5 ft. Named for the Ellis family, which lived on its shores.

Ellis Mountain, central Mitchell County between Rebel Creek and Toe River.

Ellison Branch rises in se Buncombe County and flows s into Cane Creek.

Ellison Branch rises in n Watauga County and flows w into Cove Creek.

Ellison Creek rises in sw Forsyth County and flows sw into Yadkin River.

Ellis Store, community in se Bertie County.

Elm City, town in n Wilson County. Alt. 131. Inc. 1873 as Toisnot, and post office est. there, succeeding nearby post office at Joyner's, *which see*. Named changed to Elm City, 1891; back to Toisnot, 1895; and again to Elm City, 1913.

Elmer, community in w Yancey County served by post office, 1881–1907.

Elmira Crossroads, community in se Pitt County.

Elmore, community in s central Scotland County formerly called Elmores Crossroads.

Elmore Branch rises in e Macon County and flows s into Rabbit Creek.

Elmores Crossroads, community in se Gaston County.

Elmores Crossroads. *See* Elmore.

Elm Swamp. *See* Corapeake Swamp.

Elmwood, community in se Bertie County on Salmon Creek. Named for an early plantation at the site. Was early waiting place for the ferry across the creek to Edenton and beyond.

Elmwood, community in e central Iredell County. Alt. 836. Named for elm trees in the vicinity.

Elon, town in w Alamance County. Inc. 1893. Formerly known as Mill Point for a freight depot for shipping mill products manufactured nearby. Elon College, a four-year coeducational institution, opened there in 1890. Upon the school's name change to Elon University in 2001, the town formerly known as Elon College became Elon. Its name comes from the Hebrew word for oak and was selected because of the large oak trees in the area. Alt. 716.

Elrod, community in w Robeson County.

Elrod Branch rises in s Watauga County and flows nw into Middle Fork [South Fork New River].

Elroy Store, community in e Wayne County near the head of Walnut Creek.

El-see-toss. *See* Mount Pisgah.

Elsworth Creek rises in e Davie County and flows sw into Dutchmans Creek.

Elwell Ferry, across Cape Fear River in se Bladen County.

Emaline Gap, s Macon County between Everett Mountain and Brush Creek.

Emandell, community in sw Washington County w of Van Swamp. Since the 1950s the name has not generally appeared on maps of the county.

Emanuel, community in e Caldwell County served by post office, 1880–1902.

Embro, community in central Warren County n of Reedy Creek. A post office est. there in 1889 was discontinued in 1921.

Emerald Isle, town on Bogue Banks, se Carteret County. Inc. 1957. A resort town located on the Atlantic Ocean.

Emerson, community in s Bladen County. Alt. 104. Railroad name was Portersville.

Emerson, community in sw Columbus County.

Emerson Branch rises in nw tip of Cabarrus County, where it forms a part of the head-waters of Coddle Creek.

Emit, community in n Johnston County on Little River. *See also* Flower Hill.

Emma, community in central Buncombe County w of Asheville. Alt. 2,075.

Emma Branch rises in central Buncombe County near Dryman Mountain and flows se through the community of Emma into Smith Mill Creek.

Emmons Mine, former gold mine in e Davidson County about 5 mi. n of Denton. In 1855 a large gold nugget ("123 penny-weights") was picked up in the vicinity.

Emmons Township, e central Davidson County.

Emory, community in central Warren County.

Emperor Landing, sw Chowan County in the mouth of Chowan River. Probably named for Emperor Moseley, early landowner.

Emperors Island. *See* Church Island.

Empire, community in e Randolph County served by post office, 1882–1906.

Encas, community in e Wilson County.

Endesokes. *See* Core Banks.

Endicott, community in central Montgomery County served by post office, 1886–1911.

Endicott Branch rises in nw Surry County and flows se into Fisher River.

Endor Iron Works, on Deep River n of Sanford in Lee County, large smelting furnace provided iron to Confederacy, 1862–65. Operated irregularly thereafter.

Endy, community in w Stanly County. Named for Arch Eudy who, in 1903, applied for the establishment of a post office there. The Post Office Department misread his name and assigned the name Endy instead of the requested Eudy.

Endy Township, central Stanly County.

Energy. *See* Siler City.

Enfield, town in s Halifax County. The county seat of Edgecombe County was there from 1745 until the formation of Halifax in 1759; the first Halifax court met there, but Halifax (town) was afterward the county seat. Inc. 1861. Named probably for the town of Enfield, Middlesex, England. Known originally as Huckleberry Swamp. Alt. 111.

Enfield Township, s Halifax County.

Engagement Hill, a sand hill between the ocean and sound in Nags Head, e Dare County, now covered by houses. A favorite spot for visits by young couples in former days.

Engelhard, community in e Hyde County on Far Creek. Alt. 2. Inc. 1874; charter revoked 1967. Named for Joseph A. Engelhard (1832–79), publisher of the *Wilmington Daily Journal*, 1861–70. Known earlier as Far Creek.

Engine Gap, ne Mitchell County near the Tennessee state line.

English, community in e Madison County at the head of Puncheon Fork Creek. Named for an early settler.

English Branch rises in e Madison County and flows se into Puncheon Fork Creek.

English Branch rises near Chalk Mountain in s Mitchell County and flows se into North Toe River. Named for Isaac English, an early settler.

English Branch rises in w Yancey County and flows se into Jacks Creek.

English Knob, e Mitchell County between Beaver Creek and Gouges Creek.

English Town, community in n Pender County.

Enka, community in central Buncombe County. Alt. 2,060. Home of the American Enka Corporation, est. 1929. The name is from the letters *N* and *K* taken from the firm's official name: Nederlandsche Kunstzyde Fabricken. Produces textiles and chemicals.

Enka Lake, central Buncombe County on Bill Moore Creek. Covers 40 acres; max. depth 40 ft. Owned by American Enka Corp. as a source of water for rayon manufacturing. Formed 1928.

Enloe Creek rises in ne Swain County in Great Smoky Mountains National Park and flows se into Raven Fork Creek.

Enloe Ridge, ne Swain County in Great Smoky Mountains National Park, a short spur extending e from Hughes Ridge.

Ennetts Point, w Carteret County, extending into Bogue Sound w of the mouth of Deer Creek. Named for the Ennett family.

Ennice, community in e Alleghany County. Named for Ennice Higgins, daughter of the first postmaster, 1883.

Enno. *See* Holleman's Crossroads.

Enoch Canal, e Washington County, extends ne from Lake Phelps to Mall Creek.

Enoch Mill Creek rises in s Sampson County and flows se into Black River.

Enochville, town in sw Rowan County. Inc. 1877. Named for St. Enoch's Evangelical Lutheran Church. Long inactive in municipal affairs. Served by post office, 1877–1902.

Enola, community in s Burke County. Name is "alone" spelled backwards.

Enon, community in e Yadkin County between Logan Creek and Yadkin River.

Enon Mountain, in e Transylvania County w of Lydia Creek.

Eno River rises in n Orange County and flows se across the county into w Durham County, where it flows e and joins Flat River in forming the Neuse River. Appears on the Moseley map, 1733. The name probably is from the Tuscarora Indian word *e-eno* (a great way; far off).

Enos Plotts Balsam Mountain, w Haywood County about 5 mi. w of Waynesville. Alt. 6,097. Known by the Cherokee Indians as Sunneehaw. *See also* Plott Balsam.

Eno Township, e central Orange County.

Ens Creek. *See* South Fork.

Enterprise, community in n Davidson County. Name chosen to suggest the nature of the inhabitants.

Enterprise, community in e Warren County between Stonehouse Creek and Little Stonehouse Creek.

Enterprise, former community s of town of Mount Olive in s Wayne County. Now within town limits of Mount Olive.

Entwistle, community in central Richmond County.

Eoka, community in central Columbus County served by post office, 1884–1902.

Ephesus, community in s Davie County. Named in 1890 when a post office was est. there in Miles A. Foster's store.

Ephraim Branch rises in n Haywood County and flows sw into Groundhog Creek.

Ephraim Hensley Mountain, n Madison County between Rick Branch and Big Creek.

Ephraim Place, mountain on the Mitchell County, N.C.–Unicoi County, Tenn., line.

Epping Forest, an eighteenth-century community and census district in sw Vance County. The community was located near the present town of Kittrell. In 1790 the district had 65 heads of families.

Epps Springs, community in central Swain County on Tuckasegee River. Alt. 1,662.

Epsom, community in e Vance County and n Franklin County. Known as Dukes Crossroads in 1881. When a post office was est. there in 1887, the name Duke was rejected because there was another post office by that name. According to tradition, the present name was suggested by Dr. Bennett P. Alston, who noticed a stock of Epsom salts in the local store.

Epworth, community in n Edgecombe County served by post office, 1893–1907.

Equality, community in sw Mecklenburg County served by post office, 1836–46. Later known as Dixie, *which see.*

Erastus, community in w Jackson County on Little Piney Creek.

Erect, community in se Randolph County. Name suggested to Post Office Department in 1873 by C. M. Tysor, local merchant, to compliment the posture of his neighbor, Tom Bray.

Erie Mills, community in sw Montgomery County served by post office, 1879–1905.

Erlanger, former community in central Davidson County. Est. 1914 and named for founder of local mill. Alt. 806. Now within the limits of Lexington.

Ernul, community in ne Craven County. Alt. 25. Settled about 1888. Named for James and Freeman Ernul, residents. Post office est. 1919 as successor to one at Askins.

Ervinsville. *See* Erwinsville.

Ervintown, community in nw Onslow County on the w limits of Richlands. Named for the numerous Ervins living there.

Erwin, town in se Harnett County. Est. about 1902 with the construction there of Erwin Cotton Mills. First known as Duke for the Duke family of Durham. Name changed to Erwin about 1925 for William Allen Erwin (1856–1932), operator of the local mill. Inc. 1967. Produces textiles. Alt. 195.

Erwinsville, also known as Ervinsville, a former town in sw Cleveland County (then Rutherford County). Inc. 1808; previously inc. as Burrtown in 1800. Located near the mouth of First Broad River and the South Carolina line e of Ellis Ferry. In 1800 the General Assembly authorized 50 acres there to be laid out and sold in lots. Post office est. 1813, active until 1882. Town site later abandoned.

Eskota, community in s Yancey County on Cane River. Alt. 3,101.

Eskridge Cove, the valley through which Eskridge Cove Branch flows in se Buncombe County.

Eskridge Cove Branch rises in se Buncombe County near Lookoff Gap and flows nw into Swannanoa River.

Esmeralda, community in nw Rutherford County on Broad River.

Ess-ee-daw. *See* Broad River.

Essex, town in sw Halifax County. Inc. 1891, but long inactive in municipal affairs. Prior to 1860 it was the center of a settlement of free blacks.

Essex Island. *See* Etacrewac.

Estatoe, community in s Mitchell County on Brushy Creek. Named for the daughter of an Indian chief.

Estatoe. *See* Rosman.

Estatoe Path, s Transylvania County, trading route between settlements of Cherokee Indians and their town of Estatoe, now in South Carolina.

Estatoe River. *See* Toe River.

Estelle, community in ne Caswell County. A post office operated there during the approx. period 1880–1905.

Estes Branch rises in n Swain County and flows sw into Indian Creek.

Etacrewac, appears on the White maps, 1585 and 1590, as an island that today would be bounded on the n by the community of Duck on the North Banks and on the s by a point on Bodie Island opposite Broad Creek Point on Roanoke Island, e Dare County. The name appears to have been Algonquian for "evergreen-ground." *See also* Bodie Island; North Banks. The Smith map, 1624, appears to apply the name Essex Island there.

Ether, community in ne Montgomery County. Known as Freeman's Cross Roads prior to the establishment of a post office there in 1888, when it was named by Dr. F. E. Asbury, local physician.

Etheridge Creek rises in se Halifax County and flows se on the Halifax-Edgecombe county line into Etheridge Swamp.

Etheridge's Branch rises in nw Wilson County and flows s and se into Contentnea Creek.

Etheridge Swamp receives the waters of Etheridge Creek on the Halifax-Edgecombe county line and flows se into Conoho Creek in Martin County.

Ethram Boney Bay, a large sandy loam marsh in s Duplin County.

Etna, community in n Macon County on Lakey Creek.

Etowah, community in w Henderson County. Alt. 2,101. The name comes from the Cherokee word *I'tawa* or *Et-toh-wah*, an unidentified kind of tree.

Eubanks, community in s Orange County.

Euchulla Cove, w Swain County between Wiggins Creek and Nantahala River.

Eufola, community in w Iredell County on Southern Railway. Alt. 788. Prior to 1903 known as Deep Cut; the railroad station was Plotts. May have been named for the Eufaula or Yufala Indian tribe in Georgia.

Eupeptic Springs, community and former resort (1860s–1870s), nw Iredell County. Known as Powder Springs prior to development as a resort by Dr. John Ford, who renamed it Eupeptic (good digestion).

Euphronia, community in n Moore County served by post office, 1877–1905.

Eure, town in w Gates County. Alt. 22. Inc. 1915, but no longer active in municipal affairs.

Eureka, community in central Moore County. Originally centered about Eureka Farm Life School, est. about 1915. In 1920 James Rogers McConnell Hospital was built there; later moved to Pinehurst and now known as Moore Memorial Hospital. McConnell died in World War I, serving in the Lafayette Escadrille.

Eureka, town in ne Wayne County near the head of Watery Branch. Inc. 1879 as Saul's Cross Roads; name changed 1901.

Eurins Creek rises in e central Stokes County and flows se into Rockingham County, where it enters Dan River. Perhaps a variant of the older forms Hewins, Hewings, and Hughens.

Eury Lake, central Montgomery County on Little River, approx. 8 mi. s of Troy. Constructed about 1914 by S. J. and W. G. Smitherman and J. C. Hurley to provide electric power. Covers 80 acres, with a shoreline of approx. 3 mi. Later owned by Carolina Power and Light Company but sold in 1962 to the Montgomery County Hunt Club, Inc. Known as Hurley Lake until 1916, when the present name came into use.

Euto. *See* New Salem.

Eva, community in sw Perquimans County served by post office, 1887–1905.

Evans, community in sw Chatham County.

Evans Branch rises in central Clay County and flows sw into Johnson Mill Creek.

Evans Branch rises in w Haywood County and flows s into Jonathans Creek.

Evans Creek rises in s Macon County and flows nw into Tessentee Creek.

Evansdale, community in s Wilson County. Post office, 1908–10. Named for one Evans, who operated a sawmill at the site.

Evans Gap, w Swain County between Greasy Branch and Flat Branch.

Evans Knob, se Buncombe County s of Jobs Peak near the McDowell County line.

Evans Knob, w Swain County between Fishtrap Branch and Tuckasegee River. Alt. 2,481.

Evans Mountain, w Henderson County at the head of South Fork.

Evans Ridge, n Clay County, extends ne from Shearer Creek to Chestnut Stamp Knob.

Evan's Store Crossroads. *See* Winnabow.

Evansville, community in e Bertie County served by post office, 1893–1905.

Everett Creek rises in s Onslow County and flows e and n into New River.

Everett Mountain, s Macon County between Buck Creek and Emaline Gap.

Everetts, town in w Martin County. Settled about 1877. Inc. 1891 as Everitts; reincorporated 1893 as Everetts. Named for local family; S. F. and J. A. Everetts were commissioners of the town when inc. Alt. 66.

Everett's Crossroad, community in central Beaufort County.

Everetts Creek rises in s New Hanover County and flows e into Myrtle Sound.

Everetts Mill. *See* Cedar Falls.

Everetts Mill Pond, in sw Richmond County on Marks Creek, approx. 1 mi. long.

Evergreen, town in nw Columbus County. Settled 1870; inc. 1907. Named for surrounding pine forest. Alt. 104.

Evergreen Island, Pamlico Sound just off the central section of Portsmouth Island, e Carteret County.

Evergreen Slough, inlet into e end of Portsmouth Island on Pamlico Sound side, e Carteret County.

Everitts. *See* Everetts.

Everittsville, former community near Dudley

in s Wayne County. Prior to the Civil War, a group of plantation owners built homes together there and went out daily to tend their nearby plantations. There were schools and churches and in 1851 a post office, but no stores or other businesses. Named for Joseph Everitt, early settler. Only a cemetery remains to mark the site.

Ewart, community in n Mitchell County on Big Rock Creek.

Ewing, community in w Wake County.

Exact, community in e Mecklenburg County served by post office, 1898–1903.

Excelsior, community in nw Brunswick County served by post office, 1881–1915.

Excelsior. *See* Rutherford College.

Exeter, former town in e Pender County on the e side of Northeast Cape Fear River on a high sandy bluff between Sand Hill Cove and Jumping Run. Flourished from about 1740 to 1790. Est. 1754 as New Exeter for Exeter, England, but it seems generally to have been known as Exeter. Appears on the Collet map, 1770, as Exeter. Began to decline as South Washington, *which see*, grew in importance after 1790 but appears on the Purcell map, 1792. Rutherfords Mill (later Ashe's Mill) was located nearby in the nineteenth century. In 1781, during the Revolution, British major Sir James Henry Craig constructed field fortifications there, which are still visible. Headquarters of the Holly Shelter State Game Management Area now occupy the site.

Exter, community in central Bertie County served by post office, 1886–1905.

Exum, community in nw Brunswick County.

Exum Mill Branch rises in e Wayne County and flows e and ne into The Slough. Named for early settlers who had a mill on the stream in the late eighteenth century.

Exum Store, community in ne Wayne County between Turner Swamp and Ivy Swamp.

Exway, crossroads community in n Richmond County on the Montgomery County line. The name X-Way was recommended to the Post Office Department when a post office was about to be est. in 1898. The name was accepted, but the spelling was altered.

Eye, community in nw Ashe County served by post office, 1889–1906.

Ezra, community in central Johnston County served by post office, 1881–1903.

Ezzell Mill Pond. *See* McLamb Mill Pond.

F

Face Rock, peak in the Swannanoa Mountains, s Buncombe County between Ballard Gap and Buckey Mountain.

Face Rock, peak at the w end of Bearwallow Mountain on the Buncombe-Henderson county line.

Factor Branch rises in central Haywood County and flows ne into Lake Junaluska. Named for a "factory" that once stood nearby. The structure was a large warehouse where plants and herbs were collected, graded, dried, and packed for shipment.

Factory Branch rises in w Macon County and flows sw into Nantahala River.

Factory Branch. *See* Factor Branch.

Fagansville. *See* Carthage.

Faggart Mine. *See* Nash Mine.

Faggarts, community in central Cabarrus County.

Faggarts Township. *See* Watts Cross Roads Township.

Faggs Creek rises in n Stokes County and flows s into Dan River.

Fain Cove, e Cherokee County, through which a short tributary of Slow Creek flows.

Fain Mountain, central Cherokee County, extends ne from Laurel Creek.

Fair Bluff, town in w Columbus County on a bluff overlooking Lumber River. Authorized to be laid off on the lands of John Wooton at Fair Bluff in 1807 and to be known as Wootonton. The new name apparently was not adopted, as Fair Bluff appears on the Price map, 1808, and on the MacRae map, 1833. Reincorporated in 1873 as Fair Bluff. Alt. 69.

Fair Bluff Township, w Columbus County.

Fairfax, community in nw Swain County on Lake Cheoah.

Fairfield, town on the n shore of Lake Mattamuskeet in central Hyde County. Alt. 3. Inc. 1885. Said to have been named for "fair fields" of crops grown on adjacent reclaimed swampland.

Fairfield, community in e Union County between Richardson Creek and Niggerhead Creek.

Fairfield Falls, s Jackson County on Trays Island Creek near n edge of Fairfield Lake. Alt. approx. 3,200.

Fairfield Lake, s Jackson County on Trays Island Creek formed in 1910. Covers 100 acres; max. depth 40 ft. Used for fishing, swimming, and boating and as a power source. Not open to the public. *See also* Fairfield Falls.

Fairfield Ridge, se Clay County between Scaly Ridge and Bear Pen Ridge.

Fairfield Township, n central Hyde County.

Fair Grounds, The. *See* Ellerbe.

Fair Grove, community in nw Randolph County.

Fair Grove. *See* Cedar Lodge.

Fairly, community in central Scotland County.

Fairmont, town in s Robeson County. Known first as Ashpole for nearby Ashpole Swamp. Inc. 1899 as Union City; name changed to Ashpole, 1901, and to Fairmont, 1907.

Fairmont. *See* Southmont.

Fairmont Township, s Robeson County.

Fair Mountain, s Watauga County on the head of Laurel Creek.

Fairntosh, community in n Durham County. Named for the plantation of Duncan Cameron (1777–1853); house built in 1802 still stands. Former post office nearby was named Stagville. Alt. 284.

Fairplains, community in central Wilkes County near Long Branch.

Fairport, community in e Granville County.

Fairview, community in se Buncombe County.

Fairview, community in nw Macon County on Queens Creek.

Fairview, community in s Surry County. Alt. 1,109. Formerly known as Fairview Crossroads and earlier as Alberty.

Fairview, community in n Union County between Crooked Creek and Goose Creek. Formerly known as Benton Crossroads. Inc. 2002.

Fairview Gap, s Buncombe County ne of Concord Mountain.

Fairview Township, se Buncombe County.

Faison, town in nw Duplin County. Est. as Faison's Depot about 1833 on the land of Henry Faison. Inc. as Faison's Depot in 1872

through the efforts of Elias Faison, landowner and stockholder in the Wilmington and Raleigh Railroad. Received postal service from nearby Wrightsville as early as 1822. Fruit and vegetable market; produces pickles. Alt. 166.

Faisons Old Tavern, community in central Northampton County between Corduroy and Wildcat Swamps. Named for a tavern operated there by the Faison family. The community of Odamsville, which had a post office as early as 1830, is traditionally said to have been the predecessor of Faisons Old Tavern.

Faison Township, nw Duplin County.

Faith, town in s Rowan County. Inc. 1903. Named for a granite quarry opened by J. T. Wyatt, who lacked experience in quarrying but went ahead with his work "on faith."

Falcon, town in ne Cumberland County on Mingo Swamp. Alt. 125. Known as Starling's Bridge from as early as 1863 until 1893, when a post office was est. Inc. 1913. When a name was being sought for the post office, it is said that J. A. Culbreth glanced at a box of Falcon pens on the shelf of a country store and said, "Name it Falcon."

Falkland, town in w Pitt County. Post office est. in 1813 as Bensborough, changed to Falkland in 1838. Inc. 1887. Said to have been named for Falkland, Scotland, long the home of Scottish kings; or may have been named for the Falkland Islands, which the British had long claimed but only finally occupied a few years before Bensborough was changed to Falkland. Alt. 76.

Falkland Township, nw Pitt County. Formerly named California Township.

Fall Branch rises in central Alamance County and flows ne into Haw River.

Fall Branch rises in central Avery County at Bellvue Mountain and flows sw into North Toe River.

Fall Branch rises in central Avery County near Big Elk Mountain and flows s into Plumtree Creek.

Fall Branch rises in central Avery County near Blood Camp Ridge and flows sw into North Toe River.

Fall Branch rises in w Avery County near Big Yellow Bald Mountain and flows s into Roaring Creek.

Fall Branch rises in ne Buncombe County and flows se into North Fork [Swannanoa River].

Fall Branch rises in e Cherokee County and flows se and sw into Hiwassee River.

Fall Branch rises in n Haywood County and flows nw into Cold Springs Creek.

Fall Branch rises in e Macon County and flows nw into Mica City Creek.

Fall Branch rises in w Macon County and flows ne into Burningtown Creek.

Fall Branch rises in w Madison County and flows s into Roaring Fork.

Fall Branch rises in e Wake County and flows e into Little River.

Fall Branch rises in s Yancey County and flows nw into Big Lost Cove Creek.

Fallcliff, community in w Jackson County on Cullowhee Creek.

Fall Creek rises in e Haywood County and flows sw into Crabtree Creek.

Fall Creek rises in e Lee County and flows ne into Cape Fear River.

Fall Creek rises in e Mitchell County and flows s into Little Rock Creek.

Fall Creek rises in sw Polk County and flows ne into Pacolet River.

Fall Creek rises in n Yadkin County and flows nw into Yadkin River.

Fall Creek. *See* Honeycutt Creek.

Fall Creek Township, ne Yadkin County.

Falling Branch rises in n Franklin County and flows sw into Tooles Creek.

Falling Creek rises in nw Catawba County and flows ne into Catawba River.

Falling Creek rises in sw Greene County and flows se across Lenoir County into Neuse River. Appears in local records as early as 1730–35.

Falling Creek rises in e Richmond County and flows w into Hitchcock Creek.

Falling Creek rises in ne Sampson County and flows ne into w Wayne County, where it enters Beaverdam Creek. *See also* Thoroughfare Swamp.

Falling Creek, community in n Lenoir County on the stream of the same name. The Croom family operated a store there early in the nineteenth century, and it was the site of a free public school in 1840.

Falling Creek. *See* Thoroughfare Swamp.

Falling Creek Township, central Lenoir County.

Falling Hollow, sw Watauga County on the head of Watauga River.

Falling Rock Creek rises in w Haywood County,

Great Smoky Mountains National Park, near lat. 35°36′56″ N., long. 83°10′40″ W. Flows ne to join Beech Creek in forming Palmer Creek. Named when an overhanging rock cliff on a stream where hunters, fishermen, and others camped fell after being heated by a big campfire. One person was killed and others were injured.

Falling Run. *See* Deep Creek.

Falling Water Branch rises in s Yancey County and flows w into Cane River.

Fall Line, the dividing line between Coastal Plain and Piedmont North Carolina where the soft sedimentary soils of the Coastal Plain meet the hard rocks of the Piedmont. It often is marked in streams by falls and rapids. The fall line runs w of Wilson and e of Sanford in an irregular progression n and s.

Fall Ridge, s Watauga County, extends s in Watauga Township and causes a bend in Boone Fork.

Falls, community in n Wake County on Neuse River. *See also* Falls of the Neuse.

Falls Branch rises in e Macon County and flows s into North Prong Ellijay Creek.

Falls Branch rises in s Macon County and flows s into North Fork Coweeta Creek.

Falls Branch rises in s Macon County and flows s into Rabun County, Ga., where it enters Barkers Creek.

Falls Branch rises in e Swain County and flows nw into Tuckasegee River.

Falls Branch rises in se Swain County and flows n into Yalaka Creek.

Falls Creek rises in n Avery County and flows w into Elk River.

Falls Creek rises in sw Chatham County and flows s into Moore County, where it enters Deep River.

Falls Creek rises in n Cumberland County and flows ne into Carver Creek. Named for the falls just downstream from its junction with Carver Creek.

Falls Lake was built by the U.S. Army Corps of Engineers by damming the Neuse River at the community of Falls in Wake County. Provides water supply, recreation, and flood control. Main body of 20 sq. mi. Lake is in Durham and Wake Counties.

Falls of Gouges Creek, e Mitchell County.

Falls of Gunpowder. *See* Granite Falls.

Falls of the Neuse, rapids in Neuse River, n Wake

County near the community of Falls. Name appears on the Price map, 1808.

Fallston, town in ne Cleveland County. Settled 1885. Inc. 1893, but long inactive in municipal affairs. Alt. 950. Named for John Z. Falls, sheriff of the county when the town was inc. Served by post office, 1886–1940.

Fallstown. *See* Bells Cross Roads.

Fallstown Township, sw Iredell County.

False Gap, on the Swain County, N.C.–Sevier County, Tenn., line in Great Smoky Mountains National Park between The Sawteeth and Laurel Top.

Fancy, community in s Cleveland County served by post office, 1883–1902.

Fancy Hill. *See* Loray.

Fandon, community in Mecklenburg County served by post office, 1892–95.

Fannie, community in central Haywood County served by post office, 1892–1902.

Fannie Ridge extends ne from the Henderson county line into s Buncombe County between Cole Cove and Reed Cove.

Faraby Island, a narrow sandy loam island about 1 mi. long in the mouth of North Landing River, ne Currituck County. Sometimes called Ferebee's Island.

Far Creek rises in e Hyde County near Engelhard and flows se into Pamlico Sound. Appears as Gibbs Creek on the Collet map, 1770, and as recently as 1833 on other maps. In 1862 it was called Fur Creek, and by 1882, Far Creek.

Far Creek. *See* Engelhard.

Farley Branch rises in n Graham County and flows e into Little Tennessee River.

Farley Cove follows the se course of a small stream flowing into Santeetlah Lake in w central Graham County.

Farlow Gap, nw Transylvania County between Klesee Creek and Shuck Ridge Creek. Alt. 4,559.

Farmer, town in w Randolph County. Inc. 1897, but long inactive in municipal affairs. In center of a rich farming community.

Farmer Branch rises in s Haywood County and flows nw into Richland Creek.

Farmer's Branch rises in w central Wilson County and flows s into Toisnot Swamp. Named prior to 1770 for Isaac Farmer Sr.

Farmers Creek rises in n Yadkin County and flows n into Yadkin River.

Farmers Store, community in nw Ashe County.

Farmers Turnout. *See* Maco.

Farmer Top, central Cherokee County near the headwaters of Dockery and Rose Creeks.

Farmer Top, central Cherokee County s of Hiwassee River and nw of Murphy.

Farmington, community in n Davie County. As early as 1805, former residents of Currituck County began to move into the area. Two hurricanes in 1830 and another one in 1839 caused extensive crop damage in the Currituck County area; the population of the county dropped from 7,655 in 1830 to 6,703 in 1840. The community was known as Little Currituck until 1837, when a post office was est. and named Farmington for the fertile farming land there. Alt. 758.

Farmington Township, ne Davie County.

Farmville, town in w Pitt County. Settled about 1850 and known as New Town prior to 1872, when it was inc. as Farmville, a name derived from the fact that it was in the center of rich farming land. Produces building materials. Alt. 86.

Farmville. *See* Coalglen.

Farmville Township, w Pitt County.

Farnell Bay, central Onslow County, is formed by an indentation of the e bank of New River se of Hadnot Point.

Farnell Point, central Onslow County on the mouth of Wallace Creek.

Farner Branch rises in n Cherokee County and flows w into Cook Creek.

Faro, community in ne Wayne County near the head of Beaver Branch.

Farrar, former town in central Edgecombe County on the sw limits of Tarboro and now wholly within Tarboro. The name West Tarboro was changed to Hilma in 1893, when it was inc. Name changed from Hilma to Farrar, 1899, probably for O. C. Farrar, who purchased land in Tarboro for a cotton mill. Charter repealed 1909.

Farrars Island, in the Cape Fear River at the junction of the Chatham, Harnett, and Lee county lines nw of Buckhorn Falls. Approx. 1½ mi. long. Mentioned as early as 1819 in a survey of the rivers of the state.

Farrington, community in ne Chatham County. Named for local Fearrington family at the time of the construction of the Durham and Southern Railroad.

Fate Puett Cove, e Cherokee County on the headwaters of Burl Branch se of Indian Grave Gap.

Faucette. *See* Calvander.

Faucette Township, former township in n
central Alamance County. Now township
no. 5.

Faucetts Store, community in nw Halifax
County.

Faucett Township, central Halifax County.

Faulk, community in se Union County.

Faulkner Creek rises in ne Surry County and
flows sw into Ararat River. Probably named
for William Faulkner, an eighteenth-century
resident of the county.

Faust, community in e Madison County on Big
Laurel Creek.

Fawn Branch rises near Burl Mountain in n
central Transylvania County and flows se into
King Creek.

Fawn Mountain, e Yancey County between Blue
Rock Branch and a bend in South Toe River.

Fax Creek rises in n Graham County and flows
ne into Little Tennessee River.

Fayette County was formed in July 1784 when an
act of the General Assembly divided Cumberland County into Fayette and Moore Counties. It was intended to honor Marquis de
Lafayette (1757–1834), who visited the United
States that year. Fayette County retained the
courthouse in Fayetteville. In October of the
same year, the act was amended to retain the
name Cumberland for the county.

Fayette District, at the time of the 1790 cen-
sus, was composed of Anson, Cumberland,
Moore, Richmond, Robeson, and Sampson
Counties and the town of Fayetteville.

Fayetteville, city and county seat, central
Cumberland County at the head of navigation
on the Cape Fear River. The first settlement at
the site was about 1730. Est. 1762 as Campbellton, named for Farquhard Campbell. In
1778 Campbellton, and the adjacent trading
center of Cross Creek, *which see*, were consolidated as Lower and Upper Campbellton,
respectively. Name changed to Fayetteville
in 1783 in honor of Marquis de Lafayette
(1757–1834), who assisted Americans during
the Revolutionary War. The legislature met
there 1786, 1788–90, 1793–94. Location of
Fayetteville State University and Methodist
University. Produces textiles, dairy products,
bakery products, machinery, lumber, and

soft drinks. Alt. 107. Fort Bragg, *which see*, is
nearby.

Featherston Creek rises in n Henderson County
and flows sw into Mud Creek.

Fed Cove, on a tributary of Caler Fork in e Macon
County.

Federal Point projects from the s tip of New
Hanover County between Cape Fear River and
the Atlantic Ocean.

Federal Point Township, s New Hanover County.

Fed Gap, e Macon County between Fed Cove and
Mason Mountain.

Feds Branch rises in n Yancey County and flows
s into Cane River.

Fee Branch rises in s Yancey County and flows se
into Rock Creek.

Feeding Ridge, n Mitchell County between Cook
Branch and Gouges Creek.

Feezor, community in s Davidson County.
Named for local family.

Felts, community in se Wilkes County. Named
for local family.

Fender Mountain, peak in the Peach Bottom
Mountain range, w Alleghany County. Alt.
approx. 3,600.

Fenix, community in w Cumberland County.

Fennimore, community in e Mecklenburg
County served by post office, 1892–1903.
Formerly known as Garrison.

Fentress. *See* Pleasant Garden.

Fentress Township, s central Guilford County.
Named for Frederick Fentriss.

Ferebee's Island. *See* Faraby Island.

Ferguson, community in ne Haywood County
served by post office, 1885–1905.

Ferguson, community in w Wilkes County on
Yadkin River. Named for Capt. Lindsay C.
Ferguson, a nineteenth-century resident.

Ferguson Hill, central Yancey County between Pine Swamp Branch, Cane River, and
Bowlens Creek.

Ferguson Peak, on the Buncombe-Henderson
county line se of Hickory Nut Gap.

Ferndale, community in e Rockingham County
served by post office, 1888–1903.

Fern Knob, n Swain County in Great Smoky
Mountains National Park on Suli Ridge between Jonas Creek and Huggins Creek. Alt.
3,780.

Fern Mountain, n Jackson County on the ne end
of Black Mountain. Alt. 5,200.

Fernside, community in central New Hanover

County. Est. 1908 and named for Fernside Fertilizer plant. Alt. 15.

Ferrells Creek rises in s Orange County and flows s into Chatham County, where it enters Haw River.

Ferrell's Springs Branch rises in ne Wake County and flows se into Upper Barton's Creek.

Ferrells Township, sw Nash County.

Ferrin Knob, on the Buncombe-Henderson county line between Beaverdam and Long Gap.

Ferry, community in s Rutherford County formerly known as Ferry Store.

Ferry Branch rises in w Madison County and flows ne into French Broad River.

Fetner, community in w Wake County.

Few, community in s Durham County. Formerly known as Oyama, the name taken from that of a Japanese city; a railroad station opened there about 1904. The name was changed after the attack on Pearl Harbor, December 7, 1941, to honor William P. Few (1867–1940), first president of Duke University.

Fiars Creek. *See* Fires Creek.

Fiddler Creek rises in s Forsyth County and flows sw into South Fork. Named for Fidler or Fiedler family living in the vicinity by 1777. Appears as James Creek on Collet map, 1770.

Fiddlers Run rises in central Burke County and flows n into Sandy Run Creek.

Fidelity, community in e Jackson County served by post office, 1888–1901.

Fie Creek rises in w Haywood County and flows s into Jonathans Creek.

Field Branch rises in w Hoke County on Fort Bragg Military Reservation and flows e into Rockfish Creek. Earlier known as Old Field Branch. Leslies Mill Pond, now drained, was formerly on the creek.

Fields, community in nw Lenoir County. Alt. 111. Named for a local family.

Fieldsboro. *See* Walstonburg.

Fie Top Mountain, w Haywood County. Alt. 5,060. A ski run, Cataloochee, *which see*, is now operated there.

Fifth Creek rises in n central Iredell County and flows e into South Yadkin River. A portion of the stream in the Bethany Community is known as Five Mile Branch. It is the fifth in a series of creeks crossed by early settlers from Salisbury.

Fifth Creek. *See* Deep Creek.

Fig, community in w central Ashe County. Alt. approx. 2,880.

Figure Eight Island, e New Hanover and Pender Counties between Middle Sound and the Atlantic Ocean and extending from Mason Inlet on the s to Rich Inlet on the n. In 1965 work was begun to develop the island into a private gated resort community. A 260-foot causeway and a bridge over the Intracoastal Waterway connect it with the mainland.

Fillie Gap, ne Buncombe County e of McKinney Gap.

Filmore, community in w Wilson County.

Filo. *See* Biscoe.

Finch, community in s Nash County served by post office, 1890–1903.

Finch Cove, e Haywood County on Rush Fork.

Fincher Mountain, central Haywood County on the head of McElroy Branch.

Fincher's Branch rises in ne Orange County and flows s into Buck Quarter Creek. It was named for Jonathan Fincher, who acquired land in the vicinity in 1755.

Finchs Crossroads. *See* Denton.

Finch's Mill Pond, w Wilson County on Bloomery Swamp. Formed 1875 and named for owner. Covers 30 acres; max. depth. 10 ft. Fishing, boating. Finch Mill post office, 1898–1901.

Findley Creek rises in central Henderson County and flows ne and s into Perry Creek.

Findleysville, community in Mecklenburg County served by post office, 1810–34.

Fines Creek rises in ne Haywood County and sw into Waterville Lake on Pigeon River. Named for a scout who was killed in 1783 when he and others were chasing Indians who had stolen their horses.

Fines Creek, community in n Haywood County on the creek of the same name. Settled about 1850.

Fines Creek Gap, ne Haywood County on the head of Fines Creek. Alt. 3,948.

Fines Creek Township, ne Haywood County.

Finger, community in w Stanly County.

Finger Counties, five counties in the ne corner of the state—Chowan, Perquimans, Pasquotank, Camden, and Currituck—whose collective geographical mass resembles digits on a hand.

Finley, community on the upper waters of the Yadkin River in n Caldwell County. Named for

Finley P. Curtis, who was active in securing a post office for the community.

Fire Gap Ridge, w Macon County between Roaring Fork Creek and Jarrett Creek.

Firescald Branch rises in w Avery County and flows s into Henson Creek.

Firescald Branch rises in w Yancey County and flows se into Big Creek.

Firescald Creek rises in n McDowell County on the sw slope of Betsy Ridge and flows sw into Slim Creek.

Fire Scald Knob, se Alleghany County about 3 mi. se of Bullhead Mountain.

Firescald Mountain, w Avery County.

Firescald Mountain, w Yancey County between Simms Fork and Elk Wallow Creek. Alt. 4,840.

Firescald Ridge, n Graham County, extends ne from Bearpen Gap to Little Tennessee River.

Firescald Ridge extends se from Deep Gap to Snowbird Creek in sw Graham County.

Fire Scald Ridge, s Haywood County between West Hollow and West Fork Pigeon River.

Firescald Ridge, n Jackson County between Blackrock Creek and Shut-in Creek.

Firescald Ridge, sw Macon County between Park Creek and Pat Stable Branch.

Firescald Ridge, n Swain County in Great Smoky Mountains National Park, a spur of Welch Ridge extending se between Jonas Creek and Little Jonas Creek.

Fires Creek rises in n Clay County and flows sw into Hiwassee River. Appears as Fiars Creek in the 1861 law establishing the county.

First Broad River rises in e Rutherford County and flows se into Cleveland County. There it flows se and sw into Broad River. Appears on the Collet map, 1770, as Sandy River.

First Gum Swamp. *See* Gum Swamp.

First Hurricane Branch rises in s Swain County and flows sw into Yalaka Creek.

First Potts Creek rises in w Davidson County and flows se into High Rock Lake on Yadkin River. Appears on the Collet map, 1770, as Potts Creek.

Fish Creek rises in e Guilford County and flows ne across the nw corner of Alamance County into Caswell County, where it enters Buttermilk Creek.

Fish Creek rises in w Harnett County and flows ne into Cape Fear River.

Fishcreek. *See* Mamers.

Fish Dam, community in e Durham County served by post office, 1881–1902. Spelled Fishdam after 1895.

Fishdam. *See* Fish Dam.

Fishdam Creek rises in w Wilkes County and flows se into Yadkin River. Known as Fish Trap Creek until the 1960s, when the spillway of one of the flood-control dams in connection with the W. Kerr Scott Dam emptied into it and the name was changed.

Fisher, community in sw Mecklenburg County served by post office, 1891–92. Earlier known as Kelleyville, *which see*.

Fisher Creek rises in n Jackson County and flows s into Scott Creek.

Fisher Lake, on a tributary of Watkins Creek in s Macon County.

Fisherman Bay, e Pamlico County in the Bay River estuary.

Fisherman Islands, two small tidal-marsh islands, e Pamlico County in the Bay River estuary se of Bay Point.

Fishermare Branch rises in n Cherokee County on Fishermare Ridge and flows s into Hyatt Creek.

Fishermare Ridge, n Cherokee County in the Snowbird Mountains.

Fisher Peak, mountain on the Surry County, N.C.–Carroll County, Va., line. Alt. 3,609.

Fisher River rises in Virginia and flows s into Surry County and se across the county into Yadkin River. Appears on the Collet map, 1770.

Fisher's Ford. *See* Cooleemee.

Fisher Swamp rises in ne Craven County and flows sw into Little Swift Creek.

Fisherville, community in s Forsyth County.

Fishhawk Mountain, s Macon County between Little Fishhawk Mountain and Wolf Rock. Alt. 4,684.

Fish Hawk Point, ne Carteret County extending into Rumley Bay.

Fishing Branch rises in n Person County and flows nw into Marlowe Creek.

Fishing Creek rises in e Granville County and flows s into Tar River.

Fishing Creek rises in nw New Hanover County and flows ne into Cape Fear River. *See also* Longs Island.

Fishing Creek rises in e Vance County and flows ne in Vance and Warren Counties and se and s in Warren County to the Franklin-Warren, Halifax-Nash, and Halifax-Edgecombe county lines to a point approx. 7 mi. n of Tarboro. From there, it flows s to enter Tar River. It appears as Great Fishing Creek on the Moseley map, 1733, and on the Collet map, 1770.

Fishing Creek rises in s Wilkes County in the Brushy Mountains and flows ne into Yadkin River.

Fishing Creek District. *See* Fishing Creek Township.

Fishing Creek Township, e central Granville County. Fishing Creek District had 59 heads of families in 1790.

Fishing Creek Township, se Warren County.

Fishing Creek Township, former township in central Wilkes County, now a part of Wilkesboro Township.

Fishprong Branch rises in e Clay County and flows se into Barnett Creek.

Fish Ridge, n Haywood County, extends s beside Morgan Creek.

Fishton, community in w Polk County on Green River.

Fishtown. *See* Beaufort.

Fishtrap Branch rises in e Swain County and flows ne into Tuckasegee River.

Fish Trap Creek. *See* Fishdam Creek.

Fitch, community in s Caswell County, formerly known as Fitch's Store. A post office was operated there, 1876–1926.

Fitches Knob, se Wilkes County. Alt. 1,850.

Fites Creek rises in e Gaston County and flows se into Catawba River.

Fitts, community in n central Warren County. Post office est. in 1895 but discontinued in 1905. Named for the first postmaster, Edward F. Fitts.

Fitzgerald, community in n Rockingham County served by post office, 1900–1906. Named for Thomas B. Fitzgerald, textile executive and local farmer.

Five Comb Branch rises in ne Cherokee County and flows se and sw into Valley River.

Five Forks, community in n Person County.

Five Forks, community in sw Stokes County upon boundary with Forsyth County. Located in elevated area with several springs. Served by post office beginning 1871.

Five Forks, community in n Warren County s of Lake Gaston and e of Jordans Creek. Settled about 1880. Alt. 400.

Five Forks, community in n Yadkin County.

Fivemile Branch rises in central Columbus County and flows se then n into Cedar Branch.

Five Mile Branch. *See* Fifth Creek.

Five Mile Creek rises in e Robeson County and flows sw into Saddletree Swamp.

Five Points, community in ne Cabarrus County.

Five Points, community in w Hoke County.

Flag Branch rises in se Union County and flows ne into Rays Fork.

Flaggtown, community in nw Montgomery County served by post office from 1879 until 1895, when name was changed to Pontop. Area now home to Uwharrie Point Lake and golf course community.

Flake, community in w Iredell County served by post office, 1900–1905.

Flannery Fork [South Fork New River] rises in Moses H. Cone Memorial Park approx. 2 mi. nw of town of Blowing Rock, s Watauga County. It flows w into Trout Lake and then ne to join East Fork and Middle Fork in forming South Fork New River approx. 2 mi. se of town of Boone.

Flat Branch rises in w Brunswick County and flows s into Wet Ash Swamp.

Flat Branch rises near Lookoff Gap in se Buncombe County and flows se into Rocky Fork.

Flat Branch rises in ne Cherokee County and flows nw into Collett Creek.

Flat Branch rises in ne Cherokee County and flows s into Valley River.

Flat Branch rises in nw Gates County and flows se through Jones Swamp into Hacklan Branch.

Flat Branch rises in n Haywood County and flows nw into Laurel Creek.

Flat Branch rises in s Mecklenburg County and flows se into Sixmile Creek.

Flat Branch rises in w Mitchell County and flows sw into Nolichucky River.

Flat Branch rises in w Surry County and flows e into Fisher River.

Flat Branch rises in w Swain County and flows nw into Tuckasegee River.

Flat Branch rises in s Watauga County and flows se into Buffalo Branch.

Flat Branch rises in se Watauga County and flows ne into Laurel Fork.

Flat Branch, community in e Gates County.

Flat Branch. *See* Oak Summit.

Flat Branch. *See* Sweetwater Creek.

Flat Branch Gap, on the Jackson-Macon county line.

Flat Creek rises in n Buncombe County near Watershed Ridge and flows sw into French Broad River.

Flat Creek rises in ne Buncombe County and flows sw through Montreat into Swannanoa River.

Flat Creek rises in se Buncombe County and flows se into Broad River. Appears as Upper Flat Creek on recent highway maps.

Flat Creek rises in e Granville County and flows ne into Vance County, where it enters Nutbush Creek.

Flat Creek rises on the Fort Bragg Military Reservation in n Hoke County and flows ne into Little River.

Flat Creek rises in s Jackson County and flows n into Bear Creek Lake on the Tuckasegee River.

Flat Creek rises in sw Jackson County and flows n into Mill Creek.

Flat Creek rises in se Rowan County and flows e approx. 4½ mi. into Yadkin River. Known also as Flat Swamp Creek.

Flat Creek rises in ne Swain County in Great Smoky Mountains National Park and flows se into Bunches Creek.

Flat Creek is formed in s Transylvania County by the junction of South Fork and North Fork and flows ne into West Fork French Broad River.

Flat Creek rises in w Vance County and flows ne into Kerr Lake.

Flat Creek, community in n Buncombe County. Alt. 2,161.

Flat Creek Bald, ne Swain County in Great Smoky Mountains National Park on the n end of Overlook Ridge. Alt. 5,240.

Flat Creek Falls, se Buncombe County on Flat Creek.

Flat Creek Township, n central Buncombe County.

Flat Fork Creek rises in central Anson County and flows n into Brown Creek.

Flat Gap, e central Burke County.

Flat Gap, w Haywood County on Eaglenest Ridge.

Flat Gap, on the Jackson-Haywood county line.

Flat Knob, n Macon County at the head of Rhinehart Creek.

Flat Land Branch rises in e central Avery County and flows s into Wilson Creek.

Flat Laurel Creek rises in s Haywood County and flows nw into West Fork Pigeon River.

Flat Laurel Gap, on the Haywood-Transylvania county line between Big Bald and Little Bald Mountain.

Flat Mountain, s Jackson County between East Fork Chattooga River and Whitewater River. Also called Flattop Mountain. Alt. 3,931.

Flat Mountain, se Macon County between Cullasaja River and Big Creek.

Flat River is formed in s Person County by the junction of North Flat River and South Flat River. It flows se into n Durham County and se across the county to join Eno River in forming Neuse River. Appears on the Moseley map, 1733.

Flat River, community in ne Durham County served by post office, 1881–1903.

Flat River Township, s central Person County.

Flat Rock, mountain in e central Avery County.

Flat Rock, residential community adjacent to East Flat Rock, *which see*, central Henderson County. Alt. 2,207. Settled by Charlestonians as summer resort. Home to the Flat Rock Playhouse, state theater of North Carolina, and Connemara, home of poet Carl Sandburg. A post office since 1838. Named for a smooth outcropping of granite that was a Cherokee Indian ceremonial ground centuries ago. Inc. 1996.

Flat Rock, community in w Stokes County.

Flat Rock, community in ne Surry County. Named for a nearby open-faced granite quarry, the largest in the world, at which work was begun in 1889.

Flat Rock, community in ne Vance County named for large, flat rock in old stage road.

Flat Rock Branch rises in n Nash County and flows ne into Swift Creek.

Flatrock Creek rises in n Franklin County and flows se into Sandy Creek.

Flat Rock Creek rises in sw Wilkes County and flows se through the corner of Yadkin County and into Iredell County, where it enters Hunting Creek. Sometimes known locally as North Hunting Creek.

Flats, a tourist resort and community in se

Macon County near the head of Middle
Creek. It is on an elevation that extends se
from Middle Creek in Macon County into
Rabun County, Ga.

Flat Shoal Creek rises in s central Stokes County
and flows ne into Dan River.

Flat Shoal Mountain, central Stokes County
parallel to Flat Shoal Creek.

Flat Shoals, community in s central Stokes
County.

Flat Springs, sw Yancey County at the head of
Indian Fork.

Flat Springs Creek rises in Tennessee and flows
e into n Avery County, where it enters Beech
Creek.

Flat Springs Gap, on the Buncombe-Yancey
county line between Flat Springs Knob and
Big Butt.

Flat Springs Knob, on the Buncombe-Yancey
county line ne of Flat Springs Gap at lat.
35°47'30" N., long. 82°20'30" W. Alt.
5,700–5,800. Sometimes also known as
Flattop.

Flats Township, s central Macon County.

Flat Swamp rises in s Hertford County and flows
se to join Horse Swamp in forming Bear
Swamp.

Flat Swamp rises in n Jones County and flows s
into Rattlesnake Branch.

Flat Swamp rises in w Martin County and flows
se into Tranters Creek.

Flat Swamp rises in sw Onslow County and
flows nw into Pender County, where it enters
Shaking Creek.

Flat Swamp Creek rises in e central Bertie
County and flows sw into Hoggard Mill Creek.
Flat Swamp is mentioned in local records as
early as 1724.

Flat Swamp Creek rises in e Davidson County
and flows sw into Yadkin River.

Flat Swamp Creek. *See* Flat Creek.

Flat Swamp Mountain, a long mountain in s
Davidson and e Rowan Counties through
which the Yadkin River cut a channel. Geologists indicate that the mountain is the rem-
nant of ancient lava flow.

Flatt Creek. *See* Big Flatty Creek.

Flat Top, peak on Flat Top Mountain, se
Buncombe County between Lookoff Gap
and High Hickory Knob in Swannanoa
Mountains.

Flat Top, mountain knob in central Caldwell
County.

Flattop, peak in n Yancey County n of Big Creek.
Alt. approx. 4,807.

Flattop. *See* Flat Springs Knob.

Flattop Branch rises in s Watauga County at the
sw end of Flattop Mountain and flows se into
Middle Fork [South Fork New River].

Flattop Cliffs. *See* Flattop Mountain.

Flattop Creek rises in e central Avery County and
flows n into Banner Elk Creek.

Flattop Mountain, e Avery County. Alt. approx.
5,050. Known also as Flattop Cliffs.

Flat Top Mountain, se Buncombe County between Trantham Creek and Flat Branch.

Flattop Mountain, s Watauga County nw of
Blowing Rock. Alt. 4,568.

Flattop Mountain, n Yancey County, extends ne
from the head of Deer Creek to Nolichucky
River.

Flattop Mountain. *See* Flat Mountain.

Flattop Mountain Branch rises in nw Yancey
County and flows w into Tennessee, where it
enters Spivey Creek.

Flatt's Creek. *See* Salmon Creek.

Flatty Creek. *See* Big Flatty Creek.

Flatwood Gap, nw Macon County. Alt. 1,475.

Flatwoods, The, level land at the head of Shoal
Creek in sw Henderson County. Settlers
moved from nearby mountains into The
Flatwoods in late nineteenth century.

Flax Creek rises in sw Cherokee County and
flows se into Persimmon Creek.

Flay, community in w Lincoln County.

Fleaback Mountain, s Clay County between
Needmore Branch and Hothouse Branch.
Alt. 3,165.

Flea Branch rises in e Madison County and flows
s into Laurel Creek.

Flea Mountain, central Cherokee County
between Dockery and Cook Creeks.

Fleetwood, community in s Ashe County.

Fleetwood Point extends from mainland of ne
Dare County into Croatan Sound.

Fleming's Creek. *See* Raymond's Creek.

Flemington. *See* Brassfield.

Flemington. *See* Lake Waccamaw (town).

Flemming, community in se Catawba County
served by post office, 1875–1907.

Fletcher, community in n Henderson County.
Alt. 2,112. Named for Dr. George W. Fletcher,

popular country doctor and surgeon during the Civil War. Est. about 1883 after the railroad was completed. With the development of Fletcher, Shufordsville, approx. 2 mi. n, declined, and the post office there was transferred to Fletcher and the name changed. Produced textiles.

Fletcher Branch rises in n Henderson County and flows nw into Cane Creek.

Fletcher Creek rises in nw Henderson County and flows se, where it joins Big Creek in forming North Fork.

Fletcher Knob, w Caldwell County. Named for Reuben Fletcher, Revolutionary soldier.

Flint, community in w Wake County.

Flint Gap, nw Cherokee County in the Unicoi Mountains.

Flint Gap, ne Graham County between Meetinghouse Mountain and Little Tennessee River.

Flint Hill, se Cleveland County between Jolly Mountain and Sandy Run Creek.

Flint Hill, community in n Montgomery County.

Flint Hill, community in w Randolph County.

Flint Hill, community in e Yadkin County near Yadkin River. A post office est. there in 1881 was named Shore. Inc. 1903 as Shore by A. E. Shore and others for the legal manufacture of whiskey. Charter repealed 1911. Present name adopted prior to 1924.

Flint Hill. *See* Cherry Mountain.

Flint Hill. *See* Scottville.

Flint Hill Creek rises in e Rutherford County and flows ne into Cleveland County, where it enters Hinton Creek.

Flint Knob, se Buncombe County between Miner and Sam Gaps.

Flint Level Branch rises in w Madison County and flows sw into French Broad River.

Flint Rock Gap, n Macon County near the head of Sugar Cove Creek.

Flint Spring Branch rises in n Clay County and flows se into Fires Creek.

Flinty. *See* Newdale.

Flinty Gap, on the McDowell-Yancey county line between Green Knob and Big Craggy.

Flora, community in w Burke County served by post office, 1870–1921.

Flora, community in sw Randolph County served by post office, 1883–1914.

Floral College, community in nw Robeson County. Alt. 193. Named for a woman's college that operated there, 1841–78. One of the earliest colleges for women in the South, it was named for the wildflowers growing in profusion in the area.

Florence, community in sw Guilford County near present-day Jamestown. Florence Female Seminary was there.

Florence, community in e Pamlico County on Bald Creek. Known earlier as Spring Creek; named for Florence, wife of Stanley Martin, first postmaster.

Florian, community in central Anson County served by post office, 1893–1904.

Flounder Slue Rock, two small islands in Pamlico Sound, ne Carteret County n of Portsmouth Island. In 1795 the islands were called Flounder Rocks.

Flower Cove, s Swain County on the head of Marr Branch.

Flower Gap, s Haywood County between Nigger Spring and Dina Branch.

Flower Hill, worn-down remains of an ancient mountain, n Johnston County between Emit and Moccasin Creek. Rhododendron flourishes there.

Flower Hill, community in se Randolph County served by post office, 1877–1907.

Flower Knob, s Haywood County on the head of Little East Fork Pigeon River.

Flowers Gap, at the head of Coon Creek in e Macon County.

Flowers Swamp rises in e Robeson County and flows sw into Lumber River.

Flows Store, community in s Cabarrus County named for Daniel W. Flowe, who opened a store there in 1881. Flowe's store, closed about 1925, still stands.

Flox, community in n Onslow County served by post office, 1891–1907. Formerly Purgatory, served by post office beginning in 1884.

Floyd, community in se Cumberland County served by post office, 1889–1907.

Floyds Creek rises in s Rutherford County and flows s into Broad River.

Fly, community in central Montgomery County served by post office, 1889–97.

Flynn, community in s Moore County served by post office, 1891–1901.

Flynn Ridge, s Yancey County between Setrock Creek and Whiteside Branch.

Fodderstack Mountain, nw Buncombe County

between South Turkey and North Turkey Creeks.

Fodderstack Mountain, se Macon County between Rich Gap and Satulah Mountain.

Fodderstack Mountain, e Transylvania County between Lydia Creek and French Broad River.

Fodderstack Mountain. *See* Terrapin Mountain.

Folk Hill, community in central Rockingham County named for Douglas Foucht, local sawmill owner and farmer, whose home stood on large hill. By 1920s name became Folk Hill.

Folkstone, community in sw Onslow County. Alt. 69. Believed to have been named by a retired sea captain for his native town in England. Served by post office, 1902–54.

Folly Creek rises in w Henderson County and flows nw into Little Willow Creek.

Folly Fork, community in ne Gates County. Folly post office est. prior to 1828. Frequently in the seventeenth and eighteenth centuries, the word folly was used in the sense of the French *folie* (delight; favorite abode) and it formed a part of the name of English estates.

Folly Swamp rises in ne Gates County and flows e into Dismal Swamp.

Fonta Flora. *See* Flora.

Fontana, former community in nw Swain County, est. 1902 by employees of Montvale Lumber Co. The site is now covered by the waters of Fontana Lake, *which see*. Said to have been named by Mrs. George Leidy Wood, wife of an official of the lumber company, because it was "a short word, musical, easy to spell," and it reminded her of "the waterfalls that looked like fountains, leaping from ledge to ledge" in the nearby forest.

Fontana Lake, n Graham and w and central Swain Counties on Little Tennessee River and its tributaries. Forms the s boundary of the Great Smoky Mountains National Park. Dam begun in 1941, completed in 1945, forms the lake, largest of the Tennessee Valley Authority system. Max. depth 480 ft. The lake, 30 mi. long, has a shoreline of 248 mi. and covers 10,530 acres at full lake. Provides flood control, electric power, and recreation facilities. The dam there is the highest in e America. Alt. 1,710. *See also* Fontana and Fontana Village.

Fontana Village, resort community in n Graham County in Welch Cove near Fontana Lake. Alt. 1,800. Built in 1941 as a construction village for the employees of Fontana Dam. After the dam was completed, it was leased to a private corporation for development as a resort. *See also* Welch Cove.

Fontcal. *See* Wagram.

Fontena, formerly the plantation of the Baker family, located between Little Fishing Creek and Reedy Creek near the community of Grove Hill, s Warren County. The plantation house, no longer standing, was built in 1790 by Judge Blake Baker, attorney general of North Carolina in 1794. In 1816 the library at Fontena was described as the finest in the state.

Fonville, community in s Harnett County.

Footsville, community in s Yadkin County near South Deep Creek. Known first as Footville.

Forbes, community in w Mitchell County on Toe River. Alt. 2,185.

Forbes Bay, e Pasquotank County between Cottage Point and Cobb Point on the Pasquotank River.

Forbes Millpond, central Pitt County on Greens Mill Run.

Forbush, community in central Yadkin County on Logan Creek.

Forbush Creek rises in n Yadkin County and flows se into Logan Creek.

Forbush Township, se Yadkin County.

Ford Creek rises in se Granville County and flows ne into w Franklin County, where it enters Tar River.

Forest, community in central Craven County.

Forest City, town in s central Rutherford County. Alt. 869. Inc. 1877 as Burnt Chimney; name changed to Forest City in 1887 in honor of Forest Davis, lumber merchant.

Forest Grove, community in n Watauga County on Forest Grove Creek.

Forest Grove Creek rises in n Watauga County and flows sw into Beaverdam Creek.

Forest Hill, former town in central Cabarrus County. Inc. 1887 but now a part of the city of Concord. Began as a mill settlement in the 1850s and named McDonalds Mill. Later known as Odell Mill and Locke Mills; now the site of Randolph Mill.

Forestville, community in ne Wake County s of the town of Wake Forest. Inc. 1879; charter repealed 1915.

Forge, community in e Surry County served by post office, 1888–1903.

Forge Knob, on the Swain County, N.C.–Blount County, Tenn., line in Great Smoky Mountains National Park between Rich Gap and Buck Gap.

Forge Mountain, nw Henderson County between South Fork Mills River and Boylston Creek in Pisgah National Forest. Alt. 3,280. Granted to Philip Sitton about 1806 as a "forge bounty" where he manufactured iron for many years. Adjoining it was the Gillespie gun works, where long guns were fashioned from Sitton's iron.

Fork, town in se Davie County. Inc. 1895 as Fork Church, but long inactive in municipal affairs. Developed around Fork Baptist Church, organized 1793. Alt. 824.

Forkade, community in ne Moore County served by post office, 1886–1905.

Fork Branch rises in ne Onslow County and flows ne into White Oak River.

Fork Branch rises in n Watauga County on Fork Ridge and flows sw into Little Beaverdam Creek.

Fork Church. *See* Fork.

Fork Creek rises in s Avery County and flows s into Three Mile Creek.

Fork Creek rises in s Randolph County and flows se into Deep River. Appears as Crooked Creek on the Collet map, 1770; as Pork Creek (likely a typographical error) on the Price map, 1808; and as Fork Creek on the MacRae map, 1833.

Forked Mountain, on the Henderson-Transylvania county line.

Forked Ridge, ne Buncombe County sw of Slaty Branch.

Forked Ridge, on the Henderson-Transylvania county line.

Forked Ridge, w Watauga County, extends nw between Grassy Gap and Beech Creek.

Forked Tree Mountain, ne Buncombe County between Burleson Branch and North Fork Ivy Creek.

Fork Legged Mountain, e Madison County at the head of California Creek.

Fork Mountain, central Avery County.

Fork Mountain, ne Buncombe County between Left Fork Creek and Beetree Creek.

Fork Mountain, sw Buncombe County near the headwaters of Ballard Creek.

Fork Mountain, n Caldwell County. Alt. 2,000. Named for its position near a fork in the Yadkin River.

Fork Mountain, e Haywood County between Pisgah Creek and Reed Creek.

Fork Mountain, nw Haywood County n of Conrad Branch in Great Smoky Mountains National Park. Alt. approx. 4,000.

Fork Mountain, w Haywood County in Great Smoky Mountains National Park near lat. 35°40'14" N., long. 83°07' W. on e slope of Indian Ridge.

Fork Mountain, n Macon and s Swain Counties parallel to Poplar Cove.

Fork Mountain, s Macon County between Piney Knob Fork and Turtle Pond Creek.

Fork Mountain, s Madison County. Alt. approx. 3,560.

Fork Mountain, n Mitchell County between Little Rock Creek and Roan Mountain. Alt. approx. 4,500. Named because, to an early settler, its three peaks resembled the tines of a fork.

Fork Mountain, n Rutherford County between Camp and Cane Creeks. Alt. approx. 1,750.

Fork Mountain, s Swain County between Yalaka Creek and Bowers Creek.

Fork Mountain Branch rises in central Avery County and flows s into North Toe River.

Fork Mountain Township, central Mitchell County.

Fork Point, a peninsula in w Beaufort County between Chocowinity Bay and Pamlico River.

Fork Point, point of land at the mouth of Bond Creek in se Beaufort County at Pamlico River.

Fork Point Island, in Chocowinity Bay, w Beaufort County. Approx. 1/10 mi. long.

Fork Ridge extends from central Cherokee County ne into n Cherokee County between Davis and Bald Creeks.

Fork Ridge, ne Cherokee County in the Snowbird Mountains.

Fork Ridge, n Clay County, extends ne between Little Fires Creek and Bald Spring Branch.

Fork Ridge, n Graham County between Oldfield Gap and Little Tennessee River.

Fork Ridge, w Graham County between Squally Creek and Hooper Mill Creek.

Fork Ridge, s Haywood County, extends from the head of West Fork Pigeon River to the mouth of Middle Prong.

Fork Ridge, central Jackson County between Trout Creek and Mill Creek.

Fork Ridge, between North Fork and Plott Balsams in n Jackson County.

Fork Ridge, n Jackson County between Jones Knob and Yellow Face.

Fork Ridge extends ne from Rattlesnake Ridge in ne Jackson County to Campbell Creek in w Haywood County.

Fork Ridge, w Jackson County between Dodgen Creek and Whiterock Creek.

Fork Ridge, s Macon County at the head of Peeks Creek.

Fork Ridge, s Macon County between Shope Fork and Henson Creek.

Fork Ridge, n Mitchell County between Grassy Creek and Big Rock Creek.

Fork Ridge, n Mitchell County between Right Fork and Pigeonroost Creek.

Fork Ridge, n Swain County, extends sw from Thomas Ridge between Left Fork and Right Fork to the confluence of the forks to form Indian Creek.

Fork Ridge, n Swain County in Great Smoky Mountains National Park, a spur extending se from Mount Collins.

Fork Ridge, nw Watauga County, begins near head of Little Beaverdam Creek at State Line Gap and extends s, branching sw and se to form an inverted Y. Highest point is about 4,300 ft.

Fork Ridge, n Yancey County parallel to Hensley Branch.

Fork Ridge, s Yancey County between Middle Fork Rock Creek and North Fork Rock Creek.

Fork River Bald, on the Haywood-Transylvania county line at the nw end of Fork River Ridge.

Fork River Ridge, nw Transylvania County, extends se from Fork River Bald between Daniel Ridge Creek and Right Fork Davidson River.

Forks of Ivy, community on the Buncombe-Madison county line on Ivy Creek. Named for the fact that it is near the junction of Ivy and Little Ivy Creeks. Alt. 1,978.

Forks of Pigeon. *See* Canton. Post office operated by the name, 1841–1901.

Forks of Tar River. *See* Washington.

Fork Swamp rises in sw Beaufort County in Reedy Pocosin and flows s into Craven County, where it enters Palmetta Swamp. Named because an adjacent road forks, one road leading to Pinetown and the other route to Washington, N.C.

Fork Swamp rises in central Pitt County and flows s into East Branch.

Fork Township, se Warren County.

Fork Township, w Wayne County. Named for location in fork of Neuse and Little Rivers. Designation has remained unchanged since first listed in 1838.

Former Camp Branch rises in n Madison County and flows s into Big Laurel Creek.

Forney, former community in w Swain County on Tuckasegee River at the mouth of Forney Creek. Alt. 1,537. The site is now under the waters of Fontana Lake.

Forney Creek rises in e Lincoln County and flows se into Killian Creek. Named for Jacob Forney, pioneer settler of about 1750.

Forney Creek rises in n Swain County in Great Smoky Mountains National Park and flows sw and s into Tuckasegee River.

Forney Ridge, n Swain County in Great Smoky Mountains National Park, a lofty spur extending sw from Clingmans Dome between Forney Creek and Noland Creek.

Forneys Creek Township, nw Swain County.

Forrester Ridge, nw Swain County in Great Smoky Mountains National Park, extends se from Blockhouse Mountain to the confluence of Haw Gap Branch and Hazel Creek.

Forshee, community in s Rockingham County between Troublesome Creek and Little Troublesome Creek. Served by post office, 1900–1917. Named for Annie Forshee, relative of postmaster.

Forsyth County was formed in 1849 from Stokes County. In the central part of the state, it is bounded by Guilford, Davidson, Davie, Yadkin, and Stokes Counties. It was named for Col. Benjamin Forsyth (ca. 1760–1814), a native of Stokes County who was killed on the Canadian frontier in the War of 1812. Area: 424 sq. mi. County seat: Winston-Salem, with an elevation of 858 ft. Townships are Abbotts Creek, Belews Creek, Bethania, Broadbay, Clemmonsville, Kernersville, Lewisville, Middle Fork, Old Richmond, Old Town, Salem Chapel, South Forks, Vienna, and Winston. Produces tobacco, wheat, oats, soybeans, blueberries, grapes, corn, poultry, dairy products, livestock, hogs, cigarettes and other tobacco products, hosiery, textiles, bakery products, machinery, fabricated metals, banking services, corrugated boxes, apparel, lumber, and crushed stone. *See also* Dobbs Parish; Wachovia.

Forsyth Creek rises in e central McDowell County and flows se into Lake James on the Catawba River.

Fort Anderson. *See* Brunswick.

Fort Barnwell, community in nw Craven County. Alt. 40. Settled about 1800. Named for Fort Barnwell, constructed by Col. John Barnwell of South Carolina in a campaign against the Tuscarora Indians in April 1712. Remains of the fort are on a bluff overlooking the Neuse River 2 mi. ne of the community.

Fort Bartow, Civil War fort on Roanoke Island, Dare County.

Fort Benjamin, Civil War fort on the Newport River, e Carteret County opposite town of Newport.

Fort Bragg, nw Cumberland, e Hoke and Moore, and s Harnett Counties. Est. 1918 as Camp Bragg, a U.S. Field Artillery training center; name changed to Fort Bragg in 1922. Named for Gen. Braxton Bragg (1817–76), Confederate commander. Alt. 110. Area, 200 sq. mi. Now headquarters for airborne troops and special operations. Reached a peak of 104,000 men just prior to the North African invasion in World War II. Pope Air Force Base, *which see*, is adjacent.

Fort Branch rises in nw Bertie County and flows n into Hertford County where it enters Ahoskie Creek.

Fort Branch, a Confederate fort at Rainbow Banks, nw Martin County. Built to prevent Union gunboats from going up the Roanoke River to Weldon to attack the railroad bridge. Earthworks remain.

Fort Branch. *See* Conoho Creek.

Fort Butler, s Cherokee County, military installation where Gen. Winfield Scott, in command of U.S. forces, gathered Cherokee Indians before moving them west in 1838.

Fort Butler Mountain, s Cherokee County s of Right Prong Martin Creek and w of Martin Creek. Named for the fort near the present

town of Murphy, *which see*, where Gen. Winfield Scott, in command of U.S. forces, gathered the Cherokee Indians before moving them west in 1838.

Fort Caswell, on the se tip of Oak Island in se Brunswick County. Begun by United States in 1826; seized by North Carolina troops in 1861 and abandoned by Confederates in 1865. Used also in Spanish-American War and both world wars. Well-preserved remains now in Baptist summer camp area.

Fort Clark, Civil War fort on Cape Hatteras 1 mi. up the beach from Hatteras Inlet. It was laid out by William B. Thompson and construction started about July 1861.

Fort Creek rises in ne Caldwell County e of Fort Defiance and flows n into Yadkin River.

Fort Creek rises in w Granville County and flows ne into Tar River. Shown on modern maps as Ford Creek.

Fort Defiance, ne Caldwell County. Home of William Lenoir, leader in Revolutionary War and public affairs; built 1788–92 and stands on site of frontier Fort Defiance.

Fort Dobbs, built 1755–56 to protect w counties from Indians. Site in n central Iredell County, 4½ mi. n of Statesville.

Fort Dobbs. *See* Fort Macon.

Fort Fisher, State Historic Site and former Confederate fort at the s tip of New Hanover County. Construction began in April 1861 under direction of Capt. Charles P. Bolles, who was soon transferred. The first section of the fort was named Battery Bolles. Upon completion, the fort—constructed of sand, palmetto logs, and railroad iron—was named for Capt. Charles F. Fisher (1816–61), who had been killed at the Battle of First Manassas while commanding North Carolina troops. Fort Fisher controlled the Cape Fear River and kept the port of Wilmington open. The fort was bombarded from the sea on December 23–25, 1864, and January 12–13, 1865. It fell on January 15. During World War II, the site was used in connection with coastal defense. Restoration and development as a State Historic Site began in 1960.

Fort Fisher Junction, community in s New Hanover County. Prior to 1957, when the name was changed by the county commissioners, the community was known as Monkey Junction because the proprietor of a store there once owned a great many monkeys.

Fort Hamby, a name applied to a log house fortified in 1865 at the end of the Civil War by deserters from the Union Army. Named for a woman, apparently of evil repute, who formerly owned the house. Located in sw Wilkes County near the mouth of Lewis Fork Creek in Yadkin River, it provided refuge for a band of armed men who robbed and murdered the residents of several counties. A group of local citizens, including a number of former Confederate soldiers, attacked the "fort," set it on fire, and captured a number of the men. Some were shot during the attack and others were tried and sentenced to prison.

Fort Hampton. *See* Fort Macon.

Fort Hembree. *See* Hayesville.

Fort Hill, former Confederate batteries on the Pamlico River, e central Beaufort County, which enabled Gen. D. H. Hill's forces to besiege Washington, N.C., in the spring of 1863.

Fort Hill, a Civil War fort "near Hill's Point" in Buncombe County. The exact location cannot now be determined.

Fortin Island, the westernmost of a small group of islands in Core Sound about 3 mi. se of community of Davis, se Carteret County.

Fortiscue Creek rises in sw Hyde County near Beulah and flows nw into Pungo River.

Fort Island, a large sandy area in Big Pocosin in sw Gates County about 1 mi. n of Chowan River. Named for George Fort.

Fort Johnston was located at the present town of Southport, se Brunswick County. Built 1748–64 and named for Gov. Gabriel Johnston (1699–1752); burned by Whigs, 1775. Rebuilt by U.S. government, 1794–1809. Seized by Confederate forces in 1861 and used in the Civil War. Only the officers' quarters remain.

Fort Lamb, small battery below Fort Anderson on Price Creek in se Brunswick County. Named for Col. William Lamb (1835–1909) of Fort Fisher.

Fort Landing, ne Tyrrell County at the mouth of Alligator Creek. Believed to be the oldest settlement in Tyrrell County, but date unknown. Said to have been named for an old fort that stood near the Alligator Creek landing. The Price map, 1808, shows Warington at the approx. location. Appears as Port Landing on the MacRae map, 1833, but as Fort Landing on subsequent maps.

Fort Lane, a Civil War fort, was located 3 mi. se of New Bern in Craven County.

Fort Macon, built 1826–34 on the e end of Bogue Banks, s Carteret County, to protect Beaufort Inlet. Replaced the earlier Fort Hampton and Fort Dobbs. Now a state park, est. 1924 on 390 acres. Historical museum maintained inside the brick fort; swimming, fishing, hiking, nature study. Site of Civil War battle.

Fort Macon Village, part of the Cherry Point Housing Area in se Craven County. *See also* Cherry Point.

Fort McFadden. *See* Mountain Creek.

Fort McGaughey. *See* Westminster.

Fort Raleigh, ne shore of Roanoke Island, e Dare County. The remains of the earthen fort, constructed in 1585 by Ralph Lane's colony, were reconstructed in 1950 by the National Park Service after extensive archaeological study. Appears on the Collet map, 1770. The Fort Raleigh National Historic Site and the Waterside Theatre—at which Paul Green's symphonic drama, *The Lost Colony*, has been presented in the summer since 1937—are there. An Elizabethan Garden maintained by the Garden Club of North Carolina and a museum are also nearby.

Fort Rollins. *See* Blowing Rock.

Fort Run, stream, rises in w Greene County and flows ne into Contentnea Creek. Named because an early eighteenth-century Tuscarora Indian fort was located nearby. John Lawson was killed near the head of the stream in 1711.

Fort St. Philip. *See* Brunswick.

Fort San Juan, w Burke County, camp used by Spanish expeditionary force by Juan Pardo. Explorers built fort upon site of Indian village known as Joara or Xuala in January 1567; it was destroyed by Indians, 1568. Archaeological work at what is known as Berry site each summer.

Fort Shaw, former fort on the beach of Oak Island in se Brunswick County. Used to protect Confederate blockade-runners moving in close to shore.

Fort Thompson, Civil War fort, site 5 mi. se of New Bern on Neuse River in Craven County.

Fort Totten, one of the forts built around New Bern by Union forces after they took the town in March 1862. Located in s central Craven County.

Foscoe, community in sw Watauga County on Watauga River. Alt. 2,969.

Foster, community in se Person County served by post office, 1892–1910.

Foster Cove, n Graham County between Carringer Gap and Bee Creek.

Foster Creek rises in ne Madison County and flows sw into Big Laurel Creek.

Foster Creek Township, former township in n central Madison County, now township no. 16.

Foster Knob, s Macon County between Ash Flat Branch and Rockyface Mountain.

Foster Mill Creek rises in nw Henderson County and flows se into Mills River.

Foster Mountain, central Polk County n of Columbus. Also called Chocolate Drop Mountain. Alt. 1,500.

Foster Ridge, s Macon County parallel to Ash Flat Branch.

Foster's Mill Creek. *See* Sweeten Creek.

Foundry Branch rises in central Granville County and flows se into Fishing Creek. Named for Hobgood's Foundry, which operated in Oxford during the Civil War.

Fountain, community in se Duplin County.

Fountain, town in w Pitt County. Settled about 1900 and first known as Reba for the sister of Henry Clark Bridgers, founder of the East Carolina Railway. When a post office was est., the name had to be changed, as another Reba already existed in the state. Inc. 1903; named for Robert Almon Fountain (1878–1962), local merchant.

Fountain Fork, community in e Edgecombe County.

Fountain Hill, community in w Anson and e Union Counties.

Fountain Hill, community in n Lenoir County on Contentnea Creek. Named for a local family, the first member of which, Francis Fountain, settled in the vicinity prior to 1769.

Fountain Park, community on Hickory Nut Creek in ne Henderson County.

Fountainshead, town inc. 1818 and authorized to be laid out on the Pee Dee River in Anson County on the lands of John and James Permenter, 11 mi. e of Wadesboro. No evidence exists that the town was est. *See also* Permetter Creek.

Fountain Township, w Pitt County.

Four Corners, community in nw Davie County. In 1924–25 a gasoline station and a grocery store were built at the rural crossroad, which was given the name by the owners.

Four Diamond Ridge, mountain in ne Avery County.

Four Forks, community in central Pasquotank County.

Fourmile Branch rises in s Buncombe County and flows nw into French Broad River ½ mi. s of The Lagoon.

Fourmile Branch rises in central Davidson County and flows s into Flat Swamp Creek.

Fourmile Creek rises in se Mecklenburg County and flows sw into McAlpine Creek.

Four Oaks, town in w Johnston County. Settled about 1885; inc. 1889. Named for four oaks growing from the stump of a tree that had been cut down in an opossum hunt in the yard of K. L. Barbour, first to build a house there. Alt. 208.

Fourth Creek rises in w Iredell County and flows e into Rowan County, where Third and Fourth Creeks join before entering South Yadkin River. It is the fourth creek in a series of creeks crossed by early settlers from Salisbury. The name appears on the Collet map, 1770. A settlement on the creek about 1750 later became the city of Statesville, which grew up around Fourth Creek (Presbyterian) Church.

Fourway, community in s Greene County. Community took the name of a filling station built there in the late 1920s or early 1930s.

Foust's Creek. *See* Moulder Branch.

Foust's Mill. *See* Coleridge.

Fowler Bend, formerly a sharp bend in Hiwasee River in w central Cherokee County, now a peninsula extending into Hiwassee Lake.

Fowler Cove, in n Swain County on the head of North Fork [Chambers Creek].

Fowler Creek rises in sw Jackson County between Terrapin Mountain and Coldside Mountain and flows s 4 mi. into Chattooga River at the county line.

Fowlers Mill Creek rises in e Wake County and flows e into Little River.

Fox Branch rises in s Madison County and flows nw into Ivy River.

Fox Branch rises in nw Swain County and flows se into Lake Cheoah.

Fox Cabin Gap, on the Madison County, N.C.–Greene County, Tenn., line.

Fox Creek rises in n Franklin County and flows sw into Tar River.

Fox Creek rises in w Granville County and flows s into Shelton Creek.

Fox Creek rises in e Madison County and flows s into Laurel Creek.

Fox Creek rises in w Yancey County and flows se into Bald Creek.

Foxes Island, central Harnett County in Cape Fear River nw of Lillington. Mentioned in Fulton's survey of North Carolina rivers in 1819 and appears on the MacRae map, 1833. A series of low falls or rapids there, known as Fox Island Falls, drop between 5 and 10 ft. over a distance of about a quarter of a mile.

Fox Gap, nw Swain County in Great Smoky Mountains National Park on Twentymile Ridge between the head of Fox Branch and Hamilton Hollow.

Fox Grape Branch rises in ne Brunswick County and flows w into Columbus County, where it enters Dams Creek.

Fox Island Falls. *See* Foxes Island.

Fox Knob, nw Yadkin County at the ne end of the Brushy Mountains. Alt. 1,590. Also known as Star Peak.

Fox Mountain, central Polk County ne of Columbus. Alt. 1,500.

Fox's Mountain, nw Iredell County. Named for Fox family, owners in twentieth century. Formerly known as Shumaker Mountain for early settlers. In the mid-twentieth century, "an authentic Western town" called Love Valley was constructed on the s side of the mountain.

Foxtown Mountain, w Madison County between Baltimore Branch and Spring Creek.

Foxville, community in w Buncombe County served by post office, 1880–96.

Foys Creek rises in s Pender County and flows s into Topsail Sound.

Fradey Mountain, s Buncombe County between Ducker and Blake Mountains.

Frady Creek rises in e Jackson County and flows se into Chastine Creek.

Fraley Branch. *See* Curl Tail Creek.

Francisco, community in n Stokes County between Big Creek and Dan River.

Francis Cove, in s Haywood County on the head of Raccoon Creek.

Francktown. *See* Franktown.

Frank, community in w Avery County. Said to have been named prior to 1901 for a post office official.

Franklin, a state organized in December 1784 in what had been the western territory of North Carolina. The area had been ceded by the state to the federal government briefly, but the act of cession was repealed. During the period, residents of the area organized the State of Franklin, and it was not until 1789 that North Carolina was able to reestablish jurisdiction over the area, the State of Franklin having collapsed the previous year. The area was again (and finally) ceded in 1789, and the state of Tennessee, admitted to the Union in 1796, was formed from it. *See also* Watauga Settlement; District of Washington.

Franklin, town and county seat in central Macon County on Little Tennessee River. Alt. 2,113. Settled prior to 1828; inc. 1855. Named for Jesse Franklin (1760–1823), governor of North Carolina, 1820–21. A mound there marks the site of the old Cherokee town Nikwasi. A council of Sir Alexander Cuming with the Indians there led to a treaty in 1730. Produces textiles and lumber.

Franklin, community in n Rowan County est. about 1828 as Franklinville, named for Benjamin Franklin. Named changed to Franklin in 1884.

Franklin Branch rises in w Caldwell County and flows s into Johns River near the town of Collettsville.

Franklin County was formed in 1779 from Bute County, *which see*, when that county was divided to form Franklin and Warren Counties. Located in the ne section of the state, it is bounded by Nash, Wake, Granville, Vance, and Warren Counties. It was named for Benjamin Franklin (1706–90). Area: 494 sq. mi. County seat: Louisburg, with an elevation of 280 ft. Townships, now numbered 1 to 10, were formerly Dunn, Harris, Youngsville, Franklinton, Hayesville, Sandy Creek, Gold Mine, Cedar Rock, Cypress Creek, and Louisburg. Produces corn, wheat, oats, tobacco, Irish potatoes, hogs, livestock, marble, aluminum products, pharmaceuticals, electronics, lumber, and fabricated metals.

Franklin Gap, sw Cherokee County s of Franklin Mountain.

Franklin Mountain, sw Cherokee County between Hothouse Branch and Wolf Creek.

Franklin Spring, former resort in nw Person County. Flourished in the early twentieth century. Mineral water bottled and sold.

Franklinsville. *See* Franklinville.

Franklinsville Township, e central Randolph County.

Franklinton, town in w Franklin County. Alt. 432. Est. in 1839 as Franklin Depot on land of Shemuel Kearney. Name changed to Franklinton in 1842, when it was inc. Produced textiles.

Franklinton Township, former township in w Franklin County, now township no. 4.

Franklin Township, central Macon County.

Franklin Township, ne Rowan County.

Franklin Township, s Sampson County.

Franklin Township, nw Surry County.

Franklinville, town in e Randolph County on Deep River. Inc. 1847 as Franklinsville. Named in honor of Jesse Franklin (1760–1832), governor of North Carolina, 1820–21. Site acquired in 1801 by Christian Morris, who built a gristmill there; purchased in 1820 by Elisha Coffin, who, with others, built a cotton mill there in 1838.

Franklinville. *See* Franklin.

Frank Mountain, s Henderson County near the South Carolina state line. Formerly known as Gau Mountain.

Franks Creek rises in e Graham County and flows sw between Franks Creek Lead and Bert Creek Lead into Tulula Creek.

Franks Creek Lead follows the course of Franks Creek in e Graham County.

Franks Ferry. *See* Mill Creek.

Franktown, community in nw Onslow County between Jenkins Swamp and Juniper Swamp. Formerly called Francktown for the Franck family, which owned much land in the area.

Frankum Branch rises in s Cherokee County on Poor House Mountain and flows se into Ricks Branch.

Frankum's Creek rises in nw Caldwell County and flows s into Mulberry Creek.

Fray Creek. *See* Fryes Creek.

Frazier Creek rises in e central Forsyth County and flows sw into Brush Fork Branch e of Winston-Salem.

Fraziers. *See* Progress.

Fraziers Creek, on the w end of Bogue Banks, sw Carteret County, flows w into Bogue Inlet.

Fraziers Crossroads, community in s Hertford County.

Frederick, community in sw Beaufort County. Settled 1908 and named for Frederick H. von Eberstein, local farmer.

Frederick, community in w Wilson County. Post office, 1894–95.

Fredericktown. *See* Bethany.

Freedom Hill. *See* Princeville.

Freeland, community in nw Brunswick County.

Freeman, community in ne Columbus County. Believed to have been named for free blacks living in the area before the Civil War.

Freeman Branch rises in ne Cherokee County and flows s into Beaver Creek.

Freeman Creek rises in s Henderson County and flows se into Edith Lake.

Freeman Knob, n Cherokee County in the Unicoi Mountains.

Freeman's Channel, in the tidal marshes of Brown's Sound in s Onslow County.

Freemans Creek rises in e Onslow County and flows ne into White Oak River.

Freeman's Cross Roads. *See* Ether.

Freeman's Mills, community in s Guilford County served by post office, 1870–1904.

Freemans Township. *See* Youngsville Township.

Freemason Creek rises in s Caldwell and flows s into Catawba River.

Fremont, town in n Wayne County. Inc. 1867 as Nahunta; name changed, 1869. Settled prior to 1830 and known as Narhantes and Torhunta. Named Fremont in honor of Col. S. L. Fremont, chief engineer of Wilmington and Weldon Railroad. Birthplace of Gov. Charles B. Aycock (1859–1912), 1 mi. s, has been restored as a State Historic Site. Alt. 152.

French Branch rises in central Jones County and flows n into Trent River.

French Broad River is formed in s Transylvania County near Rosman by the junction of North Fork and West Fork. It flows ne in Transylvania and into Henderson County, where it turns nw to flow through Buncombe and Madison Counties into Tennessee. From the state line, it flows w 102 mi. to join Holston River near Knoxville to form Tennessee River. One of the Cherokee names was Tah-kee-os-tee (racing waters). Others, frequently for only a part of the river, were Poe-li-co, Agiqua, and Zillicoah. Known by the English at first as Broad River and appears as such on the De Brahm manuscript map of Indian Nations in the Southern Department, 1766. By 1776 the present name was in use. Named because much of the territory that it drained w of the Blue Ridge was held by the French in the eighteenth century.

French Broad Township, nw Buncombe County.

Frenchmans Creek. *See* Frenchs Creek.

Frenchs Creek rises in se Bladen County and flows s into Cape Fear River.

Frenchs Creek rises in se Onslow County and flows nw into New River opposite Rhodes Point. Appears as Frenchmans Creek in local records as early as 1744. Took its name from the fact that Alexander Nicola, a Frenchman, settled near its mouth.

Frenchs Creek Township, se Bladen County.

Fresh Pond Hill, a sand hill near Wash Woods 4 mi. s of the Virginia state line on Currituck Banks, ne Currituck County.

Freydeck, term used by Moravians to describe "area across the Blue Mountains on New River," likely the present Watauga-Wilkes County area. By the account in Bishop Augustus Spangenberg's diary (1752), "it is very lonesome, not one man lives there." From the German *freideck*, meaning blank slate. Appears on the Bellin map, 1757.

Friars Cove, se Buncombe County between High Hickory Ridge and Eskridge Cove.

Friar Swamp rises in se Bladen County and flows s into Columbus County, where it enters Buckhead Swamp. Council Mill Pond is on Friar Swamp.

Friar Swamp rises in n Columbus County and flows sw into Lake Waccamaw.

Friday Shoals, in South Fork Catawba River, n Gaston County near Hardin. Named for Capt. Nicholas Friday, who settled there about 1760. The court for newly established Lincoln County met at his house in 1783 and 1784.

Friedberg, community in n Davidson County served by post office, first in 1860 and later from 1893 to 1903.

Friedland, community in s Forsyth County.

Settled 1770 by Moravian families from Broadbay, Mass., now Waldoboro, Maine. Name, in German, means "land of peace."

Friendship, community in w Duplin County.

Friendship, community in w Guilford County, est. 1833. Alt. 893. Named for a Friends (Quaker) meetinghouse.

Friendship, community in sw Wake County. Settled about 1800 and named for a church previously est. there. Also known as Jordans. Alt. 350.

Friendship, community in ne Yadkin County near Yadkin River.

Friendship Township, w central Guilford County.

Fries Creek rises in nw Forsyth County and flows sw into Yadkin River.

Friezeland, community in s Madison County served by post office, 1886–1905.

Friezeland Creek rises in s Madison County and flows nw into Spring Creek.

Frisbee Branch rises in s Swain County and flows sw into De Hart Branch.

Frisco, community on Hatteras Island sw of Buxton, se Dare County. Known first as Trent, but post office est. in 1898 was named Frisco, perhaps to avoid confusion with Trenton, Jones County. In 1795 three sand hills known as Stowe's Hills were described there. Later the name Creed's Hill was applied to a single large sand hill s of Frisco.

Frog Creek rises in n Rutherford County and flows s into Camp Creek.

Frog Level, community in w central Pitt County. Alt. 81.

Frog Level. *See* Clingman.

Frog Level. *See* Oakland.

Frog Level Swamp, sw Bertie County.

Frog Mountain, on Lower Trail Ridge in sw Macon County.

Frog Pond, community in e Cherokee County n of Peachtree.

Frogsboro, community in e Caswell County.

Frogtown, community in n Moore County.

Frohock Mill. *See* Grants Creek; Macay's Mill.

Frohock Sawmill appears on the Collet map, 1770, as being near the mouth of Hunting Creek in present w Davie County. Undoubtedly owned by John Frohock (d. 1772), colonial official.

Frolictown Creek rises in se Jackson County and flows ne into Panthertown Creek.

Frost Mill Creek rises in n Davie County and flows e into Dutchmans Creek. Formerly known as Sweet Creek, and as such appears in numerous early local records.

Frost's Iron Works, former community in sw Stokes County. A post office from 1829 to 1836; iron foundry flourished there about 1850–60.

Frosty Knob, mountain in w central Buncombe County. Alt. 4,576.

Frozea Creek rises in s Transylvania County and flows sw, then se into Toxaway Creek.

Frozenhead Ridge, w Watauga County, extends se from the head of East Fork [Cove Creek] to Cove Creek, s of George Gap Branch.

Frozen Knob, on the Madison County, N.C.–Unicoi County, Tenn., line.

Frozen Knob, in s Transylvania County e of Frozen Creek.

Frozen Lake, s Transylvania County on Frozen Creek.

Fruitland, community in n Henderson County on Kyles Creek. Named for large quantity of apples traditionally produced in the vicinity. Site of Fruitland Baptist Institute, training ground for Baptist ministers.

Fruitland. *See* Pores Knob.

Fruit Ridge, community in central Columbus County between Whiteville and Chadbourn.

Fruitville Township, ne Currituck County.

Fry, former community in w Swain County on Nantahala River. Site now under the waters of Fontana Lake.

Fryes Creek rises in n Davidson County and flows nw into Muddy Creek. Appears on the Collet map, 1770, as Fray Creek.

Frying Pan, The, e Tyrrell County, is a large body of water roughly shaped like a frying pan. It flows se into Alligator River. Appears on the Collet map, 1770.

Fryingpan Bend, in Roanoke River in n Martin County.

Frying Pan Creek, a bay on the n side of Pamlico River, e Beaufort County.

Fryingpan Gap, on the Haywood-Transylvania county line. Said to be so named because a frying pan was left there at a common camping ground for the use of all comers.

Frying Pan Landing, e Tyrrell County on The Frying Pan.

Fryingpan Mountain, in Haywood and Tran-

sylvania Counties. Part of Pisgah Ridge, n of Beech Knob in Pisgah National Forest.

Frying Pan Shoals, in the Atlantic Ocean immediately off Cape Fear, the s tip of New Hanover County. Appears on the Collet map, 1770.

Fry Mountain, in e Swain County at the ne end of Buckhorn Ridge.

Fuda Creek rises in se Mecklenburg County and flows ne into Cabarrus County, where it enters Back Creek. Said locally to be named for a Scottish word, sometimes spelled "foody," meaning "slightly crazy."

Fulbright Cove, central Haywood County 1 mi. n of Lake Junaluska.

Fulcher Branch rises in s Macon County and flows w into Little Tennessee River.

Fulcher Landing, s Onslow County on New River, now the principal landing at the community of Sneads Ferry, *which see*.

Fulcher Mountain, n Surry County between Fisher River and Buck Mountain.

Fulchers Creek, a stream about 1 mi. long flowing se into Core Sound about midway between Nelson Bay and Brett Bay, e Carteret County.

Fulchertown, community in s Macon County on Fulcher Branch.

Fulford, community in sw Brunswick County.

Fulford Point, peninsula extending off the nw side of Goose Creek Island into Goose Creek estuary, ne Pamlico County.

Fulk Creek rises in se Stokes County and flows se into Dan River.

Fullard Creek rises in s Onslow County and flows se into Chadwick Bay. Named for Thomas Fulwood or Fullwood, an early settler. Mentioned in local records as early as 1748.

Fuller's Creek rises in sw Caswell County and flows n into Moon Creek.

Fullwood or **Fullwood's Store**. *See* Matthews.

Fulmore, community in central Robeson County served by post office, 1880–1902.

Fulp, community in n Forsyth County and s Stokes County.

Fulp Creek rises in ne Forsyth County and flows n into Redbank Creek.

Fulton, a small community in e Davie County on the Yadkin River. Inc. 1819, but active only a short time in municipal affairs, if at all. Site laid off in town lots when attempts were made to improve navigation on the Yadkin

River. Post office est. 1822. Probably named for Hamilton Fulton (d. 1834), state engineer, who was employed in connection with many internal-improvement projects. A native of England, Fulton arrived in North Carolina in July 1819.

Fulton Township, se Davie County.

Funnel Top, a peak in w central Graham County between Santeetlah Gap and Santeetlah Lake. Alt. approx. 3,200.

Funneltop Mountain, in n Transylvania County between Billy Branch and Shooting Ridge.

Funston, community in e central Brunswick County.

Fuquay Springs. *See* Fuquay-Varina.

Fuquay-Varina, town in sw Wake County n of Harnett County line. Settled prior to 1860. Inc. 1909 as Fuquay Springs, taking its name from David and Stephen Fuquay, early settlers. In 1963 merged with nearby town of Varina, *which see*, and assumed its present name. Produces tobacco, electronics equipment, apparel, and dairy products. Alt. 350.

Furches, community on the Alleghany-Ashe county line.

Fur Creek. *See* Far Creek.

Furniss Mine adjoins the Phoenix Mine property in e Cabarrus County about 8 mi. se of city of Concord. Former gold mine (late 1800s). Extensive underground exploration in 1954-56 for tungsten.

Furr City. *See* Oakboro.

Furrs, community in se Cabarrus County.

Furr Township, sw Stanly County.

Futches Creek rises in ne New Hanover County and flows se into Topsail Sound.

G

Gabby Branch rises in n Cherokee County and flows sw into Colvard Creek.

Gabes Branch rises in s Nash County and flows ne into Henry Branch. Mentioned in local records as early as 1779.

Gabes Mountain Branch rises in e central Avery County and flows s into Wilson Creek.

Gabourel's Bluff was a name applied to an area on the w side of Cape Fear River in present ne Brunswick County. At one time, it was the property of Joshua Gabourel, attorney and a justice of the peace in New Hanover County in 1736. Known as Partridge's Bluff prior to 1735.

Gabriels Creek rises in e Madison County and flows sw into Ivy River.

Gadd Creek rises in w Polk County and flows s into Green River.

Gaddis Branch rises in s Haywood County and flows n into Jonathans Creek.

Gaddy's Goose Pond, n central Anson County near Ansonville. Est. 1934 by Lockhart Gaddy when 9 geese were offered winter protection and food. Thousands of geese now winter there.

Gaddysville, community in sw Robeson County.

Gaddy Township, s Robeson County.

Gage, community in n Rutherford County served by post office, 1898-1908.

Gage Bald, on Rich Mountain in e Jackson County on the head of Gage Creek. Alt. 5,800.

Gage Creek rises in e Jackson County and flows se into Wolf Creek.

Gailors Hammock. *See* Gaylords Island.

Gaither, community in s McDowell County served by post office, 1891-95.

Galamore Branch rises in ne Swain County and flows s into Raven Fork.

Galatia, community in n Northampton County.

Galbreath Creek rises in e Swain County and flows s into Tuckasegee River.

Gale, community in central Ashe County served by post office, 1898-1921.

Gale Creek rises in nw Pamlico County and flows se into Bay River. A part of the Intracoastal Waterway.

Gales Creek rises in w Carteret County and flows s into Bogue Sound. Appears on the Moseley map, 1733. Probably named for Christopher Gale (1680-1734).

Gallagans, community in n Madison County.

Gallant Point, a point of land in s Carteret County extending into the mouth of Newport River. Separated from Beaufort by Town Creek.

Gallants Channel, in the mouth of Newport River, central Carteret County. Named for John Galland, an early settler, but in pronunciation the *d* became a *t*. Frontage property of North Carolina Maritime Museum.

Gallatin. *See* Graham.

Gallberry Swamp rises on the Cumberland-Robeson county line and flows se to join Big Marsh Swamp in forming Big Swamp.

Galloway, community in s Transylvania County on Toxaway Creek.

Galloway Creek rises in s Transylvania County and flows se into French Broad River.

Galloway Creek. *See* West Prong [Glady Fork].

Galloway Crossroads, community in e Pitt County.

Galloway Mountain, s Clay County between Shooting Creek and the Georgia state line.

Gallows Branch, The, rises in Salisbury, e Rowan County, and flows w into Grant Creek. Named for the fact that the early site of public hangings for Rowan County was nearby.

Gambrick Branch rises in nw Burke County and flows e into Linville River.

Gamewell, community in sw Caldwell County. Alt. 1,078. Named for Gamewell Tuttle, a Methodist circuit rider who was in the area about 1840.

Gander Mountain. *See* Mount Bolus.

Ganders Fork, community in e Duplin County.

Gannaway, community in sw Caswell County. A post office operated there during the approx. period 1890–1905.

Gant Inlet. *See* Gunt Inlet.

Gants, community in sw Rockingham County served by post office, 1888–92.

Gap, community in w Stokes County at the head of East Prong Little Yadkin River.

Gap Bay, boggy area on the Pender-Sampson county line se of Newtons Crossroads. *See also* Carolina Bays.

Gap Civil Township, n central Alleghany County. Training camps were located there during the early months of the Civil War. *See also* Sparta.

Gap Creek rises in s Buncombe County and flows se into Cane Creek.

Gap Creek, community in s Ashe County. Formerly copper was mined in the vicinity.

Gap Creek. *See* Deep Gap Creek.

Gap Point, se Hyde County, extends into Pamlico Sound from the se end of Ocracoke Island.

Gapway Swamp rises in sw Columbus County and flows nw into South Carolina, where it enters Lumber River.

Garbacon Creek rises in n Carteret County and flows n into Neuse River.

Gar Creek rises in nw Mecklenburg County and flows sw into Catawba River.

Garden City, community in central New Hanover County. Alt. 15. Settled about 1912. Named for natural beauty of area.

Garden City. *See* Pleasant Gardens.

Garden Creek rises in e Haywood County and flows ne into Pigeon River. One of the earliest settlements in the county was at a wide bottom on the stream, which still is known by its earliest name, Garden Farm.

Garden Creek rises in n Wilkes County in Doughton Park and flows e into East Prong Roaring River.

Garden Farm. *See* Garden Creek.

Garden Hill, former community in s Guilford County s of Sedgefield near Groometown. Site of Gardiner Hill Gold Mine. Both the community and the mine were deserted after the 1849 gold rush in California.

Garden Township, e Wilson County. Named for Jack Gardner, prominent local merchant in the mid-nineteenth century.

Gardner's Branch rises in e Wilson County and flows n into Town Creek.

Gardners Creek rises in e Martin County and flows ne into Devils Gut.

Gardnerville, community in s Pitt County.

Garfield, community in se Rowan County served by post office, 1880–1913.

Gargales Creek. *See* Muddy Creek.

Gar Gut rises in e Beaufort County and flows s into Pamlico River.

Garland, town in sw Sampson County. Settled about 1888; inc. 1907. Named for Augustus Hill Garland (1832–99), attorney general of the United States, 1885–89. Known earlier as Sloan's Crossing. Alt. 137.

Garland Creek rises in sw Cherokee County and flows se into Rapier Mill Creek.

Garland Gap, central Mitchell County on Pumpkin Patch Mountain.

Garlington's Island, a spur of high land containing approx. 250 acres extending from the center of Camden County through North River Pocosin to a point on Crooked Creek 2 mi. from North River. Named because it was the site of the home of Capt. James S. Garlington, commander of two companies raised for service in the War of 1812. Also known as Garrenton's Island.

Garner, town in s Wake County. Settled about 1800. Inc. 1883 as Garner's Station, named for founder, H. C. Garner. Charter repealed 1891; reincorporated in 1905 as Garner.

Garner Branch rises in e Davidson County a short distance n of Denton and flows s into Yadkin River.

Garner Cove, s Haywood County on the head of Raccoon Creek.

Garner's Ford, community in ne Rutherford County served by post office, 1828–1933.

Garner's Station. *See* Garner.

Garners Store, community on the Randolph-Moore county line.

Garnett, community in w Rutherford County served by post office, 1884–96.

Garreck Creek rises in n Cherokee County and flows se and sw into Beaverdam Creek.

Garren Branch. *See* Gerren Branch.

Garren Creek rises in se Buncombe County and flows nw into Cane Creek.

Garren Mountain, se Buncombe County sw of Dyeleaf Mountain.

Garren Mountain, n Henderson County between Bank Mountain and Sand Flat Mountain.

Garrenton's Island. *See* Garlington's Island.

Garrett Creek rises in central Haywood County and flows nw into Jonathans Creek. Named for W. G. B. Garrett (ca. 1845–1925), who owned land and had a ranger's cabin there.

Garretts Gap, w Haywood County, Great Smoky Mountains National Park near lat. 35°32'55" N., long. 83°08'25" W. on Cataloochee Divide.

Garringer Branch rises in se Cherokee County and flows se into Little Brasstown Creek.

Garr Island, in the waters of Pamlico Sound off the n tip of Pea Island, e Dare County.

Garrison. *See* Fennimore.

Garrison Branch rises in w Macon County and flows sw into Nantahala Lake.

Garrison Point, point of land on the s side of Pamlico River, central Beaufort County near the mouth of Durham Creek. A fort or garrison was erected there in 1711 during the Tuscarora War. *See also* Durham Creek.

Garysburg, town in w Northampton County. Inc. 1891. Known as Garys in 1833 but changed to Garysburg after the post office there received the name in 1838. Alt. 145. Peebles Tavern and Blakely's Depot were nearby communities in the early nineteenth century, but they were supplanted by Garysburg. Strategically important during Civil War as convergence

of two railroads. Site of Camp Beauregard, *which see*.

Gash Creek rises in e Transylvania County and flows se into French Broad River.

Gashes Creek rises in central Buncombe County and flows nw into Swannanoa River.

Gasters Creek rises in s Lee County and flows se into Little River.

Gaston, former town in nw Northampton County on Roanoke River. It developed as the n terminus of the Raleigh and Gaston Railroad, chartered 1835 and completed 1840. The town began to decline after 1865 when the bridge across the Roanoke River was burned. Named for Judge William Gaston (1778–1844). The site is now under the waters of Roanoke Rapids Lake. The modern community of Thelma, across the river, is s of the site. *See also* South Gaston.

Gaston, town in nw Northampton County on Roanoke River. Inc. 1949, at which time the name was changed from Camp's Store. Named for the township and for the old town of Gaston, the site of which is about 5 mi. w.

Gaston County was formed in 1846 from Lincoln County. Located in the sw section of the state, it is bounded by the state of South Carolina and by Cleveland, Lincoln, and Mecklenburg Counties. It was named for William Gaston (1778–1844), a member of Congress and a judge of the Supreme Court of North Carolina. Area: 363 sq. mi. County seat: Gastonia, with an elevation of 825 ft. Townships are Cherryville, Crowell Mountain, Dallas, Gastonia, River Bend, and South Point. Produces corn, wheat, oats, hay, soybeans, air filters, trucking, nursery products, poultry, hogs, livestock, textiles, hosiery, machinery, corrugated boxes, chemicals, motor-vehicle parts, crushed stone, mica, and sand.

Gastonia, city and county seat, central Gaston County. Inc. 1877 and named for the county in which it was located. Replaced Dallas as the county seat, 1909. Produces textiles, hosiery, machinery, corrugated boxes, electronic components, apparel, and motor-vehicle parts. Gaston College, est. 1964, is there. Alt. 825.

Gastonia Township, s central Gaston County.

Gaston Township, nw Northampton County.

Gates, community in n Gates County. Alt. 73.

Gates County was formed in 1779 from Chowan, Hertford, and Perquimans Counties. Located in the ne section of the state, it is bounded by Camden, Pasquotank, Perquimans, Chowan, and Hertford Counties and the state of Virginia. It was named for Gen. Horatio Gates (1728?–1806), commander of Revolutionary forces that defeated Burgoyne at Saratoga, October 1777. Area: 349 sq. mi. County seat: Gatesville, with an elevation of 40 ft. Townships are Gatesville, Hall, Haslett, Holly Grove, Hunters Mill, Mintonsville, and Reynoldson. The area was explored in 1622 by John Pory, who came down from Jamestown, Va. Produces peanuts, corn, soybeans, cotton, hogs, wood products, and lumber.

Gates Courthouse. *See* Gatesville.

Gatesville, town and county seat in central Gates County. Alt. 40. Inc. 1830. Known originally as Bennetts Creek Landing and as Gates Courthouse from 1779 until 1830.

Gatesville Township, central Gates County.

Gatewood, community in nw Caswell County, named for J. M. Gatewood, local resident. A post office operated there, 1884–1907.

Gath. *See* White Cross.

Gatlington, community in nw Gates County on Chowan River. Beach there is a popular picnic area, and boat races are held on the river. Prior to the Civil War, known as Lumberton and center for the manufacture of barrel staves and sawed lumber to be shipped down the river.

Gau Mountain. *See* Frank Mountain.

Gay, community in w Jackson County on Savannah Creek.

Gaylord, community in e Beaufort County.

Gaylords Hammock. *See* Gaylords Island.

Gaylords Island, high ground in Pantego Swamp, e Beaufort County. Known as Gaylords Hammock (also spelled Gailors Hammock) as early as 1754.

Gaylors Branch rises in w Transylvania County between Indian Creek and Shoal Creek and flows s about 1 mi. to empty into Indian Creek just above its junction with Shoal Creek.

Gela, community in n Granville County. Alt. 483.

Gem, community in nw Buncombe County served by post office, 1886–1929.

Gem Creek rises in w Jackson County and flows se into Little Pine Creek.

General Assembly has met in the following places, *which see*. Bath, Edenton, Fayetteville, Halifax, Halls Creek, Hillsborough, Little River, New Bern, Perquimans County, Raleigh, Smithfield, Tarboro, Wake Court House (Raleigh), and Wilmington. It may also have met at other places, but many records of the seventeenth and eighteenth centuries have not survived.

Geneva, community in s Rockingham County served by post office, 1888–1902.

Genlee, community in s Durham County. Formerly known as Togo, the name of a Japanese city given the community when a railroad station opened there about 1904. The name was changed after the attack on Pearl Harbor, December 7, 1941, to honor Gen. Robert E. Lee. Produces bricks.

Genoa, community in s central Wayne County. Named for Genoa, Italy, the birthplace of Christopher Columbus.

Gentry, community in sw Rockingham County served by post office, 1886–1903. Named for first postmaster.

Gentry Branch rises in n Buncombe County and flows nw into Adkins Branch.

Gentry Gap, n Buncombe County between Bill Cole and Lankford Mountains.

Gentrys Store, community in n Person County.

Geographic Center of North Carolina has been determined by the Geological Survey, U.S. Department of the Interior, to be in Chatham County, 10 mi. nw of Sanford. *See also* Gulf.

George, community in e Northampton County, approx. 1 mi. sw of Woodland. Named for a local citizen, George Harrison Parker. Former post office was George; railroad station was Woodland Station.

George Branch rises on the Buncombe-Haywood county line near Grassy Top and flows se into Hominy Creek.

George Branch rises in w central Watauga County and flows sw into Brushy Fork.

George City, proposed provincial capital in what is now ne Lenoir County near Kinston. Authorized to be laid out in 1758 at Tower Hill, *which see*, but its establishment was not approved by officials in London. The name was intended to honor King George II.

George Creek rises in s Cherokee County and flows ne into Martin Creek.

George Fork rises in e Yancey County and flows n into Little Crabtree Creek.

George Gap, w Watauga County on the head of George Gap Branch.

George Gap Branch rises in w Watauga County and flows se into Cove Creek.

George Ira Creek rises in w Haywood County and flows ne into Woody Creek.

George Martin Branch rises in e Cherokee County and flows nw into Valley River.

George Orr Mountain, e Transylvania County, extends ne from the head of Boylston Creek to Bryson Creek. Named for first clerk of court in Transylvania County.

Georges Branch rises in n Swain County and flows sw into Indian Creek.

Georgetown, historically African American community in ne Davidson County between forks of Spurgeon and Abbotts Creeks.

Georgetown, community in s Jackson County served by post office, 1854–1907.

Georgetown, community in e Lenoir County near Kinston. Takes its name from George City, *which see*.

George Town, planned and begun in 1786 by George Hazard between Bear Creek and Queens Creek in se Onslow County. It did not prosper and soon was abandoned.

Georgeville, community in se Cabarrus County at junction of Dutch Buffalo Creek and Rocky River. Named for George Shinn; formerly known as Shinnville. *See also* Reed Gold Mine.

Georgia Branch rises in w Madison County and flows e into Spring Creek.

German's Hill, a ridge in ne Caldwell County on which was formerly located a small community (post office name Cilley). Named for Wellborn German, who lived there until 1848.

Germanton, community in s Stokes and n Forsyth Counties. Alt. 662. Est. 1790; charter repealed 1895. County seat of Stokes County from the creation of the county until 1849, when it was divided to form Forsyth County.

Germantown, town in sw Hyde County. Inc. 1791. Named for German Bernard, on whose land the town was laid off. County seat from about 1792 to 1820.

Germany Cove, in central Haywood County on a tributary of Hemphill Creek.

Gerren Branch rises in s Transylvania County and flows se into Glady Fork. Also spelled Garren Branch.

Gerren Creek rises in s Transylvania County and flows ne into East Fork French Broad River.

Gerton, community in ne Henderson County.

Gethsemane, community in n Edgecombe County.

Ghents Creek rises in n Person County and flows ne into Hyco River.

Ghio, community in se Richmond County. Named in the 1860s for a German engineer employed by the railroad.

Ghock Fork rises in e Richmond County and flows nw into Hitchcock Creek.

Ghormley Mountain extends ne from Thompson Branch to Quinn Creek in w Cherokee County.

Ghoul's Fork rises in central Carteret County and flows sw into Black Creek.

Gibbs, community in w Burke County served by post office, 1883–1930.

Gibbs Branch rises in nw Jackson County and flows w into Oconaluftee River.

Gibbs Creek rises in e Granville County and flows se into Tar River.

Gibbs Creek. *See* Far Creek.

Gibbs Lake, marsh in se Duplin County.

Gibbs Mountain, e Yancey County on the head of Shuford Creek. Alt. 6,224. Named for Rev. Billy Gibbs, a circuit rider.

Gibbs Point, peninsula extending into the mouth of North Landing River, ne Currituck County. A nearby community is known as Gibbs Woods. Site of the home of Capt. John Gibbs, who in 1690 claimed to be governor of Albemarle. The Moseley map, 1733, shows the area as "Gover. Gibbs's Point."

Gibbs Point, point of land extending into Pamlico Sound from s Hatteras Island n of the community of Avon, s Dare County. Probably named for Henry Gibbs, who had a grant of land on Hatteras Island in 1716.

Gibbs Point extends into Pamlico Sound from the e mainland of Hyde County.

Gibbs Woods, community near Gibbs Point in ne Currituck County. *See also* Gibbs Point.

Gibbton, community in central Pamlico County on Trent River.

Gibby Branch rises in w Macon County and flows e into Choga Creek.

Gibby Branch rises in s Swain County and flows nw into Brush Creek.

Gibby Branch rises in s central Swain County and flows se into Bucknor Branch.

Gibraltar, former community in central Union County between Richardson's and Crooked Creeks. Appears on the Shaffer map, 1886. Later known as Polk Mountain, but no longer recognized as a community.

Gibson, town in w Scotland County. Post office est. there 1846 and named for Noah Gibson, storekeeper and first postmaster. Inc. 1899. Alt. 255.

Gibson Branch rises in e Haywood County and flows sw into Wesley Creek.

Gibson Cove, in nw Jackson County between Gibson Knob and Tuckasegee River.

Gibson Cove, s Swain County e of Wesser Creek.

Gibson Cove Branch rises in central Macon County and flows se into Cartoogechaye Creek.

Gibson Knob, nw Jackson County between Gibson Cove and Peggy Gap.

Gibson Knob, central Macon County between Gibson Ridge and Mint Branch.

Gibson Millpond. *See* Blues Pond.

Gibson Pond, e central Richmond County on Ghock Fork.

Gibson Ridge, central Macon County between Wallace Branch and Gibson Cove Branch.

Gibson Ridge, se Swain County, extends n from Peaks Bald between Jones Creek and Little Laurel Creek.

Gibson's Mill, community in central Richmond County served by post office, 1878–1907.

Gibsonville, town in e Guilford and w Alamance Counties. Alt. 728. Est. 1855 and inc. 1871. Named for Joseph Gibson (1785–1857), local land and slave owner who was active in contracting and grading for the North Carolina Railroad. A station est. about 1 mi. n of his

home was named for him and became the town.

Giddensville, community in ne Sampson County on the w edge of Bear Pocosin.

Gideon, community in e Stokes County served by post office, 1898–1916.

Gideon Swamp rises in n Nash County and flows se into Sandy Creek.

Giesky Creek rises in s Clay County and flows nw into Shooting Creek.

Gift, community in s Johnston County served by post office, 1887–1903.

Gilbert, community in n Moore County served by post office, 1887–1906.

Gilberts Creek rises in s Stanly County and flows s into Rocky River.

Gilbert Town, former county seat of Rutherford County, 1781–85. Site, now abandoned, is a short distance n of Rutherfordton in the center of the county on Hollands Creek. Named for William Gilbert, owner of the land. Campsite for both sides prior to Battle of Kings Mountain, October 1780.

Gilead, community in sw Beaufort County.

Gilead Ridge, mountain ridge in South Mountains that form Burke-Cleveland county line.

Giles Creek rises in n Franklin County and flows sw into Tooles Creek.

Giles Creek rises in se Rockingham County and flows sw into Haw River.

Giles' Mills, community in nw Sampson County served by post office, 1874–1906.

Gilkey, community in n Rutherford County. Formerly known as Millwood until renamed for a local family.

Gilkey Creek rises in n Rutherford County and flows se into Mill Creek.

Gilkey Township, central Rutherford County.

Gill, community in s Vance County; named for a local family.

Gillam Gap, on the Ashe-Wilkes county line.

Gill Branch rises in n Buncombe County near Weaverville and flows sw into Reems Creek.

Gillburg, community in s Vance County on the head of Gills Little Mill Creek.

Gillespie Gap, on the McDowell-Mitchell county line. Alt. 2,800. Troops en route to the Battle of Kings Mountain passed through the gap on September 29, 1780. The North Carolina Mineral Museum is located on the Blue Ridge Parkway on the Mitchell County side of the gap.

Gillett, former community in s Onslow County e of Stones Bay. Abandoned 1941 with the establishment of Camp Lejeune Marine Corps Air Station.

Gilletts Creek rises in se Onslow County and flows se into Brown's Sound. Also known locally as Old Woman's Swamp from the fact that an elderly woman was drowned there many years ago. Now within the Camp Lejeune Marine Corps Air Station. Mentioned in local records as early as 1744.

Gilliam Branch rises in n Vance County and flows nw into Island Creek Reservoir.

Gilliam County was name proposed in 1872–73 legislature for new county to be created out of Granville, Warren, and Franklin Counties. Name selected to honor Judge Robert Gilliam of Oxford. Bill failed to pass, but in 1881 Vance County was formed with similar boundaries.

Gillikin Creek rises in e Carteret County and flows w into North Leopard Creek.

Gilliland's Creek rises in central McDowell County in the Old Fort area and flows into Crooked Creek.

Gillis Station. *See* Parkton.

Gill Mountain, s Wilkes County extending ne from Morris Knob to Owen Knob.

Gills Knob, n Caldwell County. Alt. 2,000. Probably named for Gilbert Cottrell, eighteenth-century settler in the vicinity.

Gills Little Mill Creek rises in s Vance County and flows s into n Franklin County, where it enters Lynch Creek.

Gilmer Township, central Guilford County.

Gilmore Swamp rises in ne Sampson County and flows se into Six Runs Creek.

Gilreath, community in s Wilkes County on North Rocky Creek. Formerly known as Brushy Mountain and as Dodson Store. Old Gilreath, another community, is located approx. 3 mi. nw.

Gin, community in n Cumberland County.

Gin Branch rises in central Nash County and flows s into Sapony Creek.

Gingerberry, high ground in Murphy Bay, e Bladen County.

Gingercake Creek rises in nw Burke County and flows se, e, and ne into Steels Creek.

Gingercake Mountain, nw tip of Burke County on Jonas Ridge. Alt. 4,120. A summer residential community, Gingercake Acres, is there.

Gipps Creek rises in ne Cherokee County and flows sw into Valley River.

Gladden Ridge, w Madison County parallel to Raccoon Branch.

Gladdens Creek rises in central Graham County and flows w into Cheoah River.

Glade, The, a relatively level area on Newfound Mountain on the Buncombe-Haywood county line between Grassy Gap and Beaverdam Gap.

Glade, The, loamy marsh in se Duplin County.

Glade Branch rises in e Clay County and flows ne into Buck Creek.

Glade Creek rises in central Alexander County and flows s into Lower Little River to form Bell River, *which see.*

Glade Creek rises in s central Alleghany County and flows n into Little River.

Glade Creek rises in se Buncombe County and flows se into Broad River.

Glade Creek rises in se Macon County and flows ne into Chatooga River.

Glade Creek rises in ne Transylvania County and flows se into French Broad River.

Glade Creek, community in e Alleghany County.

Glade Creek Township, ne Alleghany County.

Glade Gap, e Clay County near Glade Branch.

Glade Mountain, nw Buncombe County e of Cherry Gap.

Glade Mountain, e Haywood County between head of Thickety Creek and head of Willow Creek. Peaks are Goat Rock, Wines Top, and Point Lookout.

Glade Mountain, at the head of Glade Creek in se Macon County.

Glades Creek rises in s McDowell County and flows n into Catawba River.

Glade Top, on the Buncombe-Haywood county line.

Glade Valley, community in se Alleghany County. Glade Valley High School there operated under direction of Presbyterian Church.

Gladie Creek rises in e Jackson County and flows sw into Tuckasegee River.

Gladis, community in e Mecklenburg County.

Gladstone. *See* Misenheimer.

Glady, community in sw Buncombe County on South Hominy Creek.

Glady Branch rises in w Swain County and flows s into Tuckasegee River.

Glady Creek rises in s Rockingham County and flows se into Troublesome Creek, a tributary of Haw River. Named for glade, or swampy area, at head of creek.

Glady Fork rises on the Buncombe-Henderson county line n of Glady Fork Gap and flows nw into South Hominy Creek.

Glady Fork is formed in s Transylvania County by the confluence of West Prong and South Prong. It flows n into East Fork French Broad River.

Glady Fork Gap, on the Buncombe-Henderson county line.

Gladys Branch rises in central Transylvania County and flows sw into Spanish Oak Branch.

Gladys Fork Gap, at the head of Fletcher Creek in nw Henderson County.

Glasgow County, formed in 1791 from Dobbs County, was named in honor of James Glasgow, secretary of state of North Carolina, 1777–98. The name was changed to Greene, *which see*, in 1799 when Glasgow was convicted of land fraud. Glasgow died in Tennessee in 1820.

Glass, community in n Cabarrus County. Named for Peter Glass, an early German settler.

Glassmine Branch rises in ne Buncombe County and flows sw into North Fork [Swannanoa River].

Glassmine Gap, on Little Bald Mountain, sw Macon County.

Glassmine Mountain, w Transylvania County between Lamance and Beasley Creeks. Named for the fact that isinglass (mica) was mined in the vicinity.

Glassmine Ridge, ne Buncombe County between Sugarhouse Cove and Corner Rock Creek.

Glass Rock Knob, on the McDowell-Yancey county line.

Glassy Rock, mountain in se Henderson County overlooking Flat Rock community. According to legend, renegades hid there during the Civil War, and money and other valuables that they concealed in the caves there were later found. Trail from Connemara, the Carl Sandburg house, leads to the overlook.

Glassy Rock Creek rises in s Jackson County and flows s into Webb Lake.

Glassy Rock Mountain, on the se end of Glassy Rock Ridge, s Jackson County. Alt. approx. 4,500.

Glassy Rock Ridge, s Jackson County between Rattlesnake Knob and Glassy Rock Mountain.

Glen Alpine, town in sw Burke County. Inc. 1883. Alt. 1,206. First known as Turkey Tail because of an old tree root that resembled a turkey's tail. Later called Sigmonsburg for a local storekeeper, and finally given its present name when the railroad was built.

Glen Ayre, community in e Mitchell County on Little Green Creek. A late nineteenth-century post office there was known as Little Rock Creek.

Glen Brook, community in ne Montgomery County served by post office, 1880–1906.

Glen Burnie Falls, on New Years Creek, w edge of town of Blowing Rock in s Watauga County. Height 75 ft. Part of Blowing Rock recreation area since 1906.

Glenburnie Gardens, residential area about 3 mi. n of New Bern, central Craven County.

Glencannon Falls, e central Transylvania County in Williamson Creek.

Glencoe, community in central Alamance County. Formerly site of textile mills.

Glen Cove, the valley through which Glen Cove Branch flows in se Buncombe County.

Glen Cove Branch rises in se Buncombe County and flows nw into Swannanoa River.

Glendale, community in n Alamance County served by post office, 1884–1901.

Glendale Springs, community in se Ashe County. Alt. 2,850.

Glendon, community in ne Moore County. Named for E. F. Glenn, owner of the site. A pyrophyllite open-cut mine and processing plant operated there. Alt. 301.

Glen Falls, on East Fork Overflow Creek in se Macon County. Water drops about 75 ft.

Glenfield, community in s Greene County. Tyndal's College, located nearby, was est. about 1913, abandoned about 1929. Founded by James Tyndal and son, John, prominent Baptists. The community was settled prior to 1890.

Glenhaven, community in central Beaufort County on the n bank of Pamlico River.

Glen Inglis, community in central Buncombe County served by post office, 1890–1909.

Glen Mary Falls, in New Years Creek, w edge of town of Blowing Rock in s Watauga County. Height 100 ft. Part of Blowing Rock recreation area since 1906.

Glenmore, community in s Johnston County
served by post office, 1879–1902.

Glenn, community in nw Ashe County. Alt.
approx. 3,500.

Glenn. *See* University.

Glenn Bald, mountain peak in s Buncombe
County between Lance Mountain and Shut-in
Ridge. Alt. 2,703.

Glenn Gap, on the Monroe County, Tenn.–
Graham County, N.C., line.

Glenn Mountain, in s Person County near Flat
River.

Glenola, community in n Randolph County.
Alt. approx. 793.

Glen Raven, community in w Alamance County.
Alt. 701. Named by John Q. Gant (1847–1930),
who est. first mill at the site. He first chose
Glendale, but the name was rejected because
it was already a post office name in the state.
He kept the "Glen," however, and added
Raven because of his fondness for hunting
crows.

Glenville, town in s Jackson County between
Thorpe Reservoir and Glassy Rock Ridge. Inc.
1891. Alt. approx. 3,560.

Glenville Lake. *See* Lake Thorpe.

Glenwood, former community in central
Guilford County now within Greensboro
city limits.

Glenwood, community in s Johnston County
served by post office, 1884–1904.

Glenwood, community in s McDowell County.
Inc. 1909; ceased to be active in municipal
affairs in 1927; charter repealed 1945. A post
office there was known as Nealsville.

Glenwood Township, se McDowell County.

Gliden, community in n Chowan County.
Alt. 38.

Glisson Township, n central Duplin County.

Globe, community in nw Caldwell County. Alt.
1,325. Settled about 1775 and named because
the area cleared by the settlers was practically
round. Globe Academy operated there from
1882 until it was washed away in the flood of
1916.

Globe Mountains, a range of mountains extending across nw Caldwell County on the e side
of Johns River. Alt. from 1,500 to 3,283.

Globe Township, nw Caldwell County.

Gloucester, town authorized to be laid off in
1754 on 50 acres of land owned by John
Jenkins on the s side of the Pee Dee River in
Anson County. No evidence exists that the
town was ever est.

Gloucester, community in e Carteret County.
Alt. 10. Settled about 1800 and named for the
city in Massachusetts.

Gloucester District, one of the districts into
which Caswell County was divided at the time
of the 1790 census. It contained 211 heads of
families.

Gloucester Gap, a low gap at the heads of Shoal
Creek and Long Branch nw of Rich Mountain,
n Henderson County.

Gloucester Township, nw Transylvania County.

Glover, community in s Nash County served by
post office, 1890–1909.

Glover Creek rises in ne Carteret County and
flows s into Styron Bay between Sealevel and
Atlantic.

Glovers Crossroads, community in ne Bertie
County.

Gnat Ridge, in se Macon County between
Henson Branch and Brooks Creek.

Gneiss, community in e Macon County on
Cullasaja River. Alt. 2,115. Named for gneiss,
a laminated or foliated metamorphic rock
found in the vicinity.

G. Newby's Ferry. *See* Belvidere.

Goade Island, a name applied on the Smith
map, 1624, to the s extremity of Currituck
Banks, e Currituck County.

Goat Bald, w Macon County between Bearpen
Creek and Wine Spring Creek.

Goat Island, s central Carteret County in Bogue
Sound off Morehead City.

Goat Island, e Pasquotank County n of Elizabeth
City in the Pasquotank River.

Goat Knob, s Jackson County s of Coldside
Mountain near Chester Branch.

Goat Knob, on the Jackson-Macon county line.

Goat Neck, community in ne Tyrrell County ne
of Fort Landing.

Goat Rock, e Haywood County on Glade Mountain. Alt. approx. 4,450.

Goatrock Ridge, central Haywood County,
extends e from Jonathans Creek to Snakeden
Top.

Gobble Creek rises in w Davidson County and
flows nw into Yadkin River.

Godfrey, community in n Richmond County.

Godfrey Branch. *See* Citte Weeks Branch.

Godfrey Creek rises in s Pender County and
flows w into Harrisons Creek.

Godleys Crossroads. *See* Chocowinity.

Godley Store, community in se Beaufort County.

Godsey, community in sw Wake County served by post office, 1900–1904.

Godwin, town in ne Cumberland County. Settled 1877. Inc. 1905. Named for Isaac W. Godwin, who gave the railroad right-of-way. Alt. 156.

Godwins, community in s Johnston County.

Godwin's Branch rises in e Wilson County and flows se into Whiteoak Swamp.

Goff, community in ne Chatham County served by post office, 1881–1915.

Goff's Swamp. *See* Goss Swamp.

Goins Creek, community in nw Rockingham County settled by Melungeons in early nineteenth century. Served by local "Indian School," 1943–55.

Goins Creek rises in Virginia and flows s into Surry County, where it enters Stewart Creek.

Gold, former community in nw Burke County on Canoe Creek.

Gold Branch rises in s Cherokee County and flows sw into Nottely River.

Golden. *See* Golden Valley.

Golden Creek rises in s central Avery County and flows se into Linville River.

Goldengrove. *See* Kenansville.

Golden Ridge, n Madison County between Rocky Branch and Hurricane Creek.

Golden Valley, community in ne Rutherford County on the head of First Broad River. A post office, Golden, est. there as early as 1835. Large tracts of timber exist in the area; although worked by a lumber company many years ago, there are said to be stands of virgin timber remaining in the far reaches because it was too difficult to get it out.

Golden Valley Township, ne Rutherford County.

Gold Hill, community in sw Rockingham County. Name said to be derived from "discovery" of gold, which turned out to be only mica.

Gold Hill, town in s Rowan County. Gold was discovered there in 1824, and the community soon developed. Inc. 1859; reincorporated 1874, but long inactive in municipal affairs. Extensive mining operations carried on there over a long period of years. Alt. 764.

Gold Hill, community in central Rutherford County.

Gold Hill Township, se Rowan County.

Goldknob, community in se Rowan County served by post office, 1892–1904.

Gold Mine Branch rises in n Graham County and flows e into Cheoah River.

Goldmine Branch rises near Forge Mountain on the Henderson-Transylvania county line and flows ne into Boylston Creek.

Gold Mine Branch rises in s Macon County and flows e into Cullasaja River.

Goldmine Branch rises in w Swain County and flows s into Tuckasegee River.

Goldmine Branch rises in s Watauga County and flows w into Middle Fork [South Fork New River].

Gold Mine Township, former township in ne Franklin County, now township no. 7.

Gold Park Lake, on an unnamed stream in s central Wayne County. Formed by an artificial dam in 1940; max. depth 10 ft.; area 20 acres. Swimming facilities; open to public. First named Woodland Lake; name changed in 1954 to present name based on name of county seat, Goldsboro.

Gold Pit Creek rises in w Macon County and flows nw into Cold Spring Creek.

Gold Point, town in w Martin County on Collie Swamp. Settled about 1871. Inc. 1899 as Goldpoint, but long inactive in municipal affairs; reincorporated 1957 as Gold Point. Originally called Long Town. Alt. 74.

Gold Rock, community in ne Nash County on Swift Creek. Inc. 1875 as Whitaker's Mills, but long inactive in municipal affairs. Henry W. Whitaker was appointed first mayor. Present name selected 1886 by R. R. Gay, postmaster, when a post office was est. there and it was necessary to avoid confusion with nearby Whitakers. Alt. 110.

Goldsboro, city and county seat, central Wayne County e of Neuse River, where it is joined by Little River. Inc. 1847; became county seat in 1850, succeeding town of Waynesborough, *which see*. Named for Maj. Matthew Tilghman Goldsborough, native of Maryland, assistant engineer for Wilmington and Weldon Railroad. Includes former community of Adamsville, *which see*. Produces textiles, electronic components, primary metals, leather products, bakery products, tobacco, furniture, lumber, cottonseed oil, machinery, dairy products, and processed grain. Alt. 111.

Seymour Johnson Air Force Base, est. 1942, is there.

Goldsboro Cooling Pond, in w central Wayne County about 5 mi. w of county seat. Impounded in 1961 to cover 575 acres, with max. depth of 15 ft. and a shoreline of 4.6 mi. Used to provide supplementary cooling for the Goldsboro Steam Electric Generating Plant and named for same. Lies in a looping meander of Neuse River (though its water level is as much as 22 ft. above that of the river), and its water covers the site of an old Quaker meetinghouse. The upper meander loop forms an area known as Quaker Neck; the lower meander loop was known as The Roundabout in the 1830s.

Goldsboro Township, central Wayne County.

Goldspring Gap, s Macon County between Wolfpen Gap and Pickens Nose.

Goldston, town in s Chatham County. Settled about 1885; inc. 1907. Named for Joseph Goldston, on whose land the town developed. Alt. 424.

Gold Valley Crossroads, community in w Nash County.

Goldview Knob, central Buncombe County sw of Beard Mountain.

Gooch Gap, on the McDowell-Mitchell county line.

Gooch Peak, central Buncombe County in the w part of the Elk Mountains.

Goode Creek rises in se Rutherford County and flows s into Broad River.

Goodings Creek. *See* Goodwin Creek.

Goodluck, community in n Henderson County on Hooper Creek.

Goodman, community in nw Anson County. Named for local family; J. C. Goodman, Civil War veteran, est. a tannery there soon after the war.

Goodman Branch rises in e central Brunswick County and flows s into Town Creek.

Goodman Branch rises in n Union County and flows se into Richardson Creek.

Goodmans Island, in se Bertie County between the mouth of Cashie River and Eastmost River. Irregularly shaped, it measures approx. 1¼ mi. in width and length from its most distant points. *See also* Purchace Islands.

Goodman Swamp rises in nw Bladen County and flows sw into Robeson County, where it enters Big Swamp.

Goodman Swamp rises in s Nansemond County, Va., and flows s into Gates County, where it enters Duke Swamp.

Goodson's Store. *See* Boger City.

Goodsonville. *See* Boger City.

Good Spring, community in w Surry County served by post office, 1878–1916.

Good Spring Branch rises in w Haywood County and flows se into Pretty Hollow Creek.

Goodwill, community in ne Forsyth County served by post office, 1884–1903.

Goodwin Creek rises in w Perquimans County and flows e into Perquimans River. Named for Caleb Goodwin, who operated a mill on the creek about 1820. Appears as Cypress Swamp on the Moseley map, 1733, and generally known as Cypress Creek until renamed for the miller. Appears as Goodings Creek on the 1905 soil-survey map.

Goodwin Forest, central Moore County, a tract of 1,122 acres owned by James L. Goodwin from 1930 until his death in 1967, when it was given to North Carolina State University for use in education, research, and recreation. Net proceeds are used for scholarships. Pine and hardwoods grow in the forest.

Goodwin Hills, community on n Cedar Island in ne Carteret County.

Goodwin Mill Pond, approx. 1½ mi. long, on Goodwin Creek, w Perquimans County.

Goose Bay, off the se end of the largest island in the Hog Island group, ne Carteret County.

Goose Bay Point, at the s tip of the largest island in the Hog Island group, ne Carteret County.

Goose Branch rises in e Nash County and flows se into Tar River.

Goosecastle Point, neck of land extending from n end of Church Island into Currituck Sound in central Currituck County.

Goose Creek, forming a part of the boundary between Beaufort and Pamlico Counties, is formed on the county line by the junction of Campbell and Upper Spring Creeks. It flows n into Pamlico River. The Intracoastal Waterway connects Goose Creek and Jones Bay.

Goose Creek rises in w Carteret County and flows 3 mi. s into Bogue Sound. Appears on the Moseley map, 1733.

Goose Creek formerly rose in s Clay County and flowed nw into Hiwassee River. Its course is now covered by the waters of Chatuge Lake.

Goose Creek rises in e Gates County and flows se and e into Dismal Swamp.

Goose Creek rises in se Hertford County and flows se into Chowan River.

Goose Creek rises in e Mecklenburg County and flows se into Union County, where it turns ne to enter Rocky River.

Goose Creek rises in e Onslow County and flows se into Sanders Creek. Mentioned in local records as early as 1744.

Goose Creek rises in w Pamlico County and flows sw into Neuse River. Appears on the Moseley map, 1733.

Goose Creek rises in e Swain County and flows se into Oconaluftee River.

Goose Creek rises in e Tyrrell County and flows e into Alligator River. Appears on the Collet map, 1770.

Goose Creek Island, the ne neck of Pamlico County cut off from the mainland by the Intracoastal Waterway. Near the end of the nineteenth century, Goose Creek Island post office served the area. The North Carolina Wildlife Resources Commission maintains the Goose Creek Wildlife Management Area of 5,865 acres w of the Intracoastal Waterway in Beaufort and Pamlico Counties. *See also* Greens Land.

Goose Creek State Park, Beaufort County. Opened to the public, September 1974. The park covers 1,327 acres and fronts Pamlico River. Features six hiking trails.

Goose Creek Township, n Union County.

Goose Island, in Core Sound near Core Banks in e Carteret County.

Goose Neck Creek rises in n Granville County and flows e into Kerr Lake. Name derived from irregular course of creek. Also known as Johnson Creek.

Goose Nest. *See* Oak City.

Goose Nest Township, nw Martin County. *See also* Oak City.

Goose Pond, community in ne Bertie County. Named for the goose pond on a local plantation owned by the Holley family.

Gordens Island. *See* Wococon Island.

Gordons Mountain, sw Anson County near the head of Lick Creek. Alt. 400–500 ft.

Gordonton, community in e Davidson County. Earlier known as Gordontown.

Gordonton, community in sw Person County. A post office as early as 1830.

Gordontown, town authorized to be est. in 1824 on the lands of James Gordon on Cribs Creek, nw Anson County, but there is no evidence that the town was laid out.

Gorge, The. *See* Linville Gorge.

Gorman, community in e Durham County.

Gorvas Island, an island of uncertain identity shown on the Moll map, 1729, within the bounds of present Currituck County.

Goshen, community in w Granville County. The home of Gen. Thomas Person (1733–1800), known by biblical name of Goshen, was there. Homestead burned in 1930s. Goshen District in 1790 had 67 heads of families.

Goshen, community in ne Sampson County at the head of Goshen Swamp.

Goshen, former community in sw Wilkes County on Yadkin River. The site is now a part of the W. Kerr Scott Reservoir.

Goshen Branch rises in s Watauga County and flows ne into Storey Branch.

Goshen District. *See* Goshen.

Goshen Hill, s Watauga County between Raccoon Branch and Goshen Branch.

Goshen Swamp rises in ne Sampson County and flows se into Duplin County, where it continues se until it enters Northeast Cape Fear River. Appears on the Collet map, 1770. Holley's Mill is also shown on the Collet map as being near the headwaters of the stream.

Goss Swamp rises in se Wilson County and flows sw into Toisnot Swamp. Known earlier as Goff's Swamp.

Gouches Branch rises in sw Buncombe County near Bert Mountain and flows ne into Newfound Creek.

Gouge Branch rises n of Gouge Mountain in se Mitchell County and flows nw into Toe River.

Gouge Knob, central Mitchell County at the head of Rebel Creek.

Gouge Mountain, se Mitchell County.

Gouges Creek rises in e Mitchell County and flows se into North Toe River.

Gouges Creek rises in n Mitchell County and flows s into Little Rock Creek.

Gould, community in s Gaston County served by post office, 1888–1902.

Goulds, community in sw Wilkes County on Yadkin River at the mouth of Stony Fork Creek. Named for Andy Gould, who operated a mill on Stony Fork Creek.

Goulds Fork rises in sw Anson County and flows
n into Brown Creek.

Gourdvine Creek rises in e Union County and
flows nw into Richardson's Creek.

Gover. *See* Gibbs Point.

Governors Creek. *See* Big Governors Creek;
Crawley Creek.

Governors Island, community in e Swain County
on Johnson Branch. Takes its name from
an adjoining loamy area on the Tuckasegee
River.

Governors Island, loamy section in e Swain
County on Tuckasegee River extending se
from the mouth of Galbreath Creek to the
mouth of Johnson Branch.

Gowans Cove, nw Cherokee County, through
which an unnamed stream flows into Shuler
Creek.

Gow-ta-no. *See* Neuse River.

Grable Branch rises in central Macon County
and flows n into Owenby Branch.

Grabtown, community in sw Bertie County.

Grabur Heights, community in central Alamance County.

Grace, community in central Buncombe County
served by post office, 1889–1902.

Grade, community in nw Alexander County.
Alt. approx. 975.

Gradins Station, community in sw Granville
County.

Grady, community in w Robeson County served
by post office, 1890–1904.

Gradys, community in se Wayne County near
Buck Marsh.

Grady Township, sw Pender County.

Gragg, community in ne Avery County. Probably
named for John Gragg, Revolutionary War
soldier (buried at Montezuma) or for Gragg
Prong, *which see*, probably also named for
him.

Gragg Prong, stream, rises in e central Avery
County and flows s into Lost Cove Creek.

Graggs Fork rises in nw Caldwell County and
flows s into Anthonys Creek.

Graham, city and county seat, central Alamance
County. Laid out in 1849 with the formation
of the country to serve as county seat. Inc.
1851. Named for William A. Graham, governor, 1845–49. In the act providing for the
town, it was first named Gallatin, then Montgomery, Berry, and finally Graham, as chosen by North Carolina representative Giles

Mebane, who introduced the bill to create
Alamance County. Alt. 656. Produces textiles,
hosiery, and primary metals.

Graham Branch rises in e Cherokee County and
flows se into Slow Creek.

Graham Branch rises in n Granville County and
flows nw into Little Grass Creek.

Graham County was formed in 1872 from Cherokee County. Located in the w section of the
state, it is bounded by the state of Tennessee
and by Cherokee and Swain Counties. It was
named for William A. Graham (1804–75), U.S.
senator, governor of North Carolina, secretary
of the navy, and Confederate senator. Area:
299 sq. mi. County seat: Robbinsville, with an
elevation of 2,150 ft. Townships are Cheoah,
Stecoah, and Yellow Creek. Produces hay,
cattle, poultry, livestock, furniture, fish, and
lumber.

Graham Creek rises in central Transylvania
County and flows ne into Nicholson Creek.

Graham Mountain, on the Buncombe-
Henderson county line.

Graham's Ferry crossed the Catawba River in nw
Mecklenburg County at Lincoln County line.

Graham Top, central Cherokee County near the
headwaters of Cook Creek.

Graham Township, former township in central
Alamance County. Now township no. 6.

Graingers, town in ne Lenoir County. Alt. 74.
Inc. 1925. Named for Jesse Grainger, on
whose plantation it developed after a railroad
station was est. there.

Grampian Hills, a range of hills about 3 mi.
long in s Orange County running sw and
ne. Named for the Grampian Hills, natural
boundary between Scottish Highlands and
Scottish Lowlands in Scotland.

Granburys Crossroads. *See* Roxobel.

Grandfather, community in sw Watauga County
on Watauga River.

Grandfather Mountain, at junction of Avery,
Caldwell, and Watauga Counties. Alt. 5,964.
Tourist attraction formerly owned by Morton
family and sold to state in 2008. "Mile High

Swinging Bridge" connects two peaks. Annual "Singing on the Mountain" and "Gathering of the Scottish Clans" are held. Named for the fact that, when viewed from a distance, the outline of the mountain against the sky suggests the profile of an old man. Highest point in the Blue Ridge. Called *Tanawha* by the Cherokee Indians, meaning "a fabulous hawk or eagle."

Grandin, former town in ne Caldwell County. Inc. 1913 on the lands of the Grandin Lumber Co. Long inactive in municipal affairs and now abandoned.

Grandmother Creek rises in e central Avery County near Grandmother Gap and flows sw into Linville River.

Grandmother Gap, e Avery County.

Grandmother Mountain, e Avery County. Alt. 4,696.

Grandmother Ridge, e central Avery County.

Grandview, community in central Cherokee County at the junction of Davis and Hanging Dog Creeks.

Grand View, community in e Watauga County s of Laxon Creek.

Grandy, community in s Currituck County on the e side of North River. Post office est. 1898; closed 1932. Named for Caleb Grandy, first postmaster.

Grange. *See* Little River.

Granger Branch rises in sw Madison County and flows nw into Spring Creek.

Granger Mountain, w Madison County between Foxtown Mountain and Spring Creek.

Granite City, a formation of granite cliffs s of Devils Court House area between Blackrock Mountain and Chattooga River on the Jackson-Macon county line.

Granite Falls, a 35-ft. waterfall in Gunpowder Creek, se Caldwell County. Known first as Falls of Gunpowder. Baird's Forge or Baird Iron Works est. there, 1795, by Maj. Andrew Baird.

Granite Falls, town in se Caldwell County. Inc. 1863. Takes its name from a waterfall of the same name, *which see*, a short distance ne of the town. A former post office serving the community was Baird's Forge; renamed Lovelady in 1824 and Granite Falls in 1887. Produced textiles and pianos. Alt. 1,213.

Granite Quarry, town in s Rowan County. Inc. 1901 as Woodside; name changed in 1905 for local quarries. Post office est. as Woodside, 1891; name changed to Granite Quarry, 1902.

Granny Branch rises in n central Wayne County and flows ne into The Slough.

Granny Cove Branch rises in ne Buncombe County and flows se through Granny Cove into North Fork [Swannanoa River].

Granny Green Mountain, s Macon County between Lowery Creek and Allison Creek.

Granny Mountain, w Haywood County between Johnson Gap and Jonathans Creek.

Granny Squirrel Branch rises in ne Cherokee County and flows ne into Valley River.

Granston Lake. *See* White Lake.

Grant Branch rises in central Northampton County and flows se into Urahaw Swamp.

Grantham, community in sw Wayne County between Beaverdam Creek and Neuse River. Formerly called Grantham's Store.

Granthams, community in e Craven County.

Grantham's Store. *See* Grantham.

Grantham Township, sw Wayne County. Named for Grantham family, eighteenth-century settlers of the area.

Grant Knob, n Macon County between Mouse Mountain and Devil Den Ridge.

Grants, community in central Wayne County.

Grants. *See* Grantsboro.

Grantsboro, community in w Pamlico County. Named for an early settler. Alt. 20. Railroad name is Grants.

Grants Creek rises in ne Onslow County and flows ne into White Oak River. Named for Alexander Grant, an early settler. A 1730 reference to the stream in local records calls it Alex's Creek. Known by present name since 1744.

Grants Creek rises in s Rowan County and flows ne into Yadkin River. Named because the earliest known grants of land in the area were along the stream. Frohock Mill on Grants Creek appears on the Collet map, 1770.

Grant Township, e central Randolph County.

Grantville, community in e Madison County.

Granville County was formed in 1746 from Edgecombe County. Located in the ne section of the state, it is bounded by Vance, Franklin, Wake, Durham, and Person Counties and by the state of Virginia. It was named for John Carteret, Earl Granville (1690–1763), owner of the Granville District, *which see*, in which the new county was located. Area: 543 sq. mi. County seat: Oxford, with an elevation of 476 ft. Townships are Brassfield, Dutchville, Fishing Creek, Oak Hill, Oxford, Salem, Sassafras Fork, Tally Ho, and Walnut Grove. Produces tobacco, corn, oats, wheat, hay, sweet potatoes, poultry, livestock, hogs, dairy products, cosmetics, wood products, machinery, lumber, and apparel.

Granville District was the portion of North Carolina allotted to John Carteret, Earl Granville (1690–1763), one of the Lords Proprietors, who refused to sell his interest in North Carolina to the Crown in 1729. The upper half of present-day North Carolina was included in the district, which extended from the Virginia boundary to 35°34′, a strip 60 mi. wide. The southern line was run from the coast to Bath in 1744, to Haw River in 1746, and to Rocky River in 1766. The district was lost to the Granville estate at the time of the American Revolution.

Granville Parish, Church of England, Granville County, est. in 1758 in the w part of the county, when St. John's Parish (est. 1746 with the formation of the county and coextensive with it) was divided. After St. John's Parish in the e became Bute County in 1764, Granville Parish was coextensive with Granville County. In 1767 there were 1,022 white taxables in the parish. *See also* St. John's Parish.

Grape Branch rises in ne Duplin County and flows sw into Northeast Cape Fear River.

Grape Branch rises in s Jones County and flows se into White Oak River.

Grape Branch rises in se Nash County and flows ne into Tar River.

Grape Cove, s Swain County between Mica Knob and Marr Branch.

Grape Creek rises in central Cherokee County and flows se and sw into Hiwassee River.

Grape Creek rises in Great Dover Swamp, n Jones County, and flows ne into Craven County, where it enters Cove Creek.

Grape Creek, community in central Cherokee County near the mouth of Hanging Dog Creek.

Grapevine Bay, se Tyrrell County in Alligator River.

Grapevine Landing, se Tyrrell County on Grapevine Bay.

Grapevine Ridge, e Madison County between West Fork [Bull Creek] and Beetree Creek.

Grapevine Township, former township in central Madison County, now township no. 14.

Graphite. *See* Graphiteville.

Graphiteville, community in w McDowell County. Alt. 2,037. Named for nearby graphite mine. Also known as Graphite.

Grass Branch rises in n central Ashe County and flows s into Windfall Creek.

Grassland, community in s Avery County.

Grass Land Ridge, s Madison County between South Fork [Big Pine Creek] and Little Pine Creek. Alt. 3,884.

Grassy Bald, mountain on the Haywood-Jackson county line. Alt. 5,613.

Grassy Branch rises in central Buncombe County and flows s into Swannanoa River.

Grassy Branch rises in se Buncombe County and flows ne into Rock Creek.

Grassy Branch rises in w Cleveland County and flows ne into First Broad River.

Grassy Branch rises in central Haywood County and flows nw into Pigeon River.

Grassy Branch rises in nw Macon County and flows sw into Queens Creek.

Grassy Branch rises in e Swain County and flows nw into Raven Fork.

Grassy Branch rises in se Swain County and flows n into Connelly Creek.

Grassy Branch rises in w central Swain County and flows sw into Yalaka Creek.

Grassy Camp Creek rises in sw Jackson County and flows ne into Norton Creek.

Grassy Cove Gap, s Haywood County between Grassy Cove Ridge and Little Buckeye Cove.

Grassy Cove Ridge, s Haywood County, extends e from Grassy Cove Top to Grassy Cove Gap.

Grassy Cove Top, s Haywood County on the s end of Shining Rock Ledge.

Grassy Creek rises in n Alexander County and flows s and w into Lower Little River.

Grassy Creek rises in Grayson County, Va., and flows se into Ashe County, where it enters North Fork New River.

Grassy Creek rises in s Ashe County and flows s approx. 4 mi. into South Fork New River near the Watauga County line.

Grassy Creek rises in se Buncombe County and flows sw into Henderson County, where it enters Broad River.

Grassy Creek rises in w Granville County and flows ne into Kerr Lake.

Grassy Creek rises in sw Henderson County and flows w into Transylvania County, where it enters Little River.

Grassy Creek rises in w Jackson County and flows se into West Fork Tuckasegee River.

Grassy Creek rises in w Madison County and flows ne into French Broad River.

Grassy Creek rises in s Mitchell County and flows n into North Toe River.

Grassy Creek rises in ne Moore County and flows ne into Deep River. Appears in local records as early as 1747 and on the MacRae map, 1833.

Grassy Creek rises in e Surry County and flows s into Yadkin River. Appears on the Collet map, 1770.

Grassy Creek rises in e Transylvania County and flows w into Little River.

Grassy Creek rises in n Union County and flows ne into Rocky River.

Grassy Creek rises in e Watauga County and flows se into South Fork New River.

Grassy Creek, community in ne Ashe County. Settled about 1788.

Grassy Creek, community in n Granville County. A church there was est. in 1755.

Grassy Creek Township, ne Ashe County.

Grassy Creek Township, s Mitchell County.

Grassy Gap, on the Buncombe-Haywood county line on Newfound Mountain.

Grassy Gap, n Cherokee County in the Unicoi Mountains.

Grassy Gap, se Clay County on Chunky Gal Mountain.

Grassy Gap, on Graham-Swain county line between Grassy Top and Tyre Knob.

Grassy Gap, n Mitchell County between Grassy Knob and Right Fork Bean Creek.

Grassy Gap, sw Swain County between Silvermine Gap and Briertown Mountain.

Grassy Gap Branch rises in w Watauga County and flows nw into Buckeye Creek on the Avery-Watauga county line.

Grassy Islands, several islands in Pee Dee River n of Blewett Falls Lake on the Anson-Richmond county line. Shown on the Price map, 1808, and the MacRae map, 1833.

Grassy Knob, n Buncombe County between Salton Gap and Frosty Knob.

Grassy Knob, nw Buncombe County ne of High Knob.

Grassy Knob, s Buncombe County.

Grassy Knob, central Caldwell County.

Grassy Knob, n Haywood County between Pigeon River and Wilkins Creek.

Grassy Knob, nw Iredell County. Now covered with trees, but apparently grassland when first discovered by settlers. The first Baptist church in the county was organized at its base in 1789, and an old Masonic lodge exists in the community nearby.

Grassy Knob, s Jackson County between Round Mountain and Whitewater River.

Grassy Knob, on the Jackson-Macon county line.

Grassy Knob, central Macon County at the head of Poindexter Branch.

Grassy Knob, n Madison County between Shelton Laurel Creek and Spillcorn Creek.

Grassy Knob, a peak on Grassy Mountain on the McDowell-Mitchell county line. Alt. approx. 2,020.

Grassy Knob, n Mitchell County between Grassy Gap and Rich Branch.

Grassy Knob, w Haywood County on Eaglenest Ridge.

Grassy Knob, central Watauga County on the e slope of Rich Mountain.

Grassy Knob, w Yancey County between Price and Banks Creeks.

Grassy Knob Branch rises in s Yancey County and flows se into Upper Creek.

Grassy Knob Ridge, s Yancey County between Lower Creek and Grassy Knob Branch.

Grassy Knobs, s Macon County between Rattlesnake Ridge and Middle Creek.

Grassy Lot Gap, n Transylvania County between Thompson Creek and Bradley Creek. Alt. 3,358.

Grassy Mountain, sw Henderson County near Grassy Creek. Alt. 3,678.

Grassy Mountain, on the McDowell-Rutherford county line.

Grassy Point, e Beaufort County on Pungo River.

Grassy Ridge, on the Avery-Mitchell county line.

Grassy Ridge Bald, on the Avery-Mitchell county line. Alt. 6,200–6,300.

Grassy Ridge Bald. *See* Bald Mountain.

Grassy Ridge Branch rises in s Haywood County and flows nw into Middle Prong.

Grassy Top, on the Cherokee County, N.C.–
Monroe County, Tenn., line in the Unicoi
Mountains. Alt. 4,979.

Grassy Top, on the Graham-Swain county line
between The Jump-up and Grassy Gap.

Grassy Top, peak on Holland Mountain on
Haywood-Buncombe county line.

Gravel Creek rises in s Buncombe County and
flows se into Cane Creek.

Gravel Hill, community in e Bladen County
served by post office, 1875–1911. Spelled
Gravelhill after 1894.

Gravelhill. *See* Gravel Hill.

Gravel Knob, on the Madison County, N.C.–
Greene County, Tenn., line.

Gravelly Hill. *See* Hickory Grove Crossroads.

Gravel Spring, community in n Chatham County
served by post office, 1879–1904.

Graves Ferry appears on the Moseley map,
1733, over the Neuse River near the mouth
of Bachelor Creek, s Craven County. The
road from Bath to Wilmington crossed there.
A 1901 map shows Nelsons Old Ferry at the
site.

Graveyard Cove, in White Oak River, w Carteret
County, a short distance n of the community
of Stella. Named for nearby cemetery.

Graveyard Creek rises in s Mitchell County and
flows ne into Grassy Creek.

Graveyard Mountain, n McDowell County
between North Fork [Catawba River] and
Woodlawn. Alt. approx. 2,250.

Graveyard Ridge, w central Clay County in the
Tusquitee Mountains, runs n and s along the
Hiwassee River.

Graveyard Ridge, s Haywood County between
Yellowstone Prong and Dark Prong. A flat
area there has numerous mounds resem-
bling graves. They have been dug into but no
human remains found. A hurricane or wind-
storm likely uprooted trees and, through the
years, the old root stumps and trees rotted
out, leaving only the dirt mounds. There is a
slight depression beside each mound, which
is the hole from which the stumps came.

Graybeal, community in w Ashe County. Alt.
approx. 3,000.

Graybeard Creek rises in ne Cherokee County
and flows w into Vengeance Creek s of Brushy
Head Mountain.

Graybeard Mountain, on the Buncombe-
McDowell county line. Alt. 5,360–5,400.

Gray Camp Branch rises in nw Haywood County
and flows se into Big Creek.

Gray Gap, s Macon County between The
Pinnacle and Tessentee Creek.

Grays Branch rises in sw Caswell County and
flows se into Stony Creek.

Grays Branch rises in n Columbus County and
flows sw into Pinelog Swamp.

Grays Chapel, community in ne Randolph
County. Named for a local family. A post
office est. there as early as 1882.

Grays Creek rises in s Cumberland County and
flows se in an arc into Cape Fear River.

Grays Creek rises in sw Rutherford County and
flows w into Broad River.

Grays Creek rises in e Wilkes County and flows
ne into Yadkin River. Named for James Gray,
pre–Revolutionary War settler there.

Grays Creek, community in s central Cumberland County approx. 6 mi. s of city of
Fayetteville.

Grays Creek Township, sw Cumberland County.

Grays Landing. *See* Windsor.

Grays Mill appears on the Collet map, 1770,
near the mouth of Sawyers Creek, w Camden
County.

Grays Mountain, s Randolph County between
Needhams Mountain and Pond Mountain.

Grayson, community in nw Ashe County.

Gray's Point, central Onslow County in s Farnell
Bay.

Gray Swamp, s Pasquotank County between
Little Flatty Creek and Big Flatty Creek.

Gray Wolf Creek rises in n Swain County in Great
Smoky Mountains National Park and flows sw
into Forney Creek.

Greasy Branch rises in w Madison County and
flows e into Spring Creek.

Greasy Branch rises in w central Swain County
and flows sw into Little Tennessee River.

Greasy Corner. *See* Davie Crossroads.

Greasy Cove, nw Buncombe County se of Rogers
Gap.

Greasy Cove Prong rises in se Haywood County
and flows e into East Fork Pigeon River.

Greasy Creek rises in ne Alexander County and
flows e into South Yadkin River.

Greasy Creek rises in central Clay County in
Winchester Cove and flows nw into Tusquitee
Creek.

Greasy Creek rises in sw Clay County and flows
sw into Brasstown Creek.

Greasy Creek rises in n Mitchell County and flows s into Big Rock Creek.

Greasy Creek. *See* Abingdon Creek.

Greasy Mountain, sw Wilkes County between Long Fork of Beaver Creek and Beaver Creek.

Great Alamance Creek is formed by the junction of Little Alamance and Big Alamance Creeks in e Guilford County and flows e across Alamance County, where it enters Haw River. Appears as Aramancy River on the Moseley map, 1733. Called Aramanchy River by William Byrd, 1728.

Great Alegator Dismal Swamp appears on the Collet map, 1770, as the large swampy area in much of present Tyrrell, Dare, and n Hyde Counties.

Great Branch rises in e Beaufort County and flows e into Pungo River.

Great Branch rises in s Nash County and flows e into Tar River.

Great Branch rises in ne Pitt County and flows se into Meadow Branch.

Great Coharie Creek rises in n Sampson County and flows s to join Little Coharie Creek in forming Coharie River. Appears as Cohary Swamp on the Collet map, 1770.

Great Coneghta Pocosin. *See* Conetoe Creek.

Great Contentnea Creek. *See* Contentnea Creek.

Great Coteckney Creek. *See* Contentnea Creek.

Great Craggy Mountains, range in ne Buncombe County extending s from Balsam Gap to the Swannanoa River. Alt. 3,332. Known by the Cherokee Indians as *Sunnatee* (morning).

Great Creek rises in North River Pocosin in s Camden County and flows e into North River.

Great Creek, tidal creek in Jarrett Bay, se Carteret County.

Great Creek. *See* Deep Creek; Smith Creek.

Great Dismal Swamp. *See* Dismal Swamp.

Great Ditch, waterway between two of the e islands in the Hog Island group, ne Carteret County.

Great Dover Swamp is located in ne Jones County and sw Craven County; drains sw into Trent River and its tributaries. Mill Branch, Moseley Creek, Bachelor Creek, Grape Creek, Rollover Creek, and Cove Creek rise in Great Dover Swamp.

Great Elliby. *See* Upper Bartons Creek.

Great Falls, on the Yadkin River a short distance s of The Narrows on the Montgomery-Stanly county line.

Great Falls. *See* Roanoke Rapids.

Great Falls, The. *See* High Falls.

Great Fishing Creek. *See* Fishing Creek.

Great Hammock Swash lies between Core Beach and Core Banks (on the sound side) in e Carteret County.

Great Hogback, mountain on Jackson-Transylvania county line. Alt. 4,785.

Great Iron Mountain. *See* Bald Mountain; Great Smoky Mountains.

Great Island, in se Bertie County between Cashie River and Middle River, formed in part by the Thoroughfare. The largest of a group of 9 islands, it measures approx. 4¾ mi. long and 2½ mi. wide. *See also* Purchace Islands.

Great Island, approx. 200 acres of high land located in North River Pocosin, e Camden County about 2 mi. e of Alder Branch and near the headwaters of Hunting Creek. No longer inhabited, but at one time as many as 8 families lived there.

Great Island, in Core Sound near Core Banks in e Carteret County.

Great Island, a small marshy island in the Neuse River in se Craven County.

Great Island, in the waters of Pamlico Sound off the w coast of Hatteras Island, e Dare County sw of the community of Waves.

Great Island, s Hyde County in Pamlico Sound, 25–30 acres in area. Appears as Gul Island on the Collet map, 1770. *See also* Abigails Islands.

Great Island, ne Tyrrell County in the mouth of Alligator Creek.

Great Island Bay, in Core Sound against the Core Banks, e Carteret County.

Great Lake, a natural lake in Croatan National Forest, s Craven County. Covers approx. 2,600 acres; max. depth 4 to 5 ft. One of several lakes in Lakes Pocosin.

Great Lick Creek. *See* Lick Creek.

Great Marsh, tidal marsh covering the w portion of Knotts Island, ne Currituck County.

Great Marsh. *See* Bells Island.

Great Marsh Point. *See* Bells Point.

Great Mountain, ne Henderson County.

Great Neck Landing, e Onslow County on Queens Creek; more recently known as Reed's Landing.

Great Pee Dee River. *See* Pee Dee River.

Great Pisgah. *See* Mount Pisgah.

Great Pond, in the nw part of Hog Island on the s side of Pamlico Sound, ne Carteret County.

Great Sandy Run Pocosin, w Onslow County between Shelter Swamp and Sandy Run Swamp.

Great Shell Rock. *See* North Rock.

Great Smoky Mountains are a part of the Appalachian Mountains, *which see*, and lie along the North Carolina–Tennessee state line. Clingmans Dome, at 6,642 ft., is the highest peak. The first written reference to the name Smoky is probably that found in the act of cession, passed in 1789 by the General Assembly of North Carolina, which, in describing the boundary of North Carolina and what is now Tennessee, stated: "thence along the highest ridge of the said mountain to the place where it is called Great Iron or Smoky Mountain." *See also* Bald Mountains.

Great Smoky Mountains National Park lies in portions of Haywood and Swain Counties, N.C., and Blount, Cocke, and Sevier Counties, Tenn. Establishment authorized by Congress in 1926 was the culmination of activity for the purpose beginning in the 1880s. Administered by the National Park Service since 1931. Contains approx. 461,000 acres. Has campgrounds, museums, restorations, nature trails, and other features of interest, including a variety of wild animals, birds, and plants. Clingmans Dome, alt. 6,642, the highest point in the park, has an observation tower.

Great Swamp, in Beaufort, Martin, and Washington Counties between the Roanoke and Pamlico Rivers.

Great Swamp, swamplands covering most of central Currituck County and extending into e Camden County.

Great Swamp rises in e Johnston County, flows ne across nw Wayne County and into s Wilson County, where it enters Black Creek.

Great Swamp rises in Grindle Pocosin in n Pitt County and flows s into Johnsons Mill Run.

Great Swamp rises in n Tyrrell County and flows n into Albemarle Sound.

Great Swamp. *See* Bloomery Swamp; Starkeys Creek.

Great Swamp Branch. *See* Hall Swamp.

Great Swamp Township, nw Wayne County.

Great Trading Path. *See* Trading Path.

Great White Marsh. *See* White Marsh.

Greenback, community in n central Warren County. Post office est. 1884, discontinued 1907.

Green Banks Landing, on Cape Fear River, ne Brunswick County.

Greenbrier Knob. *See* Mount Davis.

Green Cove, valley of Nichols Branch in s Macon County.

Green Cove, community on Green Cove Creek in e Mitchell County.

Green Cove Creek rises in e Mitchell County and flows nw into Cane Creek.

Green Creek rises in s Haywood County and flows n into West Fork Pigeon River.

Green Creek rises in e Jackson County and flows nw into Panthertown Creek.

Green Creek rises in sw Jackson County on the s slope of Whiteside Mountain and flows se into Chattooga River.

Green Creek rises in e Mitchell County and flows w into Little Rock Creek.

Green Creek rises in e Pamlico County and flows s into Broad Creek.

Green Creek rises in ne Rockingham County and flows n into Wolf Island Creek.

Greene Channel, in the sw end of Topsail Sound, s Pender County.

Greene County was formed in 1799 when the name of Glasgow County, *which see*, was changed to Greene. Located in the e section of the state, it is bounded by Pitt, Lenoir, Wayne, and Wilson Counties. It was named for Gen. Nathanael Greene (1742–86), Revolutionary War leader whose action at the Battle of Guilford Courthouse led to the American victory at Yorktown. Area: 269 sq. mi. County seat: Snow Hill, with an elevation of 74 ft. Townships are Bull Head, Carrs, Hookerton, Jason, Olds, Ormonds, Shine, Snow Hill, and Speights Bridge. Produces tobacco, corn, cotton, poultry, hogs, turkeys, sweet potatoes, sorghum, oats, lumber, fiberglass products, transformers, and textiles. *See also* St. Patrick's Parish.

Greene County, now in Tennessee, was created in 1783 and named in honor of Gen. Natha-

nael Greene (1742–86). Greeneville became
the county seat. It was a part of the territory
ceded by North Carolina in 1789 to the federal government.

Greene Ridge, n Madison County between Big
Creek and Dry Creek.

Greenesville. *See* Greenville.

Greene Township, se Guilford County. Named
for Gen. Nathanael Greene.

Greenevers, town in s Duplin County. Inc. 1969.

Greenevills Rode. *See* Port Grenvil.

Greenfield Lake, a natural lake now within the
limits of city of Wilmington, w New Hanover
County. Covers 125 acres; max. depth 12 ft.
Mentioned by name in the will of Dr. Samuel
Green, original owner, about 1760. A munici-
pal park and garden surround the lake.

Greenfield Ridge, n Buncombe County between
Eller Cove and Rattlesnake Ridge.

Green Gap, in central Graham County at the
head of Mountain Creek.

Green Gap, on Yellow Creek Mountains in n
Graham County s of Fontana Village.

Green Gap, e Haywood County between Cove
Creek and Fines Creek.

Green Hill, s Watauga County n of the community of Green Park.

Green Hill, community in w Rutherford County
between Maple and Mountain Creeks.

Green Hill, an eighteenth-century community
in w Washington County on Conaby Creek
e of the town of Plymouth. The community
declined as Plymouth, on the Roanoke River,
grew in importance as a port town.

Green Hill Place, home of Maj. Green Hill (1741–
1826), central Franklin County 1 mi. e of
Louisburg. Site of the first annual conference
of the Methodist Episcopal Church, 1785.

Green Hill Township, w Rutherford County.

Green Island, in the waters of Pamlico Sound off
the n tip of Pea Island, e Dare County.

Green Knob, s Haywood County in the middle of
Fork Ridge.

Green Knob, on the Haywood-Transylvania
county line between Bennett Gap and Pisgah
Ridge. Alt. 5,150.

Green Knob, on the McDowell-Yancey county
line between Deep Gap and Flinty Gap. Alt.
5,070.

Greenland Creek rises in se Jackson County and
flows nw to join Panthertown Creek in forming Tuckasegee River.

Greenleaf, community in central Wayne County
served by post office, 1886–1912.

Greenlee, community in s central McDowell
County on Catawba River. Settled before the
Revolution.

Green Level, community in ne Alamance
County. School by the name in place by 1934.
Inc. 1990.

Green Level, community in w Wake County on
head of Whiteoak Creek, est. before 1865.

Green Mountain, a peak of Linville Mountain on
the Burke-McDowell county line.

Green Mountain, a range extending from central into ne Caldwell County. Alt. from 2,000
to 2,330. Indian name was *Oawahua.* Indian
Grave Gap there is the site of Indian burials.
Indians lived on the top of the range.

Green Mountain, n Henderson County between
Kyles Creek and Piney Mountain.

Green Mountain, n Jackson County between
Hornbuckle Creek and Open Branch.

Green Mountain extends n in ne Yancey County
from near the head of Shoal Creek to Toe
River. Alt. approx. 4,500.

Green Mountain, community in n Yancey
County on Toe River. Alt. 4,990.

Green Mountain Branch rises in s Watauga
County and flows sw into Boone Fork.

Green Mountain Gap, n central Yancey County
between Phillips Knob and Three Quarters
Creek.

Green Mountain Knob, s Watauga County s of
Martin Knob.

Green Mountain Township, ne Yancey County.

Green Oak Creek rises in e Pender County and
flows sw into Northeast Cape Fear River.

Green Park, former community in n Caldwell
County, now within the limits of Blowing
Rock, *which see.* Named for the Green family,
descendants of Richard Green, who settled
there in the late eighteenth century.

Green Point, ne Carteret County at mouth of
Lewis Creek on e side of Cedar Island.

Green Point, ne Carteret County on w side of
central Cedar Island extending into West Bay.

Green Pond. *See* Highs Crossroads.

Green Ridge, s Haywood County between Tom
Creek and Green Creek.

Green River rises in sw Henderson County and
flows ne into Polk County, where it turns se
to enter Broad River on the Polk-Rutherford
county line. Lake Summit in Henderson

County and Lake Adger in Polk County are on Green River. The Peter Guice Bridge on Interstate 26 across the river is the second-highest bridge in the eastern United States after the New River Gorge Bridge in West Virginia.

Green River, community in e Polk County between Mill Creek and Whiteoak Creek.

Green River Gap, on the Henderson-Polk county line. Alt. 2,700. Green River rises nearby.

Green River Township, s Henderson County.

Greensboro, city and county seat, central Guilford County. Alt. 838. Est. 1808 and inc. 1810. Named for Gen. Nathanael Greene (1742–86), American leader at Battle of Guilford Courthouse, 1781. Produces textiles, fabricated metals, food products, tobacco products, chemicals, drugs, aircraft parts, and electronics. The University of North Carolina at Greensboro, Bennett College, Greensboro College, Guilford College, and North Carolina Agricultural and Technical State University are located there.

Greens Branch rises in n Columbus County and flows se into West Prong Creek.

Greens Creek rises in w Jackson County and flows e into Savannah Creek.

Greens Creek rises in se Pamlico County and flows e into Neuse River. Appears as Powel's Creek on the Lawson map, 1709. Soon afterward it came to be known as Farnifold Green's Creek for Furnifold Green, who had a grant for 1,700 acres there in 1707. Green was killed by the Tuscarora Indians in 1714.

Greens Creek rises in se Polk County and flows ne into Whiteoak Creek.

Greens Creek, community in w Jackson County on Savannah Creek. Alt. 2,120.

Greens Creek Township, w Jackson County.

Greens Creek Township, se Polk County.

Green's Ferry. *See* Spring Bank.

Greens Fork, community in central Gates County.

Greens Gap, on the Jackson-Macon county line.

Green's Grove. *See* Washburns Store.

Greens Land is the name applied on the Ogilby map, 1671, to that part of present-day Pamlico County that lies between the Pamlico and Bay Rivers.

Greens Millpond, w central Gates County on Cole Creek. Covers approx. 30 acres; max. depth 8 ft. Formerly known as Lilleys Millpond.

Greens Mill Run rises in central Pitt County and flows ne into Tar River. Approx. 6½ mi. long. Perhaps the same stream as Rock Creek on the Moseley map, 1733, and the Collet map, 1770.

Greens Point, a projection of n Hatteras Island into Pamlico Sound, e Dare County beside the community of Rodanthe.

Greens Store, community in se Rutherford County.

Greens Thorofare, channel of water separated from the main body of Neuse River and bypassing a curve in the river in n Craven County. Name appears in local records as early as 1819. Land in the area was included in a 1707 grant to Furnifold Green, killed by the Tuscarora Indians in 1714.

Greenstreet Mountain, n Wilkes County parallel to East Prong Roaring River. Named for a local family.

Green Swamp, nw Brunswick and e Columbus Counties, an area of approx. 140 sq. mi. of peat and muck timberland. In 1795 the state of North Carolina granted 170,120 acres there to Benjamin Rowell, William Collins, and Stephen Williams. *See also* River View Community.

Green Swamp, n Pender County between Angola Bay and Northeast Cape Fear River, drains sw into Northeast Cape Fear River.

Green Top, mountain peak in sw Buncombe County between Rich Knob and Yellow Gap.

Green Valley, the valley through which Round Hill Branch flows in nw Buncombe County.

Green Valley, community in w Ashe County.

Greenville, city and county seat, central Pitt County on Tar River. Est. 1771 as Martinsborough, named for Josiah Martin (1737–86), last royal governor of North Carolina, serving from 1771 to 1775. Name changed in 1786 to Greensville in honor of Nathanael Greene (1742–86), Revolutionary War general. With the passage of time, the name came to be spelled as it is today. East Carolina University, est. 1908, is located there. Produces tobacco, lumber, textiles, batteries, bakery products, and boats. Alt. 64.

Greenville Sound, e New Hanover County between Middle Sound on the n and Masonboro Sound on the s.

Greenville Township, central Pitt County.

Greenwood Township, former township in s Lee County, now township no. 1.

Greenwood Township, e Moore County.

Greer Branch rises in nw Swain County in Great Smoky Mountains National Park and flows sw into Twentymile Creek.

Greer Branch rises in s Watauga County and flows e into Middle Fork [South Fork New River].

Greer Creek rises in s central Henderson County and flows nw into Mud Creek.

Greer Creek. *See* South Fork.

Greer Knob, nw Swain County in Great Smoky Mountains National Park on Twentymile Ridge between Greer Branch and Proctor Sang Branch. Alt. 4,463.

Gregg Branch rises in central Buncombe County near Jack Gap and flows se into Beetree Creek.

Gregory, community in w Currituck County. Alt. 9.

Gregory Bald, peak on the Swain County, N.C.– Blount County, Tenn., line in Great Smoky Mountains National Park between Parsons Bald and Rich Gap. Alt. 4,948. Known earlier as Bald Spot Mountain.

Gregory Branch rises in e Cherokee County and flows nw into Pipes Branch.

Gregory Branch rises in nw Haywood County and flows se into Big Creek.

Gregory Crossroads, community in nw Onslow County near New River.

Gregory's Mill, community in e Granville County served by post office, 1848–1951.

Gresham's Lake, in central Wake County on Perry Creek ne of city of Raleigh. Formed in 1939 to cover 100 acres, with a max. depth of 30 ft. Named for owner, S. T. Gresham. Used for boating and fishing.

Gretna Green, community in w Halifax County.

Grey Eagle. *See* Black Mountain.

Greystone, community in e Vance County. Alt. 493. Settled by 1835 and named for gray granite once mined there in large quantities. Quarrying done by hand until 1885.

Grice Branch rises in se Buncombe County and flows sw into Broad River.

Gridiron, community in central Halifax County served by post office, 1900–1902.

Grier Bald. *See* Big Bald.

Griffins Crossroads, community in e Chatham County.

Griffins Township, se Martin County.

Griffins Township, nw Nash County.

Griffinsville. *See* Marshville.

Griffith, community in s Mecklenburg County.

Griffith Branch rises in w Mitchell County and flows s into Brummett Creek.

Griffith's Mill Pond. *See* Worrells Mill Pond.

Griffton. *See* Grifton.

Grifton, town in s Pitt and n Lenoir Counties. Known as Peter's Ferry as early as 1756, when Presbyterian minister Hugh McAden stopped there; in 1764 it was called Blount's Ford; and in the mid-nineteenth century, it was called Bell's Ferry for the ferry operated by Warren Bell. Inc. in 1883 as Bell's Ferry. Name changed to Griffton in 1889 to honor C. M. A. Griffin, local merchant. Griffton soon came to be spelled Grifton. Produces apparel. Alt. 28.

Grifton Township, s Pitt County. Created after 1950.

Griggs Branch rises in ne Cherokee County and flows sw between Fork Ridge and Old Mattie Ridge into Welch Mill Creek.

Grill Cove, nw Swain County in Great Smoky Mountains National Park on Ekaneetlee Creek.

Grimes Crossroads, community in ne Forsyth County. Also known as Crims Crossroads.

Grimesland, town in e Pitt County. The first settlement there in the eighteenth century was known as Boyd's Ferry, a name that it retained until after 1880. (Boyd's Ferry across the Tar River, ½ mi. ne of the town, continued to operate until after 1909.) For a short while it was called Mount Calvert, and in 1885 the post office was named Nelsonville. In 1887 the name was changed to Grimesland in honor of J. Bryan Grimes (1828–80), Confederate general. Inc. 1893. Alt. 36.

Grimesland Township, e Pitt County. Created after 1950.

Grimes Millpond, e Pitt County, drains into Chicod Creek.

Grimshawes, community on the head of the Chattooga River in s Jackson County. Named for the first postmaster, Thomas Grimshawe Sr. Touted as site of "world's smallest post office."

Grimsley, community in n Ashe County served by post office, 1886–1911.

Grindle Creek rises in n Pitt County and flows

se into Tar River. Probably named for the fish *amiatus calva*, commonly known as grindle.

Grindle Pocosin, n Pitt County.

Grindool. *See* Whitehurst.

Grindstone Branch rises in central Anson County and flows n into Goulds Fork.

Grindstone Knob, e Macon County at the head of Indian Camp Creek.

Grindstone Knob, e Macon County between Ellijay Creek and Walnut Creek.

Grindstone Ridge, nw Henderson County near Bradley Creek.

Grinnel Hill, community in n Tyrrell County near town of Columbia.

Grinnell Creek, swampy low grounds of se Bertie County between Broad Creek and Middle River.

Grinnel Slough, stream and swamp in s Pitt County between Contentnea and Swift Creeks and bordered on the s by Neuse River. The stream flows nw into Contentnea Creek.

Grissettown, community in sw Brunswick County.

Grissett Swamp rises in sw Columbus County and flows se into Monie Swamp.

Grissom, community in se Granville County served by post office, 1877–1914. Formerly called Slab Town.

Grist Mountain, e Davidson County between Flat Swamp Creek and Lick Creek.

Grists, community in w Columbus County.

Grit, community in nw Pender County served by post office, 1893–1905.

Grogan Creek rises in n Transylvania County and flows ne into Davidson River.

Grogansville, town in nw Rockingham County est. on property of tobacco grower John P. Grogan. Inc. 1889 but never functioned as a municipality.

Grog Creek rises in e Rutherford County and flows s into Cleveland County, where it enters Sandy Run Creek.

Grog Creek rises in s Rutherford County and flows w into Broad River.

Groometown, community in s Guilford County. Named for local family.

Gross Mine, former gold mine in s Yadkin County on Harmon Creek.

Grotto, community in n Moore County served by post office, 1893–1905.

Groundhog Branch rises in s Watauga County and flows se into Yadkin Creek.

Groundhog Creek rises in n Haywood County and flows sw into Pigeon River.

Groundhog Ridge, nw Cherokee County in the Unicoi Mountains.

Groundnut Creek rises in nw Lenoir County and flows se into Moseley Creek. Named for the groundnut, or peanut. Groundnut Swamp appears in local records as early as 1750–60.

Grove Creek rises in central Duplin County and flows e into Northeast Cape Fear River. Appears on the Collet map, 1770, as Grove Swamp.

Grove Hill, community in s Warren County e of Buffalo Creek and s of Reedy Creek. Settled prior to 1800; post office est. 1828 but discontinued in 1954. In 1840 the post office name was temporarily changed to Owens Store. *See also* Fontena.

Grovemont, community in se Buncombe County n of Swannanoa.

Grovemont. *See* Kenansville.

Grover, town in s Cleveland County. Inc. 1885. Alt. 877. Named for Grover Cleveland (1837–1908), president of the United States, 1885–89 and 1893–97. Produces textiles.

Grovestone, community in se Buncombe County between Swannanoa and Black Mountain.

Grove Swamp. *See* Grove Creek.

Grove Township, e Harnett County. Named for Congressman William Barry Grove (1764–1818) of Fayetteville.

Gudger. *See* Newfoundland.

Gudger Knob, e Haywood County on the ne end of Crab Orchard Fields.

Gudger's Ford. *See* Azalea.

Gudger's Mills, community in nw Buncombe County served by post office, 1888–1906.

Guerilla Island, n Camden County. Used by local Confederates led by Capt. William Sanderlin. Target of Union troops under Gen. Edward Wild, 1863.

Guerrant Springs. *See* Oregon Hill.

Guffy Branch rises in s Wake County and flows s into Ditch Branch.

Guide, community in s Columbus County.

Guilders Creek rises in n central Yancey County on n slopes of Rocky Knob and Phillips Knob and flows nw into Jacks Creek.

Guilford, community in s central Beaufort County.

Guilford, community in w central Guilford County. Named for the county.

Guilford College, town in w central Guilford County. Quaker settlement founded 1750 and known as New Garden. Boarding school opened 1837; renamed Guilford College in 1888, at which time the community name also was changed. Chartered 1895. The college is now within the limits of the city of Greensboro. Alt. 949.

Guilford County was formed in 1771 from Rowan and Orange Counties. Located in the n central section of the state, it is bounded by Alamance, Randolph, Davidson, Forsyth, and Rockingham Counties. It was named for Francis North, first Earl of Guilford (1704–90), member of Parliament and intimate personal friend of George III and Queen Charlotte. Area: 652 sq. mi. County seat: Greensboro, with an elevation of 838 ft. Townships are Bruce, Center Grove, Clay, Deep River, Fentress, Friendship, Gilmer, Greene, High Point, Jamestown, Jefferson, Madison, Monroe, Morehead, Oak Ridge, Rock Creek, Sumner, and Washington. Produces tobacco, corn, wheat, oats, barley, rye, sorghum, poultry, eggs, dairy products, livestock, hogs, horses, greenhouse products, flowers, textiles, paper boxes, strawberries, soybeans, fabricated metals, aircraft parts, cigarettes, electronics, appliances, pharmaceuticals, toys, lumber, chemicals, and corrugated boxes.

Guilford Courthouse, former county seat, central Guilford County. Est. 1774; chartered as Martinville, *which see*, 1785; abandoned 1808. Battle there on March 15, 1781, between American Gen. Nathanael Greene and British general Lord Charles Cornwallis; site now a National Military Park.

Guinea Mill Run, a stream, rises in n Currituck County and flows se into Tull Creek. A part of Dismal Swamp drains into Guinea Mill Run.

Gulden Creek rises in se Craven County and flows nw into Clubfoot Creek.

Gulf, town in s central Chatham County. Inc. 1913, but long inactive in municipal affairs. Early nineteenth-century center of trade and coal mining. Alt. 275. The geographic center of the state, *which see*, is nearby.

Gulf Branch rises in nw Burke County and flows sw into Linville River.

Gulf Branch rises in s Macon County and flows n into Big Laurel Branch.

Gulf Creek rises in se Chatham County and flows sw into Cape Fear River.

Gulf Prong rises in ne Swain County and flows s to join Chasm Prong in forming Bradley Fork.

Gulf Stream is a warm current in the Atlantic Ocean that flows out of the Gulf of Mexico along the e coast of the United States and e in the North Atlantic toward Europe. Along the coast of North Carolina, it approaches Cape Hatteras and gives that part of the state a milder winter than would otherwise be the case. Winter temperatures of the surface waters there are approx. 63°, while summer temperatures are about 80°. The Gulf Stream was first described by Benjamin Franklin, and it appears on a map prepared for him in 1770 by Timothy Folger.

Gulf Township, sw Chatham County.

Gul Island. *See* Great Island.

Gulledge Township, s central Anson County.

Gulley's Mill, community in s Wake County.

Gulley's Mills, community in se Wake County served by post office, 1878–1903.

Gull Island, a tiny island in sw Carteret County in Bogue Sound.

Gull Island Bay, on the w shore of Hatteras Island in the waters of Pamlico Sound, s Dare County opposite Gull Island.

Gull Rock, community in e Hyde County on Wyesocking Bay. A former post office there was Gulrock.

Gull Shoal, a small island in Pamlico Sound off the w shore of Hatteras Island, se Dare County. The name appears in local records as early as 1794 as "Gull Shore."

Gull Shore. *See* Gull Shoal.

Gulrock. *See* Gull Rock.

Gumberry, community in n central Northampton County. Settled about 1882. Alt. 134. Name probably derived from fruit of a tree described by John Lawson in 1709 as a type of black gum, the berries of which were used by the Indians in making soup and in cooking peas and beans.

Gumberry Swamp rises in w Northampton County and flows s to join Lily Pond Creek in forming Wheeler Creek. For origin of name, *see* Gumberry.

Gum Branch rises in sw Gates County and flows ne into Taylor Millpond.

Gum Branch rises in w Hoke County and flows se into Rockfish Creek.

Gum Branch rises in w Mecklenburg County and flows w into Long Creek.

Gum Branch rises in se Wilson County and flows nw into Whiteoak Swamp.

Gum Branch, community in n Onslow County between Cowhorn Swamp and Bachelors Swamp. Mentioned in local records as early as 1748. Served by post office, 1860–1903.

Gum Corner, community in w Currituck County.

Gum Creek rises in e Stanly County and flows se into Cedar Creek.

Gumflats Creek rises in ne Cherokee County and flows nw into Taylor Creek.

Gum Fork rises in n Lee County and flows ne into Hughes Creek.

Gum Forks, community in nw Northampton County.

Gum Lake, ne Nash County on Beaverdam Swamp.

Gumlog Creek rises in Union County, Ga., and flows ne into Clay County, where it enters Brasstown Creek.

Gum Log Creek rises in s Union County and flows se into Lanes Creek.

Gum Neck, community in s Tyrrell County on a canal, which flows se into Alligator River.

Gum Neck Creek, commonly called Gum Neck Landing, rises in se Tyrrell County and flows s into Alligator River. Appears as Landing Creek on the Collet map, 1770.

Gum Neck Landing. *See* Gum Neck Creek.

Gum Neck Township, s Tyrrell County.

Gum Pond, swamp in Grindle Pocosin in n Pitt County.

Gumstand Gap, n Transylvania County on Seniard Ridge.

Gum Swamp, se Beaufort and nw Pamlico Counties.

Gum Swamp rises in w Columbus County and flows se to join Beaverdam Swamp in forming Monie Swamp.

Gum Swamp rises in e Duplin County and flows sw into Limestone Creek.

Gum Swamp rises in s Hoke County and flows se into Robeson County, where it enters Lumber River.

Gum Swamp rises in nw Jones County w of the town of Dover and flows nw into Craven County, where it enters Tracey Swamp. Formerly both were known as Gum Swamp. Two Civil War engagements took place on Gum Swamp, one on April 28, 1863, and the other on May 22, 1863. The first engagement is called by various names, including Wise's (Wyse's) Crossroads, Dover Crossroads, and First Gum Swamp.

Gum Swamp rises in se Martin County and flows s into Beaufort County, where it enters Latham Creek.

Gum Swamp rises in ne Pender County and flows s into Angola Creek.

Gum Swamp rises in w Pitt County and flows se into Swift Creek.

Gum Swamp rises in n Tyrrell County and flows ne into Albemarle Sound.

Gum Swamp Creek rises in n Lenoir County and flows sw into Falling Creek. Name appears in local records dating from before the Revolution. Named for sweet gum trees in the area; sometimes locally called Sweetgum Swamp.

Gum Swamp Creek rises in e Richmond County and nw Scotland County and flows s across Scotland County into South Carolina, where it enters Little Pee Dee River.

Gum Swamp Run rises in se Beaufort County in Gum Swamp and flows w into South Creek.

Gumtree, community in n Davidson County; named for a gum tree (cut down about 1948) at the junction of the Thomasville and Lexington roads to Winston-Salem.

Gun Creek rises in w central Alamance County and flows se into Great Alamance Creek.

Gunlock Ridge, w Swain County between Hickory Cove and Hazel Creek.

Gunna Creek rises in nw Swain County and flows sw to join Tub-Mill Creek in Great Smoky Mountains National Park to form Eagle Creek.

Gunntown, community in central Rockingham County; est. 1854 by James M. Gunn and largely populated by his descendants.

Gunpowder Creek rises in central Caldwell County and flows se into Catawba River.

Gunt, Gun, or **Gant Inlet**, from the Atlantic Ocean into Pamlico Sound through Bodie

Island, opened prior to 1733 and closed in the 1770s. Appears as Gun Inlet on the Moseley map, 1733.

Gunter Branch rises in n Madison County and flows sw into Big Laurel Creek.

Gunter Fork rises on the e slope of Luftee Knob, w Haywood County in Great Smoky Mountains National Park, and flows ne into Big Creek.

Gunter Gap, on the Jackson-Swain county line near the head of Connelly Creek in se Swain County.

Gunter Knob, s Madison County at the head of Simmons Branch.

Guntertown, community in n Madison County on Barnes Creek.

Gupton, community in Franklin County. Alt. 300. Settled about 1898. Named for J. E. Gupton, local landowner.

Gurleys Store, community in e central Rutherford County between Heaveners and Robinson Creeks.

Gurley Store, community in w Wayne County between Little River and Nahunta Swamp.

Gusher Knob, mountain in sw Avery County. Site of a plant for processing fine china clay.

Gut, The, central Craven County, a channel extending between Bachelor Creek and Neuse River forming the n boundary of Hog Island. Approx. 1 mi. long.

Gutches Creek rises in n Mitchell County and flows s into Little Rock Creek.

Guthrie, community in e Forsyth County. In 1858 Jackson Guthries and two other men from Virginia settled there and began growing tobacco.

Guthrie Point extends from the mainland of sw Carteret County into Bogue Sound.

Gutter Branch rises in w Mecklenburg County and flows w into Long Creek.

Guy Knob, s Macon County between Mashburn Branch and Hayes Mill Creek.

Guyton, community in w Bladen County served by post office, 1892–1922.

Gwaltneys Township, ne Alexander County.

Gwinns Millpond, se Richmond and w Scotland Counties on Joes Creek. Covers 75 acres; max. depth 10 ft. Formed prior to 1909.

Gwyn, community in s Yadkin County served by post office, 1900–1907.

Gypsy, community in nw Henderson County served by post office, 1880–1902.

H

Haas Creek rises in s Catawba County and flows s into Pott Creek.

Hachers Run. *See* Hatcher's Run.

Hackett, community in w Watauga County.

Hack Gap Knob, n Madison County on Colvin Creek.

Hacklan Branch rises in n Gates County and flows s, where it is joined by Buckland Mill Branch in forming Cole Creek.

Hackney, community in sw Beaufort County.

Haddock, community in central Columbus County served by post office, 1884–1903.

Haddocks Crossroads, community in s Pitt County.

Hadley, community in e Duplin County approx. 3 mi. e of town of Beulaville.

Hadleys Mill, community in central Chatham County on Landum Creek. An early nineteenth-century post office was there. Old mill still standing but not in use.

Hadley's Mill Pond. *See* Contentnea Lake.

Hadley Township, nw Chatham County.

Hadnot Creek rises in w Carteret County and flows about 5 mi. sw into White Oak River. Named for an early settler.

Hadnot Point, in central Onslow County at the junction of Wallace Creek and New River. The headquarters and hospital of Camp Lejeune Marine Corps Air Station are there. Said to have been named for Charles Hadnot, an early settler.

Hagaman, community in n central Caldwell County. Named for Hagaman family, large landowners in the vicinity.

Hagaman. *See* Brushy Fork.

Hagan Creek rises in s Surry County and flows se into Yadkin River.

Hagan Fork rises in central Catawba County and flows ne into McLin Creek.

Hagers, community in e Lincoln County served by post office, 1889–1903.

Hagers Mountain, n Person County between Fishing Branch and Mitchell Creek.

Haines Cove, e Haywood County between Conner Mill Branch and Anderson Mountain.

Haines Eyebrow, peak in nw McDowell County near the head of Buck Creek.

Hairston, town in se Stokes County. Inc. 1793 as Hairstonborough, but long inactive in municipal affairs.

Hairy Bear Mountain. *See* Big Tom.

Halcher Swamp rises in central Edgecombe County and flows nw into Harts Mill Run.

Halcombville, a town authorized in 1816 to be laid off on the lands of George D. Halcomb and Peter Dowel in Surry County. There is no evidence that the town was actually established.

Hale, community in n Avery County served by post office, 1911–15.

Hale Cove, n Buncombe County between Frosty Knob and Paint Fork.

Hales Beach, a section of outer beach in sw Brunswick County extending from Shallotte Inlet to Tubbs Inlet.

Hale Wood, community in s Madison County served by post office, 1871–1908.

Half Acre Ridge, w Haywood County in Great Smoky Mountains National Park, a short spur extending nw from Cataloochee Divide near lat. 35°37′45″ N., long. 83°04′15″ W., between Den Branch and Winding Stair Branch.

Half Moon, community in n Onslow County between Bachelors Delight Swamp and Half Moon Creek.

Half-Moon Bay, w Carteret County in White Oak River between Terrapin Run and Hill's Bay. Named for the adjacent channel.

Half Moon Branch rises in nw Craven County and flows ne into Neuse River. Appears in local records as early as 1770. *See also* Cove Creek.

Half-Moon Channel, in White Oak River, w Carteret and e Onslow Counties. The channel has gradually filled in and is no longer the main channel of the river.

Half Moon Creek rises in n Onslow County and flows w into New River. Appears as Half Moon Swamp in local records as early as 1744.

Half Moon Swamp. *See* Half Moon Creek.

Halfway Point, the southernmost point of Mackay Island, ne Currituck County. A name given by steamboat men.

Halifax, town and county seat, n Halifax County on Roanoke River. Authorized to be laid out, 1757; inc. 1760. Named for George Montagu, second Earl of Halifax (1716–71), who was president of the Board of Trade at the time the town was est. Alt. 135. The legislature met

there, 1779–81. Scene of meeting, April 12, 1775, where North Carolina representatives sanctioned American independence. *See also* Enfield.

Halifax County was formed in 1758 from Edgecombe County. Located in the ne section of the state, it is bounded by Bertie, Martin, Edgecombe, Nash, Warren, and Northampton Counties. It was named for George Montagu, second Earl of Halifax (1716–71), president of the Board of Trade and Plantations and called the "Father of the Colonies" for his success in extending American commerce. Area: 724 sq. mi. County seat: Halifax, with an elevation of 135 ft. Townships are Brinkleyville, Butterwood, Conoconnara, Enfield, Faucett, Halifax, Littleton, Palmyra, Roanoke Rapids, Roseneath, Scotland Neck, and Weldon. Produces peanuts, corn, oats, soybeans, tobacco, cotton, poultry, hogs, livestock, rubber products, textiles, paper, lumber, apparel, and sand. *See also* Roanoke County.

Halifax District, at the time of the 1790 census, was composed of Caswell, Chatham, Granville, Orange, Randolph, and Wake Counties.

Halifax Township, e Halifax County.

Hall, community on Scotts Creek in n Jackson County.

Hallback Mountain, s Yancey County approx. 1 mi. w of Mount Mitchell. Alt. 6,400 ft.

Hall Creek rises in sw tip of Burke County and flows n into Silver Creek.

Hallison. *See* Parkwood.

Hall Knob, sw Burke County. Alt. approx. 1,850.

Hall Mountain, n Macon County in a bend of Little Tennessee River.

Hallow. *See* Mount Airy.

Halloway, community in central Durham County.

Hallowing Point extends from the mainland of central Craven County at New Bern into the Neuse-Trent River estuary opposite Union Point. Appears on the Lawson map, 1709, and the Moll map, 1729.

Hall Pocosin, n Gates County.

Hall Point extends from mainland of ne Carteret County into mouth of Thorofare Bay.

Hall Pond, near the head of Little Beaverdam Creek in w Duplin County.

Halls, community in s Hertford County. Also known as Duke Hall or Dukie Hall's Crossing.

Hallsboro, town in central Columbus County. Settled 1888; inc. 1889, but long inactive in municipal affairs. Named for family of original settler. Produces lumber. Alt. 66.

Hallsborough was authorized to be laid out in se Surry County at the junction of Little Yadkin and Yadkin Rivers in 1809 on the land of John Hall. There is no evidence that the town was ever laid out.

Hallsborough. *See* Hallsville.

Hall's Branch rises in e Wake County and flows sw into Little River below Moore's Mill.

Hall's Creek rises in e Onslow County and flows sw into Queens Creek. Named for early settlers Edward and/or Thomas Hall. Also known as Hotel Creek.

Halls Creek rises in w Pasquotank County and flows sw into Little River. First North Carolina Assembly met on the banks of the creek in 1665.

Halls Crossroads, community in s Franklin County.

Halls Ferry, community in ne Davie County served by post office, 1878–1902. *See also* Siloam.

Halls Ferry Junction, community in n Stanly County. Named for the fact that railroad passengers changed trains there for the ferry over Yadkin River.

Halls Ford, s Swain County in Little Tennessee River at Horseshoe Bend.

Hall's Gut, a drain in e central Hertford County that empties into Chowan River.

Halls Harbor, a natural harbor in the s waters of Currituck Sound in s Currituck County.

Halls Knob, sw Cherokee County between the headwaters of Beech Creek and Nottely River.

Halls Marsh Branch rises in n Duplin County and flows s into Goshen Swamp.

Halls Mill Creek rises in n Wilkes County and flows sw into Mulberry Creek.

Halls Mills, community in n Wilkes County on Mulberry Creek.

Halls Point, s Onslow County, extends into New River.

Halls Township, n central Sampson County.

Hallsville, community on e side of Northeast Cape Fear River near the mouth of Limestone Creek, central Duplin County. Authorized to be laid out in 1818 on the lands of William Hall Sr. and sons and named Hallsborough. Post office est. as early as 1828.

Hall Swamp, community in w Beaufort County.

Hall Top, central Haywood County on Chestnut Flat Ridge.

Hall Township, w Gates County. Formerly known as Scratch Hall Township; origin of name unknown.

Ham, community in central Bladen County served by post office, 1885–1912.

Hambey Bend, a bend in Hiwassee River, w Cherokee County, near the mouth of Anderson Creek below Hiwassee Dam.

Hambton Creek rises in s Cherokee County and flows nw into Hiwassee River.

Hamburg Ditch flows through Dismal Swamp in ne Gates County, connecting Corapeake Swamp with Cross Canal in nw Camden County. Both canals were known as Cross Canal in 1808 and as White Oak Spring Canal in 1833.

Hamburg Gap, on the Jackson-Macon county line n of Yellow Mountain.

Hamburg Mountain, n Buncombe County e of Weaverville. Alt. 2,910. Traditionally the site of neutral hunting grounds used by Cherokee and Catawba Indians.

Hamburg Township, sw Jackson County.

Hamby Branch rises in e central Cabarrus County and flows s into Rocky River.

Hamby Mountain, w Wilkes County between Smithies Creek and North Prong Lewis Fork Creek. Probably named for William Hamby, an eighteenth-century settler on North Prong Lewis Fork Creek.

Hambys Creek rises in e Davidson County and flows sw and nw into Rich Fork Creek.

Hamer, community in n central Caswell County. A post office operated there, 1882–1904.

Hamer Creek rises in sw Montgomery County and flows se into Richmond County, where it enters Little River.

Hamilton, town in n Martin County on Roanoke River. Known as Milton prior to 1804, when the name was changed to Hamilton and the town inc. Probably named for Alexander Hamilton (1757–1804). Also in 1804 the polling place at nearby Hogtown, *which see*, was combined with that at Hamilton. Produces textiles.

Hamilton Creek. *See* Washington Creek.

Hamilton Hollow, valley in nw Swain County between Fox Gap and Twentymile Creek.

Hamilton Lakes, former town in central Guilford County est. by Alfred M. Scales. Inc. 1925; merged with city of Greensboro in 1945.

Hamiltons Crossroads, community in e Union County w of Gourdvine Creek.

Hamiltons Old Field, former community in central Rutherford County 3 mi. n of present Rutherfordton. In 1862 residents claimed to have been the first to nominate Zebulon B. Vance for governor.

Hamilton Township, nw Martin County.

Hamilton Township. *See* Catawba Township.

Hamlet, town in s Richmond County. Settled about 1875. Inc. 1897. Named by John Shortridge, local citizen, for the word then descriptive of its size. An important railroad center with maintenance shops, hump classification yard, and other facilities. Produces dairy products, apparel, and furniture. Alt. 349.

Hamlins Shoals, rapids in Roanoke River, nw Halifax County, extending from the mouth of Stonehouse Creek to Tucker Island. The name appears on the MacRae map, 1833. *See also* Tucker Island.

Hammer Branch rises in n Swain County in Great Smoky Mountains National Park and flows se into Deep Creek.

Hammers Millpond, in w Robeson and sw Scotland Counties on Little Pee Dee River.

Hammock, The, e bank of the mouth of Queens Creek in se Onslow County. Called Starkey's Hammock in the 1790s, when it was owned by Edward Starkey. Long site of summer meetings by black teachers.

Hammocks Beach, resort on Bear Island, Onslow County. A state park.

Hammond Mountain, s Henderson County between Mill Creek and Cabin Creek. Alt. 2,978.

Hammonds Creek rises in central Bladen County and flows ne into Cape Fear River. Appears on the Moseley map, 1733.

Hampstead, community in se Pender County. Alt. 56.

Hampton, former community in sw Granville County served by post office, 1879–1906. Was located near Durham-Granville county line and dated from the nineteenth century. The site now lies within the Butner area. Ceased to exist when Camp Butner was created. *See also* Butner.

Hampton. *See* Ruth.

Hampton Bay. *See* Pettivers Bay.

Hampton Branch rises in nw Macon County and flows s into Partridge Creek.

Hampton Branch rises in e Madison County and flows sw into Puncheon Fork Creek.

Hampton Branch rises in n Yancey County and flows ne into Mine Fork Creek.

Hampton Lake, in s Jackson County on Fowler Creek at High Hampton Estate about 1 mi. e of town of Cashiers. Named for Wade Hampton, South Carolina governor and Confederate general, founder of the estate. Was formed in 1918 and today covers 24 acres, with a max. depth of 25 ft. Used for recreation.

Hampton Lodge, community on n end of Church Island in central Currituck County.

Hampton Township, nw Davidson County.

Hamptonville, town in s Yadkin County near South Deep Creek. Settled about 1738; chartered 1818, but long inactive in municipal affairs. Named for Hampton family, early settlers who came from England.

Hamrick, community in se Yancey County on South Toe River.

Hams Crossroads, community in e Pitt County.

Hancock Bay, e Carteret County between Tusk Creek and Middens Creek.

Hancock Creek rises in s Craven County and flows n into Neuse River. Now within the limits of Cherry Point Marine Corps Air Station. Appears as Handcocks Creek on the Moseley map, 1733. *See also* Hancock Town.

Hancock Point, w Carteret County, extends into White Oak River.

Hancock Town appears on Moseley map, 1733, as Handcocks Town in present Craven County. It was the Tuscarora Indian village of King Hancock, who participated in the 1710 attack on New Bern.

Hancock Village, part of Cherry Point housing area in se Craven County. *See also* Cherry Point.

Handpole Branch rises in central Avery County and flows n into Kentucky Creek.

Handy, community in se Davidson County. Residents formerly received mail at Jackson Hill, 3 mi. w, and wanted a post office that would be "handy" for them. Post office est. 1889, discontinued 1931.

Handy Gap, n Wilkes County on Carters Mountain. Named for local family.

Hanes or **Hanestown**, former community in s Forsyth County. Named for Hanes family, which est. a mill village there. Now within the corporate limits of Winston-Salem. Alt. 887.

Haney Creek rises in s Yancey County and flows e into Elk Fork.

Hanging Bluff. *See* Hanging Rock State Park.

Hanging Dog, community in nw Cherokee County.

Hanging Dog Creek rises in n Cherokee County on Hanging Dog Mountain and flows sw into Hiwassee River. It was named because an Indian's hunting dog became hung in a mass of jammed logs and vines in the flooded creek.

Hanging Dog Gap, n Cherokee County in the n end of Hanging Dog Mountain.

Hanging Dog Mountain extends from central Cherokee County ne into the Snowbird Mountains in sw Graham County. Named peaks include Buzzard Roost, High Peak, and Rocky Knob.

Hanging Rock, on the Avery-Watauga county line at the sw end of Hanging Rock Ridge. Alt. 5,237. Known by the Cherokee Indians as *Yonah-wayah* (bear's paw).

Hanging Rock, e Mitchell County between Hanging Rock Branch and Gouges Creek.

Hanging Rock Branch rises in e Mitchell County and flows sw into Beaver Creek.

Hanging Rock Ridge extends ne from Hanging Rock on the Avery-Watauga county line between Dutch Creek and Watauga River to Townsend Gap in s Watauga County.

Hanging Rock State Park, central Stokes County in the Sauratown Mountain range. Named for a natural rock formation. Contains 3,865 acres. Est. 1935. Scenic, recreational; vacation cabins and tent and trailer camping; picnicking, swimming, boating, fishing, hiking, and nature study; lookout tower. *See also* Cascade Falls; Moores Knob; Tories Den. Appears as Hanging Bluff on the Kerr map, 1882.

Hangman Branch rises in Drowned Bay, sw Brunswick County, and flows s into Calabash Creek.

Hangover Creek rises in w Graham County in Saddle Tree Gap and flows nw into Slickrock Creek.

Hangover Lead, nw Graham County, extends nw from Saddle Tree Gap to Cold Spring Knob and ne from Cold Spring Knob to Yellowhammer Gap.

Hangover Mountain, w Graham County near the Tennessee line. Alt. approx. 5,180.

Hankins, community in e central McDowell County.

Hanks Branch rises in e Davidson County and flows e into Hunts Fork.

Hanlon Mountain, nw Buncombe County e of Fodderstack Mountain. Alt. 3,197.

Hannah Branch rises in e Yancey County and flows w into South Toe River.

Hannah Creek rises in w Johnston County and flows se into Mill Creek.

Hannah Mountain, s Macon County between Mulberry Gap and Norton Branch.

Hannersville, community in central Davidson County served by post office, 1859–1920.

Hanrahan, community in sw Pitt County.

Hanted Pond, The. *See* Jumping Run.

Haoe (hey-yo), mountain in w Graham County near the Tennessee line. Alt. 5,249. Named after John Stratton Sr., pioneer settler who climbed the mountain, straddled the line, and looked into Tennessee and shouted "Hey-yo." He then turned toward North Carolina and repeated the shout.

Haoe Lead, w Graham County between Saddle Tree Gap and Rock Creek Knob.

Haoe Trail encircles Joyce Kilmer Memorial Forest in w Graham County and leads through the center of the forest following the main course of Little Santeetlah Creek.

Hap Mountain, sw Madison County. Alt. 4,072.

Happy Hill, s Macon County between High Holly and Pipetrack Gap.

Happy Home, community in ne Rockingham County named for local Christian church organized in 1884.

Happy Home. *See* Connelly Springs; Rutherford College.

Happy Top, s Cherokee County s of Nottely River and w of Laudermilk Bend.

Happy Valley, the valley of the upper Yadkin River in n central Caldwell County between the town of Patterson and the Wilkes County line. Site of the homes of several prominent early settlers.

Harbinger, community on s tip of Currituck

County. Named for a steamboat that once docked there.

Harbon Cove, e Haywood County on Bald Creek.

Harbor Channel, s Carteret County in Bogue Sound between Morehead City and Sugar Loaf Island.

Harbor Island, ne Carteret County in Core Sound midway between Chainshot Island and Wainwright Island. Appears on the Moseley map, 1733. Once horseshoe-shaped, but storms have caused erosion, and much of it is now washed away. The site of fishermen's huts and anchorage. *See also* Hunting Quarter Sound.

Harbor Island, e New Hanover County w of Wrightsville Beach.

Harbour, community in s Surry County served by post office, 1889–1906.

Hardbargain Branch rises in ne Rutherford County and flows se into First Broad River.

Hardee Creek rises in s Pitt County and flows n into Tar River.

Hardin, community in ne Cherokee County nw of Andrews.

Hardin, town in n Gaston County on South Fork Catawba River. Inc. 1887 as Hardin and in 1897 as town of Hardin Cotton Mills. Prior to 1887, that portion of the town on the n side of the river was known as Worth, which is still the railroad name. Long inactive in municipal affairs. Alt. 679.

Hardin Creek rises in central Watauga County and flows se into South Fork New River.

Harding Swamp rises in w Beaufort County and flows w to join Juniper Swamp in forming East Branch Chicod Creek. Mentioned in local records as early as 1750.

Hardison Mill Creek rises in s Martin County and flows nw into Statons Pond on Sweetwater Creek.

Hard Ridge, s Haywood County, extends ne in an arc from the head of Gaddis Branch to Factor Branch.

Hardscrabble Branch rises in w Yancey County and flows ne into Cane River. Named by early settlers, who found the soil there to be so unproductive that they had a "hard scrabble" to make a living.

Hard Slate Gap, w Graham County between Hooper Mill Creek and Snowbird Creek.

Hardy, community in w Johnston County.

Hardy Creek, a short stream in n central Carteret County flowing e into South River.

Hardy Creek rises in s Stanly County and flows s into Rocky River.

Hardy Mill Branch rises in w Johnston County and flows ne into Black Creek.

Hardy Store, community in e Wayne County near West Bear Creek. Named for a family living in the area before the Revolution.

Hares Branch rises in w Hertford County and flows ne into Worrell Mill Pond.

Hares Creek rises in s Graham County and flows ne into Tulula Creek. Named for Jim Hare, early black resident of the area.

Hares Crossroads, community in n Johnston County.

Hare's Mill Pond, e Hertford County near the mouth of Deep Creek. Formed about 1736. Covers approx. 75 acres; max. depth 10 ft.

Hare Snipe Creek rises in nw Wake County and flows se into Crabtree Creek.

Hargetts Store, community in w Jones County.

Hargrove. *See* Providence.

Hargrove Crossroads, community in ne Sampson County.

Hariots Island. *See* Batts Island.

Harkers Island, se Carteret County between The Straits and Back Sound, approx. 5 mi. long and 1 mi. wide. Granted to Thomas Sparrow, March 21, 1714; later sold to Ebenezer Harker, September 15, 1730. Known as Craney Island until 1783, when three brothers who owned the island—Zachary, James, and Ebenezer Harker—divided it among themselves. In 1957 the entire island was inc. as the town of Harkers Island. Appears as Davers Island on the Smith map, 1624, and as Crane Island on the Moseley map, 1733. On the latter map, the name Harker appears to denote the owner.

Harkers Island Township, on Back Sound, The Straits, and the Atlantic Ocean in s Carteret County. Believed to have been home of Manteo, the Indian who befriended the Roanoke colonists, 1587.

Harley, community in w Wilkes County on South Prong Lewis Fork Creek. Named for Harley Thompson, nineteenth-century resident.

Harley Branch rises in e Haywood County and flows sw into East Fork Pigeon River.

Harlowe, community in n central Carteret County on Harlowe Creek.

Harlowe Canal. *See* Clubfoot Canal.

Harlowe Creek rises in central Carteret County and flows s into Newport River. A canal connects the creek with Clubfoot Creek, affording a waterway from Neuse River to Newport River.

Harlowe Township, on Newport River and Core Creek, n central Carteret County; formed from a part of Newport Township in 1917.

Harm Creek rises in e Henderson County and flows e into Polk County, where it enters Brights Creek.

Harmiller Gap, n Yancey County near the head of Howell Branch.

Harmon, community in nw Wilkes County near the head of North Fork Reddies River.

Harmon Creek rises in s Yadkin County and flows ne into South Deep Creek.

Harmon Den Mountain, n Haywood County between Cold Springs Creek and Tom Hall Branch.

Harmon Gap, n Avery County.

Harmon Knob, n Watauga County s and w of Norris Fork.

Harmon's Crossroads. *See* Aulander.

Harmony, town in ne Iredell County. Originally known as Harmony Hill because of the "protracted" or "harmony" meetings held there beginning about 1850. Inc. 1874 as Harmony Hill Camp Ground; name changed to Harmony in 1927. A late nineteenth-century academy there became the first high school in the county, 1907. Alt. 993.

Harmony Hill Camp Ground. *See* Harmony.

Harnet Cove, sw Buncombe County sw of Yellow Gap.

Harnett, community in s Harnett County. Gravel deposits are present.

Harnett County was formed in 1855 from Cumberland County. Located in the e section of the state, it is bounded by Chatham, Cumberland, Hoke, Moore, Lee, Wake, and Johnston Counties. It was named for Cornelius Harnett (1723–81), Revolutionary War patriot, president of the Provincial Council and the Council of Safety, and delegate to the Continental Congress. Area: 607 sq. mi. County seat: Lillington, with an elevation of 325 ft. Townships are Anderson Creek, Averasboro, Barbecue, Black River, Buckhorn, Duke, Grove, Hectors Creek, Johnsonville, Lillington, Neills Creek, Stewarts Creek, and Upper Little River. Produces tobacco, corn, wheat, oats, soybeans, cotton, sweet potatoes, poultry, hogs, livestock, pumpkins, mobile homes, concrete products, lumber, textiles, sand, and gravel.

Harnett Township, e New Hanover County.

Harold. *See* South Creek.

Harper Branch rises in central Jones County and flows e into Mill Run.

Harper Creek is formed in se Avery County by the junction of North Harper and South Harper creeks. It flows e into Caldwell County, where it enters Wilsons Creek.

Harper Creek rises in n Henderson County and flows se into Clear Creek.

Harpers, community in s Johnston County served by post office, 1876–1903.

Harpers Crossroads, community in sw Chatham County e of Beck Mountain.

Harpertown, community in Wilkes County on w outskirts of Lenoir. Largely African American; founded by former slaves.

Harrells, town largely in se Sampson County, although a small area of the inc. limits lies in sw Duplin County. Appears as Harrells Store on the Morse-Breese map, 1843. Inc. 1943 as Harrells Store; name changed to Harrells, 1955. Alt. 88.

Harrells Bay, swamp in sw Duplin County.

Harrells Quarter, community in se Bertie County.

Harrellsville, town in se Hertford County on Wiccacon River. Inc. 1883. Post office est. there in 1827 as Bethel. Name changed to Harrellsville in 1847 to honor Abner Harrell.

Harrellsville Township, se Hertford County.

Harrell Swamp rises in e Gates County and flows sw to join Duke Swamp and Raynor Swamp in forming Bennetts Creek.

Harrell Township, n central Mitchell County.

Harrelson Branch rises in n Duplin County and flows e into Northeast Cape Fear River.

Harrelsonville, community in central Columbus County.

Harricane, community in n Wake County. For many years the area was notorious for its distillers. The name came from a hurricane that struck the section in 1805, causing extensive damage.

Harrington, community in w Harnett County. Cornwallis camped there en route to Wilmington following the Battle of Guilford Courthouse. A post office was est. there, 1855. John McLean Harrington edited and published a handwritten newspaper there, 1858–60.

Harris, community in central Jackson County served by office, 1892–1911. Also known as Harris Mine.

Harris, community in s Moore County between Big Juniper Creek and McLendons Creek.

Harris, community in s Rutherford County. Est. about 1909 when the Carolina, Clinchfield, and Ohio Railway built a station there. Post office est. 1912 as Orenburg since there was another post office named Harris in the state. In 1914 the first Harris post office closed, and the name was then taken by the former Orenburg post office. Named for a local family.

Harris Branch rises in w Yancey County and flows s into Lickskillet Branch.

Harrisburg, community in sw Cabarrus County. First Known as Harris Depot. Alt. 610.

Harrisburg. *See* Harris Burgh.

Harris Burgh appears on the Collet map, 1770. It was the location of the Granville County courthouse for various periods between 1746 and 1764 and was located between Hachers Run and Fishing Creek se of the present town of Oxford. Named for Sherwood Harris, a local citizen. In 1778 it was described by James Iredell as containing "half a dozen straggling houses, and is a burlesque upon a town." It continued to exist, however, until Oxford was made the county seat in 1811.

Harris Creek rises in s Avery County and flows w into North Toe River.

Harris Creek rises in ne Cherokee County and flows nw into Valley River.

Harris Creek rises in n McDowell County and flows e into Tom Creek.

Harris Creek rises in w Onslow County and flows e into Southwest Creek.

Harris Creek rises in n Wilkes County and flows se into Double Creek.

Harris Crossroads, community in s Franklin County.

Harris Crossroads, community in w Vance County on the head of Crooked Run.

Harris Depot. *See* Harrisburg.

Harris Gap, w Jackson County between West Fork [Barkers Creek] and Nation Creek.

Harris Lake, se Macon County on Satulah Branch.

Harris Landing, community and landing on Chowan River, w Chowan County. Also known as Tynch Town.

Harris Millpond, s Martin County on Beargrass Swamp.

Harris Millpond, w Pitt County on Tyson Creek.

Harris Mill Run rises in w central Pitt County and flows ne into Tar River.

Harris Mine. *See* Harris.

Harris Mountain, on the McDowell-Rutherford county line. Named for John W. Harris, one of the commissioners who surveyed the line between the two counties about 1845.

Harris Mountain. *See* Shumont Mountain.

Harrison, former community in s Mecklenburg County, was visited by George Washington, May 28, 1791. Harrison Methodist Church there was organized about 1785 and named for Harrison Hood, donor of the site. With the development of Pineville, 3 mi. w, after 1873, Harrison began to decline.

Harrison Branch rises in s Watauga County and flows n into Hodges Creek.

Harrison Creek rises in s Pender County and flows nw into Merricks Creek. Named for Charles Harrison, who owned property in the vicinity as early as 1739.

Harrison Creek. *See* Dawson's Landing.

Harrison Gap, on the Graham County, N.C.– Monroe County, Tenn., line.

Harrison Gap, s Macon County at the head of Lowery Creek.

Harrisons Creek rises in s Cumberland County and flows s into Bladen County, where it enters Cape Fear River.

Harrisons Crossroads, community in e Rockingham County named for local landowner William Harrison.

Harris Swamp Branch rises in e central Brunswick County and flows e into Mills Creek.

Harriston. *See* Ayden.

Harris Top, peak on Payne Mountain in sw Cherokee County.

Harris Top, sw Cherokee County on Pack Mountain between Pack Top and Signal Pole Hill. Alt. approx. 2,815.

Harris Township, former township in s Franklin County, now township no. 2.

Harris Township, n Stanly County.

Harris View, mountain peak in se Buncombe County near the Rutherford County line.

Harrisville, community in s Montgomery County.

Harrold Mountain. *See* Herald Mountain.

Harrys Branch rises in sw Duplin County near Bearford Bay and flows sw into Rockfish Creek.

Harshaw Bottom, a sandy strip along the Hiwassee River in e Cherokee County.

Harshaw Branch rises in se Cherokee County on Poor House Mountain and flows se into Hambton Creek.

Harshaw Gap, central Cherokee County near a bend in West Prong Grape Creek before it flows into Grape Creek.

Hart Branch rises in e Transylvania County and flows ne into Little River.

Hartford. *See* Hertford.

Hartland, community in w Caldwell County. Formerly known as Tuttles Cross Roads for Andrew Hull Tuttle, early nineteenth-century merchant there.

Hartleys Creek rises in w Davidson County and flows nw into Yadkin River.

Hartman, community in central Stokes County.

Harts, community in w Rowan County served by post office, 1876–1903.

Hartsboro, community in central Edgecombe County.

Hartsease. *See* Heartsease.

Hartshorn, community in central Alamance County served by post office, 1849–1916.

Harts Mill Run rises in central Edgecombe County and flows ne into Tar River.

Hartsville, community in ne Wake County.

Harvard, community in s Yancey County.

Harvel Bay, sand-filled bay in se Sampson County at the head of Clear Run Swamp. *See also* Carolina Bays.

Harvey, community in e Lincoln County served by post office, 1891–1903.

Harvey. *See* Harveys Neck.

Harveys Neck, peninsula in e Perquimans County extending into Albemarle Sound between Perquimans and Yeopim Rivers. Home of John Harvey (d. about 1679), colonial governor, and Thomas Harvey (d. 1699), governor, 1694–99. Appears simply as Harvey on the Hack map, 1684.

Harveytown, former community n of Kinston in e Lenoir County. Now within the corporate limits of Kinston. Flourished following the Civil War when Amos Harvey and his son, Lemuel, rented property there to former slaves who moved into town from surrounding plantations.

Harwells Island, silty clay island in Roanoke River in nw Northampton County, sw of the community of Vultare. Appears as Jones Island on the Price map, 1808, but as Harwells Island on the MacRae map, 1833.

Haslett Township, n central Gates County.

Haslin, community in ne Beaufort County served by post office, 1874–1907.

Hassell, town in w Martin County. Settled about 1878 and known as Dogville Crossroads until inc. in 1903. Named for Primitive Baptist elder Sylvester Hassell (1842–1928). Alt. 78.

Hastings Corner, community in e central Camden County. Named for the Hastings family, which settled there about 1700.

Hasty, town in s Scotland County. Inc. 1889, but long inactive in municipal affairs. Named for a family that owned land there when a railroad flag stop was est. Alt. 197.

Hatchell's Point. *See* Windmill Point.

Hatcher's Run rises in w Granville County and flows s and e into Fishing Creek. Appears on 1770 Collet map as Hatches Run.

Hatch Point, s Onslow County, extends into New River. Probably named for Lemuel Hatch, who owned property in the vicinity in 1760.

Hatorask. *See* Hatteras Island.

Hatorask Inlet, from the Atlantic Ocean into Roanoke Sound through Bodie Island, opened prior to 1585 and closed prior to 1657. The site was a short distance n of present Oregon Inlet, e Dare County. At various times, Hatorask Inlet was also known as Port Fernando and under other spellings of Hatorask.

Hatrask. *See* Hatteras Island.

Hattaway Mountain, e Stanly County between Little Mountain Creek and Sugarloaf Mountain.

Hatteras, community near the s end of Hatteras Island, e Dare County. Inc. 1931, but never active in municipal affairs. The name apparently is an English rendition of the Algonquian Indian expression meaning "there is less vegetation." Post office est. there, 1858. Alt. 10.

Hatteras Bight, a cove in the Atlantic Ocean off the s shore of Hatteras Island at Cape Hatteras, s Dare County.

Hatteras Inlet, from the Atlantic Ocean into Pamlico Sound, lies between Hatteras Island, s Dare County, on the n and Ocracoke Island, s Hyde County, on the s. It was opened by a storm in 1846. Previously was closer to Ocracoke Inlet and closed in 1760s. From 1760s to 1846, Cape Hatteras was joined to Ocracoke Island.

Hatteras Island, one of the Outer Banks of e Dare County extending from Hatteras Inlet on the s to New Inlet and Oregon Inlet on the n. Appears as Hatrask on the White map, 1585, though at that time the name was not applied to as much of the Island as today. The name appears as Hattorask, though misplaced, on the Comberford map, 1657. Smith's map, 1624, calls it Hertfords Island, while the Moseley map, 1733, gives it its present name. *See also* Croatoan Island; Paquiac.

Hatteras Shoals. *See* Diamond Shoals.

Hatteras Slough. *See* Diamond Shoals.

Hatteras Township, s Hatteras Island, e Dare County on the Outer Banks.

Hatteras Woods, a heavily wooded area, 8 mi. in length n of Cape Hatteras in se Dare County. At 2,500 acres, largest maritime forest in North Carolina. Extensive stand of mixed hardwoods and pines. Also known as Cape Hatteras Woods or Buxton Woods Coastal Reserve.

Hatters Branch rises in ne Wake County and flows sw into Smiths Creek.

Hattie, community in w Watauga County named for Hattie Farthing.

Hatton Island. *See* Isle Hatton.

Haulover Point, a peninsula extending w into Albemarle Sound from the n mainland of Dare County. It is near the e tip of Durant Island.

Haunty Branch rises in s central Transylvania County and flows nw into French Broad River.

Havelock, town in se Craven County on Slocum Creek. Settled prior to 1857 and named in that year when the Atlantic and North Carolina Railroad from Goldsboro to Morehead City reached the area. Named for Sir Henry Havelock (1795–1857), British major general and noted Baptist layman who dramatically relieved British forces garrisoned at Lucknow, India, on September 25, 1857. Alt. 24. Cherry Point Marine Corps Air Station, *which see,* is adjacent.

Haw Branch rises in central Avery County and flows n into North Toe River.

Haw Branch rises in nw Beaufort County and flows sw into Tranters Creek.

Haw Branch rises in n Buncombe County near Cherry Log Gap and flows n into Dillingham Creek.

Haw Branch rises in sw Nash County and flows s into Turkey Creek.

Hawbranch, community in ne Moore County. Also spelled Haw Branch.

Haw Branch, community in nw Onslow County on New River.

Haw Cove, sw Avery County.

Haw Creek rises in central Buncombe County and flows sw into Swannanoa River. Named in 1860 for the black haw bushes growing along its banks.

Haw Creek rises in w Orange County and flows sw into Alamance County, where it enters Haw River. Appears as Jumping Run on the Moseley map, 1733.

Hawes Mill Creek. *See* Haw Mill Creek.

Haw Fields, name given by traders in the early eighteenth century to the region occupied by Saxapahaw and Sissipahaw Indians between the Haw and Eno Rivers in what is now Alamance and Orange Counties. The Indians had left by the time the first white settlers arrived, and they called the region "Haw old fields," a name mentioned in 1728 by William Byrd. Haw Fields was used in 1736 in connection with a land grant there. Edward Moseley patented 10,000 acres of land in the region on November 6, 1728.

Haw Gap, central Avery County.

Haw Gap, nw Swain County on Jenkins Trail Ridge in Great Smoky Mountains National Park.

Haw Gap Branch rises in nw Swain County in Great Smoky Mountains National Park and flows se across the park boundary for a distance of 4.5 mi. into Hazel Creek.

Hawk, community in e Mitchell County at the junction of Right Fork [Cane Creek] and Left Fork [Cane Creek]. A post office there known as Hawk Mine operated from 1872 to 1883.

Hawkbill Creek rises in ne Buncombe County and flows ne into Mineral Creek.

Hawkbill Gap, ne Buncombe County between Hawkbill Rock and Snowball Mountain.

Hawkbill Rock, prominent rock mass in ne Buncombe County near lat. 35°42′30″ N., long. 82°24′45″ W., in Pisgah National Forest. When viewed from the valley below, the rock has the appearance of a hawk's bill.

Hawk Branch, n Yancey County, is formed by the junction of South Fork Hawk Creek and Middle Fork Hawk Creek and flows w into Cane River. Sometimes known locally as Hog Branch.

Hawk Branch, community in n Yancey County between Middle Fork Hawk Branch and South Fork Hawk Branch.

Hawk Creek rises in e Mitchell County and flows sw into Left Fork [Cane Creek].

Hawkins Bay, off the n end of Huggins Island in the mouth of White Oak River, se Onslow County. Named for Bazel Hawkins.

Hawkins Branch rises in s Pender County and flows sw into Northeast Cape Fear River.

Hawkins Branch rises in e Transylvania County and flows se into Little River.

Hawkins Branch rises in n Washington County and drains w into Chappel Swamp.

Hawkins County, now in Tennessee, was created in 1787 and named in honor of Benjamin Hawkins (1754–1816). Rogersville became the county seat. The county was a part of the territory ceded by North Carolina in 1789 to the federal government.

Hawkins Island, in the e end of Brown's Sound, s Onslow County.

Hawkins Knob, e Jackson County near Caney Fork between Chastine Creek and Mull Creek.

Hawkins Mill Creek rises in n Stokes County and flows sw into Snow Creek.

Hawkins Slough, channel among the tidal-marsh islands in White Oak River w of Swansboro, e Onslow County. Named for Bazel Hawkins. Also known as Ward's Creek.

Hawk Knob, n Cherokee County on nw end of Chestnut Mountain in the Unicoi Mountains.

Hawk Knob, n Swain County in Great Smoky Mountains National Park on Welch Ridge. Alt. 4,940.

Hawk Mine. *See* Hawk.

Hawk Mountain, e Mitchell County between Big Spring Gap and Little Yellow Mountain. Alt. approx. 5,450.

Hawk Mountain, w Transylvania County on Toxaway River.

Haw Knob, on Jess Ridge in n Buncombe County near lat. 35°44′ N., long. 82°27′ W. Known as Rocky Knob until 1932, when the name was changed to eliminate duplication of names in the same vicinity.

Haw Knob, on the Graham County, N.C.–Monroe County, Tenn., line. Alt. 5,472.

Hawk Ridge, n Swain County in Great Smoky Mountains National Park, a short spur extending w from Welch Ridge between Huggins Branch and Elbow Branch.

Hawksbill Mountain, nw Burke County near the se end of Jonas Ridge. Alt. 4,020. Known by the Cherokee Indians as *Nokassa*.

Hawkside, community in n Onslow County.

Hawley's Store, community in Sampson County served by post office, 1848–1907.

Haw Mill Creek rises in w Pender County and flows s into Black River. Formerly called Hawes Mill Creek.

Hawns, town chartered in 1749 to be laid out on 36 acres in Northampton County at the plantation of Samuel Jordan on the n side of Roanoke River. "Lots of half an acre each with convenient streets and squares" were authorized but apparently never laid off. The name came from the title of one of the Lords Proprietors, Baron Carteret of Hawnes and Earl Granville. *See also* Granville District.

Haw Patch, a level area below the peak of Fork Mountain in n Mitchell County.

Haw Pocosin, nw Bertie County.

Hawra, community in sw Wilson County near the head of Lee Swamp. Post office, 1898–1903.

Haw Ridge, ne Mitchell County parallel to Holder Creek.

Haw River rises in ne Forsyth County and flows ne and se through Guilford and Rockingham Counties and across Alamance and Chatham Counties to join Deep River on the Chatham-Lee county line to form Cape Fear River. It is approx. 130 mi. in length. In 1709 John Lawson called it the Hau River and said that it was named for the Sissipahau Indians, who lived along its banks. Appears as Saxapahaw River on the Moseley map, 1733, but the Collet map, 1770, uses its present name. The town of Haywood, at the junction of Deep and Haw Rivers, was one of six sites suggested in 1788 for the location of the state capital.

Haw River, community in e Alamance County on Haw River. Founded by descendants of Adam Trollinger, a German immigrant who settled there in 1747. His son, Jacob, built a gristmill at the site, and for many years it was known as Trollinger's Crossing or Trollinger's Ford. Alt. 539. Produces textiles.

Haw River State Park, in s Rockingham and n Guilford Counties. Est. 2003. Facilities for recreation along waters of Haw River.

Haw River Township, former township in central Alamance County. Now township no. 13.

Haw River Township, se Chatham County.

Hawshore Mountain, s central Avery County.

Haws Run rises in w Onslow County and flows e into Southwest Creek.

Hawtree Creek rises in n central Warren County and flows n into Virginia, where it enters Roanoke River. Appears on the Moseley map, 1733.

Hawtree Township, n Warren County.

Haydon Top, s Cherokee County s of Murphy.

Hayes Branch rises in central Watauga County and flows s into Laurel Creek.

Hayes Cove, sw Buncombe County w of Bent Mountain.

Hayes Gap, n Cherokee County in Hanging Dog Mountain.

Hayes Mill Creek rises in s Macon County and flows w into Little Tennessee River.

Hayes Mountain, se Wilkes County near the Alexander County line.

Hayes Ridge, e Swain County between Williams Branch and Wesser Creek.

Hayes Run rises in s Madison County and flows sw into French Broad River.

Hayes Top, sw Buncombe County nw of Dix Creek Gap.

Hayesville, town and county seat, central Clay County on Hiwassee River. Alt. 1,893. Inc. 1891. Named for George W. Hayes (1804–64), a member of the General Assembly who was instrumental in the formation of the county. Fort Hembree, ¾ mi. nw, was one of the forts at which Gen. Winfield Scott, in command of U.S. forces, gathered the Cherokee Indians before moving them w in 1838. Produces lumber and apparel.

Hayesville or **Haysville Township**, former township in nw Franklin County, now township no. 5.

Hayesville Township, sw Clay County.

Hay Meadow, community in n central Wilkes County on Bee Tree Branch.

Hay Meadow Creek rises in n Wilkes County and flows s into Mulberry Creek.

Hayne, community in w Sampson County served by post office, 1887–1941. Alt. 153.

Haynes Knob, n Haywood County between Crawford Gap and Wesley Creek. Alt. approx, 3,500.

Haynes Pond, on Mingo Swamp on the Harnett-Sampson county line. A little more than ½ mi. in length.

Hays, community in n central Wilkes County between Hay Meadow Creek and the head of Camp Branch. A former post office est. there in the 1899 was named for the first postmaster, Paulina Hays Elledge; discontinued 1953.

Hayseed, community in sw Catawba County served by post office, 1892–1905.

Hays Knob, sw Cherokee County between Wildcat Cove and Potato Creek.

Hays Mill Creek rises in central Cherokee County and flows se into Valley River.

Haystack, community in w Surry County served by post office, 1831–1905. Also spelled Hay Stack.

Hay Stack. *See* Haystack.

Haystack Marshes. *See* Newport Marshes.

Haystack Point, point of land on the n shore of Pungo River, e Beaufort County.

Hayti (HAY-tie), African American business district in Durham, ca. 1900–1950. Lost to urban redevelopment and highway construction in 1960s.

Hayward Creek rises in w Craven County and flows e and sw into Trent River. Appears in early records as Haywood Creek and in the nineteenth century as both Haywood Creek and Samuel Creek.

Haywood, town in se Chatham County on Deep River. Inc. 1796 as Lyons; name changed to Haywoodsborough in 1797 and to Haywood in 1800. Long inactive in municipal affairs. Named for John Haywood (1755–1827), state treasurer. Moncure is now immediately to the nw of the site of Haywood, which, aside from a church and a few houses, is mostly wooded.

Haywood County was formed in 1808 from Buncombe County. Located in the w section of the state, it is bounded by the state of Tennessee and by Madison, Buncombe, Transylvania, Jackson, and Swain Counties. It was named for John Haywood (1755–1827), state treasurer from 1787 to 1827. Area: 544 sq. mi. County seat: Waynesville, with an elevation of 2,635 ft. Townships are Beaverdam, Cataloochee, Cecil, Clyde, Crabtree, East Fork, Fines Creek, Iron Duff, Ivy Hill, Jonathans Creeks, Pigeon, Waynesville, and White Oak. Produces apples, corn, Christmas trees, dairy products, livestock, hogs, poultry, paper, rubber goods, concrete products, chemicals, lumber, leather, textiles, tobacco, furniture, sand, and gravel.

Haywood Gap, in Newfound Mountain on the Buncombe-Haywood county line between Rocky Knob and Dry Mountain.

Haywood Gap, on the Haywood-Jackson county line. Alt. 5,225.

Haywood Gap Stream rises in s Haywood County at Sweetwater Spring and flows ne to join Buckeye Creek in forming Middle Prong [West Fork Pigeon River].

Hazanet Knob, central Graham County in the Cheoah Mountains at the head of Cochran Creek.

Hazel, former town in central Buncombe County at or near West Asheville. Inc. 1891 but soon became inactive in municipal affairs. Now within the city limits of Asheville.

Hazel, community in n Surry County served by post office, 1899–1906.

Hazel Creek rises in n Swain County on the sw slope of Silers Bald in Great Smoky Mountains National Park and flows sw into Fontana Lake. It was named for a patch of hazelnut bushes near its mouth.

Hazel Dell, community in e central Caldwell County. Formerly a post office.

Hazel Hollow, w Jackson County between Mince Branch and Dicks Creek.

Hazel Knob, on the Cherokee County, N.C.–

Monroe County, Tenn., line in the Unicoi Mountains.

Hazelnut Gap, on the McDowell-Yancey county line between Buck Creek Gap and Horse Gap.

Hazelton, community in n Gates County.

Hazel Top, peak in central Haywood County on the nw end of Teaberry Ridge.

Hazelwood, former town in s Haywood County adjacent to Waynesville. Inc. 1905. In 1953 it became a part of Waynesville. Named for hazelnuts growing in the vicinity. Alt. 2,713. *See also* Waynesville.

Headquarters Mountain, se Avery County. Alt. 4,135.

Headwater, community in sw Chatham County.

Heady Mountain, s Jackson County at s end of Chattooga Ridge. Also spelled Heddie Mountain.

Heady's Beach. *See* Bear Banks.

Healing Springs, community and springs in s Davidson County between Flat Swamp and Lick Creek at n end of Flat Swamp Mountain.

Healing Springs Township, s Davidson County.

Healthy Plain, community in w Wilson County.

Heareford, community in ne Stokes County served by post office, 1898–1907.

Heartline Creek. *See* North Fork Tar River.

Hearts Delight Pocosin, nw Bertie County.

Heartsease, community in central Edgecombe County about 8 mi. nw of Tarboro. Named by Richard Hart, who built his home there. Appears as Hartsease on U.S. Geological Survey map, 1903.

Heath, community in e Union County served by post office, 1894–1903.

Heatherly Height, high ground in se Henderson County.

Heath Mill Run rises in n Jones County and flows s into Beaver Creek.

Heathsville, community in w central Halifax County.

Heaton, community on Elk River, n Avery County. Alt. approx. 3,500. Named for Rev. James M. Heaton of Tennessee, who came to w North Carolina in 1882.

Heaveners Creek rises in e Rutherford County and flows w into Robinson Creek.

Hebo Mountain, on the Haywood-Madison county line. Alt. 4,300–4,368.

Hebron, community in nw Granville County.

Hebron, community in s Mecklenburg County.

Hebron Mountain, w Henderson County between Cantrell Mountain and North Fork. Alt. 2,966.

Heck Creek rises in central Madison County and flows sw into Walnut Creek.

Hector Creek rises in s Harnett County and flows s on the Moore-Cumberland county line into Little River. Named for Hector McNeill, an early settler.

Hector Creek rises in sw Wake County and flows sw through n Harnett County into Cape Fear River. Named for Hector McNeill, who settled along its banks, 1740.

Hector Creek Township, n Harnett County.

Heddie Mountain. *See* Heady Mountain.

Hedgecock, community in s Guilford County.

Hedricks Island, a narrow island of sand approx. 1 mi. long in Yadkin River, w Davidson County.

Heffner Gap, on the McDowell-Mitchell county line.

Heflin, community in n Johnston County served by post office, 1898–1903.

Heggie, community in n Rockingham County served by post office, 1898–1904.

Heidelburg Ferry appears on the Moseley map, 1733, on New River in what is now s Onslow County, serving the Bath–New Bern–Wilmington road.

Heights of Gowerie, high bank overlooking Yadkin River, e Rowan County. Site of the home of Albert Torrence (1752–1825), from which Cornwallis cannonaded forces of Gen. Nathanael Greene, 1781.

Heighwaree. *See* Uwharrie Mountains.

Heilig, community in s Rowan County served by post office, 1875–1903.

Heilig's Mill. *See* Heilig.

Heintooga Bald, ne Swain County in Great Smoky Mountains National Park on Overlook Ridge. Alt. 5,240.

Heintooga Creek rises in ne Swain County in Great Smoky Mountains National Park and flows sw into Bunches Creek.

Heintooga Ridge, nw Swain County in Great Smoky Mountains National Park between Heintooga Creek and Redman Creek.

Heldermans, former community in s Lincoln County on the opposite side of Leepers Creek from the community of Mariposa, but now a part of Mariposa.

Helena. *See* Timberlake.

Helens Crossroads, community in s Pitt County.

Helix, community in nw Davie County.

Hell Pocosin, a loam-filled pocosin in nw Onslow County between Purgatory Pocosin and the head of New River.

Hell's Half Acre. *See* Providence.

Hell Swamp, e Beaufort County n of Pungo Creek.

Hell Swamp, central Duplin County between North Prong Horse Branch and West Prong Horse Branch.

Helton, community in n Ashe County. Alt. 2,600. Site of iron forges, 1807–57.

Helton Creek rises in n central Ashe County and flows se into North Fork New River.

Helton Township, ne Ashe County.

Hembys Bridge, community in w Union County. Inc. 1998.

Hemlock, community in w Ashe County.

Hemlock Branch rises in s Haywood County and flows ne into Little East Fork Pigeon River.

Hemlock Knob, peak on the Swain County, N.C.–Sevier County, Tenn., line in Great Smoky Mountains National Park between Mount Davis and Cold Spring Knob.

Hemmed Island, a 75-acre island covered with hardwoods in the Tar River, central Edgecombe County.

Hemp. *See* Robbins.

Hemphill Bald, w Haywood County in Great Smoky Mountains National Park on Cataloochee Divide near lat. 35°33'50" N., long. 83°06'11" W. Alt. 5,573.

Hemphill Creek rises in central Haywood County and flows e into Jonathans Creek. Named for an early settler in area.

Hemphill Creek rises in s Yancey County and flows ne into South Toe River.

Hemphill Knob, central Buncombe County s of Lake Craig.

Hemphill Mountain, n Buncombe County between Pink Fox Cove and Pennix Cove.

Hemphill Spring, s Yancey County. Former resort on the old Mount Mitchell toll road operated by Graybeal family and used for a time during the construction of the Blue Ridge Parkway.

Hemphill's Store, community in sw Mecklenburg County served by post office, 1826–58.

Hemp Patch Branch rises in s Macon County and flows sw into Big Mooney Branch.

Henderson, former town in w Montgomery County at the junction of Yadkin and Uwharrie Rivers. Inc. 1794; "re-surveyed" in 1813. Was the site of the courthouse from soon after the establishment of the town until about 1816. By the 1850s Henderson no longer appeared on maps of the state. *See also* Tindallsville.

Henderson, city and county seat, s central Vance County. Alt. 513. Inc. 1841 and named for Leonard Henderson (1772–1833), chief justice of N.C. Supreme Court from 1829 to 1833. Originally settled in 1789 when Samuel Reavis and his sons Lewis, Samuel Jr., and Whitfield built a house there. Referred to as Lonesome Valley by a later settler, William Evans, who was homesick for Virginia. Produces textiles, hosiery, minerals, tobacco, glass products, and pickles.

Henderson Branch rises in e Haywood County and flows ne into Burnett Creek.

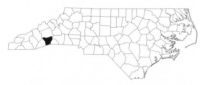

Henderson County was formed in 1838 from Buncombe County. Located in the w section of the state, it is bounded by the state of South Carolina and by Transylvania, Haywood, Buncombe, McDowell, Rutherford, and Polk Counties. It was named for Leonard Henderson (1772–1833), chief justice of the N.C. Supreme Court. Area: 382 sq. mi. County seat: Hendersonville, with an elevation of 2,146 ft. Townships are Clear Creek, Crab Creek, Edneyville, Green River, Hendersonville, Hoopers Creek, Mills River, North Blue Ridge, and South Blue Ridge. Produces apples, corn, hay, snap beans, cattle, paper products, outdoor lights, electronics, tools, limestone, granite, and clay.

Henderson Creek rises in e Henderson County and flows nw into Clear Creek.

Henderson Mountain, s Macon County between Fork Ridge and California Ridge.

Henderson's Ferry crossed Catawba River in nw Mecklenburg into Gaston County.

Henderson Shoals. *See* McAdenville.

Henderson Township, central Vance County.

Hendersonville, town and county seat, central Henderson County. Alt. 2,146. Authorized to be laid out, 1840; inc. 1847. Named for Leonard Henderson (1772–1833), chief justice of the N.C. Supreme Court, 1829–33. Produces electronic components, hosiery, textiles, and apparel.

Hendersonville Township, central Henderson County.

Hendricks Creek rises in central Edgecombe County and flows se through Tarboro into Tar River.

Hendrix, community in w Wilkes County on Stony Fork Creek.

Hen Mountain, central Caldwell County. Alt. 2,020. Formerly known as Turkey Hen Mountain. A nearby peak, Hibriten Mountain, was formerly known as Turkey Cock Mountain.

Hennessey, community in s Burke County served by post office, 1896–1903.

Henrico, community in nw Northampton County.

Henrietta, former community in s Edgecombe County. Now only a railroad crossing.

Henrietta, community in se Rutherford County on Second Broad River. Founded 1887 by Simpson B. Tanner Sr. with the establishment of Henrietta Mills. Named for Tanner's mother-in-law, Henrietta McRae Spencer.

Henry, community in nw Lincoln County.

Henry Branch rises in w Nash County and flows se into Sapony Creek. Mentioned in local records as early as 1779.

Henry Branch rises near Black Mountain in n Transylvania County and flows sw into Avery Creek.

Henry Creek rises in n Jackson County and flows s into Buff Creek.

Henry Fork rises in s Burke County and flows ne and e into Catawba County, where it joins Jacob Fork in forming South Fork Catawba River. Named for the pioneer settler Heinrich Weidner (Henry Whitener).

Henry Knob, central Haywood County between Big Spring Branch and Jonathans Creek.

Henry Mountain, s Transylvania County between Paxton Creek and Cantrell Creek.

Henry River, community in e Burke County.

Hensley Branch rises in n Madison County near Big Knob and flows se on the w side of Ephraim Hensley Mountain into Shelton Laurel Creek.

Hensley Branch rises in n Yancey County and flows ne into Bald Mountain Creek.

Hensley Ridge, n McDowell County, extends e from Betsy Ridge. Alt. approx. 2,300.

Hensley Ridge, nw Yancey County between Bald Mountain Creek and Jim Creek.

Henson Branch rises in se Macon County and flows se into Clear Creek.

Henson Cove, e Haywood County on Garden Creek.

Henson Creek rises in w Avery County and flows se into North Toe River.

Henson Creek rises in s Macon County and flows ne into Shope Fork.

Henson Gap, se Macon County between Henson Branch and Brooks Creek.

Henson Ridge, n Jackson County between Locust Creek and Cane Creek.

Hepco, former community on Waterville Lake (in Pigeon River), central Haywood County. Alt. 2,298. Was site of Haywood Electric Power Company development; the name came from the initials of the company. Now abandoned.

Herald Mountain, n Wilkes County between the head of Bee Tree Branch and Cane Creek. Named for the Harrold family, early settlers on Bee Tree Branch.

Herbert C. Bonner Bridge. *See* Oregon Inlet.

Herbert Stamp, peak in ne Clay County between Tipton Branch and Tate Branch.

Herbin's Creek rises in se Rockingham County and flows sw into Haw River. Known as High Rock Creek as early as 1754; renamed about 1800 for John and William Herbin, local landowners.

Herds Creek rises in e Moore County and flows s into Crains Creek. Named for Charles Herd, who settled at its mouth about 1760.

Heriots Island. *See* Batts Island.

Hermitage, community in nw Ashe County served by post office, 1890–1904.

Herrells, community in nw Mitchell County.

Herren Cove, the valley through which the e tributary of Pole Creek flows in sw Buncombe County.

Herring or **Herrings Crossroads**, community in n central Sampson County on the head of Merkle Swamp.

Herring Pond, stream, rises in n Carteret County and flows n into Neuse River.

Herring Run rises in central Beaufort County and flows s into Runyon Creek.

Herring's Chapel, community in sw Pender County on the e side of Long Creek.

Herring Shoal Island, small island about ½ mi. in diameter off the s end of Bodie Island in Roanoke Sound, e Dare County.

Herrings Township, n central Sampson County.

Herring Swamp rises in n Duplin County and flows se into Marsh Branch.

Herrin Knob, on the Haywood-Jackson county line.

Herron Cove, n Buncombe County sw of Little Davis Mountain.

Hertford, town and county seat, central Perquimans County on Perquimans River. Est. 1758. Named for the town of Hertford in England. Appears as Hartford on the Collet map, 1770. First known as Phelps Point for Jonathan Phelps, on whose land it was est.; appears in local records as early as 1701. Produces apparel. Alt. 15.

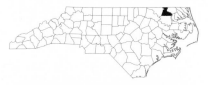

Hertford County was formed in 1759 from Chowan, Bertie, and Northampton Counties. Located in the ne section of the state, it is bounded by Gates, Chowan, Bertie, and Northampton Counties and the state of Virginia. It was named for Francis Seymour Conway (1719–94), Earl (later Marquis) of Hertford, a Lord of the Bed Chamber and Knight of the Garter. Area: 361 sq. mi. County seat: Winton, with an elevation of 45 ft. Townships are Ahoskie, Harrellsville, Maneys Neck, Murfreesboro, St. Johns, and Winton. Produces peanuts, tobacco, corn, soybeans, cotton, hogs, livestock, apparel, lumber, steel products, glass products, and wooden containers.

Hertfords Island. *See* Hatteras Island.

Hertford Township, w central Perquimans County.

Hester, community in s Granville County served by post office, 1889–1950. Named for Henry M. Hester, donor of the railroad right-of-way and station site. Alt. 384.

Hesters Pond, w Bladen County on Bareford

Swamp. Covers between 75 and 80 acres; max. depth 8 ft. at the dam.

Hester's Store, community in sw Person County served by post office, 1854–1905.

Hestertown, community in se Robeson County on Lumber River.

Hewins Creek. *See* Eurins Creek.

Hewitt, community in sw Swain County. Named for Frank R. Hewitt, talc-mine operator. Alt. 1,878.

Hewitt Gap, in sw Swain County on Nantahala Gorge.

Hewlets Creek rises in central New Hanover County and flows se into Masonboro Sound.

Hexlena, community in n central Bertie County. Inc. 1899; charter repealed 1905.

Hiawatha. *See* Watha.

Hibbard Mountain, w Cherokee County, extends ne from Bearpaw Creek.

Hibriten, community in central Caldwell County served by post office, 1886–1902.

Hibriten Mountain, central Caldwell County in the Brushy Mountains. Alt. 2,265. Formerly known as Turkey Cock Mountain but renamed in honor of Brighton, England, by Emma Baker, who moved there from England to teach school. *See also* Hen Mountain; Brushy Mountains.

Hickleberry Mountain, w Stokes County at the head of Town Fork Creek.

Hickman's Creek rises in se Caldwell County and flows s into Upper Little River.

Hickmans Crossroads, community in sw Brunswick County.

Hickory, city in nw Catawba County. Alt. 1,163. Inc. 1863 as Hickory Tavern. Named for a log tavern built at the site in the 1850s. Name changed to Hickory, 1873. West Hickory, inc. as Berryville in 1895, is now within the limits of Hickory. Highland, inc. 1905, whose charter was repealed in 1931, is also now a part of Hickory. Highland was named for Highland Academy, located within its limits. Lenoir-Rhyne University now occupies site of former Highland Academy. Produces hosiery, textiles, furniture, electronics, fabricated metals, primary metals, and lumber.

Hickory, community in ne Nash County between Beaverdam Swamp and Fishing Creek. Sometimes also known as Pittmans Store.

Hickory Basin, a depression in e Graham County at the head of Shell Stand Creek.

Hickory Bearpen Mountain, e Madison County between Roaring Fork and Little Creek.

Hickory Bottom, sandy valley in nw Swain County between Pinnacle Ridge and Hazel Creek.

Hickory Bottom Branch rises in n McDowell County and flows s into Armstrong Creek near Woodlawn.

Hickory Branch rises in n central Avery County and flows s to join Whitehead Creek before flowing into Elk River.

Hickory Branch rises in sw Cherokee County and flows se into Persimmon Creek.

Hickory Branch rises in w Macon County and flows se into Dicks Creek.

Hickory Cove, s Swain County, extends ne between Marr Branch and Brush Creek.

Hickory Cove, w Swain County between Sandy Gap Branch and Gunlock Ridge.

Hickory Cove, w Swain County between Watia Creek and Jake Branch.

Hickory Cove Creek rises in nw Clay County and flows sw into Rock House Creek.

Hickory Creek rises in se Caldwell County and flows s into Upper Little River.

Hickory Creek rises in e Cleveland County and flows sw into First Broad River.

Hickory Creek rises in s Guilford County and flows s into Deep River. Appears on the Collet map, 1770.

Hickory Creek rises in ne Stokes County and flows e into Rockingham County, where it enters Mayo River.

Hickory Crossroads, community in e Johnston County.

Hickory Cross Roads, community in n Perquimans County.

Hickory East, unincorporated outskirts of city of Hickory, nw Catawba County.

Hickory Flat Branch rises in n Swain County and flows s into Oconaluftee River.

Hickory Flat Branch rises in w central Swain County and flows sw into Tuckasegee River.

Hickory Flat Cove, s Haywood County on a tributary of West Fork Pigeon River.

Hickory Flat Creek rises near Mine Mountain in n Transylvania County and flows sw into East Fork French Broad River.

Hickory Flats, e Mitchell County between Beaver Creek and Gouges Creek.

Hickory Fork rises in n Madison County and flows se into Shelton Laurel Creek.

Hickory Gap, near the junction of the Buncombe-Madison-Yancey county lines. Alt. approx. 3,550.

Hickory Gap, s Graham County between Little Snowbird Creek and Teeseteska Ridge.

Hickory Gap, s Macon County between Rector Knob and Bennies Branch.

Hickory Grove, community in sw Chatham County.

Hickory Grove, community in e Mecklenburg County. A post office was est. there as early as 1828.

Hickory Grove, community in e Wake County.

Hickory Grove. *See* Wilson.

Hickory Grove Crossroads, community in e Bladen County on South River. Stewarts Ferry appears on the river there on the Price map, 1808. The MacRae map, 1833, shows Cromartys Ferry there, while the soil survey map, 1914, shows Cromarties Bridge across the river and the community of Gravel Hill a short distance w. Gravelly Hill had appeared on the Colton map, 1861, and on various other maps through Kerr's in 1882. Gravelly Hill post office was there as early as 1827 and operated until 1866; it became Gravelhill in 1875. The present name occurs first on the Geological Survey map, 1954.

Hickory Hill. *See* Lawrence.

Hickory Knob, at the junction of the Alexander, Caldwell, and Wilkes county lines.

Hickory Knob, sw Burke County.

Hickory Knob, on the Cherokee-Macon county line.

Hickory Knob, e Macon County between Laurel Creek and North Prong Ellijay Creek.

Hickory Knob, n Transylvania County between Presley Branch and South Prong Turkey Creek.

Hickory Knob Mountain, at junction of Alexander, Caldwell, and Wilkes Counties. Alt. 2,635.

Hickory Knoll Creek rises in s Macon County and flows sw into Little Tennessee River.

Hickory Log Branch rises in n Madison County and flows se into Shelton Laurel Creek.

Hickory Mountain, w Chatham County approx. 5 mi. e of Siler City.

Hickory Mountain, on the Henderson-Transylvania county line n of Hooker Creek.

Hickory Mountain Township, w central Chatham County.

Hickory North, unincorporated outskirts of city of Hickory, nw Catawba County.

Hickory Nut Branch rises in central Avery County and flows s into North Toe River.

Hickorynut Branch rises in e Swain County on Yalaka Mountains near Hickorynut Knob and flows s into Una Creek.

Hickory Nut Creek rises in ne Henderson County and flows se into Broad River.

Hickory Nut Falls, on Broad River near Chimney Rock, w Rutherford County. 400 ft. tall.

Hickory Nut Gap, central Avery County.

Hickory Nut Gap, on the Buncombe-Henderson county line between Tater Knob and Ferguson Peak. Alt. 2,878. Originally known as Sherrill's Gap. One of two gaps (the other being Swannanoa Gap) through which early settlers and travelers from the e reached the Asheville plateau.

Hickory Nut Gap, nw Swain County on Long Hungry Ridge in Great Smoky Mountains National Park.

Hickory Nut Gorge, w Rutherford County, through which Broad River flows. A good view of the gorge may be had from atop Chimney Rock.

Hickorynut Knob, e Swain County on Yalaka Mountains near the head of Hickorynut Branch.

Hickory Nut Mountain, in sw Burke County. Alt. 2,512.

Hickory Nut Mountain, central Jackson County, extends n from Slatten Creek to Tuckasegee River.

Hickorynut Mountain, in e Swain County between Second Hurricane Branch and Hickorynut Branch.

Hickorynut Mountains, a long ridge, s McDowell County between Crooked Creek and Cove Creek.

Hickory Point, se Beaufort County on the s side of Pamlico River at the mouth of South Creek.

Hickory Point extends from sw Carteret County into Hills Bay.

Hickory Ridge, in n Haywood County between Rube Rock Branch and Chestnut Orchard Branch.

Hickory Ridge Branch rises in w Madison County and flows s into Roaring Fork.

Hickory Run rises in w Onslow County and flows ne into Southwest Creek.

Hickory Springs. *See* Mount Vernon Springs.

Hickory Spur, peak in w Madison County between Levy Branch and French Broad River.

Hickory Tavern. *See* Hickory.

Hickory Top, s Buncombe County between Billy Cove Gap and Little Hickory Top.

Hickory Township, w Catawba County. Was Hickory Tavern Township prior to 1876.

Hicks Branch rises in ne Cherokee County and flows se into Junaluska Creek.

Hicks Branch rises in n Haywood County and flows ne into Pigeon River.

Hicks Branch rises in w Macon County and flows n into Nantahala Lake.

Hicks Creek rises in s Iredell County w of Troutman and flows s into Catawba River.

Hicks Crossroads, community in nw Mecklenburg County.

Hicks Crossroads, community in nw Vance County n of Flat Creek.

Hicks Grove, community in s Rutherford County s of Broad River.

Hicks Pond, in n Warren County on Mill Creek.

Hickstown, former town in central Durham County. Inc. 1887 on property of W. H. and Ella Hicks; charter repealed 1889. Site is now within the corporate limits of Durham.

Hicksville, community in s Rutherford County served by post office, 1845–1905.

Hicootomony River. *See* Hyco River.

Hico River. *See* Hyco River.

Hiddenite, community in e central Alexander County. Named for William Earl Hidden (1853–1918), mineralogist of New York who prospected in the area about 1880. Mines nearby produced the gem hiddenite, found only in North Carolina. Inc. 1913; charter repealed 1919. Known as White Plains prior to the arrival of Hidden and so appears on a map of 1871. Alt. 1,140. Produces poultry.

Hide Pond, a muck-filled slough in se Duplin County.

Hidetown, community in e Graham County on Stecoah Creek.

Higdon Branch rises in e Macon County and flows nw into Ellijay Creek.

Higdon Mountain, e Macon County at the head of Higdon Branch. Alt. 4,045.

Higdonville, community in e Macon County on Battle Branch.

Higgens Island, formerly a 10-acre island in Little Tennessee River in ne Graham County. Now under the waters of Fontana Lake.

Higgins, community in n central Yancey County on Cane River. Alt. 2,390. Named for John Higgins, early settler and father of a large family.

Higgins Creek rises in w Yancey County and flows nw into Cane River.

Higgins Knob, w Yancey County between Langford Branch and Higgins Creek.

Higgins Township, central McDowell County.

High Country, modern name applied to nw North Carolina, especially area around Boone and Blowing Rock, to promote tourism.

Highfall Branch rises in central Cherokee County and flows n into Valley River.

Highfall Branch rises in central Cherokee County and flows se into Morgan Creek.

High Falls, in Little River in e Transylvania County s of the mouth of Grassy Creek. Height of the falls is 50 ft.

High Falls, n Transylvania County in South Fork Mills River. Height of the falls is 30 ft.

High Falls, se Transylvania County in Little River near Cedar Mountain. Height of the falls is 75 ft.

High Falls, in Horsepasture River in sw Transylvania County between Drift Falls and Stairway Falls. Height is 150 ft.

High Falls, community in n Moore County on Deep River. William England built a mill there about 1790. Originally known as The Great Falls and The Big Falls for a 15 ft. waterfall in the river. The community of Prosperity, approx. 1 mi. e, was settled about 1862, but by 1941 it had been almost completely abandoned in favor of High Falls. Prosperity was named for the fact that it was in the center of a prosperous farming section.

High Falls of the Tuckasegee. *See* Tuckasegee Falls.

High Hampton Estate, se Jackson County on the w edge of Hampton Lake. Estate named for Gen. Wade Hampton, Confederate officer and governor of South Carolina, who had a home there. It is now a private recreation area and resort, High Hampton Inn. Alt. 3,524.

High Hickory Knob, se Buncombe County between Patton Gap and Flat Top in the Swannanoa Mountains.

High Hickory Ridge, se Buncombe County n of High Hickory Knob.

High Hill, community in n Hertford County.

High Hill Inlet between Whalebone Island in Pamlico Sound and Portsmouth Island in e Carteret County.

High Hills, The, sand dunes on Portsmouth Island about 1 mi. ne of Drum Inlet, e Carteret County.

High Holly, mountain in s Macon County between Kinley Mountain and Middle Creek.

High Knob, n Buncombe County between High Swan and Rich Knob.

High Knob, ne Buncombe County w of Pigpen Knob.

High Knob, nw Buncombe County between Robinson Mountain and Grassy Knob.

High Knob, mountain in Wilson Ridge, nw Caldwell County. Alt. 2,686.

High Knob, s Macon County between Deer Gap and Beasley Gap.

High Knob, n Madison County at the head of Duckmill Branch.

High Knob, e Mitchell County between Ivy Knob and Lightwood Mountain.

High Knob, e Mitchell County between Little Bald and Stagger Weed Creek.

High Knob, n central Transylvania County at the e end of Shutin Ridge.

High Knob, s Yancey County near the head of Banks Creek.

High Knob, sw Yancey County on Wilson Ridge.

Highland. *See* Hickory.

Highland Falls, on the headwaters of Cullasaja River in se Macon County.

Highland Lake, central Henderson County on King Creek. Constructed about 1906. Covers 20 acres; max. depth 20 ft. Site of a summer camp. Alt. 2,117.

Highland Ridge, ne Swain County in Great Smoky Mountains National Park, a spur extending se from Katalsta Ridge between Enloe Creek and Raven Fork.

Highlands, town in se Macon County. The highest town in the state, alt. 3,838. Laid out as a summer resort in 1875 by Samuel T. Kelsey and Charles Hutchinson of Kansas. They chose the location from a map when they discovered that a line drawn on it from Chicago to Savannah crossed another line at the site drawn from Baltimore to New Orleans. Inc. 1879. Named for its high elevation. Highlands has an average yearly precipitation of 79 in. Highlands Biological Station est. there 1927 as a nonprofit research and field training center for the study of plants and animals. *See also* Horse Cove.

Highlands Township, se Macon County.

High Laurel Branch rises in w Macon County and flows w into Nantahala Lake.

High Lonesome Mountain, se Jackson County between Fowler Creek and Ellicott Mountain.

High Mountain, ne Rutherford County between Oakey Mountain and Silver Creek Knob.

High Peak, on the Buncombe-Henderson county line.

High Peak, central Burke County. Alt. 2,184.

High Peak, on the Burke-Rutherford county line in the South Mountains. Alt. approx. 2,720.

High Peak, n Cherokee County on Hanging Dog Mountain. Also known as High Top. Alt. 4,053.

High Peak, ne Cherokee County on the head of Tom Thumb Creek in the Snowbird Mountains. Alt. approx. 3,800.

Highpeak, mountain on the Henderson-Transylvania county line.

High Peak, se Watauga County between Joes Creek and Triplett Creek.

High Peak, n Yancey County between the heads of Seng Branch and Bailey Branch. Alt. approx. 4,400.

High Peak, w Yancey County near the head of Wolf Branch.

High Peak, community in se Burke County approx. 5 mi. se of Morganton at foot of South Mountains.

High Pinnacle, central Buncombe County nw of Elk Wallow Gap in the Elk Mountains.

High Point, s peak of Deaver View Mountain in central Buncombe County.

High Point, peak in w Jackson County between Nation Creek and Rocky Branch.

High Point, city in sw Guilford County. Alt. 940. Laid out in 1853 and inc. 1859. Named for the fact that it was the highest point on the North Carolina Railroad. Produces textiles, hosiery, furniture, baked goods, apparel, corrugated boxes, fabricated metals, toys, lumber, and chemicals. Furniture market is operated there. Home of High Point University. *See also* Browntown.

High Point Lake, sw Guilford County, is formed at the junction of East Fork Deep River and West Fork Deep River where Deep River is formed. The lake was created by a dam constructed in 1928 and is named for and owned

by the city of High Point. Max. depth 20 ft.;
area 150 acres.

High Point Township, sw Guilford County.
Named for the town.

High Ridge, w Madison County between Davis
Branch and Murray Branch.

High Rock, mountain in central Madison
County between Hunter Creek and Brush
Creek at the n end of High Rock Ridge. Alt.
3,555.

High Rock, community in s Davidson County
on Yadkin River. Alt. 584.

High Rock, former community and post office
in se Rockingham County on Haw River.
Mentioned in local records as early as 1754;
mill operated there from as early as 1753 until
the 1920s, when the dam was broken. Gov.
William Tryon camped there, 1771; Generals
Cornwallis and Greene camped there during
the Revolutionary War. The name survives as
applied to a local farm and brick house built
about 1807.

High Rock Creek. *See* Herbin's Creek.

High Rock Lake, on Yadkin River in Davidson
and Rowan Counties. Formed in 1927 by a
dam in the river constructed for the Carolina
Aluminum Company. Covers approx. 18,000
acres; max. depth 60 to 70 ft. Named because
the dam is built from one high rock to another above the bed of the river.

High Rock Lake, on Steel Creek in s Transylvania
County. Covers 15 acres and has a max. depth
of 15 ft.

High Rock Ridge, central Madison County
between Brush Creek and Walnut Creek.

High Rock Ridge, n Swain County in Great
Smoky Mountains National Park, a spur ex-
tending w from Welch Ridge between Cold
Spring Branch and Hazel Creek.

High Rocks, peak in n Swain County in Great
Smoky Mountains National Park on Welch
Ridge. Alt. 5,188.

High Rocks, peak in n Yancey County at the ne
end of Chestnut Ridge.

High Rock Wildlife Management Area, on High
Rock Lake in sw Davidson County. Operated
by state of North Carolina on privately owned
land. Principal wildlife are deer, turkey, and
quail.

Highs Crossroads, community in s Nash County
near Bissett Mill Pond. It is now known also
as Green Pond community.

High Shoals, community on South Fork
Catawba River in n Gaston County. Settled
about 1750. Named for high, rocky shoal in
the river. Alt. 724.

High Shoals. *See* Cliffside.

High Shoals Branch rises in s Madison County
and flows e into Little Pine Creek.

High Shoals Township, se Rutherford County.
Named for a series of shoals in Second Broad
River. *See also* Cliffside.

Highsmith, community in s Pender County on
Mill Creek. Named for the Highsmith family,
which operated a large farm and sawmill at
the site.

High Swan, peak at the n end of Swan Mountain
in central Buncombe County.

High Top, se Buncombe County in the Blue
Ridge Mountains between High Windy and
Lakey Knob.

High Top, sw Buncombe County ne of Stony
Knob.

High Top, n Graham County on the e end of
Yellow Creek Mountains.

High Top, central Haywood County between
Messer Branch and Sugar Cove.

High Top, s Haywood County at the head of
Big Branch.

Hightop, n Henderson County between Baldwin
Gap and Terry Gap. Alt. 3,482.

High Top, w Jackson County at the head of
Brook Branch.

High Top, s Macon County between Low Gap
and Pine Knob.

High Top. *See* High Peak.

High Top of Bee Tree. *See* Craggy Knob.

Hightower Gap, s Swain County between Licklog
Creek and Wiggins Creek.

Hightowers, community in se Caswell County.
Named for Daniel Hightower, who moved
there from Virginia about 1795. A post office
operated there approx. 1830–1930.

Hightower Township, se Caswell County.

Hightsville, community in w New Hanover
County n of Wilmington on Smiths Creek.

Highview, community in ne Person County
served by post office, 1892–1901.

High Windy, peak in se Buncombe County
between Black Knob and High Top.

Hilda, community in w Alleghany County
served by post office, 1898–1907.

Hildebran, town in e Burke County. Inc.
1899. Alt. 1,149. Named for J. A. Hildebran,

lumber merchant. Produces textiles and hosiery.

Hildebran Creek rises in central Catawba County sw of Conover and flows s into Clark Creek.

Hildrup, former mining town in s McDowell County in the vicinity of Demming, *which see.*

Hill, community in nw Pitt County served by post office, 1892–1916.

Hill Forest, n Durham County. Contains 2,450 acres. The original tract of 275 acres was donated by George Watts Hill of Durham to North Carolina State College in 1929. He later assisted in financing additional purchases of land. Named for the original donor. The second-year class of the Department of Forestry and Environmental Resources spends 10 weeks in summer camp there doing surveying and all phases of forestry, such as timber cruising, dendrology, stand improvement, and mensuration. The camp is equipped with classrooms, dormitory, dining hall, and all necessary facilities.

Hillgirt, community in n Henderson County.

Hill Hollow, n Mitchell County on a tributary of Spring Creek.

Hilliards Mill. *See* Tippetts Mill Pond.

Hilliardston, community in n Nash County on Swift Creek. Settled about 1780. Named for John Hilliard, one of the first settlers. Alt. 200.

Hills Bay, in White Oak River, w Carteret County. Named for Edward Hill, who owned the adjacent land and Cedar Point Plantation there before and during the Civil War.

Hillsboro Store, formerly a community in e Wayne County between Hills Pond and Bear Creek.

Hillsborough, town and county seat, central Orange County on Eno River. Alt. 543. John Lawson visited the Indian town of Occaneechi there, 1701. Appears on the Moseley map, 1733. In 1754 the site came to be known as Corbinton for Francis Corbin, colonial official. Est. as Childsburgh, 1759, in honor of Thomas Childs, attorney general of the province. Name changed to Hillsborough in 1766 in honor of Wills Hill, Earl of Hillsborough (1718–93), president of the Board of Trade and Plantations, and secretary of state for the colonies. The spelling later changed unofficially to Hillsboro, but the original spelling was restored in 1965. The legislature met there in 1778 and 1782–84.

Hillsborough District was composed of Caswell, Chatham, Granville, Orange, Randolph, and Wake Counties at the time of the 1790 census.

Hillsborough Lake. *See* Ben Johnson Lake.

Hillsborough Township, central Orange County.

Hill's Bridge, nineteenth-century span across Potecasi Creek, n Hertford County between Murfreesboro and Winton. Site of a Civil War skirmish, 1863. U.S. Highway 158 now crosses at or near the site.

Hills Creek rises in sw Beaufort County and flows n into Pamlico River.

Hills Creek rises in e Rutherford County and flows sw into Second Broad River.

Hills Creek rises in n Scotland County and flows ne into Lumber River.

Hills Crossroads, community in e Halifax County. Settled prior to 1830.

Hillsdale, community in ne Davie County. Alt. 807.

Hillsdale, community in n Guilford County.

Hillside Branch rises in s Watauga County and flows se into Buffalo Branch.

Hills Mill. *See* Chiska Creek.

Hills Point, sw Beaufort County on the s side of Pamlico River.

Hill's Point. *See* Fort Hill.

Hills Pond, e Wayne County on the head of West Bear Creek.

Hill's Rock, a landing in sw Carteret County on the mainland side of Bogue Sound. Named for Edward Hill, on whose plantation it was located in the middle of the nineteenth century. Also known as White Rock.

Hills Store, community in e Lincoln County.

Hill Top, community in sw Guilford County.

Hilltop, community in s Stokes County served by post office, 1892–1903.

Hilma. *See* Farrar.

Hilton, community in n Brunswick County.

Hiltons River. *See* Brunswick River.

Hines Crossroads, community in n Halifax County. Named for Peter Hines, an early settler, a part of whose home still stands there.

Hinklesville. *See* Welcome.

Hinshaw, community in w Yadkin County. A post office once serving the community was named Randolph.

Hinson, community in w Washington County. Alt. 43.

Hinsons Crossroads, community in w Columbus County.

Hinton, community in central Guilford County served by post office, 1880–1903.

Hinton Creek rises in e Rutherford County and flows e into Cleveland County, where it enters First Broad River.

Hinton's Branch rises in e central Wake County and flows ne into Beaverdam Creek.

Hinton's Quarter, former site of Johnston County courthouse, nw Johnston County e of Clayton on the s side of Neuse River. Probably named for John Hinton, who owned much land in the area. A courthouse was est. there in 1759 or 1760 and remained until 1771, when it was moved to Smithfield, *which see*, after the formation of Wake County. Gov. William Tryon, on May 3, 1771, at Smith's Ferry a short distance e, reviewed troops from Wilmington and New Bern en route to suppress the Regulators.

Hipps Ridge, nw Cherokee County, extends ne parallel to Wolf Ridge.

Hirams Hill, a sand hill on Bogue Banks, sw Carteret County. Site of former community. Named for Hiram Moore.

Hitchcock Creek rises in e Richmond County and flows sw into Pee Dee River.

Hives, community in central Sampson County served by post office, 1884–1902.

Hiwassee Dam, resort community covering 547 acres in w Cherokee County. Privately owned. Originally served as site of construction camp from 1936 to 1940 as Hiwassee Dam was being built on Hiwassee River. Alt. 1,375.

Hiwassee Lake, nw Cherokee County, was formed at the completion of Hiwassee Dam in 1940 on Hiwassee River. Approx. 20 mi. long; covers 6,120 acres, with a max. depth of 250 ft. Owned by Tennessee Valley Authority and used for flood control, power generation, and recreation.

Hiwassee Lake State Park, former state park in w Cherokee County containing 834 acres. Est. 1948; lease from Tennessee Valley Authority terminated on December 31, 1952, and it ceased to operate as a state park. Was a scenic and recreational area; provided fishing and nature study and had vacation cabins.

Hiwassee River rises in Towns County, Ga., and flows nw into Clay County through Lake Chatuge; nw and w across the Cherokee-Clay county line; nw in Cherokee County through Hiwassee Lake and Apalachia Lake; and into Tennessee, where it enters Tennessee River approx. 30 mi. w of Athens, Tenn. Named for the Cherokee word *ayuhwá-si* (a meadow).

Hiwassee Township, s central Clay County.

Hobart. *See* Piney.

Hobbsville, community in s Gates County. Alt. 40.

Hobbton, community in n Sampson County near Wards Swamp. A post office operated there, 1881–1904.

Hobby Branch rises in se Alamance County and flows s into Haw River.

Hobby Hole, The, a deep hole in Contentnea Creek approx. 3 mi. below Ruffin's (formerly Peacock's) Bridge se of Stantonsburg on the Greene-Wilson county line. Traditionally reputed to be "bottomless." Its max. depth in 1923 was only 58 ft; by 1955 it had largely filled up.

Hobgood, town in s Halifax County. Inc. 1891. Appears as Hobgood on Gilmer map, 1863. Named for local Hobgood family. Alt. 91.

Hobson Branch rises in n Buncombe County and flows nw into Ivy Creek.

Hobson Creek rises in n Mitchell County and flows s into Little Rock Creek.

Hobton, community in n Sampson County served by post office, 1881–1904.

Hobucken, community on s Goose Creek Island, ne Pamlico County. Originally known as Jones Bay; renamed for Hoboken, N.J., to which large shipments of Irish potatoes were once sent. *See also* Secotaoc.

Hockiday Ridge, w Watauga County, extends ne from Watauga River to Rush Branch.

Hocut, community in central Bladen County served by post office, 1888–1910.

Hocutts Crossroads, community in n Johnston County.

Hodges Creek rises in se Buncombe County and flows ne into McDowell County, where it enters Crooked Creek.

Hodges Creek rises in se Hertford County and flows se into Chowan River.

Hodges Creek rises in s central Watauga County and flows e into Flannery Fork [South Fork New River].

Hodges Gap, s central Watauga County between Laurel Creek and Hodges Creek.

Hodges Gap, community in s central Watauga County on Hodges Creek.

Hodges Gap Mountain, s Watauga County 1 mi. sw of town of Boone. Alt. 3,376.

Hodges Mill Creek rises in e Wake County and flows w into Neuse River.

Hodgetown, community in e Watauga County s of Camp Branch and w of Elk Creek.

Hodgins Pond, s Hoke County on Raft Swamp, was formed in 1871 and named for Henry Hodgins. Covers 100 acres; max. depth 8 ft.

Hoe Swamp rises in n Sampson County and flows se into Six Runs Creek.

Hoffman, town in e Richmond County. Settled in the mid-1870s with the construction of Raleigh and Augusta Air Line Railroad. Inc. 1899 and reincorporated in 1913. Named for Richard C. Hoffman (1839–1926), president of the railroad. Post office est. there 1878. During World War II, Camp Mackall was adjacent to Hoffman on the e in Richmond and Scotland Counties.

Hoflers Fork, community in e Gates County.

Hofmann Forest, Onslow and Jones Counties, contains 78,000 acres. Est. in 1934 by the North Carolina Forestry Foundation. Named for Dr. Julius V. Hofmann (1882–1965), who est. the forest program at North Carolina State College in 1929 and was director of the Division of Forestry when he retired in 1948. Used as a demonstration forest by N.C. State University.

Hogan, community in w Rockingham County served by post office, 1885–89. Named for nearby Hogans Creek.

Hogan Branch rises in ne Cherokee County and flows s into Junaluska Creek.

Hogan Branch rises in se Clay County between Kimsey Bald and Marbleyard Ridge and flows sw into Buck Creek.

Hogan Creek rises in se Orange County and flows se through Hogan's Lake and into Bolin Creek.

Hogan Ridge, e Clay County between Hogan Branch and Black Branch.

Hogans Creek rises in nw Caswell County and flows ne into Dan River.

Hogans Creek rises in n Guilford County and flows n into sw Rockingham County and into Dan River.

Hogans Creek rises in se Rockingham County and flows ne into Caswell County and into Dan River.

Hogan's Lake, se Orange County 2½ mi. nw of town of Carrboro. Alt. 488. Formed in 1930 by H. C. Hogan and named for his family. Covers 17 acres, with a max. depth of 15 ft. For private recreation.

Hogback Gap, w Swain County between Cabe Branch and De Hart Creek.

Hogback Knob, w Henderson County. Alt. 3,020.

Hogback Mountain, n Graham County between Stecoah Creek and Sawyer Creek, extends ne from Big Garland Gap to Wildcat Gap. Alt. 5,200.

Hogback Mountain, nw Henderson County at the head of Foster Mill Creek.

Hogback Mountain, on the Jackson-Macon county line. Alt. 4,950.

Hogback Mountain, e Macon County between Walnut and Buck Creeks.

Hogback Mountain, w Madison County between Spring Creek and Meadow Fork.

Hog Back Mountain, ne Madison County between Bear Wallow Branch and Peter Cove Creek.

Hogback Ridge, s Buncombe County between Redmans Cove and Buckeye Cove.

Hogback Township, sw Transylvania County.

Hogback Valley, community in w Transylvania County near Lake Toxaway.

Hog Branch rises in nw Ashe County and flows s into Big Laurel Creek.

Hog Branch rises in w Orange County and flows s into Cane Creek.

Hog Branch. *See* Hawk Branch.

Hog Camp Branch rises in s Watauga County and flows se into Rockhouse Creek.

Hog Cane Branch rises in w Jackson County and flows n into Savannah Creek.

Hogeye Branch rises in nw Buncombe County and flows ne into Sandymush Creek.

Hoggard Mill Creek rises in central Bertie County and flows sw into Cashie River. Appears as Wills Quarter Creek on the Collet map, 1770, a name that was in use as late as 1882.

Hoggard's Mill, 2 mi. n of Windsor in se Bertie

County on Hoggard Mill Creek. The large pond there was the site of Lockhart Mill according to the Collet map, 1770. The surrounding community was known as Wolfington and was the county seat from 1722 until it was moved to Windsor in 1774. By 1833 the site bore its present name. *See also* Hoggard Mill Creek.

Hoggard Swamp, s Hertford County. Wiccacon River rises there.

Hogg's Folly, name formerly applied to a tract of land in w New Hanover County adjoining Wilmington on the n. John Hogg, in the eighteenth century, by means of a ditch, enclosed a tract of land on which he intended to establish a market garden. Evidently, failure of the project produced the name.

Hog Hill, se Catawba County. Named for the fact that early settlers branded their hogs and let them roam there until fall, when they were taken home to be fattened.

Hog Island, a group of islands between Back Bay and Pamlico Sound, ne Carteret County. Site of early settlement. Appears as Hog Island on Moseley map, 1733. *See also* Camp Point.

Hog Island, swampy island in central Craven County formed by Neuse River on the e and Bachelor Creek and The Gut on the w. Formerly known as Leaches Island for George M. Leach, who owned the island in 1804, and appears with that name on the Price map, 1808, the MacRae map, 1833, and the U.S. Coast Survey map, 1865. Approx. 3½ mi. long and 1 mi. wide at its widest point.

Hog Island, in Pamlico Sound near Hog Island Point on the e mainland of Hyde County.

Hog Island. *See* Lake Bay.

Hog Island Bay, name erroneously given to Cedar Island Bay, ne Carteret County, on the 1935 Soil Survey map.

Hog Island Narrows, ne Carteret County, connects Cedar Island Bay with Back Bay.

Hog Island Point, s point of Hog Island in ne Carteret County.

Hog Island Point extends off the e mainland of Hyde County into Pamlico Sound.

Hog Island Swamp, sw Sampson County s of Little Coharie Creek.

Hogjaw Gap, n Cherokee County.

Hoglot Branch rises in s Macon County and flows ne into Bates Branch.

Hogpen Bay, in the waters of Core Sound extending into Core Banks in se Carteret County.

Hogpen Branch rises in sw Buncombe County near Hogpen Gap and flows nw into Glady Fork.

Hogpen Branch rises in ne Cherokee County and flows nw into Taylor Creek.

Hogpen Branch rises in sw Johnston County and flows n into Mills Creek.

Hogpen Creek rises in se Rutherford County and flows ne into Second Broad River.

Hogpen Gap, sw Buncombe County s of Young Pisgah Mountain.

Hogpen Gap, central Cherokee County between West Prong Grape Creek and Grape Creek.

Hogpen Gap, ne Cherokee County in the Valley River Mountains. Alt. 2,353.

Hogpen Mountain, nw Rutherford County. Alt. approx. 1,900.

Hog Point, a point of land in n Carteret County extending into the waters of Turnagain Bay.

Hog Quarter. *See* Spot.

Hogsed Cove, se Clay County, through which Eagle Creek flows.

Hogs Falls, rapids in Neuse River in s Wayne County in The Roundabout. Mentioned as early as 1818 in a survey of the rivers of North Carolina.

Hogshead Creek rises in e Transylvania County and flows nw into French Broad River.

Hog Swamp rises in s Robeson County and flows s into Ashpole Swamp.

Hogtown, former town in n Martin County on Roanoke River about 1 mi. se of Hamilton, *which see*. Appears on the Collet map, 1770, and on the Price map, 1808. In 1804, however, the polling place at Hogtown was moved to Hamilton, and the former place began to decline. Probably named for the local Hogg family.

Ho-Ho Village, a modern community on the mainland side of Bogue Sound, sw Carteret County between Bogue and Morehead City.

Hoke, community in sw Washington County. Alt. 41. Known as Long Ridge from about 1857 until about 1900. The post office name was changed to Hoke in 1900 in honor of R. F. Hoke (1837–1912), the Confederate general who forced the evacuation of the Federal troops from the occupied towns of Plymouth and Washington in 1864.

Hoke County was formed in 1911 from Cumberland and Robeson Counties. Located in the se section of the state, it is bounded by Cumberland, Robeson, Scotland, Moore, and Harnett Counties. It was named for Robert F. Hoke (1837–1912) of Lincoln County, a major general in the Confederate army. Area: 382 sq. mi. County seat: Raeford, with an elevation of 262 ft. Townships are Allendale, Antioch, Blue Springs, McLauchlin, Quewhiffle, Raeford, and Stonewall. Produces corn, wheat, oats, soybeans, cotton, turkeys, livestock, hogs, watermelons, tools, concrete products, transformers, and textiles.

Holberts Cove, community in w Polk County w of Miller Mountain.

Holcombe, community in ne Madison County.

Holcombe Branch rises in e Madison County and flows nw into Little Ivy Creek.

Holcombe Cove, the valley through which Moore Creek flows in sw Buncombe County.

Holden Beach, a section of outer beach in s Brunswick County w of Lockwoods Folly Inlet and e of Big Beach. Approx. 3½ mi. long. A summer resort with cottages is there.

Holden Cove, valley in central Clay County through which Downing Creek flows.

Holden Cove, se Clay County between Big Kitchens and Little Kitchens Ridges.

Holden's Crossroads, community in e Wilson County n of White Oak Swamp. Named for W. T. Holden, local landowner.

Holder Branch rises in w Duplin County and flows sw into Maxwell Creek.

Holder Creek rises in ne Mitchell County and flows se into Charles Creek.

Holiday Island, approx. 2 mi. long in the Chowan River, nw Chowan County. Formerly about 150 acres, but now only about 40 to 50 acres. Appears on the Collet map, 1770, as Holladay Island.

Holiday Lake. *See* Pages Lake.

Holland, community in s Wake County. Est. 1900. Named for J. C. Holland. Alt. 411.

Holland Branch rises in e Madison County and flows se into Middle Fork.

Holland Branch rises in e Onslow County and flows n into Holland Mill Creek.

Holland Creek rises in s Rutherford County and flows ne into Second Broad River.

Holland Gap, e Haywood County on Glade Mountain.

Holland Mill Creek rises in e Onslow County and flows into White Oak River. Also called Holland's Creek.

Holland Mountain extends from near Canton in e Haywood County to Hooker Gap in sw Buncombe County. Its peak is known as The Pinnacle.

Hollands, community in n Pitt County on Conetoe Creek.

Hollands Creek rises in w Chatham County and flows se into Rocky River.

Hollands Creek rises in n central Rutherford County and flows se into Catheys Creek. Named for James Holland, member of the first board of trustees of the University of North Carolina. Gilbert Town, former county seat, was on the creek.

Holland's Creek. *See* Holland Mill Creek.

Hollands Crossroads, community in nw Wayne County n of Nahunta Swamp.

Holland's Point extends from e Onslow County into Queens Creek.

Hollands Sein Hole, a shallow place in Northeast Cape Fear River in central Duplin County suitable for seining.

Holleman's Crossroads, community in sw Wake County between Whiteoak Creek and Cary Branch. Known in late 1800s as Enno (post office operated by that name, 1881–1907) and in early 1900s as Collins Crossroads.

Holley Branch rises in se Mitchell County and flows se into North Toe River.

Holley's Mill. *See* Goshen Swamp.

Hollis, community in e Rutherford County on Hinton Creek.

Hollister, community in w Halifax County.

Hollow. *See* Mount Airy.

Holloway Branch rises in w Macon County and flows nw into Whiteoak Creek.

Holloway Mines, copper mines on Aarons Creek in nw Granville County. Operated from shortly prior to 1900 to about 1910 and again briefly during World War I.

Holloway Ridge, nw Yancey County between Patsy Creek and Riddle Branch.

Holloway Township, ne Person County.

Hollow Ground Swamp, in central Tyrrell County. *See also* Long Island.

Hollow Poplar. *See* Poplar.

Hollow Poplar Creek rises in nw Mitchell County and flows sw into Nolichucky River.

Hollow Rock, former rock cave on Deep River in se Chatham County near Moncure. Said to have been used for shelter by Indians. Destroyed in 1957 for gravel for road construction.

Hollow Township, nw Bladen County.

Holly Bottom Branch rises at Wildcat Spring, n Haywood County, and flows se into Groundhog Creek.

Holly Branch rises in se Macon County and flows ne into Cane Creek.

Hollybush, community in w Cleveland County served by post office, 1875–1905. Also spelled Holly Bush.

Holly Bush. *See* Hollybush.

Holly Grove, community in n central Bertie County.

Holly Grove, community in central Davidson County. *See also* Conrad Hill.

Holly Grove, community in ne Gates County.

Holly Grove, community in w Richmond County.

Holly Grove Township, ne Gates County.

Holly Meadow Branch rises in central Cabarrus County and flows s into Coddle Creek.

Holly Neck. *See* Beasley.

Holly Point, peninsula extending from w Goose Creek Island, ne Pamlico County, into Goose Creek at the mouth of Dixon Creek.

Holly Ridge, a raised strip of ground in Dismal Swamp, se Gates County.

Holly Ridge, town in s Onslow County. Alt. 66. Est. about 1890 as a wood station on the railroad. Inc. 1941. Named for a slight elevation on which holly formerly grew; at Holly Shelter Bay about 1 mi. s was Sages Ordinary (dating from the Revolution), at which George Washington spent the night, April 23, 1791. *See also* Camp Davis.

Holly Shelter Bay, a pocosin in e Pender County bounded on the ne by Shaken Creek, on the w by Northeast Cape Fear River, and on the s by Trumpeter Swamp. It is about 10 mi. long and 7 mi. wide. Appears as Holly Schelter Precoson on the Collet map, 1770 (although mistakenly applied to Angola Bay), and on the Price map, 1808. Holly Shelter Wildlife Management Area, 48,470 acres, is operated by the N.C. Wildlife Resources Commission; bear and deer abound.

Holly Shelter Creek receives the waters of Angola, Shaken, and Moores Creeks; Cane Branch; and other streams in ne Pender County and flows w approx. 30 mi. into Northeast Cape Fear River. Called Shelter River in a 1913 report by the U.S. Chief of Engineers. Appears as Holly Schelter Creek on the Collet map, 1770.

Holly Springs, community in e Carteret County on Newport River.

Holly Springs, community in w Henderson County between Boylston and Brock Creeks.

Holly Springs, community in s Rutherford County; former resort with a hotel.

Holly Springs, town in s Wake County. Settled 1826; inc. 1877. Named for holly trees growing near a spring in the vicinity. Alt. 350.

Holly Springs, community in n Yadkin County between Smithtown and Yadkin River.

Holly Springs Township, sw Wake County.

Holly Township, ne Pender County.

Hollyville, town in ne Pamlico County adjoining Vandemere. Inc. 1907, but long inactive in municipal affairs. Named for local holly trees. Known more recently as Cash Corner. *See also* Cash Corner No. 2.

Hollywood, community in central Carteret County served by post office, 1874–1915.

Hollywood Ridge, community in n central Caldwell County on a ridge parallel to and s of Yadkin River.

Holman, community in w Davie County near the headwaters of Bear Creek. Settled about 1786 and named for Holman family.

Holmans Mills, community in s Alamance County served by post office, 1878–1908.

Holmes Point, on the w side of New River in central Onslow County. Formerly known as Little Ragged Point.

Holsclaw's Creek rises in e Caldwell County and flows e into Duck Creek.

Holt Knob, se Macon County between Monger Creek and Mill Creek.

Holt Lake, central Johnston County on Black Creek. Original dam constructed prior to 1911; present dam, downstream from first, built in early 1920s. Covers approx. 400 acres; max. depth 25 ft.

Holtsburg, community in sw Davidson County served by post office, 1856–66.

Holts Mill, community in w Wayne County.

Holt's Store. *See* Albertson.

Holy Swamp rises in central Robeson County and flows se into Big Raft Swamp.

Homestead, community in nw Mecklenburg County.

Homing Creek rises in e Wake County and flows se into Little River.

Hominy, community in sw Buncombe County. Alt. 2,097.

Hominy Creek rises in e Haywood County and flows generally e into central Buncombe County, where it enters French Broad River. Said to have been visited by a South Carolina hunting party before the Revolution and given the name because they ate hominy for supper the first night.

Hominy Gap, e Haywood County. Alt. 2,678. Highway between Canton and Asheville passes through the gap.

Hominy Heights, former community in central Wilson County just w of and named for Hominy Swamp, now within the limits of the city of Wilson. Known earlier as White's Store. Capt. William White operated a store there as early as 1812.

Hominy Swamp rises in w central Wilson County and flows se into Contentnea Creek. Appears in local records as early as 1764. Said to have been named for a hominy mill operated on its waters by that date.

Honey, community in e Union County served by post office, 1892–1903.

Honeycut Cove, near the n end of the Elk Mountains, central Buncombe County e of Jump Cove.

Honeycutt, community in w Johnston County served by post office, 1899–1903.

Honeycutt, community in w Mitchell County on Big Rock Creek.

Honeycutt Branch rises in n Mitchell County and flows s into Cane Creek.

Honeycutt Creek rises in n central Wake County and flows ne into Neuse River. Formerly called Fall Creek and Big Fall Creek.

Honeycutt Mine, former gold mine on Little Buffalo Creek, ne Cabarrus County.

Honeycutts Township, central Sampson County.

Honey Hill, town in central Columbus County. Inc. 1895, but long inactive in municipal affairs.

Honey Island Swamp rises in w Brunswick and e Columbus Counties and flows sw along the Brunswick-Columbus county line through Green Swamp into Juniper Creek.

Honey Pond, community in w central Brunswick County.

Honey Pot Swamp rises in central Gates County and flows s into Bennetts Creek.

Honolulu, community in n Craven County.

Hood Creek rises in ne Brunswick County and flows n into Cape Fear River.

Hood Gap, e Haywood County at the ne end of Buck Cove.

Hoods or **Hoods Crossroads**, community in e Mecklenburg County. Morning Star Lutheran Church organized there in 1775.

Hoods Pond, e Wake County on Marks Creek.

Hoodsville. *See* Chesterfield.

Hood Swamp, community in e Wayne County near West Bear Creek. Formerly called Aaron for Aaron Parks (d. 1845), a local farmer and lay religious leader. Renamed for local Free Will Baptist church, of which Parks was a member. Name appeared in nineteenth-century records as Wood Swamp.

Hoof Inn, an early nineteenth-century tavern in w Washington County located on what is now the Plymouth-Pinetown road approx. midway between Ausbon and Hinson.

Hooker, community in e Alleghany County. Alt. approx. 2,600.

Hooker Creek rises in w Henderson County and flows sw into e Transylvania County and into Little River.

Hooker Gap, sw Buncombe County at the e end of Holland Mountain.

Hookers Knob, e Madison County between Jarvis Mountain and Gabriels Creek.

Hookerton, town in se Greene County on Contentnea Creek. Alt. 75. Inc. as Hookerton, 1817, on the lands of William Hooker. Known as Caswells Landing prior to the Revolution for Benjamin Caswell, brother of Governor Richard Caswell. Several early nineteenth-century academies flourished there, and a public library was est. in 1817.

Hookerton Township, s Greene County.

Hooks Branch rises in w Johnston County and flows s into Black Creek.

Hooper Bald, w Graham County between McGuires community and Huckleberry Knob. Alt. 5,429. Named for Enos Hooper, who moved to Graham from Jackson County and had a farm in the valley below the mountain.

Hooper Branch rises in s Graham County and flows nw into Snowbird Creek.

Hooper Branch rises in n Lincoln County and flows se into Anderson Creek.

Hooper County was authorized to be est. from Robeson and Richmond Counties in 1851 provided the people in the territory voted for its creation. The people voted against the new county, however. It was to have been named in honor of William Hooper, one of the North Carolina signers of the Declaration of Independence.

Hooper Cove, w Graham County between Cedar Top and Rattler Ford.

Hooper Creek rises in s Polk County and flows se into South Carolina, where it enters Pacolet River.

Hooper Knob, central Jackson County between Moses Creek and Wayehutta Creek. Alt. 3,719.

Hooper Mill Creek rises in w Graham County and flows se and n into Santeetlah Lake.

Hoopers Creek rises in n Henderson County and flows w into Cane Creek.

Hoopers Creek Township, n Henderson County.

Hoophole Landing, e Beaufort County on Pungo River. A small community adjoining the landing bears the same name.

Hoop Pole Creek, a waterway between several small islands near the e end of Bogue Banks, s Carteret County in Bogue Sound.

Hootentown. *See* Wootentown.

Hoot Owl Cove, nw Jackson County on Shoal Creek.

Hootowl Hollow, sw Mitchell County parallel to Roaring Branch.

Hoots Millpond, e Wilkes County on Little Elkin River. Grain and sawmill operated there by the Hoots family.

Hoover Hill, community in w Randolph County. A post office operated there, 1849–1907. In the early twentieth century, a prosperous gold mine was operated there. Ancestors of President Herbert Hoover are buried in the vicinity.

Hoover Meadow, se Yancey County between the sw end of Dovers Ridge and Sevenmile Ridge.

Hop Creek rises in nw Catawba County and flows se into Jacob Fork.

Hope. *See* Trinity.

Hopedale, community in central Alamance

County on Stony Creek at Big Falls, *which see.* Produces textiles.

Hope Mills, town in sw Cumberland County. Active antebellum textile center. Known as Rockfish before the Civil War. Inc. as Hope Mills, 1891, when new mills were built. Alt. 117.

Hope Valley Forest, n Chatham and s Durham Counties, contained 1,735 acres. Est. in 1941 when the U.S. government conveyed a rehabilitation camp area to North Carolina State College. Now part of Jordan Lake public lands.

Hopewell, community in nw Mecklenburg County. It developed around Hopewell Presbyterian Church, organized 1762.

Hopewell, community in e Rutherford County. Named for a local church.

Hopewell Branch rises in central Madison County and flows sw into French Broad River.

Hopis Branch rises in w Madison County and flows s into Meadow Fork.

Hopkins, community in n Ashe County.

Hopkins, community in e Wake County.

Hopkins Mine, former gold mine in ne Cabarrus County on Beaver Creek.

Hop Mountain, sw Madison County, a peak on Spring Creek Mountain. Alt. 4,072.

Hopper, community in ne Rockingham County served by post office, 1892–1910. Named for postmaster Ida Hopper.

Hopper's Ford. *See* Worthville.

Horace, community in e Henderson County between Little Hungry Creek and Big Hungry River.

Horn Beam Swamp rises in e Nash County and flows se into Edgecombe County, where it enters Compass Creek.

Hornblower Point, s Chowan County, extends from e side of Edenton Bay into Albemarle Sound. A railroad bridge across the sound extends from the site to the mouth of Kendricks Creek in n Washington County. Now a part of Edenton Naval Air Station property. Shown as Moseleys Point on the Collet map, 1770; as Hornblow's Point on the MacRae map, 1833; and as Skinner's Point on the Price map, 1808, and on the Kerr map, 1882. Named for the Horniblow family, which owned property there.

Hornbuckle Creek rises in n Jackson County and flows nw into Soco Creek.

Hornbuckle Ridge, w Jackson County between Sassafras Branch and Grassy Knob.

Horn Camp Swamp rises in s Robeson County and flows sw into Ashpole Swamp.

Horne Creek rises in se Surry County and flows se into Yadkin River.

Horner, community in e Granville County. Once a railroad siding; also site of Horner Military School.

Hornes Bay, a sand-filled bay in w Columbus County. *See* Carolina Bays.

Hornet, community in se Mecklenburg County served by post office, 1880–1903. *See* also Alexander's Store.

Hornet Swamp rises in w Sampson County and flows w into Little Coharie Creek.

Horneyhead Mountain, in central Jackson County on the ne end of Cedar Valley Knob. Alt. 4,060.

Horniblow. *See* Hornblower Point.

Hornpipe Creek rises in s Lenoir County and flows nw into Southwest Creek. The name appears in local records dating from before the Revolution.

Horns Branch rises in s Surry County and flows ne into King Creek.

Horn's Branch rises in w Wilson County and flows w into Shepherd's Branch.

Horn Swamp. *See* Sandy Run.

Hornytown, community in ne Davidson County at the head of Abbotts Creek.

Horsebone Gap, on the Haywood-Jackson county line on the main Balsam Range. The Blue Ridge Parkway passes through or near the gap. Named for the fact that a horse, turned out to graze in the area, died, and his bones lay bleaching in the sun for a number of years.

Horse Branch rises in sw Beaufort County and flows ne into Chocowinity Creek.

Horse Branch rises in w Lenoir County and flows se into Southwest Creek. The name appears in local records dating from before the Revolution.

Horse Branch rises in n Madison County and flows se into Shelton Laurel Creek.

Horse Branch rises in n Pender County and flows sw into Long Creek. Named for adjacent high ground to which wild horses retreated in time of flood in pre-Revolutionary days.

Horsebranch, community in central Pender County on Horse Branch.

Horse Cove, w Graham County between Little Santeetlah Creek and Rock Creek Knob.

Horse Cove, nw Henderson County between Beetree Ridge and Big Ridge.

Horse Cove, se Macon County, through which Edwards and Blackrock Creeks flow. A post office by the name served the area in the late nineteenth century. Woodrow Wilson, in a letter written from Horse Cove on July 30, 1879, reported that he spent a part of the summer there with his mother and other relatives. John R. Thompson rented summer homes and furnished meals for visitors from New Orleans, Charleston, and other coastal cities. Highlands, *which see*, was being developed nearby at about the same time.

Horse Cove, w central Swain County, extends e from Noland Creek between Andreas Branch and Massie Gap.

Horse Cove, n Transylvania County, extends ne from Cat Pen Gap to Davidson River.

Horse Cove Branch rises in n Macon County and flows ne into Burningtown Creek.

Horse Cove Ridge, w Graham County, forms the sw watershed of Little Santeetlah Creek and the sw boundary of Joyce Kilmer Memorial Forest.

Horse Creek rises in sw Grayson County, Va., and flows se into n central Ashe County, where it enters North Fork New River.

Horse Creek rises in w Avery County and flows e into North Toe River.

Horse Creek rises in Cherokee County, S.C., and flows ne into Rutherford County, where it enters Broad River.

Horse Creek rises in nw Durham County and flows s into North Fork Little River.

Horse Creek rises in w Franklin County and flows sw into n Wake County, where it enters Neuse River. Appears on the Collet map, 1770.

Horse Creek, w Haywood County in Great Smoky Mountains National Park, rises near lat. 35°35′17″ N., long. 83°10′40″ W., and flows ne to join Bear Branch in forming Rough Creek.

Horse Creek rises on Fort Bragg Military Reservation in n Hoke County and flows ne into Little River.

Horse Creek rises in s Moore County near town of Pinehurst and flows s into Deep Creek.

Horse Creek rises in w central Polk County and flows s into Pacolet River.

Horse Creek rises in s Stanly County and flows ne into Long Creek.

Horse Creek Gap, on the Haywood-Swain county line on Balsam Mountain between Chiltoes Mountain and Cataloochee Balsam. Alt. 5,575.

Horse Creek Ridge, w Avery County.

Horse Creek Township, nw Ashe County.

Horse Fork rises in nw Catawba County and flows n into Catawba River.

Horsefork Mountain, e Haywood County, extends ne from Fall Creek to Grassy Gap.

Horse Gap, on the Ashe-Wilkes county line.

Horse Gap, n Buncombe County between Sheep Knob and Ray Knob.

Horse Gap, on the McDowell-Yancey county line near the head of Left Prong Three Forks Creek.

Horse Gap, n Transylvania County between Laurel Brook and Cantrell Creek.

Horse Island, in Core Sound, ne Carteret County. Ruins of a clubhouse exist on the island, and two persons are said to have been murdered there, giving rise to ghost tales.

Horse Island, a long, narrow tidal-marsh island se of Beaufort in s Carteret County.

Horse Knob, n Transylvania County at the nw end of Huckleberry Ridge near the head of South Prong Turkey Creek.

Horselot Cove, central Clay County, s of Evans Ridge.

Horse Mountain, on the McDowell-Yancey county line.

Horse Mountain Gap, s Burke County. Alt. 2,018.

Horsepasture River rises in s Jackson County and flows se across sw Transylvania County into South Carolina, where it enters the Toxaway River.

Horse Pen Bay, swamp in nw Brunswick County. A part of Green Swamp.

Horsepen Bay, a small pocosin near the head of Horse Branch, *which see*, n Pender County.

Horse Pen Branch rises in sw Bladen County and flows w into Horse Pen Swamp.

Horsepen Branch rises in s Greene County and flows se into Rainbow Creek. The name appears in local records prior to the Revolution.

Horsepen Branch rises in s Warren County and flows se into Shocco Creek.

Horse Pen Creek rises in s central Bladen County and flows se into Brown Marsh Swamp.

Horsepen Creek rises in nw Columbus County on the Columbus-Robeson-Bladen county lines and flows w into Big Swamp.

Horsepen Creek rises in w Guilford County and flows ne into Reedy Fork Creek.

Horse Pen Mountain, at the head of Cabin Creek in s Henderson County.

Horsepen Pocosin, a sandy pocosin in sw Gates County. Alt. 28.

Horsepen Point, se Carteret County, extends from Core Banks into Core Sound.

Horsepen Point, on Ocracoke Island near the community of Ocracoke, se Hyde County.

Horse Pen Ridge, w Haywood County in Great Smoky Mountains National Park, a spur extending nw from Cataloochee Divide; its center is near lat. 35°35′40″ N., long. 83°05′07″ W.

Horsepen Swamp rises in nw Beaufort County and flows sw into Tranters Creek.

Horse Pen Swamp rises in sw Bladen County and flows w into Robeson County, where it enters Big Swamp.

Horsepen Swamp rises in w Pitt County and flows se into Swift Creek.

Horse Pool appears on the Moseley map, 1733, in what is now e Gates County in the w edge of the Dismal Swamp.

Horse Range Ridge, s Graham County, extends se from Little Snowbird Creek to Old Billy Top.

Horse Ridge, n Avery County.

Horse Ridge, s Burke County in the South Mountains. Alt. 2,800.

Horse Ridge, ne Cherokee County in the Valley River Mountains.

Horse Ridge, sw Macon County between Siler Bald Branch and Factory Branch.

Horse Ridge, ne Swain County in Great Smoky Mountains National Park, extends sw from Balsam Mountain between Stillwell Creek and Left Fork [Deep Creek].

Horse Ridge, nw Watauga County, extends n between Rube Creek and Little Beaverdam Creek.

Horse Ridge, n Yancey County between Seng Branch and Cynthia Branch.

Horse Ridge. *See* Balsam Mountain.

Horse Run rises in e Duplin County and flows se into Cabin Creek.

Horse's Creek rises in s Moore County and flows sw into Deep Creek.

Horse's Creek rises in w Moore County and flows nw into Dry Creek.

Horseshoe, community in nw Camden County. Settled shortly after 1700 and formerly known as Newfoundland.

Horse Shoe, community in w Henderson County. Named because it is situated in a sharp bend in French Broad River. Alt. 2,083.

Horseshoe, community on Deep River in ne Moore County. Named for bend in river.

Horseshoe, The, bend in Nantahala River, w Macon County.

Horseshoe, The, a ridge parallel to a deep bend in Hazel Creek, w Swain County.

Horseshoe Bend, a bend in Eagle Creek at the sw end of Big Fork Ridge, nw Swain County.

Horseshoe Bend, w Swain County in Little Tennessee River.

Horseshoe Bend. *See* Andrews Geyser.

Horse Shoe Mountain, w Henderson County between Johnsons Mill Creek and French Broad River. Alt. 2,775.

Horseshoe Mountain, se Macon County at the head of Brooks Creek.

Horseshoe Neck, a sharp bend in the Yadkin River in w Davidson and e Davie Counties. The neck of land formed by the bend is in Davidson County. Appears on the Collet map, 1770, as Horse-shoe. *See also* Boone's Cave.

Horseshoe Ridge, s Swain County between Dark Branch and Davis Branch.

Horseshoe Rock, peak on the sw end of Wolf Mountain, e Jackson County.

Horse Swamp rises in s Hertford County and flows se and ne to join Flat Swamp in forming Bear Swamp.

Horse Swamp rises in e Onslow County and flows nw into Little Northeast Creek.

Horse Swamp rises in s Robeson County and flows sw into Aaron Swamp.

Horse Swamp Pocosin, e Onslow County between Queens Creek and Little Northeast Creek.

Horse Trail Gap, on the McDowell-Yancey county line near the head of Roaring Fork.

Horse Trough Mountain, w Montgomery County near Woodrun Creek.

Horsetrough Ridge, ne Swain County in Great Smoky Mountains National Park, a spur extending sw from Overlook Ridge between Heintooga Creek and Selma Creek.

Horseway Swamp rises in e Pitt County and flows ne into Beaufort County, where it enters Chicod Creek.

Horton Bay, n central Carteret County behind Horton Point near the mouth of South River.

Horton Branch rises in n Cherokee County and flows sw into Beaverdam Creek.

Horton Branch rises in s Watauga County and flows se into Joe Creek.

Horton Creek rises in w Yancey County and flows e into Indian Creek.

Horton Hill, n Yancey County between Bee Branch and Sidney Hill.

Horton Knob, n Macon County between Allen Branch and Rose Creek.

Horton Point, n central Carteret County on e shore of South River near its mouth.

Hoskin Fork rises in nw Watauga County and flows n into sw Ashe County, where it enters North Fork New River.

Hoskins Point. *See* Palmetto Point.

Hosley Branch. *See* Hostler Branch.

Hostler Branch rises in w Caswell County and flows e into County Line Creek. Appears as Hosley Branch on early maps of the county.

Hotel. *See* Woodville.

Hotel Creek. *See* Hall's Creek.

Hothouse, community in sw Cherokee County on Persimmon Creek.

Hothouse Branch rises in sw Cherokee County and flows se into Hot House Creek. Named for the fact that the Indians had "hot houses" in which heated stones were placed for "sweat baths" to refresh fatigued warriors and hunters.

Hothouse Branch rises in s Clay County and flows nw into Shooting Creek.

Hot House Branch rises in central Hertford County and flows nw into Potecasi Creek.

Hot House Creek rises in sw Cherokee County and flows sw into Fannin County, Ga., where it enters Ocoee River.

Hot House Township, sw Cherokee County.

Hot Springs, town in w Madison County on French Broad River. Named for thermal springs in the town, discovered in 1778; a health resort since 1800. Name changed from Warm Springs, 1886; inc. 1889. Alt. 1,332. An internment camp for Germans during World War I was there. Spaightville, *which see*, inc. 1802, may have been at the site.

Hot Springs Mountain, w Madison County parallel to Mountain Island Branch.

Hot Springs Township, former township in nw Madison County, now township no. 9.

Houck, community in w Caldwell County served by post office, 1888–90. Name changed to Mortimer, *which see.*

House, community in central Pitt County, approx. 1 mi. n of Greenville.

House Creek rises in central Wake County just w of city of Raleigh and flows ne into Crabtree Creek.

House Creek Township, central Wake County.

House of Passage. *See* Old Town.

House's Mill Pond, n Sampson County on Sevenmile Swamp. A mill est. there in 1812 by William House still grinds corn.

Houston, community in sw Union County. Alt. 666.

Houston Branch rises in e Macon County and flows sw into Big Creek.

Houston Gap, e Mitchell County between Little Bear Creek and Beaver Creek.

Houston Knob, e Macon County between Moss Branch and Walnut Creek.

Houston Knob, w Yancey County between Possumtrot Creek and Indian Creek.

Houston Ridge, central Avery County.

Houston's Shop, community in se Mecklenburg County.

Houstonville, community in ne Iredell County.

Howard, community in s Bertie County served by post office, 1883–1900.

Howard Branch rises in s Macon County and flows n into Dryman Fork.

Howard Creek rises in n Watauga County and flows se into South Fork New River.

Howard Gap, s Macon County between Middle Creek and Norton Branch.

Howard Gap, w Polk County between Warrior Mountain and Miller Mountain. Named for Capt. Thomas Howard, whose men, led by Skyuka, defeated Cherokee Indians there in 1776. *See also* Skyuka Mountain.

Howard Knob, mountain in central Watauga County about ½ mi. n of town of Boone. Named during Revolutionary War when a Loyalist, Benjamin Howard, fled from American patriots to a cave on the mountain. There is no record of his discovery. Alt. 4,420. *See also* Sampson's Chimney.

Howard Reef, se Hyde County in Pamlico Sound approx. 1 nautical mi. n of Ocracoke Island; approx. 1¾ mi. long and over ½ mi. wide.

Howards Bay, s Onslow County in New River between Cedar Point and Sulliers Bay.

Howards Creek. *See* Indian Creek.

Howards Creek Township, w central Lincoln County.

Howard's Knob Gap, central Watauga County. Alt. 3,679.

Howard's Mill, community in n Moore County in an area formerly known as Noise, *which see.* Named for John Hayworth (later Howard), who operated a tannery and gristmill there. Mill operated until 1950s.

Howard Swamp rises in s Robeson County and flows sw into Indian Swamp.

Howell Branch rises in n Yancey County and flows s into Big Creek.

Howell Creek rises in central Wayne County and flows se into Stony Creek.

Howells Point, a small neck of land on the e side of Lockwoods Folly River just n of the channel of the Intracoastal Waterway in s Brunswick County.

Howellsville, community in central Robeson County served by post office, 1894–1913.

Howell Swamp rises in n Greene County and flows sw into Beaman Run. Named for the Howell family, who were living in the vicinity as early as 1769.

Howes Point, se Brunswick County on Cape Fear River. Now within the bounds of Sunny Point ammunition depot. Birthplace of Gen. Robert Howe (1732–86).

Howes Point, e New Hanover County, extends from the mainland into the n waters of Middle Sound.

Howie Mine, former gold mine in w Union County s of East Fork Twelvemile Creek.

Howland Creek rises in e Carteret County and flows approx. 2.2 mi. se into Jarrett Bay.

Howlett Creek rises in e Granville County and flows n into Little Island Creek.

Howsers Creek rises in central Gaston County and flows e into South Fork Catawba River.

Hoyle, community in nw Randolph County served by post office, 1886–1905.

Hoyles Creek rises in s Lincoln County and flows sw into n Gaston County, where it turns se to flow into South Fork Catawba River.

Hoyles Store, community in s Lincoln County between Rockdam Creek and Leonard Fork. The Hoylesville post office that existed in

1822 may have been at or near the community. *See also* Dallas.

Hoylesville. *See* Dallas.

Hoyts Stop, a short channel running into the Banks Channel in w Carteret County. Named for Hoyt Tootle, a black fisherman.

Hub. *See* Boardman.

Hubbard, former community in w Swain County on Little Tennessee River. The site is now covered by the waters of Fontana Lake.

Hubert, community in e Onslow County on Bell Swamp.

Huble Creek. *See* Hubquarter Creek.

Hubquarter Creek rises in ne Warren County and flows ne into Lake Gaston. Appears as Huble Creek on the Collet map, 1770, but with its present name on the Price map, 1808.

Huckleberry Branch rises in sw Wilson County and flows n into Black Creek.

Huckleberry Creek rises in ne Macon County and flows s into Beasley Creek.

Huckleberry Gap, n Madison County between White Rock Branch and Chimney Creek.

Huckleberry Knob, w Graham County between Hooper Bald and Little Huckleberry Knob. Alt. approx. 5,570.

Huckleberry Knob, w Haywood County between Deep Gap and Murray Gap.

Huckleberry Knob, n Madison County between Huckleberry Gap and White Oak Gap.

Huckleberry Mountain, n Henderson County between Rattlesnake Knob and Kyles Creek. Alt. 2,959.

Huckleberry Mountain, ne Rutherford County between Pot Branch and North Fork. Alt. 2,108.

Huckleberry Patch, mountain in sw Watauga County at the head of Boone Fork.

Huckleberry Ridge, s Henderson County between Cabin Creek and Rush Mountain. Cited in early county records as Whortleberry Mountain. Formerly a Girl Scout camp and later an artists' and writers' summer retreat known as Huckleberry Mountain Artists' Colony.

Huckleberry Ridge, ne Macon County between Blazed Creek and Huckleberry Creek.

Huckleberry Ridge, n Madison County parallel to Rock Branch.

Huckleberry Ridge, a sandy area on the sw side of Angola Bay, n Pender County.

Huckleberry Ridge, n Transylvania County, extends se beside South Prong Turkey Creek.

Huckleberry Springs, community in w Durham County a short distance nw of the city of Durham. Formerly a popular picnic site because of the excellent spring water.

Huckleberry Swamp. *See* Enfield.

Hudson, town in s Caldwell County. Settled in the late nineteenth century and known as Sardis for a local Baptist church. Inc. 1905 and named for David Hudson, the founder. Alt. 1,264.

Hudson Spring, community in nw Anson County on Richardson Creek.

Hudson Township, se Caldwell County.

Huey Gap, central Haywood County on the head of Dotson Branch.

Huff Island, se Bertie County between Middle River and Roanoke River. Approx. 4½ mi. long and 1 mi. wide. *See also* Purchace Islands.

Huff Island, a sandy island approx. ½ mi. long in French Broad River, w Madison County.

Huffmans Creek rises in n Davidson County and flows sw into Reedy Creek.

Huffmantown, community in nw Onslow County between Mill Swamp and Purgatory Pocosin.

Huggins Bay, a loam-filled bay in sw Columbus County. *See also* Carolina Bays.

Huggins Branch rises in n Swain County and flows nw into Hazel Creek.

Huggins Creek rises in sw Columbus County and flows s into South Carolina, where it enters Jordan Swamp.

Huggins Creek rises in n Swain County in Great Smoky Mountains National Park and flows sw into Forney Creek.

Huggins Hell, thicket of rhododendron and laurel covering between 400 and 500 acres in n Swain County in Great Smoky Mountains National Park. Named for Irving Huggins, early settler, who was trapped there for several days while herding cattle.

Huggins Island, e Onslow County between Dudley's Island and Swansboro in White Oak River. Named for Luke Huggins. Appears as Stones Island on the Moseley map, 1733. A fort or battery erected there by Confederate forces was designed to protect Bogue Inlet and West Channel from the Union fleet; it was destroyed in 1862.

Huggins Ridge, n Swain County in Great Smoky Mountains National Park, a short spur extending nw from Welch Ridge between Sawbrier Ridge and Huggins Branch.

Hugh Day's Gap, ne Caldwell and w Wilkes Counties. Alt. 1,687. Named for Hugh Day, a hatter in the area in the early nineteenth century.

Hughes, community in central Avery County.

Hughes Branch rises in e Macon County and flows sw into Watauga Creek.

Hughes Branch rises in n Mitchell County and flows se into Bean Creek.

Hughes Branch rises in central Swain County and flows n into Tuckasegee River.

Hughes Creek rises in n Lee County and flows e into Lick Creek.

Hughes Creek rises in nw Mitchell County and flows sw into Hollow Poplar Creek.

Hughes Creek rises in s Polk County and flows se into South Carolina, where it enters Pacolet River.

Hughes Creek appears on the Collet map, 1770, apparently rising in what is now ne Yadkin County n of East Bend and flowing ne into Yadkin River.

Hughes Gap, on the Mitchell County, N.C.–Carter County, Tenn., line.

Hughes Gap, w Mitchell County at the head of Cooper Branch.

Hughes Knob, w Jackson County between Bearpen Creek and Jim Creek.

Hughes Ridge, e Avery County.

Hughes Ridge, ne Swain County in Great Smoky Mountains National Park, extends approx. 11 mi. s from Pecks Corner.

Hughes Ridge, n Yancey County between Lottie Creek and Little Creek.

Hughes Ridge Branch rises in e Avery County and flows e into Rockhouse Creek.

Hugh's Creek. *See* East Buies Creek.

Hugo, community in n Lenoir County. The name may have been given in honor of French author Victor Hugo.

Huitt Bay, swamp in s central Brunswick County; a part of Green Swamp.

Hull Branch rises in se Avery County and flows e into South Harper Creek.

Hulls Crossroads, community in w Lincoln County.

Hulme Hill (Hull Hill), a low ridge in n central Caldwell County on the n side of Yadkin River.

Named for Maj. William Hulme, planter and legislator who settled there in 1807.

Humpback Mountain, on the Avery-McDowell county line at the e end of Dividing Ridge. Alt. approx. 4,200. Known by the Cherokee Indians as Koonasoga.

Humphrey, community in se Duplin County.

Hump Mountain, w Avery County. Alt. 5,587.

Hungry Creek rises in e Haywood County and flows nw into East Fork Pigeon River.

Hungry Neck. *See* Kelly.

Hunkadora. *See* Bahama.

Hunsucker, community in sw Scotland County. Formerly known as Brick Mill.

Hunsucker's Store. *See* Star.

Huntdale, community in w Mitchell County on Toe River. Alt. 2,058.

Hunter Branch rises in n central Haywood County and flows n into Stevens Creek.

Hunter Branch rises in s Madison County and flows s into Ivy River.

Hunter Creek rises in central Madison County between Watershed Mountain and High Rock and flows se into Walnut Creek.

Hunter Jim Creek rises in w Jackson County and flows se into West Fork Tuckasegee River.

Hunters Bridge, community in central Beaufort County on Bath Creek.

Hunters Creek rises at Great Lake in sw Craven County and flows sw along the Carteret-Jones county line into White Oak River. Named for the Hunter family, early settlers.

Hunters Millpond, built prior to 1720 at the junction of Raynor Swamp and Harrell Swamp at the head of Bennetts Creek, e Gates County. Was destroyed about 1922 when a new highway was built. It was about 1 mi. long. Known in later years as Cross Millpond.

Hunters Mill Township, e central Gates County.

Huntersville, town in n Mecklenburg County. Inc. 1873. Known previously as Hunter's Depot. Named for Robert Hunter, local resident about 1860. Alt. 814.

Huntersville. *See* Mount Holly.

Huntersville. *See* Murphy.

Huntersville Township, former township in ne Mecklenburg County, now township no. 15.

Hunting Branch rises in Cane Creek Mountains in s Alamance County and flows s into Cane Creek.

Hunting Branch rises in n Northampton County and flows se into Corduroy Swamp.

Hunting Creek rises in central Burke County and flows n through Morganton into Catawba River.

Hunting Creek rises in North River Pocosin, s Camden County, and flows e into North River.

Hunting Creek rises in n Rutherford County and flows s into Robinson Creek.

Hunting Creek rises in s Wilkes County in the Brushy Mountains and flows se through ne Iredell and w Davie Counties into South Yadkin River. *See also* Flat Rock Creek; Frohock Sawmill.

Hunting Creek, community in s Wilkes County on Hunting Creek.

Hunting Island, in Bogue Sound, sw Carteret County.

Hunting Island Creek rises in w Carteret County and flows s into Bogue Inlet.

Hunting Quarter Inlet appears on the Moseley map, 1733, in Core Banks of Carteret County. It was opened and closed in the 1730s.

Hunting Quarter Sound appears on the Moseley map, 1733, as the water now forming the n end of Core Sound in ne Carteret County. Four small islands extending se from the present Hog Island separated the sound from Pamlico Sound. Three of the four islands were named Chainshot, Harbour, and Shell.

Hunting Quarters Township, former township in e Carteret County. Cedar Island Township was formed from a part of Hunting Quarters, and the remainder is now Atlantic Township. The area was formerly a summer camp of the Core Indians.

Hunting Run rises in n Pitt County and flows se into Grindle Creek.

Huntley, community in central Sampson County served by post office, 1875–1922.

Hunts, community in w Nash County served by post office, 1885–1903.

Huntsboro, community in e Granville County. Named for John and Mourning Hunt, residents in 1760s.

Huntsborough, town authorized in 1814 to be laid off on the lands of Jonathan Hunt "on the waters of Little Ivey" in what was then Buncombe County but is now Madison County. The town apparently did not materialize.

Hunts Branch rises in central Transylvania County and flows se into Tucker Creek.

Hunts Fork rises in e Davidson County and flows se into Rich Fork Creek.

Hunts Pond. *See* Lake View.

Hunt's Store. *See* New Castle.

Huntsville, town in se Yadkin County near Yadkin River. Chartered 1792 by Charles Hunt of Salisbury, who sold lots there. Thomas L. Clingman, U.S. senator and Confederate general, was born there. Town rechartered 1822, but long inactive in municipal affairs.

Huntsville Mountains, a ridge in s McDowell County near Glenwood. Extensive gold-mining operations were carried on there from the mid-nineteenth century until 1909.

Huntsville Township, sw Rockingham County. Name derived from activity of sportsmen in area.

Hurdle Mills, community in sw Person County.

Hurdle Ridge, a strip of high ground in the Dismal Swamp, se Gates County.

Hurley Lake. *See* Eury Lake.

Huron, community in nw Tyrrell County served by post office, 1900–1908.

Huronian Mountain, a peak in the Cane Creek Mountains, s Alamance County.

Hurrah Ridge, s Macon County between West Fork Overflow Creek and Abe Creek.

Hurricane, The (HARRY-kin), se corner of Granville County and parts of Franklin and Wake Counties where a storm wreaked havoc in the nineteenth century.

Hurricane Branch rises in nw Ashe County and flows ne into Horse Creek.

Hurricane Branch rises in ne Cherokee County and flows s into Welch Mill Creek.

Hurricane Branch rises in nw Swain County and flows s into Ekaneetlee Creek.

Hurricane Cove, e Graham County on the headwaters of Panther Creek.

Hurricane Creek rises in central Clay County and flows nw into Tusquitee Creek.

Hurricane Creek rises in n Haywood County and flows sw into Pigeon River.

Hurricane Creek rises in sw Jackson County and flows ne into Lake Thorpe.

Hurricane Creek rises in s Macon County and flows w into Nantahala River.

Hurricane Creek rises in w Macon County and flows w into Jarrett Creek.

Hurricane Creek rises in n Madison County and flows se into Big Laurel Creek.

Hurricane Creek rises in central Wake County and flows s into Crabtree Creek.

Hurricane Gap, central Cherokee County

between Hiwassee River and West Prong Grape Creek.

Hurricane Gap, on the Madison County, N.C.–Greene County, Tenn., line.

Hurricane Gap, s Yancey County between the head of Falling Water Branch and South Fork Cattail Creek.

Hurricane Mountain, n Haywood County, extends ne from the head of Toms Branch to the head of Morgan Creek.

Hurricane Mountain, w central Swain County between Laurel Branch and Tuckasegee River.

Hurricane Ridge, n Haywood County, extends ne between Hurricane Creek and Cold Springs Creek.

Hurricane Ridge, n Mitchell County parallel to Big Branch.

Hurricane Ridge, nw Swain County, a short spur extending w from Big Grill Ridge.

Hurricane Ridge. *See* Rose Ridge.

Hurricane Top, mountain in sw Macon County between Clear Branch and Rocky Cove.

Hurricane Township, ne Ashe County.

Hurst Beach. *See* Onslow Beach.

Hurts Creek rises in n Montgomery County and flows sw into Denson Creek.

Husbands Creek rises in sw Caldwell County and flows s into Lower Creek. Named for Veazey Husband, locally noted Tory who lived in the vicinity.

Husk, community in nw Ashe County. Railroad name is Nella. Post office est. there, 1915.

Huskanaw Swamp. *See* Collie Swamp.

Huskey Creek rises in n Swain County and flows s into Beech Flats Prong.

Hyatt, community in n Anson County served by post office, 1888–1905.

Hyatt Bald, ne Swain County in Great Smoky Mountains National Park on Hyatt Ridge. Alt. 5,153.

Hyatt Branch rises in w Swain County and flows sw into Goldmine Branch.

Hyatt Cove, nw Jackson County at the head of Shoal Creek.

Hyatt Creek rises in n Cherokee County in the Snowbird Mountains and flows se into Valley River.

Hyatt Creek rises in sw Haywood County and flows e into Richland Creek.

Hyatt Creek rises in ne Swain County on Hyatt Ridge near Hyatt Bald and flows s into Straight Fork.

Hyatt Creek, community in sw Haywood County on Hyatt Creek.

Hyatt Mill Creek rises in s Clay County and flows ne into Hiwassee River.

Hyatt Ridge, ne Swain County in Great Smoky Mountains National Park, a spur extending se from Dashoga Ridge with its center near lat. 35°39′35″ N., long. 83°13′58″ W. *See also* McGee Spring.

Hyco Lake. *See* Carolina Power Lake.

Hyco-ote. *See* Hyco River.

Hyco River is formed in nw Person County by the junction of North Hyco and South Hyco Creeks. It flows ne into Virginia, where it enters Dan River. In 1728 William Byrd referred to the stream as "Hicootomony, or Turkey-Buzzard River, from the great number of those unsavoury Birds that roost on the tall Trees growing near its banks." Appears on the Moseley map, 1733, as Hyco-ote. Hyco Dam, completed in 1964, now impounds its waters to form Carolina Power Lake.

Hycotee, community in e central Caswell County. A post office was operated there during the approx. period 1880–1905.

Hyde County was formed in 1705 as Wickham Precinct, *which see*, of Bath County. The name was changed to Hyde about 1712. Located in the e section of the state, it is bounded by Pamlico Sound; Beaufort, Washington, Tyrrell, and Dare Counties; and (on the Outer Banks) the Atlantic Ocean and Dare and Carteret Counties. Named for Governor Edward Hyde, who died in 1712. Area: 1,364 sq. mi. (634, land; 730, water). County seat: Swan Quarter, with an elevation of 10 ft. Townships are Currituck, Fairfield, Lake Landing, Mattamuskeet, Ocracoke, and Swan Quarter. Produces soybeans, corn, wheat, cotton, snap beans, seafood, hogs, livestock, dairy products, lumber, and wooden boxes. *See also* Woodstock Point; Aramuskeet.

Hyde Islands, formerly two islands with a total of 10 acres in Little Tennessee River in ne

Graham County. Now under the waters of
Fontana Lake.

Hydeland, community in s Hyde County s of
Lake Mattamuskeet near the head of Juniper
Bay.

Hyde Mill Creek rises in s Graham County and
flows ne into Tulula Creek.

Hyde Parish, Church of England, Hyde County,
est. 1715, coextensive with the county. By
1767 the parish was being called St. George's
and in that year had 441 white taxables.

Hyder Mountain, e Haywood County between
Pigeon River and Long Branch.

Hydro, community in sw Montgomery County
on Pee Dee River at the dam that forms Lake
Tillery. Power-generating plant is there.

Hymans, community in central Craven County.

Hymans Ferry, former ferry across Roanoke
River, s Bertie County.

I

Icard, community in e Burke County. First
known as Bowan's Crossing. Alt. 1,172.

Icard Township, e Burke County.

Icaria, community in n Chowan County. Alt. 34.

Icemorlee. *See* West Monroe.

Ichley, community in n Orange County.

Icy Knob, on Burke-Rutherford county line.

Ida, community in w Scotland County. Named
for Ida Cotton Mills, which in turn were
named for Ida Morgan, daughter of Mark
Morgan.

Idaho, community in central Cumberland
County served by post office, 1877–1903.

Idalia, community in se Beaufort County.

Idlewild, community in s Ashe County. Alt.
2,700.

Idol, community in central Ashe County served
by post office, 1879–1906. Also known as
Idol's Mill.

Idol's Mill. *See* Idol.

Ijames Crossroads, community in w Davie
County. A Baptist church built there in 1897
on land donated by Cas Ijames was known as
Ijames Crossroads Church.

Ike Cove, s Haywood County on a tributary of
Little East Fork Pigeon River.

Ike Mountain, n Buncombe County w of
Dillingham.

Ilex, community in central Davidson County
served by post office, 1886–1902.

Immer, community in n Montgomery County
served by post office, 1888–1932.

Improvement Cove, e Swain County between
Middle Ridge and Connelly Mountain on Improvement Creek.

Improvement Creek rises in e Swain County and
flows ne into Wesser Creek.

Inadu Knob, on Haywood County, N.C.–Cocke
County, Tenn., line in Great Smoky Mountains National Park near lat. 35°43′37″ N.,
long. 83°14′27″ W. Formerly Snake Knob but,
to prevent duplication within the park, the
name was changed to *Inadu*, the Indian word
for snake. Alt. 5,941.

Inanda, former town in central Buncombe
County on French Broad River at the mouth
of Hominy Creek. Inc. 1893; charter repealed
1901. Served by post office, 1891–1904.
A church at the site still bears the name.

Independence Hill, community in n Mecklenburg County.

Index, community in se Ashe County.

Indian Branch rises in e Haywood County and
flows se into Bald Creek.

Indian Camp Bay, an arm of Big Colly Bay, ne
Bladen County.

Indian Camp Branch rises in n Buncombe
County near Jupiter and flows sw into Shepherd Branch.

Indian Camp Branch rises in central Jackson
County and flows se into West Fork [Moses
Creek].

Indian Camp Branch rises in e Macon County
and flows n into Ellijay Creek.

Indian Camp Branch rises in w Macon County
and flows sw into Wine Spring Creek.

Indian Camp Branch rises in w Madison County
and flows se into Big Pine Creek.

Indian Camp Branch rises in w central Transylvania County and flows se into Kuykendall
Creek.

Indian Camp Creek rises in n Macon County
and flows se into Burningtown Creek.

Indian Camp Gap, n Jackson County near the
heads of Allens Branch and Kitchin Branch.

Indian Camp Mountain, s Transylvania County
in the Blue Ridge Mountains e of Estatoe
Creek.

Indian Creek rises in nw Bertie County and flows s into Roanoke River. Creek was the n boundary of the Tuscarora Indian property in Indian Woods Township. Mentioned in local records as early as 1723. Appears as Deep Creek on the Collet map, 1770. *See also* Resootskeh.

Indian Creek rises in sw Catawba County, flows se across w Lincoln County, dips briefly into nw Gaston County, and flows ne back into Lincoln County, where it enters South Fork Catawba River. Appears on the Collet map, 1770, as Howards Creek but as Indian Creek on the Price map, 1808.

Indian Creek rises in s Chatham County and flows se into Deep River.

Indian Creek rises in s Cumberland County and flows s into Bladen County, where it enters Harrisons Creek.

Indian Creek, waterway in ne Currituck County between Knotts Island and Mackay Island.

Indian Creek rises in w Hertford County and flows e into Livermans Mill Pond.

Indian Creek rises in n Jackson County and flows nw into Soco Creek.

Indian Creek rises in w Stokes County and flows ne into Cascade Creek.

Indian Creek rises in n Swain County and flows s into Noland Creek.

Indian Creek, formed in n Swain County in Great Smoky Mountains National Park by the junction of Left Fork [Indian Creek] and Right Fork [Indian Creek]. It flows sw into Deep Creek.

Indian Creek rises in w Transylvania County and flows s into Toxaway River.

Indian Creek rises in w Transylvania County and flows sw and se to join Shoal Creek in forming North Fork French Broad River.

Indian Creek rises in central Vance County and flows n into Kerr Lake.

Indian Creek rises in w Yancey County and flows n into Price Creek.

Indian Creek. *See* Dillard Creek; Town Creek.

Indian Ford, shallow rock formation in Contentnea Creek, central Wilson County, ½ mi. below Contentnea Lake. Mentioned in early records as "the falls," below which the stream is navigable by boat.

Indian Fork rises in sw Yancey County and flows se into Cane River.

Indian Gap, on Swain County, N.C.–Sevier County, Tenn., line near the head of Right Fork [Deep Creek]. Alt. 5,317.

Indian Grave Creek rises in central Davidson County and flows se into Swearing Creek.

Indian Grave Gap, ne Caldwell County in the Green Mountain range. *See also* Green Mountain.

Indian Grave Gap, ne Cherokee County in the Valley River Mountains.

Indian Grave Gap, sw Cherokee County near the headwaters of Hickey Branch.

Indian Grave Gap, on the Mitchell County, N.C.–Unicoi County, Tenn., line. Alt. approx. 3,100.

Indian Grave Gap, s Swain County between Brush Creek and Little Tennessee River.

Indian Grave Gap, w central Swain County on the head of Laurel Branch.

Indian Island, in Pamlico River, se Beaufort County. Approx. 1 1/10 mi. long and 3/10 mi. wide.

Indian Island, approx. 500 acres of arable land in North River Pocosin, se Camden County, bounded on the e by North River. Island formerly was home to a thickly settled community, but it is now abandoned. Named for the large number of Indian artifacts that have been found there.

Indian Knob, peak on Indian Ridge, w Haywood County near lat. 35°40′06″ N., long. 83°07′43″ W., in Great Smoky Mountains National Park. Alt. 5,120.

Indian Landing, e Beaufort County on Pungo River.

Indian Ridge, w Haywood County in Great Smoky Mountains National Park, a spur extending s from Mount Sterling Ridge, center near lat. 35°40′ N., long. 83°07′10″ W.

Indian Ridge, sw Macon County between Big Indian Creek and Nantahala River.

Indian Ridge, w Swain County on a bend in Nantahala River; now surrounded at the sw end by the backwaters of Fontana Lake.

Indian Run rises in e Beaufort County in Pantego Swamp and flows e into Pungo River.

Indian Spring Branch rises in sw Buncombe County near the Haywood County line and flows w into South Hominy Creek.

Indian Springs, community in s Wayne County near a tributary of Smith Millpond. The site was settled as early as 1829 and named for local springs traditionally used by Saponi Indians.

Indian Springs Township, se Wayne County. First listed on county tax records in 1838.

Indian Swamp rises in s Robeson County and flows s into Ashpole Swamp.

Indian Swamp rises on the Tyrrell-Washington county line and flows n into Banton Creek.

Indian Top, central Cherokee County between West Prong Grape Creek and Rose Creek.

Indiantown, community in e central Camden County. A post office est. 1882 operated there until 1934. Settled prior to 1697. In 1704 the Governor's Council ordered a reservation to be laid off for the Yeopim Indians, and it is from the reservation that the present name derives.

Indiantown, former community in w central Currituck County approx. 5 mi. s of Shawboro. Appears in local records as early as 1764; a post office as early as 1793 and as recently as 1882. Currituck Seminary, burned during the Civil War, was there.

Indiantown Creek, a name sometimes applied to the upper course of North River, *which see*, in Camden County.

Indian Town Creek. *See* Dillard Creek.

Indian Trading Path. *See* Trading Path.

Indian Trail, town in w Union County. Inc. 1907. Located between heads of North Fork Crooked Creek and South Fork Crooked Creek. Alt. 697.

Indian Wells, indicated on the Price map, 1808, and the MacRae map, 1833, as four wells on Cape Fear River in se Bladen County. Possibly these were natural artesian wells, common to the area.

Indian Well Swamp rises in s Pitt County and flows se into Clayroot Swamp.

Indian Woods, central Bertie County, a reservation set aside in 1717 for the Tuscarora Indians remaining in North Carolina after the war of 1711–13. The Indians later joined relatives in New York, and the state sold the tract of land in 1828.

Indian Woods Township, sw Bertie County.

Indigo Branch rises in Horry County, S.C., and flows nw into sw Brunswick County, where it enters Cawcaw Swamp.

Inez, community in s Warren County e of Shocco Creek. Post office est. there in 1890, but discontinued in 1954.

Ingalls, community in sw Avery County. Named for Senator John J. Ingalls (1833–1900) of Kansas. A nineteenth-century post office serving the area was named Keenerville.

Ingles Cove, n Buncombe County n of Ingles Gap.

Ingles Field Gap, s Buncombe County between Little Hickory Top and Stradley Mountain.

Ingles Gap, n Buncombe County between Grassy Knob and Ravens Knob.

Ingleside, community in n Franklin County.

Ingles Ridge, n Buncombe County between Sugar Cove and Sawyer Cove.

Ingold, community in s Sampson County on the e side of Great Coharie Creek. Alt. 100. Settled about 1888. Inc. 1889; charter repealed 1895.

Ingraham Mountain, ne Buncombe County near Dillingham.

Ingram, community in nw Northampton County served by post office, 1882–1907.

Ingram Branch rises in ne Cherokee County and flows ne into Worm Creek.

Ingram Branch rises in w Macon County and flows se into Nantahala Lake.

Ingrams Mountain, ne Anson County. Alt. approx. 525.

Ingrams Township, s central Johnston County.

Inipta, community in w Alleghany County.

Ink. *See* Newlife.

Inland Waterway. *See* Intracoastal Waterway.

Inman, community in s Robeson County served by post office, 1896–1902.

Inman Branch rises in s Haywood County and flows se into West Fork Pigeon River.

Inner Diamond Shoal. *See* Diamond Shoals.

Institute, community in nw Lenoir County. Named for the Lenoir Collegiate Institute, which operated there for a number of years after 1855. Some of the buildings of the institute were later used as residences.

Institute Branch rises in w Hertford County and flows ne into Worrell Mill Pond.

Institute Township, nw Lenoir County.

Intelligence, community in w Rockingham County served by post office, 1901–11. Known as Bald Hill until about 1920. Between 1850 and 1900, several tobacco factories flourished there. Named because the first public school in North Carolina was there. "Danbury," plantation home of Governor Alexander Martin (1740–1807), was nearby. Sharp's Institute, operated by James Sharp, father of N.C. Supreme Court justice Susie Sharp, was there.

Intracoastal Waterway extends from Gloucester, Mass., to Key West, Fla., a distance of 1,950 mi., of which 308 are in North Carolina. It passes through sounds, rivers, and canals. The depth of the waterway is 12 ft., minimum width is 47 ft., and minimum vertical clearance is 80 ft. The oldest segment of the waterway in North Carolina was begun in 1856 as a private enterprise. In 1873 control and maintenance of the network of coastal canals was taken over by the U.S. Corps of Engineers, and work was expanded through the 1940s. Pleasure craft, towed barges, and small freight boats use the Intracoastal Waterway.

Inverness, community in central Hoke County served by post office, 1854–1912.

Invershiel, mountain resort in e Avery County near Grandfather Mountain. A village containing shops, a church, and other buildings is modeled after an old Scottish village. Named for the village in Scotland, ancestral home of the MacRae family, developers of the resort. Est. 1966.

Iola, community in e Montgomery County served by post office, 1903–15. Named for Iola gold mine.

Iona, community in central Robeson County served by post office, 1896–1902.

Iotla Branch rises in n Macon County and flows se into Iotla Creek.

Iotla Creek rises in central Macon County and flows ne into Little Tennessee River.

Iotla Gap, central Macon County near the head of Iotla Creek.

Iowa Hill, e Mitchell County between Beaver Creek and North Toe River.

Ira, community in w Wilkes County served by post office, 1899–1903.

Iredell, community in sw Brunswick County.

Iredell County was formed in 1788 from Rowan County. Located in the central section of the state, it is bounded by Rowan, Cabarrus, Mecklenburg, Lincoln, Catawba, Alexander, Wilkes, Yadkin, and Davie Counties. It was named for James Iredell (1751–99), attorney general of North Carolina during the Revolution and delegate from Edenton to the Convention of 1788, where he advocated adoption of the Federal Constitution. Area: 594 sq. mi. County seat: Statesville, with an elevation of 925 ft. Townships are Bethany, Chambersburg, Coddle Creek, Concord, Cool Spring, Davidson, Eagle Mills, Fallstown, New Hope, Olin, Sharpesburg, Shiloh, Statesville, Turnersburg, and Union Grove. Produces wheat, oats, corn, poultry, livestock, hogs, canned milk, textiles, apparel, hay, ceramics, glass products, fabricated metal, lumber, and machinery. *See also* York County.

Iredell House. *See* James Iredell House.

Iredell Station. *See* Loray.

Irena, community in central Clay County on Tusquitee Creek.

Irene, community in se Mecklenburg served by post office, 1871–80.

Irish Buffalo Creek rises in sw Rowan County and flows s into Cabarrus County, where it enters Coldwater Creek. Called Buffalo Creek on the Collet map, 1770, but Irish Buffalo Creek on the Price map, 1808. Named for Scots-Irish settlers. *See also* Dutch Buffalo Creek.

Irish Creek rises in w Burke County and flows se to join Upper Creek in forming Warrior Fork [Catawba River].

Irisquoque. *See* Clubfoot Creek.

Iron Duff, community in central Haywood County on Big Branch. Named for an early settler, Aaron MacDuff. Known as Aaron Duff until 1873, when a post office was est. An error in Washington, D.C., resulted in the use of the name Iron Duff instead of Aaron Duff.

Iron Duff Township, central Haywood County.

Ironhill, community in s Columbus County.

Iron-Lithia Springs, former resort community in s Wilkes County near Old Gilreath. Buildings destroyed by fire about 1900. Alt. approx. 1,500.

Ironmonger Mountain, s central Burke County. Alt. 1,823.

Iron Mountain, nw Mitchell County at the head of Bearwallow Creek.

Iron Mountain, community in s Randolph County.

Iron Mountain Gap, on the Mitchell County, N.C.–Unicoi County, Tenn., line. Alt. 3,725.

Iron Mountains. *See* Unaka Mountains.

Iron Ore Ridge, n Buncombe County, extends sw from Jones Knob in the Elk Mountains.

Iron Station, town in s Lincoln County. Settled about 1789. Inc. 1909. Named for the fact that many iron mines and forges were operated within a radius of 10 mi. between 1790 and 1880. Earlier known as Sharon.

Ironton Township, e central Lincoln County.

Iron Works. *See* Troublesome Creek Iron Works.

Irvin, community in e Transylvania County served by post office, 1889–1901. Later known as Blantyre, *which see.*

Irvin River. *See* Smith River.

Irvins Creek rises in e Mecklenburg County and flows sw into McAlpine Creek.

Irvins Crossroads, community in s Lenoir County.

Irvinsville, a town authorized in 1815 to be laid out in sw Cleveland County (then Rutherford County) on Broad River opposite Quinn's Ferry. The town seems not to have developed as expected and the last mention of it occurs in local records of 1828.

Irwin Creek rises in n Mecklenburg County and flows sw into Stewart Creek.

Isaac Creek rises in se Craven County and flows n into Adams Creek.

Isaac Hollow, w Watauga County, extends se n of George Gap Branch.

Isaac Parlier's Creek. *See* Purlear Creek.

Isaac Walton Lake, formerly Water Works Lake, in w Person County on Storys Creek at the mouth of Satterfield Creek. Formed prior to 1928. Covers 213 acres; max. depth 25 ft. Owned by the town of Roxboro.

Isenhour, community in ne Stanly County. Grew up around Isenhour Brick Yard in early twentieth century.

Isenhour Mine, former gold mine in ne Cabarrus County on Little Buffalo Creek.

Isinglass Creek rises in n Franklin County and flows ne into Little Shocco Creek.

Isinglass Ridge, s Graham County, extends se from Sassafras Ridge to Little Snowbird Creek. Named for isinglass or mica mined in the area.

Island Borough, former town in e Rowan County. Inc. and authorized to be laid out in 1795 on the Yadkin River opposite the e end of Big Island, *which see.* Site is about 3 mi. ne of Spencer. Intended to promote navigation on the river, the town was to be built on land owned by Edward Yarborough. Little if any development took place at the site.

Island Branch Swamp connects Resolution Branch to Musselshell Creek in nw Jones County.

Island Creek rises in se Alexander County and flows s into Catawba River.

Island Creek rises in e Anson County and flows se into Pee Dee River.

Island Creek rises in e Burke County and flows n into Catawba River.

Island Creek rises in s Duplin County and flows se into Northeast Cape Fear River. Appears as Cook Creek on the Collet map, 1770; not shown on the Price map, 1808, but shown and named Island Creek on the MacRae map, 1833.

Island Creek, a channel of Chowan River flowing n of an unnamed island ¾ mi. long in w Gates County.

Island Creek rises in ne Granville County and flows n and ne along the Granville-Vance county line until it reaches the nw corner of Vance County, where it enters Island Creek Reservoir.

Island Creek rises in e Jones County and flows n into Trent River. Appears on the Moseley map, 1733, which also shows Murfy's Ferry across the Trent River near the mouth of Island Creek.

Island Creek rises in w Montgomery County and flows n and nw into Pee Dee River.

Island Creek rises in n New Hanover County and flows nw forming the New Hanover-Pender county line before entering Northeast Cape Fear River.

Island Creek rises in se Rockingham County and flows ne into Caswell County, where it enters Dan River.

Island Creek rises in sw Rutherford County and flows ne into Broad River.

Island Creek rises in sw Stanly County and flows s into Rocky River. Called Stillwater Creek on the Kerr map, 1882.

Island Creek. *See* Lillington Creek.

Island Creek District, formerly a census precinct in what is now nw Vance County approx. 2 mi. w of the town of Williamsboro. By 1790, 107 heads of families had settled in the area.

Island Creek Reservoir, in the nw corner of Vance County, is fed by Island Creek and Little Island Creek. It is separated from Kerr Lake by a dike that prevented the flooding of nearby tungsten mines. Extends about 5 mi. along the Granville-Vance county line. Formed about 1952 after the completion of Kerr Lake.

Island Creek Township, s central Duplin County.

Island Ford, former passage over the Catawba River between Catawba and Iredell Counties near the site of the dam that forms Lookout Shoals Lake, *which see*. Appears on maps of the Revolutionary period and on the Price map, 1808, as one of the northernmost fords over the river.

Island Ford, in n Rockingham County within present city of Eden. Eighteenth-century Salem-Petersburg road crossed Smith River there.

Island Ford, across Yadkin River in w Surry County near the community of Jonesville. Mentioned in local records as early as 1778.

Island Fort, community in s Rutherford County served by post office, 1827–1907.

Island Swamp rises in e Pitt County and flows ne into Chicod Creek.

Isle Hatton, island in Pamlico Sound that cannot now be identified; appears on the Smith map, 1624.

Isothermal Belt. *See* Thermal Belt.

Ita, community in n Nash County.

Itiner, community in e Harnett County.

Itom, community in central Rutherford County served by post office, 1887–1933.

Ivanhoe, community in s Sampson County on Black River. Named in the 1880s for the hero in Sir Walter Scott's novel of the same name. Alt. 29. The Colton map, 1861, shows a community at the site named Black River. Corbetts Ferry there was taken by Gen. Richard Caswell on the eve of the Battle of Moores Creek Bridge. Corbetts Ferry appears on maps at the site through 1865. Black River Presbyterian Church, est. there in 1740, occupies a building erected in 1859.

Ivestor Gap, s Haywood County on the head of Little East Fork Pigeon River.

Ivestor Ridge, s Haywood County between Grassy Cove Prong and Dark Prong.

Ivory Crossroads, community in e Franklin County.

Ivory Ridge, w Watauga County, extends ne from Hockiday Ridge s of Rush Branch.

Ivory Swamp rises in n Wayne County and flows ne into Wilson County, where it enters Contentnea Creek.

Ivy, community in e Madison County on Little Ivy Creek. Alt. 2,150. A post office existed there from 1833. Named by early settlers because of the abundance of laurel, which they called ivy.

Ivy Creek is formed in n Buncombe County by the junction of North Fork Ivy Creek and Dillingham Creek and flows w into Madison County (doubling back into Buncombe County at one point), where it joins Little Ivy Creek at the county line to form Ivy River.

Ivy Creek rises in n Northampton County and flows ne into Jordans Mill Pond on Cypress Creek.

Ivy Gap, on the Buncombe-Yancey county line nw of Cane River Gap.

Ivy Gap, w Haywood County in Great Smoky Mountains National Park near lat. 35°43′23″ N., long. 83°05′10″ W.

Ivy Gap, on the Madison-Yancey county line near Fox Creek. Alt. approx. 3,140.

Ivy Gap, community in n Haywood County on Mount Sterling Creek.

Ivy Gap, community in w Yancey County near the Madison County line.

Ivy Hill Township, w central Haywood County.

Ivy Knob, ne Buncombe County between Little Will Branch and North Fork Ivy Creek.

Ivy Knob, w Henderson County between Brock Mountain and Cash Creek.

Ivy Knob, e Mitchell County on Laurel Branch.

Ivy Ridge, nw Swain County in Great Smoky Mountains National Park, a short spur extending e from Big Grill Ridge.

Ivy River is formed on the Buncombe-Madison county line by the junction of Ivy Creek and Little Ivy Creek. It flows w through s Madison County into French Broad River, crossing back briefly into Buncombe County at three points.

Ivy Swamp rises in ne Wayne County and flows ne into Wilson County, where it enters Contentnea Creek. Named for the Ivey family, early settlers.

Ivy Top, s Clay County near the headwaters of Webb Creek.

Ivy Township, nw Buncombe County.

J

Jack, community in ne Warren County. Post office est. there in 1901, but discontinued in 1905. Due to a shift in population, the community is dwindling, and the name is not widely known.

Jack Bradley Branch rises in n Swain County and flows s into Beech Flats Prong.

Jack Cabin Branch rises in s Jones County and flows nw into Trent River.

Jack Cove, nw Jackson County, formerly Schuler Cove. In 1956, on a 5,000-acre tract there, R. H. Kress est. the Jack Kress School and renamed Schuler Cove in honor of his late son. Operated as a trade school, there is a model farm and nursery; classes in forestry and various trades are conducted.

Jack Creek rises in central Beaufort County and flows e into Nevil Creek.

Jack Creek rises in e Beaufort County and flows nw into Pungo Creek.

Jack Creek rises in nw Jackson County and flows sw into Tuckasegee River.

Jackdaw, community in s central Stanly County.

Jacket Swamp rises in w central Halifax County and flows se into Burnt Coat Swamp.

Jackeye Creek rises in ne Brunswick County and flows ne approx. 5 mi. into Brunswick River.

Jack Gap, central Buncombe County between Pine Knob and Bartlett Mountain.

Jackie Branch rises in s Clay County and flows se into Shooting Creek.

Jackies Mill Branch rises in n Yancey County and flows se into Cane River.

Jack Island Swamp, w Duplin County on Nahunga Creek.

Jack Knob, e Macon County between Passmore Knob and Watauga Creek.

Jackrabbit Mountain, s Clay County. Now a peninsula in Chatuge Lake.

Jacks Bay, ne Carteret County on e side of Piney Island and adjacent to Long Bay.

Jacks Branch rises in w Anson County and flows se into Brown Creek.

Jacks Branch rises in s Graham County and flows s into Tulula Creek.

Jacks Branch rises in w Madison County and flows sw into French Broad River.

Jack's Branch rises in e central Wake County and flows se into Neuse River.

Jacks Creek rises in w central Yancey County and flows ne into Toe River.

Jacks Creek Township, ne Yancey County.

Jacks Fork rises in s Greene County and flows n into Tyson Marsh.

Jacks Knob, s Jackson County, is bordered on the e by Scotsman Creek. Alt. approx. 3,440.

Jack Smith Creek rises in central Craven County sw of New Bern and flows ne into Neuse River. It forms a part of the limits of New Bern.

Jackson, town and county seat, central Northampton County. Alt. 131. Inc. 1873. Settled prior to 1741 and known as Potecase Bridge. Made county seat in 1741 and known as Northampton Court House until renamed Jackson in 1826, presumably for Andrew Jackson (1767–1845), recent unsuccessful Democratic candidate for president. In 1808 the General Assembly had authorized the county seat to be named Atherton, but apparently the name was never adopted. It probably was intended to honor Maj. Jeptha Atherton, member of the Provincial Congress and the General Assembly. Produces lumber.

Jackson, town authorized in 1818 to be laid off by Isaac Medley, Eustis Hunt, Gideon Johnston, John May Sr., and Joseph Porter "on the north side of Dan river, at the Eagle falls in Rockingham county." The scheme for developing a town there was proved to be a fraud in the case *Morehead vs. Hunt*, December 1826. *See also* Eagle Falls.

Jackson, community in sw Union County between Waxhaw Creek and Cane Creek. President Andrew Jackson was born nearby.

Jackson Branch rises in central Cherokee County and flows se into Colvard Creek.

Jackson Branch rises in se Mitchell County and flows s into Middle Ridge Branch.

Jackson Corner, community in n Pasquotank County.

Jackson County was formed in 1851 from Haywood and Macon Counties. Located in the w section of the state, it is bounded by the states of South Carolina and Georgia and by Macon, Swain, Haywood, and Transylvania Counties. It was named for Andrew Jackson (1767–1845), president of the United States. Area 499 sq. mi. County seat: Sylva, with an elevation of 2,047 ft. Townships are Barkers Creek, Canada, Caney Fork, Cashiers, Cullowhee, Dillsboro, Greens Creek, Hamburg, Mountain, Qualla, River, Savannah, Scott Creek, Sylva, and Webster. Produces corn, dairy products, livestock, hogs, paper, fish, lumber, Christmas trees, textiles, mica, granite, olivine, and crushed stone.

Jackson Creek rises in se Buncombe County and flows ne into McDowell County, where it enters Crooked Creek.

Jackson Creek rises in nw Franklin County and flows n into Tar River.

Jackson Creek rises in central Granville County and flows e into Tar River.

Jackson Creek rises in w Moore County and flows s into Drowning Creek. Named for William Jackson, who settled on it about 1754.

Jackson Creek rises in w Randolph County and flows se into Uwharrie River.

Jackson Creek, community in w Randolph County.

Jackson Gap, on the McDowell-Mitchell county line.

Jackson Hamlet, a black community in s Moore County between towns of Aberdeen and Pinehurst. Est. about 1899 and named for James Jackson, an original resident.

Jackson Hill, community in s Davidson County. Said to have been named because an admirer of Andrew Jackson raised a flagstaff there to celebrate Jackson's election to the presidency, 1828. A post office as early as 1830.

Jackson Hill Township, s Davidson County.

Jackson Knob, se Gaston County approx. 1 mi. sw of Boogertown. Alt. 1,080.

Jackson Knob, on the McDowell-Mitchell county line. Alt. 3,223.

Jackson Line Mountain extends se from w central Swain County to Little Yalaka Creek in s part of the county.

Jackson's Corner, community in n Sampson County.

Jacksons Crossroads, community in central Duplin County.

Jacksons Pond, on Cypress Creek in e Franklin County. Formed 1885. Covers 65 acres; max. depth 20 ft.

Jackson Springs, town in sw Moore County on Jackson Creek. Inc. 1921; named for William Jackson, who settled nearby in 1754. The mineral spring, developed as a resort in the late nineteenth century, was patronized largely by wealthy cotton growers of North Carolina and South Carolina. The hotel there burned in 1932. Alt. 730.

Jacksons Store, crossroads community in central Lenoir County. Named for one Jackson, said to have been a Civil War veteran, who operated the store for many years prior to his death in the 1920s.

Jackson Swamp, e Beaufort County.

Jackson Swamp rises in e Robeson County and flows e into Big Swamp.

Jackson Town was laid out in Rockingham County by Virginia promoters in 1818 on n side of Dan River at Eagle Falls. Failed to develop.

Jackson Township, s Nash County.

Jackson Township, central Northampton County.

Jackson Township, sw Union County.

Jacksonville, city and county seat, central Onslow County on New River. Alt. 23. A courthouse was constructed near there about 1757 at Wantland's Ferry. A new courthouse was constructed within ½ mi. of the old one about 1819, and the county seat was called Onslow Court House. In 1843 the town of Jacksonville was authorized to be est. and inc. there, but it was not immediately done; the act was reenacted in 1849. Named for President Andrew Jackson (1767–1845). Produces lumber and apparel. Camp Lejeune is adjacent. *See also* Johnston.

Jacksonville, town authorized in 1818 to be laid off on the lands of Hezekiah Naylor and Maccajah Lassiter in Randolph County "on the road from Fayetteville to Salisbury." The exact location is not known, and the town probably never developed.

Jacksonville Township, central Onslow County.

Jacks Swamp rises in n Northampton County and flows ne into Virginia, where it enters Fountains Creek. Appears on the map of the North Carolina–Virginia line run by William Byrd and others, 1728.

Jack Swamp flourished as a community on the stream of that name in n Northampton County from about 1775, when a Quaker meetinghouse was built there, until about 1812, by which time most of the people had moved to central North Carolina and to Ohio.

Jack Trail Mountain, w Madison County between Little Creek and Meadow Fork.

Jacob Branch rises in central Macon County and flows ne into Rocky Branch.

Jacob Branch rises in w Pitt County and flows se into Black Swamp.

Jacob Branch rises in w Robeson County and flows se into Lumber River.

Jacob Creek rises in e central Stanly County and flows se into Pee Dee River.

Jacob Fork rises in s Burke County and flows ne into Catawba County, where it joins Henry Fork in forming South Fork Catawba River. Named for Jacob Shuford, a pioneer settler.

Jacobs Creek rises in central Rockingham County and flows ne into Dan River. "Danbury," the home of Governor Alexander Martin (1740–1807), was near its mouth. The Indian settlement Upper Saura Town was also nearby prior to 1710.

Jacobs Fork Township, sw Catawba County.

Jacob's Gap, w Ashe County near the Tennessee state line. Named for an Indian youth said to have been killed by a white man.

Jacobs Knob, e Macon County between Lickskillet Branch and Cullasaja River.

Jacobs Swamp rises in s Nash County and flows se into Tar River.

Jacob Swamp rises in central Robeson County and flows se into Weatherspoon Cooling Pond. Approx. 7 mi. long.

Jacocks, community in se Perquimans County served by post office, 1894–1911.

Jacocks Landing. *See* Wellington.

Jady Branch rises in w Gates County and flows sw into an unnamed swamp, which flows se into Taylor Millpond.

Jake Branch rises in se Clay County and flows nw into Muskrat Branch.

Jake Branch rises in w Swain County and flows s into Nantahala River.

Jake Cove Branch rises in w Clay County and flows s into Fires Creek.

Jake Hollow, w Mitchell County on a tributary of Pigeonroost Creek.

Jake Ridge, se Clay County between Jake Branch and Muskrat Branch.

Jalong. *See* Longhurst.

James Branch rises in e Haywood County and flows nw into Cove Creek.

James Cathey's Creek. *See* Kerr Creek; Sloans Creek.

James City, community in central Craven County on Neuse River near its junction with Trent River approx. 1½ mi. s of city of New Bern. Alt. 10. Settled 1865. Named for Capt. Horace James, former Union chaplain, who supervised a freedmen's colony at the site.

James Creek rises in se Moore County and flows ne into Little River. Named for James McNeill, an early settler.

James Creek rises in ne Pamlico County on n Goose Creek Island and flows ne into Pamlico River.

James Creek. *See* Fiddler Creek.

James Iredell House, focal point of Historic Edenton State Historic Site, s Chowan County. Situated on approx. 2 acres. The Iredell house, built about 1759, is included in the area and open to the public as a historic house museum.

James Mill Creek. *See* Staffords Creek.

Jameston. *See* Jamesville.

Jamestown, town in sw Guilford County. Settled 1752 and named for James Mendenhall, an early settler whose first name was chosen in Quaker fashion to avoid ostentation. Inc. 1816; rechartered 1947. Produces baked goods, corrugated boxes, and textiles. Home to Oakdale Cotton Mills, continuously operating since 1865. Alt. 779.

James-Town. *See* Jamesville.

Jamestown Township, sw Guilford County.

Jamesville, town in e Martin County on Roanoke River. Est. 1785 as James Town; inc. 1832 as Jameston; name changed to Jamesville, 1855. Alt. 47.

Jamesville Township, ne Martin County.

Jane Cantrell Creek rises in s Transylvania County and flows nw into South Prong [Glady Fork].

Janeiro, community in s Pamlico County on Dawson Creek, *which see*. Known as Dawson Creek until a post office was est. (since discontinued). Named by seafaring men of the community for Rio de Janeiro, Brazil.

Jane Knob, e Macon County between Brown Creek and Corbin Creek.

Jane Otter Branch rises in nw Macon County and flows nw into Otter Creek.

Jane's Bald, on the Mitchell County, N.C.–Carter County, Tenn., line. Said to have been named for a woman who lost her life there in a snowstorm but who saved her young child by covering it with her own body.

Japan, former community in ne Graham County on forks of Tobacco and Panther Creeks. Est. about 1908 as a supply center for surrounding lumbering camps. Named for "Japan clover" (*Lespedeza striata*) growing in the area. During World War II, local residents began calling it MacArthur for Gen. Douglas MacArthur, but the post office name was never changed. Inundated by waters of Fontana Lake, 1944.

Jarmantown, community in nw Onslow County between Hall Pocosin and the head of New River.

Jarrets Creek. *See* Jarrett Bay.

Jarrett Bald, w Macon County between Wine Spring Creek and High Laurel Branch.

Jarrett Bay extends into the mainland of e Carteret County from Core Sound. It appears as Jarrets Creek on the Moseley map, 1733. Named for the Jarratt family.

Jarrett Creek rises in w McDowell County and flows se into Catawba River.

Jarrett Creek. *See* Moore Creek.

Jarrett Hollow, n Mitchell County, through which an unnamed tributary of Right Fork Bean Creek flows.

Jarrett Knob, w Macon County between Moore Creek and Tyler Branch. Alt. approx. 4,500.

Jarretts Creek rises in sw Rutherford County and flows sw into Broad River.

Jarrett's Gap, sw Macon County s of Moore Creek. Alt. 2,931.

Jarrett's Point, s Onslow County, extends into New River. Named for John Jarratt. Now within the limits of Camp Lejeune Marine Base.

Jarvins Mountain, se Buncombe County near the Rutherford county line between Stone and Weedy Mountains.

Jarvis, community in se Wilkes County served by post office, 1900–1914.

Jarvis Branch rises in e Madison County and flows se into California Creek.

Jarvisburg, community in sw Currituck County on North River. Settled prior to 1750. Named for the Jarvis family, of which Governor Thomas J. Jarvis was a member. Alt. 15.

Jarvis Channel, se Currituck County in Currituck Sound.

Jarvis Mountain, e Madison County between Gabriels Creek and Sprinkle Branch.

Jason, town in sw Greene County. Inc. 1889, but long inactive in municipal affairs.

Jason Township, sw Greene County.

Jasper, community in central Craven County. Alt. 6. Settled about 1868. Named for local citizen James Spear.

Jasperfield Branch rises in sw Madison County and flows nw into Spring Creek.

Jasper's Creek. *See* Bell Bay.

Jawbone Branch rises in nw Burke County and flows s into Steels Creek.

Jaynes Cove, central Haywood County on a tributary of Jonathans Creek.

Jean Guite Creek rises on the w side of the s end of the North Banks, ne Dare County, and flows n into Currituck Sound. Also known as Martins Point Creek.

Jefferson, town and county seat, central Ashe County. Inc. 1803 and named for Thomas Jefferson, who was president of the United States at the time. Alt. 2,900. Produces chemicals and textiles.

Jefferson, town authorized to be laid out in Chatham County at Tyson's Mill on Deep River in 1796. Commissioners were appointed, but there is no evidence that the town ever developed. A warehouse was to have been erected in the town for the inspection of tobacco, beef, pork, flour, and other commodities.

Jefferson, a proposed town in what is now sw Cleveland County. A 1799 law, slightly changed in 1800, authorized the establishment of a town in s Rutherford County between the Broad River and South Carolina. A building for a warehouse and for the inspection of tobacco was to be erected there. Commissioners were authorized to purchase 50 acres of land and to lay out the town. As late as July 1803, the county court appointed a successor commissioner, but all plans for the town appear to have been abandoned when it was decided that the river could not be made navigable.

Jefferson Township, central Ashe County.

Jefferson Township, e central Guilford County.

Jeffersonville, community in Mecklenburg County served by post office, 1832–34.

Jeffreys, community in se Granville County served by post office, 1899–1903.

Jenick Branch rises in ne Cherokee County and flows nw into Graybeard Creek.

Jenkins Branch rises in se Buncombe County and flows w into Rock Creek.

Jenkins Branch rises in s Swain County and flows nw into Tuckasegee River.

Jenkins Cove, ne Cherokee County. An unnamed stream flows nw in the cove.

Jenkins Cove, e Currituck County off the w side of Currituck Banks in Currituck Sound.

Jenkins Creek is formed by junction of East Fork and West Fork in n Jackson County and flows sw into Soco Creek.

Jenkins Divide, n Jackson County between Big Witch Creek and Jenkins Creek.

Jenkins Swamp rises in n Onslow County and flows s into Cowhorn Swamp.

Jenkins Trail Ridge, nw Swain County in Great Smoky Mountains National Park, extends s across the park boundary from Thunderhead Mountain to Pickens Gap.

Jenks Branch rises in n Cherokee County at the foot of Jenks Knob and flows ne into Tipton Creek.

Jenks Knob, on the Cherokee County, N.C.–Monroe County, Tenn., line in the Unicoi Mountains.

Jenney Knob, w Jackson County between Little Savannah Creek and Savannah Creek.

Jennie's Creek rises in central Wake County and flows s into Neuse River.

Jennie Wolf Creek. *See* Schene Wolf Creek.

Jennings, community in n Iredell County on Rocky Creek.

Jenny Branch rises in w Swain County and flows se into Tuckasegee River.

Jenny Lind, community in w Lenoir County. Named for the Swedish singer (1820–87), who, according to local legend, once sang beneath a tree there.

Jennys Gut rises in central Perquimans County and flows n into Raccoon Creek.

Jepha, community in central Transylvania County served by post office, 1890–1901.

Jericho, community in s Caswell County. A post office operated there, 1904–17.

Jericho, community in s Davie County near the head of Baxter Creek. Named for the Jericho Church of Christ, est. there in 1872. A post office that operated there, 1900–1902, was known as Kurfees.

Jericho, former community in se Wayne County on the n side of Neuse River from Seven Springs (then Whitehall). Destroyed by Union forces during the Battle of Whitehall on December 16, 1862. Site now included in the corporate limits of Seven Springs, *which see.*

Jericho Run rises in e Lenoir County and flows ne into Stonyton Creek. The name appears in local records as early as the 1740s.

Jerome, community in nw Bladen County.

Jerome. *See* Micro.

Jerome Bog, a pocosin on the Bladen-Cumberland county line e of the community of Jerome. An almost perfect elliptical shape with its long axis running nw-se, it is an ancient lake now filled with peat. *See also* Carolina Bays.

Jerry. *See* Levels.

Jerry Bald, n Swain County in Great Smoky Mountains National Park at the ne end of Jerry Bald Ridge. Alt. 5,080.

Jerry Bald Ridge, n Swain County in Great Smoky Mountains National Park, a spur extending se from Andrews Bald on Forney Ridge between Mill Creek and Noland Creek.

Jerry Branch rises in w Transylvania County and flows sw into West Fork French Broad River.

Jerry Creek rises in w Avery County and flows e into Roaring River. Named for Jerry Hughes, an early settler.

Jerry Knob, central Haywood County between Jones Cove and Liner Cove.

Jerry Mountain, ne Caldwell County.

Jersey Settlement, former community on the e bank of Yadkin River near present Linwood, *which see*, in w Davidson County (formerly Rowan). So called because settlers in the 1750s arrived from New Jersey. A post office by the name existed as late as 1830.

Jerusalem, former community in s Davie County. In 1815 a union church was organized there, erected on land given by Nicholas Click, and named New Jerusalem. By the 1830s a community was growing up around the church; a post office est. in 1850 was called Jerusalem. Church still active (Baptist), but the community has ceased to exist as such. Alt. 787.

Jerusalem Township, s Davie County.

Jessama, community in w central Beaufort County. More recently known as Midway.

Jesse, community in ne Person County served by post office, 1899–1904.

Jesse Branch rises in sw Buncombe County near Rich Knob and flows nw into Beaverdam Creek.

Jesse Gap, n Buncombe County between Jess Ridge and Jess Knob.

Jesse Ridge, w Haywood County in Great Smoky Mountains National Park, center near lat. 35°38′20″ N., long. 83°06′50″ W., between Little Davidson Creek and Mossy Branch.

Jesses High Top, peak in the Swannanoa Mountains of se Buncombe County.

Jessie, community in s Cumberland County on Harrisons Creek.

Jess Knob, n Buncombe County between Bald Knob and Jess Gap. Appears as Alexander Knob on state highway maps.

Jess Ridge, n Buncombe County, extends nw from Jess Gap.

Jessup, community in n Moore County.

Jester, community in ne Avery County.

Jesup, community in n Moore County served by post office, 1891–1934.

Jeter, community in nw Rutherford County on Cedar Creek.

Jewel Branch rises in n central Alleghany County and flows se into Little River.

Jewel Hill. *See* Marshall.

Jews Quarter Island, a peninsula approx. 2½ mi. long extending into the s waters of Currituck Sound from the mainland, se Currituck County. Presently owned by the Chatham family and used as a hunting lodge. Appears as Deuces Quarters on early maps. Today known as Dews Island and operates as a hunting club.

Jim Branch rises in s Buncombe County and flows nw into Christian Creek.

Jim Branch rises in w Haywood County and flows nw into Rough Fork.

Jim Branch rises in sw Wake County and flows sw into Buckhorn Creek.

Jim Carroll Top, w Clay County, a peak of Carroll Mountain. Alt. 2,700.

Jim Creek rises near Stone Mountain in sw Henderson County and flows sw into Grassy Creek.

Jim Creek rises in n Yancey County and flows se into Bald Mountain Creek.

Jimes, community in central Davidson County served by post office, 1891–1903.

Jimmies Run rises in nw Northampton County and flows s into Roanoke River.

Jimmy Branch rises in n Buncombe County near Richland Mountain and flows w into Ox Creek.

Jimmy Gap, s Macon County between Bates Ridge and Hickory Knoll Creek.

Jim Ray Branch rises in n central Yancey County and flows s into Little Crabtree Creek.

Jims Beech Ridge, e Jackson County, between Bearwallow Creek and Chestnut Ridge Creek.

Jinnys Branch rises in sw Brunswick County and flows e and s into Shallotte Inlet.

Jinnys Branch, community in sw Brunswick County.

Joanna Bald, on the Cherokee-Graham county line near the head of Anderson Branch. Alt. 4,708.

Joanna Mountain, e Transylvania County e of Little River between Grassy Creek and Briary Creek.

Joara. *See* Fort San Juan.

Jobs Cabin Township, w Wilkes County.

Jobs Peak, se Buncombe County near the McDowell county line n of Evans Knob.

Jockey's Ridge, sand dune 80–100 ft. high a short distance n of Nags Head, Bodie Island, e Dare County. It is the highest coastal sand dune on the Atlantic or Gulf coasts. Apparently indicated by a symbol but not named on the Mouzon map, 1775; the name was in use by 1851. Designated state park 1973 and U.S. Natural Landmark 1975.

Joe, community in w Madison County on Meadow Fork. Alt. 2,649.

Joe Branch rises in sw Beaufort County and flows ne into Chocowinity Creek.

Joe Cove, valley in central Clay County through which Perry Creek flows.

Joe Creek rises in e Macon County and flows sw into Ellijay Creek.

Joe Knob, s Clay County on the sw end of Cherry Mountain.

Joel Branch rises in n central Transylvania County and flows e into Davidson River.

Joel Cove, e Clay County between Fishprong Branch and Buck Creek.

Joel Jackson Pond. *See* Williams Lake.

Joel Ridge, nw Rutherford County, extends e from the head of Buffalo Creek.

Joe Mountain, n Jackson County between North Fork and Scott Creek.

Joes Branch rises in s Vance County and flows sw into Ruin Creek.

Joes Creek rises in s Richmond County and flows se onto the Richmond-Scotland county line and se into Scotland County, where it enters Gum Swamp Creek. *See also* Rochdale.

Joes Creek rises in s Watauga County and flows se into Caldwell County.

Joes Creek, community in w Scotland County.

Joes Fork rises in s Moore County and flows ne into Nicks Creek.

Joe's Fork rises in s Watauga County and flows se into n Caldwell County, where it enters Buffalo Creek.

Joes Island Creek rises in e Pasquotank County and flows e into Pasquotank River.

Joe White Mountain, w Caldwell County. Named for Major White, Revolutionary War officer who lived on Johns River nearby.

Joe Young Ridge, s central Yancey County between Bowlens Creek and Bowlens Pyramid.

Joford, community in Duplin County served by post office, 1884–1902. A crossing point on Rockfish Creek.

John Anders Ridge, on Buncombe-Madison county line, extends sw from Moody Gap.

John Autrey Branch rises in s Yancey County and flows n into Rock Creek.

John Branch rises in sw Macon County and flows e into Little Indian Creek.

John Brown Branch rises in central Jackson County and flows w into Tuckasegee River.

John Green Bend, a bend in the Hiwassee River in w Cherokee County.

John H. Kerr Reservoir. *See* Kerr Lake.

John Ish High Top, a peak in w Cherokee County in a bend of Hiwassee River.

John Mason Branch rises in se Cherokee County and flows nw into Little Brasstown Creek.

John Newton Branch rises in central Cherokee County and flows s into Pace Branch.

Johnnies Creek rises in w Transylvania County and flows se into Tucker Creek.

John Reese Branch rises in central Clay County and flows w and nw into Downing Creek.

John Rock, mountain in nw Transylvania County between Cat Gap and Davidson River. Alt. approx. 3,220.

John Rock Branch rises in nw Transylvania County n of Cedar Rock Mountain and flows n on the w side of John Rock approx. 1 mi. into Cedar Rock Creek.

Johns, community in se Scotland County. Settled about 1875. Named for Capt. James T. John, owner of land on which the railroad station was built. Alt. 179.

Johns Branch rises in w Graham County and flows se into Santeetlah Creek.

Johns Branch rises in sw Madison County and flows nw into Spring Creek.

Johns Camp Branch rises in e Mitchell County and flows se into Fall Creek.

Johns Cove, s Haywood County on Crawford Creek.

Johns Cove, nw Swain County between Twentymile Creek and Twentymile Ridge.

Johns Creek rises in central Jackson County and flows nw into Caney Fork.

Johns Knob, on the Graham County, N.C.–Monroe County, Tenn., line.

Johns Millpond, se Scotland County on Leiths Creek. Formed 1840. Covers 150 acres; max. depth 15 ft.

Johnson Branch rises in e Clay County and flows nw into Davenport Branch.

Johnson Branch rises in w Haywood County and flows n into Campbell Creek.

Johnson Branch rises in w Macon County and flows e into Nantahala Lake.

Johnson Branch rises in n Madison County and flows w into Shelton Laurel Creek.

Johnson Branch rises in e Swain County and flows s into Tuckasegee River.

Johnson Branch rises in e Wayne County and flows ne into Exum Mill Branch.

Johnson Cove, se Buncombe County e of Turkey Ridge.

Johnson Cove, e central Yancey County between Bowlens Creek and George Fork. Said to have been named for a yodeler who walked through the region yodeling.

Johnson Creek, a tidal creek in Core Sound near the Core Banks, e Carteret County.

Johnson Creek rises in n Granville County and flows e into Grassy Creek basin of Kerr Lake.

Johnson Creek rises in s Granville County and flows se into Aycock Creek.

Johnson Creek rises in s Vance County and flows se into n Franklin County, where it enters Lynch Creek.

Johnson Drainage Ditch rises s of Hendersonville in central Henderson County and flows ne into Bat Fork near its junction with Mud Creek.

Johnson Gap, n Graham County between tributaries of Sawyer Creek and Stecoah Creek.

Johnson Gap, w Haywood County between Johnson Branch and Pine Tree Cove.

Johnson Gap, near the nw end of the Henderson-Transylvania county line.

Johnson Knob, nw Henderson County on Laurel Mountain between Sassafras Gap and Rich Gap Mountain. Alt. 5,540.

Johnson Mill Creek rises in n Clay County and flows sw into Tusquitee Creek.

Johnson Pond, n Harnett County on West Buies Creek. Approx. ½ mi. long.

Johnson Pond. *See* Watsons Pond.

Johnson Ridge, n Clay County between Evans and Julie Ridges. *See also* Matlock Bald.

Johnson's Branch. *See* Big Branch.

Johnsons Corner, community in nw Camden County. Named for Charlie Johnson, who operated a store there following the Civil War.

Johnsons Creek rises in se Lincoln County and flows s into ne Gaston County, where it enters Catawba River.

Johnsons Falls, on the Yadkin River at Donnoha, ne Forsyth County. Fall of about 4 ft. in ½ mi. A ledge of rock extends diagonally across the river, over which the water falls in a straight plunge for 2 ft.

Johnsons Island, ne Currituck County off Currituck Banks.

Johnsons Mill Creek rises in w Henderson County and flows nw into Shaws Creek. Also known locally as Battle Creek.

Johnsons Mill Run rises in n Pitt County in Grindle Pocosin and flows s into Tar River.

Johnsons Mills, community in s Pitt County. A post office was est. there in 1882.

Johnsons Pond, s Wake County on Terrible Creek.

Johnsonville, community in sw Cherokee County at the mouth of Hothouse Branch.

Johnsonville, community in w Harnett County named for Samuel Johnson, early innkeeper there. Surrounding elevated lands first known as Mount Pleasant by Highland Scots who settled there in the 1750s. Name changed later to Camerons Hill for Daniel Cameron, who lived nearby. Afterward changed to its

present name. Flora MacDonald, Scottish heroine, lived there, 1774-75. In a mound 4 mi. w are buried over 100 Indians, victims of a massacre shortly before the area was settled by Scots. The mound has been vandalized.

Johnsonville. *See* Traphill.

Johns River rises in n Caldwell County near the foot of Blowing Rock. Approx. 32 mi. long, it flows s, sw, and se across w Caldwell and into n Burke County, where it enters Catawba River. Named for John Perkins, local black landowner.

Johns River Township, w Caldwell County.

Johns Swamp rises in se Bladen County and flows s into Colly Creek.

John Station, community in s Scotland County served by post office, 1886-1955.

Johnston, former county seat is Onslow County on New River. Est. 1741; destroyed by a hurricane in September 1752 and abandoned. Named for Gabriel Johnston (1699-1752), governor of North Carolina, 1734-52.

Johnston County was formed in 1746 from Craven County. Located in the e section of the state, it is bounded by Wilson, Wayne, Sampson, Cumberland, Harnett, Wake, and Nash Counties. It was named for Gabriel Johnston (1699-1752), governor of North Carolina, 1734-52. Area: 795 sq. mi. County seat: Smithfield, with an elevation of 155 ft. Townships are Banner, Bentonville, Beulah, Boon Hill, Clayton, Cleveland, Elevation, Ingrams, Meadow, Micro, O'Neals, Pine Level, Pleasant Grove, Selma, Smithfield, Wilders, and Wilson's Mills. Produces tobacco, corn, soybeans, wheat, oats, cotton, poultry, hogs, livestock, dairy products, sweet potatoes, turkeys, lumber, watermelons, furniture, chemicals, cottonseed oil, pharmaceuticals, wood products, heavy equipment, and crushed stone.

Johnston Court House. *See* Smithfield.

Johnston Swamp rises in s Johnston County and flows ne into Stone Creek.

Johnstonville, former town est. 1788 in ne Randolph County as the county seat. Named for Governor Samuel Johnston (1733–1816), who was chief executive at the time. The town declined after 1796, when Asheboro was est. as the county seat in a more central location. The community of Brown's Crossroads is now at the site.

Johnstonville Township, sw Harnett County.

Johnstown, community in s Lincoln County on Indian Creek.

John Taylor Branch rises in w Madison County and flows e into Spring Creek.

John West Cove, in ne Cherokee County. Named for an early settler who lived in the cove.

Jolly Branch rises in sw Cleveland County and flows s beside Jolly Mountain into Broad River.

Jolly Branch rises in se Orange County about 2 mi. n of town of Carrboro and flows sw into Bolin Creek.

Jolly Gap, central Haywood County on the head of Dotson Branch.

Jolly Mountain, in sw Cleveland County on Broad River. Alt. approx. 925.

Jomeokee. *See* Pilot Mountain.

Jonas Creek rises in n Swain County in Great Smoky Mountains National Park and flows s into Forney Creek.

Jonas Ridge, mountain range in nw Burke County. Named for Jonas Braswell, an early settler who froze to death there.

Jonas Ridge, community in nw Burke County.

Jonas Ridge Township, n Burke County.

Jonathan Creek rises in nw Granville County and flows e into Goose Neck Creek.

Jonathan Crossroads, community in n Granville County.

Jonathans Creek rises in w Haywood County and flows ne across the county into Pigeon River.

Jonathans Creek Township, w-central Haywood County. Named for Jonathan McPeters, one of the first men of European descent to visit and settle in the area.

Jones, community in se Beaufort County.

Jones Bay, ne Pamlico County in Pamlico Sound on the s side of Goose Creek Island. *See also* Hobucken.

Jonesboro, former town in central Lee County a short distance se of Sanford. The courthouse was equidistant from the two towns. Jonesboro was settled about 1869 and inc. 1873. Named for L. C. Jones, who built the railroad between Wilmington and Sanford. Merged with Sanford, 1947. The former town is now known as Jonesboro Heights in Sanford.

Jonesboro Township, former township in e central Lee County, now township no. 2.

Jonesborough. *See* Camden.

Jones Branch rises in sw Buncombe County near Jones Mountain and flows w into Newfound Creek.

Jones Branch rises in ne Cherokee County and flows se into Ricket Branch.

Jones Branch rises in sw Cleveland County and flows n into Broad River.

Jones Branch rises in central Haywood County and flows nw into Pigeon River.

Jones Branch rises in w Madison County and flows ne into East Fork Shut-in Creek.

Jones Branch rises in nw Watauga County and flows s into Little Beaverdam Creek.

Jones Chapel, community in nw Martin County.

Jones Chapel, community in s Rockingham County. Historically African American, it was founded by Samuel Jones, free black. Once known as Nubbin Ridge.

Jones County was formed in 1778 from Craven County. Located in the e section of the state, it is bounded by Carteret, Craven, Duplin, Lenoir, and Onslow Counties. It was named for Willie Jones (1740–1801), Revolutionary leader, president of the Council of Safety, and later opponent of the adoption of the U.S. Constitution. The Lawson map, 1709, shows "Mr Jones 4000 Acres" at the location. The Moseley map, 1733, shows "Mr. Frederick Jones 7375 Acres." Area: 468 sq. mi. County seat: Trenton, with an elevation of 28 ft. Townships, now numbered 1 to 7, were formerly White Oak, Pollocksville, Trenton, Cypress Creek, Tuckahoe, Chinquapin, and Beaver Creek. Produces tobacco, corn, soybeans, hogs, livestock, peanuts, cotton, lumber, signs, marl, sand, and gravel.

Jones Cove, central Haywood County near the head of Jones Branch.

Jones Cove, central Macon County at the head of Jacob Branch.

Jones Cove Creek rises in central Buncombe County and flows sw through Jones Cove into Bull Creek.

Jones Creek is formed in se Anson County by the junction of North Fork Jones Creek and South Fork Jones Creek. It flows ne and s into Pee Dee River. During the Civil War, a gun factory was operated on the bank of the stream. Jones Creek was the name of a post office operated in the vicinity, 1882–1904.

Jones Creek rises in sw Avery County and flows e into North Toe River.

Jones Creek rises in se Buncombe County and flows se into Broad River.

Jones Creek rises in ne Jackson County and flows w into Dark Ridge Creek.

Jones Creek rises in s Macon County and flows n into Cartoogechaye Creek.

Jones Creek rises in e Rockingham County and flows e into Lower Hogans Creek. Appears as Pruetts Fork Creek in early records; known as Manly Mill Creek in the 1920s and more recently by its present name.

Jones Creek rises in ne Swain County and flows sw into Raven Fork.

Jones Creek rises in s Swain County and flows nw into Bowers Creek.

Jones Creek. *See* Lick Fork.

Jones Gap, s Macon County between Cadon Gap and the head of Stephens Creek.

Jones Gap, in the Blue Ridge Mountains on the Transylvania County, N.C.–Greenville County, S.C., line near Walker Creek.

Jones Island, in White Oak River, w Carteret County, near the mouth of Pettivers Creek. Named for Robert Jones.

Jones Island. *See* Harwells Island.

Jones Island. *See* Pittmans Island.

Jones Knob, n Buncombe County at the n end of Iron Ore Ridge in the Elk Mountains.

Jones Knob, sw Cherokee County between Rocky Ford Creek and Shoal Creek.

Jones Knob, on the Haywood-Jackson county line. Alt. 6,240–6,260. Formerly known as Jones's Folly because, at a time when Elisha Mitchell and Thomas Clingman were contending over the highest peak in the southern Appalachians, a man named Jones came into the area and reported the knob to be the highest mountain. Upon questioning him, his friends discovered that he had not been near the top, so they called it Jones's Folly. In the 1850s, Arnold Guyot tried to name the peak Mount Junaluska, but the name did not stick.

Jones Knob, w Jackson County between Windy Gap and Poplar Cove Knob. Alt. approx. 4,140.

Jones Knob, s Macon County at the head of Whiterock Branch. Alt. 4,600.

Jones Lake, central Bladen County, one of the Carolina Bays, *which see*. Covers 224 acres; max. depth 8.7 ft. It is part of Jones Lake State Park. Fishing, swimming, and boating. Known earlier as Woodwards Lake for Samuel Woodward, a local justice of the peace in 1734. Probably named for Isaac Jones, who later owned adjacent property.

Jones Lake State Park, central Bladen County 4 mi. n of Elizabethtown. Est. 1939 as first state park in North Carolina for blacks; integrated in 1960s. Includes 2,208 acres. A scenic and recreational area with provisions for picnicking, swimming, fishing, camping, boating, hiking, and nature study. *See also* Jones Lake; Salters Lake.

Jones Mill appears on the Collet map, 1770. It was located near the mouth of the stream in sw Camden County that is now known as Portohonk Creek.

Jones Mill, community in e Cherokee County on Peachtree Creek.

Jones Mill. *See* Barrows Mill Pond.

Jones Mill. *See* Page's Mill.

Jones Mine, community in e Davidson County served by post office, 1886–1905.

Jones Mountain, central Buncombe County w of Wilson.

Jones Mountain, sw Buncombe County ne of Rockyface Mountain.

Jones Pond, a natural lake in e Gates County fed by several small streams and emptying into the Dismal Swamp. It is about ¾ mi. long and 2 to 6 ft. deep.

Jones Pond, se Scotland County on Bridge Creek. Formed about 1810. Covers 75 acres; max. depth 8 ft.

Jones's Folly. *See* Jones Knob.

Jones Store, community in s Lenoir County.

Jones Swamp, w central Gates County drained by Flat Branch.

Jones Swamp rises in w Sampson County and flows sw into South River.

Jonesville, town in nw Yadkin County on the s side of Yadkin River. Est. about 1811 on the land of Richard Cunningham and Jesse

Lester and named Martinsborough, probably for Governor Alexander Martin of nearby Stokes County, who died in 1807. Name changed to Jonesville for local citizen Hardy Jones in 1815. Inc. 1852. Merged with Arlington, 2001. Alt. 998.

Joplar, community in nw Mecklenburg County.

Joppa, community in w Orange County served by post office, 1888–1905.

Joppa, community in n Perquimans and s Gates Counties.

Joppa Cemetery, burial ground w of Mocksville in Davie County. Graves of Squire and Sarah Boone, parents of Daniel Boone, are there.

Jordan Branch rises in w Gates County and flows nw into Lassiter Branch.

Jordan Branch rises in e Haywood County and flows nw into Fall Creek.

Jordan Creek rises in e Beaufort County and flows e into Pungo River. Appears on the Collet map, 1770. *See also* Chappel Creek.

Jordan Creek rises in s Caswell County and flows sw into n Alamance County, where it enters Stony Creek.

Jordan Creek rises in central Granville County and flows se into Coon Creek.

Jordan Island, in e Pasquotank County in Newbegun Creek near the community of Weeksville.

Jordan Lake, reservoir in Durham, Wake, and Chatham Counties. The 13,900-acre lake was created by the U.S. Corps of Engineers. Authorized 1963; construction began 1967. Name changed from New Hope Lake to B. Everett Jordan Dam and Lake in 1973 to honor former U.S. senator B. Everett Jordan. Built for recreation, water supply, and flood control.

Jordan River. *See* Cape Fear River.

Jordans. *See* Friendship.

Jordans Creek rises in n Scotland County and flows se into Juniper Creek.

Jordans Creek rises in n Warren County and flows n into Sixpound Creek.

Jordans Landing, on Roanoke River, s Bertie County. The house on the Jordan plantation there is one of the oldest in the county.

Jordans Mill Pond, n Northampton County on Cypress Creek. Ivy Creek also flows into Jordans Mill Pond. Covers approx. 135 acres, with a max. depth of 12 ft. Named for an early owner.

Joshua Branch rises in s Transylvania County and flows ne into East Fork French Broad River.

Joshua Creek rises in se Lenoir County and flows se into Jones County, where it enters Trent River. Probably the same tributary as Joshua Foy's Creek, which is mentioned in local records as early as 1763.

Joshua Foy's Creek. *See* Joshua Creek.

Joshua Lake, on Gerren Creek in s Transylvania County. Covers 60 acres and has a max. depth of 70 ft.

Joshua Mountain, s Transylvania County between the head of Joshua Branch and Middle Fork French Broad River. Alt. 3,163.

Jourghland, community in n Davidson County.

Joy, community in nw Burke County.

Joyce Creek rises in Dismal Swamp, n Camden County, and flows se and sw into Pasquotank River. Though slightly misplaced, the tributary likely is the Joys Fork shown on the Moseley map, 1733, and as Joy Creek on the Price map, 1808.

Joyce Kilmer Memorial Forest, w Graham County in Nantahala National Forest, was dedicated to poet Joyce Kilmer (1886–1918), author of *Trees and Other Poems*, on July 30, 1936. It contains 3,840 acres of virgin forest (including poplar, hemlock, and oak) and is one of the finest stands of its type in America. Little Santeetlah Creek flows through the forest.

Joycetown, community in se Caldwell County. An industrial center, it was named in 1947 by Regina Reid for Joyce Hogan, wife of James Hogan, owner of a manufacturing plant there.

Joy Fork. *See* Joyce Creek.

Joyland, community in central Durham County on the outskirts of the city of Durham.

Joyner, community in w Wayne County.

Joyner's, former town in n Wilson County. Site approx. 1 mi. n of Elm City. Inc. 1870 on Wilmington and Weldon Railroad, now Seaboard Coast Line Railroad. Depot est. 1839; post office, 1846–73. Declined after establishment of Toisnot, now Elm City, *which see*.

Joynes, community in n Wilkes County on East Prong Roaring River.

Jubilee, community in w Davidson County.

Judaculla Mountain, n Jackson County between Balsam and Willits. Judaculla (or Jutaculla) was a giant in Indian legend.

Judaculla Ridge, e Jackson County between Beechfat Creek and Mull Creek.

Judaculla Rock, central Jackson County 3½ mi. se of East Laport on Caney Fork. Large rock covered with well-preserved Indian picture writing of unknown origin and meaning.

Judd Mountain, w Wilkes County between Lewis Fork Creek and South Fork Reddies River. Named for the Judd family, which settled in the vicinity before 1778.

Judes Gap, on the Polk-Rutherford county line.

Judges Quarter, community in s Hyde County.

Judith, community in n central Union County.

Judith Island, peninsula on Bell Island in s Hyde County. *See also* Abigails Islands.

Judkins Township, e Warren County.

Judson, former community in w Swain County on Little Tennessee River. Alt. 1,563. Site now under the waters of Fontana Lake.

Judson Lake, s Transylvania County, drains n into Little River. Covers 8 acres and has a max. depth of 20 ft.

Judy Branch rises in nw Swain County and flows s into Lake Cheoah.

Juford, community in sw Duplin County served by post office, 1884–1902. Formerly Rock Fish.

Jugtown, community in sw Buncombe County.

Jugtown, former community in sw Catawba County near the Lincoln County line. An area approx. 8 mi. square in which pottery was made from the early nineteenth century. Jacob Weaver, German potter, began the work and used a secret color formula, which he never shared with anyone else. Hilton, Reinhardt, Hartsoe, Johnson, Propst, Ritchie, and Seagle families and others also worked there.

Jugtown, community in nw Moore County n of Bear Creek. Est. about 1920 by Jacques Busbee (1870–1947) and Juliana Busbee (1876–1962), artists from Raleigh. Manufactured hand-turned pottery, which has been widely distributed in the United States. Chriscoe, Cole, Craven, Luck, McNeill, Owen, and Teague families and others also worked in the vicinity.

Jugtown Branch rises in sw Buncombe County near Jugtown and flows se into Pole Creek.

Jule, community in n Forsyth County served by post office, 1899–1904.

Julian, community in s Guilford and n Randolph Counties. Alt. 772.

Julie Knob, n Clay County on Julie Ridge. Named for a slave formerly owned by Robert Henry, who built her a house at the foot of the mountain when she was freed.

Julie Ridge, n Clay County between Deadline and Johnson Ridges.

Julius Duggar's Rock House Creek. *See* Dugger Creek.

Julius Knob, n Yancey County on Cane Mountain near the head of Sampson Branch. Alt. 3,931.

Jumbo, community in e Caldwell County served by post office, 1889–1905.

Jump and Run Branch rises in central Duplin County and flows sw into Northeast Cape Fear River.

Jump Cove, n Buncombe County e of Iron Ore Ridge.

Jumping Branch rises in n Transylvania County and flows se into South Fork Mills River.

Jumping Creek rises in e Jones County and flows s into Trent River.

Jumping Off Place, peak in nw Wilkes County w of Middle Fork Reddies River. It is the steepest portion of the Blue Ridge Mountains in the county.

Jumping Run rises in e Burke County and flows n into Catawba River.

Jumping Run, a stream about 1 mi. long, rises in s Carteret County and flows e and then s into the n side of Bogue Sound about 4 mi. e of Broad Creek.

Jumping Run rises in central Franklin County and flows sw into Tar River.

Jumping Run rises in s Franklin County and flows ne into Crooked Creek.

Jumping Run rises on the Fort Bragg Military Reservation in ne Hoke County and flows ne into Little River.

Jumping Run rises in sw Johnston County and flows ne into Mill Creek.

Jumping Run rises in n Lenoir County and flows sw into Falling Creek. The woodland pond forming the headwaters of the stream has been called The Hanted Pond since 1730.

Jumping Run rises in nw Nash County and flows n into Tumbling Run.

Jumping Run rises in s New Hanover County and flows w into Greenfield Lake.

Jumping Run rises in se Onslow County and flows w into Frenchs Creek.

Jumping Run rises in e Pender County and flows w into Northeast Cape Fear River.

Jumping Run. *See* Haw Creek.

Jumping Run Creek rises in central Alexander County and flows sw into Glade Creek. Name appears in local records as early as 1790.

Jumping Run Creek is formed in w Harnett County by the confluence of Reedys Swamp and McLeod Creek, *which see*, and flows se into n Cumberland County to enter Little River.

Jumping Swamp rises in s Columbus County and flows ne and e into Grissett Swamp.

Jump Off, The. *See* Mount Kephart.

Jumpoff Gap, s central Yancey County between Bowlens Creek and Bowlens Pyramid.

Jumpoff Mountain, w Henderson County between the headwaters of Brightwater Branch and North Fork. Alt. approx. 3,150.

Jumpoff Rock, w Henderson County on Jumpoff Mountain. Used by Indians as a post for sentinels to observe the approach of enemies up French Broad River valley. During the 1920s a resort, the Fleetwood Hotel, was begun there but never completed.

Jump Run, a tidal inlet near the mouth of Middens Creek e of the community of Smyrna in e Carteret County.

Jump-up, The, peak on the Graham-Swain county line between Grassy Top and Swim Bald.

Jumpup Ridge, n Swain County in Great Smoky Mountains National Park, a spur extending se from Bald Ridge between Bear Creek and Advalorem Branch.

Junaluska Creek rises in ne Cherokee County and flows sw and nw into Valley River.

Junaluska Gap, on the Cherokee-Macon county line in the Snowbird Mountains n of Rich Knob. Alt. 3,506.

Junaluska Mountain, sw Haywood County, about 5 mi. sw of Lake Junaluska. Alt. 5,071. Named to honor Junaluska, Cherokee chief who saved Andrew Jackson's life at the Battle of Horseshoe Bend, 1812. Known for a time in the 1920s as North Eaglenest Mountain in connection with the promotion of a hotel there. *See also* Jones Knob.

Juneau, community in w Mecklenburg County.

Juney Whank Branch rises in n Swain County and flows se into Deep Creek.

Junietta. *See* East Fork Pigeon River.

Juniper, community in Cumberland County.

Juniper Bay, s Hyde County in Pamlico Sound e of Marsh Island. Appears as New Mattamuskeet Creek on the Moseley map, 1733. *See also* Cecils Harbor.

Juniper Branch rises in s Pitt County and flows ne into Chicod Creek.

Juniper Branch rises in s Wake County and flows s into Middle Creek.

Juniper Creek rises in Green Swamp in n central Brunswick County. It flows w and sw into Waccamaw River. For a distance of several mi., it forms a part of the boundary between Brunswick and Columbus Counties.

Juniper Creek rises in e Harnett County and flows sw into Cape Fear River.

Juniper Creek rises on the Fort Bragg Military Reservation in n Hoke County and flows s into Rockfish Creek.

Juniper Creek rises in s Lee County and flows ne into Little River.

Juniper Creek rises in s Nash County and flows e into nw Wilson County, where it joins Millstone Creek in forming Bloomery Swamp.

Juniper Creek rises in n Scotland County and flows se into Big Shoeheel Creek.

Juniper Creek rises in s Tyrrell County and flows ne into Northwest Fork [Alligator River].

Juniper Run rises in se Johnston County and flows se into Mill Creek.

Juniper Swamp rises in w Beaufort County and flows w to join Harding Swamp in forming East Branch Chicod Creek.

Juniper Swamp rises in s Johnston County and flows se into Hannah Creek.

Juniper Swamp rises in n Onslow County and flows s into Cowhorn Swamp.

Juniper Swamp rises in sw Onslow County and flows nw into Pender County, where it enters Shaking Creek.

Juno, community in central Buncombe County on Dix Creek.

Jupiter, town in nw Buncombe County. Inc. 1895, but long inactive in municipal affairs. Served by post office, 1885–1909.

Just, community in e Madison County on Terris Fork.

Justice, community in e Franklin County on Little Peachtree Creek. Alt. 261. Settled about 1873.

Justice Creek rises in e Mitchell County and

flows e into Avery County, where it enters North Toe River.

Justice Ridge, sw Buncombe County n of Candler Heights.

Jutts Creek rises in se Graham County and flows n into Tulula Creek. Named for Jutt Colvard.

Jutts Creek, community in se Graham County.

Jutts Gap, on the Cherokee-Graham county line in the Snowbird Mountains.

K

Kadar, community in s Wake County.

Kagle Branch rises in w central Transylvania County and flows s into Catheys Creek.

Kagle Mountain, central Transylvania County between Catheys Creek and Kuykendall Creek. Alt. 3,908.

Kaiser Lake, s Transylvania County at the head of Morgan Mill Creek. Covers 2 acres and has a max. depth of 20 ft.

Kalamazoo, community in s Madison County.

Kalmia, community in se Mitchell County. A post office operated there, 1937–54.

Kanady Creek. *See* Candy Creek.

Kanati Fork rises in n Swain County in Great Smoky Mountains National Park on the e slope of Nettle Creek Bald and flows ne into Beech Flats Prong.

Kannapolis, city in s Rowan and n Cabarrus Counties. Alt. 765. Until inc. in 1984, it was the seventeenth-largest unincorporated community in the United States and the largest in North Carolina. James William Cannon bought 600 acres there along the Southern Railway tracks in 1905; there he built houses and a mill, which began production in 1908. Cannon Mills, noted for manufacture of towels, was there. Since 2008 the site of North Carolina Research Campus, with focus on nutrition. The name comes from a form of the Cannon family name plus *polis*, the Greek word for city.

Kannapolis Township, former township in nw Cabarrus County, now township no. 4. Once named Cooks Cross Roads Township.

Kanuga Lake, central Henderson County on Little Mud Creek. Formed about 1908. Cov-

ers 12 acres; max. depth 20 ft. Summer camp owned by the Episcopal Church. Named for prehistoric Cherokee town Ka-nu-ga, on the West Fork of Pigeon River in Haywood County. The Indian name traditionally meant "Meeting Place of Many Peoples."

Kappa, community in w Davie County. In the 1870s known as Ketchie's Mill for a mill erected on Little Creek. Post office est. 1883 in the home of W. R. Ketchie, a Lutheran minister, who gave it the name Kappa, the Greek name for the letter *K*. Davie Academy opened there about 1908, and the name Davie Academy is also sometimes still used for the community.

Kapps Mill, community in w Surry County served by post office, 1878–1929.

Karrs Branch rises in sw Iredell County w of Troutman and flows sw into Hicks Creek.

Katalsta Ridge, ne Swain County in Great Smoky Mountains National Park, a spur extending s from Eagle Rock. Named for a daughter of Yonaguska, noted as a pottery maker.

Kate Gap, on the Madison County, N.C.–Cocke County, Tenn., line.

Kate Knob, s Macon County between Pine Ridge and Jones Creek.

Katesville, community in central Franklin County. Settled 1888. Named for Kate Griffin, donor of the site. Alt. 300.

Katie Creek rises in e Macon County and flows w into Walnut Creek.

Kawana, community in se Avery County.

Kaylors Knob, sw Burke County.

Kayoo-lanta. *See* Chimneytop Mountain.

Kays Crossroads, community in se Gates County.

Kayser Junction, community in w Cumberland County.

Kearney, community in n Franklin County. Alt. 300. Named in 1894 for Charlie B. Kearney.

Kearney Creek rises in se Craven County and flows e into Adams Creek.

Keasler Branch rises in central Buncombe County near Craven Gap and flows se into Bull Creek.

Keeauwee, an Indian village, appears on the Moseley map, 1733. Site was on the trading path of the Cherokee and Catawba Indians to Virginia on Deep River in present nw Randolph County. *See also* Caraway Creek.

Keel Creek rises in se Hertford County and flows

s approx. 3 mi. to enter Chowan River at the ne corner of Bertie County.

Keelsville. *See* Congleton.

Keene, community in s Durham County about 3 mi. s of the city of Durham. Site of the yards of the Norfolk and Southern Railroad.

Keener, community in n Sampson County at the head of Beaverdam Swamp. A post office est. there in 1879 was named Bass.

Keener Creek rises in central Cherokee County and flows se into Marble Creek.

Keener Knob, e Macon County between the head of Crows Branch and Ledford Branch.

Keener Mountain, e Macon County between Long Branch and Brush Creek.

Keenerville. *See* Ingalls.

Keeters Store, community in central Halifax County.

Keeversville. *See* Plateau.

Keg Drive Branch rises in n Swain County and flows se into Left Fork [Deep Creek].

Keg Island, in the Cape Fear River, w New Hanover County se of Campbell Island.

Kehukee, community in s Pasquotank County.

Kehukee Creek. *See* Kehukee Swamp.

Kehukee Swamp rises in e Halifax County and flows sw into Roanoke River. Appears as Kehukee Creek on the Collet map, 1770.

Keith, community in w Pender County on Black River.

Keiths Bay, sand-filled bay in s Sampson County on the head of Keiths Swamp. *See also* Carolina Bays.

Keiths Swamp rises in s Sampson County and flows se into Black River.

Kelford, town in nw Bertie County. Settled 1890; inc. 1893. Built on the land of Col. S. A. Norfleet, whose home, Kelford, was named for a ford in Scotland. Alt. 88.

Keller Gap, on the Watauga County, N.C.–Johnson County, Tenn., line in the Stone Mountains.

Kellogs Fork, community in e Gates County.

Kellum, community in n Onslow County.

Kellumtown, a community of African Americans in se Onslow County. Made up largely of people formerly living on land that became Camp Lejeune Marine Corps Air Station.

Kelly, community in se Bladen County. Formerly known also as Centerville and Hungry Neck.

Kelly, community in central Moore County.

Kelly Cove, n Macon County on a tributary of Burningtown Creek.

Kelly Creek rises in se Henderson County 1½ mi. sw of Saluda and flows se into Pacolet River. Lake Kelly, *which see*, is on Kelly Creek.

Kelly Mountain, s Transylvania County between Tower Creek and Cantrell Creek. Alt. approx. 2,980.

Kelly Ridge, n Macon County between Shope Cove and Kelly Cove.

Kellys Creek rises in s Pender County and flows w into Rileys Creek.

Kellys Pond, on Southwest Creek in e Lenoir County. Formed in or prior to 1738 by a man named Marshall. Covers 312 acres; max. depth 10 ft.

Kellyville, community in sw Mecklenburg County served by post office, 1876–87.

Kelsey, community in nw Caldwell and sw Watauga Counties near Boone Fork 3 mi. w of Blowing Rock. Probably named for Samuel T. Kelsey, who operated a nursery nearby in the late nineteenth century. Also known as White's Spring.

Kelvin Grove, community in nw Wake County served by post office, 1840–1903.

Kelvyn Fork rises in w Wake County and flows w into Brier Creek.

Kemps Mill, community in s Randolph County on Richland Creek.

Kems Branch rises in e Haywood County and flows n into Allens Creek.

Kenady's Branch. *See* Candy Creek.

Kenan Ditch, a drain in s Duplin County to carry the waters of Kenan Pocosin into Northeast Cape Fear River.

Kenan Pocosin, a large swamp in s Duplin County that is drained by ditches into Northeast Cape Fear River.

Kenansville, town and county seat, central Duplin County. Authorized to be laid out 1816; inc. 1852. Alt. 127. Named for Gen. James Kenan (1740–1810), member of Provincial Congress and Revolutionary officer. Site once known as Grovemont. "Goldengrove," plantation of Congressman James Gillespie, was at or near the site of Kenansville before it was laid out. Earlier Duplin Court House was approx. 2½ mi. w of present town of Warsaw on the Duplin-Sampson county line. Site of Confederate arms factory, manufacturer of swords, sabers, and accoutrements.

Kenansville Township, central Duplin County.

Kendal, community in s Wilkes County served by post office, 1895–1914.

Kendall Beach, community on Neuse River in sw Pamlico County. Developed after World War I by a man named Kendall.

Kendrick Crossroad, community in sw Mecklenburg County.

Kendricks Creek rises in East Dismal Swamp, central Washington County, and flows approx. 9 mi. n into Albemarle Sound. Formerly called Mackeys Creek. The part of Kendricks Creek that is s of the town of Roper is sometimes called Mill Creek locally.

Kenilworth, former town in central Buncombe County. Inc. 1891; became a part of Asheville, 1905.

Kenly, town in e Johnston County. Settled about 1875; inc. 1887. Named for J. I. Kenly, an official of the Atlantic Coast Line Railroad. Alt. 220.

Kennebec, community in s Wake County. Named for a county in Maine.

Kennedy Creek, central Beaufort County. A short but rather wide stream at the w limit of Washington, N.C. It flows s into Pamlico River.

Kennedy Creek rises in ne Cherokee County and flows ne and w into Worm Creek.

Kennedy Creek rises in n Mecklenburg County and flows s into Sugar Creek.

Kennedy Crossroads, community in s Wayne County w of Mount Olive.

Kennedy Falls, community in ne Cherokee County.

Kennedy Ford, ne Union County in Rocky River.

Kennedy Top, ne Cherokee County near the headwaters of Kennedy Creek.

Kennekeet Banks. See Kinnakeet Banks.

Kenneth Branch rises in s Wake County and flows se into Neill Creek.

Kenneth Creek rises in s Wake County and flows s into Harnett County, where it enters Neill Creek.

Kenricks Mounts or Kindrickers Mounts, sand dunes fixed by vegetation, are shown on the White map, 1590, somewhat s of the present community of Rodanthe on Hatteras Island, e Dare County. The dunes presumably were submerged with Cape Kenrick, which see.

Kent, community in ne Mecklenburg County served by post office, 1876–87.

Kenton Fork. See Kinton Forks.

Kentucky Creek rises in central Avery County and flows s and w into North Toe River.

Keowee. See Cowee.

Kephart Prong rises in n Swain County in Great Smoky Mountains National Park on the e slope of Mount Kephart and flows se to join Beech Flats Prong in forming Oconaluftee River. Named for Horace Kephart (1862–1931), author and authority on campcraft, who is buried in Bryson City.

Kerners Crossroads. See Kernersville.

Kerners Mill Creek rises in e Forsyth County and flows w into Salem Lake.

Kernersville, town in e Forsyth County. Inc. 1871. Site first settled in 1756 by Caleb Story, an Irishman. It was purchased about 1770 by William Dobson and came to be known as Dobson's Crossroads; Washington had breakfast at Dobson's tavern on June 2, 1791. In 1871 Joseph Kerner bought the property, and the town that developed there took his name. Formerly Kerner's Crossroads. Former Southern Pilgrim College was located there. Produces hosiery, textiles, and fabricated metals.

Kernersville Township, e Forsyth County.

Kernersville Water Reservoir, on Kerners Mill Creek, e Forsyth County. Formed 1953. Covers 120 acres; max. depth 25 ft.

Kerr, community in New Hanover County.

Kerr, community in s Sampson County. Settled about 1888. Named for John Daniel Kerr, who influenced the location of the Cape Fear & Yadkin Valley Railroad on the e side of the Cape Fear River. Alt. 91.

Kerr Creek rises in w Rowan County and flows ne into Back Creek. Appears in early records as James Cathey's Creek, named about 1749 for an early settler. See also Millbridge.

Kerr Lake was formed in 1952 with the completion of John H. Kerr Dam on Roanoke River in Virginia. Reservoir also fed by Dan River, Nutbush Creek, Island Creek, and many smaller tributaries, it extends into central Vance County, n Granville County, and nw Warren County. Normally it covers 48,900 acres and is 39 mi. long, with a shoreline of 800 mi. Max. depth 99 ft. Used for hydroelectric power generation, flood control, municipal water supply, irrigation, and recreation. Named for Congressman John H. Kerr (1873–1958). Initially known as Buggs Island Lake for an island in Roanoke River below the dam. The section of the reservoir extending into Vance County on Nutbush Creek is sometimes known as Townsville Lake. The official name is John H. Kerr Reservoir.

Kershaw, community in s Pamlico County between Greens and Kershaw Creeks.

Kershaw Creek rises in se Pamlico County and flows se into Greens Creek.

Kesiah River. *See* Cashie River.

Ketchie's Mill. *See* Kappa.

Kettle Rock, se Macon County between Big Dog Mountain and Chinquapin Mountain.

Kevin, community in central Mecklenburg County.

Key, community in se Harnett County served by post office, 1888–1903.

Keyser. *See* Addor.

Kick Shin Creek rises in central Surry County and flows e into Cody Creek.

Kidsville, community in e Lincoln County served by post office, 1882–1912.

Kies Mountain, s Randolph County.

Kiger, community in s Stokes County served by post office, 1890–1903.

Kilbart Slough, a short tidal creek in sw Brunswick County that joins the channel of the Intracoastal Waterway n of Hales Beach.

Kilby Branch rises in n Haywood County and flows se into Big Creek.

Kilby Branch rises in n Wilkes County and flows s into Reddies River. Named for William Kilby, colonial settler.

Kilby Cove, s Cherokee County. An unnamed stream flowing through the cove forms the headwaters of the e fork of Cook Creek.

Kilby Creek rises in sw Macon County and flows ne into Nantahala River.

Kilby Gap, on the Alexander-Wilkes county line in the Brushy Mountains. Named for William Kilby Jr., early nineteenth-century resident of the area. Alt. 1,540.

Kilby Gap, sw Macon County on Kilby Creek.

Kildeer Mountain, w Cherokee County between Rocky Ford Creek and Shoal Creek.

Kilgo, community in ne Chatham County served by post office, 1898–1904.

Kilkenny, community in s Tyrrell County. *See also* Warbler.

Kilkenny Landing, s Tyrrell County on Alligator River.

Kill Devil Hill, large sand hill, e Dare County, appears first on Price map, 1808. It was from

Kill Devil Hill in 1903 that the Wright Brothers made the first successful powered airplane flight. Site of 60-foot-tall monument honoring the achievement.

Kill Devil Hills, town on n Bodie Island, e Dare County. Inc. 1953. There are numerous legends concerning the origin of the name, but among the earliest was one recorded in 1728 by William Byrd of Virginia. He reported that rum consumed in that part of Carolina was shipped from New England and was of such strength that a saying arose: "That thar rum is powerful enough to kill the devil." Alt. 11.

Kill Devil Hills Coast Guard Station, on n Bodie Island in e Dare County. First est. as a life-saving station in 1878–79. Life-saving Service and Revenue Cutter Service joined to form U.S. Coast Guard in 1915.

Kill'em Swamp rises in se Hertford County and flows nw into Chinkapin Creek.

Killets Creek rises in central Moore County and flows n into McLendons Creek. Named for William Killet, who settled in the area about 1766.

Killian Branch rises near Killian Knob in central Buncombe County and flows se into Beaverdam Creek. Probably named for Daniel Killian, friend and host of Bishop Francis Asbury in his travels, 1803.

Killian Knob, central Buncombe County near Gooch Peak n of Asheville.

Killian Knob, w Haywood County between Mitchell Cove and Riddle Cove.

Killians Creek rises in s Catawba County and flows s through e Lincoln County and into ne Gaston County, where it joins Leepers Creek in forming Dutchmans Creek. Appears as Killings Creek on the Collet map, 1770.

Killings Creek. *See* Killians Creek.

Killpecker Ridge, nw Swain County in Great Smoky Mountains National Park, a spur extending se from Jenkins Trail Ridge.

Kill Quick. *See* Quick.

Killquick. *See* Lawrence.

Kill Swamp rises in n Sampson County and flows sw into Great Coharie Creek.

Kilmer Memorial Forest. *See* Joyce Kilmer Memorial Forest.

Kimbolton, community in n Chatham County served by post office, 1859–1923.

Kimesville, community in w Alamance and e

Guilford Counties. Settled about 1745; a mill there dates from about 1788. Named for the Keim (Kime) family, a pioneer German family in the area.

Kimsey Bald, on the Clay-Macon county line.

Kimsey Cove, ne Cherokee County in the Valley River Mountains. An unnamed stream flowing through the cove empties into Vengeance Creek.

Kimsey Cove, w Macon County at the head of Gibby Branch.

Kimsey Creek rises in s Buncombe County and flows sw into Henderson County, where it enters Cane Creek. A large lime deposit along Kimsey Creek is now used for crushed stone.

Kimsey Creek rises in sw Macon County and flows ne into Nantahala River.

Kimsey Gap, s Macon County between Allison Creek and Jones Creek.

Kimsey Ridge, s Clay County, extends ne in an arc from Sweetwater Gap to Sweetwater Creek.

Kinack, a name appearing on the Ogilby map, 1671, for the land now in Craven County between Upper Broad Creek and Swift Creek.

Kincaids Mill Creek. *See* Bristol's Mill Creek.

Kind, community in sw Madison County.

Kindrickers Mounts. *See* Kenricks Mounts.

King, community in sw Stokes County. Alt. 1,115. Originally known as King's Cabin for a double log cabin owned by Oscar King. The present name was adopted with the coming of the railroad.

King Blount's Town. *See* Ucohnerunt.

King Creek rises in ne Craven County and flows n into Neuse River.

King Creek rises in s Henderson County and flows ne into Bat Fork.

King Creek rises in s Surry County and flows se into Fisher River.

King Creek rises in central Transylvania County and flows se into French Broad River.

King Mountain, s Henderson County n of Zirconia.

King Mountain, sw Randolph County.

King Mountain, w central Transylvania County between Negro Prong and Catheys Creek.

Kings Bluff, United States Lock Number 1 on Cape Fear River, se Bladen County.

Kingsboro, community in central Edgecombe County. Alt. 113.

Kings Branch rises in s Mecklenburg County and flows s into Sugar Creek. Appears as Kings River on the Collet map, 1770.

King's Cabin. *See* King.

Kings Creek rises in nw Alleghany County and flows sw into South Fork New River.

Kings Creek rises in ne Caldwell County and flows n into Yadkin River. Has been known by the name since the colonial period, hence it probably honors King George III.

Kings Creek rises in se Cleveland County on Kings Mountain and flows se into South Carolina, where it enters Broad River.

Kings Creek rises in nw Guilford County and flows w into Forsyth County, where it enters East Belews Creek.

Kings Creek rises in s Onslow County and flows se into Spicers Bay.

Kings Creek rises in s Vance County and flows s into n Franklin County, where it enters Tar River.

Kings Creek, community in e Caldwell County.

Kings Creek Township, ne Caldwell County.

Kings Crossroads, community in nw Guilford County.

Kings Crossroads, community in w Pitt County.

Kingsdale, former town in se Robeson County near the head of Mill Swamp Creek. Inc. 1907, but long inactive in municipal affairs. Site of huge sawmill operations that cleared virgin longleaf pine timber in the region; operations ceased about 1918, and the site was abandoned. Some mill foundations, machine parts, and railroad fill still visible.

Kings Island, s Dare County in the waters of Pamlico Sound off Brooks Point, Hatteras Island.

Kings Mountain, a range about 3 mi. long in se Cleveland and sw Gaston Counties extending into South Carolina. The highest peak, The Pinnacle, is at the n end of the range, separated from the rest of the range by Sherrars Gap. The Battle of Kings Mountain, October 7, 1780, was fought a short distance s in South Carolina.

Kings Mountain, n Jackson County between Tuckasegee River and Cope Creek.

Kings Mountain, city in se Cleveland County. Inc. 1874. Alt. 995. Named for the mountain 7 mi. s. In 1923 East Kings Mountain, *which see*, became a part of Kings Mountain. Produces textiles, lumber, minerals, and hosiery.

Kings Mountain Township, former township in se Cleveland County, now township no. 4.

Kings Point, peninsula extending from the mainland of ne Carteret County into Brett Bay.

Kings River. *See* Kings Branch.

Kingswood, community in se Mecklenburg County served by post office, 1880–1903.

Kingville, former black community in n central Stanly County, now a part of the city of Albemarle. Named for Dr. O. D. King, on whose land it was founded in 1890.

Kingwood, community in se Mecklenburg County served by post office, 1880–1903.

Kinley Mountain, s Macon County between High Holly and the North Carolina–Georgia state line.

Kinnakeet. *See* Avon.

Kinnakeet Banks, the name commonly given to the middle section of Hatteras Island in e Dare County extending s from Chicamacomico Banks to Hatteras Woods. Also spelled Kennekeet Banks.

Kinnekeet Township, e Dare County on the Outer Banks. Also spelled Kennekeet Township.

Kinnion, community in w Cumberland County served by post office, 1895–1907.

Kinsey, community in s Cherokee County on Nottely River. Alt. 1,609.

Kinston, city and county seat, e Lenoir County on Neuse River. Site granted to Robert Atkins in 1729 and came to be known as Atkins Bank. A chapel erected there about 1748, and a tobacco warehouse built about 1757. Est. 1762 as Kingston in honor of King George III. Renamed Kinston, 1784, after the American Revolution. Name changed to Caswell in honor of Governor Richard Caswell in 1833, but changed back to Kinston the following year. Lenoir County Community College, est. 1966, is there. Alt. 44.

Kinston Township, e central Lenoir County.

Kinton Forks, community in n Granville County.

Kip, community in central Rockingham County served by post office, 1900–1902.

Kipland. *See* Kipling.

Kipling, community in n central Harnett County. Known as Bradley's Store in late nineteenth century. Railroad timetable of 1907 lists it as Kipland.

Kirby. *See* Conway.

Kirby Branch rises in nw Watauga County on the se prong of Fork Ridge and flows approx. 1½ mi. se into Cove Creek.

Kirby Grange, plantation of Christopher Gale, appointed in 1712 as the first chief justice of North Carolina; stood near Bath, central Beaufort County.

Kirby Knob, on the Jackson-Macon county line. Alt. 4,410.

Kirbys Creek is formed by the junction of Rogers Swamp and Corduroy Swamp in n Northampton County. It flows se and ne into Meherrin River, which forms the Northampton-Hertford county line.

Kirby's Gap, nw Caldwell County. Alt. 1,789.

Kirby Township, ne Northampton County.

Kirkendall Creek. *See* South Prong [Glady Fork].

Kirkland, community in ne New Hanover County.

Kirkland Creek, formed in s Swain County by the confluence of West Fork and East Fork and flows ne into Tuckasegee River.

Kirkland Creek rises in w Swain County and flows se into Fontana Lake.

Kirkland Gap, n Graham County between Yellow and Fax Creeks; the Appalachian Trail passes through the gap.

Kirklin Creek rises in central Cherokee County and flows nw into Hiwassee River.

Kirkpatrick, former community in central Guilford County, now a part of the city of Greensboro.

Kirksey, community in se McDowell County s of Marion near Rutherford county line at Cane Creek. Named for local family. Served by post office, 1895–1911.

Kitchen, community in n central Halifax County.

Kitchen Branch rises in ne Buncombe County near Sourwood Gap and flows sw through Montreat into Flat Creek.

Kitchin, community in n Halifax County served by post office, 1893–1909.

Kitchin Branch rises in n Jackson County and flows se into Scott Creek.

Kit Creek rises in w Wake County and flows nw into Chatham County, where it enters Northeast Creek.

Kits Knob, n Buncombe County nw of Jones Knob in the Elk Mountains.

Kit Swamp rises in n Craven County and flows sw into Little Swift Creek.

Kitten Creek rises in w Pitt County and flows ne into Otter Creek.

Kittrell, town in sw Vance County between Long Creek and Buffalo Creek. Alt. 372. Inc. 1885 and named for George Kittrell, who donated land for a railway station there. Confederate cemetery is there. Nearby Kittrell's Springs, *which see*, is said to have been the first summer resort in the state. Before the incorporation of the town, the community was known as Staunton. Served by post office since 1854. Kittrell College, est. 1886, was there. *See also* Epping Forest.

Kittrell's Springs, health resort and social and recreational center in the nineteenth century. Served as Confederate hospital. Springs are ½ mi. w of the town of Kittrell, sw Vance County.

Kittrell Township, s Vance County.

Kitty Fork, community in n central Sampson County near Great Coharie Creek.

Kitty Hawk, town and summer resort in e Dare County on the s boundary of the North Banks. Inc. 1981. Former site of the New Inlet. Settled before 1790. Name probably is a variation of an Indian place name, as it appears on maps as early as 1738 as Chickehauk. At nearby Kill Devil Hill, *which see*, in 1903, the Wright Brothers made the first successful powered airplane flight. Alt. 9.

Kitty Hawk Bay, ne Dare County at the e end of Albemarle Sound, *which see*. Bounded on the n by the s extremity of North Banks and on the s by Colington Island.

Klansoona. *See* Terrapin Mountain.

Klesee Creek rises in nw Transylvania County and flows sw into Court House Creek.

Klondike, community in e Bladen County served by post office, 1898–1908.

Knap of Reeds, former community in sw Granville County dating from the nineteenth century or earlier. Served by post office, 1839–1905. The site is now within the Butner area. A Knap of Reeds District in 1790 had 77 heads of families at the time of the first census.

Knap of Reeds Creek rises in w Granville County and flows s into Neuse River on the Granville-Durham county line.

Knee Branch rises in s Hertford County and flows n into Ahoskie Swamp. Probably named for the cypress knees in the area.

Knightdale, town in e Wake County on the head of Poplar Creek. Chartered in 1927 and named for its founder, H. H. Knight. Alt. 318.

Knights Crossroads, community in w Halifax County.

Knights Crossroads, community in e Wake County.

Knobbs Creek rises in e central Pasquotank County and flows se into Pasquotank River at the n limits of Elizabeth City.

Knob Creek rises in n Cleveland County and flows sw into First Broad River.

Knob Creek rises in sw Jackson County and flows e into Norton Creek.

Knob Creek rises in nw Rutherford County and flows sw into Broad River.

Knobcreek, community in n Cleveland County on Knob Creek.

Knob Creek Township, former township in ne Cleveland County, now township no. 10.

Knobs Township, nw Yadkin County.

Knoll, community in se Macon County served by post office, 1886–1905.

Knotts Island, a peninsula in n Currituck County approx. 5 by 3½ mi.; extends into North Carolina from Princess Anne County, Va. Knotts Island Channel on the e connects Currituck Sound with Back Bay (in Virginia); North Landing River on the w rises in Virginia and flows past Knott Island into Currituck Sound. Appears as Knot Isle on the Comberford map, 1657. Probably named for James Knott or a member of his family. Knott held land in s Virginia as early as 1642. *See also* Mackay Island.

Knotts Island Channel, a waterway between Knotts Island and Currituck Banks, ne Currituck County. The channel connects Currituck Sound in North Carolina with Back Bay in Virginia.

Knotts Store, community in w Anson County served by post office, 1877–1905.

Knottville, community in e central Wilkes County between Rock and Mulberry Creeks.

Knotty Pine Creek. *See* Buckland Mill Branch.

Knox, community in n Moore County served by post office, 1900–1905.

Kolasko. *See* Weatherman Bald.

Kona, community in w central Mitchell County near the junction of North Toe and South Toe Rivers. The name is said to have been coined by R. M. Lawson, first dispatcher for the railroad, simply because it was a short, easily spelled and understood word.

Konnatoga. *See* Little Pisgah Mountain.

Koonasoga. *See* Humpback Mountain.

Koonces Bay, on White Oak River, sw Carteret County between Wire Point and Balls Point. Named for the Koonce family.

Kornegay, community in e Duplin County.

Kossie, community in s Cleveland County served by post office, 1898–1902.

Kototine. *See* Little River.

Kross Keys, community in s Polk County. Settled about 1900. Named by Greenberry Sanders because of keylike intersection of roads at the site.

Krunkleton Knob, s Burke County. Alt. 2,600.

Kuhns, community in w Carteret County. Named for William Kuhn, native of Germany and later a resident of the Stella community who engaged in lumbering along the White Oak River.

Kullaughee Valley. *See* Cullowhee.

Kure Beach, town in se New Hanover County on the Atlantic Ocean. Inc. 1947. Named for the Kure family, which first settled there in 1867. Alt. 5.

Kurfees. *See* Jericho.

Ku-wa-hi. *See* Clingmans Dome.

Kuykendall Branch rises in n Buncombe County near the Madison county line and flows sw into French Broad River.

Kuykendall Creek rises in w central Transylvania County and flows se and sw into Catheys Creek.

Kyle, community in nw Macon County on White-oak Creek.

Kyles Creek rises in n Henderson County and flows se into Clear Creek.

Kyles Landing, community in ne Cumberland County served by post office, 1852–1902.

L

Laboratory, community in s central Lincoln County. Named for Confederate drug manufactory operated under the direction of Dr. A. S. Piggott. A part of the original laboratory still stands.

Lacey, community in e Rockingham County.

Lackey, community in e Alexander County.

Lackey Mountain, e Alexander County. Alt. 1,430.

Lacky Crossroads, community in central Cleveland County e of Lawndale.

Lacrosse, community in se Guilford County served by post office, 1891–1904.

Lacys Creek rises in nw Chatham County and flows ne into Rocky River.

Ladd Branch rises in central Cherokee County and flows w into Parsons Branch.

Ladonia, community in nw Surry County on Fisher River.

Lagoon, The, s Buncombe County, is separated from the French Broad River by a narrow strip of land s of city of Asheville near the Biltmore Estate.

LaGrange, town in nw Lenoir County. Known as Rantersville and Moseley Hall prior to 1869, when it was inc. as LaGrange after Lafayette's estate near Paris. Moseley Hall had been the plantation name given by Thomas Moseley of Virginia, who settled there before the Revolution. William Dunn Moseley (1795–1863), first governor of the state of Florida, was born there. Produces trailers, tobacco trucks, and cotton gins. Alt. 113. *See also* Moseley County.

Lake Adger, in n central Polk County on Green River. Built by Blue Ridge Power Company in 1925 and known as Turners Lake for nearby Turners Shoals. Duke Power Company bought the hydroelectric plant and water rights in 1927 and later renamed the lake, likely for John B. Adger, who was active in power development on Broad River in South Carolina. Covers 438 acres, with a max. depth of 86 ft. Used to generate hydroelectric power.

Lake Ashnoca, central Buncombe County on Ragsdale Creek. The property of the Asheville School, it covers 27 acres.

Lake Bay, community in se Moore County on Carrolls Branch. Formerly known as Hog Island.

Lake Benson, in s Wake County on Swift Creek. Formed in 1925 and named Rands Mill Pond for owners. Later renamed for B. B. Benson, former Raleigh city councilman. Covers 490 acres and has max. depth of 19 ft. Enlarged in 1951. Used as reservoir and for fishing.

Lake Brandt, an artificial lake in central Guilford County on Reedy Fork Creek. Max. depth 25 ft. Covers 400 acres. Formed in 1920 and named for former Greensboro mayor Leon J. Brandt (1874–1920). Municipal water supply for Greensboro and owned by the city.

Lake Burlington, central Alamance County on Stony Creek. Formed 1910; enlarged 1961. Source of water for the city of Burlington. Covers 750 acres; 7½ mi. long, with a 50 mi. shoreline. Fishing, boating. Known earlier as Stony Creek Lake.

Lake Charles, on Grassy Creek, se Buncombe County.

Lake Cheoah, nw Graham and sw Swain Counties. Formed 1928 by Aluminum Company of America in damming Little Tennessee River. Covers 648 acres; max. depth 200 ft. Used for power, swimming, and boating. Alt. 1,276.

Lake Chub. *See* Loch Lily.

Lake Comfort, community on the s shore of Lake Mattamuskeet in central Hyde County.

Lake Craig, on Swannanoa River in central Buncombe County near the e boundary of Asheville. The Asheville Recreation Park is located near the dam. Named for Governor Locke Craig (1860–1925), whose home was nearby. The lake covers approx. 55 acres. Was a source of water for the city of Asheville prior to about 1903.

Lake Creek flows se from Black Lake into South River in e Bladen County.

Lake Creek Township, in e Bladen County.

Lake Devin, central Granville County on Hatcher's Run, was formed in 1954 as a source of water for the town of Oxford. Covers 100 acres; max. depth 40 ft. Named for former chief justice of the North Carolina Supreme Court, W. A. Devin, a resident of Oxford.

Lake Drain flows e from Singletary Lake in e Bladen County into Colly Creek.

Lake Eden, on a tributary of North Fork [Swannanoa River], e Buncombe County at the former site of Black Mountain College.

Lake Emory, on Little Tennessee River in central Macon County. Covers 200 acres; max. depth 20 ft. Formed 1925. Used by Nantahala Power & Light Company to generate electricity.

Lakefield, community in e Hoke County.

Lake Fisher, ne Cabarrus County. Formed in 1946 by a dam on Cold Water Creek. Covers 277 acres; max. depth 30 ft. Named for L. A. Fisher, superintendent of Concord water and power department. Used for fishing and as a source of water for the city of Concord.

Lake Franklin, e Anson County se of Lilesville. Covers approx. 5 acres; max. depth 25 ft. Formed in 1908 when gravel was removed from the site. Named for the owner of the property from which the gravel was dug.

Lake Gaston was formed on Roanoke River about 8 mi. upstream from the city of Roanoke Rapids and extends along the Halifax-Northampton county line nw into ne Warren County and into Virginia. Gaston Dam, 3,600 ft. wide and 105 ft. high, was completed in 1963 by Virginia Electric and Power Company and lies on the upstream end of the Roanoke Rapids Lake. Lake Gaston is 34 mi. long, with max. width of 1.3 mi. Covers 20,300 acres, with a shoreline of 350 mi. and a max. depth of 97 ft. Used for generation of hydroelectric power and recreation.

Lake Gresham, in n central Wake County on Perry Creek. Formed in 1939. Covers 100 acres and has max. depth of 30 ft. Used for recreation.

Lake Hickory, on Catawba River, within Alexander and Caldwell Counties on the n and Burke and Catawba Counties on the s. Formed by a dam constructed in 1928 by Duke Power Co. Covers 4,110 acres. Source of hydroelectric power; fishing, boating, and swimming. Dam at the site of former Oxford Ford across the river; named for Samuel Oxford, pioneer settler who opened the ford. Alt. 829. Lake formerly known as Oxford Lake or Oxford Reservoir.

Lake Hunt, s Rockingham County. Built on n fork of Piney Creek in 1956. Covers approx. 175 acres. Named for George Hunt, mayor of Reidsville.

Lake James, on Catawba River, Burke and McDowell Counties. Formed when Bridgewater Dam was built, 1916–23, and formerly called Bridgewater Reservoir. Fed by North Fork [Catawba River], Linville River, and numerous smaller tributaries in addition to Catawba River. Owned by Duke Power Co. and named for James B. Duke (1856–1925). Covers 6,510 acres, with a shoreline of 150 mi. Used for recreation and generation of hydroelectric power.

Lake Johnson, in s central Wake County on Walnut Creek. Covers 160 acres and has max.

depth of 18 ft. Owned by city of Raleigh. Used for fishing, boating, and municipal water supply.

Lake Juanita. *See* Lake Louise.

Lake Junaluska, central Haywood County on Richland Creek. Formerly covered 250 acres, but silt filled it until it is much smaller. Named for the Cherokee Indian chief, Junaluska (ca. 1758–1858). The lake covers the site of the former community of Tuscola, which had a post office in the 1870s and 1880s.

Lake Junaluska, community in central Haywood County on the lake. Methodist assembly grounds and resort area. The assembly was inc. in 1909 and the community site selected soon afterward. Alt. 2,584.

Lake Kawana, se Avery County on Linville River. Two acres in area; max. depth 10 ft. Owned by Linville Resort and used for fishing, boating, swimming, and, sometimes in the winter, ice skating. Also known as Linville Lake.

Lake Kelly, water-supply reservoir in se Henderson County for town of Saluda. Located at the head of Kelly Creek.

Lake Kenilworth, central Buncombe County in the city of Asheville. Approx. ½ mi. long.

Lake Landing, community in e Hyde County on the se shore of Lake Mattamuskeet. The courthouse was there from about 1820 to 1836.

Lake Landing Township, e Hyde County.

Lake Lanier, in s Polk County, N.C., and ne Greenville County, S.C. Formed about 1916–18. Covers 127 acres, with a max. depth of 70 ft. Named for poet Sidney Lanier (1842–81), who spent his last years in Polk County. Water source for town of Tryon. Used for recreation and for commercial purposes.

Lake Lee. *See* Lake Monroe.

Lake Logan, s Haywood County on West Fork Pigeon River. Approx. 1½ mi. long and ¼ mi. wide. A water reservoir for Champion Paper and Fiber Company in Canton. Alt. 2,909.

Lake Louise, a 35-acre lake formed in 1927 in se Alleghany County on the headwaters of Laurel Branch. Owned by Roaring Gap, Inc., and open exclusively to stockholders and guests for fishing, swimming, and boating.

Lake Louise, n Buncombe County in the town of Weaverville. Covers 6 acres; max. depth 50 ft. Fed by 5 underwater springs. Built before 1907 by Charles R. Moore and named Lake Juanita for Juanita Peace, a young girl who lived in the Moore home. At Moore's death, the property was given to Weaver College and later to the town of Weaverville, when the name was changed to Lake Louise in honor of Louise Moore, the donor.

Lake Lure, w Rutherford County on Broad River. Formed in 1928 as a part of a resort development; the dam is 104 ft. high. The lake covers 1,500 acres, with a shoreline of 27 mi. Used for recreation.

Lake Lure, town in w Rutherford County on the lake of the same name. Est. 1925; inc. 1927. Alt. 1,050. The town has an immense corporate limit situating it on Buffalo Creek, Broad River, and Pool Creek.

Lake Mattamuskeet, central Hyde County, a natural lake covering approx. 30,000 acres. Alt. 3 ft. below sea level. Max. depth 5 ft. Discovered 1585 by Richard Grenville's exploring party. Appears as Paquippe on the White map, 1585, for an Indian word meaning shallow (or dry) lake; as Paquike Lake on the Comberford map, 1657; and as Mattamuskeet Lake on the Moseley map, 1733. Present name from an Indian word *Mata-mackya-t-wi* (it is a moving swamp; quaky bog). As early as 1789 efforts were made to drain the lake for farming purposes, and the most recent efforts at drainage came to an end in 1934. Now a federal wildlife refuge. *See also* Aramuskeet; Aromuskek Marshes; New Holland.

Lake Michael, w Orange County. Formed in 1953 as a municipal water supply for the town of Mebane. Covers 51 acres; max. depth 20 ft. Named for Arthur Michael, engineer for the town of Mebane at the time the lake was formed.

Lake Michie (mick-e), reservoir for the city of Durham. About 4 mi. long on Flat River, ne Durham County.

Lake Mirl, e central Wake County on Hodges Creek. Formed in 1940. Covers 5 acres, with a max. depth of 10 ft. Open to the public for recreation.

Lake Monroe, central Union County s of Monroe. It is at the junction of Richardson and Little Richardson Creeks. Formed in 1925 and known first as Lake Lee for the owners. Later acquired by city of Monroe as a municipal water source. Covers 144 acres, with a max. depth of 35 ft.

Lake Norman, on the Catawba River in Catawba, Iredell, Mecklenburg, and Lincoln Counties. Formed by the dam at Cowan's Ford, completed 1963. Covers 32,510 acres. Shoreline approx. 520 mi. Hydroelectric plant of Duke Power Co. Named for Norman A. Cocke, retired president of the company. Alt. 760. *See* Duke Power Park.

Lake Palcoy, in central Haywood County near Lake Junaluska.

Lake Park, community in nw Union County. Inc. 1993.

Lake Phelps, natural freshwater lake in e Washington County and w Tyrrell County, the bed of which is thought to have been formed by the impact of a meteor. The lake surface covers 16,600 acres, with a max. depth of 12 ft.; mean alt. 10 ft. Owned by the state of North Carolina and included in Pettigrew State Park, *which see*. Said to have been named for Josiah Phelps, one of a group of explorers who discovered it in 1775. Known for a while as Scuppernong Lake and appears as such on the Collet map, 1770. Used for fishing, swimming, and boating.

Lake Point, point of land on the sw tip of Durant Island, central Dare County.

Lake Raleigh, in central Wake County on Walnut Creek. Formed in 1900. Covers 72 acres and has max. depth of 25 ft. Used for municipal water supply.

Lake Reidsville, in Rockingham County on Troublesome Creek. Built in 1972 to serve as part of Reidsville's water supply and for recreational activities such as fishing, waterskiing, and camping. Covers 750 acres.

Lake Rogers. *See* Creedmoor Lake.

Lakers Creek. *See* Raccoon Creek.

Lake Run flows s from Little Singletary Lake, ne Bladen County, into Ellis Creek.

Lake Santeetlah. *See* Santeetlah Lake.

Lake Sapphire, central Transylvania County on Allison Creek approx. 1½ mi. n of town of Brevard. Covers 3 acres, with a max. depth of 30 ft. Used for recreation. *See also* Sapphire Lake.

Lake Scuppernong. *See* Lake Phelps.

Lake Sequoyah, se Macon County at the head of Cullasaja River. Formed about 1920. Covers approx. 150 acres, with a max. depth of 40 ft.

Owned by the town of Highlands and used as a source of power and for swimming, fishing, boating, and skating. Named for Sequoyah (1770?–1843), Indian teacher.

Lakes Pocosin, a mucky slough in the sw corner of Craven County and extending into nw Carteret and e Jones Counties. Ellis Lake, Great Lake, Little Lake, and Long Lake in Craven County, and Catfish Lake in Jones and Craven Counties, are located in the pocosin.

Lake Summit, s Henderson County on Green River. Formed in 1920 as a source of power. Covers 350 acres, with a max. depth of 100 ft. A textile mill formerly operated there, and summer homes stand along the shores of the lake.

Lake Susan, ne Buncombe County. Formed by a dam on Flat Creek in Montreat.

Lake Tabor, s Columbus County. Formed by a dam on Grissett Swamp. Covers 8 acres, with a max. depth of 15 ft. Known as Spiveys Pond in the early twentieth century, when it was used to provide waterpower to operate a gristmill. The dam broke in 1950. The site was purchased by Tabor City, the dam was rebuilt, and the name was changed in 1955.

Lake Tahoma, w McDowell County on Buck Creek and Little Buck Creek. Formed about 1927 by J. Q. Gilkey of Marion. The name, an Indian word believed to mean "mountain lake of the gods," was suggested by Mary Hudgins of Marion. Covers approx. 500 acres; max. depth 30 to 40 ft. Owned by Lake Tahoma, Inc., a landholding corporation.

Lake Thorpe, an irregular-shaped reservoir in w Jackson County formed in 1941 by a dam on the West Fork of Tuckasegee River. Originally known as Glenville Lake for the nearby community; renamed in 1951 for J. E. S. Thorpe, former president of Nantahala Power and Light Company. Also known for a time as Thorpe Reservoir. Covers 1,462 acres, with a max. depth of 135 ft. Used to generate hydroelectric power and for recreation. Alt. 3,492.

Lake Tillery, on Pee Dee River in Montgomery and Stanly Counties. Formed in 1928. Covers 5,260 acres, with a shoreline of 104 mi. and a max. depth of 89 ft. Owned by Progress Energy and used for generating hydroelectric power, boating, swimming, and fishing. Originally named Norwood Lake for nearby town of Norwood. Renamed for former president of the company, Paul A. Tillery (1880–1933).

Lake Tomahawk, se Buncombe County on Tomahawk Branch.

Lake Toxaway, resort community in w Transylvania County on Toxaway River. The original Toxaway Inn, built in 1901, became a popular resort for the wealthy. The lake, formed in 1903, covered 540 acres, with a shoreline of 15 mi. and a max depth of 50 ft. The dam was destroyed in the flood of 1916 but was rebuilt in 1961. The lake now covers 900 acres, the largest privately owned lake in w North Carolina, and is surrounded by homes. There is also a golf course and an airport in the community. The name is derived from the Cherokee word *Tortzoo-whah* (redbird).

Lake Trojan, s central Wake County on a tributary of Swift Creek. Formed about 1900 and called Yates Mill Pond for the owner of the mill. Name changed in the 1950s. Covers 20 acres, with a max. depth of 15 ft. Used as a source of power and for fishing and swimming. Mill open to the public.

Lake View, pond on Flatrock Creek in n Franklin County. Formed 1890. Known as Hunts Pond until 1931. Covers 10 acres; max. depth 12 ft.

Lakeview, community in e Moore County on Crystal Lake. Alt. 300.

Lake Waccamaw, a natural lake in ne Columbus County, 5 mi. long and 3 mi. wide. Surrounding area drains into the lake; appears on Moseley map, 1733. Named for local tribe of Indians.

Lake Waccamaw, town in n Columbus County on the n shore of Lake Waccamaw. Known as Flemington from as early as 1853 until about 1885, when the present name came into use. Inc. 1911. Alt. 62.

Lake Wheeler, s Wake County on Swift Creek. Formed in 1957. Covers 540 acres, with a max. depth of 30 ft. Named for Fred B. Wheeler, former mayor of Raleigh. Used as a recreation area and as a source of water for the city of Raleigh.

Lake William, on Little Rockfish Creek due w of city of Fayetteville in w Cumberland County near county line. Approx. ¾ mi. long.

Lake Witheranna. *See* Bull Hill Mill Pond.

Lake Wood, lake approx. 1 mi. long on Cross Creek, nw Cumberland County. Covers approx. 20 acres; max. depth 20 ft. Fishing and swimming.

Lakewood. *See* Tuxedo.

Lake Worth, small community on the mainland of Dare County on the w shore of Stumpy Point Bay.

Lake Wylie, on the Catawba River in Gaston and Mecklenburg Counties, is formed by a dam constructed in South Carolina, 1924–26. Most of the lake, which covers 12,455 acres with a shoreline of 325 mi., is in South Carolina. Known as Catawba Lake until 1960, when it was renamed Lake Wylie for Dr. Walker Gill Wylie (1848–1923), friend and associate of James B. Duke. Site of Duke Power hydroelectric plant.

Lakey Creek rises in n Macon County and flows sw into Little Tennessee River.

Lakey Gap, se Buncombe County in Blue Ridge Mountains. Alt. 3,028.

Lakey Knob, se Buncombe County between Lakey Gap and High Top.

Lamance Creek rises in w central Transylvania County approx. 2 mi. s of the community of Balsam Grove and flows se into North Fork French Broad River.

Lamance Creek Falls, on Lamance Creek in w central Transylvania County. Falls are 18 ft. high. Sometimes known as Lemon Creek Falls.

Lamar, community in e Ashe County served by post office, 1890–1912.

Lamb Branch rises in e Cherokee County and flows sw into Peachtree Creek.

Lamb Creek rises in central Transylvania County s of Shutin Ridge and flows e and then s into Allison Creek on w edge of community of Pisgah Forest.

Lambert, community in w Stanly County. Named for local family.

Lambert Branch rises in e Swain County and flows se into Oconaluftee River.

Lambert Cove, w Macon County on a tributary of Nantahala River.

Lambert Fork Creek rises in nw Alexander County and flows se into Lower Little River. Named for Alexander Lambert, early Scottish settler.

Lambert Point, peninsula extending from n Pamlico County into Bay River.

Lambeth. *See* Monticello.

Lamb Knob, w Madison County between East Fork Shut-in Creek and Stony Spur.

Lamb Mountain, e Henderson County between Lewis Creek and Mills Gap.

Lamb Mountain, s Macon County between Buck Creek and Cullasaja River. Alt. approx. 4,600.

Lambo Creek rises in central Transylvania County and flows s into French Broad River.

Lambsburg, community in n Surry County. Also known as Piper Gap.

Lambs Corner, community in w Camden County named for local family.

Lamm's, community in n Wilson County s of Bloomery Swamp. Post office, 1895–1906. Named for Thomas Ruffin Lamm.

Lamm's Crossroads, community in w Wilson County s of Contentnea Creek. Named for Haywood Lamm.

Lamms Mill Pond, on Moccasin Creek on the Johnston-Nash county line. Approx. ½ mi. long. A mill operated there until about 1930.

Lamond's Old Field. *See* Candor.

Lamont, community in se Guilford County served by post office, 1886–1907.

Lancaster, community in w Edgecombe County.

Lancaster Crossroads, community in w Nash County between Back Swamp and Peachtree Creek.

Lancaster Store, community in e Wayne County between The Slough and West Bear Creek.

Lance Creek rises in sw Watauga County, flows s to Camp Yonahlosee, then flows in a nw arc into Watauga River. About 4 mi. long.

Lance Mountain, s Buncombe County e of Reynolds Gap.

Landgrave Smith's Island. *See* Smith Island.

Landing Creek. *See* Gum Neck Creek.

Landing Ridge, a ridge of high ground in Big Pocosin, sw Gates County.

Landis, town in sw Rowan County. Inc. 1901. Named for Judge Kenesaw Mountain Landis (1866–1944), who imposed a $29 million fine on Standard Oil Company at the time the community was searching for a name. Landis Northeast is a community on the outskirts of the town.

Land of Eden, former 20,000-acre tract belonging to William Byrd (1674–1744) along the Dan River, n Rockingham County. Byrd surveyed area in 1728. Named because of its Garden of Eden qualities. An additional 6,000 acres were granted to Byrd's son in 1742. Purchased from the younger Byrd by the Farley family in 1755; by 1769 it had been divided into farms and plantations. The town of Eden, formed in 1967 by the merger of Leaksville, Spray, and Draper, took its name from Byrd's estate.

Landrum Creek rises in central Chatham County and flows se into Rocky River.

Lands Creek rises in n central Swain County and flows sw into Tuckasegee River.

Lanefield, community in w Duplin County.

Lane Pinnacle, n Buncombe County at the e end of Bull Mountain. Alt. 5,277. Named for the owner, Charles Lane, who, in the first quarter of the nineteenth century, operated an iron forge on Reems Creek. He obtained some of his ore from the mountain.

Lane River. *See* Alligator River.

Lanesboro, community in w Anson County on Lanes Creek. A post office operated there, 1825–88. Now sometimes known as Old Lanesboro.

Lanesboro Township, w central Anson County.

Lanes Creek rises in s Union County and flows e and ne into w Anson County and ne into Rocky River.

Lane's Creek, community in se Union County.

Lanes Creek Township, se Union County.

Lane's Ferry, community in s central Pender County on Northeast Cape Fear River. The river is now bridged, but a ferry operated there for most of the nineteenth century and into the twentieth. Named for Levin Lane, landowner in the vicinity. *See also* Rocky Point.

Lanes Store, community in n Rutherford County on Cane Creek.

Lane Swamp rises in ne Nash County and flows se into Swift Creek.

Langdon. *See* Waddells.

Langford Branch rises in w Yancey County and flows nw into Cane River.

Langs Mill Run rises in e Wilson and s Edgecombe Counties and flows se into Pitt County, where it enters Black Swamp.

Langston, community in e central Wayne County e of Stony Creek. Named for Langston family, which received land grants in the area as early as 1758.

Lanier, community in w Onslow County served by post office, 1884–1905.

Lanier Crossroads, community in se Duplin County.

Laniers Creek rises in w Randolph County and flows e into Uwharrie River.

Lanier Swamp rises in e Martin County and flows nw into Gardners Creek.

Lankford Mountain, n Buncombe County w of Bill Cole Mountain.

Lanning Branch rises near Lanning Ridge in nw Transylvania County and flows sw into Right Fork Davidson River.

Lanning Ridge, nw Transylvania County, extends s from Seniard Mountain.

Lansing, town in nw Ashe County. Inc. 1928. Produces electronics.

Lanvale, community ne Brunswick County.

Lapland. *See* Marshall.

Largo, former plantation in sw Warren County. The plantation house was built in 1790 by Hugh Johnson and subsequently sold to Peter R. Davis, an early Warrenton merchant (fl. 1800–1841).

Lark Knob, in ne Macon County between Beasley Creek and Mica City Creek.

Larler Creek. *See* Chadwick Creek.

Larry Brush Branch rises in nw Macon County and flows se into Cold Spring Creek.

Lash. *See* Walnut Cove.

Lashleys Island. *See* Baker Island.

Lasker, town in central Northampton County. Inc. 1895; named for Hezekiah Lasker, railroad conductor. Earlier known as Alto.

Lassiter, community in sw Randolph County served by post office, 1848–1933. Known as Lassiter's Mills until 1894.

Lassiter, community in ne Wake County. Settled 1875. Named for its founder, C. J. Lassiter. Alt. 300.

Lassiter Branch rises in w Gates County and flows nw into Somerton Creek.

Lassiter Mill Lake, artificial lake in sw Forsyth County on Blanket Creek. Formed in 1935. Built for a mill dam by Lassiter family. Covers 50 acres and has max. depth of 20 ft. Not open to the public.

Lassiters Creek rises in n Nash County and flows s into Stony Creek.

Lassiters Crossroad, community in central Northampton County.

Lassiters Mill Pond, on Crabtree Creek in central Wake County within nw city limits of Raleigh. Present dam built in 1907–1908 by Mary Lassiter; pond named for her. A mill built on the site in 1778 by Isaac Hunter burned about 1823.

Lassiters Mills, community and former post office, se Randolph County on Uwharrie River. Mill built in 1845 on the w side of the river was moved to the e side in 1925.

Lassiter's Mills. *See* Lassiter.

Latham, community in nw Beaufort County.

Latham. *See* Latham's.

Latham Creek rises in nw Beaufort County and flows se into Old Ford Swamp.

Latham's, community in nw Beaufort County served by post office, 1872–1909. Known as Latham after 1894.

Lattimore, town in w Cleveland County. Settled in 1880; a post office named Delight was est. there in 1886. Inc. 1899 as Lattimore, named for Audley M. Lattimore, Confederate veteran and first postmaster. Alt. 945.

Lauada, community in s Swain County on Pole Bridge Branch.

Laudermilk Bend, a bend in Nottely River, s Cherokee County above Cobb Bluff.

Laughlins Creek rises in s Caswell County and flows se into Alamance County, where it enters Buttermilk Creek.

Laughter Cove, se Buncombe County between Spring and Garren Mountains. Named for a family of notorious moonshiners who lived in the cove in the first half of the twentieth century.

Laughton Point extends from the mainland of central Carteret County into Newport River.

Launch, The, a narrow inlet between Tull Bay and the mouth of North Landing River in ne Currituck County. Appears on the Collet map, 1770. Site of shipbuilding operations from colonial times until the present, hence the name.

Laurel, community in n Franklin County.

Laurel, community in n Madison County on Big Laurel Creek.

Laurel Bottoms, valley in se Avery County along the Linville River n of the town of Linville.

Laurel Branch rises in se Alleghany County and flows sw then ne into Brush Creek.

Laurel Branch rises in w Avery County and flows sw into Roaring Creek.

Laurel Branch rises in ne Buncombe County in the Great Craggy Mountains and flows se into North Fork [Swannanoa River].

Laurel Branch rises in s Buncombe County and flows se into Bent Creek.

Laurel Branch rises in se Buncombe County and flows sw into Broad River.

Laurel Branch rises in se Buncombe County near Flat Top Mountain and flows s into Cane Creek.

Laurel Branch rises in ne Cherokee County on Brushy Head Mountain and flows nw into Burnt Branch.

Laurel Branch rises in s Cherokee County and flows nw into Nottely River.

Laurel Branch rises in s Clay County and flows n into Shooting Creek.

Laurel Branch rises in n central Haywood County s of Chestnut Flat Ridge and flows e to join Pigeon River opposite Solray Gap.

Laurel Branch rises in n Haywood County on e slopes of Cowpen Top and flows ne into Waterville Lake.

Laurel Branch rises in n Haywood County on s slopes of Ed Top and flows sw into se part of Waterville Lake.

Laurel Branch rises in s Haywood County e of Cold Spring Knob and flows e into West Fork Pigeon River 1½ mi. s of Lake Logan dam.

Laurel Branch rises in n Henderson County and flows se into Bold Branch.

Laurel Branch rises in w Jackson County and flows n into Tuckasegee River.

Laurel Branch rises in s Macon County and flows ne into Cullasaja River.

Laurel Branch rises in w Macon County and flows nw into Rowlin Creek.

Laurel Branch rises in w Macon County and flows se into Nantahala Lake.

Laurel Branch rises in e Mitchell County and flows s into Cane Creek.

Laurel Branch rises in n Swain County and flows sw then e into Noland Creek.

Laurel Branch rises in nw Swain County and flows se into Tub-Mill Creek.

Laurel Branch rises in w Swain County and flows w into Fontana Lake near the confluence of Hazel Creek.

Laurel Branch rises in w central Swain County and flows ne into Tuckasegee River.

Laurel Branch rises in s Transylvania County and flows sw into East Fork French Broad River.

Laurel Branch rises in w Transylvania County and flows ne into West Fork French Broad River.

Laurel Branch rises in w Transylvania County and flows w into North Fork French Broad River.

Laurel Branch rises in n Watauga County and flows se into Cove Creek.

Laurel Branch rises in s Watauga County and flows nw into Sawpit Branch.

Laurel Branch rises in s Yancey County and flows ne into South Toe River.

Laurel Branch rises in s central Yancey County and flows w into Cane River.

Laurel Branch rises in sw Yancey County and flows e into Cane River.

Laurel Brook rises in n Transylvania County and flows se into South Fork Mills River.

Laurel Creek rises in nw Ashe County and flows se into North Fork New River.

Laurel Creek rises in se Burke County and flows se parallel to Prospect Ridge into Henry Fork.

Laurel Creek rises in central Cherokee County near Fain Mountain and flows sw into Hiwassee River.

Laurel Creek rises in w Cherokee County and flows ne into Apalachia Lake.

Laurel Creek rises in se Durham County and flows ne into Lick Creek.

Laurel Creek rises in n Haywood County and flows nw into Big Creek.

Laurel Creek rises in e Macon County and flows s into Ellijay Creek.

Laurel Creek rises in ne Mitchell County and flows s into Little Rock Creek.

Laurel Creek rises in e Transylvania County and flows ne into Cascade Lake (Little River).

Laurel Creek rises in ne Transylvania County and flows se into Henderson County, where it enters South Fork.

Laurel Creek rises in sw Transylvania County and flows s into Whitewater River.

Laurel Creek rises in nw Wake County near Little Laurel Creek and flows ne into Big Lick Creek.

Laurel Creek rises in s Watauga County and flows n into Boone Fork.

Laurel Creek rises in w Watauga County and flows ne into Watauga River.

Laurel Creek Falls, in w Watauga County on Laurel Creek just before its confluence with Watauga River.

Laurel Creek Township, w Watauga County.

Laurel Fork rises in central Buncombe County and flows n into Reems Creek.

Laurel Fork rises in s Watauga County and flows ne and se into Elk Creek.

Laurel Fork Creek rises in sw Alleghany and se

Ashe Counties and flows n to join Meadow Fork Creek in forming Mulberry Creek.

Laurel Fork Creek rises in s Henderson County and flows ne into Green River.

Laurel Fork [Davidson River] rises in w Transylvania County and flows e into Davidson River.

Laurel Gap, in Locust Ridge, ne Buncombe County.

Laurel Gap, between Rocky Knob and Glade Ridge in e Haywood County.

Laurel Gap, on the Haywood-Swain county line in Great Smoky Mountains National Park on Balsam Mountain between Balsam High Top and Balsam Corner, near lat. 35°39'55" N., long. 83°11'15" W. Alt. approx. 5,400.

Laurel Gap, on the Jackson-Macon county line.

Laurel Gap, in n Transylvania County between Rich Mountain and Poundingstone Mountain.

Laurel Gap Branch rises in ne Swain County and flows sw into Balsam Corner Creek.

Laurel Hill, community in sw Buncombe County near Beaverdam.

Laurel Hill, community in nw Lincoln County.

Laurel Hill, community in w Scotland County. Named for Presbyterian church est. there, 1793, and in turn named for laurel growing on the elevated site. A post office est. there, 1807. Alt. 250.

Laurel Hills, rugged terrain s of Chapel Hill, se Orange County.

Laurel Hill Township, w central Scotland County.

Laurel Knob, mountain between Double Knob Mountain and Cowrock Mountain in s Jackson County. Alt. approx. 4,300.

Laurel Knob, s Jackson County between Hurricane Creek and Hurricane Lake. Alt. 4,014.

Laurel Lake, se Buncombe County near Black Mountain.

Laurel Mountain extends se in an arc from Sassafras Gap to Yellow Gap in nw Henderson County.

Laurel Mountain, n Transylvania County between Cantrell Creek and Laurel Gap.

Laurel Mountain, se Yancey County near the head of Roaring Fork.

Laurel Park, town in central Henderson County adjoining Hendersonville on the latter's sw line. Inc. 1925.

Laurel Patch Bald, on Jackson-Haywood county line. Alt. 5,560–5,580.

Laurel Point extends from w Dare County n of Mill Tail Creek into Alligator River.

Laurel Point extends from ne Washington County into Albemarle Sound.

Laurel Ridge, n Buncombe County between Laurel Fork and Sugarcamp Fork.

Laurel Ridge, at the se end of Laurel Mountain in nw Henderson County.

Laurel Ridge on the Madison-Yancey county line n of Big Laurel Creek.

Laurel Ridge, in ne Mitchell County between Laurel Creek and Holder Creek.

Laurel Ridge, w Mitchell County between Bird Creek and Pate Creek.

Laurel Ridge, s Yancey County between Elk Fork and Cane River.

Laurel River rises in central Carteret County and flows e into Merrimon River.

Laurel Springs, community in sw Alleghany County. Settled about 1859 and named for a spring flowing from laurel-covered rocks. Alt. 2,822.

Laurel Spur, on the Watauga-Wilkes county line e of Stony Fork Creek.

Laurelton, community in n Madison County on Foster Creek.

Laurel Top, peak on Graham County, N.C.–Monroe County, Tenn., line. Alt. approx. 5,325.

Laurel Top, peak on Swain County, N.C.–Sevier County, Tenn., line in Great Smoky Mountains National Park near the head of Gulf Prong. Alt. 5,900–5,950.

Laurel Township, w central Ashe County.

Laurenceville. *See* Lawrenceville.

Laurinburg, city and county seat, s Scotland County. Appears on maps as early as 1865. Inc. 1877 as Laurenburg; charter amended 1883 and name spelled Laurinburg. Named for McLaurin family, early Scottish settlers. Alt. 227. St. Andrews Presbyterian College, est. 1961, is there.

Lawhon, community in central Moore County served by post office, 1892–1905.

Lawndale, town in central Cleveland County on First Broad River. Alt. 843. Settled 1870; inc. 1903. Named for spreading green lawns of Maj. H. F. Schenck, owner of local mills, est. in 1888, and local power company.

Lawrence, town in ne Edgecombe County. Known as Killquick as early as 1837, the name by which it was chartered in 1883. Laid off in an area ½ mi. square from Richard H. Gatlin's "big new store." Name changed to Hickory Hill in 1885 and to Lawrence in 1889. Original Killquick charter repealed in 1893; chartered as Lawrence in 1901, but long inactive in municipal affairs.

Lawrence Run rises in w Pitt County and flows nw into Tyson Creek.

Lawrenceville, former town in w Montgomery County on Pee Dee River. Authorized to be laid out as the county seat, 1815; named Laurenceville, 1816. Post office operated as Lawrenceville from 1818 to 1850. After Stanly County was formed from Montgomery County in 1841, Lawrenceville was no longer in the center of the county and was soon replaced as the county seat by Troy. By 1860 it was no longer being shown on maps of the state. The site is now abandoned.

Laws, community in n Orange and s Person Counties. Formerly known as Laws Store.

Lawson Creek rises in central Craven County and flows ne into Trent River.

Lawson Gant Lot, bald spot on Swain County, N.C.–Sevier County, Tenn., line near lat. 35°32′45″ N., long. 83°47′38″ W.

Lawson Gant Lot Branch rises in nw Swain County in Great Smoky Mountains National Park and flows se into Tub-Mill Creek.

Lawsonville, community in e Rockingham County between Lick Fork and Jones Creeks. Named for Bobbie Lawson, early resident and subject of popular local legend. Lawson's Store post office operated there, 1817–23 and 1830–45. Site of several early tobacco factories and a carriage and wagon factory.

Lawsonville, community in n Stokes County. Alt. 1,179.

Laws Store. *See* Laws.

Lawyers. *See* Alexander's Store.

Lawyers Springs, w Anson County on a tributary of Brown Creek. So named because lawyers on the way to court used to stop there. Local tradition says a party of lawyers, spending the night there, froze to death on a snowy winter night.

Laxon, community in e Watauga County.

Laxon Creek rises in e Watauga County and flows nw into South Fork New River.

Layn Flu. *See* Alligator River.

Layton, community in central Rockingham County served by post office, 1892–1903.

Laytown, community in ne Caldwell County. Named for Thomas Lay, eighteenth-century settler.

Laytown Creek rises in n Caldwell County and flows se into Yadkin River. Originally called Linville's Mill Creek.

Leachburg, community in n Johnston County served by post office, 1854–1903. Spelled Leechburg until 1876.

Leaches Island. *See* Hog Island.

Lead, community in s Henderson County on Green River.

Leading Ridge, n Mitchell County between Shepherd Knob and Big Rock Creek.

Lead Mine Ridge, w Madison County between Doe Branch and Rocky Branch.

Leaflet, community in w Harnett County near Upper Little River.

Leak Creek rises in n Davidson County and flows nw into s Forsyth County, where it enters South Fork.

Leaksville, former town in n Rockingham County on Dan and Smith Rivers. Alt. 700. Inc. 1874. Named for Revolutionary War veteran John Leak, who owned a plantation there before 1797. A post office est. there in 1817. In 1793 the General Assembly directed that a town to be named Danville be laid out at the site as a tobacco inspection station; in 1797 commissioners were appointed "to build and improve the Town of Leaksville in accordance with the plan drawn up by Abraham Philips." Philips had been a member of the commission appointed in 1793 to lay out the town of Danville. In 1967 Leaksville was merged with Draper and Spray, *which see*, to form the town of Eden, *which see*.

Leaksville Township, n Rockingham County.

Leaman, community in n Moore County on Bear Creek.

Leander, community in nw Watauga County on Beaverdam Creek.

Leaper's Creek. *See* Leepers Creek.

Leasburg, town in e Caswell County. Est. 1788, but long inactive in municipal affairs. Named for William and James Lea, who owned part of the original site. Location of Caswell County courthouse from 1777 until 1791, when it was moved to the center of the county after Person County was formed from Caswell. Alt. 750.

Leasburg Township, e central Caswell County.

Leatherman, community on Shepherd Creek in n Macon County.

Leatherman Gap, on Macon-Swain county line between Leatherman Knob and Raven Mountain. Alt. 4,300.

Leatherman Knob, on Macon-Swain county line between Leatherman Gap and Shepherd Bald.

Leatherman Mountain, on the Macon-Swain county line.

Leathermans Fork rises in w Mitchell County and flows sw into Right Fork [Pigeon-roost Creek].

Leatherwood Branch rises in w Clay County and flows se into Fires Creek.

Leatherwood Branch rises in n Haywood County and flows e into Big Creek.

Leatherwood Cove, central Haywood County just n of Lake Junaluska.

Leatherwood Mountain, ne Cherokee County s of Andrews.

Leatherwood Top, in w Haywood County between Walker Bald and Tritt Knob. Alt. 5,000–5,020.

Leaventhorps View. *See* Shumont Mountain.

Lebanon Township, central Durham County.

Ledbetter, community in central Richmond County. Named for the family that est. a mill on Hitchcock Creek there about 1895.

Ledbetter Branch rises in ne Macon County on the slope of Tellico Ridge and flows n into Swain County, where it enters Little Tennessee River.

Ledbetter Creek rises in sw Swain County on Cheoah Bald in Nantahala National Forest and flows s into Nantahala River.

Ledbetter Lake, central Richmond County on Hitchcock Creek at the community of Ledbetter, *which see.* Covers 800 acres.

Ledford. *See* Nantahala.

Ledford Branch rises in s Cherokee County and flows nw into Nottely River.

Ledford Branch rises in sw Clay County and flows sw, nw, then sw again into Brasstown Creek.

Ledford Branch rises in e Macon County and flows se into Walnut Creek.

Ledford Creek rises in s Buncombe County and flows se into Bent Creek.

Ledford Creek. *See* Left Fork [Eagle Creek].

Ledford Gap, s Clay County near the headwaters of Hothouse Branch.

Ledge Bald, on Haywood-Swain county line in Great Smoky Mountains National Park on Balsam Mountain near lat. 35°38′35″ N., long. 83°12′05″ W. Alt. 5,175.

Ledge Creek rises in sw Granville County just nw of town of Stem, flows s through Creedmoor Lake w of town of Creedmoor, and empties into Neuse River at Durham-Wake county line. Appears as Ledge of Rocks Creek on the Collet map, 1770, and others.

Ledge Creek rises in ne Swain County in Great Smoky Mountains National Park and flows sw into Straight Fork [Raven Fork].

Ledge Gap, on Haywood-Swain county line between Beech Gap and Pin Oak Gap.

Ledge of Rocks Creek. *See* Ledge Creek.

Ledger, community in central Mitchell County on Snow Creek. Said to have been named by the Post Office Department because of a report submitted in a ledger by a local resident named Phillips. His record of mail sent and received in the community through another post office resulted in the establishment of a post office there. The "Good Will" Free Library, opened in Ledger in 1886 through the efforts of Charles Hallet Wing, is said to have been the first free public library in the state and the third county library in the United States. *See also* Wing.

Lee Branch rises in w Macon County and flows sw into Nantahala Lake.

Leechburg. *See* Leachburg.

Leechville, town in e Beaufort County on Pungo River. Inc. 1834 and name changed from Lumberton. Reincorporated 1899, but long inactive in municipal affairs.

Lee County was formed in 1907 from Moore and Chatham Counties. Located in the central section of the state, it is bounded by Harnett, Moore, and Chatham Counties. It was named for Gen. Robert E. Lee (1807–70). Area: 256 sq. mi. County seat: Sanford, with an elevation of 375 ft. Townships, now numbered 1 to 7, were formerly Greenwood, Jonesboro, Cape Fear, Deep River, East Sanford, West Sanford, and

Pocket. Produces tobacco, corn, wheat, oats, strawberries, dairy products, hogs, bricks, lumber, textiles, heavy equipment, electronics, sheet metal, apparel, industrial machinery, furniture, sand, and gravel.

Lee Creek rises in central Buncombe County near Spivey Mountain and flows ne into French Broad River.

Lee Creek rises in s Macon County and flows e into Jones Creek.

Lee Mountain, e Haywood County, extends ne between Bald Creek and Liner Creek.

Leepers Creek is formed by the junction of Sawmill and Lippard Creeks in ne Lincoln County. It flows se into Gaston County, where it joins Killians Creek in forming Dutchmans Creek. Appears as Leapers Creek on the Collet map, 1770.

Lees Branch rises in w Warren County and flows se and sw into Shocco Creek.

Leesburg. *See* Willard.

Lees Creek rises in se Beaufort County and flows nw into Pamlico River. Appears on the Collet map, 1770.

Lees Creek rises in nw Northampton County and flows sw into Roanoke River.

Lees Landing, on Upper Broad Creek in w Pamlico County.

Lees Millpond, e Scotland County on Big Shoeheel Creek. Covers 50 acres; max. depth 18 ft.

Lees Mills. *See* Roper.

Lees Mills Township, central Washington County, was formed in 1868 but was a voting precinct before that time.

Lees Point extends from w Carteret County into White Oak River.

Lees Township, se Columbus County.

Leesville, former community in s Robeson County between Hog Swamp and Oldfield Swamp. A post office existed there from ca. 1816 to 1900. The name is still used in the county with reference to the general area.

Leesville, community in nw Wake County on head of Lower Bartons Creek. Named for John Lee, who first settled there about 1800. Alt. 300.

Leesville Township, nw Wake County.

Lee Swamp rises in sw Wilson County and flows se in an arc into Black Creek. Named for local family.

Left Fork rises in ne Buncombe County and flows se into Beetree Reservoir.

Left Fork Bean Creek rises in n Mitchell County and flows se to join Right Fork Bean Creek in forming Bean Creek.

Left Fork Belews Creek. *See* West Belews Creek.

Left Fork [Cane Creek] rises in e Mitchell County and flows sw to join Right Fork [Cane Creek] in forming Cane Creek.

Left Fork [Deep Creek] rises in n Swain County in Great Smoky Mountains National Park and flows se into Deep Creek.

Left Fork [Eagle Creek] rises in se Clay County and flows sw to join Right Fork in forming Eagle Creek. Known also as Ledford Creek.

Left Fork [Indian Creek] rises in n Swain County and flows sw into Right Fork [Indian Creek] to form Indian Creek.

Left Fork [Raven Fork] rises in ne Swain County in Great Smoky Mountains National Park and flows s to join Right Fork and Middle Fork in forming Raven Fork [Oconaluftee River].

Left Fork [Redman Creek] rises in ne Swain County and flows sw to join Right Fork [Redman Creek] in forming Redman Creek.

Left Fork [Swannanoa River] rises in ne Buncombe County and flows e into North Fork [Swannanoa River]. Often known locally as Left Hand Fork.

Left Fork Webb Creek rises in ne Cherokee County near Moody Stamp and flows se to join Right Fork Webb Creek in forming Webb Creek.

Left Hand Fork. *See* Left Fork [Swannanoa River].

Left Prong Bent Creek rises in n Yancey County and flows se to join Right Prong Bent Creek in forming Bent Creek.

Left Prong [Bridge Creek] rises in n central Swain County and flows ne into Bridge Creek.

Left Prong South Toe River has its origin at Pinnacle Spring, s Yancey County, and flows e to join Right Prong South Toe River in forming South Toe River.

Left Prong Three Forks Creek rises in se Yancey County and flows sw to join Right Prong in forming Three Forks Creek.

Legal, community in central Harnett County served by post office, 1894–1908.

Legerwood, community in n central Caldwell County. Named for Samuel Legerwood Patterson (1850–1908), onetime state commissioner of agriculture, who donated his plantation, "Palmyra," for a farm school for boys there.

Leggett, town in n Edgecombe County inc. 1895 and reincorporated 1925 but not now active in municipal affairs. Post office name was Leggettsville, 1886–1913.

Leggetts Crossroads, community in nw Beaufort County.

Leggettsville. *See* Leggett.

Legion Beach, a recreation and picnic area on Albemarle Sound in n Tyrrell County 3 mi. e of Columbia. Owned by local American Legion Post. Boating, bathing, and fishing.

Legislature. *See* General Assembly.

Leicester, community in nw Buncombe County. Inc. 1859; charter repealed 1905. Named for or by Leicester Chapman, a settler from Leicester, England. Alt. 2,090.

Leicester Township, w Buncombe County.

Leiths Creek rises in central Scotland County and flows se to join Bridge Creek in forming the Little Pee Dee River.

Leland, community in nw Brunswick County.

Leman Gap, on Burke-Cleveland county line.

Lemay, community in se Wake County served by post office, 1882–1901.

Lemley's Township, former township in nw Mecklenburg County. Now township no. 10.

Lemon Creek Falls. *See* Lamance Creek Falls.

Lemon Gap, on the Madison County, N.C.– Cocke County, Tenn., line.

Lemon Springs, community in s Lee County. Was designated a railroad station in 1890. Named for mineral springs, owned by a man named Lemon, which were formerly a favorite picnic spot. Alt. 369.

Lena, community in s Cumberland County.

Lennon Crossroads, community in s central Brunswick County.

Lennon's Marsh. *See* Warwick Bay.

Lennon's Mill Pond. *See* Warwick Bay.

Lenoir, city and county seat, central Caldwell County. Laid out 1841, inc. 1851. Named in honor of Gen. William Lenoir (1751–1839), a Revolutionary War leader. A nearby forerunner of Lenoir was Tucker's Barn, a small community that developed around a tavern and blacksmith shop operated by the Tucker family. Produces furniture and textiles. Alt. 1,182.

Lenoir Branch rises in central Macon County and flows s into Cartoogechaye Creek.

Lenoir (leh-NOR) County was formed in 1791, when Dobbs County was divided to form Glasgow and Lenoir Counties. Located in the e section of the state, it is bounded by Craven, Jones, Duplin, Wayne, Greene, and Pitt Counties. It was named for William Lenoir (1751–1839), one of the heroes of the Battle of Kings Mountain. Area: 399 sq. mi. County seat: Kinston, with an elevation of 44 ft. Townships are Contentnea Neck, Falling Creek, Institute, Kinston, Moseley Hall, Neuse, Pink Hill, Sand Hill, Southwest, Trent, Vance, and Woodington. Produces tobacco, corn, wheat, oats, soybeans, cotton, hogs, turkeys, cantaloupes, dairy products, livestock, chemicals, textiles, vacuum cleaners, ceramics, pharmaceuticals, sand, and gravel. *See also* St. Patrick's Parish.

Lenoir Creek rises in s Haywood County and flows ne into East Fork Pigeon River.

Lenoir Township, s central Caldwell County.

Lenox Castle, former resort in se Rockingham County. A tavern, baths, store, and springs made it a popular spa; probably operated prior to 1800, but flourished from 1803 until after 1844. Named for John Lenox, who advertised his tavern as "The Castle of Thundertontrenck" in 1804. A post office as late as 1882.

Lenox Point extends from the mainland of s Carteret County into North River Thorofare e of the limits of Beaufort. Also once known as Titus Point.

Lenoxville, a proposed town chartered in 1816 to be laid out on the lands of James McKinlay in s Carteret County e of Beaufort at present-day Lenox Point. Apparently it was never developed. A contemporary manuscript map of Lenoxville is in the North Carolina Collection, University of North Carolina at Chapel Hill.

Lens Knob, w Surry County near Saddle Mountain Creek.

Lenton, community in s Rockingham County served by post office, 1889–90.

Lentz, community in w Rowan County served by post office, 1886–1902.

Lenzton, community in w Richmond County.

Leo, community in s Stanly County served by post office, 1858–1907.

Leo. *See* Skinnersville.

Leonard, community in central Madison County served by post office, 1889–1901.

Leonard Creek rises in central Davidson County and flows s into Abbotts Creek.

Leonard Creek rises in central Davie County near the town of Mocksville and flows e for approx. 4 mi. into Dutchmans Creek.

Leonard Fork rises in s Lincoln County and flows se into Indian Creek.

Leonards Crossroads, community in nw Columbus County.

Leonards Point extends from n Washington County into Albemarle Sound.

Leonsburg, former town in w Hyde County between Germantown and Sladesville. Inc. 1833, but now only a rural community.

Leota, community in n Chatham County served by post office, 1883–96.

Leroy Creek rises in n central Avery County and flows ne into Elk River.

Lester, community in n Wilkes County between North Fork Reddies River and Mulberry Creek.

Letha, community in n Franklin County.

Letitia, community in sw Cherokee County.

Lettered Rock Ridge, nw Burke County. Alt. 3,100.

Level Cross, community and former post office, n Randolph County. Named for the level intersection of several roads there.

Levelcross, community in se Surry County. Named for the fact that two roads cross there in comparatively level country.

Level Cross Township, n central Randolph County.

Level Plains, community in nw Randolph County served by post office, 1875–1906.

Levels, community in n central Tyrrell County at the head of Riders Creek. Alt. approx. 4. Also called Riders Creek Community. Formerly received postal service from post office named Jerry, which was located about 1 mi. sw of the community.

Levi, community in central Davidson County served by post office, 1889–1907.

Levingtons Creek. *See* Livingston Creek.

Levy Branch rises in w Madison County and flows nw into Big Pine Creek.

Lewarae, town in s Richmond County. Est. 1900; inc. 1905. No longer active in munici-

pal affairs. Name derived from parts of the names of three local families: Leak, Wall, and MacRae.

Lewellyn Cove follows the course of a stream emptying into Little Tennessee River in n Graham County.

Lewis, community in e Granville County. Named for Willis Lewis, local doctor. Alt. 545.

Lewis. *See* Atkinson.

Lewis Branch rises in e central Brunswick County and flows n into Lewis Swamp.

Lewis Branch rises in nw Jackson County and flows ne into Tuckasegee River.

Lewis Branch rises in n Madison County and flows s into Big Laurel Creek.

Lewisburg, community in n Yancey County on Cane River at the mouth of Bald Mountain Creek. Alt. 2,288.

Lewis Canal, central Washington County, drains ne from East Dismal Swamp into Main Canal.

Lewis Creek, an inlet of Core Sound into se Cedar Island in ne Carteret County.

Lewis Creek rises on se Core Banks and flows n into Core Sound in se Carteret County.

Lewis Creek rises in e Henderson County and flows nw into Clear Creek.

Lewis Creek rises in s Onslow County and flows ne into Morgan Bay. Mentioned in local records as early as 1744 as Lewis's Creek.

Lewis Creek rises in n Pender County and flows ne into Northeast Cape Fear River.

Lewis Crossroads, community in n Halifax County.

Lewis Fork, community in sw Wilkes County on South Prong Lewis Fork Creek. Lewis Fork Baptist Church there was organized in 1792.

Lewis Fork Creek is formed in sw Wilkes County by the junction of North Prong Lewis Fork Creek and South Prong Lewis Fork Creek and flows se approx. 3 mi. into W. Kerr Scott Reservoir. *See also* Fort Hamby.

Lewis Fork Township, sw Wilkes County.

Lewis Gap, central Buncombe County n of Patton Mountain.

Lewis McDaires Knob, n Buncombe County on Lankford Mountain. *See also* McDaires Cove and Ridge.

Lewis Mountain, between Henderson Creek and Lewis Creek in e Henderson County.

Lewis Point, n Tyrrell County, extends from the mainland into Albemarle Sound w of Peartree Point.

Lewis's Creek. *See* Lewis Creek.

Lewis Swamp rises in e central Brunswick County and flows e to join Rattlesnake Branch in forming Town Creek.

Lewiston, town in nw Bertie County. Inc. 1881. Named for the Watson Lewis family. A previous post office there, 1816–40, was known as Turner's Cross Roads. Post office known as Lewiston after 1872. Alt. 50. *See also* Woodville.

Lewisville, former town in se Columbus County. Inc. 1885, but long inactive in municipal affairs. Two rural service stations now mark the site.

Lewisville, community in w Forsyth County. Named in honor of Lewis Lagenauer, around whose home it developed.

Lewisville Township, sw Forsyth County.

Lewters Crossroads, community in ne Northampton County.

Lexine. *See* Washburns Store.

Lexington, city and county seat, central Davidson County. Inc. 1827. Named for the Battle of Lexington, April 19, 1775, in Massachusetts. Davidson County Community College, est. 1966, is there. Alt. 810. Produces dairy products, textiles, hosiery, lumber, furniture, apparel, and batteries.

Lexington Township, central Davidson County.

Liberia, community in s central Warren County s of Reedy Creek.

Liberty, town in ne Randolph County. Inc. 1889. Named for the nearby plantation of John Leak, who settled there in 1807. Alt. 790.

Liberty, community in se Rowan County. Named for a local church.

Liberty Hill, former community in central Guilford County, now a part of Greensboro.

Liberty Hill, community in w central Montgomery County that takes its name from local Baptist church.

Liberty Knob, w Surry County near the head of Millers Creek.

Liberty Store, community in ne Guilford County served by post office, 1877–83.

Liberty Township, ne Randolph County.

Liberty Township, se Yadkin County.

Lick, The. *See* Williamsboro.

Lick Creek rises in sw Anson County and flows n into Brown Creek.

Lick Creek rises in n Chatham County and flows n across the county line into Alamance County for a short distance before turning s again into Chatham County, where it enters Terrell Creek.

Lick Creek rises in e Davidson County and flows sw into Yadkin River.

Lick Creek rises s Durham County and flows ne into Neuse River. Once known as Great Lick Creek.

Lick Creek rises in n Forsyth County and flows ne into s Stokes County, where it enters Town Fork Creek. Probably named for a salt lick frequented by deer; the name appears in records as early as 1755.

Lick Creek rises in central Lee County and flows ne into Cape Fear River.

Lick Creek rises in e Montgomery County and flows ne into Cotton Creek.

Lick Creek rises in ne Orange County and flows ne into Person County, where it enters Byrds Creek.

Lick Fork rises in n Forsyth County and flows sw into Mill Creek. Appears as Jones Creek on the Collet map, 1770; not named on subsequent maps until it appears as Little Lick Fork on MacRae map, 1833.

Lick Fork rises in n Gaston County and flows ne into s Lincoln County, where it enters Mill Creek.

Lick Fork Creek rises in w Montgomery County and flows sw into Clarks Creek.

Lick Fork Creek rises in e Rockingham County and flows ne into Hogans Creek near Caswell County line.

Licking Branch rises in w Gates County and flows sw into Jady Branch.

Licking Creek. *See* Elisha Creek.

Licklog Branch rises in se Buncombe County and flows s into Rocky Fork.

Lick Log Creek rises in central Clay County and flows sw into Lake Chatuge. The name originated when the Davis family, early settlers, felled trees and cut notches in the logs to hold salt for their cattle.

Licklog Creek rises in n Jackson County and flows nw into Scott Creek.

Licklog Creek rises in s Jackson County on s slopes of Heady Mountain and flows s and w 1½ mi. to join Fowler Creek.

Lick Log Creek, community in s Clay County.

Licklog Gap, se Buncombe County in the Swannanoa Mountains between Lookoff Gap and Jesses High Top.

Licklog Gap, nw Burke County. Alt. 2,420.

Licklog Gap, on the Haywood-Jackson county line. Takes its name from a "licklog" formerly there, a log with boxes chopped into its upper side to hold salt for the cattle to lick.

Licklog Gap, in s Macon County between Grassy Knobs and Middle Creek.

Licklog Gap, in w Macon County at the head of Whiteoak Creek.

Lick Log Gap, on the Madison County, N.C.– Greene County, Tenn., line.

Licklog Gap, n Swain County in Great Smoky Mountains National Park between Hickory Cove and Right Fork [Cold Spring Branch] near lat. 35°29′05″ N., long. 83°39′48″ W.

Lick Meadow Branch rises in e Franklin County and flows ne into Redbud Creek.

Lick Mountain, s Caldwell County. Alt. 1,990.

Lick Mountain, w Montgomery County near Dutchmans Creek.

Lick Mountain, w Randolph County sw of Jackson Creek.

Lick Ridge, in e Mitchell County between Honeycutt Branch and Young Cove Creek.

Lick Rock, on the Madison County, N.C.–Unicoi County, Tenn., line.

Lick Run rises in central Lincoln County and flows se into Leepers Creek.

Lickskillet, community in s Macon County between the head of Tessentee Creek and Piney Knob Fork. Named by hunters who left unwashed cooking pans in camp and returned to find that they had been licked by dogs or other animals.

Lickskillet, community in s Warren County s of Shocco Creek.

Lickskillet Branch rises in w Yancey County and flows se into Bald Creek.

Lickstone Bald, on Lickstone Ridge in s Haywood County. Alt. 5,700. Named for the fact that salt for cattle was put on a large smooth rock.

Lickstone Mountain, on the Jackson-Haywood county line. Alt. 5,576.

Lickstone Ridge extends ne from Soco Creek in n Jackson County to Wolfpen Mountain in s Haywood County.

Liddell, community in w Lenoir County.

Light, community in e Davidson County.

Light Gap, ne Buncombe County near Big Andy Ridge.

Light Ground Pocosin, a muck-filled area covering approx. 4 by 5 mi., w central Pamlico County.

Lighthouse Creek. See Baldhead Creek.

Lightwood Knot Creek rises in s Richmond County and flows s into South Carolina, where it joins Beverly Creek in forming Crooked Creek.

Lightwood Mountain, e Mitchell County at the head of Laurel Branch.

Lilac, community in s Davidson County served by post office, 1895–1914.

Liledoun, community in central Alexander County on Lower Little River. Founded to produce textiles.

Liles Creek. See Lyle Creek.

Lilesville, town in e Anson County. Inc. 1874. A post office as early as 1827. Named for Nelson P. Liles, local merchant. Alt. 474.

Lilesville Township, e Anson County.

Lilleys Millpond. See Greens Millpond.

Lillian, community in n Wake County.

Lillie. See Lizzie.

Lillington, town and county seat on Cape Fear River, central Harnett County. Inc. 1859; the name was changed from Long Creek Village to Lillington in honor of the Revolutionary War patriot Alexander Lillington (1725–86). Alt. 325. Produces apparel. See also Summerville.

Lillington. See Long Creek.

Lillington County was authorized to be est. in 1859 from a portion of New Hanover County, provided that two-thirds of the qualified voters of Rocky Point Precinct approved. The act was not approved, but Pender County, which see, was later est. in approx. the same area.

Lillington Creek rises in e Pender County and flows sw into Northeast Cape Fear River. Named for Gen. Alexander Lillington (1725–86), whose plantation was nearby. Appears as Island Creek on the Collet map, 1770; as Maxwell Creek on the Price map, 1808; and as Lillington's Mill Creek on the MacRae map, 1833.

Lillington's Mill Creek. See Lillington Creek.

Lillington Township, central Harnett County.

Lilliput, the plantation of Eleazer Allen (1692–1750), councillor, judge, receiver general, and treasurer of North Carolina, was located on the n side of Lilliput Creek in e Brunswick County. Land was granted to Allen in 1725, and he named the plantation for the imaginary country in Jonathan Swift's satire *Gulliver's Travels* (1726). Part of the 300-volume library at Lilliput was inherited by a daughter of James Hasell and might have been inc. into the remarkable Hasell library. Lilliput was purchased by Gov. William Tryon as a summer residence, and he still owned the property as late as 1784. Location of Lilliput is shown on the Moseley map, 1733, under the name of "E. Allen"; on the Collet map, 1770, as "Lilliput to the G."; and on the Price map, 1808, as "Lilliput."

Lilliput Creek, e Brunswick County, flows e from McKenzie Pond into Cape Fear River. Named for Lilliput, *which see*, a nearby plantation. Shown as Allen's Creek on the MacRae map, 1833, and on the Colton map, 1861. Appears as Lilliput Creek on the 1865 U.S. Coast Survey map and on the Kerr map, 1882.

Lilly, community in ne Camden County.

Lily Branch rises in central Mitchell County and flows sw into North Toe River.

Lily Pond Creek rises in w Northampton County and flows sw to join Gumberry Swamp in forming Wheeler Creek.

Lima, community in central Craven County.

Limekiln Branch rises in w central Transylvania County and flows se into French Broad River.

Limekiln Creek rises in w Gaston County and flows sw into Long Creek.

Limekiln Creek rises in n McDowell County and flows e through Woodlawn into North Fork [Catawba River].

Lime Rock, community in s Surry County on Yadkin River. Took its name from local lime kiln operated by Martin family. Alt. 820.

Limestone Creek rises in s Buncombe County and flows s into Merrill Cove Creek.

Limestone Creek rises in e Duplin County and flows sw into Northeast Cape Fear River.

Limestone Township, s central Buncombe County. A post office named Limestone existed in Buncombe County as early as 1828.

Limestone Township, se Duplin County.

Linbank, formerly a post office and community in s Vance County approx. 4 mi. s of the town of Henderson. The building used from 1829 until 1839 as a post office is still standing, and the name survives as the name of the local road on which the building stands.

Linches Creek. *See* Lynch Creek.

Lincoln County was formed in 1779, when Tryon County was divided to form Lincoln and Rutherford Counties. Located in the sw section of the state, it is bounded by Mecklenburg, Gaston, Cleveland, Catawba, and Iredell Counties. It was named for Benjamin Lincoln (1733–1810), distinguished general of the Revolution. Area: 309 sq. mi. County seat: Lincolnton, with an elevation of 860 ft. Townships are Catawba Springs, Howards Creek, Ironton, Lincolnton, and North Brook. The Schenck-Warlick Mill, the first cotton mill in the South, was built about 1812 approx. 1 mi. w of Lincolnton. Produces corn, wheat, oats, cotton, poultry, dairy products, livestock, hogs, textiles, furniture, auto parts, apples, soybeans, machinery, hosiery, crushed stone, mica, sand, and amethyst.

Lincoln Hollow, valley in w Avery County between Teagues Ridge and Powdermill Creek.

Lincolnton, town and county seat, central Lincoln County. Est. 1785. Name honors Gen. Benjamin Lincoln (1733–1810), Revolutionary War leader. The Battle of Ramsour's Mill, a Whig victory over the Tories, was fought on June 20, 1780, at a site on the n outskirts of Lincolnton. Produces textiles, furniture, machinery, and hosiery. Alt. 860.

Lincolnton Township, central Lincoln County.

Lindell, community in nw Greene County served by post office, 1898–1907. Formerly Appletree, *which see*.

Linden, town in n Cumberland County. Settled about 1800. Inc. 1913 and named for a grove of linden trees nearby. Known as Little River Academy prior to 1910. Alt. 150. *See also* Choffington.

Linden Mountain, w Randolph County on Jackson Creek.

Lindhurst, community in central Chatham County served by post office, 1895–1916.

Lindley's Mill, on Cane Creek in s central Alamance County, a short distance w of Sutphin. The site of a battle on September 13, 1781, in which John Butler's Whigs failed to rescue Governor Thomas Burke from David Fanning's Tories. The first gristmill there was erected in 1756 by Thomas Lindley.

Lindsay, community in se Orange County served by post office, 1888–1905.

Lindsay C. Warren Bridge. *See* East Lake Landing; Sandy Point.

Lindscomb Branch rises in nw Brunswick County and flows w into Columbus County, where it enters Livingston Creek. Sometimes known locally as Linksom Branch and believed to have been named originally Lynchum Branch.

Line, community in sw Rutherford County.

Lineberry, community in n Randolph County. Named for Capt. Scott Lineberry, local resident.

Line Creek rises in s Buncombe County and flows ne into French Broad River. Forms the Buncombe-Henderson county boundary for approx. 1 mi.

Liner Cove, central Haywood County near Jerry Knob.

Liner Creek rises in e Haywood County and flows sw into Crabtree Creek.

Line Runner Lake, in s Transylvania County on Gerren Creek. Covers 11 acres and has max. depth of 28 ft. Used for recreation.

Line Runner Ridge, s Transylvania County, extends n in an arc from Blue Ridge Mountains to the head of Gerren Creek.

Linker, community in s Iredell County served by post office, 1898–1903.

Linksom Branch. *See* Lindscomb Branch.

Linn Cove, the valley through which Linn Cove Creek flows in central Buncombe County.

Linn Cove Creek rises in Elk Mountains in central Buncombe County and flows sw to join Webb Cove Creek in forming Beaverdam Creek.

Linn Cove Viaduct, elevated section of Blue Ridge Parkway around Grandfather Mountain. Opened in 1987.

Linney, community in central Ashe County served by post office, 1899–1915.

Linsters Springs. *See* Barium Springs.

Linviles Creek. *See* Blanket Creek.

Linville, town in e central Avery County on Linville River. Alt. 3,623. Summer resort. Post office est. 1883 as Clay; changed to Porcelain in 1885 and to Linville in 1888. Laid out by Samuel T. Kelsey of Kansas, who had earlier (with Charles Hutchinson) laid out High-

lands. Inc. 1891, but not now active in municipal affairs.

Linville Creek rises in e Davie County and flows ne into Yadkin River.

Linville Creek rises in central Watauga County and flows sw in an arc into Brushy Fork.

Linville Creek. *See* Carters Creek.

Linville Falls, nw Burke County on Linville River approx. 2 mi. s of the Avery-Burke county line. In 1876 there were two distinct falls, each approx. 35 ft. high. In the early 1900s, the lower ledge gave way, so that now the upper falls cascade over a smooth, 12 ft. rock shelf, and the water then drops 90 ft. at the lower falls into a rock-encircled pool at the head of Linville Gorge. Reached by foot trail near the Blue Ridge Parkway. Named for William and John Linville, killed by Indians below the falls in 1766.

Linville Falls, community on Avery-Burke county line near the nw tip of Burke County w of Linville River. Alt. 3,325. Named for falls on nearby river.

Linville Gorge, a narrow defile through which the Linville River flows in nw Burke County. Extends from Linville Falls to Lake James. Linville Gorge "wild area" in Pisgah National Forest in Burke County, set aside on February 7, 1951, contains 7,655 acres preserved in their natural state. Foot trails make it accessible, but no other development is permitted.

Linville Lake. *See* Lake Kawana.

Linville Mountain, e Avery County.

Linville River rises in e Avery County approx. 3 mi. sw of Grandfather Mountain. It flows sw in Avery County and se and s in Burke County, where it enters Lake James. Said to have been named for two brothers who hunted along its banks between 1760 and 1766 and were killed by Indians. Known by the Cherokee as *Eeseeoh* (River of Cliffs). *See also* Linville Gorge.

Linville's Mill Creek. *See* Laytown Creek.

Linville Township, central Avery County.

Linville Township, w Burke County.

Linwood, community in w Davidson County in the former Jersey Settlement, *which see*. Alt. 659. Named by Dr. William Rainey Holt (1798–1868) for his nearby plantation. Produces lumber.

Lipe, community in sw Rowan County served by post office, 1886–1902.

Lippard Creek rises in s Catawba County and flows sw into Lincoln County, where it joins Sawmill Creek in forming Leepers Creek.

Lisbon, community in s central Bladen County, was the plantation of Col. John Slingsby, Tory commander at the Battle of Elizabethtown, at which he was fatally wounded.

Lisbon, former community in s Sampson County at the junction of Six Runs Creek and Coharie River where Black River is formed. Authorized to be laid out on the land of Jesse Peacock in 1785 and named Lisburn, probably for the town of the same name in Northern Ireland, birthplace of Hugh Waddell (1734?–1773), colonial soldier. Authorized to be resurveyed in 1824, when it was called Lisbon. A post office est. there as early as 1833 and named Lisborne operated as Lisbon as late as 1882.

Lisbon Township, s central Sampson County.

Lisburn. *See* Lisbon.

Lisenbee Branch rises in n Madison County and flows s into Spillcorn Creek.

Lisenbee Ridge, central Madison County, extends sw approx. 1½ mi. between Heck Creek and Bee Branch.

Lisenberry Mountain, ne Rutherford County between First Broad River and Duncans Creek. It is said that carpetbaggers lived in a cave there during the Reconstruction period following the Civil War.

Lisha. *See* Elisha Creek.

Lisk, community in se Rowan County served by post office, 1890–1906.

Lissa, community in central Sampson County served by post office, 1894–1902.

Listen Knob, peak in central Caldwell County about 5 mi. ne of Lenoir. Named for the fact that foxhunters built fires on the top as they listened to their dogs running foxes.

Listers Corner, community in s Pasquotank County.

Litaker Township, s Rowan County.

Lithia Springs, community in central Lincoln County that was a popular nineteenth-century resort. Gen. Robert F. Hoke (1837–1912) owned the springs and marketed bottled water from them.

Little Abrams Gap, in Great Smoky Mountains National Park on the Swain County, N.C.–Blount County, Tenn., line near lat. 35°33'18" N., long. 83°46'34" W.

Little Alamance Creek rises in w Alamance County and flows se into Great Alamance Creek.

Little Alamance Creek rises in central Guilford County and flows ne to join Big Alamance Creek in forming Great Alamance Creek, *which see.*

Little Andy Creek rises in ne Buncombe County and flows w into Corner Rock Creek.

Little Andy Ridge, ne Buncombe County n of Little Andy Creek and Big Andy Ridge.

Little Bald, on the Cherokee-Graham county line in the Snowbird Mountains.

Little Bald, se Clay County. Alt. 5,030.

Little Bald, e Graham County at the head of Franks Creek.

Little Bald, e Mitchell County between High Knob and Wiggins Cove.

Little Bald, on the Yancey County, N.C.–Unicoi County, Tenn., line. Alt. approx. 5,240.

Little Bald Branch rises in w Haywood County and flows ne into Caldwell Fork.

Little Bald Branch rises in sw Madison County and flows nw into Spring Creek.

Little Bald Knob, w Haywood County in Great Smoky Mountains National Park on Cataloochee Divide between Sheepback Knob and Fie Creek, near lat. 35°33'05" N., long. 83°07'10" W.

Little Bald Knob, on the Mitchell County, N.C.–Unicoi County, Tenn., line.

Little Bald Mountain, on the Haywood-Transylvania county line on the Pisgah Ridge. Alt. 5,280–5,320.

Little Bald Mountain, sw Macon County, extends se from Runaway Knob to the head of Long Branch. Alt. 5,217.

Little Bald Mountain, on the Madison County, N.C.–Greene County, Tenn., line.

Little Bald Mountain. *See* Mount Squires.

Little Bald Rock Mountain, s Jackson County on e edge of Fairfield Lake and s of Bald Rock Mountain.

Little Balsam Gap, on the head of Plott Creek in w Haywood County.

Little Balsam Knob, on the head of Plott Creek in w Haywood County.

Little Bear Creek rises in ne Cabarrus County and flows sw into Dutch Buffalo Creek.

Little Bear Creek rises in s Mitchell County and flows sw into North Toe River.

Little Bear Creek rises in w central Stanly County and flows s into Long Creek.

Little Bearpen Gap, on the Jackson-Haywood county line.

Little Bearpen Mountain, se Macon County between Bearpen Mountain and Cullasaja River.

Little Beartrail Ridge, s Haywood County between Little Beartrap Branch and Big Beartrap Branch.

Little Beartrap Branch rises in s Haywood County and flows ne into Middle Prong.

Little Bear Wallow Creek rises in w Transylvania County and flows sw into North Fork French Broad River.

Little Bearwallow Mountain, n Henderson County between Bearwallow Mountain and Hickory Nut Creek.

Little Beaver Creek rises in w Wake County and flows nw into e Chatham County, where it enters Beaver Creek.

Little Beaverdam Creek rises in sw Duplin County and flows se into Big Beaverdam Creek.

Little Beaverdam Creek rises in nw Gaston County and flows ne into Beaverdam Creek.

Little Beaverdam Creek rises in se Granville County and flows sw into Wake County, where it enters Beaverdam Creek.

Little Beaverdam Creek rises in nw Watauga County and flows sw into Beaverdam Creek.

Little Beaverdam Swamp rises in w Sampson County and flows sw into South River.

Little Bernal Branch rises in w Johnston County and flows se into Bernal Branch.

Little Black Creek rises in s Wake County and flows se into w Johnston County, where it enters Black Creek.

Little Bottom Branch rises in w Madison County and flows ne into Spring Creek.

Little Branch rises in w Haywood County and flows se into Winchester Creek.

Little Branch rises in n Johnston County and flows se into Swift Creek.

Little Branch rises in w Wake County and flows sw into Whiteoak Creek.

Little Brasstown Creek rises in s Cherokee County and flows ne into Brasstown Creek.

Little Brier Creek rises in w Wake County and flows sw into Brier Creek.

Little Brier Ridge, spur of Brier Ridge extending ne to Dark Ridge Creek in ne Jackson County.

Little Broad Creek rises in North River Pocosin in s Camden County and flows e into North River ½ mi. below the mouth of Broad Creek.

Little Brown Creek rises in sw Anson County and flows n into Brown Creek.

Little Brown Creek rises in se Union County and flows se into Brown Creek.

Little Browns Landing, on Cape Fear River in central Bladen County.

Little Brush Creek rises in sw Chatham County and flows sw into Randolph County, where it enters Brush Creek.

Little Brush Creek rises in ne Yancey County and flows nw into Brush Creek.

Little Brush Mountain is made up of a chain of 5 or 6 peaks in w Alexander and e Caldwell Counties.

Little Brushy, peak at the s end of Brushy Mountain, ne Buncombe County.

Little Brushy Mount, a range of mountains in e Caldwell and w Alexander Counties. Alts. from 1,850 to 1,890.

Little Buck Creek rises in nw Burke County and flows ne into Steele's Creek.

Little Buck Creek rises in se Clay County and flows sw into Buck Creek.

Little Buck Creek rises in e Macon County and flows sw into Buck Creek.

Little Buck Creek rises in nw McDowell County on the s slopes of Woods Mountain and flows se into Buck Creek and Lake Tahoma.

Little Buckeye Cove, se Haywood County on the head of East Prong Pigeon River.

Little Buck Hill, mountain in w Avery County.

Little Buckle Swamp rises in se Bladen County and flows se into Buckle Swamp.

Little Buck Mountain, on Alexander-Caldwell county line. Alt. 1,890.

Little Buffalo Creek rises in e Johnston County and flows se into Little River.

Little Buffalo Creek rises in central Lee County and flows n into Deep River.

Little Buffalo Creek rises in sw Lincoln County and flows sw into Cleveland County, where it enters Buffalo Creek.

Little Buffalo Creek rises in nw Richmond County and flows sw into Buffalo Creek.

Little Buffalo Creek rises in s Rowan and n Cabarrus Counties and flows sw into Dutch Buffalo Creek.

Little Buffalo Creek rises in s Vance County and flows sw into Buffalo Creek.

Little Buffalo Creek. *See* West Buffalo Creek.

Little Bugaboo Creek rises in n Wilkes County and flows se into Big Bugaboo Creek.

Little Butt Knob, on the Buncombe-Yancey county line between Big Butt Knob and Point Misery. Alt. approx. 3,300.

Little Camp Creek rises in n Rutherford County and flows sw into Camp Creek.

Little Cane River Gap. *See* Cane River Gap.

Little Caraway Creek rises in nw Randolph County and flows s into Caraway Creek.

Little Cataloochee Creek is formed in nw Haywood County in Great Smoky Mountains National Park by the junction of Woody Branch and Conrad Branch. Flows e 2 mi. and empties into Cataloochee Creek.

Little Catawba River. *See* South Fork Catawba River.

Little Cawcaw Swamp rises in sw Brunswick County and flows w into Cawcaw Swamp at e limit of Thomas Bay.

Little Cedar Cliff, ne Buncombe County near Ingraham Mountain.

Little Cedar Mountain, s Buncombe County in the Swannanoa Mountains.

Little Celo Mountain, e Yancey County at the ne end of Celo Ridge.

Little Chestnut Bald, mountain peak in Great Smoky Mountains National Park on the Swain County, N.C.–Sevier County, Tenn., line near lat. 35°33′54″ N., long. 83°38′30″ W. Alt. 5,042.

Little Chestnut Mountain, ne Burke County and sw Caldwell Counties.

Little Chestnut Ridge, n Swain County in Great Smoky Mountains National Park, a short spur of Locust Ridge near lat. 35°32′50″ N., long. 83°39′54″ W.

Little Chimney Knob, s Macon County between Chimney Knob and Kimsey Gap.

Little Chinquapin Branch rises in w Jones County and flows e about 3½ mi. into Trent River.

Little Choga Creek rises in w Macon County and flows se into Nantahala Lake.

Little Coharie Creek rises in nw Sampson County and flows se to join Great Coharie Creek in forming Coharie River.

Little Coharie Township, w Sampson County.

Little Cokey Swamp rises in w Edgecombe County and flows se into Cokey Swamp.

Little Cold Water Creek rises in n Cabarrus County and flows s into Cold Water Creek.

Little Colington Island. *See* Colington Island.

Little Colly Creek rises in e Bladen County and flows s into Colly Creek.

Little Contentnea Creek rises in se Wilson County and flows se on the Greene-Pitt county line into Pitt County, then back to the Pitt-Greene county line, which it follows into Contentnea Creek. *See also* Contentnea Creek. Appears as Little Cotecktney Creek on the Collet map, 1770.

Little Cotecktney Creek. *See* Little Contentnea Creek.

Little Cove Creek, w Polk County flows ne and nw into Green River.

Little Crabtree Creek rises in central Yancey County and flows e into South Toe River.

Little Craggy Knob, ne Buncombe County between Sugar Fork and Left Fork.

Little Crains Creek. *See* Whiteoak Creek.

Little Creek rises in sw Alamance County and flows n into Stinking Quarter Creek.

Little Creek rises in n Anson County and flows n into Rocky River.

Little Creek rises in se Anson County and flows s into Jones Creek.

Little Creek, e Beaufort County, an inlet of Pungo Creek near the junction with Pungo River.

Little Creek rises in se Beaufort County and flows nw into South Creek.

Little Creek is shown on the Collet map, 1770, as flowing parallel to the present Broad Creek of Camden County, though s of it. The creek n of the present Broad Creek is probably intended, as there is no parallel stream s of it.

Little Creek rises in Black Swamp on the s tip of Camden County and flows n into North River.

Little Creek rises in s Carteret County and flows s into Newport River.

Little Creek rises in nw Cumberland County and flows n into Little River.

Little Creek rises in w Davie County and flows se approx. 6 mi. into South Yadkin River.

Little Creek rises in the sw section of Winston-Salem, central Forsyth County, and flows sw into Muddy Creek. Appears as Loar Creek on the Collet map, 1770; as Long Run on the Price map, 1808; and under its present name on the MacRae map, 1833.

Little Creek rises in s Franklin County and flows ne into Crooked Creek.

Little Creek rises in e Haywood County and flows sw into Bald Creek.

Little Creek rises in w Hoke County and flows sw into Lumber River.

Little Creek rises in e Johnston County and flows ne into Wilson County, where it enters Contentnea Creek.

Little Creek rises in n Johnston County and flows se into Little River. Appears on the Collet map, 1770.

Little Creek rises in nw Johnston County and flows se into Swift Creek.

Little Creek rises in n Lincoln County and flows ne into Catawba River.

Little Creek rises in se Macon County and flows se into Big Creek.

Little Creek rises in ne Madison County and flows s into Big Laurel Creek.

Little Creek rises in sw Madison County and flows ne into Spring Creek.

Little Creek rises in w Madison County and flows e into Meadow Fork.

Little Creek rises in e central Moore County and flows nw into McLendons Creek.

Little Creek rises in se Moore County and flows s into Little River.

Little Creek rises in sw Nash County and flows sw into Moccasin Creek.

Little Creek is formed in se Orange County by the junction of Booker Creek and Bolin Creek; it flows e into sw Durham County, where it flows se into New Hope Creek.

Little Creek rises in w Stanly County and flows sw into Big Bear Creek.

Little Creek rises in n Stokes County and flows sw into Peters Creek.

Little Creek rises in w Surry County and flows se into Snow Creek.

Little Creek rises in e Wake County and flows se into n Johnston County, where it enters Moccasin Creek.

Little Creek rises in n Yancey County and flows se into Cane River.

Little Creek, community on Little Creek s of Sams Gap, ne Madison County. Alt. 2,892.

Little Creek Gap, on the Haywood-Madison county line.

Little Creek Point, s Onslow County in New River.

Little Crooked Creek rises in sw McDowell County and flows e into Crooked Creek.

Little Cross Creek rises in n Cumberland County and flows se into Cross Creek. Early settlers found that Cross Creek and Little Cross Creek crossed.

Little Cub Creek. *See* East Prong Cub Creek.

Little Currituck. *See* Farmington.

Little Cypress Creek rises in e Franklin County and flows sw into Cypress Creek.

Little Cypress Creek rises in s Jones County and flows ne into Cypress Creek.

Littledals Ferry. *See* Mount Gould.

Little Dam Branch rises in n Cherokee County on Hanging Dog Mountain and flows ne into Hyatt Creek.

Little Davidson Branch rises in w Haywood County and flows nw into Davidson Branch.

Little Davis Mountain, n Buncombe County in the Elk Mountains.

Little Deep Creek rises in n central Carteret County and flows s into Deep Creek.

Little Deep Creek rises in s Halifax County and flows se into Deep Creek.

Little Deep Creek rises in w Warren County and flows ne into Ellingtons Creek.

Little Dismal Swamp, nw Johnston County, drains into Dismal Branch.

Little Dugger Creek rises in se Watauga County and flows se into Wilkes County, where it enters Dugger Creek.

Little Dugger Mountain, se Watauga County near the head of Little Dugger Creek.

Little Ease Creek, a bay on the n side of Pamlico River, e Beaufort County.

Little East Fork Pigeon River rises in s Haywood County and flows nw into West Fork Pigeon River.

Little Elk Creek rises in w Alleghany County and flows n into Elk Creek.

Little Elk Creek rises in sw Avery County and flows ne into Elk River.

Little Elkin River rises in ne Wilkes County and flows se into Yadkin River.

Little Elk Knob, n Graham County between Tuskeegee Creek and Sawyer Creek.

Little Elk Mountain, central Avery County.

Little Elk Ridge, central Avery County.

Little Elliby. *See* Upper Bartons Creek.

Little Fall Branch rises in n Haywood County and flows nw into Cold Springs Creek.

Little Fall Creek rises in n central Wake County e and flows ne into Fall Branch.

Littlefield, community in s Pitt County. Alt. 57.

Little Fires Creek rises in n Clay County and flows sw into Fires Creek.

Little Fisher River rises in n Surry County and flows se into Fisher River.

Little Fishhawk Mountain, s Macon County

between Fishhawk Mountain and Whiterock Gap. Alt. 4,706.

Little Fishing Creek is formed in e central Warren County by the junction of Walkers Creek and Big Branch. It flows se into w Halifax County, where it enters Fishing Creek on the Halifax-Nash county line. Appears as Conway Creek on the Moseley map, 1733, and as Little Fishing Creek on the Collet map, 1770.

Little Fishing Creek. *See* Mill Creek.

Little Flat Creek rises in n Buncombe County near Brittain Mountain and flows nw into Flat Creek.

Little Flatty Creek rises in se Pasquotank County and flows se into Pasquotank River.

Little Florida, artificial pond in nw Tyrrell County formed in 1946 by the digging of sand from a farm to make a fill. Covers 3 acres; max. depth 30 ft. Named by C. E. Liverman, former owner, for name of the farm.

Little Fodderstack Mountain, se Macon County at the head of Edwards Creek.

Little Fork rises in ne Buncombe County and flows nw into Right Fork. These are tributaries of Swannanoa River. Sometimes known locally as Little Right Hand Fork.

Little Fork Ridge, ne Buncombe County between Hawkbill and Mineral Creeks.

Little Fork Ridge, w Haywood County between Big Fork Ridge and Woody Creek.

Little Fork Ridge, n Mitchell County between Left Fork Bean Creek and Right Fork Bean Creek.

Little Foster Creek rises in ne Madison County and flows s into Foster Creek.

Little Gap Creek rises in n Watauga County and flows n into Ashe County, where it enters South Fork New River.

Little Glade Creek rises in se Alleghany County and flows n into Brush Creek.

Little Governors Creek rises on the Lee-Moore county line and flows nw into Big Governors Creek. Forms part of the Lee-Moore county line for its entire course. Named for Governor Gabriel Johnston, who acquired land in the vicinity in 1748.

Little Grandfather Mountain, on the Alleghany-Wilkes county line. Alt. 3,745.

Little Grassy Creek rises in n Granville County and flows n into Grassy Creek.

Little Green Creek rises in se Jackson County

n of Cold Mountain and flows 1½ mi. w into Tuckasegee River.

Little Green Mountain, in se Jackson County between Big Green Mountain and Panthertown Creek. Alt. approx. 4,100.

Little Green Swamp, ne Brunswick County. Approx. 10 mi. square.

Little Grill Ridge, w Swain County in Great Smoky Mountains National Park, a short spur from Big Grill Ridge, lat. 35°32'38" N., long. 83°47'28" W.

Little Gunpowder Creek rises in s Caldwell County and flows e into Gunpowder Creek.

Little Hamer Creek rises in s Montgomery County and flows s into Richmond County, where it enters Hamer Creek.

Little Harris Creek rises in central Cleveland County and flows se into Big Harris Creek.

Little Haw Creek rises in e Alamance County and flows sw into Haw Creek.

Little Hawk Mountain, e Mitchell County between Hawk Creek and Long Hollow.

Little Haw Knob, on the Graham County, N.C.–Monroe County, Tenn., line. Alt. 5,146.

Little Haw Mountain, central Avery County.

Little Helton Creek rises in n Ashe County and flows se into Helton Creek.

Little Hensley Branch rises in n Yancey County and flows ne into Cane River.

Little Hickory Creek rises in s Cleveland County and flows w into Hickory Creek.

Little Hickory Knob, n Transylvania County between Avery Creek and Thrift Cove Branch.

Little Hickory Top, s Buncombe County sw of Ingles Field Gap.

Little Hogback Creek rises in se Jackson County and flows s into Horsepasture River.

Little Hogback Mountain, se Jackson County between Burnt Cabin Gap and Toxaway Mountain.

Little Hogback Mountain, on the Jackson-Macon county line.

Little Hope Creek rises in sw Mecklenburg County and flows se into Little Sugar Creek.

Little Horse Creek rises near Pond Mountain in nw Ashe County and flows se into Horse Creek.

Little Horse Creek rises in w Avery County and flows se into North Toe River.

Little Hoyles Creek rises in n Gaston County and flows s into Hoyles Creek.

Little Hubquarter Creek rises in e Warren County and flows n into Hubquarter Creek.

Little Huckleberry Knob, w Graham County between Huckleberry Knob and Doc Stewart Ridge. Alt. approx. 5,380.

Little Hump Mountain, on the Avery County, N.C.–Carter County, Tenn., line.

Little Hungry Creek rises in e Henderson County and flows sw into Hungry River.

Little Hunting Creek rises in s Wilkes County and flows se into Hunting Creek.

Little Hurricane Creek rises in n Madison County and flows se into Big Laurel Creek.

Little Indian Creek rises in s Chatham County and flows e into Indian Creek.

Little Indian Creek rises in nw Lincoln County near the Catawba County line and flows se into Indian Creek.

Little Indian Creek rises in sw Macon County and flows ne into Nantahala River.

Little Inlet, former inlet from the Atlantic Ocean through Onslow Beach in s Onslow County. Appears on the Moseley map, 1733, and the Mouzon map, 1775, where the max. depth is shown to be 6 ft. Does not appear on the Price map, 1808, or on subsequent maps.

Little Island Creek rises in nw Vance County and flows n into Island Creek.

Little Ivy Creek is formed in w Madison County by the junction of California Creek and Paint Fork and flows sw to join Ivy Creek at the Buncombe-Madison county line to form Ivy River.

Little Jacobs Creek rises in s Stanly County and flows se and ne into Jacobs Creek.

Little Jacob Swamp rises in central Robeson County and flows se into Jacob Swamp.

Little John Creek rises in se Craven County and flows nw into Hancock Creek.

Little Johnson Creek. *See* Beech Creek.

Little Jonas Creek rises in n Swain County and flows se into Jonas Creek.

Little Juniper Creek rises in s Lee County and flows ne into Little River.

Little Juniper Creek rises in central Moore County and flows nw into Big Juniper Creek.

Little Kings Creek rises in ne Caldwell County and flows ne into Kings Creek.

Little Kinnekeet Coast Guard Station, decommissioned station on Hatteras Island, se Dare County. First est. as a lifesaving station in 1874. Life-saving Service and Revenue Cutter Service joined to form U.S. Coast Guard in 1915.

Little Kitchens Ridge, se Clay County between Holden Cove and Tallulah River.

Little Knob, on Haywood-Swain county line.

Little Knob, on the Madison County, N.C.–Greene County, Tenn., line.

Little Knob Creek rises in n Cleveland County and flows se into Knob Creek.

Little Lake, natural lake in Croatan National Forest, s Craven County. Covers approx. 500 acres; max. depth 4 to 5 ft. One of several lakes in Lakes Pocosin.

Little Laurel Branch rises in se Mitchell County and flows s into North Toe River.

Little Laurel Creek rises in w Ashe County and flows e into Big Laurel Creek.

Little Laurel Creek rises in w Macon County and flows ne into Whiteoak Creek.

Little Laurel Creek rises in n Madison County and flows sw and se into Shelton Laurel Creek.

Little Laurel Creek rises in se Swain County and flows ne into Yalaka Creek.

Little Laurel Creek rises in nw Wake County and flows w into Big Lick Creek.

Little Ledge Creek rises in s Granville County and flows s into Ledge Creek.

Little Lick Creek rises in s Durham County and flows ne into Neuse River.

Little Lick Creek rises in e Lee County and flows n into Lick Creek.

Little Lick Fork. *See* Lick Fork.

Little Limestone Creek rises in e Duplin County and flows se into Limestone Creek.

Little Long Creek rises in central Gaston County and flows se into Long Creek.

Little Long Mountain, sw Randolph County between King Mountain and Poison Fork.

Little Lost Cove Creek rises in e central Avery County and flows ne into Lost Cove Creek.

Little Lost Cove Creek rises in s Yancey County and flows nw into South Toe River.

Little Lyman Branch rises in sw Macon County and flows n into Kimsey Creek.

Little Manor, ne Warren County near the town of Littleton. Home of William Person Little, state senator from Warren County (1804–1806). The house was built in 1780 and is still standing.

Little Marsh Swamp rises in s Hoke County and flows se into Robeson County, where it enters Gallberry Swamp.

Little Matrimony Creek rises in n Rockingham County and flows e in an arc into Matrimony Creek, *which see.*

Little Meadow Creek rises in se Cabarrus County and flows sw into Rocky River.

Little Middle Mountain, n Buncombe County between Brank Mountain and Brittain Cove 2½ mi. ne of town of Weaverville.

Little Middle Ridge, ne Madison County between Colvin and Amos Creeks.

Little Mountain, se Clay County extending from Eagle Creek e to White Oak Stamp.

Little Mountain, between Hyatt Creek and Richland Creek, s Haywood County. It is an extended ridge approx. 1 mi. long.

Little Mountain, s Haywood County on Plott Creek.

Little Mountain, on Gash Creek in w Henderson County.

Little Mountain, s Macon County between Coweeta Creek and Little Tennessee River.

Little Mountain, e Mitchell County between Green Cove Creek and Cane Creek.

Little Mountain, sw Polk County. Alt. 1,600.

Little Mountain, n Rutherford County at the head of Hunting Creek.

Little Mountain, w Surry County between Mitchell River and South Fork.

Little Mountain, ne Transylvania County between Silver Creek and Boylston Creek.

Little Mountain, sw Wilkes County near Yadkin River.

Little Mountain, s Yancey County, extends ne from Setrock Creek to John Autrey Branch.

Little Mountain, community in e McDowell County.

Little Mountain. *See* Anderson's Mountain.

Little Mountain Creek rises in n Richmond County and flows sw into Big Mountain Creek.

Little Mountain Creek rises in ne Stanly County and flows se into Mountain Creek.

Little Mountain Creek rises in s Yancey County and flows se into South Toe River.

Little Mud Creek rises in w Henderson County and flows ne into Mud Creek.

Little Mulberry Creek, approx. 5 mi. long, rises in Pisgah National Forest, n Caldwell County, and flows first se then sw into Mulberry Creek.

Little Neatman Creek rises in s Stokes County and flows sw into Neatman Creek.

Little Nettle Branch rises in nw Haywood County and flows n into Big Creek.

Little New Mountain, central Buncombe County e of Wilson.

Little Nigger Head, peak in n Clay County between Tusquitee Gap and Tuni Creek. In 2003 state legislature directed county to rename peak.

Little Northeast Creek rises in ne Onslow County and flows sw into Northeast Creek.

Little Nutbush Creek, former stream rising in n central Vance County and flowing ne into Nutbush Creek. Now submerged by the waters of Kerr Lake.

Little Panthertail Mountain, w Transylvania County between Panthertail Mountain and Indian Creek.

Little Paw Creek rises in w Mecklenburg County and flows w into Catawba River.

Little Peachtree Creek rises in e Franklin County and flows se into Nash County, where it joins Big Peachtree Creek in forming Stony Creek.

Little Pee Dee River is formed in se Scotland County by the junction of Bridge and Leiths Creeks. It flows se across the w corner of Robeson County and into South Carolina, where it enters Pee Dee River near its mouth.

Little Permetter Creek rises in n central Anson County and flows s into Permetter Creek, *which see.*

Little Persimmon Creek rises in e Cleveland County and flows nw into Persimmon Creek.

Little Peters Creek rises in Virginia and flows sw into Stokes County, where it enters Peters Creek.

Little Pine Creek rises in e Alleghany County and flows sw into Brush Creek.

Little Pine Creek rises in w Jackson County and flows se into Pine Creek.

Little Pine Creek rises in s Madison County and flows ne into French Broad River.

Little Pine Creek Township, former township in s central Madison County, now township no. 7.

Little Pine Gap, s Madison County on the sw end of Rocky Ridge.

Little Pine Mountain, n Avery County.

Little Piney Branch rises in ne Buncombe County and flows se into Flat Creek.

Little Piney Ridge, ne Buncombe County sw of Little Piney Branch.

Little Piney Ridge, s Yancey County between Big Poplar Creek and Mitchell Creek.

Little Pinnacle, s Macon County between Pinnacle Branch and the head of Jones Creek.

Little Pisgah Mountain, on Buncombe-Haywood-Henderson county lines e of Mount Pisgah. Alt. approx. 5,320.

Little Pisgah Mountain, on the Buncombe-Henderson county line between the headwaters of Ashworth Creek and Blue Rock Knob. Alt. 4,412. Known as Konnatoga by the Cherokee Indians.

Little Pisgah Ridge, nw Henderson County, a part of Pisgah Ridge.

Little Plumtree Creek rises in central Avery County and flows s and w into Plumtree Creek.

Little Pocket Creek rises in w Lee County and flows ne into Pocket Creek.

Little Polecat Creek rises in n Randolph County and flows sw into Polecat Creek.

Little Pole Creek rises near Luther Knob in sw Buncombe County and flows s into Pole Creek.

Little Pond Branch rises in w Watauga County and flows nw into Pond Branch.

Little Porpoise Bay, in Pamlico Sound on the e side of Goose Creek Island, ne Pamlico County.

Little Prong, community in nw Brunswick County.

Little Quankey Creek rises in n Halifax County and flows se into Quankey Creek.

Little Raft Swamp rises in s Hoke County and flows se into Raft Swamp in n Robeson County.

Little Ragged Point. *See* Holmes Point.

Little Rattlesnake Branch rises in ne Buncombe County and flows s into Swannanoa River.

Little Richardson Creek rises in s Union County and flows n into Richardson Creek.

Little Richmond, community in s Surry County e of Snow Creek.

Little Rich Mountain, at the head of Queen Creek in nw Henderson County.

Little Rich Mountain, on the Transylvania County, N.C.–Greenville County, S.C., line near Wildcat Branch.

Little Ridge, w Haywood County in Great Smoky Mountains National Park, a short spur of Big Fork Ridge extending ne; center near lat. 35°35'38" N., long. 83°08'28" W.

Little Ridgepole Mountain, s Macon County between Big Laurel Branch and Betty Creek.

Little Right Hand Fork. *See* Little Fork.

Little River rises in sw Alleghany County and flows e and n into Virginia, where it enters New River.

Little River rises in s Burke County and flows s into Jacob Fork.

Little River is formed in nw Durham County by the junction of North Fork Little River and South Fork Little River; it flows se into Eno River. Appears on the Moseley map, 1733.

Little River rises in sw Franklin County near the town of Youngsville and flows se across e Wake County, across ne Johnston County, and into central Wayne County, where it splits into two branches, each entering Neuse River sw of city of Goldsboro. Shown on Collet map, 1770.

Little River rises in sw Moore County and flows se across n Hoke County into Cumberland County and along the Cumberland-Harnett county line into the Cape Fear River. Appears on the Collet map, 1770. Known also as Lower Little River.

Little River, nw Northampton County, a part of the Roanoke River that flows on the n side of Tucker Island.

Little River rises in e Perquimans and w Pasquotank Counties and flows se on the county line into Albemarle Sound. Appears on the Comberford map, 1657, as Yeopim River but is correctly shown on the Ogilby map, 1671. In 1662 the Indians in the area knew the river as Kototine. The legislature met at Little River in 1707, 1709, 1712, and 1716.

Little River rises in central Randolph County and flows s through Montgomery County into Richmond County, where it enters Pee Dee River. Appears on the Collet map, 1770.

Little River rises in se Transylvania County and flows ne then nw into French Broad River.

Little River, community in w Alexander County. Alt. approx. 1,125.

Little River, community in e Transylvania County on Little River about 2 mi. n of Cascade Lake. Now includes community of

Grange, whose post office was est. in 1882. Alt. approx. 2,120.

Little River Academy. *See* Linden.

Little River Township, n Alexander County.

Little River Township, e Caldwell County.

Little River Township, ne Montgomery County.

Little River Township, e Moore County. Transferred from Hoke to Moore County, 1958.

Little River Township, ne Orange County.

Little River Township, se Transylvania County.

Little River Township, ne Wake County.

Little Roaring Creek rises in nw Avery County and flows e into Cranberry Creek.

Little Rock, community in e Rockingham County served by post office, 1850–53. Known later as Ruffin, *which see.*

Little Rock Branch rises in sw Macon County and flows sw into Nantahala River.

Little Rock Creek rises in e Mitchell County and flows sw into Big Rock Creek.

Little Rock Creek. *See* Glen Ayre.

Little Rock Creek Township, ne Mitchell County.

Little Rockfish Creek rises in Fort Bragg Military Reservation on the Cumberland-Hoke county line and flows se along the line to Lake William, where it enters w Cumberland County and flows se to enter Rockfish Creek at town of Hope Mills.

Little Rockfish Creek rises in s Duplin County and flows s from Boney Mill Pond into Rockfish Creek on the Duplin-Pender county Line.

Little Rockhouse Creek rises in central Rockingham County and flows n and w into Dan River. Also known as Roach's Creek, *which see.*

Little Rock Knob, on the Mitchell County, N.C.–Carter County, Tenn., line. Alt. approx. 4,920.

Little Rocky Creek. *See* Olin Creek.

Little Rocky Face, a peak in e Haywood County between the head of Garden Creek and the head of Harley Branch.

Little Rocky Knob, n Buncombe County ne of Razor Mountain.

Little Rocky Knob, nw Caldwell County on sw side of Rocky Knob. Alt. approx. 2,250.

Little Rocky Mountain, e Macon County on a tributary of Little Salt Rock Creek.

Little Rose Creek rises in se Mitchell County and flows nw into Rose Creek.

Little Ruin Creek rises in w Vance County and flows se into Ruin Creek. Appears on Collet map, 1770.

Little Salt Rock Creek rises in e Macon County and flows nw into Wildcat Creek.

Little Sam Knob, s Haywood County between Bubbling Springs Branch and Flat Laurel Creek. Alt. 5,862.

Little Sandy Branch rises in s Stokes County and flows se into Town Fork Creek.

Little Sandy Creek rises in ne Wilkes County and flows s into East Prong Roaring River.

Little Sandy Gap, on the Buncombe-Madison county line e of Davidson Gap.

Little Sandy Mush Bald, peak on the Buncombe-Madison county line between Sandy Mush Bald and Chestnut Gap.

Little Sandymush Creek rises in s Madison County and flows e into Sandy Mush Creek.

Little Sandy Run Swamp rises in w Onslow County and flows se into Sandy Run Swamp.

Little Santeetlah Creek rises in w Graham County and flows se through the Joyce Kilmer Memorial Forest into Santeetlah Creek, *which see.*

Little Sapony Creek rises in w Nash County and flows se into Sapony Creek.

Little Savannah Creek rises in w Jackson County and flows nw into Savannah Creek.

Little Scaly Mountain, s Macon County between Abe Creek and Chinquapin Mountain. Alt. 4,200.

Little Shaddox Creek rises in n Lee County and flows e into Cape Fear River.

Little Sheep Cliffs, s Jackson County between Horsepasture River and Sheep Cliffs.

Little Shell Rock. *See* North Rock.

Little Shepherd Mountain, w Randolph County between Uwharrie River and Little Caraway Creek.

Little Shoal Creek rises in w Cherokee County and flows se into Shoal Creek.

Little Shocco Creek rises in e Vance County and flows se into Warren County and onto the Franklin-Warren county line before entering Shocco Creek.

Little Shocco Creek rises in sw Warren County and flows e into Shocco Creek.

Little Shuckstack, mountain in Great Smoky Mountains National Park, nw Swain County, lat. 35°29′26″ N., long. 83°48′37″ W. Alt. 3,821.

Little Silver Creek rises in sw Burke County and flows ne into Silver Creek.

Little Singletary Lake, a natural lake in n Bladen

County; approx. 1½ mi. long and ¾ mi. wide. Fishing. *See also* Carolina Bays.

Little's Mill, community in nw Richmond County on Little River. A post office operated there from 1850 to 1913.

Little's Mills, community in n Richmond County served by post office, 1850–1913.

Little Snowball Mountain, n Buncombe County between Cherry Log Gap and Snowball Gap. Alt. 4,824.

Little Snowbird Creek rises in s Graham County and flows ne and nw into Snowbird Creek.

Little Snow Creek rises in n Stokes County and flows se into Snow Creek.

Little Spivey Creek rises in n Yancey County and flows w into Tennessee, where it enters Spivey Creek.

Little Spruce Ridge, w Haywood County in Great Smoky Mountains National Park, a spur extending ne from Cataloochee Divide; center near lat. 35°33'35" N., long. 83°08'04" W., between Little Bald Branch and Bearpen Branch.

Little Steeltrap Creek rises in n Swain County and flows sw into Forney Creek.

Little Stonehouse Creek rises in e Warren County and flows ne into Lake Gaston.

Little Stone Mountain, n Wilkes County on the w side of East Prong Roaring River.

Little Sugar Creek rises in central Mecklenburg County and flows sw into South Carolina, where it enters Sugar Creek. Appears as Shugan Creek on the Collet map, 1770, but with its present name on the Price map, 1808.

Little Sugar Loaf, community in central Bladen County served by post office, 1870–1901.

Little Swamp rises in e Columbus County and flows sw into Juniper Creek.

Little Swamp rises in s Nash County and flows se into Toisnot Swamp.

Little Swamp Branch rises in sw Johnston County and flows se into Mill Swamp Branch.

Little Swift Creek rises in ne Craven County and flows sw into Swift Creek.

Little Switzerland, community and summer resort in nw McDowell County on the head of Threemile Creek. Alt. 3,500. Founded in 1910 as a summer resort by Heriot Clarkson (1863–1942). Named because of the supposed resemblance of the mountains of the area to those of Switzerland. *See also* Armstrong.

Little Tennessee River is formed in Rabun County, Ga., by the junction of Betty and Darnell Creeks. It flows n and nw into Macon County and through Lake Emory; into Swain County and along the Graham-Swain county line through Fontana Lake and Lake Cheoah; and into Tennessee, where it enters the Tennessee River. The river was long believed to have been discovered in 1540 by Hernando De Soto and as such the first tributary of the Mississippi River discovered by Europeans.

Little Terrapin Mountain, s Jackson County approx. 1½ mi. s of Hampton Lake, is bordered on the w by Fowler Creek. Alt. 3,900.

Little Timber Ridge, n Avery County.

Little Tomahawk Creek rises in w Forsyth County and flows se into Stewarts Creek. Some time prior to 1762 Stewarts Creek was known as Tomahawk Branch. *See also* Stewarts Creek.

Little Tomahawk Creek rises in s Sampson County and flows nw to join Big Tomahawk Creek in forming Tomahawk Creek.

Littleton, town in e Warren County and nw Halifax County. Alt. 389. Inc. 1877 and named for Little Manor, *which see*. Person's Ordinary, the tavern owned by Thomas Person (1733–1800), Regulator, officer of the Continental Line, and state legislator, was located there and is shown on the Collet map, 1770. The tavern, which is still standing, was called Peterson Inn on the Price map, 1808. Littleton was mentioned by name in newspapers as early as 1823, and in 1831 a post office was est. there under the present name. The MacRae map, 1833, shows Littleton as an established community.

Littleton's Store, community in central Onslow County between Rocky Run and Mott Creek.

Little Town Creek rises in s Montgomery County and flows se into Town Creek.

Littletown Township, nw Halifax County.

Little Troublesome Creek is formed in e Rockingham County in Reidsville and flows se into Haw River.

Little Trout Creek rises in central Jackson County and flows n into Mill Creek.

Little Tuni Creek rises in n Clay County between Deadline Ridge and Tuni Creek and flows s into Tusquitee Creek.

Little Tuni Creek rises in w Macon County and flows n into Big Choga Creek.

Little Turnbull Creek rises in ne Bladen County

and flows w into Turnbull Creek. Once known as Edward Jones Creek.

Little Uwharrie River rises in nw Randolph County and flows se into Uwharrie River.

Little Warrior Mountain, s Polk County w of town of Tryon. The name is a corruption of the Indian word *wayah* (wolf).

Little Webb Creek rises in s Buncombe County and flows sw into Gap Creek.

Little Whiteoak Creek rises in w Wake County and flows sw into Whiteoak Creek.

Little Whiteoak Creek rises in e Yancey County and flows nw into South Toe River.

Little Whitewater Creek rises in s Jackson County and flows se to join Silver Run Creek in forming Whitewater River.

Little Will Branch rises in ne Buncombe County and flows sw into North Fork Ivy Creek.

Little Willow Creek rises in w Henderson County and flows ne into French Broad River. A legendary Cherokee route, "Willow Trail," followed the course of the stream.

Little Yadkin River is formed in sw Stokes County by the junction of East Prong Little Yadkin River and West Prong Little Yadkin River and flows s into Forsyth County, where it enters Yadkin River.

Little Yalaka Creek rises in s Swain County and flows sw into Yalaka Creek.

Little Yellow Mountain, on the Avery-Mitchell county line. Alt. 5,000–5,100.

Little Yellow Mountain, se Macon County between Brooks Creek and Monger Creek.

Liverman. *See* Newton.

Liverman Creek rises in n Hertford County and flows se into Meherrin River.

Livermans Mill Pond, w Hertford County, 1½ mi. long, drains into Potecasi Creek.

Liverpool. *See* Cornelius.

Livingston. *See* Acme.

Livingston Creek rises in Green Swamp in n central Brunswick County and flows n across Columbus County, where it enters the Cape Fear River. Appears as Levingtons Creek on maps as early as 1844.

Livingswood Creek. *See* Carvers Creek.

Lizard Creek rises in s Brunswick County, Va., and flows se into ne Warren County, where it enters Lake Gaston.

Lizard Lick, crossroads community in e Wake County near town of Wendell. Named by a passing observer who saw many lizards sun-

ning and "licking" themselves on a rail fence there.

Lizard Ridge, community in e central Caldwell County between Zacks Fork and Blair Fork.

Lizzards Creek rises in Virginia and flows se into n Halifax County, where it enters Roanoke River.

Lizzie, community in central Greene County; a post office in the late nineteenth century. Said to have been known first as Lizzie's Store for the old lady who kept a store there. Also called Lillie during the 1890s.

Lizzie's Store. *See* Lizzie.

Lizzy Mountain, central Jackson County between Dickson Creek and Trout Creek.

Lloyd Cove, s Macon County e of Green Cove on a tributary of Tessentee Creek.

Lloyd Crossroads, community in se Hertford County.

Lloyds Meadows, an area of meadow land approx. 2 mi. long and 1 mi. wide in e Onslow County at the head of Horse Swamp.

Loafers Glory, community in central Mitchell County on Cane Creek. Named about 1890 by Jonathan Burleson because men delighted in whiling away their time on the porch of the local general store.

Loar Creek. *See* Little Creek.

Lobelia, community in se Moore County.

Loch Lily, lake on Storys Creek, nw Person County. Formed prior to 1928 and known first as Barnetts Pond, later as Lake Chub, and finally by its present name. Covers 94 acres; max. depth 12 ft.

Locke Mills. *See* Forest Hill.

Locke Township, central Rowan County. Named for Gen. Matthew Locke (1730–1801), statesman and patriot, who lived there.

Locketts Island, a clay loam island approx. 1 mi. long in Roanoke River, w Northampton County.

Lockhart Mill. *See* Hoggard's Mill.

Lockport, community in se Chatham County on Deep River w of Moncure. An earlier post office there was known as Lockville. Site of locks of Cape Fear and Deep River Navigation Co.; Progress Energy has a small power plant there that uses the lock canal as a mill race. At Ramsey's Mill there, following the Battle of Guilford Courthouse in 1781, the British general, Lord Cornwallis, built a bridge over Deep River.

Locks Creek rises in e central Cumberland County and flows sw and s into Cape Fear River. *See also* Lords Creek.

Lockville. *See* Lockport.

Lockwoods Folly Inlet, between Holden Beach and Long Beach, through which Lockwoods Folly River flows into Long Bay of the Atlantic Ocean, s central Brunswick County. Appears on the Ogilby map, 1671. The name is derived from a man named Lockwood, who built a fine boat up Lockwoods Folly River but discovered that it was too large to float into the Atlantic through the inlet. He was forced to abandon his boat, and it eventually fell to pieces. Frequently in the seventeenth century, however, the word "folly" was used in the sense of the French *folie* (delight; favorite abode), and it formed a part of the name of English estates. Lockwoods Folly River, *which see*, has been described as the second-most-beautiful river in North Carolina, and it may have been the "delight" or "favorite abode" of an early settler named Lockwood. *See also* Longs Delight.

Lockwoods Folly River is formed in central Brunswick County by the junction of Pinch Gut Creek and Red Run and flows w and s through Lockwoods Folly Inlet, *which see*, into Long Bay of the Atlantic Ocean.

Lockwoods Folly Township, s central Brunswick County.

Loco, community in n Onslow County served by post office, 1883–1903.

Locust, town in sw Stanly County. Inc. 1905, but long inactive in municipal affairs. A post office, Locust Level, opened 1869; discontinued 1919. Reestablished under present name, 1955. Named for large locust tree. Locust Level changed to Locust in 1894.

Locust Cove Gap, e Graham County on the headwaters of Stecoah Creek.

Locust Creek rises in n Jackson County and flows sw into Tuckasegee River.

Locust Creek rises in e Yancey County and flows se into South Toe River.

Locust Gap, ne Buncombe County between Pigpen Cove and Sugarhouse Cove.

Locust Gap, ne Buncombe County between Rough Hew Ridge and Forney Creek.

Locust Gap, ne Cherokee County at the end of Townhouse Ridge between Townhouse and Welch Mill Creeks.

Locust Gap, on Jackson-Haywood county line.

Locust Gap, n Swain County on Locust Ridge near the head of Big Flats Branch.

Locust Gap, on the Watauga County, N.C.–Johnson County, Tenn., line in the Stone Mountains.

Locust Grove, community in n Randolph County.

Locust Grove. *See* Satterwhite.

Locust Hill, community in w Caswell County. Named for locust trees in the vicinity. Known as Brown's Store from the early nineteenth century until the 1840s, when the name was changed. Jethro Brown operated the store. Rose Hill, home of Bedford Brown, U.S. senator from 1829 to 1840, state legislator, and opponent of secession in 1860, stands there; built about 1802.

Locust Hill, home of William Eaton, w Vance County. Built between 1740–43; served as an early religious center for the Episcopal Church, and the first Granville County Superior Court met there in 1746. Located approx. 3 mi. sw of Henderson.

Locust Hill Township, w central Caswell County.

Locust Knob, s central Avery County.

Locust Knob, ne Buncombe County in the Great Craggy Mountains. Alt. approx. 5,480.

Locust Knob, n McDowell County, a part of Pompey Ridge between O'Dear Creek and Long Branch. Alt. approx. 2,650.

Locust Knob, central Mitchell County between Toe River and Pumpkin Patch Mountain.

Locust Knob, ne Swain County on Heintooga Ridge in Great Smoky Mountains National Park, lat. 35°33′27″ N., long. 83°12′08″ W. Alt. 4,034.

Locust Level. *See* Locust.

Locust Licklog Gap, central Graham County in Cheoah Mountains between Hazanet Knob and Wauchecha Bald.

Locust Mountain, The, on Burke-McDowell county line.

Locust Ridge, ne Buncombe County s of Staire Branch.

Locust Ridge, on the Madison County, N.C.–Unicoi County, Tenn., line.

Locust Ridge, w Swain County in Great Smoky Mountains National Park extending s from Big Chestnut Bald.

Locust Ridge, e Yancey County between Whiteoak and Locust Creeks.

Locust Rough Mountain, n Yancey County at the se end of Bailey Hill.

Locust Rough Ridge, w Yancey County between Simms Fork and Lickskillet Branch.

Locust Tree Branch rises in w Macon County and flows se into Wyah Creek.

Locust Tree Gap, central Macon County between Bruce Knob and Wilkes Knob.

Locust Tree Gap, w Macon County at the head of Locust Tree Branch.

Lodo, community in w Mecklenburg County served by post office, 1884–1903. Was located on the Charlotte and Atlanta Railroad at the Steele Creek station.

Loftins Crossroads, community in e Lenoir County. Named for the Loftin family, which settled there.

Loftis. *See* Cedar Mountain.

Logan, community in n central Rutherford County. Named for a local storekeeper; the post office est. prior to 1882 but now discontinued was Logans Store.

Logan Creek rises in s Jackson County and flows s into Horsepasture River.

Logans Store Township, e Rutherford County.

Loggerhead Inlet, from the Atlantic Ocean into Pamlico Sound through Hatteras Island n of the present community of Rodanthe, e Dare County. It opened prior to 1851 and closed in the late 1870s.

Loggy Branch rises in se Clay County and flows n into Right Fork.

Loggy Gap, mountain gap in central Avery County.

Loggy Knob, n Mitchell County between Bearwallow Creek and Waterfall Branch.

Loggy Ridge, n Swain County in Great Smoky Mountains National Park, lat. 35°33′ N., long. 83°32′08″ W.

Log Hollow Branch rises in n Transylvania County and flows se into Big Bear Pen Branch.

Log Shoal, in the waters of Pamlico Sound, s Dare County, off the s part of Hatteras Island and e of Bird Islands.

Lola, community on Cedar Island in ne Carteret County.

Lomax, community in n Wilkes County between East Prong Roaring River and Big Bugaboo Creek in rich agricultural area.

Lona Creek rises in se Beaufort County and flows n into South Creek.

London Bald, on the Cherokee-Macon county line.

Lone Bald Mountain, on the Haywood-Jackson county line. Originally Lone Balsam Mountain from the fact that a single large balsam tree stood on its crest. With the disappearance of the tree, the name was shortened to Lone Bald. Alt. 5,880.

Lone Balsam Mountain. *See* Lone Bald Mountain.

Lone Hickory, community in s Yadkin County near South Deep Creek.

Lone Island Ford, in central Rockingham County on Dan River at confluence of Dan River and Upper Hogan's Creek.

Lone Knob, n Madison County between Duckmill Branch and West Prong [Hickory Fork].

Lone Mountain, ne Rutherford County between the heads of First Broad River and Cane Creek. Alt. approx. 1,650.

Lone Oak Channel, between Beasley Bay and Currituck Sound, e Currituck County.

Lone Pine Ridge, n Swain County in Great Smoky Mountains National Park, a short spur extending sw from Thomas Ridge, lat. 35°31′15″ N., long. 83°23′13″ W.

Lonesome Mountain, n Madison County on Big Laurel Creek.

Lonesome Valley. *See* Henderson.

Long Acre, an elevated area of clay loam extending s from the head of Conaby Creek in w Washington County to Pungo Creek se of the community of Pinetown in n central Beaufort County. The ridge is broken at the Tare-over in sw Washington County by Van Swamp. Appears on the Collet map, 1770. *See also* Tare-over.

Long Acre Township, n central Beaufort County. *See also* Acre.

Long Arm Mountain, nw Burke County. Alt. 4,350. Highest point in county.

Longarm Mountain, n Haywood County, extends ne from the head of Dogwood Flats Creek to the head of Stinking Camp Creek.

Long Arm Ridge, s Yancey County, extends se between Devils Den and Laurel Branch.

Long Bay, in the Atlantic Ocean off the se coast of North Carolina and ne South Carolina from Winyah Bay on the s to Cape Fear on the n. Appears on the Moseley map, 1733.

Long Bay, ne Carteret County between Cedar Island and Piney Island s of West Bay.

Long Beach, a section of outer beach in se
Brunswick County on the Atlantic Ocean w
of Caswell Beach and e of Lockwoods Folly
Inlet. Long Beach, a town there, was inc.
1955. A summer resort.

Long Bottoms, an area of approx. 50 acres
of level old-field land between 2 mountains
in sw Graham County on Snowbird
Creek.

Long Branch rises in se Alamance County and
flows e into Mary's Creek.

Long Branch rises in ne Buncombe County and
flows sw into Beetree Creek.

Long Branch rises in nw Buncombe County and
flows se into Sandy Mush Creek.

Long Branch rises in nw Buncombe County near
Graybeard Mountain and flows w into North
Fork [Swannanoa River].

Long Branch rises in s Buncombe County and
flows ne into Bent Creek.

Long Branch rises in ne Cherokee County and
flows nw into Valley River.

Long Branch rises in sw Cherokee County and
flows se into Hothouse Branch.

Long Branch rises in n Clay County and flows sw
into Fires Creek.

Long Branch rises in n Clay County and flows sw
into Tuni Creek.

Long Branch rises in s Clay County and flows se
into Crawford Creek.

Long Branch rises in se Cleveland County and
flows nw into Beason Creek.

Long Branch rises in sw Columbus County and
flows ne into Porter Swamp.

Long Branch rises in s Duplin County and flows
se into Cypress Creek.

Long Branch rises in s Durham County and
flows sw into w Wake County, where it enters
Kit Creek.

Long Branch rises in central Franklin County
and flows se into Tar River approx. 4 mi. se of
town of Louisburg.

Long Branch rises in e Franklin County and
flows sw into Cypress Creek.

Long Branch rises in se Graham County and
flows w into Sweetwater Creek.

Long Branch rises in n Guilford County and
flows sw into East Fork Deep River.

Long Branch rises in e Haywood County and
flows sw into Beaverdam Creek.

Long Branch rises in e Haywood County and
flows sw into East Fork Pigeon River.

Long Branch rises in e Haywood County and
flows w into Pigeon River.

Long Branch rises in s Haywood County and
flows ne into Cherry Cove Creek.

Long Branch rises in nw Henderson County and
flows se into North Fork.

Long Branch rises in s Hertford County and
flows se into Chinkapin Creek.

Long Branch rises in se Hertford County and
flows sw into Kill'em Swamp.

Long Branch rises in e Jackson County and flows
se into Charley Creek.

Long Branch rises in s Jackson County e of
Cowrock Mountain and flows se to enter
Trays Island Creek n of Fairfield Lake.

Long Branch rises in w Jackson County and
flows ne into Cullowhee Creek.

Long Branch rises in w Jackson County and
flows sw into Tuckasegee River s of Hazel
Hollow.

Long Branch rises on the s slopes of Jones Knob
in w Jackson County and flows sw into Savannah Creek.

Long Branch rises in n Johnston County and
flows se into Little River.

Long Branch rises in ne Jones County and flows
sw approx. 3 mi. into Trent River.

Long Branch rises in e Macon County and flows
sw into Cullasaja River.

Long Branch rises in n Macon County and flows
n into Little Tennessee River.

Long Branch rises in n Macon County and flows
se into Lakey Creek.

Long Branch rises in nw Macon County and
flows w into Whiteoak Creek.

Long Branch rises in sw Macon County and
flows w into Nantahala River.

Long Branch rises in e Madison County and
flows nw into Big Laurel Creek.

Long Branch rises in s Madison County and
flows s into Ivy River.

Long Branch rises in w Madison County and
flows e into Meadow Fork.

Long Branch rises in n McDowell County on the
s slope of Pompey Ridge and flows se into
Armstrong Creek.

Long Branch rises in ne McDowell County and
flows n into Pepper Creek.

Long Branch rises in s Mitchell County and
flows sw and w into Big Crabtree Creek.

Long Branch rises in sw Polk County and flows
nw into Pacolet River.

Long Branch rises in central Randolph County and flows nw into Back Creek.

Long Branch rises in e Robeson County and flows se into Big Swamp.

Long Branch rises in ne Rutherford County and flows se into Cleveland County, where it enters Duncans Creek.

Long Branch rises in n central Swain County and flows sw into Lands Creek.

Long Branch rises in sw Swain County and flows sw into Siles Branch approx. 1 mi. se of community of Almond.

Long Branch rises in ne Transylvania County and flows se into Sitton Creek.

Long Branch rises in w Transylvania County and flows ne into Davidson River.

Long Branch rises in w Transylvania County and flows se into North Fork French Broad River.

Long Branch rises near the e border of Vance County and flows ne into w Warren County, where it enters Matthews Creek.

Long Branch rises in central Wake County and flows s into Marsh Creek.

Long Branch rises in s Warren County and flows e into Fishing Creek.

Long Branch rises in e Watauga County and flows s into Southwest Stony Fork Creek.

Long Branch rises in n Watauga County and flows sw into Cove Creek.

Long Branch rises in s Watauga County and flows se into Caldwell County, where it enters China Creek. Approx. 1 mi. long.

Long Branch rises in central Wilkes County and flows se into Mulberry Creek.

Long Branch rises in sw Wilson County and flows se into Black Creek.

Long Branch rises in e Yancey County and flows nw into South Toe River.

Long Branch rises in n Yancey County and flows ne into Cane River.

Long Branch rises in n Yancey County and flows ne into Pigpen Creek.

Long Branch, community in se Cleveland County.

Long Branch, community in s Robeson County.

Long Brook rises in s Catawba County and flows sw into Pinch Gut Creek.

Long Bunk, ridge in w Haywood County in Great Smoky Mountains National Park extending se from Mount Sterling Ridge, with its center near lat. 35°41'10" N., long. 83°06'40" W. Lies between Andy Branch and Dude Creek.

Long Cove, n Swain County between Bearwallow Ridge and Long Cove Ridge.

Long Cove Ridge, n Swain County in Great Smoky Mountains National Park extending sw from Proctor Ridge, lat. 35°33'15" N., long. 83°36'25" W.

Long Creek rises in ne Catawba County and flows se and e into McLin Creek.

Long Creek rises in the town of Kings Mountain in se Cleveland County and flows se into Buffalo Creek.

Long Creek rises in se Craven County and flows n into Neuse River.

Long Creek rises in Great Swamp, central Currituck County, and flows s into North River.

Long Creek rises in w Gaston County and flows e into South Fork Catawba River.

Long Creek rises in s Graham County and flows n into Santeetlah Lake.

Long Creek rises in s Martin County and flows ne into Hardison Mill Creek.

Long Creek rises in n Mecklenburg County and flows sw into Catawba River. Appears as Wis's Creek on the Collet map, 1770, but with its present name on the Price map, 1808.

Long Creek rises in e Pamlico County and flows e and n into Bonner Bay.

Long Creek rises in nw Pender County and flows se into Northeast Cape Fear River. Appears on the Moseley map, 1733.

Long Creek rises in s Rowan County and flows across the ne tip of Cabarrus County; it enters n Stanly County, where it runs the entire length of the county before entering Rocky River on the border of Stanly and Anson Counties.

Long Creek rises in nw Stanly County and flows se and sw into Rocky River. Appears on the Collet map, 1770.

Long Creek rises in w Surry County and flows se into Mitchell River.

Long Creek rises in e Swain County and flows sw into Una Creek.

Long Creek rises in s Vance County and flows s into Tabbs Creek.

Long Creek, community in Mecklenburg County served by post office, 1873–74.

Long Creek, community in s Pender County on the stream of the same name. Alt. 50. Formerly known as Lillington, but the name was changed after the town of the same name was est. in Harnett County in 1859.

Long Creek Township, w central Mecklenburg County, now township no. 11.

Long Creek Township, s central Pender County.

Long Creek Village. *See* Lillington.

Long Drive Ridge, n Swain County in Great Smoky Mountains National Park, extends sw from Thomas Ridge, lat. 35°33′25″ N., long. 83°23′38″ W.

Long Fork of Beaver Creek rises in sw Wilkes County and flows e into Beaver Creek.

Long Gap, sw Buncombe County between Rich Knob and Ferrin Knob.

Long Gap, on the Buncombe-McDowell county line between Pot Cove Gap and Sourwood Gap.

Long Hill Township, ne Surry County.

Long Hollow, at the head of Left Fork [Cane Creek] in e Mitchell County.

Long Hope Creek rises in nw Watauga County and flows n into sw Ashe County, where it enters Three Top Creek.

Long Hungry Ridge, nw Swain County in Great Smoky Mountains National Park between Twentymile Creek and Moore Springs Branch, lat. 35°31′08″ N., long. 83°50′57″ W.

Longhurst, community in central Person County. Settled about 1890 and known first as Jalong for J. A. Long Sr., who est. a cotton mill there. Post office est. there in 1913; name changed to Longhurst in 1936.

Long Island, a long tidal-marsh island in Bogue Sound, sw Carteret County.

Long Island, high ground in e central Tyrrell County at the ne end of Hollow Ground Swamp.

Long Island, community in e Catawba County. Post office operated there from 1894 to 1949. Former site now covered by waters of Cowan's Ford Dam. The post office and many homes were moved to nearby higher ground. Named for an island in the Catawba River. An earlier post office approx. 1 mi. away was known as Shawnee, 1888–1904.

Long Island, community in w Iredell County on Catawba River.

Long John Mountain, central Henderson County, extends from the nw limits of Hendersonville almost to French Broad River. Named for an early whiskey distiller.

Long Lake, natural lake in Croatan National Forest, s Craven County. Covers 1,100 acres;

max. depth 4 to 5 ft. One of several lakes in Lakes Pocosin.

Longleaf, community in nw Moore County served by post office, 1886–1906.

Long Level Mountain, w central Avery County.

Long Level Mountain, e Mitchell County between Rube Green Top and Dellinger Hollow.

Long Levels, a rocky elevation approx. 1½ mi. long in e Haywood County between the head of Silvers Cove Creek and Long Levels Branch. Numerous other small unnamed streams rise there.

Long Levels Branch rises in e Haywood County and flows se into Bald Creek.

Long Mountain, sw Buncombe County; approx. 1¼ mi. long.

Long Mountain, w Madison County between John Taylor Branch and Turkey Cove Branch.

Long Mountain, w Montgomery County between Clarks Creek and Pee Dee River.

Long Mountain, a long level ridge, s Randolph County e of Poison Fork.

Long Mountain, n Rutherford County on Chalk Creek.

Long Mountain, ne Rutherford County between Molly Fork and the head of First Broad River.

Long Mountain Branch rises in w Madison County near Long Mountain and flows e into Spring Creek.

Long Neck Point, peninsula extending from w Goose Creek Island into Goose Creek at the mouth of Upper Spring Creek, ne Pamlico County.

Long Pine, community in sw Anson County. Named for local Methodist church est. 1791–95. A post office operated there from 1869 to 1906.

Long Point, on s side of Pamlico River, se Beaufort County.

Long Point, ne Carteret County, a se point of Cedar Island extending into the waters of Core Sound.

Long Point, a long, narrow point of land extending off a tidal-marsh island adjacent to Piney Island in the waters of Coinjock Bay, central Currituck County. The Intracoastal Waterway separates the small island from the parent island (Piney). Gas for lighthouses was produced there.

Long Point, peninsula extending se from a small tidal-marsh island in Currituck Sound, s Currituck County. The island lies immediately s of Rattle Snake Island and e of Poplar Branch Bay.

Long Point, a peninsula extending from the mainland of central Dare County into East Lake.

Long Point, se extremity of North Banks in ne Dare County between Kitty Hawk Bay and Currituck Sound. Long Point actually is separated from North Banks by very shallow water.

Long Point extends from the e mainland of Hyde County into Pamlico Sound.

Long Reach Sein Hole, a shallow place in Northeast Cape Fear River in central Duplin County suitable for seining.

Long Ridge, mountain in se Avery County.

Long Ridge, w Cherokee County, extends ne from Apalachia Dam on Hiwassee River. Named for its length.

Long Ridge, a sandy ridge extending from s Craven County below Great Lake into nw Carteret County.

Long Ridge, s Macon County between Barkers Creek and Commissioner Creek.

Long Ridge, ne Swain County in Great Smoky Mountains National Park extending sw from Hughs Ridge, lat. 35°37′ N., long. 83°19′ W.

Long Ridge, s Tyrrell County, is a stretch of loam surrounded by peat extending se at the head of Southwest Fork [Alligator River].

Long Ridge, an elevated area of clay loam in n Washington County extending s from the forks of Kendricks Creek to the edge of East Dismal Swamp. One of the sites of earliest settlement in Washington County. Appears on the Price map, 1808, and mentioned in local court records as early as 1718. *See also* Long Acre.

Long Ridge, w Watauga County n of Laurel Creek.

Long Ridge. *See* Hoke.

Long Run. *See* Little Creek.

Longs Delight appears on the Ogilby map, 1671, near the upper portion of the Cape Fear River. It was a name assigned probably for Capt. Anthony Long, member of an expedition led by Capt. William Hilton in 1663 to explore the lower Cape Fear region. *See also* Lockwoods Folly Inlet.

Long Shoal, in the waters of Pamlico Sound off the se mainland of Dare County. The waters of Parched Corn Bay lie between it and the mainland.

Long Shoal Bay, the mouth of Long Shoal River in s Dare County.

Long Shoal Point extends from the mainland of s Dare County into Pamlico Sound. Appears on the Moseley map, 1733.

Long Shoal Point, ne Tyrrell County, extends from the mainland into the mouth of Alligator River near the mouth of Alligator Creek.

Long Shoal River rises in the s mainland of Dare County and flows se along the Dare-Hyde county line into Long Shoal Bay in Pamlico Sound. Appears on the Moseley map, 1733.

Long Shoals, community in s Buncombe County on French Broad River.

Longshoals, community in s Lincoln County on South Fork Catawba River. Settled prior to 1901. Named for shoals in the river. Alt. 732.

Long Shoals Mill Pond, s Lincoln County on South Fork Catawba River. Formed 1901 to provide power for cotton mill. Covers 125 acres; max. depth 12 ft.

Long Shore Branch rises in e Ashe County and flows n into North Fork New River.

Longs Island, name applied on the Ogilby map, 1671, to the land now in nw New Hanover County between the Brunswick and Cape Fear Rivers n of Eagles Island. The peninsula was formerly an island when Fishing Creek flowed between the two rivers. *See also* Longs Delight.

Longs Store, community in w Person County.

Longs Store, community in n central Rutherford County.

Long's Store, community in n Union County.

Longtown, community in w Burke County.

Longtown, community in se Lincoln County.

Longtown, community in w Yadkin County on South Deep Creek.

Long Town. *See* Gold Point.

Longview, town in nw Catawba County w of Hickory. Inc. 1907. Earlier known as Penelope. Served by post office of that name, 1888–1904.

Longview, community in se Guilford County served by post office, 1891–1901.

Longwood, community in sw Brunswick County.

Longwood Park, community on the outskirts of Hamlet, s Richmond County. Known also as Northeast Hamlet.

Lonnie-Womble Creek rises in n Lee County and flows se into Cape Fear River.

Lookadoo Mountain, n Rutherford County

between Carson Mountain and the head of Duncans Creek.

Looking Glass Creek rises in n Transylvania County e of Bennett Gap on the Haywood-Transylvania county line and flows s into Davidson River. Located in Pisgah National Forest.

Looking Glass Falls, n Transylvania County on Looking Glass Creek about ½ mi. upstream from its mouth on Davidson River. The falls are 85 ft. high. Located in Pisgah National Forest.

Looking Glass Rock, n Transylvania County on the se end of Seniard Ridge in Pisgah National Forest. Named because the huge rock face of the mountain glistens like a giant mirror.

Lookoff Gap, se Buncombe County near Flat Top in the Swannanoa Mountains.

Lookout Bight, a bay in the waters of the Atlantic Ocean formed by the s end of Shackleford and Core Banks in se Carteret County in connection with a stone breakwater started before World War I but never completed.

Lookout Bight Channel. *See* Barden Inlet.

Lookout Knob, ne Catawba County.

Lookout Knob, se Yancey County near the head of Roaring Fork.

Lookout Mountain, central Buncombe County between Woodfin and Asheville.

Lookout Mountain, ne Buncombe County se of Montreat.

Lookout Point, the s tip of Cedar Island extending into the waters of Core Sound in ne Carteret County.

Lookout Shoals Lake, on Catawba River, bounded by Iredell and Alexander Counties on the n and Catawba County on the s. Formed by a dam constructed in 1915 by Duke Power Co. Covers 1,270 acres. Source of hydroelectric power; fishing, boating, and camping. *See also* Island Ford.

Loose Mountain, w Caldwell County.

Loosen Swamp. *See* Corapeake Swamp.

Loosing Swamp rises in n central Bertie County and flows ne into Stony Creek. Mentioned in local records as early as 1725.

Loosing Swamp rises in n central Lenoir County and flows e for approx. 5 mi. into Stonyton Creek. The name appears in local records as early as 1744. It is believed to be derived from Lucerne, the Swiss city, and was given to the swamp by Swiss settlers who moved into the area from New Bern in the early eighteenth century. Also appears as Louson, Lousin, and Luzern.

Lorane, community in nw Rockingham County served by post office, 1898–1904.

Loray, community in w Iredell County. Grew up around Concord Church, est. 1775. Prior to 1903, when it was given its present name by Ora Sharpe, it was known as Fancy Hill post office and Iredell Station on the railroad.

Lords Creek rises in n central Cumberland County and flows sw between Dunfields Creek and Locks Creek to empty into Cape Fear River e of the town of Fayetteville. The stream appears as both Lords Creek and Locks Creek, *which see*, on the Kerr map, 1882, but the error is corrected by the McDuffie map, 1884.

Lords Creek rises in s New Hanover County and flows w into the Cape Fear River. Named for the Lord family of Brunswick County.

Loretta, community in s Catawba County served by post office, 1893–1904.

Lost Bottom Creek, w Haywood County in Great Smoky Mountains National Park, rises near lat. 35°40′ N., long. 83°11′07″ W., and flows se into Palmer Creek.

Lost Cove, n Jackson County between Lost Cove Branch and Lickstone Ridge.

Lost Cove, n Yancey County on a short unnamed stream that flows nw into Nolichucky River.

Lost Cove, community in n Yancey County on Nolichucky River.

Lost Cove Branch rises in n Jackson County and flows se into Soco Creek.

Lost Cove Creek rises in e central Avery County and flows e into Caldwell County, where it enters Wilsons Creek.

Lost Cove Creek, in Great Smoky Mountains National Park, rises in nw Swain County and flows se into Fontana Lake.

Lost Cove Ridge, se Avery County.

Lost Cove Ridge, s Yancey County, extends ne parallel to South Toe River between Little Lost Cove Creek and Big Lost Cove Creek.

Lost Knob, e Jackson County between Lynn Gap and Deep Gap.

Lost Ridge, n Watauga County, extends ne of Forest Grove Creek.

Lotta, community in n Hertford County served by post office, 1887–1909.

Lottie Creek rises in nw Yancey County and flows se into Bald Mountain Creek.

Loudermilk Ridge, w Swain County in Great Smoky Mountains National Park, lat. 35°28′33″ N., long. 83°39′48″ W.

Louie Camp Branch rises in n Swain County and flows se into Bradley Fork.

Louisburg, town and county seat, central Franklin County on Tar River. Alt. 280. Authorized to be laid out and named Lewisburg, 1779. Named for French king Louis XVI, to whose court Benjamin Franklin (for whom the county was named) was then American representative. Both spellings occur in early records, the present form soon becoming the only one used. Home of Louisburg College. Produces lumber and fabricated metals.

Louisburg Township, former township in central Franklin County, now township no. 10.

Louise, community in s Catawba County served by post office, 1890–1903.

Louis Ray Knob, ne Buncombe County.

Louse Island, nw Washington County in the mouth of Roanoke River. In a cluster of marshy islands, Louse Island is one of the smallest, approx. 2,000 ft. long and 200 ft. wide. It lies in the river between Rice Island and the mainland. *See also* Purchace Islands.

Lousin Swamp. *See* Loosing Swamp.

Louson Swamp. *See* Loosing Swamp.

Lousy Creek rises in n central Wilkes County and flows s into Reddies River.

Louzanla Islands, area of fine sandy loam surrounded by swamp in e Washington County, sw of the community of Scuppernong.

Love Joy, community in n Montgomery County. Formerly known as Queen and had a post office by the name, 1888–1933. Often spelled Lovejoy.

Love Knob, w Watauga County at the n end of Ward Hollow.

Lovelace, community in se Wilkes County between Little Hunting Creek and Hunting Creek. Named for Archibald Lovelace, prominent early-nineteenth-century resident.

Lovelace Creek rises in s Alleghany County and flows s into Wilkes County, where it joins Basin Creek in forming Middle Prong Roaring River.

Lovelace Gap, n Buncombe County between Lovelace Knob and Jess Knob.

Lovelace Knob, n Buncombe County nw of Lovelace Gap. Alt. 4,315.

Lovelaces Creek rises in e Rockingham County and flows ne into Wolf Island Creek. Named for local landowner, John Lovelace.

Lovelace Township, se Wilkes County.

Lovelady, community in nw Mecklenburg County served by post office, 1894–1902.

Lovelady Township, e central Burke County.

Lovelady Township, se Caldwell County. Named for a projected town, Lovelady, planned by Abner Summers before the Civil War. Lovelady post office, est. 1834, served a rural area, but it was moved in 1887 and the name was changed to Granite Falls, *which see*.

Loveland. *See* Willis Creek.

Love Mountain, n Henderson County between Belmont Mountain and Clear Creek.

Lovers Leap, high point overlooking Hiwassee River in central Cherokee County.

Lovers Leap Ridge, n Madison County between Silvermine Branch and Pump Branch.

Loves Creek rises in w Chatham County and flows e into Rocky River.

Lovesfield, community in central Jackson County.

Loves Fish Lake, ne Surry County on Toms Creek. Covers 8 acres; max. depth 30 ft. Fishing. Named for J. B. Love, owner. Created 1949.

Loves Ford, n Union County in Rocky River.

Love's Level, community in n Union County.

Lovett Island, a small island in sw Carteret County in Bogue Sound. Apparently named for the family whose surname appears in the old records as Lovett, Lovitt, and Lovick. Thomas Lovett or Lovick was an early landowner in the county.

Love Valley. *See* Fox's Mountain.

Loviade Mountain, n Madison County between Wolf Branch and the head of Spillcorn Creek.

Lovill, community in central Watauga County on Brushy Fork. Named for Capt. Edward F. Lovill of Boone. Alt. 3,112.

Lovills Creek, approx. 18 mi. long, rises in Virginia and flows s into Surry County, where it enters Ararat River.

Lowder, community in se Stanly County served by post office, 1889–1907.

Lowe, community in central Robeson County served by post office, 1890–1949.

Lowell, town in central Gaston County. Settled

about 1850 when Woodlawn Mill was built on South Fork River. First known as Wrights Station for William Wright, nearest resident. Inc. 1879 as Lowell because the construction of several textile mills there suggested the name of the textile center in Massachusetts. Alt. 770.

Lowe Mountain, w Randolph County between Taylors Creek and Caraway Creek. Named for Dan Lowe.

Lower Bartons Creek rises in nw Wake County at community of Leesville and flows ne into Neuse River just e of mouth of Upper Bartons Creek, *which see.*

Lower Beaverdam Creek rises in w Scotland County and flows se into Gum Swamp Creek.

Lower Broad Creek. *See* Broad Creek.

Lower Campbellton. *See* Fayetteville.

Lower Coneto Township, former township in e central Edgecombe County, now township no. 2.

Lower Creek rises in ne Caldwell County and flows sw across the county and into n Burke County, where it enters Catawba River.

Lower Creek rises in s Transylvania County and flows sw into East Fork French Broad River.

Lower Creek rises in s Yancey County and flows se into South Toe River.

Lower Creek Township, n central Burke County.

Lower Creek Township, e central Caldwell County.

Lower Cullasaja Falls, se Macon County nw of Highlands on Cullasaja River. Water falls a total of 310 ft. in ¼ mi. *See also* Cullasaja River.

Lower Double Branch rises in w Haywood County and flows se into Cataloochee Creek.

Lower Dowry Creek rises in e Beaufort County and flows approx. 2 mi. sw into Pungo River.

Lower Falls, on the Graham County, N.C.–Monroe County, Tenn., line on Slickrock Creek. Water drops 1,200 ft.

Lower Ferry on New River. *See* Sneads Ferry.

Lower Fishing Creek, former township in ne Edgecombe County, now township no. 5.

Lower Fork Township, se Burke County.

Lower Grassy Branch rises in n Swain County and flows sw into Kephart Prong.

Lower Hominy Township, w central Buncombe County.

Lower Little River rises in sw Moore County and flows e through Moore County, forms the n boundary of Fort Bragg Military Reservation in Hoke and Cumberland Counties, and continues in part along the Cumberland-Harnett county line to Cape Fear River.

Lower Little River. *See* Little River.

Lower Norfolk County. *See* County of Norfolk.

Lower Pigeon. *See* Clyde.

Lower Sassafras Gap, n Swain County in Great Smoky Mountains National Park on Noland Divide near the head of Bridge Creek, lat. 35°31′09″ N., long. 83°27′15″ W.

Lower Saura Town, former Indian village in ne Rockingham County on Dan River. Site approx. 2 mi. e of Leaksville. Probably occupied by Saura Indians by the middle of the seventeenth century and abandoned in early eighteenth century. Saura or Sara meant "a place of tall grass or weeds." *See also* Upper Saura Town; Town Creek.

Lower Second Creek. *See* South Second Creek.

Lower Spring Creek rises in se Beaufort County and flows e into Goose Creek.

Lower Town Creek Township, former township in s Edgecombe County, now township no. 10.

Lower Trail Ridge, se Macon County between Devils Prong and Little Indian Creek.

Lowery Cove, n Buncombe County nw of Thurz Mountain.

Lowery Creek rises in s Macon County and flows ne into Cartoogechaye Creek.

Lowery Creek rises in s Macon County between Devils Prong and Little Indian Creek.

Lowery Knob, central Macon County between Dobson Branch and Salser Branch.

Lowery Mill Creek rises in n central Forsyth County and flows s and sw into Salem Lake.

Lowes Grove, community in s Durham County on w edge of Research Triangle Park.

Lowesville, community in se Lincoln County. Named for Lowe family.

Low Falls. *See* Cullasaja River.

Low Gap, w Avery County in Roan Mountain.

Low Gap, n Buncombe County at the se end of Ike Mountain.

Low Gap, e Haywood County on Lee Mountain.

Low Gap, nw Haywood County on the head of Low Gap Branch.

Low Gap, on the Haywood County, N.C.–Cocke County, Tenn., line in Great Smoky Mountains National Park near lat. 35°44′16″ N., long. 83°10′50″ W.

Low Gap, between Rich Mountain and West Fork [Dicks Creek] in nw Jackson County.

Low Gap, s Macon County between High Top and McDowell Mountain.

Low Gap, on the Macon-Swain county line near the head of Brush Creek.

Low Gap, on the Mitchell County, N.C.–Unicoi County, Tenn., line.

Low Gap, e Yancey County between Sevenmile Ridge and Crabtree Creek.

Low Gap, s central Yancey County between Bowlens Creek and Low Gap Hollow.

Lowgap, community in nw Surry County. Named for a nearby low gap in the Blue Ridge Mountains.

Low Gap, community in s central Yancey County.

Low Gap Branch rises in nw Haywood County and flows se into Big Creek.

Low Gap Hollow, s central Yancey County between Cane River and Bowlens Creek.

Low Gap Wildlife Pond, nw Surry County on North Fork Mitchell River. Covers 12 acres; max. depth 26 ft. Formed 1954 and owned by Low Gap Wildlife Club. Fishing.

Lowing Bald, sw Swain County near the head of Big Creek.

Lowland, community on w Goose Creek Island, ne Pamlico County. Post office est. 1892. Processes seafood.

Loy, community in s Alamance County served by post office, 1879–1905. Known as Loy's Shop until 1895.

Loyal Creek. *See* Riles Creek.

Loyd, community in sw Lincoln County served by post office, 1885–1906.

Loy's Store. *See* Loy.

Luart, community in central Harnett County.

Lucama, town in s Wilson County. Alt. 140. Known earlier as Lucas's Crossroads. Name derived about 1883, according to tradition, by Josephus Daniels, then editor of a newspaper in Wilson, from the initial letters of the names of three friends: Lucy, Carrie, and Mary Borden. Post office est. 1884. Inc. 1889.

Lucas Creek rises in se Bladen County and flows sw into Cape Fear River.

Lucia, community in ne Gaston County. Oak Grove, home of James Johnston, officer in the Revolutionary War and member of the Provincial Congress, the N.C. legislature, and the Convention of 1788, is 2 mi. e. The house, built in 1782, still stands.

Lucile, community in e Wilkes County served by post office, 1887–1905.

Luck, community in sw Madison County on Spring Creek.

Lucknow. *See* Dunn.

Lucks Island appears on the Comberford map, 1657, as the present Currituck Banks, e Currituck County. It was mentioned as the n limits of Carolina in the charter granted in 1663 to the 8 Lords Proprietors. *See also* Currituck Banks; Croatamung.

Lucy Branch rises in s Lenoir County and flows ne into Spring Branch.

Luftee Gap, n Swain County in Great Smoky Mountains on Thomas Ridge, lat. 35°36′30″ N., long. 83°26′23″ W. Alt. approx. 5,200.

Luftee Knob, on Haywood-Swain county line in Great Smoky Mountains National Park near lat. 35°41′34″ N., long. 83°10′30″ W., between Balsam Corner and Mount Sterling Ridge. Alt. 6,216.

Lukens, former community in n Carteret County. Abandoned following a severe storm in 1933. Church, houses, and school moved across South River to the communities of South River and Merrimon. Named for the Lukens family.

Lul, community in e Wake County.

Lumbee River. *See* Lumber River.

Lumber Bridge, across Cashie River in central Bertie County. Appears on the Collet map, 1770. The lumber bridge stood as late as 1833, and there is still a bridge across the river at the site.

Lumber Bridge, town in ne Robeson County. Alt. 192. Settled about 1776. Inc. 1891. Named for the wooden bridge across Little Marsh Swamp there.

Lumber Bridge Township, n Robeson County.

Lumber River is formed on the Moore-Richmond county line where Naked Creek enters Drowning Creek. It flows se along the Moore-Richmond and Hoke-Scotland county lines and for a short distance along the Robeson-Scotland county line. It then flows se, e, and s across Robeson County to the Columbus-Robeson county line, which it follows into South Carolina. A short distance s of the state line, Lumber River enters Little Pee Dee River. It is approx. 125 mi. long. Sometimes known locally as Lumbee River.

Lumbershed Marsh, a tidal-marsh island in the

w end of Bogue Sound, se Onslow County, between Dudleys Island and Cedar Point. Named for a lumber shed built there during a lumber-industry boom.

Lumberton, city and county seat, e central Robeson County on Lumber River. Alt. 137. Inc. 1788. Laid out on Red Bluff Plantation, owned by John Willis. Named for Lumber River. East Lumberton and West Lumberton, *which see*, formerly inc. municipalities, were made a part of the city of Lumberton in 1953.

Lumberton. *See* Gatlington.

Lumberton. *See* Leechville.

Lumberton Township, e central Robeson County.

Lump Mountain, n Rutherford County near the head of Chalk Creek.

Lumptown, community in central Madison County at the head of Revere Creek.

Lunday, community in w central Mitchell County on Toe River. Alt. 2,346.

Luneville. *See* Polkton.

Lupton, former community on the southernmost island in the Hog Island group, ne Carteret County. Named for Lupton family.

Lupton Lake, in s Jackson County ne of Cashiers on Horsepasture River. Formed in 1924; covers 15 acres and has max. depth of 40 ft. Named for owner. Used for fishing, swimming, and boating and as a power source. Open to the public.

Luster, community in ne Durham County served by post office, 1881–1903.

Luther Branch rises in ne Cherokee County on Brushy Head Mountain and flows ne into Taylor Creek.

Luther Gap, sw Buncombe County between Luther Knob and Stony Knob.

Luther Knob, sw Buncombe County between Luther Gap and Dix Creek Gap.

Luthers, community in sw Buncombe County.

Luthersville. *See* China Grove.

Lutterloh, community in central Chatham County served by post office, 1894–1907.

Lutz Creek, a marsh creek in sw Currituck County, flows sw into North River.

Lyddies Creek rises in ne Mitchell County and flows nw into Big Rock Creek.

Lydia, community in w Sampson County served by post office, 1891–1907.

Lydia Creek rises in e Transylvania County and flows se into French Broad River.

Lydie Mountain, n Buncombe County in the Elk Mountains.

Lyle Creek rises in n Catawba County and flows se into Catawba River. Appears on Collet map, 1770, as Liles Creek.

Lyle Knob, e Macon County between Mason Mountain and the head of Thompson Branch. Alt. approx. 3,600.

Lyman, community in se Duplin County.

Lynch, community in sw Madison County.

Lynchburg, community in sw Lenoir County.

Lynch Cove, se Buncombe County e of Sheep Ridge.

Lynch Creek rises in n Orange County and flows n into Caswell County, where it enters North Hyco Creek.

Lynch Creek rises in s Vance County and flows s into Franklin County, where it enters Tar River. Appears as Linches Creek on the Collet map, 1770. Said to have been named for a Major Lynch, who was sent to Bute County (now Franklin and Warren Counties) by Governor Tryon in 1768 to collect taxes but was hanged by a mob of Regulators on the bank of the stream.

Lynches Creek rises in s Union County and flows s into South Carolina, where it enters Pee Dee River. Appears on the Collet map, 1770. Also sometimes known as Lynches River.

Lynches River. *See* Lynches Creek.

Lynchs Corner, community in n Pasquotank County.

Lynchum Branch. *See* Lindscomb Branch.

Lyndover, community in nw Durham County.

Lynesville. *See* Townsville.

Lynn, town in s Polk County on Skyuka Creek. Inc. 1911, but long inactive in municipal affairs. Named for Lynn McAboy, son of Dr. L. R. McAboy, an early settler. Alt. 1,500.

Lynn Branch rises in ne Swain County and flows ne into Straight Fork [Raven Fork].

Lynn Cove, se Swain County, extends n from Shepherd Bald to Yalaka Creek.

Lynn Gap, e Jackson County between Lost Knob and High Knob.

Lynn Gap, on the McDowell-Mitchell county line.

Lynn Mountain, sw Catawba County. Alt. approx. 1,300. Believed to have been named for a pioneer settler. Sometimes also spelled Linn.

Lynn's Branch rises in nw Wake County and flows se into Sycamore Creek.

Lyon Branch rises in n Clay County and flows sw into Tusquitee Creek.

Lyon Creek. *See* Lyon Swamp Canal.

Lyons, community in sw Granville County served by post office, 1889–1928. Alt. 346.

Lyons. *See* Haywood.

Lyons Creek rises in n Franklin County and flows ne into Devil's Cradle Creek.

Lyons Landing, community in nw Bladen County served by post office, 1850–1903.

Lyon Swamp, se Bladen County e of Cape Fear River.

Lyon Swamp Canal, se Bladen County, drains se from Lyon Swamp into sw Pender County, where it is called Lyon Creek before emptying into Lyon Thorofare.

Lyon Thorofare, sw Pender County, connects Cape Fear River with Black River approx. 4 mi. above their natural junction. Approx. 3 mi. long.

Lytchs Millpond, s Scotland County on Gum Swamp Creek. Formed 1870. Covers 325 acres; max. depth 12 ft.

Lytle Cove, the valley through which Stepp Branch flows in se Buncombe County.

M

Mabel, community in n Watauga County on Cove Creek.

Mabry, community in central Stanly County served by post office, 1889–1906.

MacArthur. *See* Japan.

Macay's Mill, an early Rowan County landmark. It was used as a recruiting place for soldiers during the Revolutionary War as well as a point of discharge. It was owned for many years by Judge Spruce Macay, who taught Andrew Jackson law in Salisbury. The mill, on Grants Creek in the se section of the county, was built by Thomas Frohock and later sold to Macay. The mill was used until World War I, although the millpond was drained about 1870 because of fever epidemics. Appears on the Collet map, 1770, as Frohock Mill.

Macclesfield, town in s Edgecombe County. Inc. 1901 and named for Macclesfield, England, town of origin of the ancestors of Henry Clark Bridgers, founder of East Carolina Railroad. Alt. 100.

Mace Branch rises in n McDowell County on the s slope of Stony Knob and flows se about 1½ mi. into Rag Creek.

Macedonia, community in s Cherokee County.

Macedonia, community in w Chowan County at the mouth of Rockyhock Creek. Named for local Baptist church.

Macedonia, community in w Montgomery County served by post office, 1841–1908.

Macedonia, community in w Wake County between Swift Creek and Walnut Creek.

Macedonia, community in ne Yadkin County.

Macedonia. *See* Basnight.

Machapounga River. *See* Pungo River.

Machapunga, Machapungo. *See* Pungo.

Machapunga Bluff. *See* Bluff Point.

Machelhe Island, marsh island about ½ mi. long in the Pasquotank River, w Camden County opposite Elizabeth City. Probably named for the Macheel family, living in the area as early as 1723.

Machine Branch rises in nw Cumberland County and flows n into Little River.

Machine Creek rises in e central Polk County and flows se into Whiteoak Creek.

Machpelah, community in se Lincoln County served by post office, 1881–1908.

Mack, community in central Rutherford County served by post office, 1889–1907.

Mackay Island, a portion of sw Knotts Island, ne Currituck County. It is separated from Knotts Island by Indian Creek and Back Creek, an inlet of North Landing River. Approx. 2 mi. long and 2 mi. wide. Appears as Notts or Mackys Island on the Collet map, 1770.

Mackerel Mountain, on the Henderson County, N.C.–Greenville County, S.C., line. Alt. 3,031.

Mackey Mountain, w McDowell County. Alt. 3,994.

Mackeys, community in n Washington County w of the mouth of Kendricks Creek on Albemarle Sound. Alt. 8. Settled about 1765 near the s terminus of Mackeys Ferry, *which see*, named for Col. William Mackey, local landowner. Post office est. 1856 as Mackeys Ferry;

name changed to Mackeys in 1913. Mackeys
Ferry appears on the Collet map, 1770.

Mackeys Creek rises in w McDowell County and
flows se into Catawba River.

Mackeys Creek. *See* Kendricks Creek.

Mackeys Ferry, formerly located at the present
community of Mackeys in n Washington
County on Kendricks Creek. Shown as
T. Bells Ferry on the Moseley map, 1733;
purchased from Bell by Col. William Mackey
in 1735; was in continuous operation until
1938. At the time it was dismantled, the ferry
operated between Edenton in s Chowan
County and the s shore of Albemarle Sound
immediately n of Pleasant Grove in n
Washington County.

Mack Gap, w Jackson County on the head of Sutton Branch.

Mack Hill Gap, n Yancey County on McKinney
Branch.

Mack Perry Pond, on Fowlers Creek, ne Wake
County. Covers 38 acres; max. depth 20 ft.
Used for fishing and irrigation.

Macks, community in w Johnston County.

Mack Williams Branch rises in w Yancey County
and flows se into Jacks Creek.

Maco, community in ne Brunswick County.
Named Farmers Turnout in 1867, but about
1890 intended to be named Maraco for the
MacRae Co., which developed land in the
vicinity. The present name, easier to pro-
nounce, came into use instead. Alt. 49. Site of
the "Maco Light," an unidentified phenom-
enon that has been recurring frequently since
a train wreck there in 1867. Traditionally, the
light is said to be the lantern of Joe Baldwin,
a railroad conductor who was killed while
attempting to prevent the wreck. President
Grover Cleveland purportedly saw the light in
1889 and asked for an explanation.

Macon, town in n central Warren County on
heads of Sixpound Creek and Walkers Creek.
Alt. 285. Settled in early 1800s and shown as
Chestnut Crossroads on the MacRae map,
1833. Post office of Macon est. in 1839. Inc.
1889; named for Nathaniel Macon (1758–
1837), speaker of the U. S. House of Representatives, member of Congress from 1815
to 1828, and president of N.C. Constitutional
Convention, 1835. A Civil War training camp,
Camp Macon, was located there.

Macon County was formed in 1828 from Haywood County. Located in the w section of the
state, it is bounded by the state of Georgia
and by Clay, Cherokee, Swain, and Jackson
Counties. It was named for Nathaniel Macon
(1758–1837), speaker of the U.S. House of
Representatives and U.S. senator. Area: 520
sq. mi. County seat: Franklin, with an elevation of 2,113 ft. Townships are Burningtown,
Cartoogechaye, Cowee, Ellijay, Flats, Franklin, Highlands, Millshoal, Nantahala, Smiths
Bridge, and Sugar Rock. Produces corn, dairy
products, livestock, hogs, textiles, lumber,
heavy equipment, hay, honey, plastics, and
mica.

Madcap Branch rises in ne Swain County and
flows nw into Bunches Creek.

Madge, community in se Mecklenburg County
served by post office, 1892–1903.

Mad Inlet, tidal waterway between Bald Beach
and Bird Island in sw Brunswick County.

Madison, town in w Rockingham County at the
junction of Mayo and Dan Rivers. Alt. 577.
Chartered in 1815, first sale of lots 1818; inc.
1851. Named for President James Madison
(1751–1836).

Madison County was formed in 1851 from Buncombe and Yancey Counties. Located in the w
section of the state, it is bounded by Yancey,
Buncombe, and Haywood Counties and the
state of Tennessee. It was named for James
Madison (1751–1836), fourth president of
the United States. Area: 456 sq. mi. County
seat: Marshall, with an elevation of 1,650 ft.
Townships, now numbered 1 to 16, were formerly Marshall, Shelton Laurel, Bull Creek,
Middle Fork of Ivy, West Fork of Ivy, Sandy
Mush, Little Pine Creek, Spring Creek, Hot

Springs, Big Laurel, Upper Laurel, Big Pine Creek, Meadow Fork of Spring Creek, Grapevine, Mars Hill, and Foster Creek. Produces tobacco, corn, dairy products, livestock, hay, nursery products, pumpkins, tomatoes, textiles, and electronics.

Madison Township, ne Guilford County. Named for President James Madison and his wife Dolley Payne, who was born at the Quaker settlement of New Garden, present site of Guilford College.

Madison Township, w Rockingham County.

Magazine Branch rises in central Cherokee County and flows sw and se into Valley River.

Maggie Valley, resort center in w Haywood County. Named when the first post office was est. in 1909 for Maggie Mae Setzer (later Mrs. Ira Pylant of Hendersonville), daughter of the postmaster. Alt. 3,019.

Maggot Ridge, w Haywood County in Great Smoky Mountains National Park, extends n from Buck Knob on Cataloochee Divide, center near lat. 35°33′45″ N., long. 83°08′32″ W. For origin of the name, *see* Maggot Spring Gap.

Maggot Spring Gap, w Haywood County in Great Smoky Mountains National Park near lat. 35°33′08″ N., long. 83°07′55″ W. Named for a nearby spring used by cattle rangers that had in it the larvae of an insect that resembled a maggot.

Magness Creek rises in e Cleveland County and flows s, nw, and s into First Broad River.

Magnetic City. *See* Buladean.

Magnolia, town in w Duplin County. Alt. 108. Inc. 1855 as Stricklandsville to be laid out on the lands of Jesse Strickland. Name changed to Magnolia, 1857, for magnolia trees growing there.

Magnolia, old Pettigrew family plantation in w Tyrrell County on shores of Lake Phelps. Built in 1830 by Ebenezer Pettigrew. Birthplace of Confederate general J. J. Pettigrew. Now part of Pettigrew State Park. Plantation, around house named Bonarva, covered approx. 2,000 acres.

Magnolia Canal. *See* Bonarva Canal.

Magnolia Township, sw Duplin County.

Magnus, community in ne Person County served by post office, 1899–1904.

Maho Creek rises in e Person County and flows n into Virginia, where it enters Hyco River.

Named Mayo River in 1728 by William Byrd and his "dividing line" survey party for William Mayo, one of the surveyors.

Mahogany Knob. *See* White Hurricane Knob.

Mahogany Rock, s Watauga County e of Blowing Rock on Blue Ridge Parkway. Alt. 3,425.

Mahogany Rock, summer resort in s Alleghany County.

Maiden, town in s central Catawba County. Alt. 891. Inc. 1883. Named for Maiden Creek, on which it is located. Produces furniture and textiles.

Maiden Cane Creek rises in w Wilkes County and flows ne into Reddies River.

Maiden Creek rises in s Catawba County and flows approx. 7 mi. sw into Clark Creek. Named for profusion of maidencane (*Poaceae hemitomon*) found growing in the bottomland nearby when first seen by early settlers.

Maidenhair Falls, s Jackson County on Trays Island Creek ½ mi. n of Fairfield Lake. Alt. 3,640.

Maidenhair Falls, se Transylvania County on Hogshead Creek 2 mi. se of Brevard. Water falls 50 ft.

Maiden Point extends into Jones Bay, ne Pamlico County. Named because the shoreline on maps resembles a female breast.

Main Canal extends nw from n central Washington County, where it receives the waters drained from East Dismal Swamp by a system of canals and channels them into Kendricks Creek.

Main Channel, in Bogue Sound sw Carteret County leading s into Bogue Inlet.

Main Creek rises in ne Buncombe County and flows nw into Reems Creek.

Maine. *See* Oak Grove.

Maitland, community in central Sampson County served by post office, 1887–1904.

Majolica, community in n central Rowan County on Southern Railway. Alt. 713. It is said that while V. C. McBee, railroad superintendent, was considering a name for the termination of a siding there, his clerk, T. C. McNeely, brought in a green majolica pot filled with drinking water. McNeely suggested that the water be used for christening and that the place be named for the pot.

Major Hills, mountain in s Alamance County.

Makatoka, community in nw Brunswick County.

Makleyville, community in sw Hyde County on Pungo River near the mouth of Slade Creek.

Malee, community in w Richmond County served by post office, 1881–1906.

Mallard, community in e Mecklenburg County served by post office, 1898–1903.

Mallard Creek rises in n Mecklenburg County and flows e into Cabarrus County, where it enters Rocky River. The name appears on the Collet map, 1770, though it is slightly misplaced.

Mallard Creek. *See* Town Creek.

Mallard Creek Township, former township in e central Mecklenburg County, now township no. 8.

Mall Creek rises in e Washington County, receives drainage from Enoch Canal, and flows ne into Scuppernong River. First shown on the MacRae map, 1833.

Malloby's Branch rises in central Wake County and flows se into Beaverdam Creek.

Mallory Creek rises in e Brunswick County and flows e into Cape Fear River.

Malloy, community in central Rockingham County served by post office, 1898–1903.

Malloys Pond. *See* Richmond Millpond.

Malmo, community in ne Brunswick County.

Malones Creek rises in w Warren County and flows nw into Blue Mud Creek.

Maltby, community in central Cherokee County between the junction of Cindy Branch and Dick Branch. Alt. 1,611.

Mamers, community in w Harnett County. A short distance se was the pre–Civil War community and post office of Fishcreek, which operated from 1914 to 1954. A muster ground for the county militia was there.

Mamie, farming community in s Currituck County on Albemarle Sound. Post office est. there in 1904 and named for Mamie Crank.

Manchester, town in nw Cumberland County on Little River. Inc. 1895, but long inactive in municipal affairs. Adjacent to Spring Lake.

Manchester Township, nw Cumberland County.

Maney Branch rises in n Buncombe County near Paint Fork Gap and flows sw into Reems Creek.

Maney Gap, on the Madison-Yancey county line near the head of Indian Creek. Alt. 3,848.

Maney's Ferry. *See* Riddicksville.

Maneys Neck Township, n Hertford County.

Mangum, community in nw Richmond County.

Mangum Store, community in ne Durham County on Dry Creek about 2 mi. n of Lake Michie. Named for Willie Person Mangum, U.S. senator and area landowner.

Mangum Township, n Durham County.

Manly, community in s Moore County. Inc. 1879 as Manly Station and in 1899 as Manly; no town government was est., and the charter was repealed in 1955. Named for Charles Manly (1795–1871), governor of North Carolina, 1849–51. Alt. 444.

Manly Mill Creek. *See* Jones Creek.

Manly Station. *See* Manly.

Manndale, community in sw Orange County.

Manning, community in w Rowan County served by post office, 1887–1906.

Mannings Township, w Nash County.

Mann Point, on the w shore of n Bodie Island in Roanoke Sound between Kill Devil Hills and Nags Head, e Dare County.

Manns Harbor, community on the e shore of the mainland, central Dare County on Croatan Sound. Settled in the early nineteenth century. Known earlier as Croatan. Named for a German sea captain, Charles Mann, who harbored there during a fierce storm. He later returned, with his wife and 9 children, to live. The Indian village of Dasemunkepeuc (Algonquian word meaning "where there is an extended land surface separated by water") was located there and is shown on the White maps, 1585 and 1590, and on the Velasco map, 1611. Alt. 10.

Manor Branch rises in nw Buncombe County near Newfound Mountain and flows ne into Sandy Mush Creek.

Mansfield, community in s Carteret County w of Morehead City.

Manson, town in w Warren County near the head of Rocky Creek. Inc. 1874, but not now active in municipal affairs. Alt. 424. First known as Cheathamville; name changed to Branchville in 1858 because the Roanoke Valley Railway branch joined the Raleigh and Gaston Railroad there. Name changed to Manson in 1859 in honor of Dr. O. F. Manson (1822–88), local physician and later a Confederate surgeon.

Manteo, town and county seat, on n Roanoke Island, e Dare County. Settled 1865. Inc. 1899. Named for the Indian chief Manteo, taken to England in 1584 by Philip Amadas and Arthur

Barlowe in the service of Walter Raleigh. Alt. 12. *The Lost Colony*, an outdoor drama by Paul Green, has been presented nearby each summer since 1937.

Manus, community in n Richmond County.

Maple, community in central Currituck County. Named for the *Maple Leaf*, a federal transport that grounded on Currituck Beach with 101 Confederate prisoners during the Civil War. Alt. 7.

Maple, community in n central Washington County.

Maple Bald Creek rises in s Yancey County and flows se into Rock Creek.

Maple Branch rises in nw Beaufort County and flows sw into Tranters Creek.

Maple Branch rises in s Warren County and flows se into Fishing Creek.

Maple Camp Bald, s Yancey County on the head of Maple Bald Creek. Alt. 5,275.

Maple Camp Ridge, s Yancey County between Middle Creek and Maple Creek.

Maple Creek rises in ne Cleveland County and flows sw into First Broad River.

Maple Creek rises in s Nash County and flows se into Tar River.

Maple Creek rises in nw Rutherford County and flows se into Mountain Creek.

Maple Creek rises in s Yancey County and flows e in an arc into Rock Creek.

Maple Cypress, community in nw Craven County served by post office, 1873–1904. Named for maple tree growing from cypress knee in Neuse River.

Maple Fork Branch rises in ne Northampton County and flows se and n to join a small unnamed stream that rises in Hertford County to form Turkey Creek.

Maple Gap, s Transylvania County in Blue Ridge Mountains near the head of Abrams Branch.

Maple Grove, community in nw Caldwell County near Staircase Mountain.

Maple Hill, community in ne Pender County on Moores Creek. Alt. 50. Named by a member of the Ashe family for the trees growing at the site. A post office as early as 1879. Angola, formerly considered to be a separate community (and with a post office as early as 1882), about 1½ mi. nw, is now considered to be within the Maple Hill community.

Maple Run rises in n Duplin County and flows ne into Goshen Swamp.

Maple Spring. *See* Mapleville.

Maple Spring Branch rises in w Madison County and flows ne into Meadow Fork.

Maple Spring Branch rises in e Union County and flows se into Beaverdam Creek.

Maple Spring Gap, on the Haywood-Madison county line. Alt. 4,050.

Maple Springs, community in s Swain County between the heads of Siles Branch and Tarkiln Branch.

Maple Springs, community in w Wilkes County on South Prong Lewis Fork Creek.

Maple Swamp, central Currituck County near the w shore of Currituck Sound.

Maple Swamp rises in n Edgecombe County and flows se into Fishing Creek.

Maple Swamp Creek rises in e central Burke County and flows se into Laurel Creek.

Mapleton, town in n Hertford County. Inc. 1901, but long inactive in municipal affairs.

Mapleville, community in central Franklin County. Alt. 350. Settled about 1877. Known first as Maple Spring because a maple tree grew by the spring that furnished water for a church there.

Maplewood, community in e Watauga County.

Maraco. *See* Maco.

Marasanico, apparently an Indian village, appears on the White map, 1585, located in what is now s Craven County on the Neuse River.

Marathon, former community in n New Hanover County near Castle Hayne. An agricultural colony of Greek farmers was est. there by Hugh MacRae of Wilmington in the early twentieth century, but it was not successful.

Maraton, village of the Moratuc Indian tribe, is shown on the Smith map, 1624, as being on the Chowan River in present e Chowan County downstream from Rockyhock Creek. The Comberford map, 1657, places the village farther upstream.

Marble, community in central Cherokee County. Inc. 1911; charter revoked June 22, 1939. Alt. 1,686. Named for deposits of marble in the vicinity.

Marble Creek rises in central Cherokee County and flows se into Valley River.

Marbleyard Ridge, se Clay County between Hogan Branch and Little Buck Creek.

Marce, community in Mecklenburg County served by post office, 1894–95.

Marcus, community in se Montgomery County served by post office, 1898–1913.

Marcus, former community in w Swain County on Tuckasegee River. Site now under the waters of Fontana Lake.

Maready, community in se Duplin County.

Mare Branch rises in e Hertford County and flows s into Bertie County, where it enters Keel Creek.

Mare Branch rises in s Lee County and flows e into Juniper Creek.

Mare Branch rises in w central Wilson County and flows ne into Contentnea Creek.

Margaret, community in e Franklin County. Named by C. P. Harris for his daughter. A post office prior to 1909.

Margaret Peak, on the McDowell-Rutherford county line. Alt. 2,500.

Margaretsville, town in ne Northampton County. Post office est. 1836. Chartered 1885 as Margarettsville, but charter repealed 1891. Rechartered as Margaretsville in 1895. Named for Mrs. Margaret Ridley, an early resident. Alt. 54. The railroad name is Margaret.

Marg Mountain, s Haywood County between Camp Branch and Browning Branch.

Margrace, community in se Cleveland County.

Maria Creek rises in ne Carteret County and flows se into Core Sound.

Marianna Falls. *See* Dutch Creek Falls.

Maribel, community in n Pamlico County on Chapel Creek, known originally as Shoofly. At the establishment of a post office in 1883, long since discontinued, it was named by postmaster Fentress for his sweetheart in Georgia, a girl named Mary Belle.

Marietta, town in s Robeson County. Alt. 125. Settled about 1898. Inc 1911. Formerly known as Affinity until renamed by Augustus Marriel, a promoter of the Raleigh and Charleston Railroad, whose line formerly ran through the town.

Marietta Township, s Robeson County.

Marines, former community in s Onslow County on New River. A post office est. in 1885. Abandoned 1941 with the development of Camp Lejeune.

Marion, city and county seat, central McDowell County. Alt. 1,437. Inc. 1844. Named for Gen. Francis Marion (1732?–95), Revolutionary War leader. East Marion and West Marion are adjacent unincorporated communities.

Produces textiles, hosiery, furniture, and paper boxes.

Marion Township, w central McDowell County.

Mariposa, community in s Lincoln County on Leepers Creek. *See also* Heldermans.

Mark Creek. *See* Morgan Creek.

Markee's Creek. *See* Stewart's Town.

Mark Pine Bay, a muck-filled bay in central Columbus County.

Marks Creek rises in n Johnston County and flows sw into Neuse River.

Marks Creek rises in se Richmond County and flows sw into Pee Dee River. Reference is made to a "Markees's Creek" in the vicinity in the act of 1799 incorporating Stewart's Town.

Marks Creek rises in e Wake County and flows s into Johnston County, where it enters Neuse River.

Marks Creek Township, se Richmond County.

Marks Creek Township, e Wake County.

Marks Knob, ne Swain County in Great Smoky Mountains National Park on Dashoga Ridge. Lat. 35°40′47″ N., long. 83°14′30″ W. Alt. 6,140.

Marks Pond, approx. ½ mi. long, se Harnett County on Buffalo Creek.

Marlboro, community in s Pender County.

Marlboro, town in w Pitt County immediately s of Farmville. Inc. 1875, but long inactive in municipal affairs. Alt. 82.

Marl Branch rises in w Hertford County and flows s into Potecasi Creek.

Marler, community in w Yadkin County.

Marley's Ford, former ford through Yadkin River w Wilkes County near the mouth of Stony Fork Creek. The site is now under the waters of W. Kerr Scott Reservoir.

Marleys Mill, community in w Chatham County.

Marlins Creek. *See* Sloans Creek.

Marlowe Creek rises in central Person County in the city of Roxboro and flows n into Hyco River.

Marl Pits, on the head of Stewarts Creek in w Duplin County. Abounds in fossils, sharks' teeth, and fossilized whalebones.

Marlville. *See* East Arcadia.

Marmaduke, community in s Warren County n of Fishing Creek. A post office was est. there in 1893 but was discontinued in 1930.

Marr Branch rises in s Swain County and flows se into Brush Creek.

Marr Gap, central Cherokee County between Bates Creek and Hiwassee River.

Marrow, community in n Randolph County.

Marrow Bone River. *See* Stony Creek.

Marrow Branch rises in central Haywood County and flows ne into Pigeon River.

Marsden. *See* Chocowinity.

Marsden Creek rises in central Henderson County and flows nw into Mill Pond Creek.

Marsh, community in s Davidson County served by post office, 1883–1905.

Marshall, town and county seat, s Madison County on French Broad River. Authorized to be est. 1852; site still in dispute, 1855. Inc. 1863 and named for John Marshall (1755–1835), chief justice of the U.S. Supreme Court. Alt. 1,650. Post office est. there 1857, before the establishment of the county seat, was named Lapland. For a period before Marshall was laid, Jewel Hill (or Duel Hill), at present-day Walnut, was the seat of government. County court was held at Jewel Hill as late as the fall of 1859.

Marshallberg, community on the mainland of se Carteret County approx. 8 mi. e of town of Beaufort. Settled about 1800. Named by Matthew Marshall, a rural mail carrier, for himself. Alt. 5. Formerly known as Deep Hole Point.

Marshallberg Township, s central Carteret County.

Marshall Ridge extends se from Turkey Knob to Clear Creek in n Henderson County.

Marshall Tavern. *See* Ridgeway.

Marshall Township, former township in s central Madison County, now township no. 1.

Marsh Bay, a loam-filled bay in s Columbus County.

Marshbourns Pond, in e Wake County on Buffalo Creek.

Marsh Branch rises in central Duplin County and flows e into Grove Creek.

Marsh Creek rises in central Wake County and flows se into Crabtree Creek.

Mars Hill, town in e Madison County on Gabriels Creek. Inc. 1893; named for a hill in Athens, Greece. Alt. 2,300. Mars Hill College, est. 1856, is there.

Mars Hill Township, former township in se Madison County, now township no. 15.

Marsh Island, a peninsula extending from the s mainland of Hyde County into Pamlico Sound between Swanquarter Bay and Juniper Bay. *See also* Abigails Islands.

Marsh Point extends from the s mainland of Hyde County into Rose Bay.

Marsh Swamp rises in n Halifax County and flows se into Beech Swamp. Appears as Elk Marsh on the Collet map, 1770, and with its present name on the Price map, 1808.

Marsh Swamp rises in n Sampson County and flows se into Great Coharie Creek.

Marsh Swamp rises in nw Wilson County and flows se into Contentnea Creek.

Marsh Township, sw Surry County.

Marshville, town in e Union County. Settled in 1874. Originally known as Beaverdam for nearby Beaverdam Creek, and at the time centered around a depot on the Central Carolina Railroad. Inc. 1877 as Griffinsville; name changed to Marshville in 1897 for the Marsh family, which donated land for a school and church. Produces processed poultry, asbestos products, boxes, and staves.

Marshville Township, e Union County.

Marston, community in e Richmond County. Est. 1913. Named for Edgar L. Marston of New York, developer of local real estate. Alt. 431.

Martha, community and former post office, w Randolph County. Named for first postmaster, Martha Ingram.

Martin, community in central Yadkin County served by post office, 1887–1909.

Martin Bay, e Pitt County in Tar River.

Martin Branch rises in nw Buncombe County and flows n into Turkey Creek.

Martin Branch rises in se Durham County and flows n into Lick Creek.

Martin Branch rises in n Madison County and flows sw into Little Laurel Creek.

Martin Branch rises in n McDowell County and flows se approx. 1½ mi. into North Fork [Catawba River] near North Cove.

Martin County was formed in 1774 from Halifax and Tyrrell Counties. Located in the e section of the state, it is bounded by Washington, Beaufort, Pitt, Edgecombe, Halifax, and Bertie Counties. It was named for Josiah Martin (1737–86), last royal governor of North Carolina. The name very likely would have been changed, as were those of other counties named for royal governors, had it not been for the popularity of Alexander Martin, governor in 1782–85 and 1789–92. Area: 482 sq. mi. County seat: Williamston, with an elevation of 60 ft. Townships are Beargrass, Cross Roads, Goose Nest, Griffins, Hamilton, Jamesville, Poplar Point, Robersonville, Williams, and Williamston. Produces tobacco, peanuts, corn, cotton, Irish potatoes, hogs, livestock, poultry, apparel, canned goods, heavy equipment, chemicals, lumber, paper, and textiles.

Martin Cove, s Swain County on Yalaka Creek.

Martin Creek rises in w Avery County and flows e into Roaring Creek.

Martin Creek rises in ne Buncombe County and flows sw into North Fork Ivy Creek.

Martin Creek rises in s Cherokee County and flows ne into Hiwassee River.

Martin Creek rises in n Haywood County on Hurricane Mountain and flows s into Fines Creek.

Martin Creek rises in n Rockingham County and flows ne into Virginia, where it enters Smith River.

Martin Creek rises in se Stokes County and flows se into Town Fork Creek.

Martin Creek rises in nw Yadkin County and flows nw into Yadkin River.

Martindale, community in w Mecklenburg County served by post office, 1836–1902.

Martin Knob, s Watauga County between Green Mountain Branch and Cannon Branch.

Martin Mill Creek rises in n central Forsyth County and flows s and sw to enter Lowery Mill Creek approx. 1 mi. before it flows into Salem Lake.

Martin Ridge, w Avery County.

Martinsborough. *See* Greenville.

Martin's Crossroads. *See* Conway.

Martins Gap, n Swain County in Great Smoky Mountains National Park on Sunkota Ridge, lat. 35°31′10″ N., long. 83°24′30″ W.

Martins Mill, community on West Fork Little River in ne Montgomery County. A post office, Martin's Store, existed there as early as 1828. Named for Farquhardt Martin, who had a

store there, 1822–60. Dam at the mill site was washed out in 1927.

Martins Point, a projection in the s North Banks, ne Dare County, extending into Currituck Sound. Located at the mouth of Jean Guite Creek.

Martins Point Creek. *See* Jean Guite Creek.

Martin's Store. *See* Martins Mill.

Martinville, former town and county seat, central Guilford County. Est. 1774 as Guilford Courthouse, *which see*, and chartered as Martinville, 1785. Named for Governor Alexander Martin (1740–1807). Abandoned about 1808 with the establishment of Greensboro as county seat.

Marty's Ridge, nw Burke County. Alt. 3,625.

Marvin, community in w Union County. Inc. 1994.

Marvin. *See* Point Harbor.

Mary Branch rises in central Cherokee County and flows sw into Valley River.

Mary Branch rises in ne Cherokee County and flows sw into Stewart Branch.

Mary Gap, e Madison County at the head of Gabriels Creek.

Mary Gray Knob, between Rock Hollow Branch and Rogers Cove Creek in e Haywood County.

Mary Knob, on the Haywood-Madison county line.

Mary Sander Creek, a tidal creek in s Currituck County n of Poplar Branch Bay.

Marys Branch rises in w Avery County and flows e into Roaring Creek.

Mary's Creek rises in s Alamance County in the foothills of the Cane Creek Mountains and flows e into Haw River.

Marys Gap, e Haywood County between Rice Cove and Sassafras Knob.

Mary Simmons Ridge, e Watauga County, extends s between Boone Camp Branch and East Ridge.

Masa Knob, peak on Swain County, N.C.–Sevier County, Tenn., line in Great Smoky Mountains National Park about halfway between Mount Kephart and Charlies Bunion, lat. 35°38′10″ N., long. 83°22′40″ W. Alt. over 6,000. Named for George Masa (d. 1933), Japanese photographer whose extensive knowledge of the area, acquired through 18 years' association with it, was recognized by his appointment as a member of the Nomenclature Committee for the first map of the park.

Mascomenge, a village of the Weapemeoc Indians; shown on the White map, 1585, as being on what is now the s tip of Chowan County on Albemarle Sound.

Masequetuc, village of the Weapemeoc tribe probably situated on what is now the se tip of Pasquotank County. Shown on the White map, 1585. Variant spelling: Masquetuc.

Mashawatoc. *See* Mashoes.

Mashburn Branch rises in s Macon County and flows n into Cullasaja River.

Mashoes, community on the ne shore of the mainland of Dare County on Albemarle Sound. Legend relates that it is named for Peter Michieux or Mashows who, with his family, was shipwrecked on a nearby beach in the eighteenth century. He was washed ashore with his wife and child clinging to him. When he regained consciousness, he found both were dead. The shock of the experience shattered his reason, and 20 years later he sat with his back to a cypress tree and died. His skeleton and a board on which he had rudely carved the account of his tragic experience were discovered years later. The name, in spite of the legend, may be of Indian origin; John White's map, 1585, shows an Indian village named Mashawatoc on the e Virginia shore.

Mason Bay, n Pamlico County, in Bay River.

Masonboro, community in e New Hanover County on Masonboro Sound. Appears on the Collet map, 1770. Named because members of the order of Masons in the late eighteenth century built houses there. A popular resort in the early and middle nineteenth century.

Masonboro Inlet, e New Hanover County opposite the mouth of Hewlets Creek between the waters of Middle and Masonboro Sounds. Shole Inlet, on the Moseley map, 1733 (Shoal on the Mouzon map, 1775), was at the site, but it closed after 1775. An inlet nearby, Deep Inlet, opened by 1808 and closed after 1833. Masonboro Inlet opened by 1833 at the old Shole or Shoal Inlet site. Took its name from the resort community of Masonboro s of the mouth of Hewlets Creek.

Masonboro Sound, e New Hanover County between Greenville Sound and Myrtle Sound.

Masonboro Township, central New Hanover County.

Mason Branch rises in central Cherokee County near Mason Knob and flows se into Valley River.

Mason Branch rises in n Macon County and flows sw into Little Tennessee River.

Mason Branch rises in se Swain County on Una Mountain and flows sw into Yalaka Creek.

Mason Creek rises in w central Transylvania County and flows se into Cherryfield Creek.

Mason Inlet, ne New Hanover County between Moore Inlet on the s and Rich Inlet on the n. The waters of Topsail Sound enter the Atlantic Ocean through the inlet. Appears as Barren Inlet on the Moseley map, 1733, and on other maps as late as 1909; and as Queen Inlet during the period 1906–36.

Mason Knob, n Cherokee County.

Mason Mountain, e Macon County between Lyle Knob and Fed Gap.

Mason Mountain, n Macon County between Mason Branch and Cowee Creek.

Masons Cross, crossroads community in s Scotland County.

Masontown, community in ne Carteret County on Nelson Bay between the mouths of Broad and Salter Creeks.

Masquetuc. *See* Masequetuc.

Massey, community in w central Wake County.

Massey Branch rises in e Beaufort County and flows ne into Pungo Creek near Yeatesville.

Massie Gap, w central Swain County between Horse Cove and the head of Hickory Flat Branch.

Massy Creek rises in w central Rockingham County and flows n into Dan River.

Mast, community in n Watauga County on Cove Creek. Alt. 2,670.

Mast Knob, se Watauga County nw of Dugger Mountain.

Matakomak, a name appearing on the Ogilby map, 1671, to designate the territory presently in Chowan County between Yeopim River and Pembroke Creek.

Matchipungo. *See* Pungo.

Matecomack. *See* Edenton; Matakomak; Queen Anne's Creek.

Matherson Branch rises in w Macon County and flows se into Pine Branch.

Matherson Creek rises in ne Cherokee County and flows ne into Worm Creek.

Mathis, community in se Forsyth County. Named for a family that settled in the vicinity as early as 1757.

Matkin, community in sw Caswell County. Named in 1967 for a family long resident in the area when a plant of Burlington Industries opened there. A name was required for directing truck drivers to the rural location.

Matlock Bald, n Clay County on the n end of Johnson Ridge. Alt. 5,230.

Matlock Creek rises in n Clay County and flows se between Johnson and Julie Ridges into Tusquitee Creek.

Matney, community in w Watauga County on Craborchard Creek.

Matney Branch rises in s Watauga County and flows n into East Fork [South Fork New River].

Matrimony, community in n Rockingham County served by post office, 1881–94 and 1898–1903.

Matrimony Creek rises in nw Rockingham County at the Virginia line and flows se into Dan River. Named prior to 1728, when William Byrd recorded that it was "call'd so by an unfortunate marry'd man, because it was exceedingly noisy and impetuous."

Mattacomack Creek. *See* Queen Anne's Creek.

Mattamuskeet, former township in central Hyde County, now reported as "Unorganized Territory." Most of the area is now owned by the federal government and is a fish and wildlife reservation. Residents vote and list taxes in Lake Landing township.

Mattamuskeet Lake. *See* Lake Mattamuskeet.

Matt Branch rises in nw Swain County and flows se into Fontana Lake.

Matthews, town in se Mecklenburg County. Inc. 1879. Known as Fullwood or Fullwood's Store from 1825, when a post office existed there; in 1875 it was given its present name to honor an official of the Central Carolina Railroad. Produces textiles, electrical equipment, pottery, and tools. Alt. 729.

Matthews Branch rises in w Haywood County and flows s into Mossy Branch.

Matthews Creek rises in ne Duplin County and flows sw into Northeast Cape Fear River.

Matthews Creek rises in w Warren County and flows ne into Fishing Creek.

Matthews Crossroads, community in w Nash County near the headwaters of Pig Basket Creek.

Matthews Cross Roads. *See* Siler City.

Matthews Township, w central Chatham County.

Matt Mountain, nw Swain County between Cable Branch and Fontana Lake.

Mattock Creek rises in n Macon County and flows sw into Cowee Creek.

Maua, community in e Yadkin County.

Maufin, town inc. in 1905 in n Pitt County on the n side of Grindle Creek. Apparently it was not developed, as the charter was repealed in 1911.

Mauls Point, small tip of land in w central Beaufort County extending into Pamlico River at the ne edge of Blounts Bay. Named for Dr. Patrick Maule (d. 1736), but earlier known as Smiths Point for a family who lived there.

Mauls Swamp rises in n Craven County and flows sw into Swift Creek.

Mauney Cove, s Haywood County on the head of Mauney Cove Branch.

Mauney Cove Branch rises in central Haywood County and flows ne into Factor Branch.

Mauney Gap, central Graham County between Snowbird Creek and Long Creek.

Maury, town in e Greene County. Alt. 78. Est. late nineteenth century. Inc. 1911. Named for Matthew Fontaine Maury (1806–73), naval officer and oceanographer.

Maw Point, peninsula in e Pamlico County extending into Pamlico Sound and forming the se side of Fisherman Bay.

Max Patch Mountain, w Madison County at the sw end of Buckeye Ridge. Alt. 4,629.

Maxton, town in w Robeson County on Big Shoeheel Creek. Alt. 197. Inc. 1874 as Shoe Heel; changed to Tilden in 1877 to honor Samuel J. Tilden (1814–86), Democratic nominee for president, 1876; to Quhele in 1879, probably from a form of the Gaelic word *Caoile* (the narrow part of a stream); to Shoe Heel in 1881, for the imagined meaning of Quhele; and to Maxton in 1886. Local tradition says that the area was long known as Mackstown because of the many people of Scottish descent living there whose names begin with Mc or Mac; it was changed to Maxton by postal authorities when the first post office was est. in 1866. An earlier post office serving the community was Cowper's Hill, est. 1811 a mi. or so e of the present town. Carolina College operated there, 1908–26, and Presbyterian Junior College, 1929–60; Carolina Military Academy is there now.

Maxton Township, w Robeson County.

Maxwell, community in ne Columbus County.

Maxwell, community in ne Henderson County at the s end of Marshall Ridge.

Maxwell Branch rises in n Transylvania County and flows sw into Avery Creek.

Maxwell Creek rises in w Duplin County and flows se into Northeast Cape Fear River.

Maxwell Creek. *See* Lillington Creek.

Maxwells Mill Pond, on Burnt Coat Creek in ne Duplin County.

Maxwell's Store, community in s Mecklenburg County served by post office, 1821–49. Later known as Cluster, *which see*.

May, community in n Harnett County served by post office, 1883–1904.

Mayapple Gap, between Doubletop Mountain and Thunder Struck Mountain in n Jackson County. Named for the herb (*Podophyllum peltatum*).

Mayberry Hollow, valley in n central Avery County a short distance n of Cranberry.

May Branch rises in w Macon County and flows se into Nantahala Lake.

Mayesworth. *See* Cramerton.

Mayfield, community in ne Rockingham County served by post office, 1853–66 and 1870–1910.

Mayhew, community in sw Iredell County.

Mayhew Lake, a small body of water formed by a dam on New Years Creek w of Blowing Rock, s Watauga County.

Mayne Creek rises in w Cleveland County and flows sw into Sandy Run Creek.

Mayo, community in nw Rockingham County served by post office, 1821–40 and 1855–66. Named changed to Stoneville, *which see*.

Mayodan, town in w Rockingham County on Mayo River. Built as textile mill village. Inc. 1899. Named for nearby Mayo River and Dan River. Alt. 594. *See also* Avalon.

Mayo Mountain, on w side of Mayodan, extends 2 mi. from Beaver Island Creek toward Dan River. Rises about 300 ft.

Mayonia. *See* Whitakers.

Mayo River rises in Patrick County, Va., and flows se into Rockingham County and into Dan River. Named for William Mayo, member of William Byrd's surveying party, 1728.

Mayo River State Park, in nw Rockingham County. Est. in 2003 with plans for hiking trails and canoe access.

Mayos Crossroads, community in se Edgecombe County.

Mayo Township, nw Rockingham County.

Mays Crossroads, community in w Franklin County.

Maysville, town in s Jones County on White Oak River. Inc. 1897. A post office est. there in 1827 was known as Cross Roads. It appears to be the "Young's Cross Roads" that is mentioned frequently in Civil War official records. Alt. 41.

Mayview Hill, s Watauga County on the head of China Branch.

Mayview Lake, in s Watauga County in the headwaters of Middle Fork [South Fork New River].

Mayview Park. *See* Blowing Rock.

Maywood, community in n Alamance County served by post office, 1886–1905.

Mazeppa, community in se Iredell County. Alt. 901.

McAdams Creek rises in e Alamance County and flows w into Back Creek.

McAdenville, town in e Gaston County. First Known as Henderson Shoals for Lawson Henderson, early Lincoln County official; later as Spring Shoals for a local landowner, Adam A. Springs, graduate of the University of North Carolina in 1798. Inc. 1883 as McAdenville. Named for Rufus Yancey McAden (1833–89), speaker of the N.C. House of Representatives in 1866 and local owner of mills. Alt. 600.

McAllister Creek rises in e Cabarrus County and flows s into Adams Creek.

McAlpine Creek rises in e Mecklenburg County and flows sw into South Carolina, where it enters Sugar Creek.

McAlpine Mountain, s Henderson County at the head of King Creek.

McAlpin's Grove. *See* Rennert.

McArthurs, community in s Robeson County served by post office, 1888–1907.

McBrides Mill. *See* Amantha.

McBryde's Pond, sw Hoke County. Located on an unnamed stream that flows into Big Raft Swamp about 2 mi. nw of Antioch. Named for Thomas F. McBryde, owner.

McCain, community in w Hoke County. Formerly named Sanatorium because a state tuberculosis sanatorium was located there.

Renamed McCain in 1948 in honor of Dr. Paul P. McCain, who died in 1946. Alt. 550.

McCains, community in se Union County served by post office, 1890–1904.

McCall Branch rises in e Transylvania County and flows sw into Little River.

McCall Gap, s Mitchell County between South Fork [Carvers Branch] and Middle Fork Grassy Creek.

McCall Mountain, in n Transylvania County at the w end of Forge Mountain.

McCalls Mill Creek. *See* Staffords Creek.

McCampbell Knob, Great Smoky Mountains National Park on the Swain County, N.C.– Blount County, Tenn., line. Lat. 35°33′53″ N., long. 83°45′18″ W.

McClammy, community in w Wayne County served by post office, 1888–1902.

McClellan Creek rises in ne Cherokee County and flows n into Tatham Creek.

McClure Branch rises in s Lincoln County and flows ne into Leepers Creek.

McClure Cove, e Haywood County on Pigeon River.

McClure Creek rises in s Haywood County and flows ne into West Fork Pigeon River.

McClure Hicks Creek rises in nw Alamance County and flows s into Ridge Creek.

McClure Ridge, w Haywood County in Great Smoky Mountains National Park, a short spur extending nw from Cataloochee Divide, center near lat. 35°34′35″ N., long. 83°06′52″ W., between Big Bald Branch and Double Gap Branch.

McCollums Pond, at the head of Big Creek in e Montgomery County.

McComb Branch rises in e Cherokee County and flows nw into Hiwassee River.

McConnell, community in n Moore County. Named for James McConnell (1888–1917) of the Lafayette Escadrille in World War I. His father, Judge Samuel McConnell, operated the railroad that ran from Cameron via Carthage and terminated at McConnell on the s side of Deep River opposite High Falls. *See also* Eureka.

McCoy, community in nw Sampson County served by post office, 1886–1903.

McCoy Cove, e Buncombe County ne of the town of Black Mountain.

McCoy Creek rises in e Anson County and flows se into Pee Dee River.

McCoys Mill Pond, e Robeson County in Big Swamp. Approx. 2 mi. long.

McCrarey's Creek. *See* East Buies Creek.

McCrary Branch rises in e Transylvania County and flows se into Little River.

McCray, community in n Alamance County served by post office, 1854–1903.

McCronan Creek rises in w Craven County and flows ne into Neuse River.

McCullen, community in n Sampson County near Hoe Swamp.

McCuller, community in s Wake County. Settled 1800. Named for John McCullers, the first settler. Alt. 300.

McCullers Branch rises in w Johnston County and flows se into Black Creek.

McCullers Pond, s Wake County on a tributary of Middle Creek. Covers 4 acres and has a max. depth of 20 ft. One of the oldest ponds in the county.

McCullough Branch rises in s Mecklenburg County and flows se into Sugar Creek.

McCurdy, community in w Iredell County served by post office, 1879–1906.

McDade, community in nw Orange County.

McDaires Cove, n Buncombe County on the nw side of McDaires Ridge. *See also* Lewis McDaires Knob.

McDaires Ridge, n Buncombe County, extends sw from Bald Knob to Reems Creek. *See also* Lewis McDaires Knob.

McDaniel, community in sw Sampson County.

McDaniel Bald, on the Cherokee-Graham county line in the Unicoi Mountains. Alt. 4,662.

McDaniels Township, sw Sampson County.

McDeeds Creek rises in se Moore County and flows ne to join Mill Creek in forming Shaddock's Creek. Formerly known as Shaddock's Creek.

McDonald Ridge, w Macon County between Jarrett Bald and Middle Ridge.

McDonalds, town in s Robeson County. Alt. 175. Inc. 1911. Named for Peter McDonald, a turpentine distiller whose business was largely responsible for the opening of a railroad station there.

McDonald's Mill. *See* Forest Hill.

McDowell Branch rises in central Macon County and flows se into Little Tennessee River.

McDowell County was formed in 1842 from Rutherford and Burke Counties. Located in the w central section of the state, it is bounded by Burke, Rutherford, Henderson, Buncombe, Yancey, Mitchell, and Avery Counties. It was named for Maj. Joseph Mc-Dowell (1758–96) of Pleasant Gardens, who fought at the Battle of Kings Mountain and was a member of Congress and of the commission to settle the North Carolina–Tennessee line. Area: 447 sq. mi. County seat: Marion, with an elevation of 1,437 ft. Townships are Brackett, Crooked Creek, Dysartsville, Glenwood, Higgins, Marion, Montford Cove, Nebo, North Cove, and Old Fort. Produces corn, soybeans, dairy products, livestock, hogs, poultry, hay, honey, machinery, textiles, hosiery, furniture, paper boxes, limestone, and gravel.

McDowell Creek rises in n Henderson County and flows e and ne into French Broad River.

McDowell House. *See* Quaker Meadows.

McDowell Mountain, s Macon County between Middle Creek and Little Tennessee River.

McDowells, community in n Mecklenburg County.

McDowells Creek rises in n Mecklenburg County and flows sw into Mountain Island Lake on the Catawba River.

McDuffie Creek rises in e Hoke County and flows se into Puppy Creek.

McElroy Branch rises in central Haywood County and flows se into Factor Branch.

McElroy Cove, central Haywood County between Yates Cove and Toms Top.

McFarlan, town in se Anson County. Inc. 1885 as McFarland, but the 1900 census used the name McFarlan. Named for Allan McFarland (1819–69), president of the Cheraw and Salisbury Railroad. Post office est. there in 1883 when the post office at nearby Sneedsboro was discontinued. Alt. 297.

McFarland, community in w Hoke County.

McGalliard Creek rises in central Burke County and flows n into Catawba River.

McGee Branch rises in ne Swain County and flows se into Straight Fork [Raven Fork].

McGees Creek rises in nw Franklin County and flows ne into Taylors Creek.

McGee Spring, ne Swain County in Great Smoky Mountains National Park on w slope of Hyatt Ridge near summit at lat. 35°38'20" N., long. 83°14'20" W. Drains nw into Right Fork [Raven Fork].

McGehees Mill, community in nw Person County on Hyco River. A post office there from 1874 to 1906 was known as Woodburn.

McGill Branch rises in s Gaston County and flows se into Crowders Creek.

McGinnis Crossroads, community in se Polk County.

McGinnis Mountain. *See* McInnis Mountain.

McGinty Creek, w Haywood County in Great Smoky Mountains National Park, rises on n slope of Big Cataloochee Knob near lat. 35°40'30" N., long. 83°10'12" W., and flows ne into Swallow Fork Creek.

McGowan Creek rises in w Orange County and flows e into Eno River.

McGowans Crossroads, community in se Pitt County.

McGowen, community in n Duplin County served by post office, 1893–96.

McGrady, community in n Wilkes County on Mulberry Creek. Alt. 1,459.

McHan Branch rises in e Swain County and flows s into Oconaluftee River.

McHan Cove, a small valley heading se of De-Hart Bald, s Swain County, and draining nw into the valley of Wesser Creek.

McHan Knob, s Swain County between Pole Bridge Branch and Yalaka Creek.

McHargue Mountain, nw Iredell County.

McInnis Mountain, sw Wilkes County between Warrior Creek and Beaver Creek. Named for McGinnis family.

McIntosh Branch rises in central Yancey County and flows s into Pine Swamp Branch.

McIntosh Creek rises in w Moore County and flows n into Big Governors Creek.

McIntyre Branch rises in n Mecklenburg County and flows nw into Long Creek.

McIver. *See* Williamsburg.

McKay Island, se Chatham County in Cape Fear River. Approx. ½ mi. long and containing 65 acres, the island once was 100 acres in area.

McKee Branch, w Haywood County in Great Smoky Mountains National Park, rises near lat. 35°35′02″ N., long. 83°04′50″ W., and flows nw into Caldwell Fork.

McKee Branch rises in central Macon County and flows nw into Cartoogechaye Creek.

McKees Creek rises in e Mecklenburg County and flows ne into Reedy Creek in Cabarrus County.

McKenzie Pond, artificial pond in e Brunswick County. Formed approx. 1860; max. depth 10 ft.; covers 50 acres. Fed by Allen Creek and drained by Lilliput Creek, *which see*. Also spelled McKensie Pond.

McKinley, community in se Tyrrell County served by post office, 1897–1901.

McKinney Branch rises in central Buncombe County and flows se into Smith Mill Creek.

McKinney Branch rises in n Buncombe County and flows nw into Ivy Creek.

McKinney Branch rises in Pisgah National Forest in nw Henderson County and flows se into Boylston Creek.

McKinney Branch rises in n Yancey County and flows nw into Toe River.

McKinney Creek rises in sw Buncombe County near the Henderson County line and flows nw into Stony Fork.

McKinney Creek rises in se Polk County and flows se into Rutherford County, where it enters Broad River.

McKinney Gap, ne Buncombe County near the headwaters of Whitaker Branch.

McKinney Gap, on the McDowell-Mitchell county line near the se corner of Mitchell County.

McKinney Gap, e Mitchell County at the head of Bear Creek.

McKinney Gap, w Yancey County near the head of Elk Wallow Creek.

McKinney Lake, e Richmond County on Hitchcock Creek. Covers 65 acres.

McKinney Ridge, n central Mitchell County n of town of Bakersville and between Cub Creek and Honeycutt Branch.

McKoy, community in sw Johnston County and ne Sampson County.

McLamb Crossroads, community in n Sampson County.

McLamb Mill Pond, s Sampson County on Clear Run Swamp. Formed about 1800 and

known successively as Rackley Mill Pond, as Ezzell Mill Pond, and, since about 1949, by its present name. Covers approx. 75 acres; max. depth 14 ft.

McLauchlin Township, e Hoke County.

McLean Creek rises in s Harnett County and flows ne into Upper Little River. Named for Peter McLean, who settled along its banks about 1760.

McLeans Branch rises in e Moore County and flows s into Thagards Pond on Little River.

McLeans Creek rises in nw Montgomery County and flows se into Uwharrie River.

McLeansville, community in e Guilford County. Named for the McLean family, Ulster Scots who settled in the area.

McLendons Creek rises in w Moore County and flows ne into Deep River. From 1748 to 1754, known as Buck Creek. Named for Joel McLendon, who settled there about 1748.

McLeod, community in n Richmond County.

McLeod Creek rises in w Harnett County and flows s to join Reedys Swamp in forming Jumping Run Creek. The basin of the creek was once an inland sea 30 mi. square. Its limestone bed, composed of fossilized shells, is 8 ft. thick.

McLeods Branch rises in s Moore County and flows n into Joes Fork.

McLin Creek rises in central Catawba County and flows ne into Lyle Creek.

McMilly Swamp rises in s Brunswick County and flows w into Shallotte River.

McMullen Creek rises in s Mecklenburg County and flows sw into McAlpine Creek.

McMurray Branch rises in Forest City, s central Rutherford County, and flows n into Broad River.

McNairs Millpond, central Scotland County on Juniper Creek. Formed 1830. Covers 50 acres; max. depth 15 ft.

McNatt, community in n Robeson County served by post office, 1884–1902.

McNeely, community in n Rockingham County served by post office, 1886–1905. Named for George McNeely, local minister.

McNeills Township, se Moore County.

McNeils Pond, se Hoke County on Beaver Creek. Built in 1870 by J. A. McNeil. Covers 100 acres. Max. depth 8 ft.

McPhail Branch rises in n Sampson County and flows e into Merkle Swamp.

McPhaul's Pond, located on Little Raft Swamp in sw Hoke County. Named for owner Henry McPhaul.

McPherson Creek rises in nw Cumberland County and flows n into Little River.

McPhersons Creek. *See* Daniels Creek.

McQueen's Store. *See* Plainview.

McQueen's Store. *See* Queensdale.

McQuires, community in w Graham County between Queen Ridge and Hooper Bald.

McRae Canal. *See* Skinner Canal.

McWilliams Pond. *See* Monroes Millpond.

Meadlock Mountain, n Mitchell County between the head of Honeycutt Branch and Young Cove Creek. Originally spelled Medlock.

Meadow, The, a loamy swamp in sw Johnston County.

Meadow Branch rises in se Duplin County and flows se into Back Swamp.

Meadow Branch rises in nw Graham County and flows w into Cheoah River.

Meadow Branch rises in n Moore County and flows ne into Buffalo Creek.

Meadow Branch rises in se Nash County and flows s into Wilson County, where it enters Bloomery Swamp.

Meadow Branch rises in s Orange County and flows sw into Chatham County, where it enters Ferrells Creek.

Meadow Branch rises in ne Pitt County and flows se into Tranters Creek.

Meadow Branch rises in w Wilkes County and flows s into Cole Creek.

Meadow Creek rises in se Alamance County near the foot of Mt. Willing and flows sw into Haw River.

Meadow Creek rises in w Chatham County and flows se into Rocky River.

Meadow Creek rises in s Randolph County and flows e into Fork Creek.

Meadow Creek rises in w Stokes County and flows se into Pinch Gut Branch.

Meadow Creek rises in e Watauga County and flows n into s Ashe County, where it enters New River.

Meadow Fork rises in w Madison County and flows ne into Spring Creek.

Meadow Fork Creek rises in sw Alleghany County and flows sw into Ashe County, where it joins Laurel Fork Creek in forming Mulberry Creek.

Meadow Fork Gap, on the Haywood-Madison county line.

Meadow Fork Mountain, w Madison County parallel to Meadow Fork.

Meadow Fork of Spring Creek Township, former township in se Madison County, now township no. 13.

Meadow Gap, e Madison County between Beetree Creek and Long Branch.

Meadow Gap, nw Swain County in Great Smoky Mountains National Park on Forrester Ridge, lat. 35°33'43" N., long. 83°42'10" W.

Meadow Hill, community in n Caldwell County served by post office, 1879–1903.

Meadow Mine, w Avery County. Mica was discovered about 1870 and the mine, still being worked, is said to have produced more mica than any other mine in history.

Meadows, community in central Stokes County between Flat Shoal Creek and the head of Zilphy Creek.

Meadows, The, area of level land in n Rockingham County along n side of Dan River. Once livestock production center. Described by surveying party of William Byrd, 1728.

Meadows Store, community in w Madison County on Spring Creek.

Meadows Summit, former station on the Danville and Western Railroad, n Rockingham County. Was the high point on the railroad from Leaksville to present Eden.

Meadows Township, s central Stokes County.

Meadow Township, s Johnston County.

Meads Corner, community in s Pasquotank County.

Mears Fork Creek rises in ne Guilford County and flows ne into Haw River near the Rockingham County line.

Meat Camp, community in n Watauga County on Meat Camp Creek.

Meat Camp Creek rises in ne Watauga County and flows se into South Fork New River. Named because early hunters had a camp there, to which they took hides and salted meat.

Meat Camp Township, n central Watauga County.

Mebane, town in e Alamance and w Orange Counties. Settled about 1854 and named for a local family. Inc. 1880 as Mebanesville; name changed 1883. Mepern's [Mebane's?] Tavern in the vicinity was mentioned by Bishop A. G. Spangenberg in 1752. The Bingham School was there from 1865 to 1891. Produces bedding, furniture, textiles, and apparel. Alt. 678.

Mecca, community in sw Surry County served by post office, 1898–1913.

Mechanic, community in w Randolph County.

Mechanicks Hill. *See* Robbins.

Mechanicsville. *See* Robbins.

Mecklenburg County was formed in 1762 from Anson County. Located in the s central section of the state, it is bounded by the state of South Carolina and by Gaston, Lincoln, Iredell, Cabarrus, and Union Counties. It was named for Princess Charlotte Sophia of Mecklenburg-Strelitz (1744–1818), who married George III in 1761. Area: 549 sq. mi. County seat: Charlotte, with an elevation of 795 ft. Home to banks, corporate offices, and professional football and basketball teams. Townships, now numbered 1 to 15, were formerly Charlotte, Berryhill, Steele Creek, Sharon, Providence, Clear Creek, Crab Orchard, Mallard Creek, Dewees, Lemley, Long Creek, Paw Creek, Morning Star, Pineville, and Huntersville. Produces corn, wheat, oats, cotton, eggs, poultry, dairy products, processed meat, baked goods, fabricated metals, textiles, industrial machinery, canned foods, paper products, chemicals, hosiery, apparel, furniture, snack foods, software, soybeans, peaches, tires, computers, aircraft parts, electronics, and asbestos products.

Meck Neck is modern colloquial term used to describe area in nw Mecklenburg County surrounded by waters of Lake Norman on three sides and Lincoln County on the n.

Medford Branch rises in s Haywood County and flows nw into Browning Branch.

Medford Cove, e Haywood County between Brown Cove and Chambers Branch.

Medlin, former community in nw Swain County now within the bounds of Great Smoky Mountains National Park. Settled before 1886 and named for Marion Medlin, popular Baptist minister who lived in the vicinity. After the property was acquired for the national park, houses and stores were torn down and moved. Only local family cemeteries remain to mark the site.

Medlock Mountain. *See* Meadlock Mountain.

Medoc, community in w Halifax County between Brinkleyville and Ringwood. Named for nearby Medoc Mountain.

Medoc Mountain, a comparatively high hill on the e bank of Little Fishing Creek, w Halifax County; center of a state park. Named for a vineyard est. there in the late nineteenth century and named for Médoc, France, which contains some of that country's most famous vineyards. "Rocky Hill," the summer home of Governor Hutchins G. Burton (1774–1832), was nearby.

Medora, community in w Edgecombe County.

Meege Crossroads, community in n Chowan County. A post office operated there, 1902–25, called Meege, which was the nickname of Mrs. Miles Elliott, wife of the postmaster.

Meeksville, community in w Wilson County served by post office, 1878–1901.

Meetinghouse Branch rises in n central Sampson County and flows se into Great Coharie Creek.

Meeting House Branch rises in e central Wilson County and flows sw in an arc into Buck Branch. Name appears in local records as early as 1775.

Meetinghouse Mountain extends ne from Stecoah Creek to Little Tennessee River in ne Graham County.

Meeting of the Waters, creek in se Orange County rising just s of the town of Chapel Hill and flowing se into Morgan Creek.

Meherrin, community in ne Northampton County. An earlier community by the name is now known as Severn.

Meherrin Creek. *See* Potecasi Creek.

Meherrin River rises in Virginia and flows s into North Carolina, where it forms the Hertford-Northampton county line for approx. 9 mi. and then flows se across Hertford County into Chowan River. Appears as Pochike River on the Comberford map, 1657, and as Wayanock on the Hack map, 1684. Parker's Ferry has been operated across the Meherrin River near its mouth since the early years of the twentieth century.

Meherrin Swamp. *See* Raynor Swamp.

Meiggs, community in se Surry County served by post office, 1894–1901.

Melanchton, community in ne Randolph County served by a post office, 1894–1901.

Melrose, community in sw Polk County. A former post office serving the community was called Mimosa. Alt. 1,424.

Melrose, community in w Robeson County served by post office, 1855–1902.

Melrose Falls, sw Polk County on Big Fall Creek a short distance w of town of Tryon.

Melton Branch rises in central Clay County and flows n into Perry Creek.

Melton Branch rises in n Mitchell County and flows e into Left Fork Bean Creek.

Melton Creek rises in ne Cherokee County and flows se and sw into Valley River.

Melton Mountain, n Rutherford County between Little and Carson Mountains.

Melville, community in e Alamance County. Settled about 1845 and known at first as Burnt Shop.

Melville Township, former township in e central Alamance County, now townships nos. 10 and 13.

Melvin Hill, community in se Polk County. Settled in late nineteenth century. Named for Thomas Melvin, first postmaster.

Melvin's Mill Pond, ne Bladen County on Little Turnbull Creek.

Memminger Creek rises in central Henderson County and flows ne into King Creek. Named for C. G. Memminger (1803–88), Confederate secretary of the treasury, who had a summer home at Flat Rock.

Memory, community in e Cleveland County.

Menola, community in w Hertford County served by post office, 1886–1907.

Mentso, marked as the central part of Pamlico Sound, present-day Hyde County, on the White map, 1590, but apparently a place on the shore, as the name comes from an Indian word meaning "he cooks for the first time." The word could be the name given a stopping place for eating on travels, perhaps the end of a day's journey in the direction from Roanoke Island.

Mequopen. *See* Second Creek.

Mercer, community in s Edgecombe County.

Probably the location of Mercersville post office in 1828.

Mercers Mill Pond, a stream that rises in se Brunswick County and flows sw into tidal marshes that drain into the Atlantic Ocean through Lockwoods Folly Inlet.

Mercersville. *See* Mercer.

Merchants, community in ne Gates County served by post office, 1879–1913. Known as Merchants Mills after 1902.

Merchants Millpond, central Gates County on Bennetts Creek; center of a state park. Formed about 1857 by Rufus Williams and known as Williams Millpond until about 1910, when it was sold. The new owner built a store there, hence the name. Approx. 3 mi. long. Max. depth 8 ft. Sawmill and gristmill formerly operated there, but now a popular place for fishing.

Merchants Mills. *See* Merchants.

Meredith, community in w Orange County served by post office, 1890–1907.

Meredith Branch rises in n Yancey County and flows s into Cane River.

Meredith Township, central Wake County.

Merkle Bay, off the nw side of Cedar Island in ne Carteret County. Merkle is local pronunciation of myrtle.

Merkle Swamp rises in n Sampson County and flows se into Great Coharie Creek. Appears as Myrtle Swamp on the Kerr map, 1882.

Merricks Creek rises in s Pender County and flows nw and sw into Northeast Cape Fear River.

Merrill Cove, s Buncombe County e of Merrill Mountain.

Merrill Cove Creek rises in s Buncombe County and flows se into Cane Creek.

Merrill Creek rises near Black Knob in e Transylvania County and flows e into Cascade Lake [Little River].

Merrill Mountain, s Buncombe County between Robinson Creek and Merrill Cove.

Merrimon, community in n Carteret County.

Merrimon River rises in central Carteret County and flows s into North River.

Merrimon Township, n central Carteret County on Neuse and South Rivers and Adams Creek. At one time a part of Straits and Smyrna Townships. Previously also known as township no. 9.

Merritt, community on Trent River in central

Pamlico County. Originally known as Trent; renamed to honor Gen. Wesley Merritt (1834–1910), who captured Manila in 1898.

Merritt Mill Pond, on Bear Marsh Branch in n Duplin County.

Merry Hill, community in e central Bertie County. Named for the Webb family plantation. A post office was est. there in 1816. *See also* Society Parish.

Merry Hill Township, se Bertie County.

Merrymount. *See* Paschall.

Merry Oaks, town in se Chatham County. Inc. 1901, but long inactive in municipal affairs. Named for grove of oaks in which Indians are said to have held tribal celebrations. Alt. 246.

Mertie, community in n Wilkes County between North Fork Reddies River and Burke Mountain.

Mesic, community in ne Pamlico County on Bear Creek. First known as Bear Creek; renamed for S. R. Messick, the second postmaster. Alt. 4.

Messer Branch rises in e Cherokee County and flows s into Slow Creek.

Messer Branch rises in central Haywood County and flows ne into Cove Creek.

Messer Branch rises in n Haywood County and flows ne into Teague Branch.

Messer Branch rises in s central Swain County and flows se into Bucknor Branch.

Messer Creek, w Haywood County in Great Smoky Mountains National Park, rises near lat. 35°36′57″ N., long. 83°36′57″ W., and flows e into Rough Fork. Formerly known as Sugar Fork but changed to honor Elijah Messer, an early settler on the stream.

Messer Ridge, s Macon County, extends se into Rabun County, Ga.

Metackwem. *See* Metocuuem.

Metakquam. *See* Metocuuem.

Metal, community in s Cleveland County served by post office, 1894–1902.

Method, community in w central Wake County near the head of House Creek.

Metocuuem, an Indian village of either the Weapemeoc or Chawanoac tribes located in what is now e Bertie County between the mouths of Chowan and Roanoke Rivers near Albemarle Sound. Appears on the De Bry map, 1590, and on the Velasco map, 1611, as Metakquam. Variant spellings are

Metackwem and Mettaquen. The name may have meant "big woods" or "trees."

Mettaquen. *See* Metocuuem.

Mewborn Crossroads, community in n Lenoir County. Named for the Mewborn family, which settled there before the Revolution.

Miami. *See* Newton.

Miami Mountain, se Buncombe County near the town of Black Mountain.

Mica City Creek rises in ne Macon County and flows sw into Cowee Creek.

Mica Knob, s Swain County between Whiteoak Branch and Grape Cove.

Micaville, community in e Yancey County near the junction of Ayles and Little Crabtree Creeks. Alt. 2,504. Named for mica mined in the vicinity.

Michael, community in w Davidson County served by post office, 1880–1903. Michael was the surname of successive postmasters.

Michael Branch rises in w Alamance County and flows s into Back Creek.

Michael's Creek. *See* Carraway Creek.

Michfield, community in s Randolph County. Said to have been named for a local resident, Mrs. Michfield Wright, or for the Michell family.

Micro, town in e Johnston County. Settled about 1890; inc. 1899 as Jerome. Named for Jerome Creech, local landowner. Named changed to Micro (small) in 1905 because of confusion with the community of Jerome in Bladen County. Alt. 192.

Micro Township, e central Johnston County.

Midas Spring, w central Mecklenburg County, 9 mi. from Charlotte. Discovered 1812 by a slave. Since 1871 commercially bottled water, high in magnesium and calcium content, has been available. Spring is located on a 40-acre tract, Midas Park.

Middens Creek, a tidal creek about 1 mi. long near Smyrna, se Carteret County. It flows se into Core Sound. Named for Samuel Mittams or Middams.

Middle Bay, in Pamlico Sound on se side of Goose Creek Island, ne Pamlico County.

Middleburg, town in e Vance County between Mill Creek and Fishing Creek. Alt. 489. Inc. 1880; named for the fact that it was midway between the terminals of the Raleigh and Gaston Railroad.

Middleburg-Nutbush Township, e Vance

County. Two separate townships were merged in 1965.

Middle Cave, community in e Watauga County.

Middle Creek rises in w Cumberland County and flows se into Bones Creek.

Middle Creek rises in w Franklin County and flows ne into Tar River.

Middle Creek rises in e Hyde County at Middletown and flows se approx. 1¼ mi. into Pamlico Sound.

Middle Creek rises in s Macon County and flows sw and nw into Little Tennessee River.

Middle Creek rises in s Transylvania County se of Kelly Mountain and flows sw through Rainbow Lake into East Fork French Broad River.

Middle Creek rises in sw Wake County se of the town of Apex and flows se through Sunset Lake; it continues across s Wake County and into central Johnston County, where it enters Neuse River w of the town of Smithfield. Appears on the Collet map, 1770.

Middle Creek rises in s Yancey County and flows ne into South Toe River.

Middle Creek Falls, on Middle Creek s of Rattlesnake Ridge, s Macon County.

Middle Creek Township, s Wake County.

Middle Elk Ridge, central Avery County.

Middle Falls, in Snowbird Creek between Upper Falls and Big Falls in sw Graham County. Water drops approx. 50 ft.

Middle Fork rises in nw Henderson County and flows se into Fletcher Creek.

Middle Fork rises in sw Macon County and flows n into Kilby Creek.

Middle Fork rises in e Madison County and flows sw into Little Ivy Creek.

Middle Fork [Barkers Creek] rises in w Jackson County and flows ne to join West Fork in forming Barkers Creek.

Middle Fork French Broad River rises in s Transylvania County and flows nw into French Broad River.

Middle Fork [Grassy Creek] rises in s Mitchell County and flows ne to join East Fork [Grassy Creek] in forming Grassy Creek.

Middle Fork [Hawk Branch] rises in n Yancey County and flows sw to join South Fork [Hawk Branch] in forming Hawk Branch.

Middle Fork Little Horse Creek rises in nw Ashe County and flows e into Little Horse Creek.

Middle Fork [Lower Creek] rises in ne Caldwell County and flows sw into Zacks Fork.

Middle Fork Muddy Creek. *See* Salem Creek.

Middle Fork of Ivy Township, former township in e Madison County, now township no. 4.

Middle Fork [Raven Fork] rises in ne Swain County in Great Smoky Mountains National Park and flows sw to join Left Fork and Right Fork in forming Raven Fork [Oconaluftee River].

Middle Fork [Reddies River] rises in nw Wilkes County and flows se to join North Fork [Reddies River] in forming Reddies River.

Middle Fork Ridge, ne Swain County in Great Smoky Mountains National Park, a spur extending sw from Dashoga Ridge, lat. 35°39′15″ N., long. 83°15′30″ W.

Middle Fork [Rock Creek] rises in s Yancey County and flows e to join North Fork [Rock Creek] in forming Rock Creek.

Middle Fork [South Fork New River] rises in s Watauga County on e limits of town of Blowing Rock and flows ne and then n to join East Fork and Flannery Fork in forming South Fork New River approx. 2 mi. se of town of Boone.

Middle Fork Township, e central Forsyth County.

Middle Fork [Upper Creek] rises in s Yancey County and flows se to join South Fork [Upper Creek] in forming Upper Creek.

Middle Fourth Creek. *See* Morrison Creek.

Middle Ground, a former shoal between Oak Island and Bald Head (Smith Island) in se Brunswick County; appears on the Collet map, 1770. It is called Sea Cattle on the Price map, 1808, but the shoal had eroded and was practically gone by 1833 (MacRae map).

Middle Little River rises in e Caldwell County and flows se into Alexander County, where it enters Lake Hickory on Catawba River.

Middle Marshes, a group of tidal-marsh islands at the nw end of Back Sound in se Carteret County.

Middle Mountain, n Buncombe County between Frosty Knob and Bruce Knob.

Middle Mountain, ne Buncombe County between Flat Creek and North Fork [Swannanoa River].

Middle Mountain, e Mitchell County between Stony Valley and Soapstone Branch.

Middle Mountain, s Transylvania County between South Prong and the head of East Fork French Broad River.

Middle Peachtree Creek rises in central Swain County and flows s into Peachtree Creek.

Middle Prong rises in ne Pamlico County on the n side of Goose Creek Island and flows n into Pamlico River.

Middle Prong of Little River. *See* Perry Creek.

Middle Prong [Roaring River] is formed in n Wilkes County by the junction of Basin and Lovelace Creeks. It flows se to join North Prong [Roaring River] in forming Roaring River.

Middle Prong [West Fork Pigeon River] is formed in s Haywood County by the junction of Haywood Gap Stream and Buckeye Creek and flows n into West Fork Pigeon River.

Middle Ridge, w Haywood County in Great Smoky Mountains National Park, extends se from Canadian Top, center near lat. 35°38'20" N., long, 83°05'35" W., between Upper Double Branch and Lower Double Branch.

Middle Ridge, sw Macon County between the head of Park Creek and Kimsey Creek.

Middle Ridge, n Madison County between Lisenbee Branch and Colvin Creek.

Middle Ridge, e Mitchell County between Little Rock Creek and Green Creek.

Middle Ridge, e Swain County between Improvement Creek and Wesser Creek.

Middle Ridge, s Yancey County between Middle Creek and Colbert Creek.

Middle Ridge Branch rises in se Mitchell County and flows s into Dicks Creek.

Middle River rises in se Bertie County and flows ne into Cashie River. Named for the fact that along much of its course, it lies midway between Roanoke and Cashie Rivers.

Middlesex, town in sw Nash County, settled about 1907. Inc. 1908. Named for the English city. Produces apparel. Alt. 255.

Middle Sound, e New Hanover County between Topsail sound on the n and Greenville Sound on the s.

Middle Swamp rises in s central Bladen County and flows s and w into Elkton Swamp.

Middle Swamp rises in se Brunswick County and flows sw into Lockwoods Folly River.

Middle Swamp rises in n Gates County and flows e into Duke Swamp.

Middle Swamp rises in n Greene County and flows se on the Greene-Pitt county line into Little Contentnea Creek.

Middleton Creek rises in se Chowan County and flows ne into Yeopim River.

Middle Top, w Haywood County between Walker Bald and Germany Cove. Alt. 5,165.

Middletown, town in e Hyde County between Lake Mattamuskeet and Pamlico Sound. Est. 1787, but long inactive in municipal affairs.

Middle Township, former township in central Chowan County, now township no. 2.

Middle Trail Ridge, sw Macon County between Little Indian Creek and Nichols Branch.

Middle Watch Creek. *See* Salem Creek.

Midgett Island, in the waters of Pamlico Sound off the w coast of Hatteras Island, e Dare County.

Midland, community in s Cabarrus County. Name derived from the fact that it lies halfway between Charlotte and Norwood on the railroad. Inc. 2000.

Midstate Mill, community adjoining the w limits of Red Springs in n Robeson County. A textile mill est. there in the nineteenth century; now location of Amerotron textile mills. Known briefly as Dora or Dora Mills after that name ceased to be applied to what is now Red Springs, *which see*. Dora post office operated, 1880–84.

Midville, community in central Onslow County adjoining Jacksonville on the se.

Midway, community in s central Brunswick County.

Midway, community in n Davidson County. Inc. 2006.

Midway, community in w Robeson County. The former communities of Raemon or Raemont and Branchville are now considered to be a part of Midway community.

Midway, community in s Rockingham County. Took its name form local Methodist church.

Midway, former community in w Vance County located at the crossroads now approx. 1 mi. sw of Hicks Crossroads. Appears on the MacRae map, 1833. So named because it was located approx. midway between Williamsboro and Oxford.

Midway. *See* Eller.

Midway. *See* Jessama.

Midway Park, community in central Onslow County on the outskirts of Camp Lejeune Marine Base.

Midway Township, n central Davidson County.

Mike Branch rises in ne Cherokee County and
flows se into Morris Creek.

Mikes Knob, s Madison County between Friezeland Creek and Little Pine Creek.

Mikes Mountain, n Rutherford County between
the head of Catheys Creek and Second Broad
River.

Milam, community in sw Ashe County.

Milburnie, pond in e central Wake County on
Beaverdam Creek. Covers 50 acres and has
max. depth of 20 ft. Used for recreation.
Named for the former community of Milburnie there. A post office, 1891–92, served
the community, and a printing establishment
operated there.

Mildred, town in e Edgecombe County. Inc.
1887, but not now active in municipal affairs.
Alt. 46.

Miles, community in se Alleghany County between Bucks Peak and Stone Mountain.

Miles, community in w Orange County.

Miles Gap, n Madison County between Cutshalltown and Shelton Laurel Creek.

Miles Point, s Camden County in the mouth of
Pasquotank River. Named for Miles Jones,
who lived nearby approx. 1840–60.

Milesville, community in s Caswell County.
A post office operated there, 1882–1907.

Milk House Branch. *See* Tanyard Branch.

Milksick Cove, sw Buncombe County, the valley
through which the w tributary of Pole Creek
flows.

Milksick Cove, central Clay County near Chatuge
Lake.

Milksick Cove, central Swain County, extends s
from Tuckasegee River.

Milksick Knob, s Macon County between
Tommy Branch and Wayah Creek.

Milksick Ridge, w Jackson County between
Pressley and Tilley Creeks.

Millboro, community in n Randolph County.

Mill Branch rises in nw Bertie County and flows
n into Hertford County, where it enters
Ahoskie Creek.

Mill Branch rises in e Cherokee County and
flows sw into Peachtree Creek.

Mill Branch rises in ne Cherokee County and
flows s into Valley River.

Mill Branch rises in ne Cherokee County and
flows se into Valley River.

Mill Branch rises in e Clay County and flows nw
into Perry Creek.

Mill Branch rises in e Clay County near Boteler
Peak and flows se into Shooting Creek.

Mill Branch rises in sw Columbus County and
flows e into Gum Swamp.

Mill Branch rises in Great Dover Swamp, w Craven County, and flows e into Cove Creek.

Mill Branch rises in s Duplin County and flows
se into Pagets Branch.

Mill Branch rises in se Duplin County and flows
sw into Cypress Creek.

Mill Branch rises in n Franklin County and flows
s into Sandy Creek.

Mill Branch rises in central Hertford County and
flows nw into Potecasi Creek.

Mill Branch rises in w Johnston County and
flows s into Middle Creek.

Mill Branch rises on the Johnston-Wayne county
line and flows ne into Mill Creek.

Mill Branch rises in w Jones County and flows se
into Trent River.

Mill Branch rises in s Macon County and flows
ne into Cunningham Creek.

Mill Branch rises in n Martin County and flows n
into Conoho Creek.

Mill Branch rises in nw Swain County and flows
se into Bone Valley Creek.

Mill Branch rises in w Swain County and flows
sw into Fontana Lake.

Mill Branch rises in w Transylvania County and
flows se into West Fork French Broad River.

Mill Branch rises in nw Wilson County and flows
s into Contentnea Creek.

Mill Branch rises in s Wilson County and flows e
into Contentnea Creek.

Mill Branch rises in w Wilson County and flows
se into Shepherd's Branch. Apparently once
known as Big Branch.

Mill Branch, community in sw Brunswick County.

Millbridge, community in w Rowan County.
Named for the mill built in 1822 by Samuel
Kerr and the nearby bridge over Kerr Creek.

Mill Brook rises in n central Wake County and
flows se into Marsh Creek.

Millbrook, community in n central Wake County
approx. 3 mi. n of the city of Raleigh. Settled
prior to 1860 and named for the brook on
which a gristmill operated. Alt. 318.

Mill Cove, ne Currituck County, is formed by the
waters of Knotts Island Channel, which cuts
into the e shore of Knotts Island.

Mill Creek rises in e Alamance County and flows
w into Back Creek.

Mill Creek rises in ne Alamance County and flows s into Stag's Creek.

Mill Creek rises in ne Alexander County and flows s into South Yadkin River.

Mill Creek rises in s Anson County and flows ne into Pee Dee River.

Mill Creek rises in s Ashe County and flows s into South Fork New River.

Mill Creek rises in ne Brunswick County and flows se into Brunswick River.

Mill Creek rises in nw Cabarrus County and flows s into Coddle Creek. *See also* Mill Hill.

Mill Creek rises at the foot of the Green Mountain range in central Caldwell County and flows se into Zacks Fork Creek. Named because several mills once were operated along its course.

Mill Creek rises in se Caldwell County and flows s into Upper Little River on the Caldwell-Alexander County line.

Mill Creek rises in central Carteret County and flows s into the estuary of Newport River.

Mill Creek rises in e Carteret County and flows s and se into the headwaters of Newport River.

Mill Creek rises in w Cherokee County and flows w into Hiwassee River.

Mill Creek rises in s Clay County and flows ne into Hiwassee River.

Mill Creek rises in n Forsyth County and flows s into Muddy Creek.

Mill Creek rises in ne Henderson County and flows se into Hickory Nut Creek.

Mill Creek rises in w Henderson County and flows sw into Crab Creek.

Mill Creek rises in central Hoke County and flows ne into Rockfish Creek.

Mill Creek rises in se Hoke County and flows ne into Rockfish Creek.

Mill Creek rises in central Jackson County and flows nw into Trout Creek.

Mill Creek rises in n Jackson County and flows sw into Tuckasegee River.

Mill Creek rises in sw Jackson County and flows ne into Lake Thorpe.

Mill Creek rises in n Johnston County and flows s into Neuse River.

Mill Creek rises in s Johnston County and flows ne into Neuse River.

Mill Creek rises in s Jones County and flows n into Trent River. Appears on the Moseley map, 1733, which also shows Franks Ferry across the Trent River near the mouth of Mill Creek.

Mill Creek rises in w Lincoln County and flows se into Indian Creek.

Mill Creek rises in central Macon County and flows se into Cartoogechaye Creek.

Mill Creek rises in se Macon County and flows ne into Mirror Lake.

Mill Creek rises in n Madison County and flows sw into Shelton Laurel Creek.

Mill Creek rises in w McDowell County and flows se into Catawba River.

Mill Creek rises in se Moore County and flows e to join McDeeds Creek in forming Shaddock's Creek.

Mill Creek rises in w Moore County and flows ne into Cabin Creek. In 1754 it was originally called Smiths Mill Creek for "Sandhill" John Smith, who had a mill there. Later called Tillis's Mill Creek for Richard Tillis, who bought the mill from Smith. Still later called Sowell's Mill Creek for another owner, a name by which it is also sometimes known today.

Mill Creek rises in central Onslow County and flows s into Stones Bay.

Mill Creek rises in e Onslow County and flows se into Bear Creek.

Mill Creek rises in n Onslow County and flows sw into New River.

Mill Creek rises in s Onslow County and flows s into Alligator Bay.

Mill Creek rises in s Pender County and flows n into Long Creek.

Mill Creek rises in s Pender County and flows se into Rileys Creek.

Mill Creek rises in e Perquimans County and flows sw into Perquimans River. Known originally as Vosses Creek, named for William Voss, who owned land there before 1700. At the end of the nineteenth century, it was called Brights Mill Creek for a local mill owner. From that name the modern name derived.

Mill Creek rises in central Person County and flows ne into Maho Creek.

Mill Creek rises in w Person County and flows n into South Hyco Creek.

Mill Creek rises in central Randolph County and flows se into Deep River. Appears on the Mac-Rae map, 1833, and apparently named for Cox's Mill, *which see*, located at its junction with Deep River.

Mill Creek rises in sw Randolph County and flows nw into Uwharrie River.

Mill Creek rises in n Rutherford County and flows se into Catheys Creek.

Mill Creek rises in w Sampson County and flows s into South River.

Mill Creek rises in s Stokes County and flows se into Town Fork Creek.

Mill Creek rises in w Surry County and flows se into Mitchell River.

Mill Creek rises in n Swain County in Great Smoky Mountains National Park and flows sw into Noland Creek.

Mill Creek rises near Middle Mountain in s Transylvania County and flows n into Little River.

Mill Creek rises in s Transylvania County and flows nw into French Broad River.

Mill Creek rises in n Union County and flows se into Richardson Creek.

Mill Creek, former stream rising in e Vance County and flowing nw into Nutbush Creek; now covered by Kerr Lake.

Mill Creek rises in n Vance County and flows n into Virginia and Kerr Lake.

Mill Creek rises in nw Wake County and flows w into Big Lick Creek.

Mill Creek rises in w Wake County and flows n into Crabtree Creek.

Mill Creek rises in n Warren County and flows ne into Hawtree Creek.

Mill Creek rises in s Wilkes County and flows n into Fishing Creek near its junction with Yadkin River. Formerly known as Little Fishing Creek.

Mill Creek, community in e central Brunswick County.

Mill Creek, community in s central Carteret County at the mouth of Mill Creek on the n shore of Newport River. Formerly known as Bordensville for William Borden, an early Quaker settler who operated a shipyard there.

Mill Creek. *See* Kendricks Creek.

Mill Creek. *See* Mill Tail Creek.

Milledgeville. *See* Tuckertown.

Miller, community in e central Wayne County. Formerly known as Millers Station.

Miller Branch rises in e central Bertie County and flows n into Cricket Swamp.

Miller Branch rises in w Mitchell County and flows s into Brummett Creek.

Miller Branch rises in w Yancey County and flows s into Fox Creek.

Miller Cove, se Buncombe County near the headwaters of Broad River.

Miller Cove, sw Swain County on the n side of Nantahala Gorge.

Miller Creek rises in s Buncombe County and flows se into Tweed Creek.

Miller Gap, on the Ashe-Wilkes county line.

Miller Gap, central Avery County.

Miller Gap, central Haywood County on the head of Rabbitskin Branch.

Miller Hollow, w Macon County between Tom Bryan Cove and Deweese Creek.

Miller Mountain, central Buncombe County sw of Spivey Gap.

Miller Mountain, se Buncombe County e of Little Pisgah Mountain.

Miller Mountain, w Polk County between Howard Gap and Tryon Mountain. Alt. 2,500.

Millers Branch rises in n central Avery County and flows nw into Cranberry Creek.

Millers Creek rises in e Caldwell County and flows e into the headwaters of Upper Little River. Formerly known as Bull Branch.

Millers Creek rises in s Caldwell County and flows w into Lower Creek.

Millers Creek rises in w Duplin County and flows w into Stewarts Creek.

Millers Creek rises in w Surry County and flows se into Mitchell River.

Millers Creek rises in central Wilkes County and flows se into Yadkin River.

Millers Creek, community in central Wilkes County near the head of Millers Creek. Alt. 1,423.

Millers Landing, n Tyrrell County on Alligator Creek.

Miller's Point, a point of land extending into Pasquotank River in s Camden County. Named for Thomas Miller, who was granted land there on January 1, 1694.

Millers Station. *See* Miller.

Millers Township, s Alexander County.

Millersville, community in s central Alexander County. Named for one Miller, owner of an antebellum cotton mill there.

Millford, former community in e Vance County at Southerland Millpond. Appears on the MacRae map, 1833, but the name was out of use by 1913.

Mill Fork rises in n Caldwell County and flows

se into Yadkin River. Originally called South Fork of the Yadkin.

Mill Fork rises in sw Franklin County and flows sw into Wake County, where it enters Horse Creek.

Mill Gap, n Macon County between Matlock Creek and Shepherd Creek.

Mill Grove, country home of Carl Propst in w Cabarrus County. Originally home of Robert Harris, who ran a mill on nearby Rocky River. Later sold to Michael Cox and named Cox Mill.

Mill Grove, community about 2 mi. n of city of Durham in central Durham County.

Mill Hill, home built by Jacob Stirewalt in 1821 on Mill Creek in n Cabarrus County. Restored in 1938. Nearby creek dammed to provide power for a gristmill and tannery.

Milligan, community in s Cleveland County served by post office, 1889–1902.

Millingport, community in w Stanly County.

Mill Knob, s Macon County between North Fork Coweeta Creek and Coweeta Creek.

Mill Knob, s Yancey County between Sodom Branch and Indian Creek.

Mill Landing, e Bertie County on Salmon Creek. Site of a gristmill built in 1771 by George Ryan and operated for many years; ruins still exist. Ships loaded cargo from the mill at the landing.

Mill Mountain, e Haywood County between Big Branch and Crabtree Creek. Alt. 3,459.

Mill Mountain, e Stanly County on the w bank of Pee Dee River in Morrow Mountain State Park.

Mill Neck, community in n Hertford County on Buckhorn Creek.

Mill Point, ne Carteret County, extends into the mouth of Styron Bay.

Mill Point extends from s Pasquotank County into Little River.

Mill Point, n Tyrrell County, extends from River Neck into the mouth of Scuppernong River.

Mill Point. *See* Elon.

Mill Pond Branch rises in n Nash County and flows ne into Flat Rock Branch.

Mill Pond Creek rises in central Henderson County and flows nw into French Broad River.

Mill Pond Creek rises in n Pasquotank County and flows nw into Newland Drainage Canal.

Mill Ridge, s Avery County.

Mill Ridge, n Madison County between Little Hurricane Creek and Big Laurel Creek. Alt. 2,763.

Mill Run rises in central Greene County and flows se into Contentnea Creek. Early settlers built a gristmill and later a sawmill on the stream. Evidence of the old mill dam is still visible in the woods about 3 mi. upstream from its mouth in Contentnea Creek.

Mill Run rises in central Jones County and flows ne into Trent River.

Mill Run rises in central Onslow County and flows ne into Southwest Creek. *See also* Troublesome Creek.

Millsaps. *See* Santeetlah.

Mills Bay, a bay in the n end of Church Island in Currituck Sound in central Currituck County.

Mills Creek rises in se Brunswick County and flows n into Prices Creek.

Mills Creek rises in w Transylvania County and flows e into Toxaway River.

Millseat Branch rises in ne Cherokee County and flows sw into Valley River.

Mills Gap, on Point Lookout Mountain, e Henderson County. Named because it was used by William Mills, first-known white settler of Henderson County, when he crossed the mountains after being wounded at the Battle of Kings Mountain.

Mill Shoal Ridge, w Avery County.

Millshoal Township, ne Macon County.

Mills Mountain, between McDowell Creek and Foster Creek in n Henderson County. Alt. 2,761.

Mills Pond, lake in sw Wake County on Basal Creek. Originally named Norris Pond. Renamed in 1925 for the owner. Covers 58 acres and has a max. depth of 20 ft.

Mill Spring, town in central Polk County. Inc. 1885 as Mills Spring, but long inactive in municipal affairs. Named for a son of William Mills, pioneer settler. Alt. 1,017.

Mills Ridge, a strip of high ground in n Tyrrell County s of Big Savanna from near the community of Levels and supporting a road on its surface. Extends e to w.

Mills River is formed in nw Henderson County by the junction of South Fork and North Fork and flows ne into French Broad River. Inc. 2003.

Mills River, community on Mills River in w Henderson County; inc. 2003. Alt. 2,077. A post office operated there since 1838.

Mills River Township, nw Henderson County.

Mill Station Creek rises in nw Transylvania County and flows se into Court House Creek.

Millstone Creek rises in ne Franklin County and flows ne into Richland Creek.

Mill Stone Creek rises in n Richmond County and flows sw into Rocky Fork Creek.

Millstone Creek rises in nw Wilson County and flows e approx. 5 mi. to join Juniper Creek in forming Bloomery Swamp. Named prior to 1783 for the fact that millstones were made from a type of stone found there.

Millstone Creek. *See* Austin Creek.

Millstone Creek. *See* Big Governors Creek.

Millstone Mountain, e Haywood County between the head of Rice Cove Creek and Thickety Creek.

Millstone Mountain, n Montgomery County on Barnes Creek.

Mill Swamp rises in se Bertie County and flows ne into Roquist Creek.

Mill Swamp rises in s Duplin County and flows s into Little Rockfish Creek.

Mill Swamp rises in nw Onslow County and flows se into New River.

Mill Swamp rises in ne Sampson County and flows sw into Six Runs Creek.

Mill Swamp rises in se Sampson County and flows ne along the Duplin-Sampson County line and into Doctors Creek on the Duplin-Pender county line.

Mill Swamp rises in w Sampson County and flows sw into Little Coharie Creek.

Mill Swamp Branch rises in sw Johnston County and flows se into Mill Creek.

Mill Swamp Creek rises in e Robeson County and flows se into Lumber River.

Mill Tail Creek rises in w Dare County and flows n and w into Alligator River. Appears on the Collet map, 1770, as Mill Creek.

Mill Timber Creek rises in central Avery County and flows sw into Linville River.

Milltown, community in central Graham County on Long Creek.

Mill Town. *See* Shiloh.

Millville. *See* Rockwell.

Millwood, community in central Chatham County served by post office, 1883–1914.

Millwood. *See* Gilkey.

Milray Knob, s Watauga County e of Boone Fork and nw of Cannon Branch.

Milton, town in ne Caswell County on Dan River. Site settled by 1728; inc. 1796. Named for (a) Robert Milton, a Virginian who settled on the Dan River nearby; (b) Thomas Milton, who operated a mill where planters held community meetings; or (c) the mills operated in the community. Originally known as Thomas Mill, then as Mill Town until 1796. It was an important town in antebellum days, at one time having two newspapers, a branch of the State Bank, and considerable traffic on Dan River. Home to Thomas Day, free black craftsman.

Milton. *See* Hamilton.

Milton Township, ne Caswell County.

Milwaukee, town in e Northampton County. Inc. 1915. Settled about 1889 and known first as Bethany. Said to have been named by Hezekiah Lasker, railroad conductor, for the city in Wisconsin. Alt. 85.

Mimosa. *See* Melrose.

Mimosa Shores, community in w Beaufort County on Pamlico River.

Mince Branch rises in w Jackson County and flows sw into Long Branch.

Mine Branch rises in w Haywood County and flows n into Jonathans Creek.

Mine Branch rises in e Yancey County and flows sw into South Toe River.

Mine Creek rises in nw Alamance County and flows se into Stony Creek.

Mine Creek rises in e Mitchell County and flows nw into Cane Creek.

Mine Creek rises in n Wake County and flows s into Crabtree Creek.

Mine Fork rises in n central Yancey County and flows ne into Jacks Creek.

Mine Fork Branch rises in e Mitchell County and flows nw into Right Fork [Cane Creek].

Mine Fork Ridge, e Mitchell County between Bee Branch and Mine Fork Branch.

Mine Gap, s Henderson County between King Mountain and Butt Mountain.

Mine Hill, e Mitchell County between Buchanan Hollow and Cane Creek.

Minehole Gap, s Buncombe County between Chestnut Mountain and Cedar Cliff. Alt. 2,555. Named because in the first quarter of the nineteenth century, very crude iron ore was mined nearby.

Mine Knob, e Yancey County near the head of Shoal Creek.

Mine Mountain, se Henderson County on Pacolet River.

Mine Mountain, central Swain County between Peachtree Creek and Middle Peachtree Creek.

Mine Mountain, n Transylvania County, extends s beside North Prong Turkey Creek.

Mineola, community in nw Beaufort County; formerly known as Old Ford. Served by post office, 1898–1903.

Mineral Creek rises in ne Buncombe County and flows nw to join Carter Creek in forming Stony Creek.

Mineral Gap, in Great Smoky Mountains National Park on the Swain County, N.C.–Blount County, Tenn., line near the head of Roaring Creek, lat. 35°34′08″ N., long. 83°40′55″ W. Alt. approx. 5,280.

Mineral Springs, located approx. 4 mi. e of Hookerton on Contentnea Creek in e Greene County on the Jim Smith plantation. A high ridge rises on the s side of the creek. The springs, on the slope of the hill, formerly were quite popular as a source of supposedly healthful waters. Several acres of adjacent lowlands are covered with laurel.

Mineral Springs, town in w Union County. Inc. 1905. Post office est. as Potters, 1891. Name changed to Mineral Springs in 1900. Reincorporated 1999. Site of Queen's Cup steeplechase event. Alt. 631.

Mineral Springs Township, sw Moore County. Named for the spring at Jackson Springs.

Mineral Springs Township, n Richmond County.

Mine Ridge, n Haywood County, extends s from Wildcat Spring to Skiffley Creek.

Mine Ridge, w Madison County between Grassy Creek and Shut-in Creek.

Mine Ridge, ne Swain County in Great Smoky Mountains National Park, a spur extending sw from Hughes Ridge, lat. 35°36′20″ N., long. 83°18′38″ W.

Minersville, mining community in se McDowell County near Dysartsville.

Mines Creek rises in nw Bladen County and flows e into Cape Fear River.

Mingo, community in nw Sampson County. A post office operated there, 1875–1903. Takes its name from East Mingo Branch (or Mingo Swamp). Mingo was an Indian word for a treacherous person.

Mingo Creek rises in ne Swain County and flows nw into Raven Fork.

Mingo Mill. *See* Burnt Mill Creek.

Mingo Swamp. *See* East Mingo Branch.

Mingo Township, nw Sampson County.

Mingus Creek, in Great Smoky Mountains National Park, rises in ne Swain County and flows s and e into Oconaluftee River.

Mingus Ridge, w Haywood County, extends se between Winchester Creek and Little Branch.

Mining Branch rises in n central Transylvania County and flows se into King Creek.

Mining Ridge, nw Henderson County, extends se from Big Knob to Queen Creek.

Mink Neck, community in se Hertford County.

Minneapolis, community in central Avery County. Post office est. 1911 and named for the city in Minnesota. Inc. 1911; charter repealed 1915. An extensive deposit of asbestos was mined there at one time.

Minneapolis Ridge, central Avery County.

Minnesott Beach, resort area in s Pamlico County on Neuse River. Developed by Hardison family, largely under the direction of Naaman Hardison, after World War I. Named for an Indian word said to mean "land of sky blue water."

Minnie, community in n Mecklenburg County served by post office for about 10 years beginning in 1898. Named for Minnie Barnhardt, first postmaster.

Minor, community in w Cabarrus County served by post office, 1898–1906.

Minpro, community in s Mitchell County on North Toe River.

Mint Branch rises in central Macon County and flows sw into Mill Creek.

Mint Hill, town in se Mecklenburg County. Site of Philadelphia Presbyterian Church, organized 1770. Inc. 1899, but long inactive in municipal affairs.

Minton, former community in s Wilkes County near Smithies Creek. Named for Meridy Minton, eighteenth-century settler. The Smitheys Creek Public Use Area on W. Kerr Scott Reservoir is there.

Mintons. *See* Mintonsville.

Mintons Store, community in sw Hertford County.

Mintonsville, community in s Gates County. Post office in 1828 was Minton's, but by 1830 known as Mintonsville.

Mintonsville Township, s Gates County.

Mintz, community in w Sampson County. Named for Wm. Ashe Mintz, whose daughter Mittie was first postmaster, 1900.

Miranda, community in w Rowan County served by post office, 1830–1903.

Mirey Branch rises in ne Hertford County and flows e into Chowan River.

Mirey Branch rises in se Onslow County and flows ne into Turpentine Creek.

Mirror Lake, se Macon County on Cullasaja River. Area approx. 50 acres; max. depth 40 ft.

Miry Branch rises in ne Bladen County and flows e into South River.

Miry Branch rises in s Johnston County and flows e into Neuse River. Mentioned in local records as early as 1795.

Miry Branch rises in w Nash County and flows e into Tar River.

Miry Gut, n central Carteret County, flows e into South River.

Misenheimer, community in nw Stanly County. Alt. 675. Former resort in the 1880s and 1890s known as Misenheimer Springs, which is still the name of the railroad station. Home of Pfeiffer University. Inc. 1903 as Gladstone, but the charter was repealed in 1909, and the name later changed to Misenheimer. Reincorporated 2003.

Misenheimer Springs. *See* Misenheimer.

Miser Creek rises in w Transylvania County and flows se into Parker Creek.

Miss Creek rises in se Polk County and flows ne into Whiteoak Creek.

Mission, community in e Cherokee County near the mouth of Calhoun Creek.

Mission, community in w Stanly County. Named for a local church.

Mission Branch rises in e Cherokee County and flows sw into Hiwassee River.

Mission Mountain, e Cherokee County, extends ne from the headwaters of Suddereth Branch to the mouth of Moody Branch.

Mistletoe Creek rises in n Cherokee County and flows sw into Tellicoe River.

Mitchell, community in s Carteret County on Bogue Sound near the mouth of Spooners Creek.

Mitchell Branch rises in nw Beaufort County and flows sw into Tranters Creek.

Mitchell Branch rises in central Yancey County and flows se into Little Crabtree Creek.

Mitchell County was formed in 1861 from Yancey, Watauga, Caldwell, Burke, and McDowell Counties. Located in the w section of the state, it is bounded by the state of Tennessee and by Avery, McDowell, and Yancey Counties. It was named for Elisha Mitchell (1793–1857), professor at the University of North Carolina who was killed while exploring the peak that now bears his name—the highest point e of the Mississippi. Area: 220 sq. mi. County seat: Bakersville, with an elevation of 2,550 ft. Townships are Bakersville, Bradshaw, Cane Creek, Fork Mountain, Grassy Creek, Harrell, Little Rock Creek, Poplar, Red Hill, and Snow Creek. Produces tobacco, Christmas trees, apples, corn, hay, dairy products, livestock, textiles, apparel, hosiery, lumber, mica, gypsum, feldspar, kaolin, and quartz.

Mitchell Cove, w Haywood County on the head of Mitchell Cove Branch.

Mitchell Cove Branch rises in w Haywood County and flows se into Jonathans Creek.

Mitchell Creek rises in se Craven County and flows ne into Clubfoot Creek.

Mitchell Creek rises in n Person County and flows nw into Marlowe Creek.

Mitchell Creek rises in s Yancey County and flows ne into Timber Creek. *See also* Mitchell Falls.

Mitchell Falls, s Yancey County on Mitchell Creek. It was there that Elisha Mitchell fell to his death in June 1857.

Mitchell Lick, on Cherokee-Graham county line approx. ½ mi. from the North Carolina–Tennessee state line on the headwaters of Snowbird Creek. It is a site at which early settlers salted stock and to which wild animals also came for salt.

Mitchell Mountain, ne Henderson County.

Mitchell Ridge, s Yancey County between Mitchell and Timber Creeks.

Mitchell River rises in se Alleghany County and flows e into Surry County, where it enters Yadkin River. Appears on the Collet map, 1770.

Mitchells Fork, community in s Gates County.

Mitchell's Island, w Craven County in Trent River. Size: 361 acres, partly cultivated; the remainder is swamp.

Mitchells Township, n central Bertie County.

Mitchell Swamp rises in w Robeson County and flows s into South Carolina.

Mitcheners Pond, w Franklin County on Buffalo Creek. Formed in 1907. Covers 50 acres, with a max. depth of 12 ft.

Mitchenor's Station. *See* Selma.

Mitchiners Crossroads, community in nw Franklin County.

Mitford, community in sw Rowan County served by post office, 1891–1903.

Mix, community in nw Sampson County served by post office, 1886–1906.

Mixon Bay, e Beaufort County e of Bayview and opening into Pamlico River.

Mizell, community in nw Washington County.

Mizpah, community in s Stokes County served by post office, 1884–1932.

Moadam's Creek rises in e Alamance County and flows w into Back Creek.

Mobley Point extends from w Carteret County into White Oak River.

Moccasin Canal, e Washington County, drains from the n shore of Lake Phelps ne to Scuppernong River. Approx. 4.2 mi. long.

Moccasin Creek rises in n central Alleghany County and flows se into Little River.

Moccasin Creek rises in s Cherokee County and flows nw into Nottely River.

Moccasin Creek rises in sw Franklin County and flows se on the Franklin-Wake county line, the Johnston-Nash county line, and the Johnston-Wilson county line until it joins Turkey Creek in forming Contentnea Creek.

Moccasin Creek rises in w Johnston County and flows se into Neuse River.

Moccasin Creek rises in w Wilson County and flows s and se into Contentnea Creek.

Moccasin Gap, s Cherokee County at the se end of Moccasin Mountain near the headwaters of Moccasin Creek.

Moccasin Gap, w Madison County between Partridge Gap Ridge and Hopis Branch.

Moccasin Mountain, s Cherokee County, extends se from Sheep Knob to the Clay County line.

Moccasin River, a name sometimes applied to the lower part of Contentnea Creek after it has been joined by Little Contentnea Creek.

The section of the creek lies on the Lenoir-Pitt county line.

Moccasin Swamp rises in e Johnston County and w Wayne County and flows s on the Johnston-Wayne county line into Neuse River.

Mocksville, town and county seat, central Davie County. Named for the Mock family, owners of the land on which the town was founded. Inc. 1839. Post office est. there, 1826. Produces apparel, furniture, chemicals. Alt. 866.

Mocksville Township, central Davie County.

Moffet Branch rises in s Clay County and flows n into Shooting Creek.

Moffitt, community in se Randolph County on Richland Creek. Named for Hugh Moffitt, who operated the first flour and feed mill there. A post office est. 1823 and discontinued 1935 was known as Moffitt's Mills.

Moffitt Hill, community in sw McDowell County.

Moffitt Mountain, e Jackson County between Chastine Creek and Coward Mountain.

Moffitt's Mills. *See* Moffitt.

Mohawk, community in w Harnett County served by post office, 1891–1908.

Mojoson, community in nw Guilford County.

Molasses Creek, a tidal creek in se Brunswick County, rises in the swampy ne part of Oak Island and flows e into Elizabeth River.

Mollie, community in s Columbus County.

Mollie Branch rises in w Avery County and flow e into Roaring Creek.

Mollie Ridge, w Avery County.

Molly Fork rises in ne Rutherford County and flows se and ne into First Broad River.

Moltonville, community in e Sampson County.

Momeyer, community in w central Nash County. Est. about 1910 and named for Thomas Momeyer, local resident who est. a sawmill there. Previously the community had been known as Bass's Crossroads. Alt. 190.

Monbo, community in e Catawba County on Catawba River. Named Mont Beau by the owner of a local cotton mill, but residents of the area soon corrupted the name into its present form. *See also* East Monbo.

Moncure, community in se Chatham County on Deep River. A post office est. there in 1877. Inc. 1905; charter repealed 1935. Named for Thomas Jefferson Moncure, civil engineer, who built the railroad station. The former town of Haywood is immediately se of Moncure.

Mondine Branch rises in s Jones County and flows s into White Oak River. Probably named for the Mundine family, early settlers.

Money. *See* Etowah.

Money Island, s central Carteret County near the e end of Bogue Banks in Bogue Sound.

Money Island, e New Hanover County in Greenville Sound w of Wrightsville Beach. Several acres in area, it is the traditional hiding place of pirate treasure.

Money Island Bay, in Bogue Sound, s Carteret County between Atlantic Beach and Tar Landing Bay and opposite Morehead City.

Money Island Swamp rises in central Carteret County and flows sw into Black Creek.

Monger Creek rises in se Macon County and flows ne into Lake Sequoyah.

Monie Swamp is formed in s Columbus County by Gum Swamp and Beaverdam Swamp. It flows s to join Big Cypress Swamp in forming Seven Creeks.

Monkey Island, in Currituck Sound, n Currituck County 4 mi. e of Church Island. Approx. ½ mi. square. Site of an old hunting lodge. Appears on the Collet map, 1770.

Monkey Junction. *See* Fort Fisher Junction.

Monks Crossroads, community in n Sampson County between Mill and Craddock Swamps.

Monroe, city and county seat, central Union County. Named for President James Monroe (1758–1831). Inc. 1844. Merged with town of Benton Heights, *which see*, in 1945 and with town of West Monroe, *which see*, in 1949. William Henry Belk opened the first of his department stores there in 1888. Produces textiles, apparel, bricks, processed meat, industrial machinery, fabricated metals, and wood products. Alt. 576.

Monroe, former community in ne Warren County on Roanoke River. Grew up around Robinson's Ferry after Clack Robinson laid out a town on his lands near the ferry in 1818, named it for President James Monroe, and sold lots to prospective citizens; a post office, tavern, racetrack, tobacco warehouse, and stores soon sprang up. It was shown on the MacRae map, 1833, as a well-established community. In 1840, when the Raleigh and Gaston Railroad was completed, it began a rapid decline.

Monroe Mountain, n Cherokee County between Allen Branch and Davis Creek. Alt. 3,171.

Monroes Millpond, n Scotland County on Jordans Creek. Formed about 1825; known in the 1850s as McWilliams Pond. Covers 70 acres; max. depth 14 ft. Owned by Fayetteville Presbytery and used as a recreation area.

Monroeton, community in s Rockingham County between Troublesome Creek and Haw River. Est. prior to 1832; probably named for James Monroe (1758–1831), president of the United States. Cunningham Mill, built by James Patrick Sr. in 1818, still stands nearby. Patrick cemetery has graves dating from 1771. Cotton gin est. 1835.

Monroetown, an African American community in s Moore County approx. 4 mi. n of Pinehurst. Named for John Monroe, who est. the settlement about 1915.

Monroe Township, n central Guilford County.

Monroe Township, central Union County.

Mon Swamp, in se Tyrrell County.

Montague, community in sw Pender County. Alt. 39. Named for a local resident.

Mont Beau. *See* Monbo; East Monbo.

Monteith, community in e Mecklenburg County served by post office, 1880–1903.

Monteith Branch rises in n Jackson County and flows se into Scott Creek.

Montezuma, community in central Avery County. Known first as Bull Scrape (*see* Bullscrape Gap). Inc. 1891. Post office est. there in 1883 as Aaron; name changed to Montezuma in 1911. Named for Aztec chief of ancient Mexico (1479–1520). Long inactive in municipal affairs. Alt. 3,797.

Montford, former town in central Buncombe County. Inc. 1893; became a part of Asheville in 1905.

Montford Cove Church. *See* Whitehouse.

Montford Cove Township, s central McDowell County.

Montford Point, Onslow County. Training site for black Marines in World War II. Adjunct to Cherry Point Marine Corps Air Station. *See also* Mount Pleasant Point.

Montford Point. *See* Mount Pleasant Point.

Montgomery, community in sw Montgomery County served by post office, 1854–58.

Montgomery. *See* Graham.

Montgomery Corner, a point on the North

Carolina–Georgia state line at the se end of Sharptop Ridge, se Clay County due s of 30 Mile Post, *which see*. From the point, the state line runs w to the junction of the North Carolina–Georgia–Tennessee state lines.

Montgomery County was formed in 1779 from Anson County. Located in the s central section of the state, it is bounded by Moore, Richmond, Stanly, Davidson, and Randolph Counties. It was named for Gen. Richard Montgomery (1736–75), Revolutionary War leader who was killed in the Battle of Quebec. Area: 499 sq. mi. County seat: Troy, with an elevation of 664 ft. Townships are Biscoe, Cheek Creek, Eldorado, Little River, Mount Gilead, Ophir, Peedee, Rocky Springs, Troy, and Uwharrie. Produces peaches, oats, wheat, corn, tobacco, cotton, poultry, hogs, livestock, cantaloupes, watermelons, textiles, furniture, packaging, carpets, mobile homes, lumber, apparel, clay, slate, pyrophyllite, and sand.

Montgomery Slough, a tidal waterway in se Brunswick County located just inside Long Beach and extending 2½ mi. w to Eastern Channel.

Monticello, community in n Guilford County. Named for Thomas Jefferson's home near Charlottesville, Va. Formerly known as Lambeth for a boarding academy operated there by a minister named Lambeth.

Monticello, community in w Harnett County.

Monticello, community in central Iredell County that grew up around a school of the same name est. there in the 1920s.

Monticello, former community and post office in sw Washington County approx. 1½ mi. n of the Tare-over. Settled prior to 1886; post office, 1893–96.

Montland, community in w Alleghany County served by post office, 1892–1904.

Montpelier. *See* Wagram.

Montreat, town in ne Buncombe County on Flat Creek. Alt. 2,500. Est. by Mountain Retreat Association, chartered 1897. Montreat is

derived from the words "Mountain Retreat." Later acquired by Presbyterian Church and now operated as its Assembly Grounds (4,500 acres). Historical Foundation (library and museum) and Montreat College are there. Inc. 1967.

Montrose, community in central Chowan County.

Montrose, community in w Hoke County. Alt. 483.

Montvale, community in sw Transylvania County.

Moody Branch rises in n Buncombe County near Moody Gap and flows s into Poverty Branch.

Moody Branch rises in e Cherokee County and flows s into Peachtree Creek.

Moody Branch rises in ne Cherokee County and flows s into Webb Creek.

Moody Branch rises in central Haywood County and flows ne into Cove Creek.

Moody Branch rises in ne Swain County and flows n into Bunches Creek.

Moody Cove, n Buncombe County w of Pine Mountain.

Moody Gap, on the Buncombe-Madison county line e of Moody Knob.

Moody Knob, on the Buncombe-Madison county line.

Moody Knob, nw Jackson County between Camp Creek and Hyatt Cove.

Moody Mountain, s Yancey County between Bowlens and Cattail Creeks.

Moodys Mill Creek rises in sw Watauga County and flows ne into Spice Bottom Creek.

Moody Stamp, ne Cherokee County in the Snowbird Mountains.

Moody Top, w Haywood County between Fie Top and Hemphill Creek. Alt. 5,320.

Moon Creek rises in w Caswell County and flows ne into Dan River.

Mooney Branch rises in s Macon County and flows se into Hemp Patch Branch.

Mooney Gap, at the head of Mooney Branch in s Macon County.

Moore, community in w Orange County served by post office, 1897–1905.

Moore Branch rises in e Swain County and flows ne into Connelly Creek.

Moore Branch rises in s Watauga County and flows nw into Middle Fork [South Fork New River].

Moore County was formed in 1784 from Cumberland County. Located in the s central section of the state, it is bounded by Cumberland, Harnett, Hoke, Scotland, Richmond, Montgomery, Randolph, Chatham, and Lee Counties. It was named for Capt. Alfred Moore (1755–1810) of Brunswick County, a Revolutionary War soldier and a judge on the U.S. Supreme Court. Area: 760 sq. mi. County seat: Carthage, with an elevation of 575 ft. Townships are Carthage, Bensalem, Sheffields, Ritters, Deep River, Greenwood, McNeills, Sandhills, Mineral Springs, Little River. Produces corn, wheat, hay, oats, poultry, eggs, livestock, hogs, carpets, hosiery, textiles, canned foods, furniture, pyrophyllite, sand, clay, and gravel.

Moore Cove, between Bear Branch and Seniard Mountain in nw Henderson County.

Moore Creek rises in sw Buncombe County near Stony Knob and flows se into Hominy Creek.

Moore Creek rises in sw Macon County and flows sw into Nantahala River. Also known locally as Jarrett Creek.

Moore Gap, on the Madison-Yancey county line near the head of Possumtrot Creek. Alt. approx. 3,100.

Moore Inlet, ne New Hanover County between Mason Inlet on the n and Masonboro Inlet on the s. The waters of Middle Sound enter the Atlantic Ocean through the inlet. Sometimes known as Wrightsville Inlet.

Moore Knob, e Macon County between Ellijay Creek and North Prong Ellijay Creek.

Moore Mountain, central Avery County.

Moores Beach, community in e Beaufort County on the n shore of Pamlico River, 35°23′51″ N., 76°37′15″ W. Formerly known also as Wade Point and Wades Point.

Mooresboro, community in w Cleveland County. Alt. 970. Settled in 1780s; inc. 1885. Charter repealed 1943. Named for Lem Moore, an early settler.

Moores Branch rises in central Clay County between Church Branch and Moss Branch and flows s into Tusquitee Creek.

Moores Corner, community in s Pamlico County.

Moores Creek rises in se Brunswick County and flows e into Orton Creek.

Moores Creek rises in w Guilford County and flows ne into Reedy Fork Creek.

Moores Creek rises in ne Pender County and flows sw into Holly Shelter Creek.

Moores Creek rises in nw Pender County and flows s into Black River. Sometimes referred to as Widow Moores Creek in the eighteenth century; probably named for the "Widow Eliz Moore," who owned land adjacent as early as 1735. It was on the stream that the Battle of Moores Creek Bridge was fought on February 27, 1776, the first battle of the Revolutionary War in North Carolina. *See also* Currie.

Moores Crossroads, community in ne Johnston County.

Moores Crossroads, community in w Wilson County near the head of Lee Swamp.

Moores Knob, in the Sauratown Mountain range, w Stokes County in Hanging Rock State Park. *See also* Tories Den.

Moore's Lake, central Anson County. Formed 1948. Fed by two springs. Covers 11 acres; max. depth 24 ft. Fishing and boating. Took its name from owner Bernard W. Moore.

Moores Pond, s Franklin County on Little River. Covers 100 acres, with a max. depth of 10 ft.

Moore Springs Branch, in Great Smoky Mountains National Park, rises in nw Swain County and flows sw into Twentymile Creek.

Moores Spring, former community and resort in w Stokes County on Cascade Creek. Flourished from about 1870 until the early twentieth century. The hotel burned about 1935, and the site is now a popular campground. Bottled water from the spring was widely marketed.

Mooresville, town in s Iredell County near Lake Norman. Inc. 1873. Named for John F. Moore, first mayor and donor of land for railroad depot in 1857. Construction of the railroad began in 1860. Alt. 910. Produces apparel, textiles, and milling products.

Mooresville. *See* Warsaw.

Moose Cove, central Cherokee County.

Mooshaunee, community in n Moore County founded around railroad siding and school.

Moratock, community in w Montgomery County served by post office, 1892–1926.

Morattico River. *See* Roanoke River.

Moratuc, village of the Moratuc Indian tribe on the Roanoke River near the present junction of Bertie, Martin, and Washington Counties. Appears on the White map, 1585; the Velasco map, 1611; and the Smith map, 1624. *See also* Roanoke River.

Moravian Creek rises in s Wilkes County and flows ne into Yadkin River. Named for the fact that Moravians had a grant from Earl Granville (*see* Granville District) there in the eighteenth century.

Moravian Falls, s Wilkes County on Moravian Creek. Water falls from 30 to 35 ft. over broad, steep rock between wooded hills. Named because of its discovery by Moravian surveyors in 1752. Fishing, swimming, and picnicking.

Moravian Falls, community in s Wilkes County between Moravian and Cub Creeks. Alt. 1,206. Est. in the late eighteenth century and named for the nearby waterfall.

Moravian Falls Township, s Wilkes County.

Morehead. *See* Rudd.

Morehead Bluffs. *See* Edgewater.

Morehead City, town in s central Carteret County on Bogue Sound and Newport River. Summer resort and the only deep-sea port in the state n of Wilmington; state port facilities are there. Inc. 1861 and named for John Motley Morehead (1796–1866), governor of North Carolina, who had bought land there in 1853 as the terminus of a newly inc. railroad. Ships are built there; produces asphalt and apparel. The site was formerly known as Shepherds' Point, *which see.* Alt. 16.

Morehead Township, s Carteret County. Known for a time as township no. 2.

Morehead Township, central Guilford County. Named for Governor John Motley Morehead (1796–1866) of Greensboro. Covers most of the w half of Greensboro.

Moretz, community in ne Watauga County on Meat Camp Creek. A post office operated there, 1849–1910.

Morgan Bay, in central Onslow County in New River.

Morgan Branch rises in e central Brunswick County and flows s into Town Creek.

Morgan Branch rises in n Buncombe County and flows n into McKinney Branch.

Morgan Branch rises in ne Buncombe County and flows sw into Right Fork.

Morgan Branch rises in sw Buncombe County near Smathers Mountain and flows se into South Hominy Creek.

Morgan Branch rises in central Clay County and flows nw then sw into Cold Branch.

Morgan Cove, sw Buncombe County sw of Luthers.

Morgan Creek rises in central Cherokee County and flows se and sw into Valley River.

Morgan Creek rises in n Haywood County and flows se into Fines Creek.

Morgan Creek rises in sw Orange County and flows e into w Durham County, where it turns s into Chatham County and enters New Hope River. Formerly known as Mark Creek. Named for Mark Morgan, who owned land in the area as early as 1753.

Morgan Creek rises in s Pender County and flows sw into Long Creek.

Morgan District, at the time of the 1790 census, was composed of Burke, Lincoln, Rutherford, and Wilkes Counties.

Morgan Hill, peak in s Transylvania County near the mouth of Cherryfield Creek.

Morgan Hill, community in n Buncombe County.

Morgan Mill Creek rises in s Transylvania County and flows se then ne into French Broad River.

Morgan Mills Ford, n Union County on Rocky River. Site of a large gristmill dating from the middle of the nineteenth century. The building and machinery still stand, but the mill no longer operates.

Morgan Ridge, n Buncombe County, an extension of Bill Cole Mountain.

Morgan's Branch rises in n Wilson County and flows se into Cattail Swamp.

Morgan's Mills, community in ne Union County.

Morganton, town and county seat, central Burke County. Est. 1784 as Morgansborough. Alt. 1,182. Named for Gen. Daniel Morgan (1736?–1802), Revolutionary War leader. Western Piedmont Community College, est. 1966, is located there. Produces furniture, electronic components, hosiery, apparel, textiles, and dairy products.

Morganton Township, s central Burke County.

Morgantown, community in e Carteret County near the nw limits of Newport.

Morgan Township, se Rowan County.

Morgan Township, nw Rutherford County.

Moriah, community in se Person County.

Morlin Mountain, n Rutherford County between Cane Creek and the head of South Creek. Alt. approx. 2,100.

Morning Star, community in e Haywood County on the head of Allens Creek.

Morning Star Township, former township in se Mecklenburg County, now township no. 13.

Morris Creek rises in e Caldwell County and flows s into Cedar Creek.

Morris Creek rises in ne Cherokee County and flows se and sw into Valley River.

Morris Field Air Base, in Charlotte, central Mecklenburg County, was dedicated April 21, 1941, and used to train combat pilots during World War II. Named for Maj. William C. Morris of Cabarrus County, distinguished World War I pilot. Property returned to city of Charlotte in 1946 for use as municipal airport.

Morris Knob, s Wilkes County at the sw end of Gill Mountain.

Morris Landing, community in sw Onslow County on Stump Sound.

Morris Mountain, n Montgomery County between Bundle Mountain and Barnes Creek.

Morrison, former community in w Iredell County on Fourth Creek near the present community of Loray. William Morrison (1704–71) settled there in 1750 and by 1752 was operating a gristmill. In an Indian attack, all buildings were burned except the mill, which was saved owing to an Indian superstition that evil would befall them if they burned a mill. Appears on the Collet map, 1770, and as Morrisons Mill as recently as 1901 on a map of the county. A cemetery with eighteenth-century tombstones marks the site.

Morrison, community in s Richmond County.

Morrison Creek rises in w Iredell County and flows e into Fourth Creek. Formerly known as Middle Fourth Creek.

Morrison's Tan Yard, community in se Mecklenburg County served by post office, 1820–71.

Morris Pond, on Juniper Creek, se Lee County. Formed about 1865. Covers 25 acres; max. depth 8 ft. Formerly a millpond, now used for fishing, swimming, and boating.

Morris Run rises in sw Beaufort County and flows nw into Chocowinity Creek.

Morristown. *See* Asheville.

Morrisville, town in w Wake County on Crabtree Creek. Settled 1840; chartered in 1875 and named for Jerry Morris, who owned the town site. Charter repealed in 1933. Reincorporated in 1947. Alt. 304.

Morrosenean, community in w Robeson County served by post office, 1871–1901.

Morrow Branch rises in central Haywood County and flows se into Jonathans Creek.

Morrow Branch rises in s Madison County and flows s into Little Sandymush Creek.

Morrow Creek rises in s Rutherford County and flows ne into Second Broad River.

Morrow Gap, w Cherokee County between Shuler and Sular Creeks.

Morrow Mountain State Park, e Stanly County on Yadkin and Pee Dee Rivers. 4,135 acres. Est. 1935 on land given in large part by James McKnight Morrow. Former Naked Mountain, *which see,* renamed Morrow Mountain. Scenic, recreational area; picnicking, swimming, fishing, tent and trailer camping, boating, hiking, nature study, museum, restaurant, and recreation lodge. There are several peaks (Mill Mountain, Sugarloaf Mountain, and Tater Top Mountain) in the park, none of which is over 1,050 ft. in alt.

Morrow's Turnout, community in sw Mecklenburg County. Formerly known as Mount Moriah (post office, 1830–31, 1849–52), Mount Leer (post office, 1831–49), and since 1852 Pineville.

Morse Point, a neck of land extending from Virginia into the mouth of North Landing River in ne Currituck County.

Mortimer, town in w Caldwell County. Inc. 1907, but long inactive in municipal affairs. Alt. 1,502. Largely a ghost town. Est. in connection with a lumber mill.

Morton Creek rises in w Transylvania County and flows se into South Fork Flat Creek.

Morton Township, former township in nw Alamance County, now township no. 4.

Mortons Store, community in n Alamance County served by post office, 1852–1906.

Morven, town in se Anson County. Inc. 1883. Post office est. there in 1823 and named for Morven, Scotland, home of the mother of Hugh McKenzie, first postmaster. Alt. 341.

Morven Township, se Anson County.

Moscow, community in nw Bladen County served by post office, 1892–1907.

Moseley County. In about 1907 an unsigned petition was presented to the General Assembly proposing that a county be created from portions of Lenoir, Wayne, and Greene Counties, with the county seat at LaGrange. It was to be named for William D. Moseley (1795–1863), who was born near LaGrange and who was governor of Florida, 1845–49. The General Assembly apparently never acted on the petition.

Moseley Creek rises in Great Dover Swamp, w Craven County, and flows nw into Neuse River. For a part of its course, it forms the Craven-Lenoir county line.

Moseley Creek rises in nw Lenoir County and flows se into Falling Creek. Named for Matthew Moseley, who settled there about 1770.

Moseley Hall. *See* LaGrange.

Moseley Hall Township, nw Lenoir County. Named for plantation house of Moseley family.

Moseley's Cove, s Pender County on Northeast Cape Fear River. Adjacent land once was owned by Edward Moseley (1682–1749), colonial surveyor general and member of the governor's council.

Moseley's Creek. *See* Parrotts Creek.

Moseleys Point. *See* Hornblower Point.

Moser, community in s Surry County served by post office, 1889–1905.

Moses Branch rises in e Macon County and flows nw into Elijay Creek.

Moses Branch rises in n Yancey County and flows e into Jacks Creek.

Moses Creek formed by junction of East Fork and West Fork in n Jackson County and flows sw into Caney Fork.

Moses H. Cone Memorial Park, s Watauga County on Blue Ridge Parkway nw of Blowing Rock. Est. 1950. Former estate of textile executive Moses H. Cone (1857–1908); 3,517 acres. Flat Top Manor is now a museum and craft center at which mountain handicrafts are sold. Trails for hiking and horseback riding and lakes for fishing are there. *See also* Bass Lake.

Moses Knob, e Caldwell County. Probably named for Capt. Moses Guest, a Revolutionary soldier who lived nearby on the Yadkin River.

Moses Knob, on the Jackson-Macon county line.

Moss, community in n Cherokee County.

Moss, community in n Halifax County served by post office, 1897–1909.

Moss, community in ne Stanly County.

Moss Branch rises in central Anson County and flows e into Brush Fork Creek.

Moss Branch rises in n Cherokee County on Hanging Dog Mountain and flows se into Slickrock Branch.

Moss Branch rises in central Clay County and flows s into Tusquitee Creek.

Moss Branch rises in e Macon County and flows s into Little Buck Creek.

Mossey Islands, in Currituck Sound off the w shore of Currituck Banks, se Currituck County.

Moss Gap, on the Jackson-Macon county line.

Moss Knob, on the Jackson-Macon county line. Alt. 4,500.

Moss Neck, community in w central Robeson County.

Mossy Back Gap, sw Macon County on Clear Branch.

Mossy Branch rises in w Haywood County and flows se into Cataloochee Creek.

Motes Creek rises in se Alamance County and flows s into Haw River.

Mott Creek rises in e Onslow County and flows nw into Northeast Creek.

Motts Creek. *See* Todds Creek.

Motts Falls, rapids in the Yadkin River, s Davidson County near the mouth of Riles and Ellis Creeks. The rapids extend approx. 8/10 of a mi. and drop 13½ ft., having 6 nearly vertical falls of from 6 in. to 2 ft. each.

Mott Swamp rises in e Lenoir County and flows n into Southwest Creek.

Moulder Branch rises in s Alamance County in the Cane Creek Mountains and flows se into Cane Creek. Also known as Foust's Creek.

Moulton, community in n Franklin County.

Mountain Branch rises in n Stokes County and flows e into Snow Creek.

Mountain Canal, e Washington County, extends ne from Lake Phelps to Scuppernong River.

Mountain Creek rises in s Alexander County and flows s into Catawba River.

Mountain Creek is formed by the junction of its North and South Forks in se Catawba County. It flows se into Catawba River.

Mountain Creek rises in nw Durham County and flows se into Little River.

Mountain Creek rises in w Gaston County and flows sw into Long Creek.

Mountain Creek rises in central Graham County and flows sw into Santeetlah Lake.

Mountain Creek rises in n Granville County and flows ne into Grassy Creek.

Mountain Creek rises in w Hoke County and flows sw into Lumber River.

Mountain Creek rises in s Orange County and flows ne into New Hope Creek.

Mountain Creek rises in n Rutherford County and flows s into Broad River. Fort McFadden was located on the creek near the present site of Rutherfordton in the mid-eighteenth century.

Mountain Creek rises in n Stanly County and flows se into Pee Dee River.

Mountain Creek, community in se Catawba County.

Mountain Creek Township, se Catawba County.

Mountain Home, community in n Henderson County.

Mountain Island, town in ne Gaston County on Catawba River at Mountain Island Lake. Inc. 1891, but long inactive in municipal affairs. Formerly ferry site across Catawba River. *See also* Mountain Island Lake.

Mountain Island Branch rises in w Madison County and flows ne into French Broad River.

Mountain Island Lake, on the Catawba River, Gaston and Mecklenburg Counties. Formed 1922–24. Covers 3,235 acres, with a shoreline of 61 mi. Owned by Duke Energy and site of hydroelectric power plant. *See also* Mount Heckler.

Mountain Park, community in w Surry County est. 1913 and named for its mountain location in a parklike setting.

Mountain Region, Mountain Section, or simply **The Mountains**, terms applied to the mountainous section of w North Carolina. The e limit of the region runs generally through Surry, Wilkes, Caldwell, Burke, Rutherford, and Polk Counties. The Indians referred to the area as Ottaray (Highlands). White settlers sometimes rendered the word into English as Otaré, which they translated as "Over Hills." *See also* Appalachian Mountains.

Mountain Run rises in e Caldwell County and flows s into Upper Little River.

Mountain Run Creek rises in w Rockingham Creek and flows into Mayo River. Named for Cedar Point Mountain, where creek originates.

Mountainside Branch rises in s Macon County and flows nw into Big Mooney Branch.

Mountainside Grove, community on Falls Branch in e Macon County.

Mountain Tea Branch rises near Henry Mountain in s Transylvania County and flows s into East Fork French Broad River. Named for the abundance of wintergreen that grows near the branch, the herb from which "mountain tea" is made.

Mountain Township, sw Jackson County.

Mountain Valley, community in s McDowell County. Named for plantation owned by George Gradin.

Mountain View, community in s Stokes County between the head of Danbury Creek and Town Fork Creek. Mountain View Institute, an academy, operated there, 1895–1920.

Mountain View, former community in e Warren County. A post office was est. there in 1879 but was discontinued in 1929.

Mount Airy, town in ne Surry County. Alt. 1,104. Settled about 1850; inc. 1869. In the early nineteenth century, the vicinity was called the Hollow or Hallow. *See also* Perkinsville.

Mount Airy Township, n Surry County.

Mount Ararat. *See* Pilot Mountain.

Mount Bolus, hill in se Orange County near Bolin Creek ½ mi. n of Chapel Hill. An extinct volcano. Said to have been named by university students after "Old Diabolus" (devil), their nickname for Joseph Caldwell, president of the university, 1796–1835. Appears as Gander Mountain in local records as late as 1792.

Mount Buckley, the southernmost of three knobs, the central one of which is Clingmans Dome and the northernmost Mount Love, in Great Smoky Mountains National Park on the border of Swain County, N.C., and Sevier County, Tenn., lat. 35°33′15″ N., long. 83°30′ W. Named by Arnold H. Guyot prior to 1860 in honor of naturalist S. B. Buckley (1809–84), Guyot's friend and sometime coworker. Alt. 6,500.

Mount Calvert. *See* Grimesland.

Mount Cammerer, on the Haywood County, N.C.–Cocke County, Tenn., line in Great Smoky Mountains National Park on Cammerer Ridge about lat. 35°45′50″ N.,

long. 83°09′40″ W. Named in honor of A. B.
Cammerer, formerly of the U.S. Department
of the Interior, who was active in promoting
the park. Alt. approx. 4,928.

Mount Carmel, community in central Moore
County served by post office, 1885–1905.

Mount Carmel, community in s Vance County
on Sandy Creek. Named for a local church,
which was in turn named for the biblical
mountain in nw Palestine from which Elijah
called down fire from Heaven.

Mount Chapman, in Great Smoky Mountains
National Park on Swain County, N.C.–Sevier
County, Tenn., line, lat. 35°41′ N., long. 83°17′
W. Named for David Carpenter Chapman
(1876–1938?) of Knoxville, Tenn., whose ini-
tiative and persistent activity over many years
was largely responsible for the establishment
of the Great Smoky Mountains National Park
by the act of Congress approved on May 22,
1926. Alt. 6,425. Formerly known as Black,
Old Black, and The Black.

Mount Collier, s Orange County at ne end of
Grampian Hills.

Mount Collins, in Great Smoky Mountains National Park on the Swain County, N.C.–Sevier
County, Tenn., line, lat. 35°35′ N., long. 83°28′
W. Named for Robert Collins (1806–63), one
of the first settlers in the area and a guide for
Arnold Guyot and other explorers. Mount Collins was renamed Mount Kephart in 1928, but
that name was later given to another peak.
Alt. 6,255.

Mount Craig, peak in Mount Mitchell State Park,
s Yancey County near lat. 35°46′40″ N., long.
82°15′40″ W. Alt. 6,663. Second-highest peak
in the state. One of two peaks known as Black
Brothers until 1947, when renamed in honor
of Governor Locke Craig (1860–1924), who
was largely responsible for the establishment
of Mount Mitchell State Park. Known earlier
as Balsam Cone.

Mount Davis, in Great Smoky Mountains National Park on the Swain County, N.C.–Sevier
County, Tenn., line. Alt. approx. 5,000. Formerly named Greenbrier Knob; renamed
about 1950 for Willis P. Davis of Knoxville,
Tenn., who started the movement for the
establishment of the park. Located at lat.
35°34′15″ N., long. 83°38′03″ W.

Mount Energy, community in s Granville County
served by post office, 1877–1900.

Mount Gallant, elevation in nw Northampton
County. Alt. 250. Plantation there was owned
by William Maule and called by the name in
1723. Governor William Tryon visited Mount
Gallant in 1765 and remarked upon the fine
view from its summit. Appears on the Collet
map, 1770, and on the MacRae map, 1833.

Mount Gibbes, s Yancey County in Black Moun-
tains between Clingmans Dome and Stepps
Gap. Alt. 6,600. Named about 1852 for Dr.
Robert Wilson Gibbes (1809–66) of Columbia,
S.C., the first to measure its altitude.

Mount Gilead, community in n Cabarrus
County.

Mount Gilead, town in sw Montgomery County.
Settled by 1835, when a post office was est.
there. Inc. 1899. Originally called Providence
and was part of a 1797 land grant to William
Scarborough. Named for the biblical mountain. Alt. 421. Produces shoes, hosiery, textiles, and apparel.

Mount Gilead Township, former township in
n Cabarrus County, now township no. 5. In
1945 a part of the township was annexed to
Concord.

Mount Gilead Township, sw Montgomery
County.

Mount Glory, n Swain County in Great Smoky
Mountains National Park on Welch Ridge
near the head of White Mans Glory Creek,
lat. 35°31′22″ N., long. 83°36′08″ W. Alt. 4,965.

Mount Golland. *See* Mount Gould.

Mount Gould, community in e central Bertie
County served by post office, 1829–1907.
Developed at the site of a plantation first
known as Mount Golland and later Mount
Gould after George Gould, a surveyor, came
into possession of it. Littledals Ferry on the
Chowan River nearby appears on the Collet
map, 1770.

Mount Guyot, in Great Smoky Mountains National Park on the Haywood County, N.C.–
Sevier County, Tenn., line near lat. 35°42′20″
N., long. 83°15′30″ W. Alt. 6,621. Named by
Prof. S. B. Buckley prior to 1859 in honor of
Arnold Guyot, geographer, who made the
first comprehensive survey of the region and
did much to stimulate public interest in the
mountains. Known by the Cherokee Indians
as *Sornook*.

Mount Hardison, ne Swain County in Great
Smoky Mountains National Park at the n

end of Dashoga Ridge. Alt. 6,148. Named for James Archibald Hardison (1867–1930) of Anson County, an original member of the N.C. State Park Commission.

Mount Hardy, s Haywood County near lat. 35°18′15″ N., long. 82°55′38″ W. Named 1957–58 for Dr. James F. E. Hardy of Asheville, who, in cooperation with Arnold Guyot, explored and named many of the mountains of w North Carolina in the 1850s. Formerly known as Black Mountain. Alt. 6,110.

Mount Hardy Gap, s Haywood County near lat. 35°17′55″ N., long. 82°55′30″ W. Formerly known as Black Mountain Gap.

Mount Heckler, former mountain in ne Gaston County. Following the construction of the dam on the Catawba River at the site, it was almost covered by water. Its peak now forms an island in Mountain Island Lake. Named for Mount Hecla Mill in Greensboro. In 1848 a cotton mill was transplanted near there from Greensboro by the son-in-law of the owner of Mount Hecla Mill. *See also* Mountain Island Lake.

Mount Hermon, unincorporated community in s central Alamance County. Name derived either from biblical Mount Hermon or for a local road known as Hermon Road for Regulator leader Hermon Husband. Mount Hermon Methodist Church, est. around 1829, is there.

Mount Hermon, community in s Caldwell County. Named for Mount Hermon Church.

Mount Hermon Township, w central Pasquotank County.

Mount Holly, town in e Gaston County. Post office est. as Huntersville in 1800, named for Rev. Humphrey Hunter, postmaster. Name changed to Woodlawn in 1846. Inc. 1879 as Mount Holly, named for the town in New Jersey where fine yarns were manufactured. Produces textiles and hosiery. Alt. 621. *See also* Nims.

Mount Holly Ferry crossed the Catawba River in nw Mecklenburg into Gaston County.

Mount Ida, central McDowell County at the s limits of the town of Marion. Alt. approx. 2,000. Named for Ida Neal.

Mount Jefferson, se of and named for town of Jefferson in central Ashe County. State park of 474 acres is maintained there for sightseeing and picnicking; created 1956. Appears

in local records as Nigger Mountain as early as 1810; name changed at the creation of the park. Original name given because of the black appearance of the weathered granite of which much of the mountain is composed. A cave near the top is said to have been used by slaves fleeing to Ohio before the Civil War. Alt. 4,683.

Mount Junaluska. *See* Jones Knob.

Mount Kephart, in Great Smoky Mountains National Park on the Swain County, N.C.–Sevier County, Tenn., line, lat. 35°38′ N., long 83°24′ W. Named in 1928 for Horace Kephart (1862–1931), explorer, naturalist, and authority on campcraft who lived in the area for many years. Alt. 6,400. Mount Collins, nearby, bore the name Mount Kephart for a short while. The Jump Off, on the Tennessee side of Mount Kephart, was formerly believed to be in North Carolina. A cliff there drops vertically for almost 500 ft. and then nearly vertically for an additional 1,000 ft.

Mount Leer. *See* Morrow's Turnout.

Mount Love, in Great Smoky Mountains National Park on the Swain County, N.C.–Sevier County, Tenn., line, lat. 35°33′30″ N., long. 83°30′ W. Named by Arnold Guyot before 1860 for Dr. S. L. Love (1828–87), who accompanied T. L. Clingman and S. O. Buckley in 1858 when Clingmans Dome was first measured. Alt. approx. 6,500.

Mount Misery appears on the Collet map, 1770, as a large sand hill n of Eagle Island in w New Hanover County. A ferry across the Cape Fear River was operated there from as early as 1754 and possibly through the Revolution.

Mount Mitchell, s Yancey County in Black Mountains. Alt. 6,684, the highest peak in e United States. Formerly known as Black Dome but renamed for Professor Elisha Mitchell (1793–1857) of the University of North Carolina, who fell to his death nearby while trying to verify his claim that it was the highest mountain e of the Mississippi. Known by the Cherokee Indians as Attakulla. *See also* Mitchell Falls.

Mount Mitchell, community in s Mitchell County on East Fork Grassy Creek.

Mount Mitchell State Park, s Yancey County. Covers 1,224 acres. Est. 1915 as the first state park in North Carolina. Scenic area, tent camping, picnicking, hiking, nature study, museum, recreation lodge, and lookout tower.

Mount Mourne, town in s Iredell County. Inc. 1875, but long inactive in municipal affairs. Settled prior to the American Revolution and took its name from the home of Rufus Reid, which Reid had named Mount Mourne for the mountain in Ireland. At Torrence's Tavern there, Lt. Col. Tarleton's British cavalry routed a force of American militia, February 2, 1781. Crowfield Academy, an early classical school about a mi. s, was est. 1760 and closed by the time of the Revolution.

Mount Nebo. *See* Nebo.

Mount Night. *See* Pores Knob.

Mount Noble, e Swain County in Great Smoky Mountains National Park, lat. 35°30'20" N., long. 83°20'15" W.

Mount Olive, community in n Columbus County.

Mount Olive, community in s Stokes County; named for a church.

Mount Olive, town in s Wayne County. Inc. 1870. Named by Benjamin Oliver, local resident, for biblical Mount of Olives. Town limits now encompass former community of Enterprise, *which see*. Center for marketing produce— vegetables, strawberries, and grapes; site of a large cucumber-pickle processing plant. Mount Olive College is there.

Mount Pisgah, on the Buncombe-Haywood county line nw of Little Pisgah Mountain. Alt. 5,721. Also sometimes known as Big Pisgah and Great Pisgah. View from its top includes points in North Carolina, South Carolina, Georgia, Tennessee, and Virginia. Reached by U.S. Forest Service trail from the Blue Ridge Parkway at Pisgah Inn. Named for the biblical mountain from which Moses saw the Promised Land. Known by the Indians as *El-see-toss*.

Mount Pisgah, community in ne Alexander County.

Mount Pisgah, community in n Rutherford County on Little Camp Creek.

Mount Pleasant, community in central Avery County.

Mount Pleasant, town in e Cabarrus County. Alt. 630. Settled about 1750 by Germans from Pennsylvania. Inc. 1859. Took its name from its elevated site between Buffalo Creek and Adams Creek. Former home of 2 Lutheran Synod church schools: Mount Pleasant Collegiate Institute (male) and Mount Amoena Seminary (female).

Mount Pleasant, community in se Moore County between Crains Creek and Buffalo Creek.

Mount Pleasant, community in sw Nash County.

Mount Pleasant, community in w Rockingham County served by post office beginning in 1808. Named for plantation owned by Gov. Alexander Martin and his heirs, the Henderson family.

Mount Pleasant, community in n Yadkin County near the head of Forbush Creek.

Mount Pleasant. *See* Elliott.

Mount Pleasant. *See* Johnsonville.

Mount Pleasant Creek rises in e Randolph County and flows sw into Sandy Creek.

Mount Pleasant Point extends from e Onslow County into White Oak River about 20 ft. above the water. Named for the pre-Revolutionary plantation of Emanuel Jones. Also known as Montford Point, *which see*, in recent years.

Mount Pleasant Township, former township in e Cabarrus County, now township no. 8.

Mount Prospect. *See* Waynesville.

Mount Regis. *See* Norlina.

Mount Sequoyah, in Great Smoky Mountains National Park on the Swain County, N.C.–Sevier County, Tenn., line, lat. 35°40' N., long. 83°18'15" W. Alt. approx. 6,000. Named for Sequoyah (1770?–1843), Indian who devised a Cherokee alphabet used in teaching thousands to read and write.

Mount Squires, in Great Smoky Mountains National Park on the Swain County, N.C.–Blount County, Tenn., line between McCampbell Knob and Rocky Top near lat. 35°33'47" N., long. 83°44'30" W. Alt. 5,042. Named for state senator Mark Squires (1878–1938), a leader in the movement to establish the park. Formerly known as Little Bald.

Mount Sterling, w Haywood County in Great Smoky Mountains National Park near lat. 35°42'10" N., long. 83°07'20" W. Alt. 5,835. Said to have been named by a woodcutter and logger from the town of Sterling, Ky.

Mount Sterling, community in w Haywood County on Big Creek near lat. 35°45'42" N., long. 83°06'15" W.

Mount Sterling Creek rises in w Haywood County and flows ne into Pigeon River.

Mount Sterling Gap, w Haywood County in Great Smoky Mountains National Park near lat. 35°42′ N., long. 83°05′59″ W. Alt. 3,887.

Mount Sterling Ridge, w Haywood County in Great Smoky Mountains National Park from Balsam Mountain extending ne from lat. 35°40′17″ N., long. 83°10′55″ W., forming the watershed between Big Creek and Cataloochee Creek.

Mount Tirzah, community in s Person County. Named in 1783 by Col. Stephen Moore, Revolutionary soldier. A post office operated there, 1795–1906.

Mount Tirzah Township, se Person County.

Mount Ulla, community in w Rowan County. Said to have been named for "a place in Ireland," probably the village of Oola. Wood Grove post office est. there in 1830; named for plantation home of Capt. Thomas Cowan, which still stands. Named changed to Mount Ulla in 1842 and to Rowan for a few months in 1900. Alt. 839.

Mount Ulla Township, w central Rowan County.

Mount Vernon, community in nw Rowan County on Fourth Creek. A post office as early as 1819 and as recent as 1882.

Mount Vernon, crossroads community in central Rutherford County between Catheys Creek and Second Broad River.

Mount Vernon Springs, community in w Chatham County. The springs, a popular resort area in the early and middle nineteenth century, are approx. 1 mi. w; known earlier as Hickory Springs. The present community was inc. as Ore Hill in 1907, but the charter was repealed in 1913. Named for the home of George Washington. Alt. 500. *See also* Wilcox Iron Works.

Mount Willing, w Orange County on the head of Toms Creek.

Mount Yonaguska, on the Haywood-Swain county line between Tricorner Knob and Luftee Knob in Great Smoky Mountains National Park near lat. 35°41′40″ N., long. 83°14′53″ W. Alt. 6,150. Named for Yonaguska, chief of the Cherokee Indians.

Mount Zion, community in w Wilkes County on Stony Fork Creek. Named for a Baptist church that was organized there in 1849.

Mount Zion. *See* Chowan Beach.

Mouse Creek, w Haywood County in Great Smoky Mountains National Park, rises near lat. 35°42′22″ N., long. 83°07′17″ W., and flows nw into Big Creek. The name is an Indian one.

Mouse Harbor, bay on the e side of Goose Creek Island, ne Pamlico County in the waters of Pamlico Sound. The shape of the bay on a map vaguely suggests the shape of a mouse.

Mouse Knob, sw Graham County on Snowbird Creek. The name is a translation of the Indian name.

Mouse Mountain, n Macon County between Rickman Creek and Bradley Creek.

Mowfield, community in w Northampton County. Sir Archie, famed thoroughbred, is buried on plantation there.

Moxley, community in n Wilkes County on Middle Prong Roaring River.

Moyes Run rises in e Pitt County and flows se into Broad Run.

Moyock, community in nw Currituck County. Name appears in local records as early as 1753. Alt. 5. Rev. Thomas Coke in 1785 recorded that he visited and preached at "Mowyock."

Moyock Creek. *See* Shingle Landing Creek.

Moyock Township, nw Currituck County.

Moyton. *See* Stantonsburg.

Mucky Branch rises in n Durham County and flows ne into Little River.

Mud Castle, community in w Northampton County. Named for a pre-Revolutionary plantation there.

Mud Creek rises in sw Durham County and flows se into New Hope Creek. Formerly known as Bakers Creek.

Mud Creek rises in w Gates County and flows se into Chowan River.

Mud Creek rises in sw Henderson County and flows ne and nw into French Broad River. The Indian name was *Oklawaha* (Muddy Waters). *See also* Naples.

Mud Creek rises in n Wake County and flows s into Horse Creek. Known previously as Mutton Creek, as shown on several nineteenth-century maps.

Mudcut Branch rises in sw Swain County and flows se into Nantahala River.

Muddy Branch rises in Green Swamp in w central Brunswick County and flows ne and n into Juniper Creek.

Muddy Creek rises in se Beaufort County and flows nw into Bond Creek.

Muddy Creek rises in the s tip of Cabarrus County and flows se into Rocky River.

Muddy Creek rises in central Catawba County and flows se and sw into Henry Fork.

Muddy Creek rises in e Duplin County and flows sw into Northeast Cape Fear River.

Muddy Creek rises in nw Forsyth County and flows s into Davidson County, where it enters Yadkin River. Called Charles Creek on the Collet map, 1770.

Muddy Creek is formed in ne McDowell County by the junction of North Muddy Creek and South Muddy Creek and flows ne into the Catawba River in w Burke County.

Muddy Creek rises in s Onslow County and flows se into Stones Bay.

Muddy Creek rises in nw Randolph County and flows se into Deep River. Appears on the Collet map, 1770.

Muddy Creek rises in n Scotland County and flows ne into Lumber River.

Muddy Creek rises in sw Stokes County and flows s through w Forsyth County and into nw Davidson County, where it enters Yadkin River. Appears as Gargals Creek on the Fry-Jefferson map, 1755, and as Gargales Creek on the Collet map, 1770. The uppermost branch is shown on the Collet map as Dorithea Creek, named for Dorothea, Countess Zinzendorf, whose husband was a patron of the Moravians. Known as Dorithea Creek as early as 1756, but sometime after 1770 its entire course became known as Muddy Creek.

Muddy Creek, community in sw Forsyth County near the Davidson county line. Alt. 726.

Muddy Cross, community in s Gates County.

Muddy Fork rises in e Cleveland County and flows sw into Buffalo Creek.

Muddy Fork Creek rises in n central Alexander County and flows sw into Lower Little River.

Muddy Slue, a slough in the tidal-marsh islands in the Cape Fear River opposite Southport, se Brunswick County.

Mud Gap, in Great Smoky Mountains National Park on Swain County, N.C.–Blount County, Tenn., line, lat. 35°31′18″ N., long. 83°48′24″ W.

Mud Lick, community in nw Chatham County served by post office, 1833–1904.

Mudlick. *See* Mud Lick.

Mulatto Branch rises in s Lee County and flows se into Little Juniper Creek.

Mulatto Mountain, s Ashe County. Alt. 4,680.

Mulberry, community in n central Wilkes County at the head of Lousy Creek.

Mulberry Bay, sw Carteret County in Bogue Sound between Banks Channel and Bogue Inlet.

Mulberry Branch rises in Green Swamp, sw Brunswick County, and flows sw into Shallotte River.

Mulberry Creek is formed in se Ashe County by the junction of Meadow Fork and Laurel Fork Creeks and flows n and w to join Piney Fork Creek in forming Cranberry Creek.

Mulberry Creek rises in n Caldwell County about 2½ mi. se of Blowing Rock in Pisgah National Forest and flows approx. 12 mi. s into Johns River.

Mulberry Creek rises in n central Carteret County and flows s into South River.

Mulberry Creek rises in s Macon County and flows se into Little Tennessee River.

Mulberry Creek rises in ne Onslow County and flows se into White Oak River.

Mulberry Creek rises in n Wilkes County and flows se into Yadkin River. Appears as Mulberryfield on the Collet map, 1770.

Mulberry Fields. *See* North Wilkesboro.

Mulberry Gap, on the Alleghany-Wilkes county line.

Mulberry Gap, at the head of Howard Branch in s Macon County.

Mulberry Island was former island and plantation on n side of Dan River in Rockingham County. Owned by Thomas Settle Jr., N.C. Supreme Court justice. No longer extant.

Mulberry Point, on the s shore of the Neuse River about 5 mi. upstream from its mouth between Cedar Bay and Turnagain Bay in n Carteret County.

Mulberry Township, n central Caldwell County.

Mulcahy. *See* Peachland.

Mule Gap, n Swain County in Great Smoky Mountains National Park on Welch Ridge, lat. 35°33′02″ N., long. 83°34′15″ W. Alt. approx. 5,000.

Mull Creek rises in n Catawba County and flows ne into Lyle Creek.

Mull Creek rises in e Jackson County and flows sw into Caney Fork.

Mullet Gut, a stream that rises in w Carteret County and flows se into Starkey Creek.

Mullet Pond, a bay on the extreme w end of Shackleford Banks, s Carteret County.

Mull Grove, community in sw Catawba County served by post office, 1842–1905. Spelled as Mullgrove after 1892.

Mullgrove. *See* Mull Grove.

Mullin Hill, mountain in sw Avery County.

Mumblehead Top, e Cherokee County between the headwaters of Rattler Branch and Brooks Cove.

Mumford. *See* Mumfords.

Mumford Point, central Onslow County about 2 mi. s of the city of Jacksonville, the point of land between the junction of New River and Northeast Branch. Now within the Camp Lejeune reservation.

Mumfords, community in n Pasquotank County served by post office, 1892–1903.

Munday Cove, central Buncombe County, extends nw from Iron Ore Ridge to Reems Creek.

Murchison, community in s Yancey County on Cane River. Alt. 2,930.

Murfreesboro, town in w Hertford County on Meherrin River. Settled around 1707 and known as Murfree's Landing for William Murfree, colonial and Revolutionary leader and owner of the town site. Known as Murfree's Ferry by 1770. Est. as Murfreesboro 1787. Site of Chowan University, founded there in 1848. Alt. 75. Produces wooden containers, tobacco, peanuts, cotton, corn, and pork. *See also* Princeton.

Murfreesboro Township, nw Hertford County.

Murfree's Ferry or **Murfree's Landing**. *See* Murfreesboro.

Murphey, community in s Duplin County.

Murphy, town and county seat, central Cherokee County at the junction of Hiwassee and Valley Rivers. Alt. 1,535. Site known first as Christie Ford for an Indian named Christie who lived there. Later called Huntersville for Col. A. R. S. Hunter, who est. a trading post there with the Cherokee Indians about 1830. Inc. as Murphy, 1851, and named for Archibald Debow Murphey (1758–1832), leader for internal improvements in North Carolina. Fort Butler, site ¼ mi. sw, was one of the assembly points used by Gen. Winfield Scott in 1838 to gather Cherokees before moving them west. The fort served as a site for the first courts until a suitable building was erected in Murphy. Produces textiles and lumber.

Murphy Bay, a swamp in e Bladen County se of Black Lake. *See also* Carolina Bays.

Murphy Branch rises in s Mitchell County and flows w into Crabtree Creek.

Murphy Branch rises in e Yancey County and flows w into South Toe River.

Murphy Falls, on Big Crabtree Creek on the Mitchell-Yancey county line.

Murphy Gap, ne Graham County.

Murphy Township, central Cherokee County.

Murray Branch rises in e Haywood County in Buckeye Cove and flows s into Pigeon River.

Murray Branch rises in nw Henderson County and flows s into Boylston Creek.

Murray Branch rises in w Madison County and flows sw into French Broad River.

Murray Cove, s Haywood County on a tributary of Little East Fork Pigeon River.

Murray Creek rises in s central Henderson County and flows n into Greer Creek.

Murray Gap, w Haywood County between Huckleberry Knob and Winding Knob.

Murray Gap, e Madison County at the head of California Creek.

Murraysville, community in n New Hanover County.

Murrayville, former community on Cane Creek in n Henderson County (then Buncombe County); named for William Murray, whose home was there. Buncombe Turnpike ran nearby. A post office operated there, 1806 to ca. 1827. The Catawba grape was discovered growing in the vicinity.

Mush Island, a sandy formation about 2¼ mi. long and 1¼ mi. wide, surrounded by silty clay, on the banks of the Roanoke River se of Weldon, ne Halifax County. The Collet map, 1770, shows Raglins Ferry at the site; called Prides Ferry on the Price map, 1808.

Musketo Inlet, through present Currituck Banks, e Currituck County, opened prior to 1657 and closed in the 1670s. Appears on the Ogilby map, 1671. *See also* Denniss Island.

Muskrat Branch rises in se Clay County and flows nw into Shooting Creek.

Muskrat Creek rises in central Macon County and flows e into Cartoogechaye Creek.

Mussel Run rises in e Greene County and flows sw into Contentnea Creek.

Musselshell Creek rises in ne Jones County and flows sw into Trent River.

Muttenz, community in w Caldwell County on Johns River.

Mutton Creek. *See* Mud Creek.

Mutual Love, community in nw Mecklenburg County served by post office, 1877–79.

Myatt's Mills, community in s Wake County.

Myatts Pond, s Wake County on Black Creek. Covers 44 acres and has max. depth of 12 ft. Used for recreation and as a power source.

Myers, community in n Wilkes County near Middle Prong Roaring River.

Myers. *See* South Gastonia.

Myers Branch rises in nw Swain County and flows sw into Fontana Lake.

Myra Lake, se Wake County on Marks Creek. Formed in 1900. Covers 50 acres and has max. depth of 15 ft. Used for recreation.

Myrtle, community in central Rutherford County served by post office, 1885–1907.

Myrtle. *See* Elah.

Myrtle Grove, community in se New Hanover County on Myrtle Sound.

Myrtle Grove Island, tidal-marsh island in se Onslow County just inside Bear Inlet.

Myrtle Grove Sound. *See* Myrtle Sound.

Myrtle Island, in Bogue Sound, w Carteret County s of Burthen Channel.

Myrtle Lawn, a family seat in s Warren County near the community of Inez. Built by the Williams family in 1790 and still standing.

Myrtle Sound, se New Hanover County. Also known as Myrtle Grove Sound. *See also* Snows Cut.

Myrtle Swamp. *See* Merkle Swamp.

Myrts, community in n Duplin County served by post office, 1893–96. Named for first postmaster James Grady's daughter Myrtie.

N

Nags Head, town on n Bodie Island facing the Atlantic Ocean, e Dare County. A popular summer resort since the 1830s. Inc. 1923; charter repealed 1949; inc. again in 1961. Numerous legends exist explaining the origin of the name. One of the most popular tells of natives who tied lanterns around the necks of ponies ("nags"), which were driven up and down the beach at night. The motion of the lanterns resembled that of a vessel at anchor and lured ships at sea into the shore, where they were wrecked and easily robbed. The name appears on maps of the area as early as 1738. Nags Head as a place name appears in various parts of England, the Channel Islands, and the West Indies.

Nags Head Coast Guard Station, central Bodie Island in e Dare County. Est. in 1874 as a lifesaving station. Lifesaving Service and Revenue Cutter Service joined to form U.S. Coast Guard in 1915. The station was declared surplus and decommissioned after World War II.

Nags Head Township, e Dare County. Includes all of Roanoke Island and the town of Nags Head.

Nags Head Woods, maritime forest, e Dare County. An ecological preserve that includes 1,400 acres. Protected by Nature Conservancy and designated a U.S. Natural Landmark, 1974.

Nahunga Creek rises in w Duplin County and flows ne into Goshen Swamp.

Nahunta, community in nw Wayne County s of Nahunta Creek, from which it takes its name. Called Academy Crossroads as recently as 1915.

Nahunta. *See* Fremont and Torhunta.

Nahunta Swamp rises in e Johnston County and flows e across ne Wayne County and ne into Contentnea Creek in w Greene County. It is mentioned under various spellings as early as 1711 as Norhanty, Norrihunta, and No Honey. Appears on the Collet map, 1770, as Beaverdam Swamp in n Wayne County. It is not shown as such on subsequent maps. The name is either originally or in corrupted form a Tuscarora Indian word, perhaps from *Kahunshe Wakena* (Black Creek).

Nahunta Township, ne Wayne County.

Nain, community in sw Forsyth County served by post office, 1890–1904.

Naked Creek rises in central Ashe County and flows e into South Fork New River.

Naked Creek rises in n Catawba County and flows n into Catawba River.

Naked Creek rises in se Montgomery County and flows se into Richmond County. At the

Moore-Richmond county line, it joins Drowning Creek in forming Lumber River.

Naked Creek rises in sw Wilkes County and flows e into Lewis Fork Creek.

Naked Mountain, now Morrow Mountain State Park, *which see*, in e Stanly County. Named after a tornado stripped timber off and left it naked; renamed in 1935 to honor donor of site for a state park.

Naked Place Mountain, ne Haywood County between Bear Wallow Gap and Fines Creek.

Nakina, community in s Columbus County. Formerly known as Wattsville.

Nalls, community in w Montgomery County served by post office, 1884–1902.

Namonda. *See* Table Rock Mountain.

Nance, community in ne Rockingham County served by post office, 1884–1910.

Nancy Hawkins Branch rises in ne Cherokee County and flows nw into Graybeard Creek. Named for an Indian woman.

Nancy Mountain, s Transylvania County between the headwaters of Toxaway Creek and Shoal Creek. Alt. 3,013.

Nancys Mountain, s Randolph County between Kies Mountain and Little River.

Nane Branch rises in central Clay County and flows nw into Cold Branch.

Nanito. *See* Shingle Hollow.

Nanny Mountain, se Buncombe County near the Rutherford County line.

Nansemond Indian Town appears on the Moseley map, 1733, near the forks of Nottoway River and Blackwater River where they form the Chowan River. The site is now in ne Hertford County.

Nantahala, community in sw Swain County. A post office operated there, 1873–1905. After 1889 known as Ledford. Alt. 1,942.

Nantahala Balds, grassy areas in the Nantahala Mountain Range, *which see*, of w Macon County. Wayah Bald is the most prominent of these areas. Named for the Cherokee word *Nan-toh-ee-yah-heh-lih* (sun in the middle; noonday), as Indian runners between Valley River crossed it at midday on their way to Oconaluftee or Soco in Swain County.

Nantahala Gorge, ne Graham and sw Swain Counties, a canyon of the Nantahala River with such depth and such sheer sides that the Cherokee Indians named it "Land of the Middle Sun," believing that only the noonday sun could penetrate its depths. One of the several Cherokee legends is that the gorge was the haunt of the *Uktena* (keen-eyed), a huge horned serpent. The bright gem blazing from between its horns was called *ulstitlu* (it is on his head) and meant death to the family of any Indian who beheld it. However, when detached it became the *ulunsuti* (transparent), the great talisman that revealed the future to the possessor. When a wary hunter encased himself in leather, surprised the monster, killed it, and tore the great jewel from its head, the snake writhed from one side of the gorge to the other, shutting out the radiance of the sun and causing the perpetual twilight. The great jewel was said to be the rutile quartz, so rare that there was only one specimen among the Eastern Cherokee in 1890. In the gorge, on the left bank of the river, are caves claimed by some to have been occupied by a race that preceded the Cherokee.

Nantahala Lake, in Clay and Macon Counties on the headwaters of Nantahala River. Dam completed in 1942. Area 1,605 acres; max. depth 225 ft.; shoreline 30 mi. Owned by Nantahala Power and Light Company and used for the generation of electricity. Nantahala is an Indian word meaning "sun in the middle" and was applied to the gorge through which the river runs.

Nantahala Mountain Range lies between the Great Smoky Mountains on the n and the Blue Ridge on the s. It extends about 50 mi. across Macon County from the junction of Nantahala and Little Tennessee Rivers in Swain County to Tallulah Falls, Ga.

Nantahala National Forest, in portions of Cherokee, Clay, Graham, Jackson, Macon, Swain, and Transylvania Counties, was est. in 1911 and includes 531,286 acres. Nature trails, mountain climbing, picnicking, and other recreational uses. *See also* Joyce Kilmer Memorial Forest.

Nantahala River rises in sw Macon County and flows nw to the Clay-Macon county line, which it forms for a part of its course; it then flows into Graham County, where it enters Little Tennessee River. *See also* Camp Branch Falls.

Nantahala Township, nw Macon County.

Nantahala Township, s Swain County.

Naomi Falls. *See* Randleman.

Naples, community in n Henderson County. Alt. 2,080. A cooperative school and hospital are maintained there by Seventh-Day Adventists. Named 1901 when a post office was est. there because Mud Creek in the valley below often flooded, reminding a local resident of the Bay of Naples.

Narassa, community in ne Brunswick County. Produces lumber and fertilizers.

Narhantes. See Nahunta Swamp.

Narrow Ridge, ne Yancey County between Green Mountain and Brush Creek.

Narrows, boat channel through the narrow part of Currituck Sound near Poplar Branch. Tidal-marsh islands lie on either side of the channel in s Currituck County. Appears on the Comberford map, 1657.

Narrows, The, the final mile and a half of Newport River confined within banks before it approaches the estuary, central Carteret County.

Narrows, The, section of Green River in e Henderson County where rocks narrow to tight passageway. Favored by kayakers despite access difficulties.

Narrows, The. *See* Croatan Sound.

Narrows of the Yadkin, formerly a portion of Yadkin River in Montgomery and Stanly Counties constricted by the Uwharrie Mountains, through which the river passes. With the construction of Badin Dam in 1917, the Narrows of the Yadkin were submerged by Badin Lake. Appears on the Price map, 1808, and the MacRae map, 1833. Sometimes referred to as Yadkin Narrows.

Narrows Reservoir. *See* Badin Lake.

Narrowsville, community in nw Montgomery County near Narrows of the Yadkin. Served by post office, 1833–41.

Nash County was formed in 1777 from Edgecombe County. Located in the ne section of the state, it is bounded by Edgecombe, Wilson, Johnston, Franklin, and Halifax Counties. It was named for Gen. Francis Nash (1742–77) of Hillsborough, mortally wounded at the Battle of Germantown while

fighting under George Washington. Area: 552 sq. mi. County seat: Nashville, with an elevation of 180 ft. Townships are Bailey, Castalia, Coopers, Dry Wells, Ferrells, Griffins, Jackson, Mannings, Nashville, North Whitakers, Oak Level, Red Oak, Rocky Mount, South Whitakers, and Stony Creek. Produces tobacco, corn, wheat, oats, peanuts, cotton, poultry, hogs, livestock, machinery, computers, plastics, sweet potatoes, strawberries, cantaloupes, cucumbers, bakery products, textiles, furniture, lumber, and apparel.

Nash District, one of the districts into which Caswell County was divided at the time of the 1790 census. It contained 118 heads of families.

Nash Mine, e Cabarrus County 1½ mi. nw of Phoenix Mine Village, *which see*. Known as Faggart Mine in the mid-nineteenth century, when gold was mined there. Uranium was discovered there in 1954.

Nashville, town and county seat, central Nash County. Authorized to be laid out and est., 1815. Named for Gen. Francis Nash (1742–77), Revolutionary War officer killed at Germantown. Produces lumber and apparel. Alt. 180.

Nashville Township, central Nash County.

Nathans Creek rises in e Ashe County and flows e into South Fork New River.

Nathans Creek, community in e central Ashe County. Alt. approx. 2,800.

Nations Creek rises in w Jackson County and flows ne into Tuckasegee River.

Nat Moore, community in se Bladen County served by post office, 1875–1914.

Nattie Branch rises in s Clay County and flows n into Giesky Creek.

Natural Wells, community in sw Duplin County served by post office, 1892–1903. Name for large limestone sinkholes in the area.

Nausegoc, a name appearing on the White map, 1590, in Pamlico Sound, e Dare County approx. between the present communities of Rodanthe and Salvo on Hatteras Island. The name is believed to have been an Algonquian Indian word for "take a breathing-spell," hence a resting place for those on a long canoe journey.

Navassa, community in ne Brunswick County on Cape Fear River. Historically African American, center for Gullah Geechee culture and traditions.

Navy Yard Lake, e Anson County se of Lilesville. Covers approx. 10 acres; max. depth 15 ft. Formed early in the twentieth century when gravel was removed from the site.

Naylors Knob, central Caldwell County. Named for James Nailor, an early settler.

Nazareth, community in central Wake County s of Raleigh. Settled 1898. Named for the biblical town by Rev. Thomas Price, who est. a Roman Catholic orphanage there. Alt. 325.

Neal, community in w Bertie County.

Neal Branch rises in sw Mecklenburg County and flows nw into Stowe Branch.

Neal Branch rises in s Wake County and flows e into Swift Creek.

Neal Creek, short stream in n central Carteret County that flows ne into South River.

Neal Gut, a narrow, water-filled defile in central Franklin County that empties into Tar River.

Neals Creek rises in se Yancey County and flows nw into Big Lost Cove Creek.

Nealsville. *See* Glenwood.

Neatman, community in s central Stokes County. A post office operated there, 1857–1903.

Neatman Creek rises in s central Stokes County and flows s into Town Fork Creek.

Nebo, community in e McDowell County. Inc. 1909; charter repealed 1943. Alt. 1,282. A popular Methodist campground there before the Civil War was known as Nebo for the biblical mountain. When the North Carolina Railroad was constructed, the station there took the name of the campground.

Nebo, community in n central Yadkin County. Once known as Mount Nebo.

Nebo Township, e McDowell County.

Nebraska, town in e Hyde County. Inc. 1855, but long inactive in municipal affairs. Probably named because of the importance of the Kansas-Nebraska Act of 1854, which repealed the Missouri Compromise.

Ned Branch rises in central Haywood County and flows se into Hemphill Creek.

Neddie Creek rises in e Jackson County and flows se into Tuckasegee River.

Neddie Knob, on the ne end of Neddie Mountain in e Jackson County.

Neddie Mountain, e Jackson County, extends ne between Dismal Mountain and Neddie Knob.

Ned Gap, in sw Jackson County between Rich Mountain and West Fork [Dicks Creek].

Neds Creek rises in w Carteret County and flows w into Koonces Bay of White Oak River.

Neds Lick Gap, w Haywood County on the head of Hemphill Creek.

Neds Marsh, central Duplin County.

Needhams Mountain, s Randolph County near the head of Fork Creek.

Needmore, community in s Caldwell County between Lower and Smoky Creeks.

Needmore, community in nw Franklin County. Also known as Wilder.

Needmore, community in Moore County n of Carthage. Settled by African Americans after the Civil War.

Needmore, community in nw Rowan County.

Needmore, former community in s Swain County est. about 1880 on property of Allison McHan. A thriving trading center until after about 1912, when the site was purchased by Nantahala Power Company for a right-of-way for a proposed power project. Population in 1950 was 75, but by 1960 only one house was occupied. Post office, est. 1891 and discontinued 1953, was named Needmore because of the habit of the people constantly complaining that they "needed more of this and that." Alt. 1,830.

Needmore Branch rises in s Clay County and flows n into Shooting Creek.

Neely Gap, sw Cherokee County near the headwaters of Persimmon Creek.

Nee-oh-la. *See* Pigeon River; West Fork Pigeon River.

Negro Hammocks, formerly two islands in s Hyde County in Pamlico Sound ne of Ocracoke Island, but now submerged. Known by the name as early as 1795. One of the islands was above water as late as 1910 and was called Negro Island.

Negrohead, community in e Union County served by post office, 1888–1903.

Negro Island. *See* Negro Hammocks.

Negro Prong rises in w Transylvania County and flows ne into Catheys Creek.

Neil Gap, in n central Transylvania County on the head of Lamb Creek.

Neills Creek rises in s Wake County and flows sw in n Harnett County into Cape Fear River. Named for Red Neill McNeill, who settled along its banks in 1740.

Neills Creek Township, central Harnett County.

Nella. *See* Husk.

Nellie, former community in w Haywood County on Cataloochee Creek near the mouth of Palmer Creek near lat. 35°37'40" N., long. 83°06'10" W. Settled about 1848. Named for Nellie Palmer, who in 1907, at the age of one, won first prize in a baby contest. Site now is in the Great Smoky Mountains National Park and is abandoned.

Nellie Ridge, w Haywood County in Great Smoky Mountains National Park, a short spur of Big Fork Ridge near lat. 35°37'10" N., long. 83°06'50" W. Named for nearby community of Nellie.

Nelms, community in s Pamlico County.

Nelson, community in central Caldwell County.

Nelson, community in se Durham County.

Nelson Bay, a bay formed by waters of Core Sound in ne Carteret County.

Nelson Branch rises in central Haywood County and flows ne into Jonathans Creek.

Nelson Branch rises in n Haywood County and flows se into Whiteoak Branch.

Nelson Branch rises in w Haywood County and flows ne into Cataloochee Creek.

Nelson Branch rises in e central Union County and flows ne into Rays Fork.

Nelson Cove extends se from Sassafras Ridge to Snowbird Creek in s Graham County.

Nelson Creek. *See* East Nelson Creek; West Nelson Creek.

Nelson Ridge, central Clay County between Vineyard Mountain and Tusquitee Creek.

Nelsons Old Ferry. *See* Graves Ferry.

Nelsonville. *See* Grimesland.

Nero, community in nw Wake County served by post office, 1900–1904.

Ness Creek rises in n New Hanover County and flows sw into Cape Fear River.

Nestor, community in nw Davie County served by post office, 1886–1905.

Net, community in w Iredell County served by post office, 1894–1907.

Nettle Branch rises in s Burke County and flows n into Jacob Fork.

Nettle Creek rises in nw Haywood County and flows ne into Big Creek.

Nettle Creek, in Great Smoky Mountains National Park, rises in n Swain County and flows sw into Deep Creek.

Nettle Creek Bald, n Swain County in Great Smoky Mountains National Park, lat. 35°34'02" N., long. 83°22'55" W. Alt. 5,172.

Nettle Knob, in central Watauga County n of Howard Creek. Alt. 4,000.

Nettle Knob, community in se Ashe County.

Nettle Patch, mountain near the Blue Ridge Parkway on the McDowell-Mitchell-Yancey county line. Alt. approx. 3,950.

Nettles Cove, n Buncombe County ne of Snowball Gap.

Neuse. *See* Neuse Crossroads.

Neuse Crossroads, community in n central Wake County. Named for nearby Neuse River. Formerly known as Dunnsville and as Neuse. Produces textiles. Alt. 234.

Neuse Forest, community in e Craven County.

Neuseoco Lake, e central Wake County on Beaverdam Creek. Covers 75 acres and has a max. depth of 20 ft. Owned by a club and used for recreation.

Neuse River is formed in w Durham County by the junction of Eno and Flat Rivers. It flows se, forming in part the Durham-Granville and Durham-Wake county lines; then through Wake, Johnston, Wayne, Lenoir, and Craven Counties, forming in part the Craven-Pamlico and Carteret-Pamlico county lines before entering Pamlico Sound. Named in 1584 by Arthur Barlowe for the Neusiok Indians. The Tuscarora Indians called the river *Gow-ta-no* (pine in water).

Neuse River Township, central Wake County.

Neuse Township, central Lenoir County.

Never Mountain, an almost perfect cone, w Alexander County.

Neverson, community in nw Wilson County. Named for Neverson Williams. Post office, 1908–11.

Nevil Creek rises in central Beaufort County and flows n into Pamlico River. Appears as Turners Creek on the Collet map, 1770, but the MacRae map, 1833, calls it Nevil Creek.

Neville Creek rises in n Chatham County and flows n into Orange County, where it enters University Lake.

Nevin, community in Mecklenburg County served by post office, 1891–1902.

Newasiwac, an Indian village of the Neusiok tribe located in what is now the s tip of Craven County on the Neuse River estuary. Appears on the White map, 1585. Called Neuustooc on the De Bry map, 1590, and Nustoc on the Smith map, 1624.

New Began Creek. *See* New Begun Creek.

New Begun Creek rises in s Pasquotank County and flows se into Pasquotank River. Mentioned in records of the area as early as 1660. The name Newbiggin is a common place name in the n of England, but in this case it may represent an attempt to spell in English the Indian name. Appears as New Began Creek on the Collet map, 1770, and as New Beggin Creek on the Price map, 1808, and the MacRae map, 1833. *See also* Weeksville.

New Belden, community in e central Pitt County.

New Berlin. *See* Delco.

New Bern, city and county seat, central Craven County at the junction of Neuse and Trent Rivers. Settled in 1710; inc. 1723. Took its name from Bern, Switzerland, capital of the homeland of its founder, Baron Christoph de Graffenried. Alt. 12. New Bern was the colonial and state capital from 1746 until the est. of Raleigh in 1792, although during the period the General Assembly met in various places from time to time. It met there in 1738–40, 1744–46, 1747–51, 1754–59, 1760, 1762, 1765–78, 1784–85, 1791–93, and 1794. Produces boats, lumber, apparel, dairy products, fertilizer, and processed meat. *See also* Tryon Palace; Drysborough.

Newbern District, at the time of the 1790 census, was composed of Beaufort, Carteret, Craven, Dobbs, Hyde, Johnston, Jones, Pitt, and Wayne Counties.

Newberry Creek rises in w McDowell County and flows se into Curtis Creek.

Newbes Bridge. *See* Belvidere.

New Bethel, community in ne Orange County. Developed around New Bethel Methodist Church, est. 1859.

New Bethel Crossroads, in w Rockingham County. Area renamed Bethany.

New Bethel Township, sw Rockingham County.

New Biggin Creek. *See* New Begun Creek.

New Branch rises in n Avery County and flows ne into Buckeye Creek.

Newby's Bridge. *See* Belvidere.

New Carthage. *See* Wilmington.

New Castle, community in se Wilkes County between Osborne and Hunting Creeks. Named for the plantation of James Clemmons Hunt (1804–47), local merchant and planter. The

town of Denneysville was authorized to be laid out at the site in 1817 on land then owned by George Denny, but it apparently did not develop. Known as Hunt's Store by 1847 and by its present name by the 1850s.

New Castle Township, e Wilkes County.

New Currituck Inlet, from the Atlantic Ocean into Currituck Sound through Currituck Banks, opened in the 1730s and closed in 1828. The site is now in e Currituck County.

Newdale, community in e Yancey County on Long Branch. Flinty, former post office serving the area, is a part of Newdale.

Newell, community in e Mecklenburg County. Settled about 1880 and named for John A. Newell, local resident, in whose home the first post office was est. in 1882. Alt. 756.

New Exeter. *See* Exeter.

Newfound, community in w Buncombe County on Newfound Creek.

Newfound Creek rises on the Buncombe-Haywood county line near Newfound Gap and flows ne into French Broad River.

Newfound Gap, on the Buncombe-Haywood county line at the s end of Newfound Mountain. Alt. approx. 3,000.

Newfound Gap, in Great Smoky Mountains National Park on Swain County, N.C.–Sevier County, Tenn., line, lat. 35°37′ N., long. 83°26′ W. Alt. 5,045.

Newfoundland, community in n Tyrrell County at the head of Alligator Creek. Former post office, Gudger, operated there, 1882–1912.

Newfoundland. *See* Horseshoe.

Newfound Mountain, on the Buncombe-Haywood county line. The peak of the mountain is known as Big Butt Mountain.

New Garden. *See* Guilford College.

New Hanover County was formed in 1729 from Craven County. Located in the se section of the state, it is bounded by the Atlantic Ocean, Cape Fear River, and Brunswick and Pender Counties. It was named in honor of the royal family of England, members of the House of Hanover. Area: 225 sq. mi. County seat: Wilmington, with an elevation of 38 ft. Townships are Cape Fear, Federal Point, Harnett, Masonboro, and Wilmington. Produces miscellaneous fruits and vegetables, bulbs and flowers, seafood, ceramics, optical fiber, nuclear technology, corn, soybeans, hogs, dairy products, poultry, bakery goods, fabricated metals, lumber, wooden containers, textiles, apparel, paper boxes, chemicals, refrigeration machinery, sand, and limestone.

New Hill, community in sw Wake County. Post office est. in 1832. Inc. 1907; charter repealed 1917. Alt. 356.

New Holland, community on the s shore of Lake Mattamuskeet in central Hyde County. Alt. 3. Settled 1910 and named by a development company that attempted to drain the lake for farmland but finally gave up in 1934, when the lake was allowed to refill. Their activity suggested the Netherlands' continuous efforts to drain farmland, hence the name.

New Hope, community in s Franklin County.

New Hope, community in nw Iredell County.

New Hope, community in se Randolph County. Post office there, 1859–1934, was New Hope Academy, named for a local school; the building still stands but is used as a residence.

New Hope, community in e Wayne County. A post office was located there by 1811.

New Hope, community in nw Wilson County s of Silver Lake. Named for a local Baptist church.

New Hope. *See* Durants Neck.

New Hope Creek rises in central Orange County and flows e into w Durham County. There it turns se and flows into Chatham County, where it becomes New Hope River, *which see*. Appears as New River on the Moseley map, 1733, but by 1770 (Collet map) appears as New-hope Creek.

New Hope Lake. *See* Jordan Lake.

New Hope River, the name applied to New Hope Creek in e Chatham County from the mouth of Whiteoak Creek to its confluence with Haw River, a distance of approx. 8 mi. *See also* New Hope Creek.

New Hope Township, e Chatham County.

New Hope Township, nw Iredell County. Named for a Civil War muster ground.

New Hope Township, se Perquimans County.

New Hope Township, sw Randolph County.

New Hope Township, e Wayne County. First listed in county tax records in 1838.

New House, community in w Cleveland County.

New Inlet, from the Atlantic Ocean into Pamlico Sound s of Pea Island, se Dare County. It opened probably in the late 1720s and has closed periodically, the most recent closing being in the 1930s. Also known as Chickinacommock and as such appears on the Moll map, 1729.

New Inlet gave access from Onslow Bay and the Atlantic Ocean into the Basin at the s tip of New Hanover County. Used extensively by blockade runners under the guns of Fort Fisher. Closed by The Rocks, a great seawall constructed 1879–95.

New Institute. *See* Olin.

Newkirk Mill Pond, on Ben's Creek in w Duplin County. Built by slave labor.

New Lake. *See* Alligator Lake.

New Lake Fork flows se from the s shore of Alligator Lake in n Hyde County and along the Hyde-Tyrrell county line to empty into Alligator River. N section also known as Squyars Canal.

Newland, town and county seat, central Avery County on Linville and North Toe Rivers. Site selected by commissioners for county seat. Inc. 1913. Named for William Calhoun Newland (1860–1938), lieutenant governor, 1909–13. Site had been early muster ground in campaign against Indians and before the Battle of Kings Mountain; called Old Fields of Toe, for Toe River. Alt. 3,589. Produces textiles.

Newland Drainage Canal, in Newland Township in nw Pasquotank County, drains e into Pasquotank River.

New Lands, community in w Tyrrell County e of White Oak Island.

New Lands, e Washington County, area at the ne boundary of East Dismal Swamp, *which see*. Name appears in county records as early as 1868.

Newland Township, n Pasquotank County.

New Lebanon. *See* South Mills.

Newlife, community in n Wilkes County near North Prong Roaring River. The former community of Ink is now a part of Newlife.

New Light, community in n Wake County.

New Light Creek rises in se Granville County and flows sw into n Wake County, where it enters Neuse River. Shown on Collet map, 1770, as Newlight Creek.

New Light Township, n Wake County.

Newlin Township, former township in s central Alamance County, now township no. 8.

New Liverpool. *See* Wilmington.

New London, town in n Stanly County. Alt. 697. Prior to incorporation in 1891, it was known as Bilesville.

Newman, community in nw Warren County. A post office was located there, 1892–1906.

Newmarket, town authorized in 1801 to be est. in Orange County at or near Woody's Ferry on Haw River. It was a project of the Deep and Haw River Company designed to improve river navigation, but apparently the town was never laid out.

New Market, town in n Randolph County. Inc. 1813, but long inactive in municipal affairs.

New Market Township, nw Randolph County.

New Mattamuskeet Creek. *See* Juniper Bay.

Newport, town in w Carteret County on Newport River. Inc. 1866. Alt. 20 ft. First known as Bells Corners, but Quakers from Rhode Island settled there and changed the name to Newport for the city in their native state.

Newport, chartered 1789 to be county seat of Tyrrell County. On sw side of Scuppernong River at Back Landing. The town was never built.

Newport Marshes, a marshy island in Newport River about 1 mi. ne of Morehead City between the channel of the Intracoastal Waterway and Crab Point Thorofare in central Carteret County. Formerly Haystack Marshes.

Newport News Point, se Tyrrell County, extends from the mainland into Alligator River. Appears on the Collet map, 1770, as Nupernuse Point.

Newport River rises in w Carteret County and flows about 23 mi. e and se into the central part of the county, where it enters Bogue Sound. Appears as Coranine River on the Lawson map, 1709, but as Newport River on the Moseley map, 1733.

Newport Township, on Newport River and Broad Creek in ne Carteret County. For a time called township no. 3.

New River is formed on the Ashe-Alleghany county line by the junction of North Fork and South Fork New River. It flows ne and nw into Virginia and West Virginia and enters Kanawha River at Charleston, W.Va. In its meanderings, it crosses the North Carolina–Virginia line into Alleghany County several times. Named because of the discovery of the river in 1749, when the boundary between North Carolina and Virginia was extended 90 mi. The surveyors crossed what they thought was "a large branch of the Mississippi which runs between the ledges of the mountains," and which, in the words of Governor Gabriel Johnston, "Nobody ever drempt of before." Designated a National Scenic River in 1976; now a state park.

New River rises in nw Onslow County near the Jones County line and flows se across the county into Onslow Bay of the Atlantic Ocean. Appears as Corani River on the Moll map, 1729, and as New River on the Moseley map, 1733. Tradition says that it was originally a long lake in a swampy area, but after an extended period of torrential rain, the lake overflowed into the Atlantic Ocean and became a new river. Camp Lejeune Marine Base is near the mouth of New River.

New River Inlet, s Onslow County between Stump Sound and Onslow Beach. Appears on the Moseley map, 1733.

New River Marine Base. *See* Camp Lejeune.

New River Township, central Watauga County.

New Salem, community in n Randolph County served by post office, 1879–1906.

New Salem, community in ne Union County. Named for a local school by the State Highway Commission when it took over maintenance of local roads and a name was entered on a road map of the county. The crossroads community there was originally called Euto by returning veterans of the Battle of Eutaw Springs, S.C., during the Revolution. Served by post office, 1880–1905.

New Salem. *See* Salem.

New Salem Township, ne Union County.

Newsom, community in s Davidson County on Yadkin River. Alt. 558. Named for the family from whom land was acquired for the railroad station.

Newsome, community in e Wayne County between Walnut Creek and West Bear Creek.

Newsome Store, community in se Hertford County.

New Stirling, community in w central Iredell County.

Newstump Point, ne Carteret County, e extension of Piney Island into West Bay.

Newton, city and county seat, in central Catawba County. Alt. 996. Authorized to be laid out in 1845, inc. 1855. Named for Isaac Newton Wilson, son of Nathaniel Wilson and member of the General Assembly in 1842. He introduced the bill to create Catawba County. Produces textiles, furniture, hosiery, apparel, and paper boxes.

Newton, community in e Northampton County. Known first as Miami, later as Liverman, and finally by its present name.

Newton. *See* Wilmington.

Newton Bald, n Swain County in Great Smoky Mountains National Park, lat. 35°32′39″ N., long. 83°21′32″ W. Alt. 5,142.

Newton Grove, town in n Sampson County. Alt. 185. A post office, Coxe's Store, est. in the vicinity in 1825; discontinued 1849, when Newton Grove post office est. Inc. as Newton Grove, 1879; reincorporated, 1935.

Newton Grove Township, n Sampson County.

Newtons Crossroads, community in se Sampson County.

Newton Township, central Catawba County.

New Topsail Beach. *See* Topsail Beach.

New Topsail Inlet, s Pender County between Old Topsail Inlet and the Onslow-Pender county line, through which waters of Topsail Sound flow into the Atlantic Ocean. Appears on the Moseley map, 1733.

New Town. *See* Charles Town.

New Town. *See* Farmville.

New Town. *See* Swansboro.

New Town. *See* Wadesboro.

New Town. *See* Wilmington.

New Years Creek rises in s Watauga County on the w limits of the town of Blowing Rock and flows s into n Caldwell County, where it enters Thunderhole Creek.

Niagara, community in se Moore County est. about 1904 by northern interests. Alt. 402.

Nibb's Knob. *See* Big Cataloochee Mountain.

Nicanon, community in n Perquimans County.

Nichols Branch rises in s Macon County and flows ne into Tessentee Creek.

Nichols Branch rises in sw Macon County and flows ne into Nantahala River.

Nicholson, community in central Alamance County served by post office, 1879–1903.

Nicholson Creek rises in central Transylvania County and flows se into French Broad River.

Nicholsons Creek rises in n Hoke County and flows s into Rockfish Creek.

Nicholsons Mills, community in ne Iredell County served by post office, 1876–1905.

Nickajack Creek rises in e Macon County and flows ne into Cullasaja River.

Nickajack Gap, at the head of Nickajack Creek in e Macon County.

Nick Bottom, loamy section in e Swain County on Oconaluftee River near the mouth of Goose Creek.

Nick Branch rises in ne Cherokee County and flows n into Radder Creek.

Nick Creek rises in s Haywood County and flows se into West Fork Pigeon River.

Nick Gap, central Haywood County on the head of Messer Branch.

Nicks Creek rises in s McDowell County and flows ne into Catawba River.

Nicks Creek rises in w Moore County and flows ne into Little River. Named for Nicholas Smith, who settled there about 1768.

Nicks Creek. *See* Pheasant Creek.

Nicks Knob, s Cherokee County near the headwaters of Moccasin Creek.

Nigger Bay, between Swan Island and Currituck Banks in ne Currituck County. In 2003 state legislature directed county to rename bay.

Nigger Head, mountain on the Clay-Macon county line. Alt. approx. 4,900. In 2003 state legislature directed counties to rename mountain; now also known as Clay Knob.

Niggerhead Creek rises in e Union County and flows nw into Richardson Creek. In 2003 state legislature directed county to rename creek; now also known as Salem Creek.

Nigger Mountain. *See* Mount Jefferson.

Niggerskull Creek. *See* Cedar Valley Creek.

Nigger Skull Mountain, w Haywood County on the head of East Fork. In 2003 state legislature directed county to rename mountain.

Niggerskull Mountain. *See* Cedar Valley Knob.

Nigger Spring, s Haywood County, a spring on the head of Little East Fork Pigeon River. In 2003 state legislature directed county to rename spring.

Nigh Inlet, a point of land on Ocracoke Island about 3½ mi. from the s end of the island, se Hyde County. The inlet may be the site of Port Grenvil, *which see*, shown on the White map, 1590, but long closed.

Nikwasi. *See* Franklin.

Nile, community in n Alleghany County served by post office, 1898–1915.

Nimrod, community in sw Mecklenburg County served by post office, 1891–1902. Was on the w side of the Charlotte, Columbia, and Augusta Railroad. Site is now the Yorkmont area of Charlotte.

Nims, formerly a community in e Gaston County but now a part of the town of Mount Holly, *which see.*

Nina, community in ne Cherokee County served by post office, 1880–1911.

Nine Mile Creek. *See* Ninemile Swamp.

Ninemile Swamp rises in w Onslow County and flows sw into Duplin County, where its name becomes Nine Mile Creek and it enters Back Swamp. Named for its distance from Rich Lands Chapel, an early center of settlement.

Ninive, community in w Transylvania County.

Nin Ridge, nw Cherokee County in the Unicoi Mountains, is bounded on four sides by Bryson Lead, Groundhog Ridge, Copper Ridge, and Chestnut Orchard Ridge.

Nit Top, on the Cherokee County, N.C.–Monroe County, Tenn., line in the Unicoi Mountains.

Nix Creek rises in s Jackson County on n slopes of Sassafras Mountain and flows ne into Sapphire Lake.

Nix Mountain, s Jackson County between Nix Creek and Horsepasture River.

Nixon's. *See* Columbus.

Nixons Mill Creek flows se from Old Topsail Creek into Topsail Sound, s Pender County.

Nixon's Town. *See* Nixonton.

Nixonton, town in w Pasquotank County on Little River. The site was originally known as Windmill Point. Laid out in 1746, settled then or soon afterward, and est. 1758 as Nixon's Town. Named for Zachariah Nixon, an early settler. Appears on the Collet map, 1770; served as county seat, 1785–1800. Inc. 1818; reincorporated 1951, but not now active in municipal affairs.

Nixonton Township, s Pasquotank County.

No Ache Bay, on the w shore of Hatteras Island in the waters of Pamlico Sound, s Dare County s of the community of Salvo.

No Ache Island, a small island in No Ache Bay on the w shore of Hatteras Island in the waters of Pamlico Sound, s Dare County.

Noah Branch rises in se Buncombe County and flows se into Rutherford County, where it enters Cedar Creek.

Noah's Mountain, in the Cane Creek Mountains, s Alamance County.

Nobles Crossroads, community in s Lenoir County.

Nobles Mill Pond, on tributary of Cokey Swamp in central Edgecombe County. Est. by Nobles family for furnishing waterpower for mill. Has max. depth of 15 ft. and area of 37 acres. Now used for fishing, swimming, and boating. Open to the public.

Nobles Mill Pond, in s Lenoir County on Trent River. Formed prior to 1802 by William Williams or his son, Evan, and known as Williams Pond until 1852, when it was acquired by the Nobles family. Covers 125 acres. Max. depth 8 ft.

Noblin, community in n Granville County served by post office, 1887–1905.

Nobreeches Ridge, se Haywood County on the head of East Fork Pigeon River.

No Business Creek rises in nw Cleveland County and flows sw into First Broad River.

No Business Mountain, nw Cleveland County near the headwaters of Cox Creek. Said to be too rough to be surveyed. Local residents claim they have "no business" on it. Alt. 1,760.

Nocona, community in s Madison County. Alt. 1,585.

No Creek rises in s Davie County and flows s 4 mi. into Dutchmans Creek. It is said that an early settler bought land there, and the deed called for a creek. He complained that he found no creek on his land, but later, when he discovered one, it came to be called No Creek.

Nofat Mountain, on the Buncombe-Madison county line w of Pleasant Gap.

No Grease, riverside site in e central Hertford County on Chowan River approx. ¼ mi. n of Winton. A fishery there in the nineteenth century departed from custom when it kept no grease on hand, which meant that customers could not cook fish at the site.

No Honey Swamp. *See* Nahunta Swamp.

Noise, community in nw Moore County served by post office, 1882–1912. Ten mi. e was Quiet, *which see.*

Nokassa. *See* Hawksbill Mountain.

Noland, former community in w central Swain

County on Tuckasegee River. Alt. 1,622. Named for Andrew Noland, one of the first settlers in the area. Site now under the waters of Fontana Lake.

Noland Creek rises in e Davie County and flows approx. 1½ mi. sw into Dutchmans Creek.

Noland Creek, Great Smoky Mountains National Park, rises in n Swain County on Noland Divide and flows se then sw into Tuckasegee River. Named for Andrew Noland, first settler along its banks.

Noland Divide, mountain ridge, central Swain County in Great Smoky Mountains National Park, extending from the Tennessee state line s to Bryson City. Roundtop Knob, *which see*, a peak on the ridge, has an elevation of 5,120 ft.

Noland Gap, w Haywood County in Great Smoky Mountains National Park between Noland Mountain and Canadian Top near lat. 35°39′10″ N., long. 83°06′ W.

Noland Mountain, w Haywood County in Great Smoky Mountains National Park near lat. 35°39′35″ N., long. 83°05′18″ W. Alt. 3,951.

Nolen Creek rises in w Haywood County and flows se into Richland Creek.

Nolichucky River is formed on the Mitchell-Yancey county line by the junction of Toe River and Cane River. It flows n and w along the county line and into Tennessee, where it enters the French Broad River.

Nolton Ridge, se Graham County in the Snowbird Mountains.

Nonah, community in ne Macon County served by post office, 1883–1904.

Noratake River. *See* Roanoke River.

Norfleet, community in se Halifax County. Norfleet Ferry appears on the Collet map, 1770, ne of the present community. The ferry across the Roanoke River was operated as late as 1886 but was discontinued in 1888, when the railroad bridge was built there.

Norfolk, County of. *See* County of Norfolk.

Norhanty Swamp. *See* Nahunta Swamp.

Norlina, town in w Warren County. Inc. 1913. Alt. 438. Originally known as Mount Regis, but the name was changed after a post office was est. there in 1900 as Norlina, a contraction of "North Carolina."

Norman, town in n Richmond County. Known first as Sprouls Old Field. Post office est. 1911 and named for Flim Norman, local lumber

merchant. Inc. 1913. Long inactive in municipal affairs. Processes lumber.

Norrihunta Swamp. *See* Nahunta Swamp.

Norrington's Falls, in Cape Fear River in n central Harnett County. In an 1819 survey of the rivers of North Carolina, the n end, near the confluence of Hector Creek with the river, is called Norrington's Upper Falls; the s end, near the confluence of Neals Creek with the river, is called Norrington's Lower Falls.

Norris, community in e Watauga County.

Norris Branch rises in w Wake County and flows sw into Cary Branch.

Norris Branch rises in central Watauga County and flows se and ne into Howard Creek.

Norris Branch rises in n Yancey County and flows n into Nolichucky River.

Norris Creek rises in s Franklin County and flows se and ne into Crooked Creek.

Norris Fork rises in n Watauga County on Rich Mountain and flows se into Meat Camp Creek.

Norris Pond. *See* Mills Pond.

North Albemarle Township, e central Stanly County.

Northampton County was formed in 1741 from Bertie County. Located in the ne section of the state, it is bounded by the state of Virginia and by Hertford, Bertie, Halifax, and Warren Counties. It was named for James Compton, Earl of Northampton (1687–1754). Area: 544 sq. mi. County seat: Jackson, with an elevation of 131 ft. Townships are Gaston, Jackson, Kirby, Oconeechee, Pleasant Hill, Rich Square, Roanoke, Seaboard, and Wiccacanee. Produces peanuts, corn, soybeans, chemicals, sorghum, cotton, hogs, livestock, lumber, apparel, sand, and gravel.

Northampton Court House. *See* Jackson.

North Asheboro. *See* Balfours.

North Banks. *See* Currituck Banks.

North Bay, in the n end of Cedar Island in ne Carteret County adjacent to West Bay.

North Bay, in n Piney Island n of Rattan Bay, ne Carteret County. Approx. ½ mi. long and ½ mi. wide.

North Belmont, community in e Gaston County on the outskirts of the city of Belmont.

North Blue Ridge Township, e Henderson County.

North Brook, community in nw Lincoln County.

North Brook Township, w Lincoln County.

North Buffalo Creek rises in central Guilford County and flows ne through the city of Greensboro to join South Buffalo Creek in forming Buffalo Creek in ne Guilford County.

North Cackalacky. *See* Cackalacky.

North Carolina is bounded on the e and se by the Atlantic Ocean, on the n by Virginia, on the w by Tennessee, and on the s by Georgia and South Carolina. It is 52,712 sq. mi. in area, of which 49,067 are land and 3,645 are water. Elevation ranges from sea level in the e to 6,684 ft. at Mount Mitchell, the highest peak e of the Mississippi River. Raleigh is the state capital. The largest cities are Charlotte, Raleigh, Greensboro, Durham, Winston-Salem, Fayetteville, Cary, High Point, Wilmington, and Asheville.

> **Nicknames:** Tar Heel State; Old North State
> **Colors:** Blue and red
> **Bird:** Cardinal
> **Flower:** Dogwood
> **Tree:** Pine
> **Shell:** Scotch bonnet
> **Motto:** *Esse Quam Videri* (To Be Rather Than to Seem)

There are 100 counties in the state:

County	County Seat
Alamance	Graham
Alexander	Taylorsville
Alleghany	Sparta
Anson	Wadesboro
Ashe	Jefferson
Avery	Newland
Beaufort	Washington
Bertie	Windsor
Bladen	Elizabethtown
Brunswick	Bolivia
Buncombe	Asheville
Burke	Morganton
Cabarrus	Concord
Caldwell	Lenoir
Camden	Camden
Carteret	Beaufort
Caswell	Yanceyville
Catawba	Newton
Chatham	Pittsboro
Cherokee	Murphy
Chowan	Edenton
Clay	Hayesville
Cleveland	Shelby
Columbus	Whiteville
Craven	New Bern
Cumberland	Fayetteville
Currituck	Currituck
Dare	Manteo
Davidson	Lexington
Davie	Mocksville
Duplin	Kenansville
Durham	Durham
Edgecombe	Tarboro
Forsyth	Winston-Salem
Franklin	Louisburg
Gaston	Gastonia
Gates	Gatesville
Graham	Robbinsville
Granville	Oxford
Greene	Snow Hill
Guilford	Greensboro
Halifax	Halifax
Harnett	Lillington
Haywood	Waynesville
Henderson	Hendersonville
Hertford	Winton
Hoke	Raeford
Hyde	Swan Quarter
Iredell	Statesville
Jackson	Sylva
Johnston	Smithfield
Jones	Trenton
Lee	Sanford
Lenoir	Kinston
Lincoln	Lincolnton
Macon	Franklin
Madison	Marshall
Martin	Williamston
McDowell	Marion
Mecklenburg	Charlotte
Mitchell	Bakersville
Montgomery	Troy
Moore	Carthage
Nash	Nashville
New Hanover	Wilmington
Northampton	Jackson
Onslow	Jacksonville
Orange	Hillsborough
Pamlico	Bayboro

Pasquotank	Elizabeth City
Pender	Burgaw
Perquimans	Hertford
Person	Roxboro
Pitt	Greenville
Polk	Columbus
Randolph	Asheboro
Richmond	Rockingham
Robeson	Lumberton
Rockingham	Wentworth
Rowan	Salisbury
Rutherford	Rutherfordton
Sampson	Clinton
Scotland	Laurinburg
Stanly	Albemarle
Stokes	Danbury
Surry	Dobson
Swain	Bryson City
Transylvania	Brevard
Tyrrell	Columbia
Union	Monroe
Vance	Henderson
Wake	Raleigh
Warren	Warrenton
Washington	Plymouth
Watauga	Boone
Wayne	Goldsboro
Wilkes	Wilkesboro
Wilson	Wilson
Yadkin	Yadkinville
Yancey	Burnsville

North Catawba Township, s central Caldwell County.

North Charlotte, community in n Mecklenburg County served by post office, 1908–30.

North Clinton Township, central Sampson County.

North Cove, community in n McDowell County on North Fork [Catawba River]. Post office named Pitts served the community, 1915–24. Alt. 1,469.

North Cove Township, n McDowell County.

North Cox Creek rises in n Yancey County and flows nw into Cane Creek.

North Creek rises near Ransomville, e Beaufort County, and flows se into Pamlico River. Appears as North Dividing Creek on the Collet map, 1770.

North Deep Creek rises in n Yadkin County and flows se to join South Deep Creek in forming Deep Creek.

North Dividing Creek. *See* North Creek.

North Double Creek rises in w Stokes County and flows e into Dan River.

North Durham, former town in central Durham County at the n boundary of Durham. Inc. 1891. Now wholly within the limits of Durham.

North Eaglenest Mountain. *See* Junaluska Mountain.

North East, community in s Duplin County.

Northeast, community in ne Onslow County.

Northeast, community in n Pender County served by post office, 1900–1903.

Northeast Branch [Newport River] rises in e Carteret County and flows s into Newport River e of the town of Newport.

Northeast Branch [New River]. *See* Northeast Creek.

Northeast Cape Fear River rises in nw Duplin County about 2 mi. s of Mount Olive; flows se to form a part of the Duplin-Wayne county line; continues s through Duplin and Pender Counties; turns slightly w to form a part of the New Hanover–Pender county line; and flows s in New Hanover County, where it enters Cape Fear River at Wilmington. Appears as Northeast Fork and North East River on the Collet map, 1770.

Northeast Creek rises in sw Durham County and flows sw into Chatham County, where it enters New Hope River.

Northeast Creek rises in n Onslow County and flows sw into Morgan Bay. Also known as Northeast Branch of New River. Name appears in local records as early as 1744.

Northeast Fork. *See* Northeast Cape Fear River.

Northeast Hamlet. *See* Longwood Park.

Northeast Prong [South Lake], central Dare County.

Northeast River. *See* Northeast Cape Fear River.

North Edenton, former town in s Chowan County adjacent to Edenton. Inc. 1911; charter repealed 1917.

North Fayetteville, community in central Cumberland County on the outskirts of the city of Fayetteville.

North Flat River rises in central Person County and flows sw into Flat River.

North Fork rises in s Clay County and flows e into Blair Creek.

North Fork rises in central Forsyth County and flows sw into Muddy Creek.

North Fork rises in s Haywood County and flows se into Shining Creek.

North Fork is formed in nw Henderson County by the junction of Big and Fletcher Creeks. It flows se to join South Fork in forming Mills River. Sometimes also known as North Fork Mills River.

North Fork rises in w Henderson County and flows w into Willow Creek.

North Fork rises in s Jones County and flows se into White Oak River.

North Fork rises in ne Madison County and flows s into Big Laurel Creek.

North Fork rises in ne Rutherford County and flows sw into First Broad River.

North Fork, community in n Watauga County on North Fork [Cove Creek].

North Fork. *See* Creston.

North Fork [Big Pine Creek] rises in s Madison County on the w side of Fork Mountain and flows ne to join South Fork in forming Big Pine Creek.

North Fork [Carvers Branch] rises in s Mitchell County and flows sw into Carvers Branch.

North Fork [Catawba River] rises in ne McDowell County and flows s into Lake James on Catawba River.

North Fork Cattail Creek rises in s Yancey County and flows sw to join South Fork Cattail Creek in forming Cattail Creek.

North Fork [Chambers Creek] rises in w Swain County and flows se into Chambers Creek.

North Fork Clear Creek rises in se Mecklenburg County and flows ne into sw Cabarrus County, e through Union County, and s into Clear Creek.

North Fork [Cove Creek] rises in n Watauga County and flows se into Cove Creek.

North Fork Coweeta Creek rises in s Macon County and flows se into Coweeta Creek.

North Fork Crains Creek. *See* Whiteoak Creek.

North Fork Crooked Creek rises in se Mecklenburg County and flows e into n Union County, where it joins South Fork Crooked Creek in forming Crooked Creek.

North Fork [Duck Creek] rises in nw Alexander County and flows s into Duck Creek. Known locally as White Creek.

North Fork Flat Creek rises in w Transylvania County and flows se into Flat Creek.

North Fork French Broad River is formed in w Transylvania County by the junction of Indian and Shoal Creeks and flows se to join West Fork French Broad River in forming French Broad River.

North Fork [Grassy Creek] rises in s Mitchell County and flows se into Middle Fork Grassy Creek.

North Fork Hawk Branch rises in n Yancey County and flows sw into Hawk Branch.

North Fork Ivy Creek rises in ne Buncombe County and flows sw to join Dillingham Creek in forming Ivy Creek. Known also as Big Ivy Creek.

North Fork Jones Creek rises in sw Anson County and flows e to join South Fork Jones Creek in forming Jones Creek.

North Fork Little River rises in n Orange County and flows se into nw Durham County, where it joins South Fork Little River in forming Little River.

North Fork Mitchell River rises in nw Surry County and flows se into Mitchell River.

North Fork Mountain Creek rises in e Catawba County and flows se to join South Fork in forming Mountain Creek.

North Fork Nahunga Creek rises in w Duplin County and flows se into Nahunga Creek.

North Fork New River rises in n Watauga County and flows ne into Ashe County, where it joins South Fork New River on the Ashe-Alleghany county line to form New River.

North Fork of Rattle Snake Creek rises in central Caswell County and flows ne to join South Fork of Rattle Snake Creek in forming Rattle Snake Creek.

North Fork Reddies River rises in nw Wilkes County and flows se to join Middle Fork Reddies River in forming Reddies River.

North Fork Rock Creek rises in s Yancey County and flows se to join Middle Fork Rock Creek in forming Rock Creek.

North Fork Sawyer Creek rises in n Watauga County and flows sw into Sawyer Creek.

North Fork [Scott Creek] rises in n Jackson County and flows sw into Scott Creek.

North Fork [Skeenah Creek] rises in s Macon County near Blaine Knob and flows se to join South Fork [Skeenah Creek] in forming Skeenah Creek.

North Fork [Swannanoa River] rises in ne Buncombe County near Balsam Gap and flows s into Swannanoa River. Part of the Asheville watershed.

North Fork Tar River rises in central Granville County and flows sw into Tar River. Appears as Heartline Creek on the Collet map, 1770.

North Fork Township, sw Ashe County.

North Fork Township, n Watauga County.

North Fork Tucker Creek rises in w Transylvania County and flows se into Tucker Creek.

North Fork [Whitewater River] rises in s Jackson County and flows se into South Carolina, where it enters Whitewater River.

North Harlowe, community in se Craven County.

North Harper Creek rises in se Avery County in Boone Wildlife Management Area and flows se to join South Harper Creek in forming Harper Creek near the Caldwell County line.

North Henderson, community in central Vance County on the outskirts of the city of Henderson.

North Hominy Creek rises in e Haywood County in Worley Cove and flows sw into Hominy Creek.

North Hunting Creek. *See* Flat Rock Creek.

North Hyco Creek rises in s Caswell County and flows ne into Person County, where it joins South Hyco Creek in forming Hyco River.

North Knob, n Buncombe County ne of Windy Gap.

North Landing River rises in Princess Anne County, Va., and flows s into Currituck County, where it enters Currituck Sound. The Intracoastal Waterway connects James River and North Landing River.

North Leopard Creek rises in e Carteret County and flows nw into North River.

North Lumberton, former town in e central Robeson County. Inc. 1911. Charter repealed 1953. Now a part of Lumberton. Was a mill-owned village (Jennings Cotton Mills) until 1949–50, when houses were sold to individuals.

North Muddy Creek rises in central McDowell County and flows ne to join South Muddy Creek in forming Muddy Creek near the Burke County line.

North Pacolet River. *See* Pacolet River.

North Point. *See* Eagleton Point.

North Prong. *See* Correll Branch.

North Prong [Clarks Creek] rises in n Mecklenburg County and flows se to join South Prong in forming Clarks Creek.

North Prong Creek rises in se Guilford County and flows ne into Alamance County, where it enters Stinking Quarter Creek.

North Prong Ellijay Creek rises in e Macon County and flows sw into Ellijay Creek.

North Prong Horse Branch rises in central Duplin County and flows se into Northeast Cape Fear River.

North Prong Lewis Fork Creek rises in w Wilkes County and flows se approx. 9 mi. to join South Prong Lewis Fork Creek in forming Lewis Fork Creek. Yates Mountain lies between the two prongs.

North Prong Roaring River rises in n Wilkes County and flows se to join Middle Prong Roaring River in forming Roaring River.

North Prong Turkey Creek rises in n Transylvania County and flows s to join South Prong Turkey Creek in forming Turkey Creek.

North River rises in Dismal Swamp, e Camden County and flows s approx. 18 mi. into Albemarle Sound. For a part of its course, it forms the boundary between Camden and Currituck Counties. Above Thoroughfare Island it is sometimes known as Indiantown Creek. Shown as Potaskike River on the Comberford map, 1657, but as North River on the Ogilby map, 1671, and subsequent maps.

North River, about 10 mi. long, rises in central Carteret County and flows s into Back Sound and The Straits in se Carteret County. Appears on the Moseley map, 1733.

North River Pocosin, along the w shore of North River in s Camden County.

North River Point is the tip of s Camden Point, which extends into the mouth of North River.

North River Thorofare, between two groups of tidal-marsh islands in s Carteret County.

North Rock, island in Pamlico Sound, ne Carteret County n of Portsmouth Island. In 1795 the middle section of the island was submerged; the w end was called Great Shell Rock and the e end Little Shell Rock.

North Rocky Creek rises in s Wilkes County and flows s into Rocky Creek.

North Rodanthe. *See* Rodanthe.

North Second Creek is formed in nw Rowan County by the junction of Back and Withrow Creeks and flows ne into Yadkin River. Appears as Second Creek on the Collet map, 1770. Named because it was the second creek reached by settlers moving w from Salisbury,

Grants Creek being the first. *See also* Withrow Creek.

North Shores, community on Pamlico River, w Beaufort County.

Northside, community in sw Granville County.

North Slope Ridge, n Transylvania County extends e between Joel Branch and Davidson River.

North Stinking Quarter Creek rises in se Guilford County and flows ne into Alamance County, where it enters Stinking Quarter Creek, *which see.*

North Toe River rises in n Avery County and flows s, e, and s again across Avery into Mitchell County. It flows sw across Mitchell to the Mitchell-Yancey county line, where it joins South Toe River in forming Toe River. The last native elk shot in North Carolina is said to have been killed alongside North Toe River in 1781.

North Turkey Creek rises in sw Buncombe County near Newfound Mountain and flows ne to join South Turkey Creek in forming Turkey Creek.

Northview, community in n Lee County.

Northwest, community in ne Brunswick County.

Northwest Creek rises in e Craven County and flows s into Neuse River.

Northwest Ditch drains water from nw Camden County (Dismal Swamp) to the se into Cross Canal.

Northwest Fork [Alligator River] rises in s central Tyrrell County and flows se into Alligator River.

Northwest Parish, Church of England, Bertie County and later Northampton County, was est. in 1727 by the division of Society Parish in the nw part of the county. In 1741 the parish became Northampton County and, except for a part of the parish in the e, was renamed St. George's Parish in 1758. The following year, the remaining part of Northwest Parish became a part of Hertford County and St. Barnabas' Parish. Northwest Parish, therefore, ceased to exist.

Northwest Point, the nw tip of Roanoke Island, central Dare County, that extends into Croatan Sound.

Northwest Prong Creek rises in nw Carteret County and flows s into Newport River.

Northwest River rises in Norfolk County, Va., and flows se into Currituck County, where it empties into Tull Bay and North Landing River. Prior to the opening of the Dismal Swamp Canal, Northwest River flowed from Lake Drummond, Va., to Currituck Sound. Appears on the Ogilby map, 1671.

Northwest Township, n Brunswick County.

North Whitakers Township, ne Nash County.

North Wilkesboro, town in s central Wilkes County on Yadkin River. Alt. 1,016. Inc. 1891 and named for the county seat, Wilkesboro, across the Yadkin River to the s. The site was described as Mulberry Fields, a former Cherokee Indian area, in a report of Moravian surveyors in 1752. Appears as Mulberry Fields on the Collet map, 1770. Produces furniture, mirrors, textiles, apparel, hosiery, processed poultry, and dairy products.

North Wilkesboro Township, central Wilkes County.

Norton, community on Grassy Camp Creek and Norton Creek in sw Jackson County. Named for pioneer settler Roderick Norton. His son Richard was first postmaster.

Norton, community on Little Tennessee River in s Macon County. Also called Tryphosa.

Norton Branch rises in s Macon County near Downs Mountain and flows ne into Little Tennessee River.

Norton Branch rises in s Macon County near Plass Gap and flows w into Little Tennessee River.

Norton Branch rises in se Macon County and flows sw into Big Creek.

Norton Creek rises in sw Jackson County and flows ne into Lake Thorpe.

Norton Fork Creek rises in sw Madison County and flows nw into Spring Creek.

Norton Fork Gap, on the Buncombe-Madison county line between Chestnut Gap and Robinson Rough.

Norton Prong rises in e Macon County and flows s into Big Creek.

Norval, community in w Harnett County served by post office, 1856–1908.

Norwood, town in se Stanly County on Lake Tillery. Alt. 365. Post office est. there in 1826 and named for William C. Norwood, first postmaster. Inc. 1881.

Norwood Lake. *See* Lake Tillery.

Notla Township, s central Cherokee County.

Nottely River rises in Georgia and flows n into Cherokee County, through which it flows n, w, and ne into Hiwassee River about 2 mi. w of Murphy.

Nottoway River rises in Virginia and flows se into Hertford County, where it joins Blackwater River on the Gates-Hertford county line to form Chowan River. Nottoway, meaning "adders" or "rattlesnakes," was a name applied by Algonquian neighbors to Indians in the area. The name Nataway River appears on the Ogilby map, 1671, intended for the river but mistakenly applied to the present Wiccacon River. *See also* Weyanoke Creek.

Notts Island. *See* Mackay Island.

Nova Scotia Branch rises in sw Macon County and flows nw into Nantahala River.

Nubbin Ridge. *See* Jones Chapel.

Nubbinscuffle Creek rises in w Yancey County and flows s into Bald Creek.

Nuna Ridge, nw Swain County in Great Smoky Mountains National Park between Tub-Mill Creek and Gunna Creek.

Nunda Branch, in Great Smoky Mountains National Park, rises in nw Swain County and flows se into Bone Valley Creek.

Nunn Mountain, se Orange County on the head of Booker Creek.

Nuns, community in se Nash County served by post office, 1898–1902.

Nupernuse Point. *See* Newport News Point.

Nutbush. *See* Williamsboro.

Nutbush Creek rises in city of Henderson in central Vance County and flows n into Kerr Lake. Shown on the Moseley map, 1733.

Nutbush Township. *See* Middleburg-Nutbush Township.

Nye, community in s Robeson County served by post office, 1890–1905.

O

Oakanoahs. *See* South Mountains.

Oakboro, town in sw Stanly County. Inc. 1915. Known as Furr City until about 1905. Post office est. 1914 with the coming of the railroad and when Big Lick post office was closed.

Oak City, town in nw Martin County. Site given the name Goose Nest by a Union soldier on a raid. Inc. as Conoho, 1891. Name changed to Oak City, 1905, because of confusion with Conetoe; name selected from a calendar advertising Oak City Laundry in Raleigh.

Oakdale, community on Deep River in sw Guilford County.

Oakdale, community in sw Wilkes County between Beaver Creek and Yadkin River.

Oakes Ridge. *See* Oak Knob.

Oakey Mountain, ne Rutherford County between North Fork and Collins Creek. Alt. approx. 2,200.

Oak Forest, community in e Iredell County. Settled prior to 1800. Store there operated by James Gay. Thriving business community around 1900.

Oak Grove, community in sw Brunswick County.

Oakgrove, community in e Cleveland County.

Oak Grove, community in central Davie County between Elisha and Dutchmans Creeks. Est. prior to 1879. Also known as Maine.

Oak Grove, community on Little Lick Creek in e Durham County.

Oak Grove, community in s Jones County.

Oak Grove, community in n Macon County between Caler Cove Branch and Lakey Creek.

Oak Grove, community in nw Northampton County. The post office there, 1907–26, was known as Stancell.

Oak Grove, community in n Surry County between Wood Fork Branch and Little Fisher River.

Oakgrove, community in nw Union County.

Oak Grove, community in w Yadkin County n of Flat Rock Creek.

Oak Grove Township, e central Durham County.

Oak Hill, community in n central Burke County about 4 mi. n of Morganton.

Oak Hill, community in e Caldwell County.

Oak Hill, community in nw Granville County. A post office est. 1821 was called Young's Store, but by 1830 the present name was being used.

Oak Hill, community in central Macon County between Crawford Branch and Wallace Branch.

Oak Hill Mountain, peak in the Cane Creek Mountains, s Alamance County.

Oak Hill Township, nw Granville County.

Oak Island, a peninsula between Elizabeth River and the Atlantic Ocean at the mouth of the Cape Fear River in se Brunswick County. Site of Fort Caswell, Long Beach, and Yaupon

Beach. Appears as an island on the Collet map, 1770.

Oak Knob, on the Buncombe-Madison county line. Alt. approx. 4,400. Also appears on maps as Oakes Knob and as Oak Ridge.

Oak Knob, e Haywood County on James Branch.

Oakland, community in central Nash County served by post office, 1885–1903.

Oakland, community in s central Rutherford County near the head of Floyds Creek. Formerly known as Frog Level. A post office known as Butler operated there, 1853–1904.

Oakland, community in sw Transylvania County n of Round Mountain. Alt. 3,104.

Oakland Township, s central Chatham County.

Oak Level Township, se Nash County.

Oakley, former community se of Asheville, central Buncombe County; now within the limits of Asheville.

Oakley, town in n Pitt County. Inc. 1903.

Oak Lodge, community in e Guilford County.

Oaklog Gap, on the Haywood-Transylvania county line.

Oak Park, community in s Buncombe County.

Oak Park, community in w Cherokee County on Shoal Creek s of Hiwassee River.

Oak Ridge, town in nw Guilford County. Alt. 885. Est. in 1852 and inc. in 1897. Named for its location on an oak-grown ridge. Oak Ridge Military Institute, oldest military preparatory school in North Carolina, founded there in 1853.

Oak Ridge, community in n Stokes County.

Oak Ridge. *See* Oak Knob.

Oak Ridge Creek rises in e Jackson County and flows sw into Piney Mountain Creek.

Oak Ridge Township, nw Guilford County.

Oaks, community in sw Orange County on Cane Creek. Site of an academy as early as 1829. The Bingham School operated there, 1844–65.

Oaks Knob, w Avery County.

Oak Spring, community in central Rutherford County on Catheys Creek. A post office was there, 1855–1907.

Oak Summit, community in n Forsyth County served by post office, 1891–1903. Formerly Flat Branch.

Oak Swamp rises in e Robeson County and flows ne into Big Swamp.

Oakview, community in sw Guilford County adjacent to High Point. A portion of High Point was formerly a part of the Oakview community.

Oak Villa, community in e Hertford County. It developed on the old post road from Norfolk, Va., to Wilmington and was a point from which mail was rerouted.

Oakville, community in n Franklin County.

Oakville, community in n Warren County between Hawtree Creek and Sixpound Creek. A post office est. there in 1872 was discontinued in 1907.

Oakwood Acres, community in s Davidson County on High Rock Lake.

Oakwoods, community in s Wilkes County between Cub Creek and East Prong Cub Creek. Settled by several Scottish families.

Oaky Mountain, ne Chatham County.

Obadiah Cove, w Graham County between Fork Ridge and Hooper Mill Creek.

Obadiah Gap, on Horse Cove Ridge in w Graham County.

Oberlin, formerly a community in central Wake County nw of Raleigh but now a part of the city of Raleigh.

Obids, community in s Ashe County. Alt. approx. 2,800.

Obids Creek rises in se Ashe county and flows n into South Fork New River.

Obids Township, se Ashe County.

Obies Creek rises in n Chatham County and flows ne into Orange County, where it enters Morgan Creek.

Observer, community in sw Mecklenburg County served by post office, 1900–1915. Named for local Observer School, which in turn was named for the *Charlotte Observer.*

Ocala, community in s Jackson County on Fowler Creek.

Occacock. *See* Ocracoke.

Occam. *See* Croatan Sound.

Occaneechi Mountain, central Orange County s of the town of Hillsborough. Named for an Indian tribe mentioned frequently in seventeenth- and eighteenth-century records. The mountain is referred to in a letter of January 31, 1767, by Governor Tryon. Appears but is not named on the Collet map, 1770. Called Occaneeche Hills on the Kerr map, 1882. Alt. approx. 700. Now a local park.

Occoneechee Creek rises in w Northampton County and flows s into Roanoke River.

The name is probably from the Tutelo Indian word *yuhkañ* (man).

Occoneechee Neck, the w neck of Northampton County, is formed by a large bend in Roanoke River.

Occoneechee Township, sw Northampton County.

Ocean, community in w Carteret County served by post office, 1891–1927.

Ocean Isle Beach, town on the Atlantic Ocean, s Brunswick County. Inc. 1959.

Ochre Creek rises in n Jackson County and flows w into Scott Creek.

Oconaluftee River is formed in the Great Smoky Mountains in ne Swain County by the junction of Beech Flats Prong and Kephart Prong. For a part of its course, it forms the Jackson-Swain county line. It flows se into Tuckasegee River. The name, long written as two words (Ocona Luftee), is from the Cherokee words *Egwanulti* or *Egwani* (river) and *nulati* or *nuti* (near; beside). The Cherokee town of Oconalufte, mentioned by explorer-naturalist William Bartram about 1775, was probably on the lower course of the river at present Birdtown.

Oconalufty Township, formerly in e Swain County but inc. into the limits of Charleston Township when it was enlarged between 1934 and 1940 with the establishment of Great Smoky Mountains National Park.

Ocracoke, community on Ocracoke Island, se Hyde County. Settled in the seventeenth century. The name Ocracoke seems originally to have been Wococon, which appeared first on the White map, 1585. The Indian word apparently was *waxkahikani*, meaning "enclosed place," "fort," or "stockade," and it is believed that a fortified Indian village existed at the site. By 1676 the name Okok was used, and by 1709 it had developed into Occacock. *See also* Wococon Island.

Ocracoke Inlet, from the Atlantic Ocean into Pamlico Sound, lies between Ocracoke Island (Hyde County) on the n and Portsmouth Island (Carteret County) on the s. The pirate Blackbeard was killed in the vicinity in 1718. Once chief trade inlet for North Carolina.

Ocracoke Island, se Hyde County, one of the Outer Banks. Approx. 17 mi. long. *See also* Croatoan Island; Wococon Island.

Ocracoke Township, se Hyde County on the Outer Banks.

Odam Millpond, sw Wayne County on Thoroughfare Swamp.

Odamsville. *See* Faisons Old Tavern.

Odear Cove, e Swain County on the head of Wesser Creek.

O'Dear Creek rises in nw McDowell County and flows e on the n side of Pompey Ridge into Threemile Creek.

Odell, community in e Warren County s of Little Fishing Creek. Post office est. there in 1892 but discontinued in 1914.

Odell Mill. *See* Forest Hill.

Odell School Township, former township in nw Cabarrus County, now township no. 3. Once known as Deweese Township.

Odessa, community in w Pender County served by post office, 1891–1905.

Offen, community in n Wilkes County near Middle Prong Roaring River.

Off Island, approx. ½ mi. in diameter, lies off s Bodie Island in Roanoke Sound, e Dare County. Separated from Bodie Island by Blossie Creek.

Ogburn, community in w Johnston County. Formerly spelled Aughburn.

Ogburn's Crossroads, community in nw Guilford County.

Ogburntown, community in central Forsyth County within the urban extension of the city of Winston-Salem.

Ogden, community in sw Clay County on Crawford Creek.

Ogle Branch rises in ne Buncombe County and flows s into North Fork Ivy Creek. Named for a pioneer family.

Ogle Creek rises in s Yancey County and flows sw to join Timber Creek in forming Sugar Camp Creek.

Ogle Gap, s Yancey County at the nw end of Ogle Ridge.

Ogle Knob, s central Swain County between the head of Bucknor Branch and Davis Branch.

Ogle Meadow Knob, on the Buncombe-Yancey county line. Alt. 5,384. A grassy bald known locally simply as Ogle Meadows.

Ogle Ridge, s Yancey County near the head of Ogle Creek.

Ogreeta, community in w Cherokee County on Hiwassee Lake between the mouth of Chambers Creek and Grape Creek.

Ohanoak or **Ohaunoock**, an Indian village visited by Ralph Lane, 1585–86, on the w bank of Chowan River in what is now ne Bertie County s of Colerain. Appears on the De Bry map, 1590. On the Comberford map, 1657, it appears as Wohanoke. Modern Tuscarora Indians say the name means "old village."

Ohlanto. *See* Blowing Rock.

Oine, community in nw Warren County. Post office est. there in 1886 but discontinued in 1904.

Okay, community in ne Forsyth County served by post office, 1890–1904.

Okeewemee, community in n Montgomery County. Name derived from Indian word meaning "land between two rivers."

Okie Branch rises in s Duplin County and flows se into Northeast Cape Fear River.

Okisko, community in w Pasquotank County. Settled prior to 1890. Named for a king of the Yeopim Indians. Alt. 12.

Oklawaha. *See* Mud Creek.

Okok. *See* Ocracoke.

Ola, former community in w Haywood County near lat. 35°36′15″ N., long. 83°08′00″. The site is now within Great Smoky Mountains National Park and abandoned.

Old Apalachia, former community in nw Cherokee County below and n of Apalachia Dam near the junction of Shuler Creek with Hiwassee River.

Old Bald Creek rises in s Haywood County and flows ne into Allen Creek.

Old Bald Mountain, on Haywood-Jackson county line. Alt. 5,800. Named for bald appearance from the Jackson County side.

Old Bald Ridge extends from Chastine Creek in e central Jackson County n and ne to Allen Creek in sw Haywood County. Named for Old Bald Mountain, one of its peaks.

Old Barfields. *See* Tuscarora Beach.

Old Bear, The, point of land off e Pamlico County extending into Jones Bay.

Old Bethlehem, community in se Warren County near the Halifax-Warren county line.

Old Billy Top, on the Cherokee-Graham county line in the Snowbird Mountains.

Old Black. *See* Mount Chapman.

Old Black Mountain, at the junction of the lines of Haywood County, N.C., and Cocke and Sevier Counties, Tenn., in Great Smoky

Mountains National Park near lat. 35°42′44″ N., long. 83°15′18″ W. Alt. 6,430.

Old Catawba River rises at the Catawba River Dam on Lake James and flows se and ne into Catawba River about 1 mi. se of Linville Dam in w Burke County.

Old Cove, n Swain County on Chambers Creek.

Old Dock, community in se Columbus County on Waccamaw River 1 mi. se of Schulkens Pond. Settled about 1800. Alt. 40.

Old Field, an area in what is now Beaufort County between Pungo and Pamlico Rivers; shown on the Ogilby map, 1671.

Old Field Bald Mountain, on Ashe-Watauga county line. Alt. 4,939. Named for muster ground and drill field used by Col. Benjamin Cleveland during the Revolution.

Old Field Branch rises in ne Ashe County and flows se into Poison Branch.

Old Field Creek rises in n Caldwell County and flows ne into Buffalo Creek.

Old Field Creek rises in e Orange County and flows ne into New Hope Creek.

Oldfield Creek. *See* Redbank Creek.

Oldfield Gap, n Graham County between Yellow Creek Mountains and Fork Ridge.

Oldfield Gap, on the Madison-Yancey county line near Indian Creek.

Old Fields of Toe. *See* Newland.

Oldfields Township, sw Ashe County. Named for muster ground and drill field used by Benjamin Cleveland during the Revolution.

Old Fields Township, w Wilson County.

Oldfield Swamp rises in s Robeson County and flows se into Hog Swamp.

Old Field Top Mountain, w Haywood County between Plott Balsams and Mingus Ridge. Alt. 5,820. Sometimes called Plott's Old Field Mountain.

Old Ford. *See* Mineola.

Old Ford Swamp rises in nw Beaufort County and flows w to join Snoad Branch in forming Aggie Run.

Old Fort, town in w McDowell County on Catawba River. Alt. 1,438. Inc. 1872 as Catawba Vale by a northern land company that expected to develop a city on the David-son plantation, which it had purchased the previous year. Name changed in 1873 to Old Fort, the name by which the community had been known since 1828 or earlier, when a post office existed there. Named for Davidson's Fort, erected in 1776 by troops under the command of Gen. Griffith Rutherford, who led expedition against the Cherokee Indians.

Old Fort Township, sw McDowell County.

Old Furnace, community in s Gaston County served by post office, 1848–1902.

Old Gilreath, community in s Wilkes County 3 mi. nw of Gilreath.

Oldham, community in n Forsyth County served by post office, 1883–1901.

Old House Branch rises in se Watauga County and flows ne into Dugger Creek.

Old House Channel, a slough in the waters of Pamlico Sound immediately w of and leading to Oregon Inlet, e Dare County. Also known as Old House Slough.

Old House Creek, a short stream in n central Carteret County flowing n into South River.

Old Hundred, community in w Scotland County. Named because the 100-mile post was there when the railroad from Wilmington was built. Alt. 318.

Old Lanesboro. *See* Lanesboro.

Old Mattie Ridge, ne Cherokee County in the Snowbird Mountains.

Old Mattie Top, on the Cherokee-Graham county line in the Snowbird Mountains.

Old Mill Creek rises in n central Washington County in East Dismal Swamp ne of the town of Roper and flows nw into Kendricks Creek.

Old Mill Swamp rises in n Sampson County and flows se into Great Coharie Creek.

Old Paddy Creek, about 7/10 mi. long, rises at Paddy Creek Dam on Lake James and flows e into Old Catawba River in w Burke County about 9 mi. w of Morganton.

Old Richmond Township, nw Forsyth County. Named for the former town of Richmond, *which see*, seat of Surry County from 1774 to 1789.

Old Road Gap, on the Cherokee-Macon county line.

Old Road Ridge, n Mitchell County between Spring Creek and Greasy Creek.

Old Rock. *See* Shell Castle.

Old Rocky Mountain, e Macon County between the head of Ellijay Creek and the head of Little Salt Rock Creek. Alt. 4,825.

Olds, community in s Currituck County. Known locally as Olds Hill for a sand hill nearby.

Old Salem. *See* Salem.

Old Shatter. *See* Axtell.

Old Sheep Knob, n Cleveland County. Alt. 1,497.

Old Skinnersville. *See* Skinnersville.

Old Sneedsborough, abandoned town in se Anson County on Pee Dee River. Laid out in 1795 to be at the head of navigation on the Pee Dee River and named for Honora Sneyd, stepmother of Richard Lovell Edgeworth, founder of the town. Navigation was not developed sufficiently, and the town declined after about 30 years. Post office est. about 1803; closed 1883. Sneedsborough was famous for its inn. John J. McRae, governor of Mississippi (1854–58) and a member of U.S. and Confederate Congresses, was born there. *See also* McFarlan.

Old Sow, The, tidal-marsh island in Pamlico Sound off the se tip of Goose Creek Island, ne Pamlico Sound.

Old Sparta, town in s Edgecombe County on Tar River. Inc. as Sparta, 1876, and reincorporated as Old Sparta, 1903. No longer active in municipal affairs. Post office est. 1829; probably came to be called Old Sparta after Sparta, county seat of Alleghany County, est. 1859, began to thrive.

Old Stanhope. *See* Spring Hope.

Old Station Gap, central Madison County between Brush Creek and Walnut Creek.

Olds Township, e central Greene County. Named for the Olds family whose members moved there after 1779.

Old Topsail Creek rises in s Pender County and flows s into Topsail Sound.

Old Topsail Inlet, s Pender County, through which waters of Topsail Sound enter the Atlantic Ocean. It lies between New Topsail Inlet on the n and Rich Inlet on the s.

Old Topsail Inlet. *See* Beaufort Inlet.

Old Town, community in central Forsyth County. Settled 1753 by first Moravians to arrive at the Wachovia tract from Pennsylvania. First named Bethabara, or House of Passage, since it was intended to be a temporary settlement. After 1766, when Salem was begun, Bethabara declined. The post office, est. 1832, ceased to be called Bethabara in 1835 and was changed to Old Town.

Old Town Creek. *See* Town Creek.

Old Town Township, w central Forsyth County.

Old Trap, community in s Camden County, was probably settled as early as the 1650s. In the

eighteenth century, it was the center of much
maritime activity, and a grog shop there supplied the local trade with West India rum.
Tradition says that men carrying grain to a
local windmill tarried long at the grog shop—
it "trapped" them. By the end of the Revolution, the name The Trap was being used,
and after 1800 Old Trap came into use.

Old Tree Swamp rises in w Hertford County and
flows se into Potecasi Creek.

Old Weeksville. *See* Weeksville.

Oldwoman Branch rises in w Pitt County and
flows se into Little Contentnea Creek.

Old Woman's Swamp. *See* Gilletts Creek.

Olga, community in w Pender County served by
post office, 1900–1908.

Olin, town in n central Iredell County. Est. and
inc. 1855 as New Institute when Brantley York
and Baxter Clegg opened an academy there.
Reincorporated 1857 as Olin in honor of Stephen Olin, Methodist educator. Inc. again in
1905, but long inactive in municipal affairs.

Olin Creek rises in nw Iredell County and flows
se into Patterson Creek. Formerly known as
Little Rocky Creek.

Olin Township, n central Iredell County.

Olive Branch, community in ne Union County e
of Gourdvine Creek.

Olive Grove, community in n Cleveland County.

Olive Hill, community in central Macon County
on Iotla Creek.

Olive Hill, community in w Person County.

Olive Hill Township, w central Person County.

Olive Hollow, w Watauga County, extends north-
ward w of Laurel Creek.

Oliver, community in e Johnston County.

Oliver Reef, s Dare and e Hyde Counties in the
waters of Pamlico Sound n of Hatteras Inlet.
Presented by the state to the U.S. government
in 1874 for use in naval target practice. Returned to the state in 1965.

Olivers, community in central Jones County.

Olivers Crossroads, community in s Catawba
County.

Oliver's Crossroads, community in central Jones
County.

Olivet, community in nw Caldwell County on
Mulberry Creek. Named for Olivet Method-
ist Church, in turn named for biblical Mount
Olivet or Mount of Olives.

Olivette, community in central Buncombe
County.

Olivia, community in w Harnett County. Settled
about 1865. Known as Rock Branch until
1913, when it was renamed to honor W. J.
Olive, who in 1912 introduced cultivation
of flue-cured tobacco there.

Ollie Branch rises in central Graham County and
flows sw into East Buffalo Creek.

Olmmetta, community in e Wilkes County.

Olne, community in nw Warren County served
by post office, 1886–1904.

Olympia, community in w Pamlico County. In
1891 named for Mount Olympus when a post
office, discontinued in 1908, was est. there.

Omega, community in n Rowan County served
by post office, 1886–1904.

O'Neals Township, n Johnston County.

Oneida, community in n Alamance County
served by post office, 1900–1908.

Onetree Point, shown on Moseley map, 1733,
extending from the mainland of what is now
se Brunswick County into Cape Fear River
between Elizabeth River and Walden Creek.
Located n of and adjacent to Deep Water
Point. Not shown on modern maps.

Onion Falls, in West Fork Tuckasegee River at
the n end of Thorpe Reservoir in w Jackson
County.

Onion Knob, Alexander-Wilkes county line.

Onion Mountain, e Macon County between
the head of Cat Creek and Laurel Creek. Alt.
3,500.

Onitalooga Lake. *See* Ela Lake.

Onslow Bay, in the Atlantic Ocean off the se
coast from Cape Fear on the s to Cape Lookout on the n.

Onslow Beach, se Onslow County between New
River Inlet and Browns Inlet. Known earlier as
Hurst Beach. Now a part of the Camp Lejeune
Marine Corps Air Station and used for train-
ing for amphibious landings.

Onslow County was formed in 1734 from New
Hanover County. Located in the se section of
the state, it is bounded by the Atlantic Ocean
and by Pender, Duplin, Jones, and Carteret
Counties. It was named for Arthur Onslow

(1691–1768), member of Parliament and speaker of the House of Commons, 1728–61. Area: 806 sq. mi (756, land; 50, water). County seat: Jacksonville, with an elevation of 23 ft. Townships are Jacksonville, Richlands, Stump Sound, Swansboro, and White Oak. Produces tobacco, turkeys, cotton, corn, soybeans, hogs, livestock, lumber, apparel, marble, crushed limestone, sand, and gravel.

Onslow Court House. *See* Jacksonville.

Onvil, community in central Montgomery County near the head of Thickety Creek. Served by post office, 1883–1915.

Onward, community in sw Montgomery County served by post office, 1887–96.

Ooneroy, a Tuscarora Indian village on the Roanoke River in Bertie County shown on the Moseley map, 1733. It was a chief town of the Tuscarora; the name meant "gathered together."

Open Branch rises in n Jackson County and flows nw into Hornbuckle Creek.

Opening, The, a clay and swamp area in e Pitt County between the head of Clayroot Swamp and Chicod Creek.

Open Land or **Open Ground,** a shrub bog area of approx. 50,000 acres in Carteret County about 12 mi. ne of Beaufort. An attempt to reclaim the area in 1926 was abandoned, but much of it is now included in a large experimental farm.

Open Ridge, s Yancey County between Rock Creek and South Toe River.

Ophir, community in n Montgomery County served by post office, 1883–1933. Settled shortly after the middle of the nineteenth century in the midst of a gold-producing area and named for the land furnishing gold for King Solomon's Temple in biblical days. Now an agricultural and timber-producing community.

Ophir Township, nw Montgomery County.

Oporauck, an otherwise unidentified designation appearing on the Comberford map, 1657, shown parallel with what is now Scuppernong River in Washington and Tyrrell Counties.

Opossum Swamp rises in w Sampson County and flows s into Little Coharie Creek.

Ora, community in central Sampson County served by post office, 1886–1902.

Orange, community in w Sampson County between Caesar Swamp and Little Coharie Creek.

Orange County was formed in 1752 from Johnston, Bladen, and Granville Counties. Located in the central section of the state, it is bounded by Durham, Chatham, Alamance, Caswell, and Person Counties. It has long been said that the county was named for William III (1650–1702) of the House of Orange, who ruled England from 1689 to 1702. However, in 1752, when the county was formed, the infant William V (1748–1806) of Orange was Stadtholder, and his mother, Anne, daughter of George II of England, controlled affairs of state. It seems reasonable to assume that Orange County was named in honor of William V of Orange (and perhaps also to flatter his grandfather, George II of England) instead of for William III, who had been dead for 50 years. Area: 398 sq. mi. County seat: Hillsborough, with an elevation of 543 ft. Townships are Bingham, Cedar Grove, Chapel Hill, Cheeks, Eno, Hillsborough, and Little River. Produces corn, tobacco, wheat, oats, dairy products, barley, poultry, livestock, hogs, textiles, furniture, pyrophyllite, and crushed stone.

Orange Factory, community on Little River in n Durham County formerly known as Laura Cotton Mill. Once operated by Willard Manufacturing Company.

Orange Grove, community in sw Orange County between Cane Creek and Bear Creek.

Orange Point, e Tyrrell County, extends from the mainland into Alligator River s of the mouth of The Frying Pan.

Orapeake. *See* Corapeake.

Orapeake Creek. *See* Corapeake Swamp.

Orapeake Swamp. *See* Corapeake Swamp.

Orbit, community in s Bladen County served by post office, 1898–1911.

Orchard Branch rises in e Haywood County and flows se into Fines Creek.

Orchard Branch rises in n central Transylvania County and flows s into King Creek.

Orchard Creek rises in e Pamlico County and flows se into Neuse River. Appears on the Moseley map, 1733.

Orchard Creek. *See* Craborchard Creek.

Orchard Ridge, n Madison County between Big Laurel Creek and Little Foster Creek.

Oregon. *See* South Creek.

Oregon Hill, community in n Rockingham County served by post office, 1853–66 and 1868–1909. Located between the heads of Quaqua and Lovelace Creeks. It is said that a man stopped there early in the nineteenth century on his way to Oregon but never got any farther, so he called the site Oregonville and the name evolved. Nearby Guerrant Springs was a popular resort later in the century and into the early 1900s.

Oregon Inlet, e Dare County from Pamlico Sound into the Atlantic Ocean between s tip of Bodie Island and n tip of Pea Island. Formed by a hurricane on September 7, 1846. Named for the first vessel to pass through, the side-wheeler *Oregon*. State-operated free ferry across the inlet now replaced by the Herbert C. Bonner Bridge, approx. 2½ mi. long, which opened in December 1963; named for N.C. congressman Herbert C. Bonner (1891–1965).

Oregon Inlet Coast Guard Station, e Dare County on Pea Island near Oregon Inlet. First est. as Bodie's Island Lifesaving Station in 1874; name later changed. The Life-saving Service and Revenue Cutter Service joined in 1915 to form U.S. Coast Guard.

Oregonville Township, former township in e Rockingham County. Name changed in 1887 to Ruffin.

Ore Hill. *See* Mount Vernon Springs.

Ore Knob, n Haywood County between Fall Branch and Hurricane Creek.

Ore Knob, former town in se Ashe County. Inc. 1875. Copper mine there once employed 250 men; closed in 1886. Little evidence of buildings remains. Alt. 3,150.

Orenburg. *See* Harris.

Orfords Pond. *See* Sunset Lake.

Organ Church, community in s Rowan County served by post office, 1851–1906.

Oriental, town in s Pamlico County on Neuse River at the mouth of Smith Creek. First settled about 1870 by "Uncle Lou" Midgett and known as Smith's Creek. Later renamed for the Federal transport *Oriental*, which sank in 1862 near Bodie Island. The ship's nameplate had been found by Rebecca Midgett, wife of the town's first settler.

Orinoco, community in ne Davidson County served by post office, 1886–1904.

Orion, community in se Ashe County.

Orlando, community in s Macon County.

Orleans, community in sw Lincoln County served by post office, 1886–1906.

Ormonds Township, se Greene County. Named for the Ormond family, which settled in the Ormondsville community prior to 1769.

Ormondsville, community in e Greene County. Developed from a country crossroads store at the Ormond family plantation.

Orris's Run, swampy stream rises in n central Beaufort County and flows se into Pungo Creek. Named for Orris Waters who lived nearby.

Orrum, town in s Robeson County. Settled as early as 1832 as a community around Big Branch Church. Inc. 1903. Orton was the first choice for a name in 1903 when a post office was about to be est., but as the name was already in use in Columbus County, it was rejected. Orrum was coined as a variant of Orton.

Orrum Township, se Robeson County.

Orton, community in e central Brunswick County on Cape Fear River.

Orton, community in n Columbus County served by post office, 1883–1904.

Orton Branch rises in s Buncombe County and flows ne into French Broad River.

Orton Creek rises in se Brunswick County and flows e into Cape Fear River.

Orton Plantation, e central Brunswick County overlooking Cape Fear River. House, built about 1725 by Roger Moore and later the home of Governor Benjamin Smith, is now a tourist attraction with extensive azalea gardens. The old town of Brunswick, *which see*, was nearby.

Orton Point, point of land s of mouth of Lilliput Creek in e Brunswick County extending into Cape Fear River.

Orton Pond, artificial pond on Orton Creek in e Brunswick County. Built about 1810. Max. depth 12 ft. Surface area 500 acres.

Osage Mountain, s Macon County between West Fork Overflow Creek and Watkins Creek.

Osborn Branch rises in ne Transylvania County and flows se into Boylston Creek.

Osborne, community in s Richmond County.

Osborne Creek rises in se Wilkes County and flows s into Iredell County, where it enters Hunting Creek.

Osborn Mountain, e Watauga County between Elk Creek and Southwest Stony Fork Creek.

Osbornville, community in se Wilkes County on Osborne Creek.

Osburn Ford, shallows in Pigeon River just ne of the town of Clyde in central Haywood County.

Osceola, community in central Alamance County served by post office, 1894–1903.

Osceola, crossroads community in ne Guilford County.

Osceola Lake, central Henderson County, is fed by Findley, Perry, and Tonys Creeks and drained by Shephard Creek. It was formed about 1914 and named for an Indian chief in the area. Covers 12 acres; max. depth 20 ft.

Osgood, community in n Lee County. Inc. 1889; charter repealed 1891. Named for local family. Early known as Shakerag, traditionally because two prominent men fought there until their clothes were torn off. Alt. 242.

Osmond, community in ne Caswell County. A post office was operated there, 1883–1916.

Os-quee-ha-ha. *See* Clear Creek.

Ossipee, community in w Alamance County on the s side of Altamahaw. Developed after 1890 when a mill was est. there. Inc. 2002.

Osteen, community in sw Henderson County on Crab Creek.

Ostin Creek rises in w central Polk County at the base of Chimney Top and flows ne into Lake Adger on Green River.

Ostin Knob, se Macon County between Brown Gap and East Fork Overflow Creek.

Ostwalt, community in s Iredell County. Known as Cambridge for an Associate Reformed Presbyterian Church from the early nineteenth century until 1895, when it took its present name from J. K. Ostwalt's store when it became a post office.

Oswego, community in ne Franklin County served by post office, 1892–1903.

Otaré. *See* Mountain Region.

Oteen, community in central Buncombe County near the e limits of Asheville. Site of a veterans hospital, est. during World War I for tubercular soldiers. Name said to be an Indian word meaning "chief aim" and descriptive of the hospital's efforts to restore health to the disabled.

Othello, community in se Ashe County.

Otis, community in ne Yadkin County served by post office, 1891–1903.

Ottanola, community in ne Henderson County.

Ottaray. *See* Mountain Region.

Otter Creek rises in e Alamance County and flows s into Quaker Scrub Creek.

Otter Creek rises in e Craven County and flows n into Neuse River.

Otter Creek rises in nw Macon County and flows sw into Whiteoak Creek.

Otter Creek rises in n Rutherford County and flows se into Cove Creek.

Otter Creek rises in e Wilson County and flows e across s Edgecombe County into w Pitt County, where it enters Tar River.

Otter Creek, community in n Rutherford County on Cove Creek. A post office was there, 1854–1915.

Otter Creek Township, former township in s Edgecombe County, now township no. 9. Earlier known as Autreys Creek Township.

Otter Gap, nw Macon County between Long Branch and Otter Creek.

Otter Mountain, nw Macon County between Cold Spring Creek and the head of Jane Otter Branch.

Otters Knob. *See* Arturs Knob.

Otto, town in s Macon County. Alt. 2,060. Inc. 1909, but long inactive in municipal affairs.

Otway, community in e Carteret County near the mouth of Ward Creek. Settled about 1800. Named for Otway Burns (1775–1848), captain of a privateer vessel in the War of 1812. Alt. 5.

Ouaniche. *See* Wananish.

Outer Banks are a string of low, narrow, sandy islands extending for more than 175 mi. from the Virginia state line to below Cape Lookout. They are separated from the mainland of North Carolina by broad, shallow sounds. Narrow inlets through the Outer Banks provide access to the Atlantic Ocean from the sounds. The Outer Banks, from n to s, are Currituck Banks, Bodie Island, Pea Island, Hatteras Island, Ocracoke Island, Portsmouth Island, Core Banks, Shackleford Banks, and Bogue Banks. In 1709 John Lawson wrote of the "Sand Banks." In 1713 the term "Sea Banks" was used in describing them (*see* Shackleford Banks). *See also* Caro-larns Islands; Croatoan Island.

Outer Diamond Shoal. *See* Diamond Shoals.

Outlaws Bridge, community in ne Duplin County.

Outlaws Pond, on Halls Marsh Branch in n Duplin County.

Outlook, community in s Madison County.

Outz Creek rises in e Alexander County and flows e into Iredell County.

Oval, community in s Ashe County served by post office, 1898–1953.

Overcup Creek rises in ne Chatham County and flows se into New Hope Creek.

Overflow Creek is formed in s Macon County by the junction of East Fork Overflow Creek and West Fork Overflow Creek and flows se into Rabun County, Ga., where it enters Chattooga River.

Overhills, community in sw Harnett County. Approx. 20,000 acres developed by the Rockefeller family as a hunting and timber-growing preserve.

Over Hills. *See* Mountain Region.

Overlook Ridge, ne Swain County in Great Smoky Mountains National Park, lat. 35°33′37″ N., long. 83°10′50″ W.

Overshot, community in s Johnston County served by post office, 1893–1904.

Owenby Branch rises in central Macon County and flows ne into Little Tennessee River.

Owenby Cove, central Buncombe County between Little Cedar Mountain and Gashes Creek.

Owen Creek rises in central Granville County.

Owen Hill Landing, nw Bladen County on Cape Fear River at the site of Owen Hill plantation, home and birthplace of Governor John Owen (1787–1841), only N.C. governor from Bladen County. Foundation and basement of original house are still there on a bluff above the landing.

Owen Jones Tar Landing. *See* Tar Landing.

Owens, community in central Cumberland County.

Owens Branch rises in s Clay County and flows nw into Shooting Creek.

Owens Cove, s Buncombe County n of Face Rock.

Owen's Creek rises in ne Alamance County and flows sw into Jordan Creek.

Owens Creek rises in w Warren County and flows sw into Fishing Creek. Appears on the MacRae map, 1833.

Owens Gap, on the Jackson-Transylvania county line n of the head of West Fork French Broad River. Alt. 3,590.

Owens Knob, s Wilkes County at the ne end of Gill Mountain. Alt. 1,350. The W. Kerr Scott Dam on Yadkin River is nearby. Named for one Owen, who lived there in 1752 when Moravian surveyors arrived.

Owens Point extends from e Onslow County into White Oak River. Probably named for either Thomas Owens or Benjamin Owens, two early settlers there.

Owens Store. *See* Grove Hill.

Owensville. *See* Roseboro.

Owl Branch rises in e Swain County near Rattlesnake Mountain and flows sw parallel to Adams Creek into Oconaluftee River.

Owl Creek rises in n Cherokee County and flows sw into Hiwassee River.

Owl Creek Gap, n Cherokee County on Hanging Dog Mountain near the headwaters of Owl Creek.

Owl Knob, on the Jackson-Swain county line sw of Rattlesnake Mountain.

Owl Knob, n Macon County on Matlock Creek.

Owltown, community in sw Buncombe County n of Hooker Gap.

Ox Creek rises in central Buncombe County and flows nw into Reems Creek.

Oxear Cove, w Haywood County on the head of Hyatt Creek.

Oxford, town authorized to be laid off on the lands of Robert Fields, 1806. The Oxford Academy was to be est. there. Said to have been located on Cedar Creek, present Davie County. No evidence that the town ever existed.

Oxford, town and county seat, central Granville County. Authorized to be laid off in 1811 and inc. 1816. The land on which the town was est. had been a part of Samuel Benton's plantation, "Oxford," hence the name. Produces tobacco and textiles. Appears on the Price map, 1808. Alt. 476. *See also* Harris Burgh.

Oxford District, a section of Granville County, perhaps in the central part of the county in which Samuel Benton's plantation, "Oxford," was located. In 1790 there were 65 heads of families in the district.

Oxford Lake. *See* Lake Hickory.

Oxfords Ford, community in w Catawba County served by post office, 1873–1903.

Oxford Township, central Granville County.

Ox Pen Branch rises in s central Brunswick County and flows sw into Skipper Branch.

Oyama. *See* Few.

Oyster Creek rises in central Carteret County and flows s into Newport River. Appears on the Moseley map, 1733. Approx. ¾ mi. long.

Oyster Creek rises in e Carteret County and flows se into Core Sound. Approx. 2 mi. long.

Oyster Creek, a channel among the tidal-marsh islands on the sw shore of Roanoke Island, e Dare County in the waters of Croatan Sound. Approx. 1 mi. w of community of Wanchese.

Oyster Creek rises on nw Goose Creek Island, ne Pamlico County, and flows ne into Pamlico River.

Oyster Creek Landing, community in s Hyde County on Swanquarter Bay.

Ozark, community in ne Wilkes County served by post office, 1882–1908.

P

Pace Branch rises in central Cherokee County and flows sw into Rogers Creek.

Pacific. *See* Youngsville.

Pack Gap, sw Cherokee County on Pack Mountain.

Pack Mountain, sw Cherokee County, extends se from Pack Gap near the Polk County, Tenn., line to Signal Pole Hill. In Nantahala National Forest. Named peaks include Harris Top, Pack Top, and Signal Pole Hill.

Packs Creek rises in s Jackson County and flows nw into Robinson Creek.

Pack Top, sw Cherokee County in Nantahala National Forest at the nw end of Pack Mountain near the Tennessee state line. Alt. approx. 2,415.

Pacolet Fall, on Pacolet River in se Henderson County.

Pacolet River rises in se Henderson County near the South Carolina state line and flows ne into Polk County, where it turns se to flow into South Carolina. There it enters Broad River. Sometimes also known as North Pacolet River.

Pactolus, town in e Pitt County. Inc. 1887. Named for the ancient river in Asia Minor. Alt. 22.

Pactolus Township, e Pitt County.

Paddy Creek rises in w Burke County and flows se approx. 6½ mi. into Lake James.

Paddy Mountain, central Ashe County w of West Jefferson.

Paddys Delight Creek rises in n Northampton County and flows se into Potecasi Creek.

Padgett, community in w Onslow County on Sandy Run Swamp.

Padgett Branch rises in n Buncombe County and flows se into White Branch.

Padgett Swamp rises in w Onslow County and flows se into Sandy Run Swamp.

Page, community in nw Pender County served by post office, 1887–1903.

Page's Branch rises in e Wilson County and flows n into Cattail Swamp. Named for Thomas Page prior to 1786.

Pages Creek rises in ne New Hanover County and flows se into Topsail Sound.

Pages Lake, nw Bladen County, was formed about 1925 by a dam on Mines Creek. Max. depth 18 ft. Formerly known as Davis Mill Pond.

Page's Mill, community on East Prong Moon Creek, w Caswell County. Earlier known as Jones Mill for Richard Jones, who est. a water mill there about 1840.

Page's Siding. *See* Cary.

Page's Tavern. *See* Cary.

Page's Turnout. *See* Cary.

Paget Branch rises in s Duplin County and flows s into Boney Mill Pond.

Pailin Creek rises in e Pasquotank County and flows se into New Begun Creek.

Paine Mountain, nw Cleveland County. Alt. approx. 1,975.

Pains Bay, s Dare County in the mouth of Long Shoal River.

Paint Creek. *See* Paint Fork.

Painted Rock. *See* Paint Rock.

Painter. *See* Cullowhee.

Painter Branch rises in e Cherokee County and flows nw into Peachtree Creek.

Painter Branch rises in n Haywood County and flows sw into Pigeon River.

Painter Branch rises in w Swain County and flows se into Little Tennessee River.

Painter Knob, n Cleveland County. Alt. 2,323.

Painters Gap, n Rutherford County on the ne side of Chalk Mountain. Perhaps originally Panthers Gap.

Painter Swamp rises in w Hertford County and flows se into Potecasi Creek.

Paint Fork rises in n Buncombe County near Paint Fork Gap and flows n into Dillingham Creek. Also known as Paint Creek.

Paint Fork rises in e Madison County and flows se to join California Creek in forming Little Ivy Creek.

Paint Fork, community in n Buncombe County on the stream of the same name. Alt. 2,455.

Paint Fork, community in e Madison County on Paint Fork.

Paint Fork Gap, n Buncombe County near the headwaters of Paint Fork.

Paint Gap, on the Madison-Yancey county line.

Paint Gap, w Yancey County on Horton Creek.

Paint Gap, community in w Yancey County on Indian Creek at the mouth of Horton Creek. Alt. 2,676.

Paint Hill, se Moore County. Indians made red paint from stones found at the site, hence the name. Alt. 640.

Paint Mountain, sw Swain County between Big Creek and Right Fork [Wesser Creek].

Paint Rock, community in w Madison County on French Broad River. Inc. 1891; charter repealed 1895. Early landmark, site of a blockhouse to protect settlers from Indians, 1793. Figures on a rock cliff there appeared to early settlers to be paintings. Appears as Painted Rock on the Price map, 1808. Alt. 1,265.

Palestine, community in n Stanly County. Alt. 582.

Palm, community in ne Haywood County served by post office, 1886–1905.

Palmer Branch rises in e Cherokee County and flows sw into Valley River.

Palmer Branch rises in w Haywood County and flows nw into Caldwell Fork.

Palmer Camp Branch rises in e central Madison County and flows se into Big Laurel Creek.

Palmer Creek, w Haywood County in Great Smoky Mountains National Park, is formed by the junction of Beech Creek and Falling Rock Creek near lat. 35°38′05″ N., long. 83°09′17″ W. Flows e to join Caldwell Fork in forming Cataloochee Creek. Named for "Turkey" George Palmer, who lived on its banks.

Sheriff of Haywood County, Palmer acquired the nickname "Turkey" because he killed so many wild turkeys.

Palmer Mountain, ne Stanly County on a peninsula in Badin Lake.

Palmerville, community in ne Stanly County.

Palmetto Point extends from the mainland into Albemarle Sound in n Tyrrell County. Appears as Hoskins Point on the Tanner map, 1829.

Palmetto Swamp rises in n Craven County and flows sw into Swift Creek.

Palmyra, town in se Halifax County. Inc. 1883. A post office was est. there in 1811. Alt. 96.

Palmyra Township, se Halifax County.

Palo Alto, community in e Onslow County served by post office, 1850–1902. Birthplace and burial site of Governor Daniel Russell (1897–1901).

Pamlico, town in e Pamlico County on Broad Creek near Neuse River. Post office est. 1878. Founded by Joshua Dean, first postmaster, who was a native of Fall River, Mass., and engaged in the lumber business there as well as in his native town. Known earlier as Broad Creek. Inc. 1913, but long inactive in municipal affairs.

Pamlico Beach, resort community in e Beaufort County on the n side of Pamlico River.

Pamlico County was formed in 1872 from Craven and Beaufort Counties. Located in the e section of the state, it is bounded by Pamlico Sound, Neuse River, and by Craven and Beaufort Counties. It was named for Pamlico Sound. Area: 576 sq. mi. (341, land; 235, water). County seat: Bayboro, with an elevation of 8.5 ft. Townships are nos. 1–5. Produces corn, soybeans, Irish potatoes, turkeys, hogs, and processed seafood.

Pamlico Point, peninsula off Goose Creek Island, ne Pamlico County, extending into Pamlico River.

Pamlico River is the lower course of Tar River after it enters Beaufort County. It flows se for 33 mi. before emptying into Pamlico Sound. Explored in 1584 by Arthur Barlowe and called Cipo River, for *sipowi*, the local Indian word for river. Appears as Pamptico River on the Comberford map, 1657, and as Pamticough River on the Moll map, 1729. Named for the Pamlico Indians in the area. Bonds Ferry appears on the Collet map, 1770, as crossing the Pamlico River on the road from Bath to New Bern.

Pamlico Sound, ne and e North Carolina, is separated from the Atlantic Ocean by a part of the Outer Banks. Approx. 80 mi. long and 15 to 30 mi. wide. Shallow in the n; max. depth 21 ft. in the s. Sea level, freshwater, not affected by the tide. Waters from Albemarle Sound and Pamlico and Neuse Rivers enter the Sound, and it drains into the Atlantic Ocean through Hatteras and Ocracoke Inlets. Named for the Pamlico Indians who lived along its shores. Shown but not named on early maps; appears simply as The Sound on the Ogilby map, 1671, but as Pamticoe Sound on the Moseley map, 1733. The White map, 1590, labels the central part of the sound as Mentso, *which see*, and the n part as Nausegoc, *which see*. The largest sound on the e coast of the United States. *See also* Paquiac.

Pamptecough Precinct was created in Bath County on December 3, 1705. It took its name from Pamptecough (Pamlico) River. The name was changed to Beaufort County, *which see*, about 1712. The town of Bath was the county seat from its inc. in 1705 until 1785, when Washington became the county seat.

Pamticoe Sound. *See* Pamlico Sound.

Panacea, community in e Warren and nw Halifax Counties on Bens Creek. Named for Panacea Springs, a popular resort there in early 1900s with a large hotel and a lake near mineral springs (supposedly curative). Water formerly bottled and sold; the hotel, lake, and cottages are gone.

Panacea Springs. *See* Panacea.

Panauuaioc, Indian village site shown on the De Bry map, 1590, in what is now Beaufort County near the head of Pamlico River on its s bank.

Pancake Branch rises in w Avery County and flows nw into North Toe River.

Panhandle Creek rises in s Madison County and flows nw into French Broad River.

Pant, community in ne Haywood County served by post office, 1884–1905.

Pantego, town in ne Beaufort County on Pantego Creek. Alt. 7. A post office since 1825. Inc. 1881.

Pantego Creek rises in Dismal Swamp, e Beaufort County, and flows s and e into Pungo River. It is also fed by several canals draining from the swamp. Appears on the Moseley map, 1733.

Pantego Swamp, e Beaufort County.

Pantego Township, ne Beaufort County.

Panther Branch rises in n Buncombe County and flows sw into French Broad River.

Panther Branch rises in se Caswell County and flows n into North Hyco Creek.

Panther Branch rises in e Cherokee County and flows nw into Peachtree Creek.

Panther Branch rises in s Haywood County and flows sw into Little East Fork Pigeon River.

Panther Branch rises in w Madison County and flows e into Meadow Fork.

Panther Branch rises in s Wake County and flows s into Middle Creek.

Panther Branch Township, se Wake County.

Panther Cove, s Graham County between Little Snowbird Creek and Old Mattie Top.

Panther Creek rises in e Duplin County and flows w into Northeast Cape Fear River.

Panther Creek rises in e Durham County and flows ne into Neuse River.

Panther Creek rises in w Forsyth County and flows se into Yadkin River.

Panther Creek rises in e Graham County and flows ne into Little Tennessee River.

Panther Creek rises in central Haywood County and flows w into Pigeon River.

Panther Creek rises in w Lenoir County and flows n into Dailys Creek.

Panther Creek rises in e Pitt County and flows se into Tar River.

Panther Creek rises in e Rowan County and flows ne about 6 mi. into High Rock Lake.

Panther Creek rises in ne Sampson County and flows ne into Duplin County, where it enters Goshen Swamp.

Panther Creek rises in w Wake County and flows sw into Chatham County, where it turns nw to flow into Northeast Creek.

Panther Den Falls, on Britton Creek in ne Cherokee County. A picnic area, est. by the U.S. Forest Service, is nearby.

Panther Flat Top, mountain on Cherokee-Graham county line.

Panther Gap, s Macon County between Sheep Knob and Panther Knob.

Panther Knob, between Savannah Ridge and East Fork [Savannah Creek] in w Jackson County. Alt. 4,010.

Panther Knob, se of Cope Knob on the Jackson-Macon county line. Alt. 4,376.

Panther Knob, s Macon County at the head of Nickajack Creek. Alt. approx. 3,450.

Panther Knob, w Macon County between heads of Bryson Branch and Poplar Cove Creek. Alt. 4,621.

Panther Knob, w Madison County between Hog-back Mountain and Meadow Fork.

Panther Mountain, se Macon County between Buck Creek and Deep Gap. Alt. approx. 4,600.

Panther Mountain, s Transylvania County between Eby Creek and Cannon Creek.

Panther Ridge, ne Macon County between Beasley Creek and Mica City Creek.

Panthers Gap. *See* Painters Gap.

Panther Spring Gap, w Haywood County in Great Smoky Mountains National Park near lat. 35°36′35″ N., long. 83°03′50″ W.

Panther Swamp, e Moore County on Turkey Creek.

Panther Swamp, a sandy loam area approx. 1 mi. square in e Northampton County on the headwaters of Canal Swamp.

Panther Swamp Creek rises in central Greene County and flows sw into Contentnea Creek.

Panthertail Mountain, w Transylvania County n of Toxaway River. Alt. 4,516.

Panther Top, s Cherokee County between Beech Creek and Notelly River. Alt. 2,287.

Panthertown Creek rises in se Jackson County and flows nw then ne to join Greenland Creek in forming Tuckasegee River.

Paquiac, name given by John White on his maps of 1585 and 1590 to the section of Hatteras Island s of Cape Kenrick and extending almost to modern Cape Hatteras, se Dare County. The section lay between present Chicamacomico Banks and Kinnakeet Banks. The name *Paquiac* is an Algonquian Indian term for "it is shallow," describing the adjacent Pamlico Sound.

Paquike Lake. *See* Lake Mattamuskeet.

Paquinouc. *See* Perquimans River.

Paquippe. *See* Lake Mattamuskeet.

Paradise, community in w Richmond County served by post office, 1893–95.

Paradise Point, on the e side of New River in central Onslow County. Named for a former owner of the area. Now within Camp Lejeune Marine Base. Local tradition says that the home of David Simmons was there, and that he had several daughters widely known for their charms and beauty. Lovesick beaux called the place Paradise Point.

Parched Corn Bay, in the waters of Pamlico Sound off the se shore of the mainland of Dare County.

Parched Corn Point, land on the se mainland of Dare County extending into Pamlico Sound.

Paris, community in se Anson County served by post office, 1870–1901.

Park Creek rises in sw Macon County and flows ne into Nantahala River.

Parker, community in w Ashe County. Alt. 3,950.

Parker Branch rises in nw Buncombe County and flows se into Newfound Creek.

Parker Branch rises in ne Cherokee County on Brushy Head Mountain and flows nw into Valley River.

Parker Creek rises in central Currituck County on s Piney Island and flows se into Currituck Sound near community of Barco. Approx. ¾ mi. long.

Parker Creek rises in central Pitt County and flows se into Tar River.

Parker Creek rises in w Transylvania County and flows se into West Fork French Broad River.

Parker Gap, between Neddie Knob and Cub Branch in e Jackson County. Alt. 4,038.

Parker Knob, central Jackson County between Wayehutta Creek and Moses Creek. Alt. 4,187.

Parker Knob, on the Jackson-Haywood county line. Alt. 5,420.

Parker Mountain, w Cherokee County near Bearpaw Creek.

Parker Ridge, n Cherokee County in the Snowbird Mountains.

Parkersborough. *See* The Borough.

Parkers Branch rises in e Union County and flows e into Lanes Creek.

Parkersburg, town in w Sampson County. Settled about 1888; inc. 1891, but long inactive in municipal affairs. Named for William J. Parker, an early subscriber of stock in the railroad on which the town was located. Alt. 118.

Parkers Creek rises in e Chatham County and flows se into New Hope River.

Parkers Creek rises in n Harnett County and

flows sw into Cape Fear River. Named by Peter Parker when he settled along its banks prior to 1746.

Parker's Ferry. *See* Meherrin River.

Parkers Fork, community in ne Gates County.

Park Gap, se Clay County between Marbleyard Ridge and Little Buck Creek.

Parks, community in ne Wilkes County served by post office, 1884–1906.

Parks Branch rises in central Haywood County and flows nw into Jonathans Creek.

Parks Mountain, nw tip of Burke County. Alt. 4,066.

Park Springs, lake on Moon Creek in w Caswell County. Formerly a health resort and mineral spring. Lake, covering 8 acres and owned by the Danville, Va., Kiwanis Club, long used for fishing and swimming.

Parkstown, community in e Wayne County near the coincident boundaries of Greene, Lenoir, and Wayne Counties.

Parkton, town in ne Robeson County. Settled about 1884. Inc. 1901. Known first as Gillis Station for Mrs. John Gillis, who sold land for a railroad station. When the railroad was completed, the name was changed to Parkton, probably from the fact that farmers of the surrounding area "parked" teams at the station to take the train to Fayetteville.

Parkton Township, n Robeson County.

Parktown, community in s Warren County between Fishing Creek and Shocco Creek.

Parkville, community in nw Pasquotank County.

Parkville, community in e Perquimans County.

Parkville Township, e central Perquimans County.

Parkwood, residential community in s Durham County a few miles w of Lowes Grove. Name derived from the Research Triangle Park. Developed in the early 1960s.

Parkwood, formerly an industrial community in n Moore County. Est. before the Civil War when William Donnelly, stonemason, began making millstones there. A sawmill, brick kiln, flour mill, and other businesses developed. Bankruptcy in the 1880s forced the closing of the businesses, and the community began to decline. During World War II, the remaining buildings were dismantled and removed. In 1953 the community of Hallison, about 1¼ mi. n, changed its name to Parkwood. Hallison had been named by Maj. W. C.

Petty, a railroad man, for his deceased son, Hall Jefferson. Alt. 450.

Park Yarn, community in se Cleveland County s of the town of Kings Mountain. Park Yarn mills operated there.

Parmele, town in w Martin County. Settled about 1885; inc. 1893. Named for a partner in the Parmele-Eccleston Lumber Company, which operated at the site. Alt. 76.

Parrish Creek rises in central Macon County and flows nw into Burningtown Creek.

Parrish's Pond, formed about 1890 on Redbud Creek in e Franklin County. Covers 20 acres, with a max. depth of 15 ft. Known first as Babbit's Pond and then as Woods Pond.

Parrotts, community in n Lenoir County. Named for the Parrott family, which settled in the vicinity in the 1760s. Alt. 54.

Parrotts Creek rises in e Onslow County and flows e into Queens Creek. Named for John Parrott. Generally known locally as Parrotts Swamp but also called Moseley's Creek.

Parrotts Swamp. *See* Parrotts Creek.

Parson Bald, in Great Smoky Mountains National Park on Swain County, N.C.–Blount County, Tenn., line, lat. 35°31′25″ N., long. 83°53′ W. Alt. 4,730.

Parson Branch rises in n Yancey County and flows se into Peterson Branch.

Parsons Branch rises in ne Cherokee County on Brushy Head Mountain and flows w into Valley River.

Parsonville, community in w Wilkes County on North Prong Lewis Fork Creek.

Partee. *See* Tuttles Store.

Partins Millpond, in s Wake County on Black Creek.

Partridge Creek rises in n Macon County and flows sw into Whiteoak Creek.

Partridge Gap Ridge, w Madison County between Bluff Mountain and Pine Mountain.

Partridge's Bluff. *See* Gabourel's Bluff.

Paschall, community in n Warren County. Alt. 311. Formerly known as Merry Mount, its post office name from 1847 to 1929.

Paschalls. *See* Ridgeway.

Pasley, community in s Duplin County.

Pasley Cove, se Watauga County, extends se on the head of Dugger Creek.

Pasleys Ridge, s Watauga County, extends se between Hog Camp Branch and Joe Creek.

Pasour (PAY-sewer) Mountain, a ridge approx.

4 mi. long extending ne from Long Creek to Sulphur Branch in n Gaston County. Alt. 1,100.

Pasquotank, community in w Pasquotank County.

Pasquotank County was formed by 1681 as a precinct of Albemarle County. Located in the ne section of the state, it is bounded by Albemarle Sound and by Perquimans, Gates, and Camden Counties. The name of the county is from the Indian word *pāsk-e'tan-ki* (where the current [of the stream] divides or forks). Area: 290 sq. mi. (229, land; 61, water). County seat: Elizabeth City, with an elevation of 12 ft. Townships are Elizabeth City, Mount Hermon, Newland, Nixonton, Providence, and Salem. Produces corn, soybeans, potatoes, cabbage, miscellaneous vegetables, cotton, hogs, livestock, textiles, ships, lumber, hosiery, apparel, paper boxes, and industrial machinery.

Pasquotank River rises in nw Camden County and flows se to form the Camden-Pasquotank county line until it enters Albemarle Sound. An Indian village, Pasquenoke, is shown in the area on the De Bry map, 1590. Appears as Pacequenock on the Blaeu map, 1640, and as Prascantanck River on the Comberford map, 1657. The Intracoastal Waterway enters Pasquotank River through Dismal Swamp Canal. *See also* Shipyard.

Passmore Branch rises in ne Clay County and flows sw into Perry Creek.

Passmore Knob, e Macon County between Jack Knob and Brown Gap.

Pastook, community in s Davidson County served by post office, 1886–1901.

Pasture Branch rises in s Duplin County and flows se into Northeast Cape Fear River.

Pasture Creek, stream in Nelson Bay that cuts nw into the mainland in ne Carteret County. Approx. ¼ mi. long.

Patchet Creek rises in e Lee County and flows s into Little River.

Pate Creek rises in nw Mitchell County and flows s into Pigeonroost Creek.

Pates, community in w Robeson County. Inc. 1883, but long inactive in municipal affairs. Named for Ed Pate, a railroad employee.

Pate Store, community in e Wayne County s of the community of Cherry and n of The Slough.

Patetown, town in e Wayne County near The Slough. Inc. 1907, but no longer active in municipal affairs. Named for the Pate family living in the area.

Pat Knob, n Macon County between Sawmill Ridge and Shepherd Creek.

Patrick, community in w Cherokee County near Camp Creek.

Pat Stable Branch rises in sw Macon County and flows ne into Nantahala River.

Pat Stable Ridge, sw Macon County between Kimsey Bald and Pat Stable Branch.

Patsy Creek rises in nw Yancey County and flows se into Roaring Fork.

Patterson, town in central Caldwell County. Founded in 1851 as the site of a textile mill. Inc. 1905, but long inactive in municipal affairs. Named for Samuel Finley Patterson (1799–1874), local resident and state official. Alt. 1,253. Patterson School operated there since 1909.

Patterson Branch rises in ne Cherokee County and flows nw into Junaluska Creek.

Patterson Branch rises in central Franklin County and flows se into Fox Creek.

Patterson Branch rises in e Hoke County and flows sw into Puppy Creek.

Patterson Branch rises in n Yancey County and flows se into Jacks Creek.

Patterson Creek rises in nw Iredell County and flows e into Rocky Creek. Formerly known as Big Rocky Creek.

Patterson Creek rises in w Lee County and flows nw into Deep River.

Patterson Creek rises in s central Transylvania County and flows se into French Broad River.

Pattersons Bridge, community in sw Moore County served by post office, 1876–98.

Pattersons Mill. *See* Roberta.

Patterson Springs, community in s Cleveland County. Alt. 904. Settled in the 1880s. Named for Arthur Patterson Sr., who lived near Kings Mountain at the time of the 1780 battle.

Patterson Top, w Cherokee County n of Hiwassee Dam and e of Anderson Creek.

Patterson Township, former township in sw Alamance County, now township no. 1.

Patterson Township, n central Caldwell County.

Patterson Township, former township in sw Durham County, now combined with Cedar Fork Township to form Triangle Township.

Patton, mining town in se McDowell County near Dysartsville. Named for Patton family, local landowners.

Patton Cove, nw Buncombe County e of Hanlon Mountain.

Patton Cove, the valley through which Patton Cove Creek flows in se Buncombe County.

Patton Cove Creek rises near Patton Gap in se Buncombe County and flows n through Patton Cove into Swannanoa River.

Patton Gap, se Buncombe County between Big Flats and High Hickory Knob in the Swannanoa Mountains.

Patton Mountain, central Buncombe County near the headwaters of Ross Creek.

Patton Mountain, central Macon County at the head of Blaine Branch.

Patton Ridge, community in w Wilkes County near the head of South Prong Lewis Fork Creek.

Pattonsville, former community in Granville County w of the mouth of Tabb Creek on Tar River. Appears on the McRae map, 1833.

Paul Gamiels Hill, n end of Bodie Island in e Dare County. Site of lifesaving station est. in 1878–79. Lifesaving Service and Revenue Cutter Service joined to form U.S. Coast Guard in 1915. Active until after World War II.

Pauls Creek rises in Virginia and flows s into Surry County, where it enters Stewarts Creek. Approx. 14 mi. long.

Pauls Gap, on the Haywood-Swain county line between Cataloochee Balsam and Sugar Tree Licks. Alt. approx. 5,100.

Paw Creek rises in w Mecklenburg County and flows sw into Catawba River.

Paw Creek, community in w Mecklenburg County. Name of the railroad depot is Thrift.

Paw Creek Township, former township in w central Mecklenburg County, now township no. 12.

Pawpaw Creek rises in s Madison County and flows ne into French Broad River.

Pawpaw Creek rises in nw Rockingham County and flows sw into Mayo River.

Pawpaw Creek rises in nw Swain County and flows sw into Eagle Creek.

Paw Paw Ridge, nw Swain County in Great Smoky Mountains National Park, extends sw from Cherry Knob on Jenkins Trail Ridge, lat. 35°30′50″ N., long. 83°44′52″ W.

Paxton Creek rises in central McDowell County and flows se approx. 2 mi. into Clear Creek. Formerly known as Poplar Cove Creek.

Paxton Creek rises in s Transylvania County and flows ne into French Broad River.

Payne Branch rises in nw Swain County and flows se into Fontana Lake.

Payne Branch rises in s Watauga County and flows ne into Middle Fork [South Fork New River].

Payne Mountain, sw Cherokee County, extends ne from Wolf Pen Gap to Harris Top.

Paynes Branch rises in sw Clay County and flows ne into Brasstown Creek.

Paynes Knob, central Buncombe County ne of Rocky Knob.

Paynes Store, community in se Alexander County.

Paynes Tavern, community in s Person County near North Flat River. Cornwallis spent a night there in 1781 during the Revolutionary War. The tavern has long since ceased to exist.

Pea Branch rises in e Pitt County and flows e into Tranters Creek.

Peace, community in sw Wake County.

Peach, community in n Perquimans County.

Peach Bottom Mountains, a range of high, grass-covered mountains extending across most of Alleghany County from sw to n central. Among the named peaks are Cheek, Fender, and Doughton Mountains and Bald Knob.

Peach Knob, central Buncombe County sw of Craven Gap in Elk Mountains.

Peachland, town in w Anson County. Originally known as Mulcahy; renamed in 1888 for a large peach orchard nearby. Inc. 1895. Alt. 446.

Peach Orchard, mountain in the Cane Creek Mountains, s Alamance County.

Peach Orchard Creek rises in ne Buncombe County and flows w into Carter Creek.

Peachtree, community in e Cherokee County.

Peachtree Branch rises in se Duplin County and flows w into Mill Branch.

Peachtree Creek rises in ne Cherokee County and flows sw into Hiwassee River in the central part of the county.

Peachtree Creek rises in e Franklin County and flows se into Nash County to form Stony Creek with Little Peachtree Creek.

Peachtree Creek rises in central Swain County and flows sw into Tuckasegee River.

Peachtree Creek rises in e central Wake County and flows w into Neuse River near Milburnie.

Peachtree Creek. *See* White Oak Swamp.

Peachtree Gap, on Graham-Swain county line between Broke Yoke Gap and Round Top.

Peachtree Knob, on the Cherokee-Clay county line. Alt. 4,200.

Peacocks, community in n Columbus County. Earlier known as Peacocks Store.

Peacock's Bridge, se Wilson County over Contentnea Creek approx. 1½ mi. se of Stantonsburg. A bridge existed there by 1751 and is shown on the Price map, 1808, and on the MacRae map, 1833. There Lt. Col. Banastre Tarleton's British dragoons and Col. James Gorham's militia engaged in a skirmish, May 1781. Known for a time as Ruffin's Bridge.

Peacocks Crossroads, community in sw Johnston County.

Pea Hill Creek rises in s Virginia and flows s into Northampton County, where it enters Roanoke River. Appears on the map of the North Carolina–Virginia line run by William Byrd and others, 1728.

Pea Island, part of the Outer Banks in e Dare County. Once a separate island, but now part of Hatteras Island, bounded on the n by Oregon Inlet and on the s by Hatteras Island. Also known as Chicamacomico Banks, *which see*.

Pea Island National Waterfowl Refuge, a national wildlife refuge covering all of Pea Island and the n end of Hatteras Island to Rodanthe, e Dare County. Federally funded in 1938 as a winter preserve for migratory birds. Formerly known as Pea Island Migratory Waterfowl Refuge.

Peak, The, mountain in e Ashe County between Peak Creek and South Fork New River. Alt. approx. 3,950.

Peak, The, mountain in sw Ashe County. Alt. 5,195.

Peak, The, sw Mitchell County between Crabtree Creek and North Toe River. Alt. 3,866.

Peak Creek rises on the Ashe-Wilkes county line near Mulberry Gap and flows nw into South Fork New River.

Peak Creek Township, e Ashe County.

Peaked Knob, on the Haywood County, N.C.–Cocke County, Tenn., line. Alt. 3,370.

Peaked Top, central Caldwell County near the headwaters of Abingdon Creek.

Peak Knob, e Macon County between Grindstone Knob and the head of Moses Branch.

Peak Mountain, ne Avery County.

Peaks Bald, on the Macon-Swain county line between Davis Bald and Low Gap.

Pea Landing. *See* Calabash.

Pearce Crossroads, community in s Franklin County.

Pearce's Creek rises in n Burke County and flows e into Carroll's Creek.

Pearces Mill Township, central Cumberland County.

Pearceville, community in nw Camden County. Named for Pearce family from New England, who settled there following the Revolution. Often appears on maps as Pierceville.

Pea Ridge, elevated sandy area in n Washington County on Albemarle Sound extending ne from Leonards Point.

Pea Ridge, community in e Polk County. Alt. 1,050.

Pea Ridge. *See* Cycle.

Pea Ridge. *See* Ridgeville.

Pearsall, community in n Duplin County.

Pearson Knob, mountain in nw Alexander County. Alt. 1,898.

Pearson's Falls, sw Polk County between town of Saluda and city of Tryon on Colt Creek. Named for Charles William Pearson, former owner of the site. The falls tumble over 75 ft. of rugged rocks. The surrounding 308 acres contain a wildflower sanctuary and herbarium. There are more than 200 different varieties of flowers and woodland growth there.

Peartree Point extends from the mainland into the mouth of Alligator River in ne Tyrrell County.

Peckerwood Creek rises in n Cherokee County and flows sw into Tellicoe River.

Peckerwood Creek rises in central Clay County and flows nw into Tusquitee Creek. Named for an Indian, Jim Peckerwood, who lived near its head.

Peckerwood Ridge, n Cherokee County.

Pecks Corner, mountain on the Swain County, N.C.–Sevier County, Tenn., line at the head of Enloe Creek. Alt. approx. 5,700. Also known as Pecks Peak.

Pecks Peak. *See* Pecks Corner.

Pedlars Hill. *See* Pleasant Hill.

Peebles Tavern. *See* Garysburg.

Pee Dee, community in e Anson County.

Pee Dee, community in w Montgomery County. Produces hosiery and lumber.

Pee Dee River is formed by the junction of the Yadkin and Uwharrie Rivers in Montgomery County. It flows s along the Stanly-Montgomery and Anson-Richmond county lines into South Carolina, where it empties into Winyah Bay. Also known as Great Pee Dee River. The name may be a Catawba Indian word *pi'ri* (something good) or *pfhere* (smart; expert; capable).

Peedee Township, w Montgomery County.

Peek, community in e Madison County.

Peeks Creek rises in s Macon County and flows ne into Cullasaja River.

Peele Branch rises in ne Bertie County and flows sw into Chinkapin Swamp.

Peeler, community in e Rowan County served by post office, 1894–1904.

Peeler Creek rises in s Davie County and flows se approx. 2 mi. into Yadkin River.

Peels Top, nw Cherokee County in the Unicoi Mountains.

Peewee Branch rises in w Jackson County and flows s into Greens Creek.

Peggy Gap, on the head of Camp Creek in nw Jackson County.

Peggy Knob, s Macon County between Tessentee Creek and Bennies Branch.

Peggy Peak, sw Buncombe County at the e end of Smathers View Mountain.

Pegries, community in sw Richmond County served by post office, 1885–1904.

Pekin, community in s Montgomery County. A post office, Chisholm's Store, est. there 1824, was renamed Pekin in 1853.

Peletier, community in w Carteret County. Named for family of same name.

Peletier Creek rises in s Carteret County and flows s into Bogue Sound. Probably named

for Jerome Peletier, first of the family to settle in the vicinity.

Pelham, community in nw Caswell County. Est. during the Civil War as a station on the Piedmont Railroad; named for Maj. John Pelham, Alabamian killed in action during the war. Alt. 740.

Pelham Precinct appears on the Wimble map, 1738, between the Cape Fear and the Northeast Cape Fear Rivers at approx. what is now Pender County. Wimble's map was dedicated to Thomas Hollis Pelham, Duke of Newcastle (1693–1768), secretary of state for the Southern Department. Pelham County appears at the same location on the Mouzon map, 1775. Since there appears to be no reference to such a precinct or county in the records of North Carolina, it is possible that Wimble was simply flattering his patron and that Mouzon followed Wimble's map in making his own.

Pelham Township, nw Caswell County.

Pell Mell Pocosin, n central Bertie County.

Pembroke, town in w central Robeson County. Alt. 172. Inc. 1895. Originally called Campbell's Mill on Waterhole Swamp; later, Scuffletown, after Scoville Town in England or because it was a good place to get into a fight. Today, it is center of Lumbee Indian business and social life. Named for Pembroke Jones (1825–1910), an official of the Wilmington and Weldon Railroad, which intersected the Wilmington, Charlotte, and Rutherford Railroad there. Home of the University of North Carolina at Pembroke, founded in 1887.

Pembroke Creek rises in Pollock Swamp, e Chowan County, and flows s and se into the w side of the head of Edenton Bay. Formerly known as the w branch of Mattacomack Creek and later Queen Anne's Creek. Took its present name from Thomas Barker's plantation, Pembroke, which was named for his birthplace, Pembroke, Mass. Barker bought his property from Edmund Gale about 1751. *See also* Ramushawn River.

Pembroke Township, central Robeson County.

Pender, community immediately s of the town of Halifax, e Halifax County.

Pender County was formed in 1875 from New Hanover County. Located in the se section of the state, it is bounded by the Atlantic Ocean and by New Hanover, Brunswick, Columbus, Bladen, Sampson, Duplin, and Onslow Counties. It was named for Gen. William D. Pender (1834–63), a Confederate officer killed at Gettysburg. Area: 869 sq. mi. (857, land; 12, water). County seat: Burgaw, with an elevation of 49 ft. Townships are Burgaw, Canetuck, Caswell, Columbia, Grady, Holly, Long Creek, Rocky Point, Topsail, and Union. Produces corn, oats, soybeans, miscellaneous fruits and vegetables, peanuts, poultry, eggs, hogs, dairy products, livestock, turkeys, seafood, metal products, and lumber. *See also* Pelham Precinct; Lillington County.

Pendergrass Mountain, central Macon County between Blaine Branch and the heads of Battle Branch and Salser Branch.

Penderlea, community in nw Pender County. Land in the area had been purchased after the Civil War by E. R. Brink, a northern investor. He subdivided it, prepared a map, and sold about 50 farms to people in New York City. His mortgage with a Wilmington bank was foreclosed, and the New Yorkers lost their farms and money. Beginning in 1934, the U.S. government purchased a total of 10,500 acres, which was subdivided into tracts of about 30 acres each. Houses and other buildings were erected, and farmers who had been removed from submarginal land taken out of cultivation by the government were moved into the area. A total of 142 farm units were est., and a school, community center, and lake were built. The farms later were sold to those who lived on them.

Pender's Crossroads, community in e Wilson County near White Swamp and Town Creek. Maj. Gen. William Dorsey Pender (1834–63), a Confederate officer killed at Gettysburg, was born nearby.

Pendleton, town in ne Northampton County. Est. about 1887; inc. 1893. Known as Woodward's Crossroads until renamed to honor an employee of the railroad on the first train to pass through. Alt. 84.

Penelo, community in central Edgecombe County.

Penelope. *See* Longview.

Penland, community in s Mitchell County on North Toe River. Alt. 2,462. Named for Milton P. Penland, pioneer settler and businessman. Penland School of Crafts grew out of a school est. there in 1910.

Penland Bald, on the Clay-Macon county line at the head of Park Creek. Alt. approx. 5,000.

Penland Cove, se Cherokee County at the ne end of Poor House Mountain.

Penland Gap, on Middle Ridge in sw Macon County.

Penland Yellow. *See* Big Bald.

Penley, community in se Watauga County.

Penley Branch rises in s Watauga County and flows se into Middle Fork [South Fork New River].

Penly Cove, central Buncombe County e of Bee Ridge.

Pennington, community in n Stanly County served by post office, 1886–1909.

Pennix Cove, n Buncombe County e of Hemphill Mountain.

Penn Point, in central Carteret County extending into Newport River.

Penny, community in n Johnston County served by post office, 1884–1901.

Penny Hill, town on the Edgecombe-Pitt county line on Tar River. Inc. 1875, but no longer active in municipal affairs.

Pennys Hill, a large sand hill at the present community of Seagull on Currituck Banks, e Currituck County; has been a landmark locally since the early eighteenth century.

Penrose, community in e Transylvania County between Lydia Creek and French Broad River. Alt. 2,087.

Pensacola, community in s Yancey County on Cane River. Alt. 2,858. Name derived from an Indian word probably meaning "hair people" (those who wore their hair long).

Pensacola Township, s central Yancey County.

Penson Knob, s Macon County between Dover Knob and the Georgia state line.

Penson Mountain, s Macon County between Middle Creek and Norton Branch.

Peoria, community in nw Watauga County on the head of Stone Mountain Branch.

Pepper Creek rises in ne McDowell County and flows s into North Fork [Catawba River] near North Cove.

Peppers, community in w Mitchell County on Bee Creek.

Perch, community in se Surry County served by post office, 1894–1904.

Perfection, community in w Craven County.

Perkins Branch rises in central Watauga County and flows s into Hardin Creek.

Perkinsville, community in n Burke County on John's River.

Perkinsville, town authorized in 1819 to be laid off on the land of Constantine Perkins "on the main Hallow road" in the vicinity of modern Mount Airy, ne Surry County. There is no evidence that any building activity took place before 1848, after which the town of Mount Airy began to develop.

Perkinsville, community in central Watauga County on Perkins Branch and Hardin Creek.

Permetter Creek rises in n central Anson County and flows s into Brown Creek. Named for the Permenter family, early settlers.

Permudas Island, approx. 1½ mi. long, in s Onslow County in Stump Sound.

Pernell, community in n Wake County served by post office, 1885–1904.

Perquimans County was formed by 1679 as Berkeley Precinct in Albemarle County. Located in the ne section of the state, it is bounded by Albemarle Sound and by Chowan, Gates, and Pasquotank Counties. It was named for Indians in the vicinity. The legislature met there, 1707–16. Area: 324 sq. mi. (261, land; 63, water). County seat: Hertford, with an elevation of 15 ft. Townships are Belvidere, Bethel, Hertford, New Hope, and Parkville. Produces corn, soybeans, peanuts, cotton, hogs, livestock, apparel, sorghum, truck bodies, and sand.

Perquimans River rises in the Dismal Swamp in n Perquimans County and flows se into Albemarle Sound. Appears as Pequaimings River on the Comberford map, 1657;

as Wiquemans on the Ogilby map, 1671; and as Paquinous on the Hack map, 1684.

Perrishoes Creek. *See* Raccoon Creek.

Perry, community in nw Gaston County.

Perry Creek rises in e Clay County and flows w through Joe Cove into Tusquitee Creek.

Perry Creek rises in central Henderson County and flows ne into Osceola Lake.

Perry Creek rises in e Wake County and flows se into Little River. Formerly known as Middle Prong of Little River.

Perry Creek rises in n central Wake County and flows e through Gresham's Lake and into Neuse River. Shown as Simes Creek on Bevers map, 1870.

Perry Gap, e Clay County between the headwaters of Perry and Barnett Creeks.

Perry Knob, n Graham County between Cables Cove Creek and Tuskegee Creek.

Perry Knob. *See* Perry Top.

Perry Ridge, central Avery County.

Perrys Pond, in ne Wake County on Buffalo Creek. Formed in 1910, covers 20 acres, with a max. depth of 10 ft. Open to the public; used for recreation.

Perry Store, community in n Wake County.

Perry Top, peak in Plott Balsams in n Jackson County on the head of Monteith Branch. Also called Perry Knob. Alt. 5,080.

Perrytown, community in ne Bertie County.

Pershing. *See* Delco.

Persimmon Branch rises in central Duplin County and flows se and ne into Northeast Cape Fear River.

Persimmon Branch rises in ne Washington County and flows n and ne into Deep Creek.

Persimmon Creek rises in sw Cherokee County and flows ne into Hiwassee River. A fixed level impoundment of Persimmon Creek covers an area of 100 acres and overflows into Hiwassee Lake. It is maintained by the U.S. Forest Service.

Persimmon Creek rises in e Cleveland County and flows sw into Muddy Fork.

Persimmon Creek rises in central Lee County and flows n into Big Buffalo Creek.

Persimmon Creek, community in w Cherokee County.

Persimmon Ridge, se Avery County.

Persimmon Swamp rises in sw Brunswick County and flows n into Shingletree Swamp.

Person Branch rises in n Franklin County and flows sw into Sandy Creek.

Person County was formed in 1791 from Caswell County. Located in the n central section of the state, it is bounded by the state of Virginia and by Granville, Durham, Orange, and Caswell Counties. It was named for Gen. Thomas Person (1733–1800), Revolutionary patriot, member of the Council of Safety, and benefactor of the University of North Carolina. Area: 400 sq. mi. County seat: Roxboro, with an elevation of 671 ft. Townships are Allensville, Busby Fork, Cunningham, Flat River, Holloway, Mount Tirzah, Olive Hill, Roxboro, and Woodsdale. Produces tobacco, corn, wheat, oats, poultry, eggs, dairy products, livestock, hogs, textiles, hay, auto parts, wood products, lumber, and fabricated metals. Copper formerly was mined in the county.

Person Ordinary. *See* Littleton.

Perth, community in nw Bladen County.

Peru, community in ne Haywood County served by post office, 1852–1905.

Peru, community in s Onslow County on New River.

Pescud. *See* Thermal City.

Petche Gap, s central Burke County.

Peter Cove, s Haywood County on the head of Peter Cove Branch.

Peter Cove Branch rises in s Haywood County and flows se into Bird Creek.

Peter Cove Creek rises in ne Madison County and flows sw into Foster Creek.

Peter Cove Mountain, e Madison County between Foster Creek and Roaring Fork.

Peter Dick Gap, central Cherokee County near the head of Cook Creek and n of Flea Mountain. Named for an early settler.

Peter Mashoes Creek, a bay off the mainland of central Dare County in the waters of Croatan Sound. The community of Mashoes is located on the creek. *See* Mashoes.

Petersburg, community in s Madison County on Bull Creek. Alt. 1,972.

Petersburg, community on Jenkins Swamp in n Onslow County.

Petersburg Crossing, a crossroads community in e Duplin County.

Peters Creek rises in ne Bladen County, flows ne across se tip of Cumberland County, then flows back into Bladen County, where it enters South River.

Peters Creek rises in central Forsyth County in Winston-Salem and flows sw and s through the city into Middle Fork. Probably named for Hans Petersen, who was among the first settlers at Bethabara, 1753.

Peters Creek rises in Virginia and flows s into Stokes County, where it enters Dan River. It was the w limit of William Byrd's survey of the North Carolina–Virginia boundary in 1728.

Peters Creek, community in n central Stokes County on the Virginia line. Post office was there from 1850 until 1882, when name was changed to Elko, *which see*.

Peters Creek Township, n central Stokes County.

Peters Ferry. *See* Grifton.

Peterson, community in se Bertie County.

Peterson, community in w Mitchell County on Nolichucky River. Also known as Warrick.

Peterson Branch rises in n Yancey County and flows s into Jacks Creek.

Peterson Gap, n Mitchell County on Fork Mountain.

Peterson Inn. *See* Littleton.

Peterson Ridge, n Yancey County between Cooper Gap and Bee Branch.

Peters Point, point of land 1 mi. nw of Fort Fisher in s New Hanover County extending into the Cape Fear River near its mouth. *See also* Point Peter.

Peter Swamp rises at the se shore of Warwick Bay in e Robeson County and flows e into Big Swamp.

Peter Weaver Creek rises in s Jackson County and flows se then ne into Morgan Mill Creek.

Petra Mills. a small farming community in se Caldwell County. Also known as Petra.

Pett, community in e central Wake County.

Pettifords Creek. *See* Pettivers Creek.

Pettigrew State Park, e Washington and w Tyrrell Counties 9 mi. s of Creswell. Contains 16,828 acres, including 16,600-acre Lake Phelps. Est. 1939. Scenic, recreational, historical attraction; fishing. Somerset Place State Historic

Site House, antebellum plantation, adjacent to park. *See also* Somerset.

Pettivers Bay, at the mouth of Pettivers Creek in White Oak River, w Carteret County. Also known as Hampton Bay.

Pettivers Creek rises in w Carteret County and flows sw approx. 8 mi. into White Oak River. Named for John Pettiver, who owned land in the vicinity as early as 1728. Sometimes also called Pettifords Creek.

Petty Gulf Creek rises in e Anson County and flows s into Blewett Falls Lake.

Petty Point, peninsula extending from ne Pamlico County into Bay River.

Pettys Shore, community in e Hertford County on Chowan River at the site of an earlier Indian village. A large fishery once was operated there.

Pfafftown, community in w Forsyth County. Named for Peter Pfaff, who arrived in the Wachovia settlement in 1771.

Pharisee Swamp rises in se Sampson County and flows ne into Bulltail Swamp.

Pheasant Creek, in the tidal-marsh islands of Bear Banks, se Onslow County. Named for the pheasants formerly found there. Known also as Nicks Creek for Nick Moore.

Phelps Point. *See* Hertford.

Pheney, community in n McDowell County.

Phenoy, community in n McDowell County near present site of Little Switzerland, *which see*.

Phi, community in n Rowan County served by post office, 1884–1904.

Philadelphus, community in n Robeson County on Richland Swamp. Settled 1796–99; site of an early private academy.

Philadelphus Township, w central Robeson County.

Phillip Knob, s Swain County between Yalaka Creek and Little Yalaka Creek.

Phillips' Branch rises in w Caldwell County and flows e into Wilson's Creek.

Phillips Branch rises in e Haywood County and flows e into Fines Creek.

Phillips Branch rises in n central Henderson County and flows se into Clear Creek.

Phillips Branch rises in w Watauga County and flows se into East Fork [Cove Creek].

Phillips Creek rises in nw Bladen County and flows s into Cape Fear River.

Phillips Creek rises in ne Cherokee County and flows ne into Tatham Creek.

Phillips Creek rises in s Transylvania County and flows nw into Hogshead Creek.

Phillips Crossroads, community in n Jones County.

Phillips Gap, on the Ashe-Wilkes county line.

Phillips Knob, n Alexander County.

Phillips Knob, n central Yancey County on the head of Guilders Creek 1½ mi. n of town of Burnsville. Alt. 4,390.

Phillipsville, community in e Haywood County on the w outskirts of Canton.

Phils Creek rises in s Orange County and flows se into University Lake.

Phin's Island, in the e end of Brown's Sound in s Onslow County. Probably named for Phineas Stephens, an early landholder on Bear Creek.

Phipps Branch rises in e Yancey County and flows w into South Toe River. Named for Sidney Phipps, an early settler.

Phipps Cove, w Swain County between Yalaka Creek and Stevenson Branch; almost entirely submerged by the backwaters of Fontana Lake.

Phipps Creek rises in w Yancey County and flows nw into Cane River.

Phipps Gap, w Yancey County between Indian and Price Creeks.

Phoebes Creek rises in w Warren County and flows ne into Fishing Creek.

Phoenix, community in ne Brunswick County. A post office operated there, 1883–1938. Named for the mythical bird that, after death, rises from its ashes. Alt. 40.

Phoenix Creek rises on the e side of Phoenix Mountain, central Ashe County, and flows n into North Fork New River.

Phoenix Mine Village, former community in e Cabarrus County at site of Phoenix Mine. Period of greatest activity was from 1870 to 1907, when the chlorination process for treatment of gold ores was perfected there by Capt. Adolph Thies. At the time, the discovery was a notable step forward in metallurgy. The mine shafts were dewatered in 1955 for further ore-deposit appraisals.

Phoenix Mountain, central Ashe County. Alt. 4,673–4,700.

Pickards Mountain, sw Orange County on the head of Morgan Creek.

Pick Breeches Creek rises in ne Watauga County and flows se into Rube Creek.

Pickens Gap, nw Swain County on the s end of Jenkins Trail Ridge.

Pickens Nose, mountain in s Macon County between Betty Creek and Dryman Fork. Alt. approx. 4,900.

Picket Branch rises in ne Cherokee County and flows se and sw into Valley River.

Picketts Bay, an arm of White Oak River n of Swansboro, se Onslow County between Muddy Creek and Mount Pleasant Point.

Picks. *See* Somerset.

Pick's Sliding. *See* Somerset.

Picture Creek rises in sw Granville County and flows sw into Knap of Reeds Creek.

Piedmont or **Piedmont Plateau** extends from the Fall Line, *which see*, on the e to the Blue Ridge Mountains on the w. In elevation, the area ranges from approx. 500 ft. above sea level on the e to 1,500 ft. on the w. Rolling hills and stiff clay soil are characteristic of the Piedmont. The Indians knew the region as *Tar-ko-ee* (Catawba Land; Under Hills).

Piedmont, community in central Mecklenburg County e of Charlotte.

Piedmont Crescent is an extended area in the Piedmont section of the state from Wake County on the e through Durham, Orange, Alamance, Guilford, Randolph, Forsyth, Davidson, Rowan, Cabarrus, Mecklenburg, Gaston, and Lincoln Counties. It follows route of Interstate 85 and includes rapidly growing urban and industrial areas, most of which had their beginning along the route of the North Carolina Railroad.

Piedmont Lake, in se Transylvania County near Panther Mountain, drains s into Little River. Covers 5 acres, with a max. depth of 12 ft.

Piedmont Springs, former resort in nw Burke County. Now abandoned.

Piedmont Springs, community in central Stokes County on Dan River. A popular resort from about 1900 to 1930, when the hotel burned.

Piedmont Triad, a term used for the Greensboro, High Point, Winston-Salem area.

Pierce Creek rises in nw Macon County and flows ne into Nantahala River.

Pierce Creek rises in se Pamlico County and flows se into Neuse River. Named for Edmond Pierce, who settled there in 1708.

Pierces Crossroads, community in n Halifax County. Named for the Pierce family, which settled there in 1812.

Pierceville. *See* Pearceville.

Pig Basket Creek rises in nw Nash County and flows se into Stony Creek. Legend says that an early settler, going home with a basket of newborn pigs, dropped them into the water as he tried to cross the stream while it was swollen after a storm.

Pigeon Branch rises in n Transylvania County near Pigeon Gap and flows se into South Fork Mills River.

Pigeon Creek rises in ne Swain County and flows nw into Raven Fork.

Pigeon Creek rises in s Swain County and flows sw into Yalaka Creek.

Pigeon Flats Bay, a sand-filled bay in s Sampson County. *See also* Carolina Bays.

Pigeon Gap, s Haywood County on the head of Bird Creek.

Pigeon Gap, on the Haywood-Transylvania county line on Pisgah Ridge between Green Knob and Wagon Road Ridge.

Pigeon House Branch rises in central Wake County within the city limits of Raleigh. It rises in what is now Cameron Village and flows e into Crabtree Creek.

Pigeon Ledge, on the Haywood-Buncombe county line.

Pigeon River is formed in se Haywood County by the junction of East Fork Pigeon River and West Fork Pigeon River. It flows nw into Tennessee, where it enters French Broad River. Known as *Nee-oh-la* by the Cherokee Indians. *See also* Canton.

Pigeonroost, community in w Mitchell County on Pigeonroost Creek. Named when carrier pigeons, now extinct, were common in the area.

Pigeonroost Creek rises in nw Mitchell County and flows sw into Toe River.

Pigeonroost Creek rises in w Watauga County and flows ne into Dutch Creek. *See also* Dutch Creek Falls.

Pigeon Township, s central Haywood County.

Pigpen Bluff, ne Yancey County at the s end of Green Mountain.

Pigpen Cove, ne Buncombe County between Pinnacle Mountain and Cedar Cliff Knob.

Pigpen Creek rises in ne Yancey County and flows nw into Toe River.

Pigpen Flats, se Swain County on the head of Connelly Creek.

Pigpen Knob, ne Buncombe County between High Knob and Sheepwallow Knob.

Pigpen Knob, s Watauga County between Buck Ridge and Fall Ridge.

Pig Point extends into s waters of Currituck Sound in s Currituck County.

Pigtail, community in central Caldwell County near Hulme Hill.

Pike, community in s Cumberland County served by post office, 1877–1901.

Pike, community in n Scotland County served by post office from 1901 to 1908.

Pike Creek rises in central Pender County and flows se into Northeast Cape Fear River.

Pike Crossroads, community in w Wayne County between Little River and Nahunta Swamp. Named for Quaker family that settled in the area prior to 1758.

Pike Road, community in n Beaufort County.

Pikeville, town in n Wayne County in a region first settled by Quakers and on land originally granted to Samuel Pike in 1763. Land transferred in 1785 to Nathan Pike, for whom the town was named. Inc. in 1891. Alt. 142.

Pikeville Township, n central Wayne County.

Pilands Crossroads, community in se Hertford County.

Pile Creek rises in ne Cherokee County and flows s into Valley River.

Pilgrim, community in central Davidson County served by post office, 1892–95.

Pilkey Creek rises in w Swain County and flows sw into Fontana Lake.

Pilot, community in s Franklin County.

Pilot Cove, n Transylvania County, extends se from Slate Rock Ridge to Bradley Creek.

Pilot Creek rises in e Surry County and flows sw into Ararat River.

Pilot Gap, w Swain County on Pilot Ridge.

Pilot Knob, on Avery-Caldwell county line.

Pilot Knob, s Madison County at the head of Bailey Branch.

Pilot Knob, w Swain County in Great Smoky Mountains National Park at the se end of Pilot Ridge, lat. 35°27'53" N., long. 83°34'22" W. Alt. 2,967.

Pilot Mountain, on Burke-McDowell county line. Alt. 2,050.

Pilot Mountain, se Caldwell County. Alt. 1,486.

Pilot Mountain, on Lewis Creek in e Henderson County. Alt. 2,608.

Pilot Mountain, in central Jackson County between Shoal Creek and Betsy Branch. Alt. 4,059.

Pilot Mountain, e Randolph County.

Pilot Mountain, se Surry County. Alt. 2,700. The mountain is an isolated peak surviving from ancient mountains that have eroded away. The peak, classified as a monadnock, stands 1,500 ft. above the surrounding countryside; it served as a landmark for Indians and pioneer white settlers of the area. Appears as "Mt. Ararat or the Stonehead" on the Fry-Jefferson map, 1753, and as Mt. Ararat on the Collet map, 1770. The Price map, 1808, and subsequent maps show it with the present name. Called *Jomeokee* by the Indians, meaning "The Great Guide." The Devil's Den on Pilot Mountain is a small grotto from which a steady breeze blows at all times. *See also* Brushy Mountains.

Pilot Mountain, w Transylvania County s of Deep Gap. Alt. 5,151.

Pilot Mountain, s Wilkes County s of Hunting Creek.

Pilot Mountain, town in e Surry County. Alt. 1,100. Inc. 1889. Named for the nearby mountain.

Pilot Ridge, central Madison County parallel to Teat Branch. Walnut Knob is on the s end of this ridge.

Pilot Ridge, w Swain County in Great Smoky Mountains National Park, a spur of Welch Ridge extending se from Cherry Gap to Pilot Knob, lat. 35°28'18" N., long. 83°35'37" W.

Pilot Rock, n Transylvania County between Dividing Ridge and Pilot Cove.

Pilot Township, e Surry County.

Pilot View, community in central Yadkin County between North Deep and Forbush Creeks. Formerly known as Sugartown.

Pinchback's Tavern. *See* Clarksville.

Pinchgut Branch rises in s Duplin County and flows s into Island Creek.

Pinch Gut Branch rises in e Surry County and flows se into Stokes County, where it enters Big Creek. Said to have been named by Saura Indians in the vicinity who almost starved because of the scarcity of game.

Pinch Gut Creek rises in w Anson County and flows n into Brown Creek.

Pinch Gut Creek rises in e central Brunswick County and flows s to join Red Run in forming Lockwoods Folly River.

Pinchgut Creek rises in nw Caldwell County and flows e into Johns River. *See also* Coldass Creek.

Pinch Gut Creek rises in s Catawba County and flows sw into Maiden Creek.

Pinckton, community in nw Ashe County. Alt. approx. 3,498.

Pine Barrens. *See* Sandhills.

Pinebluff, town in s Moore County. Settled approx. 1890. Inc. 1899. Named for the longleaf pine in the vicinity. Alt. 307.

Pine Branch rises in central Avery County and flows n into Plumtree Creek.

Pine Branch rises in w Macon County and flows ne into Dicks Creek.

Pine Branch rises in e central Madison County and flows n into Big Laurel Creek.

Pine Branch rises in e Mitchell County and flows sw into North Toe River.

Pine Branch rises in n Mitchell County and flows sw into Right Fork Bean Creek.

Pine Branch rises in w Surry County and flows sw into Mitchell River.

Pine Cabbin. *See* Weaverville.

Pine Camp Branch rises in n Avery County and flows w into Tennessee, where it enters Elk River.

Pine Creek rises in w Jackson County and flows ne into Lake Thorpe.

Pinedene, community in s Moore County s of town of Southern Pines.

Pine Gap Branch rises in w Swain County and flows nw into Hazel Creek.

Pine Grove, community in se Craven County on Tucker Creek. Alt. 23.

Pine Hall, community in se Stokes County. Named for the pine trees growing there.

Pine Hammock, a tidal-marsh island approx. 1¼ mi. long in n Pamlico County.

Pine Hill, mountain in the Cane Creek Mountains, s Alamance County.

Pinehurst, town in s Moore County. Settled 1895. Inc. 1949. Named for its location in a pine forest. A popular resort founded by Tufts family and renowned for its golf courses. Alt. 536.

Pine Knob, on the Avery-Mitchell county line.

Pine Knob, central Buncombe County between Rocky Knob and Jack Gap.

Pine Knob, n Cherokee County.

Pine Knob, se Clay County at n end of Sharptop Ridge. Alt. approx. 3,650.

Pine Knob, on Cash Creek in w Henderson County.

Pine Knob, nw Jackson County between Gibbs Branch and Oconaluftee River.

Pine Knob, s Macon County between Plass Gap and High Top.

Pine Knob, w Mitchell County between Pigeonroost Creek and Brummett Creek.

Pine Knob, n Rutherford County between two unnamed branches that are the headwaters of Mountain Creek. Alt. approx. 1,555. Sometimes known as Piney Knob.

Pine Knob, se Watauga County n of Bens Ridge.

Pine Knob Branch rises in se Watauga County and flows ne into Laurel Fork.

Pine Level, town in e Johnston County. Settled about 1868; inc. 1874. Named for pine forest and level land of the area. Alt. 155. Produces cottonseed oil.

Pine Level Township, e central Johnston County.

Pinelog, community in sw Clay County on Pinelog Creek.

Pinelog, community in central Columbus County.

Pinelog Branch rises in nw Beaufort County and flows w into Tranters Creek.

Pine Log Branch rises in n Nash County and flows ne into Beaverdam Swamp.

Pinelog Branch rises in w Pitt County and flows sw into Little Contentnea Creek.

Pine Log Creek rises in w Anson County and flows n into Richardson Creek.

Pinelog Creek rises in sw Clay County and flows ne into Brasstown Creek.

Pinelog Swamp rises in n Columbus County and flows s into Soules Swamp.

Pine Mountain, n Buncombe County between Moody Cove and Maney Branch.

Pine Mountain, on the Buncombe-Henderson county line between Double Head and Cold Knob.

Pine Mountain, in the South Mountains in se Burke County. Alt. 1,821.

Pine Mountain, s Macon County between Jones Creek and South Fork [Skeenah Creek].

Pine Mountain, sw Macon County between Park Creek and Nantahala River.

Pine Mountain, sw Madison County between Norton Fork Creek and Friezeland Creek.

Pine Mountain, w Madison County between Partridge Gap Ridge and Spring Creek.

Pine Mountain, s Mitchell County between Brushy Creek and North Toe River.

Pine Mountain, e Transylvania County between Blythe Branch and Ballard Gap.

Pine Mountain, n central Transylvania County on the head of Allison Creek.

Pine Mountain, ne Transylvania County between Sitton Creek and Osborn Branch.

Pineola, community in s Avery County on Linville River. Alt. 3,538. Post office est. there in 1911 as Saginaw. Name changed to Pineola in 1914 for the pine trees growing in the vicinity and for Ola Penland, daughter of a local hotel keeper.

Pine Orchard Mountain, n Watauga County, extends ne from the head of Riddle Fork.

Pine Plains. *See* Cape Fear Section.

Pine Ridge, central Avery County.

Pine Ridge, s Buncombe County between Laurel Branch and Boyd Branch.

Pine Ridge extends from nw Burke County into w Caldwell County.

Pine Ridge, w Graham County between Cold Branch and Johns Branch.

Pine Ridge, along the n bank of the Tuckasegee River opposite Barkers Creek community in w Jackson County.

Pine Ridge, w Jackson County between Brush Fork and Sugar Fork.

Pine Ridge, s Macon County between South Fork [Skeenah Creek] and North Fork [Skeenah Creek].

Pine Ridge, e Mitchell County between Dry Branch and Left Fork [Cane Creek].

Pine Ridge, n Mitchell County between Hughes Branch and Bean Creek.

Pine Ridge, s Watauga County, extends sw parallel with Flannery Fork [South Fork New River].

Pine Ridge, se Yancey County, extends ne between South Toe River and Pine Ridge Branch.

Pine Ridge, community in e Mecklenburg County.

Pine Ridge, community in n Surry County between Little Fisher River and Stewart Creek. Alt. 1,347.

Pine Ridge Branch rises in se Yancey County and flows s into Three Forks Creek.

Pineroot Branch rises in n Mitchell County and flows w into Big Rock Creek.

Pine Run rises in e Watauga County and flows ne into South Fork New River.

Pine Stand Ridge, n Cherokee County, extends se from Copper Ridge to the junction of Beaverdam and Garreck Creeks.

Pine Station, community in s Wake County.

Pine Swamp rises in s Ashe County and flows n into South Fork New River.

Pine Swamp Branch rises in central Yancey County and flows sw into Cane River.

Pine Swamp Creek rises in s Alleghany County and flows n into Little River.

Pine Swamp Township, se Ashe County.

Pine Top, peak in w Surry County near the head of South Fork.

Pinetops, town in s Edgecombe County. Inc. 1903. Named by Henry Clark Bridgers (1876–1951), founder of the East Carolina Railway, which was completed between Tarboro and Hookerton in 1900. On the first run of the new railroad, Bridgers noticed that he could see only the tops of pine trees from the train there. Produces furniture. Alt. 100.

Pinetown, town in n central Beaufort County. Alt. 43. Inc. 1907.

Pine Tree Cove, w Haywood County on Pine Tree Cove Creek.

Pine Tree Cove Creek rises in w Haywood County and flows ne into Jonathans Creek.

Pinetree Creek, a channel of water separated from the main body of Neuse River by two small islands in central Craven County.

Pine Tree Gap, w Haywood County in Great Smoky Mountains National Park near lat. 35°33′23″ N., long. 83°06′37″ W., between Little Bald Knob and Hemphill Bald. Alt. 5,270.

Pine Tree Mountain, s Buncombe County e of the Biltmore Estate.

Pine Tree Store, community in se Hertford County.

Pine Tree Swamp rises in ne Craven County and flows nw into Little Swift Creek.

Pineview, community in w Harnett County. Formerly the center of a large area devoted to dewberry culture. Alt. 320.

Pineville, town in s Mecklenburg County. Inc. 1873. James K. Polk, eleventh president of the United States, was born 1 mi. e, 1795. Formerly Morrow's Turnout, *which see.* Alt. 575.

Pineville Township, former township in central Mecklenburg County, now township no. 14.

Piney, community in sw Caldwell County, formerly known as Hobart. Alt. 1,309.

Piney Bottom Creek rises on the Fort Bragg Military Reservation, nw Hoke County, and flows sw into Rockfish Creek.

Piney Branch rises in ne Brunswick County and flows e into Jackeye Creek.

Piney Branch rises in n Mitchell County and flows s into Little Rock Creek.

Piney Creek rises in nw Alleghany County and flows n into Virginia, where it enters New River.

Piney Creek rises in n central Ashe County and flows se into North Fork New River.

Piney Creek, an inlet on the sound side of Bogue Banks in sw Carteret County.

Piney Creek rises in s Rockingham County and flows se into Troublesome Creek. Lake Hunt, Reidsville reservoir, was built on the creek in 1956.

Piney Creek, community in nw Alleghany County.

Piney Creek Township, nw Alleghany County.

Piney Creek Township, n central Ashe County.

Piney Field Top, e Haywood Gounty between Pisgah Creek and Hungry Creek.

Piney Fork, community in central Rockingham County. Historically African American; named for local church.

Piney Fork Creek rises in sw Alleghany County and flows sw into e Ashe County, where it joins Mulberry Creek in forming Cranberry Creek.

Piney Green, community in central Onslow County between Wallace and Mott Creeks near the main gate of Camp Lejeune Marine Corps Air Station. An early post office and on the stage route from New Bern to Wilmington. Takes its name from the last eighteenth-century plantation of Joseph Marshall.

Piney Green, community in n Sampson County.

Piney Grove, community in ne Caldwell County.

Piney Grove, community in e Wayne County near the mouth of Walnut Creek in Neuse River. Named for a local church.

Piney Grove. *See* Pino.

Piney Grove Landing, on Pungo River, e Beaufort County.

Piney Grove Run rises in e Beaufort County and flows n into Pungo River.

Piney Grove Township, ne Sampson County.

Piney Island, ne Carteret County, is bounded by Neuse River on the w, Long Bay and West Bay on the e, and Pamlico Sound on the n. Approx. 8 mi. n to s, 3 mi. e to w.

Piney Island, a small island in Bogue Sound, sw Carteret County.

Piney Island, w portion of Church Island, *which see*, peninsula in central Currituck County extending into Currituck Sound. Coinjock Bay lies between the w shore and the mainland. Shown as a separate island, Pine Island, on the MacRae map, 1833.

Piney Island Bay, central Currituck County between Coinjock Bay and the sw coast of Piney Island.

Piney Knob. *See* Pine Knob.

Piney Knob Fork rises in s Macon County and flows ne into Turtle Pond Creek.

Piney Marsh, n Tyrrell County, an area of swampland on Scuppernong River opposite the town of Columbia.

Piney Mountain, central Buncombe County se of Cisco Mountain.

Piney Mountain, sw Buncombe County s of Peggy Peak.

Piney Mountain, sw Buncombe County e of Bent Mountain.

Piney Mountain, e Davidson County between the headwaters of Fourmile Branch and Flat Swamp Creek.

Piney Mountain, n Haywood County between Stevens Creek and Whiteoak Creek.

Piney Mountain, on Tumble Bug Creek in e Henderson County.

Piney Mountain, n Henderson County between Green Mountain and Clear Creek.

Piney Mountain, on the head of Whiterock Creek in w Jackson County.

Piney Mountain, sw Polk County w of town of Tryon. Alt. 1,550.

Piney Mountain, ridge across w central Polk County. Alt. approx. 1,920.

Piney Mountain, e Rutherford County between Puzzle Creek and the head of Brushy Creek.

Piney Mountain Creek rises in e Jackson County and flows se to join Rough Butt Creek in forming Caney Fork.

Piney Mountain Ridge, e Jackson County, extends ne from Rich Gap to Richland Balsam.

Piney Point, a point extending from mainland in ne Carteret County into Core Sound. *See also* Stacy.

Piney Point, sw Carteret County, extends from the w side of Bogue Banks into Bogue Sound.

Located near the mouth of Piney Creek. Appears on the Moseley map, 1733.

Piney Point, site of early settlement on e end of Bogue Banks, s Carteret County. Storms drove out early settlers until the settlement of Salter Path, *which see.*

Piney Point, peninsula in e Pamlico County extending into Pamlico Sound. Appears on the Moseley map, 1733.

Piney Prospect. *See* Point Prospect.

Piney Ridge, nw Swain County in Great Smoky Mountains National Park, a short spur extending w from Paw Paw Ridge, lat. 35°31′30″ N., long. 83°45′22″ W.

Piney Top, central Clay County at the n end of Big Pine Ridge.

Piney Wood Creek rises in e Swain County and flows sw into Una Creek.

Pin Gap, s Macon County between Foster Knob and the head of Jones Creek.

Pin Hook, community in se Duplin County.

Pin Hook, community in central Northampton County.

Pinhook Gap, on the Jackson-Transylvania county line at the head of Bee Tree Fork. Alt. 4,175.

Pink Beds, plateau area in n Transylvania County in Pisgah National Forest. Used extensively as a recreation area. Name comes from the color of rhododendron that once covered the area. Alt. 3,280.

Pink Fox Cove, n Buncombe County between Hemphill and Brank Mountains.

Pink Hill, town in se Lenoir County. A post office est. there, 1849. Inc. 1907. Named for a nearby plantation.

Pink Hill Township, s Lenoir County.

Pinkney, community in nw Wayne County n of Nahunta Swamp.

Pinkney. *See* South Gastonia.

Pink Ridge, s Avery County.

Pinkston, community in central Anson County. Named about 1911, when railroad construction reached this point on the land of John Pinkston.

Pinnacle, mountain at the intersection of the Buncombe-McDowell-Yancey county lines. Alt. 5,665. Sometimes referred to as Blue Ridge Pinnacle to distinguish it from other mountains named Pinnacle.

Pinnacle, peak in nw Swain County on the ne end of Pinnacle Ridge.

Pinnacle, community in sw Stokes County. Alt. 1,085. Inc. 1901; charter repealed 1903. Originally known as Culler for Emanuel W. Culler, who owned part of the land on which a railroad station was built. The railroad began operation in 1888, and the post office there, 1880–1900, was known as Culler. The present name was adopted in 1900.

Pinnacle, The, peak of Holland Mountain in sw Buncombe County. Alt. approx. 4,000.

Pinnacle, The, a peak on Kings Mountain, *which see,* on the Cleveland-Gaston county line. Alt. 1,705.

Pinnacle, The, mountain at the head of Dismal Creek in sw Henderson County.

Pinnacle, The, on the Jackson-Transylvania county line at the head of Miser Creek. Alt. approx. 4,145. Part of Tennessee Ridge, *which see.*

Pinnacle, The, mountain in s Macon County between Hickory Knoll Creek and Gray Gap.

Pinnacle Branch rises in s Macon County and flows e into Shope Fork.

Pinnacle Creek rises in nw Swain County on Jenkins Trail Ridge and flows sw into Eagle Creek.

Pinnacle Gap, ne Buncombe County near Craggy Pinnacle in Great Craggy Mountains.

Pinnacle Knob, at the junction of Buncombe-McDowell-Yancey county lines. Alt. 5,665.

Pinnacle Knob, central Graham County between Sweetwater Creek and Mountain Creek.

Pinnacle Knob, sw Haywood County on the ne end of Pinnacle Ridge.

Pinnacle Knob, on Macon-Swain county line s of Brush Creek.

Pinnacle Mountain, ne Buncombe County between Town Branch and Corner Rock Creek.

Pinnacle Mountain, central Henderson County overlooking Kanuga Lake. Alt. 3,662.

Pinnacle Mountain, n Jackson County between Dills Creek and Fisher Creek.

Pinnacle Mountain, s Macon County at the head of Pinnacle Branch. Alt. 5,020.

Pinnacle Mountain, on the McDowell-Rutherford county line. Alt. 3,832.

Pinnacle Ridge, sw Haywood County, extends ne from Wesner Bald to Pinnacle Knob.

Pinnacle Ridge, nw Swain County, extends ne from Eagle Creek to Pinnacle [peak].

Pinnacle Ridge, w Watauga County, extends ne between Bear Branch and Brassy Gap Branch.

Pinnacle Spring, s Yancey County, the source of Left Prong South Toe River.

Pinner Cove, the valley through which Robinson Creek flows in s Buncombe County w of Merrill Mountain.

Pinner Creek rises in s Buncombe County and flows se into Henderson County, where it enters Cane Creek.

Pinnix, community in central Davidson County served by post office, 1894–1904.

Pino, community in nw Davie County. First known as Piney Grove, but changed to Pino in 1890 when a post office was est. (closed 1906).

Pin Oak Gap, on Haywood-Swain county line on the head of Ledge Creek in Great Smoky Mountains National Park. Alt. 4,428. A prominent Indian trail passed through the gap before the coming of Europeans.

Pinoka, community in s Montgomery County; named in 1922 by local teacher who looked out the front window and saw pine trees and looked out the back window and saw oak trees.

Pinson, sw Randolph County.

Pinson Creek rises in s Caswell County and flows se into South Country Line Creek.

Pioneer Mills, community in s Cabarrus County. Gold and copper mines operated there from the 1850s until 1931.

Piper Gap. *See* Lambsburg.

Piper Hill, se Currituck County, former sand hill on s Currituck Banks. Erosion has now worn the hill down to beach level.

Pipes Branch rises in e Cherokee County in the Valley River Mountains and flows s of Tibb Ridge into Peachtree Creek.

Pipetrack Gap, s Macon County between Thomas Knob and the North Carolina–Georgia state line.

Pipkins Crossroads. *See* Savages Crossroads.

Pireway, town in s Columbus County near Waccamaw River. Inc. 1883, but long inactive in municipal affairs. Post office operated, 1855–1933, was known as Pireway Ferry after 1882.

Pisgah, community in s Randolph County. Named for nearby Pisgah Church. A post office est. there 1896, closed 1953.

Pisgah Creek rises in e Haywood County and flows nw into East Fork Pigeon River.

Pisgah Forest, community in e central Transylvania County near the confluence of Davidson

and French Broad Rivers. Includes the old communities of Davidson River and Ecusta. Produces lumber.

Pisgah Mountain, e Mitchell County parallel to the head of Green Cove Creek.

Pisgah National Forest, in portions of Avery, Buncombe, Burke, Caldwell, Haywood, Henderson, Madison, McDowell, Mitchell, Transylvania, Watauga, and Yancey Counties, was est. in 1911 and includes 510,113 acres. Nature trails, mountain climbing, picnicking, and other recreational uses.

Pisgah Ridge extends the length of the Haywood-Transylvania county line. The Blue Ridge Parkway traverses its length.

Pit Branch rises in n Yancey County and flows ne into Big Creek.

Pitch Landing, former community on Chinkapin Creek in s Hertford County. Appears on the Price map, 1808; post office est. 1801, closed 1881. Shown on maps as recently as 1916.

Pitch Landing. *See* Princeton.

Pitman Creek rises in n Carteret County and flows n into Turnagain Bay.

Pitt County was formed in 1760 from Beaufort County. Located in the e section of the state, it is bounded by Beaufort, Craven, Lenoir, Greene, Wilson, Edgecombe, and Martin Counties. It was named for William Pitt, Earl of Chatham (1708–78), secretary of state in England and virtual prime minister, whose vigorous war policies resulted in the defeat of the French in America by the British. Area: 656 sq. mi. County seat: Greenville, with an elevation of 64 ft. Townships are Arthur, Ayden, Belvoir, Bethel, Carolina, Chicod, Falkland, Farmville, Fountain, Greenville, Grifton, Grimesland, Pactolus, Swift Creek, and Winterville. Produces tobacco, corn, soybeans, oats, hay, apples, peanuts, cotton, poultry, hogs, livestock, lumber, textiles, batteries, baked goods, boats, canned foods, and apparel. *See also* Chatham County.

Pitt Crossroads, community in s Edgecombe County.

Pittman Creek rises in e Pamlico County and flows s into Broad Creek.

Pittmans Island, in White Oak River, se Onslow County. Known first as Bell Island for Ross Bell, owner from 1717 until about 1746; later known as Jones Island for Emanuel Jones, who purchased it about 1746 from Bell. Present name from John A. Pittman, a later owner.

Pittmans Store. *See* Hickory.

Pitts. *See* North Cove.

Pittsboro, town and county seat, central Chatham County. Est. 1778 as Chatham, site of the courthouse. Pittsboro authorized to be laid out on land adjacent to the courthouse in 1785, but owners would not sell the desired land. In 1787 land on another site was acquired. Named for William Pitt, Earl of Chatham (1708–78), defender of American rights in the British Parliament. Alt. 409. Produces textiles, hosiery, poultry.

Pitts Creek rises in e Chatham County and flows sw into Whiteoak Creek.

Pitt's Creek rises in e Onslow County and flows e into White Oak River. Named for Richard Pitts.

Pivers Island, s Carteret County w of the town of Beaufort. Named for the Piver family. Site of a U.S. marine biological station.

Pixie Mountain, central Avery County.

Plain, community in se Guilford County served by post office, 1879–1903. Name derived from Quaker principles.

Plainfield, community in w Alleghany County served by post office, 1898–1908.

Plain View, community in n Richmond County.

Plainview, community in w Robeson County on the nw outskirts of Rowland, *which see*. McQueen's Store, a post office est. 1811 was in the vicinity. Name changed to Queensdale, *which see*, 1820, and operation continued until 1904.

Plain View Township, nw Sampson County.

Plank Bridge. *See* Camden.

Plank Ford, n Union County across Rocky River.

Plass Gap, s Macon County between Norton Branch and Middle Creek.

Plateau, town in sw Catawba County. Inc. 1885 as Keeversville. Name changed, 1893. Long inactive in municipal affairs.

Player, community in e Pender County between Shaken Creek and Northeast Cape Fear River.

Players Swamp rises in s Pender County and flows sw into Merricks Creek.

Play Rock Hill, elevation in s Henderson County on Mud Creek.

Pleasant Branch rises in ne Swain County and flows nw into Bunches Creek.

Pleasant Gap, on the Buncombe-Madison County line between Nofat and Carter Mountains.

Pleasant Garden, community in s Guilford County. Alt. 805. Known first as Fentress for local family; renamed Pleasant Garden about 1879.

Pleasant Gardens, community in central McDowell County. Named for the home of Joseph McDowell, Patriot leader at the Battle of Kings Mountain (1780). Post office named Garden City operated nearby, 1886–1929.

Pleasant Grove, community in ne Alamance County. A post office est. there 1815 operated until 1908.

Pleasant Grove, community in e central Caswell County.

Pleasant Grove, community in n Duplin County.

Pleasant Grove, community in w Northampton County.

Pleasant Grove, community in n Washington County e of Kendricks Creek.

Pleasant Grove Township, former township in ne Alamance County, now township no. 11.

Pleasant Grove Township, w Johnston County.

Pleasant Grove Township, se Randolph County.

Pleasant Hill, community in ne Alamance County. Site of Christian Church est. about 1825. Early temperance society met there.

Pleasant Hill, community in se Chatham County. A post office there, 1828–1915, was known as Pedlars Hill.

Pleasant Hill, community in w Cherokee County between the headwaters of Little Shoal Creek and Hiwassee River.

Pleasant Hill, community in w Jones County on Trent River.

Pleasant Hill, community in n Northampton County. Alt. 118. A post office there from 1828.

Pleasant Hill, home of William Hawkins, governor, 1811–14, stands about 8 mi. n of Henderson in e Vance County.

Pleasant Hill Township, n central Northampton County.

Pleasant Knob, central Buncombe County w of Beaver Lake.

Pleasant Lodge, community in ne Randolph County.

Pleasant Plains, community in central Hertford County. A free black Baptist church said to have existed there as early as 1845.

Pleasant Ridge. *See* South Gastonia.

Pleasants, community in n Granville County served by post office, 1892–1903.

Pleasant View, crossroads community in n central Tyrrell County about 1½ mi. sw of community of Levels on s side of Riders Creek.

Pleasantville, community in w Rockingham County served by post office, 1818–1904.

Pleasure Beach, modern promotional term for Carolina Beach, Kure Beach, and Fort Fisher, all in s New Hanover County. Area also takes in Carolina Beach State Park.

Pledger Landing, n Tyrrell County on Albemarle Sound e of Lewis Point.

Plot Knob, sw Clay County between the headwaters of Suddawig and Rocky Branches. Alt. 2,390.

Plott, community in sw Haywood County served by post office, 1886–1926. Named for local Plott family.

Plott Balsam, a knob in w Haywood County on the ne end of Plott Balsams (ridge). Alt. 6,088. Named by Arnold Guyot for Amos Plott, pioneer settler. Nearby Enos Plotts Balsam Mountain (also known as Waterrock Knob) was named for his brother.

Plott Balsams, a ridge extending ne from Tuckasegee River in w Jackson County to Plott Balsam (knob) in w Haywood County. Known by the Cherokee Indians as Tunn Ensleas. Named for Henry Plott, father of Amos and Enoch Plott. Elder Plott introduced Plott Hound (now the State Dog) to North Carolina.

Plott Creek rises in w Haywood County and flows se into Richland Creek.

Plotts. *See* Eufola.

Plott's Old Field Mountain. *See* Old Field Top Mountain.

Pluck, community in n Chatham County served by post office, 1884–1903.

Plum Branch rises in se Cabarrus County and flows w into Hamby's Branch.

Plum Branch rises in e Yancey County and flows s into Little Crabtree Creek.

Plum Creek rises in nw Alamance County and flows sw into Ridge Creek.

Plummers Creek rises in e Davidson County and flows ne into Randolph County, where it enters Little Uwharrie River.

Plumtree, community on North Toe River, sw Avery County. Named for Plumtree Creek, which enters North Toe River nearby. Alt. 2,830. Mica has been mined there since 1891.

Plumtree Creek rises in central Avery County and flows s and w into North Toe River. Named for plum orchards set there by Avery and Connelly families.

Plyler, community in w Stanly County.

Plymouth, town and county seat, w Washington County on Roanoke River. Settled by 1727. Inc. 1807; named for Plymouth, Mass. Important as a shipping center and as a producer of lumber products, veneer, plywood; also the location of a paper mill and a center of grain mills. Alt. 21. Battle of Plymouth fought there, 1863.

Plymouth Township, w Washington County, was formed in 1868; was a voting precinct before that date.

Pocahontas, community in sw Swain County on Nantahala River.

Pochike River. *See* Meherrin River.

Pocket, The. *See* Pocket Township.

Pocket Creek rises in w Lee County and flows n into Deep River.

Pocket Township, former township in w Lee County (formerly Moore County), now township no. 7. A post office named The Pocket was est. there 1828 and continued to 1905. Named for the fact that it was isolated from the remainder of the county by a bend in Deep River, hence a "pocket."

Pocomoke, community in w Franklin County.

Pocosin Branch rises in s Jones County and flows n into Trent River.

Pocosin Branch rises in e Pitt County and flows se into Tranters Creek.

Pocosin Point. *See* Poquoson Point.

Poe-li-co. *See* French Broad River.

Poga Mountain, n Avery County at the n end of Beech Mountain. Alt. 3,790. Local tradition is that a man was lost on the mountain for several days, and when he returned home he explained to his friends that he had "been to Pogey." He may have been using the Englishdialect word "poggy," meaning boggy or sloppy, as a field in wet weather.

Pogey Mountain. *See* Poga Mountain.

Poindexter. *See* Smithtown.

Poindexter Branch rises in central Macon County and flows ne into Iotla Creek.

Point Bacon appears on the Smith map, 1624, as the n portion of present Currituck Banks in e Currituck County. It was shown as extending s from Cape Henry, Va., to Currituck Inlet. Undoubtedly named for Sir Francis Bacon, whose favor Smith sought to win.

Point Caswell, community in w Pender County on Black River. Named for Richard Caswell (1729–89), governor of North Carolina. Settled prior to the Civil War. Inc. in 1883 as Caswell; charter repealed 1901. Formerly a thriving shipping point on the river; now only a church and a few houses remain.

Point Corbett appears on the Smith map, 1624, as the area of ne North Carolina presently included in Camden and Currituck Counties.

Point Durant. *See* Durants Neck.

Point Harbor, community at the extreme s tip of Currituck County at Powells Point. Settled prior to 1667. Post office est. in 1906 as Marvin but changed in 1907 to Point Harbor.

Point Hezel appears on the Collet map, 1770, as a point of land in se New Hanover County between Hewlets and Bradley Creeks on the mainland w of modern Wrightsville Beach. Probably named for James Hasell (d. 1786), chief justice of the colony.

Point Lookout, e Haywood County on Glade Mountain. Alt. approx. 4,530.

Point Lookout Mountain, e Henderson County, extends ne from the w side of Big Hungry River. William Mills built a crude fort there soon after moving to the area, and it served as a haven for pioneer settlers in time of threat from the Indians. It was there, by tradition, that Polly Stepp, firing through a porthole, struck an Indian and exclaimed: "I've hit the Big Chief, darned if I ain't hit the Big Chief!" Remains of the old foundation logs can still be seen.

Point Misery, mountain peak on the Buncombe-Yancey county line at the e end of Big Andy Ridge. Alt. 5,715.

Point of Grass, nw point of Cedar Island in ne Carteret County between West Bay and Pamlico Sound.

Point of Grass Creek, a tidal creek on the Core Sound side of Core Banks near Drum Inlet, ne Carteret County.

Point of Marsh, a point of land extending into the mouth of Neuse River in the most n part of Carteret County.

Point of Woods. *See* Archie's Point.

Point Peter, point of land extending into Cape Fear River at its junction with Northeast Cape Fear River opposite Wilmington, w New Hanover County. Before the Civil War, it was a terminal for river traffic to and from Fayetteville and Averasboro. Named for Peter Mallett (b. 1744), Revolutionary leader. *See also* Peters Point.

Point Prospect, s Orange County in the town of Chapel Hill about ½ mi. e of the University of North Carolina campus, a very high ridge below which, as William R. Davie wrote in 1793, "the flat country spreads off . . . like the ocean, giving an immense hemisphere, in which the eye seems to be lost in the extent of space." The peak was owned by the university until 1894, when the U.S. Circuit Court ordered it to be sold to pay university debts. Sometimes known as Piney Prospect for the pines in the vicinity and because Point was often pronounced "pint," which evolved into Piney. Site of Gimghoul Castle.

Poison Branch rises in ne Ashe County and flows ne into North Fork New River.

Poison Branch rises in n Graham County and flows nw into Fontana Lake.

Poison Cove, e Haywood County on the head of Poison Cove Branch.

Poison Cove Branch rises in ne Buncombe County and flows nw into North Fork Ivy Creek.

Poison Cove Branch rises in e Haywood County and flows nw into Pigeon River.

Poison Cove Top, e Haywood County near the head of Poison Cove Branch.

Poison Fork rises in s Randolph County and flows sw into Montgomery County, where it enters Barnes Creek.

Poison Springs. *See* Barium Springs.

Pokeberry Creek rises in n Chatham County and flows sw into Haw River.

Pole Branch rises in w Johnston County and flows se into Black Creek.

Pole Bridge Branch rises in central Cherokee County and flows nw into Valley River.

Pole Bridge Branch rises in nw Swain County and flows s into Lake Cheoah.

Pole Bridge Branch rises in s Swain County and flows w into Little Tennessee River.

Pole Bridge Branch rises in s Transylvania County and flows ne into Little River.

Pole Bridge Creek rises in w Stanly County and flows ne into Big Bear Creek.

Pole Bridge Gap, n Wilkes County at the n end of Greenstreet Mountain.

Polecat Branch rises in ne Cherokee County and flows n into McClellan Creek.

Polecat Branch rises in ne Cherokee County and flows sw into Junaluska Creek.

Polecat Branch rises in e Greene County and flows sw into Contentnea Creek.

Polecat Branch rises in n Jackson County and flows sw into Hornbuckle Creek.

Polecat Branch rises in central Johnston County and flows sw into Neuse River.

Polecat Branch rises in n Macon County and flows sw into Lakey Creek.

Polecat Creek rises in s Guilford County and flows se into Randolph County, where it enters Deep River. The name appears in local records as early as 1762. Edward R. Murrow and O. Henry (William Sydney Porter) were born in the vicinity.

Polecat Creek rises in s Union County and flows se into South Carolina, where it enters Wildcat Creek.

Polecat Hollow, w Madison County on an unnamed tributary of French Broad River.

Polecat Ridge, n Macon County between Bradley Creek and Lakey Creek.

Pole Creek rises in sw Buncombe County from 2 branches, each rising on the s slopes of Holland Mountain. One flows se through Milksick Cove; the other flows se through Herren Cove. They join to flow se into Hominy Creek.

Pole Mountain, s Wilkes County near the head of Fishing Creek.

Polenta, community in central Johnston County served by post office, 1882–1900.

Pole Road Creek, in Great Smoky Mountains National Park, rises in n Swain County and flows se into Deep Creek.

Poley Branch rises in n Duplin County and flows s into Back Marsh.

Poley Branch rises in ne Pitt County and flows e into Tranters Creek.

Poley Branch rises in se Richmond County and flows s into Joes Creek.

Poley Swamp rises in n Duplin County and flows n from Whitfields Pond into Deavers Mill Pond. Also known as Polly Run Creek.

Polk, community in n Harnett County served by post office, 1891–1904.

Polk County was formed in 1855 from Rutherford and Henderson Counties. Located in the sw section of the state, it is bounded by the state of South Carolina and by Henderson and Rutherford Counties. It was named for Col. William Polk (1758–1834), Revolutionary War officer who was, before his death, the last surviving field officer of the North Carolina line. Area: 235 sq. mi. County seat: Columbus, with an elevation of 1,145 ft. Townships are Columbus, Cooper Gap, Greens Creek, Saluda, Tryon, and White Oak. Produces corn, wheat, oats, hay, apples, lumber, cotton, livestock, hogs, textiles, and apparel.

Polk Ditch rises in sw Mecklenburg County and flows se into Walker Branch.

Polk Mountain. *See* Gibraltar.

Polkton, town in w Anson County. With the coming of the railroad, the town was laid out on the lands of, and named for, Leonidas L. Polk (1837–92), state agricultural leader. He first proposed that it be called Luneville. Inc. 1875. Alt. 320.

Polkville, community in w Cleveland County.

Polkville Township, former township in w Cleveland County, now township no. 8.

Pollard Swamp rises in sw Beaufort County and flows sw into Creeping Swamp.

Pollock Mill Creek rises in w Duplin County and flows se into Stewarts Creek.

Pollock's Ferry. *See* Bridgers Creek.

Pollocksville, town in s Jones County on Trent River. Known as Trent Bridge as early as 1779, and a post office was est. 1809. Inc. 1834 as Pollocksville, but a municipal government was not formed at that time. Reincorporated 1849. The name Pollock appears at the location on the Collet map, 1770, and others into the nineteenth century, when Trent Bridge is shown across the river and Pollocksville at the site of the town. Produces lumber. Alt. 13.

Pollocksville Township, e Jones County.

Pollock Swamp, a marshy stream, rises in Bear Swamp, e Chowan County, and flows sw into Pembroke Creek. Pollock Swamp watershed, approx. 17 mi. long, is in the area.

Polls Gap, w Haywood County in Great Smoky Mountains National Park on Balsam Mountain near lat. 35°33'48" N., long. 83°09'42" W. Alt. 5,090. Named after Aunt Polly Moody's family cow, Poll, died, and her bones were left bleaching in the sun for many years.

Polly Hollow, e Mitchell County parallel to Laurel Branch.

Polly Middleton Gap, in central Jackson County between Double Top Mountain and Horneyhead Mountain.

Polly Mountain, s Jackson County, bordered on the e by Scotsman Creek and on the s by Chattooga River. Alt. approx. 3,150.

Polly Run Creek. *See* Poley Swamp.

Polycarp, community in s Alexander County. Alt. approx. 1,000. Named for Rev. Polycarp Henkle, Lutheran minister in the vicinity in the nineteenth century.

Pomeiock appears on the White–De Bry map, 1590, as an enclosed Indian village in present Hyde County between Lake Mattamuskeet and Wyesocking Bay.

Pomona, former community in central Guilford County now within Greensboro city limits. Alt. 868. Named for the Italian goddess of the fruit of trees; a nursery was once located there.

Pompey Ridge, nw McDowell County. Average alt. approx. 2,600. Locust Knob is on the ridge.

Pond. *See* Stokesdale.

Pond Branch rises in s Buncombe County near Stradley Mountain and flows ne into Hominy Creek.

Pond Branch rises in e Moore County and flows s into Little River.

Pond Branch rises in w Watauga County and flows n into Beech Creek.

Ponder Branch rises in se Madison County and flows n into French Broad River.

Ponder Creek rises in e Madison County and flows sw into Middle Fork.

Pond Knob, nw Swain County in Great Smoky Mountains National Park on Big Grill Ridge, lat. 35°32' N., long. 83°46'23" W. Alt. 4,148.

Pond Mountain, nw Ashe County. Alt. approx. 5,000. The top of the mountain is a large level plateau covered with bluegrass and containing several small ponds. Said to have been named by Peter Jefferson in 1749.

Pond Mountain, e McDowell County.

Pond Mountain, s Randolph County between Bachelor Creek and Fork Creek.

Pond Mountain Township, nw Ashe County.

Pond Ridge, in most w part of Burke County. Alt. 3,546.

Pontop, community in ne Montgomery County served by post office, 1858–1873. *See also* Flaggtown.

Pony Ridge, s Mitchell County at the head of Brushy Creek.

Ponzer, community in nw Hyde County on Pungo River.

Pool, community in se Rowan County served by post office, 1872–1906.

Pool Creek rises in w Rutherford County and flows ne into Lake Lure. The Bottomless Pools, *which see*, are on the creek.

Pooletown, community in e Rowan County between Cedar and Panther Creeks. A post office named Pool was est. there 1872; closed 1906.

Pool Point extends from e Pasquotank County into Pasquotank River at the mouth of New Begun Creek.

Poolville, community in se Pasquotank County on Pasquotank River.

Poor House Mountain, s Cherokee County, extends ne from Martin Creek.

Poorhouse Run rises in s Greene County and flows ne into Contentnea Creek. Earlier called Caswells Branch. Name derived from the fact that it runs by the former County Home.

Poorlith, community in w Union County.

Poors Ford, community in se Polk County served by post office, 1881–1914. Named for Green River crossing.

Poors Knob, e Watauga County between Chestnut Branch and Elk Creek. Alt. approx. 2,350.

Poors Knots, community in s Wilkes County served by post office, 1888–1916.

Poor Town, community in s Hertford County.

Pop Castle, w Vance County approx. 1 mi. w of the town of Kittrell. Popecastle Inn was est. there approx. 1734, and local usage changed the name to Pop Castle. Racetrack, cockpit, and tavern were adjuncts of the inn; use of the racetrack began during the Revolution, and the main building of the inn was dismantled after the Civil War.

Pope, community in central Robeson County.

Pope Air Force Base, nw Cumberland County, was est. during World War I and named in honor of Lt. Harley Halbert Pope, who died in a postwar aircraft accident on the Cape Fear River near Fayetteville, January 7, 1919.

Pope Branch rises in w Halifax County and flows s into Fishing Creek.

Popecastle Inn. *See* Pop Castle.

Popes Pond, slightly less than ½ mi. long, on Black River, se Harnett County.

Poplar, community in w Mitchell County on Nolichucky River. Alt. 1,993. A post office there, 1872–96, was called Hollow Poplar.

Poplar Branch rises in s Cleveland County and flows se into Beaverdam Creek.

Poplar Branch rises in central Guilford County and flows ne into Reedy Fork Creek. Appears on the Collet map, 1770.

Poplar Branch rises in s Haywood County and flows se into West Fork Pigeon River.

Poplar Branch rises in n Johnston County and flows se into Neuse River. Mentioned in local records as early as 1780.

Poplar Branch rises in s Jones County and flows nw into Trent River.

Poplar Branch rises in s Lee County and flows s into Little River.

Poplar Branch rises in n Rockingham County and flows sw into Matrimony Creek.

Poplar Branch rises in e central Wilson County and flows s into Whiteoak Swamp.

Poplar Branch rises in sw Wilson County and flows ne into Black Creek.

Poplar Branch, community on the w shore of Currituck Sound in s Currituck County. Known first as Currituck Narrows. Post office 1829. *See also* Narrows.

Poplar Branch Bay, s central Currituck County, is formed in Currituck Sound by the mainland, Rattle Snake Island, and Long Point.

Poplar Branch Township, s Currituck County.

Poplar Cove, w Graham County between Horse Cove Ridge and Little Santeetlah Creek.

Poplar Cove, e Haywood County between Turkey Cove and Bill Cove.

Poplar Cove, nw Haywood County between Rough Mountain and Big Branch.

Poplar Cove, n Macon County, extends n to the junction of Right Fork [Wesser Creek] and Wesser Creek in s Swain County.

Poplar Cove, central Macon County at the head of Mill Creek.

Poplar Cove, on a tributary of Hickory Knoll Creek in s Macon County.

Poplar Cove, s Swain County extends sw from Little Tennessee River.

Poplar Cove Branch rises in sw Macon County and flows ne into Poplar Cove Creek.

Poplar Cove Creek rises in w Macon County se of Panther Knob and flows ne into Cartoogechaye Creek.

Poplar Cove Creek. *See* Paxton Creek.

Poplar Cove Gap, central Macon County between the head of Mill Creek and Trimont Ridge.

Poplar Cove Knob, w Jackson County between Big Cove and Savannah Creek.

Poplar Cove Knob, s Macon County between Commissioner Creek and the Georgia state line.

Poplar Creek rises in n Onslow County and flows s into Little Northeast Creek. Mentioned in local records as early as 1744 as Poplar Swamp.

Poplar Creek rises in n Transylvania County s of Fryingpan Gap and flows se into South Fork Mills River.

Poplar Creek rises in w Vance County and flows sw into e Granville County, where it enters Tabbs Creek.

Poplar Creek rises in e Wake County and flows s into Neuse River.

Poplar Gap, e Haywood County between Sheep Mountain and Glade Mountain.

Poplar Grove, community in n Polk County. A post office operated there, 1875–1908.

Poplar Grove, community in ne Sampson County.

Poplar Hill, community in sw Anson County served by post office, 1825–1905.

Poplar Hollow Branch rises in ne Swain County and flows s into Raven Fork.

Poplar Lick Gap, n Transylvania County on the head of Sitton Creek.

Poplar Point, a bluff on the Roanoke River, n Martin County. Appears on the Collet map, 1770. A steamboat landing was there at one time; Poplar Point Church and a rural community are nearby. Roanoke, a post office, operated at or near the point, 1851–80.

Poplar Point Township, n central Martin County.

Poplar Springs, community in s Stokes County.

Poplar Spring Top, on the Cherokee-Graham county line in the Snowbird Mountains.

Poplar Swamp. *See* Poplar Creek.

Poplar Tent Township, former township in w Cabarrus County, now township no. 2.

Poplar Township, nw Mitchell County.

Poppaw Creek rises in sw Alamance County and flows n into Stinking Quarter Creek.

Populi, community in nw Bladen County served by post office, 1892–1929.

Poquoson Point, s Camden County in the mouth of Pasquotank River. Also sometimes called Camden Point. Name derived from an Algonquian word *pequessen*, meaning a swamp or a dismal.

Porcelain. *See* Linville.

Pores Knob, s Wilkes County, the highest peak in the Brushy Mountains. Alt. 2,680. Named for Moses Poore, an eighteenth-century resident. Appears on the Collet map, 1770, as Mt. Night. *See also* Brushy Mountains.

Pores Knob, community in s Wilkes County near the peak of the same name. Name changed at one time to Fruitland and to East Fruitland, but the original name was soon restored.

Pork Creek. *See* Fork Creek.

Porpoise Point, ne Pamlico County on the e side of Goose Creek Island between Big Porpoise Bay and Little Porpoise Bay.

P[ort] Box appears on the Smith map, 1624, in Pamlico Sound, but the feature for which this name is intended is uncertain.

Porter, community in se Stanly County. Named for an official of the railroad.

Porter Cove, central Buncombe County near Azalea.

Porter Cove, on a tributary of Cullasaja River in s Macon County.

Porter Creek rises in se Beaufort County and flows n into Durham Creek.

Porterfield Gap, on the Cherokee-Graham county line. Alt. 3,462.

Porters Gap, in Great Smoky Mountains National Park on Swain County, N.C.–Sevier County, Tenn., line, lat. 35°38′55″ N., long. 83°21′28″ W. Alt. approx. 5,500.

Portersville. *See* Emerson.

Porter Swamp rises in w Columbus County and flows nw and sw into Lumber River.

Port Fernando. *See* Hatorask Inlet.

Port Grenvil appears on the White map, 1590, as an inlet through Ocracoke Island a short distance n of the community of Ocracoke, se Hyde County. Named for Sir Richard Grenville. Appears as "Greenevills Rode" on the Smith map, 1624. There is some doubt that such an inlet actually existed, though it may have been at what is now known as Nigh Inlet, *which see*.

Portia was inc. as a town in McDowell County, 1891; charter repealed 1893. It apparently was never laid out, and the proposed site is unknown.

Portis Gold Mine, now abandoned, ne Franklin County. Shown on a map as recently as 1931.

Port Landing. *See* Fort Landing.

Port Lane, an inlet from the Atlantic Ocean into Roanoke Sound through Bodie Island opposite the se shore of Roanoke Island, e Dare County. Opened prior to 1585 and closed prior to 1657.

Portohonk Creek rises in sw Camden County and flows s into Pasquotank County. *See also* Jones Mill.

Portsmouth, formerly a thriving town in ne Carteret County at the tip of Core Banks. Settled in the early 1700s; est. 1753 and probably named for the city in England. Long inactive in municipal affairs. Alt. 8. *See also* Portsmouth Island.

Portsmouth Island, ne Carteret County, is the name applied to the ne end of Core Banks. Appears as Wococon, *which see*, on the White map, 1585. May have been a part of Croatoan Island. *See also* Portsmouth; Core Banks; Cape Lookout National Seashore Recreational Area.

Portsmouth Township, e Carteret County, is made up of Core Banks extending from Cape Lookout to Ocracoke Inlet. *See also* Portsmouth Island.

P[ort] Vaughn appears on the Smith map, 1624, in Pamlico Sound, but the feature for which this name is intended is uncertain.

Possum Branch rises in s Macon County and flows n into Tessentee Creek. Approx. 1 mi. long.

Possum Branch rises in s Macon County and

flows nw into Hickory Knoll Creek. Approx. ½ mi. long.

Possum Creek. *See* Possumquarter Creek.

Possum Hollow, s Haywood County on the e side of Bearpen Gap. An unnamed stream rises there and flows e into Haywood Gap Stream.

Possum Hollow, nw Swain County, extends se from Pinnacle Ridge to Hazel Creek.

Possum Hollow, community on the n side of Yadkin River, n central Caldwell County.

Possum Neck Swamp rises in s Craven County and flows nw into Brice Creek.

Possumquarter Creek rises in w central Warren County and flows s into Fishing Creek. Probably named for Possum Quarter, the plantation of Governor Gabriel Johnston, mentioned in his 1751 will. Appears on the Price map, 1808, as Possum Creek.

Possumtown. *See* Bethany.

Possumtrot, community in w Yancey County on Possumtrot Creek. Named by an early settler who was riding down a trail on horseback when a lone opossum entered the path ahead of him and trotted along in front of the horse for some distance.

Possumtrot Creek rises in w Yancey County and flows ne into Bald Creek.

Postell, community in w Cherokee County on Shoal Creek. Alt. 1,900. Named for Thomas Postell, an early settler.

Post Oak. *See* Blaine.

Potaskike River. *See* North River.

Potato Branch rises in sw Buncombe County near Potato Gap and flows nw into South Turkey Creek.

Potato Creek rises in nw Alleghany County and flows n into Virginia, where it enters New River.

Potato Creek rises in sw Cherokee County and flows w into Polk County, Tenn., where it turns sw and flows into Ocoee River.

Potato Field Gap, ne Buncombe County s of Snowball Mountain. The Blue Ridge Parkway passes through the gap.

Potato Gap, sw Buncombe County near the headwaters of Potato Branch.

Potato Gap, n Madison County at the sw end of Sugarloaf Mountain.

Potato Hill, s Henderson County on Mud Creek.

Potato Hill, on Jackson Line Mountain in s central Swain County between the head of Laurel Branch and the head of Davis Branch. Alt. 3,306.

Potato Hill, s Yancey County between Cattail Peak and the head of Colbert Creek.

Potato Hill. *See* Tater Hill.

Potato Hill Bald, ne Swain County in Great Smoky Mountains National Park on Chiltoskie Ridge near the se end of Ravens Roost Ridge, lat. 35°35′42″ N., long. 83°12′33″ W. Alt. 5,209.

Potato Hill Lake, artificial lake in central Watauga County on Howard Creek between Rich Mountain and Harmon Knob. Formed in 1947; max. depth 25 ft.; covers 9 acres. Open to public. Also known as Tater Hill Lake.

Potato Hill Mountain, w Randolph County on Little Caraway Creek.

Potato Knob, at the head of Brooks Branch in sw Buncombe County ne of Potato Gap.

Potato Knob, on the Buncombe-Yancey county line between Rainbow Gap and Swannanoa Gap. Alt. approx. 6,400, the highest point in Buncombe County. Known earlier as Potato Top.

Potato Knob, e Haywood County between Dutch Cove Creek and Doubletop Mountain.

Potato Lump Mountain, sw Madison County between Johns Branch and Spring Creek.

Potato Mountain, nw Buncombe County between Willow and Sandy Mush Creeks.

Potato Patch, mountain in w Haywood County on the head of a tributary of Hemphill Creek.

Potato Top. *See* Potato Knob.

Pot Branch rises in s McDowell County and flows se into Rutherford County, where it enters Briar Creek. Erosion in rocks over which it flows has made potlike holes.

Pot Cove Gap, on the Buncombe-McDowell county line near the headwaters of Flat Creek.

Potecasi (potty-casey), community in e Northampton County. Named for its location near Potecasi Creek, an Indian word meaning "parting of the waters." A post office operated there, 1839–1928.

Potecasi Bridge. *See* Jackson.

Potecasi Creek rises in central Northampton County and flows e into Hertford County, where it enters Meherrin River. Appears as Weyanok Creek on the Ogilby map, 1671. The upper portion of Potecasi Creek is marked Catawhisky on the Moseley map, 1733. Appears as Meherrin Creek on the Collet map, 1770.

Potoskite, appears on the Moseley map, 1733, in s Currituck Precinct (now Currituck County), possibly representing an Indian village.

Potrock Bald, a peak in n Clay County near the headwaters of Potrock Branch and Compass Creek. Alt. 5,200–5,250. Named for a large rock on top of the mountain that was hollowed out by an Indian medicine man and used to steep his medicinal herbs.

Potrock Branch rises in n Clay County and flows sw into Fires Creek.

Pott Creek rises in s Catawba County and flows s into Lincoln County, where it enters South Fork Catawba River.

Potter, community in sw Union County served by post office, 1891–1900.

Potters. *See* Mineral Springs.

Potters Hill, community in e Duplin County.

Potter's Hill, community in s central Lenoir County. So called for the Potter family, early settlers.

Pottertown. *See* Tamarack.

Potts Branch rises in n Macon County and flows sw into Little Tennessee River.

Potts Creek rises in se Cleveland County and flows nw into Buffalo Creek.

Potts Creek rises in central Macon County and flows ne into Cartoogechaye Creek.

Potts Creek. *See* First Potts Creek; Second Potts Creek.

Pounding Creek rises in central Clay County and flows s into Shooting Creek.

Pounding Mill Branch rises in n Cherokee County in the Snowbird Mountains and flows se into Hyatt Creek.

Pounding Mill Branch rises in n Haywood County and flows se into Cold Springs Creek.

Pounding Mill Branch rises in n Madison County and flows sw into Little Laurel Creek.

Pounding Mill Branch rises in n Transylvania County near Green Knob and flows se into Looking Glass Creek.

Pounding Mill Branch rises in n Transylvania County near Poundingstone Mountain and flows se into South Fork Mills River.

Pounding Mill Branch rises in s Watauga County and flows ne into Elk Creek.

Pounding Mill Cove, n Yancey County on Pounding Mill Creek.

Poundingmill Creek rises in ne Cleveland County and flows s into Knob Creek.

Pounding Mill Creek rises in n Yancey County and flows nw into Cane River.

Poundingstone Mountain, n Transylvania County between Pounding Mill Branch and Jumping Branch. Alt. approx. 3,450.

Pound Mill Gap, w Macon County between Burningtown Creek and Deweese Creek.

Pousville, community in n Franklin County.

Poverty Branch rises in n Buncombe County and flows sw into North Fork Ivy Creek.

Powder Burnt Creek rises in ne Cherokee County and flows nw into Valley River.

Powdermill Creek rises in w Avery County and flows se into North Toe River. Said to have been named because Lodawick and Dora Oakes, who lived along its banks, burned willow switches to make enough gunpowder to buy a slave.

Powder Springs. *See* Eupeptic Springs.

Powell Creek rises in s Buncombe County and flows w into French Broad River. Skyland Lake, *which see*, is on the stream.

Powell Creek rises in Virginia and flows sw into Northampton County, where it enters Meherrin River.

Powell Creek rises in e Wake County and flows sw into Hodges Mill Creek.

Powell Crossroads, community in s Gates County.

Powell Knob, in Great Smoky Mountains National Park on Swain County, N.C.–Blount County, Tenn., line between Buck Gap and Ekaneetlee Gap, lat. 35°32′24″ N., long. 83°49′19″ W.

Powells Creek rises in w Halifax County and flows se into Little Fishing Creek.

Powells Creek. *See* Whitaker Creek.

Powells Pocosin, nw Bertie County.

Powells Point, tip of the peninsula of s Currituck County in Albemarle Sound. Appears in local records as early as 1665 and on the Ogilby map, 1671. The community (and post office, est. 1818) of Powells Point is 6½ mi. n.

Powellsville, town in n central Bertie County. Post office est. 1879; inc. 1887. Named for a local family and originally known as Powell's Crossroads. Alt. 67.

Powellton, community in nw Richmond County. A post office operated there, 1829–1918. Named for Pleasant M. Powell.

Powelltown, community on the outskirts of Lenoir, central Caldwell County. Named for a British soldier, Elias Powell (d. 1831), who remained in the area following the Battle of Kings Mountain, 1780. Known earlier as Powellton.

Powelltown, community in s Transylvania County near the mouth of East Fork French Broad River.

Powel's Creek. *See* Greens Creek.

Powers Branch rises in e Mitchell County and flows se into Fall Creek.

Powhatan, community in n Johnston County. Alt. 294.

Poyner Hill, formerly a sand hill on s Currituck Banks, e Currituck County. Erosion has almost obliterated the hill. During World War II, a temporary Coast Guard base was located there.

Prather Gap, w Yancey County between Possumtrot and Price Creeks.

Prathers Creek rises in sw Alleghany County and flows nw into South Fork New River.

Prathers Creek Township, w central Alleghany County.

Pratt, community in w Johnston County served by post office, 1884-1901.

Prattsburg, former community in central Durham County approx. 2 mi. e of the original railroad station for Durham. In the 1850s, William Pratt refused to give a right-of-way or land for a station at Prattsburg. The railroad avoided his property, and as a result, Durham was est.

Prentiss, community in s Macon County.

Prescott, community in s central Beaufort County.

Presley Branch rises in n Transylvania County and flows sw into Avery Creek.

Presley Creek rises in w Jackson County and flows ne into Tilley Creek.

Press Cove, n Jackson County on the head of East Fork [Dicks Creek].

Pressley Gap, at the head of Rose Creek in n Macon County.

Pressly Mountain, e Haywood County on the head of Conner Mill Branch and Stamey Cove Branch.

Press Prong rises in w Nash County and flows se into Murrays Mill Pond on Turkey Creek.

Prestonville, community in ne Stokes County.

Pretty Hollow Creek, w Haywood County in Great Smoky Mountains National Park, rises near lat. 35°40′55″ N., long. 83°08′17″ W., on Mount Sterling Ridge and flows s into Palmer Creek.

Pretty Hollow Gap, w Haywood County in Great Smoky Mountains National Park on Mount Sterling Ridge near lat. 35°41′10″ N., long. 83°08′26″ W. Alt. 5,176 at the head of Pretty Hollow Creek.

Pretty Pine Branch rises in nw Cherokee County and flows se into Shuler Creek.

Pretty Pond, a natural lake in se Brunswick County. Max. depth 8 ft. Surface area, 150 acres.

Price, community in nw Rockingham County. Est. 1868. Named for John Price, on whose plantation a store and post office were built. The post office, 1870-1956, for a time was known as Price's Store.

Price Creek rises in se Brunswick County and flows e into the Cape Fear River.

Price Creek rises in s Orange County and flows ne into Neville Creek.

Price Creek rises in sw Yancey County and flows n into Cane River.

Price Creek Township, w Yancey County.

Prices Creek, community in w Yancey County served by post office, 1888-1927.

Price's Mill, community in w Union County.

Price Township, nw Rockingham County.

Prickly Ash Ridge, w Jackson County between Tarcamp Branch and Hunter Jim Creek.

Prickly Pear Mountain, w Randolph County just w of Caraway Mountain in a close group with Black Jack, Slick Rock, and Vineyard Mountains.

Prides Ferry. *See* Mush Island.

Priest Hill, community in central Moore County.

Prince George County was proposed as a name for new county by Colonial Assembly in 1762. Name, intended to honor future King George III, was rejected in favor of Bute County, *which see.*

Prince George Creek rises in n New Hanover County and flows nw into Northeast Cape Fear River. Appears in local records as early as 1744, hence probably named for Prince George (1738-1820), who became George III in 1760.

Prince's Bridge, former community in ne Chatham County on New Hope Creek.

A post office operated there, 1828–32. *See also* Cyprett's Bridge.

Princess Anne, town in se Robeson County. Inc. 1796 "on lands of Mary Griffin and William Ashley on Drowning Creek," now Lumber River. Long inactive in municipal affairs. Site approx. 2½ mi. se of the community of Barnesville.

Princeton, town in e Johnston County. Inc. 1861 as Boon Hill for the Boon family plantation in the vicinity. Named changed to Princeton in 1873. Alt. 152.

Princeton, town est. 1787 on Meherrin River in ne Northampton County. Previously known as Pitch Landing. Streets were laid off and some homes built, but it soon declined as nearby Murfreesboro (inc. at the same time) grew. A plantation on the site continues to be called Princeton. Washington Ferry crossed the river there and is shown on the Collet map, 1770.

Princeville, town in central Edgecombe County just s of the Tar River from Tarboro. Settled 1865 by former slaves and called Freedom Hill. Inc. 1885 and named for Turner Prince, a resident. Alt. 58. Scene of massive flooding, 1999, owing to Hurricane Floyd.

Print, community in n Halifax County.

Priscilla. *See* Ranlo-Rex-Priscilla.

Prissy Bay, sand-filled bay in se Sampson County at the head of Wildcat Swamp. *See also* Carolina Bays.

Pritchard Tavern. *See* Buena Vista.

Pritchett, community in se Rockingham County served by post office, 1886–1903. Named for postmaster Thomas Pritchett.

Privett, community in s Franklin County.

Procks Point extends into Jarrett Bay se of community of Davis, se Carteret County.

Proctor, former town in w Swain County on Hazel Creek. Alt. 1,735. Inc. 1911; the site is now in the Great Smoky Mountains National Park. Named for William Proctor, who was instrumental in having a post office est. there in 1886. Service discontinued, 1944.

Proctor Branch rises in nw Swain County on Twentymile Ridge and flows sw into Twentymile Creek.

Proctor Creek, in Great Smoky Mountains National Park, rises in w Swain County and flows s into Hazel Creek.

Proctor Ridge, in Great Smoky Mountains National Park, n Swain County between Proctor Creek and Long Cove, lat. 35°33′18″ N., long. 83°35′46″ W.

Proctor Sang Branch rises in nw Swain County and flows e into Ekaneetlee Creek. *See also* Seng Branch.

Proctorville, town in s Robeson County. Alt. 120. Settled about 1870. Inc. 1913. Named for Edward Knox Proctor Jr. (1862–1902), promoter of the Raleigh and Charleston Railroad.

Proffits Knob, n Watauga County sw of Laurel Branch.

Proffitt, community in sw Wilkes County served by post office, 1898–1906.

Progress, community in nw Randolph County. Formerly known as Fraziers for a local storekeeper.

Promontorium tremendum. *See* Cape Fear.

Prong, community in n Columbus County served by post office, 1889–1903.

Prophet Branch rises in nw Haywood County and flows se into Big Branch. Named for a prominent mountain family in the area.

Propst, community in sw Catawba County served by post office, 1899–1905.

Propst's Knob, sw Burke County. Alt. 3,022.

Prospect, community in w central Caswell County.

Prospect, community in nw Robeson County.

Prospect Hill, community in se Caswell County. Named for the former Warren family plantation and its elevated view. A post office was est. there, 1823.

Prospect Knob, nw Iredell County.

Prospect Ridge, a narrow loam and sandy ridge traversing Green Swamp in Brunswick and Columbus Counties from se to nw. A road between the communities of Supply and Makatoka follows this ridge.

Prospect Ridge, se Burke County between Laurel Creek and Henry Fork.

Prosperity. *See* High Falls.

Protection, community in ne Madison County.

Providence, community in nw Caswell County, sometimes known locally as "Hell's Half Acre." Post office est. there, 1953.

Providence, community in sw Chatham County served by post office, 1877–1900.

Providence, community in central Granville County. A former post office there, 1890–1922, was known as Hargrove. Alt. 431.

Providence, community in s McDowell County on the head of Nicks Creek.

Providence, community in s Mecklenburg County, grew up around Providence Presbyterian Church, organized in 1767.

Providence Inlet. *See* Caffey's Inlet.

Providence Township, former township in s Mecklenburg County, now township no. 5.

Providence Township, ne Pasquotank County.

Providence Township, ne Randolph County.

Providence Township, se Rowan County. Named, according to tradition, because an act of God (Providence) enabled Gen. Nathanael Greene to cross Yadkin River in 1781 to escape Cornwallis. *See* Trading Ford.

Proximity, formerly a cotton-mill community in central Guilford County, now a part of Greensboro. Camp for Overseas Replacement Depot located there during World War II.

Pruitts Fork Creek rises in e Rockingham County and flows e into Lower Hogan's Creek. Later known as Jones Creek, *which see*.

Public Creek rises in the highlands of Indian Island, se Camden County, and flows e into North River.

Puella, former community in central Transylvania County near confluence of Davidson and French Broad Rivers. Earlier known as Deavers and today known as Pisgah Forest.

Puett Cove, ne Cherokee County in the Valley River Mountains.

Puett Creek rises in central Cherokee County and flows n into Vengeance Creek. *See also* Will Puett Cove.

Pughs, community in n Franklin County.

Pughs Island. *See* Tucker Island.

Pug Knob, on Haywood-Madison county line. Alt. 4,245.

Pulham Creek rises w Polk County and flows sw into Green River.

Pulhams Ferry. *See* Bridgers Creek.

Pump, community in ne Madison County.

Pump Branch rises in n Madison County and flows se into French Broad River.

Pump Branch rises in n Mitchell County and flows w into Big Rock Creek.

Pumpkin Center, community in n Lincoln County.

Pumpkin Creek rises in sw Wilkes County and flows e into Warrior Creek. Maps of W. Kerr Scott Reservoir show the feature as Punkin Creek.

Pumpkin Patch Gap, n Mitchell County between Pumpkin Patch Mountain and Meadlock Mountain.

Pumpkin Patch Mountain, central Mitchell County between Cub Creek and Little Rock Creek. Alt. 4,263.

Pumpkintown, community in w Jackson County on Savannah Creek.

Pump Mountain, n Jackson County between Cope Creek and Scott Creek. Named for the fact that the first running water in the area was run through log pipes from the mountains to the home of Thaddeus Clingman Bryson, where the first court in Jackson County was held.

Punch Bowl, community in a small valley in s Macon County between Bates Mountain and the head of Bates Branch.

Punch Bowl Creek rises in s Alexander County and flows se into Catawba River.

Puncheon Branch rises in ne Cherokee County and flows nw into Valley River. Fortified Indian villages were protected by "wooden puncheons," high stakes driven into the ground, and this may be the source of the name.

Puncheon Camp Branch rises in w Madison County and flows nw into Spring Creek.

Puncheon Camp Creek rises in e Henderson County and flows ne into Clear Creek.

Puncheon Creek rises in se Transylvania County near Standingstone Mountain and flows nw into Reasonover Creek.

Puncheon Fork Creek rises in e Madison County and flows sw into Big Laurel Creek.

Pungo, community in ne Beaufort County on Indian Run near its junction with Pungo River. Alt. approx. 5.

Pungo Creek rises in Great Swamp, n central Beaufort County, and flows se into Pungo River. Appears as Machapunga Creek on the Moseley map, 1733.

Pungo Lake, natural lake in s Washington and nw Hyde Counties in East Dismal Swamp. Inaccessible except through private property; not open to the public. Owned by Roper Lumber Company. Covers 2,700 acres, with a max. depth of 5 ft. Name is shortened from name for the Machapunga Indians.

Pungo River rises in East Dismal Swamp, Washington County, and flows generally se, forming the Beaufort-Hyde county line into Pamlico River near its mouth. Appears as Machapounga River on the Comberford map,

1657, and as Machaponga on the Moseley map, 1733, and other maps until 1807, when it appears, apparently for the first time, as Pungo River on the William Tatham map. Named for the Machapunga Indians, whose name is said to have meant "bad dust" or "much dust."

Punkin Creek. *See* Pumpkin Creek.

Puppy Creek rises in e Hoke County and flows s into Rockfish Creek.

Pups Branch rises in nw McDowell County and flows se into Armstrong Creek.

Pups Branch Ridge. *See* Pups Ridge.

Pups Ridge, approx. 2 mi. long, nw McDowell County in Pisgah National Forest. Formerly known as Big Ridge and as Pups Branch Ridge.

Purcepolis, community in n Scotland County served by post office, 1883–1905.

Purchace Islands, the name given on the Smith map, 1624, to the nine islands in Roanoke and Cashie Rivers at the conjunction of Bertie, Martin, and Washington Counties. Apparently one of the islands is unnamed, but the other eight are known as Louse Island, Rice Island, Goodmans Island, Wood Island, Great Island, Huff Island, Conine Island, and Tabor Island. Smith is thought to have named the islands in honor of Samuel Purchas (1575?–1626), an English compiler of travel books.

Purchase Knob, in central Haywood County between Sugar Cove and the head of Cove Creek. It overlooks a large section of the old North Carolina Land and Lumber Company tract, and prospective buyers were taken there to get a good view of the property. Alt. 5,086.

Purgatory. *See* Flox.

Purgatory Mountain, central Randolph County, site of North Carolina Zoological Park.

Purgatory Pocosin, a sandy loam-filled pocosin in sw Jones and nw Onslow Counties at the head of Mill Swamp.

Purlear, community in w central Wilkes County on Cole Creek. Named for Isaac Parlier, who settled on nearby Purlear Creek.

Purlear Creek rises in w Wilkes County on the w side of Rendezvous Mountain and flows s into North Prong Lewis Fork Creek. Once known as Isaac Parlier's Creek.

Purley, community in n central Caswell County. Probably named for Purley Cobb, local resident. A post office operated there, 1855–1920.

Alt. 524. Bright-leaf tobacco was discovered in 1839 on the Slade farm there.

Purnell, community in n Wake County on the head of Mud Creek; formerly known as Purnell Crossroads.

Purnell Crossroads. *See* Purnell.

Purviance Creek rises in e New Hanover County and flows e into Masonboro Sound.

Purvis, community in w Robeson County.

Push, community in s Person County near Aldridge Creek.

Putnam, community in n Moore County. Called Johnson City for Harvell Johnson, local resident, until renamed for Israel Putnam (1718–90), Revolutionary War general, leader, and ancestor of local residents. Alt. 442.

Puzzle Creek rises in e Rutherford County and flows sw into Second Broad River. Quicksand in the creek made it a "puzzle" to early settlers who wondered whether their horses could cross it.

Pyatt Creek rises in sw Avery County and flows e into North Toe River.

Pyatte, community in central Avery County.

Quail Roost, community in n Durham County. Named for a former hunting club there acquired in 1925 by George Watts Hill of Durham, who turned it into a dairy farm. In 1963 the farm was given to the state of North Carolina by Hill. The large house is used as a conference center by the University of North Carolina; North Carolina State University makes use of the surrounding land, designated as Hill Forest.

Quaker, community in s Stokes County served by post office, 1876–1903. Also known as Quaker Gap.

Quaker Creek rises in ne Alamance County and flows s into Quaker Scrub Creek.

Quaker Gap. *See* Quaker.

Quaker Gap Township, w central Stokes County.

Quaker Meadows, a grassy region in w central Burke County 1 mi. nw of Morganton, lying between Canoe and Upper Creeks. Settled as early as 1752; appears on the Collet map,

1770. A frontier rendezvous, it was the home of Joseph and Charles McDowell, officers at the Battle of Kings Mountain (1780) and later public leaders. Zebulon B. Vance and his first wife, Harriet Espy, were married there.

Quaker Meadows Township, central Burke County.

Quaker Neck, w central Wayne County, is formed by a crook in Neuse River. Location of a Quaker settlement prior to 1758. *See also* Goldsboro Cooling Pond.

Quaker Scrub Creek rises in ne Alamance County and flows s into Back Creek.

Qualla, community in nw Jackson County on Shoal Creek. The name is from the Cherokee word *kwalli* (old woman), because an old Cherokee woman, Polly, lived there. Also called Quallatown. Alt. 2,250.

Qualla Boundary, home of the Eastern Band of Cherokee Indians in Swain, Jackson, and Haywood Counties in Great Smoky Mountains. Est. by the United States after the Cherokee removal of 1838. Covers 63,000 acres and is the largest Indian reservation e of the Mississippi. The reservation is divided into Big Cove Town, Wolf Town, Yellow Hill Town, Paint Town, and Bird Town townships. In addition, a number of Cherokees living off the reservation in Cheoah Township, Graham County, are under tribal jurisdiction. Land is held in common and assigned on a tenant system.

Quallatown. *See* Qualla.

Qualla Township, n Jackson County.

Qualls Creek rises in s Clay County and flows ne into Hiwassee River approx. ¾ mi. n of town of Hayesville. Named for an Indian woman.

Quankey Creek rises in n Halifax County and flows se into Roanoke River. Appears as Quountka Creek on the Moseley map, 1733; does not appear on the Collet map, 1770, or the Price map, 1808. Appears next on the MacRae map, 1833, with its present name. A Tuscarora Indian name. Indian relics have been found along its lower course.

Quaqua Creek rises in n Rockingham County and flows e into Wolf Island Creek.

Quarry, community in s Wilkes County.

Quarry Branch rises in n Alamance County and flows se into Tom's Creek.

Quarter Swamp rises in central Northampton County and flows se into Urahaw Swamp.

Quebec, community in s Transylvania County between Blue Ridge and West Fork French Board River. Alt. 2,530.

Queen. *See* Love Joy.

Queen Anne's Creek rises in s Chowan County and flows sw into the e side of Edenton Bay. Known as Mattacomack Creek prior to about 1712. The present name appears in local records as early as 1712. *See also* Pembroke Creek.

Queen Anne's Town. *See* Edenton.

Queen Branch rises in n Macon County and flows sw into Little Tennessee River.

Queen Creek rises in s Haywood County and flows e into West Fork Pigeon River.

Queen Creek rises in nw Henderson County and flows se into South Fork.

Queen Creek Mountain, nw Henderson County, extends se from Yellow Gap to Buttermilk Mountain. Alt. 3,650.

Queen Inlet. *See* Mason Inlet.

Queen Mountain, se Macon County between Sassafras Gap and Big Creek.

Queen Ridge extends ne between Snowbird and Squally Creeks in w Graham County.

Queens Creek rises in nw Macon County and flows w and n into Swain County, where it enters Nantahala River. Queens Falls on the stream was obliterated when Nantahala Power and Light Company diverted the water for a hydroelectric project.

Queens Creek rises in e Onslow County and flows se into White Oak River. Named for Queen Anne (1665–1714). Name occurs in local records as early as 1713. Appears on the Moseley map, 1733. Otway Burns (1775–1848), privateer in the War of 1812, was born on the w side of Queens Creek.

Queens Creek Lake, formed in 1948 on Queens Creek in nw Macon County. Covers 37 acres, with a max. depth of 68 ft. Owned by Nantahala Power and Light Company to generate electricity.

Queensdale, community in n Robeson County served by post office, 1820–1904. Formerly known as McQueen's Store.

Queens Falls. *See* Queens Creek.

Query's, community in e Mecklenburg County served by post office, 1859–1903. Named for James Query, first postmaster.

Quewhiffle Creek rises in w Hoke County and flows s into Lumber River. The name may be derived through faulty pronunciation from the Gaelic *Culmhutar* (pronounced "kul-vu-tar"), meaning "smuggler" or "mutineer." *See also* Cuwhiffle.

Quewhiffle Township, w Hoke County.

Quhele. *See* Maxton.

Quick, community in w Caswell County originally known as Kill Quick. Post office est. there in 1898 closed 1909.

Quiet, community in n Moore County served by post office, 1883–1905. Ten mi. w was Noise, *which see.*

Quillaree Branch rises in ne Swain County and flows se into Straight Fork.

Quillen Mountain, on the Transylvania County, N.C.–Greenville County, S.C., line near the head of Pole Ridge Branch.

Quincy, community in n Onslow County served by post office, 1893–1903.

Quinerly, community in s Pitt County.

Quinine, community in s Randolph County served by post office, 1890–1921.

Quinine Swamp rises in nw Bertie County and flows se into Roanoke River.

Quinn Creek rises in w Cherokee County and flows nw into Shoal Creek.

Quinn's Ferry. *See* Irvinsville.

Quioccosin Swamp rises in n central Bertie County and flows nw into Stony Creek.

Quitsna, community in sw Bertie County. Name formerly spelled Quitonoi, a Tuscarora Indian word meaning "strong and mighty."

Quonutka Creek. *See* Quankey Creek.

Quoracks River. *See* Trent River.

Quotankney Creek. *See* Contentnea Creek.

R

Rabbit Creek rises in e Macon County and flows sw into Lake Emory.

Rabbit Mountain, e Macon County between Cat Creek and Rabbit Creek.

Rabbit Mountain, w Montgomery County between Lick Mountain and Cedar Creek.

Rabbit Ridge, w Haywood County on Caldwell Fork.

Rabbits Crossroads, community in sw Chatham County approx. 3¼ mi. w of Bonlee.

Rabbit Shuffle, community in central Caswell County. Named because the land was said to be so poor that "a rabbit had to shuffle to get his rations."

Rabbitskin Branch rises in central Haywood County and flows n into Pigeon River.

Raby Bend, in Little Tennessee River in n Macon County.

Raccoon Bay, in Currituck Sound off the w shore of Currituck Banks, e Currituck County.

Raccoon Branch rises in w Madison County and flows ne into French Broad River.

Raccoon Branch rises in s Watauga County and flows n into East Fork [South Fork New River].

Raccoon Creek rises in s Haywood County and flows n into Richland Creek.

Raccoon Creek rises in w Lee County and flows nw into Pocket Creek.

Raccoon Creek rises in w Mitchell County and flows sw into Toe River.

Raccoon Creek rises in n Pamlico County and flows se into Bay River.

Raccoon Creek rises in sw Perquimans County in Bear Swamp and flows ne into Perquimans River. Until early in the twentieth century, it was known as Skinners Creek. In colonial days it was known as Castletons Creek (for George Castleton, a landowner there prior to 1688). Two small streams, now without names, that form the headwaters of Raccoon Creek were known in the seventeenth and eighteenth centuries as Lakers Creek (for Benjamin Laker, who owned land there in 1686) and Perrishoes Creek (for James Perishoe, who lived on the creek prior to 1688). Lakers Creek appears on the Moseley map, 1733.

Raccoon Creek rises in n Stokes County and flows sw into Snow Creek.

Raccoon Key, an island in Pamlico Sound in n end of Carteret County.

Raccoon Mountain, w Polk County. Alt. approx. 2,000.

Raccoon Ridge, w Avery County.

Raccoon Swamp rises in se Bladen County and flows w into Colly Creek.

Raccoon Swamp rises in se Johnston County and flows s into Neuse River.

Race Prong rises in ne Nash County and flows se into Beaverdam Swamp.

Rachel, community in sw Randolph County served by post office, 1890–1926.

Rackley Mill Pond. *See* McLamb Mill Pond.

Radder Creek rises in ne Cherokee County and flows ne into Worm Creek.

Radford Crossroads, community in e Johnston County.

Radical, community in n Wilkes County between Chestnut and Herald Mountains.

Radio Island, land mass between Morehead City and Beaufort, s Carteret County. Takes name from commercial radio station formerly operating on the island.

Raeford, town and county seat, central Hoke County. Settled 1867; inc. 1901. Took its name from the last syllables of two of the town's founders, J. A. MacRae and A. A. Williford. Produces textiles, lumber, concrete, rubber; processes poultry, and cotton. Alt. 262.

Raeford Township, central Hoke County.

Raft Swamp rises in s Hoke County and flows se into central Robeson County, where it enters Lumber River. Much Tory activity during the Revolution was centered there, and the name is frequently mentioned in records of the time.

Raft Swamp Township, central Robeson County.

Rag Creek rises in n McDowell County and flows approx. 2 mi. se into Cox Creek.

Ragged Point, central Onslow County, extends into n Morgan Bay.

Raglins Ferry. *See* Mush Island.

Ragsdale Creek rises in central Buncombe County and flows se into Hominy Creek.

Raider Camp Creek rises in se Avery County and flows se into Caldwell County, where it enters Harper Creek.

Raider Camp Ridge, se Avery County.

Rail Cove, ne Cherokee County at the head of Rail Cove Branch.

Rail Cove Branch rises in ne Cherokee County and flows sw and ne into Ingram Branch.

Railroad Pond, e Anson County se of Lilesville. Covers approx. 4 acres; max. depth 12 ft. Formed early in the twentieth century when gravel was removed from the site.

Rainbow Banks, steep bank of the Roanoke River, n Martin County between Poplar Point on the e and Hamilton on the w. Mentioned in an act of the General Assembly in 1729 and appears on the Collet map, 1770.

Rainbow Creek rises in s Greene County and flows ne into Contentnea Creek. The name appears in local records as early as 1730.

Rainbow Falls, in sw Transylvania County on Horsepasture River. Height of falls is 200 ft.

Rainbow Gap, ne Buncombe County between Lookout Mountain and Montreat. Alt. approx. 3,250.

Rainbow Gap, on the Buncombe-Yancey county line between Blackstock and Potato Knobs. Alt. approx. 5,860.

Rainbow Islands, areas of fine, sandy loam surrounded by swamp in e Washington County sw of the community of Scuppernong.

Rainbow Lake, in s Transylvania County on Middle Creek near its junction with East Fork French Broad River. Covers 2 acres and has a max. depth of 20 ft. Used for recreation.

Rainbow Springs, community in sw Macon County on Pat Stable Branch.

Raines Crossroads, community in e Johnston County.

Raines Mountain, Transylvania County between Carson Creek and Dunn Creek.

Rainey Knob, sw Transylvania County between Thompson River and Horsepasture River.

Rakahak. *See* Rockyhock Creek.

Raleigh, city, county seat, and state capital, central Wake County on Neuse River. Made county seat in 1771 and known as Wake Court House until the site was selected as the state capital in 1792 and named for Sir Walter Raleigh (1552?–1618), English statesman who sent the first English colonists to Roanoke Island. Inc. 1794. The legislature met at Wake Court House in 1781 and has met in Raleigh since 1794. Alt. 363. Now includes former communities of Oberlin and Caraleigh, *which see*, and West Raleigh. Home of North Carolina State University, Meredith College, Peace College, St. Mary's School, Shaw University, and St. Augustine's College. Produces farm machinery, bakery products, processed meat, paper products, fabricated metals, heavy equipment, textiles, dairy products, cottonseed oil, and printed products.

Raleigh Bay, in the Atlantic Ocean off the central coast of North Carolina from Cape Lookout on the s to Cape Hatteras on the n.

Raleigh Township, central Wake County.

Ramah Creek rises in n Mecklenburg County and flows se into Clarks Creek.

Ram Branch rises in central Buncombe County and flows nw into Swannanoa River.

Ramey Creek rises in nw Surry County and flows e into Roaring Fork.

Raminger Creek rises in s Cherokee County and flows ne into Nottely River.

Ramoth, former town in central Buncombe County. Inc. 1889; name changed to Woolsey in 1903. Became a part of Asheville in 1905.

Ramp Branch rises in n central Avery County and flows ne into Elk River.

Ramp Cove, ne Cherokee County in the Valley River Mountains. Named because ramps grow abundantly there.

Ramp Cove Branch rises in ne Cherokee County and flows nw through Ramp Cove and Big Cove into Vengeance Creek.

Ramsaytown, community in n Yancey County on Cane River s of Sugarloaf Mountain. Alt. 2,141.

Ramseur, town in e Randolph County on Deep River. Known as Allen's Fall prior to 1878; named Columbia after 1878, when Deep River Mills est. Inc. 1895 as Ramseur in honor of Stephen D. Ramseur (1837–64), Confederate major general with whom William H. Watkins, one of the local mill owners, had been associated during the Civil War. Alt. 442.

Ramsey, community in s tip of Burke County on headwaters of Jacob Fork.

Ramsey Bend, in the Hiwassee River in central Cherokee County.

Ramsey Creek rises in s Iredell County and flows w into Catawba River.

Ramsey Creek rises in nw Northampton County and flows se into Potecasi Creek.

Ramsey Gap, n Madison County at the head of Cascade Branch.

Ramsey Mountain, n Buncombe County n of Wolfpen Gap.

Ramsey's Mill. *See* Lockport.

Ramseytown Township, n Yancey County.

Ramsour's Mill. *See* Lincolnton.

Ramushawn River appears on the Comberford map, 1657, in what is now Chowan County. Its identity is uncertain, but it lay between Yeopim River and Chowan River and may have been intended to represent the present Pembroke Creek.

Ranaleburg, community in sw Mecklenburg County served by post office, 1834–1902. Originally Randlesburg for Arthur Randolph Erwin, who opened a store and cotton gin there in 1834. Company B of 13th North Carolina Troops, known as "Ranalesburg Rifles," formed there during Civil War. Served by post office, 1851–1902.

Randall Gap, central Buncombe County near the headwaters of Ross Creek.

Randall Lake, on Big Creek in se Macon County.

Randleman, town in n Randolph County on Deep River. First known as Dicks for Peter Dicks, who built a gristmill there approx. 1830; in 1848 a cotton mill was built there and the name changed to Union Factory. In 1866 the name was changed to Randleman for John B. Randleman, one of the owners of the mill. Inc. in 1880 as Randleman Mills; name changed to Randleman in 1889. Naomi Falls, low natural falls in Deep River, was there but now under the water behind a 25 ft. dam. Falls named for Naomi Wise, who was drowned there by Jonathan Lewis in 1808, giving rise to eponymous folk song.

Randleman Township, nw Randolph County.

Randolph. *See* Hinshaw.

Randolph County was formed in 1779 from Guilford County. Located in the central section of the state, it is bounded by Chatham, Moore, Montgomery, Davidson, Guilford, and Alamance Counties. It was named for Peyton Randolph (1721?–75), president of the Continental Congress. Area: 801 sq. mi. County seat: Asheboro, with an elevation of 879 ft. Townships are Asheboro, Back Creek, Brower, Cedar Grove, Coleridge, Columbia, Concord, Franklinville, Grant, Level Cross, Liberty, New Hope, New Market, Pleasant Grove, Providence, Randleman, Seagrove, and Trinity. Produces wheat, corn, oats, poultry, dairy products, hay, barley, tobacco, nursery products, hogs, livestock, hosiery, apparel, textiles, tires, batteries, toys, furniture, shoes, and electric blankets.

Randolph Courthouse, community in w Randolph County served by post office, 1794–1810. Named changed to Asheboro, *which see*.

Randolph Mill. *See* Forest Hill.

Rands Mill, community in e Wake County near Swift Creek.

Rands Mill Pond. *See* Lake Benson.

Randys Store, community in n Montgomery County on Barnes Creek.

Ranger, community in s Cherokee County on Walker Mill Creek near Nottely River. Alt. approx. 1,565.

Rankin, community in s Mecklenburg County served by post office, 1888–1903.

Ranlo-Rex-Priscilla and Smyre Mills, an industrial community in e Gaston County between Lowell and East Gastonia. Textile-manufacturing plants operated there.

Ranns Falls, rapids in Cape Fear River in central Harnett County e of the town of Lillington. Mentioned as early as 1819 in a survey of the rivers of North Carolina.

Ransom's Bridge, community at the junction of Nash, Franklin, Warren, and Halifax Counties; formerly thriving, but now sparsely settled. There is a bridge at the site over Fishing Creek. A post office by the name existed as early as 1822 and as recently as 1882. Was a center of gold-mining activity before the Civil War.

Ransom Township, e Columbus County.

Ransomville, community in e Beaufort County at the head of North Creek. Named for Confederate general Matthew W. Ransom (1826–1904).

Rantersville. *See* LaGrange.

Raoul Branch rises in s Buncombe County near the Biltmore Estate and flows sw into Fourmile Branch.

Rapid Creek Ridge, ne Swain County in Great Smoky Mountains National Park, a short spur extending s from Dashoga Ridge, lat. 35°39'10" N., long. 83°15' W.

Rapier Mill Creek rises in sw Cherokee County and flows se and ne into Nottely River.

Ratcliff Cove, central Haywood County, forms a semicircle on the head of a tributary of Raccoon Creek w of Ratcliff Mountain.

Ratcliff Mountain, central Haywood County between Bird Creek and Ratcliff Cove.

Rattan Bay, w Piney Island in ne Carteret County bounded by Neuse River and North, East, and South Bays. Approx. 1 mi. wide and ¾ mi. long.

Rattan Ridge, a strip of higher ground in the Dismal Swamp in se Gates County.

Rattler Branch rises in e Cherokee County and flows nw into Valley River.

Rattler Ford, across Santeetlah Creek in w Graham County.

Rattle Shoal Creek rises in n Gaston County and flows ne into South Fork Catawba River.

Rattlesnake Branch rises in e central Brunswick County and flows e to join Lewis Swamp in forming Town Creek.

Rattlesnake Branch rises in se Brunswick County and flows sw into River Swamp.

Rattlesnake Branch rises in nw Columbus County and flows w then n into Horsepen Creek.

Rattlesnake Branch rises in n Duplin County and flows e into Northeast Cape Fear River.

Rattlesnake Branch rises in n Jones County and flows se into Beaver Creek.

Rattlesnake Branch rises in e Macon County and flows nw into Brush Creek.

Rattlesnake Branch rises in nw McDowell County on the s slope of Woods Mountain and flows se approx. 1 mi. into Little Buck Creek.

Rattlesnake Cliff, mountain in e Swain County between Hayes Ridge and Hickorynut Knob. Alt. 4,950.

Rattle Snake Creek is formed in n Caswell County by the junction of North Fork of Rattle Snake Creek and South Fork of Rattle Snake Creek and flows n into Dan River.

Rattlesnake Creek rises in n Macon County and flows ne into Swain County, where it enters Little Tennessee River.

Rattlesnake Creek rises in w Pender County and flows se into Whiteoak Creek.

Rattle Snake Island, a small tidal-marsh island in Currituck Sound off the se shore of the mainland of Currituck County.

Rattlesnake Knob, se Buncombe County nw of Lake Charles.

Rattlesnake Knob, on the Buncombe-Haywood county line.

Rattlesnake Knob, ne Cherokee County in the Valley River Mountains.

Rattlesnake Knob, w Haywood County on the w end of Eaglenest Ridge.

Rattlesnake Knob, n Henderson County at the head of Harper Creek.

Rattlesnake Knob, between Glassy Rock Ridge and Glenville Lake in s Jackson County.

Rattlesnake Knob, on the se end of Rattlesnake Ridge in n Jackson County.

Rattlesnake Knob, on the Jackson-Macon county line.

Rattlesnake Knob, at the head of Younce Creek in n Macon County.

Rattlesnake Knob, nw Macon County between Pierce Creek and Rowlin Creek.

Rattlesnake Knob, in se Macon County between Rich Mountain and Houston Branch.

Rattlesnake Knob, sw Macon County between Bryson Branch and Moore Creek.

Rattlesnake Knob, n Swain County in Great Smoky Mountains National Park on the sw end of Long Drive Ridge, lat. 35°33'07" N., long. 83°23'50" W. Alt. 4,311.

Rattlesnake Mountain, on Jackson-Swain county line near the head of Owl Branch.

Rattlesnake Pocosin, s Duplin County on Island Creek.

Rattlesnake Ridge, n Buncombe County between Greenfield Ridge and Snowball Gap.

Rattlesnake Ridge, n Jackson County between Rocky Face and North Fork.

Rattlesnake Ridge, s Macon County parallel to Shoal Creek.

Rattlesnake Ridge, e Mitchell County between Young Cove and Rock Creek Gap.

Rattlesnake Ridge, n Swain County in Great Smoky Mountains National Park, a short spur extending nw from Welch Ridge, lat. 35°30'55" N., long. 83°37' W.

Raven Cliff Branch rises in n Haywood County and flows nw into Cold Springs Creek.

Ravencliff Mountain, e Haywood County between Crab Orchard Fields and Rush Fork Gap.

Raven Cliff Ridge, se Haywood County between Bell Collar Cove and Little Buckeye Cove.

Raven Cliffs, on the Avery-Mitchell county line.

Raven Den, peak in n Swain County on Locust Ridge near the head of Bee Gum Branch. Alt. 4,247.

Ravenel Lake, se Macon County in the e edge of the town of Highlands on Mill Creek. Approx. ½ mi. long.

Ravenel Lake, se Macon County near the head of Cullasaja River 2 mi. nw of Highlands. Approx. 2 mi. long. The body of water is probably the Stewart's Pond visited by Bradford Torrey and described in the *Atlantic Monthly*, September 1897.

Raven Fork rises in sw Yancey County and flows ne into Cane River.

Raven Fork [Oconaluftee River], ne Swain County in Great Smoky Mountains National Park, is formed by the junction of Left Fork [Raven Fork] and Right Fork [Raven Fork] and flows sw into Oconaluftee River. *See also* Straight Fork.

Raven Hollow, s Haywood County between Beartrap Knob and Beartrap Ridge.

Raven Knob, n Buncombe County between Ingles Gap and Paint Fork Gap.

Raven Knob, nw Surry County.

Raven Knob. *See* Raven Mountain.

Raven Knob Pond, nw Surry County on an unnamed tributary of Fisher River. Covers 15 acres; max. depth 20 ft. Formed in 1950. Fishing, boating, and swimming. Owned by Old Hickory Council, Boy Scouts of America.

Raven Mountain, on the Macon-Swain county line near the head of Cold Spring Branch. Alt. approx. 4,700. Sometimes also known as Raven Knob.

Raven Ridge, ne Swain County in Great Smoky Mountains National Park, lat. 35°40' N., long. 83°17' W.

Raven Rock, mountain in ne Henderson County.

Raven Rock, ne Swain County at the s end of Hyatt Ridge between Raven Fork and Straight Fork.

Ravenrock Ridge, se Clay County between Left Fork and Right Fork [Eagle Creek].

Raven Rocks, peak in s Watauga County on the head of China Creek approx. 2 mi. nw of town of Blowing Rock. Alt. 3,913.

Raven Rock State Park, in Harnett County w of Lillington. Named for rock cliffs overlooking Cape Fear River. Covers 4,667 acres. Est. 1969. Recreational area with hiking, canoeing, and camping.

Raven Roost Ridge, ne Swain County in Great Smoky Mountains National Park, a short spur extending nw from Chiltoskie Ridge, lat. 35°36'08" N., long. 83°12'55" W.

Ravens, community in ne Swain County served by post office, 1889–1915. Also spelled Ravins.

Ravensford, community in e Swain County in Great Smoky Mountains National Park on Raven Fork near where it enters Oconaluftee River. Alt. 2,100.

Ravenswood, community in s Jones County.

Ravins. *See* Ravens.

Rawlingsburgh, community in e Rockingham

County served by post office, 1821–55 and 1859–66. Named for postmaster William Rawlings.

Rawls, community in n Harnett County.

Ray, community in s Madison County served by post office, 1883–1908. Named for first postmaster.

Ray Branch rises in w Macon County and flows ne into Deweese Branch.

Ray Cove, n Buncombe County between Ray Knob and Reems Creek.

Ray Knob, n Buncombe County between Horse Gap and Vance Knob.

Raymond Island, off of w side of Currituck Banks in Currituck Sound s of South Channel, ne Currituck County.

Raymond's Creek rises in s Camden County and flows sw into Pasquotank River. Named for William Raymond, who was granted land bordering the creek on February 25, 1696. Earlier called Fleming's Creek for George Fleming, who owned a small tract along the creek and died there in 1694.

Rayner Millpond, w Wayne County on a tributary of Beaverdam Creek.

Raynham, community in s Robeson County. Alt. 125. Settled about 1884. Named for the parish in Norfolk, England, from which the local Townsend family had migrated.

Raynor, community in s Franklin County.

Raynor Pond, on Mingo Swamp in sw Johnston County and e Harnett County.

Raynors Lake, a crescent-shaped lake on Cypress Creek in se Duplin County.

Raynor Swamp rises in s Gates County and flows nw to join Harrell Swamp and Duke Swamp in forming Bennetts Creek. Recorded as Meherrin Swamp in eighteenth-century land grants and deeds.

Ray's Branch rises in ne Wake County near the Franklin County line and flows s into Neuse River.

Rays Creek rises in w Franklin County and flows ne into Cedar Creek.

Rays Fork rises in e Union County and flows nw into Richardson Creek.

Ray's Mill Creek rises at the town of Southern Pines in s Moore County and flows sw into Aberdeen Creek at the town of Aberdeen.

Raywood, community in w Union County served by post office, 1858–1903.

Razo Creek. *See* Resoe Creek.

Razorback Ridge, w Avery County.

Razor Mountain, n Buncombe County between Poverty Branch and Martin Creek.

Reading. *See* Elizabeth City.

Ready Branch rises in s Jones County and flows n into Trent River.

Ready Branch rises in s Martin County and flows se into Statons Pond on Sweetwater Creek.

Readybranch, community in sw Wilkes County near the head of Naked Creek. A post office operated there, 1876–1935.

Reas Beach. *See* Albemarle Beach.

Reasonover Creek rises in se Transylvania County and flows ne then n into Little River.

Reasonover Lake, in se Transylvania County in Reasonover Creek. Covers 16 acres and has a max. depth of 22 ft.

Reatkin River. *See* Yadkin River.

Reaves, community in n Cumberland County.

Reba, community in s central Transylvania County.

Reba. *See* Fountain.

Rebels Creek rises in central Mitchell County and flows sw into North Toe River.

Rector Branch rises in w Madison County and flows ne into Big Pine Creek.

Rector Butte, w Madison County near the head of Rector Branch.

Rector Knob, e central Burke County. Alt. 2,153.

Rector Knob, s Macon County between Cadon Branch and Cadon Gap.

Redallia, community in s Pitt County.

Redbank Branch rises in w Haywood County and flows nw into Richland Creek.

Redbank Creek rises in n Forsyth County and flows ne into s Stokes County, where it enters Town Fork Creek. Called Oldfield Creek on the Collet map, 1770, and on subsequent maps through the Kerr map, 1882. Apparently, the soil survey map of 1913 was the first to use the present name. A Redbanks Church near the creek has been in existence since 1859.

Redbank Creek rises in n Stokes County and flows s into Dan River.

Redbanks, community in w Robeson County. Alt. 179. Pembroke Farms there est. 1938 by the Farm Security Administration as a cooperative under a 99-year lease. Descendants of several members of the cooperative still operate the farms there. Redbanks is named for the relatively high clay banks of nearby Lumber River.

Red Branch rises in e Cabarrus County and flows e into Dutch Buffalo Creek.

Redbud Creek rises in ne Franklin County and flows e into Nash County, where it enters Sandy Creek. Formerly known as Redbud Swamp.

Redbud Creek rises in w Vance County and flows sw into Ruin Creek. Named for the abundance of redbud trees (*Cercis canadensis*) in the area.

Red Bug, community in sw Brunswick County.

Redbug, community in central Columbus County.

Red Creek. *See* Clear Creek.

Redcross, community in n Randolph County.

Red Cross, community in sw Stanly County. Inc. 2002.

Reddick Branch. *See* Reddix Branch.

Reddick's Creek rises in s Guilford County. Gold mine operated by John Lowder was on its banks ca. 1820.

Reddies River is formed in w Wilkes County by the junction of North Fork Reddies River and Middle Fork Reddies River. It flows se into Yadkin River.

Reddies River, community in w Wilkes County on Reddies River. The area was settled prior to the Revolutionary War.

Reddies River Township, central Wilkes County.

Redding. *See* Elizabeth City.

Redding Mountain, e Wilkes County n of Flat Rock Creek.

Reddix Branch rises in s Mitchell County near Swafford Gap and flows w into East Fork Grassy Creek. Said to have been named for the Reddix family, which camped near its head. While there, two of their children died of colic and were buried at the head of the stream. Recent maps have used the form Reddick.

Reddy Branch rises in nw Madison County and flows s into Shelton Laurel Creek.

Red Hill, community in n Duplin County.

Red Hill, community in n Edgecombe County. In 1855, when Wilson County was formed in part from Edgecombe, Red Hill was described as "Henry Horn's old place."

Red Hill, community in w Mitchell County.

Red Hill, community in n Sampson County between Merkle Swamp and Great Coharie Creek.

Red Hill Creek rises in w Surry County and flows se and ne into Fisher River.

Red Hill Knob, central Madison County. Alt. 3,180.

Red Hill Swamp, the lower course of Brown Marsh Swamp, *which see*. The name is applied at the Bladen-Columbus county line, and it flows s across Columbus County. At the junction with Western Prong, the name is changed to White Marsh, *which see*.

Red Hill Township, w central Mitchell County.

Red Horse Creek. *See* Worley Cove Branch.

Red House, community in ne Caswell County. Post office, 1806–49. Named for Red House Presbyterian Church, where Rev. Hugh McAden, eighteenth-century missionary, preached and is buried.

Redland, community in n Davie County. Originally known as Bethlehem community for a Methodist church (on the site of Old Timber Ridge Meeting House, where Moravian ministers preached as early as 1773). When a post office was est. there in 1892, the name Bethlehem could not be used, as it was already in use elsewhere in the state. Redland was chosen as descriptive of the soil thereabouts. Post office closed 1906. Alt. 875.

Red Log Gap, n Cherokee County at the sw end of State Ridge. Alt. 3,697.

Redman Creek is formed in ne Swain County by the confluence of Left Fork and Right Fork and flows sw into Bunches Creek.

Redman Ridge, ne Swain County in Great Smoky Mountains National Park, a spur extending sw from Balsam Mountain, lat. 35°34′15″ N., long. 83°12′ W.

Redmans Cove, s Buncombe County sw of Hogback Ridge.

Redmans Old Field, appears on the Collet map, 1770, as open ground on the n side of Cokey Swamp, *which see*, w central Edgecombe County s of Tarboro.

Red Marble Gap, ne Cherokee County. Alt. 2,750. *See also* Topton.

Red Marble Gap, at the head of Rowlin Creek on the Graham-Macon county line. Alt. approx. 2,750.

Redmon, community in se Madison County. Inc. 1897; charter repealed 1899. Alt. 1,603.

Redmond Creek, a tidal stream on the w side of Eagles Island in the Cape Fear River, ne Brunswick County.

Red Mountain, n Durham County.

Red Mountain. *See* Rougemont.

Red Oak, town in n Nash County. Settled about 1880 and named for a grove of red oaks at the site. Inc. 1961. Alt. 225.

Red Oak Cove, nw Haywood County on the head of Low Gap Branch in Great Smoky Mountains National Park.

Red Oak Knob, n Buncombe County near the Madison County line.

Red Oak Township, n central Nash County.

Red Ridge, nw Swain County in Great Smoky Mountains National Park, a short spur extending e from Twentymile Ridge, lat. 35°29′40″ N., long. 83°48′10″ W.

Red Ridge Gap, nw Swain County in Great Smoky Mountains National Park on Twentymile Ridge between Lost Cove Creek and Coldspring Branch, lat. 35°29′52″ N., long. 83°48′47″ W.

Red Rock Ridge, n Avery County.

Red Run rises in e central Brunswick County and flows se to join Pinch Gut Creek in forming Lockwoods Folly River.

Red Shoals, community in e central Stokes County. A post office est. there in 1813 continued through 1920.

Red Sour, mountain in nw Cleveland County.

Red Springs, town in n Robeson County. Alt. 204. Inc. 1896 but settled much earlier. At the site of former Flora MacDonald College there, Vardell Hall, a school for girls, was est. in 1964 and operated for 10 years. The town was named for the color of spring and well water there, which was red because of iron oxides. Known first as Dora but changed to Red Springs in 1885. Formerly a popular health resort. Produces textiles, fertilizer, and lumber products.

Red Springs Township, nw Robeson County.

Redstone Point, on the mainland of n Dare County extending into Croatan Sound. The William B. Umstead Bridge, approx. 3 mi. long and opened on December 22, 1956, extends from the point to Weir Point on nw Roanoke Island; named for Governor William B. Umstead (1895–1954).

Red Store Crossroads, community in w Duplin County.

Red Town. *See* Deep Run.

Redwood, community in e Durham County on Neuse River. Est. 1890. Named for red oaks

growing in the vicinity. Flourished, 1895–1917. Following the removal of a lumber mill during World War I, the community declined.

Reece Mountain, e Lincoln County near Killian Creek.

Reed Branch rises in se Buncombe County and flows sw into Ashworth Creek.

Reed Branch rises in w Jackson County and flows ne into Savannah Creek.

Reed Cove, s Buncombe County e of Fannie Ridge.

Reed Cove, e Haywood County on n side of Fork Mountain. Reed Creek flows w through the cove.

Reed Creek rises in central Buncombe County nw of Asheville near Patton Mountain and flows w through Asheville into French Broad River.

Reed Creek rises in s Buncombe County and flows se into Gap Creek.

Reed Creek rises in se Catawba County and flows se into Mountain Creek.

Reed Creek rises in e Haywood County and flows w into Pisgah Creek.

Reed Creek rises in n Lincoln County and flows s into Leepers Creek.

Reed Creek rises in e Randolph County and flows sw into Deep River.

Reed Creek rises in s Randolph County and flows se into Little River.

Reed Creek rises in e Stokes County and flows e into Rockingham County.

Reeders Creek rises in s Greene County and flows e into Tyson Marsh.

Reed Gold Mine, former gold mine in e central Cabarrus County w of community of Georgeville. Gold was found there in 1799, and the discovery of a 28-lb. nugget set off a gold rush. Mine was the site of the first authentic discovery of gold in the state. Named for John Reed, on whose farm the discovery was made. Now a State Historic Site.

Reed Marsh rises in s Nash County and flows sw into Haw Branch.

Reed Misenheimers Township. *See* Earnhardt's Township.

Reeds Creek rises in s Iredell County and flows s into Mecklenburg County, where it enters Davidson Creek.

Reeds Crossroads, community in w Davidson County at the head of Beaverdam Creek.

Reeds Hammock, an island in Pamlico River,

se Beaufort County; approx. ½ mi. long and 2/10 mi. wide. *See also* The Ditch.

Reed's Landing. *See* Great Neck Landing.

Reeds Point, a point extending from the mainland of ne Dare County into Croatan Sound.

Reedy, community in nw Davidson County served by post office, 1870–1903.

Reedy Branch rises in s Alamance County and flows ne into Cane Creek.

Reedy Branch rises in ne Caldwell County and flows n into Yadkin River.

Reedy Branch rises in nw Duplin County and flows ne into Goshen Swamp.

Reedy Branch rises in se Duplin County and flows se into Back Swamp.

Reedy Branch rises in ne Franklin County and flows ne into Little Shocco Creek.

Reedy Branch rises in n Johnston County and flows sw into Little Branch.

Reedy Branch rises in w Johnston County and flows se into Black Creek.

Reedy Branch rises on the Jones-Craven county line and flows nw into Trent River.

Reedy Branch rises in s Lee County and flows n into Thoroughfare Branch.

Reedy Branch rises in ne Northampton County and flows ne into Kirbys Creek.

Reedy Branch rises in s Robeson County and flows se into Oldfield Swamp.

Reedy Branch rises in e Wake County and flows sw into Little River.

Reedy Branch rises in s Wake County and flows s into Buck Branch.

Reedy Branch rises in w Wake County and flows sw into Beaver Creek.

Reedy Creek rises in sw Burke County and flows nw into Old Catawba River approx. 8 mi. w of town of Morganton.

Reedy Creek rises in sw Cabarrus County and flows ne into Rocky River.

Reedy Creek rises in n Davidson County and flows sw into Yadkin River. Appears on the Collet map, 1770.

Reedy Creek rises in e Mecklenburg County and flows ne into Cabarrus County, where it enters Rocky River.

Reedy Creek rises in s Rowan County and flows ne approx. 4 mi. into South Second Creek. Mentioned in local records as early as 1762 as Reedy Fork.

Reedy Creek rises in central Warren County and flows se into w Halifax County, where it enters

Little Fishing Creek. Appears on the Price map, 1808.

Reedy Creek, community in nw Davidson County.

Reedy Creek Bay, an arm of Big Colly Bay in ne Bladen County.

Reedy Creek State Park, former park in nw Wake County est. in 1,234 acres in 1943 for blacks. Consolidated in 1965 with William B. Umstead State Park, *which see*.

Reedy Creek Township, nw Davidson County.

Reedy Fork rises in e Forsyth County and flows e into w Guilford County, ne across Guilford County, and into nw Alamance County, where it enters Haw River. Mentioned in local records as early as 1755.

Reedy Fork. *See* Reedy Creek.

Reedy Fork Creek rises in central Anson County and flows s into North Fork Jones Creek.

Reedy Fork Creek rises in e Caswell County and flows ne into North Hyco Creek.

Reedy Glade, a branch, rises in e Craven County and flows e into Broad Creek.

Reedy Island, an elevated sand and loam area approx. ¼ mi. wide and ¼ mi. long in e Duplin County approx. 2 mi. se of community of Hadley.

Reedy Meadow Creek rises in w Bladen County and flows w into Bryants Pond on Black Swamp.

Reedy Patch Creek rises in e Henderson County and flows ne into Broad River.

Reedy Patch Gap, e Henderson County near the head of Reedy Patch Creek. Alt. 2,242.

Reedy Pocosin, the nw section of Big Pocosin, sw Beaufort County.

Reedy Swamp rises from several small branches in w Harnett County and flows se to join McLeod Creek in forming Jumping Run Creek. Approx. 3½ mi. long.

Reedy Swamp rises in e Robeson County and flows s into Ten Mile Swamp.

Reelsboro, community in w Pamlico County. Named for the local Reel family.

Reems Branch rises in s Madison County and flows se into Ponder Branch.

Reems Creek rises in ne Buncombe County near Snowball Mountain and flows w into French Broad River. Probably named for a pioneer settler named Reems who was killed by Indians near present Weaverville about 1785. The name also appears in local records as Rims,

Reams, and Rheims Creek. *See also* Lane Pinnacle.

Reems Creek. *See* Weaverville.

Reems Creek Township, n central Buncombe County.

Reepsville, community in w central Lincoln County.

Reese, community in nw Watauga County on Little Beaverdam Creek. Est. before 1900. Alt. 3,320.

Reese Creek rises in e Cumberland County and flows sw into Lords Creek.

Reeves, community in s Columbus County.

Refuge, community in w Robeson County served by post office, 1893–1903.

Regal Station, a stop on the Southern Railway in central Cherokee County.

Regans Crossroads, community in w Brunswick County.

Registers Creek rises in s Guilford County and flows se into Hickory Creek.

Rehoboth, community in s Northampton County on Quarter Swamp. Grew up around Rehoboth Methodist Church, est. 1798.

Reid, community in sw Transylvania County near the head of South Fork Flat Creek. Alt. 2,725.

Reids Mountain, se Rowan County near Yadkin River at the mouth of Flat Creek.

Reid's Springs. *See* Catawba Springs.

Reidsville, city in s Rockingham County. In 1814 Reuben Reid purchased a farm and his son, future governor David Settle Reid, was appointed first postmaster in 1829. In 1864 Piedmont Railroad was completed between Greensboro and Danville, boosting Reidsville. Following the war, the town became a center of tobacco manufacturing. In time, textiles became a major factor. Post office est. in 1829. Inc. 1873. Alt. 841. Appears on the Colton map, 1861.

Reidsville Township, se Rockingham County.

Reinhardt, community in e Lincoln County served by post office, 1888–1904.

Reinhardt Gap, on the Haywood-Jackson county line. Alt. 5,440.

Reinhart Knob, on the Haywood-Jackson county line. Alt. 6,100.

Relief, community in w Mitchell County on Toe River. Alt. 2,092. Named for the patent medicine Hart's Relief, a popular product with a high alcoholic content sold at John Peterson's store there after about 1870.

Rella, community in n Stokes County served by post office, 1894–1904.

Rena, community in w Yadkin County on South Deep Creek.

Rendezvous Mountain, w central Wilkes County between the heads of Purlear and Cole Creeks. Alt. 2,450. Named for the fact that militiamen from the area are believed to have gathered there to drill and that it is the traditional rendezvous site for troops that assembled before marching to the Battle of Kings Mountain, October 7, 1780. In 1926 Judge Thomas B. Finley and his wife gave the state 142 acres there for a state park. Now an Educational State Forest operated by the North Carolina Forest Service.

Renfro Knob, w Yancey County between Hardscrabble Branch and Nubbinscuffle Creek.

Rennert, community in n Robeson County. Inc. 1895; charter repealed 1947. Known as McAlpin's Grove until the Atlantic Coast Line Railroad was constructed; the name was then changed, probably to honor someone connected with the railroad. James McAlpin, for whom the community was first named, is said to have been a Scottish officer in the British army during the American Revolution. After the war, he remained in North Carolina, taking an oath of allegiance to the United States and becoming a schoolteacher in the community that came to bear his name.

Rennert Township, n Robeson County.

Rennys Creek rises in s Craven County and flows ne into Neuse River.

Renston, community in sw Pitt County. Alt. 67.

Repose, community in s Lenoir County served by post office, 1887–1909.

Reps Martin Island, 14-acre sandy island in Yadkin River, ne Yadkin County.

Republican, community in w central Bertie County. Named for the Republican Baptist Church there. The name derived from the fact that the church was a public meeting place for the neighborhood.

Resaca, community in ne Duplin County served by post office, 1853–1916. Named for Mexican War Battle of Resaca de la Palma.

Research Triangle Park, a 5,000-acre tract in se Durham and w Wake Counties. Industrial and governmental research facilities operate there in a campus-like setting. Years of planning preceded opening of first businesses in

1959. Prospects boosted by est. of IBM facility in 1964. Duke University, the University of North Carolina, and North Carolina State University loaned startup expertise and give continuing support. Success of park has made it a national and international model.

Reservoir Branch rises in nw Madison County and flows e into Spring Creek.

Resoe Creek rises in central Pender County and flows s into Rileys Creek. Also known as Razo and Rizzo Creek.

Resolution Branch rises in n Jones County and flows s into Trent River.

Resootskeh, a Tuscarora Indian village in Bertie County on Indian Creek that appears on the Moseley map, 1733. Site was the base of "King Blount," the friendly Indian chief who aided the whites during the Tuscarora Indian War, 1711–13. The modern Tuscarora spelling of the word is Resootska, meaning "to our grandfather."

Rest, community in central Stanly County served by post office, 1883–1907.

Retreat, community in s Haywood County between Inman Branch and West Fork Pigeon River. Also known as Riverside, the name of the local Baptist church.

Reuben, community in ne Union County.

Reuben Creek rises in e Mitchell County and flows sw into Little Rock Creek.

Reuben Mountain, w Stokes County at the head of East Prong Little Yadkin River.

Revere, community in central Madison County on Revere Creek.

Revere Creek rises in central Madison County and flows nw into Big Laurel Creek.

Revis Branch rises in n Buncombe County and flows nw into s Madison County, where it enters Ivy River.

Revolution, former community in central Guilford County. Est. 1899. Named because the textile plant est. there was expected to revolutionize the cotton-manufacturing industry. Now within Greensboro city limits.

Rex, community in ne Robeson County.

Rex. *See* Ranlo-Rex-Priscilla.

Reynolda Lake, seminatural lake on Silas Creek on Reynolda Estate near the Wake Forest University campus in central Forsyth County. Covers 25 acres, with a max. depth of 15 ft. Used for fishing, boating, swimming, and irrigation. Not open to the public.

Reynolds Cove, nw Buncombe County ne of Rocky Knob.

Reynolds Gap, s Buncombe County between Lancy Mountain and Grassy Knob.

Reynolds Gap, s Macon County between the head of Ball Creek and the head of Dryman Fork.

Reynoldson, community in n Gates County. Reynoldson School operated there prior to the Civil War to prepare boys for Wake Forest College. The school was opened in 1856 and operated into the twentieth century.

Reynoldson Township, nw Gates County.

Rhea Branch rises in n Cherokee County in Rhea Cove and flows se and s into Valley River.

Rhea Cove, n Cherokee County at the head of Rhea Branch.

Rheasville, community in n Halifax County on Quankey Creek.

Rhems, community in w Craven County. Alt. 38. Est. prior to 1900 as Debruhls, named for a local family. Post office was est. in 1898, closed 1907.

Rhinehardt Creek rises in n Macon County and flows ne into Little Tennessee River.

Rhoades Academy, community in s Wayne County between Thoroughfare Swamp and Beaverdam Creek.

Rhodarme Cove, e Haywood County on the head of Kems Branch.

Rhode Branch rises in w Jackson County and flows se into Savannah Creek.

Rhodes, community in nw Bertie County.

Rhodes, community in central Duplin County.

Rhodes Creek rises in e Orange County and flows ne into Eno River.

Rhodes Mill Creek rises in s Catawba County and flows se into Pott Creek.

Rhodes Point, central Onslow County in Farnell Bay in Camp Lejeune Marine Corps Air Station.

Rhodestown, community in e Onslow County.

Rhodhiss, town on Burke-Caldwell county line near the e extremity of Burke County. Settled 1875. Inc. 1903. Alt. 965. Named in 1902 for John Rhodes and George Hiss, who est. a cotton mill there. The town is divided by the Catawba River, and at one time the portion in Burke County was known as Cliffs. Produces textiles.

Rhodhiss Lake, on the Catawba River, Burke and Caldwell Counties. Formed 1924–25. Covers

3,515 acres, with a shoreline of 90 mi. Owned by Duke Power Co. and site of hydroelectric power plant.

Rhodo, community in n Cherokee County. According to local tradition, it was named for the "raw dough" biscuits once served at a local boardinghouse.

Rhody Franklin Mountain, n Madison County between Shelton Laurel Creek and the head of Martin Branch.

Rhyne. *See* Daniels-Rhyne.

Rhynes Crossroads, community in w central Pender County.

Ricahokene, a village of Weapemeoc Indian tribe in what is now s Perquimans County on Perquimans River. Shown on the White map, 1585; appears as Rickahock on the Comberford map, 1657. The name survives in adjoining Chowan County as Rockyhock, *which see*.

Rice Branch rises in central Buncombe County and flows nw into Beaverdam Creek. Named for a pioneer settler.

Rice Branch rises in central Madison County and flows sw into Ammons Branch.

Rice Cove, e Haywood County on the head of Rice Cove Creek.

Rice Cove Creek rises in e Haywood County in Rice Cove and flows se into Beaverdam Creek.

Rice Cove Creek rises in n central Madison County and flows n into Big Laurel Creek.

Rice Creek rises in sw Beaufort County and flows n into Chocowinity Bay of Pamlico River.

Rice Gap, n central Transylvania County between Shutin Ridge and Lamb Creek.

Rice Island, in se Bertie County between Roanoke River and Eastmost River. A large swampy island, it measures almost 2½ mi. from tip to tip and is approx. 1 mi. wide at its greatest width. *See also* Purchace Islands.

Rice Knob, central Buncombe County between Craven Gap and Roaring Gap.

Rice Path, site of early settlement on e end of Bogue Banks in s Carteret County. A vessel, laden with a cargo of rice, went aground there at one time. The people on the sound side made a path across the banks to the ocean side to get the rice, and so they called it Rice Path. Storms drove out early settlers until settlement of Salter Path, *which see*.

Rice Pinnacle, s Buncombe County at the n end of Stradley Mountain.

Rices Creek rises in se Brunswick County and flows n into Town Creek.

Rices Pocosin, a swamp in central Greene County.

Riceville, community in n Buncombe County on Bull Creek, *which see*. Named for family of pioneer settlers. Served by a post office, 1876–1906.

Richards. *See* Crown Stream.

Richards Mill, on the Collet map, 1770, was located on a tributary of the Pasquotank River in what is now n Pasquotank County. The stream was located approx. 12 to 15 mi. nw of the present Knobbs Creek but has long since left its streambed to become a part of the surrounding marsh.

Richardson, community in sw Bladen County.

Richardson Creek rises in s Rutherford County and flows s into Broad River. P. H. Richardson operated a gold mine on the creek in the 1830s.

Richardson Creek rises in s Union County, flows ne into nw Anson County, and enters Rocky River on the Stanly County line.

Richardson Creek, community in n Union County on the e side of Richardson Creek.

Rich Branch rises in s Buncombe County and flows ne into Bent Creek.

Rich Branch rises in n Mitchell County and flows e into Spring Creek.

Rich Cove, between Laurel Mountain and Big Creek in nw Henderson County.

Richey Gap, s Macon County between Buck Knob and Richey Knob.

Richey Knob, s Macon County between Sheep Hollow and Middle Creek.

Richfield, community in n Stanly County. Alt. 661. Inc. 1899. Named for local Ritchie family.

Rich Fork Creek rises in ne Davidson County and flows sw into Abbotts Creek.

Rich Gap, se Macon County between Fodderstack Mountain and Rich Mountain.

Rich Gap, in Great Smoky Mountains National Park on the Swain County, N.C.–Blount County, Tenn., line between Gregory Bald and Forge Knob, lat. 35°31′45″ N., long. 83°51′14″ W.

Rich Gap Mountain, nw Henderson County on Laurel Mountain between Johnson Knob and Black Mountain.

Rich Hammock, a name applied on the Moseley

map, 1733, to a neck of land (apparently especially suitable for cultivation) extending into North River, s Carteret County e of present town of Beaufort.

Rich Hill, peak on the Alleghany-Surry county line. Alt. 3,260.

Rich Hill, community in e Alleghany County.

Rich Hill Creek rises in w Ashe County and flows se into North Fork New River.

Rich Inlet, se Pender County, from Topsail Sound into Atlantic Ocean. Appears on the Moseley map, 1733.

Rich Island Gut, n central Carteret County, flows n into South River.

Rich Knob, central Buncombe County ne of Randall Gap. Alt. 3,535.

Rich Knob, n Buncombe County at the se end of Richland Mountain in Pisgah National Forest.

Rich Knob, sw Buncombe County between Green Top and Long Gap.

Rich Knob, on the Cherokee-Macon county line between Junaluska Gap and Wolf Creek Gap.

Rich Knob, on the Haywood-Madison county line.

Rich Knob, s Macon County between Commissioner Gap and Doubletop Mountain.

Rich Knob, s Mitchell County between South Fork [Carvers Branch] and North Fork [Grassy Creek].

Richland Balsam, a peak on the Haywood-Jackson county line 8 mi. s of town of Waynesville. Alt. 6,540, the highest point on Balsam Mountain, *which see.*

Richland Creek rises in n Franklin County and flows ne into Neuse River.

Richland Creek rises in w Franklin County and flows sw into Wake County, where it enters Neuse River. Appears on the Collet map, 1770, although somewhat misplaced. The name Richmond Creek is applied on the Mouzon map, 1775.

Richland Creek rises in n central Guilford County and flows ne into Reedy Fork Creek. Appears on the Collet map, 1770.

Richland Creek rises in w Haywood County and flows ne into Pigeon River.

Richland Creek rises in w Moore County and flows ne into McLendon Creek.

Richland Creek rises in w Person County and flows nw into South Hyco Creek.

Richland Creek rises in s Randolph County and flows se into Deep River.

Richland Creek rises in s Rutherford County s of Oakland and flows se into Broad River.

Richland Creek rises in w Transylvania County and flows ne into West Fork French Broad River.

Richland Creek rises in w central Wake County near Asbury and flows n into Crabtree Creek.

Richland Gap, s Haywood County on the head of Shiny Creek.

Richland Gap, at the sw end of Piney Mountain Ridge in e Jackson County.

Richland Knob, n Buncombe County on Richland Mountain in Pisgah National Forest.

Richland Lake, central Guilford County formed by dam on Richland Creek. Built in 1943 by Cone Mills and used for industrial and municipal purposes.

Richland Mountain, n Buncombe County between Courthouse Knob and Rich Knob.

Richland Mountain, n Swain County in Great Smoky Mountains National Park, a ridge extending se from Charlies Bunion between Kephart Prong and Bradley Fork, lat. 35°36′47″ N., long. 83°20′30″ W. Alt. approx. 5,600.

Richland Mountains, ne Rutherford County along Sally Queen Creek. There are several named peaks in the range.

Richlands, town in nw Onslow County between New River and Mill Swamp. Alt. 64. Settled approx. 1775; inc. 1880. Named for fertile soil of the region. Former home of Richlands Academy (1848–1904); it served as the educational center of Jones and Onslow Counties. Produces lumber. Known as Upper Richlands until it was inc. in 1880.

Richlands Township, nw Onslow County.

Richland Swamp rises in s Hoke County and flows se into Robeson County, where it enters Big Raft Swamp.

Richland Township, se Beaufort County.

Richland Township, s central Randolph County.

Richmond, former seat of Surry County, 1774–89. Est. 1779. Site now in nw Forsyth County near the community of Donnoha. Town completely destroyed by a cyclone in or soon after August 1830 and the site abandoned. Moravian diarist recorded history of the courthouse.

Richmond. *See* Bear Creek.

Richmond County was formed in 1779 from Anson County. Located in the s central section of the state, it is bounded by the state of South Carolina and by Anson, Stanly, Montgomery, Moore, and Scotland Counties. It was named for Charles Lennox (1735–1806), third Duke of Richmond, military officer, ambassador, and secretary of state who denounced British policy toward the American colonies. Area. 483 sq. mi. County seat: Rockingham, with an elevation of 211 ft. Townships are Beaverdam, Black Jack, Marks Creek, Mineral Springs, Rockingham, Steeles, and Wolf Pit. Produces cotton, corn, wheat, oats, peaches, poultry, hogs, livestock, textiles, paper, furniture, hosiery, and lumber.

Richmond Creek. *See* Richland Creek.

Richmond District, one of the districts into which Caswell County was divided at the time of the 1790 census. It contained 253 heads of families.

Richmond Hill, community on the outskirts of Burlington, central Alamance County.

Richmond Hill, community in n Yadkin County. Home of Richmond Pearson (1805–78), chief justice of North Carolina Supreme Court; he conducted a law school at his home, "Richmond Hill," which has been restored.

Richmond Millpond, nw Scotland County on Gum Swamp Creek. Formed prior to 1800 and known until 1893 as Malloys Pond for Charles Malloy, original owner. Covers 75 acres; max. depth 18 ft. Named because it was located in Richmond County when it was formed.

Richmond Mills, community in w Scotland County on Gum Swamp Creek.

Rich Mountain, on the Alleghany-Wilkes county line. Alt. 3,500.

Rich Mountain, se Davidson County on headwaters of Beaverdam Creek.

Rich Mountain extends ne from Johns Creek to the Haywood-Jackson county line in e Jackson County.

Rich Mountain, n Henderson County between Couch Mountain and Baldwin Gap.

Rich Mountain, on the Henderson-Polk county line. Alt. 2,542.

Rich Mountain, in nw Jackson County between Dicks Creek and Camp Creek.

Rich Mountain, e Macon County between Keener Mountain and Rattlesnake Knob.

Rich Mountain, in se Macon County between Big Creek and Rich Gap.

Rich Mountain, on the Madison County, N.C.–Greene County, Tenn., line.

Rich Mountain, s Madison County at the head of Little Sandymush Creek.

Rich Mountain, on the McDowell-Rutherford county line.

Rich Mountain extends sw in w Mitchell County along the course of Pigeonroost Creek.

Rich Mountain, s Swain County on the head of Pigeon Creek. Alt. 3,865.

Rich Mountain, n Transylvania County between Sunfish Cove and Laurel Gap. Alt. 3,952.

Rich Mountain, n Transylvania County, extends ne from Club Gap to Soapstone Ridge. Alt. approx. 4,100.

Rich Mountain, s Transylvania County between the head of Steel Creek and the head of Cannon Creek. Alt. 3,779.

Rich Mountain, peak on Brushy Mountain se of Gloucester Gap in w Transylvania County. Alt. approx. 3,580.

Rich Mountain, an extended ridge beginning at town of Boone in central Watauga County and running nw to head of Sharp Creek, n Watauga County, then ne to its highest point, Rich Mountain Bald, *which see*, before ending at Rich Mountain Gap. Named for its unusually fertile though rugged slopes.

Rich Mountain, s Wilkes County between Pole Mountain and Hunting Creek.

Rich Mountain, community on n side of mountain of same name in e Jackson County where Sugar Creek enters Caney Fork.

Rich Mountain Bald, a peak on Rich Mountain near the head of Charley Creek in e Jackson County.

Rich Mountain Bald, n Watauga County on Rich Mountain. Alt. 5,372.

Rich Mountain Creek rises in s Alleghany County and flows w into Bullhead Creek on the Alleghany-Wilkes county line.

Rich Mountain Gap, on the head of Johns Creek in central Jackson County.

Rich Mountain Gap, n Watauga County between Rich Mountain and Snake Mountain. Cove Creek rises on its w slope, and Meat Camp Creek rises on its e slope. Alt. 4,420.

Rich Neck. *See* Wilkinson Point.

Richneck Creek rises in sw Warren County and flows e into Fishing Creek.

Rich Ridge, w Madison County near the head of Jones Branch.

Richs Gap, w Avery County.

Rich Square, town in s Northampton County. Inc. 1869. Alt. 78. Settled about 1750 by Quakers from Virginia. Meeting organized in 1753 and Meeting House completed in 1760. A deed in 1761 to Thomas Hunter refers to "a tract of land called rich square," probably referring to the fertility of the soil. Appears as Richsquare on the Price map, 1808. Inc. 1883. Produces apparel.

Rich Square Township, se Northampton County.

Rich Top, mountain in e Haywood County between Harbon Cove and Silvers Cove Creek.

Rickman Creek rises in n Macon County and flows se into Matlock Creek.

Ricks Branch rises in se Cherokee County and flows se into Little Brasstown Creek.

Ricks Creek rises in nw Duplin County and flows sw into Goshen Swamp.

Ricky Knob, central Haywood County between Ned Branch and the head of Hemphill Creek.

Rico, community in n Columbus County.

Riddick Crossroads, community in w Gates County.

Riddicksville, community in ne Hertford County near Chowan River. Known as Maney's Ferry until 1825 for the Maney family, which had lived there since about 1750. The site was acquired by Adam Riddick in 1825 and the present name adopted soon afterward.

Riddie Cove, w Haywood County on Big Spring Branch.

Riddle, community in s Camden County. A post office est. there 1884 as Bray for Dempsey Bray, first postmaster, who removed to another community after two years. Renamed for Charles Riddle (1862–89), local schoolmaster, and operated until 1939.

Riddle Branch rises in nw Yancey County and flows se into Bald Mountain Creek.

Riddle Creek rises in n Watauga County and flows s into Meat Camp Creek.

Riddles Creek rises in se Rutherford County and flows s into Broad River.

Ridenhour Township, nw Stanly County.

Riders Creek rises in n central Tyrrell County near community of Levels and flows sw and nw into Scuppernong River.

Riders Creek Community. *See* Levels.

Ridge. *See* South Gastonia.

Ridge Creek rises in nw Alamance County and flows se into Haw River.

Ridgecrest, community in se Buncombe County. Alt. 2,530. Southern Baptist summer assembly grounds are there.

Ridgepole Mountain, s Macon County between Little Ridgepole Mountain and Gulf Branch. Alt. 5,008.

Ridge's Mountain, w Randolph County between Uwharrie River and Caraway Creek; a long, rather low, ridge.

Ridge Spring. *See* Scuffletown.

Ridgeville, community in se Caswell County. Known as Pea Ridge until 1875, when the present name was adopted for the ridge on which it is located. Alt. 750.

Ridgeway, community in w Warren County. Alt. 422. Inc. 1869; charter repealed 1879. Grew up around a series of inns, the first of which was Colers Ordinary, shown on the Collet map, 1770. By 1800 Charles Marshall had a tavern there; portions of the original building still exist in a local dwelling. In 1816 John Paschall operated a tavern there, and the community was known as Paschalls, the name under which it appears on the MacRae map, 1833. The present name was used when a post office was est. there in 1839; it is said to be derived from the ridge on the n edge of the community on which a railway was built. After the Civil War, a development company induced immigrants from Germany, Alsace, France, Switzerland, and England to settle there.

Riegelwood, community in ne Columbus County near the Cape Fear River. Developed around the Riegel Paper Corporation after it began production in 1951.

Riggsbee, community in ne Chatham County served by post office, 1858–1915. Known as Riggsbee's Store until 1894.

Riggsbee's Store. *See* Riggsbee.

Right Fork rises in ne Buncombe County on

s slopes of Craggy Knob and flows sw into Beetree Creek.

Right Fork rises on the s slopes of Potato Knob in ne Buncombe County near the Yancey County line and flows sw into North Fork [Swannanoa River]. Often referred to locally as Right Hand Fork. Part of the Asheville watershed.

Right Fork rises in ne Cherokee County in the Valley River Mountains and flows n into Bear Branch.

Right Fork Bean Creek rises in n Mitchell County and flows s to join Left Fork Bean Creek in forming Bean Creek.

Right Fork Belews Creek. *See* East Belews Creek.

Right Fork [Cane Creek] is formed in e Mitchell County by the junction of Mine Fork Branch and Stagger Weed Creek and flows nw to join Left Fork [Cane Creek] in forming Cane Creek.

Right Fork [Cold Spring Branch] rises in w Swain County and flows nw into Cold Spring Branch near its confluence with Hazel Creek.

Right Fork Cove Creek rises in central Haywood County and flows se into Cove Creek.

Right Fork Davidson River rises in nw Transylvania County and flows se into Davidson River.

Right Fork [Eagle Creek] rises in se Clay County and flows nw to join Left Fork [Eagle Creek] in forming Eagle Creek. Known also as Dave Barrett Creek.

Right Fork [Indian Creek] rises in n Swain County and flows sw to join Left Fork [Indian Creek] in forming Indian Creek.

Right Fork [Pigeonroost Creek] rises in w Mitchell County and flows sw into Pigeonroost Creek.

Right Fork [Raven Fork] rises in ne Swain County in Great Smoky Mountains National Park and flows sw to join Left Fork and Middle Fork in forming Raven Fork [Oconaluftee River]. *See also* McGee Spring.

Right Fork [Redman Creek] rises in ne Swain County and flows sw to join Left Fork [Redman Creek] in forming Redman Creek.

Right Fork Webb Creek rises in ne Cherokee County near Old Billy Top and flows sw and s to join Left Fork Webb Creek in forming Webb Creek.

Right Fork [Wesser Creek] rises in n Macon County and flows ne into Swain County, where it enters Wesser Creek.

Right Hand Fork. *See* Right Fork.

Right Hand Prong [Pigeon River] rises in s Haywood County and flows ne into Middle Prong.

Right Prong Bent Creek rises in n Yancey County and flows se to join Left Prong Bent Creek in forming Bent Creek.

Right Prong [Ledge Creek] rises in ne Swain County and flows nw into Ledge Creek.

Right Prong Martin Creek rises in s Cherokee County and flows e into Martin Creek.

Right Prong South Toe River rises in s Yancey County and flows e to join Left Prong South Toe River in forming South Toe River.

Right Prong Three Forks Creek rises in se Yancey County and flows w to join Left Prong Three Forks Creek in forming Three Forks Creek.

Riles Creek rises in se Rowan County and flows se into Stanly County, where it turns ne back into Rowan County and enters Yadkin River. The Kerr map, 1882, shows the stream as Loyal Creek.

Riley, community in s Franklin County. Post office there, 1873–1911, known as Rileys Cross Roads.

Riley Cove, e Clay County between Chunky Gal Mountain and Buck Creek.

Riley Knob, e Clay County between Riley Cove and Glade Gap.

Riley Knob, e Macon County between Higdon Mountain and Ledford Branch.

Rileys Creek rises in central Pender County and flows sw into Long Creek.

Rileys Cross Roads. *See* Riley.

Rimer, community in n Cabarrus County; known also as Rimertown.

Ring Fire Knob, se Wilkes County between Little Hunting Creek and Osborne Creek. Alt. approx. 1,300.

Ringstaff Mountains, range in the Cane Creek Mountains, s Alamance County.

Ringwood, town in sw Halifax County. Inc. 1877, but long inactive in municipal affairs. A number of homes there date from the early nineteenth century.

Rio, community in s central Transylvania County.

Rio Jordan. *See* Cape Fear River.

Ripley, former town on the w outskirts of Hendersonville in central Henderson County. Inc. 1909; charter repealed 1917.

Rippetoe Mountain, s Caldwell County. Alt. 1,298.

Named for William Rippetoe, who received the mountain in a land grant.

Rippys Township, former township in s Cleveland County, now township no. 3.

Ripshin Mountain, sw Buncombe County n of Mount Pisgah.

Rip Shin Mountain, n Caldwell County. Alt. 2,200.

Ripshin Ridge, nw Burke County, extends from se to nw between Steels Creek and Upper Creek. Alt. 2,875.

Risden. *See* Rufus.

Ritter, former community in w Swain County on Tuckasegee River. Site now under the waters of Fontana Lake.

Ritters Township, n central Moore County.

River Acres, community in central Beaufort County on the n shore of Pamlico River.

River Bend, community in ne Gaston County near Mountain Island Lake at the steam power-generating plant of the Duke Power Co.

River Bend Township, ne Gaston County.

Riverdale, community in e Craven County. Settled 1878 and named because of its location near Neuse River.

River Hill, community in e Iredell County served by post office, 1875–1907.

River Neck, community in nw Tyrrell County near the mouth of Scuppernong River. Alt. 2. Formerly called Devenport.

River Neck Landing, nw Tyrrell County on the e side of mouth of Scuppernong River.

River Side, community on South Fork New River in sw Ashe County. Alt. approx. 2,950.

Riverside, community in s Macon County on Little Tennessee River.

Riverside, community in w central Yancey County on Cane River.

Riverside. *See* Retreat.

Riverside Park, community in central Beaufort County on the n shore of Pamlico River.

River Swamp rises in se Brunswick County and flows nw into Lockwoods Folly River.

Riverton, community in e Scotland County on Lumber River. A summer resort used by residents of nearby towns and their descendants. Subject of John Charles McNeill's poetry.

River Township, former township in sw Cleveland County, now township no. 1.

River Township, central Jackson County.

River Township, ne Warren County.

River View Community, se Columbus County; formerly known as Crusoe Island. Renamed by resolution of the General Assembly, 1961. A marshy and sandy section between the Waccamaw River and the Columbus-Brunswick county line, it lies on the edge of Green Swamp, *which see*. It was named Crusoe Island by outsiders because of its isolation. French political refugees, who first settled in Haiti, are said to have arrived there in 1806; their descendants still live there. Roads now penetrate the area.

Rizzo Creek. *See* Resoe Creek.

Roachs Creek rises in central Rockingham County and flows w into Dan River. Named for Roach family, gristmill operators.

Road Ridge, e Mitchell County at the head of Bear Creek.

Roan Creek rises in e Ashe County and flows nw into South Fork New River.

Roanes Mill, community in s Macon County served by post office, 1878–1912.

Roan High Bluff, ne Mitchell County on Roan Mountain. Alt. 6,267.

Roan High Knob, on the Mitchell County, N.C.–Carter County, Tenn., line. Alt. 6,286.

Roan Island, a silt island in s Pender County approx. 4 mi. long and 1½ mi. wide; surrounded by Cape Fear River, Thoroughfare, and Black River.

Roan Mountain, ne Mitchell County, extends ne into Tennessee. Alt. approx. 6,200. Probably named for its roan (reddish) color when seen from a distance in the rhododendron blooming season. Site of Rhododendron Festival each June.

Roanoac, an Indian village formerly near the n tip of Roanoke Island, e Dare County; the site is now submerged in the waters of Albemarle Sound. Appears on the White maps of 1585 and 1590.

Roanoak Town. *See* Carteret.

Roanoke, community in nw Rockingham County served by post office, 1894–1904.

Roanoke. *See* Poplar Point.

Roanoke Canal, constructed between 1817 and 1823 and extended between 1824 and 1834 to bypass the Upper and Lower Falls of Roanoke River in n Halifax County. The canal, built by the Roanoke Navigation Company, provided a series of locks that made uninterrupted navigation of the river possible. The locks raised and lowered vessels 44 ft. from the basin to the river and could accommodate boats weighing from 30 to 50 tons. With the completion of the Raleigh and Gaston Railroad and its junction with Seaboard Railroad about 1841, the canal began a decline and was no longer used by 1865. Chockoyotte Creek Viaduct and other remnants remain.

Roanoke County was proposed as the name for the se portion of Halifax County in 1868, when there was a move to divide the county. A manuscript map of Roanoke County made by M. L. Venable is in the North Carolina Collection at the University of North Carolina at Chapel Hill.

Roanoke Inlet, former inlet from the Atlantic Ocean into Roanoke Sound through Bodie Island s of the present location of Nags Head, ne Dare County. Inlet was the original n boundary of Bodie Island. Opened prior to 1657 and closed in 1795, according to a note on the Kerr map, 1882. Appears on the Ogilby map, 1671.

Roanoke Island, approx. 11 mi. long and 2¼ mi. wide, e Dare County; it is separated by Roanoke Sound from Bodie Island (Outer Banks) on the e and from the mainland by Croatan Sound on the w. Site of Fort Raleigh, center of English exploration and settlement, 1584–87. Name believed to be of Algonquian Indian origin signifying "northern people" or "northerners," referring to the fact that the Indians lived on the n end of the island or that they had earlier migrated from an ancestral home in the n. The name Roanoke also came to be applied to shell beads. Site of freedman's colony, 1865. Fort Raleigh National Historic Site is on the n end of the island. *See also* Manteo; Carteret.

Roanoke Marshes, extensive string of low marsh islands in Croatan Sound, e central Dare County stretching from sw end of Roanoke Island to a large marshy area on the mainland. Site of a beacon est. approx. 1875; last of manually operated lights along the coast replaced by automatic beacon in 1955. The islands for the most part have washed away. Shown on the Collet map, 1770, as Daniels Marshes. Unnamed but shown prominently on the Moseley map, 1733.

Roanoke Rapids, city in n Halifax County on the Roanoke River. Founded in 1893 by John Armstrong Chaloner (1862–1935) as a cotton-mill site and named for the rapids in the river. Inc. 1897. Originally known as Great Falls. Produces paper and textiles. Alt. 169.

Roanoke Rapids Dam. *See* Lake Gaston.

Roanoke Rapids Lake is formed by a dam near the city of Roanoke Rapids in ne Halifax County on Roanoke River. The lake extends nw along the Halifax-Northampton county line to Gaston Dam. The dam there was completed in 1955, and the lake covers 4,900 acres, with a shoreline of 47 mi. and a max. depth of 90 ft. Built by Virginia Electric and Power Company to generate hydroelectric power, the lake is also used for recreation. *See also* Lake Gaston.

Roanoke Rapids Township, n Halifax County.

Roanoke River is formed in Montgomery County, Va., by the junction of North Fork and South Fork and flows se into North Carolina in ne Warren County. It flows across a corner of Warren and along the Halifax-Northampton, Halifax-Bertie, Bertie-Martin, and Bertie-Washington county lines into Batchelor Bay of Albemarle Sound. The John H. Kerr Dam on Roanoke River in Virginia creates Kerr Lake, a part of which is in Granville, Vance, and Warren Counties. Appears as Morattico River on the Comberford map, 1657, and as Noratake River on the Ogilby map, 1671. The Moseley map, 1733, specifies Roanoke River.

Roanoke Sea. *See* Albemarle Sound.

Roanoke Sound, between Roanoke Island and the Outer Banks in e Dare County. Known in the eighteenth century as Sanderson's Channel for Richard Sanderson, local landowner. The name Walter Rawleigh appears there on the Collet map, 1770, though it is uncertain whether it was intended to represent the name of the sound. *See also* Albemarle Sound.

Roanoke Township, e central Northampton County.

Roanoke Township, ne Warren County.

Roan Valley, parallel to Fall Creek in e Mitchell County.

Roaring Branch rises in s Mitchell County and flows nw into Crabtree Creek.

Roaring Creek rises in w Avery County and flows s into North Toe River.

Roaring Creek rises in nw Swain County in Great

Smoky Mountains National Park and flows se
to join Defeat Branch in forming Bone Valley
Creek.

Roaring Creek. *See* Valley.

Roaring Creek Township, sw Avery County.

Roaring Fork rises in nw Ashe County and flows
sw into Big Laurel Creek.

Roaring Fork rises in e Madison County and
flows s into Big Laurel Creek.

Roaring Fork rises in w Madison County and
flows ne into Meadow Fork.

Roaring Fork rises in nw McDowell County on
the n slope of Woods Mountain and flows n
into Armstrong Creek.

Roaring Fork rises in nw Surry County and flows
sw into Fisher River.

Roaring Fork rises in nw Yancey County and
flows se into Bald Mountain Creek.

Roaring Fork rises in se Yancey County and flows
n into Three Forks Creek.

Roaring Fork Creek rises in w Macon County
and flows sw into Nantahala River.

Roaring Fork Mountain, w Madison County parallel to Roaring Fork.

Roaring Fork Ridge, sw Macon County between
Roaring Fork Creek and the head of Rough
Fork.

Roaring Gap, at the junction of the Alleghany-
Surry-Wilkes county lines. Alt. 2,914.

Roaring Gap, central Buncombe County n of
Rice Knob in Elk Mountains.

Roaring Gap, community in se Alleghany
County. Est. in 1890 as a summer resort by
Alexander Chatham of Elkin, who bought
land there and built the first house. Named
for the fact that wind is said to rush with a
roar through a gap there. Alt. 3,800. Now
popular site for summer homes.

Roaring River is formed in central Wilkes
County by the junction of Middle Prong Roaring River and North Prong Roaring River and
flows se into Yadkin River. Named because of
an early description of the river, which said
that it "comes rushing and roaring" out of the
Blue Ridge Mountains.

Roaring River, community in e central Wilkes
County on Yadkin River at the mouth of Roaring River. Alt. 934. Settled about 1770. Inc.
1905; charter repealed 1907. A post office est.
there in 1872.

Roaring Spout Creek rises in e Yancey County
and flows e into Browns Creek.

Roaring Spout Falls, on Roaring Spout Creek,
e Yancey County.

Robbins, town in n Moore County on Bear
Creek. Known as early as 1828 as Mechanicks Hill and Mechanicsville for David Kennedy, local mechanic and gunsmith. Later
known as Elise, and inc. 1935 as Hemp. Name
changed in 1943 to Robbins for Karl Robbins,
owner of a local mill. Alt. 424.

Robbinsville, town and county seat, central
Graham County. Alt. 2,150. Post office est.
1874. Town authorized to be laid out in 1872
as Robbinsville for local Robbins family. Inc.
in 1893 as Robinsville; name changed in
1897 to Robbinsville. Produces carpets and
lumber.

Robedo, community in central Montgomery
County served by post office, 1903–1907.

Roberdel, town in central Richmond County
on Hitchcock Creek. Settled approx. 1850;
inc. 1889. Named for Robert L. Steele, textile
manufacturer. Alt. 246.

Roberdo, community in s Montgomery County.

Roberson Ridge, s Haywood County between
Bearpen Branch and Deep Gap Creek.

Roberson Store, community in se Martin County
on Harrison Mill Creek. Settled about 1898
and known as Amherst until after 1920.
Alt. 75.

Robersonville, town in w Martin County. Settled
before the Civil War. Inc. 1870 and named for
Henry D. Roberson, local landowner and Confederate veteran. Alt. 78. Produces processed
poultry and apparel.

Robersonville Township, sw Martin County.

Roberta, community in w Cabarrus County that
grew up around Pattersons Mill, a name by
which it was once known.

Robert Branch rises in s Madison County and
flows n into French Broad River.

Robert Gap, on the Haywood-Madison county
line.

Roberts Branch rises in n Cherokee County and
flows nw into Farner Branch.

Roberts Branch rises in s Cleveland County and
flows e into Buffalo Creek. Named for "Squire
Billy" Roberts, owner of the land through
which it ran.

Roberts Cove, in e Haywood County on the head
of Rush Fork.

Roberts Creek rises in n Lee County and flows ne
into Hughes Creek.

Roberts Crossroads, community in w Franklin County.

Robertson Creek rises in s central Granville County and flows s into Beaverdam Creek near the Granville-Wake county line.

Robertson Mountain, n Jackson County between Locust Creek and Mill Creek.

Robertsons Pond, e Wake County on Buffalo Creek. Formed in 1900. Covers 65 acres, with a max. depth of 15 ft. Used for recreation and as power source.

Robeson (ROB-uh-son) County was formed in 1787 from Bladen County. Located in the se section of the state, it is bounded by the state of South Carolina and by Scotland, Hoke, Cumberland, Bladen, and Columbus Counties. It was named for Col. Thomas Robeson (1740–85), Revolutionary War officer. Area: 948 sq. mi. County seat: Lumberton, with an elevation of 137 ft. Triracial population with roughly equal numbers of African Americans, Native Americans (principally Lumbee), and Caucasians. Townships are Alfordsville, Black Swamp, Britts, Burnt Swamp, East Howellsville, Fairmont, Gaddy, Lumber Bridge, Lumberton, Marietta, Maxton, Orrum, Parkton, Pembroke, Philadelphus, Raft Swamp, Red Springs, Rennert, Rowland, Saddletree, St. Pauls, Shannon, Smiths, Smyrna, Sterlings, Thompson, Union, West Howellsville, and Wishart. Produces tobacco, corn, soybeans, wheat, oats, cotton, poultry, hogs, turkeys, tomatoes, cabbage, eggs, livestock, onions, tomatoes, lumber, soup, textiles, packaging, and apparel.

Robeson Creek rises in central Chatham County and flows e into Haw River.

Robeson Point. *See* Robinson Point.

Robey's Camp Ground. *See* Rock Springs.

Robin Branch rises in w Macon County and flows sw into Jarrett Creek.

Robin Branch rises in w Wilson County and flows ne and n into Black Creek.

Robinson Cove, the valley through which Robinson Creek flows in nw Buncombe County.

Robinson Creek rises in nw Buncombe County and flows sw into Sandy Mush Creek.

Robinson Creek rises in s Buncombe County near Busbee Mountain and flows se into Cane Creek. *See also* Pinner Cove.

Robinson Creek rises in s Jackson County and flows ne into Bear Creek Lake on the Tuckasegee River.

Robinson Creek rises in e Rutherford County and flows sw into Second Broad River.

Robinson Gap, s central Swain County between Bucknor Branch and Cochran Branch.

Robinson Mountain, nw Buncombe County between Earlies Gap and High Knob.

Robinson Point extends from e Onslow County into White Oak River. Sometimes known as Robeson Point.

Robinson Point. *See* Cedar Island Point.

Robinson Rough, mountain on the Buncombe-Madison county line between Norton Fork Gap and Davidson Gap.

Robinson's Ferry. *See* Monroe.

Robinwood Lake, se Gaston County on Anthony Creek. Formed 1947. Covers 35 acres. Max. depth 25 ft. Swimming, fishing, boating.

Robson Branch rises in central Avery County and flows s into Plumtree Creek.

Robson Station, community in central Orange County.

Roby Creek rises in se Yadkin County and flows e into Turner Creek.

Rochdale, town authorized to be laid out in Richmond County (now w Scotland County) in 1816 on the land of John Marine and others on or near Joes Creek. Apparently, the town was never laid out.

Rock, community in s Rowan County served by post office, 1883–1906.

Rock Branch rises in e Alamance County and flows s into Haw Creek.

Rock Branch rises in s Macon County and flows sw into Betty Creek.

Rock Branch rises in n Madison County and flows sw into Shelton Laurel Creek.

Rock Branch. *See* Olivia.

Rockbrook Camp Branch rises in s central Transylvania County and flows nw through Rockbrook Camp into French Broad River.

Rock Camp Branch rises in ne Swain County and flows nw into Bunches Creek.

Rock Camp Branch rises in nw Swain County and flows e into Roaring Creek.

Rock Camp Run rises in ne Swain County and flows nw into Straight Fork.

Rock Creek rises in sw Alamance County and flows n into Stinking Quarter Creek.

Rock Creek rises in w Alleghany County and flows n into New River.

Rock Creek rises in w Ashe County and flows se into North Fork New River.

Rock Creek rises in se Buncombe County and flows se into w Rutherford County, where it enters Lake Lure.

Rock Creek rises in s Burke County and flows se into Catawba County, where it enters Jacob Fork.

Rock Creek rises in se Caldwell County and flows e into Upper Little River.

Rock Creek rises in central Graham County and flows ne into Atoah Creek.

Rock Creek rises in e Graham County and flows ne into Panther Creek.

Rock Creek rises in w Graham County and flows ne into Cheoah River.

Rock Creek rises in e Guilford County and flows s into Alamance Creek.

Rock Creek rises in sw Henderson County and flows se into Green River.

Rock Creek rises in central Montgomery County and flows s into Little River.

Rock Creek rises in n central Rutherford County and flows se into Second Broad River.

Rock Creek rises in e central Wilkes County and flows s into Yadkin River.

Rock Creek is formed in s Yancey County by the junction of North Fork Rock Creek and Middle Fork Rock Creek and flows ne and se into South Toe River.

Rock Creek, community in central Alamance County served by post office, 1849–1923.

Rock Creek. *See* Greens Mill Run.

Rock Creek Gap, e Mitchell County on Rock Creek Mountain.

Rock Creek Knob, w Graham County between Deep Creek and Rock Creek.

Rock Creek Mountain, e Mitchell County at the head of Little Rock Creek.

Rock Creek Township, e Guilford County.

Rock Creek Township, e central Wilkes County.

Rockdale, community in ne Cleveland County.

Rockdam Creek rises in s Lincoln County and flows ne into Howards Creek.

Rockett, community in ne Catawba County. Est. 1886 as Roseman, but the name was changed

in 1902 when a post office was est. Post office discontinued in 1903. Both names were for local families.

Rockfield Creek rises in central Graham County and flows sw into Santeetlah Lake.

Rockfish, community in e Hoke County. Settled about 1900 and named for nearby creek. Alt. 218.

Rockfish. *See* Hope Mills.

Rock Fish. *See* Juford.

Rockfish Creek rises in sw Duplin County and flows s and e into Northeast Cape Fear River on the Duplin-Pender county line. Appears on the Moseley map, 1733.

Rockfish Creek rises in se Moore County e of town of Aberdeen and flows se across Hoke County into Upchurch Pond on the w Cumberland County line. From the pond, it flows e across Cumberland County to enter Cape Fear River 1½ mi. e of community of Grays Creek. Appears on the Moseley map, 1733.

Rockfish Township, w Cumberland County.

Rockfish Township, sw Duplin County.

Rockford, town in s Surry County on Yadkin River. Est. 1790 as the county seat and so remained until 1851, when the county was divided and the county seat removed to Dobson. Alt. 838. Inc. 1819, but long inactive in municipal affairs.

Rockford Township, s central Surry County.

Rock Fork rises in n Swain County and flows se into Right Fork [Deep Creek].

Rock Fork Branch rises in se Person County and flows sw into Deep Creek.

Rock Gap, sw Macon County at the head of Little Rock Branch.

Rock Hole Creek rises in sw Stanly County and flows se into Rocky River. Called Cucumber Creek on the Kerr map, 1882.

Rock Hollow, e Haywood County between Soapstone Gap and Sheep Mountain.

Rock Hollow Branch rises in Rock Hollow in e Haywood County and flows nw into Crabtree Creek.

Rock House. *See* Sweezy Mountain.

Rockhouse Branch rises in sw Madison County and flows e into Sugar Camp Branch.

Rockhouse Creek rises in e Avery County and flows se into Caldwell County, where it enters Wilsons Creek.

Rock House Creek rises in n Clay County and flows sw into Fires Creek.

Rockhouse Creek rises in s Mitchell County and flows ne into Grassy Creek.

Rock House Creek rises in s Rockingham County and flows n into Dan River. Mentioned in local records as early as 1767.

Rockhouse Creek rises on Seniard Ridge in n Transylvania County and flows s into Davidson River.

Rockhouse Creek rises in s Watauga County and flows se into Caldwell County.

Rockhouse Knob, s Macon County between Long Ridge and Wolfpen Gap. Alt. 3,100. A weather station there has recorded in various years the greatest amount of rainfall e of the Rocky Mountains.

Rocking Chair Branch rises in s Clay County and flows s into Shooting Creek.

Rockingham, town and county seat, w Richmond County. Courthouse est. at site 1779 and known as Richmond Court House until 1784, when it was named for Charles Watson-Wentworth (1730–82), second Marquis of Rockingham, British advocate of American independence. Manufactures textiles, paper, apparel, and processes poultry. *See also* East Rockingham; West Rockingham. Alt. 211.

Rockingham County was formed in 1785 from Guilford County. Located in the n central section of the state, it is bounded by the state of Virginia and by Caswell, Guilford, and Stokes Counties. It was named for Charles Watson-Wentworth (1730–82), second Marquis of Rockingham, prime minister at the time of the repeal of the Stamp Act, and supporter of proposals to grant independence to the American colonies. Area: 572 sq. mi. County seat: Wentworth, with an elevation of approx. 900 ft. Townships are Huntsville, Leaksville, Madison, Mayo, New Bethel, Price, Reidsville, Ruffin, Simpsonville, Wentworth, and Williamsburg. Produces tobacco, corn, wheat, oats, hay, strawberries, dairy products, hogs, livestock, beer, apparel, textiles, hosiery, bricks, carpets, cigarettes, and other tobacco products.

Rockingham Lake, privately owned lake built 1939 on tributary of Lower Hogans Creek, Rockingham County.

Rockingham Township, w central Richmond County.

Rock Landing, formerly a landing and supply point on Roanoke River in n Halifax County constructed before 1818 for the purpose of landing stone and building supplies to be used in the construction of Roanoke Canal, *which see.*

Rock Level, community in n Rockingham County served by post office, 1878–1903. Also spelled Rocklevel.

Rocklevel. *See* Rock Level.

Rock Point, s Carteret County, extends n from central Bogue Banks w of community of Salter Path.

Rockrace Branch rises in e Transylvania County and flows ne into Cascade Lake (Little River).

Rock Rest, community in se Union County served by post office, 1888–1900.

Rock Ridge, community in w Wilson County near Marsh Swamp. Post office named Taylor served the community, 1882–1914; named for J. M. Taylor.

Rock Run. *See* Telfairs Creek.

Rocks, The, a great seawall constructed by the U.S. government, 1879–85, to close off New Inlet between the Atlantic Ocean and the Cape Fear River in s New Hanover County.

Rock Spring, community in w Orange County served by post office, 1845–1905. Spelled Rockspring after 1894.

Rockspring. *See* Rock Spring.

Rock Springs, community in central Craven County on Trent River.

Rock Springs, community and camp meeting ground, ne Lincoln County near Denver. Camp meetings held annually in August since 1830. The camp, 45 acres in area, succeeded an older one named Robey's near Catawba Springs.

Rock Springs, community in n Polk County.

Rockstack, a mountain on the Graham County, N.C.–Monroe County, Tenn., line.

Rockview, community in n Buncombe County near the junction of Martin Creek and North Fork Ivey Creek. Alt. 2,394.

Rockville. *See* Rockwell.

Rockwell, town in s Rowan County. Early travelers from Salisbury to Cheraw and Camden,

S.C., enjoyed good water from a rock well there, hence the name. A post office est. there 1838 as Millville, changed to Rockville in 1839 and to Rockwell in 1872. Inc. 1911. Alt. 785.

Rocky Bald, w Macon County between the head of Holloway Branch and Wine Spring Creek. Alt. 5,333.

Rocky Branch rises in s Chatham County and flows se into Deep River.

Rocky Branch rises in w Clay County and flows n into Hiwassee River.

Rocky Branch rises in e Durham County and flows ne into Neuse River.

Rocky Branch rises in se Durham County and flows ne into Lick Creek.

Rocky Branch rises in nw Guilford County and flows se into Haw River.

Rocky Branch rises in central Haywood County and flows ne into Pigeon River.

Rocky Branch rises in nw Haywood County and flows s into Big Creek.

Rocky Branch rises in s Haywood County and flows nw into West Fork Pigeon River.

Rocky Branch rises in sw Haywood County and flows ne into Allen Creek.

Rocky Branch rises in w Jackson County and flows ne into Tuckasegee River.

Rocky Branch rises in central Macon County and flows ne into Little Tennessee River.

Rocky Branch rises in w Macon County and flows w into Nantahala Lake.

Rocky Branch rises in n Madison County and flows e into Little Laurel Creek.

Rocky Branch rises in w Madison County and flows ne into Doe Branch.

Rocky Branch rises in s Mecklenburg County and flows w into Fourmile Creek.

Rocky Branch rises in e Vance County and flows ne into w Warren County, where it enters Matthews Creek.

Rocky Branch rises in e Wake County and flows e into Little River.

Rocky Branch rises in n Wake County and flows sw into Neuse River.

Rocky Branch rises in e Watauga County and flows nw into South Fork New River.

Rocky Branch Ridge, sw Haywood County parallel to Rocky Branch.

Rocky Broad River. *See* Broad River.

Rocky Butte Mountain, e Jackson County near the head of Chastine Creek.

Rocky Cove, s Buncombe County.

Rocky Cove, e Haywood County on Hominy Creek.

Rocky Cove, se Haywood County on East Prong Pigeon River.

Rocky Cove, sw Macon County on a tributary of Poplar Cove Creek.

Rocky Cove, w Macon County on a tributary of Nantahala River.

Rocky Cove Branch rises in e Haywood County and flows sw into Hominy Creek.

Rocky Cove Knob, sw Macon County at the sw end of Rocky Cove.

Rocky Creek rises in s Granville County and flows e into Tar River.

Rocky Creek rises in s Iredell County between Troutman and Oswalt and flows sw into Catawba River.

Rocky Creek rises in s Transylvania County and flows sw into Toxaway River.

Rocky Creek rises in w Warren County and flows se into Fishing Creek.

Rocky Creek rises in s Wilkes County and flows ne into Hunting Creek n of Pilot Mountain. Approx. 4 mi. long.

Rocky Creek rises near Pores Knob in se Wilkes County and flows se across the nw corner of Alexander County and into Iredell County, where it enters South Yadkin River.

Rocky Creek. *See* Stony Creek.

Rocky Face, mountain in ne Alexander County. Alt. 1,851. Extensive quarry operated there early in the twentieth century.

Rocky Face, exposed rock surface on Angelco Mountain, sw Cherokee County.

Rocky Face, n Jackson County between Cutoff Ridge and Whiterock Ridge. Alt. approx. 4,600.

Rocky Face, n Jackson County between Rocky Face Branch and Cane Creek. Alt. approx. 3,575.

Rocky Face Branch rises in n Jackson County on se slopes of Rocky Face and flows s into Wayehutta Creek.

Rocky Face Knob, on the Jackson-Macon county line.

Rocky Face Mountain, e Haywood County between the head of Harley Branch and Long Branch. Alt. approx. 4,600.

Rockyface Mountain, on the Jackson-Transylvania county line between Bald Rock and Bald Knob. Part of Tennessee Ridge. Alt. approx. 4,700.

Rockyface Mountain, s Macon County between Lee Creek and Jones Creek. Alt. approx. 4,500.

Rocky Face Mountain, n Rutherford County between Second Broad River and Box Creek.

Rocky Face Mountain, s Swain County extends ne from the head of Jenkins Branch to the forks of Kirkland Creek.

Rocky Face Ridge, n Jackson County between Wayehutta Creek and Cane Creek.

Rocky Ford, community in n Franklin County.

Rocky Ford Branch rises in nw Wilson County and flows e and ne into Town Creek.

Rocky Ford Creek rises in central Anson County and flows n into Goulds Fork.

Rocky Ford Creek rises in sw Cherokee County and flows nw into Polk County, Tenn., where it enters Ocoee River.

Rocky Fork rises in se Buncombe County near Jesses High Top and flows sw into Cane Creek.

Rocky Fork rises in sw Henderson County and flows e into North Fork.

Rocky Fork rises in s Lee County and flows w into Crane Creek.

Rocky Fork Creek rises in n Richmond County and flows sw into Falling Creek.

Rocky Fork Ridge, n Swain County in Great Smoky Mountains National Park, lat. 35°35′20″ N., long. 83°25′55″ W.

Rocky Glen. *See* Catawba Falls.

Rocky Hill. *See* Medoc Mountain.

Rockyhock, community in central Chowan County. Alt. 28. For a possible origin of the name, *see* Rockyhock Creek.

Rockyhock Creek rises in central Chowan County and flows sw into Chowan River. Appears as Rakahak on the Ogilby map, 1671, and as Rockyhock on the Moseley map, 1733. Name may be derived from an Indian village, Ricahokene, on the e side of Perquimans River at Albemarle Sound. It may have meant "where combs [rakes?] are made."

Rocky Hollow, w Watauga County between Laurel Creek and Watauga River.

Rocky Knob, central Buncombe County in Pisgah National Forest between Paynes Knob and Pine Knob. Alt. approx. 3,950.

Rocky Knob, n Buncombe County approx. 1 mi. s of Richland Knob. Named by early settlers because the peak is crowned by a mass of rock.

Rocky Knob, se Buncombe County between Sand Branch and Rush Branch.

Rocky Knob, on Newfound Mountain on the Buncombe-Haywood county line n of Haywood Gap.

Rocky Knob, on the Buncombe-McDowell county line between Graybeard Mountain and Pinnacle.

Rocky Knob, on the Buncombe-Yancey county line between Campground Gap and Coxcomb Mountain.

Rocky Knob, nw Caldwell County between head of Amos Creek and head of Anthony Bolick Branch. Alt. 3,280.

Rocky Knob, w Caldwell County between Franklin Branch and Coffey Creek. Alt. approx. 1,960.

Rocky Knob, n Cherokee County in the Unicoi Mountains. Alt. approx. 4,250.

Rocky Knob, n Cherokee County on Hanging Dog Mountain. Alt. 3,830.

Rocky Knob, central Haywood County between Rogers Cove Creek and Big Branch. Alt. approx. 3,840.

Rocky Knob, e Haywood County between Rough Creek and Laurel Gap approx. 4 mi. n of town of Canton. Alt. approx. 4,175.

Rocky Knob, s central Haywood County on the head of Peter Cove Branch.

Rocky Knob, on the head of Charley Creek in e Jackson County.

Rocky Knob, on the Jackson-Transylvania county line n of Pinhook Gap. Part of Tennessee Ridge, *which see*. Alt. approx. 4,000.

Rocky Knob, n Macon County between the head of Wildes Creek and Younce Creek.

Rocky Knob, s Macon County at the head of Peeks Creek.

Rocky Knob, s Macon County between Watkins Creek and Jake Branch.

Rocky Knob, e Madison County at the head of East Fork [Bull Creek].

Rocky Knob, n Madison County between Sapling Mountain and Spillcorn Creek.

Rocky Knob, e Swain County in Whiteoak Flats on the head of Adams Creek.

Rocky Knob, se Watauga County between Ben Ridge and Swift Ford Branch.

Rocky Knob, w Watauga County between Watauga River and School House Branch.

Rocky Knob, n central Yancey County on the head of Guilders Creek 1½ mi. n of town of Burnsville. Alt. approx. 4,100.

Rocky Knob, w Yancey County between Elk Wallow Creek and Lickskillet Branch. Alt. approx. 3,880.

Rocky Knob, w Yancey County between Possumtrot and Horton Creeks. Alt. approx. 3,960.

Rocky Knob. *See* Haw Knob.

Rocky Knob Creek rises in e Watauga County and flows nw into South Fork New River.

Rocky Knob Gap, between Wolf Creek and Tanasee Creek in e Jackson County.

Rockyknob Mountain, w Yancey County between Dryspring Branch and Slickrock Mountain.

Rocky Knob Ridge, s Haywood County on the head of Mauney Cove Branch.

Rocky Knob Ridge, e Macon County between Dalton Creek and Tippet Creek.

Rocky Knobs, two knobs s of Horsepasture River, sw Transylvania County.

Rocky Mount, city in e Nash and w Edgecombe Counties. Est. 1816; inc. 1867. Named for the rocky mounds and ledges on the site near the falls of the Tar River. Home of North Carolina Wesleyan College. Produces tobacco, furniture, and fabricated metals. Alt. 121.

Rocky Mount. *See* Bear Poplar.

Rocky Mountain, between Featherston Creek and Harper Creek in n Henderson County.

Rocky Mountain, s Jackson County between Chimneytop and Horsepasture River. Alt. 4,427.

Rocky Mountain, s Transylvania County between Laurel Branch and Bradley Creek.

Rocky Mountain, s Transylvania County between Woodruff Branch and Browns Mill Creek.

Rocky Mountain, w Transylvania County between Morton Creek and Indian Creek. Alt. 3,527.

Rocky Mountain, e central Watauga County between Rocky Branch and Rocky Knob Creek.

Rocky Mount Township, former township in w central Edgecombe County, now township no. 12.

Rocky Mount Township, se Nash County.

Rocky Pen Ridge, central Cherokee County, extends ne from Nottely River to Hiwassee River near Murphy.

Rocky Point, community in s Pender County. Alt. 39. Inc. 1905; charter repealed 1945. Name applied to the area by Barbadian explorers in 1663 for an unusual outcropping of rock near Lane's Ferry in the otherwise flat country. The community was settled in the late eighteenth century. Clayton Hall, home of Francis Clayton, native of Scotland and member of the Wilmington Safety Committee, 1774, was there. Produces lumber. *See also* Lillington County.

Rocky Point Township, s central Pender County.

Rocky Ridge, between Jim Creek and The Flatwoods in sw Henderson County.

Rocky Ridge, s Madison County parallel to Little Pine Creek.

Rocky River rises in se Iredell County near Mooresville and flows s along the Cabarrus-Mecklenburg county line for a short distance; across Cabarrus to the Cabarrus-Stanly county line, which it forms for a short distance; and to the Stanly-Union and Anson-Stanly county lines, which it forms before entering Pee Dee River. Appears on the Collet map, 1770.

Rocky River rises in ne Randolph County and flows sw across Chatham County into Deep River.

Rocky River Springs, community and former resort in s Stanly County. Mineral springs there said to have been known to Indians as the "place of healing waters." Hotel and places of amusement in operation from the 1830s until 1920s.

Rocky River Springs. *See* Silver.

Rocky River Township, former township in sw Cabarrus County, now township no. 1.

Rocky Run rises in se Alamance County and flows sw into Hobby Branch.

Rocky Run rises in w Craven County and flows ne into Hayward Creek.

Rocky Run rises in e Onslow County and flows nw into Little Northeast Creek.

Rocky Shoal Branch rises in s Ashe County and flows se into South Fork New River.

Rocky Springs, community in ne Alexander County. Alt. approx. 1,150. York Collegiate Institute was operated there 1856–58 by Brantley York, one of the founders of Trinity College in Randolph County, which later became Duke University.

Rocky Springs, community in sw Rockingham County. Name in use during Revolutionary War when soldiers mustered there. A post office est. there 1810; closed 1905.

Rocky Springs Township, se Montgomery County.

Rocky Spring Top, on the Cherokee-Graham county line in the Snowbird Mountains.

Rocky Swamp rises in w Halifax County and flows se into Fishing Creek. Appears on the Collet map, 1770.

Rocky Top, on the Cherokee County, N.C.–Monroe County, Tenn., line.

Rocky Top, on the Swain County, N.C.–Blount County, Tenn., line in Great Smoky Mountains National Park between Mount Squires and Thunderhead Mountain.

Rocquis Creek. *See* Roquist Creek.

Rod, community in e Iredell County served by post office, 1899–1905.

Rodanthe, community in e Dare County on Hatteras Island. Formerly known as North Rodanthe. A post office there operated as Chicamacomico until 1874, when it took present name.

Rodanthe S Curves. *See* S Curves.

Rodman's Creek rises in w Beaufort County and flows e into Pamlico River.

Rodman's Point, near the mouth of Rodman's Creek, w Beaufort County on the s side of Pamlico River.

Rodney, community in ne Person County served by post office, 1898–1901.

Roduco, community in w Gates County near Flat Branch in Jones Swamp. Alt. 35.

Roe, community on Cedar Island in ne Carteret County. Alt. 12.

Rogers or **Rogers Quarter**, community in n Northampton County.

Rogers Branch rises in central Haywood County and flows nw into Pigeon River.

Rogers Cove, central Haywood County on a tributary of Richland Creek.

Rogers Cove, e Haywood County on the head of Rogers Cove Creek.

Rogers Cove Creek rises in e Haywood County and flows nw into Crabtree Creek.

Rogers Creek rises in central Cherokee County and flows nw into Valley River.

Rogers Creek. *See* Beech Swamp.

Rogers Crossroads, community in e Wake County n of Powell Creek.

Rogers Gap, nw Buncombe County in Fodderstack Mountain near Greasy Cove.

Rogers Gap, w Cherokee County between Wehutty Mountain and Shoal Creek.

Rogers Mountain, w Yancey County between Indian and Price Creeks.

Rogers Ridge, s Avery County.

Rogers Store, community in n central Wake County. Settled prior to 1840 and named for Col. Ransome Rogers, first storekeeper. Alt. 300.

Rogers Swamp rises in n Northampton County and flows se to join Corduroy Swamp in forming Kirbys Creek.

Rogues Creek rises in nw Clay County and flows sw and se into Rock House Creek.

Roland Branch rises in w central Yancey County and flows se into Cane River. Believed to have been named for a black settler. *See also* Roland Hollow; Roland Knob.

Roland Creek Canal rises in nw Currituck County and flows e into Guinea Mill Run.

Roland Hollow, w central Yancey County on w side of Cane Mountain. Contains a tributary of Higgins Creek.

Roland Knob, w central Yancey County between head of Roland Branch and head of Bailey Branch approx. 2 mi. w of town of Burnsville. Alt. approx. 3,620.

Roland Ridge, e Haywood County parallel to Ugly Creek.

Rolesville, town in e Wake County near the head of Cedar Fork. Settled in the early nineteenth century and named for William Roles, original settler. Inc. 1837; reincorporated 1941.

Rollins, community in s Burke County served by post office, 1881–1905.

Rollins, community in s Madison County on French Broad River.

Rollinson Channel, se Dare County, provides access through Pamlico Sound from Hatteras Inlet to the town of Hatteras. Dredged to a depth of 10 ft.; 10 ft. wide.

Rollover Creek rises in Great Dover Swamp in w Craven County and flows se into Bachelor Creek.

Rome, community in s Johnston County served by post office, 1882–1904.

Rominger, community in w Watauga County on Laurel Creek. Named for Rev. W. Smith Rominger, a Methodist minister in whose home the first post office was est. in 1903.

Ronda, town in e Wilkes County on Yadkin River. Alt. 934. Inc. 1907. Est. on Col. Benjamin Cleveland's estate, "Roundabout," named for a sharp bend in Yadkin River there. The town's name is a shortened form of the plantation name. Produces furniture.

Rooks, community in w Pender County.

Roosevelt, community in ne Henderson County between Whiteside Mountain and Chickasaw Knobs. Named for President Theodore Roosevelt (1858–1919).

Rooty Branch rises in e Craven County and flows e into Broad Creek.

Roper, town in n central Washington County on Kendricks Creek. Alt. 13. Settled in 1706 by Thomas Blount, who built a dam there. Upon his death, his widow married Col. Thomas Lee, who built a mill at the site; the designations "S. Lee, Saw Mills" appear on the Moseley map, 1733. The mill, which began operation in 1709, was destroyed in an explosion in 1921. The town served as county seat from 1800 to 1823 (*see also* Cabin Ridge Plantation). Post office est. 1802; post office name changed to Union in 1851. In 1820 the town of Duckettsville was authorized to be laid out there but never developed. Lees Mills was renamed Roper in 1889 for John L. Roper, who est. a lumber industry there, and the town was inc. in 1907.

Roper Knob, n Macon County between the head of Rose Creek and Little Tennessee River.

Roper's Knob, s Burke County. Alt. 2,200.

Roper Springs, community in nw Halifax County. A mineral spring there was the site of an Indian camp before the arrival of white settlers. A man named Roper later operated a tavern there, hence the name.

Roquist Creek rises in w Bertie County and flows se into Cashie River. Many spellings (Rocquis, Rakwis, Rocquist, Roquewhist, etc.) have been used in the past, but Roquist is the accepted spelling. The word is Tuscarora for "turtle." Mentioned in local records as early as 1723.

Roquist Pocosin, sw Bertie County.

Roscoe, community in central Chatham County served by post office, 1883–1926.

Rose, community in n Chatham County served by post office, 1892–1904.

Rose. *See* Rosewood.

Rose Bay, in Pamlico Sound w of Bell Island in s Hyde County. *See also* Cecils Harbor.

Rose Bay, community in s Hyde County at the head of Rose Bay.

Roseboro, town in w Sampson County. Inc. 1891 and named for George McNeil Rose (1846–

1924), chief counsel of the Cape Fear and Yadkin Valley Railroad. Alt. 137. Owensville (Owenville post office), est. prior to 1839 on Little Coharie Creek a short distance w of the site of Roseboro, declined with the growth of Roseboro.

Roseborough, community in se Avery County.

Rose Branch rises in central Mitchell County near Burns Mountain and flows w into North Toe River.

Rose Branch rises in w Nash County and flows s into Sapony Creek.

Rosebud, community in se Stokes County.

Rosebud, community in n Wilson County between the head of White Swamp and Cattail Swamp.

Rose Creek rises in nw Burke County on Rose Mountain and flows se into Irish Creek. Named for pioneer Rose family.

Rose Creek rises in central Cherokee County and flows se into Dockery Creek.

Rose Creek rises in se Mitchell County and flows s and nw into North Toe River.

Rose Creek rises in ne Yancey County near Chestnut Mountain and flows n into North Toe River.

Rosedale, community in ne Pasquotank County. Settled prior to 1890.

Rose Hill, town in sw Duplin County. Alt. 89. Settled approx. 1847; inc. 1875. Named for wild roses growing in the vicinity. Produces hogs, lumber, poultry, and wine.

Rose Hill Township, sw Duplin County.

Roseland, community in sw Moore County. Est. around 1896 as a rival resort to Southern Pines and Pinehurst. At one time there were a number of homes there, as well as a hotel, lake, stores, and a weekly newspaper, but now it is only a rural community.

Roseman. *See* Rockett.

Rosemary, former community in n Halifax County, now within the limits of Roanoke Rapids. Served by post office, 1902–32.

Rosemead, community in ne Bertie County served by post office, 1891–1905.

Rosemont. *See* Bertie.

Rose Mountain extends along nw Burke County. Alt. 2,600.

Roseneath, community in s Halifax County served by post office, 1823–51.

Roseneath Township, se Halifax County.

Rose Ridge, a spur of Big Yellow Mountain in

w Avery County. Named for Rose family. Also called Hurricane Ridge.

Roses Branch rises in central Mitchell County and flows w into Toe River.

Roses Branch rises in ne Swain County and flows se into Straight Fork.

Roses Branch rises in ne Yancey County and flows ne into Toe River.

Roses Branch, community in central Mitchell County on Toe River.

Roses Creek rises in nw Burke County and flows se into Irish Creek.

Roses Creek rises in nw McDowell County and flows se between Pompey Ridge and Pups Ridge into Armstrong Creek.

Roses Gap, ne Swain County between Thicket Branch and Roses Branch in Great Smoky Mountains National Park near lat. 35°39′34″ N., long. 83°13′29″ W.

Roseville, community in sw Person County served by post office, 1889–1906. Named for Duncan Rose, local Tory leader during the Revolutionary War.

Rosewood, community in w central Wayne County. Formerly known as Rose. Alt. 133.

Rosindale, community in se Bladen County. Alt. 120. Settled in 1866 by George C. McDougald, who produced turpentine and rosin (from which the name was taken).

Rosin Hill, community in n Sampson County on Sevenmile Swamp. Named for the fact that rosin was produced in the pine forests there.

Roslin, community in s Cumberland County served by post office, 1869–1903. Alt. 179.

Rosman, town in s Transylvania County on French Broad River between its junction with East Fork and North Fork. Named by industrialist J. S. Silverstern, who compounded the word from the names of two associates, Rosenthal and Ormansky. Inc. 1901 as Toxaway; name changed to Estatoe in 1903 and to Rosman in 1905. A NASA satellite-tracking station was built nearby in 1962. Produces lumber. Alt. 2,188.

Ross Creek rises in central Buncombe County near Patton Mountain and flows s into Swannanoa River. Named for an early settler. Often called Chunn Cove Creek.

Rosser, community in ne Lee County.

Ross Falls, former waterfalls (8.1 ft. drop in a distance of 0.9 mi.) in Catawba River a short distance n of the South Carolina state line

in sw Mecklenburg and se Gaston Counties. The site is now under the waters of Lake Wylie.

Rosy, community in s central Transylvania County.

Roten, community in w Ashe County. Alt. approx. 3,050.

Rougemont, community in nw Durham County. Named for nearby Red Mountain. French *rouge* (red) and *mont* (mountain). Alt. 561. Effort to incorporate in 2005 failed.

Rough Branch rises in n Jackson County and flows nw into Hornbuckle Creek.

Rough Butt Bald, on the Jackson-Haywood county line. Alt. 6,010.

Rough Butt Creek rises in e Jackson County and flows nw to join Piney Mountain Creek in forming Caney Fork.

Rough Creek rises in e Haywood County and flows se into Beaverdam Creek.

Rough Fork, w Haywood County in Great Smoky Mountains National Park, is formed by the junction of Bear Branch and Horse Creek near lat. 35°36′10″ N., long. 83°09′43″ W., and flows ne into Palmer Creek.

Rough Fork rises in s Macon County and flows ne into Wayah Creek.

Rough-hew Ridge, n Swain County between Bee Gum Branch and Board Camp Creek in Great Smoky Mountains National Park near lat. 35°30′18″ N., long. 83°32′30″ W., a short spur extending w from Forney Ridge.

Rough Knob, on the Haywood-Madison county line.

Rough Knob, e Macon County between Burgoin Gap and Riley Knob.

Rough Mountain, w Haywood County in Great Smoky Mountains National Park between Low Gap Branch and Big Branch; center near lat. 35°44′27″ N., long. 83°10′ W.

Rough Ridge, e Avery County.

Rough Ridge, w Haywood County in Great Smoky Mountains National Park, a short spur extending se from Mount Sterling Ridge between Andy Branch and Woody Branch; center near lat. 35°40′55″ N., long. 83°07′10″ W.

Rough Run rises in w Jackson County and flows se into West Fork Tuckasegee River.

Rough Run Falls, just above the mouth of Rough Run in w Jackson County.

Roundabout. *See* Ronda.

Roundabout, The. *See* Goldsboro Cooling Pond.

Roundabout Creek rises in w Ashe County and flows se into North Fork New River.

Round Bald, on the Mitchell County, N.C.–Carter County, Tenn., line.

Round Bottom Creek rises in ne Swain County and flows nw into Straight Fork.

Round Cove, ne Cherokee County in the Valley River Mountains.

Round Hill, w central Swain County near the head of Greasy Branch.

Round Hill Branch rises in nw Buncombe County and flows ne through Green Valley into Newfound Creek.

Round Knob, sw McDowell County. Alt. approx. 3,500. The Southern Railway winds around the mountain.

Round Knob, community in s Haywood County between Sam Branch and Inman Branch. Alt. 4,265.

Round Mountain, on the Buncombe-Haywood county line se of Twelve O'clock Top.

Round Mountain, sw Caldwell County. Alt. approx. 1,800.

Round Mountain, n Cherokee County in the Unicoi Mountains.

Round Mountain, se corner of Jackson County between East Fork [Chattooga River] and Whitewater River. Alt. approx. 3,700.

Round Mountain, on the Jackson-Transylvania county line n of the head of West Fork French Broad River and approx. 1½ mi. e of Tuckasegee River. Alt. approx. 4,220. Southernmost peak of Tennessee Ridge, *which see*.

Round Mountain, e Macon County between Deep Gap and Brush Creek.

Round Mountain, ne Mitchell County between Charles Creek and Roan Valley.

Round Mountain, sw Polk County e of Tryon. Site of Battle of Round Mountain between Rangers from both Carolinas under Capt. Thomas Howard and Cherokee Indians under Big Wayah in the spring of 1776. Alt. 1,831. *See also* Skyuka Creek; Skyuka Mountain.

Round Mountain, a ridge in nw Swain County in Great Smoky Mountains National Park. It is a spur extending se in an arc from Twentymile Ridge to Lost Creek, with its center near lat. 35°30′57″ N., long. 83°47′20″ W.

Round Mountain, e central Wilkes County between Camp Branch and the head of Rock Creek.

Round Mountain, community in central Wilkes County served by post office, 1884–1943.

Round Mountain. *See* Roundtop.

Round Mountain Knob, nw Swain County in Great Smoky Mountains National Park at the se end of Round Mountain Ridge near lat. 35°29′43″ N., long. 83°46′38″ W. Alt. 3,033.

Round Peak Mountain, n Surry County between Camp Branch and the head of Little Fisher River. Alt. 2,094.

Round Top, mountain in ne Alexander County; an almost perfect cone. Alt. 1,750.

Round Top, on the Buncombe-Henderson county line.

Round Top, w Cherokee County w of Shoal Creek. Alt. approx. 2,130.

Round Top, on the Cherokee County, N.C.–Monroe County, Tenn., line. Alt. approx. 3,700.

Round Top, on the Graham-Swain county line near the head of Ammons Branch. Alt. 3,080.

Roundtop, mountain in sw Transylvania County n of Horsepasture River. Also known as Round Mountain. Alt. approx. 3,500.

Roundtop Knob, n Swain County in Great Smoky Mountains National Park on Noland Divide. Alt. 5,120.

Round Top Mountain, central Chatham County.

Round Top Mountain, se Clay County n of Sharptop Ridge near the Towns County, Ga., line. Alt. approx. 3,560.

Round Top Mountain, n Madison County between Silvermine Branch and Cascade Branch.

Round Top Mountain, w Rutherford County s of Rumbling Bald Mountain.

Roundtree, community in sw Pitt County served by post office, 1888–1902. Named for Jesse Roundtree (1765–1831), Irish immigrant and soldier in the Revolutionary War who settled there after the war. He served as sheriff from 1818 to 1820.

Rouse Pond, on the head of Grape Branch in n Duplin County.

Rover, community in w Beaufort County served by post office, 1900–1907.

Rowan. *See* Mount Ulla.

Rowan Branch rises in e Sampson County and flows e into Six Runs Creek.

Rowan Branch rises in w Swain County and flows ne into Hazel Creek.

Rowan (ROW-an) County was formed in 1753 from Anson County. Located in the central section of the state, it is bounded by Davidson, Stanly, Cabarrus, Iredell, and Davie Counties. Named for Matthew Rowan (d. 1760), acting governor at the time the county was formed. Area: 527 sq. mi. County seat: Salisbury, with an elevation of 764 ft. Townships are Atwell, China Grove, Cleveland, Franklin, Gold Hill, Litaker, Locke, Morgan, Mount Ulla, Providence, Salisbury, Scotch Irish, Steele, and Unity. Produces corn, wheat, hay, nursery products, tomatoes, oats, cotton, poultry, dairy products, livestock, hogs, refrigeration equipment, bakery products, textiles, rubber products, chemicals, furniture, apparel, industrial machinery, millstones, trucking, taxidermy supplies, concrete products, and crushed stone.

Rowan Creek rises in se Bladen County and flows se into Black River.

Rowan Mills, community on the sw outskirts of city of Salisbury, e central Rowan County.

Row Branch rises in central Avery County and flows n into North Toe River.

Rowell, community in n Davidson County served by post office, 1895–96.

Rowland, town in w Robeson County. Alt. 150. Inc. 1889. Named for Col. Alfred Rowland II, a Confederate officer. Ashpole Presbyterian Church there organized 1796. *See also* Plainview.

Rowland Branch rises in w Macon County and flows nw into Nantahala River.

Rowland Township, sw Robeson County.

Rowlin Creek rises in nw Macon County and flows ne into Nantahala River.

Rowsypock, area w of present town of Kill Devil Hills, e of Little Colington Island in e Dare County.

Roxboro, town and county seat, central Person County. Est. as county seat, 1793. Named for Roxburgh, Scotland. Inc. 1855. Produces lumber, fabricated metals, textiles, processed poultry, and tobacco. Alt. 671.

Roxboro Lake. *See* Carolina Power Lake.

Roxboro Township, central Person County.

Roxobel, town in nw Bertie County. Settled about 1800; inc. 1895. The early settlement was known as Cotten's Cross Roads; around 1808 the name was changed to Granberrys Cross Roads; and in 1816 a post office there was called Brittons Store. Roxobel appears as the post office name in 1847. The name was selected by Frances Norfleet for the popular three-volume novel *Roxobel*, written by Mary Martha Sherwood. The final change was necessary to avoid confusion with Britton's Neck, S.C.

Roxobel Township, nw Bertie County.

Royal, community in se Beaufort County est. 1908 and known first as Dublin for the city in Ireland. Renamed for George E. Royal, a railroad official.

Royal, community in s Franklin County.

Royal Cotton Mills, community in ne Wake County. Named for the mills est. there. Chartered 1907; charter repealed 1943.

Royal Creek, a short stream in n central Carteret County flowing e into South River.

Royal Oak appears on the Price map, 1808, and on the MacRae map, 1833, on the Jones-Onslow county line where a slight change in direction is made. Said to have been named after a British soldier was found hiding in the tree's top to spy on Americans; he was hanged from a limb of the tree. The decayed stump of the tree was removed about 1916 when the road from Richlands to Comfort was widened.

Royal Oak Swamp rises in Green Swamp in central Brunswick County and flows e into Lockwoods Folly River.

Royal Point, on the Pamlico Sound side of Portsmouth Island approx. 3 mi. from Drum Inlet, e Carteret County.

Royal Shoal, in Pamlico Sound in ne Carteret and se Hyde Counties. Extends nw in an arc from Beacon Island and obstructs the passage through Ocracoke Inlet. Appears as Ryals Shoal on the Moseley map, 1733, but by its present name on the Collet map, 1770.

Rozier, community in e Robeson County served by post office, 1888–1902.

Rube Creek rises in n Watauga County and flows sw into Beaverdam Creek.

Rube Green Top, e Mitchell County between Middle Mountain and the Avery County line.

Rube Rock Branch rises in n Haywood County and flows sw into Pigeon River.

Rubicon, community in central Moore County served by post office, 1890–1907.

Rubyatt, community in sw Montgomery County served by post office, 1912–14. Named for H. O. Ruby, early settler of area.

Rudd, community in n Guilford County served by post office, 1902–1907. Alt. 826. Est. 1898 as Sippanaw; later named Morehead. Because of a delay in shipment of merchandise consigned to Morehead City, railroad officials renamed the community to avoid confusion and to honor Senaca and Cicero Rudd, local residents.

Rudisill, community in s Catawba County served by post office, 1894–1903.

Rufe, former town in w Greene County near the head of Fort Run. Inc. 1887 and name changed from Shine. Shine family prominent in the vicinity as early as 1750. A public school near the site operated as Shine School.

Ruffin, community in e Rockingham County. Settled prior to 1860 and known first as Stubblefield for a local family. Name changed to honor Thomas Ruffin (1787–1870), chief justice of the N.C. Supreme Court. Inc. 1887; new charter issued 1891; charter repealed 1897. Alt. 712.

Ruffin's Bridge. *See* Peacock's Bridge.

Ruffin Township, ne Rockingham County.

Rufus, community in nw Caldwell County on Mulberry Creek in Pisgah National Forest. Formerly known as Risden; the present name honors W. Rufus Coffey, a nineteenth-century merchant there.

Rugby, community in n Henderson County on Mill Pond Creek served by post office, 1892–1905.

Ruggles, community in e Halifax County.

Ruin Creek rises in w Vance County and flows s into Tabbs Creek. Appears on the Collet map, 1770.

Rumbling Bald Mountain, nw Rutherford County on a ridge extending se from Shumont Mountain. Alt. approx. 3,020. There are numerous caves in the mountain, and boulders sometimes fall in them, making a rumbling noise. Known by the Cherokee Indians as *Sokassa*. A series of earthquakes occurred there from February 10 until April 17, 1874.

There were between 50 and 75 shocks. *See also* The Caves.

Rumley Bay, a small bay in se Cedar Island, ne Carteret County. Named for the Rumley family.

Rumley Marsh, a tidal-marsh peninsula approx. 1¾ mi. long and ¾ mi. wide on the n shore of Pamlico River s of Jackson Swamp, e Beaufort County. Appears as Rumneys Marsh on the Collet map, 1770.

Rumneys Marsh. *See* Rumley Marsh.

Runaway Knob, on the se end of Runaway Ridge in sw Macon County.

Runaway Ridge, sw Macon County between the head of Allison Creek and the head of Ash Flat Branch.

Run Branch rises in s Lee County and flows ne into Thoroughfare Branch.

Run Hill, sand hill in Kill Devil Hills, e Dare County.

Runion, community in w Madison County on French Broad River approx. 3 mi. e of Hot Springs.

Running Creek rises in w Stanly County and flows ne into Big Bear Creek.

Runnymede, former town in central Edgecombe County. Inc. 1907 as the site of the county fair; charter repealed 1909. The site is now within the limits of Tarboro, and the name survives only as the name of a mill.

Run of Swamp, a canal that drains the Big Pocosin in sw Gates County and empties into Chowan River.

Run of the Mill Pond, a stream that rises in se Duplin County and flows n into Jump and Run Branch.

Run Swamp Canal rises in w Currituck County and flows se into Indiantown Creek. It forms a part of the boundary between Camden and Currituck Counties.

Runyon Creek is formed by the junction of several small unnamed streams ne of Washington, w Beaufort County, and flows s into Pamlico River.

Runyon Creek rises in n Haywood County and flows sw into Pigeon River.

Runyon Gap, n Haywood County on Snowbird Creek.

Runyon Ridge, n Haywood County parallel to Snowbird Creek.

Rural Hall, community in n Forsyth County. Earliest settler apparently was Ludwig

Bitting, former German soldier in Gen. Nathanael Greene's army who liked the area when passing through and returned after the Revolutionary War to settle. Several of his descendants still live in the county. Rural Hall, however, developed after the Cape Fear and Yadkin Valley Railroad erected a station there in 1887. Produces furniture and lumber. Alt. 1,002.

Rush Branch rises in ne Buncombe County and flows se into Broad River.

Rush Branch rises in nw Henderson County and flows ne into North Fork Mills River.

Rush Branch rises in w Watauga County and flows sw into Watauga River.

Rush Creek rises in nw Caldwell County and flows sw into Mulberry Creek.

Rush Fork rises in e Haywood County and flows sw into Crabtree Creek.

Rush Fork Gap, e Haywood County on the head of James Branch.

Rushing, community in se Union County served by post office, 1883–1903.

Rush Mountain, s Henderson County between Huckleberry Ridge and McAlpine Mountain.

Rush Mountain, s Lincoln County. Named for a local family.

Rusk, community in sw Surry County served by post office, 1851–1951.

Ruskin, community in nw Bladen County served by post office, 1902–26.

Russell, community in sw Chatham County.

Russell, community in sw Rowan County served by post office, 1886–1903.

Russellborough, se Brunswick County on the Cape Fear River just n of the location of the former town of Brunswick, site of the home of royal governors Arthur Dobbs and William Tryon. A house there, begun by Capt. John Russell of His Majesty's Sloop *Scorpion*, was purchased in 1758 by Dobbs; renamed Castle Dobbs after his marriage in 1762. At Dobbs's death in 1765, Tryon occupied the house and named it Castle Tryon. When Tryon left the house in 1770, it was purchased by William Dry and renamed Bellfont. It burned in 1776. The site was excavated in 1967 by the N.C. Department of Archives and History, and eighteenth-century artifacts were discovered, many of which are on display at Brunswick State Historic Site.

Russell Branch rises in Union County, Ga., and flows ne into Clay County, where it enters Pinelog Creek.

Russell Gap, on the Alexander-Wilkes county line. Alt. 1,550.

Russell Gap, w Clay County near the headwaters of Trout Cove Branch.

Russells Creek rises in e central Brunswick County and flows e and n into Town Creek.

Russells Creek rises in central Carteret County and flows s into Newport River.

Russellville, community in central Anson County served by post office for six months in 1901.

Russtown, community in sw Brunswick County.

Ruth, community in n Forsyth County served by post office, 1885–1903.

Ruth, town in w central Rutherford County. Inc. 1893 as Hampton. Named for S. D. Hampton, first mayor. Name changed to Ruth (first part of the county name) in 1906.

Rutherford College, former town and college in e Burke County. The school was founded by R. L. Abernathy in 1853, and the 400-acre site was inc. as village of Excelsior in 1872; inc. as town of Rutherford College in 1881. Alt. 1,210. The school merged with Weaver College in 1932 and was moved to Brevard, *which see*, and renamed Brevard College. Town charter repealed in 1933. Now a residential community approx. 2 mi. e of town of Valdese. Named for John Rutherford, who donated the land for the school in 1853. Original post office, 1857–86, was named Happy Home; it also served Connelly Springs, *which see*.

Rutherford County was formed in 1779 from Tryon County when it was divided to form Rutherford and Lincoln Counties. Located in the sw section of the state, it is bounded by the state of South Carolina and by Polk, Henderson, Buncombe, McDowell, Burke, and Cleveland Counties. It was named for Griffith Rutherford (1731–1800), leader of 1776 expedition against the Cherokee, member of the Provincial Congress, and Revolutionary

War general. Area: 568 sq. mi. County seat: Rutherfordton, with an elevation of 1,096 ft. Townships are Camp Creek, Chimney Rock, Colfax, Cool Spring, Duncans Creek, Gilkey, Golden Valley, Green Hill, High Shoals, Logan Store, Morgan, Rutherfordton, Sulphur Springs, and Union. Produces corn, wheat, oats, cotton, hay, soybeans, boats, dairy products, livestock, hogs, textiles, apparel, lumber, sand, and gravel.

Rutherfords Mill. *See* Exeter.

Rutherfordton, town and county seat, w central Rutherford County. Served by post office since 1798. Est. 1787. Alt. 1,096. Town and county named for Gen. Griffith Rutherford (1731–1800), Revolutionary War leader. *See also* Gilbert Town; Mountain Creek.

Rutherfordton Township, central Rutherford County.

Rutherwood, community in e Watauga County s of South Fork New River.

Rutledge Creek rises in ne Surry County and flows se into Ararat River.

Ryan, community in n Robeson County served by post office, 1888–1902.

Ryders Pond, e Warren County on Little Fishing Creek. Covers approx. 10 acres, with a max. depth of 4 ft.

Rye Mountain, e Jackson County on the head of Flat Creek. Alt. 4,542.

Rye Patch Branch rises in nw Swain County and flows se into Twentymile Creek.

Rye Ridge, w Avery County.

Ryes, community in w Harnett County.

Rye Swamp rises in w Sampson County and flows sw into Little Coharie Creek.

Ryland, community in n Chowan County. Site of an early Quaker settlement. Post office est. there 1888 and named for a railroad official.

S

Saconon, community in e Henderson County on Little Hungry Creek served by post office, 1913–23.

Saddleback, ridge in nw Swain County in Great Smoky Mountains National Park between Roaring Creek and Desolation Branch.

Its center is near lat. 35°33′26″ N., long. 83°40′48″ W.

Saddle Gap, n Transylvania County between Looking Glass Creek and Avery Creek.

Saddle Mountain, on the Alleghany-Surry county line.

Saddle Mountain Creek rises in w Surry County and flows se into Mitchell River.

Saddle Tree Gap, w Graham County between the headwaters of Hangover Creek and Deep Creek.

Saddletree Swamp rises in n Robeson County and flows s into Lumber River.

Saddletree Township, central Robeson County.

Sadler, community in e Rockingham County served by post office, 1898–1910.

Safe, community in sw Duplin County served by post office, 1888–1903. Name derived from the fact that the first postmaster, Jacob Carr, operated a store and therein had a large safe, the only one in the area.

Sag Branch rises in w Haywood County and flows nw into Caldwell Fork.

Sage Path, site of early settlement on the e end of Bogue Banks, s Carteret County. Storms drove out early settlers until the settlement of Salter Path, *which see*.

Sage Rock, peak in w Yancey County on Sevenmile Ridge near the head of Murphy Branch.

Sages Ordinary. *See* Holly Ridge.

Saginaw. *See* Pineola.

Sago, community in central Mecklenburg County served by post office, 1891–1902.

Sahara of North Carolina. *See* Sandhills.

Sahlee Creek rises in n Swain County and flows se into Deep Creek.

Sains, community in w Lincoln County served by post office, 1886–1905.

St. Andrew's Parish, Church of England, Tyrrell County, est. 1729 with the formation of the county and coextensive with it. Previous to the formation of the county, the territory had been South Shore Parish (est. 1722), Chowan County. In 1767 St. Andrew's Parish had 594 white taxables. *See also* St. Paul's Parish.

St. Asaph's District, one of the districts into which Orange County was divided at the time of the 1790 census. It contained 199 heads of families.

St. Barnabas' Parish, Church of England, Hertford County, est. 1759 with the formation of the county and coextensive with it. The parish in 1767 had 900 white taxables.

St. Bartholomew's Parish, Church of England, Chatham County, est. with the formation of the county in 1770 and coextensive with it. St. Bartholomew's Parish of the Episcopal Church still functions in Pittsboro.

St. Clair Creek rises in Jackson Swamp, e Beaufort County, and flows se into Pamlico River.

St. Colomb Parish. *See* Donegal County.

St. David's District, one of the districts into which Caswell County was divided at the time of the 1790 census. It contained 166 heads of families.

St. David's Parish, Church of England, Cumberland County, est. 1754 with the formation of the county and coextensive with it. In 1767 the parish had 899 white taxables, described as "mostly Scotch—Support a Presbyterian Minister."

St. Gabriel's Parish, Church of England, Duplin County, est. 1750 with the formation of the county and coextensive with it. In 1767 there were 1,071 white taxables in the parish. St. Gabriel's Parish of the Episcopal Church functions in Faison at present, though there is some question of its unbroken descent from the colonial parish.

St. George's Parish, Church of England, Anson County, est. in 1750 when the county was formed and coextensive with it. Composed of 969 white taxable inhabitants in 1767, who were described as "in general poor & incapable to support a Minister."

St. George's Parish, Church of England, Northampton County, est. 1758 when Northwest Parish was divided. The w part became St. George's and, after 1759, when the e part of Northampton became a part of Hertford County, the parish was coextensive with the county. In 1767 there were 1,600 white taxables living in the parish. Records of St. George's Parish, 1773–1814, are in the North Carolina State Archives, Raleigh.

St. George's Parish. *See* Hyde Parish.

St. Helena, community in central Pender County. Alt. 55. Settled 1908 by a colony of Italian farmers. Saint Helena (d. about 330) was the mother of Constantine the Great, Roman emperor. Hugh MacRae, Wilmington entrepreneur, developed the community as an agricultural colony for immigrants.

St. James District, one of the districts into which Caswell County was divided at the time of the 1790 census. It contained 111 heads of families.

St. James' Parish, Church of England, New Hanover County, probably est. in 1729 with the creation of the county and coextensive with it. The parish is mentioned as early as 1734. In 1741 St. James's Parish was divided to form St. Philip's Parish on the s side of the Cape Fear River. With the creation of Brunswick County in 1764, St. Philip's Parish became coextensive with it and St. James's Parish with New Hanover. St. James' Parish of the Episcopal Church still functions in Wilmington.

St. Johns, community in sw Hertford County at the head of Chapel Branch. Mentioned in local records as early as 1722. Douglas Ordinary appears on the Collet map, 1770, at the site.

St. Johns, community in s Pitt County.

St. John's Parish, Church of England, Carteret County, probably was est. with the formation of the county in 1722. It is mentioned as early as 1724. Coextensive with the county. In 1767 there were 470 white taxables in the parish. The vestry book of St. John's Parish, 1742–43, in 3 volumes, is in the North Carolina State Archives, Raleigh.

St. John's Parish, Church of England, Granville (later Bute) County, est. in 1746 with the formation of Granville County. Coextensive with the county. In 1758 the parish was divided, creating Granville Parish in the w; St. John's Parish was in the e. Bute County, created in 1764, and the parish were coextensive. In 1767 there were 1,299 white taxables in St. John's Parish. Warren and Franklin Counties were formed from Bute County in 1779.

St. John's Parish, Church of England, Onslow County, was est. in 1734 with the formation of the county and coextensive with it. In 1767 the parish had 716 white taxables described as "willing to receive tho' hardly capable of making provisions for Minister."

St. John's Parish, Church of England, Pasquotank County, est. in 1701. In 1715 the parish was divided, leaving St. John's on the sw side of the Pasquotank River and creating St. Peter's Parish on the ne side. In 1756 the two parishes were consolidated to form St. John's

Parish. In 1767 the parish had 433 white taxables and was described as a "weak parish."

St. Johns Township, sw Hertford County.

St. Jude's Parish, Church of England, Surry
County, est. 1771 with the formation of the
county and coextensive with it.

St. Lawrence District, one of the districts into
which Caswell County was divided at the time
of the 1790 census. It contained 215 heads of
families.

St. Lewis, town in s Edgecombe County served
by post office, 1886–1904. Inc. 1895, but not
now active in municipal affairs. Named for
first postmaster, John I. Lewis.

St. Lukes District, one of the districts into which
Caswell County was divided at the time of
the 1790 census. It contained 137 heads of
families.

St. Luke's Parish, Church of England, Rowan
County, est. 1753 with the formation of the
county and coextensive with it. In 1767 the
parish had 3,000 white taxables. Dobbs
Parish, organized by the Moravians in the
Wachovia settlement, was created from St.
Luke's Parish in 1755. St. Luke's Parish of the
Episcopal Church still functions in Salisbury.

St. Margaret's Parish, Church of England, Wake
County, est. with the formation of the county
in 1770 and coextensive with it. (The parish probably was named for Saint Margaret
because the county was named for Margaret
Wake, wife of Governor William Tryon.)

St. Mark's District, one of the districts into
which Orange County was divided at the time
of the 1790 census. It contained 138 heads of
families.

St. Martin, community in s Stanly County between Big Bear Creek and Little Bear Creek.
Named for a local Lutheran church.

St. Martin's Parish, Church of England, Bladen
County, est. in 1734 when the county was
formed and coextensive with the county.
The parish had 791 white taxables in
1767, described as being "in middling
circumstances."

St. Martin's Parish, Church of England, Martin
County, est. 1774 with the formation of the
county and coextensive with it.

St. Martin's Parish, Church of England, Mecklenburg County, est. 1762 with the formation of the county and coextensive with it.
The parish in 1767 had 1,600 white taxables,

described as "mostly Presbyterians." St.
Martin's Episcopal Church still exists in
Charlotte.

St. Mary's District, one of the districts into
which Orange County was divided at the time
of the 1790 census. It contained 237 heads of
families.

St. Mary's Parish, Church of England, Edgecombe County, est. 1756 by the division of
the Parish of Edgecombe. St. Mary's Parish
was in the s and the Parish of Edgecombe in
the n. With the creation of Halifax County
from Edgecombe County in 1758, the Parish
of Edgecombe (est. 1741 with the formation
of Edgecombe County) became coextensive
with the new county. St. Mary's Parish then
became coextensive with Edgecombe County.
In 1767 St. Mary's Parish had 1,200 white
taxables.

St. Marys Township, e Wake County.

St. Matthew's Parish, Church of England, Orange County, est. in 1752 with the formation
of the county and coextensive with it. In 1767
the parish had 3,573 white taxables, making
it the most populous parish in the colony. Reestablished in 1824, St. Matthew's Parish of
the Episcopal Church continues to function
in Hillsborough.

St. Matthews Township, e central Wake County.

St. Michael's Parish, Church of England, Pitt
County, est. 1760 with the formation of the
county and coextensive with it. In 1767 the
parish had 775 white taxables and was described as a "small county—willing to make
provision for a Minister."

St. Patrick's Parish, Church of England, Johnston (later Dobbs) County, est. 1746 with the
formation of Johnston County. It was coextensive with the county but divided in 1756 to
form St. Stephen's Parish in the w part of the
county. St. Patrick's was in the e. With the creation of Dobbs County in 1758, St. Patrick's
Parish became coextensive with that county.
In 1767 the parish had 1,268 white taxables.
The present counties of Wayne, Lenoir, and
Greene are made up wholly or in part of territory that was once St. Patrick's Parish.

St. Pauls, town in ne Robeson County. Inc.
1909. Named for local Presbyterian church.
Post office est. there in 1832 was named
Tutons for first postmaster Oliver Tuton;
changed to St. Pauls about 4 years later.

Originally the settlement centered on a stage depot on the Fayetteville-Lumberton road about 3 mi. from present site. When the railroad came through about 1900, the settlement drifted s to center around the depot. Produces textiles.

St. Paul's Parish, Church of England, Chowan County, est. in 1701. In 1715 the parish was divided to create South West Parish in the w part of the county. The area became Bertie County in 1722, and coextensive with it was Society Parish. In 1722 St. Paul's Parish was further divided to create South Shore Parish in the s part of the county on the s shore of Albemarle Sound. With the creation of Tyrrell County in 1729, South Shore Parish became St. Andrew's Parish, coextensive with the county. In 1767 St. Paul's Parish had 900 white taxables. St. Paul's Parish of the Episcopal Church still functions in Edenton. St. Paul's Church there was begun in 1736.

St. Pauls Township, ne Robeson County.

St. Peter's Parish. *See* St. John's Parish.

St. Philip's Parish, Church of England, New Hanover, later Brunswick County, est. in 1741 when St. James' Parish, *which see*, was divided. St. Philip's Parish was that part of the county s of the Cape Fear River. With the creation of Brunswick County in 1764, St. Philip's Parish became coextensive with the new county. The parish had 224 white taxable inhabitants in 1767, described as being "mostly Gentlemen." The ruins of St. Philip's Church, completed in 1765, begun a number of years earlier, still stand near Orton Plantation, Brunswick County, at the site of the old town of Brunswick.

St. Stephen's Parish, Church of England, Johnston County, est. 1756 in the w part of the county upon the division of St. Patrick's Parish. When Dobbs County was formed from Johnston County in 1758, St. Patrick's became coextensive with the new county. St. Stephen's Parish then was coextensive with Johnston County. In 1767 the parish had 1,229 white taxables, described as "able to make provision for a minister."

St. Thomas District, one of the districts into which Orange County was divided at the time of the 1790 census. It contained 139 heads of families.

St. Thomas' Parish, Church of England, Beaufort County, organized 1701. St. Thomas' Church in Bath (oldest church building in North Carolina) was constructed in 1734. The parish had 110 white taxables in 1767. St. Thomas' Parish of the Episcopal Church still functions in Bath.

St. Thomas Parish, Church of England, Tryon County, est. 1768 with the formation of the county and coextensive with it. In 1767 the parish was described as "too unsettled to make provision for a Minister."

Sa-koh-na-gas. *See* Blue Ridge Mountains.

Saldeer Gap, n Macon County between Burningtown Creek and Rose Creek.

Salem, community in se Burke County.

Salem, formerly an independent city in central Forsyth County; inc. 1856, but since 1913 consolidated with Winston as Winston-Salem, *which see*. Salem was laid out and settled in 1766 by Moravians; its name, meaning "peace," is said to have been selected by Count Nikolaus Zinzendorf, patron and leader of the Moravian Church, prior to his death in 1760. Records of the Moravians from 1752 to 1876 have been published in 10 volumes. Old Salem has been largely restored as a living history museum, with shops, homes, a tavern (where George Washington was entertained in 1791), and other buildings open to the public.

Salem, community in s Lincoln County.

Salem, community in n Randolph County. Authorized to be laid off as New Salem, 1818; inc. 1831, but long inactive in municipal affairs. Came to be known as Salem after 1882. Long the site of a popular camp meeting in the summer.

Salem, community in n Surry County between Lovills Creek and Ararat River.

Salemburg, town in w Sampson County. Settled about 1870. Inc. 1905 and took its name from Salem Academy, est. there by Rev. Isham Royal in 1874. The academy developed into Pineland College and Edwards Military Institute, which merged in 1965 to form Southwood College; it closed in 1973.

Salem Chapel. *See* Dennis.

Salem Chapel Township, ne Forsyth County.

Salem Church, community in sw Randolph County served by post office, 1840–1918.

Salem Creek rises in e Forsyth County and flows sw through the city of Winston-Salem into

Muddy Creek in the sw corner of the county. Appears as Wack Creek on the Collet map, 1770; as "Middle Watch Creek" on the Price map, 1808; and finally as Middle Fork on the MacRae map, 1833. Known as Middle Fork or Middle Fork Muddy Creek until 1966, when the present name was adopted. Wack and Watch undoubtedly are derived from the name Wachovia, *which see.*

Salem Creek. *See* Niggerhead Creek.

Salem Lake, ne Forsyth County, is fed by Lowery Mill Creek, Kerners Mill Creek, and other streams. Formed 1942. Covers 400 acres, with a max. depth of 35 ft. Source of water for Winston-Salem.

Salem Township, e central Granville County.

Salem Township, s Pasquotank County.

Sales Branch rises in central Cherokee County and flows nw into Valley River.

Sales Ford, community in central Cherokee County on Valley River.

Salisbury, city and county seat, e central Rowan County. Est. 1755. Presumably named for the town in England but possibly for the town in Maryland, the point of origin of some of the earliest settlers in Rowan County. Catawba and Livingstone Colleges are there. Produces textiles, processed food, corrugated boxes, furniture, chemicals, machinery, structural steel, and wire cloth. Alt. 764.

Salisbury District, at the time of the 1790 census, was composed of Guilford, Iredell, Mecklenburg, Montgomery, Rockingham, Rowan, Stokes, and Surry Counties.

Salisbury Township, e Rowan County.

Salisbury West, unincorporated outskirts of city of Salisbury, e central Rowan County.

Sally Archer Crossroads, community in se Hertford County.

Sally Branch rises in e Franklin County and flows n into Lick Meadow Branch.

Sally Branch rises in e Haywood County and flows sw into Fines Creek.

Sally Cove Branch rises in nw Macon County and flows n into Whiteoak Creek.

Sally Gap, s Swain County between Yalaka Creek and Little Yalaka Creek.

Sally Haines Branch rises in e Haywood County and flows n into Pigeon River.

Sally Mountain, e Madison County between Middle Fork and Ponder Creek.

Sally Queen Creek rises in ne Rutherford County

near the Burke County line and flows sw into North Fork.

Sally's Creek rises in w Caldwell County and flows se into Johns River.

Salmon Creek rises in e Bertie County and flows se into Chowan River. Appears as Flatt's Creek on the Comberford map, 1657, but as Salmon Creek on the Ogilby map, 1671. Probably named for an early settler. Area known as "Seedbed of the Colony" due to residence of early settlers, such as Nathaniel Batts, and leaders, such as Charles Eden, royal governor.

Salmon Creek. *See* Southwest Creek.

Salola. *See* Sugarloaf Mountain.

Salola Branch rises in n Swain County s of Clingmans Dome and flows se into Noland Creek. *Salola* was the Cherokee Indian word for squirrel.

Sal Patch Gap, w Haywood County in Great Smoky Mountains National Park near lat. 35°38′24″ N., long. 83°03′28″ W.

Sals Creek rises in s Transylvania County and flows ne into Glady Fork.

Sal's Creek rises in central Wake County and flows ne into Crabtree Creek.

Salser Branch rises in central Macon County and flows e into McDowell Branch.

Salt Branch rises in s Onslow County and flows e into Chadwick Bay.

Salter Creek rises in ne Carteret County and flows se into Nelson Bay.

Salter Path, community near the center of Bogue Banks, s Carteret County. Settlement begun about 1900 on property owned by John A. Royall of Boston, Mass. A court judgment in 1923 restricted the settlement to 84 acres and declared that only persons then resident at Salter Path and their descendants could occupy the land. *See also* Rice Path.

Salters Lake, a natural lake in central Bladen County on Ellis Creek 6 mi. n of Elizabethtown. Covers 315 acres, with a max. depth of 10 ft. State owned and open to the public. Fishing, swimming, and boating. Part of Jones Lake State Park, *which see.*

Salters Lumps, two small islands in Brett Bay off Piney Point, ne Carteret County.

Salton Gap, n Buncombe County between North Knob and Grassy Knob.

Saltrock Branch rises in ne Buncombe County and flows se into North Fork [Swannanoa River].

Saltrock Branch rises in se Macon County and flows nw into Cullasaja River.

Saltrock Gap, s Macon County on Tennessee Valley Divide.

Salt Rock Gap, s Yancey County on Buncombe Horse Range Ridge.

Saluda, town in sw Polk County. Settled 1878 after the construction of the railroad. Inc. 1881. Took its name from the Indian word *salutah* (corn river). Alt. 2,097.

Saluda Mountain, s Henderson County along the South Carolina state line. Approx. 5 mi. long.

Saluda Township, sw Polk County.

Salvage Island. *See* Core Banks.

Salvo, community on Hatteras Island, e Dare County. Formerly known as Clarks or Clarksville.

Salyer's Bay. *See* Sulliers Bay.

Samarcand, community in w Moore County. Named in 1916 by Raphael W. Pumpelly Jr. for the town in Asia Minor, which he had visited in his travels. A state home and industrial school for girls opened there in 1918. Alt. 698.

Samaria, community in sw Nash County served by post office, 1902–1907. Named for local Baptist church.

Sam Branch rises in central Cherokee County and flows nw into Valley River.

Sam Branch rises in s Haywood County and flows nw into West Fork Pigeon River.

Sam Branch rises in s Haywood County and flows se into Nick Creek.

Sam Cove, nw Graham County on Deep Creek.

Sam Doane Mountain, on Madison-Yancey County line between Moore Gap and Paint Gap. Named for an early settler.

Sam Gap, se Buncombe County between Flint Knob and Round Mountain.

Sam Knob, s Haywood County between Sam Branch and Flat Laurel Creek. Alt. 6,030.

Sam Newton Branch rises in central Cherokee County and flows nw into Valley River.

Sampson, community in n central Caldwell County on the headwaters of the Yadkin River near Blowing Rock.

Sampson Branch rises in n Yancey County and flows se into Jacks Creek. Named for Sampson Honeycutt, an early settler who died and was buried nearby about 1891.

Sampson County was formed in 1784 from Duplin County. Located in the e section of the state, it is bounded by Wayne, Duplin, Pender, Bladen, Cumberland, Johnston, and Harnett Counties. It was named for Col. John Sampson (d. 1784), member of the House of Commons and the governor's council under royal governors Dobbs, Tryon, and Martin. Area: 963 sq. mi. County seat: Clinton, with an elevation of 158 ft. Townships are Belvoir, Dismal, Franklin, Hales, Herrings, Honeycutts, Lisbon, Little Coharie, McDaniels, Mingo, Newton Grove, North Clinton, Piney Grove, Plain View, South Clinton, South River, Taylors Bridge, Turkey, and Westbrook. Produces corn, soybeans, wheat, oats, hay, peanuts, tobacco, cotton, cucumbers, pepper, squash, watermelons, cantaloupe, collards, honey, nursery products, miscellaneous vegetables and fruit, poultry, hogs, livestock, turkeys, sweet potatoes, lumber, processed meat, electronics, apparel, concrete products, and textiles.

Sampson Creek rises in s Catawba County and flows ne into Pott Creek.

Sampson Gap, ne Transylvania County ne of Sharpy Mountain near the Haywood County line.

Sampson Gap, w Yancey County on Sampson Mountain near the head of Simms Fork.

Sampson Mountain, se Watauga County. Alt. 4,716.

Sampson Mountain, w Yancey County, extends se from the head of Simms Fork to Slickrock Knob. Alt. 4,826 at Sampson Peak on the mountain.

Sampson Point, s Currituck County e of community of Point Harbor, extends into Albemarle Sound. Shown on U.S. Coast Survey map, 1865.

Sampson's Chimney, rock formation on Howard Knob, central Watauga County.

Sams Branch rises in sw Buncombe County near Twelve O'clock Top and flows w into South Hominy Creek.

Sams Branch rises in w Mitchell County and flows sw into Nolichucky River.

Sams Branch rises in w Pitt County and flows ne into Tar River.

Sams Gap, on the Madison County, N.C.–Unicoi County, Tenn., line.

Sams Gap, on the Swain County, N.C.–Sevier County, Tenn., line in Great Smoky Mountains National Park near lat. 35°34′02″ N., long. 83°38′12″ W.

Samuel, community in se Surry County served by post office, 1894–1905.

Samuel Creek. *See* Hayward Creek.

Sanatorium. *See* McCain.

Sandbank Creek rises in w Avery County and flows sw into Roaring Creek.

Sandbank Ridge, w Avery County.

Sandbluff, community in central Bladen County.

Sand Branch rises in se Buncombe County and flows s into Broad River.

Sand Creek rises in se Granville County and flows n into Tar River.

Sanders Creek rises in w Carteret County and flows s into Goose Creek. Appears as Smiths Creek on the Moseley map, 1733.

Sanders Creek, a tidal inlet on the n side of Bogue Sound approx. 2 mi. w of Broad Creek, w Carteret County. It is formed by the junction of Sikes Branch and East Prong.

Sanders Creek, e Onslow County, flows from the n of Queens Creek sw into the mouth of Bear Creek. Mentioned in local records as early as 1744.

Sanders Island, e Onslow County in Brown's Sound between the mouths of Bear and Sanders Creeks.

Sanders Knob, on McDowell Branch in central Macon County.

Sanders Knob, s Macon County between Shope Fork and North Fork Coweeta Creek.

Sanderson Fish Pond, on a tributary of Cabin Creek in e central Duplin County.

Sanderson's Channel. *See* Roanoke Sound.

Sanders Point, w Carteret County, extends into Bogue Sound w of the mouth of Goose Creek.

Sand Flat Mountain, n Henderson County between Garren Mountain and Hooper Creek.

Sand Hill, community in central Buncombe County served by post office, 1873–74.

Sandhill, community in n Pamlico County.

Sand Hill Cove, e Pender County on Northeast Cape Fear River.

Sand Hill Creek rises in e central Brunswick County and flows ne into Cape Fear River.

Sandhills, a series of rolling hills between the Cape Fear and Pee Dee Rivers covering portions of Richmond, Scotland, Moore, Cumberland, and Harnett Counties. Includes approx. 1,110 sq. mi. The surrounding area is approx. 600 ft. above sea level, but, within the Sandhills, there are ridges rising 300 to 400 ft. higher. Little River, Drowning Creek, and Rockfish Creek are the principal streams. Coarse sandy soil is characteristic of the area. The Basset map, 1676, marks the area "Deserta Arenosa." It has also been called Deserta Montana, Sandy Barrens, Pine Barrens, and the Sahara of North Carolina. William Hooper, in a letter of June 15, 1779, to James Iredell, used the term sandhills. The climate of the region has been classed as "Humid Subtropical," and it has an average annual temperature of approx. 61.5°. The area was settled by Scottish Highlanders beginning about 1740. They found the region covered by a stand of longleaf pines ranging in height from 100 to 120 ft. and with diameters up to 36 inches. Beneath the pines, wire grass covered the ground. Most of the pines were cut between 1875 and 1895 (for an exception, *see* Weymouth Woods Sandhills Nature Preserve), and the region is now covered with smaller longleaf pines, scrub oak (chiefly Turkey and Black Jack), and wire grass. Extensive peach orchards have flourished in the Sandhills since 1892. The resort towns of Pinehurst and Southern Pines, *which see*, have developed there.

Sandhills Township, s Moore County.

Sand Hill Township, e Lenoir County.

Sandifer, community in central Mecklenburg County served by post office, 1885–1909.

Sand Mountain, w Caldwell County. Alt. 1,500.

Sand Point, ne Carteret County, extends from w side of central Cedar Island into West Bay.

Sand Point, on nw shore of Roanoke Island, extends w into Croatan Sound, ne Dare County.

Sands, community in e central Watauga County between Howard Creek and Meat Camp Creek.

Sandy Barrens. *See* Sandhills.

Sandy Bay, in the waters of Pamlico Sound off the se mainland of Dare County between Sandy Point on the n and Parched Corn Point on the s.

Sandy Bay, a bay in the waters of Pamlico Sound off the coast of Hatteras Island, se Dare County. It lies between Durant Point, near the town of Hatteras, and Frisco.

Sandy Bottom, a sandy strip approx. ½ mi. long along the w bank of French Broad River in s Buncombe County between Bent Creek and Orton Branch.

Sandy Bottom, community in w Lenoir County. The site is mentioned by name in local records beginning in the 1760s. In December 1862 invading Union forces gave the more sophisticated name Sandy Foundation to the community, and a post office there bore the name, 1847–82. Also known as Sandy Ridge during the Civil War.

Sandy Bottom, community in w Madison County on French Broad River served by post office, 1887–1911.

Sandy Branch rises in e Mitchell County and flows se into Cane Creek.

Sandy Branch rises in s Stokes County and flows se into Town Fork Creek.

Sandy Creek rises near Buckingham Mountain in sw Alamance County and flows n into Rock Creek.

Sandy Creek rises in e Cumberland County and flows e into South River.

Sandy Creek rises in w Davidson County and flows nw into Hartleys Creek.

Sandy Creek rises in central Durham County and flows sw into New Hope Creek.

Sandy Creek rises in central Granville County and flows se into Redbud Creek in Nash County.

Sandy Creek rises in ne Randolph County and flows sw into Deep River.

Sandy Creek rises in se Vance County and flows se across Warren and Franklin Counties and into Nash County, where, in Hilliardston community, the name is changed to Swift Creek, *which see.*

Sandy Creek, community in ne Randolph County served by post office, 1884–1906. Sandy Creek Baptist Church there was founded in 1755. There, in 1766, the first attempt was made to organize the Regulators.

Sandy Creek Township, former township in n Franklin County, now township no. 6.

Sandy Creek Township, se Vance County.

Sandy Creek Township, sw Warren County.

Sandycross, community in se Gates County served by post office, 1884–1906.

Sandy Cross, crossroads community in s Nash County. Named because of sandy soil in the vicinity.

Sandy Cross, community in central Rockingham County; center of productive tobacco country.

Sandy Foundation. *See* Sandy Bottom.

Sandy Gap, central Cherokee County between West Prong Grape Creek and Rose Creek.

Sandy Gap, ne Cherokee County in the Snowbird Mountains.

Sandy Gap, nw Cherokee County in the Unicoi Mountains.

Sandy Gap, sw Cherokee County near the headwaters of Buck Creek.

Sandy Gap, on the McDowell-Mitchell county line.

Sandy Gap, n Transylvania County near the head of Cedar Rock Creek.

Sandy Gap Branch rises in w Swain County on Welch Ridge and flows nw into Hazel Creek.

Sandy Grove, community in se Hoke County served by post office, 1826–96.

Sandy Huss Creek rises in n Carteret County and flows approx. 1 mi. sw into Adams Creek on the Craven County line. Perhaps named for the fish, *amiatus calva*, a dogfish sometimes also known as huss.

Sandy Inlet, former inlet between Topsail Sound and Atlantic Ocean, se Pender County. Appears on the Moseley map, 1733; closed soon after 1775.

Sandy John Ridge, n Haywood County between Big Creek and Pigeon River.

Sandy Landing, se Beaufort County on the w side of South Creek.

Sandy Mush, community in nw Buncombe County near the junction of Clark Branch and Sandy Mush Creek. Took its name from the creek.

Sandy Mush, community in s Rutherford County near the head of Holland Creek.

Sandy Mush Bald, on Newfound Mountain at the junction of Buncombe, Haywood, and Madison county lines. Alt. 5,152. Took its name from the nearby creek.

Sandy Mush Creek rises near Wade Gap in nw

Buncombe County and flows ne into French Broad River, forming a part of the Buncombe-Madison county line. Named by an early hunting party when sand from the creek water got into the mush they were cooking for supper.

Sandy Mush Township, w Buncombe County.

Sandy Mush Township, former township in sw Madison County, now township no. 6.

Sandy Plains, community in s Polk County served by post office, 1887–94.

Sandy Point appears on the Gascoyne map, 1682, as the point of land presently in se Bertie County between Salmon Creek and Roanoke River. It also appears on the Hack map, 1684.

Sandy Point extends from the n mainland of Carteret County into Neuse River.

Sandy Point, point of s Chowan County extending into Albemarle Sound. Appears on the Hack map, 1684, and the Moseley map, 1733.

Sandy Point extends from the mainland of s Dare County into Pamlico Sound. It separates Sandy Bay on the s from Stumpy Point Bay on the n. Appears on the Moseley map, 1733.

Sandy Point extends e from the mainland of ne Tyrrell County into Alligator River. Shown on the Price map, 1808. State-operated ferry from the point to East Lake Landing in nw Dare County replaced by the Lindsay C. Warren Bridge, 2.83 mi. long and opened in May 1962; named for Lindsay C. Warren (1889–1976), U.S. congressman and comptroller general.

Sandy Point, community on Morse Point in ne Currituck County.

Sandy Ridge, community in n Stokes County near Buffalo Creek.

Sandy Ridge. *See* Sandy Bottom.

Sandy Ridge Township, w Union County.

Sandy River. *See* First Broad River.

Sandy Run rises in s Cumberland County and flows se into Rockfish Creek.

Sandy Run rises in ne Duplin County and flows se on the Duplin-Wayne county line until it enters Northeast Cape Fear River.

Sandy Run rises in n Greene County and flows se into Middle Swamp. Appears on the Collet map, 1770. Known as Horn Swamp until some time between 1760 and 1767.

Sandy Run rises in s Moore County and flows sw into Deep Creek.

Sandy Run rises in se Northampton County and flows se into Roanoke River. For a part of its course, it forms the boundary between Northampton and Bertie Counties. Mentioned in local records as early as 1722.

Sandy Run Branch rises in n Duplin County and flows sw into Northeast Cape Fear River.

Sandy Run Creek rises in central Burke County and flows n into Hunting Creek.

Sandy Run Creek rises in e Rutherford County and flows se into Cleveland County, where it enters Broad River.

Sandy Run Swamp rises in w Onslow County and flows sw into Pender County, where it enters Holly Shelter Creek.

Sandy Run Township, former township in sw Cleveland County, now township no. 7.

Sandy Springs, community in sw Rutherford and se Polk Counties. A post office operated there, 1876–1908.

Sanford, city and county seat, central Lee County. Laid out about 1872. Inc. 1874. Said to have been named for Col. C. O. Sanford, engineer for the Chatham Railroad. Jonesboro, *which see*, merged with Sanford in 1947. Produces bricks, pottery, lumber, electrical parts, primary metals, sheet-metal working, apparel, industrial machinery, furniture, insecticides, and cosmetics. Alt. 375.

Sans Souci, community in se Bertie County. The name of an early plantation, which in French means "without care or worry." Long site of cable-drawn ferry.

Santeetlah, community in central Graham County on Santeetlah Lake. The former post office there, 1906–30, was called Millsaps.

Santeetlah Creek rises in w Graham County and flows e into Santeetlah Lake. Name said to have meant "blue waters" in Cherokee, but Mooney's glossary says the Indians did not recognize or understand the name, insisting it was given to the creek by white men. They called the creek *Nayuhi geyuni* (sandplace stream), and Little Santeetlah Creek was known by them as *Tsundaniltiyi*.

Santeetlah Gap, w central Graham County approx. ¾ mi. w of Funnel Top.

Santeetlah Lake, central Graham County, was formed in 1928 by a dam on Cheoah River. Covers 2,580 acres, with a shoreline of 105 mi. Max. depth 240 ft. Alt. 1,940. Used for power, fishing, and boating.

Santeetlah Wildlife Management Area, in w Graham County. 37,168 acres, operated by the state of North Carolina on U.S. Forest Service lands. Principal wildlife: bear, boar, deer, raccoon, and trout.

Sapling Mountain, n Madison County between Shelton Laurel Creek and Spillcorn Creek.

Sapona, community in sw Davidson County served by post office, 1885–1903.

Sapona River. *See* Yadkin River.

Sapony Creek rises in w Nash County and flows se into Tar River. Probably named for a stopping place of the Saponi Indians as they moved from the Yadkin River area in the w soon after 1701 to join the Tuscarora in the e.

Sapphire, community in sw Transylvania County s of Horsepasture River. Named because sapphires are found in the vicinity or for the vivid blue of the sky and water.

Sapphire Country, a descriptive name applied to the area around Fairfield, Sapphire, and Toxaway Lakes in s Jackson and w Transylvania Counties. It probably came into use in commercial promotion for Mountain Lodge, Fairfield Inn, and Sapphire Inn about 1898. Name derived from the blue of the mountains as well as sapphire gems found in the area.

Sapphire Lake, s Jackson County on Horsepasture River and Nix Creek. Formed by 1916; covers 50 acres, with a max. depth of 20 ft. Part of "Sapphire Country," *which see*. Used for fishing, swimming, and boating; not open to the public. *See also* Lake Sapphire.

Sapsucker Branch rises in central Clay County and flows nw into Peckerwood Branch.

Saratoga, town in se Wilson County between White Oak Swamp and Goss Swamp. Settled prior to 1839; inc. 1874.

Saratoga Township, se Wilson County.

Sardis, community in s Mecklenburg County. Sardis Presbyterian Church was organized there in 1790.

Sardis. *See* Hudson.

Sarecta, area in central Duplin County on Northeast Cape Fear River. Settled about 1736 under the direction of Henry McCulloch of London. Est. 1787 as Sarecto; long inactive in municipal affairs. Alt. 67. Named for Soracte Mountain in Italy, near Rome, on which a temple to Apollo stood in ancient times. Often referred to as Soracte in colonial records. Served by post office, 1830–1903.

Sarem, community in w central Gates County; named for the ancient name for Salisbury, England. Alt. 34. A school for Indians was in operation there in 1712, and it was a preaching station for Rev. Clement Hall of Edenton in the 1750s.

Sarem Creek rises in s Gates County and flows se into Chowan River. Appears on the Collet map, 1770, where the modern Cole Creek is shown with the same name.

Sarvis Gap, ne Mitchell County between Wiles Creek and Lyddies Creek.

Sarvis Ridge, ne Mitchell County between Wiles Creek and Lyddies Creek.

Sasnett Mill Branch rises in central Edgecombe County and flows sw into Cokey Swamp.

Sassafras Branch rises in central Cherokee County and flows se into Colvard Creek.

Sassafras Branch rises in se Clay County and flows se into Tallulah River.

Sassafras Branch rises in w Jackson County and flows n into Savannah Creek.

Sassafras Creek rises in e central Avery County and flows s into Lost Cove Creek.

Sassafras Creek rises in sw Graham County in the Snowbird Mountains and flows ne into Snowbird Creek.

Sassafras Falls, in Sassafras Creek, sw Graham County. Water drops approx. 70 ft.

Sassafras Fork. *See* Stovall.

Sassafras Fork Township, ne Granville County.

Sassafras Gap, central Buncombe County e of Buzzard Rock.

Sassafras Gap, on the Graham-Swain county line between Cheoah Bald and Swim Bald in Nantahala National Forest. Alt. approx. 4,380.

Sassafras Gap, on Laurel Mountain w of Johnson Knob in nw Henderson County near the Transylvania County line. Alt. approx. 4,060.

Sassafras Gap, in e Jackson County on Old Bald Ridge.

Sassafras Gap, on the Jackson-Macon County line. Alt. approx. 4,100.

Sassafras Gap, se Macon County between Clear Creek and Queen Mountain. Alt. approx. 2,860.

Sassafras Gap, nw Swain County on Twentymile Ridge in Great Smoky Mountains National Park near lat. 35°29′22″ N., long. 83°48′55″ W. Alt. approx. 3,650.

Sassafras Gap, on the North Carolina–South Carolina line at the junction of Transylvania

County, N.C., and Greenville and Pickens Counties, S.C. Alt. 2,774.

Sassafras Knob, on the Cherokee-Clay County line in the Valley River Mountains.

Sassafras Knob, e Haywood County on the n end of Sassafras Ridge.

Sassafras Knob, se Macon County between Brushy Face and Monger Creek.

Sassafras Knob, on Noland Divide, n Swain County in Great Smoky Mountains National Park between Lower and Upper Sassafras Gaps near lat. 35°32′03″ N., long. 83°27′10″ W. Alt. 4,665.

Sassafras Knob, nw Transylvania County s of Farlow Gap.

Sassafras Mountain, on the Jackson-Transylvania County line sw of Bearpen Mountain. Alt. 4,347.

Sassafras Mountain, on the Transylvania County, N.C.–Pickens County, S.C., line s of the head of South Prong [Glady Fork]. Alt. 3,554.

Sassafras Ridge extends ne from Bee Gap to Willie Knob in sw Graham County.

Sassafras Ridge, e Haywood County between Buckeye Cove and Beaverdam Creek.

Sassafras Ridge, s Macon County between Nantahala River and Nantahala Mountains.

Sassafras Ridge, elevated ground in e Washington County sw of the community of Scuppernong. The name appears in county records as early as 1868.

Sassarixa Swamp rises in w Johnston County and flows se into Black Creek.

Sasseenohla. *See* Big Bald.

Sassers Mill, community in nw Jones County on Heath Mill Run.

Sassers Millpond, n Wayne County on Great Swamp near Aycock Millpond. Fishing, boating; open to public.

Satterfield Creek rises in w Person County and flows ne into Storys Creek.

Satterthwaite Creek rises in e Beaufort County and flows e into Pungo River. *See also* Chappel Creek.

Satterwhite, community in n Granville County, formerly known as Locust Grove. Name derived from home of the Satterwhite family.

Satterwhite Creek rises in sw Burke County and flows n into Silver Creek.

Satulah Branch rises in se Macon County and flows n into Mill Creek.

Satulah Falls, se Macon County near the head of Clear Creek.

Satulah Mountain, se Macon County between Satulah Falls and Little Fodderstack Mountain. Alt. 4,490.

Saucepan Creek rises in sw Brunswick County and flows e into Shallotte River.

Sauls Creek rises in n Warren County and flows ne into Hawtree Creek.

Sauls Crossroads. *See* Eureka.

Saulston, community in e Wayne County s of The Slough and n of the head of West Bear Creek.

Saulston Township, e Wayne County.

Saunders, community in w Cabarrus County served by post office, 1891–1902. Named for North Carolina secretary of state William L. Saunders (1835–91).

Saunders Bay, in Currituck Sound off the w shore of Currituck Banks and n of Mossey Islands, se Currituck County.

Saunder's Hill. *See* Abner.

Saunders Point, peninsula extending from ne Pamlico County into Bay River.

Saunders' Store, community in sw Caswell County.

Saunook, community in w Haywood County. Alt. 3,206. Said to have been named for a Cherokee Indian who lived in the vicinity.

Saurat. *See* Upper Saura Town.

Sauratown, former community in se Stokes County near the mouth of Town Fork Creek on Dan River. A post office operated there, 1876–87. Earlier post office, named Saura Town, operated 1833–39.

Saura Town. *See* Lower Saura Town; Upper Saura Town.

Sauratown Mountain, a range extending from w Stokes County into the center of the county. Alt. 2,465. Appears on the Collet map, 1770. Named for the Saura Indians, who lived in the area. The Indians were mentioned by William Byrd, 1728.

Sauratown Township, se Stokes County.

Savage, community in e Gates County served by post office, 1904–35. Alt. 33. Settled prior to Civil War and named for G. W. Savage, local landowner.

Savages Crossroads, community in n Gates County. Known first as Pipkin's Crossroads, then as Brickhouse.

Savannah, community on Savannah Creek in w Jackson County.

Savannah Creek rises in e Anson County and flows ne into Blewett Falls Lake.

Savannah Creek rises in w Jackson County and flows n into Tuckasegee River.

Savannah Ridge, in w Jackson County between Little Savannah Creek and Savannah Creek.

Savannah Township, w Jackson County.

Saw, community in sw Rowan County served by post office, 1886–1903.

Saw Branch rises in sw Buncombe County near Saw Mountain and flows nw into South Hominy Creek.

Sawbrier Ridge, n Swain County in Great Smoky Mountains National Park, a short spur extending nw from High Rocks on Welch Ridge; center near lat. 35°31′ N., long. 83°38′02″ W.

Saw Mill, community in s Caldwell County.

Sawmill Branch rises in ne Buncombe County and flows n into Carter Creek.

Sawmill Branch rises in central Cherokee County and flows se into Colvard Creek.

Saw Mill Branch rises in n Davie County and flows s into Dutchmans Creek.

Sawmill Creek rises in n Lincoln County and flows se to join Lippard Creek in forming Leepers Creek.

Sawmill Creek rises in s Swain County and flows nw and then sw into Little Tennessee River.

Sawmill Creek rises in w Transylvania County and flows se into Cherryfield Creek.

Sawmill Ridge, n Macon County between Shepherd Creek and Matlock Creek.

Saw Mountain, sw Buncombe County between Saw Branch and Stony Fork.

Sawpit Branch rises in s Watauga County and flows se into East Fork [South Fork New River].

Sawteeth, The, broken, pointed summits along the Swain County, N.C.–Sevier County, Tenn., line in Great Smoky Mountains National Park near lat. 35°38′30″ N., long. 83°21′50″ W. Alt. approx. 5,450.

Sawyer Cove, n Buncombe County e of Ingles Ridge.

Sawyer Creek rises in n central Graham County and flows ne into Little Tennessee River.

Sawyer Creek rises in n Watauga County and flows w into Cove Creek.

Sawyers Creek rises in n central Camden County and flows s into Pasquotank River. Settlements existed at its mouth prior to 1677. *See also* Grays Mill.

Sawyers Creek rises in n Pender County and flows n into Rockfish Creek.

Sawyers Ferry appears on the Moseley map, 1733, on Pasquotank River in what is now Camden County n of Sawyers Creek. Site was in Pasquotank Precinct of Albemarle County. Later Shipyard Ferry operated nearby. *See also* Shipyard.

Sawyers Landing, e Beaufort County on Pungo River.

Sawyersville, community in w Randolph County served by post office, 1849–1905.

Saxapahaw, community in se Alamance County on Haw River. Named for the Sissipahaw Indians, who once lived in the area. A yarn mill was est. there in 1849.

Saxapahaw River. *See* Haw River.

Saxon, community in e Stokes County served by post office, 1891–1912.

Scale Creek rises in ne Onslow County and flows sw into Northeast Creek.

Scalesville, community in n Guilford County. Named for the Scales family of Guilford and Rockingham Counties.

Scaly Mountain, s Macon County between the head of Middle Creek and the head of Piney Knob Fork. Alt. 4,804.

Scaly Mountain, community in s Macon County on Middle Creek.

Scaly Ridge, se Clay County between Tallulah River and Beech Creek.

Scapecat Branch rises in s Haywood County and flows w into Little East Fork Pigeon River.

Scarboro, community in sw Montgomery County served by post office, 1880–1901.

Scarlet Ridge, n Swain County in Great Smoky Mountains National Park extending se from Welch Ridge to Forney Creek. Near lat. 35°31′54″ N., long. 83°34′40″ W.

Scarlet Ridge Creek rises in n Swain County in Great Smoky Mountains National Park and flows se into Jonas Creek.

Schenck Forest. *See* Carl Alwin Schenck Forest.

Schencks Station, community in s Cleveland County.

Schene Wolf Creek rises near Organ and Lower Stone Churches approx. 5 mi. sw of Rockwell, se Rowan County, and flows s into ne Cabarrus County, where it enters Dutch Buffalo Creek. Probably named by early German settlers, Schene being derived from *schön* (beautiful). Sometimes also called Jennie Wolf Creek.

Schley, community in e Orange County served by post office, 1898–1907.

Schlosstown, community in n Franklin County. Known locally as "Slosh."

Scholl, community in w Scotland County.

School House Branch rises in w Carteret County and flows sw into Hadnot Creek.

Schoolhouse Branch rises in central Cherokee County and flows se into Marble Creek.

Schoolhouse Branch rises in ne Cherokee County and flows se into Junaluska Creek.

Schoolhouse Branch rises in s Haywood County and flows sw into Little East Fork Pigeon River.

Schoolhouse Branch rises in central Pitt County and flows ne into Tar River.

School House Branch rises in w Watauga County and flows sw into Watauga River.

Schoolhouse Flats, e Haywood County on Glade Mountain.

Schoolpath Branch rises in s central Transylvania County and flows ne into West Fork French Broad River.

Schooner Creek rises in se Beaufort County and flows n into South Creek.

Schooners Bay. *See* Spooners Bay.

Schuler Cove. *See* Jack Cove.

Schulkens Pond, a natural lake in se Columbus County approx. 7 mi. sw of Lake Waccamaw and 1 mi. w of Waccamaw River. Bear Branch drains Schulkens Pond into Waccamaw River.

Science, community in sw Randolph County.

Scippco Swamp rises in Cawcaw Bay, sw Brunswick County, and flows w into Waccamaw River.

Scotch Grove, community in n central Scotland County.

Scotch Hall. *See* Bonarva.

Scotch-Irish Township, n Rowan County.

Scotia, community in n central Tyrrell County at the head of Second Creek.

Scotland County was formed in 1899 from Richmond County. Located in the se section of the state, it is bounded by the state of South Carolina and by Richmond, Moore, Hoke, and Robeson Counties. It was named for Scotland in the British Isles, from which many of the early settlers of the region emigrated. Area: 317 sq. mi. County seat: Laurinburg, with an elevation of 227 ft. Townships are Laurel Hill, Spring Hill, Stewartsville, and Williamsons. Produces cotton, corn, soybeans, peanuts, oats, watermelons, cantaloupes, hogs, livestock, processed meat, textiles, automobile parts, and lumber.

Scotland Neck, town in se Halifax County. Named for region settled 1722 by Scottish colonists. Inc. 1867. Produces textiles. Alt. 103.

Scotland Neck, a name formerly applied to a tract of land approx. 40 sq. mi. in area in se Halifax County. It lay e of Kehukee Swamp and w of Roanoke River and extended s through the present Buzzard Point. It was settled in 1722 by Scottish colonists. Appears on the Collet map, 1770, and the Price map, 1808.

Scotland Neck Township, se Halifax County.

Scotland Village. *See* East Laurinburg.

Scotsman Creek rises in s Jackson County and flows sw into Chattooga River.

Scott, community in nw Warren County.

Scott Branch rises in e Macon County and flows sw into Cullasaja River.

Scott Creek rises in central Alexander County and flows w into Glade Creek.

Scott Creek rises in e Beaufort County and flows se into Pungo Creek.

Scott Creek rises in central Craven County and flows n into Neuse River at James City.

Scott Creek rises in ne Jackson County n of Judaculla Mountain and flows sw through the towns of Sylva and Dillsboro to empty into Tuckasegee River just w of Dillsboro.

Scott Creek rises in e Jones County and flows e into Trent River.

Scott Creek Township, ne Jackson County. Named for John Scott, a trader among the Cherokees.

Scottish Mountain, w Haywood County in Great Smoky Mountains National Park near lat. 35°41′34″ N., long. 83°05′08″ W. Named for Scottish Mountain Lumber Co., which operated in the area in the 1920s. Alt. 4,290.

Scott Knob, s Swain County between the head of Welch Branch and Yalaka Creek.

Scott Mountain, s Buncombe County e of Enka Lake.

Scott Reservoir. *See* W. Kerr Scott Reservoir.

Scotts, community in w central Iredell County.

Scott's, formerly Scott's Store, community in w Wilson County s of Contentnea Creek. Named for S. H. Scott.

Scotts Creek rises in nw Rutherford County and flows se into Cove Creek.

Scotts Hill, community in se Pender County served by post office, 1876–1943. Alt. 50.

Scott's Pond, w Wilson County on Robin Branch. Formed 1954 and named for Exum Scott, owner. Covers 10 acres; max. depth 12 ft. Fishing, swimming, boating, irrigation.

Scotts Store, community in n Duplin County. Named for local storeowner, A. J. Scott.

Scotts Store, community in w Pamlico County.

Scottville, community on Alleghany-Ashe county line. Alt. approx. 2,950. Settled about 1830 and known first as Flint Hill. Post office est. 1855 as Scottville; believed to have been named for Elizabeth Scott (1799–1856), local citizen. Post office closed, 1954.

Scottsville. *See* Belfast.

Scranton, community in w Hyde County on Scranton Creek near Pungo River. Alt. 3. Originally known as Clark for the owner of a lumber mill there. Later renamed Scranton for another lumber mill that relocated from Scranton, Pa. Near the site of an old Indian village, Aquascogoc, *which see.*

Scranton Creek rises in w Hyde County and flows w approx. 3.3 mi. into Pungo River. Formerly known as Broad Creek.

Scratch Hall Swamp rises in w Gates County and flows w into Chowan River.

Scratch Hall Township. *See* Hall Township.

Scream Ridge, s Macon County parallel to Yellow Patch Creek.

Scrougetown, community in s Clay County. The site is now partially covered by the waters of Chatuge Lake.

Scuffleton. *See* Scuffletown.

Scuffletown, town in e Greene County on Little Contentnea Creek served by post office, 1837–42. Also spelled Scuffleton. Inc. 1885, but long inactive in municipal affairs. Settled prior to 1756; served by post office, 1837–42. Name said to be derived from disagreement among members of the local Free Will Baptist church. In recent years generally known as Ridge Spring.

Scuffletown. *See* Pembroke.

Scull Camp. *See* Skull Camp Mountain.

Scuppernong, community in e Washington County. Post office est. 1849, discontinued 1908. Location formerly known as Cool Spring.

Scuppernong Lake. *See* Lake Phelps.

Scuppernong River rises in e Washington County in East Dismal Swamp and flows e into w Tyrrell County, where it turns to flow nw into Albemarle Sound. Appears on the Moseley map, 1733, as Cascoponung River. It appears as Cuscopang River on a 1788 map. Approx. 22 mi. long.

Scuppernong Township, nw Tyrrell County.

Scuppernong Township, se Washington County, formed in 1868 and incorporates within its limits the old voting precinct of Cool Springs.

S Curves, section of N.C. Highway 12 n of Rodanthe on Hatteras Island, e Dare County. Term adopted by N.C. Department of Transportation because of frequent need to repair damage due to washouts. Also called Rodanthe S Curves.

Sea Banks. *See* Outer Banks; Shackleford Banks.

Seaboard, town in n Northampton County. Alt. 126. Settled about 1750 and known first as Concord. Inc. 1877. Named for the Seaboard Air Line Railroad. Post office since 1853.

Seaboard Township, n central Northampton County.

Sea Breeze, resort community in s New Hanover County near the s end of Myrtle Sound. Est. to serve African Americans.

Sea Cattle. *See* Middle Ground.

Seaforth, community in e Chatham County. The site is now under the waters of Jordan Lake.

Seagate, community in e New Hanover County on the s side of Bradleys Creek. Alt. 10. Served by post office, 1910–32. Settled about 1890. Named for the fact that it is located on an inlet of Wrightsville Sound, with access thereby to the sea.

Seago's Lake, e Anson County se of Lilesville. Covers approx. 10 acres; max. depth 20 ft. Formed early in the twentieth century when gravel was removed from the site. Named for owner.

Seagrove, town in s Randolph County. Inc. 1913. Named for a railroad official. Alt. 716. Post office since 1897. Home to North Carolina Pottery Center.

Seagull, community on Currituck Banks, e Currituck County. A lifesaving station there originally was called Old Currituck Inlet. A Coast Guard station there was decommissioned following World War II. Post office operated from 1908 to 1924.

Sealevel, community in ne Carteret County on Core Sound.

Sea Level Township, ne Carteret County on Nelson Bay and Core Sound.

Sealeys Creek. *See* Celia Creek.

Sea of Rawnocke. *See* Albemarle Sound.

Searcy Creek rises in w central Transylvania County and flows ne into Davidson River.

Seaside, community in sw Brunswick County.

Seay Mountain, central Haywood County between Jonathans Creek and Pigeon River. Alt. 3,358.

Secession, community in sw Brunswick County.

Seco, an Indian village shown on John White's map of 1585 located in what is now central Beaufort County. The name is associated with American discoveries dating from 1536, though located on different maps from the Chesapeake Bay s to Florida. De Bry's version of White's map, printed in 1590, changes Seco to Cotan. *See also* Secotan.

Second Broad River rises in s McDowell County and flows se into Rutherford County, which it crosses to the Cleveland County line and enters Broad River.

Second Creek rises in w Randolph County and flows e into Uwharrie River.

Second Creek rises in e Tyrrell County and flows se into Alligator River. Called Third Creek on the Collet map, 1770. Approx. 4½ mi. long and ¾ mi. wide at its mouth.

Second Creek rises in n central Tyrrell County s of community of Pleasant View and flows w into Scuppernong River approx. 2¼ mi. s of town of Columbia. An old Indian village of uncertain tribal affiliation, Mequopen, is shown at the mouth of the creek on the De Bry map, 1590. Name means "red tribes" or "where there are red tribes."

Second Creek, community on the creek of the same name in n central Tyrrell County.

Second Creek. *See* North Second Creek; South Second Creek; Back Creek.

Second Creek Bluff, at the mouth of Second Creek in e Tyrrell County.

Second Creek Point, e Tyrrell County, extends from the mainland into Alligator River near the mouth of Second Creek.

Second Falls, the middle of a series of three waterfalls on Yellowstone Prong, s Haywood County.

Second Hurricane Branch rises in e Swain County and flows sw into Yalaka Creek.

Second Potts Creek rises in w Davidson County and flows s into High Rock Lake on Yadkin River. Appears on the Collet map, 1770, as Potts Creek.

Secotan, an Indian village once located on the s side of Pamlico River in what is now e Beaufort County in the vicinity of Hobucken; visited by John White and other explorers based on Roanoke Island in the sixteenth century. The name meant "town at the bend of a river." Appears as Secoton on the White map, 1585; as Secota on the De Bry map, 1590; and as Secotan on the Velasco map, 1611. *See also* Seco.

Sedalia, community in e Guilford County. The Alice Freeman Palmer Memorial Institute, a junior college and high school for African American women est. 1901, operated there until 1960s. Campus now a State Historic Site.

Sedgefield, community in w central Guilford County. Named for the fields of sedge (grasslike plants) in the vicinity. English-style inn opened 1927. Golf course hosts national tournaments.

Sedges Garden, community in n central Forsyth County.

Seedbed of the Colony. *See* Salmon Creek.

Seed Cane Creek rises in e Surry County and flows sw into Ararat River.

See-noh-ya. *See* Black Mountains.

Seeoff, community in se Transylvania County.

See Off Mountain, s central Transylvania County between Dunn Creek and Haunty Branch. Alt. 3,080.

Seeshore, community in s Transylvania County on a tributary of Carson Creek.

Sega Lake, in central Transylvania County on Graham Creek. Covers ¼ acre, with a max. depth of 10 ft.

Seibold Branch rises in e Cherokee County and flows se into Fall Branch.

Seigle Creek rises in ne Lincoln County and flows s into Forney Creek.

Selah, community in n Johnston County served by post office, 1892–95.

Selena. *See* Center.

Selica, community in w central Transylvania County between Wilson Mill Creek and Catheys Creek. Alt. 2,179.

Selma, town in central Johnston County. Known first as Mitchenor's Station for John Mitchenor. Inc. as Selma, 1873; named for the town of the same name in Alabama. Town of Selma Cotton Mills, inc. 1915 and long inactive in municipal affairs, is now within the w section of Selma. Alt. 179. Produces textiles, furniture, milled grain, and chemicals.

Selma Cotton Mills. *See* Selma.

Selma Creek rises in ne Swain County and flows sw into Bunches Creek.

Selma Township, central Johnston County.

Selwin, community in s Gates County.

Seminole, community in w Harnett County.

Semora, community in ne Caswell County. Settled prior to the Revolution and known as Campbell's Crossroads. Post office, est. 1877, named Semora for the daughter of the first postmaster, James M. McAden.

Seng Branch rises in nw Yancey County and flows nw into Cane River. Named for the herb ginseng, which was gathered in large quantities in the vicinity beginning about 1837.

Seng Gap, n Madison County at the head of Little Laurel Creek.

Seng Ridge, nw Madison County between Alum Ridge and Camp Creek Bald.

Senia, community in w Avery County. Named for a local resident, Senia Pritchard.

Seniard Creek rises in nw Henderson County and flows s into North Fork in Pisgah National Forest.

Seniard Mountain, on the Haywood-Transylvania County line at the n end of Lanning Ridge. Alt. 5,025.

Seniard Ridge, n Transylvania County, extends se from Seniard Mountain to Looking Glass Rock.

Service Ridge, w Haywood County in Great Smoky Mountains National Park, a spur extending nw from Cataloochee Divide; center near lat. 35°33′27″ N., long. 83°07′15″ W., between Big Bald Branch and Little Bald Branch.

Servis Creek rises in central Alamance County and flows e into Haw River.

Sessoms Mill Pond, on Chinkapin Creek in se Hertford County; approx. ½ mi. long.

Setrock Creek rises in s Yancey County and flows se into South Toe River.

Settle, community in ne Iredell County served by post office, 1873–1906. Alt. 700. A weather station from the 1880s until mid-twentieth century.

Setzer Mountain, w Haywood County parallel to Campbell Creek. Named for a prominent family of early settlers. Maggie Setzer, for whom the community of Maggie was named, was a descendant of the family. The highest peak of the ridge, which is 2½ mi. long, is 4,810 ft. in elevation.

Setzer's Creek rises in n central Caldwell County and flows se into Warrior Creek. Named for John Setzer, who settled nearby about 1830.

Setzers Depot. *See* Claremont.

Setzers Gap, central Caldwell County. Alt. 1,342.

Seven Bridges, community in w Robeson County.

Seven Creeks is formed in s Columbus County by Big Cypress Swamp and Monie Swamp. It flows se into Waccamaw River.

Seven Devils, commercially developed recreation area opened in 1966 in e Avery and w Watauga Counties on a 1,288-acre tract.

Seven Mile Creek rises in e Orange County and flows se into w Durham County, where it enters Eno River.

Sevenmile Creek rises in w Orange County and flows ne into Eno River w of town of Hillsborough.

Seven Mile Ridge, n Haywood County, extends n parallel to McGinty Creek.

Seven Mile Ridge extends from e Madison County into the s part of the county and is parallel to Bull Creek and West Fork [Bull Creek]. Named for its length.

Sevenmile Ridge, e Yancey County, extends ne from Stones Knob to Crabtree Creek near Cox Knob. Alt. approx. 4,400.

Sevenmile Swamp rises in nw Sampson County and flows se into Great Coharie Creek.

Seven Paths, community in e Franklin County.

Seven Sisters, sand hills a short distance s of Nags Head on Bodie Island, e Dare County.

Seven Springs, town in se Wayne County on Neuse River. Inc. 1855 as Whitehall; reincorporated as White Hall, 1881; named for the plantation home of William Whitefield, who

built there about 1741. Post office est. 1881
as Jericho; name changed to Seven Springs,
1894. Named for seven mineral springs,
around which a resort operated from 1881
until 1944. The hotel and springhouse still
stand. The Confederate ironclad *Neuse* was
built there. A Civil War skirmish occurred
there in December 1862. Alt. 75.

Seven Springs Gap, w Graham County between
Hooper Mill Creek and Wright Creek in Nantahala National Forest. Alt. approx. 3,700.

Seventy-First Township, w Cumberland County.
Named for the 71st Highland Scots Regiment.

Severn, town in ne Northampton County served
by post office, 1889–1939. Alt. 59. Settled
about 1833 and known first as Meherrin for
an Indian tribe that had lived in the vicinity.
Inc. 1919. Named for Severn Ayers, a stockholder in the Seaboard Air Line Railroad.

Sevier, community in n McDowell County on
North Fork [Catawba River]. Served by post
office, 1892–1903. Alt. 1,401.

Seward, community in w Forsyth County.

Sexton, community in s Madison County on Bull
Creek. Served by post office, 1892–1905.

Sexton's Branch rises in ne Wake County and
flows se into Upper Bartons Creek.

Seymour Johnson Air Force Base, central Wayne
County at Goldsboro. Est. 1941 as an Army Air
Forces Technical Training School and named
for Lt. Seymour Johnson (1904–41), Navy test
pilot from Goldsboro.

Shacklefoot Island. *See* Brown's Island.

Shackleford Banks, one of the Outer Banks, se
Carteret County; approx. 8½ mi. long. Named
for John Shackleford, who, with Enoch Ward,
purchased the "Sea Banks" in 1713. *See also*
Cape Lookout National Seashore.

Shackleford Point, the w tip of Shackleford
Banks, se Carteret County, extending into
Beaufort Inlet. The community of Shackle-
ford formerly existed near the point.

Shacktown, community in se Yadkin County
between North Deep Creek and South Deep
Creek. Named for B. G. "Shack" Colvard, local
businessman. Previously produced tobacco
baskets.

Shad Coye, central Craven County in se end of
Hog Island adjacent to Neuse River. Approx.
¼ mi. wide.

Shaddock's Creek is formed in se Moore County
by the junction of McDeeds and Mill Creeks.

It flows e through Crystal Lake into Little
River. The name was originally applied also to
present McDeeds Creek. Named for Thomas
Shaddock, an eighteenth-century settler.

Shaddox Creek rises in se Chatham County and
flows s into Cape Fear River.

Shade Branch rises in n Madison County and
flows sw into Martin Branch.

Shadepen Branch rises in nw Buncombe County
and flows se into North Fork [Swannanoa
River].

Shad Point, on the ne mainland of Hyde County
extending into the mouth of Long Shoal Bay.

Shadrick Creek rises in e McDowell County and
flows e approx. 5 mi. into Old Catawba River
in sw Burke County.

Shady Banks, community in central Beaufort
County on the n bank of Pamlico River.

Shady Grove, community in nw Caswell County.

Shadygrove, community in nw Sampson County.

Shady Grove, community in n Yadkin County.
Named for a Baptist church.

Shady Grove. *See* Advance.

Shady Grove Township, e Davie County. Named
for Shady Grove Methodist Church, est. prior
to or in 1816.

Shaftesbury Precinct was formed by 1668 as a division of Albemarle County. It was named for
Anthony Ashley Cooper, Earl of Shaftesbury
(1621–83), one of the original Lords Proprietors of Carolina. Renamed Chowan Precinct
about 1681. *See also* Chowan County.

Shaken, community in ne Pender County on
Shaken Creek e of its junction with Holly
Shelter Creek. Served by post office, 1907–18.

Shaken Creek rises in e Pender County and flows
nw into Holly Shelter Creek.

Shakerag. *See* Osgood.

Shaleville, community in w Madison County on
Ferry Branch.

Shallop's Landing. *See* Columbia.

Shallotte, town in sw Brunswick County served
by post office since 1837. Appears on the
Morse-Breese map, 1843. Inc. 1899. Named
for Shallotte River, on which it is located.
Alt. 33.

Shallotte Creek rises in s Brunswick County and
flows w into Shallotte River.

Shallotte Inlet, sw Brunswick County between
Big Beach and Hales Beach connecting Long
Bay in the Atlantic Ocean with the mouths of
Shallotte River, Shallotte Creek, and Sauce-

pan Creek. Provides access to the Intracoastal Waterway from the Atlantic Ocean.

Shallotte River rises in sw Brunswick County and flows ne and s into the Atlantic Ocean through Shallotte Inlet. Appears on the Moseley map, 1733. May have been named for shallot, an onionlike plant growing in the vicinity.

Shallotte Sound, sw Brunswick County between Brantley Island on the mainland and Hales Beach running parallel to and s of the Intracoastal Waterway. Narrow and approx. 1½ mi. long.

Shallotte Township, sw Brunswick County.

Shallowbag Bay, a bay in Roanoke Sound off the ne shore of Roanoke Island, e Dare County. The bay forms the harbor at the town of Manteo. In the late eighteenth century, it was referred to as Shalon-bas Bay (French *chalon-bas*, "low trawl net"). Roanoke voyages–period vessel *Elizabeth II*, a reproduction, rests in bay.

Shallow Ford, in Little Tennessee River in n Macon County.

Shallow Ford, passage through the Yadkin River, se Yadkin County and sw Forsyth County. The main w road from the early Moravian settlements crossed there, and it is mentioned in records as early as 1767. Site of military encounters in both Revolutionary and Civil Wars.

Shallow Ford, community in n Alamance County served by post office, 1849–1903.

Shalon-bas Bay. *See* Shallowbag Bay.

Shamrock, community in se Mecklenburg County served by post office, 1894–1903.

Shanghai, community in se Sampson County.

Shankle Mountain, se Stanly County. Named for local family.

Shannon, community in n Robeson County on Big Raft Swamp served by post office since 1884.

Shannon Township, n Robeson County.

Shanty Cove, e Cherokee County on the headwaters of Seibold Branch.

Shanty Gap, in central Graham County between Mountain Creek and Sweetwater Creek.

Shanty Mountain, w Haywood County in Great Smoky Mountains National Park, a spur extending ne from Balsam Mountain between Sugar Fork and Palmer Creek; centers near lat. 35°37′15″ N., long. 83°09′35″ W. Alt. 4,812.

Shanty Spring Branch rises in e Avery County

and flows n into Watauga County, where it enters Watauga River.

Shark Shoal, in the waters of Pamlico Sound n of Hatteras Inlet, s Dare County.

Sharon, community in nw Camden County. Named for a Methodist church erected there in 1894. Previously known as Slab Ridge. Alt. 18.

Sharon, community in s Cleveland County.

Sharon, community in w Iredell County.

Sharon. *See* Iron Station.

Sharon Township, former township in s central Mecklenburg County, now township no. 4.

Sharp, community in w Rockingham County. In 1884 Thomas Sharp built gristmill and sawmill on his plantation. Area later became part of Spray, then Eden.

Sharp Branch rises in ne Cherokee County and flows nw into Valley River.

Sharp Creek rises in n Watauga County and flows w into Cove Creek.

Sharper Mountain, w Wilkes County near the head of Cole Creek.

Sharpesburg Township, nw Iredell County. Named for the Sharpe family.

Sharpes Township, se Alexander County.

Sharp Point, community in w Pitt County.

Sharps, community in w Rockingham County. Named for John Sharp, local landowner.

Sharpsburg, town at the coincident corners of Edgecombe, Nash, and Wilson Counties. Inc. 1883. Settled about 1851. Named for John Jay Sharp, who moved there in 1844 and was later representative in the General Assembly. Alt. 143.

Sharp Top, mountain in central Swain County in Great Smoky Mountains National Park on Noland Divide near lat. 35°28′05″ N., long. 83°27′27″ W. Alt. 3,430.

Sharptop, peak in s Yancey County n of Little Creek. Alt. approx. 5,500.

Sharptop Ridge, se Clay County nw of Hightower Bald, Ga. *See also* Montgomery Corner.

Sharpy Mountain, n Transylvania County between Sandy Gap and Sampson Gap in Pisgah National Forest. Alt. 3,383.

Sharron Branch rises in s central Brunswick County and flows sw into Sharron Creek.

Sharron Creek rises in s central Brunswick County and flows sw into Shallotte River.

Shateen Branch rises in sw Yancey County and flows e into Cane River.

Shate Gap, s Yancey County near Cane River.

Shatley Springs, community in e Ashe County.

Shatter Muster Ground. *See* Axtell.

Shaw, community in central Cumberland County. Alt. 227.

Shawano Ridge, ne Swain County in Great Smoky Mountains National Park, extends sw from Balsam Mountain near lat. 35°40′ N., long. 83°12′33″ W.

Shawboro, community in w Currituck County. Settled about 1775 and first known as Bayley. Perhaps to avoid confusion with Bailey in Nash County, it was renamed Shaw's Corner after the Civil War in honor of Col. Henry Shaw, Confederate officer. Name later changed to Shawboro by the Norfolk and Southern Railroad. Alt. 15.

Shaw Creek rises in sw Anson County and flows s into Deadfall Creek.

Shaw Creek rises in central Henderson County and flows nw into French Broad River.

Shawnee. *See* Long Island.

Shawneehaw. *See* Banner Elk.

Shawneehaw Creek rises in w Watauga County and flows sw into ne Avery County, where it enters Elk River.

Shawneehaw Township, sw Watauga County.

Shaws, community in e Scotland County.

Shaw's Corner. *See* Shawboro.

Shearer Creek rises in n Clay County and flows sw into Johnson Mill Creek.

Shearer's Hill, a low ridge on the n side of Yadkin River, ne Caldwell County. Named for John Shearer, who settled there about the end of the Revolution. A black cemetery there has been in use since before the Civil War, when the slaves of a number of wealthy planters in the neighborhood were interred.

Shear Knob, w Swain County between Yalaka Creek and a bend in Little Tennessee River.

Sheehan Creek rises in nw McDowell County and flows se into Little Buck Creek.

Sheepback Knob, w Haywood County in Great Smoky Mountains National Park on Cataloochee Divide, near lat. 35°33′10″ N., long. 83°07′33″ W., between Little Bald Knob and Little Spruce Ridge. Alt. 5,520.

Sheepback Mountain, n Jackson County between Rich Mountain and Plott Balsams. Alt. 4,700.

Sheep Cliffs Creek rises in s Jackson County and flows n into Webb Lake.

Sheep Cliffs Mountain, between Little Sheep Cliffs and Sheep Cliffs Creek in s Jackson County. Alt. 4,681.

Sheep Hollow, s Macon County between Richey Knob and Richey Gap.

Sheep Island, a tidal-marsh island just inside Lockwoods Folly Inlet, s central Brunswick County.

Sheep Island, in Pamlico Sound off Portsmouth Island and separated from it by Baymarsh Thorofare, e Carteret County.

Sheep Knob, n Buncombe County nw of Courthouse Knob.

Sheep Knob, s Cherokee County on the nw end of Moccasin Mountain.

Sheep Knob, n Cleveland County.

Sheep Knob, w Jackson County near the head of East Fork [Savannah Creek]. Alt. 4,784.

Sheep Knob, e Macon County between Caler Fork and Cowee Creek.

Sheep Knob, s Macon County at the head of Rough Fork.

Sheep Knob, nw Swain County in Great Smoky Mountains National Park on Twentymile Ridge near lat. 35°28′50″ N., long. 83°49′30″ W. Alt. 3,852.

Sheep Mountain, e Haywood County between Rock Hollow and Jordan Branch.

Sheep Mountain, n Jackson County between Black Mountain and Moses Creek.

Sheep Mountain, e Transylvania County between Laurel Creek and Little River.

Sheep Pen Gap, on Swain County, N.C.–Sevier County, Tenn., line in Great Smoky Mountains National Park near lat. 35°31′13″ N., long. 83°52′27″ W.

Sheep Ridge, se Buncombe County in the Blue Ridge Mountains, extends n from High Top to Swannanoa River s of town of Black Mountain.

Sheep Rock, mountain in sw Buncombe County s of Browns Knob.

Sheepwallow Knob, ne Buncombe County between Cedar Cliff Knob and Pigpen Knob.

Sheep Wallow Knob, on the Swain County, N.C.–Blount County, Tenn., line at the nw end of Dalton Ridge.

Sheffield, community in nw Davie County. Named by Thomas M. Smith, postmaster, in whose store the post office was est. in 1893; service discontinued 1907.

Sheffields Township, nw Moore County.

Shehan, community in n Henderson County.

Shehan Crossroads, community in ne Polk County at the Rutherford County line.

Shelby, city and county seat in central Cleveland County. Alt. 853. Inc. 1843; charter repealed 1847. Reincorporated 1849. Named for Col. Isaac Shelby (1750–1826), Revolutionary War commander. Produces textiles, bakery products, hosiery, apparel, fiberglass, chemicals, and glass products.

Shelby Township, former township in s central Cleveland County, now township no. 6.

Shellback Island, a tidal-marsh island in the Cape Fear River opposite Southport, se Brunswick County.

Shellbank Point, peninsula extending from the w shore of n Bodie Island into Kitty Hawk Bay and Currituck Sound, nw Dare County. Named for mound of shells found at the site by early settlers.

Shell Branch rises in w Jackson County and flows sw into Savannah Creek.

Shell Castle, ne Carteret County, an island in Pamlico Sound between Casey Island and North Rock near the tip of Portsmouth Island at Ocracoke Inlet. Built by John Gray Blount and John Wallace in 1790 on an earlier island known as Old Rock. At one time a dwelling house, a tavern, warehouses, a lumberyard, a wharf, and a notary public's office were there. Appears on the Price map, 1808.

Shelley Branch rises in nw Nash County and flows se into Sandy Creek.

Shell Island, ne Carteret County in Core Sound between Wainwright Island and Core Banks. Named as early as the Moseley map, 1733. *See also* Hunting Quarter Sound.

Shell Knob, on the Buncombe-Henderson county line ne of Glady Fork Gap. Alt. approx. 4,020.

Shell Point, the se point of Harkers Island in se Carteret County. Mound of shells, apparently left by Indians, gave the point its name. Indian remains have been found there.

Shell Point, community in sw Brunswick County on e side of Shallotte River.

Shell Ridge, ne Mitchell County between Blevins Branch and Broad Branch.

Shell Rock Channel, se Onslow County, flows s out of Bear Inlet.

Shell Stand Creek rises in e Graham County and flows ne into Panther Creek.

Shelly Point extends from the mainland of sw Carteret County into Bogue Sound.

Shelly Point, se Onslow County on The Hammock, extends into White Oak River.

Shelmerdine, town in s Pitt County.

Shelter Mountain, w Montgomery County between Clark's Creek and Pee Dee River.

Shelter Neck, community in n central Pender County on the e side of Northeast Cape Fear River near DeRossett Creek.

Shelter River. *See* Holly Shelter Creek.

Shelter Swamp rises in s Onslow County and flows w into Pender County, where it enters Holly Shelter Creek.

Shelton Branch rises in n Buncombe County and flows nw into Paint Fork. *See also* Anderson Cove.

Shelton Branch rises in s Haywood County and flows ne into Richland Creek.

Shelton Creek rises in w Granville County and flows se into Tar River. Appears as Charlone Creek on the Collet map, 1770.

Shelton Laurel, community in n Madison County. Alt. 1,849. Settled by Martin and David Shelton about 1790 near the junction of Shelton Laurel Creek and Big Laurel Creek. There, on January 19, 1863, 13 Union supporters (12 men and a boy) were shot by a detail of Confederate soldiers in what has become known as the Shelton Laurel Massacre. White Rock, a post office from 1851 to 1936, was in the center of the Shelton Laurel community.

Shelton Laurel Creek rises in n Madison County and flows sw into Big Laurel Creek.

Shelton Laurel Township, former township in n Madison County, now township no. 2.

Shelton's Store, community in n Stokes County. Later known as Ziglar's Store.

Shelton Town, community in ne Surry County between Rutledge Creek and Ararat River.

Shepards Mill, community in central Stokes County on Snow Creek. A mill, still standing, operated there as early as 1819 and as recently as 1957. Snow Creek Ironworks was started there in 1770 by Col. James Martin. Limestone for ironworks at Danbury mined there.

Shephard Creek drains Osceola Lake in central Henderson County and flows w into Mud Creek.

Shephard Ditch, nw Pasquotank County, drains ne into Pasquotank River.

Shepherd Bald, on Macon-Swain County line between Davis Bald and Leatherman Knob.

Shepherd Branch rises in n Buncombe County and flows sw into Flat Creek.

Shepherd Branch rises in w Yancey County and flows se into Bald Creek.

Shepherd Creek rises in n Macon County and flows s into Cowee Creek.

Shepherd Creek rises in e Swain County and flows nw into Kirkland Creek.

Shepherd Knob, n Mitchell County on Shepherd Mountain.

Shepherd Millpond, on Briery Swamp in ne Pitt County.

Shepherd Mountain, w Henderson County on South Fork.

Shepherd Mountain, n Mitchell County between Bean Creek and Spring Creek.

Shepherd Mountain, w Randolph County between Little Caraway Creek and Uwharrie River. Alt. 1,390.

Shepherd Run rises in s Greene County and flows ne into Contentnea Creek. Named for the Sheppard family, which has lived in the vicinity since the colonial period.

Shepherds, community in s Iredell County. Known as Shepherds Cross Roads in the early and middle nineteenth century.

Shepherd's Branch rises in w central Wilson County and flows se into Contentnea Creek.

Shepherdsburgh. *See* Snow Hill.

Shepherd's Point, a name formerly applied to the point of land on the w side of Newport River on which Morehead City now stands. Appears on the Moseley map, 1733.

Sherard. *See* Cherry.

Sherards Crossroads. *See* Cherry.

Sheridan Mountains, e Madison County between California Creek and Bailey Branch.

Sherman, community in nw Wilkes County near the head of Middle Fork Reddies River.

Sherrars Gap, in Kings Mountain, sw Gaston County. The gap is s of The Pinnacle. *See also* Kings Mountain.

Sherrill Cove Branch rises in e Swain County and flows n into Raven Fork.

Sherrill Gap, central Swain County between Bryson Branch and Lands Creek.

Sherrill Gap, s Swain County between Rich Mountain and Will Knob.

Sherrills Ford, across Catawba River between Catawba and Iredell Counties. Named for

Adam Sherrill, trailblazer in the settlement of w North Carolina who crossed the Catawba River there in 1747. The passage over the river was used by troops during the Revolutionary War. The site is now under the waters of Lake Norman. The name appears on various maps dating from the eighteenth century through 1963.

Sherrills Ford, community in se Catawba County; known earlier as Sherrills Mill. Named for Adam Sherrill, a pioneer settler who crossed the Catawba River at Sherrills Ford, *which see*, a short distance e. A post office was est. there in 1842.

Sherrill's Gap. *See* Hickory Nut Gap.

Sherrills Mill. *See* Sherrills Ford.

Sherrills Springs, community in s Cabarrus County. Mineral springs there still in use. Also known as Sossamon's Spring.

Sherron Acres, community in central Durham County approx. 1 mi. se of the city of Durham.

Sherwood, community in s Cumberland County served by post office, 1883–1907.

Sherwood, community in w Watauga County at the junction of Vanderpool and Cove Creeks. Post office est. in 1913 as Doughton to honor Congressman Robert L. Doughton. Name changed at his request to Sherwood.

Sheva, community in nw Mecklenburg County served by post office, 1892–1903.

Shewbird Mountain, s Clay County near the sw end of Cherry Mountain.

Shields, community in sw Cherokee County.

Shields Ridge, n Yancey County between Charlie Creek and Cove Branch.

Shiloh, town in sw Camden County. Inc. 1883, but no long active in municipal affairs. Daniel Billet settled there before 1694, and the name "Billet's Bridge" is still known locally at the site of a bridge that he built. Named Danson's Manor after 1696, when 3,640 acres were granted to John Danson, son-in-law of Governor John Archdale. Danson never lived there, but his heirs held the property until 1739. In the middle of the eighteenth century, the place came to be called Mill Town for a group of watermills erected on a bluff overlooking the Pasquotank River. Shortly after 1800, the local Baptist church (organized 1729), the oldest Baptist church in the state, changed its name to Shiloh, and the name came to be applied to the community.

Shiloh, community in nw Rockingham County. Named for Shiloh Primitive Baptist Church. Earlier name for the area was Spring Garden, *which see*.

Shiloh, community in sw Rutherford County near the headwaters of Jarretts Creek.

Shiloh Mills, community in e Edgecombe County.

Shiloh Township, s Camden County.

Shiloh Township, se Iredell County. Named for Shiloh Presbyterian Church, near its center.

Shinbone Creek rises in nw Mitchell County and flows se into Hollow Poplar Creek.

Shinbone Ridge, n Clay County between Fires Creek and Long Branch.

Shinbone Ridge, n Madison County between Wolf Branch and Orchard Ridge.

Shine. *See* Rufe.

Shines Crossroads, community in w Greene County. *See also* Rufe.

Shine Township, w central Greene County. Named for the Shine family. *See also* Rufe.

Shingle Cove, s Haywood County on Richland Creek.

Shingle Creek, a tidal creek in the waters of Pamlico Sound on n Ocracoke Island, se Hyde County.

Shingle Hollow, community in w central Rutherford County s of Toms Mountain. Post office serving the community, 1897–1906, was named Nanito.

Shingle Landing Creek rises in Norfolk County, Va., and flows se through nw Currituck County and into Northwest River. Appears on the Moseley map, 1733, and others as recent as MacRae, 1833, as Moyock Creek. Apparently named Shingle Landing about 1800.

Shingle Pile Creek rises in e Yancey County and flows w into Little Whiteoak Creek.

Shingle Point, the w side of an unnamed island off Core Banks in Core Sound, e Carteret County. The island is between Goose Island on the s and Duges Island on the n.

Shingle Top, s Cherokee County between Cane, Martin, and Moccasin Creeks.

Shingletree Branch rises in central Macon County and flows s into Wayah Creek.

Shingletree Swamp rises in sw Brunswick County and flows nw into Cawcaw Swamp on w edge of Thomas Bay.

Shining Creek rises in s Haywood County and flows e into East Fork Pigeon River.

Shining Creek Gap, se Haywood County on the mouth of Shining Creek.

Shining Rock Creek rises in s Haywood County and flows w into Little East Fork Pigeon River.

Shining Rock Gap, s Haywood County on the head of North Fork.

Shining Rock Ledge, s Haywood County, extends n from Black Balsam Knob to Cold Mountain.

Shining Rock Mountain, s Haywood County between Shining Rock Gap and Buck Spring Gap. Alt. 5,940.

Shinnsville, community in se Iredell County.

Shinnville. *See* Georgeville.

Shiny Creek rises in s Haywood County e of Spruce Ridge and flows n and then nw into Allen Creek.

Ship Channel. *See* Blair Channel.

Ship Point, n Tyrrell County, extends from the mainland into Albemarle Sound.

Shipyard, community on the Pasquotank River in w Camden County. In the eighteenth century, the area was a center for the construction of small commercial sailing vessels. The river there is straight and narrow for more than a mi., and it is now a popular spot for motorboat races.

Shit-Britches Creek rises in se Buncombe County on Burney Mountain and flows nw into Cane Creek. Named by early settlers who saw an Indian washing himself in the stream after an "accident" in his britches. The name appears frequently in early deeds but also is called Dirty Britches Creek.

Shoal Creek rises in se Buncombe County and flows nw into Cane Creek.

Shoal Creek rises in ne Burke County and flows n into Catawba River.

Shoal Creek rises in w Cherokee County between Signal Pole Hill and Arp Gap and flows ne into Apalachia Lake on Hiwassee River. Sometimes known as South Shoal Creek.

Shoal Creek rises in s Cleveland County and flows w into First Broad River.

Shoal Creek rises in sw Henderson County and flows nw into Crab Creek.

Shoal Creek rises in nw Jackson County and flows nw into Soco Creek.

Shoal Creek rises in s Jackson County and flows nw into West Fork Tuckasegee River.

Shoal Creek rises in s Macon County and flows sw into Middle Creek.

Shoal Creek rises in s Transylvania County and flows ne into Middle Fork French Broad River.

Shoal Creek rises in w Transylvania County and flows sw to join Indian Creek in forming North Fork French Broad River.

Shoal Creek rises in e Yancey County and flows s into Little Crabtree Creek.

Shoal Creek Falls, on Shoal Creek in sw Henderson County.

Shoal Creek Gap, e Yancey County near the head of Shoal Creek.

Shoal Creek Township, w central Cherokee County.

Shoal Inlet. *See* Masonboro Inlet.

Shoal Mountain, w Jackson County between Thorpe Reservoir and Shoal Creek.

Shoal Mountain, ne Rutherford County near the head of Hardbargain Branch. Alt. 2,340.

Shoals, community in se Surry County between Grassy Creek and Yadkin River. Named for Bean Shoals in Yadkin River.

Shoals Township, se Surry County.

Shocco, community in n Franklin County. Site of popular nineteenth-century springs and resort.

Shocco Creek rises in e Vance County and flows se through Warren County onto the Franklin-Warren County line, where it enters Fishing Creek. Shown on the Price map, 1808. Named for the Shoccoree Indian tribe.

Shocco Springs, former health resort in s Warren County on Shocco Creek. Located approx. 9 mi. s of Warrenton, it was popular in the nineteenth century as a social, recreational, and health resort built around mineral springs. Shocco Male Academy was located there. Neither is in existence any longer. Shocco Springs had a post office from 1832 until 1866 and was shown on the Price map, 1808.

Shocco Township, s Warren County.

Shoe, community in w Wilkes County between North Prong Lewis Fork Creek and South Fork Reddies River.

Shoe Branch rises in n central Carteret County and flows s into Newport River.

Shoe Heel. *See* Maxton.

Shoeheel Creek rises in e Scotland County and flows s into Big Shoeheel Creek. *See also* Maxton.

Sholars Crossroads, community in s Duplin County.

Shole Inlet. *See* Masonboro Inlet.

Sholes of Hatteras. *See* Diamond Shoals.

Shoofly, community in w Granville County between Culbreth and Stem.

Shoofly. *See* Maribel.

Shook Branch rises in e central Madison County and flows w into Big Laurel Creek.

Shook Brook rises in s Catawba County and flows se into Rhodes Mill Creek.

Shook Gap, central Haywood County between Colman Gap and Cansadie Top. Alt. 2,800.

Shookville, community on Little Buck Creek in e Macon County.

Shooting Creek rises in se Clay County and flows w into Lake Chatuge on the Hiwassee River. The name is believed to be a translation of the Cherokee *du-stagalan'yi* (where it made a great noise), applied to the stream.

Shooting Creek, community in s Clay County on Shooting Creek.

Shooting Creek Bald, s central Clay County. Alt. 5,010.

Shooting Creek Township, e Clay County.

Shooting Ridge, n Transylvania County, extends ne from Funneltop Mountain to Bradley Creek.

Shop Branch rises in ne Cherokee County and flows nw into Worm Creek.

Shop Branch rises in w Johnston County and flows se into Middle Creek.

Shop Branch rises in w Mitchell County and flows nw into Nolichucky River.

Shop Cove, on the Beaufort-Pitt County line at the confluence of Tar River and Tranters Creek.

Shop Creek rises in w Macon County and flows s into Little Choga Creek.

Shope Branch rises in s Macon County and flows se into North Fork [Skennah Creek].

Shope Cove, n Macon County on a tributary of Burningtown Creek.

Shope Creek rises in n Buncombe County and flows se into Bull Creek.

Shope Fork rises in s Macon County and flows ne into Coweeta Creek.

Shope Knob, s Swain County between Cullasaja Branch and Jones Creek.

Shopton, community in sw Mecklenburg County on the head of Steele Creek. Around 1880 J. R. Hays started a general store there. By 1890 several shops operated there, and the area became known as Shop Town or Shopton.

Shore. *See* Flint Hill.

Shore Ridge Mountain, ne Rutherford County between Lump and Chalk Mountains.

Short Bunk, ridge in w Haywood County between Conrad Branch and Coggins Branch.

Short Creek rises in se Beaufort County and flows n into South Creek.

Short Off, peak in nw Clay County near the Cherokee-Clay county line. Probably named for C. W. Short (1794–1863), American botanist.

Short Off, community in se Macon County near the mountain of the same name. Served by post office, 1880–1920.

Shortoff Gap, on the Jackson-Macon County line.

Shortoff Mountain, w Burke County. Alt. approx. 3,115.

Shortoff Mountain, on the Jackson-Macon County line. Alt. 5,054.

Short Swamp Branch rises in nw Nash County and flows s into Sandy Creek.

Shorty Top, central Cherokee County near the headwaters of Dockery and Rose Creeks.

Shot Beech Ridge, n Swain County in Great Smoky Mountains National Park extending s from Thomas Ridge near lat. 35°35' N., long. 83°25' W.

Shot Pouch Creek rises in w Macon County and flows se into Wayah Creek.

Shot Pouch Knob, on the Jackson-Haywood County line.

Shotwell, community in e Wake County between Marks and Poplar Creeks. Served by post office, 1883–1900. Named for Randolph Abbott Shotwell (1844–85), Confederate soldier and Democratic editor in Rutherford County.

Shoups Ford, in s Burke County crosses Jacob Fork.

Shuckpen Gap, on the Buncombe-Haywood County line between Doubletop Mountain and Thompson Knob.

Shuck Ridge Creek, rises in nw Transylvania County and flows se into Daniel Ridge Creek.

Shuckstack Mountain, w Swain County in Great Smoky Mountains National Park on Twentymile Ridge near lat. 35°29'08" N., long. 83°48'55" W. Alt. 4,100.

Shuckstack Ridge, nw Swain County, extends se from Shuckstack Mountain to Fontana Lake.

Shuford Creek rises in e Yancey County and flows se into Whiteoak Creek.

Shuford Mountain, e Transylvania County near the head of McCall Branch.

Shufordsville. *See* Arden.

Shugan Creek. *See* Little Sugar Creek.

Shular Gap, s Swain County n of Little Yalaka Creek.

Shuler Creek rises in nw Cherokee County and flows sw into Hiwassee River on the Polk County, Tenn., line.

Shuler Mountain, sw Cherokee County near the headwaters of Dickey Branch.

Shulls Mill, community in s Watauga County on Watauga River. Est. as a post office in 1870 (closed 1955); named for Joseph Shulls, settler, whose daughter eloped with the local sheriff, Cobb McCandless. The couple went to the West, where McCandless joined the Jesse James gang and was killed by a member of the Jones gang, a rival group.

Shumaker Mountain. *See* Fox's Mountain.

Shumont, community in se Buncombe County.

Shumont Mountain, on the Buncombe-Rutherford County line approx. 2 mi. n of Chimney Rock. Alt. approx. 3,839. Formerly known also as Harris Mountain and Leaventhorps View.

Shunkawakan Falls, on Whiteoak Creek, central Polk County. Water originally fell for a total of 500 ft., but blasting for road construction broke the falls into two sections.

Shute, community in central Union County nw of the city of Monroe.

Shute Branch rises in ne Buncombe County and flows se into North Fork [Swannanoa River].

Shutin Branch rises in n central Transylvania County and flows ne into Davidson River.

Shut-in Creek rises in n Jackson County on n slopes of Bald Mountain and flows n into Soco Creek.

Shut-in Creek is formed in w Madison County by the junction of West Fork Shut-in Creek and East Fork Shut-in Creek and flows ne into French Broad River.

Shut-in Ridge, s Buncombe County between Bent Creek and French Broad River.

Shutin Ridge, n central Transylvania County, extends e along the course of Joel Branch.

Sid Hill, n Yancey County between Peterson Branch and Whitson Branch.

Sidney, community in e Beaufort County.

Sidney, town in sw Columbus County. Inc. 1881, but long inactive in municipal affairs.

Sigmonsburg. *See* Glen Alpine.

Signal Bald, peak on the Clay-Macon County line. Alt. 5,275.

Signal Pole Hill, sw Cherokee County on se end of Pack Mountain. Alt. 3,459.

Sikes Branch rises in w Carteret County and flows approx. 2 mi. s and e to join East Prong in forming Sanders Creek.

Silas Creek rises in nw Ashe County and flows se into North Fork New River.

Silas Creek rises in sw Beaufort County and flows n into Chocowinity Bay, Pamlico River.

Silas Creek rises in nw Forsyth County and flows sw into Muddy Creek. Known earlier as Spangenberg Creek for Bishop August G. Spangenberg, who led a surveying party from Edenton to the Blue Ridge Mountains in 1752 in search of a suitable site for a Moravian settlement. Spangenberg Creek appears as Strangenbergs Creek on the Collet map, 1770, and as Spanking Back on the Price map, 1808. By 1833, when the MacRae map appeared, it was called Silas Creek. Reynolda Lake is on Silas Creek.

Silas Creek, community in n Ashe County. Alt. approx. 2,740.

Siler Bald, sw Macon County at the head of Roaring Fork Creek approx. 1 mi. s of Wayah Gap. Alt. 5,216. Part of Nantahala Mountain Range. Named for Jesse Richardson Siler, pioneer settler in the area. *See also* Silers Bald.

Siler Bald Branch rises on the s side of Siler Bald in sw Macon County and flows se into Bryson Branch.

Siler City, town in w Chatham County. Known first as Matthews Cross Roads because it was at the junction of the Raleigh-Salisbury and Fayetteville-Greensboro plank roads. Later known as Siler's Store and Siler's Station. Post office est. there in 1880 as Energy; changed to Siler City in 1884. Inc. 1887. Alt. 598. Produces furniture, textiles, processed grain, and poultry.

Silers Bald, mountain on the Swain County, N.C.–Sevier County, Tenn., line in Great Smoky Mountains National Park on Welch Ridge near lat. 35°33'58" N., long. 83°33'56" W. Alt. 5,620. Named for Jesse Richardson Siler (1793–1876) of Franklin, who owned the mountain and kept large herds of cattle on it.

Siles Branch rises in w Swain County and flows nw into Nantahala River.

Siles Gap, s Swain County between the head of Tarkiln Branch and the head of Siles Branch.

Silk Hope, community in nw Chatham County. Probably named in antebellum period at a time when there was an interest in producing homegrown silk.

Sills Creek rises in n Pender County and flows ne into Sawyers Creek.

Sills Creek rises in w Rowan County and flows ne into Back Creek. Named for John Sill, who settled there in 1749.

Siloam, community in s Surry County on Yadkin River. Alt. 811. Halls Ferry across the river was operated there as late as the 1930s.

Siloam Township, se Surry County.

Silver, community in se Stanly County served by post office, 1884–1906. Later known as Rocky River Springs.

Silver Bluff, community in s Haywood County on Pigeon River.

Silverboro. *See* Boyette.

Silver City, community in central Hoke County n of town of Raeford.

Silver Creek rises in nw Burke County and flows se into Rose Creek.

Silver Creek rises in sw Burke County and flows ne into Catawba River.

Silver Creek rises in se Caldwell County and flows se into Gunpowder Creek.

Silver Creek rises in central Polk County and flows n into Lake Adger on Green River.

Silver Creek rises in n Transylvania County and flows se into Turkey Creek.

Silver Creek Gap, in n Transylvania County on Sitton Mountain.

Silver Creek Knob, on the Burke-Rutherford county line. Alt. 2,838.

Silver Creek Township, sw Burke County.

Silverdale, community in e Onslow County between Freemans Creek and Webb Creek.

Silver Hill, community in s central Davidson County between Fourmile Branch and head of Battle Branch. A mine operated there almost continuously from about 1838 until 1860; produced lead, gold, and silver.

Silver Hill, community in w Pamlico County. Named for local Silver family.

Silver Hill, community in n Scotland County near Monroes Millpond.

Silver Hill Pocosin, a muck-filled area approx. 4 mi. by 4½ mi. in nw Pamlico County.

Silver Hill Township, central Davidson County.

Silver Knob, nw McDowell County near Limekiln Creek.

Silver Lake, tidal basin or boat harbor, 700 yds. long, at the community of Ocracoke on Ocracoke Island, se Hyde County.

Silver Lake, a natural lake fed by springs, sw New Hanover County between Todds and Barnards Creeks near the Cape Fear River. Covers approx. 16 acres; max. depth 30 ft.

Silver Lake, nw Wilson County on Toisnot Swamp. Covers 175 acres; max. depth 12 ft. Fishing, swimming, boating, and municipal water supply. Formed in 1785 by John Dew and known as Dew's Mill until about 1847. Called by the name of various owners until about 1922, when present name was applied.

Silvermine Bald, on the Haywood-Transylvania county line ne of Chestnut Bald.

Silvermine Branch rises in ne Cherokee County and flows se into Valley River.

Silvermine Branch rises in n Madison County and flows sw into French Broad River.

Silvermine Branch rises in central Swain County and flows sw into Lands Creek.

Silvermine Creek rises in sw Swain County and flows ne into Nantahala River.

Silvermine Gap, sw Swain County on the head of Silvermine Creek.

Silver Run rises in e Cumberland County and flows nw into Cape Fear River.

Silver Run rises in s Mitchell County and flows e into Grassy Creek.

Silver Run Creek rises in s Jackson County on the se slope of Chimneytop Mountain and flows sw 3 mi. to join Little Whitewater Creek in forming Whitewater River.

Silver Run Creek rises in w Randolph County and flows sw into Uwharrie River.

Silver Run Falls, in Cape Fear River at its junction with Silver Run approx. 3 mi. s of the mouth of Little River, ne Cumberland County. A series of small falls or rapids drop approx. 5 ft. in 300 yards. Mentioned in Fulton's survey of North Carolina rivers in 1819 and appears on the MacRae map, 1833.

Silvers Cove, e Haywood County on the head of Silvers Cove Creek.

Silvers Cove Creek rises in e Haywood County in Silvers Cove and flows sw into Rush Fork.

Silver Springs, community in central Gates County on the s side of Merchants Millpond.

Named for an artesian spring. Formerly a popular spot for picnics.

Silverstone, community in n Watauga County on Sharp Creek.

Silver Town, community in sw Brunswick County.

Silver Valley, community in e Davidson County.

Sim, community in e Robeson County served by post office, 1888–1903.

Simes Creek. *See* Perry Creek.

Simmon Grove, community in n Chatham County served by post office, 1861–1904.

Simmons Branch rises in s Madison County and flows se into Sandy Mush Creek.

Simmons Branch rises in ne Swain County and flows se into Raven Fork.

Simmons Branch rises in w Wilkes County and flows e into Dugger Creek.

Simmons Cove, n Buncombe County w of Paint Fork community.

Simmons Knob, e Yancey County between the head of Mine Branch and Crabtree Creek.

Simmons Landing, nw Tyrrell County on Scuppernong River.

Simmons Ridge, se Avery County.

Simms Fork rises in w Yancey County and flows s into Elk Wallow Creek.

Simon Branch rises in central Cherokee County and flows se into Morgan Creek.

Simon Branch rises in n Macon County and flows sw into Little Tennessee River.

Simpson, town in e Pitt County. Inc. 1923; post office est. 1888 as Chicod. Name changed in 1960. Alt. 63.

Simpson Branch rises in sw Union County and flows s into South Carolina, where it enters Cane Creek.

Simpsons Store, community in w Rockingham County served by post office, 1879–1902, which operated in Patrick Simpson's store.

Simpsonville Township, s Rockingham County.

Sims, town in nw Wilson County, was settled before 1908, when a post office was est. Inc. 1913 as Simms; named for W. W. Simms. Reincorporated in 1923 as Sims. A large stone quarry is nearby.

Sims Creek rises in s Watauga County and flows sw into Boone Fork.

Sincerity, community in ne Union County on Richardson Creek.

Singecat Ridge, nw McDowell County near the head of Buck Creek.

Singletary Lake, e Bladen County, a 572-acre natural lake with a max. depth of 11 ft., 8 in. Named for Richard Singletary, who received a grant of land in Bladen County in 1729. Part of Singletary Lake State Park. Fishing, boating, swimming, and camping. *See also* Carolina Bays.

Singletons Bay, loam-filled bay in se Hoke County between Big Marsh Swamp and Little Marsh Swamp.

Singleton Swamp rises in nw Beaufort County and flows nw and w into Old Ford Swamp.

Sings Creek rises in w Moore County and flows ne into Wet Creek.

Sinking Creek rises in nw Haywood County and flows ne into Big Creek.

Sioux, community in n Yancey County on Big Creek. Served by post office, 1887–1955. Alt. 2,109.

Sippanaw. *See* Rudd.

Sippihaw, community in s Wake County served by post office, 1900–1902.

Sites, community in s Bladen County in Carvers Creek Township served by post office, 1902–17.

Sitting Bear Mountain, nw Burke County. Alt. approx. 4,100.

Sitton, community in nw Henderson County on South Fork. Served by post office, 1888–1904, named for postmaster Silas Sitton.

Sitton Creek rises in nw Henderson County and flows sw into Seniard Creek.

Sitton Creek rises in n Transylvania County and flows se into Boylston Creek.

Sitton Knob, n Transylvania County at the se end of Sitton Mountain.

Sitton Mountain, n Transylvania County, extends se between North Prong Turkey Creek and Sitton Creek.

Six Forks, community in n Wake County near the head of Mine Creek where six roads come together; formerly called Tippers Crossroads.

Sixmile Creek rises in se Mecklenburg County and flows sw on the Mecklenburg-Union county line into South Carolina, where it enters Sugar Creek.

Sixpound Creek rises in n central Warren County and flows n then ne into Lake Gaston. Appears on the Moseley map, 1733.

Sixpound Township, n Warren County.

Six Runs, community in e Sampson County.

Six Runs Creek rises in ne Sampson County and flows s and sw to join Coharie River in forming Black River. Appears on the Collet map, 1770.

Skalley Branch rises in n Avery County and flows w into Elk River.

Skalley Knob, n Avery County.

Skeenah Creek is formed in s Macon County by the junction of North Fork [Skeenah Creek] and South Fork [Skeenah Creek] and flows e into Little Tennessee River. The name is said to be an Indian word meaning "the abode of satan."

Skeenah Gap, s Macon County between Black Mountain Branch and Jones Creek.

Skewarky. *See* Williamston.

Skibo or **Skibow (Sky-bow)**, community in central Cumberland County. Alt. 221.

Skidder Branch rises in ne Swain County and flows se into Straight Fork.

Skiffley Creek rises in n Haywood County and flows se into Pigeon River.

Skiffly Branch rises in w Madison County and flows s into Roaring Fork.

Skin Cabin Creek rises in s Surry County and flows se into Ararat River.

Skinner Canal, n Washington County, drains n from East Dismal Swamp to Kendricks Creek. Known in 1868 as McRae Canal.

Skinner's Point. *See* Hornblower Point.

Skinnersville, community in n Washington County. Post office est. in 1808 with service until 1908. Name was changed to Leo. The site of the community having moved to the ne, the old site became known locally as Old Skinnersville.

Skinnersville Township, ne Washington County, was formed in 1868.

Skipper Branch rises in s central Brunswick County and flows s into Shallotte Creek.

Skitty Creek rises in e Macon County and flows s into Cullasaja River.

Skull Camp Mountain, nw Surry County. Alt. 2,082. A post office, Scull Camp, served the area, 1800–1856. The name appears on the U.S. Coast Survey map, 1865.

Skunk Creek rises in central Lee County and flows nw into Big Buffalo Creek.

Skyco, former community and steamboat landing on the sw shore of Roanoke Island, e Dare County. It was on Ashby Harbor. Named for Skiko, son of the chief of the Choanoke Indians, who was taken prisoner by Ralph Lane in 1586. Skyco was a post office from 1892 until 1913.

Skyland, community in s Buncombe County. Alt. 2,257. Est. 1888 by Otis A. Miller as a resort. Produces electronic components.

Skyland Lake, s Buncombe County on Powell Creek, was formed in 1963 by Carolina Power and Light Company with the construction of an e dam and concrete spillway. It covers 320 acres, with a max. depth of 100 ft. and a shoreline of 9 mi. Used to condense turbine-exhaust steam at a steam power-generating plant and for public recreation.

Skyuka Creek rises in s Polk County e of Tryon Mountain and flows s into Pacolet River. Named for the Cherokee brave who, about 1774, showed his friendship for the whites by revealing to them an unknown route through the mountains. Knowledge of the route enabled Capt. Thomas Howard to defeat the Indians at Round Mountain, *which see.*

Skyuka Mountain, sw Polk County rising above the town of Tryon. Said to be named for Skyuka, son of a Cherokee chief. Skyuka was thrown from his horse and broke his leg when the horse became frightened by a snake. Capt. Thomas Howard found Skyuka and set his leg, and the two became friends. *See also* Howard Gap.

Sky View Pond, spring-fed lake in ne Iredell County. Formed in 1950; covers 38 acres, with a max. depth of 35 ft. Fishing, swimming, boating.

Slab Camp Branch rises in n Swain County in Great Smoky Mountains National Park and flows e into Forney Creek.

Slab Ridge. *See* Sharon.

Slab Town. *See* Grissom.

Slade Creek rises in sw Hyde County and flows nw and sw into Pungo River. Appears on the Collet map, 1770.

Slade Creek. *See* Blounts Creek.

Slades Swamp rises in s Bladen County and flows nw along the Bladen-Columbus county line into Brown Marsh Swamp.

Sladesville, town in sw Hyde County on Slade Creek. Inc. 1849, but long inactive in municipal affairs.

Slap Swamp rises in n Columbus County and flows se into Friar Swamp.

Slashes, The, a large marsh approx. 4 mi. wide in e Halifax County between Conoconnara Swamp and Roanoke River.

Slate, community in w Stokes County served by post office, 1884–1905.

Slate Creek rises in nw Cherokee County and flows se into Shuler Creek.

Slate Mountain, ne Surry County between Ararat River and Archies Creek.

Slate Rock Creek rises between Laurel Mountain and Slate Rock Ridge in w Transylvania County and flows se into Henderson County, where it enters Bradley Creek in Pisgah National Forest.

Slate Rock Ridge, n Transylvania County, extends se from the nw end of Dividing Ridge to the nw end of Pilot Cove.

Slatestone, community in n central Beaufort County. Alt. 40.

Slatten Creek rises in central Jackson County and flows se into Robinson Creek.

Slaty Branch rises in ne Buncombe County and flows se into Flat Creek.

Slaty Knob, w Madison County between Rector Branch and French Broad River. Alt. 2,790.

Sled Runner Gap, in the Unicoi Mountains on the Cherokee County, N.C.–Monroe County, Tenn., line near the headwaters of Garreck Creek. Alt. approx. 3,850.

Sleepy Creek rises in se Carteret County between the communities of Gloucester and Marshallberg and flows s approx. 1½ mi. into The Straits. Appears on the Collet map, 1770.

Sleepy Creek rises in s Wayne County and flows ne into Neuse River. Saponi Indians lived along its banks, and many arrowheads and artifacts have been found there. Tradition says that the Indians believed the waters of the creek had medicinal values. Sick Indians came to drink the water and later would lie along the creek banks to sleep, hence the name.

Sleepy Gap, s Buncombe County between Grassy Knob and Truckwheel Mountain.

Slek Creek. *See* Town Fork Creek.

Slickens Creek rises in e Jackson County and flows ne into Tuckasegee River.

Slicking Gap, on the Transylvania County, N.C.–Greenville County, S.C., line in the Blue Ridge Mountains near the head of Bursted Rock Creek. Sometimes known as Slick Gap or Slicken Gap. Alt. 2,873.

Slick Rock, elevation between the head of

Norton Branch and the head of Cane Creek in se Macon County approx. 3 mi. se of town of Highlands. Alt. approx. 3,340.

Slick Rock, elevation in s Macon County between Stephens Creek and Gold Mine Branch. Alt. approx. 3,860.

Slickrock Branch rises in n Cherokee County near Bearpen Gap and flows ne into Hyatt Creek.

Slickrock Branch rises in n Haywood County and flows se into Pigeon River.

Slickrock Branch rises in ne Henderson County approx. 2 mi. sw of Bat Cave community and flows approx. 1 mi. se into Reedy Patch Creek. Named for the appearance of rocks in the stream.

Slickrock Creek rises in nw Graham County and flows ne to the Graham County, N.C.–Monroe County, Tenn., line, which it follows into Little Tennessee River.

Slick Rock Falls, n Transylvania County in a branch of Rockhouse Creek.

Slickrock Knob, w Yancey County at the s end of Sampson Mountain.

Slick Rock Mountain, w Randolph County w of Caraway Mountain and in close proximity to Black Jack, Vineyard, and Prickly Pear Mountains.

Slickrock Mountain, w central Yancey County between Phipps and Baker Creeks.

Slide Branch rises in nw Haywood County and flows n into Big Creek.

Sliding Knob Creek rises in sw Madison County and flows w into Spring Creek.

Sligo, community in n Currituck County on the w side of Tull Creek. Served by post office, 1854–1910. Named by a Methodist circuit rider from Sligo, Ireland, who visited the area in 1783. Also known as Cowell's Bridge.

Slim Creek rises in n McDowell County on the w slope of Betsy Ridge and flows s into Little Buck Creek.

Slipoff Branch rises in e Swain County and flows ne into Connelly Creek.

Slipoff Knob, e Swain County between the head of Connelly Creek and the head of Slipoff Branch.

Slippery Hill Ridge, w Avery County.

Sloan, community in se Duplin County served by post office, 1884–1920. Alt. 50.

Sloan or **Sloans Station**. *See* Stony Point.

Sloans Creek rises in w Rowan County and flows

n approx. 3 mi. into Kerr Creek, *which see*. Known first as South Fork of James Cathey's Mill Creek and later as Marlins Creek.

Sloan's Crossing. *See* Garland.

Slocomb, community in n Cumberland County.

Slocomb Crossroads. *See* Turlington.

Slocum Creek rises in se Craven County and flows n into Neuse River. Appears on the Moseley map, 1733, as Slocumbs Creek.

Sloop Point extends from the mainland of s Pender County into Virginia Creek estuary in Topsail Sound. Named for the fact that sloops entering the sound moored there. Sloop Point post office, 1879–1936, was located at what is now Barlowes, *which see*. Site of oldest house in North Carolina, "Sloop Point" (ca. 1726).

Slosh. *See* Schlosstown.

Slough, The, stream, rises in n Wayne County and flows e into Nahunta Swamp.

Slow Creek rises in e Cherokee County and flows sw into Peachtree Creek.

Sluder Branch rises in nw Buncombe County on e slopes of Hanlon Mountain and flows ne and then se into Newfound Creek.

Sluice Gap, on the Swain County, N.C.–Sevier County, Tenn., line between Mount Kephart and The Sawteeth.

Sly, community in w Ashe County.

Small, community in s central Beaufort County.

Smallwood Island, a silty clay-loam island approx. 1¼ mi. long in Roanoke River, w Northampton County.

Smart Branch rises in s Macon County and flows sw into Middle Creek.

Smathers View Mountain extends e from Thompson Knob, *which see*, to Peggy Peak in sw Buncombe County.

Smethport, community in central Ashe County. Named for the town in Pennsylvania from which a local tanning extract plant had moved.

Smileys Falls, s Harnett County in Cape Fear River at the mouth of Upper Little River. A succession of ledges of rock there drops the water from 6 to 18 inches in most cases, but there is one fall of 4 ft. and another of 5 ft. Mentioned in Fulton's survey of North Carolina rivers in 1819.

Smith, community in n Forsyth County served by post office, 1883–1925.

Smith Branch rises in s central Cabarrus County and flows ne into Coddle Creek.

Smith Branch rises in e Madison County and flows s into Little Creek.

Smith Branch rises in se Mitchell County and flows n into Rose Creek.

Smith Branch rises in n Swain County and flows sw into Oconaluftee River.

Smith Creek rises in e Anson County near the town of Lilesville and flows ne into Blewett Falls Lake.

Smith Creek rises in e Beaufort County and flows se into Pungo Creek.

Smith Creek rises in central Buncombe County and flows ne into French Broad River.

Smith Creek rises in se Granville County and flows w 7 mi. into Beaverdam Creek at the Granville-Wake county line.

Smith Creek rises in w Hyde County and flows n into Pungo River. Appears as Smiths Creek on the Collet map, 1770.

Smith Creek rises in n Pamlico County and flows se into Bay River.

Smith Creek rises in se Pamlico County and flows s into the Greens Creek estuary at Neuse River. Appears on the Moseley map, 1733.

Smith Creek rises in w Warren County and flows ne into Mecklenburg County, Va., where it enters Roanoke River. Shown on the Moseley map, 1733, as Great Creek but appears by the present name on the Price map, 1808.

Smith Creek Township, nw Warren County.

Smitheys Creek rises in w Wilkes County and flows s into W. Kerr Scott Reservoir. Prior to 1962 the spelling was Smithies Creek.

Smithfield, town and county seat, central Johnston County on Neuse River. County court first held at the site in August 1771, when it became the county seat. Known as Johnston Court House until 1777, when it was est. as Smithfield. Named for John Smith, owner of land on which the town developed. The legislature met there in 1779. Produces textiles, apparel, lumber, electronic components, and processed meat. Alt. 155. *See also* Hinton's Quarter. Home of Ava Gardner Museum.

Smithfield Township, central Johnston County.

Smith Gap, e Haywood County between Big Branch and Crabtree Creek.

Smith Grove, community in central Davie County approx. 6 mi. ne of town of Mocksville. Named for a Methodist campground est. there in 1826. Post office est. 1834. Alt. 824.

Smithies Creek. *See* Smitheys Creek.

Smith Island, se Brunswick County at the mouth of Cape Fear River and bounded on the n by Corncake Inlet. Also known as Bald Head Island. The se tip is Cape Fear, and the sw portion is known as Bald Head because of its round, sandy surface. The island is approx. 17,000 acres in area and contains palmetto trees and other interesting vegetation and wildlife. Named for Landgrave Thomas Smith, who acquired it in 1690. Appears as Landgrave Thomas Smith's Island on the Moseley map, 1733, on which the present Bald Head is marked Barren Head. The Collet map, 1770, shows only "Bald Head." When Thomas Smith willed the island to his four sons in 1738, he said that its old name was Cedar Island. Scene of World War II training as auxiliary site of Camp Davis. Island developed in 1974. Access by ferry; no state-maintained roads or motorized traffic.

Smith Mill Creek rises in central Buncombe County near Deaver View Mountain and flows w through the city of Asheville into French Broad River.

Smith Millpond, s Wayne County on Sleepy Creek.

Smith Mountain, e Burke County. Alt. approx. 2,000.

Smith River rises in w Virginia and flows ne to a point approx. 3 mi. n of the North Carolina–Virginia state line, where it turns s and flows se into n Rockingham County. It enters Dan River at Eden. Called Irvin River by William Byrd in 1728 and appears as Irvine River on the Moseley map, 1733. Named for Alexander Irvine, professor of mathematics at the College of William and Mary and a member of Byrd's survey party of the North Carolina–Virginia line. Over time came to be known as Smith River for hunters Gideon and Daniel Smith, who settled on the upper waters of the river. Appears as Smith River on the Price map, 1808.

Smiths, community in s central Brunswick County.

Smiths Bridge Township, sw Macon County.

Smith's Corner, community in s central Camden County. Named for a physician who practiced there about 1840–70. Alt. 10.

Smiths Corner. *See* Smyrna.

Smiths Creek rises in ne Davie County and flows e approx. 6 mi. into Carters Creek.

Smiths Creek rises in w Lee County and flows n into Deep River.

Smiths Creek rises in n New Hanover County and flows sw into Cape Fear River.

Smiths Creek rises in ne Wake County and flows sw into Neuse River.

Smith's Creek. *See* Oriental.

Smith's Creek. *See* Sanders Creek.

Smith's Ferry. *See* Hinton's Quarter.

Smiths Mill Creek. *See* Mill Creek.

Smiths Mill Pond, e Robeson County on Oak Swamp. Covers 50 acres; max. depth 8 ft.

Smith's Point. *See* Mauls Point.

Smiths Pond, an artificial pond in ne Bladen County built about 1883. Max. depth approx. 10 ft. Fishing.

Smiths Store, community in e Alexander County.

Smiths Store, community in nw Cabarrus County.

Smiths Store, community in s Lincoln County.

Smith's Store. *See* Albemarle.

Smiths Township, former township in e Cabarrus County, now township no. 9.

Smiths Township, w Robeson County.

Smithtown, town in n Yadkin County, inc. 1924 and named for Columbus Smith, who settled there about 1894 to operate a cabinet shop and small furniture factory. Post office named Poindexter served the community, 1885–1907. No longer active in municipal affairs.

Smith Township, e central Duplin County.

Smithville. *See* Southport.

Smithville Township, s Brunswick County.

Smith Walker Mountain, sw Wilkes County between Warrior and Beaver Creeks. Named for a nineteenth-century resident of the area.

Smithwick, community in s Martin County on Long Creek.

Smithwick Creek rises in s Martin County and flows n into Statons Pond on Sweetwater Creek.

Smokemont, community in ne Swain County in Great Smoky Mountains National Park on Oconaluftee River. Alt. 2,188.

Smokey Gap, n central Avery County.

Smoky. *See* Bald Mountains.

Smoky Cove, s Haywood County on Dix Creek.

Smoky Creek rises in s Caldwell County and flows s into n Burke County, where it enters Catawba River.

Smoky Creek Township, n central Burke County.

Smoky Dome. *See* Clingmans Dome.

Smoky Mountain, se Henderson County between Butler and Blake Mountains.

Smoky Mountains. *See* Great Smoky Mountains.

Smyre Creek rises in central Catawba County and flows w and then s into Clark Creek.

Smyre Mills. *See* Ranlo-Rex-Priscilla.

Smyrna, community in e Carteret County on Middens Creek. First called Wit and later Smiths Corner. Post office est. 1853.

Smyrna Creek rises in e Carteret County and flows se into Jarrett Bay.

Smyrna Township, on Core Sound and Jarrett Bay in e Carteret County. At one time, parts of Smyrna made up Carteret and no. 6 and 7 townships.

Smyrna Township, se Robeson County.

Smyth. *See* Balfour.

Snaggy Bald, e Jackson County between Thunder Struck Mountain and Deep Gap. Alt. 5,538.

Snaggy Point, peak in w Madison County between Hogback Mountain and Meadow Fork.

Snaggy Ridge, s Haywood County between Cold Spring Branch and Deep Gap Branch.

Snake Bite Township, central Bertie County.

Snake Branch rises in w Haywood County and flows nw into Caldwell Fork.

Snake Branch rises in s Hertford County and flows ne into Ahoskie Swamp.

Snakeden Knob, s Macon County between Dryman Fork and Ball Creek.

Snakeden Mountain, s central Avery County.

Snake·Den Mountain, ne Madison County between Little Foster Creek and Foster Creek.

Snakeden Ridge, w Swain County, extends e from Pinnacle Creek to Pinnacle Ridge.

Snakeden Ridge, w Swain County, extends se between Birchfield Branch and Lost Cove Creek from Shuckstack Mountain to Eagle Creek.

Snakeden Top, central Haywood County on the e end of Goatrock Ridge.

Snake Island, a long, narrow, tidal-marsh island in sw Carteret County in Bogue Sound.

Snake Knob, n central Avery County.

Snake Knob, n Yancey County between Little Creek and Bald Mountain Creek.

Snake Knob. *See* Inadu Knob.

Snake Mountain, n Watauga County, extends n from Rich Mountain. Alt. 5,574.

Snake Ridge, w Haywood County in Great Smoky Mountains National Park, a short spur extending nw from Cataloochee Divide; center near lat. 35°36′10″ N., 83°04′54″ W.

Snapp, community in w Gaston County served by post office, 1883–1902.

Snatchet, community in e Duplin County later known as Beulaville, *which see.*

Snead Branch rises in e Cherokee County and flows se into Slow Creek.

Sneads Creek rises in s Onslow County and flows se into New River.

Sneads Ferry, community in s Onslow County on New River. Alt. 10. Originally called Lower Ferry on New River when the first ferry was licensed and operated there by Edmund Ennett in 1725. Robert W. Snead settled there about 1760 and operated the ferry and a tavern. The name of the community was then changed to Sneads Ferry. Post office est. 1842. The ferry ceased to operate in 1939 when a bridge was opened a short distance up the river. Appears on the Collet map, 1770. *See also* Fulcher Landing.

Sneads Grove, community in central Scotland County. Known earlier as Sneads Grove Church.

Sneed Branch rises in central Cherokee County and flows sw parallel to Rocky Pen Ridge into Nottely River.

Sneedsborough. *See* Old Sneedsborough.

Sneeky Creek rose in s Clay County and flowed ne into Hiwassee River. Its course is now covered by the waters of Chatuge Lake.

Snider, community in s Davidson County.

Snipe Creek rises in w Person County and flows nw into Mill Creek.

Snoad Branch rises in nw Beaufort County and flows se to join Old Ford Swamp in forming Aggie Run.

Snodes Creek rises in se Beaufort County and flows e into Goose Creek.

Snowball Gap, n Buncombe County se of Little Snowball Mountain.

Snowball Mountain, ne Buncombe County at the s end of Little Fork Ridge. Also known as Big Snowball Mountain. Alt. 5,494. Named for the fact that in winter the peak is frequently covered at its crest by a low cloud, giving the appearance of a large snowball.

Snowbird Creek rises in sw Graham County and flows se and ne into Santeetlah Lake. Called *Titiyi* (snowbird place) by Indians.

Snowbird Creek rises in n Haywood County and flows sw into Pigeon River.

Snowbird Gap, central Graham County between Snowbird Creek and Atoah Creek.

Snowbird Mountain, on the Jackson-Macon county line.

Snowbird Mountains extend across the e half of the Cherokee-Graham county line between Hawk Knob and Nantahala River. Max. alt. 4,743 at Teyahalee Bald.

Snowbird Top, on the Cherokee-Graham county line in the Snowbird Mountains. Alt. 3,882.

Snow Camp, community in sw Alamance County on Cane Creek. Dixon's Mill there dates from 1753. An iron foundry was est. there about 1800 and, as late as 1879, was still in operation. Legend says the name Snow Camp was given the community by Cornwallis's soldiers, who camped there after the Battle of Guilford Courthouse during a heavy snow.

Snow Creek rises on Asbury Mountain, ne Alexander County, and flows se into w central Iredell County, where it enters South Yadkin River.

Snow Creek rises in n Catawba County and flows ne into Catawba River.

Snow Creek rises in central Mitchell County and flows sw into North Toe River. Named for snow-white rocks in its bed.

Snow Creek rises in n Stokes County and flows se into Dan River.

Snow Creek rises in w Surry County and flows se and s into Mitchell River.

Snow Creek, community in n central Iredell County. Developed around a Methodist church founded there in 1802 at a cemetery begun in the 1780s.

Snow Creek, community in sw Mitchell County. Alt. approx. 2,600.

Snow Creek Township, s central Mitchell County.

Snow Creek Township, ne Stokes County.

Snowden, community in n Currituck County. Post office est. 1883; named for second postmaster, Milton Snowden. Service discontinued, 1966. Alt. 9.

Snow Hill, community in n Chowan County.

Snow Hill, county seat and town, central Greene County. Alt. 74. Authorized to be laid off 1811; inc. 1828. Named for a nearby plantation of the same name, which probably was named

---

for a hill of white sand. John Becton in 1753 willed lands "called the Snow Hills" in the county to his son Michael. Shortly after the Revolution, the Shepherd family tried without success to promote a town at the site to be called Shepherdsburgh. The ancient Tuscarora Indian town Catechna was located nearby. Today the town produces lumber, milling, and textile products.

Snow Hill Crossroads, community in n Duplin County.

Snow Hill Township, central Greene County.

Snow Marsh, a series of small tidal marshes, se Brunswick County in the Cape Fear River below Sunny Point.

Snow Mountain, n Avery County. Alt. 5,332.

Snow Point, se Brunswick County, extends se from the mainland into Cape Fear River at the mouth of Walden Creek and on the w side of Snow Marsh. Appears on the Collet map, 1770.

Snows Cut, canal in s New Hanover County approx. 1 3/5 mi. long, connects Myrtle Sound with Cape Fear River. It forms a part of the Intracoastal Waterway.

Snyder Creek rises in ne Cherokee County and flows nw into Tatham Creek.

Snyder Creek rises in n Lincoln County and flows se into Anderson Creek.

Soakas Creek rises in n Davidson County and flows w into s Forsyth County, where it enters South Fork Muddy Creek.

Soapstone Branch rises in nw Henderson County in Pisgah National Forest and flows e into McDowell Creek.

Soapstone Branch rises in e Mitchell County and flows w into Left Fork [Cane Creek].

Soapstone Branch rises in nw Swain County and flows sw into Eagle Creek at Horseshoe Bend.

Soapstone Creek rises in n Jackson County and flows n into Scott Creek.

Soapstone Gap, e Haywood County between Mary Gray Knob and Wines Top. Alt. 3,640.

Soapstone Gap, n Jackson County on the ne end of Rocky Face Ridge.

Soapstone Knob, s Swain County near Marr Branch and Brush Creek.

Soapstone Mount, formerly a large pyrophyllite formation in ne Randolph County; for a number of years, the mineral was mined, crushed at nearby Staley, and shipped away for refining and use in talc products. A post office by the name operated there, 1851–1901.

Soapstone Ridge extends se from Three Forks Mountain in w Transylvania County to Catheys Creek in w central Transylvania County.

Soapstone Ridge, n Transylvania County, extends ne from Rich Mountain to South Fork Mills River.

Society Parish, Church of England, Bertie County, est. with the formation of the county in 1722 and coextensive with it. Named for the Society for the Propagation of the Gospel. Previously the territory had been in South-West Parish, Chowan County, est. 1715. The parish had 930 white taxable inhabitants in 1767, described as "capable to maintain & willing to receive a Minister." Divided in 1727 to form Northwest Parish, which became Northampton County in 1741. The church for Society Parish was in the Merry Hill section of the county on Duckenfield land.

Soco Bald, on the Jackson-Swain county line near the head of Madcap Branch.

Soco Creek rises near Soco Gap, w Haywood County, and flows ne into Jonathans Creek.

Soco Creek rises in n Jackson County and flows sw into Oconaluftee River on the Jackson-Swain county line.

Soco Falls, on Soco Creek, w Haywood County. Water falls in a double stream over a series of rocky ledges for about 60 ft. into a cuplike basin. Said to have been named by the Cherokees for their word *Sog-wah* (one).

Soco Falls, on the head of Soco Creek in n Jackson County.

Soco Gap, on the Haywood-Jackson county line. Alt. 4,344. The most important passageway through Balsam Mountain for the Indians before the arrival of Europeans.

Soco Ridge, s Macon County between North Fork Coweeta Creek and the head of Hoglot Branch.

Soda Hill, community in ne Watauga County.

Sodom, community in n Madison County served by post office, 1898–1901. Laurel River and its tributaries drain the area. Local legend is that, after Presbyterian missionaries visited, name was changed to Revere, *which see.*

Sodom Branch rises in nw Madison County near

Sodom Mountain and flows n into Big Laurel Creek.

Sodom Branch rises in sw Yancey County and flows nw into Indian Creek. Named for an early sawmill camp, at which prostitution, violence of all kinds, and drunkenness were common. Nearby settlers drew upon the Bible for an appropriate name for the camp.

Sodom Hollow, central Buncombe County, the valley through which French Broad River flows nw of Asheville toward Dryman Mountain. Named by an early circuit rider, who compared the rough pioneers living there with the inhabitants of the biblical Sodom and Gomorrah.

Sodom Mountain, central Madison County between Walnut Gap and Lumptown.

Soggy Hill Branch rises in ne Swain County and flows s into Raven Fork.

Sokassa. *See* Rumbling Bald Mountain.

Solitude. *See* Ashland.

Solola Valley, community in n central Swain County on Noland Creek. The name comes from *salola*, the Cherokee Indian word for squirrel.

Solomons Creek rises in s Richmond County and flows w into Pee Dee River.

Solray Gap, central Haywood County between Little Pine Mountain and Pigeon River.

Sols Creek rises in e Jackson County and flows sw into Bear Creek Lake on the Tuckasegee River.

Somerset, community in se Chowan County served by post office, 1888–1903.

Somerset, community in central Person County. Est. 1895–1900 as Pick's or Pick's Siding, where lumber was brought by tramroad to be transferred to the railroad.

Somerset, plantation of Josiah Collins on Lake Phelps in Washington and Tyrrell Counties, developed between 1780 and 1788. At one time the plantation comprised more than 100,000 acres, 880 slaves, and about 20 buildings. The main house, Somerset Place, was built about 1830. The estate was abandoned and ruined before the end of the Civil War, and the property passed through various owners before it was sold at public auction in 1946. The state previously had purchased the mansion house and 16,628 acres in 1939. Somerset House has been restored and is open to the public as a State Historic Site. *See also* Pettigrew State Park.

Somerset Canal, se Washington County, drains the waters of Lake Phelps into Scuppernong River and forms a portion of the Washington-Tyrrell county line. The canal, built by slave labor in 1787 at a cost of $30,000, was 20 ft. wide, 6 ft. deep, and 6 mi. long. Known for almost a century as Collins Canal for Josiah Collins, the plantation owner.

Somers Township, se Wilkes County.

Somerton Creek rises in Virginia and flows sw into nw Gates County, where it enters Chowan River.

Somey Creek. *See* Sumey Creek.

Sommey Creek. *See* Sumey Creek.

Sonoma, community in s Haywood County served by post office, 1878–1905.

Sophia, community in n Randolph County. Settled prior to 1779. Post office est. 1891. Probably named for Sophia Clement, local resident. Alt. 801.

Soracte. *See* Sarecta.

Sornook. *See* Mount Guyot.

Sorrell Creek rises in s Haywood County and flows nw into Little East Fork Pigeon River.

Sorrells Cove, e Haywood County between Brown Cove and Thickety Creek.

Sorrell's Creek rises in w Wake County and flows nw into Black Creek.

Sorrow Creek appears on the Collet map, 1770, apparently rising in what is now n Davidson County and flowing w into South Fork in s Forsyth County.

Sossamon's Spring. *See* Sherrills Springs.

Soules Swamp rises in n Columbus County and flows ne then se into White Marsh.

Sound, community in ne Washington County served by post office, 1903–1908.

Sound, The. *See* Pamlico Sound.

Soundside, community in n Tyrrell County on the s side of Albemarle by post office, 1900–1901.

Sourwood Gap, on the Buncombe-McDowell county line ne of Montreat.

South Albemarle Township, e central Stanly County.

South Bay, in n Piney Island s of Rattan Bay, ne Carteret County. Approx. 1¾ mi. long and ½ mi. wide.

South Belmont, unincorporated outskirts of city of Belmont, se Gaston County.

South Biltmore, former town in central Buncombe County; inc. 1895 but now within the corporate limits of Asheville. *See also* Biltmore.

South Blue Ridge Township, e Henderson County.

South Branch Cartledges Creek rises in n Richmond County and flows sw into Cartledges Creek.

South Buffalo Creek rises in s central Guilford County and flows ne to join North Buffalo Creek in ne Guilford County to form Buffalo Creek.

South Channel, ne Currituck County.

South Clinton Township, central Sampson County.

South Country Line Creek rises in s Caswell County and flows nw into Country Line Creek.

South Cox Creek rises in n Yancey County and flows se into Jacks Creek.

South Creek rises in se Beaufort County and flows n and e into Pamlico River. Appears as Chickorack River on the Comberford map, 1657, and as South Dividing Creek on the Collet map, 1770.

South Creek rises in e Chatham County and flows e and s into Wake County, where it enters Big White Oak Creek near the Chatham County line.

South Creek rises in ne Rutherford County and flows ne into First Broad River.

South Creek, town in se Beaufort County on a peninsula formed by the mouths of Bond and Muddy Creeks as they enter Pamlico River. Settled prior to 1794, when it was known as Stanton-Harrold for two men who operated a sawmill there. Apparently known as Harold in the early nineteenth century and as Oregon (for the first steamboat to come up the Pamlico River—*see* Oregon Inlet) about the middle of the century. Post office, 1851–1954, operated as South Creek. Inc. 1883 as Stanton. Inc. 1925 as South Creek, but no longer active in municipal affairs.

South Crowders Creek rises in s Gaston County and flows se into Crowders Creek.

South Deep Creek rises in w Yadkin County and flows se and e to join North Deep Creek in forming Deep Creek.

South Dividing Creek. *See* South Creek.

South Double Creek rises in w Stokes County and flows ne into Dan River.

Southeast Muddy Creek rises in se McDowell County and flows ne into South Muddy Creek.

Southerlands Millpond, in e Vance County on Sandy Creek. Area 30 acres; max. depth 10 ft. Now used by the city of Henderson as a reservoir. *See also* Millford.

Southern City. *See* East Spencer.

Southerne Virginia Sea appears on the Comberford map, 1657, as the area of the Atlantic Ocean off the Outer Banks of modern North Carolina, roughly between the coast and the Gulf Stream.

Southern Mountain, central Transylvania County between Brushy Creek and Burl Mountain.

Southern Pines, town in s Moore County. Inc. 1887. Known earlier as Vineland, but the Post Office Department would not accept the name because of possible confusion with the town of the same name in New Jersey. Named for its location on the edge of the longleafpine belt. A popular winter resort. West Southern Pines, inc. 1923, became a part of Southern Pines in 1931. Alt. 516. Sandhills Community College, est. 1965, is located there.

Southern Plantation. *See* South Virginia.

Southern Shores, town and resort community in ne Dare County on the s coast of North Banks between Kitty Hawk and Duck. Inc. 1969.

South Fayetteville, unincorporated outskirts of city of Fayetteville in central Cumberland County.

South Flat River rises in sw Person County and flows se into Flat River.

South Fork rises in s Forsyth County and flows sw into Davidson County, where it enters Muddy Creek a short distance s of the county line. Early Moravian settlers called it Ens Creek, and it appears as such on the Collet map, 1770. On the Price map, 1808, it is marked "Ens or South Fork."

South Fork rises in s Henderson County and flows nw into Willow Creek. Also known locally as Greer Creek.

South Fork rises in n McDowell County near Betsy and Hensley Ridges and flows se into Toms Creek.

South Fork rises in nw McDowell County on the n slope of Pups Ridge and flows se into Roses Creek.

South Fork rises in w Surry County and flows se into Mitchell River.

South Fork rises in e Transylvania County and

flows se into w Henderson County, where it flows ne to join North Fork in forming Mills River. Sometimes also known as South Fork Mills River.

South Fork. *See* South Fork Catawba River.

South Fork Beech Creek rises in e Graham County and flows nw into Beech Creek.

South Fork [Big Pine Creek] rises in s Madison County and flows n to join North Fork in forming Big Pine Creek.

South Fork [Cane Creek] rises in n Chatham County and flows ne into s Alamance County, where it enters Cane Creek. Known also as South Fork Creek.

South Fork [Carvers Branch] rises in s Mitchell County and flows sw into Carvers Branch.

South Fork Catawba River is formed in central Catawba County by the junction of Jacob Fork and Henry Fork. It flows s through Catawba County, s across central Lincoln County, and se through central Gaston County to enter Catawba River in se Gaston County. Also known locally in various places as South Fork, South Fork River, and Little Catawba River. Appears as South Fork of the Catawba River on the Collet map, 1770.

South Fork Cattail Creek rises in s Yancey County and flows nw to join North Fork Cattail Creek in forming Cattail Creek.

South Fork Creek rises in w Tyrrell County and flows n into Scuppernong River.

South Fork Creek. *See* South Fork [Cane Creek].

South Fork Crooked Creek rises in w Union County and flows ne to join North Fork Crooked Creek in forming Crooked Creek.

South Fork Flat Creek rises in s Transylvania County and flows ne into Flat Creek.

South Fork Hawk Branch rises in n Yancey County and flows w to join Middle Fork Hawk Branch in forming Hawk Branch.

South Fork [James Cathey's Mill Creek]. *See* Sloans Creek.

South Fork Jones Creek rises in sw Anson County and flows ne to join North Fork Jones Creek in forming Jones Creek.

South Fork Little Horse Creek rises near Apple Grove in nw Ashe County and flows e into Little Horse Creek.

South Fork Little River rises in n Orange County and flows se into nw Durham County, where it joins North Fork Little River in forming Little River.

South Fork Mountain Creek rises in e Catawba County and flows e to join North Fork Mountain Creek in forming Mountain Creek.

South Fork New River is formed in s Watauga County approx. 2 mi. se of Boone by the confluence of East Fork, Flannery Fork, and Middle Fork. It meanders ne to join North Fork New River in forming New River on the Ashe-Alleghany county line. *See also* East Fork [South Fork New River]; Flannery Fork [South Fork New River]; Middle Fork [South Fork New River].

South Fork Rapier Mill Creek rises in sw Cherokee County and flows se and ne into Rapier Mill Creek after dipping into Fanin County, Ga.

South Fork [Rattle Snake Creek] rises in central Caswell County and flows nw to join North Fork of Rattle Snake Creek in forming Rattle Snake Creek.

South Fork Reddies River rises in w Wilkes County and flows se into Middle Fork Reddies River.

South Fork River. *See* South Fork Catawba River.

South Fork Rock Creek rises in s Yancey County and flows ne into Rock Creek.

South Fork [Second Creek]. *See* Back Creek.

South Fork [Skeenah Creek] rises in s Macon County and flows ne to join North Fork [Skeenah Creek] in forming Skeenah Creek.

South Fork Township, s Forsyth County.

South Fork Township, w Tyrrell County.

South Fork Upper Creek rises in s Yancey County and flows se to join Middle Fork Upper Creek in forming Upper Creek.

South Fork Yadkin River. *See* Mill Fork; South Yadkin River.

South Gaston, former town in nw Halifax County on Roanoke River. Chartered 1895; charter repealed 1907. Appears as So. Gaston on the Colton map, 1861, but as Gaston on the Kerr map, 1882. It was at South Gaston that passengers on the Raleigh and Gaston Railroad took a ferry across the Roanoke River to the town of Gaston before a railroad bridge spanned the river. The community of Thelma is now at the site.

South Gastonia, community in s Gaston County adjacent to the city of Gastonia. The former communities of Myers, Pinkney, and Ridge

(originally Pleasant Ridge) are now considered to be parts of South Gastonia. Alt. 772.

South Harper Creek rises in se Avery County
in Boone Wildlife Management Area and
flows se to join North Harper Creek near the
Caldwell County line to form Harper Creek.

South Henderson, unincorporated outskirts of
city of Henderson in s central Vance County.

South Hominy, community in sw Buncombe
County near the junction of Glady Fork and
South Hominy Creek.

South Hominy Creek rises in sw Buncombe
County near Brooks Gap and flows ne into
Hominy Creek.

South Hyco Creek rises in n Orange and se
Caswell Counties and flows ne into Person
County, where it joins North Hyco Creek in
forming Hyco River. The part of South Hyco
Creek that lies in Caswell County is some-
times called Sugartree Creek.

South Lake, nw mainland of Dare County. It
drains into Alligator River.

South Lake, artificial pond on Long Creek in
s Vance County. Covers 14 acres, with max.
depth of 15 ft. Originally named Beckham
Millpond and was formed sometime in the
nineteenth century. Name was changed in
early 1940s, when the lake was bought by a
social club. The mill is still standing; lake is
used for recreation (fishing, swimming, boating). The name appeared on the soil survey
map of 1913 as Beckon Mill.

South Leopard Creek, an inlet of North River
into the mainland s of North Leopard Creek
in e Carteret County.

South Lowell, community in nw Durham County
between Buffalo and Horse Creeks on the n
side of North Fork Little River.

South Mills, town in nw Camden County; inc.
1883, but not active in municipal affairs. Prior
to 1800 the community was known as New
Lebanon because the junipers that formerly
grew in the area adjacent to the Dismal
Swamp suggested the biblical reference to
the tall cedars of Lebanon. Post office was
New Lebanon from 1797 until 1839, when the
name was changed to South Mills because
waters from a spillway at the s end of the
Dismal Swamp Canal were used to turn
wheels of mills there.

South Mills Township, n Camden County.

Southmont, community in s Davidson County
on High Rock Lake and the Winston-Salem
Southbound Railway. Post office there, 1883–
1906, was known as Fairmont. Reestablished
as Southmont in 1910; probably named for
the new Winston-Salem Southbound Railway.
Alt. 669.

South Mountains, a range of mountains extending from ne Rutherford County into sw Burke
and n Cleveland Counties. Known by the
Cherokee Indians as *Oakanoahs*.

South Mountains Wildlife Management Area, in
se Burke County. 17,700 acres. Jointly owned
by private interests and the town of Morganton. Est. 1952–53.

South Muddy Creek rises in se McDowell County
and flows ne to join North Muddy Creek near
the Burke County line to form Muddy Creek.

South Point, n extremity of Pea Island in e Dare
County. Lies at junction of Oregon Inlet and
Atlantic Ocean.

South Point, community in se Gaston County
served by post office, 1846–1902.

South Point Township, se Gaston County.

Southport, town, se Brunswick County on Cape
Fear River. Fort Johnston, *which see*, built
there, 1748–64. The town began to develop by
1792 and was named Smithville for Gen. Benjamin Smith (1751–1826). Inc. in 1805 and
made county seat in 1808; remained so until
a new government center opened near Bolivia
in 1978. Name changed to Southport in 1889
because it was the southernmost seaport in
the state. Alt. 26.

South Prong, stream, rises in s Haywood County
and flows ne into Shining Creek.

South Prong rises in s Transylvania County and
flows ne into Little River.

South Prong [Clarks Creek] rises in n Mecklenburg County and flows e to join North Prong
in forming Clarks Creek.

South Prong Creek rises in e Guilford County
and flows ne into sw Alamance County, where
it enters Stinking Quarter Creek.

South Prong [Glady Fork] rises in s Transylvania
County on n slopes of Sassafras Mountain
and flows ne and then nw to join West Prong
[Glady Fork] in forming Glady Fork. Also
known as Kirkendall Creek.

South Prong Lewis Fork Creek rises in w Wilkes
County and flows se approx. 9 mi. to join

North Prong Lewis Fork Creek in forming Lewis Fork Creek. Yates Mountain lies between the two prongs.

South Prong Stanley Creek rises in ne Gaston County and flows se into Dutchmans Creek.

South Prong Turkey Creek rises in n Transylvania County and flows se to join North Prong Turkey Creek in forming Turkey Creek.

South Prong West Branch rises in n Mecklenburg County and flows se into Rocky River.

South Prong [Wet Ash Swamp] rises in Green Swamp, w Brunswick County, and flows nw into Wet Ash Swamp.

South River rises in n Carteret County and flows n approx. 9½ mi. into Neuse River. Appears on the Moseley map, 1733.

South River is formed on the Cumberland-Sampson county line by the junction of Black River and East Mingo Branch. It flows se along the Cumberland-Sampson and Bladen-Sampson county lines into Black River near the Pender County line.

South River, community on the w side of South River near its mouth, n Carteret County.

South River, community in n Rowan County on South Fork Yadkin River. Settled about 1800. Served by post office, 1860–1907.

South River Township, sw Sampson County.

South Rocky Mount, the s part of Rocky Mount in w Edgecombe County.

South Rodanthe. *See* Waves.

South Salisbury, unincorporated outskirts of city of Salisbury, e central Rowan County.

South Second Creek rises in s Rowan County and flows ne into High Rock Lake. Appears as Lower Second Creek on the Collet map, 1770; as Dutch Second Creek on the Price map, 1808, and the MacRae map, 1833; as Second Creek on the Kerr map, 1882; and as South Second Creek on recent maps.

South Shoal Creek. *See* Shoal Creek.

South Shore Parish. *See* St. Andrew's Parish; St. Paul's Parish.

Southside, community in central Lincoln County. Named for a mill built on the s side of Lincolnton in 1891. Alt. 753.

South Skitty Branch rises in e Macon County and flows sw into Cliffside Lake.

South Spring Top, on the Haywood-Transylvania county line.

South Stony Fork Creek rises in e Watauga County and flows se into Wilkes County and into Stony Fork Creek.

South Sunbury, community in central Gates County on Raynor Swamp.

South Toe River is formed in s Yancey County by the junction of Left Prong South Toe River and Right Prong South Toe River. It flows n to join North Toe River on the Mitchell-Yancey county line to form Toe River.

South Toe Township, s Yancey County.

South Tunis, community in e Hertford County.

South Turkey Creek rises on the Buncombe-Haywood county line near Turkey Creek Gap and flows ne to join North Turkey Creek in forming Turkey Creek.

South Virginia, a name frequently applied from about 1612 to about 1663 to the area that subsequently became the County of Albemarle in the colony of Carolina. William Strachey's *The Historie of Travell into Virginia Britannia* (1612) contains a brief description of South Virginia. After the region began to be settled (ca. 1650), it was also referred to as the Southern Plantation. In 1662 Samuel Stephens was made commander of the Southern Plantation by the Virginia Council.

South Wadesboro, town in central Anson County. Wadesboro Cotton Mill built there in 1892. Town inc. in 1893, but long inactive in municipal affairs.

South Washington, former town in n central Pender County on Washington Creek near its mouth in Northeast Cape Fear River. Laid out about 1740 by Malatiah Hamilton as the center of trade for the Welsh Tract, *which see*. Inc. 1791 as South Washington. About 1840 moved approx. 1½ mi. sw to a site on the newly completed railroad and came to be called Hiawatha, corrupted into Watha, *which see*.

Southwest Creek rises in n Carteret County and flows ne into South River.

Southwest Creek rises in sw Lenoir County and flows ne into Neuse River. Appears as Salmon Creek on the Moseley map, 1733; called Canterbury Creek by Governor Arthur Dobbs; and appears as Southwest Creek on the Collet map, 1770. Scene of 1863 Battle of Wyse Fork, *which see*.

Southwest Creek rises in w Onslow County and flows se into New River. Appears on the Collet map, 1770.

South Westfield Township, e Surry County.

Southwest Fork [Alligator River] rises in s Tyrrell County near Alligator Lake and flows ne into Northwest Fork [Alligator River].

South West Parish. *See* St. Paul's Parish; Society Parish.

Southwest Prong Branch rises in w central Carteret County and flows n into Moon Creek.

Southwest Stony Fork Creek rises in e Watauga County and flows se into w Wilkes County to enter Stony Fork Creek.

South West Township, e Lenoir County.

South Whitakers Township, ne Nash County.

South Williams Township, s Columbus County.

South Wilmington, unincorporated outskirts of the city of Wilmington, w New Hanover County on the Cape Fear River.

Southwood, community in s Bladen County in Carvers Creek Township.

South Yadkin River rises in ne Alexander County and flows se across Iredell County and to the Davie-Rowan county line, which it forms to its junction with Yadkin River. Also sometimes known as South Fork Yadkin River. Appears as "Sapona or Yatkin River" on the Moseley map, 1733. *See also* Cedar Run Creek; Mill Fork.

Sowell Run rises in s Greene County and flows ne into Rainbow Creek. Named for the Sowell family, which settled in the vicinity before the Revolution.

Sowell's Mill Creek. *See* Mill Creek.

Spaightville, a town inc. 1802 and authorized to be laid out on the "ne side of French Broad River . . . opposite, or a little above the upper Warm Springs" to accommodate visitors to the springs. It is not known whether the town ever existed, but it is reasonable to assume that the present Hot Springs, *which see,* in w Madison County is its "descendant." Spaightville was undoubtedly named for Governor Richard Dobbs Spaight (1758–1802), who died approx. 2 months before the act was passed.

Spain Branch rises in s Buncombe County and flows se into Avery Creek.

Spainhour Creek rises in central Caldwell County and flows sw approx. 4 mi. into Lower Creek.

Spains Creek rises in se Onslow County and flows sw into Sulliers Bay.

Spangenberg Creek. *See* Silas Creek.

Spanish Oak Branch rises in w central Transylvania County and flows s into Catheys Creek.

Spanish Oak Branch rises in n Watauga County and flows s into Buffalo Branch.

Spanish Oak Gap, s Haywood County on Shining Creek.

Spanish Oak Hill, sw Alamance County.

Spanish Oak Mountain, central Avery County.

Spanking Back Creek. *See* Silas Creek.

Sparkling Catawba Springs. *See* Catawba Springs.

Sparkman, community in w Onslow County served by post office, 1888–1909.

Sparks Creek appears on the Collet map, 1770, in nw Davidson County n of Fryes Creek. It flows w into Muddy Creek.

Sparks Gap, central Mitchell County on Pumpkin Patch Mountain.

Sparks Ridge, e Mitchell County between Bear Creek and Bailey Meadows.

Sparta, town and county seat, central Alleghany County. Post office est. there as Bower's Store, 1825; name changed to Gap Civil, 1846, and to Sparta, 1879. Inc. 1879. Named for the ancient city in Greece. Alt. 2,939. Produces apparel and textiles. *See also* Gap Civil Township.

Sparta. *See* Old Sparta.

Sparta Mill Pond, central Alleghany County on Little River. Formed in 1920. Covers 8 acres; max. depth 10 ft. Fishing and swimming.

Sparta Township, former township in se Edgecombe County, now township no. 8.

Spear, community in w Avery County; settled 1815–30. Named for nearby Spear Tops Mountain.

Spear Tops Mountain, on Avery-Mitchell county line. Named because of its two spear-shaped peaks.

Speculation Land, massive tract in w Polk and e Henderson Counties acquired in 1790s by Speculation Land Company organized by Tench Coxe of Philadelphia. Some property remained unclaimed into the mid-twentieth century. In time, land was managed by Carolina Power Company (later Duke Power) and today is part of the Green River wildlife management area.

Speed, town in e Edgecombe County; inc. 1901. Named for E. T. Speed.

Speedwell, community in w Jackson County on Tilley Creek.

Speights Bridge, former community in n Greene County on Contentnea Creek. Settled about 1751 by Speight family, some of whom operated a toll bridge there. Civil War muster grounds a short distance n. When Fieldsboro (now Walstonburg) developed during the 1880s, Speights Bridge declined.

Speights Bridge Township, n Greene County.

Spence Field, bald spot on the Swain County, N.C.–Sevier County, Tenn., line in Great Smoky Mountains National Park near lat. 35°33'48" N., long. 83°43'58" W. Alt. 4,886.

Spencer, town in e Rowan County. Construction of shops for the Southern Railway was begun there in 1896. Inc. in 1901 and named for Samuel Spencer (1847–1906), president of Southern Railway. Whiteheads Mill appears on Grants Creek near present site of Spencer on the Collet map, 1770. Alt. 747. Home to North Carolina Transportation Museum, a State Historic Site.

Spencer. *See* Spencerville.

Spencer Mountain, e central Gaston County. Broadcast towers are there. Named for Zachariah Spencer, local Loyalist (Tory) who was captured during Revolutionary War, tried, and condemned to be shot. He turned "Whig," promising allegiance to the new republic; having no Bible, he took an oath on an almanac and was released. Alt. 1,304.

Spencer Mountain, community immediately n of the mountain of the same name, e central Gaston County. Inc. 1895 as town of Spencer Mountain Mills. Charter repealed 1909.

Spencers Fork rises in ne Caldwell County and flows sw into Brumleys Creek.

Spencerville, community in nw Moore County served by post office, 1888–1907. Known as Spencer until 1897.

Spences Corner, community in w Camden County; named for a pioneer family in the area and dates from about 1700.

Spero. *See* Balfours.

Spewmarrow Creek rises in n Granville County and flows nw into Grassy Creek.

Spice Bottom Creek rises in sw Watauga County and flows ne into Watauga River.

Spice Cove, the valley through which Spice Cove Branch flows in n Buncombe County.

Spice Cove Branch rises near Louis Ray Knob in ne Buncombe County and flows nw through Spice Cove into North Fork Ivy Creek.

Spice Cove Branch rises in w Transylvania County and flows se into North Fork French Broad River.

Spice Creek rises in w Watauga County and flows ne into Laurel Creek.

Spicers Bay, s Onslow County in Stump Sound. Named for John Spicer.

Spices Cove, ne Buncombe County between Pinnacle Mountain and Dillingham Creek.

Spies (speece), community in nw Moore County.

Spikes Creek rises in sw Gates County and flows se into Chowan River.

Spillcorn Creek rises in n Madison County and flows sw into Big Laurel Creek. Said to have been named because an early settler spilled a load of corn in the creek.

Spilona, community in central Johnston County served by post office, 1882–1903.

Spindale, town in central Rutherford County. Est. 1916 by K. S. Tanner and named by him for its location in a valley where cotton mills were est. Inc. 1923. Isothermal Community College, est. 1966, is located there.

Spit Bay, between Davis Island and Davis Shore in Core Sound in e Carteret County.

Spivey Creek rises in nw Yancey County and flows nw into Tennessee, where it enters Indian Creek.

Spivey Gap, central Buncombe County between Spivey and Miller Mountains.

Spivey Mountain, central Buncombe County n of Deaver View Mountain. Alt. 3,317.

Spiveys Corner, community in n Sampson County near Little Coharie Creek. Formerly known also as West Crossroads.

Spiveys Pond. *See* Lake Tabor.

Splash Dam Lake, e Transylvania County, drains sw into Cascade Lake. Covers 5 acres and has a max. depth of 30 ft.

Splashy. *See* Spray.

Splendor, community in s Henderson County served by post office, 1887–1905.

Split Mountain, e Haywood County between Fines Creek and the county line.

Split Whiteoak Ridge, w Macon County between Whiteoak Creek and Gold Pit Creek.

Spooks Branch rises in central Buncombe County near Lewis Gap and flows nw into Beaverdam Creek.

Spooners Bay, in Brown's Sound, s Onslow County. Probably named for Jabez Spooner, landowner in the vicinity by 1743. Sometimes mistakenly called Schooners Bay.

Spooners Creek rises in s Carteret County and flows s into Bogue Sound.

Spoonwater Creek rises in ne Person County and flows nw into Maho Creek. Said to have received its name because it is so shallow that anyone wanting water from it would have to use a spoon to dip it up.

Spot, community on Currituck Sound, s Currituck County. Formerly Hog Quarter, but renamed when a post office was est. there about 1920 (spot is a fish that is caught locally).

Spot Knob, on Haywood-Jackson county line. Alt. 5,900–6,000.

Spout Branch rises in w Avery County and flows e into Roaring Creek.

Spout Branch rises in sw Madison County and flows se into Little Creek.

Spout Springs, community in sw Harnett County. Once the center of a lumber and naval-stores industry. Alt. approx. 330.

Sprawls Old Field. *See* Norman.

Spray, former town in n Rockingham County on Smith River. Settled about 1813, when James Burnett est. gristmill at falls of Smith River. Site of cotton mill founded by future governor John M. Morehead; later operated by his son J. Turner Morehead. Known first as Splashy from the water thrown up by a waterwheel at a local mill; name later changed in 1890 to the more sophisticated Spray. Inc. 1951; merged with Leaksville and Draper in 1967 to form Eden, *which see*. Alt. 625.

Spread Branch rises in ne Swain County and flows n into Bunches Creek.

Spread Eagle Branch rises in ne Cherokee County and flows sw into Pile Creek.

Spring, community in se Iredell County served by post office, 1898–1903.

Spring Bank, former plantation and ferry, central Wayne County on Neuse River midway between the mouths of Stoney and Sleepy Creeks. Owned by Joseph Green Sr., largest slave owner in the county in 1790 and a member of the General Assembly. In 1784 Spring Bank was designated as a location for the receipt and inspection of tobacco. The Price map, 1808, shows only Green's Ferry at the location.

Spring Branch rises in e Craven County and flows se into Broad Creek.

Spring Branch rises in w Franklin County and flows se into Little River.

Spring Branch rises in s Greene County and flows e into Tyson Marsh.

Spring Branch rises in e Johnston County and flows sw into Little River.

Spring Branch rises in s Lenoir County and flows nw into Southwest Creek.

Spring Branch rises in ne Onslow County and flows ne into Grants Creek.

Spring Branch rises in central Wake County and flows nw into House Creek.

Spring Branch rises in sw Wilson County and flows se into Black Creek.

Spring Creek rises in w Alexander County and flows sw into Lower Little River.

Spring Creek rises in se Brunswick County and flows se into Walden Creek.

Spring Creek rises in nw Columbus County near the Bladen County line and flows ne into Horsepen Creek.

Spring Creek rises in sw Madison County and flows ne into French Broad River.

Spring Creek rises in n Mitchell County and flows se into Big Rock Creek.

Spring Creek rises in e Pamlico County and flows ne into Bonner Bay.

Spring Creek, community in se Beaufort County.

Spring Creek, community in w Madison County on Spring Creek.

Spring Creek. *See* Florence.

Spring Creek Gap, on the Haywood-Madison county line.

Spring Creek Mountain extends ne from Friezeland Creek in s Madison County to Rector Branch. Hop Mountain, with an alt. of 4,072 ft., is a peak on the mountain.

Spring Creek Township, former township in sw Madison County, now township no. 8.

Springdale, community in se Haywood County served by post office, 1876–1923.

Springer, community in w Onslow County served by post office, 1890–1917.

Springers Point, point of land from Ocracoke Island, near community of Ocracoke, extending into Pamlico Sound, se Hyde County.

Springfield, community in w Scotland County on Gum Swamp Creek.

Springfield, community in n Wilkes County on North Prong Roaring River.

Spring Garden, community in nw Craven County on Neuse River. A farming area that has retained the name of the plantation of Governor Richard Dobbs Spaight.

Spring Garden, former community in n Rockingham County named for Gallaway and Scales plantation. Served by post office, 1823–40.

Spring Garden. *See* Castle Hayne.

Springhill, community in Cumberland County near present Fayetteville; active trading center in mid-eighteenth century. Mentioned in Moravian records.

Spring Hill, community in e Halifax County. Alt. 70.

Spring Hill, community in e Haywood County on Garden Creek.

Spring Hill Plantation. *See* East Spencer.

Spring Hill Township, ne Scotland County.

Springhill Township, sw Wilson County.

Spring Hope, community in e Craven County.

Spring Hope, town in w Nash County. Inc. 1889. Previously located approx. 4 mi. se, but moved after a railroad was constructed in 1886–87. Said to have been named by early settlers who hoped a spring nearby would always provide water for the community. Produces lumber and apparel. Alt. 261.

Springhouse Ridge, e Clay County between Arch and Bruce Ridges.

Spring Lake, town in nw Cumberland County near e limits of Fort Bragg Military Reservation. Inc. 1951. *See also* Manchester.

Spring Mountain, ne Alexander County. Alt. 1,620.

Spring Mountain, se Buncombe County between Laughter Cove and Cane Creek.

Spring Mountain, sw Buncombe County ne of Twelve O'Clock Top.

Spring Mountain, on the Madison County, N.C.–Greene County, Tenn., line.

Spring Mountain Branch rises in se Buncombe County and flows sw into Cane Creek.

Spring Point, central Onslow County in Farnell Bay of New River.

Spring Shoals. *See* McAdenville.

Sprinkle Branch rises in central Madison County on the w slope of High Rock Ridge and flows se 1½ mi. to empty into Walnut Creek at the community of Walnut Creek.

Sprinkle Cove, ne Buncombe County near the junction of Walker and Dillingham Creeks.

Sprinkle Creek rises in e Madison County and flows se into California Creek.

Spruce Fork rises in ne Buncombe County and flows sw into Beetree Creek.

Spruce Knob, s Watauga County nw of White Rock Ridge.

Spruce Mountain, Haywood and Swain Counties in Great Smoky Mountains National Park on Balsam Mountain near lat. 35°36′48″ N., long. 83°10′34″ W. Alt. 5,590.

Spruce Mountain Ridge, w Haywood County in Great Smoky Mountains National Park, a spur extending e from Spruce Mountain on Balsam Mountain; center near lat. 35°36′40″ N., long. 83°09′05″ W.

Spruce Pine, town in s Mitchell County on North Toe River. Alt. 2,620. Inc. 1907. Named for a large Carolina hemlock, locally called spruce pine, which grew near a tavern operated by Isaac English. Produces apparel, hosiery, textiles, minerals, and lumber.

Spruce Pine Cove, n Buncombe County between Wiley Mountain and Coles Cove.

Spruce Pine Mountain, sw Avery County.

Spruce Pine Ridge, ne Buncombe County between Waterfall and Carter Creeks.

Spruce Pinnacle, ne Buncombe County on Big Fork Ridge.

Spruce Ridge, s Haywood County between Cherry Cove Creek and Shiny Creek.

Spruills Bridge, e Washington County se of Creswell. First known as Samuel Spruills Landing; designated by the General Assembly in 1740 as a point for a warehouse for receipt and shipping of crown quitrents. Called Spruills Landing as late as 1812.

Spurgeon, community in s Wilkes County near Hunting Creek.

Spurgeon Creek rises in ne Davidson County and flows s into Abbotts Creek.

Spur Ridge, e Mitchell County parallel to Green Cove Creek.

Spurrier, community in w Mecklenburg County.

Squally Creek rises in w Graham County and flows e into West Buffalo Creek.

Squhawky. *See* Williamston.

Squirrel Branch rises in sw Gaston County and flows ne into Crowders Creek.

Squirrel Branch rises in n Guilford County and flows e into Reedy Fork Creek.

Squirrel Branch rises in w Madison County near Squirrels Gap and flows w into Spring Creek.

Squirrel Creek rises in central Avery County and flows w into North Toe River.

Squirrel Creek rises in w Lenoir County and flows n into Neuse River.

Squirrel Gap, n Transylvania County between Laurel Brook and South Fork Mills River.

Squirrels Gap, w Madison County on the sw end of Hot Springs Mountain.

Squyars Canal. *See* New Lake Fork.

Stacey Creek rises in se Avery County and flows nw into Linville River.

Staceyville. *See* Stacy.

Stackhouse, community in n Madison County on French Broad River at the mouth of Woolsey Branch. Alt. 1,418.

Stacy, community in ne Carteret County on a point of land extending into Core Sound from the mainland. Was called Piney Point prior to 1888.

Stacy, community and railroad flag stop in e Rockingham County. Named for local landowner Iverson Stacy. Appears as Staceyville on an 1860 map.

Stafford Hill, peak in the Cane Creek Mountains, s Alamance County.

Staffords Creek rises in s Caldwell County and flows s into Catawba River on the Burke-Caldwell county line. Formerly also known as James Mill Creek and McCalls Mill Creek.

Staffords Mill, community in nw Guilford County near Oak Ridge. Called Saunders Mill during the American Revolution. Cornwallis's troops ground corn there.

Stag Creek rises in ne Alamance County and flows s into Back Creek.

Stagg Creek rises in nw Ashe County and flows se into North Fork New River.

Stagger Weed Creek rises in e Mitchell County and flows nw to join Mine Fork Branch in forming Right Fork [Cane Creek].

Stag Park, community and former plantation, central Pender County on the Northeast Cape Fear River. Named in 1663 by Barbadian explorers for parklike terrain on which they saw deer feeding. Appears on the Ogilby map, 1671. Governor George Burrington in about 1730 acquired 10,000 acres there and built a summer home.

Stagville. *See* Fairntosh.

Staircase Mountain, nw Caldwell County near Maple Grove.

Staire Branch rises in ne Buncombe County and flows nw into Walker Branch.

Stairs Mountain, s Haywood County on the head of Crawford Creek. Alt. 5,869.

Stairwalk Ridge, se Buncombe County e of Potato Knob.

Stairway Falls, sw Transylvania County in Horsepasture River downstream from High Falls.

Stalcup Top, s Cherokee County near the headwaters of Little Brasstown Creek.

Staley, town in e Randolph County. Post office est. there in 1883 as Staleyville. Inc. 1901 as Staley. Named for Col. John W. Staley, Confederate soldier. Alt. 725.

Staley Creek rises in central Alamance County and flows ne into Servis Creek.

Staleyville. *See* Staley.

Stallings, community in e Franklin County. Alt. 347. Est. 1880. Named for J. M. Stallings, who est. a cotton gin and sawmill there.

Stallings, community in nw Union County.

Stallings Crossroads, community in nw Beaufort County.

Stallings Station. *See* Clayton.

Stamey Cove, e Haywood County on the head of Stamey Cove Branch.

Stamey Cove Branch rises in e Haywood County and flows se into Pigeon River.

Stamey Cove Gap, e Haywood County on the sw end of Anderson Mountain.

Stamper, community in s Halifax County.

Stamy Knob, central Clay County between Peckerwood Creek and Cold Branch.

Stancell. *See* Oak Grove.

Standard, community in w Pitt County. Alt. 74.

Standhill Mountain, sw Buncombe County n of Buzzard Knob.

Standing Indian, peak on the Clay-Macon county line. The Indian name was *Yunwitsulenunyi* (where the man stood). Alt. 5,500. The peak has been called "the grandstand of the southern Appalachians."

Standing Indian Wildlife Management Area, se Clay County.

Standingstone Mountain, at the junction of the lines of Henderson and Transylvania Counties, N.C., and Greenville County, S.C.

Stanfield, town in sw Stanly County. Inc. 1955.

Stanfield Branch rises in n Buncombe County and flows w into Dick Branch.

Stanford. *See* Burgaw.

Stanhope, community in s Nash County. Was site of pre–Civil War Stanhope Academy. Community of Old Stanhope, about 2 mi. w, was a stop on the Raleigh-Tarboro stage line.

Named for Stanhope Crenshaw who operated the stage line prior to 1896.

Stanley, town in n Gaston County. Inc. 1897 as Brevard Station and named for Robert Alexander Brevard, who gave land in 1861 for railroad station. Renamed Stanley Creek, 1893, and Stanley, 1911. Produces zippers and textiles. Alt. 852.

Stanley Branch rises in n Buncombe County near Lankford Mountain and flows w into Dick Branch.

Stanley Creek rises in ne Gaston County and flows se into Dutchmans Creek.

Stanley Creek. *See* Stanley.

Stanleyville, community in n central Forsyth County.

Stanly County was formed in 1841 from Montgomery County. Located in the central section of the state, it is bounded by Montgomery, Richmond, Anson, Union, Cabarrus, and Rowan Counties. It was named for John Stanly (1774–1834), member of the General Assembly, several times speaker of the House of Commons, and member of Congress. Area: 406 sq. mi. County seat: Albemarle, with an elevation of 505 ft. Townships are Almond, Big Lick, Center, Endy, Furr, Harris, North Albemarle, Ridenhour, South Albemarle, and Tyson. Produces wheat, oats, corn, barley, lespedeza, poultry, eggs, dairy products, hogs, livestock, textiles, bakery products, mobile homes, tires, wood products, furniture, aluminum, lumber, brick, and crushed stone.

Stansbury, community in s central Brunswick County.

Stansfield Branch rises in e Macon County and flows n into Cullasaja River.

Stanton, community in w Wilkes County served by post office, 1898–1915.

Stanton. *See* South Creek.

Stanton-Harrold. *See* South Creek.

Stantonsburg, town in se Wilson County on Contentnea Creek. Alt. 92. Inc. 1817. Post office name in 1828 was Stantonburgh. Named for Willie J. Stanton, one on the first com-

missioners, or James Stanton, first mayor. The former community of Moyton, named for Francis M. Moye, on the e outskirts of the town, is now a part of Stantonsburg.

Stantonsburg Township, s Wilson County.

Stanton's Gut, stream, begins in se Wilson County at the ne outskirts of Stantonsburg and runs sw into Contentnea Creek after a course of approx. 2 mi.

Stanton Township, w Wilkes County.

Star, town in e Montgomery County. Inc. 1897. Named by Angus Leach, local merchant, because of the high elevation of the site, visible from all directions. Known first as Hunsucker's Store. Alt. 637. Produces textiles and hosiery.

Star Branch rises near Oaks Knob, w Avery County, and flows ne into Roaring Creek.

Star Branch rises in n central Yancey County and flows nw into Jacks Creek.

Star Hollow, valley of Star Branch, w Avery County.

Starkey Gap, on the Swain County, N.C.–Sevier County, Tenn., line in Great Smoky Mountains National Park near lat. 35°34′12″ N., long. 83°40′15″ W.

Starkey Ridge, n Swain County in Great Smoky Mountains National Park near lat. 35°32′58″ N., long. 83°37′47″ W.

Starkeys Creek rises in w Carteret County and flows s approx. 3 mi. into Pettivers Creek. Named for John Starkey, colonial treasurer and member of the Assembly.

Starkeys Creek rises in ne Onslow County and flows se into White Oak River. Formerly called Great Swamp. Probably named for John Starkey, pioneer settler.

Starkey's Hammock. *See* The Hammock.

Starlight, community in sw Wayne County served by post office, 1894–1905.

Starling, community in se Onslow County near the head of Queens Creek. Named for Sam Starling.

Starling's Bridge. *See* Falcon.

Starnes Branch rises in central Transylvania County and flows s into Davidson River.

Starnes Cove, central Buncombe County nw of Starnes Ridge.

Starnes Ridge, central Buncombe County w of Ragsdale Creek.

Star Peak. *See* Fox Knob.

Starretts Meadows, e Onslow County between

the head of Wallace Creek and the head of Bear Creek.

Starsburg, community in s Cumberland County served by post office, 1885–1906.

Startown, community in central Catawba County. Named for pioneer Starr family. Earlier known as Danville.

Stateline. *See* Collinstown.

State Line Gap, on the Watauga County, N.C.–Johnson County, Tenn., line near the head of Little Beaverdam Creek. Alt. 3,738.

State Line Ridge, on the Watauga County, N.C.–Johnson County, Tenn., line, extends se from State Line Gap to the head of Cove Creek.

State Ridge, in the n tip of Cherokee County along the North Carolina-Tennessee state line.

State Road, community in w Surry County near the head of Camp Creek. Said to have taken its name from a "state road camp" est. there temporarily during the construction of a highway.

Statesville, city and county seat, central Iredell County. Authorized to be laid out in 1789 and probably named in honor of the fact that North Carolina had approved the federal Constitution a few weeks previously and thus had become a state. Inc. 1847. Settlement grew up around Fourth Creek Presbyterian Church, organized there in 1753. Home of Mitchell Community College. Produces textiles, apparel, fabricated metals, furniture, flour, lumber, and machinery. Alt. 925. *See also* Fourth Creek.

Statesville Township, central Iredell County.

Staton, community in n Pitt County. Alt. 42.

Statons Pond, central Martin County, is fed by the waters of several streams: Hardison Mill Creek, Ready Branch, and Smithwick Creek. It is drained by Sweetwater Creek. The pond is approx. 2 mi. long.

Stauken's Quarter Creek. *See* Stinking Quarter Creek.

Staunton, community in w Wilkes County on North Prong Lewis Fork Creek.

Staunton. *See* Kittrell.

Steadmans Creek rises in central Stokes County and flows n into Dan River.

Steadmans Lake is formed by a dam across Steadmans Creek, central Stokes County. Covers about 15 acres; max. depth 30 ft. Owned by Izaak Walton League of America.

Stearns, community in w central Polk County.

Stecoah, community in e Graham County on Stecoah Creek. Alt. 2,030. Name derived from Cherokee word *stika'yi*, the meaning of which ethnologist James Mooney believed to be lost, though it is thought by local residents to mean "lean" in the sense of "no game."

Stecoah Creek rises in e Graham County and flows ne into Little Tennessee River.

Stecoah Gap, e Graham County between the headwaters of Sweetwater Creek and Stecoah Creek.

Stecoah Township, ne Graham County.

Stedman, town in e Cumberland County. Inc. 1913. Named for Charles M. Stedman (1841–1930), president of the North Carolina Railroad and last Confederate veteran to serve in Congress. The nineteenth-century community (with a post office) of Blocker's or Blockersville was at or near the site of Stedman.

Steeds, community in ne Montgomery County served by post office, 1897–1953. Named in 1898 for J. W. Steeds, local merchant. Alt. 662.

Steel Creek rises in s Transylvania County and flows sw into Little River.

Steel Creek. *See* Steele Creek.

Steele Creek rises in w Mecklenburg County and flows s into South Carolina, where it enters Catawba River. The name appears on the Collet map, 1770, but is applied to the head of present Kings Branch. Named for Moses Steele, beaver hunter.

Steele Creek, community in sw Mecklenburg County. Steele Creek Presbyterian Church there was organized in 1760. A post office was est. there as early as 1828. Often spelled as Steel Creek on early maps.

Steele Creek Township, former township in sw Mecklenburg County, now township no. 3.

Steeles Mill. *See* Cordova.

Steeles Township, nw Richmond County.

Steele Township, w central Rowan County. Named for Gen. John Steele (1764–1815).

Steelman Creek rises in s Yadkin County and flows se into n Davie County, where it enters Dutchmans Creek.

Steels Creek rises in nw Burke County and flows se into Upper Creek. Flows between Tettered Rock Ridge and Rip Skin Ridge.

Steels Ridge, community in s Bertie County.

Steeltrap Creek rises in n Swain County in Great

Smoky Mountains National Park and flows sw into Forney Creek.

Steeltrap Knob, in s Macon County between Bearpen Mountain and Mooney Branch.

Steel Trap Ridge extends from central Cherokee County ne to n Cherokee County between Bald and Hanging Dog Creeks.

Steep Hill Branch rises in w Carteret County and flows w approx. 3 mi. into White Oak River.

Steep Hill Branch rises in w Johnston County and flows se into Middle Creek. Mentioned in local records as early as 1770.

Steep Point extends from the mainland of ne Carteret County into Core Sound.

Steep Rock Mountain, peak in w Randolph County.

Steer Gap, e Haywood County between Hungry Creek and Pisgah Creek.

Steestachee Bald, on the Haywood-Jackson county line. Alt. 5,700. Named for the Indian word for rats or nest of rats. Indian hunters are said to have found and destroyed a nest of rats there.

Steestachee Branch rises near Steestachee Bald in sw Haywood County and flows e into Allen Creek.

Stella, community in w Carteret County on White Oak River. Alt. 30, the highest point in the county. Originally named Barkers Bridge in honor of a local doctor, but when a post office was est. in 1866, the Post Office Department declined to accept the name.

Stem, town in s Granville County. Inc. 1911. Named for W. T. Stem, local landowner. The area was first served by the Tally Ho post office, 1 mi. ne. In 1889, however, the post office was moved there and the name changed. Alt. 470. *See also* Tally Ho.

Stephens Creek rises in s Macon County and flows ne into Cullasaja River.

Stephens Crossroads, community in e Rockingham County served by Confederate post office. Named for Hiram Stephens, who migrated from New York in 1876.

Stephenson, community in w Johnston County served by post office, 1893–1903.

Stephenson's Lake, a spring-fed lake covering 35 acres 2 mi. e of Garysburg, w Northampton County. Numerous wild ducks and geese winter there each year.

Stephens Swamp rises in e Duplin County and flows sw into Muddy Creek.

Stepp Branch rises in se Buncombe County and flows nw into Swannanoa River.

Stepp's Cove, on the s side of Point Lookout in ne Henderson County about 1½ mi. e of community of Edneyville. Named for Fannie Stepp, who, according to legend, was scalped there by Cherokee warriors in 1779.

Stepps Gap, on Kings Mountain on Cleveland-Gaston county line. Alt. 1,040.

Stepps Gap, s Yancey County in the Black Mountains between Mount Gibbes and Mount Mitchell. Named for Jesse Stepp, who guided the geographer Arnold Guyot through the area when Guyot mapped it in 1860.

Sterlings Township, se Robeson County.

Steve Branch rises in n Clay County and flows se into Tuni Creek.

Steve Branch rises in w Madison County and flows se into Spring Creek.

Stevens, community in w Union County served by post office, 1865–1905.

Stevens. *See* Stevens Mill.

Stevens Branch rises in ne Clay County and flows e into Clear Creek.

Stevens Cove, s Madison County at the head of Little Pine Creek.

Stevens Creek rises in n Haywood County and flows ne into Pigeon River.

Stevens Creek rises in se Mecklenburg County and flows s into Union County, where it enters Duck Creek.

Stevens Creek rises in e Onslow County and flows se into White Oak River.

Stevens Mill, community in nw Union County on Goose Creek served by post office, 1852–68. Formerly called Stevens.

Stevens Mill, community in w Wayne County on Thoroughfare Swamp.

Stevenson Branch rises in w central Swain County on Cooper Mountain and flows sw into Greasy Branch.

Stevensons Point, community in se Perquimans County.

Steward Millpond, in nw Union County in Goose Creek.

Stewards Creek. *See* Stewart Creek.

Stewart, community in s Scotland County served by post office, 1894–1905.

Stewart Branch rises in ne Cherokee County and flows sw into Valley River.

Stewart Cove, e Macon County between Buck Creek and Little Buck Creek.

Stewart Creek rises se of the town of Warsaw in w Duplin County and flows sw into Six Runs Creek in e Sampson County. Appears as Stewards Creek on the Collet map, 1770.

Stewart Creek rises in n Mecklenburg County and flows s to join Taggart Creek in forming Sugar Creek.

Stewart Creek rises in Virginia and flows se into Surry County, where it enters Ararat River.

Stewart Mountain, sw Cherokee County, extends se into Fannin County, Ga.

Stewart Ridge, ne Cherokee County in the Snowbird Mountains.

Stewarts Creek rises in w Cumberland County and flows se into Beaver Creek.

Stewarts Creek rises in w Forsyth County and flows se into Muddy Creek. Until some time prior to 1762, it was known as Tomahawk Branch. In that year, Joseph Stewart settled near its banks, and it presumably took his name. It appears as Stewarts Creek on the Collet map, 1770, but small streams flowing into it are still known as Tomahawk Creek and Little Tomahawk Creek.

Stewarts Creek rises in s Harnett County and flows se into Little River.

Stewarts Creek rises in e Hoke County and flows se onto Cumberland-Hoke county line and into Rockfish Creek.

Stewarts Creek rises in n central Union County and flows se and ne into Richardson Creek.

Stewarts Creek Township, s Harnett County.

Stewarts Creek Township, n Surry County.

Stewarts Ferry. *See* Hickory Grove Crossroads.

Stewart's Pond. *See* Ravenel Lake.

Stewart's Town, town inc. in 1799 "between Peedee and Markees's Creek" in Richmond County to encourage navigation on the Pee Dee River. Apparently it was never laid out.

Stewartsville, former community in se Scotland County. A post office by the name existed as early as 1833. In the 1890s, Stewart was a station on what is now the Seaboard Coast Line Railroad. A cemetery called "Stewartsville" in the vicinity was "Founded 1785." *See also* Stewart's Town.

Stewartsville Township, se Scotland County.

Stice, community in s Cleveland County served by post office, 1847–1902.

Stice Dam, on Broad River, s Cleveland County,

provides power for mills in Shelby. Stice's Shoal community was served by post office, 1847–1902.

Stice's Shoal. *See* Stice Dam.

Stiff Knee Knob, sw Madison County at the head of Sugar Camp Branch.

Stiles, community in n Macon County between Bird Branch and Burningtown Creek. Served by post office, 1901–51.

Still Bluff, community in sw Pender County on a bluff overlooking Black River. Named for the fact that it is a quiet spot on a bluff.

Still Branch rises in se Yancey County and flows ne into Roaring Fork.

Still Creek rises in w Carteret County and flows w into White Oak River. Named because a whiskey still was once located on the creek.

Stilley, community s Beaufort County.

Stillhouse Branch rises in s Avery County and flows nw into Whiteoak Branch.

Stillhouse Branch rises in central Cherokee County and flows se into Valley River.

Stillhouse Branch rises in n Macon County and flows w into Rose Creek.

Stillhouse Branch rises in s Macon County and flows sw into Tessentee Creek.

Stillhouse Branch rises in s Madison County and flows s into Ivy River.

Stillhouse Creek rises in central McDowell County and flows s into Paxton Creek.

Stillwater Branch rises in w central Transylvania County and flows n into Davidson River.

Stillwater Creek. *See* Island Creek.

Stillwell Creek rises in ne Swain County in Great Smoky Mountains National Park and flows sw into Straight Fork of Raven Fork Creek.

Stinking Creek rises in s Chatham County and flows se into Haw River.

Stinking Quarter Creek rises in s Guilford County and flows ne into Alamance County, where it enters Great Alamance Creek. Appears on the Collet map, 1770. Name said to have been derived from the fact that Indians cleaned animals there and left quarters of meat to spoil. Eli Caruthers, writing in 1856, said it was formerly known as Stauken's Quarter Creek, presumably named for a grant of land to a pioneer settler.

Stirewalt Creek rises in central Alexander County a short distance s of Taylorsville and flows s into Lower Little River.

Stirrup Iron Creek rises in se Durham County

and flows se into w Wake County, where it enters Crabtree Creek.

Stockade Mountain, sw Cherokee County along the Nottely River se of Die Bend.

Stocking Head Creek rises in central Duplin County and flows se into Northeast Cape Fear River.

Stocksville, community in n Buncombe County. A post office est. there 1836; closed 1958.

Stockton Cove, n Buncombe County between Morgan Ridge and Morgan Branch.

Stokes, town in n Pitt County. Settled about 1880. Inc. 1903. Named for William G. Stokes, local landowner. Alt. 56.

Stokesbury. *See* Walnut Cove.

Stokes County was formed in 1789 from Surry County. Located in the n central section of the state, it is bounded by the state of Virginia and by Rockingham, Forsyth, and Surry Counties. It was named for Capt. John Stokes (1756–90), Revolutionary War officer and member of the House of Commons and the Convention of 1789. Area: 458 sq. mi. County seat: Danbury, with an elevation of 825 ft. Townships are Beaver Island, Big Creek, Danbury, Meadows, Peters Creek, Quaker Gap, Sauratown, Snow Creek, and Yadkin. Produces tobacco, corn, wheat, hay, oats, poultry, eggs, dairy products, hogs, livestock, motor vehicle parts, brick, crushed stone. copper products, lumber, apples, and printed materials.

Stokesdale, town in nw Guilford County. Alt. 950. Inc. 1907. Known until 1887 as Pond; renamed probably for Governor Montford Stokes (1762–1842). Post office est. 1879.

Stokes Mill Run rises in e Sampson County and flows e into Duplin County, where it enters Stewart Creek.

Stone Creek rises in sw Henderson County and flows se into Rock Creek.

Stone Creek rises in sw Johnston County and flows e into Mill Creek.

Stonecutter Creek rises in central Rutherford County and flows sw into Cleghorn Creek.

Named for a stonecutter who lived along its banks and cut millstones.

Stonehead. *See* Pilot Mountain.

Stonehouse, home of William Person, member of the Provincial Congress, in ne Warren County on Stonehouse Creek. The house, which is still standing, dates from 1746.

Stonehouse Creek rises in e Warren County near the town of Vaughn and flows ne into Lake Gaston. Appears on the Price map, 1808, and the MacRae map, 1833. Sometimes referred to locally as Big Stonehouse Creek.

Stone Mountain, on the Alleghany-Wilkes county line. Alt. 3,879.

Stone Mountain, se Buncombe County n of Jarvis Mountain. Alt. 3,700.

Stone Mountain, at the head of Jim Creek in sw Henderson County. Alt. 3,647.

Stone Mountain, w Transylvania County s of Butter Gap. Alt. 3,698.

Stone Mountain, ne Watauga County e of Grassy Creek.

Stone Mountain, community in s McDowell County served by post office, 1848–1905.

Stone Mountain Bald, on the Watauga County, N.C.–Johnson County, Tenn., line at the n end of Stone Mountains, *which see*. Alt. 4,657.

Stone Mountain Branch rises in nw Watauga County in the Stone Mountains and flows sw into Watauga River.

Stone Mountain Creek rises in s Alleghany County and flows sw into n Wilkes County, where it enters Bullhead Creek.

Stone Mountain Gap, se Buncombe County between Stone and Round Mountains.

Stone Mountains, a chain of mountains in w Ashe and Watauga Counties, N.C., and Johnson County, Tenn., from the Watauga River near lat. 36°17′30″ N., long. 81°55′ W., to the nw corner of North Carolina and thence into Virginia to Whitetop Mountain. They form the common boundary line of North Carolina and Tennessee. The name dates from as early as 1795.

Stones Bay, in New River in s Onslow County. Mentioned in local records as early as 1748 as Stones Creek Bay. Named for William Stone, an early surveyor in the county.

Stones Creek rises in s Onslow County and flows ne approx. 10 mi. into Stones Bay. Mentioned in local records as early as 1744. Named for William Stone, an early surveyor in the county.

Stones Creek Bay. *See* Stones Bay.

Stones Island. *See* Huggins Island.

Stones Knob, se Yancey County between Clear and Crabtree Creeks.

Stoneville, town in nw Rockingham County. Founded in 1858 by Rev. Frank J. Stone and Pinckney M. Stone, the latter of whom operated a general store at the site. Inc. 1877. Became a trading center for Rockingham County. Several buildings demolished by tornado, 1998. Alt. 823.

Stonewall, town in central Pamlico County on Bay River. Inc. 1857 as Jackson and apparently named for the owner of a local mill. Name changed to Stonewall, 1871, to honor Gen. T. J. "Stonewall" Jackson (1824–63). Post office est. 1877. Long inactive in municipal affairs. Alt. 10.

Stonewall Township, se Hoke County.

Stoney Creek rises in s Hertford County and flows in an inverted arc into Ahoskie Swamp. Stony Bridge appears on the Moseley map, 1733, as spanning the stream s of the present town of Ahoskie. Appears as Stony Creek Bridge on the Collet map, 1770; as Bonner Bridge on the MacRae map, 1833; and as Jernigan's Bridge on the soil survey map, 1916.

Stoney Creek rises in ne Mecklenburg County and flows se into Mallard Creek.

Stoney Mountain, central Henderson County between Mill Pond Creek and Mud Creek. Alt. 2,843.

Stoney Run rises in w Cleveland County and flows se into First Broad River.

Stoney Town Creek. *See* Stonyton Creek.

Stonington Creek. *See* Stonyton Creek.

Stony Bald, on the Buncombe-Henderson county line ne of Cutthroat Gap. Alt. 4,563.

Stony Creek rises in n central Bertie County and flows n into Hertford County, where it enters Ahoskie Creek.

Stony Creek is formed in ne Buncombe County by the junction of Carter and Mineral Creeks. It flows n into Dillingham Creek.

Stony Creek rises in s Caswell County and flows s into Alamance County, where it enters Haw River. Appears as Marrow Bone River on the Moseley map, 1733.

Stony Creek rises in e Lee County and flows nw into Lick Creek.

Stony Creek is formed in w Nash County by the junction of Big and Little Peachtree Creeks and flows se into Tar River. Appears on the Collet map, 1770.

Stony Creek rises in e Orange County and flows ne into Eno River.

Stony Creek rises in e Surry County and flows sw into Ararat River.

Stony Creek rises in central Wayne County and flows sw into Neuse River. Named in local records as early as 1756. The name appears as Rocky Creek on the Price map, 1808.

Stony Creek, community in s Caswell County. A post office operated there, 1836–1905.

Stony Creek. *See* Stony Fork Creek.

Stony Creek Lake. *See* Lake Burlington.

Stony Creek Mountain, high grounds on the Caswell-Alamance county line.

Stony Creek Township, sw Caswell County.

Stony Creek Township, e Nash County.

Stony Creek Township, central Wayne County.

Stony Fork rises in sw Buncombe County near Little Pisgah Mountain and flows n into Warren Creek.

Stony Fork rises in w Johnston County and flows se into Hannah Creek.

Stony Fork, community in sw Buncombe County on Stony Fork near the mouth of McKinney Creek. Alt. 2,368.

Stony Fork, community in e Watauga County near the head of Stony Fork Creek.

Stony Fork Branch rises in ne Buncombe County and flows sw into North Fork [Swannanoa River].

Stony Fork Creek rises in e Watauga County and flows se into w Wilkes County to enter Yadkin River. Also known as Stony Creek.

Stony Fork Township, e Watauga County.

Stony Hill, community in nw Wilkes County on North Prong Lewis Fork Creek.

Stony Knob, n Buncombe County between Wagner Branch and Reems Creek.

Stony Knob, on the Buncombe-Henderson county line between High Top and Luther Gap.

Stony Knob, on the McDowell-Mitchell county line between Gillespie Gap and Little Switzerland. Alt. approx. 3,330.

Stony Knoll, community in s Surry County between Fisher River and West Double Creek. Served by post office, 1893–1906. Formerly known as Butcher. Alt. 1,194.

Stony Mountain, e Madison County between

Chandler Creek and the head of California Creek.

Stony Mountain, a range about 1½ mi. long in e Stanly County on w bank of Pee Dee River.

Stony Mountain Ridge, ne Swain County, in the shape of an inverted "S" between Poplar Hollow Branch and a bend in Raven Fork.

Stony Point, community in se Alexander County. Site settled 1789. Stony Point post office est. 1826 but operated in different homes, stores, etc., within a radius of about 2 mi. In 1887 a railroad station, Sloan or Sloans Station, was opened, but the community soon came to be known by the official post office name, Stony Point. Named for rocky formation at the site. Alt. 1,090.

Stony Point, community in e Cleveland County.

Stony Ridge, se Surry County, extends ne between Yadkin River and Grassy Creek.

Stony Run rises in w Stanly County and flows se into Big Bear Creek.

Stony Spur, w Madison County between Little Bottom Branch and John Taylor Branch.

Stonyton Creek rises in n Lenoir County and flows se into Neuse River. Now frequently appears as Stonington Creek but first called the Stoney Town Creek in the 1730s because it was near an Indian town on a hill with outcroppings of slate and sandstone.

Stony Valley, in e Mitchell County between Bee Ridge and Middle Mountain.

Store Point, peninsula extending off the w side of Goose Creek Island into Goose Creek, ne Pamlico County.

Storey Branch rises in s Watauga County and flows nw into Days Creek.

Story, community in w Gates County; formerly known as Storys Crossroads. Served by post office, 1884–85. Named for Euclid Story, postmaster.

Story Mountain, n Caldwell County. Named for the Storie family, local residents.

Storys Creek rises in central Person County and flows ne into Marlowe Creek.

Storys Crossroads. *See* Story.

Stott Knob, central Surry County between Turner Mountain and Beaver Creek. Alt. 1,550.

Stotts Crossroads, community in nw Wilson County e of Marsh Swamp. Named for Godfrey Stott.

Stouts, community in w Union County 2 mi. se

of town of Indian Trail. Inc. 1907; charter repealed 1917. Alt. 658.

Stovall, town in ne Granville County. Inc. 1883 as Sassafras Fork, named for large sassafras trees at the crossroads. Post office since 1887. Name changed in 1887 to honor John W. Stovall, who gave land for the railroad station. Alt. 478. Produces lumber.

Stover Ridge, mountain in central Avery County.

Stowe's Hills. *See* Frisco.

Strabane, community in w Lenoir County. Named for home in Ireland of early settler. Served by post office, 1828–1905.

Stradley Mountain, s Buncombe County, extends from Little Hickory Top to Rice Pinnacle.

Straight Creek rises in ne Buncombe County and flows nw into North Fork Ivy Creek.

Straight Creek, w Haywood County in Great Smoky Mountains National Park, rises near lat. 35°34′37″ N., long. 83°09′36″ W., and flows e into Caldwell Fork.

Straight Fork rises in ne Swain County in Great Smoky Mountain National Park and flows s and sw into Raven Fork.

Straits, community in se Carteret County on a point of land extending into the mouth of North River.

Straits, The, straits in the waters between North River and Core Sound in se Carteret County between Harkers Island and the mainland.

Straits Township, on The Straits in central Carteret County. At one time, a portion of Straits was called no. 5 township. From Straits were formed Carteret and no. 9 townships (both now abolished) and Merrimon.

Strange Branch rises in ne Cherokee County and flows se into Big Cove Branch.

Strangenbergs Creek. *See* Silas Creek.

Stratford, community in w central Alleghany County.

Stratton Bald, w Graham County at nw end of Horse Cove Ridge. Alt. approx. 5,380.

Stratton Branch rises in nw Swain County and flows se into Lake Cheoah.

Straw, community in s Wilkes County near East Prong Cub Creek.

Strawberry Branch rises in e Lenoir County in the n part of Ball Pocosin and flows n into Southwest Creek.

Strawberry Knob, on the Graham County, N.C.– Monroe County, Tenn., line.

Strawberry Knob, on the Haywood-Swain county line in Great Smoky Mountains National Park near lat. 35°32′54″ N., long. 83°09′35″ W., between Whim Knob and Black Camp Gap. Alt. 5,340.

Street Gap, on the Madison County, N.C.–Unicoi County, Tenn., line.

Streets Ferry, est. over the Neuse River by Richard Graves before 1730; location was 7 mi. s of Vanceboro, central Craven County. Ceased operation, 1962.

Strickland Crossroads, community in s Johnston County.

Stricklandsville. *See* Magnolia.

Strieby, community in sw Randolph County. Named for a philanthropist who helped est. a church and school for blacks there in 1880. Served by post office, 1883–1940.

Striking Island, a tidal-marsh island in the Cape Fear River opposite Southport, se Brunswick County.

Stringfellow Branch rises in s Watauga County in Moses H. Cone Memorial Park and flows e through Bass Lake and into Chetola Lake on Middle Fork [South Fork New River].

Strouds Creek rises in n Orange County and flows se into Eno River.

Strouph Gap, on the sw end of Burney Mountain on the Buncombe-Henderson county line.

Stuards Reach appears on the Smith map, 1624, in what is now the Roanoke River between Halifax and Northampton Counties.

Stuart Creek rises in nw Henderson County in Pisgah National Forest and flows ne into North Fork.

Stubblefield, community in nw Caswell County. Named for a local family.

Stubblefield. *See* Ruffin.

Stubbs, community in e Cleveland County on Buffalo Creek. Alt. 950. Settled about 1885. Named for Col. Seth W. Stubbs, who made the clock for the Lincoln County Courthouse, 1856.

Stump Inlet or **Stumpy Inlet**, former inlet from the Atlantic Ocean to Stump Sound, se Onslow County. Appears on the Moseley map, 1733, and on other maps through 1882. Apparently closed by 1912.

Stump Sound skirts the s edge of Onslow County between the Onslow-Pender county line and Alligator Bay in s Onslow County. The sound is filled with tidal-marsh islands and is separated from the Atlantic Ocean by a barrier beach.

Stump Sound Township, sw Onslow County.

Stumpy Creek rises in s Iredell County and flows sw into Cornelius Creek.

Stumpy Inlet. *See* Stump Inlet.

Stumpy Point, peninsula extending s from the e mainland of Dare County into Pamlico Sound and Stumpy Point Bay. Appears on the Moseley map, 1733.

Stumpy Point, community on the e mainland of Dare County on Stumpy Point Bay. Alt. 3.

Stumpy Point Bay, an almost round bay on the e mainland of Dare County. It has a narrow entrance into Pamlico Sound on the se side. Formerly a lake, it appears as Stumpy Point Lake on the Moseley map, 1733. Erosion opened the lake into Pamlico Sound.

Stumpy Point Lake. *See* Stumpy Point Bay.

Sturdivants Cross Roads, community in se Union County s of Lanes Creek.

Sturgeon Creek rises in ne Brunswick County and flows e into Mill Creek.

Sturgeons Point, on Moseley map, 1733, in what is now se Brunswick County between Elizabeth River and Walden Creek.

Sturgills, community in n Ashe County. Named for Sheriff B. Sturgills, who helped to obtain a post office that operated 1887–1953.

Styron Bay, on the w side of Core Sound about 1.3 mi. sw of the town of Atlantic and e of Nelson Bay, ne Carteret County. Named for a local family.

Suburb, community in se Brunswick County served by post office, 1898–1915.

Suck, community in Rutherford County served by post office, 1854–66.

Suddawig Branch rises in sw Clay County and flows nw into Hiwassee River.

Suddereth Branch rises in e Cherokee County on Mission Mountain and flows se into Hiwassee River.

Sue, community in e Columbus County served by post office, 1894–1901.

Sugar Branch rises in w Jackson County and flows se then ne into Savannah Creek.

Sugar Camp Branch rises in sw Madison County and flows ne into Spring Creek.

Sugar Camp Creek is formed in s Yancey County by the junction of Ogle and Timber Creeks and flows sw and nw into Cane River.

Sugarcamp Fork rises in n Buncombe County and flows nw into Main Creek.

Sugarcamp Ridge, mountain in w Avery County.

Sugar Cove, n Buncombe County w of Ingles Ridge.

Sugar Cove, se Clay County.

Sugar Cove, s Haywood County on the head of Right Hand Prong [Pigeon River].

Sugar Cove, sw Macon County between Firescald Ridge and Nantahala River.

Sugar Cove Branch rises in s Haywood County and flows nw into Sorrell Creek.

Sugar Cove Creek rises near Tellico Bald in n Macon County and flows ne into Tellico Creek.

Sugar Cove Creek rises in se Yancey County and flows sw into Three Forks Creek.

Sugar Cove Gap, on the Haywood-Madison county line.

Sugar Cove Gap, se Yancey County near the head of Sugar Cove Creek.

Sugar Creek rises in n Buncombe County near Watershed Ridge and flows n into Ivy Creek.

Sugar Creek rises in nw Buncombe County near Newfound Mountain and flows ne into Sandy Mush Creek.

Sugar Creek rises in ne Davie County and flows se 2 mi. into Cedar Creek w of Smith Grove. Referred to in early local records as Sugar Tree Creek.

Sugar Creek rises in e Jackson County and flows ne into Caney Fork.

Sugar Creek rises in s Lee County and flows nw into Pocket Creek.

Sugar Creek is formed in central Mecklenburg County by the junction of Stewart and Taggart Creeks and flows sw into South Carolina, where it enters Catawba River. Appears on the Collet map, 1770. Name derived from an Indian word apparently meaning "group of huts."

Sugar Creek Ridge, e Jackson County between Sugar Creek and Rough Butt Creek.

Sugar Fork rises in ne Buncombe County and flows se into North Fork [Swannanoa River].

Sugar Fork rises in w Jackson County and flows ne into Greens Creek.

Sugar Fork rises in nw Swain County in Great Smoky Mountains National Park and flows 1.5 mi. se into Haw Gap Branch.

Sugar Fork. *See* Messer Creek.

Sugar Fork Township, se Macon County.

Sugar Gap, central Avery County.

Sugar Grove, community in w Watauga County on Cove Creek. Settled 1837; named for sugar maple trees in vicinity. Alt. 2,775. Post office est. 1849.

Sugar Hill, community in s McDowell County on Cove Creek. Served by post office, 1846–1917.

Sugar Hollow, se Buncombe County between Ashworth Creek and Reed Branch.

Sugar Hollow, e central Yancey County between Jim Ray Branch and Three Quarters Creek. Named for sugar maples growing there.

Sugarhouse Cove, ne Buncombe County between Glassmine Ridge and Locust Gap.

Sugar Loaf, mountain in n Alexander County. Named for its resemblance to an old-fashioned loaf of sugar.

Sugarloaf, community in n central Watauga County.

Sugar Loaf. *See* Carolina Beach.

Sugarloaf Bluff, on Cape Fear River in central Bladen County. Probably named for the white, sandy beach across the river from the bluff. The river makes a 45° turn at the bluff.

Sugarloaf Creek rises in e Henderson County and flows n into Reedy Patch Creek.

Sugarloaf Creek rises in n Jackson County and flows nw into Scott Creek.

Sugar Loaf Island, in Bogue Sound off Morehead City in s Carteret County.

Sugarloaf Knob, n Madison County at the ne end of Sugarloaf Mountain. Alt. 4,540.

Sugarloaf Mountain, on the Henderson-Rutherford county line about 1 mi. nw from the coincident corners of Henderson, Polk, and Rutherford Counties. Alt. 3,965. The Indian name for the mountain was *Salola* (squirrel).

Sugarloaf Mountain, on the head of Sugarloaf Creek in n Jackson County.

Sugarloaf Mountain, n Madison County between Shelton Laurel Creek and Colvin Creek.

Sugarloaf Mountain, e Stanly County in Morrow Mountain State Park.

Sugar Loaf Mountain, central Transylvania County between curves in the French Broad River.

Sugarloaf Mountain, central Watauga County, extends nw from Howard Creek. Alt. 4,705.

Sugarloaf Mountain, n Yancey County, extends se parallel to and s of Big Creek. Alt. 3,202.

Sugarloaf Ridge, n Jackson County, extends se from Blanton Branch to Black Mountain.

Sugar Loaf Township, n Alexander County.

Sugar Mountain, central Avery County. Alt. 5,240.

Sugar Springs Cove, ne Buncombe County between Little Craggy Knob and North Fork [Swannanoa River].

Sugar Top, mountain in e Haywood County near the head of Garden Creek. Alt. 4,400.

Sugar Town. *See* Cullasaja.

Sugartown. *See* Pilot View.

Sugar Town Creek. *See* Cullasaja River.

Sugar Tree Branch rises in nw Ashe County and flows s into North Fork New River.

Sugartree Branch rises in e Mitchell County and flows nw into Mine Fork Branch.

Sugartree Creek. *See* South Hyco Creek.

Sugar Tree Creek. *See* Sugar Creek.

Sugartree Gap, on the Buncombe-Madison county line w of Campground Knob.

Sugartree Gap, on the Haywood-Swain county line.

Sugartree Gap, on the Swain County, N.C.–Sevier County, Tenn., line in Great Smoky Mountains National Park near lat. 35°34′12″ N., long. 83°39′28″ W.

Sugartree Licks, on the Haywood-Swain county line in Great Smoky Mountains National Park on Balsam Mountain near lat. 35°33′23″ N., long. 83°09′28″ W. Alt. approx. 5,160. The name comes from the days of cattle ranging in the area and a salting place. Salt for cattle was spread on the roots of a sugar maple tree.

Sugartree Ridge, e Mitchell County between Mine Fork Branch and Dobson Branch.

Sugartree Ridge, n Watauga County, extends se from Cove Creek to Snake Mountain.

Suggs Bridge, community in ne Montgomery County served by post office, 1831–43.

Suggs Creek rises in se Edgecombe County and flows s, forming the Edgecombe-Pitt county line until it flows into the Tar River.

Suggs Creek rises in ne Montgomery County and flows se into Little River.

Suggs Landing, s Edgecombe County, on Tar River.

Suggs Mill Pond, a natural pond in n Bladen County. Named for Aligood Suggs. Has decreased in size considerably since 1914. The pond is one of the Carolina Bays, *which see.*

Suit, community in sw Cherokee County on the headwaters of Bearpaw Creek. Served by post office, 1886–1955.

Sukey Young Crossroads, community in n Franklin County.

Sular Creek rises in nw Cherokee County and flows sw into Hiwassee River between Apalachia and Hiwassee Dams.

Suli Knob, n Swain County in Great Smoky Mountains National Park near lat. 35°33′13″ N., long. 83°33′02″ W. Alt. 4,920.

Suli Ridge, n Swain County in Great Smoky Mountains National Park between Jonas and Huggins Creeks near lat. 35°32′53″ N., long. 83°32′50″ W.

Sulliers Bay, se Onslow County between Howards Bay and Craigs Point. Appears in early county records as Salyer's Bay.

Sullins Branch rises in e Mitchell County and flows sw into North Toe River.

Sullivan County, now in Tennessee, was created in 1779 and named in honor of Gen. John Sullivan (1740–95). Blountsville became the county seat. Part of the territory was ceded by North Carolina in 1789 to the federal government.

Sulphur Branch rises in n central Gaston County just nw of Pasour Mountain and flows ne to empty into South Fork River near the community of High Shoals.

Sulphur Springs, community in central Buncombe County between Acton and Boswell.

Sulphur Springs, community in se Montgomery County served by post office, 1869–1920.

Sulphur Springs, community in n Surry County on Ararat River. Formerly a popular resort.

Sulphur Springs. *See* Davis White Sulphur Springs.

Sulphur Springs Township, s Rutherford County.

Sumey Creek rises in ne Rutherford County and flows s into First Broad River. The name is variously spelled as Summy, Somey, and Sommey. Named for the Sumey family, early settlers.

Summerfield, community in n Guilford County. Inc. 1996. Alt. 881. Settled about 1769 by Charles Bruce, later a Revolutionary War patriot, and known as Bruce's Crossroads until 1812, when a post office was est. and the community was renamed in honor of evangelist John Summerfield (1798–1825). Site, according to tradition, of Revolutionary War skirmish between Lee and Tarleton; campsite of British army under Gen. Charles O'Hara of the Coldstream Guards, February 12, 1781.

Summer Haven, community in central Beaufort County on the n shore of Pamlico River.

Summerhaven, community in ne Buncombe County on Spruce Fork Creek.

Summerlins Crossroads, community in n Duplin County.

Summerville, community in central Harnett County served by post office, 1850–1908. The law creating Harnett County in 1855 directed that the first courts were to be held there until a county seat could be est. Continued as seat of government until 1860. First called Toomer for Judge J. D. Toomer (1784–1856).

Summit, community in nw Halifax County. Since the elevation is considerably higher than that of the surrounding region, Easter sunrise services are frequently held there. Alt. 312.

Summit, community in w Wilkes County between Lewis Fork Creek and North Prong Lewis Fork Creek.

Summit. *See* Elliott.

Summy Creek. *See* Sumey Creek.

Sumner, community in s Rowan County.

Sumner's Mill, community in s Guilford County served by post office, 1853–59.

Sumner Township, s central Guilford County. Named for Gen. Jethro Sumner (1733–85).

Sumpter Cabin Branch rises in s Watauga County and flows s into Middle Fork [South Fork New River].

Sun, community in e Wilson County between Toisnot Swamp and Whiteoak Swamp. Served by post office, 1898–1905.

Sunburst, community in s Haywood County on Lake Logan. Named because the sun rises suddenly from behind a mountain ridge. Served by post office, 1906–28.

Sunbury, community in e central Gates County. Alt. 39. Had its origin at nearby site of Costens Mill, which appears as Constants Mill on the Collet map, 1770. Owner of the mill moved to present site of Sunbury when the road was rerouted. Probably named for the city in Pennsylvania.

Sunday Branch rises in e central Clay County and flows nw into Tusquitee Creek.

Sunfish Cove, in n Transylvania County just s of Shooting Ridge.

Sunk Branch rises in ne Cherokee County and flows se into Dan Holland Creek.

Sunkoto Ridge, n Swain County in Great Smoky Mountains National Park, a long spur extending sw from Thomas Ridge with its center near lat. 35°31′40″ N., long. 83°24′28″ W.

Sunnatee. *See* Great Craggy Mountains.

Sunneehaw. *See* Enos Plotts Balsam Mountain.

Sunny Point, on the w bank of Cape Fear River in se Brunswick County. Now an ammunition loading depot.

Sunnyside, community in nw Cabarrus County.

Sunnyside, community in w Gaston County.

Sunnyside, community in nw Pender County.

Sunnyside, community in sw Rowan County served by post office, 1894–1902. Formerly known as Edmiston.

Sunny Vale, community in nw McDowell County on Buck Creek.

Sunny View, community in n Polk County on Walnut Creek.

Sunset, community in central Granville County served by post office, 1892–1905.

Sunset Beach, town in sw Brunswick County. Inc. in 1963.

Sunset Lake, s Wake County on Middle Creek at the junction of Basal Creek; formerly known as Orfords Pond. Covers 100 acres; max. depth 20 ft. Used for fishing and boating.

Sunset Mountain, central Buncombe County ne of Asheville.

Sunset Park, former town in central Buncombe County, now wholly within the corporate limits of Asheville. Inc. 1891; charter repealed 1897. It lay n of the town limits and w of Charlotte Street extension.

Sunset Rock, on Satulah Branch in se Macon County.

Sunshine, community in ne Rutherford County on Robinson Creek. Served by post office, 1881–1908. Named prior to 1881 by J. W. Biggerstaff, who had a store there. The site is shaded in the early morning by Cherry Mountain, but it acquired its name because local residents could see the sunshine on the top of the mountain.

Sunup Knob, on Haywood County, N.C.–Cocke County, Tenn., line in Great Smoky Mountains National Park near lat. 35°44′45″ N., long. 83°10′14″ W. Alt. 5,050–5,100.

Supply, community in s central Brunswick County on Lockwoods Folly River. From 1805 until 1810, the county courthouse was at the site.

Surf City, town in se Pender County on the
Atlantic Ocean. Inc. 1949.

Surl, community in e Person County served by
post office, 1883–1909.

Surry. *See* White Post.

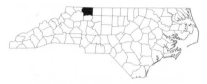

Surry County was formed in 1771 from
Rowan County. Located in the n central
section of the state, it is bounded by the
state of Virginia and by Stokes, Yadkin,
Wilkes, and Alleghany Counties. Named for
the County of Surrey in England, birthplace
of then-incumbent governor William Tryon.
The fact that the name is similar to Saura,
the Indian tribe that had recently inhabited
the region, may have had some influence
in the choice. Area: 538 sq. mi. County
seat: Dobson, with an elevation of 1,265 ft.
Townships are Bryan, Dobson, Eldora, Elkin,
Franklin, Long Hill, Marsh, Mount Airy, Pilot,
Rockford, Shoals, Siloam, South Westfield,
Stewarts, and Westfield. Produces tobacco,
corn, wheat, poultry, barley, grapes, honey,
wine, dairy products, hogs, livestock, textiles,
hosiery, apparel, furniture, granite, and
crushed stone.

Sussex, community in n Ashe County.

Sutherland, community in w Ashe County.
Alt. approx. 3,150.

Sutphin, community in s Alamance County
served by post office, 1891–1905. *See also*
Lindley's Mill.

Sutton, community in s Duplin County.

Sutton, community in s Franklin County on
Norris Creek.

Sutton Branch rises in w Jackson County and
flows se into Savannah Creek.

Suttons Creek rises in e Perquimans County and
flows s into Perquimans River. Named for the
Sutton family, which owned land there before
1700.

Suttons Mill Pond, approx. ½ mi. long, on Bear
Creek in w Lenoir County.

Suttontown, community in ne Sampson County
near Goshen Swamp.

Swafford Gap, on the McDowell-Mitchell county

line. The Blue Ridge Parkway passes through
the gap. Alt. 2,852. Named for Marcus Swafford (1856–1943), who lived there.

Swag Cove, ne Cherokee County on Buckhorn
Ridge in the Valley River Mountains.

Swain, community in n Washington County near
the head of Bakers Swamp.

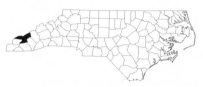

Swain County was formed in 1871 from Jackson
and Macon Counties. Located in the sw section of the state, it is bounded by the state of
Tennessee and by Graham, Cherokee, Macon,
Jackson, and Haywood Counties. It was
named for David L. Swain (1801–68), governor
of the state and president of the University
of North Carolina. Area: 544 sq. mi. County
seat: Bryson City, with an elevation of 1,736
ft. Townships are Charleston, Forneys Creek,
and Nantahala. The Qualla Boundary of the
Cherokee Indians, Great Smoky Mountains
National Park, Nantahala National Forest,
and Fontana Lake occupy much of Swain
County. Produces corn, poultry, livestock,
furniture, textiles, apparel, leather goods,
gaming proceeds, hay, candy, crushed stone,
and feldspar.

Swains Mill Pond, approx. 2 mi. long, on Deep
Swamp Branch just before it enters the
Chowan River in se Hertford County. For-
merly Taylor Pond. Est. ca. 1720.

Swallow Fork, w Haywood County in Great
Smoky Mountains National Park, rises near
lat. 35°42′11″ N., long. 83°07′47″ W., and
flows nw into Big Creek.

Swamp Creek rises in se Bertie County and flows
ne into Cashie River.

Swamp Creek rises in sw Dare County and flows
sw into Alligator River. Appears on the Collet
map, 1770.

Swampy River. *See* Black River.

Swan Corner, community in n Pamlico County
on Chapel Creek. Named for local Swan
family.

Swan Creek rises in e Pamlico County and flows
se into Pamlico Sound.

Swan Creek is formed in e Wilkes County by the

junction of East Swan Creek and West Swan Creek and flows n into Yadkin River.

Swancreek, community in w Yadkin County. Named for the fact that wild geese, erroneously called swans, once lived on nearby streams.

Swan Island, ne Currituck Sound 2 mi. s of Knotts Island, n Currituck County. Approx. ½ by ¼ mi. in size. Site of Swan Island Club, duck- and goose-shooting club owned by wealthy Bostonians.

Swan Island, tidal-marsh island in the mouth of Swan Creek, e Pamlico County.

Swan Islands, three islands in Pamlico Sound in n end of Carteret County.

Swan Mountain, central Buncombe County, extends from the junction of Swope and Bull Creeks to High Swan (peak).

Swann, town in se Lee County. Inc. 1875 as Swann's Station; charter repealed 1877. Reincorporated as Swann's, 1911, but long inactive in municipal affairs. Named for Frederick Jones Swann, who settled there about 1815. Alt. 278.

Swannanoa, community in se Buncombe County. Named for the river on which it is located. Known first as Cooper for A. D. Cooper, owner of the land on which it developed. Produces textiles and wearing apparel. Warren Wilson College is there. Alt. 2,220.

Swannanoa Creek rises in w McDowell County and flows e into Mill Creek.

Swannanoa Gap, in the Blue Ridge Mountains on the Buncombe-McDowell county line at the w end of Youngs Ridge. Lat. 35°37′20″ N., long. 82°16′20″ W. One of the two gaps (the other being Hickory Nut Gap) through which early settlers and travelers from the e reached the Asheville plateau. *See also* Black Mountain Gap.

Swannanoa Gap, on the Buncombe-Yancey county line between Potato Knob and Bald Knob.

Swannanoa Mountains, range of mountains in se Buncombe County s of the community of Swannanoa and parallel to the Swannanoa River.

Swannanoa River rises near Swannanoa Gap on the Buncombe-McDowell county line and flows w into French Broad River s of Asheville. Name is a corruption of *Suwali-Nunna*, the Cherokee word for "trail of the Suwali tribe."

Swannanoa Township, e central Buncombe County.

Swannanoa Tunnel, on the Southern Railway, se Buncombe County near Ridgecrest. Cut in 1879 at a cost of $600,000 and 120 lives, the tunnel marked the completion of a section of the railroad. An early use of nitroglycerine in engineering occurred there.

Swanner, community in nw Alexander County.

Swann Point. *See* Swan Point.

Swann's. *See* Swann.

Swannsborough. *See* Swansboro.

Swann's Station. *See* Swann.

Swan Point, the nw point of Cedar Island in ne Carteret County.

Swan Point extends from Bell Island in s Hyde County into Rose Bay.

Swan Point, s Onslow County, extends into n Chadwick Bay. Appears as Swann Point in early county records.

Swan Pond, a natural pond about 1½ mi. long in the Neuse River low grounds of se Johnston County.

Swan Quarter, former town and present county seat, s Hyde County. Alt. 10. Settled prior to 1836, when it was made the county seat. Inc. 1903; charter repealed 1929. Believed to have been named for Samuel F. Swann, an early owner of the site.

Swan Quarter Bay, in Pamlico Sound e of Bell Island in s Hyde County. *See also* Cecils Harbor.

Swan Quarter Island, a marsh island in Pamlico Sound, s Hyde County. Approx. 10 to 15 acres in area. *See also* Abigails Islands.

Swan Quarter Township, se Hyde County.

Swansboro, town in se Onslow County on White Oak River. Earlier names had been Bogue, Weeks Point, The Wharf, and New Town. Est. as Swannsborough in 1783; named for Samuel Swann (1704–72), who represented the county in the Assembly, 1739–62. Inc. in 1877 as Swansboro.

Swansboro Township, se Onslow County.

Swansee Gap, w Cherokee County between an arm of Hiwassee River and Sular Creek.

Swash, The, a narrow channel between Horse Island and Core Banks, ne Carteret County.

Swayney, community in ne Swain County at the junction of Straight Fork with Raven Fork in Qualla Boundary.

Swearing Creek rises in n Davidson County and flows sw into Yadkin River. Named for Swearingen family. Appears on the Collet map, 1770, as Swaring Creek.

Sweet Branch rises in nw Swain County and flows s into Lake Cheoah.

Sweet Branch rises in w Yancey County and flows nw into Cane River.

Sweet Creek rises in central Mitchell County and flows se into Cub Creek.

Sweet Creek. *See* Frost Mill Creek.

Sweeten Creek rises in s Buncombe County and flows nw into Swannanoa River. Named for the Sweiton family, early settlers. Name later changed to Foster's Mill Creek and then back to Sweeten Creek.

Sweetgum, community in s Graham County.

Sweetwater, community in w Watauga County on Beaverdam Creek.

Sweetwater Branch rises in n central Henderson County and flows se into North Fork.

Sweetwater Branch rises in s Madison County and flows se into French Broad River.

Sweetwater Branch rises near Black Mountain in n Transylvania County and flows ne into South Fork Mills.

Sweetwater Branch rises in n Yancey County and flows se into Sampson Branch.

Sweetwater Creek rises in w Clay County and flows sw and nw into Hiwassee River.

Sweetwater Creek rises in e Graham County and flows sw and nw, where it joins Tulula Creek in forming Cheoah River.

Sweetwater Creek drains Statons Pond, *which see*, in central Martin County and flows n into Roanoke River. Appears as Flat Branch on the Collet map, 1770.

Sweetwater Gap, s Clay County between Kimsey Ridge and Ivy Top.

Sweetwater Gap, in e Graham County at the head of Sweetwater Creek.

Sweetwater Spring, in the headwaters of Haywood Gap Stream in s Haywood County.

Sweetwater Township, w Clay County.

Sweezy Mountain, a peak on Cherry Mountain, e Rutherford County. A large pile of rocks on the w side is known as the Rock House.

Swepsonville, community in central Alamance County. Named for George W. Swepson (1811–83), who built a cotton mill there in 1868. Inc. 1887; charter repealed 1901.

Swift Creek, name given Sandy Creek in Hilliardston community, n Nash County. Sandy Creek, *which see*, rises in se Vance County. As

Swift Creek, it flows se across Nash County and into Edgecombe County, where it enters Tar River. Swift Creek appears on the Moseley map, 1733.

Swift Creek rises in s central Pitt County and flows se into n Craven County, where it enters Neuse River. Appears on the Moseley map, 1733.

Swift Creek rises in s Wake County and flows se into Johnston County, where it enters Neuse River. Appears on the Collet map, 1770.

Swift Creek. *See* Vanceboro.

Swift Creek Township, former township in nw Edgecombe County, now township no. 7.

Swift Creek Township, s Pitt County.

Swift Creek Township, s central Wake County.

Swift Fork Branch rises in se Watauga County and flows se into Elk Creek.

Swift Island, community in sw Montgomery County served by post office, 1850–83. Site of hydroelectric plant, 1926, forming Lake Tillery.

Swim Bald, on the Graham-Swain county line between Sassafras Gap and The Jump-up.

Swimmer Branch rises in n Jackson County and flows s into Wrights Creek.

Swindell, community in s Hyde County. A post office operated there, 1830–39.

Swindell Fork, community in central Hyde County.

Swinging Lick Gap, sw Macon County between Winding Stair Gap and Bryson Branch.

Swinton, community in n Moore County served by post office, 1888–1908.

Swiss, community in w Yancey County on Bald Creek. Alt. 2,681. Named because the surrounding countryside suggested that of Switzerland.

Swopes Branch rises in e Cabarrus County and flows se into Little Buffalo Creek.

Sycamore Creek rises in central Franklin County and flows sw into Tar River.

Sycamore Creek rises in nw Wake County and flows w and s along the Durham-Wake county line for a part of its course and then se in Wake County into Turkey Creek.

Sylva, town and county seat, central Jackson County. Inc. 1889. Settled in 1861; named for William D. Sylva, a Dane employed as a carpenter by Gen. E. R. Hampton, who constructed buildings at the site. Produces paper, electronics, and textiles. Alt. 2,047.

See also Webster, which was the county seat until 1913.

Sylvania, community in sw Rockingham County.

Sylvasla, community in central Wake County.

Sylva Township, n central Jackson County.

Sylvester, community in n Chatham County served by post office, 1890–96.

Symonds Creek rises in s Pasquotank County and flows s into Little River.

T

Tabbs Creek rises in e Granville County and flows se across sw Vance County into Tar River on the Vance-Franklin county line. Appears on the Collet map, 1770, as Tans Creek, probably as an engraver's error. For a time prior to 1764, the Granville County Courthouse was located on Tabbs Creek. Tabb's Creek District had 57 heads of families at the time of the 1790 census.

Tabernacle, community in se Guilford County served by post office, 1880–1903; the mail was sent to Climax after 1903.

Tabernacle Township, w central Randolph County.

Tablerock, community in nw Burke County.

Table Rock Branch rises in ne Swain County and flows sw into Straight Fork.

Table Rock Mountain, nw Burke County in Pisgah National Forest. Alt. 3,918. Summit accessible by foot trail. Appears on the Collet map, 1770, as Table Mountain. Known by the Cherokee Indians as *Namonda*.

Tabor Branch rises in n Swain County and flows se into Bradley Fork.

Tabor City, town in sw Columbus County. Settled 1886. Inc. 1905 as Tabor; name changed to Tabor City, 1935. Named for Mt. Tabor Presbyterian Church. Produces lumber, processed food. Alt. 50.

Tabor Island, in Roanoke River in se Bertie County at the sw end of Bluff Island. Known by the name since the mid-nineteenth century. Approx. ¾ mi. long and ⅛ mi. wide. *See also* Purchace Islands.

Tackett Branch rises in n Rockingham County and flows se into Smith River.

Tadmore, community in the nw tip of Pasquotank County.

Taggart Creek rises in central Mecklenburg County and flows se to join Stewart Creek in forming Sugar Creek.

Tah-kee-os-tee. *See* French Broad River.

Talbot, community in w Wilson County. Post office est. there 1892 but moved a few years later to another nearby community and discontinued in 1902.

Talc Mountain, community in sw Swain County on Nantahala River.

Talc Mountain Branch rises in sw Swain County and flows se into Nantahala River.

Tali Gap, in nw Swain County between Pickens Gap and Haw Gap Branch.

Talley Mill Creek rises in se Macon County and flows se into Rabun County, Ga., where it enters Big Creek.

Talleys Crossing, community in e Forsyth County.

Tallulah River rises in se Clay County and flows se into Towns County, Ga., where it enters Tugaloo River.

Tally Ho, community in w Granville County. A post office est. there 1830 was moved to Stem in 1889, and the name was changed. Alt. 500. Named for the traditional call of fox hunters when the quarry is sighted. Fox hunting was a popular sport in the area in the eighteenth and early nineteenth centuries.

Tally Ho Township, w central Granville County.

Ta-loh-na. *See* Yellow Mountain.

Tamarack, community in n Watauga County on Hoskin Fork. Post Office est. 1902 and closed 1966; surrounding community generally known as Pottertown. Named for tamarisk tree.

Tamban Branch rises in central Duplin County and flows w into Northeast Cape Fear River.

Tampa, community in s Mecklenburg County served by post office, 1888–1903.

Tanasee Bald, mountain peak on the Haywood-Transylvania county line at the junction of Pisgah Ridge and Tanasee Ridge in Pisgah National Forest. Lat. 35°17′30″ N., long. 82°55′03″ W. Alt. 5,560. The Cherokee name for the peak was *Tsul-ka-lu-tsu-na-gun-yi*.

Tanasee Creek rises in e Jackson County at Mount Hardy Gap and flows approx. 9 mi. sw to enter Tuckasegee River.

Tanasee Gap, in Tanasee Ridge on the Jackson-Transylvania county line in Pisgah and Nantahala National Forests.

Tanasee Ridge, on the Jackson-Transylvania county line, forms the boundary between Nantahala and Pisgah National Forests. It is approx. 11 mi. long and extends nw from the Blue Ridge.

Tanawha. *See* Grandfather Mountain.

Tanbark Gap, sw Cherokee County between Pack Top and Potato Creek.

Tanbark Ridge, central Buncombe County between Jones Cove and Bull Creek.

Tandaquomuc, an Indian village of either the Weapemeoc or Chowanoac tribes located in what is now se Bertie County between the mouths of Chowan and Roanoke Rivers. Appears on the De Bry map, 1590. The name may have meant "where the road goes by the big evergreens."

Tank Creek rises in nw Cumberland County and flows ne into Little River.

Tantram Branch rises in se Buncombe County near Patton Gap in the Swannanoa Mountains and flows s into Trantham Creek.

Tantroft Branch. *See* Tantrough Branch.

Tantrough Branch rises in e central Yancey County and flows n into Little Crabtree Creek. Named for the wooden trough used in tanning hides that an early settler had there. The spelling Tantroft is also used.

Tan Yard. *See* Eldorado.

Tanyard Branch rises in central Rutherford County nw of Rutherfordton and flows se into Cleghorn Creek. At one time it was known as Milk House Branch.

Tanyard Creek rises in n Yadkin County and flows ne into Yadkin River.

Tanyard Gap, n Madison County at the head of Silvermine Branch.

Tapoco, resort community in nw Graham County on Cheoah River. Served by post office, 1916–36. Alt. 1,110. Name coined by the Tallassee Power Company using the first two letters of the three words in the company name.

Tarawa Terrace, residential area of Camp Lejeune Marine Base, central Onslow County. Named for the Pacific Island on which a battle was fought against the Japanese, November 21–24, 1943.

Tarboro, town and county seat, central Edge-combe County. Settled in 1732 and est. 1760. Inc. 1772. Named for Tar River, on which it is situated. Town commons, created by legislative act of 1760, is still maintained. The legislature met there in 1787. Produces textiles, lumber, machinery, toys, and paper products. In early records, the name sometimes appears as Tawboro. Alt. 58. *See also* Runnymeade; West Tarboro.

Tarboro Township, former township in central Edgecombe County, now township no. 1.

Tarcamp Branch rises in w Jackson County and flows e into West Fork Tuckasegee River.

Tar Corner, community in ne Camden County. Name said to derive from a barn painted with tar that stood at intersection of two roads.

Tar Creek rises in e Pamlico County and flows n into Broad Creek.

Tare-over, sw Washington County, a bridge and straight stretch of the road from Plymouth to Leachville crossing the headwaters of Flat Swamp at the ne end of Van Swamp. The name appears on the Price map, 1808, and is thought to have originated as the name for the grassy, swampy depression that cuts into Long Acre, *which see.*

Tar Heel, a town in nw Bladen County. Settled 1875. Inc. 1963. Alt. 100. Named either for the appellation said to have been given, by Confederates from other states, to North Carolina troops who emerged from a river with tar adhering to their heels, or for tar produced in the vicinity taken to the Cape Fear River and then by raft to Wilmington. Along the riverfront, the ground was covered with tar, and so were the feet that passed over it.

Tarkiln Branch rises in w Swain County and flows se into Little Tennessee River.

Tarkiln Branch rises in w Transylvania County and flows ne into Catheys Creek.

Tar Kiln Creek rises in s Pamlico County and flows s into Dawson Creek.

Tarkiln Gap, ne Cherokee County in the Valley River Mountains.

Tarkiln Mountain, peak on Forge Mountain in w Henderson County.

Tarkiln Mountain, in w Transylvania County between Tarkiln Branch and King Mountain.

Tarkiln Neck, peninsula at the junction of Pamlico and Pungo Rivers, e Beaufort County.

Tar Kiln Ridge, nw Clay County, extends from Short Off to the Tusquitee Mountains.

Tarkiln Ridge, central Macon County parallel to Poplar Cove.

Tar-ko-ee. *See* Piedmont.

Tar Landing, community in n Onslow County between Blue Creek and New River. Early deeds refer to the landing on New River as Owen Jones's Tar Landing.

Tar Landing Bay, in the extreme e end of Bogue Banks on the sound side, s Carteret County.

Tarpleys Pond, se Wake County on Little River. Covers 50 acres and has a max. depth of 15 ft. Used for irrigation and recreation.

Tar Ridge, s Watauga County, extends se from the head of Days Creek.

Tar River rises in w central Person County and flows se through Granville, Franklin, Nash, Edgecombe, and Pitt Counties to Beaufort County, where it becomes the Pamlico River. It is 179 mi. long. Appears on the Moseley map, 1733, apparently for the first time; previously known as Pampticough and other spellings of the modern Pamlico. There are many explanations of the origin of the name. It may be from an Indian word, *Tau*, meaning "river of health"; named for the Taw River in Devonshire, England; or named because of the tar produced in the counties through which it flows.

Tar River, community in s Granville County.

Tarts Store, community in s Johnston County.

Tartt Path, pre–Civil War path still in use in e central Wilson County. It runs n from the community of Sun to the vicinity of modern N.C. Highway 42 e of Wilson. Enos Tartt operated Tartt's Mill on Bear Branch in the mid-nineteenth century.

Tate, community in n Rutherford County on Second Broad River.

Tate Branch rises in ne Clay County and flows ne into Nantahala River.

Tate Gap, e Clay County between the headwaters of Passmore Branch and Fishprong Branch.

Tater Hill, in s Macon County between Poplar Cove and Rocky Knob.

Tater Hill, in s Macon County between Rattlesnake Ridge and Licklog Gap.

Tater Hill, peak in n Watauga County on Rich Mountain approx. ¾ mi. s of Rich Mountain Bald. Also known in recent years as Potato Hill. Named because it resembles a large storage hill for potatoes. Alt. 5,194.

Tater Hill Lake. *See* Potato Hill Lake.

Tater Top Mountain, in Morrow Mountain State Park, e Stanly County.

Tate's Knob, a small, sharp-top mountain in ne Caldwell County. Named for Andrew Tate, eighteenth-century settler.

Tatham Creek rises in ne Cherokee County and flows nw through Andrews into Valley River.

Tatham Creek rises in w Jackson County and flows nw into Savannah Creek.

Tatham Gap, on the Cherokee-Graham county line in the Snowbird Mountains. Alt. 3,500–3,639.

Tatter Knob, se Buncombe County nw of Hickorynut Gap.

Tatums Township, nw Columbus County.

Tava Cove, n Cherokee County in the Snowbird Mountains.

Taylor. *See* Rock Ridge.

Taylor Bay, in Bogue Sound, w Carteret County s of community of Bogue.

Taylor Bay, central Currituck County at s tip of Great Swamp.

Taylor Creek, a waterway separating Carrot Island from the mainland in s central Carteret County; flows from Lenox Point on the e to the mouth of Newport River on the w.

Taylor Creek rises in ne Cherokee County and flows nw into Valley River.

Taylor Creek rises in n Craven County and flows se into Neuse River.

Taylor Crossroads, community in s Nash County.

Taylor Millpond, sw Gates County, receives waters of a number of small streams and flows se into Big Pocosin.

Taylor Pond. *See* Swains Mill Pond.

Taylors Branch rises in ne Columbus County and flows ne into Livingston Creek.

Taylors Bridge, community in se Sampson County on Cuwhiffle Swamp.

Taylors Bridge Township, se Sampson County.

Taylors Corner, community in w Jones County.

Taylors Creek rises in the w tip of Carteret County and flows sw approx. 1 mi. into White Oak River.

Taylors Creek rises in sw Duplin County and flows se into Duffs Creek.

Taylors Creek rises in nw Franklin County and flows n into Tar River.

Taylors Creek rises in e Gaston County and flows se into Dutchmans Creek.

Taylors Creek rises in s central Randolph County and flows w into Caraway Creek.

Taylors Ferry operated across the Roanoke River between Bertie County and Martin County. Appears on the Collet map, 1770, and known to have been in operation as late as 1833.

Taylors Mill. *See* Tippetts Mill Pond.

Taylors Mill Pond, on the head of Corduroy Swamp in central Northampton County; approx. ¾ mi. long.

Taylors Pond, on the head of Reedy Branch in nw Duplin County.

Taylors Store, community in nw Nash County.

Taylorsville, town and county seat, central Alexander County. Settled 1847; inc. 1851. Probably named for Zachary Taylor (1784–1850), whose defeat of Santa Anna early in 1847 ended the war in n Mexico; Taylor was president of the United States, 1849–50. Alt. 1,247. Produces textiles, furniture, and paper boxes.

Taylorsville, an African American community in s Moore County. Named for Robert L. Taylor, educator, who founded a school and a store there in 1908.

Taylorsville, town authorized in 1818 to be laid off on the lands of George Taylor on Black River in Sampson County. Probably never developed, and the exact site is unknown.

Taylorsville Township, central Alexander County.

Taylor Township, n Wilson County.

Taywa Creek rises in ne Swain County in Great Smoky Mountains National Park on Hughes Ridge and flows sw into Bradley Fork. Named for a Cherokee Indian chief.

Teaberry Ridge, central Haywood County between Right Fork Cove Creek and Wright Branch.

Teaches Hole, a navigable channel running ne and sw from Ocracoke Inlet, se Hyde County. Traditionally named for Edward Teach, or Blackbeard, the notorious pirate killed nearby in 1718. Appears as Thatches Hole on the Moseley map, 1733, and shown as being closed at the ne end.

Teachey, town in se Duplin County. Inc. 1874; charter repealed 1897; reincorporated 1903. Alt. 71.

Teague Branch rises in central Haywood County and flows nw into Pigeon River.

Teague Branch rises in s Macon County on the n side of Turkey Knob and flows n into Tellico Creek.

Teagues Ridge, mountain in w Avery County.

Teaguetown, community in ne Davidson County between the headwaters of Spurgeon and Abbotts Creeks. Named for a local family.

Tearshirt. *See* Dunn.

Tea Swamp rises in central Duplin County and flows ne into Grove Creek.

Teat Branch rises in central Madison County and flows nw into Big Laurel Creek.

Teds Branch rises in ne Swain County and flows s into Straight Fork.

Teer, community in sw Orange County on Cane Creek.

Teeseteska Ridge, s Graham County, extends n from Atoah Gap.

Telephone, community in ne Person County served by post office, 1882–1907.

Telfairs Creek rises in s New Hanover County and flows se into Cape Fear River. Called Rock Run on a coastal survey map made in 1851–53.

Tellico Bald, n Macon County at the head of Cold Spring Creek. Alt. 5,130.

Tellico Creek rises in n Macon County and flows ne into Little Tennessee River.

Tellico River rises in n Cherokee County and flows w into Monroe County, Tenn., where it turns n to flow into Tennessee River.

Tempa Mountain, s Mitchell County between Beaver Creek and North Toe River.

Temples Creek rises in n Davidson County and flows n into Reedy Creek.

Tempting, community in n Moore County served by post office, 1886–1905.

Teneriffe Mountain, on Mud Creek in central Henderson County.

Ten Mile Fork, community in e Jones County.

Tenmile Swamp rises in w Onslow County and flows nw into Ninemile Swamp. Named for its distance from Rich Lands Chapel, an early center of settlement.

Ten Mile Swamp rises in n Robeson County and flows se and ne into Big Swamp.

Tenmile Swamp rises in e Sampson County and flows sw into Six Runs Creek.

Tennelina, community in w Madison County served by post office, 1903–34. The name is a combination of parts of the words Tennessee and Carolina.

Tennent Mountain, se Haywood County in Pisgah National Forest near lat. 35°20′15″ N., long. 82°52′10″ W. Named for Gaillard Stoney

Tennent (1872–1953) in recognition of his lifelong interest in studying and preserving the beauty of the w North Carolina mountains. Alt. over 6,040.

Tennessee, a state formed from w territory formerly a part of North Carolina that was ceded to the federal government in 1789. *See also* Watauga Settlement; District of Washington; Franklin; Davidson County; Greene County; Hawkins County; Sullivan County; Tennessee County; Washington County.

Tennessee Bald, most n peak on Tennessee Ridge on Haywood-Transylvania county line near Jackson County line. Alt. approx. 5,575.

Tennessee Branch rises in n Swain County and flows se into Bradley Fork.

Tennessee County, former county in what is now the state of Tennessee, was formed in 1788 and named for a Cherokee Indian word whose meaning is not now known. Clarksville became the county seat, but the county was divided into Montgomery and Robertson Counties in 1796, when Tennessee County gave its name to the new state. Part of the territory ceded by North Carolina in 1789 to the federal government.

Tennessee Ridge extends from n to s along the Jackson-Transylvania county line between Haywood County line and head of West Fork French Broad River. Named peaks include Balk Knob, Bald Rock, The Pinnacle, Rockyface Mountain, Round Mountain, and Tennessee Bald.

Tennyson, community in s Davie County served by post office, 1891–1906.

Terebinthe. *See* Cedar Creek.

Teresita, community in s Macon County on Jones Creek.

Terrace Fork. *See* Terris Fork.

Terra Ceia, community in n central Beaufort County. Alt. 16. Settled in the early 1920s by Dutch bulb growers; the community's name means "heavenly land."

Terra Cotta, former community in central Guilford County, now within the bounds of Greensboro. Name is Latin for "cooked earth." Named for the hard-baked clay plant there. Alt. 889.

Terrapin, community in w Halifax County served by post office, 1893–1911.

Terrapin Creek rises in e Catawba County and flows e into Catawba River.

Terrapin Creek rises in w Warren County and flows n into Blue Mud Creek.

Terrapin Island, tidal-marsh island in Pamlico Sound, ne Pamlico County.

Terrapin Mountain, in s Jackson County between Chattooga Ridge and Chattooga River. Also called Fodderstack Mountain. Alt. 4,510. Known by the Cherokee Indians as *Klansoona* (terrapin).

Terrapin Point, in se Bertie County extending into Batchelor Bay at the n side of Cashie River.

Terrapin Point, community in w Halifax County.

Terrapin Run, a bay in White Oak River, w Carteret County, that empties into Croaker Channel. Named for the fact that fishermen catch numerous terrapins there.

Terrazzo Switch, community in ne Cherokee County in Nantahala National Forest on Southern Railway. Named for terrazzo flooring made from locally mined marble chips.

Terrell, community in se Catawba County. Named for an early Methodist minister in the vicinity.

Terrell Creek rises in n Chatham County and flows ne into Haw River.

Terrell Gap, e Swain County on Williams Branch.

Terrell Mountain, n Chatham County 7 mi. sw of town of Chapel Hill. Alt. 849. Broadcast transmitting towers are there.

Terrible Creek rises in sw Wake County n of town of Fuquay-Varina and flows e through Johnsons Pond and into Middle Creek.

Terris Fork rises in e Madison County and flows w into Paint Fork. Appears as Terry Fork and Terrace Fork on various maps.

Terry Branch rises in nw Nash County and flows e into Tumbling Run.

Terry Creek rises in s Henderson County and flows n into Green River.

Terry Fork. *See* Terris Fork.

Terry Gap, in n Henderson County at the head of Kyles Creek.

Tessentee Creek rises in s Macon County and flows w into Little Tennessee River.

Texana, community in central Cherokee County n of Murphy.

Teyahalee Bald, on the Cherokee-Graham county line in the Snowbird Mountains. Alt. 4,743.

Thagards Pond, on Little River in e Moore

County. Covers approx. 100 acres. Named
for William C. Thagard, who owned it from
1854 until about 1900. Was the site of
Nicholas Smith's mill from as early as 1769.
A residential community, Whispering Pines
and a golf course were developed there about
1901.

Thanksgiving, community in n Johnston
County; named for Baptist church founded
there on Thanksgiving Day, 1899.

Tharon, community in e Duplin County on the
head of Limestone Creek.

Tharp Mountain, ne Buncombe County between
Martin and North Fork Ivy Creeks.

Thatches Hole. *See* Teaches Hole.

Thaxton, community in nw Ashe County. Alt.
approx. 3,700.

Thelma, community in nw Halifax County near
Roanoke River and s of the site of the old
town of Gaston, *which see.* The town of South
Gaston, *which see,* was chartered in 1895, but
the charter was repealed in 1907. Alt. 224.

Theoff Point, projection from s Bodie Island
into Roanoke Sound, e Dare County approx.
½ mi. n of Cedar Island.

Thermal Belt (also called Isothermal Belt),
verdant zone largely in Polk and Rutherford
Counties—though to a lesser extent also
in Caldwell, Mitchell, and other mountain
counties—in which on certain cool nights,
the temperature may be 20° or more higher
on the slope of a mountain than at the base.
In these areas, fruit growing is a successful
undertaking, and at Tryon (Polk County) the
thermal belt has contributed to resort prosperity. The thermal belt was first described
by Silas McDowell in 1858.

Thermal City, community in n Rutherford
County on Second Broad River. A post office
est. there in 1888 was named Pescud; name
changed to Thermal City for the Thermal
Belt, *which see,* in 1891. Post office discontinued 1926.

Thermo Knob, w Haywood County in Great
Smoky Mountains National Park on Balsam Mountain near lat. 35°41′39″ N., long.
83°13′34″ W. Alt. 6,120. Formerly known as
Thermometer Knob.

Theta, community in ne Madison County served
by post office, 1886–1900.

Thicket Branch rises in ne Swain County and
flows sw into Right Fork [Raven Fork].

Thickety Creek rises in e Haywood County and
flows s into Pigeon River.

Thickety Creek rises in s Montgomery County
and flows sw into Little River.

Third Creek rises in e Alexander County and
flows se across Iredell County and into Rowan
County, where it enters Fourth Creek. It is the
third creek in a series of creeks crossed by
early settlers moving w from Salisbury. Appears on the Collet map, 1770.

Third Creek. *See* Cleveland.

Third Creek. *See* Second Creek.

Third Fork Creek rises in s Durham County and
flows sw into New Hope Creek.

Thirty Foot Canal, e Washington County, extends ne between Lake Phelps and Scuppernong River.

30 Mile Post, marked corner on the North Carolina–Georgia state line, se Clay County 30 mi.
w of Ellicott Rock, *which see.* Survey completed to the corner in 1819. There the state
line turns due s for 1,983 ft. to Montgomery
Corner, *which see.*

Thomas Bay, s extension of Cawcaw Swamp in
sw Brunswick County between its junctions
with Little Cawcaw Swamp and Shingletree
Swamp.

Thomasboro, community in sw Brunswick
County. Named for Cornelius Thomas
(1889–1961).

Thomas Branch rises in sw Macon County and
flows nw into Nantahala River.

Thomas Branch rises in central Madison County
and flows sw into Hopewell Branch.

Thomas Creek rises in w Wake County and flows
se into Little Whiteoak Creek.

Thomas Knob, s Macon County between Pipetrack Gap and Watkins Creek.

Thomas Landing, community in s Onslow
County on Spicers Bay.

Thomas Peak, nw Jackson County between
Camp Creek and Shoal Creek.

Thomas Ridge, n Swain County in Great Smoky
Mountains National Park, extends in a
semicircle from Deep Creek n following the
general curve of Oconaluftee River with its
center near lat. 35°32′30″ N., long. 83°22′03″
W. Named for Col. William Holland Thomas
(1805–93), native of Haywood County and
chief of the Cherokee Indians.

Thomasville, city in ne Davidson County.
Founded 1852; inc. 1857. Named for John

Warwick Thomas (1800–1871), founder. Produces furniture, textiles, hosiery, apparel, lumber, and concrete pipe.

Thomasville Township, ne Davidson County.

Thompkins Knob, at the junction of the Ashe-Watauga-Wilkes county lines in the Blue Ridge Mountains. Alt. 4,100. Also spelled Tomkins Knob.

Thompson. *See* Westover.

Thompson Branch rises in w Cherokee County on Ghormley Mountain and flows nw into Shoal Creek.

Thompson Branch rises in e Macon County and flows s into Watauga Creek.

Thompson Branch rises in s Swain County and flows n into Sawmill Creek.

Thompson Creek rises in n Transylvania County and flows s into South Fork Mills River.

Thompson Knob, n of Shuckpen Gap on the Buncombe-Haywood county line on Smathers View Mountain. Alt. 4,192.

Thompson River rises in sw Transylvania County and flows se into Oconee County, S.C., where it enters Whitewater River.

Thompson's Branch rises in n Greene County and flows e into Sandy Run. Named for a pioneer family.

Thompson's Bromine-Arsenic Springs. *See* Crumpler.

Thompsons Gap, e Alleghany County.

Thompsons Gut rises in w Bertie County and flows w into Roanoke River.

Thompsons Millpond, n Wake County in Horse Creek.

Thompson Store, community in ne Mecklenburg County.

Thompson Township, former township in se Alamance County, now township no. 9.

Thompson Township, sw Robeson County.

Thompsonville. *See* Williamsburg.

Thorn Mountain, sw Macon County between Siler Bald Branch and Bryson Branch.

Thorntons Creek rises in e Harnett County and flows sw into Cape Fear River.

Thorofare, channel in ne Carteret County connecting Thorofare Bay with West Thorofare Bay and forming the s boundary of Cedar Island.

Thorofare Bay, on the s side of Cedar Island emptying into Core Sound, ne Carteret County.

Thorofare Swamp rises in e Pitt County and flows se into Clayroot Swamp.

Thoroughfare, portion of Pee Dee River flowing s of Youngs Island, n Anson County.

Thoroughfare, a waterway approx. 2 mi. long in se Bertie County connecting Cashie and Roanoke Rivers.

Thoroughfare, a waterway connecting Black River and Cape Fear River, sw Pender County.

Thoroughfare Branch rises in s Lee County and flows ne into Juniper Creek.

Thoroughfare Island, a small island in North River, w Currituck County. North of the island, the river is sometimes known as Indiantown Creek.

Thoroughfare Swamp rises in sw Wayne County and flows ne and n into Neuse River. Formerly known as Falling Creek, and so designated on the Price map, 1808, and by Dr. Elisha Mitchell in his 1827 journal.

Thorpe Reservoir. *See* Lake Thorpe.

Thrash Branch rises in central Transylvania County and flows sw into French Broad River.

Thrash Creek rises in ne Cherokee County on Old Mattie Ridge and flows se and sw into Valley River. *See also* Wood Lake.

Three Forks. *See* Busick.

Three Forks Creek, formed in se Yancey County by the junction of Left Prong and Right Prong and flows nw into South Toe River.

Three Forks Mountain, w central Transylvania County at the nw end of Big Mountain Ridge and the w end of Soapstone Ridge. Alt. 3,774.

Three Hat Mountain, e Davidson County on the headwaters of Flat Swamp Creek.

Three Knobs, s Avery County.

Three Knobs, on the McDowell-Yancey county line.

Three Mile, community in s Avery County.

Three Mile Branch rises in n Cabarrus County and flows se into Cold Water Creek.

Three Mile Creek rises in s Avery County and flows sw into North Toe River.

Threemile Creek rises in nw McDowell County near Little Switzerland and flows s into Armstrong Creek.

Threemile Creek rises in w Orange County and flows se into Sevenmile Creek.

Three Point Gap, nw Cherokee County below Hazel Knob and near Bryson Lead.

Three Quarters Creek rises in e central Yancey County and flows s into Little Crabtree Creek.

Three Top Creek rises in s central Ashe County and flows n into North Fork New River.

Three Top Mountain, w Ashe County. Alt. 5,029.

Three Top Ridge, in s Haywood County between Nick Creek and McClure Creek.

Thrift, railroad depot name for the Mecklenburg County community of Paw Creek, *which see.*

Thrift Cove Branch rises in n Transylvania County and flows s into Davidson River.

Thumb Swamp, ne Bladen County. Approx. 2 mi. long; drains w into Turnbull Creek.

Thumb Swamp rises in se Bladen County and flows e into Colly Creek approx. 5 mi. se of Singletary Lake.

Thumping Branch rises in se Clay County on Little Mountain and flows sw into Eagle Creek.

Thunderbolt Landing, on Cashie River, se Bertie County.

Thunderhead Mountain, on the Swain County, N.C.–Blount County, Tenn., line in Great Smoky Mountains National Park near lat. 35°34′08″ N., long. 83°42′24″ W. Alt. 5,530.

Thunder Hill, s Watauga County near the head of Groundhog Branch.

Thunderhole Creek rises in s Watauga County approx. 2 mi. w of the town of Blowing Rock and flows s into n Caldwell County, where it enters Johns River.

Thunderstruck Knob, in e Yancey County at the e end of Bee Ridge.

Thunderstruck Knob, in nw Yancey County at the s end of Fork Ridge between Hensley Branch and Cane River.

Thunder Struck Mountain, e Jackson County between Snaggy Bald and Mayapple Gap.

Thunderstruck Ridge, n Jackson County between Polecat Branch and Soco Creek.

Thunder Swamp rises in s Wayne County and flows nw into Thoroughfare Swamp.

Thundertontrenck. *See* Lenox Castle.

Thurman, community in e Craven County on Neuse River. Alt. 26. Settled about 1850 and named for Allen G. Thurman (1813–95), member of Congress (1845–47) and later a senator from Ohio. His mother was the daughter of Nathaniel Allen, nephew and adopted son of Joseph Hewes of Edenton.

Thurmond, community in ne Wilkes County at the Surry County line.

Thurston, community in se Alexander County served by post office, 1881–1902.

Thurz Mountain, n Buncombe County nw of Wiley Mountain.

Tiancok, an Indian village of the Chawanoac tribe; appears on the Comberford map, 1657, located in what is now n Hertford County between Potecasi Creek and Meherrin River near the Chowan River. *See also* Cokey Swamp.

Tibb Ridge, e Cherokee County in the Valley River Mountains.

Tibbs Run rises in e Randolph County and flows se into Richland Creek.

Ticer Branch rises in w Mecklenburg County and flows sw into Paw Creek.

Tick Creek rises in w Chatham County and flows ne into Rocky River.

Tickle Creek rises in e Guilford County and flows se into Alamance County, where it enters Traverse Creek.

Tidewater Area, a portion of the Coastal Plain, *which see,* from 30 to 80 mi. wide on the mainland side of the sounds in e North Carolina. Much of the area is swampland, known locally as "dismals" and "pocosins." There also are a number of natural lakes there, as well as many areas of savanna with a thick growth of grass and many wildflowers.

Tiger, community in nw Rutherford County on Buffalo Creek.

Tilden, community in se Yadkin County served by post office, 1897–1904.

Tilden. *See* Maxton.

Tillery, town in e Halifax County. Inc. 1889, but long inactive in municipal affairs. Named for Tillery family, who settled there before 1790. Site of federal resettlement project, 1935. Alt. 64.

Tillery Branch rises in s Madison County and flows w into French Broad River.

Tilley Creek rises in w Jackson County and flows ne into Cullowhee Creek.

Tillis's Mill Creek. *See* Mill Creek.

Tillman, community in sw Chatham County served by post office, 1892–1905.

Timber Creek rises in s Yancey County and flows w to join Ogle Creek in forming Sugar Camp Creek.

Timbered Ridge, mountain in se Avery County.

Timberlake, community in s Person County. Settled about 1890. Named for William Timberlake Sr., first postmaster. The railroad station there is known as Helena, named for the wife of an official of the railroad. Alt. 570.

Timberland, community in w Hoke County.

Timber Ridge, mountain in e central Avery County.

Timber Ridge, sw Jackson County between Cashier Valley and Chattooga River.

Timber Ridge, s Macon County parallel to Gulf Branch.

Timber Ridge, nw McDowell County near the head of Armstrong Creek.

Timber Ridge, s Yancey County between Timber and Ogle Creeks.

Tim Creek rises in n Cleveland County and flows sw into Ward Creek.

Timothy, community in n Sampson County on Sevenmile Swamp.

Timothy Knob, s Watauga County on the head of Clark Creek.

Tims Creek rises in se Burke County near Smith Mountain and flows se into Henry Fork.

Tin Cap Knob, w Macon County between Tyler Branch and Nantahala River.

Tin City, community in s Duplin County.

Tincoco. *See* Cokey Swamp.

Tindallsville, former town in e Stanly County on Pee Dee River in what is now Morrow Mountain State Park. Inc. 1795. Served as a county seat of Montgomery County for a brief time. Site long since abandoned. *See also* Henderson.

Tinoco Creek. *See* Cokey Swamp.

Tinsley Creek rises in n central Transylvania County and flows se into King Creek.

Tippecanoe, community in n Sampson County served by post office, 1890–1904.

Tippers Crossroads. *See* Six Forks.

Tippet Branch rises in e Macon County and flows sw into Little Tennessee River.

Tippet Creek rises in e Macon County and flows nw into Caler Fork.

Tippetts Mill Pond, on Moccasin Creek at the Johnston-Nash county line. Approx. ½ mi. long. Formed before the Civil War and known first as Taylor's Mill, later as Hilliard's Mill, and since about 1949 as Tippetts Mill. In the past a sawmill, cotton gin, and corn and wheat mills have been operated there. Wagons known as Moccasin Wagons were made there.

Tipton Branch rises in ne Clay County and flows ne into Nantahala River.

Tipton Creek rises in n Cherokee County in the Unicoi Mountains and flows nw through Tipton Gap into Tellico River.

Tipton Gap, n Cherokee County in the Unicoi Mountains.

Tipton Hill, community in w Mitchell County on Raccoon Creek.

Tipton Knob, n Cherokee County in the Unicoi Mountains.

Tiptop, community in s Transylvania County served by post office, 1886–1904.

Titepano appears on White map, 1585, in what is now Currituck Sound, e Currituck County. The name may have applied to the sound and seems to have been *tetep-anwi-wi* (there is a swirling current; it swirls around).

Titus Point. *See* Lenox Point.

Toast, community in n Surry County.

Tobacco Branch rises in ne Graham County and flows ne into Wolf Creek.

Tobacco Branch rises in n central Union County and flows se into Chinkapin Creek.

Tobaccoville, community in n Forsyth County. Post office est. 1879 and named for a chewing-tobacco factory built there. Alt. 994.

Tobermory, community in nw Bladen County served by post office, 1917–25. Named for the village in w Scotland.

Tobie's Branch rises in ne Wilson County and flows se into Town Creek.

Todd, town on the Ashe-Watauga county line at the junction of Big Elk Creek with South Fork New River. Inc. 1915 in Ashe County, but that same year the county line was changed so that the town came to lie partially in Watauga County. No longer active in municipal affairs. A post office est. there as Elk Crossroads in 1837 but changed to Todd in 1894. Alt. approx. 3,000.

Todds Creek rises in s New Hanover County and flows sw into Cape Fear River. Called Motts Creek on a coastal survey map made in 1851–53.

Todds Crossroads, community in e central Bertie County.

Toddy, community in w Pitt County. The community was known as Tugwell and the railroad name was Toddy Station in the early twentieth century. Named for the fact that a drink of whiskey could be had at a local store.

Toecane, community in central Mitchell County at the junction of Toe River and Cane Creek. Alt. 2,058.

Toe River is formed on the Mitchell-Yancey county line near Boonford by the junction of

North Toe and South Toe Rivers. It flows nw along the line to join Cane River in forming Nolichucky River. Tradition says the name is derived from Estatoe, the name of an Indian princess who drowned herself in the river when her lover was killed by her kinsmen.

Toe River Township, s Avery County.

Togo. *See* Genlee.

Toisnot. *See* Elm City and *see* Toisnot Swamp.

Toisnot Swamp rises in s Nash County and flows se into n Wilson County. It flows across the county and enters Contentnea Creek in s Wilson County. The name Toisnot is from the Iroquoian language base of the Tuscarora *tosneoc*, meaning "close to two rivers." The name is properly applied not to a single village but to around a dozen different sites occupied by the Tuscarora in what is now e Wilson County. Until about the 1850s, the name was spelled Tosneot and appears that way in local records dating from 1741 and on the Collet map, 1770.

Toisnot Township, n Wilson County.

Tokay, community just outside the n limits of the city of Fayetteville, central Cumberland County.

Tolar Landing, United States Lock Number 3, on Cape Fear River in nw Bladen County.

Tolarsville, community in e Robeson County served by post office, 1876–1911.

Toledo, community in ne Yancey County served by post office, 1905–54.

Tolers, community in w Orange County served by post office, 1890–1905.

Toliver, community in sw Ashe County served by post office, 1902–53.

Toluca, community in ne Cleveland County at the Lincoln County line.

Tomahawk, community in s Sampson County. Settled about 1888. Alt. 99.

Tomahawk Branch rises in ne Buncombe County and flows s into Lake Tomahawk then sw into Swannanoa River.

Tomahawk Branch. *See* Stewarts Creek.

Tomahawk Creek rises in w Forsyth County and flows se into Stewarts Creek, *which see*.

Tomahawk Creek is formed in s Sampson County by the junction of Little Tomahawk and Big Tomahawk Creeks and flows w into South River.

Tomblin Branch rises in e central Brunswick County and flows ne into Lewis Swamp.

Tom Branch rises in ne Cherokee County and flows ne into Taylor Creek.

Tom Branch rises in se Macon County and flows sw into Brooks Creek.

Tom Bryan Cove, n Macon County between Miller Hollow and Fall Branch.

Tom Creek rises in se Buncombe County and flows se into Broad River.

Tom Creek rises in s Haywood County and flows n into West Fork Pigeon River.

Tom Creek rises in n Mitchell County and flows s into Spring Creek.

Tom Creek rises in e Transylvania County and flows s then abruptly ne into Little River.

Tomcreek. *See* Tom's Creek.

Tom Hall Branch rises in n Haywood County and flows w into Pigeon River.

Tom Jack Creek rises in s Wake County and flows s into ne Lee County, where it joins Whiteoak Creek.

Tomkins Knob. *See* Thompkins Knob.

Tom Knob, w Watauga County near the head of Spice Creek. Alt. 4,293.

Tom Mann Creek, a bay on the n shore of Durant Island, central Dare County.

Tommy Branch rises in s Macon County and flows ne into Wayah Creek.

Tommy Knob, n Graham County between the headwaters of Yellow Creek and Cables Cove Creek.

Tomotla, community in central Cherokee County. Alt. 1,575.

Toms Branch rises in n Haywood County and flows s into Fines Creek.

Tom's Creek rises in s Caswell County and flows s into Alamance County, where it enters Stony Creek.

Toms Creek rises in ne Henderson County and flows se into Mill Creek.

Toms Creek rises in w McDowell County and flows se into Catawba River. Toms Creek Falls are n of Marion.

Toms Creek rises in w Orange County and flows se into Cane Creek.

Toms Creek rises in w Randolph County and flows ne and se into Uwharrie River.

Toms Creek rises in e Surry County and flows sw into Ararat River.

Toms Creek rises in e Wake County and flows w into Neuse River.

Tom's Creek, community in central McDowell County served by post office, 1886–1905.

Toms Creek, community in n McDowell County s of Woodlawn. Named for creek of the same name.

Toms Creek. *See* Westfield.

Toms Devil Knob, se Alleghany County between Bullhead and Stone Mountains.

Toms Fork, stream rises in s Columbus County and flows n into Grissett Swamp.

Toms Mountain, a double-topped peak in nw Rutherford County near the headwaters of Cove Creek. Alt. approx. 1,920. Sometimes known as Chalk Mountain.

Toms Top, central Haywood County between Snakeden Top and Colman Gap.

Tom Thumb Creek rises on s slopes of High Peak in the Snowbird Mountains, ne Cherokee County, and flows sw and se into Valley River approx. 3 mi. ne of Andrews.

Tony, community in s Caswell County. A post office was operated there, 1890–1908.

Tonys Branch rises in se Watauga County and flows se into Joes Creek.

Toodies Creek rises in s Yancey County and flows ne into Cane River.

Tooles Creek rises in n Franklin County and flows sw into Lynch Creek.

Tooleys Creek rises in se Beaufort County and flows s into South Creek.

Tooleys Point, point of land in e Beaufort County on the n side of Pungo River at the mouth of Pantego Creek, se limits of Belhaven.

Tools Ford, former passage across Catawba River between Gaston and Mecklenburg Counties e of the present site of Mount Holly. Named for Matthew Tool, who had a grant of land in the vicinity in 1750. The ford was used by troops crossing the Catawba River during the Revolutionary War.

Toomer. *See* Summerville.

Toot Hollow Branch rises in central Swain County and flows s through Bryson City into Tuckasegee River.

Topnot, community in central Caswell County. A post office operated there, 1883–1936.

Topsail, community in s Pender County. Alt. 40.

Topsail Beach, town in se Pender County on the Atlantic Ocean side of Topsail Island. Inc. 1963. Known prior to 1963 as New Topsail Beach.

Topsail Inlet. *See* Beaufort Inlet.

Topsail Island, e Pender County. Barrier beach lying between Topsail Sound and the Atlantic Ocean. Approx. 8½ mi. long.

Topsail Sound extends ne from Mason Inlet, ne New Hanover County, across Pender County to Stump Inlet on the Onslow-Pender county line. It is separated from the Atlantic Ocean by a barrier beach. The sound, about 17 mi. in length, is filled with tidal-marsh islands. Named for the fact that local residents watched from there for the appearance of topsails of approaching vessels.

Topsail Township, se Pender County.

Topsy, community in w Gates County served by post office, 1901–10. Alt. 33. Settled about 1870.

Topton, community in ne Cherokee County. Alt. 2,599. Named because it is at the top of a pass, Red Marble Gap. It is located very near the junction of Cherokee, Graham, and Macon Counties, and residents of all three counties consider themselves citizens of the community.

Torhunta, a village of the Tuscarora Indians, appears on the Moseley map, 1733, at the head of Contentnea Creek in what is now w Wilson County. Many variant spellings include Tarhunta, Taughoutnith, Nahunta, Narhantes. Derives from Indian term meaning "it stays overnight."

Tories Den, cave beneath Moores Knob on Sauratown Mountain in Hanging Rock State Park, w Stokes County. Entrance 12 ft. high and 10 ft. wide; cave about 25 ft. deep. Said to have been occupied by a band of Tories during the Revolutionary War.

Torrence Creek rises in n Mecklenburg County and flows w into McDowells Creek.

Tory Hole. *See* Elizabethtown.

Tosneoc. *See* Toisnot Swamp.

Tosnot Depot. *See* Wilson.

Totero Fork appears on the Moseley map, 1733, as being between Uwharrie and Caraway Creek in what is now w Randolph County. Named for Totero or Tutelo Indians, who lived in the foothills of the Blue Ridge in the seventeenth century but who subsequently migrated to e Virginia and later to Pennsylvania and elsewhere.

Totherrow Branch rises in ne Cherokee County and flows sw into Valley River.

Tottering Bridge, w central Washington County over Skinner Canal near the community of

Basnight. Known by the name as early as 1868.

Tough Ridge, w Haywood County in Great Smoky Mountains National Park, a spur extending nw from Cataloochee Divide; center near lat. 35°35′05″ N., long. 83°05′54″ W., between Clontz Branch and McKee Branch.

Tower Hill, former plantation of Governor Arthur Dobbs in what is now ne Lenoir County. He purchased 850 acres there in 1755 as a possible site for a provincial capital. By an act of the Assembly in 1758, the site was purchased for a capital to be named George City in honor of King George II. The capital was not approved by authorities in London, and the property eventually was sold by the state in 1799. Tower Hill appears on the Collet map, 1770. The name apparently originated because an "old redoubt tower" remained there from a fort constructed during the Tuscarora War, 1711–13. *See also* George City.

Tower Hill Branch rises in ne Lenoir County near Georgetown and flows n into Jericho Run.

Town Branch rises in ne Buncombe County and flows sw into Dillingham Creek.

Town Branch rises in ne Cherokee County and flows nw through Andrews into Valley River.

Town Branch rises in s central Yadkin County and flows se just s of Yadkinville into North Deep Creek.

Town Creek is formed in e central Brunswick County by the junction of Rattlesnake Branch and Lewis Swamp and flows se into Cape Fear River just above Campbell Island. Named Indian Creek by William Hilton in 1663 but appears as Old Town Creek on the Moseley map, 1733. *See also* Charles Town.

Town Creek rises in s central Carteret County and flows w into Newport River. It forms the n limits of the town of Beaufort.

Town Creek rises in central Catawba County and flows sw into Clark Creek.

Town Creek rises in s Clay County and flows se and ne into Hiwassee River.

Town Creek rises in s Montgomery County and flows se into Little River.

Town Creek rises in se Nash County and flows sw across Wilson County into sw Edgecombe County, where it flows ne and se into Tar River. Called Mallard Creek on Moseley map,

1733, but appears as Town Creek on Collet map, 1770.

Town Creek rises in central Onslow County and flows ne into Farnell Bay. Land taken up along the river beginning about 1706.

Town Creek rises in central Rockingham County and flows n into Dan River. Named for the fact that Lower Saura Town, *which see*, an Indian village, was near its mouth. Discovered by William Byrd and his surveying party in 1728.

Town Creek rises in n Stanly County and flows s into Long Creek.

Town Creek, town in ne Wilson County near the stream of the same name. Inc. 1899, but long inactive in municipal affairs. A Baptist church there was est. in 1802.

Town Creek. *See also* Crane Creek.

Town Creek Indian Mound, State Historic Site, s Montgomery County. Area: 53 acres. Est. 1937. Contains excavated and restored Indian mound dating from early sixteenth century and a museum.

Town Creek Township, central Brunswick County.

Town Fork Creek rises in w Stokes County and flows se and then ne across the s part of the county, entering Forsyth County for a short distance and then flowing into Dan River. The headwaters are labeled Slek Creek on the Collet map, 1770, and the lower course simply Town Fork. An iron forge was operated along the banks of the creek by 1796.

Townhouse Branch rises in sw Swain County and flows se into Nantahala River.

Townhouse Creek rises in ne Cherokee County below Old Mattie Ridge and flows s into Welch Mill Creek.

Townhouse Ridge, ne Cherokee County between Welch Mill Creek and Townhouse Creek. Alt. 2,523.

Town Marsh, a tidal-marsh island sw of Beaufort in s Carteret County.

Town Mountain Gap, central Buncombe County in the Elk Mountains.

Town Point, central Onslow County at the n end of Farnell Bay and the s end of Morgan Bay. Now within the Camp Lejeune Marine Corps Air Station.

Townsend, community in se Cumberland County.

Townsend, community in sw Watauga County.

Townsend Gap, s Watauga County near the head of Clark Creek.

Townsville, town in n Vance County between Little Island Creek and se prong of Kerr Lake. Alt. 421. James Lyne operated a store there about 1780, and the surrounding community was named Lynesville, the name by which it appears on the MacRae map, 1833. Inc. in 1857 and named for Edmund Towne, who donated land for a railway station. Served by post office since 1855.

Townsville Lake. *See* Kerr Lake.

Townsville Township, n Vance County.

Town Swamp, sw Bertie County, a part of the larger Broadneck Swamp. Probably named for a Tuscarora Indian town in the vicinity, abandoned before 1800.

Tow String Creek rises in ne Swain County and flows sw into Oconaluftee River. Named because an old woman who lived on the creek made tow strings for the settlers.

Toxaway. *See* Lake Toxaway; Rosman.

Toxaway Creek rises in s Transylvania County and flows sw into Toxaway River.

Toxaway Falls, sw Transylvania County on Toxaway River s of community of Lake Toxaway. The falls, which cascade 123 ft., are crossed by a highway bridge.

Toxaway Mountain, on the Jackson-Transylvania county line n of Horsepasture River.

Toxaway River rises in sw Transylvania County and flows n for a short distance then se and sw into South Carolina, where it joins Whitewater River in forming Keowee River. The name is derived from the Cherokee word *Tor-tzoo-whah* (redbird).

Tracadia. *See* Baltimore.

Trace Branch rises in n Jones County and flows s into Beaver Creek.

Trace Ridge extends se from Beaverdam Gap in nw Henderson County to the junction of Wash Creek and North Fork Mills River.

Tracey Swamp rises in n Jones County and flows n along the Craven-Lenoir county line into Neuse River. *See also* Gum Swamp.

Tracy, community in n Watauga County on North Fork New River.

Tracy Grove, community in e Henderson County.

Trading Ford, former ford across the Yadkin River, Rowan and Davidson Counties. The e end of Big Island was one terminus of the ford. In 1701 John Lawson visited the site, which was on a trading path maintained by Indians across central North Carolina. Gen. Nathanael Greene's American army made a crossing there, February 1, 1781, when almost caught by Cornwallis. High water prevented the British from overtaking the exhausted Americans. A Confederate fort and earthworks nearby protected the railroad and a toll bridge during the Civil War.

Trading Path, a colonial trading route dating from the seventeenth century from Petersburg, Va., to the Catawba and Waxhaw Indians. One branch entered North Carolina in Granville County and another in Warren County. They converged near the present site of Oxford and followed a sw route through Granville, Durham, Orange, Alamance, Guilford, Randolph, Davidson, Rowan, and Cabarrus Counties. At about the present site of Concord, the road split, with a w branch leading through present Charlotte to the Catawba Indians. The e branch led almost directly s through Union County to the Waxhaw Indians. The Trading Path appears on the Collet map, 1770, and the Mouzon map, 1775.

Trafalgar, Cabo de. *See* Cape Fear.

Trail Branch rises in ne Cherokee County and flows nw into McClellan Creek.

Trailbranch, community in se Madison County. A post office operated there, 1876–1905.

Trail Ridge, a twisting mountain ridge in n Clay County extending n from Tusquitee Ridge to Wolf Ridge.

Trail Ridge, w Haywood County, extends e from the county line to Palmer Creek.

Trail Ridge, nw Macon County between Long Branch and Otter Creek.

Trail Ridge, s Macon County between Cunningham Creek and Henson Creek.

Tramaskecooc, Indian village, appears on the White map, 1585, at or near the present location of Cherry Ridge Landing, *which see*, s Tyrrell or n Hyde County near the head of Alligator River. The tribal affiliation of the Indians is uncertain, although the Secotan Indians were active in the area. The name of the village is said to have meant either "beavers" or "people of the white-cedar swamps."

Tramble Gap, se Henderson County near the North Carolina–South Carolina line.

Tramway, community in w Lee County. Named because it was the terminus of a tramroad from Cameron. A Civil War drill ground was approx. 1 mi. s of Tramway.

Tranquility, community in s Granville County served by post office, 1839–56.

Transon, community in e Ashe County served by post office, 1888–1926 and 1937–53. Alt. 3,300.

Transylvania County was formed in 1861 from Henderson and Jackson Counties. Located in the w section of the state, it is bounded by the state of South Carolina and by Jackson, Haywood, and Henderson Counties. Its name is a combination of two Latin words, *trans* (across) and *sylva* (woods). Area: 379 sq. mi. County seat: Brevard, with an elevation of 2,230 ft. Townships are Boyd, Brevard, Catheys Creek, Dunns Rock, Estatoe, Gloucester, Hogback, and Little River. Produces corn, hay, Christmas trees, apples and other fruits and vegetables, poultry, dairy products, livestock, hogs, lumber, paper products, wood products, baked goods, chemicals, textiles, crushed stone, asbestos, sand, and mica.

Tranters Creek rises in sw Martin County and flows se on the Pitt-Martin county line and s on the Pitt-Beaufort county line into Tar River near the point at which it becomes the Pamlico River. Appears on the Moseley map, 1733. The creek was the site of a Civil War battle, June 5, 1862.

Trantham Creek rises in se Buncombe County near Flat Top Mountain and flows sw into Cane Creek.

Trantus, community in sw Martin County served by post office, 1901–1904.

Trap, community in ne Bertie County. Named because a local tavern about 1860 "trapped" men of the community, according to their wives.

Trap Branch rises in ne Swain County and flows w into Straight Fork.

Traphill, community in n Wilkes County e of Little Sandy Creek. Area settled by 1775. In 1833 a town to be named Johnsonville (for an

invalid Revolutionary War veteran wounded at Kings Mountain, Capt. Samuel Johnson, who died the next year) was authorized to be laid out at Trap Hill but never developed. A post office to serve the community was est. there in 1837 and named Trap Hill for hunter William Blackburn's rail-pen snare, which he frequently set on a nearby hill to catch wild turkeys.

Trap Hill Township, ne Wilkes County.

Traps Bay, s Onslow County on the e side of New River nears its mouth. Named for Capt. Cornelius Trap, who was living in the county in 1746.

Traps Creek rises in se Onslow County and flows sw into Traps Bay.

Traverse Creek rises in e Guilford County and flows ne into Alamance County, where it enters Haw River.

Travis, community in nw Tyrrell County n of Scuppernong River.

Trays Island Creek rises in s Jackson County on the n slope of Bald Rock Mountain. It flows n and w around the mountain and then s through Fairfield Lake into Horsepasture River.

Treeland. *See* Whitnel.

Treetop, community in central Ashe County.

Trenholm Mountain, central Henderson County on Memminger Creek. Named for the family of George H. Trenholm of Flat Rock. Trenholm became Confederate secretary of the treasury after C. G. Memminger in 1864.

Trent. *See* Frisco; Merritt; Trenton.

Trent Branch rises in central Buncombe County and flows ne into Hominy Creek.

Trent Branch rises in n Madison County and flows sw into French Broad River.

Trent Bridge. *See* Pollocksville.

Trenton, town and county seat, central Jones County. Courthouse apparently est. at the site in or soon after 1779, when the county was formed. Apparently known as Trent until 1784, when a town to be known as Trenton was authorized to be laid off at the site of the courthouse. Inc. 1874. Took its name from the Trent River, on which it is located. Alt. 28.

Trenton Township, central Jones County.

Trent River rises in s Lenoir County and flows se across Jones County and into Craven County, where it enters Neuse River at New Bern. Appears as Quoracks River on the Comberford map, 1657; apparently first called Trent River by John Lawson, 1709, probably for the river of that name in England. Appears as Trent River on the Moseley map, 1733.

Trent River rises in central Pamlico County and flows n into Bay River. Often known locally as Trent Creek.

Trent Township, sw Lenoir County.

Trent Woods, town in central Craven County on Trent River s of New Bern. Inc. 1959.

Triad. *See* Piedmont Triad.

Triangle, community in e Lincoln County served by post office, 1878–1903. Settled 1902. Named for triangle formed by roads at the site.

Triangle, term used for the Raleigh–Durham–Chapel Hill area. *See also* Research Triangle Park.

Triangle Township, se Durham County. Named for Research Triangle Park, *which see*.

Trickum Creek rises in n Forsyth County and flows n into Buffalo Creek.

Tricorner Knob, on the line separating Haywood and Swain Counties in North Carolina from Sevier County in Tennessee. Alt. more than 6,100. Named for its location at the coincidence of three counties.

Trilby. *See* Allensville.

Trim Cove, ne Cherokee County, through which an unnamed stream flows se into Valley River.

Trimont Branch rises in central Macon County and flows se into Wallace Branch.

Trimont Mountain, central Macon County at the head of Jacob Branch. Alt. approx. 3,700.

Trimont Ridge extends from White Oak Ridge in w Macon County to Jacob Branch in central Macon County.

Trinity, town in nw Randolph County. Union Institute, a school, was est. there in 1838. Located midway between the neighborhoods of Hopewell on the s and Springfield on the n, it took its name from the fact that it was expected to serve to unite the two. Twelve years later the school was reorganized as Trinity College, and the town took its name from the college. Inc. 1869. In 1892 the college moved to Durham, becoming Duke University in 1924.

Trinity, community in s Union County on Buffalo Creek; named for a local church. Former Hope community was located just e.

Trinity Harbor, a former inlet from the Atlantic

Ocean into Albemarle Sound through North Banks s of the present community of Duck. It opened prior to 1585 and closed prior to 1657. Appears on the White map, 1590. The Smith map, 1624, labels it Worcester Inlet. Probably named because it was discovered on one of the Sundays after Trinity (either the 1st or 8th of August, 1585). The site is now in ne Dare County.

Trinity Township, nw Randolph County.

Trio, community in n Rutherford County served by post office, 1888–1906.

Triple Falls, e Transylvania County in Little River between the mouth of Hooker Creek and the mouth of Grassy Creek. Height of the falls is 50 ft.

Triplett, community in e Watauga County served by post office since 1881.

Triplett Creek rises in s Watauga County and flows sw into Joes Creek.

Tritt Knob, central Haywood County on Jonathans Creek. Alt. 3,600.

Tri-Villages, term used by local residents of Hatteras Island, e Dare County, to refer to Rodanthe, Waves, and Salvo, three communities formerly known collectively as Chicamacomico.

Trollinger's Crossing or **Ford**. *See* Haw River.

Trotman Creek rises in s Gates County and flows w and s into Warwick Creek to form Catherine Creek.

Trotters Creek rises in w Lenoir County and flows nw then n into Dailys Creek. Davis Mill Pond, *which see*, is on the creek.

Trotville, community in s Gates County. Alt. 39.

Troublefield Run Creek rises in w Northampton County and flows s into Roanoke River.

Troublesome, community in s Rockingham County served by post office, 1834–83.

Troublesome Creek rises in n Guilford County and flows ne into Rockingham County, where it enters Haw River. Sometimes also known as Big Troublesome Creek.

Troublesome Creek appears on the Kerr map, 1882, and on the 1865 coastal survey map as rising in w Onslow County and flowing ne into New River or Southwest Creek. The name Troublesome Run is applied to the stream on the Price map, 1808, and on the MacRae map, 1833.

Troublesome Creek Iron Works, used during Revolutionary War. Built on Troublesome

Creek, sw Rockingham County, by William Patrick, 1770. Nathanael Greene camped there, 1781; George Washington had breakfast there, June 3, 1791.

Troublesome Point extends into the mouth of the North Landing River in ne Currituck County.

Trout, community in w central Ashe County. Alt. approx. 2,900.

Trout Cove Branch rises in sw Clay County and flows sw into Brasstown Creek.

Trout Creek, a slough in the w end of Bogue Sound, sw Carteret County. Named by fishermen for the trout caught there.

Trout Creek rises in central Jackson County and flows w into West Fork Tuckasegee River.

Trout Creek rises in s Watauga County and flows ne into Elk Creek.

Trout Lake, artificial lake in central Watauga County on Flannery Fork. Formed in 1954, it has a max. depth of 20 ft. and an area of approx. 13 acres. Open to the public.

Troutman, town in s Iredell County. Settled about 1859 and inc. 1905. Named for Mrs. Annie Troutman and her sons, Sydney and Jacob, who settled there and operated a wagon shop. Post office est. 1872 known as Troutman's, 1889–1956. Produces apparel and furniture. Alt. 955.

Troutman Mine, former gold mine in ne Cabarrus County.

Troy, town and county seat in central Montgomery County. Laid out as the county seat in 1843 and inc. 1852. Alt. 664. Accounts vary on origin of name. May have been named for Robert Troy, member of the House of Commons in 1802 and 1806 from Anson County and trustee of the University of North Carolina, 1804–1807, who died in 1807; for John B. Troy, member of the General Assembly from Randolph County, who died before 1837; or for the ancient city of Troy. Produces furniture, carpets, textiles, mobile homes, and lumber.

Troy's Store, community in ne Randolph County. A post office operated there, 1826–84. John B. Troy operated a school there in 1837.

Troy Township, central Montgomery County.

Troyville. *See* Coats.

Truckwheel Mountain, s Buncombe County between Chestnut Cove and Sleepy Gap.

Truda, community in w Richmond County.

Truebloods Point, w Pasquotank County, extends into Little River just s of Nixonton.

Truett Branch rises in ne Cherokee County and flows se into Morris Creek.

Trull Cove, e Cherokee County, through which a short tributary of Slow Creek flows.

Trumpet Branch rises in n central Iredell County and flows s into Rocky Creek just n of Olin. Before the Civil War, Joseph Weisner had an iron foundry there known as Trumpet Branch. It is believed that machinery for antebellum cotton factories in the se was made there.

Trumpeters Swamp rises in s Pender County and flows nw into Merricks Creek.

Trust, community in sw Madison County on Spring Creek. Alt. 2,411.

Truth, community in se Chatham County.

Truvine, community in e Wayne County served by post office, 1891–92.

Tryon, town in sw Polk County. Inc. 1885 as Tryon City. Named for nearby Tryon Mountain, *which see*. Post office, est. 1855, known as Tryon City. Alt 1,075.

Tryon City. *See* Tryon.

Tryon County was formed from Mecklenburg County in 1769 and named in honor of William Tryon (1729–88), governor of North Carolina, 1765–71. The county was abolished in 1779 and divided into Lincoln and Rutherford Counties, *which see*.

Tryon Mountain, w Polk County above the town of Tryon between Skyuka Creek and Little Cove Creek. Named for William Tryon (1729–88), governor of North Carolina, 1765–71. Named by the Cherokee for the governor in 1767 when a boundary was being est. between white and Cherokee lands. Appears on the Collet map, 1770. Alt. 3,231.

Tryon Palace, State Historic Site in New Bern, central Craven County. Est. 1952. Contains restored and reconstructed "Tryon's Palace," completed in 1770 for royal governor William Tryon. Partly burned, 1798. First capitol of state of North Carolina. Reconstruction began, 1952; palace opened to public, 1959.

Tryon Township, sw Polk County.

Tsiyahi. *See* Cheoah.

Tubbs Inlet, a tidal waterway in sw Brunswick County between Bald Beach and Hales Beach.

Tub-Mill Creek rises in nw Swain County and flows s to join Gunna Creek in Great Smoky

Mountains National Park to form Eagle Creek.

Tuckahoe, community in w Jones County served by post office, 1836–1902. Mentioned in a letter from James Iredell to his wife dated May 17, 1782. Named for a plant (*Peltandra virginica* or *Orontium aquaticum*) whose roots were cooked and eaten by the Indians.

Tuckahoe Creek rises in nw Hoke County and flows nw into James Creek.

Tuckahoe Creek rises from Tuckahoe Swamp in w Jones County and flows e into Trent River. Appears on the Collet map, 1770.

Tuckahoe Creek rises in w Pender County and flows ne into Moores Creek.

Tuckahoe Swamp rises in s Lenoir County and flows se into w Jones County, where it becomes less well defined and more of a true swamp. The swamp is drained to the e by Tuckahoe Creek.

Tuckahoe Township, w Jones County.

Tuckasege, community in e Gaston County on Catawba River. Tuckasege Ford over the river was nearby. It is mentioned in local records as early as 1780 and appears on the Price map, 1808. Tuckasege Ferry there was in operation in the early years of the twentieth century.

Tuckasegee, community in central Jackson County at junction of West Fork Tuckasegee River with Tuckasegee River. Named for Cherokee Indian word meaning "crawling terrapin." Alt. 2,184.

Tuckasegee Falls, w Jackson County on West Fork Tuckasegee River. The construction of Lake Thorpe stopped the flow of water, and the falls are no longer noticeable. Formerly the water plunged 60 ft. and then split into two 25 ft. cataracts. Also known as High Falls of the Tuckasegee.

Tuckasegee Lake, in central Jackson County on West Fork Tuckasegee River. Formed in 1950; covers 2 acres and has max. depth of 90 ft. Used for fishing, boating, and as a power source. Open to the public.

Tuckasegee River is formed in se Jackson County by the junction of Panthertown and Greenland Creeks and flows nw through central Jackson County and into Swain County, where it enters Little Tennessee River. Named for the Cherokee Indian town *Tsiksitsi*, which stood beside the river; the word means

"crawling terrapin," referring to the sluggish movement of the water.

Tuck Creek rises in sw Cleveland County and flows n into Broad River.

Tucker Creek rises in s Craven County and flows ne into mouth of Slocum Creek.

Tucker Creek rises near Brevard in central Transylvania County and flows se into Nicholson Creek.

Tucker Creek rises in w Transylvania County and flows se into North Fork French Broad River.

Tuckerdale, community in nw Ashe County.

Tucker Gap, central Graham County between Mountain Creek and Sweetwater Creek.

Tucker Hollow, mountain valley in n central Avery County.

Tucker Island, a silty clay and loam island in Roanoke River, nw Northampton County. Formerly approx. 2 mi. long, but now largely covered by the waters of Roanoke Rapids Lake. Appears as Pughs Island on the Price map, 1808, and as a part of Hamlins Shoals on the MacRae map, 1833.

Tucker's Barn. *See* Lenoir.

Tuckertown, former community in nw Montgomery County. Served by post office, 1910–30. Site now covered by waters of Tuckertown Lake, a reservoir for Carolina Aluminum Company completed in 1962. Originally named Milledgeville; renamed about 1900 for an official of a northern firm that operated a rope-manufacturing plant there. The mill was abandoned and houses were moved from the site when construction of the dam for the lake began.

Tuckertown Lake, on Yadkin River in Davidson, Montgomery, Rowan, and Stanly Counties. Covers 3,000 acres, with a shoreline of 40 mi. Max. depth 50 ft. Named for a former community in Montgomery County whose site it now covers. Completed in 1962 by Carolina Aluminum Company; used as a reservoir, to generate hydroelectric power, and for recreation.

Tugman Mountain, w Wilkes County between Stony Fork Creek and Yadkin River.

Tugwell. *See* Toddy.

Tulin, community in nw Cabarrus County.

Tulip Jewel, community in n Stokes County served by post office, 1888–1905.

Tull Bay, an inland bay in n Currituck County in the mouth of the Northwest River.

Tull Creek rises in central and e Currituck County and flows nw and ne into Tull Bay. Appears on the Collet map, 1770. Named for the Tull family, living there by 1710.

Tull Creek rises in e Onslow County and flows e into Bear Creek.

Tull Mill Pond, on the head of Southwest Creek in sw Lenoir County. Formed approx. 1875. Covers 180 acres; max. depth 14 ft.

Tulls Creek, community in n Currituck County served by post office, 1826–74.

Tully Gap, ne Yancey County at the sw end of Buck Ridge.

Tulula, community in s Graham County on Tulula Creek, *which see.*

Tulula Creek rises in se Graham County and flows nw, where it joins Sweetwater Creek in forming Cheoah River. Named for the Cherokee word for the cry of the frog, *talulu.*

Tumblebug Creek rises in e Henderson County and flows sw into Little Hungry Creek.

Tumblerville, community in s Macon County s of Bristle Ridge.

Tumbling Run rises in nw Nash County and flows ne into Sandy Creek.

Tump Island, ne Carteret County in West Bay off Tump Point on Cedar Island. A tump is defined as a low hill or mound or as a clump of grass, especially one forming a dry spot in a swamp.

Tump Point, ne Carteret County on w side of Cedar Island extending into West Bay.

Tuneigh Branch rises in ne Swain County and flows sw into Bunches Creek.

Tungsten, community in nw Vance County near Little Island Creek. Named for the nearby tungsten deposits, reputedly the second largest in the world. Served by post office, 1949–59.

Tuni Creek rises in n Clay County and flows e and sw into Tusquitee Creek.

Tuni Gap, on the Clay-Macon county line e of Bearpen Gap at the head of Little Tuni Creek. Alt. 3,526.

Tunis, community in e Hertford County served by post office, 1884–1943. Inc. 1909. Charter repealed 1935. Alt. 17.

Tunnel Branch rises in w Swain County and flows w into Goldmine Branch.

Tunnel Falls, se Haywood County on West Fork of Pigeon River. Water drops approx. 50 ft.

Named because a small hole goes into the rock behind the falls, suggesting the entrance to a tunnel.

Tunnel Gap, se Haywood County on the head of East Fork Pigeon River.

Tunnel Ridge, w Swain County, extends se from Forney Ridge to Tunnel Branch.

Tunn Ensleas. *See* Plott Balsams.

Turkey, town in e Sampson County served by post office since 1889. Settled about 1847; inc. 1913. Named for Turkey Creek, which flows a short distance n of the town. Alt. 153.

Turkey Branch rises in w central Halifax County and flows e approx. 1½ mi. into Jacket Swamp.

Turkey Branch rises in central Jackson County and flows ne into Tuckasegee River.

Turkey Branch rises in w Scotland County and flows s into Gum Swamp Creek.

Turkey-Buzzard River. *See* Hyco River.

Turkey Cock Mountain. *See* Hibriten Mountain; Hen Mountain.

Turkey Cove, e Haywood County on the head of Cove Creek.

Turkey Cove, nw McDowell County.

Turkey Cove, nw Swain County between Twentymile Creek and Twentymile Ridge.

Turkey Cove Branch rises in w Madison County and flows se into Spring Creek.

Turkey Cove Gap, w Madison County between Turkey Cove Branch and East Fork Shut-in Creek.

Turkey Cove Gap, nw Swain County on Twentymile Ridge in Great Smoky Mountains National Park near lat. 35°28′09″ N., long. 83°50′07″ W.

Turkey Creek rises in nw Bertie County and flows nw into Hertford County and into Ahoskie Creek.

Turkey Creek is formed in nw Buncombe County by the junction of North and South Turkey Creeks and flows ne and n into Sandy Mush Creek on the Madison County line.

Turkey Creek rises in w Duplin County and flows sw into Sampson County, where it enters Six Runs Creek. Appears as Turkey Branch on the Collet map, 1770. Called Turkey Swamp on the 1959 Duplin County soil survey map.

Turkey Creek rises in e Haywood County and flows sw into Fines Creek.

Turkey Creek is formed on the Hertford-Northampton county line by the junction of

Maple Fork Branch and a small unnamed stream that rises in Hertford County. It flows n along the county line into Kirbys Creek.

Turkey Creek rises in se Moore County and flows s into Little River.

Turkey Creek rises in sw Nash County and flows s into Wilson County, where it joins Moccasin Creek in forming Contentnea Creek.

Turkey Creek rises in s Onslow County and flows s into Spicers Bay.

Turkey Creek rises in s Pender County and flows sw into Northeast Cape Fear River.

Turkey Creek rises in w Swain County and flows ne into Nantahala River.

Turkey Creek is formed in n Transylvania County by the junction of South Prong Turkey Creek and North Prong Turkey Creek and flows sw into Davidson River.

Turkey Creek rises in nw Wake County and flows s into Crabtree Creek.

Turkey Creek Gap, on the Buncombe-Haywood county line n of Big Butt Mountain near the headwaters of South Turkey Creek.

Turkeyfoot, community in w Davie County. Viewed from the air or in aerial photographs, local road intersections resemble a gobbler's appendage.

Turkey Gap, on the Haywood County, N.C.–Cocke County, Tenn., line.

Turkey Hen Mountain. *See* Hen Mountain.

Turkey Hill Creek rises in w Orange County and flows se into Cane Creek.

Turkey Hole, The, a deep slough on the e side of Contentnea Creek, e Greene County. So called from early times, probably from the abundance of wild turkeys in the vicinity.

Turkey Knob, n Henderson County near the head of Laurel Branch. Alt. approx. 3,600.

Turkey Knob, on Slickens Creek in e Jackson County.

Turkey Knob, on the Jackson-Macon county line. Alt. 4,540.

Turkey Knob, s Macon County between Board Gap and Wolf Gap.

Turkey Mountain, w Madison County between Baltimore Branch and Spring Creek.

Turkey Mountain, se McDowell County. Alt. approx. 1,900.

Turkey Pen, community in sw Cherokee County between Wolfe and Hot House Creeks.

Turkeypen Branch rises in ne Cherokee County and flows s into Pile Creek.

Turkeypen Branch rises in s Watauga County and flows ne into Trout Creek.

Turkey Pen Cove, w Macon County between Pierce Creek and Nantahala River.

Turkey Pen Gap, on Forge Mountain in w Henderson County.

Turkey Pen Hollow, nw Cherokee County, through which an unnamed stream flows se into Copper Creek.

Turkeypen Ridge, e Madison County at the head of West Fork [Bull Creek].

Turkey Point, s Onslow County at the mouth of Turkey Creek. Appears in local records as early as 1734.

Turkey Quarter Creek, nw Craven County, a channel of water separated from the main body of Neuse River by a large swampy island.

Turkey Quarters, name applied to a portion of what is now Pender County by Barbadian explorers in 1663 because of the many turkeys killed there. Appears on the Ogilby map, 1671, but otherwise no longer used.

Turkey Ridge, se Buncombe County between Johnson Cove and Briar Branch.

Turkey Swamp rises in s Martin County and flows s into Tranters Creek.

Turkey Swamp. *See* Turkey Creek.

Turkey Tail. *See* Glen Alpine.

Turkey Township, e Sampson County.

Turlington, community in e Harnett County. Slocomb Crossroads, formerly recognized as a separate community, is now a part of the Turlington community.

Turnagain Bay, ne Carteret County emptying into Neuse River. Known as The Bay until about 1775.

Turnagain Creek, ne Carteret County flows n to empty into Turnagain Bay. Known as The Bay Creek until around 1775. Said to have been named by Joseph Pittman, who ran an Indian out of his sweet potato patch. The Indian fled, swam the creek, and emerged on the opposite shore, where he turned to make an insulting remark to Pittman. Pittman told him to "turn again" and repeat what he had said. The Indian did, and Pittman shot him.

Turnage, community in s Edgecombe County.

Turnbull Creek rises in White Pond Bay in s Cumberland County and flows se into ne Bladen County, where it enters Cape Fear River in central Bladen County. Named for Thomas Turnbull, an early colonial resident.

Turnbull Township, in ne Bladen County.

Turner Branch rises in w Haywood County and flows nw into Jonathans Creek.

Turner Creek rises in s central Carteret County a short distance e of Beaufort and flows e approx. 1 mi. into Cheny Bay and North River.

Turner Creek rises in s Yadkin County and flows se into Yadkin River.

Turner Crossroads, community in e Cleveland County. Alt. 985.

Turner Crossroads, community in n Northampton County n of Cypress Creek.

Turner Crossroads, community in s central Northampton County s of Bear Swamp.

Turner Mountain, central Surry County. Alt. approx. 2,100.

Turners, community in n Polk County between Green River and Walnut Creek.

Turnersburg, community in ne Iredell County on Rocky Creek. Settled 1849 and named for Wilford Turner, local landowner. A nineteenth-century textile mill on Rocky Creek there was the first in the county; it was burned before 1900, but it was rebuilt and is still in operation. Alt. 791.

Turnersburg Township, ne Iredell County.

Turners Creek. *See* Nevil Creek.

Turner's Crossroads. *See* Lewiston.

Turners Cut, an extension of the Dismal Swamp Canal, w Camden County, from near the canal's former mouth in the Pasquotank River to a point farther downstream, bypassing a very narrow section of the river. The Intracoastal Waterway passes through Turners Cut.

Turners Lake. *See* Lake Adger.

Turner Swamp rises in ne Wayne County and flows n into Wilson County, where it enters Black Creek.

Turner Top, nw Cherokee County between Copper and Sular Creeks.

Turnout, community in w Robeson County.

Turnpike, community in sw Buncombe County near the Haywood County line. Named for the fact that it was the site of the first tollgate w of Asheville on the old turnpike between Asheville and Murphy. In the early 1860s, a tavern for the accommodation of stagecoach passengers was opened there by John C. Smathers; with the coming of the railroad in 1882, Smathers enlarged his building, serving meals to railway passengers and taking in summer tourists. A post office operated there, 1858–1908.

Turnpike Branch rises in e Hertford County and flows se into Hoggard Swamp.

Turnpike Creek rises in ne Cherokee County and flows nw into Valley River.

Turnpike Creek rises in s Haywood County and flows sw into West Fork Pigeon River.

Turpentine Creek rises in se Onslow County and flows se through tidal marsh into the Atlantic Ocean through Browns Inlet.

Turtle Pond Creek rises in s Macon County and flows n into Cullasaja River.

Turtletown, community in w Cherokee County on the Tennessee line near Copperhill, Tenn. Served by post office, 1847–1912.

Tuscarora, community in w Craven County. Settled 1825. Named for the Indians who formerly lived in the area. Alt. 39.

Tuscarora Beach, summer resort in e Hertford County near the town of Winton on Chowan River. Originally a Tuscarora Indian village; settled about 1710 by John Cotton of Virginia and known as Cotton's Crossing as late as 1759, when it was authorized to be laid out as the county seat. Later known as Old Barfields and Barfields.

Tuscola. *See* Lake Junaluska.

Tusk Creek, a tidal creek about 1 mi. n of Marshallberg in the waters of Core Sound, e Carteret County. Formerly known also as Wolfert Creek.

Tuskee Gap, n Swain County on Thomas Ridge in Great Smoky Mountains National Park near lat. 35°33′32″ N., long. 83°22′25″ W.

Tuskeegee, community in n Graham County on Tuskeegee Creek.

Tuskeegee Creek rises in n Graham County and flows ne into Little Tennessee River.

Tusquitee, community in central Clay County on Johnson Mill Creek. Served by post office, 1861–1907. Alt. 2,050.

Tusquitee Bald, n Clay County near the headwaters of Compass Creek. Alt. 5,200–5,250.

Tusquitee Creek rises in ne Clay County and flows sw into Hiwassee River.

Tusquitee Gap, n Clay County near the headwaters of Clear Creek. Alt. approx. 3,800.

Tusquitee Mountains, nw Clay County extending ne from Leatherwood Branch to the Clay-Macon county line. Named for the Cherokee word *Tusquittee* or *Tusquitta* (rafters) because the spurs of the range suggest the rafters of a roof.

Tusquitee Township, n Clay County.

Tussock Bay, in e Bladen County.

Tuton. *See* St. Pauls.

Tuttles, community in se Stokes County served by post office, 1898–1904.

Tuttles Cross Roads. *See* Hartland.

Tuttles Store, community in w Alexander County. Alt. approx. 1,100. A former post office, Partee, served the community, 1887–1906.

Tuxedo, community in s Henderson County on Lake Summit. Alt. 2,187. Post office est. 1908 as Lakewood, but name later changed in 1910 to avoid confusion with another Lakewood in North Carolina. Tuxedo chosen simply because it was considered euphonious.

Tweed Branch rises in se Cherokee County and flows se into Little Brasstown Creek.

Tweed Creek rises in s Buncombe County and flows s into Cane Creek.

Twelvemile Creek is formed in w Union County by the confluence of East Fork Twelvemile Creek and West Fork Twelvemile Creek and flows sw into Catawba River in South Carolina.

Twelve O'Clock Top, knob on the Buncombe-Haywood county line between the head of Dutch Cove Creek and Rocky Face Mountain. Alt. approx. 4,640.

Twentymile Creek rises in nw Swain County in Great Smoky Mountains National Park and flows sw into Little Tennessee River. Named because it is 20 mi. from the junction of Tuckasegee and Little Tennessee Rivers.

Twentymile Ridge, nw Swain County in Great Smoky Mountains National Park. Its center is near lat. 35°28′50″ N., long. 83°50′15″ W.

Twin Falls, in s Jackson County on Long Branch mi. n of Fairfield Lake. Alt. approx. 3,420.

Twin Knobs, n Wilkes County between East Prong Roaring River and Little Sandy Creek.

Twin Oaks, community in n central Alleghany County. Alt. 2,624.

Twin Poplars, mound and trees 4 mi. n of Lenoir, central Caldwell County. According to local tradition, the Cherokee and Catawba Indians fought there for almost a week, until they became exhausted. They then made a pact declaring that thereafter, the two tribes would live in peace. As a token, they con-structed a mound of rocks and tied two young poplar trees together. The trees, now giants of the forest, stand approx. 12 ft. apart at the base, and approx. 20 ft. above the ground they join to form a single tree.

Twin Springs, springs near Cedar Knob in se Buncombe County; the source of a small unnamed stream that flows nw into Grassy Creek.

Twitty, community in w Rutherford County served by post office, 1884–1907.

Twomile Creek rises in sw Guilford County and flows e into Deep River. Appears as Third Creek on the Collet map, 1770.

Twomile Swamp rises in w Sampson County and flows se into Caesar Swamp.

Tyancoka Creek. *See* Cokey Swamp.

Tyler Branch rises in w Macon County and flows sw into Nantahala River.

Tynch Town. *See* Harris Landing.

Tyndall Point, se Beaufort County, extends into Goose Creek.

Tyner. *See* Centre Hill.

Tyre Knob, on the Graham-Swain county line between Grassy Gap and Broke Yoke Gap. Named for the biblical city on the Mediterranean Sea that was famous throughout the classical world for its costly, royal purple. Called Tyre Top on some maps.

Tyre Top. *See* Tyre Knob.

Tyro Shops, community in w Davidson County served by post office, 1883–1903.

Tyro Township, w central Davidson County.

Tyrrell (TIR-ehl) County was formed in 1729 from Chowan, Bertie, Currituck, and Pasquotank Counties. Located in the e section of the state, it is bounded by the Albemarle Sound and by Dare, Hyde, and Washington Counties. It was named for Sir John Tyrrell (1685–1729), one of the Lords Proprietors of North Carolina. Area: 583 sq. mi. County seat: Columbia, with an elevation of 10 ft. Townships are Alligator, Columbia, Gum Neck, Scuppernong, and South Fork. Produces soybeans, corn, peanuts, hogs, seafood,

Irish potatoes, tools, wheat, livestock, and lumber.

Tyson Creek rises in w Pitt County and flows ne into Tar River.

Tyson Marsh, stream, rises in s Greene County and flows ne into Contentnea Creek.

Tyson's Mill. *See* Jefferson.

Tyson Township, s central Stanly County.

Tysonville, community in central Wake County named for Tyson's Chapel and long known by that name.

U

U-Alta Lake, w Randolph County, is formed by a dam on Caraway Creek. Covers 20–25 acres. Named for Eula Alta Farlow, wife of Arthur Farlow, who developed the lake.

Ucohnerunt, a Tuscarora Indian town shown on the Moseley map, 1733, as situated on the mouth of Town Creek in what is now central Edgecombe County. Also called King Blount's Town for the chief under whom the Tuscarora Indians began their removal to the Roanoke River in 1732.

Ugly Creek rises in s Stanly County and flows se into Hardy Creek.

Ugly Fork rises in w Haywood County near the Swain County line on the n side of Big Fork Ridge and flows e and ne into Rough Fork.

Ulah, community in s Randolph County served by post office, 1889–1953. Originally Uhla; probably named for the daughter of M. R. Moffitt, first postmaster.

Umbra, community in ne Durham County served by post office, 1891–1903.

Umstead Bridge. *See* Redstone Point; Weir Point.

Umstead State Park. *See* William B. Umstead State Park.

Una Creek rises in se Swain County and flows w into Yalaka Creek.

Una Gap, se Swain County on Una Mountain near the head of Mason Branch.

Unahala, community in s Swain County on Yalaka Creek and Una Creek.

Unaka, community in nw Cherokee County near the junction of Copper and Beaverdam Creeks.

Unaka Mountain, on the Mitchell County, N.C.–Unicoi County, Tenn., line. Alt. approx. 5,190. *See also* Unicoi Mountains.

Unaka Mountains, in Avery and Mitchell Counties, N.C., and Unicoi and Carter Counties, Tenn., form the common boundary line between the two states from the Nolichucky River to the Doe River (in Tennessee). Of 40 miscellaneous maps dating from 1795 to 1930, 22 called the ridge, in whole or in part, Iron Mountains; others divide between Iron and Yellow Mountains; and 5 call them Unaka Mountains the entire distance. Unaka is a corruption of *Unega*, meaning "white"; it is used in the 1789 act passed by the General Assembly of North Carolina that ceded what is now the state of Tennessee to the U.S. government.

Una Mountain, se Swain County on the head of Una Creek.

Uncas, community in e Mecklenburg County served by post office, 1893–1903.

Under Hills. *See* Piedmont.

Underwood Branch rises in ne Cherokee County and flows se into Webb Creek.

Underwood Mountain, w Henderson County, extends e in an arc between Little Willow Creek and South Fork. Alt. approx. 3,250.

Unicoi Gap, on the Cherokee County, N.C.–Monroe County, Tenn., line in the Unicoi Mountains.

Unicoi Mountains, in Cherokee and Graham Counties, N.C., and Monroe and Polk Counties, Tenn., form in part the common boundary line of the two states between the Little Tennessee River and Hiwassee River. The name is one of those in common use; it was suggested by Horace Kephart and approved by the nomenclature committees of the Great Smoky Mountains Park Commissions of North Carolina and Tennessee. The name—which, like Unaka, is a corruption of *Unega*, meaning "white"—was used in the 1789 act passed by the General Assembly of North Carolina that ceded what is now the state of Tennessee to the U.S. government: "where it is called Unicoy or Unaka Mountain between the Indian towns of Cowee and Old Chota."

Union, community in s Hertford County. Inc. 1889; charter repealed 1939. Brittle Ordinary appears at the location on the Collet map, 1770; in 1808 it was called Brickle Inn.

A post office with the name Union operated, 1878–1906.

Union, community in s Macon County on Dowdle Branch.

Union City. *See* Fairmont.

Union Copper Mine, former mine in ne Cabarrus County, operated extensively from the early 1900s until 1914. Further explorations made in 1960, but mine not reopened for work.

Union County was formed in 1842 from Anson and Mecklenburg Counties. Located in the s central section of the state, it is bounded by the state of South Carolina and by Mecklenburg, Cabarrus, Stanly, and Anson Counties. At the time the county was formed, there was a dispute between local Whigs and Democrats as to whether it should be named Clay or Jackson. The name Union was suggested and adopted as a compromise and because the new county was created from parts of two others. Area: 643 sq. mi. County seat: Monroe, with an elevation of 576 ft. Townships are Buford, Goose Creek, Jackson, Lanes Creek, Marshville, Monroe, New Salem, Sandy Ridge, and Vance. Produces oats, wheat, corn, cotton, lespedeza, poultry, turkeys, hogs, dairy products, livestock, textiles, apparel, bricks, pipes, processed meat, industrial machinery, wood products, asbestos, and crushed stone.

Union Cross, community in se Forsyth County.

Union Cross, community in central Yadkin County. Named for Union Cross Friends Meeting, organized in 1883.

Union Factory. *See* Randleman.

Union Grove, community in n Iredell County. Settled prior to 1847, when a Methodist church was built. Named for a grove of trees in which union camp meetings were held. Alt. 850.

Union Grove, community in n Yadkin County near the head of Fall Creek.

Union Grove Township, n central Iredell County.

Union Hill, community in w Surry County between Little Mountain and South Fork.

Union Hill, community in ne Yadkin County.

Union Hope, community in sw Nash County.

Union Mills, community in n Rutherford County. Est. 1892. Inc. 1907; charter repealed 1924. Named for the consolidation of several small sawmills in the period 1885–90.

Union Ridge, community in n Alamance County. Named for an old church that stood on the ridge there between Tom's Creek and Jordan Creek.

Union Ridge, community in s Forsyth County; now within the urban extension of the city of Winston-Salem.

Union Township, n Pender County.

Union Township, s central Randolph County.

Union Township, sw Robeson County.

Union Township, sw Rutherford County.

Union Township, w Wilkes County.

Unionville, town in n Union County at the head of Chinkapin Creek. Inc. 1911; reincorporated 1998.

Unity, community in ne Mecklenburg County served by post office, 1891–1902.

Unity Parish, Church of England, Guilford County, est. 1771 with the formation of the county and coextensive with it.

Unity Township, n Rowan County. Named for local Presbyterian church.

University, community in e Orange County on Southern Railway approx. 9 mi. n of Chapel Hill; a former rail station serving the University of North Carolina. Railroad name for the station is Glenn. Alt. 471.

University Lake, on Morgan Creek in s Orange County. Formed 1932 as a municipal water supply for Chapel Hill–Carrboro. Covers 219 acres; max. depth 30 ft.

Uno, community in central Henderson County on Clear Creek.

"Unorganized Territory," former designation for most of the area formerly in Mattamuskeet Township, central Hyde County. Owned by the federal government and used as a fish and wildlife reservation. Residents vote and list taxes in Lake Landing Township.

Upchurch, community in w Wake County. Named for William B. Upchurch, around whose farm the community grew after a railway station was built there. Upchurch is said to have built first flue-cure tobacco barn in Wake County.

Upchurch Pond, on Rockfish Creek, e Hoke and w Cumberland Counties. Approx. 5 mi. long.

Upland, community in sw Chatham County.

Upper Bartons Creek rises in nw Wake County nw of community of Leesville and flows ne into Neuse River w of mouth of Lower Bartons Creek. Formerly called Great Elliby and Little Elliby.

Upper Beaverdam Creek rises in w Scotland County and flows se into Richmond Millpond (Gum Swamp Creek).

Upper Broad Creek rises in ne Craven County on the Craven-Pamlico county line and flows sw along the line into Neuse River. Appears as Broad Creek on the Moseley map, 1733; mentioned in local records as early as 1723. Sometimes referred to in eighteenth century local records as Ashes Creek.

Upper Campbellton. *See* Fayetteville.

Upper Conetoe Township, former township in e Edgecombe County, now township no. 3.

Upper Creek rises in nw Burke County and flows s and se to join Irish Creek in forming Warrior Fork [Catawba River].

Upper Creek rises in s Transylvania County and flows sw into East Fork French Broad River.

Upper Creek is formed in s Yancey County by the junction of Middle Fork Upper Creek and South Fork Upper Creek. It flows ne into South Toe River.

Upper Creek Township, n Burke County.

Upper Dowry Creek rises in e Beaufort County and flows approx. 1½ mi. s into Pungo River.

Upper Falls, in Snowbird Creek in sw Graham County. Water pours over a steep rock for 75 to 100 ft.

Upper Falls, the first of a series of three waterfalls on Yellowstone Prong, s Haywood County.

Upper Falls, in sw Transylvania County in Laurel Creek. Height of the falls is 40 ft.

Upper Falls, se Yancey County near the head of Crabtree Creek. Water falls approx. 75 ft.

Upper Fishing Creek Township, former township in n Edgecombe County, now township no. 6.

Upper Flat Creek. *See* Flat Creek.

Upper Flats, area of stony loam in nw Swain County on Greer Branch covering approx. 1.45 sq. mi.; level except the e end, which is hilly from n to s.

Upper Fork Township, sw Burke County.

Upper Goose Creek rises in central Beaufort County and flows s into Pamlico River.

Upper Haw Knob, on the Madison-Yancey county line in the Walnut Mountains.

Upper Hominy Township, sw Buncombe County.

Upper Laurel Township, former township in ne Madison County, now township no. 11.

Upper Little River is formed in se Caldwell County by a number of small streams. It flows se, forming a part of the Alexander-Caldwell county line before flowing into Catawba River. Formerly known as Clarks Little River.

Upper Little River rises in s Lee County and flows se into Harnett County, where it enters Cape Fear River. Scottish Highlanders settled the fertile lands along its banks during the period 1740–60. Appears on the Collet map, 1770.

Upper Little River Township, nw Harnett County.

Upper Long Creek rises in se Swain County and flows sw into Yalaka Creek.

Upper Pigeonroost, community on Right Fork [Pigeonroost Creek] in w Mitchell County.

Upper Poplar, community on Hollow Poplar Creek in nw Mitchell County.

Upper Richlands. *See* Richlands.

Upper Sassafras Gap, n Swain County in Great Smoky Mountains National Park on Noland Divide near lat. 35°31′56″ N., long. 83°27′15″ W.

Upper Saura Town, former Indian village in Stokes County on Dan River. Site approx. 4 mi. e of Madison. Probably occupied by Saura Indians by the middle of the seventeenth century and abandoned in the early eighteenth century. *Saura* or *Sara* meant "a place of tall grass or weeds." The site, occupied by descendants of Europeans, was still known as Sauratown as late as 1894. Appears on the Collet map, 1770, as Upper Sawra and on the Price map, 1808, as Saurat, but it does not appear on later maps.

Upper Spring Creek rises in nw Goose Creek Island, nw Pamlico County, and flows n to join Campbell Creek at the Beaufort-Pamlico county line to form Goose Creek.

Upper Town Creek Township, former township in w Edgecombe County, now township no. 11.

Upper Township, former township in n Chowan County, now township no. 3.

Upper Trail Ridge, sw Macon County between Nichols Branch and Big Shoal Branch.

Upton, community in nw Caldwell County. Alt. 1,420.

Upward, community in e Henderson County served by post office, 1877–1905. First called Crossroads, being at junction of Ridge Road and Howard Gap Road. Took present name from a local estate of a South Carolina summer resident.

Urahaw Swamp rises in s Northampton County and flows ne into Potecasi Creek. The name appears in local records as early as 1719.

Uree, community in nw Rutherford County on Broad River.

Utah Mountain, central Haywood County between Snakeden Top and Fulbright Cove. Named for the fact that a band of Mormons lived there in the 1880s and 1890s. Their practice of polygamy made them unpopular with their neighbors, and the Mormons were forced to leave North Carolina. Their houses, barns, fences, and other property were abandoned, and the ruins still exist. Orchards and vineyards, as well as ornamental flowering shrubs, are now growing wild in the vicinity.

Utley's Creek rises in s Wake County near Holly Springs and flows sw into Big White Oak Creek.

Uwharrie (u-whar-ee), community in nw Montgomery County served by post office, 1876–1914.

Uwharrie Mountains extend ne–sw across Montgomery, Randolph, and Stanly Counties. The Yadkin River flows through the sw end. Geologists describe the mountains as isolated, residual knobs that have resisted erosion and weathering better than the surrounding countryside. Probably formed several hundred million years ago by a number of explosive-type volcanoes. John Lawson visited the area in 1701 and used the name Heighwaree. Morrow Mountain State Park and Town Creek Indian Mound Historic Site are there. There are many named peaks, particularly in Montgomery and Randolph Counties. Alts. are not over 1,800 ft.

Uwharrie National Forest, largely in w Montgomery County but also in sw Randolph, se Davidson, and nw Stanly Counties. Covers 204,682 acres, with headquarters in Troy. Originally laid out as a purchase unit in 1934 and made a National Forest in 1961.

Uwharrie River rises in nw Randolph County, flows s into Montgomery County, then flows sw to join the Yadkin River in forming the Pee Dee River. The source of the Uwharrie River is approx. 840 ft. above sea level, and the elevation at the junction of the Uwharrie and Yadkin Rivers is approx. 280 ft. Appears as Uharie River on the Moseley map, 1733, but is incorrectly placed and out of proportion. The Collet map, 1770, makes the necessary corrections but calls it Voharee Creek.

Uwharrie Township, w Montgomery County.

V

Vade Mecum, former resort and present Episcopal Church summer camp at the junction of Vade Mecum Creek and South Double Creek in w Stokes County. Alt. 1,800. Local mineral springs accredited with curative powers by Saura Indians; about 1860 the site was acquired by Sparks family, circus operators, who built a resort hotel. It was later acquired by the Episcopal Church. Name from Latin phrase meaning "go with me," attributed to an Indian legend involving a planned elopement.

Vade Mecum Creek rises in w Stokes County and flows ne into South Double Creek.

Valda. *See* Val Dor.

Valdese, town in e central Burke County. Alt. 1,203. Settled in 1893 by a group of Waldensians from n Italy. Inc. 1920. Name is Italian for "Valley of Our Lord." Produces hosiery, textiles, furniture, and bakery products.

Val Dor, former rural post office, 1904–1905, located in a country store on the headwaters of Silver Creek in sw Burke County. Probably named for a gold mine on the Hodge plantation approx. 1 mi. away.

Vale, community in central Avery County.

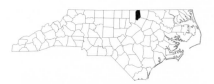

Vale, community in nw Lincoln County. Noted for the apple orchards in the vicinity. Post office est. in 1924.

Valhalla, community in central Chowan County. Alt. 39.

Valhalla, community in sw Polk County served by post office, 1923–50. Settled about 1885. Named for the Norse mythological Hall of Odin, where the souls of heroes slain in battle were received; the name is said to have been applied in commemoration of the battle at Round Mountain, *which see*, in 1776.

Valhalla Dome, peak on the ne end of Rich Mountain, w Mitchell County. Alt. over 4,060 ft.

Valle Crucis, community in central Watauga County near the junction of Dutch Creek and Watauga River. Est. in 1842 as an Episcopal mission. The name, Latin for "Valley of the Cross," was adopted because of the shape of the Watauga River valley there. The valley has an area of approx. 600 acres. Alt. 3,000.

Valley, community on Roaring Creek in w Avery County. Also called Roaring Creek.

Valley Creek rises in sw Watauga County and flows e in an arc into Watauga River.

Valley River rises in ne Cherokee County and flows sw into Hiwassee River at Murphy.

Valley River Mountains extend along the Cherokee-Clay county line to Macon County.

Valley Springs, community in s Buncombe County.

Valley Squirrel Gap, ne Cherokee County between Andrews and Rhodo.

Valley Town, community in ne Cherokee County on the outskirts of Andrews, *which see*. A post office operated there, 1846–91.

Valley Town Township, ne Cherokee County.

Valmead, community in central Caldwell County. A large part of the community was annexed to the city of Lenoir prior to 1960. Named for its location in a valley meadow. Alt. 1,131.

Vanceboro, town in n Craven County on Swift Creek. Settled about 1750 and known as Durgantown. Name changed by 1850 to Swift Creek. Inc. 1877 as Vanceboro in honor of Governor Zebulon B. Vance (1830–94) after he made a campaign speech there in 1876 while running for second term as governor. Alt. 24.

Vance County was formed in 1881 from Granville, Warren, and Franklin Counties. Located in the ne section of the state, it is bounded by the state of Virginia and by Warren, Franklin, and Granville Counties. It was named for Zebulon Baird Vance (1830–94), governor of North Carolina, congressman, and senator. Area. 268 sq. mi. County seat: Henderson, with an elevation of 513 ft. Townships are Dabney, Henderson, Kittrell, Middleburg, Nutbush, Sandy Creek, Townsville, Watkins, and Williamsboro. Produces tobacco, corn, wheat, oats, cotton, poultry, hogs, dairy products, livestock, cantaloupes, peanuts, soybeans, mobile homes, textiles, hosiery, glass products, pickles, tungsten, crushed stone, and sand.

Vance Knob, n Buncombe County between Ray Knob and the junction of Ox and Reems Creeks.

Vance Mountain, sw Cherokee County between Hot House and Rapier Mill Creeks. Probably named for Governor Zebulon B. Vance (1830–94).

Vance Mountain, on the Henderson County, N.C.–Greenville County, S.C., line. Named for Governor Zebulon B. Vance (1830–94). The scene of the 1829 duel between Robert Brank Vance and Samuel Price Carson.

Vance Township, w Union County.

Vandalia, former community in s Guilford County; now within the Greensboro city limits.

Vandemere, town in n Pamlico County on Bay River. A Dr. Abbott, former Union army surgeon, settled there in the 1870s, and his wife gave the community its name—a Dutch word meaning "from the sea." Inc. 1874; charter repealed 1893 but renewed two years later. From the formation of Pamlico County in 1872 until 1876, Vandemere served as the county seat. Alt. 4.

Vandemere Creek rises in n Pamlico County and flows se into Bay River.

Vander, community in central Cumberland County. Alt. 151.

Vanderpool Creek rises in central Watauga County and flows nw into Cove Creek.

Van Eeden, community in n Pender County. Est. on land purchased in 1909 by Frederik van Eeden (1860–1932) and Hugh MacRae for a colony of Dutch farmers. In 1939 the remaining land was purchased by a New York corporation as a refuge for Jews fleeing Germany. The last Dutch family left in 1949.

Vann, community in w Union County served by post office, 1892–1903.

Vannoy, community in nw Wilkes County on North Fork Reddies River.

Van Noy Branch rises in ne McDowell County and flows e into Long Branch.

Van Swamp extends ne from n Beaufort County into sw Washington County. Area. approx. 12,000 acres.

Vanteen, community in n central Wake County served by post office, 1891–1904.

Varina, former town in sw Wake County. Settled about 1890 and named for first postmaster's wife, who used the fanciful name, Varina, in her courtship correspondence. Alt. 426. Merged with Fuquay Springs to become part of Fuquay-Varina, *which see*, in 1963.

Varnals Creek rises in the Cane Creek Mountains, s Alamance County, and flows ne into Haw River.

Varnum, community in s central Brunswick County on Lockwoods Folly River.

Vashti, community in ne Alexander County. Known as Cedar Run in the 1880s, when Cedar Academy operated there. Alt. approx. 1,240.

Vass, town in e Moore County. Known as Winder, for an official of the Raleigh and Augusta Air Line Railroad, prior to 1907, when it was inc. with its present name. Named for William Worrell Vass (1820–96), treasurer of the Raleigh and Gaston Railroad, 1845–90. Alt. 320.

Vaughan, town in e central Warren County. Alt. 353. Founded in 1851 as Brown's Siding or Brown's Turnout by Dr. Ridley Browne. Name changed to Vaughn in 1881 in honor of John F. Vaughn, local merchant and first postmaster. Inc. 1893.

Vaughan Creek rises in South Carolina and flows n into Polk County, where it enters Lake Lanier.

Vaughan Hill, an elevation on the Fort Bragg Military Reservation, nw Cumberland County.

Vaughan's Springs, se Surry County, mineral springs resort developed by the Gid Y. Vaughan family in the early twentieth century; in recent years, the site of Camp Wilson, a private summer camp for boys.

Vaught Gap, w Watauga County in Stone Mountains near the head of Beaverdam Creek.

Veecaune Creek. *See* Wiccacon River.

Vein Mountain, community in s McDowell County. Named for the fact that it lies in a former gold-mining area.

Velna, community in se Randolph County served by post office, 1888–1916.

Venable, community in s Surry County served by post office, 1880–1905.

Venable. *See* Carrboro.

Vengeance Creek rises in ne Cherokee County and flows nw into Valley River.

Veni, community in sw Halifax County served by post office, 1889–1907.

Venters, community in s Pitt County.

Venus, community in se Ashe County served by post office, 1889–1905.

Vera Cruz Shoal, ne Carteret County, partly obstructs Ocracoke Inlet. Known during the eighteenth century as Dry Sand Shoal for the fact that it was never covered by water except during a hurricane.

Verd, community in sw Madison County.

Vernon, community in n Ashe County served by post office, 1892–1907.

Verona, community in central Onslow County. Named as a means of honoring Vera McIntyre, whose husband was one of the builders of the Wilmington and Onslow Railroad. A post office, Aman's Store, was est. in 1854. With the construction of the railroad and the establishment of Verona, the post office was moved there in 1894 and the name was changed. Alt. 49.

Vests, community in w Cherokee County sw of Hiwassee Lake. Named for first postmaster, George Vest.

Veto, community in nw Wake County served by post office, 1893–1900.

Viands, community in central Wilkes County s of the junction of Middle and North Prongs Roaring River. The name means "food" or "provisions."

Vicksboro, community in e Vance and w Warren Counties. Known prior to 1885, and until after 1913, as Coleys Crossroads.

Victoria, former town in central Buncombe County. Inc. 1887; became a part of Asheville, 1905.

Vienna, town in w Forsyth County; inc. 1794, but not now active in municipal affairs.

Vienna Township, w Forsyth County.

Vilas, community in w central Watauga County on Linville Creek. Served by post office since 1885. Alt. 2,811.

Village Creek rises in n Craven County and flows ne into Neuse River.

Villanow. *See* White Hill.

Vincent, community in n Alamance County served by post office, 1889–96.

Vinegar Hill, community in se Beaufort County.

Vineland. *See* Southern Pines; Whiteville.

Vine Swamp rises in e Lenoir County and flows e into Jones County, where it enters Beaver Creek. Named prior to the Revolution for the Vine family, which settled nearby.

Vineyard Creek rises in e Clay County and flows s into Shooting Creek.

Vineyard Mountain, s Clay County. Alt. approx. 4,900. An Englishman is said to have covered the mountain with grapevines, but his vineyard failed to prosper and he returned to England.

Vineyard Mountain, w Randolph County just w of Caraway Mountain in a close group with Black Jack, Slick Rock, and Prickly Pear Mountains.

Vinson Store, former community in e Wayne County near West Bear Creek.

Viola, community in s Pender County served by post office, 1882–1901.

Violet, community in w Cherokee County on Sular Creek between Swansee and Morrow Gaps. Served by post office, 1909–33.

Virgil, community in e Watauga County.

Virgilina, town in nw Granville County on the Virginia–North Carolina border, hence its name. Inc. 1899 in North Carolina and 1900 in Virginia.

Virginia, the name applied to the American territory granted by Queen Elizabeth to Walter Raleigh and explored in 1584 by Philip Amadas and Arthur Barlowe. The earliest evidence of the use of the name occurs before March 25, 1585, in Raleigh's seal as Lord and Governor of Virginia, which is now in the British Museum. The name honored Elizabeth, the "Virgin Queen," and was applied in the sixteenth century to the area explored from bases on Roanoke Island. In the seventeenth century, it came to be applied to the permanent settlement around Jamestown, and, after the granting of the Carolina Charter in 1663, it no longer was applied correctly to the territory that was soon to become North Carolina. *See also* South Virginia.

Virginia Creek rises in se Pender County and flows se into Topsail Sound.

Virgin's Inlet, apparently a short-lived inlet in se Onslow County from Brown's Sound into the Atlantic Ocean. It was described in records of 1784–85 as being near Gillets Creek.

Vista, community in s Pender County on Virginia Creek. Served by post office, 1893–1913.

Vivian, community in s Gates County on Bennett Creek.

Vixen, community in central Yancey County. Served by post office, 1915–54. Alt. 2,278.

Voharee Creek. *See* Uwharrie River.

Volga, community in n Buncombe County on French Broad River. Served by post office, 1902–13. Alt. 1,721.

Voline, community in central Robeson County served by post office, 1893–1905.

Vosses Creek. *See* Mill Creek.

Vox, community in n Alleghany County served by post office, 1900–1932.

Vultare, community in nw Northampton County served by post office, 1894–1928.

W

Waccamaw River rises in Lake Waccamaw, ne Columbus County, and flows s and sw in part along the Brunswick-Columbus county line into South Carolina, where it enters Winyah Bay. Appears on the Collet map, 1770.

Waccamaw Township, w Brunswick County.

Waccamaw Township, n Columbus County.

Wach. *See* Wachovia; Salem Creek.

Wachovia, a tract of land laid off by the General

Assembly in 1755 in ne Rowan County (now Forsyth) as an area for settlement by Moravians. The Parish of Dobbs was est. at the same time, coextensive with Wachovia. Wachovia, or Wachau-the-Aue (meadow land) along the Wach or Wack (principal stream), received its name from the fact that its water course and meadow land bore some resemblance to a valley in Austria of the same name that formerly belonged to the Zinzendorf family, prominent Moravian leaders. The parish was named Dobbs in honor of Governor Arthur Dobbs. *See also* Dobbs Parish.

Wack. *See* Wachovia; Salem Creek.

Waco, town in e Cleveland County. Alt. 916. Settled 1857. Inc. 1887. Named by George W. Hendrick for Waco, Tex.

Waddells, community in central Rockingham County served by post office, 1876–1903. Known as Langdon after 1890.

Wade, town in ne Cumberland County. Settled about 1886. Inc. 1889; reincorporated 1913, but long inactive in municipal affairs. Named for N. G. Wade, who donated the railroad right-of-way. Alt. 141.

Wade Creek rises in e Carteret County and flows s approx. 1 mi. into Jarrett Bay. Formerly also known as Willis Creek.

Wade Gap, in Newfound Mountain on Buncombe-Haywood county line near the headwaters of Sandy Mush Creek.

Wade Point extends from s Pasquotank County into Albemarle Sound. Appears as Wades Point on the Moseley map, 1733. It lies between Big Flatty Creek and the Pasquotank River.

Wadesboro, town and county seat, central Anson County. Authorized to be est. 1783 as county seat. Called New Town until 1787, when it was changed to Wadesboro to honor Col. Thomas Wade, Revolutionary War patriot and brother-in-law of Patrick Boggan, pioneer settler. Alt. 423. Scientists from all over the United States and Europe gathered there in 1900 to view a total eclipse of the sun. Produces hosiery, textiles, wooden boxes, bricks, hoists, medical supplies, and food products.

Wadesboro City Pond, s central Anson County on Jones Creek. Formed 1938. Covers 75 acres, with a max. depth of 25 ft. Municipal water supply, fishing, and boating.

Wadesboro Township, central Anson County.

Wades Point, point of land in e Beaufort County on the n side of Pamlico River at the w side of the mouth of Pungo River, lat. 35°23′18″ N., long. 76°34′35″ W. *See also* Moores Beach. Appears as Battis Point on the Comberford map, 1657.

Wade's Shore, a bay on the n side of Shackleford Banks, s Carteret County. A former whaling settlement by the same name existed there.

Wadeville, community in s Montgomery County. Est. 1872 and named for Wade brothers, who operated a store there in which the first post office was est. in 1878. Post office closed 1955. Alt. 558.

Wading Branch Ridge, n Haywood County parallel to Dicks Branch.

Wading Place Creek rises in e central Bertie County and flows s into Cashie River.

Wads Creek rises in central Moore County and flows se into Little River. Named for William Wadsworth, who settled on its banks in 1756.

Wagner Branch rises in central Buncombe County near Beard Mountain and flows nw into Reems Creek.

Wagoner, community in e central Ashe County.

Wagoner, community in w Yadkin County near South Deep Creek.

Wagon Road Gap, on the Haywood-Transylvania county line at the nw tip of Wagon Road Ridge. Began as a foot trail for man and horse on way to Brevard; later was widened for 2-wheeled wagons to haul salt and other provisions and eventually to accommodate large, 4-wheeled wagons, hence the name. The Blue Ridge Parkway now crosses the Wagon Road there. Alt. 4,535.

Wagon Road Gap, in nw Transylvania County between Poplar Lick Gap and Sandy Gap n of Pine Mountain.

Wagon Road Ridge extends se in n Transylvania County from Pisgah Ridge on the Haywood-Transylvania county line to the confluence of the forks of Bearwallow Brook.

Wagon Timber Branch rises in central Cherokee County and flows se into Colvard Creek.

Wagram, town in e Scotland County. Known first as Montpelier, then (around 1900) as Fontcal. Inc. 1911 as Wagram. Probably named for the Austrian town where a battle was fought in 1809 during the Napoleonic Wars. Alt. 250.

Wagstaff Store, community in w Person County.

Wahoo, community in nw Alexander County on Middle Little River.

Wahtom Pocosin, nw Bertie County.

Wahtom Swamp rises in nw Bertie County and flows se into Cashie River.

Wailes, community in sw Mecklenburg County served by post office, 1892–1902.

Wainwright Island, in Core Sound, ne Carteret County; approx. ⅔ mi. long. Probably named for James Winwright or Wainwright.

Wake County was formed in 1771 from Johnston, Cumberland, and Orange Counties. Located in the e central section of the state, it is bounded by Johnston, Harnett, Chatham, Durham, Granville, and Franklin Counties. It was named for Margaret Wake (1733–1819), wife of Governor William Tryon. Area: 867 sq. mi. County seat: Raleigh, with an elevation of 363 ft. Raleigh is also the state capital. Townships are Barton Creek, Buckhorn, Cary, Cedar Fork, Holly Springs, House Creek, Leesville, Little River, Marks Creek, Meredith, Middle Creek, Neuse River, New Light, Panther Branch, Raleigh, St. Marys, St. Matthews, Swift Creek, Wake Forest, and White Oak. Produces tobacco, corn, wheat, oats, cotton, poultry, dairy products, hogs, livestock, farm machinery, concrete products, baked goods, textiles, cottonseed oil, apparel, furniture, pharmaceuticals, packaged foods, software, nursery products, strawberries, pumpkins, crushed stone, and fabricated metals.

Wake Court House. *See* Raleigh.

Wakefield, community in e Wake County 1 mi. n of Zebulon. Inc. 1899; charter repealed 1913. Named for its location on a field in Wake County. The failure of local citizens to sell land for a right-of-way resulted in the location of a railroad a short distance s, where the town of Zebulon soon developed. Alt. 338.

Wake Forest, town in ne Wake County between Hatters Branch and Richland Creek. Settled 1823. Inc. 1880 as "town of Wake Forest College," but referred to after the turn of the century as Wake Forest. Named for large

wooded areas of n Wake County. Home of Wake Forest College (1834–1956) until it was moved to Winston-Salem. Home of Southeastern Baptist Theological Seminary since 1951. Produces textiles. Alt. 400.

Wake Forest Township, ne Wake County.

Wakelon, community in ne Bertie County.

Wake Station, community in n Wake County.

Wakulla, community in nw Robeson County. Alt. 208. Settled about 1860. Named by Col. Peter P. Smith for the Indian word meaning "clear water" because of numerous springs in the vicinity.

Walden Creek rises in se Brunswick County and flows e into Cape Fear River.

Waldrop Branch rises in ne Cherokee County and flows s into Valley River.

Walker, community in w Polk County on Harm Creek. Served by post office, 1894–1918.

Walker Bald, w Haywood County se of Potato Patch. Alt. 5,420. Named for Felix Walker (1753–1828), land speculator and member of Congress, whose cabin dwelling was at its base on upper Jonathan Creek.

Walker Branch rises in ne Buncombe County and flows w to join Corner Rock Creek in forming Dillingham Creek. Walker Falls are on the stream.

Walker Branch rises in ne Buncombe County near Brushy Knob and flows w through Walkertown into North Fork [Swannanoa River].

Walker Branch rises in central Lincoln and flows sw into Clark Creek.

Walker Branch rises in sw Mecklenburg County and flows se into Steele Creek.

Walker Creek rises in s Transylvania County and flows nw into Little River.

Walker Creek rises in sw Brunswick County, Va., and flows s into ne Warren County, N.C., where it enters Lake Gaston.

Walker Falls, waterfalls in ne Buncombe County on Walker Branch.

Walker Gap, in Yellow Creek Mountains in n Graham County.

Walker Gap, w Swain County between the head of Mill Branch and Rowan Branch.

Walker Knob, ne Buncombe County near Balsam Gap in the Great Craggy Mountains.

Walker Knob, mountain in sw Burke County. Alt. 2,919.

Walker Low Gap, e Haywood County on Glades Mountain.

Walker Mill Creek rises in sw Cherokee County and flows se into Nottely River.

Walker Mountain, w Montgomery County between Woodrun Creek and Dennis Mountain.

Walker Ridge, ne Buncombe County w of Walker Knob.

Walkers, community in e central Pender County on Burgaw Creek. Formerly known as Walkers Store.

Walkers Bluff, on Cape Fear River in e Bladen County 5 mi. above White Hall Landing.

Walkers Branch rises in sw Yadkin County and flows e into North Hunting Creek.

Walkersburg, town in se Brunswick County at Deep Water Point. Est. 1784 on lands of John Walker, for whom it was named. Courthouse and other public buildings were to be est. there but apparently never built.

Walkers Creek rises in n Swain County in Great Smoky Mountains National Park on the s slope of Mount Davis and flows s on the e side of Locust Ridge into Hazel Creek.

Walkers Creek rises in central Warren County and flows se to join Big Branch in forming Little Fishing Creek.

Walkersville, community in s central Union County on the e side of Cane Creek. Formerly known as Wilson's Old Store community. Shown on maps as Walkersville as early as 1886.

Walker Top, on the Buncombe-Haywood county line.

Walkertown, community in ne Buncombe County.

Walkertown, community in e Forsyth County. Robert Walker was living there as early as 1771; the community was named for him. Love's Meeting House (Methodist), built there in 1797, was visited by Bishop Francis Asbury in 1799. He was greatly impressed by its glass windows. Alt. 980.

Walkeys, community in sw Union County.

Walks, The, series of immovable natural stepping stones below Flat Shoals of Watauga River near the Tennessee line in nw Watauga County. They are regularly placed across the river, and one may walk over them even when the stream is swollen, hence the name.

Walkup, community in sw Union County served by post office, 1885–1908. Also spelled Wauchope. William R. Davie's assault on Tories took place, 1780, on Wauchope plantation.

Wallace, town in s Duplin County. Post office est. 1866. Alt. 51. Inc. 1873 as Duplin Roads. Name changed to Wallace in honor of Stephen D. Wallace, vice president of the Atlantic Coast Line Railroad, prior to 1899, in which year the town was reincorporated. Produces textiles.

Wallace Branch rises in central Lee County and flows ne into Lick Creek.

Wallace Branch rises in central Macon County and flows se into Cartoogechaye Creek.

Wallace Branch rises in se Union County and flows ne into Little Brown Creek.

Wallace Channel, ne Carteret County, a navigable lane in Ocracoke Inlet running nw and se. Appears by the name on the Price survey of Ocracoke Inlet, 1795. Named for David Wallace Jr., whose house on Portsmouth Island was used as a sighting point by pilots using the channel entering the Atlantic Ocean. Sometimes referred to as Beacon Island Road in the eighteenth century.

Wallace Creek rises in ne Alexander County and flows s in Greasy Creek. Probably named for Richard Wallace, pioneer Baptist minister.

Wallace Creek rises in ne Mecklenburg County and flows ne into Cabarrus County, where it enters Reedy Creek.

Wallace Creek rises in e Onslow County and flows se into Morgan Bay. Named in local records as early as 1744 as Wallace's Creek.

Wallace Gap, sw Macon County between the head of Allison Creek and Nantahala River.

Wallace Gap, s Transylvania County between the head of Boring Creek and the head of West Prong [Glady Fork].

Wallace Mountain, ne Buncombe County near Walkertown.

Wallace's Creek. *See* Wallace Creek.

Walla Watta, community in n central Beaufort County, lat. 35°35′ N., long. 76°52′15″ W. Named by Surry Parker, local lumberman, for Wallace and Waters families, who lived here. Alt. 34.

Wallburg, community in ne Davidson County served by post office, 1891–1946. Named for Sam W. Wall, state senator in 1895. Inc. 2004.

Wallnut-Tree Creek. *See* Walnut Creek.

Walnut, community in central Madison County between Brush Creek and Hopewell Branch. Inc. 1905; charter repealed 1917. Named for walnut trees in the vicinity. *See also* Marshall.

Walnut Bottom, in nw Haywood County on Big Creek in Great Smoky Mountains National Park. Named for the fact that numerous walnut trees formerly grew in the narrow bottomland there.

Walnut Branch rises in w Alleghany County and flows e into Elk Creek.

Walnut Cove, w Macon County on a tributary of Nantahala River.

Walnut Cove, town in s Stokes County. Settled 1883 and known as Lash until 1889, when it was inc. under its present name. Named for a grove of walnut trees. Alt. 634. Stokesbury, formerly a separate community just s of Walnut Cove, is now within the corporate limits.

Walnut Cove Branch rises in s Madison County and flows se into Little Sandymush Creek.

Walnut Cove Branch rises in w central Transylvania County and flows s into Catheys Creek.

Walnut Creek rises in e Macon County and flows sw into Cullasaja River.

Walnut Creek rises in central Madison County and flows sw into French Broad River.

Walnut Creek rises in n Polk County and flows se into Green River. *See* Bizzell Millpond.

Walnut Creek rises in w Wake County on the e edge of the town of Cary; s of the city of Raleigh, it flows e into Neuse River. Appears as Wallnut-Tree Creek on the Collet map, 1770.

Walnut Creek rises in e Wayne County and flows se then sw into Neuse River.

Walnut Creek, community in central Madison County on Walnut Creek.

Walnut Creek Gap, between Walnut Creek and the head of Moss Branch in e Macon County.

Walnut Creek Township, former township in central Edgecombe County, now township no. 11.

Walnut Gap, on the Macon-Jackson county line. Alt. 4,150.

Walnut Gap, n Madison County at the head of Walnut Creek.

Walnut Gap, n Madison County at the head of Woolsey Branch.

Walnut Grove Township, w central Granville County.

Walnut Grove Township, n Wilkes County.

Walnut Hill, mountain in ne Ashe County. Alt. approx. 2,700.

Walnut Hill Township, ne Ashe County.

Walnut Hollow Gap, in n Graham County on Tuskeegee Creek.

Walnut Knob, on the Alexander-Wilkes county line. Alt. approx. 1,990.

Walnut Knob, central Madison County on the s end of Pilot Ridge.

Walnut Knob, n Madison County between Big Laurel Creek and Walnut Gap.

Walnut Mountains extend e through central Madison County from French Broad River into w Yancey County. Alt. 4,335.

Walnut Run, community in n Madison County served by post office, 1872–1911.

Walsh, community in w Wilkes County on North Prong Lewis Fork Creek.

Walstonburg, town in n Greene County. Lands there acquired after 1775 by John Chester, whose plantation house, "Chesterfield," still stands. His son-in-law, Bennett Fields, after 1845 changed the name to Fieldsboro. The latter name was, and still is, used as the name of the railroad station. Fields's cousin, Seth Walston, acquired the property after the Civil War, and the name Walstonburg came to be applied. Inc. in 1908 as Walstonburg.

Walter, community in central Wayne County served by post office, 1882–1903.

Walter Rawleigh. *See* Roanoke Sound.

Walter Slough, in the waters of Pamlico Sound nw of Oregon Inlet, e Dare County.

Walters Mill, community in nw Caswell County named for the mill on Hogans Creek.

Walters Mill Pond, nw Lenoir County, was originally formed about 1755; rebuilt about 1900. Fed by springs and wells and drains into nearby Moseley Creek. Covers 32 acres; max. depth 12 ft.

Walthall. *See* Wilbon.

Walton County was created by the state of Georgia partly in territory claimed by that state but which a subsequent survey made in 1807 revealed to be in Buncombe County, N.C. Riots and bloodshed occurred during the "Walton War" over disputed land grants made by the two states in the area.

Walton Crossroads, community in s Gates County.

Walton Pond, a swamp, rises in s Gates County and drains se into Trotman Creek. Watton Mill appears on the stream on the Collet map, 1770, and the name is derived from the mill that existed as late as 1833 but had disappeared by 1862.

Wampler. *See* Elk Shoal.

Wananish, community in n Columbus County served by post office, 1899–1972. Now within the limits of the town of Lake Waccamaw. It was to have been named Ouaniche for the Indian word meaning "land-locked salmon," but the spelling Wananish was preferred for the post office name.

Wanchese, community on the s end of Roanoke Island, e Dare County. Named for one of the two Indians taken to England by Philip Amadas and Arthur Barlowe in 1584. Produces packaged seafood. Alt. 10.

Wantland's Ferry. *See* Jacksonville.

Warbler, former community in s Tyrrell County between Kilkenny and Kilkenny Landing. Now absorbed into the community of Kilkenny. Served by post office, 1917–32.

Ward Creek rises in e Carteret County and flows s into North River. Appears on the Moseley map, 1733.

Ward Creek rises in n Cleveland County and flows sw into First Broad River.

Ward Gap, on the Burke-Cleveland county line.

Ward Gap, w Watauga County on the head of Phillips Branch.

Ward Hollow, w Watauga County, extends sw from Love Gap to Watauga River.

Ward Mine, a gold mine in e Davidson County, was worked as early as 1842 and shown on maps as recently as 1915. Ward Gold-Mine Co., chartered 1852, purchased 400-acre tract from John Ward.

Ward Mountain, n Henderson County on Featherston Creek.

Ward Run rises in se Wilson County and flows se into Pitt County, where it turns sw and enters Little Contentnea Creek.

Wards, community in central Columbus County.

Wards Corner, community in w Pender County at the intersection of two highways.

Wards Creek. *See* Hawkins Slough.

Wards Mill, community in central Onslow County served by post office, 1866–1906.

Wards Mountain, n Avery County.

Wards Mountain, sw Orange County between Toms Creek and Cane Creek.

Wards Store, community in se Randolph County.

Ward Swamp rises in n Sampson County and flows sw into Great Coharie Creek.

Wardville, community in e Gates County. Name changed from Bosley about 1936.

Ware Creek rises in central Carteret County and flows sw into the mouth of Newport River.

Wareiock. *See* Beaufort.

Warington. *See* Fort Landing.

Warlick, community in e Burke County served by post office, 1882–1905.

Warlick Township, former township in e Cleveland County, now township no. 5.

Warm Cove Branch rises in w Haywood County in Great Smoky Mountains National Park and flows se into Caldwell Fork.

Warm Springs. *See* Hot Springs.

Warne, community in s Clay County between Crawford and Brasstown Creeks. Alt. 1,800. Named for the Warrens, an English family who mined gold there; the name was corrupted to Warne by the Indians.

Warnersville, community settled by African Americans in what is now the se section of Greensboro. Named for Yardley Warner, Quaker missionary.

Warowtani appears on the White map, 1585, as a village of the Weapemeoc Indians, located in what is now s Chowan County on Albemarle Sound near Edenton.

Warren, community in n Craven County. Settled after 1910. Named for James and Ben Warren, local residents. Alt. 11.

Warren Bridge. *See* East Lake Landing; Sandy Point.

Warren County was formed in 1779 from Bute County, which was divided to form Warren and Franklin Counties. Located in the ne section of the state, it is bounded by Northampton, Halifax, Franklin, and Vance Counties. It was named for Gen. Joseph Warren (1741–75), Revolutionary War patriot and physician killed at Bunker Hill. Area: 445 sq. mi. County seat: Warrenton, with an elevation of 451 ft. Townships are Fishing Creek, Fork, Hawtree, Judkins, Nutbush, River, Roanoke, Sandy Creek, Shocco, Sixpound, Smith Creek, and Warrenton. Produces tobacco, corn, wheat, oats, cotton, poultry, lumber, boxes, soybeans, dairy products, hogs, livestock, lumber products, textiles.

Warren Creek rises in sw Buncombe County near the Haywood County line and flows nw into South Hominy Creek.

Warren Hollow, n Watauga County, extends sw from State Line Ridge to North Fork of Cove Creek.

Warren Plains, community in central Warren County. Alt. 450. The site of a post office since 1857.

Warren Ridge, sw Buncombe County between Warren and Curtis Creeks.

Warren's Station. *See* Conetoe.

Warrensville, town in central Ashe County. Inc. 1931, but not now active in municipal affairs. Settled about 1826 and known as Buffalo Creek until renamed for the builder of first gristmill and sawmill.

Warrenton, city and county seat, in w central Warren County. Est. 1779. Alt. 451. Named for the county, which was in turn named for Joseph Warren, killed at Bunker Hill. Produces lumber products, and textiles.

Warrenton Township, central Warren County.

Warrick. *See* Peterson.

Warrick Branch rises in w Mitchell County and flows s into Toe River.

Warrington. *See* Fort Landing.

Warrior, African American community in central Caldwell County.

Warrior Creek rises in central Caldwell County and flows ne into Yadkin River in w end of Happy Valley.

Warrior Creek rises in s Wilkes County and flows n into W. Kerr Scott Reservoir. Originally known as Bear Creek. Daniel Boone's wilderness trail into Kentucky passed nearby.

Warrior Creek. *See* Boomer.

Warrior Fork [Catawba River] is formed in w central Burke County by the junction of Irish and Upper Creeks and flows se into Catawba River.

Warrior Gap, central Caldwell County.

Warrior Mountain, central Caldwell County. Alt. approx. 2,000.

Warrior Mountain, s Polk County. *See* Big Warrior Mountain and Little Warrior Mountain.

Warrior Mountain, nw Surry County. Alt. 1,805.

Warsaw, town in w Duplin County. Alt. 160. Settled about 1825. Inc. 1855. Early known

as Mooresville. Renamed by the conductor of the first train to run through what was then a crossroads community because he was reading a popular novel, *Thaddeus of Warsaw* by Jane Porter (1776–1850).

Warsaw Township, w central Duplin County.

Warwick Bay, a natural lake in e Robeson County. One of the Carolina Bays, *which see.* Approx. 1¾ mi. long and 1 mi. wide. Drained from the se by Peter Swamp. Known also as Lennon's Marsh and Lennon's Mill Pond. Now a privately owned wildfowl refuge with ducks, egrets, and cranes.

Warwick County. On December 4, 1771, in the General Assembly, a bill for establishing the n part of Orange County as Warwick County and St. Stephens Parish was read for the second time and rejected.

Warwick Creek rises on the Chowan-Gates county line and flows sw through Welsh Pond, where it joins Trotman Creek in forming Catherine Creek. Appears on the Collet map, 1770. A brick house, still standing, built on the creek in 1746 was an early trading center.

Warwick Mill Pond, e Robeson County on Jacob Swamp. Covers 10 acres; max. depth 10 ft.

Washburn, community in w Cleveland County. Alt. 960. Settled 1875. Named for W. W. Washburn, a county commissioner.

Washburn Creek rises in s Rutherford County and flows sw into Cleghorn Creek.

Washburns Store, community in e Rutherford County between Puzzle and Heaveners Creeks. Formerly known as Green's Grove and, when a post office from 1889 to 1906, as Lexine, named for Lexine Pruett, daughter of General Assembly member Greenbury Pruett.

Wash Creek rises in central Henderson County and flows se into Mud Creek.

Wash Creek rises in nw Henderson County and flows se into North Fork.

Wash Hollow, s Haywood County on Sam Branch.

Washington, city and county seat, w Beaufort County on Pamlico River. Alt. 11. Est. 1782. Known originally as Forks of Tar River but called Washington as early as 1776. Named by Col. James Bonner, founder of the town and friend of George Washington. Produces lumber, tobacco, textiles, and apparel. Known as "the original Washington" and commonly as "Little Washington" to distinguish it from the District of Columbia. Latter nickname not favored by town citizens.

Washington, District of. *See* District of Washington.

Washington County was formed in 1799 from Tyrrell County. Located in the e section of the state, it is bounded by Tyrrell, Hyde, Beaufort, Martin, and Bertie Counties and by Albemarle Sound. It was named for George Washington (1732–99). Area: 420 sq. mi. (336, land; 84, water). County seat: Plymouth, with an elevation of 21 ft. Townships are Lees Mills, Plymouth, Scuppernong, and Skinnersville. Produces tobacco, peanuts, corn, soybeans, wheat, Irish potatoes, wood products, seafood, hogs, livestock, lumber, and paper.

Washington County, now in Tennessee, was created from the District of Washington, *which see*, in 1777. North Carolina ceded its sw territory to the federal government in 1789.

Washington Creek rises in n Jackson County and flows n into Soco Creek.

Washington Creek rises in n Pender County and flows ne into Northeast Cape Fear River. First known as Hamilton Creek for Malatiah Hamilton, who laid out a town near its mouth about 1740; the town became South Washington, *which see.*

Washington Ferry. *See* Princeton.

Washington Forks, community in central Craven County.

Washington Heights, community in w Beaufort County adjacent to and ne of the city of Washington.

Washington Park, town in w Beaufort County. Inc. 1923. Adjoins the city of Washington on the e.

Washington Township, nw Beaufort County.

Washington Township, ne Guilford County. Named for George Washington.

Wash Ridge, w Haywood County in Great Smoky Mountains National Park, a short spur ex-

tending se from Shanty Mountain; center near lat. 35°37'07" N., long. 83°08'15" W.

Wash Woods, community and former Life Saving Station 4 mi. s of the Virginia line on Currituck Banks, ne Currituck County. Named for hundreds of old stumps there, exposed at low tide. A post office operated there, 1907–17, named Deals.

Wasp, community in ne Craven County served by post office, 1900–1903.

Wasulu Ridge, n Swain County in Great Smoky Mountains National Park, a short spur extending nw from Welch Ridge near lat. 35°29'22" N., long. 83°38'32" W.

Watauga (wah-TAW-guh) County was formed in 1849 from Ashe, Wilkes, Caldwell, and Yancey Counties. Located in the nw section of the state, it is bounded by the state of Tennessee and by Ashe, Wilkes, Caldwell, and Avery Counties. It was named for Watauga River. Area: 320 sq. mi. County seat: Boone, with an elevation of 3,266 ft. Townships are Bald Mountain, Beaverdam, Blowing Rock, Blue Ridge, Boone, Brushy Fork, Cove Creek, Elk, Laurel Creek, Meat Camp, New River, North Fork, Shawneehaw, Stony Fork, and Watauga. Produces tobacco, corn, dairy products, livestock, candy, baked goods, printed items, Christmas trees, electronics, apparel, and gravel.

Watauga Creek rises in e Macon County and flows sw into Lake Emory.

Watauga Falls, on Watauga River in w Watauga County near Laurel Creek Falls at mouth of Laurel Creek.

Watauga Falls, community in w Watauga County on Laurel Creek near its confluence with Watauga River.

Watauga Gap, on the Jackson-Macon county line. Alt. 3,280.

Watauga River rises in sw Watauga County near Grandfather Mountain and flows n, forming a short section of the Avery-Watauga county line before flowing into Tennessee, where it enters Holston River. Took its name from an Indian word meaning "beautiful water."

Watauga Settlement began to develop in 1769 in what was then w North Carolina but is now Tennessee with the arrival of settlers on the Watauga and Nolichucky Rivers. A government was formed in 1772, and in 1776 its leaders asked to be annexed to North Carolina. The District of Washington, *which see*, was formed to include the Watauga Settlement. *See also* Franklin.

Watauga Township, sw Watauga County.

Watch Knob, central Buncombe County near the junction of Beetree Creek and Swannanoa River.

Water Creek rises in s Scotland County and flows sw into Gum Swamp Creek.

Waterfall Branch rises in n Mitchell County and flows s into Right Fork Bean Creek.

Waterfall Creek rises in ne Buncombe County and flows nw into Carter Creek.

Water Fork rises in w Orange County and flows s into Bear Creek.

Water Fork rises in n Wake County and flows s into Horse Creek.

Water Gap, central Graham County between Mountain Creek and Sweetwater Creek.

Waterhole Mine, mica and feldspar mine, sw Avery County.

Watering Hole Swamp rises in w Robeson County and flows s into Wilkinson Swamp. Also sometimes known as Waterhole Swamp.

Waterlily, community on the s end of Church Island, e Currituck County. Settled about 1750. Named for water lilies growing in ponds and ditches there.

Waterloo, community in s Union County near the present Prospect School between the head of Cane Creek and Polecat Creek.

Waterloo Branch rises in s Macon County and flows se into Little Tennessee River.

Watermelon Branch rises in n central Madison County and flows ne into Big Laurel Creek.

Wateroak Creek rises in se Clay County and flows se into Tallulah River.

Wateroak Gap, se Clay County between Chunky Gal and Yellow Mountains.

Water Oak Gap, n Swain County in Great Smoky Mountains National Park on Welch Ridge near lat. 35°30′32″ N., long. 83°36′21″ W.

Waterrock Knob, on the Haywood-Jackson county line. Alt. 6,292. Named Amos Plott Balsam in 1858 by Arnold Guyot for a pioneer settler at its base. Wood cutters and loggers knew it as Waterrock Knob because there was a good spring running out over a smooth rock near its top. Also spelled Water Rock Knob.

Waters, community in n Burke County.

Watershed Mountain, central Madison County between Walnut and Hunter Creeks. Alt. approx. 3,100.

Watershed Ridge, n Buncombe County between North Knob and Wildcat Mountain.

Water Tank Branch rises in ne Cherokee County and flows se into Valley River. Named because the Southern Railway used it as a source of water for its steam locomotives.

Waterville, community in n Haywood County on Big Creek. Alt. 1,440. Named for the lake and dam built there in 1929. *See* Waterville Lake.

Waterville Lake, on Pigeon River in n Haywood County in Pisgah National Forest. Alt. 2,258. Constructed in 1929 for hydroelectric power. Covers 340 acres; max. depth 180 ft.

Watery Branch rises in w Johnston County and flows e into Juniper Swamp.

Watery Branch rises in n Scotland County and flows ne into Lumber River.

Watery Branch rises in ne Wayne County near the town of Eureka and flows ne into Greene County, where it enters Contentnea Creek.

Watery Branch, community in ne Wayne County. Settled as early as 1887.

Watery Swamp rises in central Gates County and flows s into Bennetts Creek.

Watha, town in n central Pender County. Alt. 60. Inc. 1909. About 1840, with the construction of the railroad, the old town of South Washington, *which see*, moved to the site from a point approx. 1½ mi. ne. The railroad station originally was named Hiawatha, from which the present name was corrupted. For about two years after the formation of Pender County, Waterville served as a temporary county seat. *See also* Welsh Tract.

Watia Creek rises in w Swain County and flows e into Nantahala River.

Watkins, community in w Vance County on Little Ruin Creek. Named for Samuel Watkins, Henderson merchant.

Watkins Branch rises in ne Cherokee County and flows nw into Valley River.

Watkins Creek rises in s Macon County and flows nw into Middle Creek.

Watkins Township, w Vance County.

Watkinsville, community in ne Stokes County nw of Sandy Ridge served by post office, 1878–1904.

Watson. *See* Watsonville.

Watson Creek rises in n Union County and flows se into Richardson Creek.

Watson Crossroads, community in nw Wayne County near a tributary of Great Swamp.

Watson Gap, w Jackson County on Cox Branch.

Watson Gap, se Watauga County on the head of Dugger Creek.

Watson's Mill. *See* Worrell Mill Pond.

Watsons Pond, s Hoke County on Little Raft Swamp. Formed 1865 and known first as Edens Pond and later as Johnsons Pond. Covers 50 acres; max. depth 7 ft.

Watsonville, community in central Rowan County served by post office, 1874–1903.

Watts Creek rises in se Stokes County and flows se into Town Fork Creek.

Watts Cross Roads, community in ne Cabarrus County.

Watts Cross Roads Township, former township in n Cabarrus County, now township no. 6.

Watts Landing, community in se Pender County on Intracoastal Waterway.

Wattsville. *See* Nakina.

Wauchecha Bald, central Graham County in Cheoah Mountains at the head of Bee Creek. Alt. 4,400.

Wauchope. *See* Walkup.

Waughtown, former town in s Forsyth County; inc. 1891. First called Charlestown or Charleston for Charles Bagge, who first settled there and opened a store. When the store was sold to James Waugh, the scattered settlement surrounding it came to be called Waugh's Store or Waughtown. Post office was Waughtown by 1828. Now within the corporate limits of Winston-Salem.

Waumans Creek rises in ne Columbus County and flows ne into Cape Fear River.

Waverly, community in e Madison County on Paint Fork.

Waves, community on Hatteras Island, e Dare County, formerly known as South Rodanthe.

Waxhaw, town in w Union County between East Fork Twelvemile Creek and Waxhaw Creek. Inc. 1889. Named for Waxhaw settlements made by Scots-Irish and Germans in 1740. The name Waxhaw comes from the Waxhaw Indians, who once claimed the region between Rocky River and Catawba River. President Andrew Jackson was born nearby. Produces textiles.

Waxhaw Creek rises in w Union County and flows sw into Catawba River in South Carolina.

Waxhaws, The, an area generally recognized as including much of Anson, Mecklenburg, and Union Counties in North Carolina and Chester, Lancaster, and York Counties in South Carolina. Catawba River forms the w limits. Waxhaw Creek flows through the area, forming what has been called "a rich oasis in a region of pine barrens." President Andrew Jackson was born in the area in 1767. The name came from the Waxhaw Indians of the region, whose chief village, Wisacky, was visited in 1670 by John Lederer.

Wayah Bald, w Macon County at the head of Camp Branch. Alt. 5,385. Named for a Cherokee youth who, according to legend, visited the mountain with his grandfather to listen to the message of the stars. Young Wayah's name meant "wolf."

Wayah Branch rises in sw Buncombe County and flows ne into Stony Fork.

Wayah Creek rises in w Macon County and flows se into Cartoogechaye Creek.

Wayah Gap, w Macon County at the head of Wayah Creek.

Wayanock. *See* Meherrin River.

Waycross, community in e Sampson County.

Wayehutta Creek rises in central Jackson County and flows sw into Tuckasegee River.

Wayne County was formed in 1779 from Dobbs County. Located in the e section of the state, it is bounded by Greene, Lenoir, Duplin, Sampson, Johnston, and Wilson Counties. It was named for Gen. Anthony Wayne (1745–96), Revolutionary War leader. Area: 555 sq. mi. County seat: Goldsboro, with an elevation of 111 ft. Townships are Brogden, Buck

Swamp, Fork, Goldsboro, Grantham, Great Swamp, Indian Springs, Nahunta, New Hope, Pikeville, Saulston, and Stony Creek. Produces tobacco, corn, soybeans, wheat, oats, cotton, poultry, dairy products, baked goods, wood products, sweet potatoes, cantaloupes, pickles, hogs, livestock, and cucumbers. *See also* St. Patrick's Parish.

Waynesborough, first county seat of Wayne County, est. 1787. The town died after the county seat was moved to Goldsboro in 1850. Waynesborough was located on land formerly owned by Andrew Bass, delegate to the Provincial Congress of 1775, at the sw edge of the present county seat on Neuse River. After 1847 many houses were moved from the old town to the new. The old courthouse, built by Col. William McKinne, was destroyed prior to 1917.

Waynesville, town and county seat, s Haywood County. Settled about 1800 and known first as Mount Prospect. Inc. 1810. Said to have been named by Col. Robert Love (1760–1845), one of the founders and owner of part of the site, for Gen. Anthony Wayne, whom he knew during the Revolutionary War. Produces rubber, shoes, and paper products. In 1953 the adjacent town of Hazelwood, *which see*, was inc. into the limits of Waynesville. Alt. 2,635.

Waynesville Township, sw Haywood County.

Wayside, community in central Hoke County between Beaver Creek and Black Branch.

Wayside, former community in w Swain County on Little Tennessee River. A post office, 1880–1922. Site now submerged by Fontana Lake.

Weapemeoc, the principal town of the Weapemeoc Indians visited by Ralph Lane and fellow explorers in 1585–86, was near present-day Edenton, s Chowan County. The word was also the Indian name for Albemarle Sound and may be an Algonquian word for "where shelter from the wind is sought."

Weasel, community in nw Ashe County. Alt. 2,790.

Wease Mountain, ne Rutherford County between the head of South Creek and Molly Fork. Alt. approx. 2,100.

Weatherman Bald, on the Cherokee-Clay county line in the Valley River Mountains. Alt. 4,700. Known by the Indians as *Kolasko*.

Weatherspoon Cooling Pond, in e Robeson County at the junction of Lumber River and Jacob Swamp. Approx. 3 mi. se of city of Lumberton. Formed in 1955 to cover 231 acres, with a max. depth of 5 ft.; shoreline is 4 mi. Named for W. Herbert Weatherspoon, longtime official of Carolina Power and Light Company. Used to cool steam condensers.

Weaver, community in central Durham County.

Weaver Branch rises in ne Cherokee County and flows sw into Junaluska Creek.

Weaver Branch rises in ne Swain County and flows se into Breedlove Branch.

Weaver Creek rises in e Chatham County and flows nw into Beaver Creek.

Weaver Creek rises in e Vance County and flows s into Southerlands Millpond on Sandy Creek.

Weaversford, community in ne Ashe County. Alt. approx. 2,500.

Weaverville, town in n central Buncombe County. The site was referred to as Pine Cabbin in eighteenth-century records of the county and a little later as Salem Camp Ground. A post office est. there in 1850 was named Reems Creek and changed to Weaverville in 1873. Inc. 1875. Named for Rev. Montraville Weaver, who gave land and money in 1872 to est. Weaver College (closed in 1933). From 1919 until 1921, the town was named Elkwood. Alt. 2,300. Produces textiles.

Weaverville Reservoir, n Buncombe County on Ox Creek near Bull Mountain.

Webb, community in w Mitchell County on Brummett Creek.

Webb Branch rises in sw Buncombe County near Holland Mountain and flows sw into Hominy Creek.

Webb Branch rises in s Macon County and flows ne into West Fork Overflow Creek.

Webb Cove, the valley through which Webb Cove Creek flows in central Buncombe County.

Webb Cove Creek rises in the Elk Mountains in central Buncombe County and flows sw to join Linn Cove Creek in forming Beaverdam Creek.

Webb Creek rises in e central Avery County and flows se into Gragg Prong.

Webb Creek rises in s Buncombe County and flows sw into Gap Creek.

Webb Creek is formed in ne Cherokee County by the junction of Left Fork Webb Creek and Right Fork Webb Creek and flows se into Valley River.

Webb Creek rises in s Clay County and flows sw into Crawford Creek.

Webb Creek rises in e Onslow County and flows e into White Oak River. Named for Thomas Webb.

Webb Lake, s Jackson County on Cedar Creek. Formed before 1946; covers 5 acres and has max. depth of 12 ft. Used for fishing. Not open to the public.

Webbs, community in s Edgecombe County near headwaters of Otter Creek.

Webbs, community in ne Lincoln County.

Webbs Creek rises in e Rutherford County and flows s into Second Broad River.

Webbs Mill Branch rises in se Halifax County and flows se into Kehukee Swamp.

Webster, town in central Jackson County just n of Tuckasegee River and 2 mi. s of town of Sylva. Inc. 1859. Named for Daniel Webster. Alt. 2,203. The town was the county seat from its establishment as such in 1852 until 1913.

Webster Creek, a short tidal creek and inlet, rises on the w side of the mainland of s Currituck County and flows e into Currituck Sound.

Webster Creek rises in central Jackson County and flows n into Tuckasegee River.

Webster Station. *See* Dillsboro.

Webster Township, central Jackson County.

Weddington, community in w Union County between Sixmile Creek and West Fork Twelvemile Creek. Inc. 1983.

Weecaunse Creek. *See* Wiccacon River.

Weed Patch Mountain, on the Henderson-Rutherford county line.

Weedy Mountain, se Buncombe County near the Rutherford County line se of Jarvis Mountain.

Weeks Point. *See* Swansboro.

Weeksville, community in s Pasquotank County on New Begun Creek. Named for families of James and Charles Weeks, local landowners. Known as New Begun Creek until about 1890. Older w section of the community sometimes is known as Old Weeksville.

Wehutty, community in w Cherokee County on Rocky Ford Creek.

Wehutty Mountain, w Cherokee County between Rocky Ford and Shoal Creeks.

Weightman Branch rises in central Davidson County and flows s into Swearing Creek.

Weil, former community in central Wayne County near the junction of Little and Neuse Rivers. Site of a brickyard and a railroad station near the site of the old county seat of Waynesboro.

Weir Point, point of land on nw end of Roanoke Island, ne Dare County. The William B. Umstead Bridge, approx. 3 mi. long and opened on December 22, 1956, extends from the point to Redstone Point on the n Dare County mainland; named for N.C. governor William B. Umstead (1895–1954).

Weitock River. *See* White Oak River.

Weitzel's Mill, site on Reedy Fork Creek, n central Guilford County. A skirmish occurred there on March 6, 1781, between American and British forces.

Welch Bald, n Swain County on Welch Ridge near the ne end of Big Fork Ridge. Alt. 5,087.

Welch Branch rises in n Swain County and flows se into Bear Creek.

Welch Branch rises in s Swain County and flows nw into Yalaka Creek.

Welch Branch rises in w Swain County and flows se into Fontana Lake.

Welch Cove, n Graham County w of Fontana, follows the ne course of a stream that empties into Little Tennessee River. Formerly known as Brooks Cove. *See also* Fontana Village.

Welch Creek rises in n Beaufort County and flows ne on the Martin-Washington county line into Roanoke River. Name appears as Welches Creek throughout the nineteenth century.

Welch Creek Township, n Columbus County.

Welches Creek. *See* Welch Creek.

Welch Mill Creek rises in ne Cherokee County and flows se into Valley River.

Welch Ridge, n Swain County in Great Smoky Mountains National Park, extends sw from Silers Bald to Little Tennessee River. Its center is near lat. 35°31'40" N., long. 83°35'30" W.

Welch's Bluff appears on the Moseley map, 1733, on the w side of Cape Fear River in present Brunswick County between the mouth of Indian Creek and Eagle Island. Possibly named for James Welch, who owned land in the vicinity.

Welch's Millpond, formed by a dam across Warwick Creek on the Chowan-Gates county line.

Welcome, community in n Davidson County. Alt. 860. Formerly called Hinklesville for the Hinkle family residing there. Disagreement arose over selection of a name for the new railroad depot; ultimately, Welcome was selected, either because the decision makers were impressed by the "Welcome" sign over the door of the community store or because, during the dispute over the name, one man declared, "Everybody's welcome here."

Welcome, community in w Surry County served by post office, 1899–1908.

Weldon, town in n Halifax County on Roanoke River. Inc. 1843. The Collet map, 1770, shows "Weldans," perhaps referring to the family name of the owner of the land. Town site settled prior to 1830, when it was known as Weldon's Orchard or Weldon's Place for Daniel Weldon, owner. In 1834 it became the terminus of a railroad from Virginia. Lumber and apparel produced there. Alt. 81. *See also* Blakely.

Weldons Millpond, on Sandy Creek in e Vance County. Covers 10 acres, with a max. depth of 6 ft. Named for Obed W. Weldon, owner. Known prior to 1913 as Amos Millpond. The mill there is still used for grinding corn; the pond is used for fishing, swimming, and boating.

Weldon's Orchard; Weldon's Place. *See* Weldon.

Weldon Township, ne Halifax County.

Wellington, name given the former Jacocks Landing on Cashie River, se Bertie County, for a brief time when it was the s terminus of a short railroad. Wellington is shown on the 1892 Rand McNally map, as well as on the 1897 North Carolina Railroad Commission map. The Carolina Southern Railroad was inc. as the Wellington and Powellsville Railroad in 1893.

Wells Bay, in Currituck Sound off Mossey Islands, se Currituck County.

Wells Creek rises in s Alamance County and flows sw into Cane Creek.

Wells Creek, a channel between Currituck Banks and several small tidal-marsh islands in Currituck Sound, e Currituck County.

Wells Creek rises in e Vance County and flows s into w Warren County, where it enters Sandy Creek.

Wells Knob, ne Wilkes County between Little Elkin River and Elkin River. Alt. 1,810.

Wells Mineral Spring, s Nash County on a tributary of Sapony Creek. A popular recreation spot in the early 1900s; water thought to have curative qualities.

Wells Mountain, on the Cherokee-Clay county line from Coleman Gap to the mouth of Little Brasstown Creek.

Welsh Pond, on Warwick Creek on the Chowan-Gates county line, covers approx. 75 acres and is from 2 to 15 ft. in depth. Named for owners, the Welch family.

Welsh Tract, an area between the Northeast Cape Fear and Cape Fear Rivers, now largely in central Pender County, on which a number of Welsh families from Pennsylvania settled in 1730 and shortly afterward. The first grant was made in 1731 to David Evans for 640 acres. Apparently no single large block of land was granted to the Welsh; instead, individuals acquired their own land. Appears on the Moseley map, 1733, as Welch Settlement. Rev. Hugh McAden mentioned the Welsh Tract during his visit to the area in 1755, and the name was still in use in 1775. Persons other than those of Welsh descent soon moved into the area, and the tract lost its identity. About 1740 the Welsh laid out a town that became South Washington, *which see*.

Wendell (win-DELL), town in e Wake County. Settled 1895. Inc. 1903. Named for Oliver Wendell Holmes (1809–94), American writer and father of the U.S. Supreme Court justice of the same name. Produces tobacco, apparel, and furniture.

Wenona, community in s Washington County on the n shoulder of Dogwood Ridge on East Dismal Swamp. Est. after A. E. Rice purchased 160 acres of land there and built a house in 1912. Other settlers then purchased land from Roper Lumber Company and settled; by 1914, a school was built. A post office was est. there in 1913; closed 1955. Settlers came there from Pennsylvania, West Virginia, Illinois, and Ohio.

Wentworth, county seat, central Rockingham County. Courthouse authorized to be est. 1787; first court held there 1799. Post office operated there, 1794–1827, as Rockingham Courthouse. Named for Charles Watson-Wentworth, Duke of Rockingham and prime minister of England when the Stamp Act was repealed; on March 9 and 17, 1778, Watson-Wentworth spoke on behalf of immediate recognition of the independence of the American colonies. Rockingham Community

College, est. 1966, is there. Inc. 1998. Alt. approx. 900.

Wentworth Township, central Rockingham County.

Wesley, community in se Surry County served by post office, 1894–1905.

Wesley Chapel, community in w central Union County. Inc. 1998.

Wesley Creek rises in s Buncombe County and flows se into Bent Creek.

Wesley Creek rises in ne Haywood County and flows s into Fines Creek.

Wesley Martin Branch rises in e Cherokee County and flows nw into Valley River.

Wesner Bald, on Haywood-Jackson county line. Alt. 5,600. Named for David Wesner of Cabarrus County, who obtained a grant for 100 acres in the vicinity in 1808. Wesner froze to death while hunting deer about 1812 on the mountain that now bears his name.

Wesser, community in sw Swain County near Nantahala Gorge. Alt. 1,714. Named for the nearby Wesser Creek.

Wesser Bald, n Macon County at head of Tellico Creek. Alt. 4,800.

Wesser Creek rises in n Macon County and flows nw into Swain County, where it enters Nantahala River. Named for a hunter who lived on its banks.

Wesser Creek rises in e Swain County and flows ne into Connelly Creek.

Wesser Gap, se Swain County on the head of Connelly Creek.

West Alliance. *See* Alliance.

West Asheville, former town in central Buncombe County on the w side of the French Broad River. Inc. 1889; became a part of Asheville, 1897.

West Bald, peak in the Tusquitee Mountains, n Clay County.

West Bay, s extension of Pamlico Sound between Piney Island and Cedar Island in ne Carteret County.

West Bear Creek rises in e Wayne County and flows se into Bear Creek.

West Beaver Creek rises in s Ashe County and flows se into Beaver Creek.

West Belews Creek rises in e Forsyth County and flows ne into s Stokes County and into Belews Creek. Also known as Left Fork Belews Creek and, in Stokes County, as Little Belews Creek.

West Bend, community in w Forsyth County in a bend of Yadkin River.

West Bladenboro, town in sw Bladen County adjacent to Bladenboro, *which see*. Inc. 1913, but no longer active in municipal affairs.

West Bluff Bay, in Pamlico Sound w of Bluff Point in s Hyde County.

West Branch rises in central Madison County and flows se into Walnut Creek.

West Branch rises in n Mecklenburg County and flows se into Rocky River.

West Branch rises in w Warren County and flows n into Malones Creek.

Westbrook, community in se Bladen County. Named for early colonial family of Westbrook.

Westbrooks Township, n Sampson County.

West Buffalo Creek rises in sw Graham County and flows ne into Hooper Mill Creek. Also known as Little Buffalo Creek.

West Buies Creek rises in n Harnett County and flows s and se into Buies Creek.

West Canton, suburban area of the city of Canton in e Haywood County.

West Concord, unincorporated outskirts of city of Concord, central Cabarrus County.

West Cove extends sw in e Haywood County between Wilson Cove and Long Branch.

West Crossroads. *See* Spiveys Corner.

West Double Creek rises in s Surry County and flows se to join East Double Creek in forming Double Creek.

West End, community in s Moore County. Named for the fact that it was the w terminus of a railroad from Aberdeen (about 1890–98) that later became a part of the Norfolk and Southern Railway. Alt. 604.

Western Branch of Queen Anne's Creek. *See* Pembroke Creek.

Western Cliffs, e Macon County between Houston Branch and the head of Brush Creek.

Western Point, ne Carteret County; nw point of Cedar Island extending into West Bay.

Western Prong rises in n Columbus County and flows ne and se into Red Hill Swamp, after which it is known as White Marsh.

Western Prong Township, n Columbus County.

Westfield, community in ne Surry County. Grew up around a Quaker mission est. there in 1760 and known first as Tom's Creek. Renamed for the fact that it was a w missionary field for the New Garden [Guilford County] Quakers. Served by post office since 1834.

Westfield Township, ne Surry County.

West Fork rises in central Avery County and flows s into Linville River.

West Fork [Barkers Creek] rises in w Jackson County and flows ne to join Middle Fork [Barkers Creek] in forming Barkers Creek.

West Fork [Bull Creek] rises in n Madison County near Bull Creek Gap and flows s to join East Fork [Bull Creek] in forming Bull Creek.

West Fork Campbell Creek rises in w Haywood County and flows ne into Campbell Creek.

West Fork Deep River rises in w central Guilford County and flows se into High Point Lake, where it joins East Fork Deep River.

West Fork [Dicks Creek] rises in n Jackson County and flows s to join East Fork [Dicks Creek] in forming Dicks Creek.

West Fork French Broad River rises in w Transylvania County and flows se to join North Fork French Broad River in forming French Broad River.

West Fork [Goose Creek] rises in nw Pamlico County and flows se into Goose Creek.

West Fork [Jenkins Creek] rises in n Jackson County and flows s to join East Fork [Jenkins Creek] in forming Jenkins Creek.

West Fork [Kirkland Creek] rises in s Swain County and flows n to join East Fork [Kirkland Creek] in forming Kirkland Creek.

West Fork Little River rises in s Randolph County and flows se into Montgomery County, where it enters Little River.

West Fork [Moses Creek] rises in n Jackson County and flows sw to join East Fork [Moses Creek] in forming Moses Creek.

West Fork of Ivy Township, former township in e Madison County, now township no. 5.

West Fork Overflow Creek rises in s Macon County and flows se to join East Fork Overflow Creek in forming Overflow Creek.

West Fork Pigeon River rises in s Haywood County near the Jackson-Transylvania county line and flows ne to join East Fork Pigeon River in forming Pigeon River. Known by the Cherokee Indians as *Neeoh-la*, the name that they applied to the main river formed by the junction of East and West Forks Pigeon River.

West Fork Rocky River rises in s Iredell County and flows se into Mecklenburg County, where it enters Rocky River on the Mecklenburg-Cabarrus county line.

West Fork [Rube Creek] rises in nw Watauga County and flows se into Rube Creek.

West Fork Sandy Branch rises in s Stokes County and flows s into Sandy Branch.

West Fork Shut-in Creek rises in w Madison County and flows ne to join East Fork Shut-in Creek in forming Shut-in Creek.

West Fork [South River], a short stream at the headwaters of South River in n central Carteret County.

West Fork Tuckasegee River rises in w Jackson County at n end of Thorpe Lake and flows ne to enter Tuckasegee River approx. 8 mi. away at the community of Tuckasegee.

West Fork Twelvemile Creek rises in w Union County and flows se to join East Fork Twelvemile Creek in forming Twelvemile Creek.

West Haven, community in s Buncombe County on the e limit of Pisgah National Forest.

West Hillsborough, unincorporated outskirts of town of Hillsborough, central Orange County.

West Howellsville Township, e Robeson County.

West Jefferson, town in central Ashe County. Inc. 1915. Named for its location in relation to Jefferson, the county seat. Produces hosiery and furniture.

West Jefferson Township, central Ashe County.

West Knob, on the Buncombe-Henderson county line between Double Knob and Graham Mountain.

West Littleton Branch rises in e Warren County near the town of Littleton and flows nw into Little Stonehouse Creek.

Westminster, community in w Guilford County served by post office, 1843–1904.

Westminster, community in n central Rutherford County that grew up around Fort McGaughey; built approx. 1765 and used through the Revolutionary War. Sometimes known also as Brittain for Little Brittain Presbyterian Church, est. there in 1768. Present name is taken from Westminster School, founded there in 1901 by 10 Presbyterian churches in Cleveland, Polk, and Rutherford Counties; the school closed in 1923.

West Monroe, former town in central Union County. Inc. 1909 as Icemorlee, a mill village named for three major stockholders: Iceman, Morrow, and Lee. Later renamed. Merged with the city of Monroe in 1949.

West Mountain, w Cherokee County between Camp and Shoal Creeks.

Westmouth Bay, between Browns and Harkers Island in The Straits, se Carteret County.

West Nelson Creek rises in ne Cherokee County and flows se into Valley River.

West Norman, community in Lincoln County on w shore of Lake Norman. Effort to incorporate failed in 2001.

Weston Knob, s Buncombe County s of Merrill Mountain.

Westover, community in w central Wake County; formerly the site of Thompson, a railroad station. Settled 1917 and named for Westover, Md. Alt. 325.

Westover, community in nw Washington County. Alt. 17. A post office, White Marsh, was est. there in 1878 and continued until 1886. A 450-acre tract of land there owned by Surveyor General Edward Moseley (1682–1749) was known as White Marsh, a name that appears on the Moseley map, 1733.

Westover, community in ne Wilson County. A post office operated there, March–December 1900.

West Philadelphia, community in nw Moore County.

West Point, former plantation, tavern, and ferry in w Wayne County at the junction of Thoroughfare Swamp and Neuse River; owned by Andrew Bass, delegate to the Provincial Congress of 1775, whose lands included site of Waynesborough, *which see*. Wayne County court met there during 1785. Later known as Bass Ferry. West Point was location for receipt and inspection of tobacco in 1784.

West Prong [Glady Fork] rises in s Transylvania County and flows se and then ne to join South Prong [Glady Fork] in forming Glady Fork. Also known as Galloway Creek.

West Prong Grape Creek rises in central Cherokee County and flows se and sw into Grape Creek.

West Prong [Hickory Fork] rises in n Madison County and flows se into Hickory Fork.

West Prong Horse Branch rises in central Duplin County and flows se into Northeast Cape Fear River.

West Prong Little Yadkin River rises in w Stokes County and flows se to join East Prong Little Yadkin River in forming Little Yadkin River.

West Prong Roaring River. *See* North Prong Roaring River.

West Ridge Branch rises in n Transylvania County and flows sw into South Fork Mills River.

West Rockingham, unincorporated outskirts of town of Rockingham, w Richmond County.

Westry, town in e central Nash County. Settled about 1880; inc. 1909. Named for an early settler. Alt. 125.

West Sanford Township, former township in w central Lee County, now township no. 6.

Wests Branch rises in n Macon County and flows s into Matlock Creek.

Wests Cove, on a tributary of Cowee Creek in n Macon County.

Wests Crossroads, community in e Lenoir County.

Wests Mill, community on Cowee Creek in n Macon County. In 1767 Thomas Griffiths, a South Carolina planter, shipped several tons of fine white clay, taken from a nearby pit, to the Wedgwood potteries in England.

West Swan Creek rises in e Wilkes County and flows ne to join East Swan Creek in forming Swan Creek.

West Tarboro, former town in central Edgecombe County on the nw limits of Tarboro. Inc. 1903. Charter repealed in 1909, when it became a part of Tarboro. A former West Tarboro community on the sw limits of Tarboro was inc. in 1893 and the name was changed to Hilma. *See also* Farrar.

West Thorofare Bay, ne Carteret County w of Cedar Island and adjacent to Long Bay. Connected with Thorofare Bay via Thorofare, a channel forming the s boundary of Cedar Island.

Wet Ash Swamp rises in Green Swamp in w Brunswick County and flows w into Waccamaw River.

Wet Creek rises in w Moore County and flows n into Cabin Creek.

Wethero Mountain, between Cox Creek and Clear Creek in n Henderson County.

Wet Hollow, s Cherokee County; a mountain valley sw of Rocky Pen Ridge near the mouth of Crane Creek.

Weyanok Creek. *See* Potecasi Creek.

Weyanoke Creek is mentioned in the Carolina Charter of 1665, in which the n boundary of the province is described as lying "within or about the degrees of 36 and 30 minutes northern latitude." It is shown on one version of the Comberford map, 1657, as Weyanoke River and on the other as Wepanoke River, one of several rivers flowing into Chowan River. Name soon fell out of use. Virginians thought it was intended to refer to Wiccacon River, while North Carolinians thought it was Nottoway River. Owing to the disagreement, a strip 15 mi. wide was long in dispute.

Weymouth Woods Sandhills Nature Preserve, a 403-acre tract of forest land se of Southern Pines, se Moore County. Vegetation varies from dense hardwood swamp forest to open stands of longleaf pine. Given to the state of North Carolina by Katharine (Mrs. James) Boyd in 1963. Alt. 350 to 500 ft.

Whalebone, commercial intersection on Bodie Island, e Dare County about 2½ mi. s of the town of Nags Head. Began around 1930 as intersection of then-existing sand trails and roads. Originally important commercial center. Named for whalebones in front of service station once located there. Also known as Whalebone Junction.

Whalebone Inlet. *See* Drum Inlet.

Whale Camp Point. *See* Camp Point.

Whale Head Bay, in Currituck Sound off the w shore of Currituck Banks, e Currituck County a short distance s of Corolla.

Whaley, community in n Avery County. Said to have been named for one Whaley, who became frightened by a screech owl and hid in a hollow log until morning.

Whaley Branch rises in w Haywood County near the Tennessee state line and flows sw into Big Creek.

Wharf, community in n Anson County served by post office, 1889–1907.

Wharf, The. *See* Swansboro.

Wharton, community in nw Beaufort County. Alt. 19. Named for Lt. Col. Rufus W. Wharton, Washington resident and Confederate officer.

Wheat Creek rises in e Polk County and flows se into Green River.

Wheatfield Branch rises in s Macon County and flows sw into Tessentee Creek.

Wheat Swamp rises in n Lenoir County and flows ne on the Lenoir-Greene county line into Contentnea Creek. Named for John Wheat, who had an early grant of land there.

Wheat Swamp rises in sw Wilson County and flows se into Wayne County, where it enters Great Swamp.

Wheeler Creek is formed in w Northampton County by the junction of Gumberry Swamp and Lily Pond Creek and flows s into Roanoke River. The Collet map, 1770, shows Baker Mill at the mouth of the creek.

Wheeler's Mill. *See* Barrows Mill Pond.

Whetstone, community in n Granville County served by post office, 1889–1903.

Whetstone Branch rises in s Davie County and flows e into Peeler Creek.

Whetstone Creek rises in n Rockingham County and flows ne into Dan River. Tradition attributes the name to the fact that early white settlers found the Indians used stones from the stream to whet their knives.

Whetstone Ridge, s Transylvania County, extends ne from Blue Ridge to West Fork French Broad River.

Whichard, community in ne Pitt County served by post office, 1891–1926.

Whigg Branch rises in w Graham County and flows ne into Santeetlah Creek.

Whim Knob, on the Haywood-Swain county line between Sugar Tree Lick and Strawberry Knob. Alt. approx. 5,400. Named for the fact that a whim, a horsepowered winch used to draw logs out of the valley, was operated on the peak for several years.

Whipping Creek rises in sw Dare County and flows sw into Long Shoal River. Appears as Aquascog River on the Comberford map, 1657, and under its present name on the Collet map, 1770. Aquascogoc was an Algonquian Indian village near the head of the Pungo River estuary; the name is believed to have meant "where a place for disembarking exists."

Whispering Pines, residential community on Thagards Pond, e Moore County. Developed about 1962. *See also* Thagards Pond.

Whistling Gap, nw Yancey County between Chestnut Ridge and the head of Whistling Gap Branch.

Whistling Gap Branch rises in nw Yancey County and flows se into Little Creek.

Whitaker. *See* Grover.

Whitaker Branch rises in w Avery County and flows se into North Toe River.

Whitaker Branch rises in ne Buncombe County and flows s into Town Branch.

Whitaker Branch rises in ne Cherokee County and flows nw into Valley River.

Whitaker Creek rises in e Cleveland County and flows s into Buffalo Creek.

Whitaker Creek rises in se Pamlico County between Smith Creek and Pierce Creek and flows se into Neuse River. First named Powells Creek for William Powell, who settled there in 1703. Appears as Powells Creek on Lawson map, 1709.

Whitaker Crossroads, community in s Surry County near the head of Hagan Creek.

Whitaker Mountain, s Cleveland County.

Whitakers, town on the Edgecombe-Nash county line. Settled approx. 1840; post office est. 1866. Post office name changed to Mayonia for approx. 3 months in 1886. Inc. 1872. Named for Richard and Henry Whitaker, local landowners who supplied wood to the railroad when it was being built. First known as Whitaker's Turnout. Alt. 134.

Whitaker's Mills. *See* Gold Rock.

White Branch rises in n Buncombe County and flows sw into Flat Creek.

White Branch rises in ne Cherokee County and flows s into Junaluska Creek.

White Branch rises in n Franklin County and flows ne into Little Shocco Creek.

White Creek rises in s central Avery County and flows se into Linville River.

White Creek rises in s Buncombe County and flows ne into French Broad River.

White Creek. *See* North Fork [Duck Creek].

White Creek Township, in s Bladen County.

White Cross, community in s Orange County. A post office there, 1880–1906, was known as Gath.

Whiteface Mountain, at the junction of the Caldwell-Watauga-Wilkes county lines. Alt. 2,450.

White Hall, community in central Cabarrus County.

Whitehall. *See* Seven Springs.

White Hall Landing, in se Bladen County on the Cape Fear River. An important early trading center.

Whitehead, community in central Alleghany County. Named for D. C. Whithead, early settler. Post office est. 1883. Alt. 3,026.

Whitehead Creek rises in n central Avery County and flows s, joining Hickory Branch before flowing into Elk River.

Whiteheads Mill. *See* Spencer.

Whitehead Township, s central Alleghany County.

White Hill, community in sw Lee County at the Moore County line. Took its name from a Presbyterian church there on a small knoll of very white sand. A former post office there, 1887–1906, was known as Villanow. The community has also been known as Caviness Crossroads.

White Horse Branch rises in s Lee County and flows s into Little River.

White House, community in sw Randolph County served by post office, 1849–1908.

Whitehouse, community in n Rutherford County between Cove and Otter Creeks. A stockade for the protection of settlers against Indians was erected in the vicinity of nearby Montford Cove Church in the eighteenth century.

White Hurricane Knob, on the Buncombe-Yancey county line se of Cane River Gap. Appears on recent State Highway Commission maps as Mahogany Knob.

Whitehurst, community in n Pitt County served by post office, 1900–1906. Settled about 1890 and known as Grindool (post office operated by that name, 1890–1910) until early in the twentieth century, when the name was changed to honor S. C. Whitehurst, local farmer. Alt. 68.

Whitehurst Creek rises in se Beaufort County and flows e into South Creek.

Whitehurst Creek rises in central Onslow County and flows e into New River.

Whitelace Creek rises in w Lenoir County and flows n into Neuse River.

White Lake, a natural lake in e central Bladen County. Covers 1,068 acres; max. depth 10½ ft. Appears as Granston Lake on the Collet map, 1770; later known as Bartrams Lake for William Bartram, who owned adjacent property and operated a gristmill near the lake. Apparently appears first as White Lake on the Shaffer township map of 1886; named for its white, sandy bottom and clear water. It first attracted outside interest about 1922 after roads made it accessible. Boating, fishing, and swimming. *See also* Carolina Bays.

White Lake, town in e central Bladen County. Originally chartered in 1923; repealed in 1925. Chartered again in 1951.

White Mans Glory Creek rises in n Swain County in Great Smoky Mountains National Park on Welch Ridge and flows se into Forney Creek.

White Marsh, stream in the lower course of Red Hill Swamp after it is joined by Western Prong, n Columbus County. It flows se into Waccamaw River. Appears on the Moseley map, 1733, as Great White Marsh in the vicinity of Waccamaw River. *See also* Brown Meadow.

White Marsh rises in s Pender County and flows w into Godfrey Creek.

White Marsh. *See* Westover.

Whitener, community in w Catawba County served by post office, 1893–1903.

Whitener Creek rises in s Burke County and flows s into Rock Creek.

White Oak, community in nw Bladen County. Alt. 46. Post office est. 1853. Named for John Whiteoak, a colonial resident. Once called Winnie for Jefferson Davis's daughter.

White Oak, community in w central Gates County.

White Oak, former community in central Guilford County; now a part of Greensboro.

White Oak, community in sw Halifax County.

Whiteoak, community in n Onslow County.

White Oak, community in s Wake County. Settled 1900 and named for the white oaks in the vicinity. Alt. 300.

Whiteoak Bald, ne Cherokee County in the Valley River Mountains.

Whiteoak Bottoms, sw Macon County between Kimsey Creek and Nantahala River.

Whiteoak Branch rises in s Avery County and flows w into North Toe River.

Whiteoak Branch rises in e Duplin County and flows s into Little Limestone Creek.

Whiteoak Branch rises in nw Duplin County and flows s into Goshen Swamp.

Whiteoak Branch rises in n Haywood County and flows ne into Pigeon River.

Whiteoak Branch rises in s Johnston County and flows se into Stone Creek.

Whiteoak Branch rises in s Macon County and flows sw into Tessentee Creek.

Whiteoak Branch rises in e Montgomery County and flows e into Little River.

Whiteoak Branch rises in n Swain County and flows sw into Forney Creek.

Whiteoak Creek rises in central Avery County and flows s into Fall Branch.

White Oak Creek rises in sw Avery County and flows se into North Toe River.

Whiteoak Creek rises in s tip of Burke County and flows ne into Jacob Fork.

Whiteoak Creek rises in w Macon County and flows nw into Nantahala River.

Whiteoak Creek rises in s Madison County and flows sw into Ivy River.

Whiteoak Creek rises in central Mitchell County and flows nw into Cane Creek.

Whiteoak Creek is formed in e Moore County by the junction of Crains Creek and Dry Fork Branch, both of which rise in Lee County. Whiteoak Creek flows s into Crains Creek (the lower course of Dunhams Creek). It formerly was known as North Fork Crains Creek and Little Crains Creek.

Whiteoak Creek rises in w Pender County and flows e into Moores Creek.

Whiteoak Creek rises in central Polk County and flows e into Green River.

Whiteoak Creek rises in n Rockingham County and flows ne into Virginia, where it enters Dan River.

White Oak Creek rises in n Rockingham County and flows ne into Dan River.

Whiteoak Creek rises in e Wake County and flows s into Johnston County, where it enters Swift Creek.

Whiteoak Creek rises in sw Wake County and flows sw into Chatham County, where it enters Buckhorn Creek.

Whiteoak Creek rises in w Wake County and flows sw into Chatham County, where it enters New Hope River.

Whiteoak Creek rises in e Yancey County and flows e into South Toe River.

Whiteoak Creek rises in n Yancey County and flows se into Nolichucky River.

Whiteoak Creek Falls, more accurately a cascade, near the mouth of Whiteoak Creek at Nantahala River, nw Macon County.

Whiteoak Flats, an area of stony loam in e Swain County n of Rocky Knob near the head of Adams Creek.

Whiteoak Flats, community in n Yancey County on Whiteoak Creek.

Whiteoak Gap, n Madison County at the head of East Prong [Hickory Fork].

White Oak Island, in w Tyrrell County, is a loamy section surrounded by swampland. Deer and bear hunting.

Whiteoak Knob, on the Cherokee-Clay county line.

White Oak Knob, w Graham County in the Snowbird Mountains. Alt. 4,301.

White Oak Landing, on the Cape Fear River in nw Bladen County.

Whiteoak Limb Ridge, s Graham County in the Snowbird Mountains between Rocky Spring Top and Poplar Spring Top.

Whiteoak Mountain, n Haywood County, extends ne along the course of Whiteoak Branch.

Whiteoak Mountain, w central Polk County. Alt. 3,102.

White Oak Mountain, on the Transylvania County, N.C.–Greenville County, S.C., line e of Sassafras Gap.

Whiteoak Pocosin, w Gates County. Alt. 26 to 38.

Whiteoak Ridge, w Macon County parallel to Big Laurel Creek.

Whiteoak Ridge, n Swain County in Great Smoky Mountains National Park, a short spur extending w from Forney Ridge and forming an arc between Bee Gum Branch and Whiteoak Branch. Its center is near lat. 35°28′38″ N., long. 83°33′12″ W.

White Oak River rises in n Onslow and s Jones Counties and flows se on the Jones-Onslow county line to the Carteret-Onslow county line and into the Atlantic Ocean through Bogue Inlet. It is approx. 20 mi. long. Name derived from the Weetock Indian tribe. Appears as Weetock on the Lawson map, 1709; as Weitock River on the Moseley map, 1733; and as White Oak River on the Collet map, 1770.

Whiteoak Spring, ne Haywood County on the head of Raven Cliff Branch.

White Oak Spring Canal. *See* Hamburg Ditch.

White Oak Stamp, a peak in se Clay County at the se end of Little Mountain.

Whiteoak Swamp rises in central Bertie County and flows s into Cashie River.

White Oak Swamp rises in se Bladen County and flows se into Cape Fear River.

White Oak Swamp rises in ne Edgecombe County near the town of Whitakers and flows se into Swift Creek. Appears on the Collet map, 1770, as Peachtree Creek.

White Oak Swamp rises in ne Franklin County and flows se into Nash County, where it turns ne to flow into Fishing Creek.

Whiteoak Swamp rises in the town of Ahoskie, s Hertford County, and flows e into Bear Swamp.

White Oak Swamp rises in s Nash County and flows ne into Toisnot Swamp.

Whiteoak Swamp rises in w central Sampson County and flows sw into Great Coharie Creek.

Whiteoak Swamp rises in e Wilson County and flows sw into Toisnot Swamp. Mentioned in local records as early as 1740.

White Oak Township, n Bladen County.

White Oak Township, w Carteret County on White Oak River and Bogue Sound. For a time called township no. 1.

White Oak Township, n central Haywood County.

White Oak Township, se Jones County.

White Oak Township, ne Onslow County.

White Oak Township, central Polk County.

White Oak Township, w Wake County.

White Owl Falls, sw Transylvania County in Thompson River. Height of falls is 80 ft.

White Plains, community in se Hertford County.

White Plains, community in n central Surry County. Alt. 1,150. Settled in the 1850s and named for the white, sandy loam soil in the vicinity. Eng and Chang Bunker (1811–74), famed Siamese twins, moved there in 1854 and are buried in a local churchyard.

White Plains. *See* Hiddenite.

White Point extends from the mainland of ne Carteret County into Core Sound.

White Pond, community in s Robeson County.

White Pond Bay, a sand-filled bay in s Cumberland and n Bladen Counties.

White Post, community in central Beaufort County. Formerly known as Surry.

White Road, community in ne Forsyth County served by post office, 1850–1904.

White Rock, mountain on Haywood County, N.C.–Cocke County, Tenn., line near lat. 35°45′30″ N., long. 83°10′ W. Known in Tennessee as Sharp Top for its appearance from that state. A white appearance on the North Carolina side gives it its name. Alt. 5,025.

White Rock, peak in s Watauga County between Pigeonroost and Dutch Creeks.

White Rock. *See* Hill's Rock.

White Rock. *See* Shelton Laurel.

White Rock Branch rises in sw Buncombe County near White Rock Mountain and flows ne into Warren Creek.

White Rock Branch rises in n Madison County and flows s into Hickory Fork.

White Rock Cliffs, n Madison County at the head of White Rock Branch.

Whiterock Creek rises in w Jackson County and flows se into Dodgen Creek.

Whiterock Gap, s Macon County between Jones Knob and the head of Crow Creek.

White Rock Mountain, sw Buncombe County se of Spring Mountain.

Whiterock Mountain, s Macon County between Whiterock Gap and Conley Ridge.

Whiterock Ridge, n Jackson County near the headwaters of Buff Creek.

Whiterock Ridge, w Jackson County between Wilson and Whiterock Creeks.

White Rock Ridge, e Mitchell County between Stagger Weed Creek and Sugartree Branch.

White Rock Ridge, s Watauga County, extends nw from Hillside Branch w of Buffalo Creek.

White Rocks, mountain on the Avery-Mitchell county line.

White Rocks, sw Watauga County between Bench Mountain and the head of Boone Fork.

Whites Branch rises in n Mecklenburg County and flows ne into Clarks Creek.

Whites Creek rises in s central Bladen County and flows n into Hammonds Creek.

Whites Creek rises in n Washington County in Chappel Swamp and flows nw and ne into Albemarle Sound.

Whites Creek rises in sw Wilkes County and flows nw into W. Kerr Scott Reservoir.

Whites Crossroads, community in ne Bertie County.

Whites Fork, community in sw Pasquotank County.

Whiteside Branch rises in s Yancey County and flows se into South Toe River.

Whiteside Cove, e Swain County between East Fork [Kirkland Creek] and Shepherd Creek.

Whiteside Cove, community near Whiteside Mountain in sw Jackson County.

Whiteside Creek rises in w Swain County on Welch Ridge and flows sw into Fontana Lake.

Whiteside Mountain, on Clear Creek in n Henderson County.

Whiteside Mountain, sw Jackson County 3½ mi. ne of the town of Highlands in the Blue Ridge; ne slopes are head of Chattooga River. Near the top is a sheer rock precipice 1,800 ft. high from which the mountain takes its name.

Called *Sanigilagi* by the Cherokee Indians; the meaning is unknown. In 1950 a Spanish inscription of unknown origin was discovered there. A connected peak on the n is known as Devil's Courthouse, *which see*.

Whiteside Ridge, s Yancey County between Camp Creek and Whiteside Branch.

Whites Island. *See* Church Island.

Whites Knob, sw Burke County. Alt. approx. 1,800.

Whites Mill Creek. *See* Bristol's Mill Creek.

Whites Point, se Onslow County on the w side of Queens Creek.

White's Spring. *See* Kelsey.

White's Store. *See* Hominy Heights.

White Store, community in sw Anson County. Est. about 1770 and named for Col. Joseph White Jr., who owned and operated a store there. A post office, 1837–1917.

White Store Township, sw Anson County.

Whites Township, e central Bertie County.

White Sulphur Springs, former popular resort in ne Surry County. Ceased operation about 1935.

White Sulphur Springs. *See* Catawba Springs.

White Swamp rises in central Wilson County and flows ne into Cattail Swamp.

Whiteville, town and county seat, central Columbus County. Authorized to be laid out in 1810 on the lands of James B. White. Originally known as White's Crossing; inc. 1832 as Whiteville but appeared on many maps as Whitesville. Named for the man on whose land it was est. and who was a state senator, 1809–10. The former community of Vineland is now included in the s part of the town. Southeastern Community College, est. 1966, is located there. Produces lumber, apparel, tobacco, textiles. Alt. 59.

Whiteville Township, central Columbus County.

White Walnut Branch rises in n Swain County and flows sw into Bone Valley Creek.

Whitewater Falls is located on Whitewater River along the Jackson-Transylvania county line near the North Carolina–South Carolina line. The falls, among the highest in the e United States, cascade 411 ft. from an alt. of approx. 2,560. Known as *Contara* or *Contaroga* (meaning unknown) by the Cherokee Indians.

Whitewater River is formed in s Jackson County by the junction of Silver Run and Little Whitewater Creeks and flows se on the Jackson-

Transylvania county line into South Carolina, where it is joined by Toxaway River to form Keowee River.

Whitfields Crossroads, community in e Lenoir County. Named for a prominent family that settled there before the Revolution.

Whitfields Pond, on the headwaters of Poley Swamp in n Duplin County. Alt. 118.

Whitford, community in e Jones County. Named for local Whitford family.

Whiting Spur, mountain on the McDowell-Mitchell county line.

Whitley, community in central Stanly County served by post office, 1881–1910.

Whitleys Crossroads, community in sw Nash County.

Whitnel, community in central Caldwell County. Named for J. O. White and J. L. Nelson, local mill owners. Formerly known as Treeland. Produces textiles.

Whitney, community in ne Stanly County on Badin Lake. Alt. 516.

Whitney Mines, former gold mine in ne Cabarrus County on Little Buffalo Creek.

Whitsett, community in e Guilford County. Est. 1884. Named for Whitsett Institute, successor of Fairview Academy, of which W. T. Whitsett was principal in 1888. Post office est. 1895.

Whitson Branch rises in w Mitchell County and flows sw into Toe River.

Whitson Branch rises in n Yancey County and flows se into Jacks Creek.

Whitted Knob, n Buncombe County between Brittain Cove and Charlie Ridge.

Whittemore Creek rises in n Buncombe County near the Madison County line and flows sw into Ivy Creek.

Whittier, town in e Swain and nw Jackson Counties on Tuckasegee River. Alt. 1,839. Est. 1885 by Dr. Clarke Whittier of California, who purchased 60,000 acres, including the town site. Chartered 1887; charter repealed 1895. Rechartered 1897, 1899, and 1907.

Whittier Branch rises in n Buncombe County and flows ne into French Broad River.

Whittier Creek rises in s Surry County and flows ne into Bull Run Creek.

Whittington, community in w Wilkes County on Reddies River.

Whittle Creek rises in nw Alamance County and flows w into Buttermilk Creek.

Whortleberry Creek rises in se Anson County and flows se into Pee Dee River.

Whortleberry Mountain. *See* Huckleberry Ridge.

Whortonsville, community in e Pamlico County on Brown Creek. Called Bethel until a post office was est. in 1904, at which time the name of the first postmaster was adopted (pronounced as if written "Hortonsville"). Post office closed 1959.

Whynot, community in s Randolph County est. late in the nineteenth century. A group of local citizens, meeting in 1860 to select a name for the post office about to be est. there, heard many suggestions phrased as "Why not name it for so-and-so?" Finally, someone in desperation said, "Why not name it Why not?" The group thought this was as good as any of the suggested names, and, since it removed any element of further controversy, the place was so named. Originally spelled as two words.

Wiccacanee Township, n central Northampton County.

Wiccacon River is formed by the junction of several small streams in Hoggard Swamp in s Hertford County. It flows e into Chowan River. Approx. 17 mi. long. Appears as Weecaunse Creek on the Moseley map, 1733; as Veecaune Creek on the Collet map, 1770; and as Wiccacon Creek on the Richardson map, 1808. *See also* Weyanoke Creek.

Wickacon, community in s Hertford County.

Wicker, community in w Cumberland County served by post office, 1887–1903.

Wickham Precinct, formed on December 3, 1705, from Bath County, was named for the manor of Temple Wycombe, the home of the Archdale family in Buckinghamshire, England. John Archdale had been governor in 1694–96. In 1712 Wickham Precinct became Hyde County, *which see.*

Wide Bay, swamp in w central Brunswick County; a part of Green Swamp.

Widow Moores Creek. *See* Moores Creek.

Widow Mountain, n Wilkes County between Cane Creek and North Prong Roaring River.

Wiel, community in s Onslow County on the n side of the mouth of Duck Creek.

Wiggins Branch rises in n Swain County and flows se into Cooper Creek.

Wiggins Cove, e Mitchell County at the head of Beaver Creek.

Wiggins Creek rises in w Swain County and flows ne into Little Tennessee River.

Wiggins Crossroads, community in s Edgecombe County.

Wiggins Crossroads, community in ne Gates County served by post office, 1878–1907. Alt. 30. Settled in the eighteenth century and named for a local family.

Wiggins Lake, w Edgecombe County, was formed in 1953 by a dam on Deloach Branch. Covers 52 acres, with a max. depth of 15 ft. Fishing, swimming, boating, and irrigation. Open to the public.

Wiggins Pond. *See* Contentnea Lake.

Wiggins Top, sw Clay County at the ne end of Chasteen Mountain.

Wikles Store, community in se Macon County served by post office, 1869–1905.

Wilbanks, community in e Wilson County. A post office operated there, 1895–1906.

Wilbar, community in w Wilkes County on South Fork Reddies River. Alt. 2,000. Named for Henry T. Wilbar, nineteenth-century resident.

Wilbon, community in s Wake County. Also called Walthall.

Wilcox Iron Works, remains of a large stone blast furnace located at the foot of Ore Hill near Mount Vernon Springs, w central Chatham County. One of at least 3 ironworks built in the area by John Willcox (1728–93), ironmaster and landowner, during the Revolutionary era.

Wild Boar Creek formerly rose near the e shore of the mainland of Dare County s of Stumpy Point Bay and flowed e into Pamlico Sound. Erosion that opened Stumpy Point Lake into the Sound also removed all evidence of the creek. Appears on the Moseley map, 1733, and on the Collet map, 1770.

Wild Branch rises in central Madison County and flows ¾ mi. se into Hunter Creek.

Wild Branch rises in n central Madison County and flows s into Big Laurel Creek.

Wildcat Branch rises in e Franklin County and flows e into Big Peachtree Creek.

Wildcat Branch rises in s Macon County and flows se into Betty Creek.

Wildcat Branch rises in s Swain County and flows s into Brush Creek.

Wildcat Branch rises in se Transylvania County and flows nw into Reasonover Creek.

Wildcat Branch rises in central Wake County in Raleigh and flows n into Walnut Creek.

Wildcat Cliffs, on the Jackson-Macon county line se of Whiteside Mountain.

Wild Cat Cove, on the Cherokee County, N.C.–Polk County, Tenn., line between Angelica Mountain and Hays Knob.

Wildcat Creek rises in n central Avery County and flows n into Elk River.

Wildcat Creek rises in e Macon County and flows sw into North Prong Ellijay Creek.

Wildcat Gap, n Graham County at the ne end of Hogback Mountain between Sawyer Creek and Stecoah Creek.

Wildcat Gap, on the Jackson-Macon county line.

Wildcat Hollow, n Yancey County between Seng Branch and Cane River.

Wildcat Knob, n Buncombe County between Haw Knob and Carson Mountain.

Wildcat Knob, on Sassafras Ridge in s Graham County.

Wildcat Knob, on the Jackson-Macon county line.

Wildcat Knob, central Macon County between Tarkiln Ridge and Trimont Ridge.

Wildcat Knob, sw McDowell County. Alt. approx. 2,600.

Wildcat Lake, n Avery County on the campus of Lees-McRae College, Banner Elk, on Wildcat Creek. Covers 3 acres, with a max. depth of 12 ft. Fishing, swimming, and boating.

Wildcat Mountain, n Buncombe County n of Watershed Ridge between Sugar Creek and Paint Fork.

Wildcat Mountain, s Cherokee County e of Cane Creek. Almost right-angled in shape, it extends n and ne.

Wild Cat Mountain, e Davidson County between Flat Swamp Creek and Lick Creek.

Wildcat Pond, marsh in se Duplin County.

Wild Cat Rock, a rugged precipice in sw Alleghany County near Doughton Park.

Wildcat Rock, w Henderson County at the head of South Fork.

Wildcat Spring, n Haywood County on the head of Holly Bottom Branch.

Wildcat Spur, peak in nw Polk County at the head of Brights Creek.

Wildcat Swamp rises in central Bertie County and flows nw into Loosing Swamp.

Wildcat Swamp rises in central Northampton County and flows se into Potecasi Creek.

Wildcat Swamp rises in se Sampson County and flows nw into Black River.

Wildcat Top, peak on the Haywood County, N.C.–Cocke County, Tenn., line. Alt. 4,201. The Appalachian Trail passes there.

Wild Cherry Creek rises in n Swain County and flows ne into Beech Flats Prong.

Wild Cherry Ridge, n Swain County in Great Smoky Mountains National Park, a short spur of Loggy Ridge near lat. 35°32′35″ N., long. 83°31′25″ W.

Wilder. *See* Needmore.

Wilders Grove, community in e central Wake County n of Crabtree Creek.

Wilders Township, n Johnston County.

Wildes Creek rises in n Macon County and flows se into Burningtown Creek.

Wildes Knob, n Macon County at the head of Wildes Creek.

Wild Rock Mountain, se Watauga County between Joes Creek and Old House Branch.

Wild Side, The. *See* Big Pocosin.

Wildwood, community in w central Carteret County between Morehead Bluffs and Newport. Alt. 19 ft.

Wiles Creek rises in n Mitchell County and flows nw into Big Rock Creek.

Wiley Knob, s Madison County at the head of Robert Branch.

Wiley Mountain, n Buncombe County between Thurz Mountain and Chestnut Knob.

Wilgrove, community in e Mecklenburg County.

Wilhite, community in w Yancey County served by post office, 1880–1915.

Wilkerson Creek rises in w Hyde County and flows nw approx. 1½ mi. into Pungo River. Its lower course forms part of the channel of the Intracoastal Waterway.

Wilkerson Crossroads, community in w Wilson County n of Contentnea Creek.

Wilkesboro, town and county seat in s central Wilkes County on Yadkin River. North Wilkesboro, *which see*, lies just across the river. Laid out by 1801; inc. 1847. Took its name from the county. Wilkes Community College, est. 1967, is there. Alt. 1,042.

Wilkesboro Reservoir. *See* W. Kerr Scott Reservoir.

Wilkesboro Township, central Wilkes County.

Wilkes County was formed in 1778 from Surry County and the District of Washington. Located in the nw section of the state, it is bounded by Yadkin, Iredell, Alexander, Caldwell, Watauga, Ashe, Alleghany, and Surry Counties. It was named for John Wilkes (1727–97), English political leader who championed American rights at the time of the Revolution. Area: 765 sq. mi. County seat: Wilkesboro, with an elevation of 1,042 ft. Townships are Antioch, Beaver Creek, Boomer, Brushy Mountains, Edwards, Elk, Jobs Cabin, Lewis Fork, Lovelace, Moravian Falls, Mulberry, New Castle, North Wilkesboro, Reddies River, Rock Creek, Somers, Stanton, Trap Hill, Union, Walnut Grove, and Wilkesboro. Produces corn, wheat, oats, tobacco, apples, peaches, glass products, hay, poultry, livestock, hogs, furniture, mirrors, textiles, apparel, hosiery, and crushed stone.

Wilkes Cove, at the head of Iotla Creek in central Macon County.

Wilkes Gap, central Macon County at the head of Iotla Creek.

Wilkes Mill Pond in e Richmond County drains into Gum Swamp Creek.

Wilkie Gap, s Swain County on Licklog Creek.

Wilkins, community in sw Granville County served by post office, 1890–1905. Named for L. A. Wilkins, first postmaster and donor of right-of-way for railroad and land for the station. Alt. 360.

Wilkins Bluff, s Onslow County, extends into New River.

Wilkins Creek rises in n Haywood County and flows sw into Pigeon River.

Wilkinson, community in e Beaufort County.

Wilkinson Creek rises in n Chatham County and flows sw into Haw River.

Wilkinson Point, the s tip of Pamlico County extending into Neuse River. Appears on the Lawson map, 1709; called Rich Neck in local records of 1706.

Wilkinson's Lake. *See* Bakers Lake.

Wilkinson Swamp rises in w Robeson County

and flows sw into South Carolina, where it enters Little Pee Dee River.

Wilksville, community in w Robeson County served by post office, 1890–1902.

Willard, community in n Pender County served by post office since 1883. Formerly known as Camera. Alt. 50. Also known as Leesburg until renamed for the Willard family, local lumber dealers.

Willardville, community in n Durham County served by post office, 1891–1904. Alt. 438.

Will Branch rises in n Swain County and flows sw into Oconaluftee River.

Will Creek rises in n Cherokee County in the Snowbird Mountains and flows s into Hanging Dog Creek.

Willeyton, community in ne Gates County served by post office, 1886–1907.

Will Gap, s Swain County between Will Knob and the head of Little Yalaka Creek.

William B. Umstead Bridge. *See* Redstone Point; Weir Point.

William B. Umstead State Park, w Wake County 10 mi. nw of Raleigh. Est. 1943 as Crabtree Creek State Park; name changed 1955 to honor the late governor William B. Umstead (1895–1954). Contains 5,080 acres. Nature trail; camping, fishing, and boating. *See also* Reedy Creek State Park.

Williams, community in s Wayne County near Williams Millpond.

Williams, formerly an inc. town in e Yadkin County, the site now being in w Forsyth County. A whiskey distillery was operated at the site by the Williams family (who settled there about 1765) from shortly after the Revolution until 1908. On February 26, 1903, the General Assembly passed a bill prohibiting the operation of whiskey distilleries outside of inc. towns. On March 3, 1903, the town of Williams was inc. With the coming of statewide prohibition in 1908, the Williams distillery closed and the "town" ceased to exist.

Williamsboro, town in n Vance County near the head of Little Island Creek. It was authorized to be laid out in 1786 and inc. 1808. Long inactive in municipal affairs. The place was first called The Lick for a salt lick in the vicinity. It was later known as Nutbush for the creek named by William Byrd's dividing-line party in 1728 because of the profusion

of hazelnuts there. Williamsboro was named in honor of Judge John Williams (1732–99). St. John's Episcopal Church there, dating from 1757, has been restored to its original condition.

Williamsboro Township, nw Vance County.

Williams Branch rises in ne Buncombe County near Ingraham Mountain and flows sw into Dillingham Creek.

Williams Branch rises in e Swain County and flows e into Wesser Creek.

Williamsburg, former town in ne Iredell County. Commissioners appointed and town laid out 1815. Long inactive in municipal affairs.

Williamsburg, community in se Rockingham County. Known first as Thompsonville for Thomas Thompson, wagon maker. Post office by that name existed from 1848 to 1907, when the name was changed to McIver because of confusion with Thomasville. The community name remained unchanged, however, until 1960, when it became Williamsburg. In January 1840 Williamsburg School, the first public school in the state, opened here.

Williamsburg Township, se Rockingham County.

Williams Creek rises in central Cleveland County and flows sw into First Broad River.

Williams Creek rises in ne Montgomery County and flows se into Moore County, where it enters Wolf Creek.

Williams Creek rises in w Wake County and flows se into Swift Creek.

Williams Crossroads, community in s Wake County near the head of Neal Branch.

Williams Lake, nw Sampson County on Caesar Swamp. Formed about 1855 as a millpond. Covers 30 acres; max. depth 12 ft. First owned by Joel Jackson and known as Joel Jackson Pond; acquired by his daughter, who married a Williams, hence the present name.

Williams Mill Creek rises in e Anson County and flows se into Jones Creek.

Williams Millpond, s Wayne County on a tributary of Northeast Cape Fear River. Dam and corn mill built there prior to 1915 by Robert Williams, for whom it is named. Max. depth 10 ft.; area 25 acres. Fishing and boating; open to the public. Owned by Elizabeth Wooten Holmes, granddaughter of builder.

Williams Millpond. *See* Merchants Millpond.

Williams Mountain, e Haywood County, extends ne from Beaverdam Creek to Big Butte Mountain.

Williams Mountain, s Polk County. Alt. approx. 1,450.

Williams Old Mill Branch rises in central Sampson County and flows sw into Great Coharie Creek.

Williamson Branch rises in ne Wilson County and flows se into Edgecombe County, where it enters Town Creek.

Williamson Creek rises in n Rockingham County and flows ne into Dan River.

Williamson Creek rises in e Transylvania County and flows nw into French Broad River.

Williamson Crossroads, community in nw Columbus County.

Williamsons Township, sw Scotland County.

Williams Pond. *See* Nobles Mill Pond.

Williams Store, community in w Halifax County.

Williamston, town and county seat, n central Martin County on the Roanoke River. Est. 1779 as Williamstown on Thomas Hunter's plantation, Skewarky (also commonly spelled Squhawky). Named in honor of William Williams, colonel in the Revolution. Produces canned foods, chemicals, tobacco, lumber, and apparel. Alt. 60.

Williamston Township, central Martin County.

Williamstown. *See* Williamston.

Williams Township, ne Chatham County.

Williams Township, s central Columbus County.

Williams Township, ne Martin County.

Willie Knob, s Graham County between Snowbird Creek and Little Snowbird Creek.

Willis Branch rises in sw Cleveland County and flows n into Broad River.

Willis Cove, e Haywood County. An unnamed stream that rises at Big Butte Mountain flows se through the cove into North Hominy Creek.

Willis Cove, on a tributary of Iotla Creek in central Macon County.

Willis Creek, a tidal creek approx. 1 mi. long, flows e into Nelson Bay in e Carteret County.

Willis Creek, community in nw Bladen County served by post office, 1877–1908. Formerly Loveland.

Willis Creek. *See* Wade Creek.

Williston, a community in e Carteret County on Williston Creek. Named for a local family, possibly that of John Williston, who settled there in 1745.

Williston Creek rises in e Carteret County and flows se approx. 2½ mi. into Jarrett Bay.

Willits, community on Scott Creek in n Jackson County.

Will King Gap, ne Cherokee County in the Valley River Mountains near the Clay County line.

Will Mason Branch rises in sw Clay County and flows ne into Brasstown Creek. Named for a farmer who lived nearby.

Will Mason Gap, sw Clay County in Wells Mountain.

Willow, community in s Gates County on a branch of Trotman Creek. Post office est. 1878 as Willow Branch; closed 1913.

Willowbies Island. *See* Bell Island.

Willow Branch rises in e Bertie County and flows se into Chowan River.

Willow Branch. *See* Willow.

Willow Creek rises on the Buncombe-Haywood county line and flows ne across Buncombe County into Sandy Mush Creek.

Willow Creek rises in w Henderson County and flows nw into French Broad River.

Willow Falls, rapids in Cape Fear River in central Harnett County ne of the town of Lillington. Mentioned as early as 1819 in a survey of the rivers.

Willow Green, community in e Greene County. Settled prior to 1890.

Willow Point extends from the s mainland of Hyde County into Bell Bay.

Willow Springs, community in s Wake County. Settled about 1800; named for weeping willows in the vicinity. Alt. 275. Post office est. 1899.

Will Puett Cove, central Cherokee County near the headwaters of Puett Creek. Named for Will Puett, who lived in the cove in the 1860s.

Will Quarter Creek. *See* Hoggard Mill Creek.

Will Scott Creek rises in central Cherokee County and flows s and sw into Hiwassee River.

Will Scott Mountain, central Cherokee County, extends ne from Murphy.

Wills Creek rises in s Cumberland County and flows se into Cape Fear River.

Willy Knob, n central Alleghany County between Doughton and Black (formerly Carson) Mountains.

Wilmar, community in sw Beaufort and nw Craven Counties. Alt. 57.

Wilmer Branch rises in se Richmond County and flows se into Poley Branch.

Wilmet, community in nw Jackson County. Alt. 1,866.

Wilmington, city and county seat, w New Hanover County on Cape Fear River. A port for oceangoing vessels, it is approx. 30 mi. from the Atlantic Ocean. Est. 1739-40. The town had a succession of names in its earliest years. Apparently settled and first known as New Carthage about 1733. New Liverpool seems to have been used briefly, followed by New Town or Newton, the name by which it was chartered in 1739-40, and finally Wilmington. Named for Spencer Compton (1673?-1743), Earl of Wilmington, patron of Governor Gabriel Johnston, during whose administration the town was chartered. Inc. 1760. The legislature met there, 1741, 1746, 1754, 1759-60, 1760-61, and 1764. Scene of coup d'état and racial violence, 1898. Alt. 38. Produces baked goods, fabricated metals, lumber, wooden containers, textiles, apparel, dairy products, paper boxes, chemicals, and refrigeration machinery. University of North Carolina at Wilmington is there.

Wilmington Beach, s New Hanover County on the Atlantic Ocean. Est. approx. 1913.

Wilmington District, at the time of the 1790 census, was composed of Bladen, Brunswick, Duplin, New Hanover, and Onslow Counties.

Wilmington Township, w central New Hanover County, coextensive with the city of Wilmington.

Wilmot, community in n Jackson County served by post office, 1886-1922.

Wilson, community in central Buncombe County.

Wilson, city and county seat, central Wilson County. Alt. 147. An early community at the site that developed around Toisnot Baptist Church (est. 1803) was known as Hickory Grove. Tosnot Depot, est. on the railroad there about 1840, became the post office name. In 1849 Tosnot Depot and Hickory Grove were inc. as Wilson, named in honor of Capt. Louis D. Wilson (1789-1847), who died at Vera Cruz during the War with Mexico. Barton College is there. Long the site of large

tobacco market. Produces textiles, apparel, concrete pipe, lumber products, processed meat, and grain. *See also* Hominy Heights.

Wilson. *See* Yadkinville.

Wilson Branch rises in central Cherokee County and flows se into Morgan Creek.

Wilson Branch rises in e Madison County and flows s into Big Laurel Creek.

Wilson County was formed in 1855 from Edgecombe, Nash, Johnston, and Wayne Counties. Located in the e central section of the state, it is bounded by Pitt, Greene, Wayne, Johnston, Nash, and Edgecombe Counties. It was named for Louis D. Wilson (1789-1847), delegate to the Constitutional Convention of 1835 and an officer in the War with Mexico. Area: 373 sq. mi. County seat: Wilson, with an elevation of 147 ft. Townships are Black Creek, Cross Roads, Gardner, Old Fields, Saratoga, Springhill, Stantonsburg, Taylor, Toisnot, and Wilson. Produces tobacco, corn, wheat, oats, soybeans, cotton, poultry, tobacco products, textiles, apparel, tires, sweet potatoes, concrete pipe, motor-vehicle parts, lumber products, and processed meat.

Wilson Creek rises in e Avery County near Grandfather Mountain and flows se into Caldwell County, where it enters Johns River at the Burke County line.

Wilson Creek rises in central Craven County and flows s into Trent River.

Wilson Creek rises in w Jackson County and flows e into Cullowhee Creek.

Wilson Creek Township, w Caldwell County.

Wilson Gap, se Macon County between Clear Creek and Little Creek.

Wilson Hollow, nw Watauga County, extends e from Little Beaverdam Creek.

Wilson Knob, e Mitchell County at the head of Bear Creek.

Wilson Knob Mountain. *See* Big Butte.

Wilson Mill Creek rises in w central Transylvania County and flows se into Catheys Creek.

Wilson Mountain extends ne in n Watauga County n of North Fork River.

Wilson Ridge, n Avery County.

Wilson Ridge extends from se Avery County into nw Caldwell County. Alt. varies from 2,500 to 2,696.

Wilson Ridge, s Yancey County near the head of Big Poplar Creek and the head of Beech Nursery Creek.

Wilsons Bay, central Onslow County in New River s of the city of Jacksonville.

Wilsons Creek Township, e Avery County.

Wilson's Factory, town inc. 1883 to be laid out on the bank of the South Fork of Catawba River in Gaston County. There is no evidence that it ever existed as a town.

Wilson's Mills, town in n Johnston County. Settled about 1868; inc. 1927 and named for local family. Alt. 228.

Wilson's Mills Township, n central Johnston County.

Wilson's Old Store. *See* Walkersville.

Wilson's Pond, nw Wilson County on Marsh Swamp. Formed about 1900. Covers 15 acres; max. depth 12 ft. Named for Sanford Wilson, owner. Used for fishing, swimming, boating, and irrigation.

Wilsons Store, community in ne Orange County.

Wilson Township, central Wilson County.

Wilsonville, community in e central Chatham County. Named for Cecil Wilson, owner of a store there.

Wilton, community in se Granville County at the head of Sand Creek. A post office operated there, 1826–1907.

Wilton, town authorized by the General Assembly in 1818 to be est. on the lands of Sias Billingsby Sr. at the mouth of Clarks Creek, sw Montgomery County. There is no evidence that the town was ever laid out.

Wimberly. *See* Coniott Landing.

Wimble Shoals, in the Atlantic Ocean off the community of Salvo on Hatteras Island, e Dare County. The shoals are at the approx. site of the former Cape Kenrick, *which see*. They were charted and given the present name by James Wimble in, or shortly prior to, 1738.

Winchester, former community in w Union County between West Fork Twelvemile Creek and East Fork Twelvemile Creek.

Winchester Cove, central Clay County near the headwaters of Greasy Creek.

Winchester Creek rises in Towns County, Ga., and flows nw into Clay County, where it enters Brasstown Creek.

Winchester Creek rises in w Haywood County and flows se into Richland Creek.

Wind Blow, community in se Montgomery County. Named about 1920 by S. R. Gaddy because it was believed that the wind would blow there if it blew anywhere in the area.

Winder. *See* Vass.

Winders Crossroads, community in sw Yadkin County.

Windfall Creek rises in n Ashe County and flows se into Horse Creek.

Wind Hill, community in nw Montgomery County served by post office, 1832–66.

Winding Knob, w Haywood County on the e end of Balsam Ridge.

Winding Stair Branch, w Haywood County in Great Smoky Mountains National Park, rises near lat. 35°38'13" N., long. 83°02'55" W., and flows nw into Cataloochee Creek.

Winding Stair Gap, at the head of Poplar Cove Branch in sw Macon County.

Windingstair Knob, nw Burke County. Alt. 3,473.

Winding Stairs, section of road in nw Macon County between Queens Creek and the Macon-Swain county line; winds about 5 mi. down a ½ mi. drop and gives the appearance of winding stairs. Present road laid out about 1923 along a pioneer or Indian trail that, before the Civil War, was sometimes referred to as the Cat's Stairs.

Wind Mill Creek. *See* Jacks Creek.

Windmill Point extends from w Carteret County into White Oak River. Named for the fact that a wind-powered gristmill was once operated there. Also known as Hatchell's Point for Armistead Hatchell, who settled there in the eighteenth century.

Windmill Point, point of land at the entrance to Silver Lake, Ocracoke Island in se Hyde County.

Windmill Point extends into Bay River in n Pamlico County.

Windmill Point. *See* Nixonton.

Windom, community in e central Yancey County on Little Crabtree Creek.

Windsor, town and county seat, central Bertie County. Settled 1722; est. 1768; became county seat 1774. Built on the family estate of William Gray and was known originally as Gray's Landing. Windsor was named for the royal castle near London, England. Post office est. 1794. In 1959 Windsor annexed Bertie, a small town across the Cashie River. The site is head of navigation for the Cashie River. Alt. 10. *See also* Hoggard's Mill.

Windsors, community in e Wilkes County named for Isaac Windsor, early settler.

Windsor Township, s central Bertie County.

Windy Gap, n Buncombe County between North Knob and Chestnut Knob.

Windy Gap, e Haywood County on the e end of Chestnut Mountain.

Windy Gap, w Jackson County on the head of Tatham Creek.

Windy Gap, at the head of Rocky Branch in central Macon County.

Windy Gap, on the Madison-Yancey county line in the Walnut Mountains.

Windy Gap, s Swain County s of Licklog Creek near Little Tennessee River.

Windy Gap, community in se Wilkes County on Little Hunting Creek.

Windy Point, on the n side of Pettivers Creek at its junction with White Oak River.

Wine Spring Bald, w Macon County between Middle Ridge and Rocky Bald. Alt. 5,445.

Wine Spring Creek rises on McDonald Ridge, w Macon County, and flows nw into Nantahala Lake.

Wines Top, peak at sw end of Glade Mountain in e Haywood County. Alt. approx. 4,375.

Winfall, town in central Perquimans County. Inc. 1887. Alt. 16.

Winfrey Gap, on the Cherokee-Clay county line. Alt. 3,493.

Wing, community in w central Mitchell County on Snow Creek. Named for Charles Hallet Wing (1836–1915), professor at Massachusetts Institute of Technology, who settled nearby and in 1887 opened a lending library of about 15,000 volumes. It was the first free public library in the state and the third county library in the United States. *See also* Ledger.

Wingate, town in e central Union County; post office, 1896. Formerly known as Ames. Inc.

1901 as Wingate. Home of Wingate University. Produces wood products. Alt. 575.

Winkler Creek rises in s Watauga County and flows ne into Flannery Fork [South Fork New River].

Winklertown, community in ne Caldwell County on Donahues Creek.

Winnabow, community in e central Brunswick County. Named for the plantation of Governor Daniel Russell, which, in turn, had an Indian name of unknown meaning. Called Evans Store Crossroads during the Civil War. Alt. 40.

Winnie. *See* White Oak.

Winona, community in n Richmond County served by post office, 1892–94.

Winslow, community in n Harnett County served by post office, 1858–1904.

Winstead, community in w central Person County served by post office, 1873–1910.

Winstead Crossroads, community in s Nash County.

Winsteadville, community in e Beaufort County served by post office, 1892–1909.

Winston, formerly an independent city in central Forsyth County. Authorized by act of 1849 creating Forsyth County and named the county seat in 1851. Since 1913 it has been consolidated with Salem as Winston-Salem, *which see*. Named for Maj. Joseph Winston (1746–1814), Revolutionary War leader.

Winston Lake, central Forsyth County on Brushy Fork Branch. Known earlier as City Lake. Covers 100 acres, with a max. depth of 20 ft. Used for fishing and municipal water supply. Owned by the city of Winston-Salem; open to the public.

Winston-Salem, city and county seat, central Forsyth County. Formed in 1913 by the consolidation of Winston and Salem, *which see*, previously independent towns. Winston-Salem State University, Salem College, Wake Forest University, and the University of North Carolina School of the Arts are there. Produces tobacco, textiles, hosiery, bakery products, machinery, fabricated metals, furniture, corrugated boxes, apparel, and processed meat. Alt. 858.

Winston Township, central Forsyth County, coextensive with the city of Winston-Salem.

Winter Park, community on the e outskirts

of the city of Wilmington, w New Hanover County. Alt. 45.

Winter Star Ridge, s Yancey County between South Fork Cattail Creek and North Fork Cattail Creek.

Winterville, town in s Pitt County. Inc. 1897. Alt. 72.

Winterville Township, s central Pitt County; formerly Contentnea Township.

Winthrop, community in ne Carteret County served by post office, 1888–1908.

Winton, town and county seat, e Hertford County on Chowan River. Authorized to be laid out and est. 1768 on the land of Benjamin Wynns, for whom it was named. Appears as Wynnton in eighteenth-century records and as recently as on the Tanner map, 1827. Produces aluminum castings. Alt. 45.

Winton Township, e Hertford County.

Wiquemans. *See* Perquimans River.

Wisaoky. *See* Waxhaws, The.

Wise, community in n Warren County between Malones Creek and Sauls Creek. Alt. 392. Settled in 1890s and named for Henry Wise, local resident. A post office was est. there in 1891 but was discontinued in 1951.

Wise Branch rises in sw Buncombe County and flows ne into Bill Moore Creek.

Wise Forks. *See* Wyse Forks.

Wise Knob, sw Buncombe County near the headwaters of Bill Moore Creek.

Wiseman's View, an overlook for Linville Gorge in nw Burke County. Named for William Wiseman, early settler who migrated from London in the eighteenth century.

Wise's Crossroads. *See* Gum Swamp; Wise Forks.

Wishart Township, se Robeson County.

Wis's Creek. *See* Long Creek.

Wit. *See* Smyrna.

Withers, community in se Stokes County served by post office, 1884–1905.

Withrow Creek rises in s Iredell County and flows ne into Rowan County, where it joins Back Creek in forming North Second Creek. Appears as North Fork [Second Creek] on the Collet Map, 1770.

Witness Rock Ridge, n McDowell County on the s side of Armstrong Creek.

Wittenburg, community in s Alexander County. Named for Daniel Wittenburg, who settled in the vicinity about 1830. A post office, 1807–1909.

Wittenburg Township, sw Alexander County.

Wittys Crossroads, community in s Rockingham County. Aspen Grove was a nearby post office, 1899–1902.

W. Kerr Scott Reservoir, sw Wilkes County on Yadkin River. Formed by a dam completed in 1962. Covers 1,470 acres, with a shoreline of 55 mi. Alt. 1,030. Named for William Kerr Scott (1896–1958), governor of North Carolina and U.S. senator. Constructed for flood control and public recreation.

Wococon Inlet. *See* Wococon Island.

Wococon Island appears on the White map, 1585, as composed of parts of the present Ocracoke and Portsmouth Islands in Hyde and Carteret Counties. Port Grenvil, *which see*, formed its n limit and Wococon Inlet (an inlet, now closed, in Portsmouth Island) the s limit. Name probably derived from the Indian word *wahkahikani* (enclosed place; stockade). Appears as Gordens Island on the Smith map, 1624. *See also* Portsmouth Island.

Wohanoke. *See* Ohanoak.

Wolf, community in central Person County served by post office, 1900–1902.

Wolf Bald, on the Haywood-Jackson county line.

Wolf Branch rises in se Alamance County and flows sw into Motes Creek.

Wolf Branch rises in s central Alleghany County and flows e into Glade Creek.

Wolf Branch rises in central Buncombe County near Wolf Knob and flows se into Shope Creek.

Wolf Branch rises in ne Buncombe County and flows w into Beetree Creek.

Wolf Branch rises in s Cleveland County and flows nw into Long Branch.

Wolf Branch rises in n Madison County and flows s into Big Laurel Creek.

Wolf Branch rises in s Montgomery County and flows se into Little Hamer Creek.

Wolf Branch rises in w Yancey County and flows s into Fox Creek.

Wolf Cove, the valley through which Wolf Cove Branch flows in central Buncombe County.

Wolf Cove Branch rises in central Buncombe County near Asheville and flows nw into Beaverdam Creek.

Wolf Creek rises in s Buncombe County near Stradley Mountain and flows se into Bent Creek.

Wolf Creek rises in se Cherokee County and flows sw into Fannin County, Ga., where it enters Ocoee River.

Wolf Creek rises in ne Graham County and flows ne into Little Tennessee River.

Wolf Creek rises in e Jackson County and flows sw into Tuckasegee River.

Wolf Creek rises in w Jackson County and flows nw into Cullowhee Creek.

Wolf Creek rises in w Macon County and flows se into Nantahala Lake.

Wolf Creek rises in ne Montgomery County near the town of Star and flows e into n Moore County, where it enters Bear Creek.

Wolf Creek rises in e Surry County and flows n into Chinquapin Creek.

Wolf Creek, community in sw Cherokee County on Wolf Creek. Served by post office, 1858–1904.

Wolf Creek Falls, on Wolf Creek in Canada Township of e Jackson County. Consists of a series of five separate falls, one being approx. 85 ft. high and the others averaging 35 ft. Located above Wolf Creek Lake.

Wolf Creek Gap, on the Cherokee-Macon county line.

Wolf Creek Lake, in central Jackson County on Wolf Creek. Formed in 1955 as a reservoir for Nantahala Power and Light Co. Covers 183 acres, with a max. depth of 170 ft. Shoreline is 6.9 mi. Used for generation of hydroelectric power. Named for Wolf Creek. *See also* East Fork Lake.

Wolfden Branch rises in s Watauga County and flows sw into Buffalo Creek.

Wolfden Knob, n Buncombe County between Rich Knob and Lane Pinnacle.

Wolfden Ridge, e Mitchell County at the head of Little Bear Creek.

Wolfert Creek. *See* Tusk Creek.

Wolf Gap, s Macon County between Turkey Knob and Buck Knob.

Wolfharbor Branch rises in s Franklin County and flows se into Nash County, where it enters Turkey Creek.

Wolf House Point, neck of land extending into waters of Currituck Sound on the w side of Church Island in e Currituck County.

Wolfington. *See* Hoggard's Mill.

Wolf Island Creek rises in s central Rockingham County and flows ne into nw Caswell County, where it turns n to flow into Dan River.

Wolf Knob, central Buncombe County ne of Swan Mountain.

Wolf Knob, central Cherokee County near the head of Rose Creek.

Wolf Knob, on the Jackson-Macon county line.

Wolf Knob, on Jackson-Swain county line near the head of Yalaka Creek. Alt. approx. 4,900.

Wolf Knob, on the Watauga-Wilkes county line e of the head of Stony Fork Creek.

Wolf Laurel Basin, depression between Fork Ridge and nw end of Horse Cove Ridge in w Graham County.

Wolf Laurel Branch rises in w central Haywood County and flows e into Jonathan's Creek.

Wolf Mountain, s Henderson County at the head of South Fork.

Wolf Mountain extends ne in e Jackson County between Wolf Creek and Tanasee Creek.

Wolf Mountain, n Madison County between Lewis Branch and Wolf Branch.

Wolf Mountain, community in se Jackson County on Tanasee Creek served by post office, 1876–1903.

Wolf Pen Branch rises in central Franklin County and flows se into Tar River. Now generally called Wolf Pit Branch.

Wolfpen Creek rises in central Henderson County and flows nw into Clear Creek. Also known locally as Bengle Creek.

Wolfpen Gap, n Buncombe County between Ramsey Mountain and Bruce Knob.

Wolf Pen Gap, sw Cherokee County on the headwaters of Persimmon Creek.

Wolfpen Gap, n Jackson County between Black Mountain and West Fork [Moses Creek].

Wolfpen Gap, n Jackson County between East Fork [Dicks Creek] and Dills Creek.

Wolfpen Gap, s Haywood County in Wolfpen Mountain.

Wolfpen Gap, central Macon County between Willis Cove and Trimont Ridge.

Wolfpen Gap, s Macon County between Rockhouse Knob and Dryman Fork.

Wolf Pen Mountain, e Caldwell County. Alt. 2,137.

Wolfpen Mountain, s Haywood County on the head of Farmer Branch and the head of Camp Branch. Alt. approx. 3,200.

Wolfpit Branch rises in se Buncombe County and flows nw into Swannanoa River.

Wolf Pit Branch. *See* Wolf Pen Branch.

Wolf Pit Creek rises on the Fort Bragg Military

Reservation in w Hoke County and flows ne into Rockfish Creek.

Wolf Pit Gap, e Haywood County between Millstone Mountain and Buck Cove Mountain.

Wolfpit Gap, w central Yancey County near the head of Jacks Creek.

Wolf Pit Township, sw Richmond County. In colonial times, it is said, the area was overrun with wolves. A trap was constructed for them, but the first animal to fall into it was a mule owned by a prominent farmer. Scottish settlers were so amused they gave the region the name of Wolf Pit.

Wolf Pond, community in s Union County.

Wolf Ridge, nw Cherokee County, extends ne between Gowans Cove and Hipps Ridge.

Wolf Ridge, n Clay County, extends ne from Tar Kiln Ridge to Trail Ridge.

Wolf Ridge, e Mitchell County between Charlies Ridge and Rube Green Top.

Wolf Ridge, n Mitchell County between the forks of Gouges Creek.

Wolf Ridge, nw Swain County in Great Smoky Mountains National Park, a spur extending se from Parson Bald.

Wolf Ridge, central Watauga County, extends ne from Rich Mountain to Howard Creek.

Wolf Rock, peak in s Macon County between Fishhawk Mountain and Tater Hill.

Wolfscrape Township, nw Duplin County.

Wolfsville, community in s Union County.

Wolf Swamp rises in n Onslow County and flows se into Northeast Creek.

Womacks Mill, community in central Caswell County; named for the mill on Country Line Creek.

Wood, community in ne Franklin County served by post office, 1900–1957. Alt. 350. Settled about 1893 and known as Woods Store until 1913. Inc. as Wood in 1917; charter repealed 1961.

Wood, community in central Rockingham County served by post office, 1891–95.

Woodard, community in se Bertie County served by post office, 1893–1945.

Woodard Mountains, e Madison County between California Creek and Middle Fork.

Woodard's Pond, e Wilson County, was formed in 1954 by the construction of a dam across a natural hollow between two hills. Covers 12 acres; max. depth 14 ft. Named for W. D.

Woodard, owner. Used for fishing, swimming, boating, and irrigation.

Woodburn, community in ne Brunswick County.

Woodburn. *See* McGehees Mill.

Woodby Gap, n Yancey County between Hawk Branch and Byrds Branch.

Woodcock Knob, w Caldwell County. Alt. approx. 2,500.

Wood Cove, swamp in central Pender County on Northeast Cape Fear River.

Woodenton. *See* Woodington.

Woodfin, community in central Buncombe County on the e bank of French Broad River nw of Asheville.

Woodford, community in nw Ashe County.

Wood Fork Branch rises in n Surry County and flows se into Beaverdam Creek.

Wood Grove. *See* Mount Ulla.

Woodington, community in s Lenoir County. Named by Richard Caswell, who acquired a plantation there about 1767 before becoming governor. Name sometimes appears as Woodenton in nineteenth-century records.

Woodington Township, se Lenoir County.

Wood Island, in the mouth of Cashie River in se Bertie County. Approx. 2,000 ft. long and 200 ft. wide. *See also* Purchace Islands.

Wood Island, a small island in sw Carteret County in Bogue Sound.

Wood Lake, ne Cherokee County, is formed by a dam on Thrash Creek. Covers approx. 8 acres, with a max. depth of 35 ft.

Woodland, town in e Northampton County. Alt. 72. Inc. 1883. Settled about 1835. Named for the Wood family, early Quaker settlers. Produces lumber. *See also* George.

Woodlawn, community in nw McDowell County in Turkey Cove and on Limekiln Creek. Site of Cathey's Fort, a rendezvous point for the state militia led by Gen. Griffith Rutherford against the Cherokee Indians in 1776.

Woodlawn. *See* Mount Holly.

Woodleaf, town in n Rowan County. Inc. 1909, but long inactive in municipal affairs. A post office was est. there in 1855 with Daniel Wood as first postmaster. Alt. 711. A large gravel pit is worked there.

Woodleigh, community on Knotts Island in ne Currituck County.

Woodley, community in nw Tyrrell County between Scuppernong River and the Tyrrell-Washington county line. Originated as a depot, but tracks and depot no longer in use.

Wood Mountain, between Mill Creek and Pine Creek in sw Jackson County.

Woodpin Creek rises in n Jackson County and flows sw into Scott Creek.

Woodpin Falls, in the headwaters of Woodpin Creek in n Jackson County.

Woodrow, community in s Haywood County. Alt. 2,700. Named for President Woodrow Wilson.

Woodruff Branch rises in s Transylvania County and flows ne into West Fork French Broad River.

Woodrun Creek rises in w Montgomery County and flows sw into Pee Dee River.

Woods Branch rises in central Jackson County and flows sw into Tuckasegee River.

Woodsdale, community in n Person County. Settled about 1800. Named for the Hugh Woods family, early residents. Alt. 482.

Woodsdale Township, n central Person County.

Wood's Ferry formerly crossed the Haw River in se Alamance County approx. 2 mi. below Saxapahaw. Mentioned in local records prior to the Revolution.

Woods Gap, ne Rutherford County at the ne end of the Richland Mountains.

Woodside, community in s Pender County.

Woodside. *See* Granite Quarry.

Woods Knob, s Mitchell County between Pony Ridge and South Fork [Carvers Branch]. Alt. 2,248.

Woods Millpond, e Wayne County on a tributary of West Bear Creek.

Woods Mountain, nw McDowell County, a series of small peaks. Max. alt. 3,646.

Woodson Branch rises in w central Madison County and flows n into Big Laurel Creek.

Woods Pond. *See* Parrish's Pond.

Woods Store. *See* Wood.

Woodstock Point, e Beaufort County on Pungo River. In 1739 a town named Woodstock was laid out there to serve as the county seat of Hyde County. The courthouse burned in 1789, and the following year the county seat was moved. Remains of the old courthouse may still be seen at low tide off Woodstock Point. A post office at Woodstock operated until 1825.

Woodstock Savanna, e Beaufort County between Pungo Creek and Pamlico River.

Wood Swamp. *See* Hood Swamp.

Woodsworth, community in n Vance County.

Woodville, town in nw Bertie County. Appears on the MacRae map, 1833, as Hotel, which was the post office name from 1840 through 1865. Inc. as Woodville 1911, taking the name of the Whitmell Hill Pugh home, which had been named for an estate in England. Adjacent to Lewiston, *which see*; Lewiston is the railroad name for Woodville. Post office operated as Woodville, 1912–65.

Woodville, community in ne Cherokee County in Nantahala National Forest.

Woodville, community in e Perquimans County on Little River. An early Quaker settlement. A post office operated there, 1820–1910.

Woodville, community in ne Surry County near Big Creek.

Woodville Township, w Bertie County.

Woodward Knob, nw Swain County in Great Smoky Mountains National Park on Jenkins Trail Ridge near lat. 35°31′ N., long. 83°43′02″ W. Alt. 3,939.

Woodward's Crossroads. *See* Pendleton.

Woodworth, community in n Vance County served by post office, 1831–1914.

Woody Branch rises in n Cherokee County in the Snowbird Mountains and flows sw into Will Creek.

Woody Branch rises in nw Haywood County at n end of Fork Mountain and flows 1½ mi. se to join Conrad Creek in forming Little Cataloochee Creek.

Woody Branch rises in n central Henderson County and flows se into Boylston Creek.

Woody Creek, w Haywood County in Great Smoky Mountains National Park, rises near lat. 35°35′ N., long. 83°10′20″ W., and flows ne into Ugly Fork.

Woody Ridge, w Haywood County in Great Smoky Mountains National Park, a short spur extending ne from Balsam Mountain; center near lat. 35°35′30″ N., long. 83°10′ W.

Woody's Ferry. *See* Newmarket.

Woolard Crossroads, community in nw Beaufort County.

Wooleyshot Branch rises in sw Madison County w of Hap Mountain and flows s and w into Spring Creek.

Woolly Ridge, nw Swain County in Great Smoky Mountains National Park, a short spur extending se from Blockhouse Ridge. Its center is near lat. 35°32′58″ N., long. 83°41′37″ W.

Woolsey. *See* Ramoth.

Woolsey Branch rises in n Madison County on the s slope of Walnut Knob and flows s and w into French Broad River at Stackhouse.

Wooly Ridge Branch rises in w Swain County in Great Smoky Mountains National Park and flows se into Nunda Branch.

Wooten Millpond, e Wayne County on Walnut Creek. Named for Shadrach Wooten, Revolutionary War soldier, who moved to Columbus County in 1805. Descendants still live in the area.

Wooten Mountain, e Macon County between Cat Creek and Rabbit Creek.

Wootens Creek rises in n Wilkes County and flows se into Mulberry Creek.

Wootens Crossroads, community in n central Greene County. Named for the Wooten family, which ran a store there in the 1920s and 1930s.

Wootens Crossroads, community in n Lenoir County. Named for a family that long operated a store there.

Wootentown, community in central Beaufort County 1 mi. e of Washington Park. Alt. 14. Misspelled Hootentown frequently because that is the way the name is pronounced locally. An African American community on land originally owned by Harkness Wooten, a free black in the antebellum period. Many inhabitants are descended from him.

Wootonton. *See* Fair Bluff.

Worcester Inlet. *See* Trinity Harbor.

Worlds Edge, high bluff s of Chinquapin Gap, nw Polk County. Views to e extend 40 mi. to Forest City. Property, adjacent to Chimney Rock State Park tract, under conservation easement.

Worley, community in s Madison County on Big Pine Creek.

Worley Branch rises in e Swain County and flows se into Galbreath Creek.

Worley Cove, nw Buncombe County near the Madison County line.

Worley Cove, e Haywood County on the head of North Hominy Creek.

Worley Cove Branch rises in s Madison County and flows se into Sandy Mush Creek. The name Red Horse Creek is also applied to the stream.

Worley Knob, e Swain County on the head of Worley Branch.

Worm Creek rises in ne Cherokee County and flows sw and nw into Valley River.

Worrell Mill Pond, ne Northampton County on Kirbys Creek. Prior to about 1916, when M. E. Worrell purchased the mill, it was known as Watson's Mill. For a time, a generator there produced electricity for the town of Murfreesboro, 3 mi. s. A marl cliff near the millrace has yielded evidence of at least ten species of marine life.

Worrells Mill Pond, w Hertford County at the junction of Hares and Institute Branches. Formed prior to 1842 and known first as Griffith's Mill Pond. Covers 75 acres, with a max. depth of 17 ft.

Worry, community in n central Burke County about 6 mi. nw of town of Morganton. Named by Jane Elizabeth Caldwell, who, according to local legend, had submitted several names that were rejected; troubled by the dilemma, she proposed Worry, which was selected.

Worsley Creek. *See* Chocowinity Creek.

Worth. *See* Hardin.

Worth's Mill. *See* Worthville.

Worthville, community in n Randolph County on Deep River. Settled approx. 1810 and known as Hopper's Ford for Charles Hopper, local resident. With the est. of a cotton mill by J. M. and Hal M. Worth about 1881, it came to be called Worth's Mill. Inc. 1895 as Worthville; charter repealed 1920.

Wrendale, community in n Edgecombe County served by post office, 1888–1902.

Wright Branch rises in central Haywood County and flows se into Jonathan Creek.

Wright Brothers National Memorial, on n Bodie Island, e Dare County. Includes the Kill Devil Hills Monument National Memorial, the reconstructed Wright hangar and workshop, and visitor center. Occupies 314 acres.

Wright Cove, s Buncombe County sw of Ballard Gap.

Wright Cove, the valley through which Crawford Creek flows in s Clay County.

Wright Creek rises in e Beaufort County and flows n into Pungo River near Pamlico Beach.

Wright Creek rises in ne Cherokee County and flows se into Valley River.

Wright Creek rises in w Graham County and flows ne into Santeetlah Creek.

Wright Knob, central Haywood County between Morrow Branch and Wright Branch.

Wright Memorial Bridge. *See* Currituck Sound; Kitty Hawk.

Wrightsboro, community in n New Hanover County. Alt. approx. 35.

Wrights Creek rises in n Jackson County and flows sw into Soco Creek.

Wrights Island, s Onslow County on the ne side of New River Inlet.

Wrights Station. *See* Lowell.

Wrightsville, former community in nw Duplin County near the present site of Faison, *which see*. Appears on the MacRae map, 1833, but apparently declined after the est. of Faison.

Wrightsville, community on the mainland of e New Hanover County near the mouth of Bradleys Creek and Middle Sound. Settled about 1780. Known at one time as Wrightsville Sound. Named for Joshua G. Wright (1840–94) of Wilmington, organizer of a real estate agency.

Wrightsville Beach, island approx. 4 mi. long, e New Hanover County between Atlantic Ocean and Wrightsville Sound.

Wrightsville Beach, town in e New Hanover County on Wrightsville Beach island between the Atlantic Ocean and Wrightsville Sound. Settled about 1889; inc. 1899. Alt. 5. Summer resort.

Wrightsville Inlet. *See* Moore Inlet.

Wrightsville Sound, e New Hanover County w of Wrightsville Beach island. *See also* Wrightsville.

Wriston, community in w Mecklenburg County served by post office, 1899–1902.

Wyanoke, community in nw Gates County on Chowan River.

Wyant Branch rises in sw Macon County and flows sw into Long Branch.

Wyatt, community in n Wake County near Smiths Creek. Served by post office, 1891–1910.

Wycle Creek rises in w central Haywood County and flows e into Jonathans Creek.

Wye, community in e Harnett County 1 mi. ne of Erwin; there, the railroad has a "Y" connection, with one line leading to Erwin and the other to Dunn.

Wyesocking Bay, in Pamlico Sound, e Hyde County, bounded by Long Point on the ne and by Hog Island Point on the sw. The Collet map, 1770, shows Yesocking Creek flowing into the bay, unnamed on the map. The creek named by Collet no longer exists since a canal has been dug at or near its course. The Indian word from which Wyesocking has developed is believed to have been *wayäci*, which, in combination with another word, meant "directly" or "straightaway," referring to a landing place.

Wykle Hill, n Macon County between the head of Hampton Branch and Queens Creek.

Wynn Creek rises in se Alamance County and flows w into Haw Creek.

Wynn Ferry, formerly in n Tyrrell County on Scuppernong River s of Columbia.

Wynnton. *See* Winton.

Wyo, community on the Davie-Yadkin county line. Named for local church. Served by post office, 1891–1907.

Wyse Forks, community in nw Jones County. Named for local family. Known as Wyse's Crossroads in 1863, when a Civil War engagement took place there on April 28. The battle is referred to variously as Wyse's Crossroads, Dover Crossroads, and First Gum Swamp. *See also* Gum Swamp.

Wysner Mountain, n Montgomery County near Barnes Creek.

Wythe, community in central Harnett County served by post office, 1890–1905.

Xenia, community in central Duplin County served by post office, 1891–1903. Name derived from Greek word meaning hospitality.

Xuala. *See* Fort San Juan.

X-Way. *See* Exway.

Yadkin, community in e Rowan County at Yadkin River. A large textile mill is there.

Yadkin College, town in w Davidson County on Yadkin River. Inc. 1875, but long inactive in municipal affairs. Named for the Methodist Protestant college opened there in 1865, closed in 1924. One college building and the ruins of another remain.

Yadkin College Township, w central Davidson County.

Yadkin County was formed in 1850 from Surry County. Located in the n central section of the state, it is bounded by Forsyth, Davie, Iredell, Wilkes, and Surry Counties. It was named for Yadkin River, *which see*. Area: 335 sq. mi. County seat: Yadkinville, with an elevation of 960 ft. Townships are Boonville, Buck Shoal, Deep Creek, East Bend, Fall Creek, Forbush, Knobs, and Liberty. Produces tobacco, corn, wheat, oats, poultry, textiles, machinery, plastics, barley, crushed granite, and limestone.

Yadkin Creek rises in s Watauga County and flows s into Caldwell County.

Yadkin Narrows. *See* Narrows of the Yadkin.

Yadkin River rises in s Watauga County near Blowing Rock and flows se into Caldwell County, where it turns ne to flow through Wilkes County and along the Surry-Yadkin, Yadkin-Forsyth, Davie-Forsyth, Davie-David-son, Davidson-Rowan, and a part of the Mont-gomery-Stanly county lines. It is then joined by the Uwharrie River in forming the Pee Dee River. Called Sapona River by John Lawson in 1709. Appears as "Sapona or Yadkin River" on the Moseley map, 1733. The Sapona Indians lived in the area, but the origin or meaning of Yadkin is uncertain. It was also spelled Yatkin, Atkin, Reatkin, and other ways in the eighteenth century.

Yadkin Township, sw Stokes County.

Yadkin Valley, community in ne Caldwell County served by post office, 1884–1953.

Yadkin Valley, community in ne Davie County.

Yadkin Valley Township, ne Caldwell County.

Yadkinville, town and county seat, central Yadkin County. Commissioners in 1850 authorized to select site and lay off county seat to be named Wilson. Name changed to Yadkinville 1852; town chartered 1857. Alt. 960.

Yalaka Creek rises in se Swain County and flows nw into Little Tennessee River. Sometimes also called Alarka Creek.

Yalaka Mountains extend se from the head of East Fork [Kirkland Creek] in s Swain County to the head of Upper Long Creek in se Swain County. Sometimes also called Alarka Mountains.

Yale, community in w Henderson County. Alt. 2,104.

Yamacraw, community in w Pender County.

Yancey, community in e Person County served by post office, 1894–1903.

Yancey Branch rises in s Cleveland County and flows se into First Broad River.

Yancey County was formed in 1833 from Burke and Buncombe Counties. Located in the w section of the state, it is bounded by the state of Tennessee and by Mitchell, McDowell, Buncombe, and Madison Counties. It was named for Bartlett Yancey (1785–1828), member of the General Assembly and Congress. Area: 311 sq. mi. County seat: Burnsville, with an elevation of 2,817 ft. Townships are Brush Creek, Burnsville, Cane River, Crab-tree, Egypt, Green Mountain, Jacks Creek, Pensacola, Price Creek, Ramseytown, and South Toe. Produces corn, oats, poultry, dairy products, livestock, hogs, hosiery, carpets, lumber, hay, textiles, mica, feldspar, olivine, sand, and gravel.

Yancey Ridge, e Avery County.

Yanceyville, community and county seat in central Caswell County. Est. 1791 as Caswell Court House; name changed to Yanceyville in 1833 to honor Bartlett Yancey (1785–1828), congressman and presiding officer of the state senate. Inc. 1877; charter repealed 1915. Produces textiles and lumber. Alt. 619.

Yanceyville Township, central Caswell County.

Yanu Ridge, n Swain County in Great Smoky Mountains National Park, a short spur extending se from Welch Ridge with its center near lat. 35°32′ N., long. 83°34′40″ W.

Yarbro, community in ne Caswell County. Named for Capt. Joseph Yarbrough, superintendent of ammunition manufacturing in Salisbury during the Civil War. A post office operated there, 1887–1904.

Yarnall Knob, s Watauga County n of Goldmine Branch. Alt. approx. 3,900.

Yates Cove, central Haywood County between Fincher Mountain and McElroy Cove.

Yates Mill Pond. *See* Lake Trojan.

Yates Mountain, w Wilkes County, extends from e to w between North and South Prongs Lewis Fork Creek.

Yates Top, s Cherokee County s of Shingle Top and between Cane, Martin, and Moccasin Creeks.

Yaupon Beach, town in se Brunswick County. Inc. 1955. Named for a species of holly that grows in the area.

Yaupon Creek, a bay in e Pamlico County in the waters of Bay River.

Yawpim appears on the Moseley map, 1733, as a community in e Pasquotank Precinct, now Camden County, on North River. The name survives elsewhere as Yeopim, *which see*.

Yeates Knob. *See* Big Butte.

Yeatesville, town in e Beaufort County on Pungo Creek. Inc. 1881, but long inactive in municipal affairs. Named for Jesse J. Yeates (1829–92), Confederate officer and member of Congress.

Yellow Bald, s Macon County between Hurricane Creek and Bearpen Creek.

Yellow Branch rises in ne Swain County and flows se into Raven Fork.

Yellow Buck Ridge, n Caldwell County. Named by Bryson Coffey for a large yellow buck that he killed there. Alt. approx. 1,500.

Yellow Creek rises in n Graham County and flows w into Cheoah River.

Yellow Creek rises in nw Haywood County and flows se into Big Creek.

Yellowcreek, community in n Graham County on Yellow Creek. Served by post office, 1878–1953. Alt. 1,800.

Yellow Creek Gap, n Graham County between the headwaters of Yellow Creek and Tuskeegee Creek.

Yellow Creek Mountains extend from Cheoah River in nw Graham County e along the

course of Yellow Creek to the headwaters of Mountain Creek.

Yellow Creek Township, nw Graham County.

Yellow Face, peak in n Jackson County on Plott Balsams. Alt. 6,032.

Yellow Gap, sw Buncombe County between Green Top and Billy Cove Knob.

Yellow Gap, s central Burke County.

Yellow Gap, nw Henderson County on the se end of Laurel Mountain. Alt. approx. 3,202.

Yellowhammer Branch rises in nw Graham County and flows e into Cheoah River.

Yellowhammer Gap, nw Graham County between Hangover Lead and Little Tennessee River.

Yellow Hill, mountain in w Wilkes County between Lewis Fork Creek and North Prong Lewis Fork Creek. Alt. approx. 1,300.

Yellow Jacket Lake, s Wilkes County on Moravian Creek. Covers approx. 2 acres; max. depth 15 ft. Built by R. Don Laws and named for his newspaper, the *Yellow Jacket*, which was est. in Moravian Falls in 1895.

Yellow Mountain, w Avery County near the Tennessee state line. Alt. 5,269.

Yellow Mountain, nw Buncombe County se of Davidson Gap.

Yellow Mountain, se Clay County between the forks of Little Buck and Buck Creeks to Water Oak Gap. Alt. 5,000–5,050.

Yellow Mountain, on the Jackson-Macon county line. Alt. 5,145. Known by the Indians as *Ta-loh-na* or *Da-loh-no-geh* (yellow).

Yellow Mountains. *See* Unaka Mountains.

Yellow Patch Branch rises in e Jackson County and flows sw into Wolf Creek.

Yellow Patch Branch rises in s Macon County and flows nw into Hemp Patch Branch.

Yellow Spot, mountain in n Mitchell County. Alt. 5,112.

Yellowstone Falls, the final of a series of three waterfalls on Yellowstone Prong, s Haywood County.

Yellowstone Prong rises in s Haywood County on the s slope of Black Balsam Knob and flows e into East Fork Pigeon River. Named because of the yellow color of mosses growing on stones in the stream. Upper Falls, Second Falls, and Yellowstone Falls are located on the stream.

Yellow Swamp rises in s Wayne County and flows w into Thoroughfare Swamp.

Yeopim, community in sw Perquimans County served by post office, 1884–88. Named for the Yeopim Indian tribe, which inhabited the region in the seventeenth century. Alt. 15.

Yeopim Creek rises in s Perquimans County and flows se into the mouth of Yeopim River. Appears as Clargeons Creek on the Collet map, 1770.

Yeopim River rises in Bear Swamp on the Chowan-Perquimans county line and flows se along the line into Albemarle Sound. Named for the Yeopim Indian tribe. Appears on the Comberford map, 1657, at the location of present Little River on the Pasquotank-Perquimans county line, an error that was corrected on the Ogilby map, 1671. Appears as Yeopim Creek on the Collet map, 1770.

Yeopim Township, former township in se Chowan County, now township no. 4.

Yerger, community in n central Watauga County served by post office, 1892–1905.

Yesocking Creek. *See* Wyesocking Bay.

Yoder, community in w Catawba County served by post office, 1894–1903.

Yokley, community in n Davidson County served by post office, 1880–1905.

Yonah-wayah. *See* Hanging Rock.

Yorick, community in central Bladen County served by post office, 1902–20.

York, former community in nw Warren County. A post office was est. there in 1902 but discontinued in 1905.

York Collegiate Institute, community in n Alexander County served by post office, 1855–1908.

York County. On December 7, 1771, in the General Assembly, a bill for dividing the w part of Rowan County and erecting York County and St. James Parish was read for the second time and passed. Rejected on December 10 by the Council. Iredell County, *which see*, was created from w Rowan County in 1788. St. James Episcopal Church, in the s part of Iredell County, was est. about 1800.

York Creek rises in sw Carteret County and flows w into White Oak River.

York Institute. *See* York Collegiate Institute.

Yorkville, community in nw Bladen County served by post office, 1869–89.

Yost, community in s Rowan County served by post office, 1888–1906.

Younce Creek rises in n Macon County and flows se into Burningtown Creek.

Young Cove, sw Buncombe County e of Peggy Peak.

Young Cove, e Macon County on a tributary of Watauga Creek.

Young Cove, at the head of Young Cove Creek in e Mitchell County.

Young Cove Creek rises in e Mitchell County and flows sw into Cane Creek.

Young Gap, on the ne end of Burney Mountain on the Buncombe-Henderson county line.

Young Mountain, w Cherokee County between Camp and Shoal Creeks.

Young Mountain, w Rowan County between Third and Withrow Creeks. Alt. 1,092.

Young Pisgah Mountain, sw Buncombe County between Hogpen Gap and Berrys Gap. Alt. 4,017.

Youngs, community in central Davidson County served by post office, 1900–1903.

Youngs Creek rises in s Iredell County s of Troutman and flows sw into Rocky Creek. Now largely covered by Lake Norman.

Youngs Creek rises in nw Rutherford County and flows e into Cedar Creek.

Youngs Cross Roads. *See* Maysville.

Youngs Island, a loam island approx. 2 mi. long and ¾ mi. wide, in Pee Dee River, n Anson County.

Youngs Mountain, nw Rutherford County, extends ne parallel to Buffalo Creek. Alt. approx. 2,700.

Youngs Springs, community in se Rockingham County; once a favorite rest area for liquid refreshment during horse-and-buggy days. Named for spring owner Robert Young.

Young's Store. *See* Oak Hill.

Youngs Swamp rises in ne Sampson County and flows ne into Goshen Swamp.

Youngsville, town in w Franklin County. Railroad name was Youngville. Alt. 449. Settled about 1839 and first known as Pacific. Inc. 1875. Named for John Young, local landowner. Produces apparel and furniture.

Youngsville Township, former township in sw Franklin County, now township no. 3. Earlier called Freemans Township.

Youngville. *See* Youngsville.

Yuma. *See* Deep Gap.

Z

Zachary's, community in s Transylvania County near Rosman.

Zacho, community in se Granville County served by post office, 1892–1903.

Zacks Fork Creek rises in ne Caldwell County and flows sw approx. 10 mi. into Lower Creek.

Zade Knob, n Madison County between Bull Creek Gap and Arington Branch.

Zara, community in se Bladen County served by post office, 1901–20.

Zeb, community in e Rowan County served by post office, 1884–1903. Named for Zebulon B. Vance, Civil War governor and later U.S. senator.

Zebra, community in n Wilkes County near East Prong Roaring River.

Zebulon, town in e Wake County. Inc. 1907. Named for Zebulon B. Vance (1830–94), governor of North Carolina and U.S. senator. Produces apparel and lumber products. Alt. 323.

Zeke Island, sandy island in the Cape Fear River opposite Snow Marsh in se Brunswick County.

Zephyr, community in w Surry County between Mitchell River and Little Creek. Served by post office, 1900–1909.

Ziglar's Store. *See* Shelton's Store.

Zillicoah. *See* French Broad River.

Zilphy Creek rises in s central Stokes County and flows e into Dan River.

Zion, community in sw Lincoln County served by post office, 1900–1901.

Zion, community in sw Yadkin County served by post office, 1856–95.

Zionville, community in n Watauga County on Cove Creek. Alt. 3,159.

Zirconia, community in s Henderson County. Alt. 2,084. Named for zircon mines operated there in the 1880s. Zircon discovered there in 1869.

Zircon Mountain, s Henderson County near Freeman Creek.

Zoar, community in se Union County near Lanes Creek. Served by post office, 1876–1900.

Zorah, community in ne Craven County served by post office, 1888–1904. Now known as Caton for David Caton, donor of land for local school.